Foreign National Pr

law and practice

Laura Dubinsky is a barrister at Doughty Street Chambers. She practices in public law, specialising in immigration law, prison law and challenges to administrative detention; and is also frequently instructed in civil actions against detaining authorities.

Hamish Arnott is a partner at Bhatt Murphy solicitors in London specialising in public law and human rights with a particular focus on the civil liberties of prisoners and those detained under immigration laws. He is the co-author of the leading prison law text, *Prisoners: law and practice* (LAG, 2009).

Alasdair Mackenzie is a barrister at Doughty Street Chambers who practises in public law, with a specialism in immigration and asylum. From 1990 to 2002 he was Co-ordinator of the charity Asylum Aid.

Available as an ebook at www.lag.org.uk/ebooks

LAG eBook

The purpose of the Legal Action Group is to promote equal access to justice for all members of society who are socially, economically or otherwise disadvantaged. To this end, it seeks to improve law and practice, the administration of justice and legal services.

Foreign National Prisoners

law and practice

Laura Dubinsky

with Hamish Arnott and Alasdair Mackenzie

LAG Legal Action Group
2012

This edition published in Great Britain 2012
by LAG Education and Service Trust Limited
242 Pentonville Road, London N1 9UN
www.lag.org.uk

© Laura Dubinsky and Legal Action Group 2012

While every effort has been made to ensure that the details in this text are correct, readers must be aware that the law changes and that the accuracy of the material cannot be guaranteed and the author and the publisher accept no responsibility for any loss or damage sustained.

The rights of the author to be identified as author of this work has been asserted by her in accordance with the Copyright, Designs and Patents Act 1988.

All rights reserved. No part of this publication may be reproduced, stored in a retrieval system or transmitted in any form or by any means, without permission from the publisher.

British Library Cataloguing in Publication Data
a CIP catalogue record for this book is available from the British Library.

Crown copyright material is produced with the permission of the Controller of HMSO and the Queen's Printer for Scotland.

This book has been produced using Forest Stewardship Council® (FSC®) certified paper. The wood used to produce FSC certified products with a 'Mixed Sources' label comes from FSC certified well-managed forests, controlled sources and/or recycled material.

Print ISBN   978 1 903307 66 3
ebook ISBN   978 1 908407 01 6

Typeset by Regent Typesetting, London
Printed in Great Britain by Hobbs the Printers, Totton, Hampshire

'Even the most wicked of men are entitled to justice at the hands of the state.'

Lord Steyn, *R (Roberts) v Parole Board* [2005] UKHL 45, [2005] 2 AC 738, para 84

Foreword

by Sir Nicholas Blake, Judge of the High Court and President of the Upper Tribunal (Immigration and Asylum Chamber)

The right to liberty and personal security is one of the most fundamental of rights whose history long predates the modern era of human rights law. Imprisonment of anyone, irrespective of nationality, with a view to prosecution and punishment for substantial criminal wrongdoing is a well-established exemption to this right that is regulated by the criminal courts. Whereas the liability to detention of a British citizen ends with the conclusion of the criminal process and service of any sentence imposed, different considerations apply for a foreign national and detention pending deportation or removal may follow on the criminal process. Indeed, detention unrelated to criminal proceedings may be imposed immediately on arrival to the United Kingdom whilst a claim to asylum is investigated and determined.

The treatment of foreign national prisoners is the theme of this ambitious new work. It takes the reader on a journey through the process of deportation and the exemptions to deportation that may arise in the case of those exercising European Union Treaty rights, those who are refugees or entitled to subsidiary forms or protection and those whose family and private life recognised by article 8 of the European Convention on Human Rights makes deportation disproportionate. It addresses the parallel processes under the Special Immigration Appeals Commission for those whose presence is considered to undermine national security. It then turns to prison and mental health law itself to examine how foreign nationals are treated distinctly by reason of their nationality, before returning to the field of immigration law and examining the power to detain a foreign national and the remedies available to challenge the exercise of any such power.

Fifty years ago such a survey would primarily be concerned with the distinction between aliens and British subjects and the broad exercise of prerogative powers available in respect of the former class. As such, it would have been a slim volume, on the understanding that subject to the requirements of good faith the Home Secretary could do pretty much as he or she wanted for good reason or not (see *Schmidt v Secretary of State for Home Affairs* [1969] 2 Ch 149). Today the language, law and the very nature of the discourse is fundamentally different and this exposition of law and practice takes up 44 chapters and over 800 pages. The detention of foreign nationals is an emotive subject. It can also be a costly one. As this book goes to press, the *Guardian* newspaper on 7 January 2012 reported a six figure settlement of a compensation claim by a family of four Turkish Kurdish children detained for 13 months in a detention centre in 2002.

This book will be an up to date source of information for detainees, their advisers and others concerned with making and reviewing decisions to detain and remove. I would particularly commend chapter 20 on preparing evidence and representations at immigration appeals and chapter 41 on applying for bail as important practical guidance to ensure that judges make the appropriate decisions in disputed cases.

The authors also point out a number of topics where the domestic case law may need re-examination in the light of decisions in the Supreme Court and the courts of the European institutions that are now such an important source of legal principle in this field.

It is a racing certainty that the law on this topic will not remain static, but judges will need to continue to make difficult judgments between public concern at foreigners who pose a danger as a result of the commission of crimes on one hand and those who have a good claim to remain by reason of asylum law, long residence, family ties, or the special considerations that impact of the welfare of children on the other.

It is useful to have all aspects of the law relating to the detention of foreigners in one place. The authors are to be congratulated and it is likely that this book will join the body of long-established works in the libraries of those concerned with questions relating to the imprisonment of foreign nationals.

Sir Nicholas Blake
January 2012

Preface

Spring 2006: 'a toxic mix'

... from April 2006 to September 2008 the Home Office applied an unpublished detention policy to all foreign national prisoners following the completion of their prison sentences pending their deportation. This followed the revelation on 25 April 2006 that during the past seven years over 1,000 such prisoners had been released from prison on completion of their sentences without being considered for deportation or deported. *'Illegal migrants and paedophiles, a toxic mix. The tabloids will go bananas'*. The words of a contemporary diarist, Chris Mullin, *Decline and Fall* (2010), p94, capture the atmosphere of disaster that was engendered among ministers by this announcement.

A few days later Charles Clarke was removed from his post and was replaced on 4 May 2006 as Home Secretary by Dr John Reid. A practice of blanket detention was then instituted with a ruthless determination that precluded consideration of the merits of any individual case and was wholly at odds with the presumption in the published policy in favour of temporary admission or temporary release. It remained in place until November 2007 when it was replaced by another unpublished policy which permitted release only in exceptional circumstances. It was not until 9 September 2008 that a revised detention policy was published.

The damning words are Lord Hope's, giving judgment in the Supreme Court in *R (Shepherd Masimba Kambadzi) v SSHD*.[1] The governmental response to the disclosure of its earlier failures to systematically consider foreign national prisoners for deportation prior to release was a secret policy of lockdown. In the chaotic early months of that policy's application, many foreign national prisoners (and a number of British citizens caught up because they 'looked foreign'[2]) were

1 [2011] UKSC 23, [2011] 1 WLR 1299 para 27.
2 As Her Majesty's Inspector of Prisons observed in her Thematic Report on Foreign National Prisoners dated July 2006, para 6.33 prisoners' nationalities were routinely misidentified: 'We usually found one or two of the sample of 12 prisoners spoken to in each prison who were mistakenly identified as foreign

denied release from prison on sentence completion without warning, reasons or documentation. Those foreign nationals who had been released from prison, some considerable periods earlier, were abruptly rounded up and re-detained, again often without individuated consideration of likelihood of deportation ensuing or rehabilitative progress in the community. When prison overcrowding prompted a minor relaxation of that policy of blanket post-sentence administrative detention, the Government still did not publish its true detention policy. It appears that the Government withheld publication partly in concern that this would disclose to lawyers and the courts the secret underlying policy, but primarily in fear that a policy that permitted any releases might be seen as too soft by the popular press. In the words of one contemporaneous internal memo, the government preferred to allow the courts to 'take the hit' in the tabloid press and popular eye for the release of foreign national former prisoners from immigration detention.[3] If society is measured by how it treats its least popular, the events of Spring 2006 marked a failure. The terms 'moral panic', used by some sociologists to describe popular fear of people or issues believed to threaten social order, and 'folk devils' to describe its targets, are apposite for the particular place that foreign national offenders came to occupy in the public imagination.

Many of the legislative and policy changes described in this book, including a new 'automatic' statutory regime for deportation in which the Secretary of State for the Home Department (SSHD) surrendered discretion over many decisions to deport, the devoting of certain prisons partially or wholly to hold foreign national prisoners, and the expanded use of immigration detention, form part of the longer-term parliamentary and governmental response to those events of late April 2006.

However, the difficulties facing foreign national prisoners and former prisoners (FNPs) run deeper and long pre-date that period. FNPs occupy a peculiar place in the law, their often unmet or inadequately addressed legal needs straddling multiple disciplines (in particular immigration law, prison law and, in the context of immigration detention, the law of false imprisonment). The impetus for this book was to attempt to provide a multi-disciplinary overview of the law as it affects them.

---

nationals; however in the juvenile establishment, 5 of the 12 people identified as foreign nationals by the prison were in fact British'.

3 Cited in *Lumba and Mighty v SSHD* [2011] UKSC 12, [2011] 2 WLR 671, per Lord Collins at para 220.

Why a book about FNPs

In the (long) course of writing this book, the need for an overview of the law as it is commonly applied to FNPs has, if anything, intensified. The law touching on FNPs continues to expand in span and complexity (for example, as the domestic courts increasingly apply EU law protections and concepts to expulsion challenges; or as the courts have re-examined, in the context of claims brought by FNPs, the law governing liability and quantum for false imprisonment). The prolonged administrative detention of FNPs after sentence completion pending deportation continues to be widespread. On 27 October 2011, the Independent Chief Inspector of the UK Border Agency reported that 97 per cent of the sample of foreign national prisoners interviewed for his thematic inspection had been detained upon completion of their custodial sentence and:

> By January 2011, over 1,600 foreign national prisoners were detained under immigration powers at the end of their custodial sentence, pending deportation. The average length of detention had increased from 143 days in February 2010 to 190 days in January 2011, and 27 per cent of all foreign national prisoners who were detained after their custodial sentence had been detained for longer than 12 months.[4]

The Home Office has disclosed, in response to a request for information under the Freedom of Information Act 2000, that on 30 June 2011 one detainee had spent nearly five and a half years detained solely under Immigration Act powers; three others had been detained for periods of over four years; a further sixteen had been detained for more than three years.[5]

At the same time, FNPs are faced by structural impediments in access to justice (such as a lack of familiarity with legal rights or sometimes with English language; and the fact that many will bring their cases while detained either under criminal sentences or under Immigration Act powers).

Those difficulties are likely to be significantly compounded by legal aid cuts and in particular the closure of Britain's two major not-for-profit providers of publicly funded legal services for immigrants,

---

4 A thematic inspection of how the UK Border Agency manages foreign national prisoners, February – May 2011, Executive Summary paras 7 to 8.

5 The figures, given broken down according to sex (all were male) do not indicate whether the detainees are FNPs. The length of detention makes it highly likely that all are FNPs.

both of which provided legal services in Immigration Removal Centres nationwide.[6]

A lack of funding for appeals against expulsion decisions and a lack of available legal representation for bail applications is of all the more concern against a backdrop of deficient Home Office decision-making. In his thematic report on the UK Border Agency's management of foreign national prisoners, the Independent Chief Inspector of the UK Border Agency observed:

> We found a significant disparity between the Agency's and the courts' interpretation of whether a foreign national prisoner should be entitled to remain in the UK on human rights grounds. Between March and December 2010, the Agency's decisions to deport had been overturned in 425 cases by the First-Tier Tribunal – the overwhelming majority on human rights grounds. This contrasted with figures showing 151 foreign national prisoners being granted permission to remain on initial consideration by the Agency. In the 12 months to February 2011, 32 per cent of appeals lodged by foreign national prisoners against deportation had been successful.[7]

Likewise,

> There was also a disparity between the number of people released from detention by the Agency and the number released on bail by the courts. Between February 2010 and January 2011, the Agency released 109 foreign national prisoners from detention compared with 1,102 released on bail by the courts.[8]

And the report also noted:

> In 11 of the cases sampled (8 per cent), information relating to people other than the foreign national prisoner was held on file with no explanation as to why this had happened.[9]

Drawing the line: where unlawful discrimination begins

The law on FNPs also throws into particularly sharp relief the moral and legal controversies concerning the treatment of migrants. International and domestic law permit, in very significant aspects, the differential treatment of a British national and foreign national convicted of the same offence and posing identical levels of danger to the

---

6 Refugee and Migrant Justice (closed in 2010) and Immigration Advisory Service (closed in 2011).
7 A thematic inspection of how the UK Border Agency manages foreign national prisoners, February – May 2011, Executive Summary para 4.
8 Executive Summary para 9.
9 Executive Summary para 11.

community. A British citizen is entitled to release into the community on completion of the custodial part of the sentence. But a foreign national may be recommended for deportation as part of his sentence; may, irrespective of whether so recommended, be deported; and may be administratively detained prior to deportation.

Simultaneously, the cardinal principle of the rule of law, equality before the law, prohibits differentiation between immigrants and British nationals *in areas irrelevant to expulsion*. That principle found its highest domestic expression in *A and others v SSHD* ('the Belmarsh case')[10] when the House of Lords found unlawful a statutory regime which indefinitely detained foreign nationals suspected of involvement in international terrorism who could not be deported, but which made no analogous provision for the detention of British citizens suspected of posing the same threat. As Lord Bingham subsequently wrote extra-judicially:

> The position of a non-national with no right of abode in this country differs from that of a national with a right of abode in the obvious and important respect that the one is subject to removal and the other is not. That is the crucial distinction, and differentiation relevant to it is unobjectionable and indeed inevitable. But it does not warrant differentiation irrelevant to that distinction ... [11]

An important legal question affecting FNPs is where legally permissible differential treatment based on liability to expulsion ends, and where unlawful discrimination begins. That arises, specifically, in the context of prison law, where FNPs may face differential treatment and obstacles to ordinary sentence progression and release some of which are only nominally associated with their potential expulsion. So, for example, in *R (Clift and Hindawi) v SSHD*,[12] the House of Lords found that a differential statutory release regime (under which the final decision over whether to release foreign nationals 'liable to removal' rested with the Secretary of State for the Home Department rather than with the Parole Board) unlawfully discriminated against FNPs under articles 14 and 5 ECHR. Conversely, in *R (Brooke) v Secretary of State for Justice*[13] the Divisional Court rejected a discrimination claim by a British prisoner who complained, among other points, over the difference between the Early Removal Scheme for foreign national fixed term prisoners who were 'liable to removal' (which

---

10 [2004] UKHL 56, [2005] 2 AC 68.
11 Sixth Sir David Williams lecture, *The Rule of Law*, 16 November 2006.
12 [2006] UKHL 54, [2007] 1 AC 484.
13 [2009] EWHC 1396 (Admin).

allows removal up to 270 days before the completion of the requisite custodial period) and the Home Detention Curfew (for which prisoners 'liable to removal' are ineligible, but the period for which opens only 135 days before the completion of the requisite custodial term). In *Brooke*, the Divisional Court found that the difference in regime was permissible because it centred on expulsion. There was a fundamental difference between those prisoners who were liable to be removed from the UK and those who were not: the former group faced a different sanction for their criminal offending.

Contents and structure of the book

Part I, necessarily comprising a large portion of this book, concerns expulsion (the umbrella term we use to refer to administrative removal and deportation) and deportation in particular. We begin with an examination of the relevant statutory powers for both 'discretionary' deportation under the Immigration Act 1971 and 'automatic' deportation under the UK Borders Act 2007. We review also the policies, Immigration Rules and principles applicable to 'discretionary' deportation; the mechanisms for deportation generally and the circumstances in which a deportation order may be revoked.

We go on to consider the different grounds on which FNPs may resist expulsion, beginning with the special EU law protections for EEA nationals and their family members. We then look at 'intentional harm' grounds, by which we mean claims that expulsion would amount to 'refoulement' of a person facing a substantial risk of serious harm, contrary to the Refugee Convention grounds, ECHR article 3 or article 15(c) of the Qualification Directive. We use this shorthand for claims concerning harm arising from the intentional acts of state or non-state agents (although the harm may be neither targeted nor intended). The focus of our examination is on the circumstances in which protection is lost (or a person is altogether excluded from protection) as a consequence of past offending. We then consider other ECHR grounds for resisting expulsion. Because so many FNPs have accrued long periods of residence before the start of deportation proceedings and article 8 ECHR arises so commonly in their cases, we devote particular detail to the application of ECHR article 8 in deportation cases. We examine here also the ECHR article 3 and 8 grounds on which mentally or physically ill immigrants may rely to resist expulsion. This section of the book includes an examination of the consequences of past offending for immigration status where a person succeeds in resisting expulsion.

Part I of the book closes with a review of statutory appeals to the Immigration and Asylum Chamber of the First-tier and Upper Tribunals and, in national security cases, to the Special Immigration Appeals Commission (SIAC). Here, we also provide checklists for collecting evidence, making representations and preparing appeals.

Part II of the book turns to a distinct field, prison law. We provide an overview of the institutional, statutory and policy context, available complaints mechanisms and also sentencing. We then focus on the particular obstacles to ordinary sentence progression and release which confront FNPs as they serve their sentences, and the mechanisms by which FNPs may be removed to their home countries before sentence completion, or transferred to finish their sentences there. This part of the book also includes a chapter on detention under Mental Health Act powers as it applies to both serving prisoners and immigration detainees.

Part III of the book concerns immigration detention. Although much of what is said in principle applies to the administrative detention of all immigrants, FNPs are particularly likely to detained, and detained for longer periods. Immigration detention is, again, an issue arising so commonly for FNPs that we attempt to address it as comprehensively as possible. We examine the statutory powers of immigration detention, common law and ECHR protections applicable to administrative detention, and applicable policies. We also provide specific and practical guidance on bail applications in the IAC.

Finally, Part IV provides an outline of available remedies (other than the statutory appeals processes already discussed) with an overview of legal avenues of redress and causes of action of wide application to FNPs. We end with a discussion of the damages available in false imprisonment claims.

In trying to provide a cross-disciplinary overview, it has been a temptation (and we have probably in places succumbed to it) to write an encyclopaedic book of 'everything about everything'. We have tried, as much as possible, to focus on, and reserve the detail of the book for issues that specifically affect FNPs. On topics which are of very widespread application to FNPs, such as article 8 ECHR in the expulsion context and immigration detention, we have aimed to provide a full picture even though many of the points discussed may also affect, albeit sometimes somewhat differently, other categories of immigrant or detainee.

Conversely, in certain areas, such as EU law, protection law or prison law, we provide general introductions to a very broad topic as a prelude to more detailed discussions of points particularly affecting

FNPs. In others, such as appeals procedures and remedies, we provide an outline only of mechanisms for seeking redress. In those broad summary chapters, we emphasise that practitioners should refer for detail to specialist texts for detail which is beyond the scope of this book.

This book does not touch on extradition, which would need a book in its own right and of course has many. Nor, unusually in a LAG book, do we discuss public funding: the swingeing further cuts to legal aid now proposed are likely to transform the field and it remains too early to anticipate the shape of things to come.

We have continued to amend and update the text of this book until early January 2012. However, this is a highly fast-moving area, and readers should always, particularly when dealing with government policy which is continually amended, check for fresh legal developments.

Laura Dubinsky
Doughty Street Chambers
January 2012

Acknowledgments

Enormous thanks are due to Hamish Arnott and Alasdair Mackenzie, whose thought, creativity and efficiency have proved so valuable. Hamish has written Part II of this book, on prison law and the majority of Part IV on remedies. Alasdair has written Part IC on 'intentional harm' grounds for resisting expulsion and chapter 19 on immigration status for FNPs who cannot be deported. Very great thanks also to Judith Farbey QC for all her work: Judith wrote chapter 23 on the Special Immigration Appeals Commission. Esther Pilger at LAG, has been a fantastic publisher, combining kindness, patience and firmness and artfully concealing, with only minor and necessary exceptions, what she must have thought about the time it took to complete this book. Parts of this book have been read by Shamik Dutta, Paul Bowen, Aswini Weereratne, Richard Thomas, Jonathan Glasson, Peter Melleney and Joanna Dawson to whom many thanks are owed. Simon Cox has been a generous, funny and brilliant mentor. Immense thanks to my great friend David Chirico who has read and commented on swathes of the book. My love and gratitude to Raza for doing the same, even when he might have thought we were on holiday, and for putting up with me.

This book is for my beloved parents, Helene and Alex, who I think are perfect.

Contents

Foreword   vii
Preface   ix
Acknowledgements   xvii
Table of cases   xxxiii
Table of statutes   lxvii
Table of statutory instruments   lxxix
Table of EU and international legislation   xci
Abbreviations   ci

Part I: Deportation   1

Section A: Powers and process of deportation   3
Introduction to deportation   5

1   Deportation powers under the Immigration Act 1971   7
Introduction   9
'Conducive' deportation   10
The deportation of family members   13
The deportation of certain overstayers   16
Exemption from deportation   17
Timing and effect of a deportation order in cases governed by IA 1971   20

2   Criminal court recommendations for deportation   23
Introduction   24
Which courts can recommend deportation   24
Who may be the subject of a criminal court recommendation for deportation   25
Procedural requirements   26
Relevant and irrelevant considerations for the sentencing court   27
Recommendations for deportation for passport offences   28
Challenging a recommendation for deportation   30
The approach to be taken by the SSHD to a criminal court's recommendation for deportation   30

xix

3   The Secretary of State's decision-making in deportation cases under the Immigration Act 1971   33
Introduction   35
Who is considered for deportation   35
The process of consideration for deportation   36
Sources of guidance: Immigration Rules and Home Office policies   38
Immigration Rules paragraph 364   40
Home Office policies applicable to deportation under the Immigration Act 1971   43
Home Office policies previously applicable to deportation under the Immigration Act 1971   46
Issuing a decision to deport in deportation cases under Immigration Act 1971   49

4   Deportation cases involving minors: relevant legislation and policy   51
Introduction   53
Statutory powers of deportation directly applicable to minors   53
Borders, Citizenship and Immigration Act 2009 s55 and the best interests of the child   54
Home Office policies relevant to the deportation of children   63

5   'Automatic' deportation under the UK Borders Act 2007   67
Introduction   69
Differences between the two statutory deportation regimes   70
Timetable for entry into force   70
Who is liable to 'automatic' deportation under UKBA 2007   71
No private law action for failure to issue an 'automatic' deportation order   74
Exemptions from all deportation   74
The numbered exceptions to 'automatic' deportation under UKBA 2007   75
Deportation under IA 1971 for family members and others who do not meet the criteria for 'automatic' deportation under UKBA 2007   76
When an 'automatic' deportation order can be made   77
When an 'automatic' deportation order takes effect   78
Appeal to the FTT-IAC against a decision that the criteria for 'automatic' deportation are met   79
In-country appeal to the FTT-IAC against an 'automatic' deportation order   80
Out-of-country appeal to the FTT- IAC against an 'automatic' deportation order and other remedies   81

6   **Departure: voluntary departure and deportation arrangements   83**
    Introduction   84
    A deportation order can only be signed against a person still in the UK   84
    Incentives to voluntary departure and other forms of co-operation   84
    Voluntary departure as an alternative to deportation   86
    Co-operation with deportation or administrative removal   87
    Deportation arrangements   88
    Paying for deportation   89
    Delays to deportation for medical treatment   89

7   **Revocation and other forms of termination of deportation orders in non-EEA cases   91**
    Introduction   92
    Circumstances in which a deportation order ceases to have effect or is invalid from the outset   92
    Revocation of a deportation order made under IA 1971   93
    Circumstances in which a deportation order may be revoked after enforcement   94
    In-country revocation of a deportation order made under UKBA 2007   95
    Out-of-country revocation of a deportation order made under UKBA 2007   96
    Representations for revocation   97
    Consequences of revocation   97
    Notification of revocation   98
    Appeal against a refusal to revoke a deportation order   98
    Entry in breach of a deportation order   99

    Section B: EU law grounds for restricting deportation   101
    Introduction to EU law   103

8   **The Citizens Directive and the EEA Regs 2006   107**
    Introduction   108
    EU citizens and EEA nationals   108
    Who is entitled to reside in the UK by operation of the Citizens Directive and EEA Regs 2006   109
    'Family members'   112
    Other relatives   114
    Right of residence for family members   117
    Acquisition of permanent rights of residence in the UK by an EEA national   120

Right of permanent residence for family members   121

9 The expulsion of EEA nationals and their family members under the Citizens Directive and EEA Regs 2006   123
Introduction   126
General principles   127
The first level of protection   128
The second level of protection: protections for EEA nationals and family members who have acquired a right of permanent residence in the UK   132
The third and highest level of protection: protections for EEA nationals and family members who are minors or who are long-term (ten years or more) residents in the UK   134
The calculation of the qualifying periods   136
Procedure and practice in EEA expulsion cases   142
Home Office policy on the deportation of EEA nationals and their family members   154

10 Other EU law protections from expulsion   157
Introduction   158
TFEU article 20, *Zambrano, Dereci* and the expulsion of the third-country national family members of citizens of the European Union   158
Turkish Association Agreement cases   163

Section C: 'Intentional harm' grounds for resisting deportation   167
Introduction to claims concerning 'intentional harm' on expulsion   169

11 The Refugee Convention   173
Introduction   175
A very brief history of the Refugee Convention   175
A very brief overview of the contents of the Refugee Convention   176
The UNHCR   176
The Qualification Directive and its relationship with the Refugee Convention   177
The partial incorporation of the Refugee Convention in domestic law   181
Recognition as a refugee   182
The refugee definition   184
The date at which refugee status is to be assessed   194
Burden and standard of proof   195
The duty of non-refoulement   197

12 Exclusion, loss of protection and cessation under the Refugee Convention 199
Introduction   201
The exclusion clauses   202
Article 1F   203
Procedure   204
Article 1F(a)   206
Article 1F(b)   207
Article 1F(c)   211
Complicity for exclusion purposes   216
Loss of protection from refoulement   219
Procedure on appeal to the IAC or SIAC in exclusion and loss of protection cases   227
Cessation   230

13 Relying on the ECHR in claims concerning 'intentional harm' 237
Introduction   238
ECHR article 3   239
Reliance on other ECHR rights   249

14 Article 15(c) of the Qualification Directive 253
Introduction   254
Definition   254
Approach of the ECJ   256
Approach of the domestic courts   257
Practical issues arising   258

Section D: Other ECHR grounds for resisting deportation 263
Introduction to other ECHR grounds for resisting deportation   265

15 The approach to be taken to ECHR article 8 by decision-makers 269
Introduction   270
The Razgar five-step test   270
The role of the tribunal in ECHR article 8 appeals   276
Interaction between ECHR article 8 and Immigration Rules para 364   276
Burden and standard of proof   277

16 ECHR article 8 and family and private life 279
Introduction   280
Family life   280
Private life   289

xxiii

17 Proportionality in ECHR article 8 expulsion cases   293
Introduction   295
The proportionality assessment in family life expulsion cases generally   295
Factors relevant in proportionality assessment in both private and family life cases   305
Additional proportionality considerations in criminal deportation cases   311

18 Resisting deportation on grounds of physical or mental illness under ECHR articles 3 and 8; *Quaquah* claims   323
Introduction   325
ECHR article 3 and health   325
ECHR article 3 claims based on physical ill-health and deprivation of care in the expulsion context   326
Exceptions to the N approach in HIV/AIDS cases and other cases of severe physical ill-health   330
ECHR article 3, mental ill-health and suicide risk   333
Possible exceptions to the *D v UK* and *N* approach in mental illness and suicide cases   336
Anxious scrutiny in mental health and suicide cases generally   340
Further issues arising in mental health and suicide risk cases   341
ECHR article 8 and mental and physical illness   343
MSS v Belgium and Greece and Sufi and Elmi v UK: a modified approach?   345
ECHR article 6 and '*Quaquah* claims'   345

Section E: Immigration status for FNPs who cannot be deported   347

19 Immigration status for FNPs who cannot be deported   349
Introduction   350
Humanitarian protection and discretionary leave   350
Humanitarian protection (HP)   351
Discretionary Leave (DL)   359
Leave outside the Rules   369
Special Immigration Status   370
Revocation of indefinite leave to remain where individual cannot be deported   372
Power to deprive a dual national of citizenship   375

Section F: Representations, evidence and appeals   377
Introduction to representations, evidence and appeals   379

20 Representations, evidence and preparing appeals   381
Introduction   382
Making representations against deportation   382
Evidence   386
Instructing experts   395
Preparing a trial bundle for an appeal in the IAC   397

21 Appeals in the IAC   399
Introduction   401
The statutory framework   401
Statutory grounds of appeal to the IAC   402
In-country and out-of country appeals   405
One-stop notices and one-stop statements   407
Suspensory nature of an appeal   408
The First-tier Tribunal and the Upper Tribunal   409
Starting an appeal in the FTT-IAC   409
Evidence and procedure in the FTT-IAC: a brief summary   411
Appeal hearings in the FTT-IAC   414
Challenging a determination of the FTT-IAC on a point of law   417
Review by the FTT-IAC of its own decision   418
'Excluded decisions'   418
Applying to the FTT-IAC for permission to appeal to the UT-IAC   419
Renewing the application for permission to appeal to the UT-IAC ('second applications')   420
Challenging a refusal of permission to appeal by the UT-IAC   422
Powers of the UT-IAC on determining an appeal   425
Procedure of the UT-IAC on appeal   426
Grounds of appeal in the UT-IAC   428
Hearings in the UT-IAC   429
Seeking permission to appeal from the UT-IAC on a second appeal   430
Review by the UT-IAC of its own decisions   433
Procedure after a grant of permission by UT-IAC to appeal to the Court of Appeal   433
Making an application for permission to appeal in the Court of Appeal   434
Abandonment and 'final determination' of appeals   435

22 Restriction and loss of appeal rights in deportation and revocation cases   437
Introduction   438
Loss of in-country appeal rights   438

Loss of all appeal rights   441
Summary   444

23 The Special Immigration Appeals Commission and its procedures   445
Introduction   447
The establishment of SIAC   447
SIAC's jurisdiction   449
In-country and out-of-country appeals   454
Closed material and special advocates   455
Legality of the use of closed evidence in substantive deportation appeals   460
The procedure for disclosure   464
Exculpatory review   466
Burden and standard of proof   467
Detainee reporting   467
The progress of deportation appeals in SIAC   468
Consideration of deportation appeals   472
SIAC's determination   475
Bail   476
Appeal from SIAC   481

Part II: Prison law   483

Section G: The prison and sentencing system   485
Introduction to the prison and sentencing system   487

24 Prison institutions, legislation and policy   489
Introduction   490
The organisation of the prison and probation systems   490
Statutory and policy framework   491
Prisons and other places of detention   493
Risk assessment: OASys   494
Multi-Agency Public Protection Arrangements   495

25 Complaints and supervision   499
Introduction   500
Complaints   500
The Prisons and Probation Ombudsman   501
Supervision of prisons   503

26 Sentences   507
Introduction   508
Types of prison sentence   508
Determinate sentences   509
Indeterminate sentences   510

Extended sentences 512
The meaning of the term 'liable to removal from the UK' 513
Procedures for release 514
New legislative proposals for FNPs 'liable to removal' 519

Section H: Foreign national (serving) prisoners 521
Introduction to foreign national (serving) prisoners 523

27 Management of FNPs in prisons 525
Introduction 526
The Service Level Agreement 526
Local policies for managing FNPs 527
FNPs held on remand 527
Categorisation and allocation 527
Categorisation 528
Allocation 532
Communication between prisons and the UK Border Agency 534
The IS91 detention authority form 536
Release of FNPs 536
Communication with embassies 537

28 Temporary and early release, early removal 539
Introduction 540
Release on Temporary Licence (ROTL) 540
Early release from sentence into the community – Home Detention Curfew (HDC) 542
The Early Removal Scheme (ERS) 549
The Facilitated Returns Scheme (FRS) 553

29 Repatriation of prisoners 555
Introduction 556
Repatriation of Prisoners Act 1984 556
Bi-lateral and multi-lateral prisoner transfer agreements 557
Consent of the prisoner 559
Criteria for repatriation 559
Applying for repatriation 560
The basis of the transfer 560
Additional Protocol to the Council of Europe Convention on the Transfer of Sentenced Persons 562
The EU Framework Decision 563
Challenges to repatriation decisions 564
Foreign national prisoners transferred to the UK 565

30 Mental health legislation and FNPs 567
Introduction 568

The Mental Health Act 1983   568
Hospital orders and interim hospital orders   569
Restriction orders   570
Hospital directions and limitation directions   571
Transfer directions: prisoners   572
Transfer directions: immigration detainees   573
Restriction directions   574
Remittal from hospital to prison or to a detention facility: prisoners   574
Remittal from hospital to prison or to a detention facility: prisoners   575
Access to the First-tier Tribunal (Mental Health)   576
Restricted patients   576
After-care   579
The relationship between MHA 1983 and deportation   580

Part III: Immigration detention   583

Section I: The power to detain   585
Introduction to the power to detain   587

31 Statutory powers of immigration detention   589
Introduction   590
Detention powers under the IA 1971   591
Deportation and detention powers under the UKBA 2007   594
No dual detention for deportation under the IA 1971 or under the UKBA 2007   601
R (Khadir) and statutory powers of detention   602

Section J: Restrictions on the power to detain   605
Introduction to limitations on the power to detain   607

32 Core common law principles generally applicable to detention   609
Introduction   611
Equal protection of the law for immigrants   611
The burden is on the detainer to justify the detention in legal proceedings   612
The executive's powers of detention must be strictly construed   613
The legality of a decision to detain or maintain detention is vitiated by a material public law error   614
The tort of false imprisonment is established without proof of special damage   615

No causation defence in liability for the detainer 616
Material and non-material public law error 617
Causation and damages 618
Duty to give reasons for detention 619
There is no good faith defence for the detainer 622
Whether the Immigration Acts contain a presumption of detention 622
The courts' role when assessing the lawfulness of administrative detention 627

33 The *Hardial Singh* principles 629
Introduction 630
The landmark case and the four principles 630
Factors bearing on the reasonable duration of detention for *Hardial Singh* purposes 638

34 Home Office detention policy 651
Introduction 653
The legal status of policy 654
The question of causation in the policy context 655
The detail of Home Office detention policy 656
The policy referred to below 657
General principles, applicable to all detainees (whether Criminal Casework Directorate cases or not) 658
Special criteria for detention in CCD cases 667
Other common examples of policy breaches in FNP cases 672

35 Procedural requirements in immigration detention 673
Introduction 674
Initial detention authorisation 674
Reasons for detention 675
Notification of entitlement to bail 678
Risk assessment in all immigration detention cases 679
Detention reviews 680
Authorisation before release 682
Medical reviews 682

36 The ECHR and detention 683
Introduction 685
ECHR article 5 685
ECHR article 5(1) 686
ECHR article 5(1)(f) detention 689
ECHR article 5(2) 694
ECHR article 5(4) 695

ECHR article 5(5)   696
ECHR article 3   697
ECHR article 8   704
ECHR article 14   709
Breaches of the ECHR resulting from a detention contractor's actions or omissions   711

37 Detention in CCD cases involving children   713
Introduction   714
The BCIA 2009 s55 duty and the *Every Child Matters* statutory guidance   714
Family Returns Panel   716
Children's Champion   716
Split families   717
Unaccompanied minor FNPs   719
Families with children   720

Section K: Places and conditions of detention; complaints   723
Introduction to places and conditions of detention   725

38 Places of immigration detention   727
Introduction   728
Places of detention permitted under the Immigration (Places of Detention) Direction 2009   729
Detention in prisons for those held under sole Immigration Act powers   730
Decisions over transfer   734
Detention in police stations   735

39 Conditions of detention in Immigration Removal Centres and complaints   737
Conditions of detention   740
Complaints   752

Section L: Bail   761
Introduction to bail   763

40 Powers of immigration bail and release on a restriction order   765
Introduction   766
Statutory powers of bail   766
Sureties   769
Conditions of bail   769
Breach of conditions   772

Bail from immigration judges of the Immigration and Asylum
    Chamber of the Upper Tribunal   774
Bail powers of the Administrative Court and Court of
    Appeal   774
Release directed by the criminal courts   775
Release on a restriction order   775
Home Office policy concerning authorisation for bail and
    restriction orders   777

41 Applying for bail or release on a restriction order   779
Introduction   781
Applications to the Home Office for release   781
Bail applications in the FTT-IAC   784
Challenging a refusal of bail   800
Further bail applications   800
Bail renewal   801
Bail variation   801

Part IV: Remedies   803

Section M: Remedies   805
Introduction to remedies   807

42 Choice of jurisdiction   809
Introduction   811
Litigation generally   812
Judicial review   815
Habeas corpus   830
Private law claims   833
Choosing between a civil claim for damages and judicial
    review   838

43 Causes of action   839
Introduction   840
Trespass to the person   840
Misfeasance in public office   842
Negligence   843
Breach of statutory duty   844
Human rights claims   845
Claims under the Data Protection Act 1998   846
Discrimination claims   847

44 Damages   849
Introduction   850
Nominal or substantive damages?   851

The basic award for loss of liberty 853
Aggravated damages 856
Exemplary damages 858
Settlements in civil actions 860

Index 861

Table of cases

A (Afghanistan) v Secretary of State for the Home Department [2009] EWCA Civ 825	16.20
A and others v Secretary of State for the Home Department (No 2) [2005] UKHL 71, [2006] AC 221	13.17, 23.58
A and others v Secretary of State for the Home Department [2004] UKHL 56, [2005] AC 68 (The Belmarsh Case)	23.9, 33.1, 33.4, 33.21, 36.99, 36.102, 36.103
A and others v Secretary of State for the Home Department SC/33/34/35/36/37/38/39, 20 October 2005	23.85, 23.90–23.93
A and others v UK (2009) 49 EHRR 29	13.15, 13.20, 13.21, 23.10, 23.42, 36.15, 36.20, 36.23, 36.30, 36.42, 36.46
A v Australia CCPR/C/59/D/560/1993, 30 April 1997	36.31
A v Bottrill [2003] 1 AC 449	44.40
A v Hoare [2008] 1 AC 844	42.91
AA (Afghanistan) v Secretary of State for the Home Department [2007] EWCA Civ 12	3.17, 15.10
AA (Exclusion clauses) Palestine [2005] UKIAT 00104	12.114
AA v Greece No 12186/08 22 July 2010	36.60
AA v UK app no 8000/08, judgment 20 September 2011	5.39, 17.51, 17.65, 17.66, 17.81, 17.85, 17.86
AB (Democratic Republic Congo) v Secretary of State for the Home Department [2007] EWCA Civ 1422	17.22
AB (Jamaica) v Secretary of State for the Home Department [2007] EWCA Civ 1302	15.10, 15.11, 17.39, 21.12
AB v The Netherlands (2003) 37 EHRR 48	36.81
Abbassi and others v Secretary of State for the Home Department [2011] EWCA Civ 814	4.40, 4.41, 4.42
Abdolkhani and Karimnia v Turkey App No 30471/08, judgment 22 September 2009	36.24
Abdulaziz, Cabales and Balkandali v UK (1985) 7 EHRR 330, (1984) 6 EHRR 28	16.11, 16.20, 16.22, 17.2, 17.37

xxxiii

xxxiv *Foreign national prisoners / Table of cases*

Abdulla v Bundesrepublik Deutschland, Joined Cases
  C-175/08, C176/08, C-178/08 and C-179/08, 2 March
  2010   12.134
Abel Oge-Denge v Secretary of State for Justice [2011]
  EWHC 266 (Admin)   27.20
AC (Turkey) v Secretary of State for the Home
  Department [2009] EWCA Civ 377   16.12, 17.72
Adan v Secretary of State for the Home Department
  [1999] 1 AC 293   11.38, 11.52, 11.68,
                                                                14.9
Adoui and Cornaille [1982] ECR 1665, [1982] CMLR 631   9.13
Advic v UK (1995) 20 EHRR CD 125   16.29
AE (Libya) [2011] EWHC 154 (Admin)   32.38, 38.9, 38.19,
                                                                38.21, 38.22
Aerts v Belgium (1986) 9 EHRR 297   36.15, 36.17
AF (Jamaica) v Secretary of State for the Home
  Department [2009] EWCA Civ 240   4.40, 4.43, 17.23
AG (Eritrea) v Secretary of State for the Home
  Department [2007] EWCA Civ 801   15.3, 15.7
AG (Kosovo) v Secretary of State for the Home
  Department [2007] UKAIT 00082   15.11
AH (Sudan) v Secretary of State for the Home
  Department [2007] UKHL 49, [2007] 3 WLR 832,
  [2008] 1 AC 678.   11.50, 23.100
Ahmed v Austria (1997) 24 EHRR 278   13.9
Ahmed v Secretary of State for the Home Department
  [2000] INLR 1   11.59
Ahmut v The Netherlands (1997) 24 EHRR 62   16.15
AJ (Liberia) v Secretary of State for the Home
  Department [2006] EWCA Civ 1736   18.36, 18.44, 18.45,
                                                                18.47, 18.54, 18.56
Akaeke v Secretary of State for the Home Department
  [2005] EWCA Civ 947   17.41
Aksoy v Turkey (1997) 23 EHRR 553   13.16, 13.18
Al Jedda v Secretary of State for the Home Department
  (SC/66/2008) 22 October 2008.   23.45
Al Nashif v Bulgaria (2002) 36 EHRR 37   3.17
Al Rawi v Security Service [2011] UKSC 34, [2011] 3 WLR
  388   23.26
Aleksanyan v Russia (2011) 52 EHRR 18   36.74
Al-Fayed v Commissioner of Police for the Metropolis
  [2004] EWCA Civ 1579   32.4
Alipour and Hosseinzagdan v Turkey App Nos 6909/08,
  12792/08, 28960/08, judgment 13 July 2010   36.24
Al-Jedda v Secretary of State for the Home Department
  [2010] EWCA Civ 212   23.18
Almrei, Re 2009 FC 1263, [2009] FCJ No 1579   23.27
Al-Saadoon v UK (2010) 51 EHRR 9   13.29–13.31
Al-Sabah v IAT [1992] Imm AR 223   9.18

Table of cases xxxv

Al-Sirri v Secretary of State for the Home Department [2009] EWCA Civ 222, [2009] INLR 586	12.21–12.23, 12.48, 12.57–12.60, 12.65
AM (Somalia) v Secretary of State for the Home Department [2009] EWCA Civ 114	9.65
AM and AM (armed conflict: risk categories) Somalia CG v Secretary of State for the Home Department [2008] UKAIT 00091	3.39, 14.20
American Cyanamid v Ethicon (No 1) [1975] AC 396	42.65
Amrollahi v Denmark App No 56811/00, 11 July 2002	17.11
Amuur v France (1996) 22 EHRR 533	36.7, 36.13
Anisminic Ltd v Foreign Compensation Commission [1969] 2 AC 147, [1969] WLR 163	32.5
Antonissen Case C-292/89 [1991] ECR I-745	9.6
AP (Trinidad and Tobago) v Secretary of State for the Home Department [2011] EWCA Civ 551	17.76
AR (Pakistan) v Secretary of State for the Home Department [2010] EWCA Civ 816	4.18, 15.7, 17.20, 17.64
AS (Afghanistan) v Secretary of State for the Home Department [2009] EWCA Civ 1076	11.27
AS (Libya) v Secretary of State for the Home Department [2008] EWCA Civ 289, [2008] HRLR 28	11.69, 13.9, 13.11, 23.4, 23.56, 23.79, 23.80, 23.100
AS (Pakistan) v Secretary of State for the Home Department [2008] EWCA Civ 1118	15.6, 15.7, 15.14, 17.23, 17.54, 17.70, 17.91
AS (Sudan) v Secretary of State for the Home Department [2009] EWCA Civ 1518	32.43, 33.27
AS and DD (Libya) v Secretary of State for the Home Department [2008] EWCA Civ 289	11.69
AS Somalia v Secretary of State for the Home Department [2009] EWCA Civ 114	22.9, 22.12
Ashley v Chief Constable of Sussex Police [2006] EWCA Civ 1085	43.7
Associated Provincial Picture Houses Ltd v Wednesbury Corporation [1948] 1 KB 223, [1947] 2 All ER 680	22.7, 22.8, 23.96, 32.13, 42.25, 42.64
AT (Pakistan) and JT (Pakistan) v Secretary of State for the Home Department [2010] EWCA Civ 567	5.11, 31.15
Aydin v Turkey (1998) 25 EHRR 251	13.18
Aydinli v Land Baden-Wurttemberg Case C-373/03 [2005] 3 CMLR 43.	10.18, 10.21
B v UK (1990) 64 DR 278	16.24
B, In Re; R v Special Adjudicator ex p Hoxha [2005] UKHL 19	11.9, 11.24, 12.134
BA (Demonstrators in Britain – risk on return) Iran CG [2011] UKUT 36 (IAC)	11.40

BA (Nigeria) and PE (Cameroon) v Secretary of State for
  the Home Department [2009] UKSC 7, [2010] 1 AC
  444   5.48, 5.49, 21.17,
                                                                   21.23
Babar Ahmad v UK (2010) 51 EHRR SE6   13.21
Bader v Sweden (2008) 46 EHRR 13   13.28
Baghli v France No 34374/97   17.59
Batayav v Secretary of State for the Home Department
  [2003] EWCA Civ 1489, [2004] INLR 126   11.73, 13.22
Baumbast Case 413/99 [2002] ECR I-7091, [2002] 3
  CMLR 23   9.11
Bazorkina v Russia (2008) 46 EHRR 15   36.71
BE (Iran) v Secretary of State for the Home Department
  [2008] EWCA Civ 540; [2009] INLR 1   11.66
Belgian Linguistic Case (1968) 1 EHRR 252   36.101
Belgium v Royer Case 48/75 [1976] ECR 497, [1976] 2
  CMLR 619   9.70
Beljoudi v France (1992) 14 EHRR 801   17.2, 17.47, 17.57
Benham v UK (1996) 22 EHRR 293   36.10
Benhebba v France App No 53441/99, 10 July 2003   16.29, 17.50, 17.58,
                                                                   17.89
Bensaid v UK (2001) 33 EHRR 10   13.33, 18.29, 18.30,
                                                                   18.33, 18.35, 18.40,
                                                                   18.42, 18.54–18.56
Beoku-Betts (FC) v Secretary of State for the Home
  Department [2008] UKHL 39, [2009] 1 AC 115   16.4, 17.23, 18.28
Berrehab v The Netherlands (1998) 11 EHRR 322   16.15
BF (Portugal) v Secretary of State for the Home
  Department [2009] EWCA Civ 923   9.12
Bigia v Entry Clearance Officer [2009] EWCA Civ 79,
  [2009] 2 CMLR 42   8.11, 8.22, 8.23,
                                                                   8.25
Birden v Stadtgemeinde Bremen Case C-1/97 [1998] ECR
  I-7747   10.19
BK (Zimbabwe) v Secretary of State for the Home
  Department [2008] EWCA Civ 510   18.26, 18.58
Bonsignore v Stadt Koln Case 67/74 [1975] ECR 297   9.6, 9.15, 17.71
Bouamar v Belgium (1988) 11 EHRR 1   36.15
Bouchelkia v France judgment of 29 January 1997   16.38
Boughanemi v France (1996) 22 EHRR 228   15.14, 16.16, 16.28,
                                                                   17.50, 17.55, 17.58
Boujlifa v France (2000) 30 EHRR 419   16.28, 17.50, 17.57
Boultif v Switzerland (2001) 33 EHRR 50   15.7, 17.2, 17.4,
                                                                   17.24, 17.47
Bousarra v France App No 25672/07, judgment 23
  September 2010   16.30, 17.57
Boyle v UK (1988) 10 EHRR 425   16.23, 16.34
Bozano v France (1986) 9 EHRR 297   1.10, 36.10, 36.26
Bozkurt v Staatssecretaris van Justitie Case C-434/93
  [1995] ECR I-1475   10.19

BP (Macedonia) [2008] UKAIT 00045	3.46
British Oxygen v Board of Trade [1971] AC 610	42.28
Brogan v UK (1988) 11 EHRR 117	36.46
Bronda v Italy (1998) 33 EHRR 81	16.33
Bundesrepublik Deutschland v B and D Joined Cases C-57/09 and C-101/09 [2011] Imm AR 190, [2011] INLR 133	11.11, 12.15, 12.17, 12.24, 12.25, 12.49, 12.60, 12.61, 12.69
CA v Secretary of State for the Home Department [2004] EWCA Civ 1165, [2004] Imm AR 640	18.27
Calfa Case C-348/96 [1999] ECR I-11	9.7, 9.14, 9.15, 17.71
Carpenter Case C-60/00 [2002] ECR I-6279	9.8
Cesar C v Secretary of State for the Home Department [2010] EWCA Civ 1406	9.37, 9.43
Cetinkaya v Land Baden-Wurttenberg Case C-467/02 [2004] ECR I-10895	10.18, 10.21
Chahal v UK (1996) 23 EHRR 413	13.9, 13.11, 13.13, 23.2, 23.3, 23.36, 23.56, 36.13, 36.19, 36.23, 36.25, 36.27
Charahili v Turkey App No 46605/07, judgment 13 April 2010,	36.24
Charkaoui v Canada (Citizenship and Immigration) [2007] SCR 350, 2007 SCC 9	23.27
Chenge Miao v Secretary of State for the Home Department [2006] EWCA Civ 75	15.27
Chorfi v Belgium 7 August 1996	16.38
Christie and Leachinsky [1947] AC 573	32.27, 32.28, 35.12, 35.17
Ciliz v The Netherlands [2000] 2 FLR 469	16.11, 16.12, 36.84
CM (Somalia) v Secretary of State for the Home Department [2010] EWHC 640 (Admin)	33.28
CN (Burundi) v Secretary of State for the Home Department [2007] EWCA Civ 587	18.34, 18.44, 18.47, 18.54
Collins v Wilcock [1984] 1 WLR 1772	43.5, 43.8
Commission v Belgium Case C-344/95 [1997] ECR I-1035	9.6
Commission v Germany Case C-441/02	9.8
Commission v The Netherlands Case C-50/06	9.6
Conka v Belgium (2002) 34 EHRR 1298	36.38
Co-operative Group (CES) Ltd v Pritchard [2011] EWCA Civ 329	43.5
Cruz Varas v Sweden (1992) 14 EHRR 1	13.9
Cyprus v Turkey (1982) 4 EHRR 482	36.59
D v Home Office [2005] EWCA Civ 38, [2006] 1 WLR 1003	31.39, 34.1

D v UK (1997) 24 EHRR 423	13.34, 18.6–18.11, 18.13, 18.14, 18.21, 18.22, 18.29, 18.33, 18.35, 18.36, 18.38, 18.40, 18.43, 18.59
DA (Colombia) [2009] EWCA Civ 682	2.22
Da Silva and Hoogkamer v The Netherlands (2007) 44 EHRR 34	17.7
Dalia v France, judgment of 19 February 1998	17.59
Danian v Secretary of State for the Home Department [2000] Imm AR 96	11.41
Dbouba v Turkey App No 15916/09, judgment 13 July 2010	36.24
DD (Afghanistan) v Secretary of State for the Home Department [2010] EWCA Civ 1407	12.60, 12.62
DD and AS v Secretary of State for the Home Department (SC/42 and 50/2005), 27 April 2007	23.52, 23.58, 23.78, 23.79
de Boucherville v Mauritius [2008] UKPC 37, 25 BHRC 433	13.21, 13.25
de Freitas v Permanent Secretary of Ministry of Agriculture, Fisheries, Lands and Housing [1999] 1 AC 69	15.18
De Wilde, Ooms and Versyp v Belgium, judgment of 18 June 1971, Series A no 12	36.41
Dereci and Others v Bundesministerium fur Inneres Case C-256/11	8.36, 10.2, 10.4, 10.10, 10.13
Devaseelan v Secretary of State for the Home Department [2002] UKIAT 00702, [2003] Imm AR 1	13.47
Dey Sri Kumar v Secretary of State for the Home Department [1996] Imm AR 521, CA	1.50
DH v Czech Republic (2008) 47 EHRR 3	36.97–36.99
Diatta Case 267/83 [1985] ECR 567, [1986] CMLR 164	8.15
Dickson v UK (2008) 44 EHRR 419	36.86, 36.88, 36.94
Dogan v Sicherheitsdirektion Für Das Bundesland Vorarlberg Case C-383/03 [2005] ECR I-6237, [2005] 3 CMLR 45	9.45, 10.19, 10.20
Dougoz v Greece (2002) 34 EHRR 61	13.22
Douiyeb v The Netherlands (2000) 30 EHRR 790	36.43
DPP v Humphreys [1977] AC 1	1.14
DS (Afghanistan) v Secretary of State for the Home Department [2011] EWCA Civ 305	4.32
DS (India) v Secretary of State for the Home Department [2009] EWCA Civ 544, [2010] Imm AR 81	4.18, 17.21, 17.72
Dudgeon v UK (1981) 4 EHRR 149	15.9
E v Home Office, Claim No 9CL01651, 10 June 2010	39.32, 44.37, 44.47
E and R v Secretary of State for the Home Department [2004] EWCA Civ 49, [2004] QB 1044	21.72, 21.105

EB (Kosovo) v Secretary of State for the Home Department [2008] UKHL 4, [2008] WLR 178	5.39, 17.8, 17.18, 17.19, 17.39, 17.41
Eba v Advocate General for Scotland [2011] UKSC 29, [2011] 3 WLR 179	21.94
El Boujaidi v France (2000) 30 EHRR 223	16.28, 17.50, 17.58
El Boujaidi v France 26 September 1997	16.38
El-Ali v Secretary of State for the Home Department [2002] EWCA Civ 1103; [2003] 1 WLR 95	12.8
Elgafaji v Staatssecretaris van Justitie Case C-465/07 [2009] 1 WLR 2100	14.11, 14.12, 14.14, 14.18
EM (Lebanon) v Secretary of State for the Home Department [2008] UKHL 64, [2009] AC 1198	4.21, 13.49, 16.5
EM and others (Returnees) Zimbabwe CG [2011] UKUT 98 (IAC)	4.44
EN (Serbia) v Secretary of State for the Home Department [2009] EWCA Civ 630, [2010] QB 633	5.17, 11.12, 11.22, 11.24, 12.33, 12.81, 12.89, 12.92, 12.96, 12.105, 19.24, 19.61
Engel v The Netherlands (No 1) (1976) 1 EHRR 647	36.6, 36.16
Enhorn v Sweden (2005) 41 EHRR 30	36.15
EO (Turkey) v Secretary of State for the Home Department [2007] UKAIT 00062	3.22, 15.25, 17.62
Ergat v Stadt Ulm Case C-329/97 [2000] ECR I-1487	10.18, 10.21
Estevez v Spain (App No 56501/00) 10 May 2001	16.24
EV v Secretary of State for the Home Department (SC/67/2008) 7 April 2009	23.1
FA (Iraq) v Secretary of State for the Home Department [2010] EWCA Civ 827	21.129
FA (Iraq) v Secretary of State for the Home Department [2011] UKSC 22	9.70
Farbtuhs v Lithuania App No 4672/02, judgment 2 December 2004	36.64
Fitzpatrick v Sterling Housing Association Ltd [2001] 1 AC 27	16.25
Fouzia Baig v Secretary of State for the Home Department [2005] EWCA Civ 1246	15.10, 21.12
Fox, Campbell and Hartley (1990) 13 EHRR 157	36.38
FS and others (Iran – Christian Converts) Iran CG [2004] UKIAT 00303	11.63
G v Secretary of State for the Home Department [2006] EWCA Civ 771	18.36
Garcia Alva v Germany App No 23541/94, 13 February 2001	35.19, 36.40, 36.42, 36.45
Gaskin v UK (1979) 2 EHRR 245	16.19
Gaygusuz v Austria (1997) 23 EHRR 364	36.99

xl Foreign national prisoners / Table of cases

Gebhard Case C-55 /94 [1995] ECR I-4165	9.20
Germany v Sagulo [1977] ECR 1495; [1977] 2 CMLR 585; (1977) *Times* 3 August	19.64
Ghaidan v Godin-Mendoza [2004] UKHL 30, [2004] 2 AC 557	16.25
GHB v UK [2000] EHRLR 545	16.33
Gillan and Quinton v UK (2010) 50 EHRR 45	15.12
GN (EEA Regulations: Five years' residence) Hungary [2007] UKAIT 00073	9.36
Golder v UK (1975) 1 EHRR 524	36.86
Goremsandu v Secretary of State for the Home Department [1996] Imm AR 250.	9.18
Grant v South-West Trains (1998) BHRC 578	16.24
Greens [2011] CSOH 79	36.59
GS (article 15(c): indiscriminate violence) Afghanistan CG [2009] UKAIT 00044	14.16–14.18
Gul v Switzerland (1996) 22 EHRR 93	16.15, 16.16, 17.2
Gurung (Refugee exclusion clauses especially 1F(b)) Nepal CG [2002] UKIAT 04870, [2003] INLR 133	12.15, 12.16, 12.23, 12.72, 12.114
Guzzardi v Italy (1980) 3 EHRR 333	36.7
GW (EEA Regulation 21 'fundamental interests') [2009] UKAIT 00050	9.12
Hartshorn v Home Office [1999] Prison LR 4	43.16
HB v Secretary of State for the Home Department [2008] EWCA Civ 806	9.18, 9.23, 9.43, 17.60
Herczegfalvy v Austria (1993) 15 EHRR 437, (1993) 15 EHRR 137	36.81
HH (Iraq) [2008] UKAIT 00051	3.38, 3.39
HH (Iraq) v Secretary of State for the Home Department [2009] EWCA Civ 727	3.35, 3.39, 15.10
Hirst v UK (2006) 42 EHRR 41	36.86, 36.88
HJ (Iran) and HT (Cameroon) v Secretary of State for the Home Department [2010] UKSC 31, [2010] 3 WLR 386	11.45, 11.58, 11.59, 11.63, 11.72, 16.26
HK (Turkey) v Secretary of State for the Home Department [2007] EWCA Civ 1357	34.33
HK (Turkey) v Secretary of State for the Home Department [2010] EWCA Civ 583	9.81, 16.30, 16.32, 17.20, 17.49, 17.63
HK and others (minors – indiscriminate violence – forced recruitment by Taliban – contact with family members) Afghanistan CG [2010] UKUT 378 (IAC)	14.19
HLR v France (1998) 26 EHRR 29	13.9, 13.23
HM (Iraq) v Secretary of State for the Home Department [2010] EWCA Civ 1322	17.45, 17.87
HM and others (article 15(c)) Iraq CG [2010] UKUT 331 (IAC)	14.16
Hokkanen v Finland judgment of 23 September 1994, Series A no 299-A, p19, para 54	16.15

Home Office v Mohammed [2011] EWCA Civ 351	42.7, 43.18
Horvath v Secretary of State for the Home Department [2001] 1 AC 489	11.48
HR (Portugal) v Secretary of State for the Home Department [2009] EWCA Civ 371	9.30, 9.32, 9.37, 9.44, 9.47
Huang and Kashmiri v Secretary of State for the Home Department [2007] UKHL 11, [2007] 2 AC 167	10.16, 15.3, 15.19, 15.22, 17.3, 17.13, 17.72
Huang v Secretary of State for the Home Department [2005] EWCA Civ 105, [2006] QB 1	15.15, 17.36
Hurtado v Switzerland, Series A No. A-280, 26 January 2004	36.66
I and others v Secretary of State for the Home Department [2010] EWCA Civ 727	42.52
ID and others v the Home Office [2005] EWCA Civ 38, [2006] 1 WLR 1003	32.2, 42.3
IH (s72; 'Particularly Serious Crime') Eritrea [2009] UKAIT 00012	12.79, 12.82, 12.95
Ilascu v Moldova and Russia (2005) 40 EHRR 46 (Grand Chamber)	36.52, 36.54, 36.58, 36.59
IM (Zambia) v Secretary of State for the Home Department [2008] EWCA Civ 944	17.48
INS v Cardozo-Fonseca (1987) 34 LEd2d 434	11.73
Iqbal v Prison Officers Association [2010] 2 WLR 1054	43.10, 43.11
IR (Sri Lanka) v Secretary of State for the Home Department [2011] EWCA Civ 704, (2011) *Times* 26 August	23.44
Ireland v UK (1979–80) 2 EHRR 25	13.15, 13.16, 36.56
Islam v Secretary of State for the Home Department; R v Immigration Appeal Tribunal ex p Shah [1999] 2 AC 629	11.44, 11.51, 11.52, 11.58, 11.64
Ismoilov and others v Russia (2009) 49 EHRR 1128	36.24
Iwanczuk v Poland (2004) 38 EHRR 8	36.59
J v Secretary of State for the Home Department [2005] EWCA Civ 629, [2005] All ER (D) 359 (May)	13.33, 18.31–18.34, 18.37, 18.41, 18.42, 18.48, 18.50, 18.52
JA (Ivory Coast) v Secretary of State for the Home Department [2009] EWCA Civ 1353, [2010] Imm AR 381	18.21–18.23, 18.57
Jabari v Turkey [2001] INLR 136	13.9
Jain v Secretary of State for the Home Department [2000] Imm AR 76	11.62
Jakupovic v Austria (2003) 38 EHRR 595	17.24, 17.59
Jankov v Germany (dec) No 35112/92	17.89
Jansons v Latvia [2009] EWHC 1845 (Admin)	18.34

Januzi v Secretary of State for the Home Department
  [2006] UKHL 5, [2006] 2 AC 426 — 11.8, 11.50
JB (India) v ECO [2009] EWCA Civ 234 — 16.29
JM v UK [2011] 1 FLR 491, [2010] FCR 648 — 16.24
JN (Cameroon) v Secretary of State for the Home
  Department [2009] EWCA Civ 307 — 3.47
JO (Uganda) and JT (Ivory Coast) v Secretary of State for
  the Home Department [2010] EWCA Civ 10 — 17.9, 17.20, 17.45, 17.46, 17.83
Joseph Grant v UK App No 10606/07, 5 June 1999 — 17.14, 17.58, 17.79
JS (Colombia) v Secretary of State for the Home
  Department [2008] EWCA Civ 1238 — 17.72
Jucius and Juciuviene v Lithuania (2008) 49 EHRR 70 — 16.34
K and Fornah v Secretary of State for the Home
  Department [2007] 1 AC 412 — 11.49, 11.53, 11.58, 12.104
Kacaj v Secretary of State for the Home Department
  [2002] Imm AR 213; [2001] INLR 354 — 11.72, 13.40
Kadiman v Freistaat Bayern Case C-351/95 [1997] ECR I-2133 — 10.21
Kafkaris v Cyprus (2009) 49 EHRR 35 — 13.21
Kaja v Secretary of State for the Home Department [1995]
  Imm AR 1 — 11.74, 11.75
Kalashnikov v Russia (2003) 36 EHRR 34 — 36.59
Karagozlu v Commissioner of Police for the Metropolis
  [2007] 1 WLR 1881 — 43.14
Karanakaran v Secretary of State for the Home
  Department [2000] 3 All ER 449, CA — 11.69, 11.70, 11.74
Kaya v Germany [2007] 2 FCR 527, [2007] Imm AR 802 — 17.50
Kazim Kus v Landeshauptstadt Wiesbaden Case C-237/91 [1993] 2 CMLR 887 — 10.19
KB (Trinidad and Tobago) v Secretary of State for the
  Home Department [2010] EWCA Civ 11 — 15.20, 17.9, 17.19, 17.55
KD (Sri Lanka) v Secretary of State for the Home
  Department [2007] EWCA Civ 1384 — 15.7, 17.37
Keenan v UK (2001) 33 EHRR 38 — 36.48, 36.51, 36.52, 36.64, 36.68, 36.72, 36.73, 43.7
Kehayov v Bulgaria App No 41035/98, judgment 18
  January 2005 — 36.59
KG (Sri Lanka) v Secretary of State for the Home
  Department [2008] EWCA Civ 13 — 8.22, 8.23
KH (Afghanistan) v Secretary of State for the Home
  Department [2009] EWCA Civ 1354 — 18.42
KH (article 15(c) Qualification Directive) Iraq CG [2008]
  UKAIT 00023 — 14.12
Khan v UK (2010) 50 EHRR 47 — 16.17, 16.29, 16.36, 17.38, 17.47, 17.65, 17.89

Khawaja v Secretary of State for the Home Department [1984] AC 74	1.12
Khudobin v Russia (2009) 48 EHRR 22	36.64
KJ (Sri Lanka) v Secretary of State for the Home Department [2009] EWCA Civ 292	12.28, 12.61, 12.64, 12.69, 12.71
KK (Article 1F(c) Turkey) [2004] UKIAT 00101	11.9, 12.25, 12.36, 12.37, 12.48
Kolompar v Belgium (1992) 16 EHRR 197	36.25
Konstatinov v The Netherlands 16351/03, 26 April 2007, [2006] ECHR 336	17.7
KR (Iraq) v Secretary of State for the Home Department [2007] EWCA Civ 514	15.7
Krasniqi v Secretary of State for the Home Department [2006] EWCA Civ 391	16.10, 16.26, 16.36, 16.39, 17.39
Kuddus v Chief Constable of Leicestershire [2002] AC 122	44.40
Kudla v Poland (2002) 35 EHRR 11	13.22
Kudla v Poland App No 30210/96, judgment 26 October 2000	36.54, 36.64
Kugathas v Secretary of State for the Home Department [2003] EWCA Civ 31	16.29, 16.31
Ladd v Marshall [1954] 3 All ER 745, [1954] 1 WLR 1489	21.105
Land Baden-Württemberg v Panagiotis Tsakouridis Case C-145/09 [2011] 2 CMLR 11	9.27, 9.28, 9.45
LB (Jamaica) (judgment given ex tempore on 5 October 2011) [2011] EWCA Civ 1420	21.141
LD (Zimbabwe) v Secretary of State for the Home Department [2010] UKUT 278 (IAC)	17.14, 17.27, 17.52
Lebbink v The Netherlands (2004) 40 EHRR 417	16.5, 16.15, 16.23
Lebon [1987] ECR 2811	8.25
Lee v Secretary of State for the Home Department [2011] EWCA Civ 348	4.16, 4.18, 17.20, 17.30
Levez v TH Jennings Case C-326/96 [1999] All ER (EC) 1, [1998] ECR I-7835	9.70
Lewis v Chief Constable of South Wales Constabulary [1991] 1 All ER 206	32.29
LG (Italy) v Secretary of State for the Home Department [2008] EWCA Civ 190	9.27, 9.28, 9.83
LG and CC (Italy) (EEA Regs) [2009] UKAIT 00024	8.42, 9.20, 9.23, 9.29–9.31, 9.43, 9.44
Lister v Hesley Hall Ltd [2002] 1 AC 214	42.86
Liversidge v Anderson [1942] AC 206	32.3
LO (Jordan) v Secretary of State for the Home Department [2011] EWCA Civ 164	23.18
LO v Secretary of State for the Home Department (SC/73/2009) 4 March 2010	23.34, 23.35

M v Bulgaria App No 41416/08, judgment 26 July 2011	36.21
M v Secretary of State for the Home Department [2003] EWCA Civ 146, [2003] 1 WLR 1980	2.21
M v Secretary of State for Work and Pensions [2006] UKHL 11, [2006] 2 AC 91	16.25
M1 v Secretary of State for the Home Department SC/101/10, 28 February 2011	23.87
MA (Somalia) v Secretary of State for the Home Department [2010] UKSC 49	13.40
Maaouia v France (2001) 33 EHRR 42	23.39, 23.44
MAH (dual nationality-permanent residence) Canada [2010] UKUT 445 (IAC)	8.31
Mahmood v Secretary of State for the Home Department [2001] 1 WLR 861	17.7, 17.37
Malcolm v Home Office [2010] EWHC 3389 (QB)	43.13
Malechkov v Bulgaria App No 57830/00, judgment 28 September 2007	36.59
Malik v Manchester Crown Court [2008] EWHC 1362 (Admin), [2008] 4 All ER 403	23.26
Marcic v Thames Water Utilities Ltd [2003] UKHL 66, [2004] 2 AC 42	15.27
Marckx v Belgium (1979) 2 EHRR 330	16.18, 16.33
Mario Mendes Machado v Secretary of State for the Home Department [2005] EWCA Civ 597	9.8
Marleasing SA v La Comercial Internacional de Alimentación SA (Case C-106/89) [1990] ECR I-4135, [1992] 1 CMLR 305	11.14
Maslov v Austria [2009] INLR 47	16.30, 16.37, 17.24–17.26, 17.43, 17.46, 17.59, 17.65, 17.80, 17.82, 17.86, 17.89
Mason v Ministry of Justice [2008] EWHC 1787 (QB)	28.26
Massoud v Malta App No 24340/08, judgment 27 July 2010	36.21, 36.24, 36.32
Matadeen v Pointu [1999] 1 AC 98	3.27
Mayeka v Belgium (2008) 46 EHRR 23	36.15, 36.48, 36.63
McCarthy v Secretary of State for the Home Department [2008] EWCA Civ 641	8.40, 9.44
McCarthy v Secretary of State for the Home Department Case C-434/09 [2011] 3 CMLR 10	8.40, 9.36, 9.37, 10.8, 10.13
McCotter v UK (1993) 15 EHRR CD 98	36.80
McFarland, Re [2004] UKHL 17, [2004] 1 WLR 1289	34.6
McFeeley v UK (1981) 3 EHHR 161	36.76, 36.77
McMichael v UK (1995) 20 EHRR 205	16.12
McVeigh and others v UK (1981) 5 EHRR 71	36.15, 36.16
Mehemi v France 26 September 1997 (2000) 21 EHRR 801	16.38, 17.47, 17.57
Mehmet v Secretary of State for the Home Department [1977] Imm AR 68, CA	1.37

Mendizabal v France App No 51431/99	19.69
Messina No 2 v Italy App No 25498/94, 28 December 2000	36.80, 36.83
Metock and others v Minister for Justice, Equality and Law Reform Case C-127/08 [2008] ECR I-6241, [2009] QB 318	8.12, 8.22, 8.23, 9.70
MG and VC (EEA Regulations 2006, conducive deportation) Ireland [2006] UKAIT 00053	9.18, 9.27
MH (Iraq) v Secretary of State for the Home Department [2007] EWCA Civ 852	11.72
MH (Syria) v Secretary of State for the Home Department [2009] EWCA Civ 226	12.61, 12.114, 12.115
MI (Fair Trial – Pre-Trial Conditions) Pakistan CG [2002] UKIAT 02239	11.63
MI (Iraq) and AO (Iraq) v Secretary of State for the Home Department [2010] EWHC 764 (Admin)	32.5, 33.32, 33.49
Miller v Independent Assessor [2009] EWCA Civ 609	44.17, 44.28
Milolenko v Estonia (App No 10664/05, 8 October 2009)	33.39, 36.21, 36.32
Minister for Immigration and Multicultural Affairs v Singh [2002] HCA 7	12.37
Mitunga v Belgium App No 13178/03	36.13, 36.17
MJ (Angola) v Secretary of State for the Home Department [2010] EWCA Civ 557, [2010] 1 WLR 2699	17.45, 17.84, 30.38, 30.44
MK (Algeria) v Secretary of State for the Home Department [2010] EWCA Civ 980	44.8, 44.17, 44.22, 44.26, 44.29, 44.34
MNM v Secretary of State for the Home Department [2000] INLR 576	23.39
Modarca v Moldova App No 14437/05 10 August 2007	36.59
Mohammed-Holgate v Duke [1984] AC 437	32.10
Moisejevs v Latvia, App No 64846/01, 15 June 2006	36.59
Moiusel v France (2004) 38 EHRR 34	36.63
Mokrani v France (2003) 40 EHRR 123	16.29
Moustaquim v Belgium (1991) 13 EHRR 802	16.28, 17.47, 17.80
MS (Ivory Coast) v Secretary of State for the Home Department [2007] EWCA Civ 133, [2007] Imm AR 538	16.12, 19.40, 36.84
MSS v Belgium and Greece (2011) 53 EHRR 2, App No 30696/09, 21 January 2011	13.35–13.38, 18.1, 18.59, 36.60–36.62
MT (Ahmadi – HJ (Iran)) Pakistan [2011] UKUT 00277 (IAC)	11.59
MT (Algeria), RB (Algeria) and U (Algeria) v Secretary of State for the Home Department [2007] EWCA Civ 808, [2008] QB 533	23.35, 23.36, 23.52, 23.56

MT (Zimbabwe) v Secretary of State for the Home
  Department [2007] EWCA Civ 455   16.7, 16.29, 16.31,
                                                    16.34
Mugwagwa (s72 – applying statutory presumptions)
  Zimbabwe [2011] UKUT 00338 (IAC)   12.119
Muminov v Russia App No 42502/06, judgment 11
  December 200   36.24
Murray v Ministry of Defence [1988] 1 WLR 692   32.15, 43.9
Muskhadzhiyeva v Belgium App No 41442/07, judgment
  19 January 2010   36.63
Muuse v Home Office [2009] EWHC 1886 (QB)   44.27, 44.46
Muuse v Secretary of State for the Home Department
  [2010] EWCA Civ 453   43.13, 43.28, 44.17,
                                                    44.35, 44.41, 44.42
MW (Democratic Republic of the Congo) v Secretary of
  State for the Home Department [2011] EWCA Civ
  1240   17.45, 44.27
N (Kenya) v Secretary of State for the Home Department
  [2004] EWCA Civ 1094   15.14, 17.55, 17.68,
                                                    17.69, 17.72
N (Uganda) v Secretary of State for the Home
  Department   18.12
N v Secretary of State for the Home Department [2005]
  UKHL 31; [2005] 2 AC 296   18.11–18.15,
                                                    18.18–18.21,
                                                    18.35, 18.36, 18.38,
                                                    18.43, 18.58
N v UK (2008) 47 EHRR 39   13.34, 13.38, 18.12,
                                                    18.16–18.22, 18.35,
                                                    18.36, 18.38–18.40,
                                                    18.43, 18.59, 19.14,
                                                    19.15
NA v UK (2009) 48 EHRR 15   13.41
Nadarajah and Amirthanathan v Secretary of State for the
  Home Department [2003] EWCA Civ 1768, [2004]
  INLR 139   3.18, 15.9, 15.11,
                                                    34.1, 34.2, 34.7,
                                                    36.11
Nasri v France (1996) 21 EHRR 458   16.38, 17.47, 17.57
Nazli v Stadt Nurnberg Case C-340/97 [2000] ECR I-957 9.14, 9.15, 9.17,
                                                    9.18, 9.47, 10.18,
                                                    10.19, 17.71
NB (Jamaica) v Secretary of State for the Home
  Department [2010] EWCA Civ 824   17.91
NF (Ghana) v Secretary of State for the Home
  Department [2008] EWCA Civ 906   4.42
Nhundhu and Chiwera v Secretary of State for the Home
  Department 01TH00613 – CC-21729-2000, 1 June
  2001   16.38, 17.52
Niemietz v Germany (1992) 16 EHRR 97   16.37
Nikolova v Bulgaria App No 31195/96   36.46

Case	Reference
Nowicka v Poland App No 30218/96, judgment 3 December 2002	36.80
Nunez v Norway App No 55597/09 judgment 28 June 2011	17.7, 17.15, 17.29, 17.40, 17.67
Nylund v Finland App No 7110/95	16.11
O v Secretary of State for the Home Department (SC/15/2005) 8 May 2008	23.88, 23.90
Öcalan v Turkey (2005) 41 EHRR 45	13.28
Odawey v ECO [2011] EWCA Civ 840	16.29
Odelola v Secretary of State for the Home Department [2009] UKHL 25	3.15
OH (Serbia) v Secretary of State for the Home Department [2008] EWCA Civ 694, [2009] INLR 109	17.69, 17.72, 17.76
Okafor v Secretary of State for the Home Department [2011] EWCA Civ 499, [2011] 3 CMLR 8	8.6
Olazabal (C100/01) [2002] ECR I-10981	9.13, 9.20
OM (Algeria) v Secretary of State for the Home Department [2010] EWHC 65 (Admin)	31.33
OM (Cuba) v Secretary of State for the Home Department [2004] UKIAT 00120	11.43
Omojudi v UK (2010) 51 EHRR 10	17.14, 17.61, 17.66, 17.79, 17.85, 17.89
Omoregie and others v Norway [2009] Imm AR 170	17.7, 17.37, 17.79
Omotunde (best interests – Zambrano applied – Razgar) Nigeria [2011] UKUT 249 (IAC)	4.25, 4.26, 10.9, 10.14, 17.16, 17.75, 17.77, 17.78
Onur v UK (2009) 49 EHRR 38	15.26, 16.29, 16.36, 16.37, 17.7, 17.14, 17.38, 17.88
OO v Secretary of State for the Home Department (Preliminary Issue (MB) judgment) (SC/51/2006), 27 June 2008	23.39
OP (Colombia) [2008] UKAIT 00074	9.38
OP (Jamaica) [2008] EWCA Civ 440	17.72
O'Reilly v Mackman [1983] 2 AC 237	42.3
Orfanopolous Case C-348/96 [2004] ECR I-5257, [2005] 1 CMLR 18	9.7, 9.8, 9.15, 9.17, 9.18, 9.20, 9.45
Osman v Denmark App No 38058/09, judgment 14 June 2011	16.30, 17.44
Osman v UK (1998) 29 EHRR 245	13.23.
Othman v Secretary of State for the Home Department (SC/15/2005) 26 February	23.58, 23.78, 23.79, 23.84, 23.85, 36.44, 40.26
Ouinas v France (1990) 65 DR 265	36.80
Paladi v Moldova App No 39806/05, judgment 10 March 2009	36.65
PB v Secretary of State for the Home Department [2008] EWHC 364	42.69

xlviii *Foreign national prisoners / Table of cases*

Peers v Greece (2001) 33 EHRR 1192	13.22
Pini et al v Romania (unreported, decision of 22 June 2004)	16.11
Pini et al v Romania [2005] 2 FLR 596, (2005) 40 EHRR 13	16.19
PK (Sri Lanka – risk on return – exclusion clause) Sri Lanka [2004] UKIAT 00089	12.28
Poku v UK (1996) 22 EHRR CD 94	17.7
Polat v Stadt Russelsheim Case C-349/06 [2008] 1 CMLR 9	9.7, 10.18
PR (Sri Lanka), SS (Bangladesh) and TC (Zimbabwe) v Secretary of State for the Home Department [2011] EWCA Civ 988	21.95–21.98
Practice Statement (Administrative Court: Listing and urgent cases) [2002] 1 WLR 810	42.63, 42.66
Pretty v UK (2002) 35 EHRR 1	16.37, 18.4, 36.56
Price v UK App No 33394/96, judgment 10 October 2001	36.63
Principal Reporter v K [2010] UKSC 56, [2011] 1 WLR 18	16.13, 16.14, 16.33
Pushpanathan v Canada (1998) 6 BHRC 387, [1999] INLR 36	12.36, 12.47
QD (Iraq) v Secretary of State for the Home Department (UNHCR intervening) [2009] EWCA Civ 620, [2011] 1 WLR 689	14.11–14.15, 19.10
QJ (Algeria) v Secretary of State for the Home Department [2010] EWCA Civ 1478	1.10, 4.10, 4.18, 17.20
Quaquah CO/4738/98, 15 December 1999	18.2, 18.60, 18.61, 42.87
Quaquah v Group 4 TLQ 340/01 23 May 2001	36.106
Quaquah v Group 4 Securities Ltd (No 2) [2001] Prison LR 318	43.22, 43.24
Quijano v Secretary of State for the Home Department [1997] Imm AR 227	11.58
Quinn v France (1995) 21 EHRR 529	36.14, 36.19, 36.23, 36.25
R (A) Somalia v Secretary of State for the Home Department [2007] EWCA Civ 804, (2007) *Times* 5 September	32.41, 33.9, 33.15, 33.16, 33.20, 33.21, 33.23, 33.34, 33.38, 33.40, 42.64
R (A) v Secretary of State for Health [2009] EWCA Civ 225, [2010] 1 WLR 279	1.39
R (A) v Secretary of State for the Home Department [2007] EWCA Civ 804	32.41, 33.38, 42.64
R (A) v Secretary of State for the Home Department [2008] EWHC 2844 (Admin)	4.42
R (A) v Secretary of State for the Home Department [2010] EWHC 808 (Admin)	33.28
R (A, MA, B, ME) v Secretary of State for the Home Department [2007] EWHC 142 (Admin)	33.15, 33.17, 33.26, 33.41, 33.42
R (AA) v Secretary of State for the Home Department [2010] EWHC 2265 (Admin)	33.7, 33.46

Case	Reference
R (Abbassi) v Secretary of State for Foreign and Commonwealth Affairs [2002] EWCA Civ 1598, [2003] UKHRR 76	32.3
R (Abdi) and others v Secretary of State for the Home Department [2008] EWHC 3166 (Admin)	32.19, 32.34, 34.14, 33.22, 33.27, 34.47
R (Abdi) v Secretary of State for the Home Department [2011] EWCA Civ 242	33.22, 33.27, 33.28
R (Acan) v IAT [2004] EWHC 297 (Admin)	19.56
R (Aitouaret) v Secretary of State for the Home Department [2010] EWHC 3136 (Admin)	31.36
R (Al-Sweady) v Secretary of State for the Home Department [2009] EWHC 2387 (Admin)	42.62
R (Anam) v Secretary of State for the Home Department [2010] EWCA Civ 1140	32.19, 34.27, 34.29
R (Anufrijeva) v Secretary of State for the Home Department and Secretary of State for Work and Pensions [2003] UKHL 36, [2004] 1 AC 604	1.50, 42.7
R (AR) v Secretary of State for the Home Department [2011] EWCA Civ 857	33.28
R (Asghar and another) v Governor of Richmond Remand Centre [1971] 1 WLR 129	33.7
R (B) v Crown Court at Stafford [2006] EWHC 1645 (Admin), [2007] 1 WLR 1524	16.12
R (B) v Secretary of State for the Home Department [2008] EWHC 364 (Admin)	34.2, 34.33, 34.35, 39.34, 44.28, 44.36
R (BA) v Secretary of State for the Home Department [2011] EWHC 2748 (Admin)	32.35, 32.39, 32.40, 33.44, 34.4, 34.31, 36.70, 44.15
R (Bagdanavicius) v Secretary of State for the Home Department [2005] UKHL 38, [2005] 2 AC 668	13.9, 13.23
R (Banda) v Secretary of State for the Home Department [2010] EWHC 2471 (Admin)	4.25, 4.44
R (Bary) v Secretary of State for Justice and Governor of HMP Long Lartin [2010] EWHC 587 (Admin)	36.77
R (Bary) v Secretary of State for the Home Department [2009] EWHC 2068 (Admin)	13.32
R (Bashir) v Secretary of State for the Home Department [2007] EWHC 3017 (Admin)	33.9, 33.15, 33.26, 33.32, 33.49
R (BB (Algeria)) v SIAC [2011] EWHC 2129 (Admin), [2011] UKHRR 997	23.84, 23.96
R (BB (Algeria)) v SIAC [2011] EWHC 336 (Admin), [2011] ACD 48	23.84
R (BE) v Secretary of State for the Home Department [2011] EWHC 690 (Admin)	33.38, 33.48, 34.27, 34.32
R (Belmihoub) v Secretary of State for the Home Department [2011] EWHC 2044 (Admin)	33.18, 33.43

| *Foreign national prisoners / Table of cases*

Case	Reference
R (Bizimana) v Secretary of State for the Home Department [2011] EWHC 1200 (Admin)	37.11
R (Black) v Secretary of State for Justice [2009] UKHL 1	26.11
R (Boroumand) v Secretary of State for the Home Department [2010] EWHC 225 (Admin)	19.47
R (C) v Secretary of State for Justice [2008] EWCA Civ 882, [2009] QB 657	36.53, 36.78, 43.30
R (C) v Secretary of State for the Home Department [2008] EWHC 2448 (Admin)	19.47
R (C) v Secretary of State for the Home Department [2010] EWHC 1089 (Admin)	32.5
R (Cart) v Upper Tribunal [2009] EWHC 3052 (Admin), [2010] 2 WLR 1012	36.34
R (Cart) v Upper Tribunal [2011] UKSC 28, [2011] 2 WLR 36	21.91, 21.92, 21.94, 21.95, 23.2, 23.84, 23.96
R (Choy) v Secretary of State for the Home Department [2011] EWHC 365 (Admin)	32.35, 32.38
R (Christian) v Secretary of State for the Home Department [2006] EWHC 2152 (Admin)	28.43
R (Corner House Research) v SS for Trade and Industry [2005] 1 WLR 260	42.58
R (D and K) v Secretary of State for the Home Department [2006] EWHC 980 (Admin)	34.2, 34.33, 34.35, 39.31, 39.34, 42.20
R (D) v Secretary of State for the Home Department [2004] EWHC 2857 (Admin), [2005] MHLR 17	30.14, 30.16
R (Daley-Murdock) v Secretary of State for the Home Department [2011] EWCA Civ 161	4.43
R (Daly) v Secretary of State for the Home Department [2001] UKHL 26, [2001] 2 AC 532, [2001] 2 WLR 1622	15.18, 36.87, 42.31
R (Daq) v Secretary of State for the Home Department [2009] EWHC 1655 (Admin)	33.26, 33.43
R (Davies) v Secretary of State for the Home Department [2010] EWHC 2656 (Admin)	33.9
R (Doku) v Secretary of State for the Home Department C/2000/3360, 30 November unreported, CA	42.64
R (E) v Secretary of State for the Home Department [2006] EWHC 2500 Admin	44.24
R (EHRC) v Secretary of State for Justice and Secretary of State for the Home Department [2010] EWHC 147 (Admin)	27.26, 27.27
R (Etame) v Secretary of State for the Home Department [2008] EWHC 1140 (Admin), [2008] All ER 798	5.49, 21.23
R (European Roma Rights Centre) v Immigration Officer at Prague Airport [2004] UKHL 55, [2005] 2 AC 1	11.8, 11.21, 11.60
R (Faizovas) v Secretary of State for Justice [2009] EWCA Civ 373	36.63
R (Faulkner) v Secretary of State for Justice [2011] EWCA Civ 349	26.11

R (Faulkner) v Secretary of State for the Home Department [2005] EWHC 2567 (Admin)	32.27, 35.12
R (Fawad and Zia Ahmadi) v Secretary of State for the Home Department [2005] EWCA Civ 1721	16.11
R (Fitzroy George) v Secretary of State for the Home Department [2011] EWHC 3247 (Admin)	7.25, 11.29
R (FM) v Secretary of State for the Home Department [2011] EWCA Civ 807	6.24, 34.2, 34.40, 37.5
R (FR) Iran v Secretary of State for the Home Department [2009] EWHC 2094 (QB)	33.38
R (Francis) v Secretary of State for Justice and Secretary of State for the Home Department [2011] EWHC 1271 (Admin)	28.26, 28.29, 31.36, 36.93
R (Gillan) v Commissioner of Police of the Metropolis [2006] UKHL 12, [2006] 2 AC 307	15.12
R (Graham) v Secretary of State for the Home Department [2007] EWHC 2940 (Admin)	36.63
R (Greenfield) v Secretary of State for the Home Department [2005] UKHL 14	43.26
R (Gyamfi) v Secretary of State for Justice [2010] EWHC 349 (Admin)	27.20
R (H) v London North and East Region Mental Health Review Tribunal [2001] EWCA Civ 415, [2002] QB 1	30.6, 30.27
R (H) v Secretary of State for the Home Department [2005] EWHC 1702 (Admin)	33.22, 33.41
R (Headley and Hindawi) v Secretary of State for the Home Department [2006] UKHL 54	26.13
R (Hicks) v Secretary of State for the Home Department [2005] EWHC 2818 (Admin), [2006] ACD 47	23.13
R (Hindawi) v Secretary of State for Justice [2011] EWHC 830 (QB)	26.16
R (HM Malawi) v Secretary of State for the Home Department [2010] EWHC 1407 (Admin)	16.39, 17.85
R (Hoxha) v Special Adjudicator; R (B) v Immigration Appeal Tribunal [2005] UKHL 19, [2005] 1 WLR 1063	12.136
R (Hussein) v Secretary of State for the Home Department [2009] EWHC 2492 (Admin)	5.11, 31.15, 31.18, 31.19, 31.23, 31.26–31.28, 33.6
R (HXA) v Secretary of State for the Home Department [2010] EWHC 1177 (QB)	3.10, 33.7, 33.28, 33.49, 33.50
R (HY) v Secretary of State for the Home Department [2010] EWHC 1678	33.38
R (I and O) v Secretary of State for the Home Department [2005] EWHC 1025 (Admin)	34.2

R (I) v Secretary of State for the Home Department [2002] EWCA Civ 888, [2003] INLR 196	32.43, 33.4, 33.10, 33.11, 33.14, 33.15, 33.18, 33.20, 33.23, 33.24, 33.31, 33.36, 33.38, 42.81
R (IO) v Secretary of State for the Home Department [2008] EWHC 2596 (Admin)	33.15, 33.17
R (IR) v Shetty [2003] EWHC 3022 (Admin)	30.14, 30.20
R (Iran) v Secretary of State for the Home Department [2005] EWCA Civ 982, [Imm AR 535	21.72–21.74
R (Ismailaj) v Parole Board [2011] EWHC 1020 (Admin)	26.16
R (J) v Secretary of State for the Home Department [2009] EWHC 705 (Admin)	22.19–22.21
R (Jammeh) v Secretary of State for the Home Department [2010] EWHC 1091 (Admin)	33.17
R (Jaswinder Singh) v Secretary of State for the Home Department [2011] EWHC 1402 (Admin)	32.37–32.39
R (Jav) v Secretary of State for the Home Department [2009] EWHC 1779 (Admin).	4.43
R (Jeneba Boima) v Secretary of State for the Home Department [2007] EWHC 2579 (Admin)	17.37
R (Jisha) v Secretary of State for the Home Department [2010] EWHC 2043 (Admin)	20.6, 21.22
R (JJ) v Secretary of State for the Home Department [2007] UKHL 45, [2008] 1 AC 385	23.26, 36.5
R (JS (Sri Lanka)) v Secretary of State for the Home Department [2010] UKSC 15	12.15, 12.16, 12.21, 12.22, 12.26, 12.54, 12.64, 12.66–12.68, 12.71–12.73
R (Kambadzi) v Secretary of State for the Home Department [2011] UKSC 23, [2011] 1 WLR 1299	32.10–32.12, 32.14, 32.20–32.23, 32.27, 32.37, 32.40, 33.1, 33.4, 33.18, 34.2, 34.6–34.10, 34.35, 34.36, 35.5, 35.17, 35.27, 35.30–35.33
R (Kanidagli) v Secretary of State for the Home Department [2004] EWHC 1585 (Admin)	43.18
R (Karas and Miladinovic) v Secretary of State for the Home Department [2006] EWHC 747 (Admin)	33.7
R (Khadir) v Secretary of State for the Home Department [2005] UKHL 39, [2006] 1 AC 207	31.4, 31.10, 31.37–31.39, 33.1, 33.4, 42.77
R (Khan) v Secretary of State for the Home Department and the Upper Tribunal [2011] EWHC 2763 (Admin)	21.96

R (Kluxen, Rostas, Adam) v Secretary of State for the Home Department [2010] EWCA Crim 1081, [2011] 1 WLR 218	2.2, 2.4, 2.12, 2.14, 9.10, 9.18, 9.24, 9.49
R (Konan) v Secretary of State for the Home Department [2004] EWHC 22 (Admin)	34.2, 36.44
R (Krstic) v Secretary of State for Justice [2010] EWHC 2125 (Admin)	29.30
R (Kullas) v Secretary of State for the Home Department [2009] EWHC 735 (Admin)	31.33
R (L) v Secretary of State for the Home Department [2003] EWCA Civ 25, [2003] 1 WLR 1230	22.5
R (Lekstaka) v IAT [2005] EWHC 745 (Admin)	16.34
R (Limbu) v Secretary of State for the Home Department [2008] EWHC 2261 (Admin)	3.17, 15.9
R (Limbuela) v Secretary of State for the Home Department [2005] UKHL 66, [2006] 1 AC 396	13.10, 36.67
R (Lumba and Mighty) v Secretary of State for the Home Department [2011] UKSC 12, [2011] 2 WLR 671	3.18, 4.34, 15.9, 15.10, 15.11, 31.33, 31.34, 31.39, 32.3–32.6, 32.10–32.12, 32.14, 32.19, 32.21, 32.24, 32.25, 32.27, 32.28, 32.31, 32.32, 32.35–32.38, 32.40, 32.43, 33.4, 33.5, 33.8, 33.11, 33.14, 33.16, 33.17, 33.20, 33.21, 33.23, 33.24, 33.27, 33.29–33.34, 33.36, 33.37, 33.43, 33.44, 33.50, 34.1, 34.2, 34.6–34.9, 34.12–34.14, 34.27, 34.29, 34.35, 34.51, 34.55, 35.5, 35.17, 35.33, 38.9, 40.11, 42.27, 42.28, 42.77, 42.83, 44.9, 44.11, 44.14, 44.32, 44.43, 44.44
R (M) v London Borough of Hammersmith and Fulham and others [2010] EWHC 562 (Admin)	30.36
R (M) v Nottinghamshire Healthcare NHS Trust [2002] EWCA Civ 1728, [2003] 1 All ER 784	30.20
R (M) v Secretary of State for the Home Department [2008] EWCA Civ 307	32.43, 33.15, 33.20, 33.23, 33.25, 33.27, 33.43

R (M) v Secretary of State for the Home Department
  [2010] EWHC 357 (Admin) — 6.24
R (MA and TT) v Secretary of State for the Home
  Department [2010] EWHC 2350 (Admin) — 33.15, 33.50
R (Madan) v Secretary of State for the Home Department
  [2007] EWCA Civ 770 — 42.65
R (Malcolm) v Secretary of State for Justice [2011] EWCA
  Civ 1538 — 36.78
R (Manhire) v Secretary of State for Justice [2009] EWHC
  1788 (Admin) — 27.18, 27.20
R (Mansoor) v Secretary of State for the Home
  Department [2011] EWHC 832 (Admin) — 15.14, 17.16
R (Mayaya and others) v Secretary of State for the Home
  Department [2011] EWHC 3088 (Admin) — 19.24, 19.45, 19.47
R (MC) Algeria v Secretary of State for the Home
  Department [2010] EWCA Civ 347 — 33.44, 34.27, 34.29
R (McAlinden) v Secretary of State for Justice [2010]
  EWHC 1557 (Admin) — 28.26
R (McFarlane) v Secretary of State for the Home
  Department [2010] EWHC 3081 (Admin) — 38.11, 38.16, 38.22
R (MD and others) v Secretary of State for the Home
  Department [2011] EWCA Civ 1238 — 33.47, 34.4, 34.30, 36.66

R (Medical Justice) v Secretary of State for the Home
  Department [2010] EWHC 1925 (Admin) — 42.28, 42.33
R (MH) v Secretary of State for the Home Department
  [2010] EWCA Civ 1112, [2009] EWHC 2506 (Admin) — 32.42, 33.9, 33.15–33.17, 38.16, 42.62
R (Mithokozisi) v Secretary of State for the Home
  Department [2004] EWHC 2964 (Admin) — 16.19
R (MM Somalia) v Secretary of State for the Home
  Department [2009] EWHC 2353 (Admin) — 33.28
R (MM) v Secretary of State for the Home Department
  [2010] EWHC 3288 (Admin) — 33.15
R (MMH) v Secretary of State for the Home Department
  [2007] EWHC 2134 (Admin) — 33.15, 33.43, 34.2, 34.27

R (Mounir Raki) v Secretary of State for the Home
  Department [2011] EWHC 2421(Admin) — 33.17. 33.30, 33.37
R (Mount Cook Land Ltd) v Westminster CC [2003]
  EWCA Civ 1346 — 42.57
R (MR (Pakistan)) v Same [2011] UKSC 28; [2011] 3 WLR
  107 — 23.2
R (MS) v AIT and Secretary of State for the Home
  Department [2011] EWCA Civ 938 — 32.4, 32.28, 35.17
R (MT) v Secretary of State for the Home Department
  and others [2008] EWHC 1788 (Admin) — 43.23
R (Munjaz) v Mersey Care NHS Trust [2005] UKHL 58,
  [2006] 2 AC 148 — 3.18, 15.11, 34.7
R (Murungaru) v Secretary of State for the Home
  Department [2008] EWCA Civ 1015, [2009] INLR 180 — 23.23, 23.26

R (Mwanza) v London Borough of Greenwich and London Borough of Bromley [2010] EWHC 1462 (Admin)	30.35, 30.36
R (MXL and others) v Secretary of State for the Home Department [2010] EWHC 2397 (Admin)	4.10, 32.38, 36.79, 37.5, 37.11
R (N) v Secretary of State for the Home Department [2009] EWHC 1581 (Admin)	19.45, 19.46, 36.59, 36.69
R (NAB) v Secretary of State for the Home Department [2010] EWHC 3137 (Admin)	33.9, 33.18, 33.38, 44.29
R (Nasseri) v Secretary of State for the Home Department [2009] UKHL 23 [2010] 1 AC 1.	13.9
R (Noone) v Governor of HMP Drake Hall and another [2010] UKSC 30	26.4
R (Nukajam) v Secretary of State for the Home Department [2010] EWHC 20 (Admin)	6.24, 34.2
R (NXT) v Secretary of State for the Home Department [2011] EWHC 969 (Admin)	4.32, 31.18, 32.42, 37.3, 37.11
R (OM) v Secretary of State for the Home Department [2011] EWCA Civ 909	34.27, 34.28, 42.69, 44.12, 44.15
R (Omoregbee) v Secretary of State for Justice and another [2011] EWCA Civ 559	27.19, 28.9
R (Oppong) v Secretary of State for the Home Department [2008] EWHC 2596 (Admin)	33.38
R (Oswald Thomas) v Secretary of State for the Home Department [2009] EWHC 1008 (Admin)	31.11
R (P and Q) v Secretary of State for the Home Department [2001] EWCA Civ 1151, [2001] 1 WLR 2002	36.80, 36.93
R (Pankina and Others) v Secretary of State for the Home Department [2010] EWCA Civ 719, [2010] 3 WLR 1526	3.15, 3.18
R (Polanco) v Secretary of State for the Home Department [2009] EWHC 826 (Admin)	42.64
R (Prosser) v Secretary of State for the Home Department [2010] EWHC 845 (Admin), [2010] ACD 57	18.34
R (Q) v Secretary of State for the Home Department and Governor of HMP Long Lartin [2006] EWHC 2690 (Admin)	33.22
R (Qaderi) v Secretary of State for the Home Department [2008] EWHC 1033 (Admin)	33.15
R (Quila) v Secretary of State for the Home Department [2011] UKSC 45, [2011] 3 WLR 836	15.7, 15.22, 15.27, 15.28, 17.72
R (Raed Salah Mahajna) v Secretary of State for the Home Department [2011] EWHC 2481 (Admin)	1.8, 32.29, 33.8, 35.12, 35.17

lvi *Foreign national prisoners / Table of cases*

R (Rangwani) v Secretary of State for the Home Department [2011] EWHC 516 (Admin)	32.38, 33.49, 38.6, 38.18, 38.22
R (Razai and others) v Secretary of State for the Home Department [2010] EWHC 3151 (Admin)	41.18, 41.22, 41.23
R (Razgar) v Secretary of State for the Home Department [2004] UKHL 27, [2004] 2 AC 368	15.1, 15.2, 15.4, 15.16, 15.19, 18.53, 18.54, 18.56, 22.7
R (RD) v Secretary of State for the Home Department [2008] EWCA Civ 676	36.81
R (Reece-Davis) v Secretary of State for the Home Department [2011] EWHC 561 (Admin)	4.24
R (Roberts) v Parole Board [2005] UKHL 45, [2005] AC 738	23.26
R (S Afghanistan) v Secretary of State for the Home Department [2007] EWCA Civ 546	15.11
R (S) v Chief Constable of the South Yorkshire Police [2004] 1 WLR 2196	36.103, 36.104
R (S) v Secretary of State for the Home Department [2011] EWHC 2120 (Admin)	1.50, 31.7, 31.11, 33.26, 33.44, 34.2, 34.27–34.29, 34.31, 34.36, 36.67, 36.70, 42.27
R (S, C and D) v Secretary of State for the Home Department [2007] EWHC 1654 (Admin)	33.1, 34.2, 36.78, 36.105, 37.7
R (S, H, Q) v Secretary of State for the Home Department [2009] EWCA Civ 334	15.10
R (Saadi) v Secretary of State for the Home Department [2001] EWCA Civ 1512, [2002] 1 WLR 356	34.6
R (Schmelz) v IAT [2003] EWHC 1859 (Admin)	24.15
R (Sezek) v Secretary of State for the Home Department [2001] EWCA Civ 795, [2002] 1 WLR 348, [2001] INLR 675	40.35, 42.64
R (Sezek and Samaroo) v Secretary of State for the Home Department [2001] EWCA Civ 1139, [2002] INLR 55, [2001] UKHRR 1150	10.19, 15.14, 17.20, 17.55
R (Shaheen) v Secretary of State for Justice [2008] EWHC 1195 (Admin)	29.9, 29.22
R (Shields) v Secretary of State for Justice [2008] EWHC 3102 (Admin)	29.14
R (Sino) v Secretary of State for the Home Department [2011] EWHC 2249 (Admin)	33.9, 33.16, 33.18, 33.37, 42.45, 42.52, 42.69, 44.13, 44.15
R (Sivakumar) v Secretary of State for the Home Department [2001] EWCA Civ 1196, [2002] INLR 310	11.56

R (SK) v Secretary of State for the Home Department [2008] EWCA Civ 1204, [2008] EWHC 98 (Admin), [2009] 1 WLR 1527	32.4, 33.38
R (SM) v Secretary of State for the Home Department [2011] EWHC 338 (Admin)	4.22, 37.6
R (Smith and West) v Parole Board [2005] UKHL 1	26.11
R (Solomon) v Secretary of State for the Home Department [2011] EWHC 3075 (Admin)	32.38
R (South West London and St George's Mental Health NHS Trust) v W [2002] All ER (D) 62 (Aug)	30.14
R (Spinks) v Secretary of State for the Home Department [2005] EWCA Civ 275	36.63
R (Suppiah) v Secretary of State for the Home Department [2011] EWHC 2 (Admin)	4.10, 4.18, 4.27, 34.2, 36.89, 37.5, 37.7, 37.8
R (T) v Secretary of State for the Home Department [2007] EWHC 3074 (Admin)	38.10
R (T) v Secretary of State for the Home Department [2010] EWHC 668 (Admin)	33.47, 34.2, 34.27
R (Thanigaikumaran) v Secretary of State for the Home Department [2011] EWHC 1701 (Admin)	11.28
R (Tientchu) v IAT [2000] EWCA Civ 385	11.63
R (TN) Vietnam v Secretary of State for the Home Department [2010] EWHC 2184 (Admin)	34.27
R (Tozlukaya) v Secretary of State for the Home Department [2006] EWCA Civ 379, [2006] Imm AR 417	15.11, 18.34, 18.37, 18.41, 18.42, 18.50, 18.56
R (TS) v Secretary of State for the Home Department [2010] EWHC 2614 (Admin)	4.30, 37.5
R (Turkoglu) v Secretary of State for the Home Department [1988] QB 398	40.33
R (U) v Special Immigration Appeals Commission; R (C) v Same [2009] EWHC 3052 (Admin), [2010] 2 WLR 1012	23.2, 23.84, 23.96
R (Ullah) v Secretary of State for the Home Department [2003] EWCA Civ 1366	1.12
R (Ullah) v Special Adjudicator [2004] UKHL 26, [2004] 2 AC 323	13.9, 13.42–13.48, 13.50, 23.56
R (V) v AIT [2009] EWHC 1902 (Admin)	1.13, 1.14, 3.29
R (Vallaj) v Special Adjudicator [2001] EWCA Civ 782, [2001] INLR 342	11.49
R (Vovk and Datta) v Secretary of State for the Home Department [2006] EWHC 3386 (Admin)	32.34, 32.39, 33.49
R (Wang) v Secretary of State for the Home Department [2009] EWHC 1578 (Admin)	33.9, 33.26, 33.38, 33.43
R (Wellington) v Secretary of State for the Home Department [2008] UKHL 72 [2009] 1 AC 335	13.9, 13.21, 13.25

R (Wilkinson) v RMO Broadmoor Hospital and others [2002] 1 WLR 419	42.62
R (Willcox) v Secretary of State for Justice [2009] EWHC 1483 (Admin)	29.12
R (Wood) v Commissioner of Police of the Metropolis [2009] HRLR 25	36.76
R (X) v Secretary of State for the Home Department [2001] WLR 740	30.44
R (X) v Secretary of State for the Home Department [2006] EWHC 1208 (Admin)	16.39
R (Yogathas) v Secretary of State for the Home Department [2003] 1 AC 920	22.5
R v Araoye [2007] EWCA Crim 1922	2.17
R v Asfaw [2008] UKHL 31; [2008] 1 AC 1061	2.18, 11.21
R v Bennabas [2005] EWCA Crim 2113; [2006] 1 Cr App R (S) 94	2.13, 2.16, 2.17
R v Birch (1990) 90 Cr App R 78	30.11
R v Bouchereau [1978] QB 732, [1978] 2 WLR 250, (1978) 66 Cr App R 202	2.11, 9.10, 9.14, 9.17, 9.18
R v Bozat [1997] 1 Cr App R (S) 270	2.10
R v Carmona [2006] EWCA Crim 508, [2006] 1 WLR 2264	2.12, 2.20, 2.22, 2.23
R v Chapman [2000] Cr App R 77	26.7
R v Chief Constable Thames Valley Police ex p Cotton [1990] IRLR 344	44.14
R v Cooper [2010] EWCA Crim 2335	30.13
R v Deputy Governor of Parkhurst Prison ex p Hague, Weldon v Home Office [1992] 1 AC 58	43.11, 43.19
R v Drew [2003] UKHL 25	30.10
R v Gladys Frimpong [2011] EWCA Crim 1705	2.2, 2.17
R v Governor of Brixton Prison ex p Soblen [1963] 2 QB 243	1.10
R v Governor of Brockhill Prison ex p Evans [1999] QB 1043	44.22
R v Governor of Brockhill Prison ex p Evans (No 2) [2001] 2 AC 19	32.30, 36.8, 36.12, 43.10, 44.29
R v Governor of Durham Prison ex p Hardial Singh [1984] 1 WLR 704	23.7, 23.87, 31.3, 31.27, 31.30, 31.39, 32.1, 32.5, 32.12, 32.36, 32.38–32.40, 33.1, 33.3–33.5, 33.8–33.10, 33.13, 33.14, 33.17–33.19, 33.26, 33.32, 33.43, 33.45, 33.47, 33.48, 34.13, 34.40, 36.34, 36.34, 42.77, 42.78, 43.12

R v Governor of Pentonville Prison ex p Fernandez [1971] 1 WLR 987	11.72
R v Home Secretary ex p Khawaja [1984] AC 74	32.2, 32.3, 32.7
R v IAT ex p Jonah [1985] Imm AR 7	11.44
R v IAT ex p Martinez-Tobon [1988] Imm AR 319, CA	1.10
R v IAT ex p Patel [1988] AC 910, HL	1.11
R v IAT ex p Singh [1986] 1 WLR 910	3.10
R v Inland Revenue Commissioners ex p Rossminster Ltd [1980] AC 952	32.3
R v Kandhari (unreported), 24 April 1979, CA (Crim Div)	2.13
R v LAB ex p Hughes (1992) 5 Admin L Rep 623	42.53
R v Lang and others [2005] EWCA Crim 2864	26.7
R v Liban Abdi [2007] EWCA Crim 1913, [2008] 1 Cr App R (S) 87	2.8, 2.21
R v Mabengo and others [2008] EWCA Crim 1699	2.10
R v Momodu [2008] EWCA Crim 1882	2.17
R v Mullen [2000] QB 520, [1999] 3 WLR 777, CA	1.10
R v Nazari and others [1980] 1 WLR 1366	2.9, 2.11
R v Ntlemo [2006] EWCA Crim 2514	2.17
R v Offen (No 2) [2000] WLR 253	26.7
R v Oldham Justices ex p Cawley [1997] QB 1	42.74, 42.79
R v Ovieriakhi [2009] EWCA Crim 452, [2009] 2 Cr App R (S) 91	2.17
R v Parole Board ex p Bradley [1991] 1 WLR 134	26.22
R v Parole Board ex p White (1994) *Times* 30 December QBD	26.22
R v Refugee Convention ex p Sivakumaran [1988] AC 958	11.77
R v Rodney [1996] 2 Cr App R (S) 230	2.10
R v Romeka Brown [2010] EWCA Crim 1807, [2011] 1 Cr App R (S) 79	2.4, 2.11, 2.17
R v Secretary of State for Foreign and Commonwealth Affairs ex p Rees Mogg [1994] QB 552	42.33
R v Secretary of State for the Home Department ex p Adan [2001] 2 AC 477	11.5
R v Secretary of State for the Home Department ex p Alabi [1998] COD 103	42.61
R v Secretary of State for the Home Department ex p Brezinski and Glowacka (unreported), judgment 19 July 1996	41.55
R v Secretary of State for the Home Department ex p Cheblak [1991] 1 WLR 890	42.77
R v Secretary of State for the Home Department ex p Dinc [1999] Imm AR 380	2.21
R v Secretary of State for the Home Department ex p Doody [1993] 1 AC 531	42.30
R v Secretary of State for the Home Department ex p Figueriredo [1993] Imm AR 606 QBD	2.21
R v Secretary of State for the Home Department ex p Hargreaves [1997] WLR 906	24.9
R v Secretary of State for the Home Department ex p Hosenball [1977] 1 WLR 766	1.8

R v Secretary of State for the Home Department ex p Jeyeanthan [2000] 1 WLR 354, [1999] 3 All ER 231	3.47
R v Secretary of State for the Home Department ex p Kelso [1998] INLR 603, QBD	42.64
R v Secretary of State for the Home Department ex p Leech (No 2) [1994] QB 198	24.8
R v Secretary of State for the Home Department ex p Marchon [1993] Imm AR 384	9.18
R v Secretary of State for the Home Department ex p Mbanza [1996] Imm AR 136	11.42
R v Secretary of State for the Home Department ex p Minteh (Lamin) (unreported) Judgment 8 March 1997, CA	41.55
R v Secretary of State for the Home Department ex p Mobin Jagot (2000) Imm AR 414	16.33
R v Secretary of State for the Home Department ex p Muboyayi [1991] 3 WLR 704	42.76
R v Secretary of State for the Home Department ex p Obi [1997] 1 WLR 1498, [1997] Imm AR 420, QBD	1.28
R v Secretary of State for the Home Department ex p Oladehinde [1991] 2 AC 254	3.13
R v Secretary of State for the Home Department ex p Read [1989] AC 1014	29.12
R v Secretary of State for the Home Department ex p Robinson [1997] 3 WLR 1162	21.111
R v Secretary of State for the Home Department ex p Robinson [1998] QB 929	11.50, 12.114
R v Secretary of State for the Home Department ex p Sayed Nasser Alavi-Veighoe, [1990] COD 39, (1989) *Times* 22 August	3.27
R v Secretary of State for the Home Department ex p Turkoglu [1998] 1 QB 398	42.64
R v Secretary of State for Transport ex p Factortame (No 2) [1991] 1 AC 603.	8.2, 42.24
R v Servite Houses ex p Goldsmith (2001) 33 HLR 35	42.20
R v Special Adjudicator and Secretary of State for the Home Department ex p B [1998] Imm AR 182, [1998] INLR 315	33.18
R v Staines Magistrates Court ex p Westfallen [1998] 1 WLR 652	1.10
R v Thomas Clarke [2008] EWCA Crim 3023	2.10
R v Uxbridge Magistrates' Courts and Another ex p Adimi [2000] WLR 434	2.18
RA (Sri Lanka) v Secretary of State for the Home Department [2008] EWCA Civ 1210	18.38, 18.41, 18.42, 18.47, 18.58
Racz v Home Office [1994] AC 45	43.14
Radovanovic v Austria (2005) 41 EHRR 6	17.45, 17.61, 17.80, 17.89
Ramirez v Minister of Employment and Immigration [1992] FC 306 (FCA)	12.23

Table of cases lxi

Case	References
Raninen v Finland (1998) 26 EHRR 563	13.15, 36.50, 36.63, 36.76, 36.85
Rashford v Home Office [2010] EWHC 2200 (QB)	38.20, 38.21
Ravichandran v Secretary of State for the Home Department [1996] Imm AR 97, CA	11.69, 11.70
Raza v Bulgaria App No 31465/08, 11 February 2010	36.32
RB (Algeria) and others v Secretary of State for the Home Department [2009] UKHL 10, [2010] 2 AC 110, [2009] 2 WLR 512	12.74, 13.14, 23.40, 23.41, 23.44, 23.99
RC v Sweden App No 41827/07, 9 March 2010	13.41
Reid v Secretary of State for the Home Department [2010] EWCA Civ 138	17.91
Reinprecht v Austria App No 67175/01	36.42
RG (Nepal) v Secretary of State for the Home Department [2010] UKUT 273 (IAC)	16.4, 16.30, 16.36, 17.67, 17.70, 17.77
Ribitsch v Austria (1996) 21 EHRR 573	36.49
RK (India) v Secretary of State for the Home Department [2010] UKUT 421 (IAC)	8.25
Roberts v Nottinghamshire Healthcare NHS Trust [2008] EWHC 1934	23.26
Rohde v Denmark (2006) 43 EHRR 17	13.15
Rookes v Barnard [1964] AC 1129	44.31, 44.39, 44.40
Roosli v Germany App No 28118/95, 15 May 1996	16.24
Rose (Automatic deportation- exception 3) Jamaica [2011] UKUT 276 (IAC)	8.29
RS (Zimbabwe) v Secretary of State for the Home Department [2010] UKUT 363 (IAC)	18.26
RT (Zimbabwe) v Secretary of State for the Home Department [2010] EWCA Civ 1285	11.59
RU (Bangladesh) v Secretary of State for the Home Department [2011] EWCA Civ 651	3.20, 5.13, 17.69, 17.73, 17.74, 17.76
RU (Sri Lanka) v Secretary of State for the Home Department [2008] EWCA Civ 753	17.37
Rusu v Austria (2009) 49 EHRR 28	36.32, 36.33
Rutili v Minister for the Interior Case 36/75 [1975] ECR 1219	8.2
S v UK (1986) 47 DR 274	16.24, 16.29
S and others v Secretary of State for the Home Department [2007] EWHC 1654 (Admin)	43.23
Saad, Diriye and Osorio v Secretary of State for the Home Department [2001] EWCA Civ 2008	11.6, 11.69, 12.122
Saadi v Italy (2009) 49 EHRR 30, [2008] Imm AR 519	13.9, 13.11, 13.41, 23.56, 32.28
Saadi v Secretary of State for the Home Department [2002] UKHL 41, [2002] 1 WLR 3131	32.27, 32.31, 35.17

Saadi v UK App No 13229/03 (2008) 47 EHRR 17, 29 January 2008	35.13, 35.18, 35.20, 36.13, 36.15, 36.19, 36.22, 36.28, 36.30, 36.37, 36.38
SB (Cessation and exclusion) Haiti [2005] UKIAT 00036	12.83, 12.95, 12.97, 12.134
SC (Mental Patient: Habeas Corpus), In Re [1996] QB 599	31.21
Schmelz v IAT [2004] EWCA Civ 29	9.18
SD v Greece No 53541/07 11 June 2009	36.60
Secretary of State for Education and Science v Tameside Metropolitan Borough Council [1977] AC 1014	3.10
Secretary of State for the Home Department v AF (No 3) [2009] UKHL 28, [2010] 2 AC 269	23.26, 23.42, 23.43
Secretary of State for the Home Department v BC [2009] EWHC 2927 (Admin), [2010] 1 WLR 1542	23.42
Secretary of State for the Home Department v BK [2010] UKUT 328	17.75
Secretary of State for the Home Department v Hicks [2006] EWCA Civ 400, [2006] INLR 203	23.13
Secretary of State for the Home Department v K; Fornah v Secretary of State for the Home Department [2006] UKHL 46, [2007] 1 AC 412	11.11, 11.53, 11.58
Secretary of State for the Home Department v M [2004] EWCA Civ 324, [2004] 2 All ER 863	23.4
Secretary of State for the Home Department v MB [2007] UKHL 46, [2008] 1 AC 440	23.26, 23.38, 23.39, 23.41, 23.84
Secretary of State for the Home Department v MK [2010] UKUT 281	5.13, 17.75
Secretary of State for the Home Department v Rehman [2003] AC 153 (CA)	23.4, 23.16, 23.73, 23.74, 23.76, 23.77, 23.80, 23.99
Secretary of State for the Home Department v ST (Eritrea) [2010] EWCA Civ 643	12.77
Secretary of State for Work and Pensions v Maria Dias Case C-325/09 [2011] 3 CMLR 40	8.10, 9.34, 9.36, 9.45
Secretary of State for Work and Pensions v Taous-Lassal Case C-162/09	8.42, 9.37, 9.38
Sedrati, Buitrago-Lopez and Arangatu v Secretary of State for the Home Department [2001] EWHC (Admin) 418	31.34, 32.34, 32.36, 32.37
Selmouni v France (2000) 29 EHRR 403	13.18, 13.19, 36.71, 43.7
Sen v The Netherlands (2003) 36 EHRR 7	15.1, 16.16
Senthuran v Secretary of State for the Home Department [2004] EWCA Civ 950	16.8, 16.30

Sepet v Secretary of State for the Home Department [2003] UKHL 15, [2003] 1 WLR 856	11.5, 11.8, 11.65, 11.67
Sevince v Staatssecretaris van Justitie Case C-192/89 [1992] 2 CMLR 57	10.19, 10.20
Sezen v The Netherlands (2006) 43 EHRR 30	5.39, 10.19, 17.12, 17.14, 17.57, 17.86
Shah v Barnet London Borough Council [1983] 2 AC 309	1.38
Sheekh v The Netherlands (2007) 45 EHRR 50	13.9
Singh v ECO (New Delhi) [2004] EWCA Civ 1075, [2005] QB 608	16.11, 16.15, 16.19, 16.20, 16.23
Singh v Minister of Citizenship and Immigration [2005] FCA 125, (2005) 253 DLR (4th) 606	12.23
Sisojeva v Latvia (2007) 45 EHRR 33	19.69
Sivakumaran v Secretary of State for the Home Department [1988] AC 958	11.8, 11.20, 11.21, 11.39, 11.71, 11.72, 11.73, 13.40
SK (Article 1F(a) – exclusion) Zimbabwe [2010] UKUT 327 (IAC)	12.27
SK (Zimbabwe) v Secretary of State for the Home Department [2008] EWHC 98 (Admin), [2008] EWCA Civ 1204, [2009] 1 WLR 1527	32.5, 32.19, 35.31
SL (Vietnam) v Secretary of State for the Home Department [2010] EWCA Civ 225	3.35, 4.39, 15.10
Slivenko v Latvia (2004) 39 EHRR 24	16.29, 16.37, 36.19, 36.41
SM (India) [2009] EWCA Civ 1426	8.25
Soering v UK (1989) 11 EHRR 439	13.7–13.9, 13.15, 13.17, 13.27, 13.28, 13.40, 13.46, 18.11
Soyege, Re [2005] EWHC 2648 (QB)	29.13
SS (India) v Secretary of State for the Home Department [2010] EWCA Civ 388	4.42, 4.43, 15.20, 17.9, 17.19
SS (Libya) v Secretary of State for the Home Department SC/56/2009	12.57, 12.60
Stafford v UK (2002) 35 EHRR 32	26.6, 26.11
Stenning v Home Office [2002] EWCA Civ 793	43.16
Storozhenko v Secretary of State for the Home Department [2001] EWCA Civ 895, [2002] Imm AR 329.	11.56
Sufi and Elmi v UK App Nos 8319/07 and 11449/07 28 June 2011	13.10, 13.38, 14.7, 14.20, 18.1, 18.59
Sunday Times v UK (1979) EHRR 245	36.12
Surendran v Secretary of State for the Home Department, 12 July 1999 HX/70901/98, reproduced in MNM (Surendran guidelines for Adjudicators) Kenya 00TH02423, [2000] UKIAT 00005	21.60

T (Wardship: Impact of Police Intelligence), Re [2009] EWHC 2440 (Fam), [2010] FLR 1048	23.26
T v Immigration Officer [1996] AC 742	12.30
T v Secretary of State for the Home Department (SC/31/2005) 22 March 2010	23.1
Tabesh v Greece No 8256/07 26 November 2009	36.60
Taliadorou and Stylianou v Cyprus App Nos 39627/05 and 39631/05, judgment 16 October 2008	36.84
Tan Te Lam and others v Superintendant of Tai A Chau Detention Centre [1997] AC 97.	31.21, 32.4, 32.9, 32.43, 33.4, 33.34, 42.77
Tariq v Home Office [2011] UKSC 35, [2011] 3 WLR 322	23.23, 23.26
Taylor v Chief Constable of Thames Valley [2004] 1 WLR 3155	32.29
TB (Jamaica) v Secretary of State for the Home Department [2008] EWCA Civ 977	12.111
Tehrani and others v Turkey App Nos 32940/08, 41626/08, 43616/08, 13 April 2010,	36.24
Teixera Case 480/08 [2010] 2 CMLR 50	8.8, 9.37
Thompson and Hsu v Commissioner of Police for the Metropolis [1998] QB 498	44.8, 44.17, 44.20, 44.22, 44.25, 44.29, 44.30, 44.32, 44.33, 44.45
Three Rivers District Council and others v Governor and Company of the Bank of England [2003] 2 AC 1	43.13
TL and Others (sur place activities – risk) Burma CG [2009] UKAIT 00017	11.40
TM (Zimbabwe) v Secretary of State for the Home Department [2010] EWCA Civ 916	11.59
Tozlukaya v Secretary of State for the Home Department [2006] EWCA Civ 379, [2006] Imm AR 417	18.36, 18.50
TR (reg 8(3) EEA Regs 2006) Sri Lanka [2008] UKAIT 4	8.26
TS v Secretary of State for the Home Department and Northamptonshire CC [2010] EWHC 2614 (Admin)	4.25, 4.28, 4.29
Tsakouridis Case C-145/ 09 [2011] CMLR 11	9.31, 9.45
Tsirlis and Kouloumpas v Greece (1997) 25 EHRR 198	36.16
Tyrer v UK (1979–80) 2 EHRR 1	13.19, 13.28
Tysiac v Poland (2007) 45 EHRR 42	36.84
U v Secretary of State for the Home Department (SC/32/2005) 29 July 2011	23.83
U, XC, UF v Secretary of State for the Home Department SC/77/2009, SC/80/2009, SC/32/2005, 21 December	23.86
Udu and Nyenty, Re [2008] NIQB 157	44.25
UE (Nigeria) and others v Secretary of State for the Home Department [2010] EWCA Civ 795	17.54
Uner v The Netherlands (2007) 45 EHRR 14, [2006] ECHR 873	17.4, 17.24, 17.25, 17.44, 17.50, 17.56, 17.58, 17.89

Uphill v BRB (Residuary) Ltd [2005] EWCA Civ 60	21.97
V v UK (1999) 30 EHRR 121	36.56
Valentin Batista v Secretary of State for the Home Department [2010] EWCA Civ 896	9.43, 17.5, 17.6
Van der Leer v The Netherlands (1990) 12 EHRR 567	36.14
Van Duyn Case 41/74 [1974] ECR 1337	9.6
Vasileva v Denmark (2003) 40 EHRR 27	36.15, 36.16
Vento v Chief Constable of West Yorkshire Police [2002] EWCA Civ 1871	43.34
Vilvarajah v Secretary of State for the Home Department [1990] Imm AR 457	42.64
VP (Italy) v Secretary of State for the Home Department [2010] EWCA Civ 806	9.29
VW (Uganda) and AB (Somalia) v Secretary of State for the Home Department [2009] EWCA Civ 5	15.13, 17.6, 17.8
W (Algeria) v Secretary of State for the Home Department [2010] EWCA Civ 898	23.2, 23.43, 23.45
W v Home Office [1997] Imm AR 302	43.17
W v UK (1987) 10 EHRR 29	16.15, 16.16
Wainwright v Home Office [2003] UKHL 53	43.8, 43.9
Wasfi Suleman Mahmod, In Re [1995] Imm AR 311	31.21, 32.8, 33.10, 42.77
Wassink v The Netherlands (Series A/185-A) 1990, (1990) EHRR 22820	35.20, 36.10, 36.14, 36.46
Watkins v Secretary of State for the Home Department and others [2006] AC 395	43.14
Weeks v UK (1987) 10 EHRR 293	36.10
Whiten v Pilot insurance Co [2002] 1 SCR 595, 2002 SCC 18	44.40
Winterwerp v The Netherlands (1979) 2 EHRR 387	36.10, 36.13, 36.15
Witold Litwa v Poland (2000) 33 EHRR 1267	36.14, 36.16
WL and KM v Secretary of State for the Home Department [2010] EWCA Civ 111, [2010] 1 WLR 2168	32.19, 32.35, 32.38
WN (DRC) v Secretary of State for the Home Department [2004] UKIAT 00213	21.60
X v Belgium and The Netherlands (1975) 7 D&R 75	16.19
X v Croatia App No 11223/04, judgment 17 July 2008	36.84
X v France (1982) 31 D&R 241	16.19
X v UK (1975) 2 DR 105	36.80
X v UK (1977) 12 DR 207 ECommHR	36.25
X v UK (1983) 32 DR 220	16.24
X, Y and Z v UK (1997) 24 EHRR 143	16.21
XX v Secretary of State for the Home Department (SC/61/2007) 10 September 2010.	23.58, 23.78
Y (Shi Lanka) and Z (Sri Lanka) v Secretary of State for the Home Department [2009] EWCA Civ 362, [2009] HRLR 22, (2009) *Times* 5 May	13.33, 18.41, 18.43–18.46, 18.48, 18.49, 18.51

Y v Secretary of State for the Home Department SC/36/2005 24 August 2006	23.75, 23.78
YB (EEA reg 17(4) – proper approach) Ivory Coast [2008] UKAIT 62	8.27
YD (Togo) v Secretary of State for the Home Department [2010] EWCA Civ 214	17.9
Yiadom Case C-357/98 [2000] ECR I-9265	9.6
Yildiz v Austria (2003) 36 EHRR 553	17.61
Yilmaz v Germany No 52853/99	17.89
Youssef v Home Office [2004] EWHC 1884 (QB)	32.41, 32.42
Yousuf v Secretary of State for the Home Department [2008] EWCA Civ 394	17.48, 17.72, 17.87, 33.22
Z v The Netherlands (1984) 38 DR 145 ECommHR	36.25
Z v UK (2002) 34 EHRR 3	36.48
Zambrano (Ruiz) v Office National de l'emploi Case C-34/09, [2011] 2 CMLR 46	4.23, 8.39, 10.2, 10.4–10.9, 10.12–10.14, 17.31–17.35
Zamir v UK (1983) 40 DR 42, ECommHR	33.50, 36.12, 36.25, 36.44
Zarb Adami v Malta (2006) 44 EHRR 49	36.100
Zatoon Bi (Pakistan) v Secretary of State for the Home Department [2009] EWCA Civ 834	16.4, 16.29, 16.31
ZH (Afghanistan) v Secretary of State for the Home Department [2009] EWCA Civ 1060	8.11
ZH (Tanzania) v Secretary of State for the Home Department [2011] UKSC 4, [2011] 2 WLR 148	1.24, 4.7, 4.10, 4.14–4.16, 4.18–4.24, 4.29, 4.32, 10.14, 15.15, 17.20, 17.25–17.31, 17.40, 37.3, 37.5
ZNS v Turkey App No 21896/08, judgment 19 January 2010	36.24
ZT (Kosovo) v Secretary of State for the Home Department [2009] UKHL 6, [2009] 1 WLR 348	22.5, 22.8
ZT (Zimbabwe) v Secretary of State for the Home Department [2005] EWCA Civ 1421	18.21, 18.24–18.26
ZZ v Secretary of State for the Home Department [2011] EWCA Civ 440	23.44

Table of statutes

Access to Justice Act 1999		Borders, Citizenship and	
s55	21.97	Immigration Act 2009	
Anti-terrorism, Crime and Security			20.10
Act 2001	23.5, 23.8–	s53	42.18
	23.10, 23.42,	s55	1.3, 4.2, 4.7–
	36.20		4.9, 4.11, 4.18,
Pt IV	38.4		4.27, 4.29, 4.30,
Pt 4	23.5, 23.6, 23.8,		4.32, 4.33, 4.44,
	23.9, 23.42		17.26–17.28,
s21	23.8		20.10, 21.12,
s23	23.8, 23.9		37.3–37.5, 37.7,
s24	23.8		37.8, 37.10,
s25	23.8		37.11, 37.16,
s26	23.8		41.9
s35	23.2	s55(1)	4.9
Asylum and Immigration Appeals		s55(1)(a)	4.29
Act 1993		s55(3)	4.11, 4.29
s2	11.19, 11.22,	s55(6)	4.8
	21.15	British Nationality Act 1981	
Asylum and Immigration (Treatment			1.30, 23.14
of Claimants etc) Act 2004		s3(1)	4.26
	6.7, 40.18	s39(2)	1.30
s34	40.29	s40	19.76, 23.13,
s35	33.42		23.15
s35(3)	6.7	s40A	21.4, 23.11
s35(4)(a)	6.7	Children Act 2004	
s35(5)(b)	6.7	s11	4.7, 4.12
s36	40.36	Children and Young Persons Act	
s36(2)	40.18, 40.24	1933	38.4
s36(3)	40.18, 40.24	Children (Scotland) Act 1995	
s36(4)	40.18		38.4
s36(5)	40.19	Civil Evidence Act 1968	
Sch 3 Pt 2	22.11, 22.12	ss11–13	1.14
Sch 3 para 5(2)	22.11	Colonial Prisoners Removal Act 1884	
Sch 3 para 5(3)	22.11		29.27
Sch 3 para 5(4)	22.6, 22.11	Constitutional Reform Act 2005	
Sch 3 para 5(5)	22.11	Pt 3	23.4
Bail Act 1976	41.42	County Courts Act 1984	
Sch 1 para 2	40.26	s38	42.100

lxvii

County Courts Act 1984 *continued*		Criminal Justice Act 2003 *continued*	
s64(3)	42.92	s226(2)	26.7
Crime and Disorder Act 1988		s226(3)	26.7
	28.12	s227	26.8
s39	24.11	s228	26.8
s41	24.13	s237	26.4
Crime (Sentences) Act 1997		s244(3)(a)	26.4
s28(5)	26.6, 26.11, 26.22	s246(1)	28.19
		s246(2)	28.18, 28.19
s28(6)	26.6, 26.11	s247(2)	26.8
s28(7)	26.6, 26.22	s249(1)	26.4
s31A	26.7	ss254–256A	26.11
s32	26.22	s254	26.19
s32(5)	26.11	s255	28.25
Criminal Justice Act 1991		s259	26.9, 28.14, 28.29
	28.12–28.15, 28.18, 28.19, 28.33, 28.39	s260	28.31
		s260(1)	28.32
s33(1)(a)	26.4	s260(2)	28.34
s33(1)(b)	26.4	s261	28.44
s33(2)	26.4	s269	26.6
s33(1A)	26.4	s273	29.13
s35	26.13	s325	24.22
s35(1A)	26.4	s325(3)	24.22
s33(1B)	26.4	s325(6)	24.22
s34A(3)	28.19	s325(8)	24.23
s34A(4)	28.19	s326	24.22
s34A(4)(a)	28.18	Sch 15	24.23, 26.4, 26.7, 26.8, 28.39
s35(1)	26.4		
s37(1)	26.4		
s37ZA(1)	26.4	Sch 19	26.11
s38A	28.25	Sch 21	26.6
s44(3)	26.8	Criminal Justice and Courts Services Act 2000	
s46	26.9, 28.14		
s46(4)	28.31	s6	25.18
s46A(1)	28.32	Criminal Justice and Immigration Act 2008	26.8
s46A(5)	28.33		
s46B	28.44	Pt 10	19.61
s84	24.6, 24.12	s130(2)	19.61
s85(1)	24.6	s130(3)	19.61
s87(2)	24.6	s130(4)	19.63
s88	24.6	s130(5)	19.63
Criminal Justice Act 2003		s131(1)(a)	19.61
	20.13, 26.7, 26.11, 28.13, 28.14, 28.16, 28.18, 28.19, 28.31, 28.34, 38.9	s131(2)	19.61
		s131(3)(a)	19.61
		s131(3)(b)	19.61
		s131(4)	19.61
s224(2)(b)	26.8	s131(5)	19.62
s225(2)	26.7	s132(1)	19.64
s225(3)	26.7	s132(2)(b)	19.64

Table of statutes lxix

Criminal Justice and Immigration Act 2008 *continued*	
s132(2)(c)	19.64
s133(1)	19.64
s133(2)	19.64
s133(3)	19.64
s133(4)	19.64
s133(6)	19.64
s134	19.64
s135	19.64
s136(1)(a)	19.64
s136(1)(b)	19.64
s136(1)(c)	19.64
s136(1)(d)	19.63, 19.64

Crown Proceedings Act 1947
| s17(1) | 42.85 |
| s17(3) | 42.85 |

Data Protection Act 1998
	20.13, 23.26, 39.56, 42.12–42.14, 43.2, 43.17, 43.28
s7	39.79, 42.12
s7(10)	42.12
s13(1)	43.28
s13(2)	43.28
s13(3)	43.28
s15(1)	43.28
Sch 1, Pt 1 para 4	43.28

Diplomatic Privileges Act 1964
| | 1.41 |

Disability Discrimination Act 2005
| s49A | 27.27, 34.32 |

Education Act 2002
| s175 | 4.7 |

Equality Act 2010 43.29–43.34
s4	43.31
s13	43.32
s19	43.32
s20	43.32
s113(3)(a)	42.89, 43.34
s114	42.89, 43.34
s115	42.89
s118(1)	43.33
s118(4)	43.33
s119(2)	43.34
s119(4)	43.34
s149	43.30

Freedom of Information Act 2000
| | 39.79, 42.15 |
| s1 | 42.15 |

Human Rights Act 1998
	15.25, 21.8, 21.14, 36.39, 36.106, 42.22, 42.29, 42.31, 42.33, 42.46, 43.2, 43.20–43.26, 44.7
s3	32.34
s4	42.24
s4(2)	23.9
s6	21.11, 23.7, 41.50, 42.31
s6(1)	43.22
s6(3)(b)	43.22, 43.25
s6(5)	43.22
s7(1)	43.21
s7(5)	43.25
s8	43.26

Identity Cards Act 2006
| | 1.31 |

Immigration Act 1971
	1.1–1.4, 1.6, 1.7, 1.16, 1.30, 1.43, 1.45, 1.48, 2.1, 2.2, 2.7, 3.1–3.3, 3.5, 3.9, 3.13, 3.20, 3.23, 3.24, 3.28, 3.34, 3.35, 3.47, 4.1, 4.4, 4.5, 4.10, 5.1, 5.5, 5.6, 5.31–5.36, 5.45, 6.3, 6.6, 6.15, 7.2–7.4, 7.6, 7.11, 7.12, 7.22, 9.48, 9.50, 9.64, 9.75–9.77, 12.119, 15.23, 15.24, 17.72, 17.75, 20.3, 20.10, 21.4, 21.19, 21.31, 21.37, 21.39, 22.24, 23.8, 23.83, 27.38, 27.39, 30.1, 30.4, 30.17, 30.39, 30.42, 30.44, 30.45, 31.4, 31.6, 31.7, 31.10, 31.11, 31.21–31.37, 32.31–32.34, 35.1, 35.3, 37.1, 38.12, 39.34, 40.3, 40.12, 40.15, 40.25, 40.36, 40.39, 41.17, 44.5, 44.24
s1(1)	1.5, 1.29
s2	1.30
s2(1)(b)	30.41
s2(1)(d)	1.30
s2(2)	1.29, 1.30, 2.7
s2A	1.33
s3	19.72
s3(1)	19.24

Immigration Act 1971 continued		Immigration Act 1971 continued	
s3(2)	3.15, 3.17, 11.12	s7(3)	1.36, 1.40
		s7(4)(b)	1.40
s3(5)	1.1, 1.5, 1.24, 1.25, 1.27, 5.12, 5.42, 19.67, 19.72, 20.10, 26.9	s7(4)(c)(i)	1.40
		s7(4)(c)(ii)	1.40
		s8	1.22, 5.23, 7.21, 9.50, 31.21, 31.22
s3(5)(a)	1.1, 1.7, 2.21, 4.4, 9.1, 9.9, 9.48, 9.50, 23.1	s8(3)	1.5, 1.41, 1.42, 2.7
		s8(5)	1.22
s3(5)(b)	1.1, 1.15–1.17, 4.5, 5.31, 7.8, 9.16	s8(5A)	1.22
		s9	1.28
		s24	7.30
s3(6)	1.1, 2.5, 2.7, 4.4, 19.67, 19.72, 20.10, 26.9	s24(1)(e)	40.24
		s33(1)	26.9
		s33(1)(b)	7.30
		s33(2A)	1.22
s3(8)	1.28, 1.31	Sch 2	3.18, 9.75, 9.79, 23.83, 31.1, 33.1, 40.3
s3(9)	1.31		
s3C	23.15		
s3D	23.15	Sch 2 para 1(3)	3.17
s5	1.16, 5.42, 7.7, 9.1, 9.48–9.50, 9.58, 19.64, 19.72	Sch 2 para 2(5)	40.41
		Sch 2 para 8	31.6
		Sch 2 para 9	31.6
		Sch 2 paras 12–14	31.6
s5(1)	1.2, 1.43, 1.48, 1.49, 5.3, 6.3, 6.4, 21.31	Sch 2 para 16	1.39, 31.37
		Sch 2 para 16(1)	31.6
s5(2)	1.20, 1.27, 7.7, 7.11	Sch 2 para 16(1A)	31.6
s5(3)	1.18, 1.20, 7.8	Sch 2 para 16(2)	31.6, 31.37
s5(4)	1.17	Sch 2, para 17	40.30
s5(6)	6.9	Sch 2 para 17(1)	31.8
s6(1)	2.4	Sch 2 para 18(1)	38.3
s6(2)	1.5, 1.27, 2.8	Sch 2 para 21	1.39, 31.37
s6(3)	2.6	Sch 2 para 21(1)	40.42
s6(3)(a)	2.5	Sch 2 para 22(1A)	40.4, 40.5, 40.15
s6(3)(b)	2.5		
s6(4)	2.6	Sch 2 para 22(1B)	40.4
s6(5)	2.19		
s6(6)	1.4, 1.46	Sch 2 para 22(2)	40.13, 40.16
s7	1.5, 1.34, 1.39, 1.40, 5.23, 7.21, 9.50, 9.86, 20.10, 31.21, 31.22	Sch 2 para 22(3)	40.8
		Sch 2 para 24	40.26
		Sch 2 para 24(1)	40.25
		Sch 2 para 29(1)	40.9
		Sch 2 para 29(2)	40.9, 40.15
s7(1)	9.51	Sch 2 para 29(3)	40.9
s7(1)(b)	2.7, 5.24	Sch 2 para 29(5)	40.9, 40.16
s7(2)	1.39	Sch 2 para 29(6)	40.9

Table of statutes lxxi

Immigration Act 1971 *continued*		Immigration and Asylum Act 1999 *continued*	
Sch 2 para 30(1)	40.12		
Sch 2 para 30(2)	40.11, 41.47	s4(1)(c)	41.17
Sch 2 para 33	40.26	s4(2)	41.16
Sch 2 para 33(1)	40.25	s4(3)	41.16
Sch 3	9.48, 9.75, 31.1, 31.7, 31.11, 31.19, 33.1, 33.5, 33.32, 36,25, 38.4, 40.3	s9	1.26
		s10	1.11, 1.25, 9.2, 26.9
		s10(1)	31.6
		s10(7)	31.6
		s31	2.18
Sch 3 para 1(1)	6.18	s54	40.4
Sch 3 para 1(4)	6.22	s55	12.112
Sch 3 para 2	9.77, 9.78, 31.9, 31.34, 31.36, 32.34, 40.39	s67	6.20
		s98	41.16
		s147	38.4
Sch 3 para 2(1)	31.5–31.7, 31.34, 31.36, 32.1, 32.32, 32.34, 32.35, 32.37–32.40, 33.5, 35.4, 40.29, 40.36	s148	39.2
		s148(3)	39.2
		s149(6)	39.2
		s152	39.85
		s152(2)	39.2
		s152(3)	39.2
		s153	39.2
Sch 3 para 2(1A)	40.36	s166(3)	39.2
Sch 3 para 2(2)	31.6, 31.7, 31.36, 33.5, 35.3, 40.29	s169	1.1, 1.25
		Sch 11	39.2
		Sch 12, para 1	39.2
Sch 3 para 2(3)	31.6, 31.7, 31.11, 32.32, 31.34, 32.35, 32.38, 33.5, 35.3, 40.29	Sch 12, para 2	39.2, 39.51
		Sch 12, para 3	39.2
		Sch 13, para 2	39.2
		Sch 14 para 43	1.1, 1.25
		Sch 14 para 44	1.1, 1.25
Sch 3 para 2(4)	31.7, 31.8, 38.3, 40.30	Immigration Asylum and Nationality Act 2006	23.19
Sch 3 para 2(4A)	40.5, 40.8, 40.13, 40.15, 40.16, 40.25, 40.26	s7(1)	23.19
		s12	21.23
		s12(1)	20.6, 21.22
		s12(2)	20.6, 21.22
Sch 3 para 2(5)	40.39	s30	1.31
Sch 3 para 2(6)	40.39	s40(3)	19.78
Sch 3 para 3	40.9, 40.11, 40.12, 40.15, 40.16, 40.25, 40.26, 41.47	s40(4)	19.77
		s53	31.8
		s54	12.52
		s54(2)	12.58
Sch 3 para 4	40.36	s55	12.110
Sch 3 para 5	40.5	s56	19.76
Sch 3 para 6	40.5	s57	1.33
Sch 15 para 12	1.26	Immigration and Refugee Protection Act 2001 (Canada)	
Immigration and Asylum Act 1999	39.2, 39.85		
s4	41.23		23.27

International Criminal Court Act		Mental Health Act 1983 *continued*	
2001	29.28	s47	30.3, 30.14,
ss 42–48	29.28		30.15, 30.17,
s42(1)	29.29		30.29, 30.34,
s42(4)	29.30		30.37
s77	29.28	s48	30.3, 30.17,
s77A	29.28		30.18, 30.29,
Sch 7, para 3	29.31		30.34
Limitation Act 1980	42.90, 42.91	s48(1)(b)	30.17
s2	42.91	s48(2)(d)	30.17
s2(4)	42.91	s49	30.19
s33	42.91	s49(1)	30.19
s39	42.90	ss50–53	30.19
Mental Capacity Act 2005		s50	30.20
	30.6	s50(2)	30.22
Mental Capacity Act 2007		s50(3)	30.22
	30.6	s50(4)	30.22
Mental Health Act 1983		s50(5)	30.13
	30.3–30.5, 30.8,	s53	30.23
	30.10, 30.39,	s54	30.7
	30.44	s55(5)	30.3
Pt II	30.3, 30.11	s66	30.11
Pt III	30.3, 30.5, 30.7,	s69	30.11
	30.46	s71	30.25
s1	30.5	s72(1)	30.25
s1(2A)	30.5	s72(1)(b)	30.27, 30.28,
s2	30.18		30.30, 30.31
s3	30.27, 30.34	s72(7)	30.25
s23	30.11, 30.24	s73	30.25–30.29,
s25	30.24		30.32, 30.33
s34(1)	30.3	s73(3)–(6)	30.33
s34(2)	30.3	s73(7)	30.26
s35	30.7	s74	30.25, 30.26,
s36	30.7		30.29, 30.33
s37	30.7, 30.8,	s74(1)(b)	30.30–30.32
	30.15, 30.27,	s74(5)	30.30
	30.37	s75(5A)	30.31
s37(1)	30.7	s74(6)	30.26
s38	30.9	s75	30.26
s41	30.11, 30.13,	s79	30.25
	30.19, 30.27	s86	30.41–30.46
s41(1)	30.11	s86(3)	30.41
s41(2)	30.11	s91	30.46
s41(3)	30.11	s117	30.34, 30.35
s42(1)	30.12	s117(2)	30.36
s42(2)	30.12, 30.24,	s117(3)	30.36
	30.38	s118	30.3
s45A	30.13, 30.37	s145(1)	30.3, 30.36
s45B(2)	30.13	Sch 1, Pt II	30.11

Table of statutes lxxiii

Murder (Abolition of Death Penalty) Act 1965		Nationality, Immigration and Asylum Act 2002 *continued*	
s1	26.7	s76(6)	12.132
Nationality, Immigration and Asylum Act 2002		s77	11.15
		s77(4)(a)	40.12
	1.4, 6.20, 9.56, 21.38, 23.15	s78	21.30, 23.15
Pt V	38.4, 40.6, 40.10	s78(3)(a)	40.12
		s79	1.4, 1.45, 23.15
s53	31.7	s79(1)(a)	21.31
s54	30.36	s79(1)(b)	21.31
s54(3)	31.7	s79(3)	21.32
s62	30.17	s79(4)	5.40, 5.41, 6.6
s62(4)	40.42	s81	22.23
s68	40.5, 40.7, 40.9	s82	9.56, 11.27, 21.121, 21.140, 21.141, 22.19, 23.1
s69	41.17		
s72	5.16, 5.17, 5.27, 12.3, 12.34, 12.84, 12.91, 12.93, 12.94, 12.111, 12.119, 12.120, 19.23, 19.24, 19.62, 19.68, 20.11	s82(1)	9.64, 9.65, 21.30–21.32, 23.13, 23.15
		s82(2)	6.20
		s82(2)(b)	21.4
		s82(2)(f)	19.75, 21.4, 21.142
s72(2)	12.86, 12.90, 12.92, 19.61	s82(2)(g)	21.4
		s82(2)(h)	21.4
s72(2)(a)	19.61, 19.62	s82(2)(k)	7.29, 21.4 40.10
s72(2)(b)	19.61, 19.62	s82(2)(j)	1.4, 1.43, 3.48, 21.4, 23.59, 31.14, 40.10
s72(3)	12.87, 19.61		
s72(3)(a)–(c)	19.61, 19.62		
s72(4)	12.89, 19.61	s82(2)(s)	7.29
s72(4)(a)	19.61	s82(3A)	5.45, 21.4, 21.21, 40.10
s72(4)(b)	19.61		
s72(6)	12.91, 12.93	s83	9.73, 21.7
s72(7)	12.94	s83(2)	23.13, 23.15
s72(9)	12.111, 12.112	s83A	23.13, 23.15
s72(10)	12.111	ss84–86	11.27
s72(11)(b)(i)	12.88	s84	9.57, 21.8, 21.24, 21.29, 23.15
s72(11)(b)(ia)	12.88		
s72(11)(b)(ii)	12.88		
s72(11)(b)(iii)	12.88	s84(1)	3.15
s76	12.131, 12.133, 19.66, 19.70, 19.73, 21.4	s84(1)(a)	21.8, 21.11, 21.15
		s84(1)(b)	21.8, 21.11
s76(1)	19.66, 19.68, 19.72	s84(1)(c)	21.8, 21.11, 21.14, 21.16
s76(2)	19.70, 19.73	s84(1)(d)	21.8, 21.11
s76(3)	12.130, 12.131, 19.71, 19.73	s84(1)(e)	3.26, 4.32, 15.10, 21.8, 21.12, 21.15
s76(3)(a)–(d)	12.142		
s76(4)	19.67		

Nationality, Immigration and Asylum Act 2002 *continued*		Nationality, Immigration and Asylum Act 2002 *continued*	
s84(1)(f)	3.26, 21.8, 21.10	s104(1)	1.45, 21.33
s84(1)(g)	21.8, 21.13, 21.16	s104(2)(a)	1.45, 21.33
		s104(2)(b)	1.45, 21.33
		s104(2)(c)	1.45, 21.33
s86	23.15	s104(4)	21.140, 23.68
s85(2)	21.29	s104(4A)	21.141, 23.68
s85(3)	21.29	s104(4B)	21.141, 23.68
s86	23.15	s104(4C)	21.141, 23.68
s86(3)	3.15	s104(5)	21.142, 23.68
s87	23.15	s105	23.15
s92	21.18	s113	20.6, 21.22, 21.23
s92(2)	1.43		
s92(4)	5.48, 5.49, 9.69, 9.70, 20.7	s120	11.27, 22.17, 22.19
s92(4)(b)	21.20	s120(1)(a)	21.26
s94	9.65, 20.9, 21.38, 22.4, 22.8, 22.9	s120(1)(b)	21.26
		s120(1)(c)	21.26
		Sch 3	30.36
s94(2)	22.1, 22.6	Offender Management Act 2007	
s94(4)	22.6		24.10
s94(4)(a)	21.20	s2	24.2
s94(7)	22.13	s2(1)	24.10
s96	5.52, 20.9, 21.18, 21.19, 21.21, 21.33, 22.1, 22.2, 22.14, 22.16, 22.17, 22.19–22.22, 22.25, 23.15	Police and Justice Act 2006	
		s44	29.7
		Powers of Criminal Courts (Sentencing) Act 2000	
		s80	26.7
		s82A	26.6
		s85	26.8
		s90	26.7
s96(1)	22.17, 22.19	s93	26.7
s96(1)(a)	9.66	s96	26.4
s96(1)(b)	22.19	s100	26.5
s96(1)(c)	22.18, 22.19	s109	26.7
s96(2)	21.27, 22.17, 22.19	s109(5)	26.7
		Prevention of Terrorism Act 2005	
			23.26, 23.38
s96(2)(c)	22.18, 22.19		
s96(7)	22.22	s16	23.9
s97	1.44, 21.33, 23.11, 23.60	Prison Act 1952	24.5
		s1	24.2, 24.5
s97(2)(a)	21.31	s2	24.2
s97(4)	23.14	s4	24.5
s97A	1.44, 23.19	s5(5A)	25.16
s97A(2)	23.15	s5(5B)	25.16
s97A(3)	23.19	s5A(2)	25.16
s98	21.33	s5A(4)	25.16
s99	21.33, 23.14	s6(2)	25.15
s104	1.19, 23.15, 40.9	s6(3)	25.15
		s7	24.5

Prison Act 1952 *continued*		Special Immigration Appeals		
s12	24.5	Commission Act 1997		
s13	24.5	*continued*		
ss39–40F	24.5	s2(5)	23.19	
s47	24.7, 38.3	s2B	23.13	
Protection from Harassment Act		s3	23.4, 23.83	
1997	38.9	s5	23.4	
Race Relations Act 1976		s5(3)	23.20	
	21.141	s5(6)(b)	23.46	
s19B	21.8, 21.11	s6	23.20, 23.22	
s71	27.27	s6(4)	23.25	
Rehabilitation of Offenders Act 1974		s7	23.18, 23.97	
	3.6, 3.29, 7.15	s7(1)	23.80	
s7(3)	3.29	s8	23.98	
Rent Act 1977	16.25	Sch 1, para 1	23.4	
Repatriation of Prisoners Act 1984		Sch 1, para 2	23.4	
	29.3, 29.4, 29.7,	Sch 1, para 6	23.4	
	29.13, 29.15,	Sch 3	23.83	
	29.16, 29.19	Terrorism Act 2000	12.55, 12.56,	
s1(1)	29.3		12.58	
s1(4)	29.4	s1	12.52, 12.55,	
s1(5)	29.4		12.56, 12.58	
s1(6)	29.4	s1(3)	12.55	
s2(1)	29.5	Theft Act 1978	5.17	
s2(2)	29.5	Tribunals, Courts and Enforcement		
s2(4)	29.5	Act 2007	21.110, 42.18	
s4A	29.15, 29.16	s3	21.34	
s4D	29.16	s3(5)	21.91	
s4E	29.16	s4(1)(c)	40.32	
Sch 1	29.13	s9(1)	21.75	
Senior Courts Act 1981		s9(4)(a)	21.77	
s15(3)	40.34, 42.64	s9(4)(b)	21.77	
s16	40.33	s9(4)(c)	21.77	
s31	42.17, 42.36	s9(9)	21.75, 21.78	
s31(3)	42.32	s10(1)	21.131	
s31(4)	42.37	s10(2)	21.131	
s31(6)	42.38	s10(4)(a)	21.133	
s31A	42.18	s10(4)(b)	21.133	
s37	42.100	s10(4)(c)	21.133	
s69(1)	42.92	s10(5)	21.133	
Special Immigration Appeals		s10(6)	21.133	
Commission Act 1997		s11	21.69	
	23.2, 23.4,	s11(1)	21.70, 21.110	
	23.19, 23.20,	s11(5)(d)(i)	21.78	
	23.40, 38.4	s11(5)(d)(ii)	21.78	
s1	23.2	s11(5)(d)(iii)	21.78	
s1(3)	23.2	s11(5)(d)(vi)	21.78	
s2	23.13, 23.14	s11(5)(e)	21.78	
s2(2)(e)	23.15	s12	21.119	
s2(2)(i)	22.2	s12(2)(a)	21.114	
s2(4)	23.15, 23.68	s12(2)(b)(i)	21.99	

Tribunals, Courts and Enforcement Act 2007 *continued*		UK Borders Act 2007 *continued*	
s12(2)(b)(ii)	21.99	s32(6)(a)	20.7
s12(3)(a)	21.99	s32(6)(b)	7.22
s12(4)(a)	21.99	s32(6A)	5.36
s12(4)(b)	21.99	s32(7)	5.22
s13	21.120	s33	5.25, 7.21, 12.144, 17.75, 20.2, 20.3, 20.7, 31.21, 31.27, 33.6
s13(5)	21.122		
s13(8)(c)	21.121		
s13(8)(d)	21.121		
s13(8)(e)	21.121	s33(1)	7.21, 30.37, 31.32
ss15–19	42.18		
s37(1)	21.102	s33(1)(a)	31.21
s37(2)	21.102	s33(1)(b)	5.23, 31.21, 31.22
UK Borders Act 2007	1.16, 3.20, 4.6, 4.33, 5.1, 5.3–5.5, 5.7, 5.8, 5.10–5.12, 5.17, 5.21, 5.24, 5.25, 5.31, 5.33, 5.34, 5.43, 6.3, 6.6, 7.2, 7.4, 7.6, 7.7, 7.12, 7.19, 7.22, 9.48, 9.49, 9.64, 9.77, 9.78, 17.73, 17.75, 17.76, 20.2, 20.5, 20.7, 20.10, 21.4, 21.10, 21.21, 22.24, 28.28, 30.4, 30.37, 31.1, 31.4, 31.12, 31.13, 31.15, 31.33, 31.35, 32.32, 32.38, 35.3, 40.3, 40.10, 40.37, 40.40	s33(2)	5.35, 7.21, 31.21, 31.33
		s33(2)(a)	20.10, 31.14
		s33(2)(b)	31.14, 31.33
		s33(3)	4.6, 5.28, 7.21, 9.49, 20.10, 31.21, 31.33
		s33(4)	7.21, 31.14, 31.21, 31.33
		s33(5)	7.21, 20.10, 31.21, 31.33
		s33(6)	7.21, 20.10, 30.37, 31.21, 31.33
s21	4.7, 4.11		
s32	2.2, 5.21, 20.4	s34(1)	5.38, 20.3, 31.30
s32(1)	5.14, 5.32, 31.13, 31.21, 31.32	s34(2)(a)	5.37
		s34(4)	20.8
s32(2)	5.15, 5.26, 31.21	s34(4)(a)	7.20
		s34(4)(b)	7.20
s32(2)(b)	5.37	s35	31.14
s32(3)	5.16	s35(2)	5.38, 5.40, 5.41, 6.6
s32(4)	5.12, 17.73, 30.37, 31.21	s35(3)	5.45, 40.10
s32(5)	1.16, 1.19, 5.12, 5.24, 5.43, 5.45, 7.19, 7.20, 12.144, 17.75, 21.4, 21.10, 21.32, 30.37, 31.14, 31.17, 31.21, 31.28–31.30, 31.32	s35(4)	31.14
		s36	31.17, 31.18, 31.36, 33.1, 36,25
		s36(1)	30.17, 31.18, 31.21, 31.23, 38.3, 38.4, 40.16, 40.25, 40.37, 40.41, 41.47
s32(6)	7.21		

UK Borders Act 2007 *continued*		UK Borders Act 2007 *continued*	
s36(1)(a)	9.77, 20.4, 31.17, 31.19–31.27, 31.31, 33.6, 35.3, 40.40	s36(5)	31.17, 31.21, 40.40, 40.41
		s36(6)	31.17, 31.21
		s36(7)	31.17, 31.21
s36(1)(b)	31.17, 31.28–31.33, 33.6, 35.3, 40.40	s37	1.16
		s37(1)	1.19
		s37(2)	1.19
s36(2)	31.17, 31.21, 31.33, 31.34, 32.32, 32.38, 33.6, 35.3, 38.3, 40.37, 40.40	s37(3)	1.19
		s37(4)	1.19
		s38(1)	5.20
		s38(1)(a)	5.18
		s38(1)(b)	5.19
s36(3)	31.17, 31.21, 40.37	s38(2)(a)	5.18
		s38(4)(c)	1.16, 5.42, 6.3, 7.7
s36(4)	31.17, 31.21, 38.3, 40.3, 40.5, 40.8, 40.9, 40.11–40.13, 40.15, 40.16, 40.25, 40.26, 40.30, 41.47	s59(4)(i)	5.21
		s82(2)(j)	5.45
		s82(3A)	5.43
		s92(2)	5.44
		s92(4)	5.44

Table of statutory instruments

Anti-terrorism, Crime and Security Act 2001 (Continuance in force of sections 21 to 23) Order 2004 SI No 751	23.9
Appeals (Excluded Decisions) Order 2009 SI No 275	21.78
art 3(m)	21.121
Appeals from the Upper Tribunal to the Court of Appeal Order 2008 SI No 2834	21.93
Asylum and Immigration Tribunal (Procedure) Rules 2005 SI No 230	21.50, 21.55, 40.17, 41.36
r2	21.80
r6(1)	21.37, 21.38
r6(3)(b)	21.39
r6(5)	21.39
r7(1)(a)	21.37
r7(1)(b)	21.37
r7(2)(a)(i)	21.38
r7(2)(a)(ii)	21.38
r8(1)	21.42
r8(2)	21.42
r8(3)	21.42
r10(5)	21.41, 23.60
r14	21.43
r19(1)	21.52
r21(1)	21.55
r21(2)	21.55
r21(3)	21.55
r24(2)	21.80
r24(3)	21.80
r24(4)(a)	21.80
r24(5)	21.79
r25(2)	21.81
r25(3)	21.76
r26(1)	21.76
r38(2)	41.32
r38(2)(d)	40.17
r38(3)	41.32
r39(2)	41.36
r39(3)	41.64
r39(4)	41.65

Asylum and Immigration Tribunal (Procedure) Rules 2005 SI No 230
    continued

r39(5)	41.66
r41	41.65
r45(e)	21.46
r45(4)(c)	21.50
r45(4)(d)(i)	21.53
r45(4)(d)(ii)	21.51
r45(5)	21.48
r51(1)	1.14
r57(1)(a)	21.40
r51(3)	21.45
r51(4)	21.49
r54	21.57
r57(1)(b)	21.80
r57(2)	21.40

Channel Tunnel (International Arrangements Order) 1993 SI No 1813   38.4

Channel Tunnel (Miscellaneous Provisions) Order 1994 SI No 1405   38.4

Children (Northern Ireland) Order 1995   38.4
    Pt VII   38.4

Civil Procedure Rules 1998 SI No 3132   18.61, 20.16, 42.5, 42.6, 42.9, 42.11, 42.17, 42.34, 42.35, 42.44, 42.50, 42.63, 42.93, 42.98, 42.101

r1.1(1)	42.5
r1.1(2)	18.61, 42.5
r3.1(2)(a)	21.136
r3.1(2)(f)	42.96
Pt 7	42.94, 42.95
r7.4	42.96
r7.5	42.96
r7.6	42.96
PD 7A	42.88
Pt 8	23.26
Pt 15	42.98
Pt 18	42.98, 42.101
Pt 25	42.37, 42.63
r26.11	42.92
Pt 31	42.98, 42.101
Pt 32	42.101
r32.18	42.101
Pt 34	42.98
Pt 35	42.98
Pt 36	42.11
r36.14	42.11
r39.2(4)	42.97
r40.20	42.100

Civil Procedure Rules 1998 SI No 3132 *continued*

Pt 52	20.16, 23.98, 42.70
r52.3(2)	42.70
r52.3(4)(a)	21.138
r52.3(5)	21.137
r52.3(6)	21.129
r52.4(2)(b)	42.70
r52.15	42.56, 42.70
PD 52, para 4.14A	21.137
PD 52 para 4.3A(1)	42.70
PD 52, para 5.6(2)(a)–(f)	21.135
PD 52, para 15.4	20.16
PD 52, para 21.7(3)	21.135, 21.136
PD 52, para 21.7(4)	21.135
PD 52, para 21.7(5)	21.135
Pt 54	42.17
r54.1(2)	42.23
r54.2	42.36, 42.37
r54.2(1)(f)	42.34
r54.3	42.36, 42.37
r54.5(1)	42.44
r54.5(2)	42.44
r54.7	42.48
r54.8(2)(a)	42.50
r54.8(2)(b)	42.50
r54.10(2)	42.63
r54.12(2)	42.54
r54.14	42.59
r54.15	42.60
r54.17	42.35
r54.20	42.69
PD 54 para 5.3	42.46
PD 54 para 5.7	42.46
PD 54 para 8.4	42.53
PD 54 para 8.6	42.57
PD 54 para 13.5	42.35
PD 54 para 15.1	42.67
PD 54 para 15.3	42.67
PD 54 para 65.1	42.67
PD 54 para 21.1	42.62
PD 54A para 5.6	42.46, 42.48
PD 54A para 5.7	42.48
PD 54A para 5.8	42.48
PD 54A para 5.9	42.48
PD 54A para 18.2	42.49
PD 54A	42.49
r57(b)	42.34
Sch 1	42.72
Co-operation in Public Protection Arrangements (UK Border Agency) Order 2011 SI No 1733	24.22

Data Protection (Subject Access) (Fees and Miscellaneous Provisions) Regulations 2000 SI No 191	42.12
Detention Centre Rules 2001 SI No 238	34.2, 34.26, 35.11, 39.2, 39.6, 39.14, 39.33, 39.54, 42.20, 42.24
r3(1)	39.6
r3(2)	39.6
r6	39.12
r7(1)	39.11
r7(2)	39.11
r7(3)	39.11
r9	35.11, 36.39
r12(1)	39.13
r12(2)	39.13
r15(2)	39.14
r16(2)	39.16
r17(1)	39.17
r17(3)	39.18
r17(4)	39.18
r17(6)	39.18
r17(7)	39.18
r17(8)	39.18
r18(1)	39.19
r18(2)	39.19
r19	39.41
r26(1)	39.20
r26(2)	39.20
r27(1)	39.22
r27(2)	39.22
r27(4)	39.22
r27(5)	39.22
r28(1)	39.23
r28(2)	39.23
r28(3)	39.23
r30	39.23
r33(1)	34.26, 39.24, 39.31
r33(1)	39.24
r33(7)	39.28
r33(8)	39.27
r33(9)	39.23
r33(11)	39.28
r34	32.22, 34.26, 34.35
r34(1)	34.26, 39.31
r35	34.26, 39.32
r35(1)	34.26, 39.32
r35(2)	34.26, 39.32
r35(3)	34.26, 39.32
r35(4)	39.32

Detention Centre Rules 2001 SI No 238 *continued*

r35(5)	39.33
r38	39.54
r38(1)	39.89
r39(1)	39.7
r40(1)	39.42
r40(2)	39.42
r40(3)	39.42
r40(4)	39.42
r40(5)	39.42
r40(7)	39.42
r40(9)	39.42
r41(1)	39.47
r41(3)	39.47
r42(1)	39.45
r42(2)	39.45
r42(3)	39.45
r42(4)	39.45
r42(5)	39.45
r42(8)	39.45
r43(1)	39.48, 39.50
r43(2)	39.50
r43(3)	39.50
r43(4)	39.50
r43(5)	39.50
r43(6)	39.50
r43(7)	39.50
r43(9)	39.50
r43(10)	39.48
r43(11)	39.50
r43(12)	39.49
r44(3)	39.51
r45(4)	39.36
r61(4)	39.89
r61(5)	39.89
r61(6)	39.89
r62(1)	39.87
r62(1)(a)	39.87
r62(1)(b)	39.87
r62(1)(c)	39.87
r62(2)	39.89
r62(4)	39.87
r63(1)	39.86
r63(2)	39.86

High Court and County Courts Jurisdiction Order 1991

art 4A	42.88
art 5	42.88

Human Rights Act 1998 (Designated Derogation) Order 2001 SI No 3644   23.6

Immigration, Asylum and Nationality Act
 (Commencement No 2) Order 2006 SI No 2226
 Art 3 23.19
 Sch 1 23.19
Immigration and Asylum Act 1999 (Commencement
 No 6, Transitional and Consequential
 Provisions) Order 2000 SI No 2444
 Sch 2 para 1 1.26
Immigration and Asylum (Provision of Accommodation
 to Failed Asylum Seekers) Regulations 2005 SI
 No 930
 reg 3(2) 41.16
Immigration (European Economic Area) (Amendment)
 Regulations 2009 SI No 117 9.76
Immigration (European Economic Area) Regulations
 2000 SI No 2326 9.72, 9.79
Immigration (European Economic Area) Regulations
 2006 SI No 1003 5.29, 5.47, 5.51,
 8.2–8.6, 8.8, 8.9, 8.11, 8.12, 8.14, 8.15, 8.20–8.22, 8.28, 8.32, 8.33, 8.37,
 8.38, 8.42, 8.44, 9.1, 9.3–9.5, 9.9, 9.17, 9.30, 9.31, 9.33, 9.37–9.39, 9.48–
 9.50, 9.52, 9.54–9.56, 9.60, 9.63–9.68, 9.72–9.74, 9.76, 9.78, 9.79, 9.88,
 10.2, 20.11, 21.4, 21.10, 22.23
 Pt 6 9.55
 reg 2 23.13
 reg 2(1) 8.15, 8.37, 9.48,
  21.4
 reg 3(2) 9.39
 reg 3(3) 9.41
 reg 4(1)(c) 8.6
 reg 4(1)(d) 8.6
 reg 4(4) 8.6
 reg 5(2)(a) 8.44
 reg 5(2)(a)(i) 8.44
 reg 5(2)(b) 8.44
 reg 5(2)(c) 8.44
 reg 5(3)(b)(i) 8.44
 reg 5(3)(b)(ii) 8.44
 reg 5(4) 8.44
 reg 5(6) 8.45
 reg 6 8.9
 reg 6(1)(b) 8.6
 reg 6(1)(c) 8.6
 reg 6(1)(d) 8.6
 reg 6(1)(e) 8.6
 reg 6(2)(a) 8.7
 reg 6(2)(b) 8.7
 reg 6(2)(b)(ii) 8.7
 reg 6(2)(c) 8.7
 reg 6(2)(d) 8.7
 reg 6(3) 8.7

Immigration (European Economic Area) Regulations 2006 SI No 1003
continued

reg 6(4)	8.6
reg 7	9.55
reg 7(1)	8.6
reg 7(1)(a)	8.13, 20.11
reg 7(1)(b)(i)	8.13
reg 7(1)(b)(ii)	8.13
reg 7(1)(c)	8.13
reg 7(2)	8.6
reg 7(2)(a)	8.16
reg 7(2)(b)	8.17
reg 7(3)	8.6, 8.28, 9.63
reg 7(4)	8.28
reg 8	8.20, 20.11
reg 8(2)	8.19, 8.25, 20.11
reg 8(3)	8.19, 8.26, 20.11
reg 8(4)	8.21
reg 8(5)	8.19, 8.27, 20.11
reg 9(1)	8.38
reg 9(2)	8.38
reg 10	8.6
reg 10(3)	8.32
reg 10(4)	8.32
reg 10(7)	8.33
reg 12(1)(b)(i)	8.12, 8.22
reg 12(2)(a)	8.22
reg 13	8.6
reg 14(1)	8.6, 8.9
reg 14(2)	8.6, 8.30, 8.31
reg 14(3)	8.6
reg 15	8.6
reg 15(1)	9.30, 9.33
reg 15(1)(a)	8.41, 9.39
reg 15(1)(b)	9.39
reg 15(1)(c)	8.44
reg 15(1)(d)	8.6, 8.46
reg 15(1)(e)	8.6
reg 15(1)(f)	8.46
reg 15(1)(f)(ii)	8.48
reg 15(2)	8.42, 9.39
reg 15(3)	8.42
reg 17(4)	8.20
reg 19(1)(1B)	9.3
reg 19(3)(a)	9.2, 9.9
reg 19(3)(b)	8.6, 8.42, 9.9, 9.76
reg 21	2.14, 9.24
reg 21(2)	9.11
reg 21(3)	9.30
reg 21(4)	9.30

Immigration (European Economic Area) Regulations 2006 SI No 1003
    continued

reg 21(4)(a)	9.31
reg 21(5)(a)	9.14, 9.19
reg 21(5)(b)	9.15, 17.71
reg 21(5)(c)	9.12
reg 21(5)(d)	9.15, 17.71
reg 21(6)	9.19
reg 24(1)	9.76, 9.77
reg 24(2)	9.2, 9.9
reg 24(3)	9.1, 9.9, 9.48, 9.50, 9.76
reg 24(4)	7.30, 9.79
reg 24(5)	9.74
reg 24(6)(b)	9.52
reg 24(6)(c)	9.52
reg 24A(3)	9.67–9.70, 9.88
reg 24A(4)	9.67
reg 24A(5)	9.67
reg 26	21.121
reg 26(1)	9.48, 9.68
reg 26(2)	9.63
reg 26(3)	9.63
reg 26(4)	9.65
reg 26(4)(a)	9.61
reg 26(4)(b)	9.61
reg 26(4)(c)	9.61
reg 26(5)	9.65, 21.18, 21.19, 21.21, 22.23, 22.25
reg 27(1)(b)	9.68–9.70
reg 27(1)(d)	9.59
reg 27(3)	9.59
reg 28	23.11, 23.13, 23.14
reg 28(2)	9.60
reg 28(3)(a)	9.60
reg 28(3)(b)	9.60
reg 28(5)	23.14
reg 28(8)	23.4
reg 29(3)	9.58
reg 29(4)	9.75
reg 29(6)	9.58
reg 29(7)	9.75
Sch 1	9.57
Sch 2 para 4	9.56
Sch 2 para 4(3)	9.73
Sch 2 para 4(4)	9.73
Sch 2 para 4(5)	9.73
Sch 2 para 4(7)	9.66
Sch 4 para 4(3)	9.72, 9.73

Table of statutory instruments lxxxvii

Immigration (Leave to Enter and Remain) Order 2000 SI No 1161	
art 13	19.47, 19.53
Immigration (Notices) Regulations 2003 SI No 658	3.47, 7.28
Nationality, Immigration and Asylum Act 2002 (Juxtaposed Controls) Order 2003 SI No 2818	38.4
Nationality, Immigration and Asylum Act 2002 (Specification of Particularly Serious Crimes) Order 2004 SI No 1910	5.17, 12.89
Parole Board (Amendment) Rules 2009 SI No 408	26.21
Prison Rules 1999 SI No 728	24.7, 24.8, 25.15, 28.4, 29.30, 38.3, 42.24, 43.19
r7	24.7, 27.11
r7(a)	38.14
r7(b)	38.13
r7(2)	27.21
r8	24.7
r9	28.4
r11	25.3
rr13–19	24.7
rr20–22	24.7
rr34–39	24.7
r39	43.14
r41	24.7
rr45–49	24.7
rr51–61	24.7
r77	25.15
r78	25.15
Race Relations (Northern Ireland) Order 1997	
Art 20A	21.8
Refugee or Person in Need of International Protection (Qualification) Regulations 2006 SI No 2170	11.13, 11.14, 11.16, 11.54
reg 2	11.17, 19.11
reg 4	11.49
reg 5	11.46
reg 6(1)(e)	11.58
reg 7(1)	12.10
reg 7(2)	12.41
reg 7(2)(a)	12.31
reg 7(2)(b)	12.42, 12.43, 12.45
Rules of the Supreme Court	42.72
Secretary of State for Justice Order 2007 SI No 2128	24.2
Special Immigration Appeals Commission Act 1997 (Commencement No 2) Order 1998 SI No 1892	23.2
art 2	23.2
Special Immigration Appeals Commission (Procedure) Rules 2003 SI No 1034	23.4, 23.64, 23.70, 23.89
Pt 6	23.88
r2	23.52

Special Immigration Appeals Commission (Procedure) Rules 2003 SI No 1034
  continued

r4	23.40, 23.43, 23.46, 23.48
r4(3)	23.34, 23.47
r5	23.17
r8	23.60
r8(5)	23.60
r9	23.61
r9A	23.62
r9A(1)	23.62
r10	23.53
r10A	23.53
r10A(3)	23.54
r10A(5)	23.63
r10A(10)	23.55
r10A(11)	23.55
r11	23.61
r11A	23.67
r11B	23.67
r12	23.68
r27	23.98
r29	23.88
r30	23.89
r30(4)	23.89
r30(6)	23.91
r32	23.25
r34	23.22
r35	23.20
r36(3)	23.28
r36(4)	23.29
r36(5)	23.29
r36(6)	23.25
r36(6)(b)	23.32
r37	23.20, 23.50, 23.55, 23.89
r37(2)	23.20
r37(3)(b)	23.20
r37(4A)	23.65
r38	23.43, 23.50, 23.55, 23.62, 23.63, 23.66, 23.89
r38(4)(c)	23.51
r38(5)	23.66
r38(6)–(9)	23.51
r38(8)	23.49
r38A	23.49
r39	23.64
r40	23.64
r41	23.69

Special Immigration Appeals Commission (Procedure) Rules 2003 SI No 1034 *continued*

r42	23.64
r43	23.69
r44	23.71
r45	23.70
r46	23.69
r47	23.82
r47(3)	23.81
r47(4)	23.81
r48	23.81
r53	23.64
r54	23.82
r59	23.70
r51	23.70

Tribunals, Courts and Enforcement Act 2007 (Miscellaneous Provisions) Order 2010 SI No 41

Art 2(b)	21.78
Art 3(m)	21.78

Tribunal Procedure (Upper Tribunal) Rules 2008 SI No 2698   21.110

r3	21.123
r3A	21.123
r3B(a)(i)	21.124
r3B(a)(ii)	21.125
r3B(b)	21.126
r3C(a)	21.124
r3C(b)	21.125
r3C(c)	21.126
r5(3)(a)	21.87, 21.127
r5(3)(d)	21.102
r5(3)(f)	21.51
r5(3)(h)	21.108
r6	21.103
r7(1)	21.103
r14	21.102
r15(1)	21.102
r15(2)(a)(i)	21.104
r15(2)(a)(ii)	21.104
r15(2)(b)(i)	21.103
r15(2A)(a)	21.106
r15(2A)(a)(ii)	21.107
r15(2A)(b)	21.106
r16(1)	21.102
r21(2)	21.82
r21(3)(aa)(i)	21.85
r21(3)(ab)	21.86
r21(3A)(a)	21.85
r21(3A)(c)	21.86
r21(4)	21.83, 21.84

Tribunal Procedure (Upper Tribunal) Rules 2008 SI No 2698 *continued*
r21(6)(a)	21.87
r22(2)(a)	21.110
r24(1A)	21.88
r24(2)	21.88
r24(3)	21.88
r24(4)	21.88
r25	21.89
r44(1)	21.128
r44(6)(a)	21.127
r44(7)	21.128
r45(1)(a)	21.132
r45(1)(b)	21.132
r45(5)	21.134

UK Borders Act 2007 (Commencement No 3 and   5.9, 5.10, 5.15,
    Transitional Provisions) Order 2008 SI No 1818   31.13, 31.15
Young Offender Institution Rules 2000 SI No 3371   24.7, 28.4
r4	27.11
r5	28.4
r8	25.3

Table of EU and international legislation

Agreement on the European Economic Area 1992
    Art 7 — 8.5
    Art 28 — 8.5
    Annex V — 8.5
Charter of Fundamental Rights of the European Union
    Art 7 — 10.15
Charter of the United Nations — 12.13, 12.58, 12.60
    Art 1 — 12.58, 12.60, 19.18
    Art 2 — 12.58, 12.60, 19.18
Convention against Trafficking in Human Beings — 5.30, 5.36, 20.10
Convention on the Prevention and Punishment of the Crime of Genocide 1948 — 12.26
Convention for the Prevention of Torture and Inhuman or Degrading Treatment or Punishment — 25.19
    Art 1 — 25.19
Convention on the Transfer of Sentenced Persons — 29.6, 29.7, 29.9, 29.13–29.15
    Art 3 — 29.9
    Art 9 — 29.12
    Art 11 — 29.12
    Art 12 — 29.14
    Art 13 — 29.14
Convention on the Transfer of Sentenced Persons Additional Protocol — 29.7, 29.16–29.19, 29.23
    Art 2 — 29.15
    Art 2(3) — 29.16
    Art 3 — 29.17
    Art 3(6) — 29.17
Convention Relating to the Status of Refugees 1951 — 1.10, 3.23, 3.24, 5.26, 5.27, 5.35, 7.15, 7.16, 7.21, 9.59, 9.69, 11.1, 11.3–11.6, 11.8, 11.10–11.12, 11.15–11.23, 11.35, 11.36, 11.38, 11.41, 11.45, 11.48, 11.51, 11.52, 11.55, 11.57, 11.59–11.61, 11.68, 11.72, 11.77, 12.1, 12.4–12.6, 12.12, 12.15, 12.18, 12.21, 12.24, 12.31, 12.40, 12.44, 12.45, 12.47, 12.52–12.54, 12.78, 12.84, 12.104, 12.106–12.109, 12.112, 12.125, 13.12, 13.40, 14.1, 14.18, 15.25, 18.26, 18.32, 19.1, 19.3, 19.5, 19.13, 19.16, 19.20, 19.29, 19.31, 19.39, 19.61, 19.63, 19.67, 20.10, 21.8, 21.13, 21.16, 21.111, 22.11, 22.13, 23.16, 23.57, 30.45, 31.14, 33.40
    Art 1 — 11.6, 11.77

Art 1A	11.17, 11.35, 11.46, 11.77, 12.1, 12.137, 19.13
Art 1C	12.123, 12.125–12.127, 12.130, 12.131, 12.141, 19.29
Art 1C(5)	12.136, 12.141, 19.28
Art 1D	12.1, 12.7, 12.8
Art 1E	12.1, 12.7, 12.9, 12.34
Art 1F	11.31, 12.1, 12.2, 12.11, 12.12, 12.15, 12.16, 12.18, 12.20, 12.23, 12.54, 12.58, 12.66, 12.67, 12.110, 12.127, 13.12, 19.33, 19.48, 19.50, 19.61
Art 1F(a)	12.26, 12.29, 12.47, 12.65, 19.20
Art 1F(b)	12.30, 12.32, 12.36, 12.37, 12.65, 12.80, 19.20, 19.23
Art 1F(c)	12.17, 12.46–12.49, 12.52, 12.59, 12.61, 12.62, 12.65, 12.74, 19.20
Arts 2–31	11.6
Art 3	12.101
Art 4	12.101
Art 16	12.101
Art 22	12.101
Art 28	11.30
Art 31	12.101
Art 31(1)	2.18
Art 32	12.76, 12.77, 12.101
Art 33	5.17, 11.6, 11.77, 12.76, 12.77, 12.101
Art 33(1)	11.17, 11.76, 12.78, 19.31
Art 33(2)	5.27, 11.17, 11.77, 12.3, 12.34, 12.36, 12.76, 12.78, 12.80–12.83, 12.85, 12.97, 12.103, 12.106, 12.110, 12.111, 12.119, 12.127, 13.12, 19.20, 19.31, 20.11, 23.57
Art 34	11.6

Table of EU and international legislation xciii

Convention Relating to the Status of Refugees 1951 *continued*
- Art 42(1)   11.77
- Sch   11.30

Convention Relating to the Status of Refugees Protocol 1967   1.10, 3.23, 9.59, 11.5, 11.8, 21.8, 22.11, 23.16, 31.14

Decision 1/80 of the Association Council of 19 September 1980 on the development of the association   10.21
- Art 6   10.19
- Art 6(1)   10.18–10.20
- Art 7   10.18, 10.21
- Art 14(1)   10.18

Directive 64/221   9.10

Directive 2004/38/EC on the right of citizens of the Union and their family members to move and reside freely within the territory of the member states (Citizens Directive)   5.29, 8.1–8.6, 8.8, 8.11, 8.18, 8.19, 8.21–8.23, 8.29, 8.32, 8.33, 8.36, 8.37, 8.40, 8.42, 8.43, 9.1, 9.4, 9.5, 9.9, 9.10, 9.17, 9.18, 9.25, 9.30–9.34, 9.36, 9.37, 9.39, 9.45, 9.46, 9.52–9.54, 9.67, 9.70, 9.71, 9.77, 9.78, 10.1, 17.71, 20.11, 23.44
- Art 2   5.29
- Art 2(2)   5.47, 5.51, 8.13, 20.11
- Art 2(2)(a)   8.13
- Art 2(2)(b)   8.13
- Art 2(2)(c)   8.13
- Art 2(2)(d)   8.13
- Art 3   9.36
- Art 3(1)   8.37
- Art 3(2)   5.47, 5.51, 8.19, 20.11
- Art 3(2)(a)   8.19, 8.25, 8.26
- Art 3(2)(b)   8.19, 8.27
- Art 6   8.6
- Art 7(1)   8.48
- Art 7(1)(a)   8.6
- Art 7(1)(b)   8.6
- Art 7(1)(c)   8.6
- Art 7(1)(d)   8.6, 8.17
- Art 7(3)(a)   8.7
- Art 7(3)(b)   8.7
- Art 7(3)(c)   8.7
- Art 7(3)(d)   8.7
- Art 7(4)   8.6, 8.16
- Art 8(4)   8.6
- Art 8(5)   8.29
- Art 8(5)(e)   8.6, 8.29
- Art 8(5)(f)   8.6, 8.29
- Art 9(1)   8.6
- Art 10   8.6, 8.29

Directive 2004/38/EC (Citizens Directive) *continued*
Art 10(2)(e)	8.29
Art 10(2)(f)	8.29
Art 11	8.6
Art 12(1)	8.48
Art 12(2)	8.32, 8.48
Art 12(2)(b)	19.20
Art 12(3)	8.32
Art 13(1)	8.48
Art 13(2)	8.48
Art 13(2)(a)	8.32
Art 13(2)(c)	8.32
Art 13(2)(d)	8.32
Art 14(4)(a)	8.6
Art 14(4)(b)	8.6
Art 15(1)	9.9
Art 15(3)	9.9
Art 16	8.6, 9.32, 9.36
Art 16(1)	8.41, 8.43, 8.46, 9.30, 9.39
Art 16(2)	8.43, 8.46, 9.30
Art 16(3)	9.39
Art 16(4)	8.42, 9.39
Art 17	8.6
Art 17(1)	8.46
Art 17(1)(a)	8.44
Art 17(1)(b)	8.44
Art 17(1)(c)	8.44
Art 17(3)	8.46
Art 18	8.6, 9.32
Art 21	9.41
Art 24	9.70, 9.78
Art 25(1)	8.10
Art 27	8.29
Art 27(1)	9.11, 9.19
Art 27(2)	9.11, 9.12, 9.14, 9.15
Art 28	2.14, 9.24
Art 28(1)	9.19
Art 28(2)	9.22, 9.24
Art 28(3)	9.30
Art 28(3)(a)	9.26, 9.31
Art 28(3)(b)	9.26
Art 30(1)	9.52
Art 30(2)	9.52
Art 30(3)	9.52
Art 31(1)	9.53
Art 31(2)	9.53
Art 31(3)	9.53
Art 31(4)	9.54

Table of EU and international legislation xcv

Directive 2004/38/EC (Citizens Directive) *continued*
 Art 32(1) 9.67
 Art 32(2) 9.67
 Art 33(1) 9.24
 Art 33(2) 9.74
 Art 35 8.15
 Art 37 9.70, 9.78
Directive 2004/83/EC on minimum standards for the qualification and status of third country nationals or stateless persons as refugees or as persons who otherwise need international protection and the content of the protection granted (Qualification Directive) 11.1, 11.3, 11.10–11.14, 11.18, 11.23, 11.24, 11.32, 11.41, 11.49, 11.54–11.56, 11.63, 12.13, 12.38, 12.40, 12.42, 12.44, 12.45, 12.103, 12.104, 13.5, 14.1, 14.11, 14.12, 19.2, 19.5, 19.7, 19.11, 19.15, 19.16, 19.19, 19.20, 19.22, 19.27, 19.31, 23.16
 Art 2(c) 11.17
 Art 2(e) 14.5, 14.13, 19.7, 19.13
 Art 3 11.11
 Art 4 11.12, 11.39, 19.16
 Art 4(3) 14.11
 Art 4(4) 11.38
 Arts 5–12 11.12
 Art 5 19.16
 Art 5(1) 11.40
 Art 5(2) 11.40
 Art 5(3) 11.41
 Art 6 11.47, 19.16
 Art 7 11.49, 19.16
 Art 12(2)(b) 12.31, 12.39
 Art 8 11.50, 19.16
 Art 8(1) 14.16
 Art 9 11.46, 19.13
 Art 9(1) 11.46
 Art 9(2) 11.46
 Art 9(2)(c) 11.63
 Art 9(2)(d) 11.63
 Art 9(3) 11.54
 Art 10(1)(b) 11.55
 Art 10(1)(d) 11.58
 Art 10(2) 11.56
 Art 11 12.126, 19.29
 Art 11(1)(e) 19.28
 Art 11(2) 12.126, 12.134
 Art 12 12.15, 12.60
 Art 12(1) 12.10
 Art 12(2) 11.46, 12.13
 Art 12(2)(c) 12.58

Directive 2004/83/EC (Qualification Directive) *continued*

Art 12(3)	12.14
Art 14(2)	12.134
Art 14(3)(a)	12.74
Art 14(3)(b)	12.127
Art 14(4)	12.92, 12.99– 12.101, 12.103– 12.106, 19.24
Art 14(4)(a)	11.17
Art 14(4)(b)	11.17
Art 14(5)	12.100, 12.101, 12.103, 12.105, 12.106
Art 14(6)	12.101, 12.106
Arts 15–18	11.12
Art 15	14.5–14.7, 14.11, 19.7, 19.9, 19.14
Art 15(a)	14.7, 19.10, 19.13
Art 15(b)	14.7, 19.15
Art 15(c)	11.52, 14.1–14.4, 14.7–14.14, 14.16– 14.21, 19.3, 19.12, 19.13, 20.11
Art 16	19.28
Art 16(1)	19.29
Art 17	19.8, 19.18, 19.20, 19.21, 19.35
Art 17(1)	14.5, 19.7
Art 17(1)(b)	19.20
Art 17(1)(d)	19.20
Art 17(2)	14.5, 19.7
Art 17(3)	19.19
Art 20	19.26
Art 21	12.102, 19.68
Art 21(1)	12.108
Art 21(2)	12.108, 12.109
Art 21(3)	12.103, 12.108
Art 23	11.31
Art 23(5)	11.32
Art 24	11.28, 19.68
Art 24(1)	12.108, 12.109
Art 25	11.30
Art 26(1)	11.30
Art 26(2)	11.30
Art 26(3)	19.27
Art 27	11.30
Art 28	11.30
Art 28(2)	19.27
Art 29	11.30
Art 30	23.44

Directive 2004/83/EC (Qualification Directive) *continued*
　Art 31　　　　　　　　　　　　　　　　　　　23.44
　Art 32　　　　　　　　　　　　　　　　　　　11.30
　Art 33　　　　　　　　　　　　　　　　　　　11.30
　Art 63　　　　　　　　　　　　　　　　　　　11.11
EC Treaty　　　　　　　　　　　　　　　　　　5.29, 19.63
European Convention on the Protection of Human
　Rights and Fundamental Freedoms　　　　　　1.10, 1.44, 2.12,
　2.23, 3.17, 3.18, 3.23, 3.24, 4.18, 4.38, 5.26, 5.35, 5.44, 5.46, 5.47, 5.49,
　5.51, 5.54, 7.15, 7.16, 7.21, 7.26, 9.8, 9.59, 9.69, 11.5, 11.38, 11.46,
　11.52, 11.72, 12.108, 12.119, 13.1–13.5, 13.7, 13.8, 13.19, 13.27, 13.28,
　13.43, 13.44, 14.7, 14.9, 15.1, 15.9, 15.11, 15.19, 16.2, 16.5, 18.1, 18.50,
　18.59, 19.2, 19.15, 19.31, 19.33, 19.34, 19.39, 19.56, 19.59, 19.67, 19.68,
　20.5–20.10, 21.8, 21.14–21.16, 21.20, 21.22, 21.23, 21.111, 22.6, 22.10,
　22.11, 22.13, 22.20, 23.16, 23.19, 23.40, 23.43, 23.44, 23.56, 30.40,
　30.45, 31.3, 31.26, 33.40, 34.7, 36.1–36.4, 36.11, 36.39, 36.53, 36.88,
　36.95, 36.97, 37.7, 41.16, 41.40, 41.50, 42.24, 42.31, 43.23, 43.26, 43.27
　Art 1　　　　　　　　　　　　　　　　　　　13.7
　Art 2　　　　　　　　　　　　　　　　　　　11.47, 12.5, 13.1,
　　　　　　　　　　　　　　　　　　　　　　　13.24, 13.28, 13.31,
　　　　　　　　　　　　　　　　　　　　　　　13.42, 13.44, 14.7,
　　　　　　　　　　　　　　　　　　　　　　　14.8, 19.10, 19.19,
　　　　　　　　　　　　　　　　　　　　　　　19.25, 25.14, 39.71
　Art 2(1)　　　　　　　　　　　　　　　　　　13.27
　Art 3　　　　　　　　　　　　　　　　　　　11.47, 11.52, 12.4,
　12.5, 12.15, 12.24, 12.107, 12.112, 13.1, 13.4, 13.6, 13.8–13.13, 13.15–
　13.17, 13.20–13.24, 13.26–13.28, 13.31, 13.33–13.38, 13.40–13.42,
　13.44, 14.2, 14.7, 14.8, 14.11, 14.20, 16.39, 17.52, 18.1, 18.3–18.9, 18.11,
　18.13, 18.15, 18.16, 18.18, 18.25–18.27, 18.29, 18.31–18.33, 18.38,
　18.40, 18.44, 18.45, 18.49, 18.50, 18.56–18.59, 19.10, 19.14, 19.15,
　19.19, 19.25, 19.31, 19.33, 19.48, 20.11, 22.20, 22.21, 23.3, 23.5, 23.7–
　23.9, 23.36, 23.52, 23.56, 23.77, 23.80, 30.10, 33.40, 34.31, 36.3, 36.20,
　36.47, 36.48, 36.50, 36.53, 36.55, 36.57–36.61, 36.63–36.68, 36.70,
　36.71, 36.73, 36.74, 36.85, 36.104, 43.27
　Art 4　　　　　　　　　　　　　　　　　　　13.1, 13.44
　Art 4(1)　　　　　　　　　　　　　　　　　　11.47
　Art 5　　　　　　　　　　　　　　　　　　　23.9, 23.44, 23.56,
　　　　　　　　　　　　　　　　　　　　　　　26.13, 28.43, 32.34,
　　　　　　　　　　　　　　　　　　　　　　　32.36, 34.51, 35.21,
　　　　　　　　　　　　　　　　　　　　　　　36.2, 36.4–36.6,
　　　　　　　　　　　　　　　　　　　　　　　36.31, 36.46, 36.83,
　　　　　　　　　　　　　　　　　　　　　　　36.86, 37.7, 40.31,
　　　　　　　　　　　　　　　　　　　　　　　41.50, 43.27
　Art 5(1)　　　　　　　　　　　　　　　　　　15.11, 23.6–23.8,
　　　　　　　　　　　　　　　　　　　　　　　23.10, 23.91, 28.26,
　　　　　　　　　　　　　　　　　　　　　　　34.7, 36.5, 36.8,
　　　　　　　　　　　　　　　　　　　　　　　36.10–36.17, 36.21,
　　　　　　　　　　　　　　　　　　　　　　　36.23, 36.29, 36.33,
　　　　　　　　　　　　　　　　　　　　　　　36.43, 36.46, 42.78
　Art 5(1)(a)　　　　　　　　　　　　　　　　30.14
　Art 5(1)(e)　　　　　　　　　　　　　　　　30.5, 30.14

European Convention on the Protection of Human
Rights and Fundamental Freedoms *continued*

Art 5(1)(f)	23.7, 31.19, 33.39, 36.16, 36.18, 36.19, 36.23–36.30, 36.32–36.34, 36.36
Art 5(2)	35.13, 35.18, 35.20, 36.37–36.39, 36.46
Art 5(3)	36.46
Art 5(4)	23.2, 23.10, 23.42, 23.44, 23.84, 26.11, 28.26, 33.50, 35.19, 35.20, 35.24, 36.37, 36.40–36.46
Art 5(5)	23.10, 26.11, 35.20, 36.46
Art 6	13.46, 18.2, 18.60, 23.38–23.40, 23.44, 23.45, 23.56, 23.84
Art 6(1)	23.39, 23.84
Art 6(3)(b)	18.61
Art 7	11.47, 13.46
Art 8	4.3, 4.18, 4.29, 4.32, 5.39, 5.43, 9.8, 10.12, 10.15, 10.16, 13.4, 13.43, 13.47, 13.49, 13.50, 15.1–15.3, 15.5–15.9, 15.11, 15.17, 15.21, 15.22, 15.24–15.27, 16.5, 16.10–16.12, 16.18, 16.19, 16.25, 16.29, 16.35, 16.37–16.39, 17.1–17.3, 17.7, 17.8, 17.10, 17.11, 17.14, 17.20, 17.23, 17.24, 17.27–17.29, 17.32, 17.36, 17.38–17.41, 17.44, 17.46, 17.51, 17.52, 17.57, 17.64, 17.65, 17.67, 17.72, 17.74, 17.81, 17.88, 18.1, 18.3, 18.22, 18.28, 18.32, 18.53–18.58, 19.31, 19.33, 19.39, 19.47, 19.69, 20.10, 20.11, 23.44, 23.56, 23.87, 28.26, 30.10, 31.33, 34.31, 34.51, 36.3, 36.75, 36.77, 36.78, 36.80–36.82, 36.84–36.86, 36.89, 36.91, 36.93, 36.94, 36.104, 36.105, 37.11, 43.11, 43.27
Art 8(1)	16.1, 16.3, 16.4, 16.13, 16.21, 16.28, 17.39, 36.84
Art 8(2)	5.39, 10.16, 15.8, 15.11, 15.13, 15.22, 15.28, 17.27, 17.28, 17.34, 17.35, 17.54, 17.65, 34.7
Art 9	13.45, 13.47, 13.48
Art 10	13.48
Art 11	13.48
Art 13	23.2, 23.3
Art 14	4.42, 23.9, 26.13, 36.95–36.103, 43.27
Art 15	23.9, 36.5
Art 15(1)	23.5, 23.9
Art 15(2)	11.46

European Convention on the Protection of Human Rights and Fundamental Freedoms Protocol 13	13.29
Art 1	13.25
Framework Decision 2008/909/JHA3	29.18–29.21, 29.23, 29.24
Art 3(1)	29.24
Art 6(1)	29.19
Art 6(3)	29.21
Art 8	29.20
Art 9	29.20
Art 12	29.23
Art 15	29.23
Art 26(1)	29.18
Geneva Conventions for the Protection of Victims of War 1949	12.26
International Covenant of Civil and Political Rights	
Art 9	36.31
Optional Protocol to the UN Convention against Torture	25.20
Regulation (EC) 343/2003 of 18 February 2003 establishing the criteria and mechanisms for determining the Member State responsible for examining an asylum application lodged in one of the Member States by a third-country national (OJ L 50, 25 February 2003 (Dublin Regulation)	11.15
Statute of the International Criminal Court (Rome)	12.26
Art 7	12.27
Art 7(1)(k)	12.27
Art 8	12.27
Treaty of Lisbon 2007	11.10
Treaty on the European Community	
Art 12	9.70, 9.78
Art 39	10.19
Art 310	10.17
Treaty on the Functioning of the European Union	8.1, 9.6, 9.70, 9.78, 10.2, 10.4, 11.10
Art 18	9.70, 9.78
Art 20	4.23, 8.39, 10.4, 10.5, 10.8–10.11, 10.13–10.16, 17.33, 17.35
Art 20(2)(a)	10.16
Art 21	10.8
Art 45	10.19
Art 63(1)	11.10
Art 78	11.10
Art 78(1)	11.10
Art 217	10.17
United Nations Convention against Torture and Other Cruel, Inhuman or Degrading Treatment or Punishment	
Art 1	13.16

c *Foreign national prisoners / EU and international legislation*

United Nations Convention on the Rights of the Child	4.7, 4.13, 4.18, 4.28, 9.26, 37.7
Art 3	4.7, 4.14, 17.26, 37.7
United Nations Convention on the Rights of the Child *continued*	
Art 3(1)	17.81
Art 6(2)	4.28
Art 19	4.28
Art 20(3)	4.28
Art 24	4.28
Art 27	4.28
Art 28	4.28
Art 34	4.28
Art 27(b)	4.28
Art 39	4.28
Art 40(1)	17.81
Vienna Convention on Consular Relations 1962	27.43, 27.46
Art 36(1)(b)	27.46
Art 36(1)(c)	27.46

Abbreviations

1964 Directive	Council Directive 64/221/EEC of 25 February 1964 on the co-ordination of special measures concerning the movement and residence of foreign nationals which are justified on grounds of public policy, public security or public health
ACDT	Assessment Care in Detention and Teamwork
AIAA 1993	Asylum and Immigration Appeals Act 1993
AIT	Asylum and Immigration Tribunal
AITCA 2004	Asylum and Immigration (Treatment of Claimants etc) Act 2004
APIs	Asylum Policy Instructions
ASU	Asylum Screening Unit
ATCSA 2001	Anti-terrorism, Crime and Security Act 2001
AVR	Assisted Voluntary Return
AVRFC	Assisted Voluntary Return for Families and Children
AVRIM	Assisted Voluntary Return for Irregular Migrants
BCIA 2009	Borders, Citizenship and Immigration Act 2009
BNA 1981	British Nationality Act 1981
CCA 1984	County Courts Act 1984
CCD	Criminal Casework Directorate
CIO	Chief Immigration Officer
CIPU	Country Information Policy Unit
Citizens Directive	Directive 2004/38/EC on the right of citizens of the European Union and their family members to move and reside freely within the territory of the EU
CJA 1991	Criminal Justice Act 1991
CJA 2003	Criminal Justice Act 2003
CJEU	Court of Justice of the European Union
CJIA 2008	Criminal Justice and Immigration Act 2008
CMRH	Case Management Review Hearing
CPR	Civil Procedure Rules 1998
CPT	Committee for the Prevention of Torture
CRB	Criminal Records Bureau
C(S)A 1997	Crime (Sentences) Act 1997
DEPMU	Detainee Escorting and Population Management Unit
DL	Discretionary Leave
DoH	Department of Health
DPA 1998	Data Protection Act 1998
DS CSU	Detention Services Customer Service Unit

DSO	Detention Service Order
DTO	Detention and Training Order
EA 2010	Equality Act 2010
EC	European Community
ECHR	European Convention on Human Rights
ECJ	European Court of Justice
ECommHR	European Commission of Human Rights
ECtHR	European Court of Human Rights
EEA	European Economic Area
EEA Regs 2000	Immigration (European Economic Area) Regulations 2000 SI No 2326
EEA Regs 2006	Immigration (European Economic Area) Regulations 2006 SI No 1003
EFTA	European Free Trade Association
EHRC	Equality and Human Rights Commission
EIG	Enforcement Instructions and Guidance
ELR	Exceptional Leave to Remain
EPU	Enforcement Policy Unit
ERS	Early Removal Scheme
EU	European Union
ExCom	Executive Committee of the High Commissioner's Programme
FCO	Foreign and Commonwealth Office
FNPs	Foreign national prisoners and former prisoners
FIA 2000	Freedom of Information Act 2000
FRS	Facilitated Returns Scheme
FTT-IAC	Immigration and Asylum Chamber of the First-tier Tribunal
FTT-MH	Mental Health Chamber of the First-tier Tribunal
HDC	Home Detention Curfew
HMCIP	Her Majesty's Chief Inspector of Prisons
HMP	Her Majesty's Prison
HOPO	Home Office Presenting Officer
HP	Humanitarian Protection
HRA 1998	Human Rights Act 1998
IA 1971	Immigration Act 1971
IAA	Immigration Appellate Authority
IAA 1999	Immigration and Asylum Act 1999
IAC	Immigration and Asylum Chamber of the First-tier Tribunal and/or Upper Tribunal
IANA 2006	Immigration Asylum and Nationality Act 2006
ICC	International Criminal Court
ICCA 2001	International Criminal Court Act 2001
ICCPR	International Covenant of Civil and Political Rights
IDIs	Immigration Directorate Instructions
IEPs	Incentives and earned privileges
IHL	International humanitarian law
ILPA	Immigration Law Practitioners' Association
ILR	Indefinite Leave to Remain
IMB	Independent Monitoring Board

IOM	International Organization for Migration
IPP	Indeterminate Sentence for Public Protection
IRC	Immigration Removal Centre
ISA	Independent Safeguarding Authority
ISAF	International Special Assistance Force
JR	Judicial review
LA 1980	Limitation Act 1980
LOTR	Leave outside the Rules
LSC	Legal Services Commission
MAPPA	Multi-Agency Public Protection Arrangements
MHA 1983	Mental Health Act 1983
MoJ	Ministry of Justice
NASS	National Asylum Support Service
NIAA 2002	Nationality, Immigration and Asylum Act 2002
NIC	Nominal Index Card
NOMS	National Offender Management Service
NPM	National preventive mechanism
OASys	Offender Assessment System
OEM	Operational Enforcement Manual
OGP	OASys General re-offending Predictor
OGRS3	Offender Group Reconviction Scale
OISC	Office of the Immigration Services Commissioner
OM	Offender Manager
OMA 2007	Offender Management Act 2007
OPCAT	Optional Protocol to the UN Convention against Torture
OVP	OASys Violence Predictor
PA 1952	Prison Act 1952
PC	Probation Circular
PCC(S)A 2000	Powers of the Criminal Courts (Sentencing) Act 2000
PD	Practice Direction
PI	Probation Instruction
PMS	Population Management Section
PMU	Population Management Unit
PPO	Prisons and Probation Ombudsman
PR 1999	Prison Rules 1999 SI No 728
PSI	Prison Service Instruction
PSO	Prison Service Order
PSU	Professional Standards Unit
PTA 2005	Prevention of Terrorism Act 2005
Qualification Directive	Council Directive 2004/83/EC on minimum standards for the qualification and status of third country nationals or stateless persons as refugees or as persons who otherwise need international protection and the content of the protection granted
Refugee Convention	The 1951 Convention Relating to the Status of Refugees and its 1967 Protocol
Return Directive	Directive 2008/115 on common standards and procedures in member states for returning illegally staying third country nationals

RFRL	Reasons for refusal letter
ROTL	Release on Temporary Licence
RPA 1984	Repatriation of Prisoners Act 1984
RPNIP Regs 2006	Refugee or Person in Need of International Protection (Qualification) Regulations 2006 SI No 2170
RRA 1976	Race Relations Act 1976
RRLO	Race relations liaison officer
SACU	Security and Anti Corruption Unit
SASO	Special Advocates Support Office
SCA 1981	Senior Courts Act 1981
SIAC	Special Immigration Appeals Commission
SIACA 1997	Special Immigration Appeals Commission Act 1997
SIRC	Security and Intelligence Review Committee
SLA	Service Level Agreement
SSHD	Secretary of State for the Home Department
SSJ	Secretary of State for Justice
SSWP	Secretary of State for Work and Pensions
STC	Secure training centre
STHF	Short term holding facilities
TA 2000	Terrorism Act 2000
TCEA 2007	Tribunals, Courts and Enforcement Act 2007
TEC	Treaty establishing the European Community
TEU	Treaty on European Union
TFEU	Treaty on the Functioning of the European Union
UASCs	Unaccompanied asylum-seeking children
UKBA	UK Border Agency
UKBA 2007	UK Borders Act 2007
UNCRC	UN Convention on the Rights of the Child
UNHCR	UN High Commissioner for Refugees
UNHCR Handbook	Handbook on Procedures and Criteria for Determining Refugee Status under the 1951 Convention and the 1967 Protocol relating to the Status of Refugees
UNRWA	United Nations Relief and Works Agency
UT-IAC	Immigration and Asylum Chamber of the Upper Tribunal
VARRP	Voluntary Assisted Return and Reintegration Programme
ViSOR	Violent and Sexual Offenders Register
YJB	Youth Justice Board
YOI	Young Offender Institution
YOI Rules 2000	Young Offender Institution Rules 2000 SI No 3371
YOT	Youth Offending Team

PART I

Deportation

SECTION A

Powers and process of deportation

Chapter 1: Deportation powers under the Immigration Act 1971   7

Chapter 2: Criminal court recommendations for deportation   23

Chapter 3: The Secretary of State's decision-making in deportation cases under the Immigration Act 1971   33

Chapter 4: Deportation cases involving minors: relevant legislation and policy   51

Chapter 5: 'Automatic' deportation under the UK Borders Act 2007   67

Chapter 6: Departure: voluntary departure and deportation arrangements   83

Chapter 7: Revocation and other forms of termination of deportation orders in non-EEA cases   91

Introduction to deportation

Deportation and administrative removal

There are two ways in which foreign nationals can be expelled from the UK under Immigration Act powers:

- A *deportation order* cancels any existing leave to enter or remain. Deportation can therefore be used against those who have limited leave, or who have indefinite leave to enter or remain in the UK as well as against those who have no leave. Those expelled under a deportation order are prohibited from re-entering the UK while the deportation order remains in force.
- *Administrative removal* may only be used for the expulsion of those with no existing leave to remain. Although those who have been subject to administrative removal face considerable obstacles to re-entering the UK, there is no prohibition in primary legislation on their re-entry.

We refer in this book to 'expulsion' to mean both deportation and administrative removal. Where foreign national prisoners and former prisoners (FNPs) face expulsion this will, in the vast majority of cases, involve deportation rather than administrative removal. In cases of criminal conviction, deportation is often used even against foreign nationals who have no existing leave to remain and so would also be liable to administrative removal (as well as against those who have existing leave).

Two parallel statutory regimes of deportation

There are two parallel statutory regimes governing deportation. The long-standing statutory regime for deportation was established by the Immigration Act (IA) 1971. Under the IA 1971, the Secretary of State for the Home Department (SSHD) has a discretion over whether to pursue the deportation of foreign nationals who have been recommended for deportation by a court or whose deportation is believed by the SSHD to be conducive to the public good, and their non-British family members.

In late April 2006, however, it transpired that the Home Office had not been considering deportation before releasing many FNPs at the end of their custodial term. The government's response to the revelation of the Home Office's failure to consider or exercise its wide power to deport was to introduce new legislation, the UK

Borders Act (UKBA) 2007, under which the SSHD surrendered her discretion over whether to deport in most cases (so that deportation orders were 'automatic').

Most deportation now occurs under the 'automatic' deportation provisions of the UKBA 2007. However, those who do not meet the criteria for 'automatic' deportation under the UKBA 2007, and in particular family members of criminal offenders, may still face 'discretionary' deportation under IA 1971.

CHAPTER 1

Deportation powers under the Immigration Act 1971

1.1	Introduction
1.7	**'Conducive' deportation**
1.9	'Conducive' deportation without a criminal conviction
	'Conducive' deportation based on offences committed abroad • 'Conducive' deportation where leave has been obtained by deception • 'Conducive' deportation on the basis of 'character and associations' • Allegations and evidence which resulted in acquittal at a criminal trial abroad
1.15	**The deportation of family members**
1.17	The definition of 'family member' for the purposes of deportation under IA 1971 s3(5)(b)
1.18	Time limits on the deportation of family members
1.20	Circumstances in which a deportation order made against a family member will cease to have effect
1.21	The Immigration Rules and limitations on the power to deport family members
	Meaning of 'settled' in the United Kingdom
1.23	Relevant factors in the decision whether to deport a family member
1.25	**The deportation of certain overstayers**
1.27	**Exemption from deportation**
1.27	British citizens
1.29	Others with a right of abode

continued

1.34	Long-resident Irish and Commonwealth nationals
	Meaning of 'ordinarily resident'
1.41	Diplomats and international functionaries
1.43	**Timing and effect of a deportation order in cases governed by the Immigration Act 1971**
1.43	In-country rights of appeal against decisions to deport made under the Immigration Act 1971
1.45	When a deportation order can be made under the Immigration Act 1971
1.48	When a deportation order under the Immigration Act 1971 takes effect

Introduction

1.1 Four categories of foreign nationals are liable to deportation under the Immigration Act (IA) 1971:
- those whose deportation is deemed by the Secretary of State for the Home Department (SSHD) to be conducive to the public good[1] (referred to in this book as 'conducive' deportation);
- those recommended for deportation by a court;[2]
- the non-British family members of a person who has been ordered to be deported;[3] and
- increasingly rarely, certain overstayers.[4]

1.2 The SSHD always has a discretion as to whether to make a deportation order against those liable for deportation under the IA 1971 (she 'may' make a deportation order[5]). We therefore refer in this book to 'discretionary' deportation under the IA 1971.

1.3 Parts of the Immigration Rules and a wide array of policies outside the Rules give guidance as to how that discretion to deport should be exercised; in deportation cases involving children, an important statutory duty (Borders, Citizenship and Immigration Act (BCIA) 2009 s55) also applies. The decision-making process in IA 1971 deportation cases generally is discussed in chapter 3; and statutory duties and policies relevant in IA 1971 cases involving children are discussed in chapter 4.

1.4 In cases governed by the IA 1971, it is the SSHD's decision to make a deportation order which triggers statutory rights of appeal to the Immigration and Asylum Chamber of the First Tier Tribunal (FTT-IAC) under the Nationality, Immigration and Asylum Act (NIAA) 2002.[6] Only once any appeal rights against that decision (and, in court recommendation cases, any appeal against the recommendation or conviction) are exhausted may the deportation order be made.[7] The deportation order has the effect of cancelling any existing leave to remain.

---

1 IA 1971 s3(5)(a).
2 IA 1971 s3(6).
3 IA 1971 s3(5)(b).
4 Under the old IA 1971 s3(5), which was amended by Immigration and Asylum Act (IAA) 1999 s169 and Sch 14 paras 43 and 44.
5 IA 1971 s5(1).
6 NIAA 2002 s82(2)(j).
7 NIAA 2002 s79 and IA 1971 s6(6).

1.5   Aside from British Citizens who cannot be deported,[8] there are important statutory exemptions from deportation for others with a right of abode in the UK;[9] for long-resident Irish and Commonwealth nationals[10] and for diplomats and international functionaries.[11]

1.6   This chapter reviews three groups liable for deportation under the IA 1971, namely those whose deportation is deemed conducive to the public good; family members; and certain overstayers. A further category of person liable for such deportation, those recommended for deportation by a sentencing court, is dealt with separately in chapter 2. We then discuss the statutory exemptions from deportation under the IA 1971. This chapter ends with a discussion of the timing and effects of deportation orders made in cases governed by the IA 1971.

'Conducive' deportation

1.7   The SSHD may deport those whose deportation is deemed conducive to the public good.[12] The most common use of this power is where a person has been convicted of one or more criminal offences in the UK. At paras 3.6–3.7, we discuss the criteria commonly applied by the SSHD in determining which offences and sentences should attract 'conducive' deportation under the IA 1971.

1.8   However, 'conducive' deportation has a wide ambit, and may be used in the absence of any criminal conduct at all.[13]

---

8   IA 1971 ss3(5) and 6(2).
9   IA 1971 s1(1).
10 IA 1971 s7.
11 IA 1971 s8(3).
12 IA 1971 s3(5)(a).
13 See, for example, *R v Secretary of State for the Home Department ex p Hosenball* [1977] 1 WLR 766 in which an American investigative journalist was made the subject of a deportation order after publishing an article discussing the UK government's surveillance techniques. See also the facts of *R (Raed Salah Mahjana) v Secretary of State for the Home Department* [2011] EWHC 2481 (Admin) in which the SSHD sought to deport an Arab-Israeli citizen visiting the UK to address, among others, the House of Lords. The SSHD proceeded on the basis of allegations that he had publicly expressed anti-Semitic views and views supportive of violence, and on grounds that his presence might foster inter-community violence.

'Conducive' deportation without a criminal conviction

1.9 Home Office policy refers to the following instances in which a person may be deported on conducive grounds notwithstanding that they have not been convicted of any offence in the UK:[14]

- national security cases;
- where the person has 'involvement or complicity in war crimes, crimes against humanity or genocide';
- exceptionally, 'individuals who have committed serious offences in their own country';
- where 'the person has engaged in unacceptable behaviour'; and
- where indefinite leave to remain (ILR) has been obtained by deception.

Conducive deportation in the absence of a conviction is most frequently used in national security cases, which are discussed in chapter 23 of this book. Below, we discuss other examples.

'Conducive' deportation based on offences committed abroad

1.10 The SSHD may deport on conducive grounds on the basis of offences committed abroad.[15] A number of cases have considered the relationship between deportation in these circumstances and extradition. It is lawful to deport for an extraditable offence.[16] The fact that a person will, after deportation, be prosecuted in his or her home country, is irrelevant to the lawfulness of deportation save in so far as that prosecution might breach the European Convention on Human Rights (ECHR) or Refugee Convention[17] and even where the home country prosecution would amount to double jeopardy.[18] However deportation with the *purpose* of avoiding the safeguards of the extradition procedure is an abuse of process at common law[19] and is impermissible under the ECHR.[20]

---

14 Enforcement Instructions and Guidance (EIG) chapter 13 paras 12.2 and 13.2; Immigration Directorate's Instructions (IDIs) chapter 13 para 2.1.
15 *R v IAT ex p Martinez-Tobon* [1988] Imm AR 319, CA.
16 *R v Governor of Brixton Prison ex p Soblen* [1963] 2 QB 243; *R v Staines Magistrates Court ex p Westfallen* [1998] 1 WLR 652.
17 The 1951 Convention Relating to the Status of Refugees and its 1967 Protocol ('Refugee Convention'). *QJ (Algeria) v Secretary of State for the Home Department* [2010] EWCA Civ 1478 para 21.
18 *QJ (Algeria) v Secretary of State for the Home Department* para 22.
19 *R v Mullen* [2000] QB 520, [1999] 3 WLR 777, CA.
20 *Bozano v France* (1986) 9 EHRR 297.

'Conducive' deportation where leave has been obtained by deception

1.11 The SSHD may deport on conducive grounds where leave has been obtained as a consequence of deception.[21] However, deportation is now relatively rare in such cases because obtaining leave by deception is also a ground of administrative removal[22] and it is Home Office policy to use deportation procedures for those who obtained ILR by deception prior to 1 October 1996 but to use administrative removal for those who obtained ILR by deception subsequently.[23]

1.12 Where alleged deception results in deportation or administrative removal or in an immigrant being treated as an illegal entrant, the deception must be established by the SSHD to a high degree of probability.[24]

'Conducive' deportation on the basis of 'character and associations'

1.13 'Conducive' deportation on the basis of character and associations remains relatively rare outside the national security context. However, the Home Office's 'Operation Alliance' targeted alleged gang members for deportation action in the absence of criminal conviction.[25]

Allegations and evidence which resulted in acquittal at a criminal trial abroad

1.14 It is not an abuse of process for the SSHD to rely in deportation cases, at the initial decision-making stage or on appeal, on allegations and evidence which had resulted in an acquittal at a criminal trial.[26] A criminal acquittal is not conclusive of future civil proceedings because of the lower standard of proof in civil proceedings and because 'res judicata' estoppel (the doctrine that the same matter cannot be re-litigated) does not apply to a verdict in criminal

---

21 *R v IAT ex p Patel* [1988] AC 910, HL.
22 IAA 1999 s10.
23 IDIs chapter 13 para 2.1.
24 *Khawaja v Secretary of State for the Home Department* [1984] AC 74; *R (Ullah) v Secretary of State for the Home Department* [2003] EWCA Civ 1366; see also IDIs chapter 13 para 2.1.
25 See discussion in *R (V) v AIT* [2009] EWHC 1902 (Admin).
26 *R (V) v AIT* [2009] EWHC 1902 (Admin).

proceedings.[27] Moreover, strict rules of evidence do not apply in the Immigration and Asylum Chamber of the First Tier and Upper Tribunals (referred to collectively in this book as 'IAC')[28] so that the IAC may admit evidence inadmissible in a criminal court, albeit the weight to be given to such evidence may be limited.[29]

The deportation of family members

1.15 Under IA 1971 s3(5)(b), a person who is not a British citizen is liable to be deported if another person to whose family he or she belongs is or has been ordered to be deported.

1.16 Family members can only be deported under the discretionary deportation provisions of the IA 1971. There is no 'automatic' deportation of family members under the UK Borders Act (UKBA) 2007, although the family members of a person who is 'automatically' deported under the UKBA 2007 may be subject to 'discretionary' deportation under the IA 1971.[30]

The definition of 'family member' for the purposes of deportation under IA 1971 s3(5)(b)

1.17 The definition of 'family member' for these purposes is provided at IA 1971 s5(4). The principal deportee's spouse or civil partner and the children aged under 18 of the principal deportee or his or her spouse or civil partner are family members for these purposes. An adopted child, whether legally adopted or not, may be treated as the child of the adopter and, if legally adopted must be regarded as the child only of the adopter. Subject to that rule on adoption, an 'illegitimate' child is regarded as the child of the mother. The term 'wife' includes a marriage in which there are two or more wives[31].

---

27 *DPP v Humphreys* [1977] AC 1; see also Civil Evidence Act 1968 ss11–13 which makes a conviction only prima facie evidence in proceedings other than defamation.
28 Asylum and Immigration Tribunal (Procedure) Rules 2005 SI No 230 r51(1).
29 *R (V) v AIT* [2009] EWHC 1902 (Admin) para 65.
30 By UKBA 2007 ss37 and 38(4)(c), an 'automatic' deportation order made pursuant to UKBA 2007 s32(5) is treated as a deportation order made under IA 1971 s5. Therefore, IA 1971 s3(5)(b) which permits the deportation of family members of a principal who is or has been ordered to be deported also applies to the family members of 'automatic' deportees.
31 IA 1971 s5(4).

Time limits on the deportation of family members

1.18 Under IA 1971 s5(3), a deportation order may not be made against a family member if more than eight weeks have elapsed since the principal left the UK after the making of the deportation order.

1.19 Where the principal is the subject of an 'automatic' deportation order made under UKBA 2007 s32(5),[32] different time limits apply to the making of a deportation order against a family member. Where the principal has not appealed, a deportation order may not be made against the family member of an 'automatic' deportee after the end of eight weeks from the date when an in-time appeal could no longer be brought by the principal.[33] Where the principal has appealed, a deportation order may not be made against the family member of an 'automatic' deportee after the end of eight weeks from the date when an appeal is no longer pending.[34]

Circumstances in which a deportation order made against a family member will cease to have effect

1.20 Under IA 1971 s5(3), where a deportation order is made against a family member, that deportation order will cease to have effect if the deportation order against the principal ceases to have effect or if the family member ceases to be a family member of the principal. Note too that, as with any other deportation order, a deportation order against a family member will cease to have effect if he or she becomes a British citizen.[35]

The Immigration Rules and limitations on the power to deport family members

1.21 Paragraphs 365 and 366 of the Immigration Rules set out important limitations on the exercise of the SSHD's power to deport family members. The SSHD will not normally decide to deport:

- the spouse or civil partner of a deportee who has qualified for settlement in his or her own right (Immigration Rules para 365(i));

---

32 See para 5.12.
33 UKBA 2007 s37(1), (2), (3).
34 UKBA 2007 s37(1), (2), (4). The term 'pending' is defined in NIAA 2002 s104 as covering the period from when an appeal is instituted to when it is finally determined, withdrawn or abandoned.
35 IA 1971 s5(2).

- the spouse or civil partner of a deportee who has been living apart from the deportee (Immigration Rules para 365(ii));
- the child of a deportee where the child and the child's mother or father are living apart from a deportee (Immigration Rules para 366(i));
- the child of a deportee where the child has left home and established him/herself on an independent basis (Immigration Rules para 366(ii)); or
- the child of a deportee, where the child has married or formed a civil partnership before deportation came into prospect (Immigration Rules para 366(iii)).

Meaning of 'settled' in the United Kingdom

1.22 'Settled in the United Kingdom' is defined in the IA 1971 s33(2A) as 'being ordinarily resident there without being subject under the immigration laws to any restriction on the period for which he may remain'.[36] See paras 1.38–1.40 below for the meaning of 'ordinarily resident'. 'Settled' is also defined in Immigration Rules para 6:

'settled in the United Kingdom' means that the person concerned:
(a) is free from any restriction on the period for which he may remain save that a person entitled to an exemption under Section 8 of the Immigration Act 1971 (otherwise than as a member of the home forces) is not to be regarded as settled in the United Kingdom except in so far as Section 8(5A) so provides; and
(b) is either:
   (i) ordinarily resident in the United Kingdom without having entered or remained in breach of the immigration laws; or
   (ii) despite having entered or remained in breach of the immigration laws, has subsequently entered lawfully or has been granted leave to remain and is ordinarily resident.

Relevant factors in the decision whether to deport a family member

1.23 Immigration Rules para 367 sets out a non-exhaustive list of 'relevant factors' which the SSHD will consider when deciding whether to deport a family member:
   (i) the ability of the spouse or civil partner to maintain himself and any children in the United Kingdom, or to be maintained by

---

36 Subject to IA 1971 s8(5) which provides that certain international diplomats and members of foreign armed forces posted in the UK are not to be regarded as settled.

relatives or friends without charge to public funds, not merely for a short period but for the foreseeable future; and
(ii) in the case of a child of school age, the effect of removal on his education; and
(iii) the practicality of any plans for a child's care and maintenance in this country if one or both of his parents were deported; and
(iv) any representations made on behalf of the spouse or child.

1.24 Note that it is important to check the citizenship of family members. British citizens cannot be deported[37] yet the SSHD on occasions has made decisions to deport family members who are in fact British.[38]

The deportation of certain overstayers

1.25 Until 2 October 2000, the mechanism for expelling a person who had overstayed his or her limited leave to enter or remain in the UK was deportation. On 2 October 2000, new legislation came into force under which overstayers became liable to administrative removal[39] and IA 1971 s3(5) was amended[40] to reserve deportation for more serious categories of misconduct.

1.26 However, under transitional provisions deportation is still used for a shrinking, residual group of overstayers:[41]

- overstayers who were notified before 2 October 2000 of a decision to deport them; and
- overstayers who had applied for leave to remain under a regularisation scheme for overstayers under the IAA 1999 s9[42] and whose application was refused.

---

37 IA 1971 s3(5).
38 See, for example, the comments of Baroness Hale in *ZH (Tanzania) v Secretary of State for the Home Department* [2011] UKSC 4, [2011] 2 WLR 148 para 4.
39 IAA 1999 s10.
40 IAA 1999 s169 and Sch 14 paras 43 and 44.
41 Immigration and Asylum Act 1999 (Commencement No 6, Transitional and Consequential Provisions) Order 2000 SI No 2444 Sch 2 para 1. Reflected in Immigration Rules HC 395 para 363A.
42 Applicants for this regularisation scheme for overstayers had to seek leave to remain in the period of 8 February to 1 October 2000. The consequence of refusal under this scheme was that the overstayer became liable to deportation. The transitional arrangements for this group are set out in IA 1971 Sch 15 para 12.

Exemption from deportation

British citizens

1.27 British citizens cannot be deported.[43] Where a deportation order is already in force, it will cease to have effect if the person becomes a British citizen.[44]

1.28 It is for the person claiming to be a British citizen to prove that status.[45] A British passport or a certificate of entitlement (if genuine documents) are proof of British citizenship (IA 1971 s9). Likewise it has been held that the production of a genuine British passport issued to the person discharges the burden of proof.[46]

Others with a right of abode

1.29 Those with a right of abode in the UK are free from immigration control.[47] They cannot be deported or administratively removed from the UK.[48] They do not require leave to enter the UK (although they can be required to produce a passport on arrival).

1.30 Other than British citizens, certain Commonwealth citizens have a right of abode in the UK. A Commonwealth citizen who had the right of abode in the UK[49] prior to 1 January 1983 retains the right of abode, is treated under the IA 1971 as if he or she were a British citizen[50] and is therefore exempt from deportation. The right of abode for these Commonwealth citizens derives from citizenship and nationality law and is a relic of the UK's relations with its former colonies.[51]

1.31 The onus is on the person asserting a right of abode to prove it.[52] On seeking to enter the UK, the right of abode is proved by a UK

---

43 IA 1971 ss3(5) and 6(2).
44 IA 1971 s5(2).
45 IA 1971 s3(8).
46 *R v Secretary of State for the Home Department ex p Obi* [1997] 1 WLR 1498, [1997] Imm AR 420, QBD.
47 IA 1971 s1(1).
48 IA 1971 s2(2).
49 By operation of IA 1971 s2(1)(d) or (2) as it was before its amendment by the British Nationality Act 1981, that is, prior to 1 January 1983.
50 IA 1971 s2 as amended by British Nationality Act 1981 s39(2).
51 For further detail, see Ian Macdonald QC and Ronan Toal, *Macdonald's immigration law and practice*, LexisNexis, 8th edn, ch 2; and Laurie Fransman QC, *British nationality law*, Bloomsbury Professional, 3rd edn.
52 IA 1971 s3(8).

passport describing a person as a British citizen or as a British subject having the right of abode in the UK; a certificate of entitlement of a right of abode; or an identity card issued under the Identity Cards Act 2006 describing a person as a British citizen or as a British subject with a right of abode in the UK.[53]

1.32 The right of abode should not be confused with indefinite leave to remain in the UK: those with the latter are subject to immigration control and thus to deportation.

1.33 Note, however, that the right of abode may be stripped where that person is the citizen of another Commonwealth country and it is deemed conducive to the public good to exclude that person from the UK.[54] See paras 19.76–19.77.

Long-resident Irish and Commonwealth nationals

1.34 Further exemptions from deportation are set out at IA 1971 s7 for long-resident Irish and Commonwealth citizens.

1.35 A Commonwealth citizen or citizen of the Republic of Ireland is exempt from deportation if he or she:

- was a Commonwealth citizen or citizen of the Republic of the Ireland on 1 January 1973;
- was ordinarily resident in the UK on 1 January 1973; and
- in the case of a 'conducive' or family deportation, at the time of the SSHD's decision to deport him or her, had been ordinarily resident for the last five years in the UK.

1.36 Likewise, a court may not on convicting a person of an offence recommend a person for deportation if he or she:

- was a Commonwealth citizen or citizen of the Republic of the Ireland on 1 January 1973;
- was ordinarily resident[55] in the UK on 1 January 1973; and
- at the time of the conviction had for the last five years been ordinarily resident in the UK.

1.37 The five years must have been completed at the time of the decision to make a deportation order or the date of the conviction, not the date of the deportation order.[56]

---

53 IA 1971 s3(9) as amended by Immigration Asylum and Nationality Act (IANA) 2006 s30.
54 IA 1971 s2A as amended by IANA 2006 s57.
55 IA 1971 s7(3).
56 *Mehmet v Secretary of State for the Home Department* [1977] Imm AR 68, CA.

Meaning of 'ordinarily resident'

1.38 The term 'ordinarily resident' was held by the House of Lords in *Shah v Barnet London Borough Council*[57] to mean a person's voluntarily adopted abode in a particular place or country, whether of short or long duration.

1.39 A person who has at any time become ordinarily resident in the UK will not, for the purposes of IA 1971 s7, be treated as having ceased to be ordinarily resident because he or she remained in the UK in breach of the immigration laws.[58] However, a person who is on temporary release or temporary admission under IA 1971 Sch 2 para 21 while liable to detention under IA 1971 Sch 2 para 16 is not treated as 'ordinarily resident'.[59]

1.40 The period of ordinary residence for the purposes of exemption under IA 1971 s7 does *not* include time during which the person was serving a period of imprisonment or detention by virtue of a sentence of imprisonment of six months or more, passed in the UK.[60] When calculating whether a person has served a period of imprisonment or detention by virtue of a sentence of six months or more:

- two or more sentences for consecutive or partly consecutive terms are treated as a single sentence;[61]
- time spent unlawfully at large when liable to imprisonment or detention is treated as a period of imprisonment or detention;[62] and
- any period of custody (unless the sentence is passed after that time) during which the term to be served under the sentence is reduced is treated as a period of imprisonment or detention.[63]

Diplomats and international functionaries

1.41 Certain diplomats and international functionaries are also immune from deportation (IA 1971 s8(3)) because they are exempt from immigration control altogether. The following are exempt from deportation:

---

57 [1983] 2 AC 309.
58 IA 1971 s7(2).
59 *R (A) v Secretary of State for Health* [2009] EWCA Civ 225, [2010] 1 WLR 279.
60 IA 1971 s7(3).
61 IA 1971 s7(4)(b).
62 IA 1971 s7(4)(c)(i).
63 IA 1971 s7(4)(c)(ii).

- a person who is a member of a diplomatic mission (within the meaning of Diplomatic Privileges Act 1964);
- members of his or her family who form part of his or her household; and
- a person who is otherwise entitled, under the Diplomatic Privileges Act 1964, to the immunity from jurisdiction conferred on diplomatic agents.

1.42 For the purposes of exemption under IA 1971 s8(3), other than diplomatic agents, a person will not count as a member of a diplomatic mission unless he or she was resident outside the UK and was outside the UK when offered the post and did not cease to be a member of the mission after taking up the post.

Timing and effect of a deportation order in cases governed by the Immigration Act 1971

In-country rights of appeal against decisions to deport made under the Immigration Act 1971

1.43 Where the SSHD has taken a 'discretionary' decision to make a deportation order under IA 1971 s5(1) the proposed deportee has a right of appeal to the Immigration and Asylum Chamber of the First-tier Tribunal (FTT-IAC) against the decision to deport. The right of appeal arises under NIAA 2002 s82(2)(j). The appeal is exercisable in-country, whatever the grounds of appeal.[64] Appeals to the FTT-IAC are discussed in chapter 21.

1.44 However, where the SSHD certifies that a decision to deport a person is made in the interests of national security, the appeal lies to the Special Immigration Appeals Commission (SIAC).[65] In national security cases, an appeal to SIAC may only be brought while the proposed deportee is still in the UK if he or she is an EEA national or the family member of an EEA national and has made a claim that deportation would breach EU law, or if he or she has made a human rights claim (unless the SSHD has issued a certificate that the deportation would not breach the person's rights under the ECHR, in which case an appeal to SIAC lies against that certification and this appeal can

---

64 NIAA 2002 s92(2).
65 NIAA 2002 ss97 and 97A.

be brought while still in the UK).[66] Appeals to SIAC are discussed in chapter 23.

When a deportation order can be made under the Immigration Act 1971

1.45 Where a decision to deport has been made under IA 1971, no deportation order may be made while an appeal against the decision to deport could still be brought in time, or is pending.[67] An appeal is pending from the time it is lodged until it is finally determined, withdrawn or abandoned.[68] The appeal is not finally determined while an application for permission to appeal to the Immigration and Asylum Chamber of the Upper Tribunal (UT-IAC) or the Court of Appeal could be made or is awaiting determination[69] or has been granted and the full appeal is awaiting determination;[70] or an appeal has been remitted by the UT-IAC or the Court of Appeal and is awaiting determination.[71]

1.46 Where there is a court recommendation to deport, no deportation order may be made so long as an appeal or further appeal (ie in the criminal courts) is pending against the recommendation or against the conviction on which the recommendation was made. An appeal is treated as pending until the expiry of the time within which such an appeal could still be brought, or, in Scotland, until 28 days have passed from the date of the recommendation.[72]

1.47 Time limits on deportation orders for family members have already been discussed at paras 1.18–1.19 above.

When a deportation order under the Immigration Act 1971 takes effect

1.48 A deportation order made under IA 1971 s5(1) invalidates any leave to enter or remain given to the deportee. The subject of a deportation order is prohibited from entering the UK while it is in force.[73]

---

66 NIAA 2002 s97A.
67 NIAA 2002 s79; Immigration Rules para 378.
68 NIAA 2002 s104(1).
69 NIAA 2002 s104(2)(a).
70 NIAA 2002 s104(2)(b).
71 NIAA 2002 s104(2)(c).
72 IA 1971 s6(6); Immigration Rules para 378.
73 And entry clearance must be refused to a person who is the subject of a deportation order – Immigration Rules HC 395 para 320(2).

1.49 A deportation order is normally signed by the Home Office Immigration Minister but in contentious cases may be referred to the SSHD personally for signature. A deportation order may only be signed while a person is still in the UK.[74] It is Home Office policy not to make a deportation order in respect of a person with whom it is not in contact.[75]

1.50 The Home Office takes the view that a deportation order comes into force as soon as it is signed[76] and authority pre-dating *Anufrijeva* supports this view.[77] However, in light of the House of Lords' judgment in *R (Anufrijeva) v Secretary of State for the Home Department and Secretary of State for Work and Pensions*[78] (finding that an administrative decision adverse to an individual must be communicated to him or her before it can have legal effect) we suggest that a deportation order comes into force only when served on the deportee. Recent Administrative Court authority holds that a deportation order is only 'in force' once served on the individual.[79] But, until the Home Office amends its stance, a person who left the UK voluntarily after a deportation order was signed, but before it was served, is likely to have to make representations to the Home Office challenging the validity of the deportation order before attempting to return to the UK.

---

74 IA 1971 s5(1); see also EIG chapter 15 para 15.6.
75 EIG chapter 15 para 15.10.
76 IDIs chapter 13 section 1 para 6.
77 *Dey Sri Kumar v Secretary of State for the Home Department* [1996] Imm AR 521, CA.
78 [2003] UKHL 36, [2004] 1 AC 604.
79 *R (S) v Secretary of State for the Home Department* [2011] EWHC 2120 (Admin) paras 151–159.

CHAPTER 2
Criminal court recommendations for deportation

2.1	Introduction
2.4	Which courts can recommend deportation
2.5	Who may be the subject of a criminal court recommendation for deportation
2.8	Procedural requirements
2.8	Written notice (the IM3)
2.9	Full inquiry by the sentencing court
2.10	Reasons from the sentencing court
2.11	Relevant and irrelevant considerations for the sentencing court
2.11	The essential test: whether the offender's continued presence is to the detriment of the UK
2.12	Irrelevant considerations
2.14	Special considerations in EEA cases
2.15	Recommendations for deportation for passport offences
2.19	Challenging a recommendation for deportation
2.21	The approach to be taken by the SSHD to a criminal court's recommendation for deportation

Introduction

2.1 As we have already seen at para 1.1, one route to liability for deportation under the Immigration Act (IA) 1971 is the recommendation of the sentencing criminal court that a foreign national offender should be deported.

2.2 Criminal court recommendations for deportation are diminishing sharply in relevance and prevalence. The Court of Appeal has held in *Kluxen* that recommendations for deportation will:

- be 'no longer appropriate' where the sentence is such (12 months' imprisonment or over[1]) that the foreign national would in any event be the subject of an 'automatic' deportation order by the Secretary of State for the Home Department (SSHD); and
- 'rarely be appropriate' in the residual category of cases where the sentence is below 12 months' imprisonment so that the deportee could only be the subject of 'discretionary' deportation under IA 1971.[2] And, the Court of Appeal added, 'that is so whether or not the offender is a citizen of the EU'.[3]

2.3 Nonetheless, recommendations for deportation continue to be upheld in the Court of Appeal Criminal Division since *Kluxen*.[4] This chapter reviews which courts can recommend deportation; who may be recommended for deportation; the procedural requirements for criminal court recommendations for deportation; relevant factors for a court considering making such a recommendation; and special considerations in cases concerning false documents. We finish by looking at challenges to recommendations for deportation and the approach to be taken by the SSHD to a criminal court's recommendation for deportation.

Which courts can recommend deportation

2.4 A recommendation for deportation may be made by any court with power to sentence the offender (that is, the magistrates' court, Crown

---

1 On the parts of UK Borders Act (UKBA) 2007 s32 currently in force.
2 *R (Kluxen, Rostas, Adam) v Secretary of State for the Home Department* [2010] EWCA Crim 1081, [2011] 1 WLR 218 paras 9 and 28; for an example of the application of this approach, see *R v Gladys Frimpong* [2011] EWCA Crim 1705.
3 *R (Kluxen, Rostas, Adam) v Secretary of State for the Home Department* [2010] EWCA Crim 1081, [2011] 1 WLR 218 para 28.
4 For example, *R v Romeka Brown* [2010] EWCA Crim 1807, [2011] 1 Cr App R (S) 79.

Court or Court of Appeal) unless the court commits the offender to be sentenced or further dealt with for that offence by another court.[5] In Scotland, the power to recommend a person for deportation can only be exercised by the sheriff or the High Court of Justiciary, and can only be exercised by the latter if the appeal is against a conviction on indictment or against a sentence on such a conviction.[6]

Who may be the subject of a criminal court recommendation for deportation

2.5 Recommendations for deportation may only be made against persons convicted when aged 17 or over of an offence punishable with imprisonment.[7] A person 'shall be' deemed to have reached the age of 17 at the time of conviction if, on consideration of any available evidence, he or she appears to have done so to the court making or considering a recommendation for deportation.[8] The question of whether an offence is punishable with imprisonment must be determined without regard to any statute which restricts the imprisonment of young offenders or the imprisonment of persons not previously sentenced to imprisonment.[9]

2.6 A recommendation for deportation may be made against a person sentenced to life imprisonment.[10] A person found to have committed an offence but sentenced to a conditional or absolute discharge is in principle still eligible for a court recommendation for deportation,[11] although it is difficult to conceive of circumstances in which the detriment test (see para 2.11 below) would be met and a recommendation would be appropriate notwithstanding a discharge.

2.7 There is no power to recommend for deportation British citizens[12] or persons who are otherwise exempt from deportation under IA 1971.[13] Exemptions from deportation under IA 1971 have been discussed at paras 1.27–1.42.

---

5 IA 1971 s6(1).
6 IA 1971 s6(1).
7 IA 1971 s3(6).
8 IA 1971 s6(3)(a).
9 IA 1971 s6(3)(b).
10 IA 1971 s6(4).
11 IA 1971 s6(3).
12 IA 1971 s3(6).
13 IA 1971 ss2(2), 7(1)(b), 8(3).

Procedural requirements

Written notice (the IM3)

2.8 At least seven days before recommendation for deportation, the offender must have been served with a written notice (form IM3) stating that he or she is not liable for deportation if he or she is a British citizen or otherwise exempt from deportation.[14] The mere fact that the notice has not been given will not be sufficient to invalidate a court recommendation for deportation.[15] Arguably the recommendation will be unlawful where the result of the failure to serve the IM3 was that offender did not anticipate the possibility of a recommendation and was unprepared to resist it; in any event such a failure may be the subject of representations to the SSHD or, in an appeal against the decision to deport, to the FTT-IAC, as to why the recommendation should be given lesser weight.[16]

Full inquiry by the sentencing court

2.9 Where a recommendation for deportation is considered, the warning from the Court of Appeal in *R v Nazari* remains apposite:

> ... no court should make an order recommending deportation without full inquiry into all the circumstances. It should not be done, as sometimes happened in the past, by adding a sentence as if by an afterthought, at the end of observations about any sentence of imprisonment. It would be advisable for judges to invite counsel to address them specifically on the possibility of a recommendation for deportation being made.[17]

Reasons from the sentencing court

2.10 The sentencing court should give reasons for recommending deportation.[18] A failure to give reasons may lead to the quashing of the recommendation for deportation,[19] but, if sufficient information is

---

14 IA 1971 s6(2).
15 *R v Liban Abdi* [2007] EWCA Crim 1913, [2008] 1 Cr App R (S) 87.
16 *R v Liban Abdi* [2007] EWCA Crim 1913, [2008] 1 Cr App R (S) 87, paras 30 to 31.
17 *R v Nazari and others* [1980] 1 WLR 1366, p 1373.
18 *R v Rodney* [1996] 2 Cr App R (S) 230.
19 See, for example, *R v Mabengo and others* [2008] EWCA Crim 1699 para 13.

Relevant and irrelevant considerations for the sentencing court

The essential test: whether the offender's continued presence is to the detriment of the UK

2.11 In determining whether to recommend deportation, the sentencing court must consider whether the continued presence of the offender is to the detriment of the UK.[21] This has been said to be substantially the same as the test that is set down in EU jurisprudence (the case of *R v Bouchereau*[22]) for the expulsion of EU nationals from member states: 'under both tests the bar that must be cleared before a recommendation is made is at a relatively high level'.[23] The test in *R v Bouchereau* is that there must be:

> ... a genuine and sufficiently serious threat to the requirements of public policy affecting one of the fundamental interests of society.[24]

Irrelevant considerations

2.12 Since those facing deportation will have a right of appeal to an independent tribunal against a decision to deport, in which asylum and human rights grounds can be raised, it has been held by the Court of Appeal in *Carmona* that it is neither necessary nor appropriate for the sentencing court to assess:

- the impact of deportation on third parties;
- whether the proposed deportee's rights under the European Convention on Human Rights (ECHR) would be breached by deportation; or
- the conditions that the offender would face in his or her home country if deported.[25]

---

20 *R v Bozat* [1997] 1 Cr App R (S) 270, *R v Thomas Clarke* [2008] EWCA Crim 3023 para 6.
21 *R v Nazari and others* [1980] 1 WLR 1366, 1373.
22 [1978] QB 732.
23 *R v Romeka Brown* [2010] EWCA Crim 1807 para 10.
24 *R v Bouchereau* [1978] QB 732 para 35.
25 *R v Carmona* [2006] EWCA Crim 508, [2006] 1 WLR 2264 paras 25–22; see also *R (Kluxen, Rostas, Adam) v Secretary of State for the Home Department* [2010] EWCA Crim 1081, [2011] 1 WLR 218 para 29.

2.13 The immigration status of the offender (how long he or she has been in the UK and whether lawfully or not) is irrelevant to the decision whether to recommend for deportation,[26] save insofar as this may be relevant to the circumstances of the offence itself – for example, an immigration offence.[27]

Special considerations in EEA cases

2.14 It has been held by the Court of Appeal in *Kluxen* that the particular considerations and safeguards from expulsion applicable to the expulsion of European Economic Area (EEA) nationals and their family members by operation of article 28 of the EC Directive 2004/38 on the right of citizens of the Union and their family members to move and reside freely within the territory of the member states ('the Citizens Directive') and regulation 21 of the Immigration (European Economic Area) Regulations 2006[28] apply only to the SSHD's decision to deport and do not apply to the decision of a criminal court to make a recommendation to deport.[29] We respectfully suggest that this is questionable. This is discussed at para 9.4.

Recommendations for deportation for passport offences

2.15 Below, we consider the approach to recommendations for deportation in a particularly prevalent category of offences in this context: passport offences.

2.16 The leading case on the fraudulent use of passports remains *Bennabas* in which the Court of Appeal held that:

> ... the public interest in preventing the fraudulent use of passports to gain entry or support residence is of considerable importance and deserves protection ... detriment is intimately bound up with the protection of public order afforded by confidence in a system of passports.[30]

---

26 *R v Kandhari* (unreported), 24 April 1979, CA (Crim Div).
27 *R v Bennabas* [2005] EWCA Crim 2113, [2006] 1 Cr App R (S) 94.
28 SI No 1003.
29 *R (Kluxen, Rostas and Adam) v Secretary of State for the Home Department* [2010] EWCA Crim 1081, paras 30–32.
30 *R v Bennabas* [2005] EWCA Crim 2113, [2006] 1 Cr App R (S) 94 para 41.

2.17 The use of a false passport to gain entry to the UK is more serious than the use of a false passport to gain employment.[31] Thus, an important factor in determining whether to recommend deportation in such cases is whether a false passport was used to gain entry[32] although the approach will always be fact-specific. In a number of cases where overstayers had relied on false passports to obtain employment[33] or to open a bank account in order to be able to earn money,[34] recommendations for deportation have been quashed. Conversely, the use of a counterfeit stamp in a passport and a counterfeit letter, not only in order to obtain employment but to obtain entry to the UK and to obtain benefits to which the individual was not entitled by her immigration status, has been found to justify a recommendation for deportation even where custodial part of the sentence amounted to ten months.[35]

2.18 It should be noted in this context that those travelling from a country of feared persecution for the purpose of seeking asylum should not be prosecuted for entering the UK on false documents.[36] Nor should they be prosecuted for seeking to exit the UK on such documents where they are in transit to another country with the intention of seeking asylum there.[37] This is because article 31(1) of the Refugee Convention, partially reflected in Immigration and Asylum Act (IAA) 1999 s31, prohibits the imposition of penalties on refugees who, coming directly from a territory where their life or freedom was threatened, enter or are present without authorisation, provided that they present themselves without delay to the authorities and show good reason for their illegal entry or presence.

---

31 *R v Ovieriakhi* [2009] EWCA Crim 452, [2009] 2 Cr App R (S) 91 paras 15–16.
32 See, for example, *R v Bennaba*s [2005] EWCA Crim 2113, [2006] 1 Cr App R (S) 94 para 45 in which although not charged with use of a forged passport to gain entry, the court found it 'overwhelmingly likely' that he had done so.
33 *R v Araoye* [2007] EWCA Crim 1922; *R v Momodu* [2008] EWCA Crim 1882; *R v Gladys Frimpong* [2011] EWCA Crim 1705.
34 *R v Ntlemo* [2006] EWCA Crim 2514.
35 *R v Romeka Brown* [2010] EWCA Crim 1807.
36 *R v Uxbridge Magistrates' Courts and Another ex p Adimi* [2000] 3 WLR 434.
37 *R v Asfaw* [2008] UKHL 31, [2008] 1 AC 1061.

Challenging a recommendation for deportation

2.19 A criminal court's recommendation to deport is part of a person's sentence and can only be challenged by way of an appeal against sentence.[38]

2.20 However, a recommendation for deportation is not part of the punishment imposed on the offender and the making of a recommendation for deportation does not justify a reduction in the sentence otherwise appropriate.[39]

The approach to be taken by the SSHD to a criminal court's recommendation for deportation

2.21 The recommendation for deportation is a recommendation only: the final decision over whether to deport lies with the SSHD.[40] The fact that a person has been recommended for deportation by a court carries weight but does not bind the SSHD to pursue deportation.[41] Conversely, the fact that a person has been sentenced by a court and not recommended for deportation does not debar the SSHD from then considering deportation on conducive grounds, though it is a relevant factor to be taken into account by the SSHD.[42] Even where the Court of Appeal has quashed the sentencing court's recommendation for deportation, the SSHD may still exercise her own discretionary power to deport,[43] though the SSHD must give her reasons for disagreeing with the Court of Appeal's decision.[44]

2.22 Where the sentencing judge has declined to recommend deportation for reasons connected to the criminal offences committed or offending risk, those are matters within the criminal court's expertise and the SSHD should, in making her own decision on deportation, expressly address her mind to the criminal court's reasons, however shortly. However, if the sentencing judge has strayed beyond the *Carmona* limitations (see para 2.12 above) and declined to grant a

---

38 IA 1971 s6(5).
39 *R v Carmona* [2006] EWCA Crim 508.
40 *R v Liban Abdi* [2007] EWCA Crim 1913, [2008] 1 Cr App R (S) 87 para 31.
41 *R v Secretary of State for the Home Department ex p Dinc* [1999] Imm AR 380.
42 *R v Secretary of State for the Home Department ex p Figueriredo* [1993] Imm AR 606 QBD.
43 Under IA 1971 s3(5)(a).
44 *M v Secretary of State for the Home Department* [2003] EWCA Civ 146, [2003] 1 WLR 1980.

recommendation for deportation, for example because of the foreign national offender's family ties, there is no such requirement for the SSHD to have explicit regard to the criminal court's reasons.[45]

2.23 Many of the matters which the SSHD must consider when forming her own judgment on whether to deport will not have been considered by the sentencing court. This is, first, because the SSHD's practice is to decide on deportation near the end of a prisoner's custodial term (see para 9.80 below), by which time circumstances (such as family circumstances or the risk level posed by the prisoner) may have changed significantly since the original court recommendation. Second, because at least post-*Carmona*, the sentencing court will not have taken asylum or ECHR issues into account when recommending deportation.

---

45 *DA (Colombia)* [2009] EWCA Civ 682.

CHAPTER 3
The Secretary of State's decision-making in deportation cases under the Immigration Act 1971

3.1	Introduction
3.5	Who is considered for deportation
3.9	The process of consideration for deportation
3.15	Sources of guidance: Immigration Rules and Home Office policies
3.17	Home Office policies as 'law' for the purposes of the European Convention on Human Rights
3.20	**Immigration Rules paragraph 364**
3.21	The old paragraph 364 of the Immigration Rules
3.23	The amended paragraph 364 of the Immigration Rules
3.25	'Relevant factors' in paragraph 364 of the Immigration Rules
3.27	Requirement of consistency in paragraph 364 of the Immigration Rules
3.28	**Home Office policies applicable to deportation under the Immigration Act 1971**
3.28	Different types of offences and convictions (including spent convictions)
3.30	Relevant factors and exceptional circumstances

continued

3.32 Deportation of the elderly

3.34 Home Office policies previously applicable to deportation under the IA 1971

3.35 The legal consequences of a policy which has been withdrawn

3.37 War zones policy

3.40 DP3/96

3.47 Issuing a decision to deport in deportation cases under Immigration Act 1971

Introduction

3.1 This chapter concerns the criteria and processes that govern the Secretary of State for the Home Department's (SSHD's) exercise of her discretion in Immigration Act (IA) 1971 deportation cases.

3.2 We start with a brief discussion of the criteria determining which cases will be referred for consideration by the SSHD for deportation under the IA 1971 and the ensuing steps in the decision-making process.

3.3 We then review in more detail the Immigration Rules and Home Office policies which set out guidance for decision-making in deportation cases under the IA 1971. We end this chapter with a brief review of how individuals are notified of a decision to deport.

3.4 Policies applicable to the deportation of minors are dealt with separately in chapter 4.

Who is considered for deportation

3.5 The unit within the Home Office which takes decisions on deportation in most non-national security cases is the Criminal Casework Directorate (CCD). The first step in the assessment of whether to deport under the IA 1971 is referral to the CCD for deportation consideration.

3.6 The Home Office has published criteria stipulating which cases are sufficiently serious to warrant referral. It is Home Office policy as set out in the Enforcement Instructions and Guidance (EIG)[1] that non-EEA national offenders will be 'liable to deportation consideration' if they satisfy one or more of the following criteria:

- a court recommendation to deport;
- a single custodial sentence of 12 months or more (regardless of when that sentence was passed, save where the conviction is spent under the Rehabilitation of Offenders Act 1974[2]);
- an aggregate of two or three sentences over a period of five years (counting backwards from the date of the last conviction) amounting to 12 months or more in total; and/or

---

1 EIG chapter 11 para 11.2.1.
2 EIG chapter 55 para 55.1.2.

- a custodial sentence of any length for one of a series of listed drugs offences deemed serious (these cover a wide gamut of drugs offences, save for simple possession).[3]

3.7 While the above criteria provide an important indication of where the SSHD believes the threshold of seriousness for consideration for deportation lies, the policy makes clear that the SSHD may still consider foreign nationals for deportation even if they do not meet these criteria. The EIG[4] states that in addition to those meeting the above criteria, if there are 'other circumstances where deportation is considered to be conducive to the public good', a case should still be referred to the CCD for action and states also that 'deportation action outside of this guidance can be taken on a case by case basis if it is considered to be conducive to the public good'.

3.8 Distinct considerations apply to the threshold of seriousness for EEA nationals and their family members and these are set out at para 9.82.

The process of consideration for deportation

3.9 Under the IA 1971 deportation regime, in all potential deportation cases (whether a person has been recommended for deportation by a court or the SSHD has initiated consideration in a 'conducive' deportation or family case) the SSHD must consider whether deportation is the right course on the merits.

3.10 In exercising her discretion over the pursuit of deportation, as in all other decision-making, the SSHD must take into account all relevant considerations,[5] ask himself or herself the right questions and 'take reasonable steps to acquaint [herself] with the relevant information to enable [her] to answer it correctly'.[6]

3.11 The European Casework Instructions[7] set out the documents to which the SSHD should have regard when deciding whether deportation action should be taken:

3 Since 1 August 2008: see the note in EIG chapter 14 'Important changes to our deportation policy'.
4 EIG chapter 11 paras 11.2.2 and 11.4.1.
5 *R v IAT ex p Singh* [1986] 1 WLR 910, 919B.
6 *Secretary of State for Education and Science v Tameside Metropolitan Borough Council* [1977] AC 1014, 1065B ; and applied in the context of discretionary deportation in *R (HXA) v Secretary of State for the Home Department* [2010] EWHC 1177 (QB) paras 44 and 73.
7 European Casework Instructions chapter 8 section 3 para 3.

The following information will usually be required before making a decision on whether or not to deport.
- person's current address, including prison if in custody;
- confirmation as to whether an appeal has been lodged against the conviction or sentence (inc the recommendation to deport);
- Nominal Index Card (NIC) relating to the prisoner's reception in custody and release date;
- court certificate confirming the offences and length of imprisonment;
- police report confirming the circumstances of the offence(s); or
- Custom and Excise report if they were the prosecuting authority;
- judge's sentencing remarks;
- details of any previous convictions;
- whereabouts of any passport they hold;
- CCT 2 referral from prison (form); and
- parole and probation reports.

3.12 Although the above list refers only to EEA nationals, we suggest that (for reasons of good administration, consistency and fairness) there is no reason why the same documentation should not be considered by the SSHD in relation to non-EEA nationals. As the EIG acknowledges in respect of all foreign nationals:

> Before a decision to deport is reached the Secretary of State must take into account all relevant factors known to him. It is imperative, therefore, that all the person's circumstances are reported.[8]

3.13 Prior to a decision under IA 1971 to make a deportation order, individuals potentially facing deportation may be issued with a form (ICD 0350) warning them that a deportation decision is contemplated and asking the individual to submit a 'statement of additional grounds'. This provides an opportunity for an individual potentially facing deportation to set out his or her length of residence, family ties, etc.[9]

3.14 The practice of formally inviting individuals to make representations is at best erratically followed by the Home Office. A failure to provide prospective deportees with such an opportunity to make representations is unlikely to found a successful challenge to the decision to deport, since there is a right of appeal against the decision

---

8 EIG chapter 11 para 11.2.
9 The importance of taking into consideration any individual representations concerning deportation was emphasised by Lord Griffiths in *R v Secretary of State for the Home Department ex p Oladehinde* [1991] 2 AC 254 at 301: 'It seems to me that it would be much more satisfactory if whoever is responsible for taking the decision had the opportunity to consider a written report including any representations on behalf of the immigrant before taking the decision. It is after all a grave decision affecting the future welfare of the immigrant ...'.

to the Immigration and Asylum Chamber of the First-tier Tribunal (FTT-IAC) at which point the proposed deportee has an opportunity to make his or her case (however, such a failure to invite representations may, for example, be relevant in a detention challenge where a decision was taken by the SSHD to deport based on inadequate or erroneous information and was subsequently withdrawn).

Sources of guidance: Immigration Rules and Home Office policies

3.15 The Immigration Rules are guidance in the administration of immigration control, published as House of Commons papers (currently HC395), and subject to a negative resolution procedure in parliament.[10] The Immigration Rules are not delegated legislation or rules of law but rules of practice.[11] The Immigration Rules bind the SSHD and are enforceable by the FTT-IAC.[12]

3.16 The SSHD also operates various policies and concessions on deportation which have not been incorporated to the Immigration Rules. Many, although not all, of these policies are to be found in

10 IA 1971 s3(2).
11 For a detailed discussion of the status of the Immigration Rules, see Macdonald's immigration law & practice 8th edn, paras 1.31–1.38. See also Lord Hope in *Odelola v Secretary of State for the Home Department* [2009] UKHL 25 para 6: 'The status of the immigration rules is rather unusual. They are not subordinate legislation but detailed statements by a minister of the Crown as to how the Crown proposes to exercise its executive power to control immigration. But they create legal rights: under Nationality, Immigration and Asylum Act (NIAA) 2002 s84(1), one may appeal against an immigration decision on the ground that it is not in accordance with the immigration rules'. See also Sedley LJ in *R (Pankina and Others) v Secretary of State for the Home Department* [2010] EWCA Civ 719, [2010] 3 WLR 1526 para 17: 'In my judgment the time has come to recognise that, by a combination of legislative recognition and executive practice, the rules made by Home Secretaries for regulating immigration have ceased to be policies and have acquired a status akin to that of law. Because they derive from no empowering primary legislation, they cannot be subordinate legislation or therefore open to conventional ultra vires challenges. But as an exercise of public power, which they undoubtedly are, they be no more immune to challenge for abuse of power or for violation of human rights than any other exercise of the prerogative power ...'. For an up-to-date version of the Immigration Rules, see the Border and Immigration Agency website: www.bia.homeoffice.gov.uk/policyandlaw/immigrationlaw/immigrationrules.
12 Under NIAA 2002 s86(3) the IAC must allow an appeal against an immigration decision (including a decision to deport) if the decision was not in accordance with the immigration rules.

the EIG formerly known as the Operational Enforcement Manual (OEM); and in the Immigration Directorate Instructions (IDIs).[13]

Home Office policies as 'law' for the purposes of the European Convention on Human Rights

3.17 The status of the Immigration Rules and Home Office policies was summarised by Blake J in *R (Limbu) v Secretary of State for the Home Department*:[14]

> Both the Immigration Rules and instructions to immigration officers are formal pronouncements of pertinent policy binding on immigration officials, immigration judges and applicants. They are made pursuant to statutory powers under s3(2) and Schedule 2 paragraph 1(3) Immigration Act 1971 respectively. Although the rules have not been considered to be subordinate legislation, they are considered to be part of the law for determining whether a decision is taken in accordance with the law *AA (Afghanistan) v SSHD* [2007] EWCA Civ 12. They are also part of the law for the purpose of justifying any interference with rights afforded under the ECHR and a failure to adhere to them would prevent any such interference being justified (see *Al Nashif v Bulgaria* (2002) 36 EHRR 37 at 128–129).

3.18 Home Office policies are not 'law' in the sense of a requirement of strict compliance[15] since the executive may, with good reason, depart from its own policy. But the term 'law' has an autonomous meaning in the European Convention on Human Rights (ECHR) jurisprudence. Home Office policies form part of 'domestic law' for the purposes of the requirement of justification under the ECHR: a decision which, without good reason, contravenes stated policy, or is taken in disregard of stated policy, is not in accordance with domestic law.[16]

---

13 For up-to-date versions of the EIG and IDIs, see www.bia.homeoffice.gov.uk/policyandlaw/guidance.
14 [2008] EWHC 2261 (Admin) para 44.
15 See the discussion of status of policy in *R (Pankina and Others) v Secretary of State for the Home Department* [2010] EWCA Civ 719, [2010] 3 WLR 1526 para 15.
16 As Lord Phillips MR held in *Nadarajah and Amirthanathan v Secretary of State for the Home Department* [2003] EWCA Civ 1768, [2004] INLR 139 para 54: 'Our domestic law comprehends both the provisions of Schedule 2 to the Immigration Act 1971 and the Secretary of State's published policy, which, under principles of public law, he is obliged to follow.' Approved in *R (Lumba and Mighty) v Secretary of State for the Home Department* [2011] UKSC 12, [2011] 2 WLR 671 para 30 per Lord Dyson. See also *R (Munjaz) v Mersey Care NHS Trust* [2005] UKHL 58, [2006] 2 AC 148 paras 34, 91–92, 98, 103.

3.19 The general consequences on appeal of a failure by the SSHD, in making an immigration decision, to properly apply the Immigration Rules or her own policies are discussed at para 21.12.

Immigration Rules paragraph 364

3.20 Paragraph 364 of the Immigration Rules sets out guidance for the SSHD's exercise of her discretion over whether to pursue deportation in court-recommended and conducive deportation cases under the IA 1971. Paragraph 364 of the Immigration Rules does not apply in 'automatic' deportation cases under the UK Borders Act (UKBA) 2007.[17]

The old paragraph 364 of the Immigration Rules

3.21 Paragraph 364 of the Immigration Rules underwent a significant amendment on 20 July 2006.[18] The 'old' paragraph 364 provided:

> Subject to paragraph 380 in considering whether deportation is the right course on the merits, the public interest will be balanced against any compassionate circumstances of the case. While each case will be considered in the light of the particular circumstances, the aim is an exercise of the power of deportation which will be consistent and fair as between one person and another, although one case will rarely be identical with another in all material respects. In the cases detailed in paragraph 363A deportation will normally be the proper course where a person has failed to comply with or has contravened a condition or has remained without authority. Before a decision to deport is reached, the Secretary of State will take into account all relevant factors known to him including:
>
> (a) age;
> (b) length of residence in the United Kingdom;
> (c) strength of connections with the United Kingdom;
> (d) personal history, including character, conduct and employment records;
> (e) domestic circumstances;
> (f) previous criminal record and the nature of any offence of which the person has been convicted;
> (g) compassionate circumstances;
> (h) any representations received on the person's behalf.

---

17 Immigration Rules HC395 para 364A. See also discussion in *RU (Bangladesh) v Secretary of State for the Home Department* [2011] EWCA Civ 651 para 11.
18 The new para 364 of the Immigration Rules was substituted by Statement of Changes HC 1337.

3.22 The 'old' paragraph 364 applies in any case where the decision to deport was taken before 20 July 2006 and must be applied by the IAC in any subsequent appeal (even if the appeal takes place after 20 July 2006).[19]

The amended paragraph 364 of the Immigration Rules

3.23 The amended paragraph 364 of the Immigration Rules, which applies to decisions taken on or after 20 July 2006 under IA 1971, provides:

> Subject to paragraph 380, while each case will be considered on its merits, where a person is liable to deportation the presumption shall be that the public interest requires deportation. The Secretary of State will consider all relevant factors in considering whether the presumption is outweighed in any particular case, although it will only be in exceptional circumstances that the public interest in deportation will be outweighed in a case where it would not be contrary to the Human Rights Convention and the Convention and Protocol relating to the Status of Refugees to deport. The aim is an exercise of the power of deportation which is consistent and fair as between one person and another, although one case will rarely be identical with another in all material respects. In the cases detailed in paragraph 363A deportation will normally be the proper course where a person has failed to comply with or has contravened a condition or has remained without authority.

3.24 Both old and amended versions of paragraph 364 therefore require the SSHD, when exercising her discretion over whether to deport under IA 1971, to balance the public interest in deportation against the rights of the individuals involved. However, the amended paragraph 364 shifts the balance, introducing a presumption that the public interest requires deportation, and providing that it is only in 'exceptional circumstances' that this public interest will be outweighed, where deportation would not breach the Refugee Convention or ECHR. It is now difficult and unusual for a foreign national to succeed in establishing that deportation would be unlawful under paragraph 364 of the Immigration Rules where he or she cannot succeed under the Refugee Convention or ECHR. Note, however, that the 'exceptionality test' applies only *after* Refugee Convention and ECHR matters have been considered.

---

19 *EO (Turkey) v Secretary of State for the Home Department* [2007] UKAIT 00062.

'Relevant factors' in paragraph 364 of the Immigration Rules

3.25 Although the amended paragraph 364 of the Immigration Rules no longer lists those 'relevant factors' to be considered by the SSHD in deciding whether to deport, the SSHD is still required to have regard to 'all relevant factors' (both under the terms of the amended paragraph 364 and as a matter of public law principle – see para 3.10 above). The 'old' paragraph 364 provides guidance as to what those relevant factors are.[20]

3.26 Paragraph 364 is a provision which confers discretion on the SSHD within the Immigration Rules. The importance of this is that the IAC has jurisdiction to review the merits of that discretion. So, even where the SSHD has considered all relevant factors and reached a view which is reasonable in public law terms, the IAC may allow an appeal because it considers that the discretion conferred by the Immigration Rules should have been exercised differently.[21] Where the SSHD has failed to have regard to relevant considerations, the decision will additionally not be in accordance with the law and the IAC may either choose to allow and remit the appeal[22] for further consideration by the SSHD or proceed to consider the substantive merits itself. The latter course would appear more consonant with the one-stop appeals system. Appeals in the IAC are discussed in detail in chapter 21.

Requirement of consistency in paragraph 364 of the Immigration Rules

3.27 Both versions of paragraph 364 of the Immigration Rules require that the exercise of the power to deport be 'consistent and fair as between one case and another'. It will usually be difficult to show that the power to deport has been exercised inconsistently or unfairly because, as the Immigration Rules emphasise, two cases are rarely materially identical. However, it may be contrary to paragraph 364 (as well as contrary to general public law principles of rationality and

---

20 The continuing importance of that list of relevant factors is reinforced by the fact that an identical list of 'relevant factors' appears at para 395C of the current Immigration Rules (concerning decisions over administrative removal) and also in published Home Office policy on deportation (see para 3.30 below).
21 NIAA 2002 s84(1)(f).
22 NIAA 2002 s84(1)(e).

of like treatment in like cases[23]), for example, in a multi-defendant criminal case, to deport a person with more minor involvement but not another foreign national defendant in the same case, unless there are other significant differences between the two cases.[24]

Home Office policies applicable to deportation under the Immigration Act 1971

Different types of offences and convictions (including spent convictions)

3.28 The EIG sets out those offences which are 'considered more serious than other offences'. This does not preclude the SSHD from considering for deportation or from deporting those who have committed lesser offences, but the list provides an important indication of the SSHD's assessment of where the public interest lies:
- murder;
- a terrorism offence;
- a drug trafficking offence;
- a serious immigration offence;
- a serious sexual or violent offence;
- [an offence carrying] a maximum penalty of 10 years or more.[25]

3.29 The EIG[26] also sets out the approach to be taken by the SSHD to convictions other than non-spent adult full convictions, and to police cautions:
- Where the proposed deportee has multiple convictions, the SSHD may consider offences committed before the proposed deportee's 21st birthday.
- Police cautions may be considered, but only at the stage of deciding whether deportation is conducive to the public good – not at the prior stage of deciding whether to consider deportation at all. Less weight will be given to police cautions than to criminal convictions.

23 *Matadeen v Pointu* [1999] 1 AC 98, per Lord Hoffmann: 'their Lordships would ... say that treating like cases alike and unlike cases differently is a general axiom of rational behaviour'.
24 Eg *R v Secretary of State for the Home Department ex p Sayed Nasser Alavi-Veighoe* [1990] COD 39, (1989) *Times* 22 August, applying an identical provision in the former Immigration Rules.
25 EIG chapter 11 para 11.1.1.
26 EIG chapter 11 para 11.4.1.

- A conviction which, under the Rehabilitation of Offenders Act 1974, is a spent conviction, normally cannot be taken into account when determining whether the criteria for consideration for deportation are met. However, if there are exceptional circumstances (the example given in the EIG is a person who has considerably delayed deportation action by going to ground), then the spent conviction may be taken into account.[27]

Relevant factors and exceptional circumstances

3.30 The EIG[28] lists factors that 'will be taken into account' by the SSHD when deciding whether to deport:

- age;
- length of residence in the UK;
- strength of connections to the UK;
- personal history, including character, conduct and employment record;
- domestic circumstances;
- previous criminal record and the nature of any offence of which the person has been convicted;
- compassionate circumstances;
- any representations received on the person's behalf.

3.31 The above relevant factors are followed in the EIG[29] by lists of more restrictive criteria. We suggest that the policy, which is opaquely drafted,[30] must be interpreted to mean that the relevant factors (eg length of residence) must always be considered, but if the more restrictive criteria are met (eg residence for 25 years or more in the absence of a serious offence) then these may constitute exceptional circumstances in which the public interest will be outweighed by compassionate circumstances and deportation would be unlawful under paragraph 364 of the Immigration Rules. The more restrictive

---

27 See also *R (V) v Secretary of State for the Home Department* [2009] EWHC 1902 (Admin) para 48 finding that it is not an abuse of process per se for the SSHD to rely on spent convictions since these may fall within the exception at Rehabilitation of Offenders Act 1974 s7(3).
28 EIG chapter 11 para 11.4.
29 EIG chapter 11 para 11.5 for EEA nationals and again at chapter 12 para 12.3.1 for non-EEA nationals.
30 For example, in chapter 11 of the EIG para 11.5 these comments bizarrely combine reference to EEA nationals and to the presumption of deportation (which does not apply to EEA nationals).

criteria (which we suggest constitute 'exceptional circumstances' for the purposes of paragraph 364 of the Immigration Rules) are:

- 'where a person has been resident in the UK for 25 years or more (not counting periods in custody), unless he has been convicted of a serious offence';
- 'where the person has spent the majority of their formative years (from 0–10 years) in the UK and has been resident here since';
- 'where the person has no family in their country of origin, doesn't speak the language and has not lived in that country for a significant period';
- 'where the person is married or in a civil partnership or has children (including children living with or in regular contact with the person) and there are insurmountable obstacles';
- 'where the person has an illness that "has reached such a critical stage (ie he is dying) that it would be inhuman treatment to deprive him of the care he is currently receiving and send him home to an early death, unless there is care available there to enable him to meet that fate with dignity"'.

Deportation of the elderly

3.32 Until September 2004, it was Home Office policy that as a general rule those aged 65 or over would not be removed or deported.

3.33 The revised Home Office policy provides that age is a relevant factor but that the decision of whether a person is too frail to expel is made on a case-by-case basis. The EIG now states:[31]

> In terms of removal, Ministers have agreed that a person's age is not, by itself, a realistic or reliable indicator of a person's health, mobility or ability to care for himself/herself. Many older people are able to enjoy active and independent lives. Cases must be assessed on their individual merits.
>
> The onus is on the applicant to show that there are extenuating circumstances, such as particularly poor health, close dependency on family members in the UK, coupled with a lack of family and care facilities in the country of origin which might warrant a grant of leave.

---

31 EIG chapter 53 para 53.7.

46 Foreign national prisoners / chapter 3

Home Office policies previously applicable to deportation under the IA 1971

3.34 Three policies which were of importance in deportation cases were withdrawn in 2008: the seven-year policy applicable to children, DP5/96 and the war zones policy. The seven-year policy is discussed at paras 4.40–4.44; the latter two policies are discussed in more detail below.

The legal consequences of a policy which has been withdrawn

3.35 Home Office policies remain significant to deportation in certain cases despite their withdrawal. Past prejudice to an individual in consequence of a failure to apply a relevant policy may be a relevant factor to be taken into account even when that policy is no longer applicable.[32] In addition, where a decision to deport is made under the IA 1971 without consideration of an applicable policy, then, even if the policy is subsequently withdrawn:

- where there is an ongoing appeal against the decision to deport, the appeal should be allowed on grounds that the decision was not in accordance with the law, at least to the extent that the matter is remitted to the SSHD;[33] and
- we suggest that where appeal rights have been exhausted without consideration of the policy and the deportation order has been signed and served, proposed deportees and their legal representatives may be in a strong position to make representations for revocation on grounds that the original decision was unlawful.

3.36 The implications for cases where a policy was still in force at the time of enforcement action, that is, the decision to deport, but had been withdrawn by the time the case came to appeal, are considered in more detail in paras 3.38–3.39 and 4.40.

War zones policy

3.37 The OEM, which was the predecessor to the EIG, contained an exemption from deportation from those from countries currently active war zones. The old OEM stated at paragraph 2.3:

32 *SL (Vietnam)* [2010] EWCA Civ 225 para 33.
33 *HH (Iraq)* v *Secretary of State for the Home Department* [2009] EWCA Civ 727.

The following are exempt from deportation:

...

Enforcement action should not be taken against Nationals who originate from countries which are currently active war zones. Country Information Policy Unit (CIPU) or Enforcement Policy Unit (EPU) will provide advice on this.

3.38 This policy was in force from at least June 2005 but was withdrawn on 14 January 2008. Long before the policy was withdrawn, the SSHD was failing to apply it. As the Asylum and Immigration Tribunal (AIT), the predecessor tribunal to the IAC, has noted:

... the position is that in an official statement of instructions the Secretary of State treated a group of people as exempt from deportation and immune from enforcement action in connexion with proposed deportation. That statement then appears to have been forgotten by those who had the job of applying it. The consequence may be that a number of deportation decisions made before the withdrawal of this policy on 14 January 2008 will have to be held to have been made otherwise than in accordance with the law.[34]

3.39 Where a decision to deport was taken at the time that the 'active war zone' policy was in force and while the proposed deportee's country of origin was an active war zone and the decision was taken without regard to the policy, the decision to deport will not be accordance with the law.[35] Iraq has been found to be an active war zone[36] as have Southern and central Somalia.[37]

DP3/96

3.40 On 24 April 2008, DP3/96 and DP2/93, relating to enforcement actions against those in relationships with persons settled in the UK, were withdrawn.

3.41 DP2/93 applied only to relationships made known to the Home Office on or before 13 March 1996 (the date on which the policy was replaced by DP3/96). DP2/93 concerned enforcement action against both married and unmarried partners. DP 3/96, the successor policy, concerned enforcement actions against married partners only but was supplemented since its inception by an additional policy on unmarried partners. We discuss only DP3/96 in detail here.

---

34 *HH (Iraq)* [2008] UKAIT 00051 at para 26.
35 *HH (Iraq) v Secretary of State for the Home Department* [2009] EWCA Civ 727.
36 *HH (Iraq)* [2008] UKAIT 00051.
37 *AM and AM (armed conflict: risk categories) Somalia CG* [2008] UKAIT 00091.

3.42 DP3/96 stated that 'as a general rule' in non-criminal deportation cases and in illegal entrant cases, enforcement action should not normally be initiated where the subject had a genuine and subsisting marriage with a person settled in the UK before the commencement of enforcement action; the couple had lived together in the UK continuously for at least two years before the commencement of enforcement action; and it was 'unreasonable' to expect the settled spouse to accompany the other spouse on removal. A list of factors was set out for the assessment of whether it would be 'unreasonable' to expect the settled spouse to accompany the other spouse on removal: older children from a previous relationship forming part of the family unit; where the settled spouse had been settled and living in the UK for at least the preceding ten years; or where the settled spouse suffered from ill health and medical evidence 'conclusively' showed that his or her life would be significantly impaired or endangered by relocation. The policy also set out specific considerations where children had a right of abode in the UK: in such cases, the policy stated, 'the crucial question is whether it is reasonable for the child to accompany his/her parents abroad'. The policy went on to state that in most cases involving a child of ten years old or younger, the child could reasonably be expected to adapt to life abroad but went on to list as a further consideration serious ill-health for which treatment was not available in the country to which the family were going'. Note that, in the light of the UK government's seven-year concessionary policy for children (also since withdrawn – see paras 4.40–4.44), it is doubtful whether it would still be appropriate to treat ten years as the benchmark for whether a child could reasonably be expected to adapt to life abroad.

3.43 Under DP3/96, where the person potentially liable to enforcement action had criminal convictions 'the severity of the offence should be balanced against the strength of family ties' and 'serious crimes which are punishable with imprisonment or a series of lesser crimes which show a propensity to re-offend would normally outweigh the family ties. A very poor immigration history may also be taken into account'.

3.44 Enforcement action was defined in DP3/96 as an instruction to leave with a warning of liability to deportation if the subject failed to leave; service of a notice of intention to deport; or a court recommendation to deport.

3.45 Since its inception in 1996, DP3/96 was accompanied by separate instructions which applied to unmarried partners.[38] The instructions on unmarried partners were that 'enforcement action should not

---

38 EIG chapter 53 para 53.4.1.

normally be initiated' where the subject had a genuine and subsisting relationship akin to marriage with a person present and settled in the UK and the couple had lived together in the UK for at least two years before the commencement of enforcement action and any previous marriage of either partner, or relationship akin to marriage had permanently broken down, and it was unreasonable to expect the settled partner to accompany the other partner on removal.

3.46 The EIG sets out 'transitional arrangements' and states that where an individual's case had begun to be considered under one of the policies before 24 April 2008, the relevant policy will still be applied. The EIG also suggests that in an appeal case where the decision under challenge was taken before 24 April 2008, and there was a decision not to apply one of the policies to that individual or a decision that the individual could not succeed even under the policies, the relevant policy will continue to apply to the case (if the individual should have been allowed to benefit under the policy).[39] As has been discussed earlier in this chapter (see para 3.35 above) where an immigration decision (eg a decision to deport or a refusal to revoke a deportation order) was taken before the policy's withdrawal and the facts were such that one of the policies clearly applied but the decision-maker failed to have regard to or misdirected himself as to the relevant policy, the decision may be found not to be in accordance with the law notwithstanding the policy's withdrawal.[40] However, given the wide discretion under DP3/96 for Home Office caseworkers in cases involving criminal convictions, this may be difficult to establish in many FNP cases.

Issuing a decision to deport in deportation cases under Immigration Act 1971

3.47 The decision to make a deportation order must be notified[41] in accordance with the Immigration (Notices) Regulations 2003.[42] The notice must include or be accompanied by a statement of reasons for the decision; indicate the country to which it is proposed to deport; and set out the deportee's rights of appeal. However, at least in respect of a failure to specify the country of proposed deportation,

---

39 EIG chapter 53 para 53.3.
40 See eg *BP (Macedonia)* [2008] UKAIT 00045.
41 See also Immigration Rules HC395 para 382.
42 SI No 658.

non-compliance with the procedural requirement does not invalidate the decision to deport or deprive the IAC of jurisdiction to hear an appeal against that decision.[43] For procedural defects generally, the appellant may waive the right to be given a valid notice by pursuing the appeal regardless of the defect.[44]

3.48 It is this decision to make a deportation order which triggers the right of appeal to the FTT-IAC, under NIAA 2002 s82(2)(j). Appeals to the FTT-IAC are discussed in chapter 21.

---

43 *JN (Cameroon) v Secretary of State for the Home Department* [2009] EWCA Civ 307.
44 *R v Secretary of State for the Home Department ex p Jeyeanthan* [2000] 1 WLR 354, [1999] 3 All ER 231.

CHAPTER 4
Deportation cases involving minors: relevant legislation and policy

4.1	Introduction
4.4	Statutory powers of deportation directly applicable to minors
4.7	Borders, Citizenship and Immigration Act 2009 s55 and the best interests of the child
4.7	The introduction of the new statutory duty
4.8	Borders, Citizenship and Immigration Act 2009 s55
4.11	The statutory code of practice, *Every Child Matters*
4.14	Meaning of 'primary consideration'
4.19	Meaning of 'best interests of the child'
4.20	Ascertaining the best interests of the child
4.22	Best interests of a British citizen child
4.23	*Zambrano* and the expulsion of parents of British children
4.24	Effect of parent's wrongdoing
4.25	Meaning of 'safeguarding and promoting the welfare of the child'
4.27	Reliance on other aspects of the UNCRC
4.29	Meaning of 'have regard to'
4.30	Consequences of a failure to have regard to BCIA 2009 s55 and *Every Child Matters* considerations
4.33	Timely resolution of applications made by children

continued

4.34	**Home Office policies relevant to the deportation of children**
4.34	Splitting families
4.37	Unaccompanied minors
4.40	The former seven-year concession

Introduction

4.1 This chapter is concerned with the Secretary of State for the Home Department's (SSHD's) decision-making processes in three specific types of deportation cases under the Immigration Act (IA) 1971:
- cases in which the SSHD decides to deport a minor (a person aged under 18) directly, whether as a principal or as the family member of a principal;
- cases in which a decision is taken to deport an adult which will indirectly affect a minor; and
- cases in which a decision is taken to deport an adult who was formerly in the UK as an unaccompanied minor.

4.2 We begin by reviewing the statutory powers under which the SSHD may directly proceed with deportation against a minor. We then turn to the new statutory duty under Borders, Citizenship and Immigration Act (BCIA) 2009 s55 applicable to all immigration, nationality and asylum decisions concerning minors, including deportation decisions directly or indirectly concerning minors. Finally, we consider Home Office policies which affect all three types of case.

4.3 Special considerations applicable to minors who are EEA nationals or the family members of EEA nationals are discussed separately at paras 9.25–9.29. ECHR article 8 claims in deportation cases involving minors are discussed at paras 17.24–17.35. Detention cases involving minors are discussed separately in chapter 37.

Statutory powers of deportation directly applicable to minors

4.4 Minors may be deported under the IA 1971 as principals on grounds that their deportation is conducive to the public good,[1] or, if convicted after the age of 17, following a court recommendation for deportation.[2]

4.5 More commonly, minors may also be deported under the IA 1971 as dependants.[3]

---

1 Under IA 1971 s3(5)(a).
2 Under IA 1971 s3(6). The definition of 'family members' including minors who are liable to deportation as dependants has been discussed at para 1.17.
3 Under IA 1971 s3(5)(b).

4.6 Minors cannot be deported under the 'automatic' deportation provisions of the UK Borders Act (UKBA) 2007 (since the UKBA 2007 exempts those aged under 18 at the age of conviction from 'automatic' deportation[4] and makes no provision for the 'automatic' deportation of family members).

Borders, Citizenship and Immigration Act 2009 s55 and the best interests of the child

The introduction of the new statutory duty

4.7 On 22 September 2008 the UK withdrew its general reservation on immigration matters from the UN Convention on the Rights of the Child (UNCRC).[5] UNCRC article 3 requires the best interests of the child to be treated as a primary consideration in actions concerning children[6] and other international instruments contain identical or similar obligations.[7] The withdrawal of the UK's reservation to the UNCRC paved the way for an obligation, identically worded to those already imposed on other public authorities by Education Act 2002 s175 and Children Act 2004 s11, to be imposed on the SSHD in her immigration, asylum and nationality functions.[8]

Borders, Citizenship and Immigration Act 2009 s55

4.8 BCIA 2009 s55 came into force on 2 November 2009. It imposes an important new statutory duty on the SSHD when she makes immigration, asylum or nationality decisions concerning children (defined as persons under the age of 18[9]). In summary, whenever taking

---

4 UKBA 2007 s33(3).
5 The reservations related to immigration functions and to children being held in custody with adults.
6 'In all actions concerning children, whether undertaken by public or private social welfare institutions, courts of law, administrative authorities or legislative bodies, the best interests of the child shall be a primary consideration.'
7 See summary in *ZH (Tanzania) v Secretary of State for the Home Department* [2011] UKSC 4, [2011] 2 WLR 148 para 22.
8 The first step was the adoption on 6 January 2009 of new guidance given under UKBA 2007 s21 entitled 'Keeping children safe from harm'. This stated at paragraph 1.6 that 'the best interests of the children will be a primary consideration (although not necessarily the only consideration) when making decisions about his or her future'.
9 BCIA 2009 s55(6).

immigration, asylum or nationality decisions concerning children, the SSHD must have regard to the need to safeguard and promote the welfare of children who are in the UK and (by reference to a statutory code of practice, *Every Child Matters*[10]) to the need to treat the best interests of the child as a primary consideration.

4.9 BCIA 2009 s55 also requires the SSHD to make arrangements to ensure that any of her functions, including contracted-out functions, in relation to immigration asylum or nationality are discharged having regard to the need to safeguard and promote the welfare of children who are in the UK.[11]

4.10 The decisions covered include:

- a decision to administratively remove or deport a child;
- a decision to administratively remove or deport an adult which will affect a child (whether the child will follow a parent who is being deported or be separated from the deported parent);[12]
- a decision to detain a child under Immigration Act powers;[13] and
- a decision to detain an adult where a child will be affected (whether the child will be detained with the parent or separated from the detained parent[14]).

The statutory code of practice, *Every Child Matters*

4.11 Following earlier interim measures,[15] BCIA 2009 s55 stipulates that a person exercising any of the SSHD's functions in relation to immigration asylum or nationality 'must' 'have regard to'[16] a statutory Code of Practice, *Every Child Matters*.

10 Not to be confused with the *Every Child Matters* green paper of September 2003, in response to the Victoria Climbié inquiry.
11 BCIA 2009 s55 (1).
12 *ZH (Tanzania) v Secretary of State for the Home Department* [2011] UKSC 4, [2011] 2 WLR 148; *R (MXL) v Secretary of State for the Home Department* [2010] EWHC 2397 (Admin); *QJ (Algeria) v Secretary of State for the Home Department* [2010] EWCA Civ 1478.
13 See, for example, *R (Suppiah) v Secretary of State for the Home Department* [2011] EWHC 2 (Admin).
14 See, for example, *R (MXL) v Secretary of State for the Home Department* [2010] EWHC 2397 (Admin).
15 From 9 January 2009, the UK Border Agency was required, by UKBA 2007 s21, to have regard to the UK Border Agency *Code of Practice for Keeping Children Safe from Harm*. That guidance was replaced, on 2 November 2009, by the *Every Child Matters Guidance*, to which the SSHD must have regard by operation of BCIA 2009 s55.
16 BCIA 2009 s55(3).

4.12 The *Every Child Matters* Code of Practice (like earlier guidance applying to other public bodies and made under Children Act 2004 s11) defines 'safeguarding and promoting the welfare of children' as:

- protecting children from maltreatment;
- preventing impairment of children's health or development (where health means 'physical or mental health' and development means 'physical, intellectual, emotional, social or behavioural development');
- ensuring that children are growing up in circumstances consistent with the provision of safe and effective care; and
- undertaking that role so as to enable those children to have optimum life chances and to enter adulthood successfully.[17]

4.13 The *Every Child Matters* Code of Practice also states that the UK Border Agency 'must act in accordance with' the principle that:

> In accordance with the UN Convention on the Rights of the Child the best interests of the child will be a primary consideration (although not necessarily the only consideration) when making decisions affecting children.[18]

Meaning of 'primary consideration'

4.14 The Supreme Court gave powerful guidance in *ZH (Tanzania) v Secretary of State for the Home Department*[19] on the best interests requirement. As Lady Hale held, giving the leading judgment, the best interests of the child must be considered first in decisions affecting the child. The best interests of the child are the starting point before turning to countervailing considerations,[20] although the best interests of the child are not the only[21] or the paramount

---

17 *Every Child Matters*, statutory guidance to the UK Border Agency on making arrangements to safeguard and promote the welfare of children, para 1.4.
18 *Every Child Matters*, statutory guidance para 2.7.
19 [2011] UKSC 4, [2011] 2 WLR 148.
20 *ZH (Tanzania) v Secretary of State for the Home Department* [2011] UKSC 4, [2011] 2 WLR 148 paras 26 and 33 per Lady Hale, see also para 44 per Lord Hope.
21 As Thomas Hammarberg, Commissioner for Human Rights, Council of Europe, explained of the drafting of article 3 of the UNCRC: 'The broad scope of Article 3 naturally had a price in the drafting process. There was considerable discussion on whether the formulation should be "a" or "the" primary consideration. In the end it was recognized that given the widened scope of Article 3, situations would arise when other legitimate and competing interests could not be ignored. The conclusion was to settle for the somewhat less decisive wording "a primary consideration". Thus, the best interests of

consideration.[22] Lady Hale's judgment indicates, moreover, that where a decision directly affects a child's upbringing the best interests of the child carry greater weight:[23] arguably, this imposes a higher test in circumstances where a decision to deport is directed against the child rather than the parent.

4.15 Lord Kerr's judgment in *ZH (Tanzania)* stated that while it not always decisive, the best interests of the child are a factor:

> ... that must rank higher than any other. It is not merely one consideration that weighs in the balance alongside other competing factors. Where the best interests of the child clearly favour a certain course, that course should be followed unless countervailing reasons of considerable force displace them.[24]

4.16 The judgments of Lord Kerr and the other members of the Court in *ZH (Tanzania)* have been said to be consistent (though to the extent that they differ, it is the majority that must be followed).[25]

4.17 We suggest the following synthesis: the best interests of a child must be considered first but are not the only or the paramount consideration. The best interests of the child may be displaced by countervailing reasons of considerable force.

4.18 The best interests of the child may, for example, be outweighed by the public interest in deportation, as has been held both in the context of ECHR article 8 cases relying on the UNCRC as informing the ECHR protections before the introduction of the section 55 duty[26] and more recently in the context of the section 55 duty itself.[27] However, we suggest that those cases which predate *ZH (Tanzania)* should be treated with caution.

> the child cannot normally be the only consideration, but should be among the first aspects to be considered and should be given considerable weight in all decisions affecting children' (Warsaw, 30 May 2008, CommDH/Speech(2008)10).

22 *ZH (Tanzania) v Secretary of State for the Home Department* [2011] UKSC 4, [2011] 2 WLR 148 para 25, per Lady Hale, giving the leading judgment.
23 *ZH (Tanzania) v Secretary of State for the Home Department* [2011] UKSC 4, [2011] 2 WLR 148 para 25.
24 *ZH (Tanzania) v Secretary of State for the Home Department* [2011] UKSC 4, [2011] 2 WLR 148 para 46 per Lord Kerr.
25 *Lee v Secretary of State for the Home Department* [2011] EWCA Civ 348 para 15.
26 *DS (India) v Secretary of State for the Home Department* [2009] EWCA Civ 544, [2010] Imm AR 81 para 35; *AR (Pakistan) v Secretary of State for the Home Department* [2010] EWCA Civ 816 para 18.
27 *QJ (Algeria) v Secretary of State for the Home Department* [2010] EWCA Civ 1478 para 11; *R (Suppiah) v Secretary of State for the Home Department* [2011] EWHC 2 (Admin) para 144; *Lee v Secretary of State for the Home Department* [2011] EWCA Civ 348 para 27.

Meaning of 'best interests of the child'

4.19 The 'best interests of the child' means, broadly, the well-being of the child. Where a parent faces expulsion, this includes the question of whether it is reasonable to expect the child to live in another country, relevant to which will be:

> ... the level of the child's integration in this country and the length of his or her absence from the other country, where and with whom the child is to live and the arrangements for looking after the child in the other country; and the strength of the child's relationships with parents or other family members which will be severed if the child has to move away.[28]

Ascertaining the best interests of the child

4.20 UNCRC article 12 requires that in any judicial and administrative proceedings affecting a child, a child who is capable of forming his or her own views 'shall' be given the opportunity to be heard, either directly or through a representative or appropriate body. Therefore, as Lady Hale stated in *ZH (Tanzania)* that 'the immigration authorities must be prepared at least to consider hearing directly from a child who wishes to express a view and is old enough to do so'.[29]

4.21 However, as Lady Hale noted in *EM (Lebanon)*[30] and reiterated in *ZH (Tanzania)*,[31] while separate consideration of the best interests of the child will always be necessary where the child is potentially affected and it should not be assumed that the interests of all family members are identical, separate consideration is different from separate representation. Separate representation will rarely be necessary in immigration cases, the exception being the unusual cases in which the interests of different family members conflict.

Best interests of a British citizen child

4.22 *ZH (Tanzania)* concerned the proposed administrative removal of a single mother of two British citizen children: the removal of the mother would inevitably entail the departure of the children from the

---

28 *ZH (Tanzania) v Secretary of State for the Home Department* [2011] UKSC 4, [2011] 2 WLR 148 para 29 per Lady Hale.
29 *ZH (Tanzania) v Secretary of State for the Home Department* [2011] UKSC 4, [2011] 2 WLR 148 para 37 per Lady Hale.
30 [2008] UKHL 64, [2009] AC 1198 para 49.
31 Para 35.

Deportation cases involving minors: relevant legislation and policy 59

UK. That is, *ZH (Tanzania)* was a case of constructive deportation of a British citizen child. The Supreme Court was emphatic that while not a trump card, the British citizenship of a child is of particular importance in assessing the child's best interests in an expulsion case.[32] This is because citizenship confers rights which the child will not be able to exercise if moved to another country: 'They will lose the advantages of growing up and being educated in their own country, their own culture and their own language.'[33] British citizenship 'will hardly ever be less than a very significant and weighty factor against moving children who have that status to another country'.[34] This is not limited to administrative removal cases, nor is it limited to cases in which (as in *ZH (Tanzania)*) one of the parents is British. The same principles have been applied in the context of a British citizen child neither of whose parents had leave to remain in the UK and where it was proposed to deport the father in consequence of a serious violent offence.[35]

Zambrano and the expulsion of parents of British children

4.23 The rights accorded to British children and their parents (as well as the rights of certain other family members of British citizens) have been further expanded by the landmark judgment of the Grand Chamber of the Court of Justice of the European Union (CJEU) in *Zambrano v Office National de l'emploi*[36] which post-dates *ZH (Tanzania)*. *Zambrano* holds that it is a breach of EU law (article 20 of the Treaty on the Functioning of the European Union (TFEU)) to deny a right of residence in an EU member state to the parent of a minor child who is dependent on that parent and is the citizen of that member state, where that would lead to the European child having to leave the territory of the European Union. *Zambrano* is discussed in detail at paras 10.4–10.16.

---

32 *ZH (Tanzania) v Secretary of State for the Home Department* [2011] UKSC 4, [2011] 2 WLR 148 para 30 per Lady Hale.
33 *ZH (Tanzania) v Secretary of State for the Home Department* [2011] UKSC 4, [2011] 2 WLR 148 para 32 per Lady Hale.
34 *ZH (Tanzania) v Secretary of State for the Home Department* [2011] UKSC 4, [2011] 2 WLR 148 para 41 per Lord Hope.
35 *R (SM) v Secretary of State for the Home Department* [2011] EWHC 338 (Admin).
36 Case C-34/09 [2011] 2 CMLR 46.

Effect of parent's wrongdoing

4.24 The Supreme Court in *ZH (Tanzania)* has also clearly stated that the best interests of the child should not be devalued by reference to the parent's wrongdoing.[37] *ZH (Tanzania)* was an administrative removal case in which the SSHD sought to remove the primary carer who had an 'appalling immigration history' and knew her immigration status to be precarious before the birth of her child.[38]

Meaning of 'safeguarding and promoting the welfare of the child'

4.25 The safeguarding and promoting duty extends beyond protecting children from harm: it encompasses a duty to promote optimum life chances,[39] including, for example, considerations of educational continuity.[40]

4.26 Note that where a child has undergone discretionary registration as a British citizen under British Nationality Act 1981 s3(1), this is an indication that the SSHD at that time considered that the child's future lay in the UK and that the child had close connections in the UK.[41]

Reliance on other aspects of the UNCRC

4.27 The UNCRC has not formally been incorporated to domestic law. However, the *Every Child Matters* Code of Practice stipulates that the UK Border Agency 'must' fulfil the requirements of the UNCRC and it has been held that the proper application of BCIA 2009 s55 requires compliance with that convention.[42]

---

37 *ZH (Tanzania) v Secretary of State for the Home Department* [2011] UKSC 4, [2011] 2 WLR 148 para 44 per Lord Hope, para 33 per Lady Hale.
38 See *R (Reece-Davis) v Secretary of State for the Home Department* [2011] EWHC 561 (Admin) for a further example of the application of that principle.
39 *Every Child Matters*, statutory code of practice, para 1.4 and *TS v Secretary of State for the Home Department and Northamptonshire CC* [2010] EWHC 2614 (Admin) para 29.
40 *R (Banda) v Secretary of State for the Home Department* [2010] EWHC 2471 (Admin) paras 21–22; *Omotunde (best interests – Zambrano applied– Razgar) Nigeria* [2011] UKUT 249 (IAC) para 26 per Blake J sitting as President of the Immigration and Asylum Chamber of the Upper Tribunal.
41 *Omotunde (best interests – Zambrano applied – Razgar) Nigeria* [2011] UKUT 249 (IAC) para 23 per Blake J sitting as President of UT-IAC.
42 *R (Suppiah) v Secretary of State for the Home Department* [2011] EWHC 2 (Admin) para 148.

Deportation cases involving minors: relevant legislation and policy 61

4.28 We therefore suggest that other articles of the UNCRC provide valuable guidance as to the 'best interests of the child' and the 'safeguarding and protecting' duty, including:
- article 6(2) (duty of States parties to ensure to the maximum extent possible the survival and development of the child);
- article 19 (protection from all forms of physical or mental violence, injury or abuse or negligent treatment, maltreatment or exploitation);
- article 20(3) (due regard to the desirability of continuity in a child's upbringing);
- article 24 (recognition of the right of the child to the highest attainable standard of health);[43]
- article 27 (recognition of the right of the child to a standard of living adequate for the child's physical, mental, spiritual, moral and social development);
- article 28 (recognition of the right of the child to education);
- article 34 (undertaking by States parties to protect the child from all forms of sexual exploitation and sexual abuse);
- article 37(b) (protection from unlawful or arbitrary deprivation of liberty and the detention of children only as a measure of last resort and for the shortest appropriate period of time);
- article 39 (duty of States parties to take all appropriate measures to promote physical and psychological recovery and social reintegration of child victims of any form of neglect, exploitation or abuse, torture or any other form of cruel, inhuman or degrading treatment or punishment, or armed conflict. Such recovery and reintegration 'shall' take place in an environment which fosters the health, self-respect and dignity of the child).

Meaning of 'have regard to'

4.29 BCIA 2009 s55(1)(a) requires that decision-makers 'have regard to' the duty to the need to safeguard and promote the welfare of children who are in the UK. BCIA 2009 s55(3) likewise requires decision-makers to 'have regard' to the Code of Practice. Meanwhile the *Every Child Matters* Code of Practice itself envisages that it may be departed from with good reason.[44] In the context of the SSHD's obligations

---

43 *TS v Secretary of State for the Home Department and Northamptonshire County Council* [2010] EWHC 2614 (Admin) para 32 for example accepts that the interpretation of 'best interests' is informed by UNCRC articles 20 and 24.
44 *Every Child Matters*, Introduction, para 6.

under BCIA 2009 s55 it has therefore been held by the Administrative Court (before *ZH (Tanzania)*) that the best interests of the child need not be treated as a primary consideration if there are cogent reasons for not so doing.[45] It is difficult to conceive of circumstances in which the SSHD could lawfully disregard the need to treat the best interests of the child as a primary consideration. In any event, as we see at paras 17.24–17.26, where ECHR article 8 is engaged, it is mandatory that the decision-maker treat the best interests of the child as a primary consideration.[46]

Consequences of a failure to have regard to BCIA 2009 s55 and *Every Child Matters* considerations

4.30 A decision-maker need not expressly refer to the statutory duty imposed by BCIA 2009 s55, but the terms of the decision must make it clear that the duty has been discharged.[47]

4.31 A relevant decision affecting a child made without regard to the statutory duty is marred by public law error (failure to have regard to a relevant consideration) and susceptible to judicial review.

4.32 A failure to consider BCIA 2009 s55 should be challenged in the FTT-IAC rather than in the Administrative Court where an in-country right of appeal exists.[48] An immigration decision which is taken without regard to the section 55 considerations will not be in accordance with the law[49] and an appeal against that decision must be allowed[50] at least to the extent of remittal for the taking of a lawful decision. The IAC must also itself have regard to those considerations when hearing deportation and other appeals in which children are involved, even where the BCIA 2009 s55 duty was not in force when the immigration decision was taken.[51] See para 17.27 for the

---

45 *TS v Secretary of State for the Home Department and Northamptonshire County Council* [2010] EWHC 2614 (Admin) paras 34 and 36.
46 *ZH (Tanzania) v Secretary of State for the Home Department* para 17; *R (MXL) v Secretary of State for the Home Department* [2010] EWHC 2397 (Admin) para 83.
47 *R (TS) v Secretary of State for the Home Department* [2010] EWHC 2614 (Admin) para 24.
48 *R (NXT) v Secretary of State for the Home Department* [2011] EWHC 969 (Admin) paras 151–154.
49 *ZH (Tanzania) v Secretary of State for the Home Department* para 24.
50 Under NIAA 2002 s84(1)(e).
51 *DS (Afghanistan) v Secretary of State for the Home Department* [2011] EWCA Civ 305 para 82.

ECHR article 8 consequences of a failure to have regard to the statutory duty.

Timely resolution of applications made by children

4.33 BCIA 2009 s55 and the *Every Child Matters* Code of Practice also impose other duties on the SSHD, including the requirement that the UKBA 2007 act according to the principle that 'Children should have their applications dealt with in a timely way and that minimizes the uncertainty that they may experience'.[52]

Home Office policies relevant to the deportation of children

Splitting families

4.34 An internal Criminal Casework Directorate (CCD) Process Instruction, PC 0/11 of 10 January 2011, valid until 10 July 2011, 'Parental responsibilities and continued detention of foreign national prisoners' (FNPs) addresses deportation decisions which have the result of splitting families. At time of writing, this CCD Process Instruction is unpublished: we suggest that the Home Office's failure to publish this instruction, setting out as it does the criteria by which deportation (and also detention) decisions are made, is unlawful.[53]

4.35 The internal CCD Process Instruction states:

> The Case Owner must not deport or remove a parent without either ensuring that any relevant children are being deported with the parent or, where the children are remaining in the UK, that they have some type of leave to remain in the UK and that they are either in the care of their other parent or Social Services or that they are the subject of a residency order. Arrangements for these children must be formalised on a case by case basis prior to the deportation or removal of the parent.

4.36 As the same Process Instruction stipulates, any decision to deport which will have the effect of splitting a family must be referred to the Office of the Children's Champion (whose role we discuss at para 37.11) for advice and then be approved by the CCD Director.

---

52 *Every Child Matters* para 2.7.
53 See *R (Lumba and Mighty) v Secretary of State for the Home Department* [2011] UKSC 12, [2011] 2 WLR 671 per Lord Dyson paras 34–35 on the duty to publish such policies.

Unaccompanied minors

4.37 Where a foreign national is under 18 and is unaccompanied (or has family in the UK with indefinite leave to remain) and no adequate reception and accommodation arrangements exist in the country of origin, it is Home Office policy that 'deportation should normally be deferred until the person turns 18'.[54]

4.38 It is Home Office policy that an unaccompanied minor whose asylum and ECHR claim is refused but who cannot be removed because of a lack of adequate reception arrangements will be given leave to remain.[55]

4.39 Where, in breach of stated policy, an unaccompanied minor is not given leave to remain and subsequently (even in adulthood) faces criminal deportation, the decision-maker must have regard to the fact that the minor was deprived of a period of lawful residence. This may, for example, have resulted in the individual being unable to establish himself or herself lawfully and consequently being vulnerable to criminal exploitation.[56]

The former seven-year concession

4.40 The Home Office previously operated a concessionary policy, also known as DP069/99 or DP5/96, concerning children who had lived in the UK for seven years or more, and their family members. The seven-year concession was withdrawn on 9 December 2008 but remains relevant in a number of cases:

- where a child had reached the age of seven by the time of the relevant immigration decision (for example, a decision to deport) but the policy was not applied. As we have already seen,[57] prejudice caused by the SSHD's unlawful failure to operate an applicable policy is relevant;

---

54 Enforcement Instructions and Guidance (EIG) chapter 12 para 12.3.1.
55 In cases decided before 1 April 2007, for three years (or 12 months for certain countries) or until the child's 18th birthday, whichever period was shorter. In cases decided on or after that date, for three years (or 12 months for certain countries) or until the child reached 17-and-a-half, whichever period is shorter. Note, however, that exclusions from discretionary leave may apply – see the Asylum Policy Instruction on Discretionary Leave. See also discussion at para 19.41.
56 *SL (Vietnam) v Secretary of State for the Home Department* [2010] EWCA Civ 225.
57 At para 3.35 and also para 3.38 above.

- where the policy was considered at an appeal (even if the child only reached the age of seven at the time of that appeal) and the challenge by either party to the determination of that appeal is still ongoing;[58]
- where the Asylum and Immigration Tribunal (AIT) or IAC has made a final determination allowing an appeal on the basis of DP5/96 (either outright or directing the SSHD to consider the policy afresh);[59] and
- where the UKBA has acknowledged in writing that it has received an application relying on DP5/96 or has indicated prior to the withdrawal of the policy that it has already considered DP5/96.[60]

4.41 However, the seven-year concession does not apply where, though the child had already reached the age of seven, no application to regularise the family's status or no immigration decision had been made prior to the withdrawal of the policy[61]. Still less can the policy apply where the child had not reached the age of seven by the time the policy was withdrawn.[62]

4.42 There has been considerable debate as to the actual terms of the seven-year concession. For reasons best known to the Home Office, this concession was never incorporated to the Immigration Rules, which, arguably, it should have been,[63] nor was it incorporated to the main statements of Home Office policy. It was previously thought that the concession imposed only a presumption of non-removal.[64] In *R (A) v Secretary of State for the Home Department*[65] it was clarified that the seven-year concession (erratically applied) established a presumption that where a person liable to expulsion had a child living with them who had resided in the UK for seven years or more, the adult and child a) would not be removed; and b) would be granted

---

58 *AF (Jamaica) v Secretary of State for the Home Department* [2009] EWCA Civ 240 para 21.
59 Transitional arrangements listed in EIG chapter 53 para 53.6.1.
60 Transitional arrangements listed in EIG chapter 53 para 53.6.1.
61 *Abbassi and Others v Secretary of State for the Home Department* [2011] EWCA Civ 814, case of Rahman, para 45.
62 *Abbassi and Others v Secretary of State for the Home Department* [2011] EWCA Civ 814, cases of Abbassi and Munir, para 48.
63 *Abbassi and Others v Secretary of State for the Home Department* [2011] EWCA Civ 814 para 39.
64 *NF (Ghana) v Secretary of State for the Home Department* [2008] EWCA Civ 906.
65 [2008] EWHC 2844 (Admin).

indefinite leave to remain.⁶⁶ The seven-year concession applied to families whose children had an entitlement to remain in the UK (including British citizenship) as it did to families whose children had no such entitlement.⁶⁷

4.43 The seven-year concession may apply in the context of criminal deportation.⁶⁸ However, the SSHD retained a wide discretion under the seven-year concession. Where the principal has a very poor immigration history,⁶⁹ has committed a serious criminal offence and/or where there is no proposal to deport the child (and the child has another parent who proposes to remain in the UK) such that the child would not be uprooted, the presumption of non-removal and of the grant of indefinite leave to remain, while still a relevant consideration⁷⁰, may be outweighed.

4.44 Note that the seven-year concession reflects the SSHD's recognition of the difficulties that expulsion causes for children who have spent seven or more years in the UK.⁷¹ BCIA 2009 s55 arguably imposes on the SSHD a higher threshold for the expulsion of a child than the earlier policy.⁷²

---

66 The court also found in *R (A) v Secretary of State for the Home Department* that the policy should be applied even to children whose family members did not require leave to remain: it was discriminatory, contrary to ECHR article 14 read with article 8, to treat children differently according to whether their family members required leave to remain. A child who had lived in the UK for seven years or more but was not living with a person liable to expulsion would still normally be granted indefinite leave to remain.

67 *SS (India) v Secretary of State for the Home Department* [2010] EWCA Civ 388 para 42.

68 *AF (Jamaica) v Secretary of State for the Home Department* [2009] EWCA Civ 240; *SS (India) v Secretary of State for the Home Department* [2010] EWCA Civ 388 paras 38 and 44.

69 See, for example, *R (Daley-Murdock) v Secretary of State for the Home Department* [2011] EWCA Civ 161, *R (Jav) v Secretary of State for the Home Department* [2009] EWHC 1779 (Admin).

70 *AF (Jamaica) v Secretary of State for the Home Department* [2009] EWCA Civ 240.

71 See, for example, the comments of Blake J, sitting as President of UT-IAC in *EM and others (Returnees) Zimbabwe CG* [2011] UKUT 98 (IAC): 'In the absence of any other policy guidance from the Secretary of State, it remains legitimate for Immigration Judges to give some regard to the previous policy that seven years residence by a child under 18 would afford a basis for regularising the position of the child and parent in the absence of conduct reasons to the contrary, in making a judicial assessment of whether removal is proportionate to the legitimate aim having regard to the best interests of the child.'

72 *R (Banda) v Secretary of State for the Home Department* [2010] EWHC 2471 (Admin) paras 21–22.

CHAPTER 5
'Automatic' deportation under the UK Borders Act 2007

5.1	Introduction
5.6	Differences between the two statutory deportation regimes
5.8	Timetable for entry into force
5.10	Transitional provisions
5.12	**Who is liable to 'automatic' deportation under UKBA 2007**
5.12	The definition of 'foreign criminal'
	Condition 1 • Condition 2
5.18	Which custodial sentences do and do not trigger 'automatic' deportation
	Suspended sentences • Consecutive sentences • Detention (hospitals and YOIs) • Meaning of 'is convicted' and 'is sentenced'
5.22	**No private law action for failure to issue an 'automatic' deportation order**
5.23	**Exemptions from all deportation**
5.24	The exemption for long-resident Commonwealth and Irish nationals in 'automatic' deportation cases
5.25	**The numbered exceptions to 'automatic' deportation under the UKBA 2007**

continued

5.31	**Deportation under IA 1971 for family members and others who do not meet the criteria for 'automatic' deportation under UKBA 2007**
5.31	Family members
5.32	Others who do not qualify as 'foreign criminals'
5.34	'Foreign criminals' who fall in the numbered exceptions to 'automatic' deportation
5.37	**When an 'automatic' deportation order can be made**
5.40	**When an 'automatic' deportation order takes effect**
5.43	**Appeal to the FTT-IAC against a decision that the criteria for 'automatic' deportation are met**
5.44	Obstacles to in-country appeal rights in 'automatic' deportation cases
5.47	**In-country appeal to the FTT-IAC against an 'automatic' deportation order**
5.51	**Out-of-country appeal to the FTT- IAC against an 'automatic' deportation order and other remedies**

Introduction

5.1 The UK Borders Act (UKBA) 2007 introduces the most important changes to the UK's system of deportation for foreign national offenders since the Immigration Act (IA) 1971.

5.2 The 'automatic' deportation provisions are the legislative response to the political furore that erupted in late April 2006 when it emerged that, in 1,013 cases, the Home Office had not considered whether to deport foreign national prisoners (FNPs) before releasing them at the end of their custodial terms. Notwithstanding that the crisis had arisen out of the Home Office's administrative failure to exercise or consider the wide powers of deportation which it already had, the result was a public promise of new legislation. On 17 May 2006, the then Prime Minister Tony Blair announced: 'there will be an automatic presumption to deport, and the vast bulk of those people will, indeed, be deported, irrespective of any claim that they have that the country to which they are returning may not be safe'; the then leader of the opposition, David Cameron, accused Tony Blair of 'making it up as he goes along'.[1]

5.3 'Automatic' deportation is a misnomer. The UKBA 2007 deportation provisions do not establish a system of 'automatic' deportation (still less a system that allows foreign nationals to be deported irrespective of any claim they may have of risk on return). Nor does the UKBA 2007 create a new power to deport: the deportation order is still made under IA 1971 s5(1).

5.4 What the UKBA 2007 does do in relation to deportation is:

- remove the discretion of the Secretary of State for the Home Department (SSHD) in many cases as to whether to pursue deportation. The SSHD is required in many cases to pursue deportation regardless of mitigating or compassionate circumstances;
- erect new obstacles to in-country rights of appeal for those facing deportation; and
- expand the SSHD's administrative detention powers.

5.5 In this chapter, we begin with an overview of the differences between the parallel deportation regimes under the IA 1971 and UKBA 2007 and the timetable for the entry into force of the UKBA 2007 deportation provisions. We then go on to consider liability and exceptions to liability for 'automatic' deportation, the timing and effect of an 'automatic' deportation order, and appeal rights in deportation cases governed by the UKBA 2007.

1 *Hansard* HC Debates col 990, 17 May 2006.

Differences between the two statutory deportation regimes

5.6 As we have seen at paras 1.2–1.3 above, in deportation cases pursued under the IA 1971, the SSHD exercises a discretion over whether to decide to deport a non-exempt foreign national. A right of appeal to the Immigration and Asylum Chamber of the First-tier Tribunal (FTT-IAC) lies against the SSHD's decision to make a deportation order. That right of appeal is always in-country, regardless of the grounds on which the appeal is brought. The deportation order may only be signed after the exhaustion of in-time appeals.

5.7 By contrast, under the UKBA 2007, the SSHD must make a deportation order against a foreign national who satisfies specified criteria unless certain exemptions or exceptions are made out. The 'automatic' deportation order may be made at any time, although the deportation order will not have the effect of invalidating extant leave until in-country appeal rights have been exhausted. The appeal to the FTT-IAC lies against the SSHD's decision that the conditions for 'automatic' deportation are met. That appeal may only be brought in-country if it is brought on specified grounds.

Timetable for entry into force

5.8 As will be seen in more detail further below, the UKBA 2007 contains provision for 'automatic' deportation orders to be made in respect of two classes of FNP (save for specified exceptions). The two classes are foreign nationals who are convicted in the UK of an offence and sentenced to either:

- Condition 1, a period of imprisonment of at least 12 months; or
- Condition 2, a period of imprisonment of any length for an offence defined by secondary legislation as 'particularly serious'.

5.9 The legislative provisions relating to the first group of FNPs (Condition 1) came into force on 1 August 2008.[2] The provisions relating to the second group of foreign national offenders (Condition 2) are not in force.

---

2 UK Borders Act 2007 (Commencement No 3 and Transitional Provisions) Order 2008 SI No 1818 para 2.

Transitional provisions

5.10 The 'automatic' deportation provisions (in relation to Condition 1) have retrospective effect. The SSHD may impose 'automatic' deportation orders on those convicted before the passing of the UKBA 2007 who were in custody or subject to a suspended sentence at the time of commencement on 1 August 2008.[3]

5.11 There is an apparent lacuna in the transitional provisions. They make no express provision for the application of the UKBA 2007 to those convicted after the passing of the Act but before it comes into force. The Administrative Court[4] and Court of Appeal[5] have, however, rejected arguments that the 'automatic' deportation and associated detention powers do not apply to those convicted between the passing of the UKBA 2007 and its entry into force.

Who is liable to 'automatic' deportation under UKBA 2007

The definition of 'foreign criminal'

5.12 Under UKBA 2007, the SSHD 'must' make a deportation order in respect of a person defined as a 'foreign criminal' subject to certain exceptions.[6] Where a person meets the criteria for definition as a 'foreign criminal', the person's deportation is deemed to be 'conducive to the public good' for the purposes of IA 1971 s3(5).[7]

5.13 Thus, it is not open to a person who is a 'foreign criminal' to argue that his or her deportation is not conducive to the public good, nor does the SSHD need to prove that deportation of a 'foreign criminal' is conducive to the public good.[8]

---

3 UK Borders Act 2007 (Commencement No 3 and Transitional Provisions) Order 2008 para 3.
4 *Rashid Hussein v Secretary of State for the Home Department* [2009] EWHC 2492 (Admin).
5 *AT (Pakistan) and JT (Pakistan) v Secretary of State for the Home Department* [2010] EWCA Civ 567.
6 UKBA 2007 s32(5).
7 UKBA 2007 s32(4).
8 *Secretary of State for the Home Department v MK* [2010] UKUT 281 at para 24, case presided over by Sedley LJ; endorsed by the Court of Appeal in *RU (Bangladesh) v Secretary of State for the Home Department* [2011] EWCA Civ 651 para 34.

5.14 A person is defined as a 'foreign criminal' if he or she is not a British citizen, and was convicted in the UK of an offence and meets one of two conditions.[9]

Condition 1

5.15 Condition 1 came into effect on 1 August 2008[10] and requires the SSHD to make a deportation order in respect of a person who is not a British citizen and who is convicted in the UK of an offence and who is sentenced to a period of imprisonment of at least 12 months.[11] In practice, the Home Office since May 2006 had already been pursing deportation in almost all cases where non European Economic Area (EEA) national offenders have been sentenced to 12 months or more of imprisonment[12] (and in some cases, was pursuing deportation where there had been considerably lower sentences of imprisonment).

Condition 2

5.16 If brought into force, Condition 2 will require the SSHD to make a deportation order in respect of a person who is not a British citizen, is convicted in the UK of an offence, is convicted of an offence specified as particularly serious by an order made under the Nationality, Immigration and Asylum Act (NIAA) 2002 s72, and is sentenced to a period of imprisonment of any length.[13]

5.17 Condition 2 leaves a striking latitude to the SSHD to define by secondary legislation who exactly will be affected by the 'automatic' deportation provisions: new secondary legislation defining the relevant offences will be necessary before Condition 2 can be brought into force.[14]

---

9 UKBA 2007 s32(1).
10 UK Borders Act 2007 (Commencement No 3 and Transitional Provisions) Order 2008 para 2.
11 UKBA 2007 s32(2).
12 Enforcement Instructions and Guidance (EIG) chapter 11 para 11.2.1.
13 UKBA 2007 s32(3).
14 At the time that the UKBA 2007 was passed, 'particularly serious crimes' were defined in the NIAA 2002 (Specification of Particularly Serious Crimes) Order 2004 SI No 1910. That secondary legislation had been drafted under NIAA 2002 s72 for a distinct purpose: to set out those who should not benefit from protection from refoulement under article 33 of the Refugee Convention (even though the law or policy may prohibit their removal from the UK). It covered a very wide range of offences, some of which are uncontroversially particularly serious (such as possession of a nuclear weapon) others far less serious (such as shoplifting offences under the Theft Act or reckless damage to another's

Which custodial sentences do and do not trigger 'automatic' deportation

Suspended sentences

5.18 A person does not become liable to 'automatic' deportation as a consequence of a non-activated suspended sentence. This is because, for the purposes of ascertaining whether a person meets the criteria for 'automatic' deportation (under Condition 1, or, if and when it comes into force, Condition 2), a sentence of imprisonment does *not* include a suspended sentence (unless a court subsequently orders that the sentence, or any part of it, is to take effect).[15]

Consecutive sentences

5.19 A person does not become liable to 'automatic' deportation under Condition 1 if his or her imprisonment only exceeds 12 months as a consequence of being sentenced to consecutive sentences amounting in aggregate to more than 12 months. This is because, for the purposes of ascertaining whether a person meets the criteria for 'automatic' deportation, a period of imprisonment of at least 12 months does not include a person who would reach over 12 months purely by aggregation of consecutive sentences.[16]

Detention (hospitals and YOIs)

5.20 However, a person will become liable for 'automatic' deportation where the qualifying sentence was to detention in a hospital or in a Young Offenders Institution (YOI) (under Condition 1 or, if and when it comes into effect, under Condition 2).[17] The effect of this is that 'automatic' deportation does apply to those aged under 21; and does apply to those found responsible in law for their offending but who are suffering from a treatable mental illness. However, see para 5.28 below concerning those under 18 at the time of conviction.

Meaning of 'is convicted' and 'is sentenced'

5.21 We suggest that the criteria 'is convicted' and 'is sentenced' for the purposes of the conditions for 'automatic' deportation under UKBA

    property). That secondary legislation was found to be ultra vires in *EN (Serbia) v Secretary of State for the Home Department* [2009] EWCA Civ 630, [2010] QB 633.
15 UKBA 2007 s38(1)(a) and (2)(a).
16 UKBA 2007 s38(1)(b).
17 UKBA 2007 s38(1).

2007 s32 refer only to the most recent conviction or sentence. That interpretation is supported by the repeated use of the present tense in UKBA 2007 s32 and the limited extent of the transitional provision in UKBA 2007 s59(4)(i) (allowing the Act to take retrospective effect for those convicted before the passing of the Act but only if the proposed deportee is in custody or subject to a suspended sentence at commencement).

No private law action for failure to issue an 'automatic' deportation order

5.22 There is no right of private action by an individual seeking to challenge the SSHD's failure to issue an 'automatic' deportation order[18] (meaning that an individual cannot sue the Home Office for failing, for example, to make an 'automatic' deportation order against a particular FNP).

Exemptions from all deportation

5.23 The exemptions from deportation contained in IA 1971 ss7 and 8 also apply to automatic deportation,[19] covering long-resident Irish and Commonwealth citizens and certain diplomatic and international functionaries. These exemptions have been discussed in detail at paras 1.27–1.42.

The exemption for long-resident Commonwealth and Irish nationals in 'automatic' deportation cases

5.24 IA 1971 s7(1)(b) provides that a Commonwealth citizen or citizen of the Republic of Ireland who was a Commonwealth citizen or citizen of the Republic of the Ireland on 1 January 1973; was ordinarily resident in the UK on 1 January 1973; and at the time of the SSHD's decision had been ordinarily resident for the last 5 years in the UK is not liable to deportation. Although not specified in UKBA 2007, the logical construction is that for the purposes of this exemption from 'automatic' deportation, the date of 'decision' will be the date of the decision as to whether UKBA 2007 s32(5) applies.

18 UKBA 2007 s32(7).
19 UKBA 2007 s33(1)(b).

The numbered exceptions to 'automatic' deportation under the UKBA 2007

5.25 A list of numbered exceptions to the 'automatic' deportation regime is set out in UKBA 2007 s33. The first three are of widest application.

5.26 Exception 1[20] is where removal of the 'foreign criminal' in pursuance of the deportation order would breach the person's rights under the European Convention on Human Rights (ECHR) or the Refugee Convention.

5.27 Because of the special safeguards applicable to the withdrawal of refugee status, we suggest that no 'automatic' deportation order can be made against the recipient of a grant of ongoing leave to enter or remain on the basis of refugee status, unless:

- the person has been convicted of a 'particularly serious crime' and constitutes 'a danger to the community of the United Kingdom' applies so that he or she is stripped of protection from refoulement under the Refugee Convention (see the discussion of NIAA 2002 s72 and of article 33(2) of the Refugee Convention at paras 12.78–12.96); or
- refugee status is first terminated as a consequence of cessation or revocation proceedings.[21]

5.28 Exception 2 is where the SSHD 'thinks' that the 'foreign criminal' was under the age of 18 at the time of conviction.[22]

5.29 Exception 3 is where the removal of the 'foreign criminal' in pursuance of the deportation order would breach his or her rights under the EC Treaties. The special protections from deportation applicable to EEA nationals and their family members are discussed in detail in chapter 9. As we discuss there at para 9.49, arguably, it is never lawful to make an 'automatic' deportation order against an EEA national or his or her family members.[23]

5.30 Exception 4 relates to 'foreign criminals' who are already the subject of extradition proceedings. Exception 5 relates to 'foreign criminals' who are the subject of specified orders and directions

---

20 UKBA 2007 s33(2).
21 See Immigration Rules paras 339A and 339G for provision on revocation of refugee status and humanitarian protection respectively. Revocation and cessation is discussed at paras 12.121–12.143 below.
22 UKBA 2007 s33(3).
23 Family members as defined in the Immigration (European Economic Area) Regulations (EEA Regs) 2006 SI No 1003 para 7.

under mental health legislation.[24] Exception 6 is where the SSHD 'thinks that' 'automatic' deportation would contravene the UK's obligations under the Council of Europe Convention against Trafficking in Human Beings. The law of extradition and trafficking lie outside the scope of this book and specialist texts should be consulted.[25]

Deportation under IA 1971 for family members and others who do not meet the criteria for 'automatic' deportation under UKBA 2007

Family members

5.31 Family members of principal deportees are not covered by the 'automatic' deportation provisions: the deportation of family members continues to be governed by IA 1971 s3(5)(b): see para 1.16.

Others who do not qualify as 'foreign criminals'

5.32 The SSHD retains a power to decide to deport as principals under IA 1971 those foreign nationals who are not 'foreign criminals' as defined in UKBA 2007 s32(1) (for example, a foreign national offender who was convicted of an offence but sentenced to less than 12 months' imprisonment) provided that they are not exempt from deportation under the IA 1971.

5.33 However, the UKBA 2007 legislation provides a weighty indication of where parliament considers the threshold of seriousness to lie for deportation, which is broadly consistent with the SSHD's own policy on the criteria for deportation under IA 1971.[26] Arguably, in such cases, deportation should not be pursued under IA 1971 save in exceptional circumstances.

---

24 See chapter 30 of this book for a discussion of orders and directions made under mental health legislation.
25 For a specialist text on extradition, see *Extradition and mutual assistance handbook*, 2nd edition, Oxford University Press, 2011. For a specialist text on trafficking, see Sandhya Drew, *Human Trafficking – Human Rights: law and practice*, LAG, 2009.
26 See also EIG chapter 11 para 11.2.1 which sets the threshold for consideration for deportation in most non-EEA national criminal deportation cases under IA 1971 where there is no court recommendation for deportation at a sentence of imprisonment of 12 months or over (or an aggregate of two or three sentences over a five-year period totalling 12 months or more; or a custodial sentence of any length for a listed drugs offence).

'Foreign criminals' who fall in the numbered exceptions to 'automatic' deportation

5.34 'Foreign criminals' who are not exempt from deportation under IA 1971 but who fall within certain of the numbered exceptions to 'automatic' deportation under UKBA 2007 can still be deported under IA 1971, namely:

- those whom the SSHD believes to have been under 18 at the date of conviction;
- those for whom a valid extradition request has been received; and
- certain mentally disordered offenders.

5.35 However, where a person falls within an exception to 'automatic' deportation because the SSHD believes that the person's deportation would breach his or her rights under the Refugee Convention or the ECHR,[27] deportation under IA 1971 is also precluded. The Immigration Rules prohibit the making of any deportation order against a person whose deportation would be contrary to the UK's obligations under the Refugee Convention or the ECHR.[28]

5.36 It is likewise strongly arguable that UKBA 2007 s32(6A) partially incorporates the Council of Europe Convention against Trafficking in Human Beings, so that, where the SSHD applies numbered exception 6 to an individual (because the SSHD thinks that the application of the 'automatic' deportation provisions would contravene the UK's obligations under that Convention) a decision to deport that person under IA 1971 would not be in accordance with the law. See para 21.11 on appeals to the FTT-IAC on grounds that a decision is not in accordance with the law.

When an 'automatic' deportation order can be made

5.37 An 'automatic' deportation order cannot be made while an appeal against the relevant criminal conviction or sentence is pending.[29] Likewise, an 'automatic' deportation order cannot be made while an in-time appeal could still be brought against conviction or sentence

---

27 UKBA 2007 s33(2).
28 Immigration Rules para 380.
29 UKBA 2007 s34(2)(a).

and the individual has not notified the SSHD in writing that they do not intend to bring such an appeal.[30]

5.38 Other than the above limitations, an 'automatic' deportation order can be made at any time.[31] An 'automatic' deportation order can be made while the person still has an appeal pending against the decision that the 'automatic' deportation provisions apply,[32] although see para 5.40 below on its suspended effects.

5.39 On the face of the legislation, nothing prevents the SSHD from making an 'automatic' deportation order long after the proposed deportee has completed his or her custodial sentence. However, in cases where ECHR article 8 is engaged, extensive delays by the Secretary of State in making an 'automatic' deportation order are likely to weigh against deportation in the proportionality balancing exercise under ECHR article 8(2).[33] See paras 17.86–17.88 on ECHR article 8 and delay in criminal deportation cases.

When an 'automatic' deportation order takes effect

5.40 As long as a person is still in the UK and has an appeal pending, an 'automatic' deportation order does not invalidate existing leave to enter or remain in the UK.[34] See para 1.45 for the definition of a pending appeal.

5.41 Where a person exercises his or her appeal rights to the FTT-IAC from *outside* the UK, the appeal has no such suspensive effect and, the 'automatic' deportation order takes the immediate effect of invalidating a person's leave to enter or remain.[35]

5.42 An 'automatic' deportation order is treated as being an order made under IA 1971 ss5 and 3(5).[36]

---

30 UKBA 2007 s32(2)(b).
31 UKBA 2007 s34(1).
32 UKBA 2007 s35(2).
33 See *EB (Kosovo) v Secretary of State for the Home Department* [2008] UKHL 4, [2008] 3 WLR 178 on delay and ECHR article 8 generally; see *Sezen v The Netherlands* (2006) 43 EHRR 30 and *AA v UK* app no 8000/08, judgment 20 September 2011 on delay in the criminal expulsion context.
34 UKBA 2007 s35(2) which amends NIAA 2002 s79(4).
35 UKBA 2007 s35(2) which amends NIAA 2002 s79(4).
36 UKBA 2007 s38(4)(c).

Appeal to the FTT-IAC against a decision that the criteria for 'automatic' deportation are met

5.43 In UKBA 2007 deportation cases, the appeal to the FTT-IAC lies against the decision that the criteria are met for 'automatic' deportation, that is, the SSHD's decision that UKBA 2007 s32(5) applies.[37] One of the significant changes brought about by the UKBA 2007 'automatic' deportation regime is that it imposes restrictions on in-country appeal rights in 'automatic' deportation cases. In this context, it is important to note that where ECHR article 8 is engaged, an immigration decision which is 'not in accordance with the law' will breach article 8. In 'automatic' deportation cases, it is particularly important that article 8 should be pleaded (rather than simply a challenge to the immigration decision as not in accordance with the law) in order to found in-country rights of appeal. We discuss appeal rights generally in chapter 21, and article 8 in chapters 15–18.

Obstacles to in-country appeal rights in 'automatic' deportation cases

5.44 The statutory background is as follows. An appeal can only be brought to the FTT-IAC against an immigration decision while a person is still in the UK where:

- the immigration decision is of a type which attracts an in-country right of appeal regardless of the grounds on which it is brought;[38] or
- the appeal is brought on the basis of certain types of claims. That is, the person 'has made an asylum or ECHR claim in the UK' or, being an EEA national or the family member of an EEA national has made a claim that the immigration decision breaches his or her EU law rights.[39]

5.45 A decision to deport under IA 1971 is one of the immigration decisions which attracts an in-country right of appeal regardless of the grounds on which the appeal is brought.[40] However, a decision that

---

37 NIAA 2002 s82(3A).
38 NIAA 2002 s92(2).
39 NIAA 2002 s92(4).
40 NIAA 2002 s82(2)(j).

the criteria are met for 'automatic' deportation (that is, a decision that UKBA 2007 s32(5) applies) is not such an immigration decision.[41]

5.46 Therefore, an appeal against a decision that the criteria for 'automatic' deportation are met may only be brought in-country where a non-certified asylum or ECHR claim has been made or where an EU law claim has been made by an EEA national or family member.

In-country appeal to the FTT-IAC against an 'automatic' deportation order

5.47 Provided that he or she has made a non-certified asylum or ECHR claim in the UK, or is an EEA national or the family member[42] of an EEA national who claims that the 'automatic' deportation order is in breach of his or her EU law rights, a person has an in-country right of appeal to the FTT-IAC against an 'automatic' deportation order.

5.48 In *BA (Nigeria) and PE (Cameroon) v Secretary of State for the Home Department*,[43] the Supreme Court confirmed that the right of appeal under NIAA 2002 s92(4) for a person who is making a second asylum or human rights claim does not require that the new claim meet the 'fresh claim' threshold of paragraph 353 of the Immigration Rules.

5.49 However, the person cannot rely on an old asylum or ECHR claim against which appeal rights have been exhausted: there must be a nexus between the 'automatic' deportation order under challenge and the asylum or ECHR claim relied on to found an in-country right of appeal under NIAA 2002 s92(4).[44]

5.50 For details on appeals to the FTT-IAC, see chapter 21.

---

41 NIAA 2002 s82(3A) as inserted by UKBA 2007 s35(3).
42 Family member as defined in EEA Regs 2006 para 7.
43 [2009] UKSC 7, [2010] 1 AC 444.
44 A finding in *R (Etame) v Secretary of State for the Home Department* [2008] EWHC 1140 (Admin), [2008] 4 All ER 798 which was not appealed and so remained undisturbed in the subsequent appeals to the Court of Appeal and Supreme Court, *BA (Nigeria) and PE (Cameroon) v Secretary of State for the Home Department* [2009] UKSC 7, [2010] 1 AC 444.

Out-of-country appeal to the FTT- IAC against an 'automatic' deportation order and other remedies

5.51 Where the subject of an 'automatic' deportation order has not made a non-certified asylum or ECHR claim, and is not an EEA national or family member[45] who has made a claim that the 'automatic' deportation order would breach his or her EU law right, there will be no in-country right of appeal against a decision that the criteria for 'automatic' deportation are met.

5.52 In the above cases, the person has the right to bring an appeal to the FTT-IAC against the 'automatic' deportation order only from outside the UK (unless the appeal is certified under NIAA 2002 s96 which curtails all rights of appeal: see paras 22.14–22.22).

5.53 There is a lacuna in the legislation. If a person succeeds in his or her out-of-country appeal against an 'automatic' deportation order, his or her leave to enter or remain will already have been invalidated by the (unlawful) 'automatic' deportation order. In such cases, we suggest the proper course must be a fresh grant of leave to restore the *status quo* as it was before the unlawful 'automatic' deportation order was made. But is unclear what measures, if any, the Home Office or Foreign and Commonwealth Office have put in place to deal with such a scenario.

5.54 Where there is no in-country right of appeal (or no right of appeal at all), the proposed deportee's only in-country remedy against the 'automatic' deportation order is by way of judicial review challenging:

- a certificate on his or her asylum and/or ECHR claims;
- a refusal to treat him or her as an EEA national or the family member of an EEA national; and/or
- the 'automatic' deportation order itself.

5.55 Certificates are discussed in chapter 22 and judicial review remedies including procedures in urgent cases are discussed at paras 42.16–42.71.

5.56 The revocation of 'automatic' deportation orders is discussed in detail at paras 7.19–7.22. The right of appeal to the FTT-IAC against a refusal to revoke a deportation order is discussed in chapter 21.

---

45 Family member as defined in EEA Regs 2006 para 7.

CHAPTER 6

Departure: voluntary departure and deportation arrangements

6.1	Introduction
6.4	A deportation order can only be signed against a person still in the UK
6.5	Incentives to voluntary departure and other forms of co-operation
6.8	**Voluntary departure as an alternative to deportation**
6.9	Supervised departure
6.10	Assisted voluntary return through the International Organization for Migration
6.13	**Co-operation with deportation or administrative removal**
6.13	Facilitated Returns Scheme
6.17	**Deportation arrangements**
6.22	**Paying for deportation**
6.23	**Delays to deportation for medical treatment**

83

Introduction

6.1 This chapter considers the various schemes under which foreign national former prisoners (FNPs) who are not serving a prison sentence can voluntarily leave the UK or co-operate with the deportation process; and deportation arrangements.

6.2 The early removal scheme for serving prisoners is discussed separately at paras 28.31–28.44; and prisoner repatriation is discussed in chapter 29.

6.3 The topics discussed in this chapter apply equally to 'discretionary' deportation cases under the Immigration Act (IA) 1971 and to 'automatic' deportation cases under the UK Borders Act (UKBA) 2007. Note that a deportation order made as a consequence of the 'automatic' deportation provisions of the UKBA 2007 is treated as being a deportation order made under IA 1971 s5(1).[1]

A deportation order can only be signed against a person still in the UK

6.4 A deportation order can only be signed against a person who is still in the UK.[2] Once the deportation order has been signed (and, we suggest, served[3]) it takes effect in the same way regardless of whether the subject of the order is then forcibly expelled or leaves the UK voluntarily.

Incentives to voluntary departure and other forms of co-operation

6.5 Prospective deportees therefore have an incentive to voluntarily leave the UK before the deportation order is signed and served so that they are under no prohibition on return to the UK. However, it is critical to note that:
- participation in any voluntary departure scheme requires the abandonment of appeal rights;

---

1 UKBA 2007 s38(4)(c).
2 IA 1971 s5(1). See also Enforcement Instructions and Guidance (EIG) chapter 15 para 15.6.
3 See discussion at para 1.50.

Departure: voluntary departure and deportation arrangements 85

- the main 'co-operation' scheme for FNPs, the Facilitated Returns Scheme (FRS) is not an alternative to the signature of a deportation order, see para 6.13 below; and in any event;
- departure before the signature of a deportation order is no guarantee of an ability to return to the UK. Those with criminal convictions, particularly visa nationals, face very significant barriers to re-entry even if they are not the subject of a deportation order.

6.6 In practice, the option of voluntary departure *before* the signing of the deportation order will arise more commonly in IA 1971 deportation cases (where the signature of the deportation order is deferred until the exhaustion of appeal rights). In UKBA 2007 'automatic' deportation cases, FNPs are normally served with the 'automatic' deportation order at an early stage (albeit the effect of the order is stayed until the exhaustion of in-country appeal rights,[4] see para 5.40).

6.7 Even once a deportation order is signed and served, there remain significant incentives to co-operation and disincentives to obstruction:

- The FRS, which is open to many FNPs, offers financial incentives to co-operation with deportation.
- It is a criminal offence to fail, without reasonable excuse, to take action required by the Secretary of State for the Home Department (SSHD) which the SSHD thinks will or may enable a travel document to be obtained, where possession of the travel document will facilitate deportation or removal from the UK.[5] The offence is punishable on indictment by a term of imprisonment of up to two years a fine or both[6] and on summary conviction by imprisonment of up to 12 months, a fine up to the statutory minimum or both.[7]
- A refusal by an immigration detainee to co-operate with the expulsion process after the exhaustion of appeal rights is likely to be taken to justify a longer period of detention, by the UK Border Agency, by immigration judges of the Immigration and Asylum Chamber of the First-tier Tribunal (FTT-IAC) hearing bail applications, and by the courts hearing challenges to the legality of detention. See paras 33.29–33.42.

4 Nationality, Immigration and Asylum Act 2002 (NIAA) 2002 s79(4) as amended by UKBA 2007 s35(2).
5 Asylum and Immigration (Treatment of Claimants etc) Act 2004 (AITCA) 2004 s35(3).
6 AITCA 2004 s35(4)(a).
7 AITCA 2004 s35(5)(b).

Voluntary departure as an alternative to deportation

6.8　An FNP who is at liberty may depart voluntarily at his or her own expense before the deportation order is signed. There are also limited means by which an FNP can receive assistance to depart the UK before the signing of a deportation order.

Supervised departure

6.9　Voluntary departure can be effected via a supervised departure, usually conducted following negotiations (in which the subject waives appeal rights and is allowed to leave before the signature of the deportation order). Although the reference to supervised departure has been excised from the Immigration Rules, published Home Office policy continues to refer to the availability of supervised departure.[8] Supervised departure may be paid for by the deportee. The SSHD also has the power to pay for a supervised departure.[9]

Assisted voluntary return through the International Organization for Migration

6.10　Assisted voluntary return (AVR) can be effected through the International Organization for Migration (IOM), a non-governmental organisation. Those returning through AVR are eligible for financial and logistical 'reintegration assistance' on arrival in their home countries. However, the eligibility criteria for AVR exclude most FNPs.

6.11　There are three AVR programmes operated by the IOM. The first is the Voluntary Assisted Return and Reintegration Programme (VARRP) for those who have made an asylum claim which has been refused or is still pending at the initial or appeals stage. The second is Assisted Voluntary Return for Irregular Migrants (AVRIM) for those who have entered the UK illegally or breached one or more conditions of their leave to enter or remain. The third is Assisted Voluntary Return for Families and Children (AVRFC).[10]

6.12　The eligibility criteria for the AVR programmes are stringent. A person will be ineligible for any of the AVR programmes if:

8　Immigration Inspectorate Instructions (IDIs) chapter 13 section 1 para 10.2.
9　IA 1971 s5(6).
10　For details, see EIG chapter 46.

- a deportation order has been made against him or her;
- prior to the IOM receiving the application, the applicant had received custodial sentences in the UK totalling in excess of 12 months; or
- the applicant has been granted humanitarian protection, indefinite leave to remain and/or refugee status.

Co-operation with deportation or administrative removal

Facilitated Returns Scheme

6.13 The FRS is a scheme which provides financial incentives to non-EEA national FNPs for co-operation with deportation or administrative removal. A proposed deportee can join the FRS before or after the signature of a deportation order. However, the FRS is not an alternative to deportation for a person who is the subject of deportation action: a condition of acceptance of the scheme is that a deportation order will be made prior to departure.

6.14 The FRS is open only to:

- non-EEA nationals;
- convicted of a criminal offence;
- who have served a custodial sentence of any length;
- who are liable to deportation or administrative removal; and
- for whom deportation arrangements or removal directions have not yet been set.

6.15 The FRS is open to those non-EEA national FNPs who are:

- detained solely under Immigration Act powers;
- still serving a sentence but eligible for the Early Removal Scheme (ERS, discussed at paras 28.31–28.44); or
- still serving a sentence and from a country with which the UK has a Prison Transfer Agreement (see the discussion in chapter 29 these will serve the rest of their sentence in the home country).[11]

6.16 Those on the FRS are either administratively removed or deported. The FRS offers both cash and incentives in kind to voluntary return. The earlier the scheme is taken up, the higher the financial incentives, although the cash component has been significantly reduced

11 Prison Service Instruction (PSI) 52/2011 para 2.104.

since 1 October 2010. See also the discussion of FRS specifically in the prison context at paras 28.45–28.53.

Deportation arrangements

6.17 After a deportation order has been signed and a travel document obtained if necessary (a stage which may involved protracted delays depending on the arrangements of the FNPs country of nationality), the next step is the making of 'deportation arrangements' that is, directions for deportation. (In administrative removal cases these are known as 'removal directions'.) These will specify the destination, and often also the date, time and method of expulsion.

6.18 These directions may be to:[12]
- a country of which the deportee is a national or citizen; or
- a country or territory to which there is reason to believe he or she will be admitted.

6.19 The Immigration Rules provide[13] that deportation will be to the country of which the deportee is a national or which has most recently provided the deportee with a travel document unless the deportee can show that another country will receive him or her. However, 'in considering any departure from the normal arrangements, regard will be had to the public interest generally, and to any additional expense that may fall on public funds'.

6.20 Under the NIAA 2002,[14] unlike its predecessor legislation,[15] there is no right of appeal against the destination in deportation arrangements or removal directions.

6.21 However, there may be cases in which the disclosure of the actual destination in the deportation arrangements give rise to a fresh asylum or human rights claim or give grounds for a challenge by judicial review to the destination.

---

12 IA 1971 Sch 3 para 1(1).
13 Immigration Rules HC 395 para 385.
14 NIAA 2002 s82(2) sets out an exclusive list of appealable immigration decisions.
15 For those who were the subject of deportation arrangements made prior to 1 April 2003, there was a right of appeal against destination under Immigration and Asylum Act 1999 s67.

Paying for deportation

6.22 Deportation is usually at public expense. Although the SSHD has the power to use a deportee's money to pay for deportation (or for the maintenance of the deportee and his or her dependants before deportation)[16] it is Home Office policy not to use a deportee's money for the trip unless the deportee asks to pay.[17]

Delays to deportation for medical treatment

6.23 It is stated Home Office policy that sufficient time should be given between the exhaustion of appeal rights and final expulsion to allow medical advice to be taken and any necessary treatment completed.[18] Once deportation arrangements have been set, requests to delay removal 'for a short period' to permit preventative treatment should be considered on their merits: medical evidence will be needed.[19]

6.24 In particular, it is Home Office policy that where a pregnant woman or child under the age of five is being removed to a malarial area, sufficient time before removal should be allowed for a course of treatment with malaria prophylaxis, and for the treatment to take effect and also for the treatment of any adverse side-effects, unless malaria prophylaxis is declined by the proposed deportee.[20] A list of malarial areas and recommended treatment can be found in the IDIs chapter 1 section 8.[21] We suggest that a refusal to provide *any* vulnerable detainee (including older children) with malaria prophylaxis treatment, and sufficient time for that treatment to take effect, before expulsion would be susceptible to challenge.

---

16 IA 1971 Sch 3 para 1(4).
17 EIG chapter 15 para 15.13.
18 EIG chapter 53 para 53.9.2.
19 EIG chapter 53 chapter 53 para 53.9.2.
20 IDIs chapter 1 section 8; EIG chapter 53 para 53.9.2. For the application of that policy in the detention context, see *R (Nukajam) v Secretary of State for the Home Department* [2010] EWHC 20 (Admin) in which detention without proper reference to that policy was held to be unlawful, but see also *R (M) v Secretary of State for the Home Department* [2010] EWHC 357 (Admin), *R (FM) v Secretary of State for the Home Department* [2011] EWCA Civ 807 in which a failure to comply with the policy and consequent delay did not render the detention unlawful.
21 See www.ukba.homeoffice.gov.uk/sitecontent/documents/policyandlaw/IDIs/idischapter1/section8/section8.pdf?view=Binary.

6.25 In addition, infectious tuberculosis patients should not be required to travel by air until at least two weeks of adequate medical treatment have been completed. Patients with multiple-drug-resistant tuberculosis should not be required to travel until proven by a laboratory culture to no longer be infectious.[22]

---

22 IDIs chapter 1 section 8; EIG chapter 53 para 53.9.2.

CHAPTER 7

Revocation and other forms of termination of deportation orders in non-EEA cases

7.1   Introduction

7.6   Circumstances in which a deportation order ceases to have effect or is invalid from the outset

7.11 Revocation of a deportation order made under IA 1971

7.12 Circumstances in which a deportation order may be revoked after enforcement

7.13 Old Immigration Rules

7.14 Current Immigration Rules

7.19 In-country revocation of a deportation order made under UKBA 2007

7.22 Out-of-country revocation of a deportation order made under UKBA 2007

7.23 Representations for revocation

7.25 Consequences of revocation

7.27 Notification of revocation

7.29 Appeal against a refusal to revoke a deportation order

7.30 Entry in breach of a deportation order

Introduction

7.1 This chapter first addresses circumstances in which deportation orders will automatically lapse or may be invalid from the outset. In these cases, formal revocation by the Secretary of State for the Home Department (SSHD) is not required, although representations to the SSHD are likely to be a pragmatic necessity.

7.2 We then go on to consider the criteria for revocation of a deportation order by the SSHD. The provisions for revocation differ between those deportation orders made under the 'discretionary' deportation provisions of the Immigration Act (IA) 1971 and those made under the 'automatic' deportation provisions of the UK Borders Act (UKBA) 2007.

7.3 Where a deportation order has been made under IA 1971, there are no statutory restrictions on the circumstances in which it can be revoked. The SSHD has a general discretion[1] to revoke a deportation order for change of circumstances while the proposed deportee is still in the UK. But, once deportation has been enforced, that discretion is greatly restricted by criteria laid down in the Immigration Rules.[2]

7.4 However, where a deportation order has been made under UKBA 2007, there is a statutory restriction on the circumstances in which the SSHD can grant revocation while the proposed deportee remains in the UK. Once deportation has been effected, the same considerations apply in UKBA 2007 cases as in IA 1971 cases.

7.5 Deportation orders made on public policy, public security or public health grounds against EEA nationals or their family members are dealt with separately in chapter 9.

Circumstances in which a deportation order ceases to have effect or is invalid from the outset

7.6 Paragraphs 7.7–7.10 below apply equally to deportation orders made in consequence of 'discretionary' deportation decisions under IA 1971 and to 'automatic' deportation decisions under UKBA 2007.

---

1 For which guidance is given in the Immigration Rules para 390 and in the Enforcement Instructions and Guidance (EIG) chapter 15.
2 By Immigration Rules HC395 para 391.

7.7 A deportation order automatically ceases to have effect if the deportee becomes a British citizen.[3]

7.8 For those deported under IA 1971 s3(5)(b) as family members of a principal, the deportation order will also automatically cease to have effect:

- if the deportation order against the principal ceases to have effect;[4] or
- if the person ceases to be a family member of the principal. That is, for a child when he or she reaches 18; and for a spouse or civil partner, if the marriage or civil partnership comes to an end.[5]

7.9 A deportation order may cease to have effect if a person becomes the family member of an EEA national exercising treaty rights in the UK.[6]

7.10 A deportation order may be invalid for procedural reasons (eg, it was signed while the deportee was outside the UK[7] or was never signed or served).

Revocation of a deportation order made under IA 1971

7.11 The SSHD has the statutory power to revoke a deportation order made under IA 1971 at any time.[8] Those against whom a deportation order has been made under IA 1971 but who have not in fact been deported are not subject to any minimum period under the Immigration Rules before revocation will may be granted.[9]

---

3 IA 1971 s5(2). This applies also in UKBA 2007 automatic deportation cases since an 'automatic' deportation order is treated as having being made under IA 1971 s5 by UKBA 2007 s38(4)(c).
4 IA 1971 s5(3).
5 IA 1971 s5(3) and Immigration Rules HC 395 para 389.
6 Recognised in EIG chapter 15 para 15.6.
7 The EIG specifically accepts that such a deportation order would be invalid, EIG chapter 15 para 15.6.
8 IA 1971 s5(2). But see the restrictions in the Immigration Rules, discussed at paras 7.12–7.18 below, for revocation of a deportation order in the case of those who have been deported.
9 The restrictions on minimum periods before revocation are contained in the Immigration Rules at para 391 which refers to 'an applicant who has been deported following conviction for a criminal offence'. The Immigration Inspectorate's Instructions (IDIs) suggest at chapter 13 section 5 para 3.2.2 that the exclusion periods now contained in Immigration Rules para 391 apply also where the deportation order has not yet been enforced. We suggest that the Home Office interpretation is incorrect.

Circumstances in which a deportation order may be revoked after enforcement

7.12 Paragraph 391 of the Immigration Rules, concerning revocation after the enforcement of the deportation order, applies both to IA 1971 cases and to 'automatic' deportation cases under the UKBA 2007.

Old Immigration Rules

7.13 In the past, revocation could be sought in any deportation case on the basis of passage of time. The SSHD took a different approach to:
- cases where the deportee has a 'serious criminal record', in which case revocation would normally be refused until a 'long term of years' (taken to be at least ten years) has elapsed; and
- other cases, where 'save in very exceptional circumstances', revocation would be refused unless the deportee has been outside the UK for at least three years since the deportation order was made.[10]

Current Immigration Rules

7.14 The Immigration Rules were amended on 9 June 2008,[11] placing new restrictions on the revocation of deportation orders which have been made following a criminal offence once the deportation order has been enforced.

7.15 Since 9 June 2008, a person who has been deported from the UK following a criminal offence will be normally be refused revocation of the deportation order:[12]
- if the conviction is one capable of rehabilitation under the Rehabilitation of Offenders Act 1974, until the conviction is spent, or, if the conviction is spent in less than ten years, until ten years have elapsed since the making of the deportation order; or
- if the conviction is incapable of being spent under the Rehabilitation of Offenders Act 1974, permanently unless a refusal of revocation would breach the deportee's rights under the ECHR or under the Refugee Convention.

---

10 Immigration Rules HC 395 para 391 in their previous form.
11 Statement of Changes in the Immigration Rules HC 607.
12 Immigration Rules HC 395 para 391 in its amended form.

Revocation and other forms of termination of deportation orders 95

7.16 In short, under the amended Immigration Rules, even for lesser offences, the exclusion period will be at least ten years. Meanwhile, more serious offenders now face permanent exclusion as the norm. An offence carrying a sentence of 30 months' imprisonment or more is incapable of rehabilitation. Therefore, a person who has been deported in consequence of a conviction for which the person was sentenced to 30 months' or more imprisonment will now normally only be able to obtain revocation of the deportation order if it can be shown that a refusal of revocation would breach his or her rights under the ECHR or the Refugee Convention.

7.17 However, it is Home Office policy[13] that 'other exceptional circumstances' may lead to the minimum periods before revocation being disregarded, for example 'if the situation has materially altered, either by a change in circumstances since the order was made, or by fresh information coming to light which was not available at the time the order was made'.

7.18 Conversely, it is also Home Office policy that 'where a person considerably delayed the enforcement of a deportation order through non-compliance' consideration should be given to prolonging the exclusion period.[14] The Immigration Directorate's Instructions (IDIs) also specify that the fact that a conviction has become spent (although the ten-year minimum exclusion period for a conviction capable of becoming spent has not elapsed) does not constitute an exceptional case for consideration outside the normal ten-year minimum period.[15]

In-country revocation of a deportation order made under UKBA 2007

7.19 The UKBA 2007 imposes statutory restrictions on the circumstances in which an 'automatic' deportation order (made in consequence of a decision that UKBA 2007 s32(5) applies) may be revoked while the proposed deportee is in the UK.

7.20 A decision that UKBA 2007 s32(5) applies (requiring 'automatic' deportation) may be withdrawn and an 'automatic' deportation order revoked for the purposes of the SSHD taking action under

---

13 IDIs chapter 13 section 5 para 3.2.2.
14 IDIs chapter 13 section 5 para 3.2.2.
15 IDIs chapter 13 section 5 para 3.2.2.

the Immigration Acts or Immigration Rules[16] and then issuing a fresh decision that UKBA 2007 s32(5) applies and a fresh deportation order.[17] This permits, in practice, the SSHD's certification of claims, restricting appeal rights (see the discussion of certification in chapter 22).

7.21 Other than the above circumstances, an 'automatic' deportation order can only be revoked while the proposed deportee is in the UK on grounds that he or she is exempt from deportation or falls within one of the numbered exceptions to 'automatic' deportation under UKBA 2007 s33.[18] That is, an in-country application for revocation of an 'automatic' deportation order can only succeed on grounds that:

- the person is exempt from deportation as a long-resident Commonwealth or Irish national or diplomat or international functionary;[19]
- deportation would breach the person's rights under the Refugee Convention or ECHR;[20]
- the person was under 18 at the time of his or her conviction giving rise to the 'automatic' deportation order;[21]
- deportation would breach the person's rights under EU law;[22]
- the person is subject to extradition proceedings;[23] or
- the person is subject to certain measures under mental health legislation.[24]

Out-of-country revocation of a deportation order made under UKBA 2007

7.22 There are no *statutory* limitations on the grounds on which an out-of-country application for revocation of an 'automatic' deportation order can succeed.[25] The general considerations set out in paragraph 391 of the Immigration Rules and already discussed at paras

---

16 UKBA 2007 s34(4)(a).
17 UKBA 2007 s34(4)(b).
18 UKBA 2007 s32(6).
19 UKBA 2007 s33(1) and IA 1971 ss7–8.
20 UKBA 2007 s33(2).
21 UKBA 2007 s33(3).
22 UKBA 2007 s33(4).
23 UKBA 2007 s33(5).
24 UKBA 2007 s33(6).
25 UKBA 2007 s32(6)(b).

7.14–7.16 above apply to out-of-country revocation of an 'automatic' deportation order made under UKBA 2007, as they do to deportation orders made under IA 1971.

Representations for revocation

7.23 Representations on revocation can be made directly to the Home Office's Managed Migration Directorate or can be made to an Entry Clearance Officer overseas.[26] There is no specified form for these representations.

7.24 The Immigration Rules at para 390 provide guidance for the Secretary of State in the exercise of her power to revoke a deportation order:

An application for revocation of a deportation order will be considered in the light of all the circumstances including the following:
(i) the grounds on which the order was made;
(ii) any representations made in support of revocation;
(iii) the interests of the community, including the maintenance of an effective immigration control;
(iv) the interests of the applicant, including any compassionate circumstances.

Consequences of revocation

7.25 Where a deportation order has been revoked, this does not automatically entitle the former deportee to re-enter the UK: it simply entitles the former deportee to apply for admission.[27] Nor does it automatically require the SSHD to reinstate any indefinite leave to remain held before the deportation order.[28]

7.26 Former deportees who have had their deportation order revoked, and who are non-EEA nationals, may encounter significant difficulties in obtaining entry clearance or leave to enter the UK. The law governing entry and re-entry to the UK lies outside the scope of this book, but it should be noted that there is in the Immigration Rules, for example, a general discretionary ground for the refusal of entry clearance or leave to enter the UK to a person who has been convicted in any country, including the UK, of an offence which if committed

---

26 Immigration Rules HC 395 para 392.
27 Immigration Rules HC 395 para 392.
28 *R (Fitzroy George) v SSHD* [2011] EWHC 3247 (Admin).

in the UK would be punishable with a sentence of 12 months' or more imprisonment 'save where the immigration officer is satisfied that admission would be justified for strong compassionate reasons'.[29] There is likewise a discretion to refuse leave to enter where 'from information available', 'it seems right' to do so, on grounds that exclusion is 'conducive to the public good; if, for example, in light of the character, conduct or associations of the person seeking leave to enter it is undesirable to give him leave to enter'.[30] If, of course, the deportation order has been revoked on ECHR grounds while the FNP is outside the UK, those same ECHR grounds should themselves compel the grant of entry clearance or leave enter to the FNP.

Notification of revocation

7.27 Where the SSHD revokes a deportation order, the individual will be informed by letter and the back of the original deportation order will be endorsed to the effect that it has been revoked.

7.28 Notification of a refusal to revoke a deportation order must conform with the requirements of the Immigration (Notices) Regulations 2003.[31] That is, the notice must be communicated in writing, must include or be accompanied by a statement of reasons for the decision and must inform the individual of his or her rights of appeal.

Appeal against a refusal to revoke a deportation order

7.29 There is a right of appeal to the Immigration and Asylum Chamber of the First-tier Tribunal (FTT-IAC) against a refusal to revoke a deportation order, under the Nationality, Immigration and Asylum Act (NIAA) 2002 s82(2)(k). However, there are restrictions on the circumstances in which the right of appeal against a refusal to revoke a deportation order can be exercised while the person is still in the UK. In summary, an in-country appeal against a refusal to revoke a deportation order may only be brought where an individual has made a non-certified asylum or ECHR claim or is an EEA national or the family member of an EEA national who has made a claim that

29 Immigration Rules HC 395 para 320(18).
30 Immigration Rules HC 395 para 320(19).
31 SI No 658.

the decision breaches his or her rights under EU law. Appeals to the FTT-IAC, against a refusal to revoke a deportation order and other immigration decisions, are discussed in chapter 21. Limitations on in-country appeal rights are discussed in chapter 22.

Entry in breach of a deportation order

7.30 A person who enters the UK while a deportation order is in force against him or her is an illegal entrant.[32] Knowingly entering the UK in breach of a deportation order is a criminal offence punishable on summary conviction with a fine of up to level 5 or imprisonment of up to six months or both.[33] Note that this is the case even if the deportee is an EEA national: an EEA national who enters in breach of a deportation order may be detained and administratively removed as an illegal entrant.[34]

7.31 In practice, a person who is encountered having entered in breach of a deportation order is likely to be immediately re-deported rather than prosecuted.[35] A person who enters the UK while a deportation order is in force against him or her may be deported under the original order, though the SSHD is obliged to consider the case in light of all relevant circumstances before deciding whether to enforce the order.[36]

---

32 IA 1971 s33(1)(b).
33 IA 1971 s24.
34 Immigration (European Economic Area) Regulations 2006, SI No 1003 reg 24(4).
35 IDIs chapter 13, section 1, para 8.
36 Immigration Rules HC 395 para 388.

SECTION B
EU law grounds for restricting deportation

Chapter 8:   The Citizens Directive and the EEA Regs 2006   107

Chapter 9:   The expulsion of EEA nationals and their family members under the Citizens Directive and EEA Regs 2006   123

Chapter 10: Other EU law protections from expulsion   157

Introduction to EU law

Below, we provide a very brief background on European Union (EU) law to provide a context for the discussion in this section of the book of the protections enjoyed by European Economic Area (EEA) nationals and their family members from deportation or other expulsion. We use the term 'EU law' to refer to the law made under the treaties[1] and as interpreted by the European Court of Justice (ECJ), now the Court of Justice of the European Union (CJEU).

The EEA and the Swiss

The EEA is made up of all 27 EU member states as well as three states from the European Free Trade Association (EFTA) – Iceland, Liechtenstein and Norway.[2] From 1 January 1994, the free movement rights enjoyed by EU nationals were extended to all EEA nationals.[3]

Although Switzerland is not a member of the EU or EEA, Swiss nationals enjoy similar rights of freedom of movement to EEA nationals.[4] Where 'EEA nationals' are referred to below, the same applies to Swiss nationals.

Effect of EU law in domestic law

The EU member states are required to give precedence to EU law over any conflicting national rules[5]. Since the UK became a member state of what is now the EU on 1 January 1973, the following are

---

1 Since the Treaty of Lisbon of 1 December 2009, there are now two consolidated treaties. The first is the Treaty on the Functioning of the European Union (TFEU); the second is the Treaty on European Union (TEU), that is, the Maastricht Treaty, made in 1993 as subsequently amended.
2 The following countries are now in the EEA: Austria; Belgium, Bulgaria, Cyprus, Czech Republic, Denmark, Estonia, Finland; France, Germany, Greece, Hungary, Iceland, Ireland, Italy, Liechtenstein, Latvia, Lithuania, Luxembourg, Malta, Netherlands, Norway, Poland, Portugal, Romania, Slovakia, Slovenia, Spain, Sweden and the UK.
3 By operation of the Agreement on the European Economic Area 1992, article 28, given domestic effect by the European Economic Area Act 1993.
4 By operation of the Agreement between the European Community and the Swiss Confederation on the Free Movement of Persons 2002. These were given domestic effect initially by the Immigration (Swiss Free Movement of Person) No 3 Regulations 2002 SI No 1241 and now by the Immigration (European Economic Area) Regulations (EEA Regs) 2006 SI No 1003.
5 *Costa v ENEL* Case C-6/64 [1964] ECR 585 at 593–594.

binding on the UK, with the executive and courts required to give them effect:[6]

- the Treaty on the Functioning of the European Union (TFEU);
- the Treaty of European Union (TEU);
- EU directives (other than where the UK has an opt-out);
- EU regulations (other than where the UK has an opt-out); and
- the decisions and interpretations of the above sources of law by the ECJ and CJEU.

The EU law doctrine of direct effect moreover allows individuals (as well as institutions) to rely directly on EU law measures in national courts. To have direct effect, the measure must create clear and precise obligations. Certain articles of the TFEU have direct effect, including article 20 (formerly article 17 of the Treaty of the European Community (TEC)) which creates a status of Citizen of the European Union, and article 21 (formerly TEC article 18) which confers rights of free movement on EU citizens.[7] Regulations are binding and take direct effect in their entirety;[8] while directives are binding as to the result to be achieved and may in some cases have direct effect.[9] The direct effect of directives enables individuals and institutions to rely on a directive against a member state which has failed to implement a provision of a Directive correctly or at all within the required timetable.[10]

In addition, the UK has enacted secondary legislation intended to transpose EU Directives into domestic law. In reading such domestic legislation, it is vital to refer back to the EU legislation to ensure that the EU law measures have in fact been fully and correctly transposed. Precedence must be given to EU law over conflicting domestic law. For the purposes of this book, the Immigration (European Economic Area) Regulations (EEA Regs) 2006[11] are now the most important domestic legislation. Like their predecessor, the Immigration (European Economic Area) Regulations (EEA Regs) 2000,[12] these regulations seek to consolidate the UK's obligations towards EEA nationals.

6 European Communities Act 1972 ss2–3.
7 *Baumbast* Case 413/99 [2002] ECR I-7091, [2002] 3 CMLR 23 paras 84–86.
8 TFEU article 288 (formerly EC Treaty article 249).
9 TFEU article 288 (formerly EC Treaty article 249); see also *Van Duyn v Home Office (No 2)* [1974] ECR 1337.
10 *Van Gend and Loos* Case 26/62 [1963] ECR 1.
11 SI 2006 No 1003.
12 SI 2000 No 2326.

The CJEU (formerly ECJ)

The CJEU is the ultimate interpreter of EU law. But there is no right for individuals dissatisfied with the approach taken by the domestic courts to apply to the CJEU for the determination of their case following the exhaustion of domestic remedies.[13] Rather, national courts and tribunals can seek the CJEU's guidance by making a reference, requesting a preliminary ruling[14] and a final court of appeal must do so where EU law is not clear and a decision on the question is necessary to enable the national court to give judgment.

Free movement rights

The TFEU

Under the TFEU, the freedom of movement of workers; freedom of establishment; and freedom to provide services for EU citizens may be limited only on grounds of public policy, public security or public health.[15]

Council Directive 64/221/EEC

Council Directive 64/221/EEC of 25 February 1964 on the co-ordination of special measures concerning the movement and residence of foreign nationals which are justified on grounds of public policy, public security or public health ('the 1964 Directive') set out limitations on the way in which member states could rely on these grounds to take measures restricting free movement rights for EU citizens and their family members.[16]

The 1964 Directive was repealed and replaced by Directive 2004/38/EC on the right of citizens of the EU and their family members to move and reside freely within the territory of the EU ('Citizens Directive') on 30 April 2006.[17] The Citizens Directive, as we shall see in chapter 9, grants increased protections from expulsion.

---

13 Although individuals may apply to the CJEU for the annulment of acts of EU institutions, TFEU article 263.
14 TFEU article 267.
15 TFEU articles 45, 52, 62 (formerly TEC articles 39, 46 and 55).
16 1964 Directive articles 2 and 3.
17 Citizens Directive article 38(2).

EEA Regs 2000

The UK sought to implement the 1964 Directive along with other European measures through the EEA Regs 2000.

We do not discuss the EEA Regs 2000 in any detail here because they have been entirely repealed and replaced by the EEA Regs 2006. From 30 April 2006, any decision to remove or deport and any deportation order made under the EEA Regs 2000 is treated as having been made under the EEA Regs 2006.[18] Where an appeal was pending on 30 April 2006 against an immigration decision made under the EEA Regs 2000, the appeal must, from 30 April 2006, proceed as if the decision appealed against had been made under the EEA Regs 2006.[19]

The important effect of this lack of any saving provisions is that a measure taken lawfully under the EEA Regs 2000 (such as a decision to deport or a deportation order) may now have become unlawful by virtue of the considerably higher protections contained in the Citizens Directive and the EEA Regs 2006. Where a decision to deport an EEA national or family member was made under the EEA Regs 2000, the Immigration and Asylum Chamber of the First-tier and Upper Tribunals (FTT-IAC and UT-IAC) or higher courts must apply the Citizens Directive and EEA Regs 2006 in determining whether deportation in consequence of that decision would be lawful. Likewise, even where a deportation order was made under the EEA Regs 2000, the correct test to be applied in considering whether to revoke the deportation order is now that set out in the EEA Regs 2006.

---

18 EEA Regs 2006 Sch 4 para 4.
19 EEA Regs 2006 Sch 4 para 5.

CHAPTER 8
The Citizens Directive and the EEA Regs 2006

8.1	Introduction
8.5	EU citizens and EEA nationals
8.6	Who is entitled to reside in the UK by operation of the Citizens Directive and EEA Regs 2006
8.9	'Qualified persons'
8.10	Administrative formalities
8.11	**'Family members'**
8.16	Students and their family members
8.18	**Other relatives**
8.19	Extended family members
	'Dependants', 'personal care' and 'durability' • *The rights of extended family members*
8.30	**Right of residence for family members**
8.32	Protections for family members where the EEA national with the principal right of residence dies, leaves the country or terminates the marriage or registered partnership
8.36	Family members of British citizens
8.40	Family members of dual nationals
8.41	**Acquisition of permanent rights of residence in the UK by an EEA national**
8.46	**Right of permanent residence for family members**

Introduction

8.1 EU law protections from expulsion for EEA nationals are now set down in the Citizens Directive[1] as well as in the Treaty on the Functioning of the European Union (TFEU). The Citizens Directive was signed on 29 April 2004 and came into force on 30 April 2006. The Citizens Directive sets out minimum protections: it does not preclude EEA member states from adopting measures which are more favourable to the free movement rights of EEA nationals or their family members.[2]

8.2 In domestic law, the UK has sought to implement the Citizens Directive through the Immigration (European Economic Area) Regulations (EEA Regs) 2006,[3] which also came into force on 30 April 2006. As in all other areas of EU law, where domestic law conflicts with and offers lower protections than EU law, it is EU law which must prevail.[4]

8.3 This chapter examines how rights of residence operate and how family members are defined under the Citizens Directive and EEA Regs 2006, as a prelude to our discussion in the next chapter of protections from expulsion. We do not discuss those parts of the Citizens Directive or EEA Regs 2006 which have no bearing on expulsion.

8.4 Because the provisions of the Citizens Directive and the EEA Regs 2006 are often materially identical, unless otherwise stated, the protections described below are contained in both the EU and domestic legislation. We also set out related developments in the European Court of Justice (ECJ), Court of Justice of the European Union (CJEU) and domestic case-law and Home Office policy concerning protections from expulsion for EEA nationals and their family members.

EU citizens and EEA nationals

8.5 Though the Citizens Directive refers only to EU citizens and their family members, the free movement rights applicable to EU citizens

---

1 Directive 2004/38/EC on the right of citizens of the European Union and their family members to move and reside freely within the territory of the EU.
2 Citizens Directive, preamble recital 29.
3 SI No 1003.
4 For the principle of precedence of EC law over national law, see eg Case 36/75 *Rutili v Minister for the Interior* [1975] ECR 1219; *R v Secretary of State for Transport ex p Factortame (No 2)* [1991] 1 AC 603.

The Citizens Directive and the EEA Regs 2006

and their family members under this Directive also extend to EEA nationals and their family members.[5] Hence the EEA Regs 2006 specifically refer to EEA nationals (other than British citizens[6]) and their family members as the beneficiaries of the protections contained in the EEA Regs 2006.

Who is entitled to reside in the UK by operation of the Citizens Directive and EEA Regs 2006

8.6 The following are entitled to reside in the UK by operation of the Citizens Directive and EEA Regs:
- an EEA national worker and his or her family members;[7]
- an EEA national self-employed person and his or her family members;[8]
- an EEA national who entered the UK in order to seek employment, for as long as the EEA national can show that he or she is continuing to seek employment and has a genuine chance of being engaged, and his or her family members;[9]
- an EEA national self-sufficient-person and his or her family members.[10] That is, the EEA national has sufficient resources[11] for themselves and their family members not to become a burden on

---

5 By operation of the Agreement on the European Economic Area 1992, Articles 7 and 28 and Annex V.
6 EEA Regs 2006 para 2(1).
7 Citizens Directive articles 7(1)–(a), (d), 14(4)(a); EEA Regs 2006 regs 6(1)(b), 7(1), 14(1)–(2) and 19(3)(b).
8 Citizens Directive articles 7(1)(a), (d), 14(4)(a); EEA Regs 2006 regs 6(1)(c), 7(1), 14(1)–(2) and 19(3)(b).
9 Citizens Directive article 14(4)(b); EEA Regs 2006 regs 6(1)(a), 6(4), 14(1)–(2) and 19(3)(b).
10 Citizens Directive article 7(1)(b), (d); EEA Regs 2006 regs 6(1)(d), 7(1), 14(1)–(2) and 19(3)(b).
11 The EEA Regs 2006 define sufficient resources not to become a burden on the UK's social assistance system as an assurance to the Secretary of State that the EEA national and his or her family members have resources exceeding the maximum level which a UK and his or her family members could possess to qualify for social assistance in the UK (EEA Regs 2006 reg 4(4)). This requirement in the EEA Regs 2006 may well be contrary to the provision in the Citizens Directive that member states may not lay down a fixed amount which they regard as 'sufficient resources' but must take into account the personal situation of the person concerned (Citizens Directive article 8(4)).

the UK's social assistance system and has comprehensive sickness insurance in the UK;[12]
- an EEA national student and[13] his or her spouse or registered civil partner; and the dependent children of the student or his or her spouse or civil partner;[14]
- a family member who has retained a right to reside in the UK under the Citizens Directive notwithstanding the death, departure or breakdown of the relationship with the principal EEA national;[15]
- an EEA national and his or her family members with a right of permanent residence acquired under the Citizens Directive even if the above economic activity or relationships have ceased;[16]
- the extended family member of an EEA national who has a valid EEA family permit, registration certificate or residence card;[17]
- an EEA national and his or her family member residing in the UK for three months or under who has not become an 'unreasonable burden' on the UK's social assistance system.[18]

8.7 An EEA national who is no longer a worker or a self-employed person still retains the status of worker or self-employed person (and hence retains a right of residence in the UK) if he or she:

- is temporarily unable to work as the result of an illness or accident;[19]

---

12 Citizens Directive article 7(1)(b); EEA Regs 2006 reg 4(1)(c).
13 The conditions are that the EEA national is enrolled in a public or accredited private establishment in the UK for the principal purpose of following a course of study including vocational training. The student must have comprehensive sickness insurance and assure the UK immigration authorities by means of a declaration or equivalent means that the student may choose that they have sufficient means for themselves and their family members not to become burdens on the UK's social assistance system during their residence (Citizens Directive article 7(1)(c); EEA Regs 2006 regs 4(1)(d) and 6(1)(e)).
14 Citizens Directive article 7(1)(c), (d), (4); EEA Regs 2006 regs 6(1)(e), 7(2), 14(1)–(2) and 19(3)(b).
15 Citizens Directive articles 12 and 13; EEA Regs 2006 regs 10, 14(3), 15(d)–(e). However, note that this does not in itself found a right to permanent residence if the family member then manages to accrue five years, see *Okafor v Secretary of State for the Home Department* [2011] EWCA Civ 499, [2011] 3 CMLR 8.
16 Citizens Directive articles 16–18; EEA Regs 2006 reg 15.
17 Citizens Directive articles 8(5)(e)–(f), 9(1), 10, 11; EEA Regs 2006 reg 7(3).
18 Citizens Directive article 6; EEA Regs 2006 reg 13.
19 Citizens Directive article 7(3)(a); EEA Regs 2006 reg 6(2)(a) and (3).

- is in duly recorded involuntary unemployment after having been employed for more than one year and has registered as a jobseeker in the UK;[20]
- is in duly recorded involuntary unemployment after completing a fixed-term contract of less than a year or after having become involuntarily unemployed during the first 12 months and has registered as a jobseeker in the UK. In this case, the status of worker is retained for at least six months for EU law purposes;[21] or
- embarks on vocational training. Unless the EEA national is involuntarily unemployed, the training must be related to the previous employment.[22]

8.8 Note that the Citizens Directive (and consequently the EEA Regs 2006) do not exhaustively define who is entitled to reside in the UK as a matter of EU law: the treaties themselves may confer wider rights.[23]

'Qualified persons'

8.9 The EEA Regs 2006 categorise a 'qualified person' as an EEA national who is in the UK as a jobseeker, worker, self-employed person, self-sufficient person or student.[24] Qualified persons have the right to remain in the UK for as long as they remain qualified persons.[25]

Administrative formalities

8.10 The free movement rights of EEA nationals in the UK are *not* conditional on their having actually obtained documents recording their entitlement to reside in the UK.[26] For example, an EEA national who can show that he or she has spent the required time in the UK to acquire a right of permanent residence enjoys special protections from expulsion *regardless* of whether they have actually complied with the administrative formalities of obtaining or applying for a residence document. Conversely, the CJEU has held that a person

---

20 Citizens Directive article 7(3)(b); EEA Regs 2006 reg 6(2)(b).
21 Citizens Directive article 7(3)(c); but note distinct definition in EEA Regs 2006 reg 6(2)(b)(ii).
22 Citizens Directive article 7(3)(d); EEA Regs 2006 reg 6(2)(c)–(d).
23 *Teixera* Case 480-08 [2010] CMLR 50 paras 55–60.
24 EEA Regs 2006 reg 6.
25 EEA Regs 2006 reg 14(1).
26 Citizens Directive preamble para (11); article 25(1).

who, before acquiring a right of permanent residence, held a valid residence permit but did not in fact satisfy the conditions of 'legal' residence under EU law was not 'legally resident'.[27]

'Family members'

8.11 The free movement rights and protections for EEA nationals set out in the Citizens Directive and in the EEA Regs 2006 also apply to the 'family members' of EEA nationals regardless of the family member's nationality.[28] The conditions of entry and residence of the family members of EEA nationals are a question of EU law: additional requirements cannot be imposed by the Immigration Rules.[29]

8.12 Free movement rights and protections apply to non-EEA national family members regardless of whether the family member lived lawfully in another EEA member state previously, or arrived in the UK directly from outside the EEA.[30] In a marriage case, these protections apply regardless of when and where the marriage took place. This was clarified by the ECJ Grand Chamber in *Metock and others v Minister for Justice, Equality and Law Reform*.[31] The provisions in the EEA Regs 2006 which suggest otherwise inaccurately transpose the Citizens Directive and should not be followed.[32]

8.13 For these purposes, a family member is defined[33] as:
- the spouse[34] or civil partner;[35]
- the direct descendants, aged under 21, of the EEA national, and/or of his or her spouse or civil partner;[36]
- the direct descendants, who are dependants, of the EEA national, and/or of his or her spouse or civil partner;[37] and

---

27 *Maria Dias* Case C-325/09.
28 Citizens Directive preamble para (5).
29 *ZH (Afghanistan) v Secretary of State for the Home Department* [2009] EWCA Civ 1060 para 42; *Bigia v Entry Clearance Officer* [2009] EWCA Civ 79.
30 *Metock and others v Minister for Justice, Equality and Law Reform* Case C-127/08 [2009] QB 318.
31 Case C-127/08, [2009] QB 318.
32 EEA Regs 2006 reg 12(b)(i).
33 Citizens Directive article 2(2); EEA Regs 2006 reg 7(1)(a).
34 Citizens Directive article 2(2)(a).
35 Citizens Directive preamble para (5) and article 2(b).
36 Citizens Directive article 2(2)(c); EEA Regs 2006 reg 7(1)(b)(i).
37 Citizens Directive article 2(2)(c); EEA Regs 2006 reg 7(1)(b)(ii).

- the dependent direct relatives in the ascending line of the EEA national or his or her spouse or civil partner.[38]

8.14 Where the UK recognises that a child has been validly adopted by an EEA national, the adopted child will be treated as a family member under the EEA Regs 2006.[39]

8.15 A spouse need not be living with the principal.[40] However, the EEA Regs 2006 specify that 'spouse' and 'civil partner' do not include those who have entered into a partnership or marriage of convenience.[41] The Citizens Directive permits member states to adopt necessary measures to guard against abuse of rights or fraud, in particular marriages or other relationships formed for the sole purpose of enjoying EU law rights, provided that these measures are proportionate and taken only on public policy, public health or public security grounds.[42]

Students and their family members

8.16 There is a more restrictive definition of family members for students. Where the principal EEA national with the right of residence is a student and more than three months have elapsed since the student was admitted to the UK, only the following will qualify as the student's family members:

- the spouse or civil partner; and
- the dependent children of the student or his or her spouse or civil partner.[43]

8.17 However, if the student is also a jobseeker, worker, self-employed person or self-sufficient person, then the general rules concerning the definition of 'family member' apply.[44]

---

38 Citizens Directive article 2(2)(d); EEA Regs 2006 reg 7(1)(c).
39 European Casework Instructions chapter 2 para 2.3.1.
40 *Diatta* Case 267/83 [1985] ECR 567, [1986] CMLR 164.
41 EEA Regs 2006 reg 2(1).
42 Citizens Directive preamble para (28) and article 35.
43 Citizens Directive article 7(4); EEA Regs 2006 reg 7(2)(a).
44 Citizens Directive article 7(1)(d); EEA Regs 2006 reg 7(2)(b).

Other relatives

8.18 Where a person is related to an EEA national but does not meet the definition of 'family member', his or her position is regulated by national legislation (in the UK, the Immigration Rules). In making decisions concerning entry and residence for those who are related to EEA nationals but do not qualify as 'family members', regard must be had to the relationship with the EEA national or any other circumstances such as their financial or physical dependence on the EEA national.[45]

Extended family members

8.19 The Citizens Directive requires that member states must, in accordance with their national legislation, facilitate entry and residence for those relatives who do not qualify as 'family members', but who meet certain criteria.[46] These are:

- relatives of the EEA national or his or her spouse or civil partner, who, in the country from which they have come, are dependants or members of the household of the EEA national having the primary right of residence;[47] or
- relatives of the EEA national or his or her spouse or civil partner, who, on serious health grounds, strictly require personal care by the EEA national;[48] or
- a partner with whom the EEA national has a durable relationship, duly attested.[49]

8.20 The EEA Regs 2006 define this category as 'extended family members'[50] and give the Secretary of State for the Home Department (SSHD) a discretionary power to issue extended family members with residence cards.[51]

8.21 The EEA Regs 2006 also expand 'extended family members' to include a group not covered in the Citizens Directive. A relative of an EEA national is an 'extended family member' if he or she would meet the requirements in the Immigration Rules (other than the

---

45 Citizens Directive preamble para (6).
46 Citizens Directive article 3(2).
47 Citizens Directive article 3(2)(a); EEA Regs 2006 reg 8(2).
48 Citizens Directive article 3(2)(a); EEA Regs 2006 reg 8(3).
49 Citizens Directive article 3(2)(b); EEA Regs 2006 reg 8(5).
50 EEA Regs 2006 reg 8.
51 EEA Regs 2006 reg 17(4).

8.22 requirement of entry clearance) for indefinite leave to enter or remain in the UK as a dependant relative of the EEA relative national were the EEA national a person present and settled in the UK.[52]

8.22 There is no requirement that the extended family member should have established prior lawful residence in another EEA member state.[53] The provisions in the EEA Regs 2006 which require extended family members to establish prior lawful residence in another member state[54] do not accurately transpose the Citizens Directive[55] and should not be followed.

8.23 The Court of Appeal has held, since the ECJ Grand Chamber's judgment in *Metock*, that the extended family member must have been present with the EEA national in the country from which the EEA national has most recently come (and the relationship of dependency or household membership very recently extant there).[56] We respectfully suggest that the Court of Appeal's approach is difficult to reconcile with the ECJ Grand Chamber's conclusion in *Metock* that no provision of the Citizens Directive makes the application of the directive conditional on a family member's 'having previously resided in a member state' and (in a marriage case) that the marriage may post-date the EEA national's move to the host state.[57]

8.24 A detailed examination of the expanding jurisprudence around the criteria for 'extended family members' is beyond the scope of this book. Here we mention briefly a number of points.

'Dependants', 'personal care' and 'durability'

8.25 For the purposes of Citizens Directive article 3(2)(a), EEA Regs 2006 reg 8(2), dependency entails economic dependency in fact, but does not require that the dependant is fully and solely supported by the

---

52 EEA Regs 2006 reg 8(4).
53 The conclusions reached by the Grand Chamber of the ECJ in *Metock and others v Minister for Justice, Equality and Law Reform* Case C-127/08 [2009] QB 318, in relation to 'family members' apply also to 'extended family members'.
54 EEA Regs 2006 reg 12(1)(b)(i) and (2)(a).
55 *Bigia and others v Entry Clearance Officer* [2009] EWCA Civ 79 para 41. The obiter dicta to the contrary in *KG (Sri Lanka) v Secretary of State for the Home Department* [2008] EWCA Civ 13 para 68 conflict with the subsequent judgment of the ECJ in *Metock* and, we suggest, are not good law.
56 *Bigia and others v Entry Clearance Officer* [2009] EWCA Civ 79 para 43, following the ratio of *KG (Sri Lanka) v Secretary of State for the Home Department* [2008] EWCA Civ 13 at 65, 77 and 79.
57 *Metock and others v Minister for Justice, Equality and Law Reform* Case C-127/08 [2009] QB 318 paras 49, 88–90.

principal.[58] The dependency can be in another EEA member state or in the dependant's country of origin.[59] The Court of Appeal has indicated that the dependency requirement entails very recent dependency, after the EEA national principal was exercising his or her rights of free movement in the home state;[60] but that has been doubted by the Immigration and Asylum Chamber of the Upper Tribunal (UT-IAC).[61]

8.26 'Personal care' for the purposes of Citizens Directive article 3(2)(a), EEA Regs 2006 reg 8(3) has been held to mean care relating to day-to-day physical tasks and needs, but the EEA national need not be the only person capable of providing that care.[62]

8.27 A 'durable' relationship for the purposes of Citizens Directive article 3(2)(b), EEA Regs 2006 reg 8(5) does not mean that the relationship need have lasted for at least two years.[63]

The rights of extended family members

8.28 The EEA Regs 2006 provide that where an extended family member of an EEA national has been issued with an EEA family permit, registration certificate or residence card, he or she is entitled to be treated as would any other 'family member' of an EEA national.[64] This entitlement to be treated as a 'family member' lasts for only so long as the person continues to meet the definition of extended family member and for only so long as the family permit, registration certificate or residence card remains valid and has not been revoked.[65] Where the EEA national with the principal right of residence is a student, an extended family member is only entitled to be treated as a 'family member' in somewhat more limited circumstances.[66]

8.29 Importantly for FNPs, the UT-IAC has held that 'extended family members' are *not* 'family members' for the purposes of the special protections from expulsion under article 27 of the Citizens

---

58 *Lebon* [1987] ECR 2811, *SM (India)* [2009] EWCA Civ 1426.
59 *RK (India) v Secretary of State for the Home Department* [2010] UKUT 421 (IAC) para 20.
60 *Bigia and others v Entry Clearance Officer* [2009] EWCA Civ 79, [2009] 2 CMLR 42, para 43.
61 *RK (India) v Secretary of State for the Home Department* [2010] UKUT 421 (IAC) para 22.
62 *TR (reg 8(3) EEA Regs 2006) Sri Lanka* [2008] UKAIT 4.
63 *YB (EEA reg 17(4) – proper approach) Ivory Coast* [2008] UKAIT 62 para 34.
64 EEA Regs 2006 reg 7(3).
65 EEA Regs 2006 reg 7(3).
66 EEA Regs 2006 reg 7(4).

Directive.⁶⁷ The UT-IAC considered that an 'extended family member' would only enjoy special protections from expulsion if issued by the SSHD with EEA residence documentation.⁶⁸ This is arguably incorrect since a) certain provisions of the Citizens Directive clearly do refer jointly to core and 'extended' family members as 'family members'⁶⁹ so that article 27 may be similarly interpreted; and b) the UT-IAC's restrictive interpretation is inconsistent with the Citizens Directive's objective of facilitating integration and maintaining family unity, including 'the family in the broader sense'.⁷⁰

Right of residence for family members

8.30 The family member of a qualified person is entitled to remain the UK as long as he or she remains the family member of a qualified person.⁷¹

8.31 Likewise, the family member of an EEA national with a permanent right of residence in the UK is entitled to remain in the UK as long as he or she remains the family member of the EEA national with the principal right of residence.⁷² A person who marries an EEA national after the EEA national has acquired a right of residence acquires the same right of residence.⁷³

Protections for family members where the EEA national with the principal right of residence dies, leaves the country or terminates the marriage or registered partnership

8.32 The Citizens Directive and EEA Regs 2006 seek to ensure that the rights of residence of non-EEA family members are not automatically lost in the event of the EEA national with the principal right of

---

67 *Rose (Automatic deportation- exception 3) Jamaica* [2011] UKUT 276 (IAC) para 17.
68 *Rose (Automatic deportation- exception 3) Jamaica* [2011] UKUT 276 (IAC) para 19.
69 Citizens Directive article 8(5), see in particular 8(5)(e) and (f); and article 10, see in particular 10(2)(e) and (f).
70 Citizens Directive preamble recital 6.
71 EEA Regs 2006 reg 14(2).
72 EEA Regs 2006 reg 14(2).
73 *MAH (dual nationality-permanent residence) Canada* [2010] UKUT 445 (IAC).

residence dying,[74] leaving the country[75] or (for spouses and partners) terminating the marriage or registered partnership.[76]

8.33 The EEA Regs 2006 define more restrictively than the Citizens Directive the circumstances in which the right of residence is retained.[77] Where, as here, the domestic regulations provide lesser protections than the EU law measures they seek to transpose, the more generous EU law definition should prevail.

8.34 A non-EEA national family member who has retained a right of residence in the UK (eg despite the death of the principal EEA national) also retains the protections from expulsion discussed further below.

74 Where the EEA national with the principal right of residence dies, the family members of the EEA national living in the UK do not lose their right of residence provided that they were living in the UK as family members for at least one year before the EEA national's death: Citizens Directive article 12(2).
75 Where the EEA national with the principal right of residence leaves the UK or dies, then his or her children, and a non-EEA national parent of the children who has actual custody of the children, will not lose their right of residence in the UK if certain conditions are met. The conditions are that the children reside in the UK and are enrolled here in an educational establishment for the purpose of studies. In these circumstances, the right of residence is retained until the completion of the children's studies. There is no minimum duration of residence before this protection can be invoked. See the Citizens Directive article 12(3); EEA Regs 2006 regs 10(3)–(4).
76 Where the EEA national with the principal right of residence ends his or her marriage through divorce or annulment, or terminates a registered partnership with a non-EEA national, non-EEA national family members will not lose their right of residence as a consequence, provided that one of the conditions below is met:
 • prior to the initiation of the divorce or annulment proceedings or prior to the termination of the registered partnership, the marriage or registered partnership had lasted for three years, including one year in the UK (Citizens Directive article 13(2)(a));
 • by agreement between the spouses or registered partners or by court order, the non-EEA national spouse or partner has custody of the EEA national's children;
 • where this is warranted by 'particularly difficult circumstances' such as domestic violence while the marriage or registered partnership was subsisting (Citizens Directive article 13(2)(c));
 • by agreement between the spouses or registered partner, or by court order, the non-EEA national spouse or partner has a right of access to a minor child, provided that a court has ruled that the right of access must be in the UK (Citizens Directive article 13(2)(d)).
77 EEA Regs 2006 reg 10(6) impose additional requirements for the retention of rights of residence by family members which, in the Citizens Directive apply only to the acquisition of permanent residence by family members retaining the right of residence.

8.35 We deal with the right to permanent residence for family members further below at paras 8.46–8.48.

Family members of British citizens

8.36 The Citizens Directive generally does not apply to an EEA national who has never moved from the member state of which he or she is a national or exercised free movement rights, or to his or her family members[78].

8.37 Thus, UK nationals and their non-EEA national family members living in the UK are *not* covered by the three levels of protection from expulsion contained in the Citizens Directive and in the EEA Regs 2006, discussed further below in chapter 9, unless certain conditions, set out in the EEA Regs 2006, are met.[79]

8.38 The EEA Regs 2006 provide that the family member of a UK national, living in the UK, will be protected from expulsion in the same way as the family members of other EEA nationals living in the UK only if:

- the UK national was living in an EEA state (not the UK) as a worker or self-employed person before returning to the UK; and
- the family member is the UK national's spouse or civil partner, the couple had entered into the marriage or civil partnership and were living together in the EEA state (not the UK) before the UK national returned to the UK.[80]

8.39 Distinct protections are conferred on British Citizen children and other dependants and their non-EU national primary carers by TFEU article 20. Those protections and the seminal judgment of the Grand Chamber of the CJEU in *Zambrano v Office National de l'emploi*[81] are discussed at paras 10.4–10.16 below.

---

78 *Dereci and Others v Bundesministerium fur Inneres*, C-256/11, paras 54 to 55
79 The Citizens Directive's scope is said to apply to all EU Citizens (and hence applies to all EEA nationals – see para 8.5 above) 'who move to or reside in a member state other than that of which they are a member, and to their family members': Citizens Directive article 3(1). Likewise, the EEA Regs 2006 define 'EEA states' as member states of the EEA 'other than the United Kingdom': EEA Regs 2006 reg 2(1).
80 EEA Regs 2006 reg 9(1)–(2).
81 C-34/09.

Family members of dual nationals

8.40 In *McCarthy v Secretary of State for the Home Department*,[82] the CJEU held that where the principal holds British citizenship and a further EEA nationality, the second EEA nationality cannot by itself be relied upon to invoke the benefits of the Citizens Directive.

Acquisition of permanent rights of residence in the UK by an EEA national

8.41 An EEA national who has lived in the UK legally for a continuous period of five years automatically acquires a right of permanent residence in the UK.[83]

8.42 Once acquired, the right of permanent residence for an EEA national can only be lost through an absence from the UK for a period exceeding two years[84] or, as is specifically stated in the EEA Regs 2006, by expulsion on grounds of public policy, public security or public health.[85] It does not matter whether those absences occurred before or after the transposition date for the Directive of 30 April 2006.[86] Thus, once a permanent right of residence has been acquired it is not lost purely as a result of imprisonment[87] or cessation of the exercise of EU law rights.

8.43 Under the Citizens Directive, the EEA national or family member should have been living 'legally' in the host state to acquire a right of permanent residence.[88] The meaning of 'legal residence' is discussed at paras 9.32–9.47.

8.44 In certain circumstances, an EEA national may acquire a right of permanent residence in the UK before completing five years of continuous legal residence. The right to permanent residence is acquired before five years of continuous legal residence in the following cases (defined in the EEA Regs 2006 as workers or self-employed persons who have ceased activity[89]):

---

82 C-434/09 paras 39–40.
83 Citizens Directive article 16(1); EEA Regs 2006 reg 15(1)(a).
84 Citizens Directive article 16(4); EEA Regs 2006 reg 15(2).
85 EEA Regs 2006 regs 15(3) and 19(3)(b).
86 *Secretary of State for Work and Pensions v Taous-Lassal* Case C-162/09.
87 *LG and CC (EEA Regs)* [2009] UKAIT 00024 para 81.
88 Citizens Directive article 16(1)–(2).
89 EEA Regs 2006 reg 15(1)(c).

- workers or self-employed persons who, at the time of stopping working, have reached the UK retirement age;[90]
- workers who take early retirement provided that they have been working in the UK for at least the preceding 12 months and have resided there continuously for more than three years;[91]
- workers or self-employed persons who have resided continuously in the UK for more than two years and stop working in the UK as a result of permanent incapacity;[92]
- workers who have resided in the UK for any period but who have stopped working as a result of permanent incapacity caused by an accident at work or an occupational disease which entitles them to a benefit payable by a UK institution;[93]
- workers or self-employed persons who, after three years of continuous employment or residence in the UK, work in an employed or self-employed capacity in another EEA member state, but retain their place of residence in the UK and return to the UK as a rule at least once a week.[94]

8.45 The requirements of length of residence and activity as a worker or self-employed person set out above at para 8.41 do not apply if the EEA national is the spouse or civil partner of a UK national.[95]

Right of permanent residence for family members

8.46 Family members (of any nationality) normally acquire a right of permanent residence after living legally in the UK for a continuous period of five years with the EEA national who has the principal right of residence in the UK.[96] Where the EEA national with the principal right of residence acquired a right of permanent residence before five years on the basis of the exceptions set out at para 8.44 above, his or her family members also simultaneously acquire a right of permanent residence.[97]

---

90 Citizens Directive article 17(1)(a); EEA Regs 2006 reg 5(2)(a)(i).
91 Citizens Directive article 17(1)(a) ; EEA Regs 2006 reg 5(2)(a)–(c).
92 Citizens Directive article 17(1)(b); EEA Regs 2005 reg 5(3)(b)(i).
93 Citizens Directive article 17(1)(b); EEA Regs 2006 reg 5(3)(b)(ii).
94 Citizens Directive article 17(1)(c); EEA Regs 2006 reg 5(4).
95 EEA Regs 2006 reg 5(6).
96 Citizens Directive article 16(1)–(2); EEA Regs 2006 reg 15(1)(f).
97 Citizens Directive article 17(1), (3); EEA Regs 2006 reg 15(1)(d).

8.47 Once the family member has acquired a right of permanent residence in the UK, his or her legal stay in the UK is not dependent on the EEA national with the principal right of residence.

8.48 Where the EEA national with the principal right of residence has left the country, died, or ended the marriage or registered partnership with the family member before the right of permanent residence was acquired by the family members, then the family member can only acquire a right to permanent residence in the UK if certain conditions are satisfied.[98]

---

98 Those conditions are set out at Citizens Directive articles 7(1), 12(1)–(2) and 13(1)–(2). Arguably the EEA Regs 2006 at reg 15(f)(ii) are more generous.

CHAPTER 9

The expulsion of EEA nationals and their family members under the Citizens Directive and EEA Regs 2006

9.1	Introduction
9.6	General principles
9.9	**The first level of protection**
9.9	Public security, public security or public health grounds
9.12	Genuine, present and sufficiently serious threat affecting one of the fundamental interests of society
9.14	Measures based exclusively on personal conduct
9.17	Particularly serious past offences
9.19	Proportionality
9.21	**The second level of protection: protections for EEA nationals and family members who have acquired a right of permanent residence in the UK**
9.22	Serious grounds of public policy or public security
9.24	Application in criminal court recommendation cases
9.25	**The third and highest level of protection: protections for EEA nationals and family members who are minors or who are long-term (ten years or more) residents in the UK**
9.26	Imperative grounds of public security

continued

9.30		A requirement of legal residence?
9.31		'Previous' ten years
9.32		**The calculation of the qualifying periods**
9.32		The meaning of 'legal residence'
		Brief litigation history on 'legal residence' •
9.38		Calculating the duration of 'legal' residence: starting point
9.39		Continuity of residence
9.42		Time spent in prison
9.48		**Procedure and practice in EEA expulsion cases**
9.48		The interrelationship between the EEA Regs 2006, the IA 1971 and the UKBA 2007
9.50		Exemptions from deportation under IA 1971
		Irish nationals
9.52		Notification of decisions
9.53		Judicial remedies required under EU law in expulsion cases
9.55		Appeals brought under the EEA Regs 2006 against expulsion measures
		Grounds of appeal • *In-country and out of country appeals* • *Appeals to SIAC* • *Proof that the appellant is an EEA national or the family member of an EEA national* • *Certification*
9.67		Revocation of a deportation order
		In-country applications and appeals in revocation cases • *Circumstances in which a deportation order made against an EEA national or family member should be immediately revoked or automatically becomes invalid*
9.73		Appeal against the refusal of an asylum claim by an EEA national or family member with a right to reside
9.74		Delay in enforcing a deportation order
9.75		Immigration detention of EEA nationals and their family members against whom deportation action is being taken
9.79		Entry in breach of a deportation order by an EEA national or family member
9.80		**Home Office policy on the deportation of EEA nationals and their family members**
9.80		When deportation consideration begins

9.81	What information will be sought
9.82	Which cases will be referred
9.83	Home Office interpretation of the upper two levels of protection from expulsion
9.84	Home Office incorporation of a presumption of deportation
9.85	Home Office policy concerning the deportation of Irish nationals in particular
9.87	Home Office policy on revocation of deportation orders made against EEA nationals and their family members

Introduction

9.1 Expulsion is the generic term used in the Citizens Directive[1] for a measure to eject a person from the host state.[2] Our focus is on expulsion on grounds of public policy, public security or public health. An expulsion decision of this type is treated, under the Immigration (European Economic Area) Regulations (EEA Regs) 2006,[3] as if it was a decision to deport under the Immigration Act (IA) 1971 s3(5)(a) so that the person is liable to have a deportation order made against him under IA 1971 s5.[4]

9.2 There is a second form of expulsion of EEA nationals and family members which enables them to be administratively removed under the Immigration and Asylum Act (IAA) 1999 s10.[5] This is of little application to foreign national prisoners and former prisoners (FNPs) and is beyond the scope of this book.

9.3 Exclusion is the generic term used by the Citizens Directive for a measure which prohibits entry to the host state: a deportation order is an order for both expulsion and exclusion. The EEA Regulations 2006 also confer a distinct power on the Secretary of State for the Home Department (SSHD) to make an 'exclusion order' against an EEA national or family member on public policy, public security or public health grounds who is outside the UK.[6]

9.4 The first part of this chapter considers the principles that apply under the Citizens Directive and EEA Regs 2006 to the expulsion of EEA nationals and their family members. We start by reviewing the general principles applicable to measures limiting the right to freedom of movement of an EEA national or family member. We then discuss three escalating levels of protection applicable to EEA nationals and their family members who are expelled or excluded from a host member state. The greater the degree of integration of the EEA national or family member, the higher the level of protection. The first level of protection is applicable to all EEA nationals and family members who are being deported or excluded. The second and higher level of protection applies to those who, usually by spending five years' continuous legal residence in the UK, have acquired a right

---

1 Directive 2004/38/EC on the right of citizens of the European Union and their family members to move and reside freely within the territory of the EU.
2 The EEA Regs 2006 use the corresponding generic term 'remove'.
3 SI No 1003.
4 EEA Regs 2006 reg 24(3).
5 Under EEA Regs 2006 regs 19(3)(a) and 24(2).
6 EEA Regs 2006 reg 19(1B).

of permanent residence under EU law. The third and highest level of protection applies to those EEA nationals and family members who have spent the previous ten years in the UK (or are minors). The acquisition of a right of permanent residence under EU law has been discussed at paras 8.41–8.48 and 'family members' of EEA nationals have been discussed at paras 8.11–8.29.

9.5 The second part of this chapter examines how the regime for the expulsion of EEA nationals and their family members operates in practice. We consider how the provisions of the Citizens Directive and EEA Regs 2006 fit with the pre-existing domestic regime set down in primary legislation for deportation. We go on to consider the procedures by which EEA nationals and their family members are notified of expulsion measures; may bring appeals; and may obtain revocation of a deportation order. We then turn to the power to detain EEA nationals and their family members for expulsion, and powers of removal applicable to EEA nationals and their family members who re-enter the UK in breach of a deportation order. The chapter finishes with an overview of Home Office policy concerning the deportation of EEA nationals and their family members.

General principles

9.6 The right to freedom of movement for those exercising EU Treaty rights must be broadly construed[7] while derogations from those rights must be interpreted restrictively.[8]

9.7 Expulsion and exclusion measures abrogate the right of EEA nationals to enter and reside freely in a member state under the same conditions as nationals of the member state. Therefore the power of member states to take such measures must be restrictively interpreted.[9]

9.8 EU law protects not only rights flowing from the EU Treaties but also those rights set out in the European Convention on Human Rights (ECHR) including the right to respect for family and private life under ECHR article 8.[10] Thus, a measure taken on public policy

---

7 *Antonissen* Case C-292/89 [1991] ECR I-745 para 11; *Commission v Belgium* Case C-344/95 [1997] ECR I-1035; *Commission v The Netherlands* Case C-50/06 para 42.
8 *Van Duyn* Case 41/74 [1974] ECR 1337 para 18; *Bonsignore* Case 67/74 [1975] ECR 297 para 6; *Yiadom* Case C-357/98 [2000] ECR I-9265 para 24.
9 *Orfanopolous* Case C-348/96 [2004] ECR I-5257, [2005] 1 CMLR 18 paras 64, 65 and 79; *Calfa* [1999] ECR I-11 para 23; *Polat* Case C-349/06 para 33.
10 *Carpenter* Case C-60/00 [2002] ECR I-6279 para 40.

or public security grounds to restrict free movement rights will only be justified under EU law if it is ECHR compliant.[11] Where a decision to deport is made which engages both EU law rights and article 8, the correct approach for decision-makers is to deal with EU law rights and ECHR article 8 together: ECHR article 8 issues should be included when assessing the proportionality of the interference with the EU law right.[12]

The first level of protection

Public security, public security or public health grounds

9.9 An EEA national or the family member of an EEA national may only be deported or excluded from the UK on public policy, public security or public health grounds. This is because under the Citizens Directive, an expulsion order which imposes a ban on re-entry can only be made on these specified grounds against EEA nationals and family members.[13]

9.10 Where (as in any decision to deport an EEA national or family member and consequent deportation order) a 'measure' is taken on public policy, public security or public health grounds, certain further protections apply. A criminal court recommendation to deport is a 'measure' and so, we suggest may not be made against an EEA national or family member unless the public policy, public security or public health criteria are met.[14]

11 *Orfanopoulous* [2004] ECR I-5257, [2005] 1 CMLR 18, paras 97–99; *Commission v Germany* Case C-441/02 paras 108–109.
12 *Mario Mendes Machado v Secretary of State for the Home Department* [2005] EWCA Civ 597.
13 Under the Citizens Directive, no ban on entry may be imposed on EU citizens and their family members in the context of a decision taken on grounds other than public policy, public security or public health: Citizens Directive article 15(1), (3). Under the EEA Regs 2006, those whose expulsion is not justified on public policy, public security or public health grounds are administratively removed as if overstayers (EEA Regs 2006 regs 19(3)(a) and 24(2)) whereas those whose expulsion is justified on public policy, public security or public health grounds are treated as persons to whom the 'discretionary' deportation provision of IA 1971 s3(5)(a) applies (EEA Regs 2006 regs 19(3)(b) and 24(3)). This is also recognised in Home Office policy, see Enforcement Instructions and Guidance (EIG) chapter 11 para 11.5.
14 *R v Bouchereau* [1978] QB 732, applying the predecessor Directive 64/221; see also *R (Kluxen and others) v Secretary of State for the Home Department* [2010] EWCA Crim 1081 para 22 finding that the *Boucheareau* conclusion applies equally to the Citizens Directive. However, see paras 2.14 and 9.24 of this book.

9.11 The public policy, public security and public health grounds cannot be relied on to serve economic ends.[15] Measures taken on grounds of public policy or public security must comply with the principle of proportionality.[16] Restrictions on the right of residence must be proportionate even where the measure is in strict compliance with EU law.[17]

Genuine, present and sufficiently serious threat affecting one of the fundamental interests of society

9.12 For measures to be justified on grounds of public policy or public security, the personal conduct of the person involved must represent a genuine, present and sufficiently serious threat affecting one of the fundamental interests of society.[18] The Asylum and Immigration Tribunal (AIT) has held that, for the purposes of EEA Regs 2006 reg 21(5)(c), a prospective activity will only threaten one of the fundamental interests of society if it is prohibited in law (encompassing not only offences under criminal law but, for example, breach of the peace).[19] The threat must be 'present' as of the date of the hearing.[20]

9.13 Likewise, the ECJ has held that the public policy exception can only justify a measure where the individual has engaged in conduct which, if engaged in by the member state's own nationals, would lead to punitive or other genuine and effective measures intended to combat such conduct.[21]

Measures based exclusively on personal conduct

9.14 Measures taken on grounds of public policy or public security must be based exclusively on the personal conduct of the individual concerned. Previous criminal convictions in themselves cannot constitute grounds for taking public policy or public security measures.[22] The individual's past criminal convictions are solely relevant in so

---

15 Citizens Directive article 27(1); EEA Regs 2006 reg 21(2).
16 Citizens Directive article 27(2).
17 *Baumbast* Case 413/99, [2002] ECR I-7091, [2002] 3 CMLR 23 para 91.
18 Citizens Directive article 27(2); EEA Regs 2006 reg 21(5)(c).
19 *GW (EEA Regulation 21 'fundamental interests')* [2009] UKAIT 00050.
20 *BF (Portugal) v Secretary of State for the Home Department* [2009] EWCA Civ 923 para 11.
21 *Adoui and Cornaille* [1982] ECR 1665, [1982] 3 CMLR 631 para 9; *Olazabal* Case C-100/01 [2002] ECR I-10981 para 42.
22 Citizens Directive article 27(2); EEA Regs 2006 reg 21(5)(a).

far as they manifest a present or future propensity to act in a manner contrary to public policy or public security.[23]

9.15 Justifications that are isolated from the particulars of the case or that rely on considerations of general prevention are impermissible.[24] The ECJ has repeatedly held that expulsion of EEA nationals or their family members to deter offending by others is impermissible.[25] Likewise, it is impermissible for a state automatically to take steps to expel EEA nationals or their family members as an automatic consequence of criminal convictions, without any account being taken of the personal conduct of the offender or of the danger that person represents for the requirements of public policy.[26]

9.16 Therefore, unlike other foreign nationals (who can be deported under IA 1971 s3(5)(b)), EEA nationals and the family members of EEA nationals cannot be deported owing to the conduct of a relative. This is recognised in Home Office policy.[27]

Particularly serious past offences

9.17 There has been controversy over whether particularly serious past offences could in themselves justify expulsion on public policy grounds or whether, conversely, there must be a threat of further offending to justify deportation or exclusion. We suggest that the Citizens Directive and EEA Regs 2006 now make clear that, as earlier indicated by the ECJ in *Nazli*[28] and *Orfanopolous*,[29] what is required, both in public policy and public security cases, is a serious threat of *further* conduct contrary to public policy or public security: this is a change from the test previously set out by the ECJ in *Bouchereau*.

9.18 We briefly set out the litigation history around the *Boucheareau* point here. The ECJ held in *Bouchereau* that it was possible that past conduct alone might constitute a sufficient threat to the requirements

---

23 *R v Bouchereau* [1978] QB 732, [1978] 2 WLR 250, (1978) 66 Cr App R 202 para 25; *Nazli v Stadt Nurnberg* Case C-340/97 [2000] ECR I-957 para 58; *Calfa* Case C-348/96 [1999] ECR I-11 paras 22–24.
24 Citizens Directive article 27(2); EEA Regs 2006 reg 21(5)(b) and (d).
25 *Nazli v Stadt Nurnberg* Case C-340/97 [2000] ECR I-957 para 59; *Bonsignore v Stadt Koln* Case C-67/74 [1975] ECR 297; *Calfa* Case C-348/96 [1999] ECR I-11.
26 *Nazli v Stadt Nurnberg* Case C-340/97 [2000] ECR I-957 para 59, *Calfa* Case C-348/96 [1999] ECR I-11 para 27; *Orfanopoulos* [2004] ECR I-5257, [2005] 1 CMLR 18 para 67.
27 European Casework Instructions chapter 8 section 3 para 2.3.
28 Case C-340/97, [2000] ECR I-957.
29 [2004] ECR I-5257, [2005] 1 CMLR 18.

of public policy to justify expulsion.[30] However, ECJ case-law since *Bouchereau* has indicated that what is required is an ongoing threat. In *Nazli* the ECJ held that what was required was a 'specific risk of new and serious prejudice to the requirements of public policy'[31] and in *Orfanopolous* the ECJ found that what was required was a 'present threat to the requirements of public policy'.[32] Court of Appeal authorities have been divided as to the correct test.[33] In *R (Kluxen, Rostas and Adam) v Secretary of State for the Home Department*, the Court of Appeal held that the *Bouchereau* test had survived the introduction of Directive 2004/38,[34] however, the Court of Appeal did not refer to the aspect of the *Bouchereau* test which suggests that expulsion on grounds of past conduct alone is permissible.[35] Nor did the Court of Appeal refer in *Kluxen* to *Nazli*. We suggest that *Kluxen* is not authority that this aspect of *Bouchereau* has survived. We suggest too that Home Office guidance to caseworkers is inaccurate in suggesting that past conduct alone may constitute a threat.[36] We suggest that the position to be followed is that of the AIT in *MG and VC Ireland*, to the effect that *Nazli* overrules *Bouchereau*.[37]

30 *R v Bouchereau* [1978] QB 732, [1987] 2 WLR 251, (1977) 66 Cr App R 2002 para 29. This was followed in domestic law eg in *R v Secretary of State for the Home Department ex p Marchon* [1993] Imm AR 384; *Al-Sabah v IAT* [1992] Imm AR 223; *Goremsandu v Secretary of State for the Home Department* [1996] Imm AR 250.
31 *Nazli v Stadt Nurnberg* Case C-340/97 [2000] ECR I-957 para 61.
32 *Orfanopoulos* Case C/482/01 [2004] ECR I-5257, [2005] 1 CMLR 18 para 67.
33 *HB v Secretary of State for the Home Department* [2008] EWCA Civ 806 para 16 finding that what is required is a present threat: past criminal conduct is insufficient; but in *Schmelz v IAT* [2004] EWCA Civ 29 para 15 finding that in exceptional circumstances past criminal conduct could justify the public policy deportation of an EEA national. Neither case contains reference to *Boucheareau* or *Nazli*.
34 [2010] EWCA Civ 1081, [2011] 1 WLR 218 at para 24.
35 Rather, the court cited *Bouchereau* for the general principle that previous criminal convictions may only be taken into account as evidence of personal conduct constituting a present threat to the requirements of public policy. *R (Kluxen, Rostas and Adam) v Secretary of State for the Home Department* [2010] EWCA Civ 1081, [2011] 1 WLR 218 paras 13 and 15.
36 EIG chapter 11 para 11.5.
37 In *MG and VC Ireland* [2006] UKAIT 00053 para 12.

Proportionality

9.19 The expulsion or exclusion of an EEA national or family member on grounds of public policy or public security must be proportionate.[38] Before expelling or excluding an EEA national or family member on the grounds of public policy or public security, the UK immigration authorities must take account of considerations[39] such as the individual's:

- length of residence in the UK;
- age;
- state of health;
- family situation;
- economic situation;
- social and cultural integration into the UK; and
- extent of links with his or her country of origin.

9.20 Additional considerations for decision-makers are indicated in the ECJ's jurisprudence:

> To assess whether the interference envisaged is proportionate to the legitimate aim pursued ... [such as the protection of public policy] ... account must be taken, particularly, of the nature and seriousness of the offences committed by the person concerned, the length of his residence in the host member state, the period which has elapsed since the commission of the offence, the family circumstances of the person concerned and the seriousness of the difficulties which the spouse and any of the children risk facing in the country of origin of the person concerned.[40]

The second level of protection: protections for EEA nationals and family members who have acquired a right of permanent residence in the UK

9.21 The protections are still higher for an EEA national or family member who has acquired the right of permanent residence in the UK. For a discussion of the requirements for the acquisition of a right of permanent residence, see paras 8.41–8.48.

---

38 Citizens Directive article 27(1); EEA Regs 2006 reg 21(5)(a).
39 Citizens Directive article 28(1); EEA Regs 2006 reg 21(6).
40 *Orfanopoulos* Case C/482/01 [2004] ECR I-5257, [2005] 1 CMLR 18 para 99; see also *Olazabal* para 43 and *Gebhard* Case C-55 /94 [1995] ECR I-4165, para 37; and *LG and CC (EEA Regs)* [2009] UKAIT 00024 para 105.

Serious grounds of public policy or public security

9.22 In addition to the safeguards already set out above, no expulsion or exclusion decision may be taken against an EEA national or family member who has acquired a right of permanent residence in the UK 'except on serious grounds of public policy or public security'.[41]

9.23 The Court of Appeal has found that where an EEA national had committed a series of offences including robbery as part of a gang, and showed a high risk of committing future robberies of some seriousness, deportation on serious grounds of public policy was warranted.[42] However, each case is fact-specific: an AIT panel chaired by Carnwath LJ found that a repeat offender whose most recent offence was for robbery and grievous bodily harm with intent, leading to a sentence of nine years' imprisonment was not justified on serious grounds of public policy or public security because he had long residence in the UK and had no significant links with his home country.[43]

Application in criminal court recommendation cases

9.24 A question arises over how these additional protections may impinge on the power of a criminal court to recommend deportation. The Court of Appeal in *R (Kluxen, Rostas and Adam) v Secretary of State for the Home Department* has held that Citizens Directive article 28 (which at 28(2) imposes the top two levels of the hierarchy of protections) and EEA Regs 2006 reg 21 (transposing that provision) apply only to the SSHD's expulsion decisions, not to a sentencing court's recommendation for deportation.[44] We respectfully suggest that this interpretation is questionable in the light of article 33(1) of the Citizens Directive, which provides that an expulsion order may not be issued as a legal consequence of a custodial penalty unless the order conforms with, among other protections, article 28 of the Directive. If *Kluxen* is correct, then a recommendation for deportation could lawfully be made by a criminal court against, for example, an EEA national with a right of permanent residence. However, that court recommendation would be incapable of lawful enforcement by the SSHD because articles 28 and 33(1) of the Directive prohibit the making of the deportation order in consequence of the recommendation.

41 Citizens Directive article 28(2).
42 *HB v Secretary of State for the Home Department* [2008] EWCA Civ 806.
43 *LG and CC (EEA Regs)* [2009] UKAIT 00024 para 117.
44 [2010] EWCA Civ 1081, [2011] 1 WLR 218 at paras 31–32.

The third and highest level of protection: protections for EEA nationals and family members who are minors or who are long-term (ten years or more) residents in the UK

9.25 The highest level of protection from expulsion or exclusion applies to an EEA national or family member who is a minor or who is a long-term resident in the UK. The Citizens Directive states in its preamble that:

> ... the greater the degree of integration of [EEA nationals] and their family member in the host member state, the greater the degree of protection against expulsion should be. Only in exceptional circumstances, where there are imperative grounds of public security, should an expulsion measure be taken against [EEA nationals] who have resided for many years in the territory of the host member state, in particular when they were born there and have resided there throughout their life.[45]

Imperative grounds of public security

9.26 No expulsion or exclusion decision may be taken other than on 'imperative grounds of public security' if the EEA national or family member who is the subject of the decision:

- has resided in the UK for the previous ten years;[46] or
- is a minor (ie aged under 18), except if the decision is necessary for the best interests of the child pursuant to the UN Convention on the Rights of the Child (UNCRC).[47]

9.27 The Grand Chamber of the ECJ has confirmed that measures may only be taken on 'imperative grounds of public security' in 'exceptional circumstances'.[48] The Court of Appeal has emphasised that:

> ... weight must be given to different tests within the new hierarchy. The words 'imperative grounds of public security' at the third level are clearly intended to embody a test which is both more stringent and narrower in scope than 'serious grounds of public policy or public security' at the second level.

---

45 Citizens Directive preamble para (24).
46 Citizens Directive article 28(3)(a).
47 Citizens Directive article 28(3)(b).
48 *Land Baden-Württemberg v Panagiotis Tsakouridis* Case C-145/09 [2011] 2 CMLR 11 para 40.

Thus 'imperative' must 'connote a very high threshold'.[49] Likewise, the AIT has held that the top of the hierarchy of protections from expulsion must be qualitatively and quantitatively more serious than the next level down. The AIT suggested that the term 'imperative grounds of public security' must therefore require something more than 'even a serious risk of the commission of even quite serious criminal offences'.[50]

9.28 The concept of public security is not confined to national security.[51] It includes 'the functioning of the institutions and public services and survival of the population and the risk of serious disturbance to foreign relations or to the peaceful coexistence of nations or a threat to military interests'.[52] A measure taken against an organised group trafficking in narcotics may be justified on imperative grounds of public security.[53]

9.29 Public security considerations will carry considerably less weight in cases of very long residence where there are few links with the country of origin.[54]

A requirement of legal residence?

9.30 Neither the Citizens Directive[55] nor the EEA Regs 2006[56] state that the minor or long-term resident must be exercising EU law rights or otherwise living 'legally' in the UK to acquire this highest level of protections from expulsion. This is by contrast to the second protections from expulsion (to acquire rights of permanent residence and the attendant protections from expulsion, EEA nationals and their family members must have been exercising EU law rights or at least living *legally* in the UK[57]). The Court of Appeal has nonetheless held that the same requirement of 'legal' residence applies for the third

---

49 *LG (Italy)* [2008] EWCA Civ 190 para 32.
50 *MG and VC (EEA Regulations 2006, conducive deportation) Ireland* [2006] UKAIT 00053 para 26.
51 *LG (Italy)* [2008] EWCA Civ 190 para 32(2).
52 Grand Chamber of the ECJ, in *Land Baden-Württemberg v Panagiotis Tsakouridis* Case C-145/09 [2011] 2 CMLR 11 para 44.
53 *Land Baden-Württemberg v Panagiotis Tsakouridis* Case C-145/09 [2011] 2 CMLR 11 para 47.
54 *LG and CC (EEA Regs)* [2009] UKAIT 00024 para 117; *VP (Italy) v Secretary of State for the Home Department* [2010] EWCA Civ 806 paras 21 and 25.
55 Citizens Directive article 28(3).
56 EEA Regs 2006 reg 21(4).
57 Citizens Directive articles 16(1)–(2) and 28(2); EEA Regs 2006 regs 15(1) and 21(3).

level of protection as for the second[58] and has rejected the proposition that 'resided' means no more than 'been present in' for the purpose of the ten-year qualifying period. The Court of Appeal's approach is, we respectfully suggest, difficult to reconcile with the requirement that any derogation to EU law rights be read restrictively and is likely to require resolution by the Court of Justice of the European Union (CJEU). See paras 9.32–9.47 for the definition of 'legal' residence.

'Previous' ten years

9.31 For the purposes of the third and highest level of protection, the Citizens Directive refers to those who have resided in the host state or UK 'for the previous ten years'.[59] The EEA Regs 2006 refer to an EEA national who 'has resided in the United Kingdom for a continuous period of at least ten years prior to the relevant decision'.[60] The Grand Chamber of the ECJ has held that the question of whether ten years' continuous legal residence have been accrued is to be determined as of the date of the expulsion decision.[61] The AIT has held that the continuous ten years' residence must immediately precede the expulsion decision.[62]

The calculation of the qualifying periods

The meaning of 'legal residence'

9.32 Certain rights are specifically stated in the Citizens Directive to apply only to those EEA nationals and family members who 'legally' reside in the host country.[63] In addition, as we have seen above, the highest level of protection from expulsion or exclusion has been found by the domestic courts (by implication rather than by express provision in the Citizens Directive) to apply only to those EEA nationals and family members who are legally resident in the host state.[64]

---

58 *HR (Portugal) v Secretary of State for the Home Department* [2009] EWCA Civ 371 paras 21–22; see also *LG and CC* [2009] UKAIT 00024 para 42.
59 Citizens Directive article 28(3)(a).
60 EEA Regs 2006 reg 21(4)(a).
61 *Tsakouridis* case C-145/09, [2011] CMLR 11 para 32.
62 *LG and CC (EEA Regs)* [2009] UKAIT 00024.
63 Eg the right to permanent residence after five continuous years of residing 'legally', Citizens Directive article 16; the analogous right for family members at article 18.
64 *HR (Portugal)v Secretary of State for the Home Department* [2009] EWCA Civ 371.

9.33 The main body of the Citizens Directive does not define 'legal' residence, although the preamble refers to a right of permanent residence for those who have 'resided in the host member state in compliance with the conditions laid down in this Directive'.[65] Under the EEA Regs 2006, a person must have 'resided in the United Kingdom in accordance with the Regulations' to acquire a right of permanent residence.[66]

9.34 The CJEU has held that a period of residence which was lawful only by reason of national legal provisions is not 'legal' residence for these purposes.[67] In addition, residence permits in EU law are declaratory rather than constitutive of the right to reside: that is, the right to reside flows from satisfaction of the conditions for residence (irrespective of whether a residence permit was issued) and cannot be based solely on the fact of a residence permit. Thus, a period in which an individual had a valid residence permit issued under an earlier EU Directive (not permanent residence) but did not in fact satisfy the conditions in EU law governing residence, is not a period of 'legal residence'.[68].

9.35 Since aspects of the 'legal residence' point remain contentious, we give below a brief summary of the litigation history to date.

Brief litigation history on 'legal residence'

9.36 In *McCarthy v Secretary of State for the Home Department*,[69] the Court of Appeal held that that:

> ... the lawful residence contemplated in article 16 [of the Citizens Directive] is residence which complies with community law requirements specified in the Directive and does not cover residence lawful under domestic law by reason of United Kingdom nationality.[70]

The claimant in *McCarthy* was a British Citizen with dual nationality who had never exercised the right of free movement and had always lived in the UK. She sought EEA residence documents for her Jamaican husband. The Supreme Court referred to the CJEU the

---

65 Citizens Directive preamble, recital 17.
66 EEA Regs 2006 reg 15(1).
67 *Secretary of State for Work and Pensions v Maria Dias* Case C-325/09 [2011] 3 CMLR 40.
68 *Secretary of State for Work and Pensions v Maria Dias* Case C-325/09 [2011] 3 CMLR 40, para 54.
69 [2008] EWCA Civ 641 para 31.
70 The same conclusion was reached by the AIT in *GN (EEA Regulations: Five years' residence) Hungary* [2007] UKAIT 00073.

questions of whether 1) a person of dual Irish and UK nationality who had always resided in the UK was a beneficiary of the Citizens Directive;[71] and 2) whether such a person had resided 'legally' for the purposes of the Citizens Directive. The CJEU answered the first question in the negative[72] and therefore decided that there was no need to answer the second question.[73] The remaining question was then effectively answered in *Maria Dias*.[74] Here the CJEU held that a period of residence in conformity with national law requirements (and even while holding a valid EU residence permit issued under an earlier directive) would not amount to 'legal residence' where the individual did not in fact satisfy the EU law conditions for such residence.

9.37 In *HR Portugal*,[75] the Court of Appeal held that the same quality of 'legal' residence was required for the acquisition of higher protections from expulsion for those resident in the host state for ten years or more as for permanent residence, but took an arguably more flexible view of the 'legal residence' test, finding that the requirement of 'legal' residence entailed residence 'in the exercise of the rights and freedoms conferred on them by the Treaty'.[76] That more flexible definition of 'legal residence' was subsequently endorsed by the Court of Appeal in *Cesar C v Secretary of State for the Home Department* in the context of the qualifying period for permanent residence.[77] This approach to 'legal residence' is also supported by the CJEU's judgment in *Taous-Lassal*[78] (see the discussion of that case at para 9.38 below) to the effect that the requirement of 'legal residence' is

71 Citizens Directive article 3.
72 *McCarthy v Secretary of State for the Home Department* Case C-434-09 [2011] 3 CMLR 10, paras 39–40, 57.
73 *McCarthy v Secretary of State for the Home Department* Case C-434-09 [2011] 3 CMLR 10, para 58.
74 Case C-325/09 [2011] 3 CMLR 40.
75 [2009] EWCA Civ 371 para 22.
76 The divergent interpretations between *McCarthy* and *HR Portugal* arise from reliance on different recitals within the preamble to the Citizens Directive. Recital 17 (relating to the acquisition of a right of permanent residence) refers to those who have resided 'in accordance with the conditions laid down in this Directive'. However, recital 16 (relating to protections to expulsion on public policy or public security grounds) refers to 'workers, self-employed persons or job seekers as defined by the Court of Justice'. And recital 23 (relating to expulsion on public policy, public security or public health grounds) refers to those who have 'availed themselves of the rights and freedoms conferred on them by the Treaty'.
77 [2010] EWCA Civ 1406 paras 7–8.
78 Case 162/09.

satisfied by periods of residence before the entry into force of the Citizens Directive. Note too that the Citizens Directive and consequently the EEA Regs 2006 do not exhaustively define rights of residence for EEA nationals: those set out in the Treaties may be wider.[79]

Calculating the duration of 'legal' residence: starting point

9.38 'Legal' residence may be accrued before the EEA Regs 2006 came into force on 30 April 2006. The CJEU confirmed in *Secretary of State for Work and Pensions v Taous Lassal*[80] that 'legal' residence for the purposes of the acquisition of a right of permanent residence included residence in accordance with conditions laid down in earlier EC directives. Earlier AIT authority to the contrary[81] is wrongly decided.

Continuity of residence

9.39 As we have seen above at paras 8.41–8.48, to qualify for permanent residence, an EEA national or family member must have spent (normally) five years of continuous legal residence in the host state.[82] The Citizens Directive and EEA Regs 2006 specify that continuity of residence is not affected by temporary absences not exceeding a total of six months in one year, or by absences of a longer duration for compulsory military service; or by one absence of a maximum of 12 consecutive months for important reasons such as pregnancy and childbirth, serious illness, study, vocational training or a posting in another country.[83] In addition, once permanent residence is acquired, it can be lost only through absence from the host member state for a period exceeding two consecutive years.[84]

9.40 In *Maria Dias*,[85] the CJEU considered the position of a Portuguese national living in the UK who had accrued a period of legal residence, followed by a period of less than two consecutive years in which (though she had a valid residence permit and remained in the UK) she did not in fact satisfy the conditions for residence,

---

79 *Teixera* Case C-480/08 [2010] 2 CMLR 50 paras 55–60.
80 Case 162/09.
81 *OP (Colombia)* [2008] UKAIT 00074.
82 Citizens Directive article 16(1); EEA Regs 2006 reg 15(1)(a)-(b).
83 Citizens Directive article 16(3); EEA Regs 2006 reg 3(2).
84 Citizens Directive article 16(4); EEA Regs 2006 reg 15(2).
85 Case C-325/09 [2011] 3 CMLR 40.

followed by a further period of legal residence. The CJEU held that the intervening period of less than two years of residence which were not 'legal' did not break continuity. The implication is that had the break in 'legal residence' exceeded two years, it would have broken continuity.

9.41 Expulsion (whether administrative removal or deportation) does break continuity of residence.[86] It is expulsion itself – not a decision to expel – which breaks continuity of residence. Arguably, therefore, an EEA national (or family member) who is the subject of an unenforced decision to deport or deportation order and continues to satisfy the factual requirements of legal residence continues to accrue such residence time subject to the considerations further below.

Time spent in prison

9.42 An important question for FNPs is whether time spent in prison can be counted when assessing whether an EEA national or family member a) has acquired a right of permanent residence and so can invoke the second level of protections from expulsion or exclusion, or b) has resided in the UK for ten years or more and thus can invoke the third and highest level of protection from expulsion.

9.43 Domestic authority holds that a period in prison or other penal institution following a criminal conviction does not count for the purposes of computing the five-year qualifying period for permanent residence.[87]

9.44 As we have already seen at para 9.30, the Court of Appeal has read in a requirement of 'legal' residence for the ten year qualifying period for the third and highest level of protection from expulsion or exclusion.[88] The AIT, presided over by Carnwath LJ, has held that even where the person had, before the period of imprisonment, already acquired a right of permanent residence under EU law, the period of imprisonment does not count towards the attainment of ten years'

---

86 Citizens Directive article 21; EEA Regs 2006 reg 3(3).
87 The Court of Appeal in *Cesar C v Secretary of State for the Home Department* [2010] EWCA Civ 1406 held that time spent serving a period of imprisonment in the UK could not count as 'legal residence' for the purposes of accruing a permanent right of residence after five years. See also *LG and CC (Italy)* [2009] UKAIT 00024 and the obiter dicta in *HB v Secretary of State for the Home Department* [2008] EWCA Civ 806 and *Valentin Batista v Secretary of State for the Home Department* [2010] EWCA Civ 896.
88 *McCarthy* [2008] EWCA Civ 641; *HR (Portugal)* [2009] EWCA Civ 371.

residence and so the highest level of protection from expulsion[89] a position which has obiter support from the Court of Appeal.[90]

9.45 However, the approach of the domestic courts to periods of imprisonment is likely to require resolution by the CJEU. The finding that time spent serving a criminal sentence does not count towards the ten year qualifying period for the highest level of protection is difficult to reconcile with the judgment of the Grand Chamber of the ECJ in *Tsakouridis*, where time spent in prison was treated as a relevant, but not decisive, factor in determining whether 'the integrating links' with the host state were broken and enhanced protections previous accrued lost.[91] The ECJ has also held (albeit not in the context of the rights and protections of the Citizens Directive) that a person who has previously exercised rights of freedom of movement does not forfeit EU law rights, nor does his or her residence cease to be legal purely by reason of imprisonment – even for lengthy period – after a criminal conviction.[92] On the other hand, as we have seen at para 9.40 above, the CJEU's judgment in *Maria Dias* takes a restrictive approach, appearing to suggest that residence ceases to be 'legal' for periods in which the individual is no longer exercising rights of freedom of movement.

9.46 We suggest that it cannot be correct that a) time spent serving a criminal sentence is not 'legal residence' (see paras 9.43–9.44 above); b) the ten-year qualifying period for the highest level of protection requires 'legal residence' (see para 3.30 above) *and* that c) the ten-year qualifying period is the period immediately preceding the expulsion decision. This would disqualify many long-resident integrated EEA nationals from the highest level of protection in deportation cases. This is because the deportation of longer resident EEA nationals is almost invariably associated with serious offences and lengthy prison sentences and it is standard Home Office practice to issue decisions to deport near or at the end of the custodial sentence (see para 9.80 below). That result would be contrary to the objectives of the Citizens Directive (which include the protection of those genuinely integrated to the host state).[93] It would moreover be arbitrary in its effects (an

---

89 *LG and CC (Italy)* [2009] UKAIT 00024.
90 The Court of Appeal in *HR (Portugal)* [2009] EWCA Civ 371 found that the same requirement of legal residence applied to accruing ten years' residence as to accruing permanent residence after five years.
91 Grand Chamber of the ECJ, in *Land Baden-Württemberg v Panagiotis Tsakouridis* Case C-145/09 [2011] 2 CMLR 11.
92 *Orfanopoulos* Case C/482/01 [2004] ECR I-5257, [2005] 1 CMLR 18; *Dogan* Case C-383/03 [2005] ECR I-6237, [2005] 3 CMLR 45.
93 Citizens Directive preamble, recital 24.

EEA national with 30 years' 'legal' residence who then served a two-year prison sentence, would be unable to rely on the highest level of protection from expulsion if he received notice of intention to deport at the end of the sentence but would be able to rely on it if he received the same notice at the start of the sentence).

9.47 In any event, even if the domestic approach is correct, we suggest that where a person has spent time on remand in prison only to be acquitted, or has spent time in prison post conviction only to succeed on appeal, such time should not be discounted when computing residence nor should it be considered to interrupt continuity of residence. The ECJ has found that when calculating whether a person was exercising his or her rights as an EEA national worker, time spent on remand pending trial where subsequently acquitted of the offence is not an interruption of working.[94] In obiter comments in *HR Portugal*, Sedley LJ expressed strong sympathy for this position.[95]

Procedure and practice in EEA expulsion cases

The interrelationship between the EEA Regs 2006, the IA 1971 and the UKBA 2007

9.48 The process of deportation of EEA nationals and family members weaves aspects of the pre-existing deportation regime under the IA 1971 into the new regime under the EEA Regs 2006. Where a decision is made to expel an EEA national or family member on grounds of public policy, public security or public health, this is 'an EEA decision'[96] but the proposed deportee is treated under the EEA Regulations 'as if he were' a person to whom the conducive deportation provisions of the IA 1971 (s3(5)(a)) applied. An appeal to the Immigration and Asylum Chamber of the First-tier Tribunal (FTT-IAC) against an 'EEA decision' is brought 'under the Regulations'.[97] The powers of detention under IA 1971 Sch 3 apply to that EEA national at each step in the deportation process.[98] On exhaustion of any appeals, the power to make a deportation order (under IA 1971 s5) then applies to that that person.[99]

94 *Nazli v Stadt Nurnberg* Case C-340/97 [2000] ECR I-957 para 49.
95 [2009] EWCA Civ 371 para 45.
96 EEA Regs 2006 reg 2(1).
97 EEA Regs 2006 reg 26(1).
98 EEA Regs 2006 reg 24(3).
99 EEA Regs 2006 reg 24(3).

9.49 We suggest that there is no power to make an 'automatic' deportation order against an EEA national or family member under the UK Borders Act (UKBA) 2007. The decision to deport an EEA national or family member can now only be taken on public policy, public security or public health grounds[100] *for which the UKBA 2007 makes no provision*. We suggest that although the deportation order is still a deportation order under IA 1971 s5, the decision-making process for EEA nationals and their family members is exclusively governed by the EEA Regs 2006. This does not render otiose UKBA 2007 s33(3) ('the EU law exception') since that enables nationals of Association Agreement countries[101] to rely on EU law rights in resisting 'automatic' deportation. Note that the Court of Appeal has assumed that an EEA national or family member may be the subject of 'automatic' deportation under the UKBA 2007 although argument does not appear to have been heard on the point.[102]

Exemptions from deportation under IA 1971

9.50 As we have seen at para 9.1 above, an EEA national or family member against whom an expulsion decision has been taken under the EEA Regs 2006 on public policy, public security or public health grounds is treated as being a person to whom IA 1971 s3(5)(a) applies and the consequent order is a deportation order under IA 1971 s5.[103] The exemptions from deportation in the IA 1971 (ss7 and 8) therefore also apply to EEA nationals. This is accepted in Home Office policy.[104] The exemptions to deportation have been discussed in detail at paras 1.27–1.42

Irish nationals

9.51 It is therefore important to remember that a long resident Irish national may, quite apart from possibly benefiting from the highest level of EU law protection from expulsion (paras 9.25–9.31 above) and special Home Office policies applicable to Irish nationals (para 9.85 below) be exempt from deportation under IA 1971 s7(1).

---

100 See para 9.9.
101 See para 10.17.
102 *R (Kluxen and others) v Secretary of State for the Home Department* [2010] EWCA Crim 1081.
103 EEA Regs 2006 reg 24(3).
104 European Casework Instructions chapter 8 section 1 chapter 1.

Notification of decisions

9.52 Any EEA national or family member who is the subject of a measure taken on public policy, public security or public health grounds must be informed of the decision in writing in such a way that they are able to understand the content and its implications.[105] They must be informed precisely and fully of the public policy, public security or public health grounds unless to do so would be contrary to the interests of state security.[106] The notification of the decision must specify the court or tribunal with which the person concerned can lodge an appeal and time limits for appeal.[107] Where relevant, the notification should also inform the person of the time he or she has to leave the UK. Under the Citizens Directive, save in 'substantiated cases of urgency' this should not be less than one month from the date of notification.[108] However, the EEA Regs 2006 also provide that an EEA national may be given less than a month to leave the UK where he or she has entered the country or sought to do so in breach of a deportation order or is detained pursuant to the sentence or order of any court.[109]

Judicial remedies required under EU law in expulsion cases

9.53 The Citizens Directive requires that an EEA national or family member who is the subject of a decision taken on public policy, public security or public health grounds must have access to judicial or administrative remedies[110] by which a full examination of the facts, and of the legality and proportionality of the decision can take place.[111] Where an EEA national or family member has, in addition to seeking a judicial remedy, sought an interim order to suspend enforcement of the expulsion decision, no expulsion can be taken until a decision has been taken on that application for an interim order unless:

- the expulsion decision is based on a previous judicial decision; or
- the persons concerned have had previous access to judicial review; or

---

105 Citizens Directive article 30(1).
106 Citizens Directive article 30(2).
107 Citizens Directive article 30(3).
108 Citizens Directive article 30(3).
109 EEA Regs 2006 reg 24(6)(b)–(c).
110 Citizens Directive article 31(1).
111 Citizens Directive article 31(3).

- the expulsion decision is based on imperative grounds of public security.[112]

9.54 Under the Citizens Directive, an individual may be excluded from a member state pending the judicial or administrative examination of the expulsion decision but must be allowed to return to present his or her case in person except where this 'may cause serious troubles to public policy or public security or when the appeal or judicial review concerns a denial of entry to the territory'.[113]

Appeals brought under the EEA Regs 2006 against expulsion measures

9.55 In the UK, the EU law requirements of a suspensive remedy against an expulsion decision of an EEA national or EEA family member[114] are met by Part 6 of the EEA Regs 2006.

9.56 There is a right of appeal against EEA decisions under the EEA Regs 2006[115] rather than under the Nationality Immigration and Asylum Act (NIAA) 2002.[116] This right of appeal can be exercised against a decision to deport an EEA national or his or her family member taken on public policy, public security or public health grounds. An appeal under the EEA Regs 2006 against an EEA decision to deport normally lies to the FTT-IAC.

Grounds of appeal

9.57 Where an appeal is brought in the FTT-IAC against an EEA decision to deport, the appellant can rely on any of the grounds set out in NIAA 2002 s84. The exception is that (since the immigration rules do not apply to EEA decisions) no appeal can be brought on grounds that the EEA decision is contrary to the immigration rules.[117] The standard procedures and reconsideration and appeals system for IAC appeals then apply.[118]

---

112 Citizens Directive article 31(2).
113 Citizens Directive article 31(4).
114 Family member as defined in EEA Regs 2006 reg 7 and Citizens Directive articles 2(2) and 3(2).
115 EEA Regs 2006 reg 26(1).
116 EEA Regs 2006 Sch 2 para 4 specifically provides that an EEA decision to expel a person under the regulations is not an immigration decision for the purposes of NIAA 2002 s82.
117 EEA Regs 2006 Sch 1.
118 EEA Regs 2006 Sch 1.

In-country and out of country appeals

9.58 Where a person who is still in the UK has an appeal pending against an EEA decision to deport, no deportation order can be made under IA 1971 s5[119] and no arrangements for deportation can be issued while the appeal is pending.[120] Any directions already given for removal or deportation which have not yet been enforced will be invalidated where an appeal is lodged against an expulsion decision.[121]

9.59 The exception is that there is no in-country right of appeal for an EEA national or family member who has entered the UK in breach of a deportation order and is challenging a subsequent decision to expel him or her[122] unless that person has made a non-certified claim that the decision to deport was in breach of his or her ECHR or Refugee Convention[123] rights.[124]

Appeals to SIAC

9.60 In EEA cases related to national security the appeal lies to the Special Immigration Appeals Commission (SIAC). The appeal under the EEA Regs 2006 against an EEA decision lies to SIAC where the SSHD certifies that the EEA decision was taken wholly or partly on the following grounds, or was taken in accordance with a direction of the SSHD which identifies the person to whom the decision relates and is given wholly or partly on the following grounds:

- on the basis that the person's exclusion or removal from the UK is in the interests of national security;[125]
- on the basis that the person's exclusion or removal from the UK in the interests of the relationship between the UK and another country.[126]

9.61 Likewise, the appeal lies to SIAC where the SSHD certifies that the EEA decision was taken wholly or partly in reliance on information which in the SSHD's opinion should not be made public:

---

119 EEA Regs 2006 reg 29(6).
120 EEA Regs 2006 reg 29(3).
121 EEA Regs 2009 reg 29(3).
122 EEA Regs 2006 reg 27(1)(d).
123 The 1951 Convention Relating to the Status of Refugees and its 1967 Protocol ('Refugee Convention').
124 EEA Regs 2006 reg 27(3).
125 EEA Regs 2006 regs 28(2) and 3(a).
126 EEA Regs 2006 regs 28(2) and 3(b).

- in the interests of national security;[127]
- in the interests of the relationship between the UK and another country;[128] or
- otherwise in the public interest.[129]

9.62 Appeals to SIAC are discussed in detail in chapter 23.

Proof that the appellant is an EEA national or the family member of an EEA national

9.63 For a right of appeal to arise under the EEA Regs 2006, the prospective appellant must produce proof of his or her EEA status:
- if the appellant claims to be an EEA national, he or she must produce a valid national identity card or passport issued by an EEA state;[130]
- if the appellant claims to be the family member of an EEA national, he or she must produce an EEA family permit or other proof that he or she is related as claimed to an EEA national;[131]
- and by implication, if the appellant claims to be an extended family member of an EEA national who is entitled by virtue of documentation to be treated in the same way as a family member, a valid EEA family permit, registration certificate or residence card.[132]

9.64 Where the SSHD does not accept that the subject of the decision (ie the proposed deportee) is an EEA national or family member, the right of appeal will not arise under the EEA Regs 2006. In these circumstances, an appeal against a discretionary decision to deport under IA 1971 or an 'automatic' deportation order under UKBA 2007 will arise under NIAA 2002 s82(1) and it will be for the proposed deportee to establish nationality and/or relevant family ties in the course of his or her appeal.

Certification

9.65 Where an appeal is brought under the EEA Regs 2006 against an EEA decision, the SSHD has the power to certify a ground, on the basis that the ground has already been considered in a previous appeal

---

127 EEA Regs 2006 reg 26(4)(a).
128 EEA Regs 2006 reg 26(4)(b).
129 EEA Regs 2006 reg 26(4)(c).
130 EEA Regs 2006 reg 26(2).
131 EEA Regs 2006 reg 26(3).
132 EEA Regs 2006 reg 7(3).

brought under the EEA Regs 2006 or under NIAA 2002 s82(1).[133] The effect of such certification is that the person may not bring an appeal under the EEA Regs 2006 on this ground nor rely on this ground in an appeal brought under the EEA Regs 2006.[134] We suggest that by analogy with the language of NIAA 2002 s94, the SSHD may not certify once the appeal under the EEA Regs has been lodged.[135]

9.66 In addition, the SSHD retains the power to certify appeals which are brought under the EEA Regs 2006 under NIAA 2002 s96(1)(a).[136] NIAA 2002 s96(1)(a) allows the SSHD to impose a certificate where a person was notified of a right of appeal against an earlier immigration decision (whether or not such an appeal was brought or determined) and the claim or application relates to a matter which could have been raised in the appeal against the earlier decision and in the opinion of the SSHD or immigration officer there is no satisfactory reason for that matter not having been raised in an appeal against the earlier decision. The effect of a certificate under NIAA 2002 s96(1)(a) is that no appeal can be brought in reliance of the certified claim.

Revocation of a deportation order

9.67 The Citizens Directive stipulates that an EEA national or family member who has been excluded on grounds of public policy or public security may apply for revocation on the basis of a material change of circumstances 'after a reasonable period', and in any event, after three years from enforcement of the final expulsion order.[137] Both the Citizens Directive and the EEA Regs 2006 provide that an application for revocation of an exclusion or deportation order made by an EEA national or family member must be decided within six months of the application being submitted.[138] The application must set out the material change of circumstances relied on by the applicant.[139] The EEA Regs 2006 stipulate that the SSHD 'shall' revoke the order if she considers that it can no longer be justified on grounds of public policy, public security or public health.[140] The Citizens Directive

---

133 EEA Regs 2006 reg 26(5).
134 EEA Regs 2006 reg 26(4).
135 See para 22.9 and *AM (Somalia) v Secretary of State for the Home Department* [2009] EWCA Civ 114.
136 EEA Regs 2006 Sch 2 para 4(7).
137 Citizens Directive article 32(1).
138 Citizens Directive article 32(1); EEA Regs 2006 reg 24A(5).
139 Citizens Directive article 32(1); EEA Regs 2006 reg 24A(3).
140 EEA Regs 2006 reg 24A(4).

also provides that an EEA national or family member who has been excluded does not have a right to enter the UK while his or her application for revocation is pending.[141] The above applies to a deportation order which had been validly made under EU and domestic law.[142] We deal separately with invalid deportation orders further below at paras 9.71–9.72.

In-country applications and appeals in revocation cases

9.68 A controversial issue is whether (save for lapsed or invalid deportation orders) an application for revocation of a deportation order against an EEA national or family member and any consequent appeal can be brought from within the UK before enforcement of the order. The Citizens Directive does not expressly deal with this question. But the EEA Regs 2006 as amended prohibit the making of an in-country application for revocation of a deportation order [143] (see also paras 9.87–9.88 below on exceptions recognised in Home Office policy). And, while there is a right of appeal under the EEA Regs 2006 against a refusal by the SSHD to revoke a deportation order against an EEA national or family member,[144] this right of appeal against a refusal to revoke a deportation order can only be exercised from outside the UK.[145] The slim exception to that prohibition in the EEA Regs 2006 on in-country applications for revocation and consequent appeals, as we see at para 9.73 below, is where an asylum claim has been made.

9.69 The prohibition on in-country revocation applications and appeals imposed by EEA Regs 2006 regs 24A(3) and 27(1)(b) is controversial because no such restrictions apply in non-EEA cases. There is no restriction on in-country applications for revocation of a deportation order by other foreign nationals. And, as we have seen at para 7.29 above, domestic primary legislation confers an in-country right of appeal against a refusal to revoke a deportation order where a non-certified claim has been made that deportation breach would the Refugee Convention or the ECHR, or the applicant is an EEA national or family member who claims that deportation would breach their rights under EU law.[146]

---

141 Citizens Directive article 32(2).
142 Citizens Directive article 32(1).
143 EEA Regs 2006 reg 24A(3).
144 EEA Regs 2006 reg 26(1).
145 EEA Regs 2006 reg 27(1)(b).
146 NIAA 2002 s92(4).

9.70 We suggest that the EEA Regs 2006 regs 24A(3) and 27(1)(b) are unlawful on grounds that:

- the Citizens Directive has been inaccurately transposed;
- these provisions impermissibly place EEA nationals and their family members seeking revocation at a disadvantage in relation to other foreign nationals in the UK.[147] It is long established in EU law that 'the rules of procedure laid down by domestic law for the exercise of rights derived from Community law must not be less favourable than those governing similar domestic actions';[148]
- these provisions impermissibly place the third country family members of EEA nationals at a disadvantage in relation to the third country family members of UK nationals;[149] and
- they impermissibly restrict the procedural rights of EEA nationals and family members by contrast to those they enjoyed[150] before the entry into force of the Citizens Directive, which is contrary both to the objectives of the Citizens Directive[151] and to the express provisions of the Citizens Directive.[152]

Circumstances in which a deportation order made against an EEA national or family member should be immediately revoked or automatically becomes invalid

9.71 Home Office policy acknowledges[153] that a deportation order made against an EEA national or family member should be immediately 'revoked' (including where the application is made while the proposed deportee is still in the UK) if:

---

147 Contrary to EU law principles of non-discrimination and to the prohibition of discrimination on grounds of nationality in the Treaty on the Functioning of the European Union (TFEU) itself (TFEU article 18, ex article 12) and long established in the ECJ's jurisprudence.
148 *Levez v TH Jennings* Case C326/96, [1999] All ER (EC) 1, [1998] ECR I-7835 para 21. See also *Belgium v Royer* Case 48/75 [1976] ECR 497, [1976] 2 CMLR 619. See also the Supreme Court's discussion of the principle of equivalence in *FA (Iraq) v Secretary of State for the Home Department* [2011] UKSC 22.
149 In breach of the equal treatment proviso of the Citizens Directive article 24.
150 Under NIAA 2002 s92(4).
151 The Grand Chamber of the ECJ has held that the Citizens Directive was intended to strengthen the rights of EU citizens and their family members and cannot confer fewer rights than the legislation it replaced: *Metock* Case C-127/08 [2008] ECR I-6241, [2009] QB 318, para 62.
152 Citizens Directive article 37 provides that the Directive 'shall not affect any laws ... laid down by a member state which would be more favourable to the persons covered by this Directive'.
153 European Casework Instructions chapter 8 section 3 para 8.3.

- the deportation order was made at a time that the person was neither an EEA national nor the family member of an EEA national and the person has since acquired a right of residence in the UK under EU law; or
- the deportation order otherwise fails to comply with the Citizens Directive.

The better view may be that such orders do not technically require revocation but lapse or are invalid.

9.72 The EEA Regs 2006 completely repeal and replace the EEA Regs 2000 and require any deportation order made under EEA Regs 2000 to be treated as if it had been made under the EEA Regs 2006.[154] A deportation order made under the EEA Regs 2000 (and made lawfully at the time) may not meet the more exacting tests for deportation now required by the EEA Regs 2006.

Appeal against the refusal of an asylum claim by an EEA national or family member with a right to reside

9.73 The EEA Regs 2006 establish a distinct right of appeal against the refusal of an asylum claim made by an EEA national or family member where he or she has a right to reside in the UK under the regulations.[155] Where an EEA national or family member with a right to reside in the UK under the EEA Regs 2006 and who is the subject of a deportation order makes an asylum claim, the refusal of asylum claim, unless the claim was certified as clearly unfounded, attracts a right of appeal which may be exercised while the person is still in the UK.[156] This may create an in-country right of appeal even where a deportation order has already been made. However, it is unlikely to have wide application: the EEA Regs 2006 also provide that any asylum claim made by an EEA national or family member under these provisions must be certified as clearly unfounded unless the SSHD is satisfied that the claim is not clearly unfounded;[157] the effect of such a clearly unfounded certificate is that there is no right of appeal against the refusal of the asylum claim.[158]

---

154 EEA Regs 2006 Sch 4 para 4(3).
155 EEA Regs 2006 Sch 2 para 4(3).
156 EEA Regs 2006 Sch 2 para 4(3); NIAA 2002 s83.
157 EEA Regs 2006 Sch 2 para 4(5).
158 EEA Regs 2006 Sch 2 para 4(4).

Delay in enforcing a deportation order

9.74 Where a deportation order is made under either set of EEA Regs but is not enforced during the two-year period beginning on the date on which the deportation order as made, special protections apply. In these circumstances of delayed deportation, the SSHD may only enforce the deportation order if, having assessed whether there has been any material change in circumstances since the deportation order was made, the SSHD considers that the deportation is still justified on grounds of public policy, public security or public health.[159]

Immigration detention of EEA nationals and their family members against whom deportation action is being taken

9.75 As with other foreign nationals facing discretionary deportation under IA 1971, EEA nationals and their family members can be detained under IA 1971 Sch 3 pending the steps in the deportation procedure.[160] The same provisions of the IA 1971 Sch 2 in respect of applications for bail also apply.[161]

9.76 However, that power of detention in the EEA Regs 2006 has been expanded.[162] The EEA Regs 2006 as amended now also permit the detention of an EEA national or family member 'if there are reasonable grounds for suspecting that a person is someone who may be removed from the United Kingdom' on grounds of public policy, public security or public health'.[163] In short, the EEA Regs permit a person who is otherwise treated as being subject to deportation under the IA 1971[164] to be detained where no steps have yet been taken in the deportation process, provided that the reasonable grounds for suspicion exist.

9.77 We suggest that the expanded detention power in the EEA Regs 2006 reg 24(1), which has no parallel in the Citizens Directive, is susceptible to challenge. As is discussed in more detail at para 31.7, in non-EEA 'discretionary' deportation cases, the IA 1971 only permits the detention of a person against whom the deportation machinery

---

159 Citizens Directive article 33(2); EEA Regs 2006 reg 24(5).
160 EEA Regs 2006 reg 29(4).
161 EEA Regs 2006 reg 29(7).
162 By the Immigration (European Economic Area) (Amendment) Regulations 2009 SI No 117.
163 EEA Regs 2006 regs 19(3)(b) and 24(1).
164 EEA Regs 2006 reg 24(3).

9.78 is already in motion, that is, who is the subject of a court recommendation to deport, a decision to deport or a deportation order.[165] By contrast, in 'automatic' deportation cases, the UKBA 2007 permits the detention of a person while the SSHD considers whether the 'automatic' deportation provisions apply or where the SSHD thinks that they apply.[166]

9.78 Arguably, the expanded detention power conferred by the EEA Regulations 2006 a) impermissibly places EEA nationals and their family members at a disadvantage in relation to other foreign nationals in the UK who are not liable to 'automatic' deportation under the UKBA 2007;[167] b) impermissibly places the third country family members of EEA nationals at a disadvantage in relation to the third country family members of UK nationals who are not liable to 'automatic' deportation under the UKBA 2007;[168] and c) impermissibly restricts the rights of EEA nationals and family members by contrast to those they enjoyed[169] before the entry into force of the Citizens Directive, which is contrary both to the objectives of the Citizens Directive[170] and to the express provisions of the Citizens Directive.[171]

Entry in breach of a deportation order by an EEA national or family member

9.79 An EEA national or his or her family member who enters or seeks to enter the UK in breach of a deportation order made under the EEA Regs 2000 or 2006 is an illegal entrant and liable to removal under IA 1971 Sch 2.[172]

---

165 IA 1971 Sch 3 para 2.
166 UKBA 2007 s36(1)(a).
167 Contrary to EU law principles of non-discrimination and to the prohibition of discrimination on grounds of nationality in the TFEU itself (TFEU article 18, ex article 12).
168 In breach of the equal treatment proviso of the Citizens Directive article 24.
169 Under IA 1971 Sch 3 para 2.
170 The Citizens Directive cannot confer fewer rights than the legislation it replaced: see note 152 above.
171 Citizens Directive article 37 provides that the Directive 'shall not affect any laws ... laid down by a member state which would be more favourable to the persons covered by this Directive'.
172 EEA Regs 2006 reg 24(4).

Home Office policy on the deportation of EEA nationals and their family members

When deportation consideration begins

9.80 It is Home Office policy not to begin action to obtain a deportation order, at least in an EEA case, more than 18 months before the earliest date of release.[173]

What information will be sought

9.81 It is published Home Office policy to normally obtain information before taking a decision to deport an EEA national or family member including:[174]

- police report confirming the circumstances of offence(s) or Custom and Excise report if they were the prosecuting authority;
- judge's sentencing remarks;[175]
- details of any previous convictions;
- parole and probation reports.

Which cases will be referred

9.82 It is Home Office policy as set out in the Enforcement Instructions and Guidance (EIG)[176] that EEA nationals and their third-country family members will be 'liable to deportation consideration' if they satisfy one or more of the following criteria:

- a court recommendation for deportation;
- a custodial sentence of 12 months or more where the conviction was for one of a list of specified drugs, sex and violent offences; and/or
- a custodial sentence of 24 months or more for other offences.[177]

---

173 European Casework Instructions chapter 8 section 3 para 3.2.
174 European Casework Instructions chapter 8 section 3 para 3.1. The full list is reproduced at para 3.11 above.
175 For judicial comment on the importance of the sentencing remarks as an indicator of the gravity of the offence, see *HK (Turkey) v Secretary of State for the Home Department* [2010] EWCA Civ 583 paras 28 and 34.
176 EIG chapter 11 para 11.2.1; European Casework Instructions chapter 8 section 3 para 2.2.6.
177 However, see PSI 52/2011 para 2.8 which now indicates that EEA nationals, as well as non-EEA nationals, should be referred by prisons to the UK Border Agency's Criminal Casework Directorate when sentenced to 12 months' or

Home Office interpretation of the upper two levels of protection from expulsion

9.83 For the second and third levels of protection from expulsion, the EIG states that what must be shown is the commission of 'crimes that pose a particularly serious risk to the safety of the public or a section of the public and having a propensity to reoffend'.[178] The EIG goes on to suggest that both for 'serious grounds of public policy or public security' or for 'imperative grounds of public security' this will entail conviction of an offence that carries a maximum penalty of at least ten years and moreover, for the latter (the highest level of protection) a custodial sentence for the individual of at least five years. This attempt by the Home Office to quantify the length of a sentence that will trigger deportation in an EEA case has been the subject of criticism by the Court of Appeal.[179]

Home Office incorporation of a presumption of deportation

9.84 Home Office policy states that once it is established that a person poses a threat sufficient in principle to justify deportation on grounds of public policy or security, 'there will be a presumption that the public interest requires deportation'.[180] We suggest that this Home Office guidance is unlawful: it has no basis in EU law nor in domestic law (it seems to have its origins in paragraph 364 of the Immigration Rules which do not apply to EEA nationals or their family members).

Home Office policy concerning the deportation of Irish nationals in particular

9.85 On 19 February 2007, the government announced that Irish nationals would only be considered for deportation where there was a court recommendation for deportation or where the SSHD concluded that 'due to the exceptional circumstances of the case, the public interest

more imprisonment, save for Irish nationals who should only be referred where there has been a court recommendation for deportation or 'exceptional circumstances'.
178 EIG chapter 11 para 11.5.
179 *LG Italy v Secretary of State for the Home Department* [2008] EWCA Civ 90 para 32.
180 EIG chapter 11 para 11.5.

requires deportation'.[181] The EIG provides a gloss on 'exceptional circumstances':

> These cases, by definition will be rare. However, as a guide, deportation may be considered where an offence involves national security matters or crimes that pose a serious risk to the safety of the public or a section of the public. This might be where a person has been convicted of a terrorism offence, murder or a serious sexual or violent offence and is serving a sentence of 10 years or more (a custodial period of 5 years or more).[182]

9.86 That policy is additional to and subject to the EU law protections applicable to Irish nationals and to the exemptions for long-resident Irish nationals under IA 1971 s7: see paras 9.25–9.31 and 1.34–1.40 respectively.

Home Office policy on revocation of deportation orders made against EEA nationals and their family members

9.87 Home Office policy also states that if a deportation order was made against an EEA national or family member on conducive grounds or on the recommendation of a court but not on public policy or public security grounds, the deportation order may be maintained if this can be justified on public policy or public security grounds.[183] We suggest that the policy is incorrect and that an unlawful deportation order cannot be salvaged through belated application of the correct test.

9.88 Home Office policy further states that an application for revocation of a deportation order against an EEA national or family member may be made from within the UK on the basis of a material change of circumstances,[184] although this is difficult to reconcile with the EEA Regs 2006.[185]

---

181 *Hansard* HL WS 53-54, 19 February 2007. See also EIG chapter 15 para 15.9 and Immigration Directorate's Instructions (IDIs) chapter 13 section 1 para 2.6.
182 EIG chapter 15 para 15.9.
183 European Casework Instructions chapter 8 section 3 para 9.1.
184 European Casework Instructions chapter 8 section 3 para 9.
185 EEA Regs 2006 reg 24A(3).

CHAPTER 10
Other EU law protections from expulsion

10.1	Introduction
10.4	**TFEU article 20, *Zambrano*, *Dereci* and the expulsion of the third-country national family members of citizens of the European Union**
10.4	TFEU article 20
10.5	The *Ruiz Zambrano* judgment and third-country national parents of children who are British or other EU citizens
10.7	*Zambrano* and other third-country national family members of British or other EU citizens
10.12	When does a citizen of the EU 'have to' leave?
10.13	Countervailing considerations?
10.15	TFEU article 20 and ECHR article 8
10.17	**Turkish Association Agreement cases**
	Workers • Family members

Introduction

10.1 This chapter considers expulsion in cases where EU law protections other than the Citizens Directive[1] apply.

10.2 We first consider the special protections for the third country (that is, non-EU) national primary carers of British citizens and other citizens of the EU. These are protections which arise neither under the Citizens Directive nor (at least as currently drafted[2]) the Immigration (European Economic Area) Regulations (EEA Regs) 2006[3] but directly under the Treaty on the Functioning of the European Union (TFEU) article 20. The fast-developing law on this point is, at the time of writing, in its initial stages, the judgments of the Grand Chamber of the Court of Justice of the European Union (CJEU) in *Ruiz Zambrano v Office National de l'emploi*[4] and *Dereci and others v Bundesministerium fur Inneres*[5] having raised more questions than they answer.

10.3 We then briefly summarise protections from expulsion that apply in cases where Turkish workers and their family members derive rights under the Turkish Association Agreement. The detail of the Turkish Association Agreement lies outside the scope of this book and we do not address aspects of the Turkish Association Agreement which have no direct bearing on expulsion cases.

TFEU article 20, *Zambrano*, *Dereci* and the expulsion of the third-country national family members of citizens of the European Union

TFEU article 20

10.4 Article 20 of the TFEU provides that every national of the member states is also a citizen of the EU. TFEU article 20 sets out a non-exhaustive list of rights of citizens of the EU, most importantly the right to move and reside freely within the territory of the member

---

1 Directive 2004/38/EC on the right of citizens of the European Union and their family members to move and reside freely within the territory of the EU.
2 The UK Border Agency in September 2011 indicated its intention to amend the EEA Regs 2006 to take account of *Zambrano v Office National de l'emploi* Case C-34/09 [2011] 2 CMLR 46. See http://ukba.homeoffice.gov.uk/sitecontent/newsarticles/2011/september/48-british-carers.
3 SI No 1003.
4 *Zambrano v Office National de l'emploi* Case C-34/09 [2011] 2 CMLR 46.
5 Case C-256/11.

states, to be exercised according to the conditions and limits set out in the treaties and the measures adopted under the treaties.

The *Ruiz Zambrano* judgment and third-country national parents of children who are British or other EU citizens

10.5 *Ruiz Zambrano v Office National de l'emploi*[6] holds that a child who is a citizen of an EU member state enjoys the fundamental status of citizen of the EU. A refusal to accord a right of residence in a member state to the third country (meaning non-EU) national parent of a minor dependent child who is a citizen of that member state and dependent on that parent would breach TFEU article 20 where this would lead to a situation in which the child had to leave the EU area to accompany his or her parents. TFEU article 20 prohibits national measures depriving citizens of the EU of the genuine enjoyment of the substance of the rights conferred by that status. This is so regardless of whether any rights of freedom of movement within the EU have been exercised by the child.[7]

10.6 *Zambrano* concerned the failed asylum-seeking Colombian parents of minor Belgian children. In *Zambrano*, the Grand Chamber of the CJEU accepted that the Belgian children would 'have to leave the territory of the Union' if the Colombian parents were denied a residence permit or a right to work.[8] The succinct Grand Chamber Judgment in *Zambrano* left open important questions, the answers to which have yet to be provided by the higher courts or CJEU. Below, we consider four primary questions.

Zambrano and other third-country national family members of British or other EU citizens

10.7 The first question is whether, and in what circumstances, the *Zambrano* principle protects third country national family members other than the parents of minor dependent EU Citizen children. Below, we set out a brief history of how *Zambrano* has been interpreted and applied to date before providing a synthesis. We refer to 'constructive expulsion' to mean a situation in which a person, although not the

---

6 *Zambrano v Office National de l'emploi* Case C-34/09 [2011] 2 CMLR 46.
7 *Zambrano v Office National de l'emploi* Case C-34/09 [2011] 2 CMLR 46, paras 40–45.
8 *Zambrano v Office National de l'emploi* Case C-34/09 [2011] 2 CMLR 46, para 44.

10.8 In *McCarthy*, the CJEU found that a dual British-Irish national who had never exercised free movement rights could not rely on TFEU articles 20 and 21 to claim an EEA residence permit for her Jamaican husband.[9] The CJEU distinguished *Zambrano* on the basis that while in *Zambrano*, the Belgian children would be forced to follow their parents to Colombia if the parents were refused a right of residence or a work permit, Ms McCarthy would not be required to leave the territory of the EU.[10]

10.9 Blake J, sitting as President of the Immigration and Asylum Chamber of the Upper Tribunal (UT-IAC) found in *Omotunde* that the application of *Zambrano* were not limited to constructive expulsion: a British citizen child's rights under TFEU article 20 would also be breached by being left behind in the UK and separated from his primary carer.[11]

10.10 The Grand Chamber of the CJEU then gave judgment in *Dereci and others v Bundesministerium fur Inneres* in which it was asked to consider the application of TFEU article 20 in the context of a number of different family relationships (spouse of an Austrian citizen; spouse and father of Austrian citizens; adult children dependent on Austrian citizens). The Grand Chamber in *Dereci* reaffirmed that TFEU article 20 precludes measures which have the effect of depriving EU citizens of the genuine enjoyment of the substance of the rights conferred by that citizenship status[12] and held that this referred to 'situations in which the Union Citizen has, in fact, to leave not only the territory of the member state of which he is a national but also the territory of the Union as a whole'.[13] TFEU article 20 did not preclude an EU member state from refusing to allow a third-country national to reside in its territory where the third-country national wished to reside with a family member who was a citizen of the EU, provided that this did not deny the EU citizen the genuine enjoyment of the substance of the rights conferred by that citizenship status.[14]

9 *McCarthy v Secretary of State for the Home Department* Case C-434-09 [2011] 3 CMLR 10, paras 49–57.
10 *McCarthy v Secretary of State for the Home Department* Case C-434-09 [2011] 3 CMLR 10 para 50.
11 *Omotunde (best interests – Zambrano applied – Razgar) Nigeria* [2011] UKUT 247 (IAC) paras 8 and 32.
12 Case C-256/11 para 64.
13 Case C-256/11 para 66.
14 Case C-256/11 para 74.

10.11 At the time of writing, the law on the TFEU article 20 protections as they affect third-country national family members can be summarised as follows:

- TFEU article 20 precludes the refusal of a right of residence or a work permit to the third-country national family member of an EU citizen where that refusal would lead to the EU citizen having to leave the territories of the EU. That is, TFEU article 20 precludes the constructive expulsion of citizens of the EU from the EU area.
- This applies not only to minor children, but to adult citizens of the EU who would have to leave the EU area to follow their third-country national primary carer. This is recognised in Home Office policy.[15]
- This logically applies not only to an EU citizen who is residing in the EU member state of which he or she is a national, but also to EU citizens residing in other member states who, if their third-country national family member were refused a right of residence or a right to work, would have to leave the EU area altogether.
- It remains to be determined by the CJEU and the higher courts whether and if so in what circumstances there may be measures falling short of constructive expulsion which may impair or deny the genuine enjoyment of the substance of the rights conferred on citizens of the EU by TFEU article 20. It also remains to be seen whether the constructive expulsion of a citizen of the European Union from his or her state of nationality *to another member state of the European Union* may be considered to impair or deny the genuine enjoyment of those rights.

When does a citizen of the EU 'have to' leave?

10.12 The second question is in what circumstances a citizen of the EU should be treated as having to leave the territory of the EU. In *Zambrano*, the Grand Chamber of the CJEU may have applied a humane (or ECHR article 8 compliant) approach to assessing whether the children would 'have to' leave the territory of the EU, disregarding, for example, the options that the parents might remain in Belgium in a state of destitution, or that the children might be taken into care in Belgium if the parents left.

---

15 UK Border Agency statement of 21 September 2011 'Judgment on carers of British Citizens', http://ukba.homeoffice.gov.uk/sitecontent/newsarticles/2011/september/48-british-carers.

Countervailing considerations?

10.13 The third question, of particular importance to FNPs, is whether the rights of the citizen of the EU are to be balanced against countervailing considerations (such as the past misconduct of or risk posed by the third-country national). The CJEU's judgments in *Zambrano*, *McCarthy* and *Dereci* make no mention of any countervailing considerations relating to the conduct of the third-country national family member or carer. In short, the Grand Chamber of the CJEU has left open the possibility that TFEU article 20 affords *absolute* protection for citizens of the EU from constructive expulsion from the EU area because such expulsion amounts to a complete denial of the enjoyment of the substantive rights flowing from citizenship status.

10.14 *Omotunde* was not a constructive expulsion case (on the evidence, the British citizen child would in fact remain in the UK if his primary carer father were deported[16]). In *Omotunde*, Blake J doubted that there was a substantial difference between the *Zambrano* approach required by EU law and the human rights-based approach in *ZH (Tanzania)*. Blake J found that the right of residence of the third country national facing expulsion or a denial of residence was not absolute but subject to the EU law principle of proportionality and is to be weighed against the public interest in deportation.[17] It has yet to be seen whether the *Omotunde* proportionality approach has any application in TFEU article 20 claims, and specifically whether it may remain good law for cases in which the interference with the rights of the citizen of the EU falls short of constructive expulsion from the territory of the EU.

TFEU article 20 and ECHR article 8

10.15 The fourth question is the relationship between TFEU article 20 and the right to respect for family life protected under ECHR article 8 (which has its corresponding protection in article 7 of the Charter of Fundamental Rights of the European Union).

10.16 As we discuss in more detail at para 17.3, in family life ECHR article 8 cases, a key question in assessing proportionality is whether

---

16 *Omotunde (best interests – Zambrano applied – Razgar) Nigeria* [2011] UKUT 247 (IAC) paras 8 and 32.
17 *Omotunde (best interests – Zambrano applied – Razgar) Nigeria* [2011] UKUT 247 (IAC) para 32.

family life can reasonably be expected to be enjoyed elsewhere.[18] At a minimum, we suggest that TFEU article 20 has the consequence that, in a family life case under article 8 where the settled family member is a citizen of the EU, it is never reasonable to expect a citizen of the EU to leave the territory of the EU altogether to follow his or her third country national family member. In these circumstances, the answer to the critical proportionality question under article 8 of whether family life can reasonably be expected to be enjoyed elsewhere must necessarily be *no*. We suggest also that since TFEU article 20(2)(a) protects rights of citizens of the EU to 'move and reside freely within the territory of the member states', it may also be unreasonable to expect a citizen of the EU to leave his or her country of nationality to follow a third-country national family member, even to another member state of the EU. Where the rights of a citizen of the EU under TFEU article 20 would be breached by the expulsion of a third country national, we suggest that it must also follow that the interference would not be in accordance with the law for the purposes of ECHR article 8(2).

Turkish Association Agreement cases

10.17 TFEU article 217 (formerly Treaty of the European Community (TEC) article 310) permits the EU to enter into an agreement with one or more third countries or international organisations agreements establishing an association involving reciprocal rights and obligations, common action and special procedure. After many former Association Agreement states joined the EU, the sole important remaining such Agreement is the Turkish Association Agreement signed at Ankara on 12 September 1963 and in effect since 12 December 1964 (often referred to as 'the Ankara Agreement').

10.18 It is important to note that the rights derived by Turkish workers and their legally resident family members from Decision 1/80 of the Association Council of 19 September 1980 ('Decision 1/80') may only be restricted on public policy, public security and public health grounds.[19] Thus the legal principles concerning the interpretation of the public policy, public security and public health limitations on

---

18 *Huang and Kashmiri v Secretary of State for the Home Department* [2007] UKHL 11, [2007] 2 AC 167 para 20.
19 By operation of Decision 1/80 of the Association Council of 19 September 1980 on the development of the association, articles 6(1), 7 and 14(1).

expulsion which were described at paras 9.9–9.20 above also apply to Turkish workers[20] and their family members[21] who derive rights under that instrument and are facing deportation from an EU member state.

Workers

10.19 The relevant provision for Turkish workers for these purposes is article 6 of Decision 1/80, the first paragraph of which has direct effect.[22] 'Worker' is to be interpreted in the same way as the term 'worker' in TFEU article 45 (formerly TEC article 39). 'Worker' status is not lost by temporary periods without work provided employment is found within a reasonable period[23] or by temporary incapacity to work.[24] Article 6(1) requires the worker to be 'duly registered as belonging to the labour force' but this means simply that the worker has complied with the legislation of the host state governing entry and the pursuit of employment, and does not depend on the possession of an administrative document.[25] Importantly for FNPs, a Turkish national may continue to be duly registered as belonging to the labour force notwithstanding periods of detention or imprisonment[26] unless the Turkish national 'objectively ... no longer has any chance

---

20 See for example *Nazli v Stadt Nurnberg* Case C-340/97 [2000] ECR I-957, paras 55–56; *Polat v Stadt Russelsheim* Case C-349/06 [2008] 1 CMLR 9, para 29.
21 See for example *Ergat v Stadt Ulm* Case C-329/97 [2000] ECR I-1487; *Cetinkaya v Land Baden-Wurttenberg* Case C-467/02 [2004] ECR I-10895; *Aydinli v Land Baden-Wurttemberg* Case C-373/03 [2005] 3 CMLR 43.
22 *Sevince v Staatssecretaris van Justitie* Case C-192/89 [1992] 2 CMLR 57 para 26, *Kazim Kus v Landeshauptstadt Wiesbaden* Case C-237/91 [1993] 2 CMLR 887, para 28.
23 *R(Samaroo) v Secretary of State for the Home Department* [2001] EWCA Civ 1139, [2002] INLR 55 paras 57 and 60.
24 See *Bozkurt v Staatssecretaris van Justitie* Case C-434/93 [1995] ECR I-1475, paras 29-30; *Birden v Stadtgemeinde Bremen* Case C-1/97 [1998] ECR I-7747 paras 38–39.
25 *Nazli v Stadt Nurnberg* Case C-340/97 [2000] ECR I-957, paras 31–39.
26 *Nazli v Stadt Nurnberg* Case C-340/97 [2000] ECR I-957, paras 40 to 41, concerning imprisonment on remand; *Dogan v Sicherheitsdirektion Für Das Bundesland Vorarlberg* Case C-383/03 [2005] 3 CMLR 45, paras 21–23, concerning imprisonment after conviction. However, see *R (Samaroo) v Secretary of State for the Home Department* [2001] EWCA Civ 1139, [2002] INLR 55, case of *Sezek*, paras 56–60 for an example of a case in which the Court of Appeal found that worker status was lost on commencing a lengthy period of imprisonment. We respectfully suggest that this aspect of *Sezek* may need to be revisited in light of the subsequent jurisprudence of the ECJ, for example in *Dogan*.

of rejoining the labour force or has exceeded a reasonable time-limit for finding new employment after the end of his prison term'.[27]

10.20 The 'indents' of article 6(1) provide an escalating hierarchy of rights of access to the labour market for Turkish nationals, based on their length of lawful employment. Most significantly, at the apex of that hierarchy, on completion of the fourth year of lawful employment, a Turkish national has a right of 'free access to any employment of his choice', which carries with it a concomitant right of residence.[28]

Family members

10.21 The relevant provision for family members for these purposes is article 7 of Decision 1/80, which also has direct effect.[29] Family members must have been authorised to join the Turkish worker,[30] or have been born in the EU member state[31]. The host state may insist on a period of cohabitation of the family member with the Turkish worker.[32] After three years' legal residence with the principal Turkish worker, a family member is entitled to take up paid employment, subject to priority to be given to EU national workers. After five years of legal residence with the principal Turkish worker, a family member is entitled to take up any paid employment of their choice without any need to give priority to EU national workers.[33] A concomitant independent right of residence exists for the family members of Turkish workers 'at the very least' after five years of such legal residence.[34] Once acquired under article 7 of Decision 1/80, the rights of the family member for these purposes may only be lost by a significant absence from the EU member state without legitimate

---

27 *Dogan v Sicherheitsdirektion Für Das Bundesland Vorarlberg* Case C-383/03 [2005] 3 CMLR 45, para 23.
28 *Sevince v Staatssecretaris van Justitie* Case C-192/89 [1992] 2 CMLR 57 para 29, *Dogan v Sicherheitsdirektion Für Das Bundesland Vorarlberg* Case C-383/03 [2005] 3 CMLR 45, para 14.
29 *Ergat v Stadt Ulm* Case C-329/97 [2000] ECR I-1487, para 34.
30 Decision 1/80 of the Association Council of 19 September 1980 on the development of the association, article 7.
31 *Cetinkaya v Land Baden-Wurttenberg* Case C-467/02 [2004] ECR I-10895 para 26; *Aydinli v Land Baden-Wurttemberg* Case C-373/03 [2005] 3 CMLR 43.
32 *Kadiman v Freistaat Bayern* Case C-351/95 [1997] ECR I-2133, paras 33, 37, 40, 41 and 44.
33 Decision 1/80 of the Association Council of 19 September 1980 on the development of the association, article 7, second indent.
34 *Ergat v Stadt Ulm* Case C-329/97 [2000] ECR I-1487 para 40.

reason,[35] or by operation of the public policy, public security and public health provisos. For these purposes, 'family member' status is not lost because of other changes of circumstances, for example a sentence of imprisonment[36] or where a minor child of a Turkish worker reaches adulthood.[37]

---

35 *Ergat v Stadt Ulm* Case C-329/97 [2000] ECR I-1487, paras 45–46; *Cetinkaya v Land Baden-Wurttenberg* Case C-467/02 [2004] ECR I-10895, para 36; *Aydinli v Land Baden-Wurttemberg* Case C-373/03 [2005] 3 CMLR 43, para 27.
36 *Cetinkaya v Land Baden-Wurttenberg* Case C-467/02 [2004] ECR I-10895 para 39.
37 *Ergat v Stadt Ulm* Case C-329/97 [2000] ECR I-1487, paras 26–27; *Cetinkaya v Land Baden-Wurttenberg* Case C-467/02 [2004] ECR I-10895, para 34; *Aydinli v Land Baden-Wurttemberg* Case C-373/03 [2005] 3 CMLR 43, paras 22–25.

SECTION C
'Intentional harm' grounds for resisting deportation

Chapter 11: The Refugee Convention   173

Chapter 12: Exclusion, loss of protection and cessation under the Refugee Convention   199

Chapter 13: Relying on the ECHR in claims concerning 'intentional harm'   237

Chapter 14: Article 15(c) of the Qualification Directive   253

Introduction to claims concerning 'intentional harm' on expulsion

This section concerns the legal obligations on states to provide surrogate protection for foreign nationals who, in their countries of origin or habitual residence, are at real risk of serious harm arising out of intentional acts or omissions by state or non-state agents. We refer to claims made in reliance on those obligations by the shorthand of 'intentional harm' claims, although in some instances the acts in question will not be targeted, or the harm may not be intended.

Our focus is on aspects of the law which are of specific application to foreign national prisoners and former prisoners (FNPs). We give particular attention to the circumstances in which individuals may be excluded from or lose protection under the Refugee Convention[1] by reason of their past acts or the danger they may pose to the community in the receiving state (paras 12.1–12.120).

We emphasise that our chapters on the conditions for the *grant* of protection are overviews only, forming preludes to more detailed discussions in subsequent chapters on exclusion from protection, loss of protection, and limited immigration status. In particular, for the detail of the law under the Refugee Convention and Qualification Directive, practitioners should consult specialist texts on immigration, asylum and EU law.[2]

Below, we provide a brief overview of the principal sources of law that will be referred to, before explaining the organisation of the following chapters.

Sources of law

The European Convention on Human Rights (ECHR) 1950 prohibits the expulsion of anyone to a country in which he or she will be subject to the death penalty or unlawful killing contrary to article 2 of the ECHR; torture or inhuman or degrading punishment or treatment contrary to article 3 of the ECHR; or where he or she will suffer

---

1 The 1951 Convention Relating to the Status of Refugees and its 1967 Protocol ('Refugee Convention').
2 For instance, Ian Macdonald QC and Ronan Toal, *Macdonald's immigration law and practice*, LexisNexis Butterworths, 8th edn, 2010; Mark Symes and Peter Jorro, *Asylum law and practice*, Bloomsbury Professional, 2nd edn, 2010; James Hathaway, *The law of refugee status*, Butterworths, 1991 (available at www.refugeecaselaw.org); Guy Goodwin Gill, *The refugee in international law*, OUP, 2007.

flagrant breaches of other ECHR rights. The protections afforded by articles 2 and 3 are absolute: they prohibit the expulsion of an individual to a country where he or she is at real risk of serious harm regardless of the individual's past acts or the danger posed by the individual to the community of the receiving state.

The Refugee Convention (1951 Convention Relating to the Status of Refugees[3] and its 1967 Protocol[4]) is the foundation of modern refugee law.

The Refugee Convention defines who is a refugee, affords general protection against expulsion to those who satisfy the refugee definition (known as the prohibition of refoulement) and also requires signatory states to confer other important rights and benefits on refugees. In certain circumstances, those who have themselves committed egregious past acts may be excluded from Refugee Convention protection altogether; and those who have been convicted of particularly serious crimes and who pose a danger to the community of the receiving state may, even if recognised as refugees, lose protection from refoulement.

On 20 April 2004, the EU adopted the Qualification Directive, the full title of which is Council Directive 2004/83/EC on minimum standards for the qualification and status of third country nationals or stateless persons as refugees or as persons who otherwise need international protection and the content of the protection granted. The Qualification Directive provides a legal framework for protecting migrants against expulsion to conditions of ill-treatment, based largely on, but also supplementing, the provisions of the Refugee Convention and the ECHR. The Qualification Directive confers a protection on those at real risk of indiscriminate violence in armed conflict (article 15(c) of the Qualification Directive) which is not afforded by the Refugee Convention. The Qualification Directive also stipulates the circumstances in which individuals may be excluded from certain forms of immigration status by reason of their past acts.

The UK has partially incorporated the Refugee Convention into domestic law, as we discuss at paras 11.18–11.23. Parliament has also attempted to impose, through primary legislation, certain interpretations on aspects of the Refugee Convention.[5] The UK has also incorporated much of the ECHR into domestic law through the

---

3 Commonly also known as the Geneva Convention because it was formally adopted there on 28 July 1951.
4 The convention and protocol are referred to in this book together as 'the Refugee Convention', in line with common practice among practitioners.
5 See paras 12.52–12.54 and 12.84–12.87.

Human Rights Act (HRA) 1998 and has also sought to transpose the Qualification Directive in domestic law by a combination of secondary legislation and Immigration Rules. As we explain at para 11.12, at least parts of the Qualification Directive are in any event directly effective and must be followed if there is any conflict with domestic law. Primary legislation, immigration rules and Home Office policy also define the circumstances in which a person who cannot be removed from the UK because of the UK's legal obligations will be subject to restrictions on his or her immigration status because of his or her past acts.

Finally, as we shall see in the coming chapters, Home Office policy on international protection, which is largely contained in the Asylum Policy Instructions (APIs), attempts to give guidance and also sets down certain safeguards supplementing those expressly contained in law. Home Office policy documents not infrequently offer incorrect guidance, and must be treated with caution as statements of the law.

Organisation of this section

Chapter 11 summarises the circumstances in which Refugee Convention protection will be granted, and relevant related provisions in the Qualification Directive. This is a prelude to the fuller discussion in chapter 12 of the circumstances in which individuals are excluded from or lose Refugee Convention protection, or, although refugees, will lose protection from refoulement.

Chapter 13 provides a brief overview of ECHR article 3 in the context of what we call 'intentional harm' claims. We deal separately at paras 18.6–18.52 with article 3 claims concerning the adverse effects to mental and physical health that may be caused by expulsion.

Chapter 14 briefly addresses the additional protection provided to certain victims of armed conflict by article 15(c) of the Qualification Directive.

Later in this book, in chapter 19, we will consider the different forms of immigration status available to those whose expulsion is barred by the ECHR or Qualification Directive, and the differential status that may be granted as a consequence of a person's past misconduct.

CHAPTER 11
The Refugee Convention

11.1	Introduction
11.4	A very brief history of the Refugee Convention
11.6	A very brief overview of the contents of the Refugee Convention
11.7	The UNHCR
11.10	The Qualification Directive and its relationship with the Refugee Convention
11.13	Measures aiming to transpose the Qualification Directive in domestic law
11.18	The partial incorporation of the Refugee Convention in domestic law
11.24	**Recognition as a refugee**
11.25	Domestic procedures
11.28	Grants of leave consequent on recognition as a refugee
11.35	**The refugee definition**
11.36	The elements of the refugee definition
	'Fear' • Protection rooted in future risk • 'Well-founded' • Refugees 'sur place' • 'Persecution' • Convention reasons for persecution • 'Outside country of his nationality'
11.61	The refugee definition and criminal conduct
	Prosecution and persecution • Military service

continued

11.68 The date at which refugee status is to be assessed
11.70 Burden and standard of proof
11.76 The duty of non-refoulement

Introduction

11.1 This chapter focuses on the contents and meaning of the Refugee Convention,[1] and on related provisions in the Qualification Directive[2] and domestic law.

11.2 A detailed analysis of the Refugee Convention lies outside the scope of this book. What follows is necessarily only an introduction to the main issues arising in the assessment of asylum claims. It serves as a prelude to our discussion in chapter 12 of exclusion and protection issues which are of more specific application to FNPs.

11.3 In this chapter, we first consider, briefly, the history and the contents of the Refugee Convention, then turn to the relationship between the Refugee Convention and the Qualification Directive. We look at the definition of key terms and concepts in the Refugee Convention, give an overview of the process of assessing future risk and finally consider the prohibition on refoulement which forms one of the central pillars of the Refugee Convention.

A very brief history of the Refugee Convention

11.4 As the key European instrument on protection, the Qualification Directive, recognises in its preamble, the Refugee Convention provides the 'cornerstone of the international legal regime for the protection of refugees'.[3]

11.5 The Refugee Convention adopted by a Conference of the United Nations on 28 July 1951 and came into force on 22 April 1954. At that time, it applied only to individuals whose fear of persecution was the result of events occurring before 1 January 1951. This reflected the Refugee Convention's historical origins as an international response to the persecution and displacement of people in the Second World War. The Protocol relating to the Status of Refugees, which came into force on 4 October 1967, removed the requirement that the relevant

---

1 Its full title is the 1951 Convention Relating to the Status of Refugees. It is sometimes – although not in this book – referred to as the 'United Nations Refugee Convention' or the '1951 Convention', while the Qualification Directive refers to it as the 'Geneva Convention'.
2 Council Directive 2004/83/EC on minimum standards for the qualification and status of third country nationals or stateless persons as refugees or as persons who otherwise need international protection and the content of the protection granted.
3 Third recital.

events had to have occurred before 1 January 1951.[4] In this way, the Refugee Convention covers modern instances of persecution and may evolve still further:

> It is clear that the signatory states intended that the Convention should afford continuing protection for refugees in the changing circumstances of the present and future world. In our view the Convention has to be regarded as a living instrument: just as, by the Strasbourg jurisprudence, the European Convention on Human Rights is so regarded.[5]

A very brief overview of the contents of the Refugee Convention

11.6 The Refugee Convention defines who is a refugee,[6] lays down a general duty on states not to expel refugees to countries in which they will be persecuted[7] and stipulates minimum standards for the treatment of refugees in host countries. These minimum standards relate to matters such as the practice of religion, employment rights, housing, education and various other benefits and entitlements.[8] It follows that, if a person is recognised as a refugee, he or she gains not only protection from expulsion but also a positive civil status which in turn can be viewed as part of the states parties' obligations to facilitate the assimilation and naturalisation of refugees under article 34 of the Refugee Convention.

The UNHCR

11.7 In 1951, the United Nations set up the Office of the UN High Commissioner for Refugees (UNHCR).[9] The organisation has responsibility within the structure of the UN for providing refugees with protection

---

4 In common with general usage by the courts, practitioners and the Home Office, references here to the Refugee Convention are to the convention as amended by the protocol.
5 *R v Secretary of State for the Home Department ex p Adan* [2001] 2 AC 477, 500G-H; cited with approval in *Sepet v Secretary of State for the Home Department* [2003] UKHL 15, [2003] 1 WLR 856 at 6.
6 Article 1.
7 Article 33.
8 Articles 2–31; see *Saad, Diriye and Osorio v Secretary of State for the Home Department* [2001] EWCA Civ 2008
9 General Assembly Resolution 319(IV): Provisions for the functioning of the High Commissioner's Office for Refugees; available at www.unhcr.org.

and facilitating their voluntary repatriation or their assimilation in their new host country. UNHCR is entitled to have access to all asylum applicants in the UK and to information on individual applications for asylum, and to present its views to the Secretary of State for the Home Department (SSHD) on individual asylum applications at any stage of the procedure.[10]

11.8 UNHCR has published a 'Handbook on Procedures and Criteria for Determining Refugee Status under the 1951 Convention and the 1967 Protocol relating to the Status of Refugees' (the 'UNHCR Handbook').[11] The Handbook provides authoritative guidance on the application of the convention but does not have the status of binding law. The higher courts have on numerous occasions cited passages of the Handbook with approval.[12]

11.9 UNHCR also publishes guidelines intended to assist decision-makers and others who interpret the convention.[13] UNHCR policy documents set out the organisation's views on particular aspects of refugee status determination. In addition, the Executive Committee of the High Commissioner's Programme (ExCom) publishes its 'Conclusions' on issues relating to the protection of refugees.[14]

The Qualification Directive and its relationship with the Refugee Convention

11.10 Title V of the Treaty on the Functioning of the European Union (TFEU) establishes the EU as an area of freedom, security and justice.[15] The TFEU is the successor of the Treaty Establishing the

---

10 Immigration Rules HC 395 para 358C.
11 HCR/IP/4/Eng/REV.1; re-edited, Geneva, January 1992, UNHCR 1979; available at www.unhcr.org.
12 See, for instance, *Januzi v Secretary of State for the Home Department* [2006] UKHL 5, [2006] 2 AC 426; *R (European Roma Rights Centre) v Immigration Officer at Prague Airport* [2004] UKHL 55, [2005] 2 AC 1 at 16; *Sepet v Secretary of State for the Home Department* [2003] UKHL 15, [2003] 1 WLR 856; although see *Sivakumaran v Secretary of State for the Home Department* [1988] AC 958 at 999–1000 for an example of a case where the Handbook was not followed.
13 Also often quoted with approval by the courts and tribunal, as in *In re B; R v Special Adjudicator ex p Hoxha* [2005] UKHL 19; but see *KK (Article 1F(c) Turkey)* [2004] UKIAT 00101 for a case where UNHCR guidance was rejected.
14 They are conveniently found on UNHCR's website: www.unhcr.org.
15 For a history of asylum provisions in European law, see E Guild 'The Europeanisation of Europe's Asylum Policy' 18 IJRL (2006) 630.

European Community (TEEC) as amended by the Lisbon Treaty.[16] The TFEU includes provisions on border checks, asylum and immigration. Under the TFEU article 78, the EU will develop a common policy on asylum, subsidiary protection and temporary protection. Prior to the TFEU, the member states of the EU had already formulated a common policy on significant areas of asylum law. Article 78(1) of the TFEU succeeds article 63(1) of the TEEC which made provision for the Council of the European Community to adopt various measures on asylum including minimum standards with respect to the qualification of third country nationals as refugees.

11.11 Among the measures adopted under article 63 was the Qualification Directive. The minimum standards contained in the Directive should 'guide the competent national bodies of member states in the application of the Geneva Convention'[17] and do not prevent member states from introducing or retaining more favourable standards provided that these are compatible with the Qualification Directive.[18] In *Bundesrepublik Deutschland v B and D*[19] the Grand Chamber of the Court of Justice of the European Union (CJEU) explained that this meant that member states were not entitled to grant refugee status under the Qualification Directive to those excluded by article 12 of that Directive, but were entitled to grant a different form of protection under domestic law. The Grand Chamber of the CJEU appeared to indicate that two forms of refugee status might co-exist, one under the Qualification Directive, and, potentially, another more generous one under domestic law. Consistently with that approach, the House of Lords has suggested, in strong terms, that the Qualification Directive cannot detract from the scope of protection afforded by the Refugee Convention.[20]

11.12 At least parts of the Qualification Directive are directly effective under principles of EU law.[21] It provides definitions of some of the

---

16 The Lisbon Treaty was signed on 13 December 2007 and entered into force on 1 December 2009.
17 Qualification Directive preamble, sixteenth recital.
18 Qualification Directive article 3.
19 Joined Cases C-57/09 and C-101/09 [2011] Imm AR 190, [2011] INLR 133.
20 See *Secretary of State for the Home Department v K; Fornah v Secretary of State for the Home Department* [2006] UKHL 46, [2007] 1 AC 412 at para 118 (per Lord Brown, the Qualification Directive and any regulations brought into force under it would have to be interpreted consistently with the UNHCR definition of 'particular social group').
21 *EN (Serbia) v Secretary of State for the Home Department* [2009] EWCA Civ 630, [2010] QB 633, para 62.

principal concepts of international refugee law[22] as well as setting down (in article 4) minimum standards for the assessment of the facts of an asylum application, which have been transposed into English law by amendments to the Immigration Rules.[23] It also contains criteria for subsidiary protection (known as humanitarian protection in the UK), which provides for those who do not meet the Refugee Convention criteria but would be at risk of serious abuses of human rights if returned:[24] see further chapter 19.

Measures aiming to transpose the Qualification Directive in domestic law

11.13 The UK Government introduced measures aimed at transposing the Qualification Directive into English law, where equivalent provision was not already made. First, the Immigration Rules were amended.[25] (The legal status of the Immigration Rules has been discussed at paras 3.15–3.17). Second, delegated legislation, the Refugee or Person in Need of International Protection (Qualification) Regulations (RPNIP Regs) 2006[26] were brought into force.

11.14 In applying national law, a national court must interpret it, as far as possible, in the light of the wording and purpose of any relevant EU directive, whether the national law originated before or after adoption of the directive.[27] Where the domestic measures – the Immigration Rules and the RPNIP Regs 2006 – fail properly to transpose the Qualification Directive, the directive must prevail.

11.15 The Immigration Rules stipulate that every person has the right to apply for asylum.[28] Nor will a person be removed from the UK while his or her asylum application is pending.[29] However, not all those who claim asylum in the UK will have their applications examined substantively under the Refugee Convention, because of provisions

22 Qualification Directive articles 5–12.
23 Immigration Rules HC 395 paras 339I, 339J, 339K and 339L; the Immigration Rules are, in essence, rules of practice laid before parliament by the SSHD under Immigration Act (IA) 1971 s3(2) for purposes of implementing the SSHD's powers to regulate the entry into and stay in the UK of foreign nationals.
24 Articles 15–18.
25 Cm 6918, laid before parliament on 18 September 2006.
26 SI No 2170.
27 *Marleasing SA v La Comercial Internacional de Alimentación SA* Case C-106/89 [1990] ECR I-4135, [1992] 1 CMLR 305, para 8.
28 HC 395 para 327A.
29 Nationality, Immigration and Asylum Act (NIAA) 2002 s77; HC 395 para 329.

within the so-called Dublin Regulation,[30] which provides a framework for determining which of the EU member states has responsibility for deciding any particular asylum application. This provision is highly unlikely to affect any FNP and is therefore dealt with only very briefly at paras 22.10–22.13.

11.16 Through the Immigration Rules and the RPNIP Regs 2006, the principles of the Refugee Convention are applied to all asylum claims determined substantively in the UK. Parts 11 and 11B of the Immigration Rules deal with asylum applications.

11.17 In particular, paragraph 334 deals with the grant of asylum and states that an asylum applicant will be granted asylum if SSHD is satisfied that:

- the applicant is in the UK or has arrived at a port of entry in the UK;[31]
- the applicant is a refugee, as defined in reg 2 of the RPNIP Regs 2006;[32]
- there are no reasonable grounds for regarding him as a danger to the security of the UK;[33]
- having been convicted by a final judgment of a particularly serious crime, the applicant does not constitute a danger to the community of the UK;[34] and
- refusing the application would result in the applicant being required to go (whether immediately or after the time limited by any existing leave to enter or remain) in breach of the Refugee Convention, to a country in which his or her life or freedom would threatened on account of his or her race, religion, nationality, political opinion or membership of a particular social group.[35]

---

30 Council Regulation (EC) 343/2003 of 18 February 2003 establishing the criteria and mechanisms for determining the member state responsible for examining an asylum application lodged in one of the member states by a third-country national (OJ L 50, 25 February 2003, p1).
31 Immigration Rules para 334(i), reflecting Qualification Directive articles 2(c) and 13.
32 Immigration Rules para 334(ii); RPNIP Regs 2006 reg 2 itself effectively applies the definition in the Refugee Convention, dealt with below; and see Qualification Directive article 2(c).
33 Immigration Rules para 334(iii); Qualification Directive article 14(4)(a).
34 Immigration Rules para 334(iv); Qualification Directive article 14(4)(b); this and the previous provision reflect Refugee Convention article 33(2), which is dealt with at paras 12.78–12.83.
35 Immigration Rules para 334(v), reflecting Refugee Convention articles 1A and 33(1) and Qualification Directive article 2(c).

The partial incorporation of the Refugee Convention in domestic law

11.18 Quite apart from the Qualification Directive, and long before its adoption, the UK had taken measures which partially incorporate the Refugee Convention in domestic law.

11.19 All the terms and concepts contained in paragraph 334 and elsewhere in the Immigration Rules on asylum must be interpreted consistently with the Refugee Convention and its jurisprudence. This consequence flows from Asylum and Immigration Appeals Act (AIAA) 1993 s2 which states:

> Nothing in the immigration rules ... shall lay down any practice which would be contrary to the Convention.[36]

11.20 It was said in *Sivakumaran*[37] that the provisions of the Refugee Convention have 'for all practical purposes been incorporated into United Kingdom law'.

11.21 Despite this, however, the Refugee Convention has not been formally incorporated into UK law. In *Asfaw*[38] it was said by Lord Bingham, after referring to *Sivakumaran* and to *Roma Rights Centre*:[39]

> It is plain from these authorities that the British regime for handling applications for asylum has been closely assimilated to the Convention model. But it is also plain (as I think) that the Convention as a whole has never been formally incorporated or given effect in domestic law.

11.22 In *EN (Serbia)*[40] Stanley Burnton LJ said: 'I fully accept that the Refugee Convention has been incorporated into our law for some purposes', one of those purposes being that it 'defines a claim for asylum under our law'. But he noted that AIAA 1993 s2 does not go as far as giving the Refugee Convention 'the force of statute for all purposes'.

11.23 Accordingly, although it is not permissible for administrative arrangements to be made contrary to the Refugee Convention,[41] it

---

36 See also HC 395 para 328: 'All asylum applications will be determined by the Secretary of State in accordance with the Geneva Convention.'
37 *R v Secretary of State for the Home Department ex p Sivakumaran* [1988] AC 958 at 990.
38 *R v Asfaw* [2008] 1 AC 1061.
39 *R (European Roma Rights Centre) v Immigration Officer at Prague Airport* [2005] 2 AC 1.
40 *EN (Serbia) v Secretary of State for the Home Department* [2009] EWCA Civ 630; [2010] QB 633 para 59.
41 *R (European Roma Rights Centre) v Immigration Officer at Prague Airport* [2005] 2 AC 1 para 41.

was, prior to the adoption of the Qualification Directive, in theory possible for parliament to legislate contrary to it.[42] Now, however, that is subject to the UK's obligations to comply with and implement EU law, including the Qualification Directive, which itself confers rights on refugees.

Recognition as a refugee

11.24 A person is a refugee as soon as he or she fulfils the refugee definition, and therefore the grant of refugee status recognises that a person is a refugee, rather than bestowing a new status.[43]

Domestic procedures

11.25 A person who claims asylum in the UK will undergo the Home Office's procedures for refugee status determination. If successful, he or she will be recognised as a refugee.

11.26 The Home Office generally requires applicants for asylum who have already entered the UK to attend at the Asylum Screening Unit (ASU) in Croydon.[44] They are then interviewed to establish their identity, their route to the UK and the basic facts of their asylum claims. At a later date, they are interviewed substantively about their claim[45] and given an opportunity – usually limited in time – to submit evidence in support of their claims before a decision is made. (Issues of evidence are dealt with in chapter 20.)

11.27 FNPs who are detained may claim asylum to an immigration officer,[46] or may do so in a written statement of additional grounds served on the SSHD under NIAA 2002 s120,[47] or as part of their grounds of appeal against a decision to deport or remove them from the UK[48] (see chapter 21 for the appeals process).

42 *EN (Serbia) v Secretary of State for the Home Department* [2009] EWCA Civ 630, [2010] QB 633 para 60.
43 UNHCR Handbook para 28; Qualification Directive, fourteenth recital; *In re B; R v Special Adjudicator ex p Hoxha* [2005] UKHL 19.
44 Asylum Policy Instructions (API) on Handling Claims.
45 Immigration Rules paras 339NA–339ND.
46 See, for example, API on Handling Claims, sections headed 'After entry cases' and 'Port cases'; compare Home Office Enforcement Instructions and Guidance chapter 23 paras 23.1–23.2.
47 Compare *AS (Afghanistan) v Secretary of State for the Home Department* [2009] EWCA Civ 1076.
48 NIAA 2002 ss82, 84–86.

Grants of leave consequent on recognition as a refugee

11.28 Until 30 August 2005, those recognised as refugees were normally granted indefinite leave to remain (ILR), ie permanent residency. In the UK, those recognised as refugees are now normally issued with a residence permit valid for five years, after which the refugee may apply for ILR.[49] However, there is scope for a grant of a longer period of leave, including an immediate grant of ILR, in exceptional cases, for those who are vulnerable and are assessed to have special needs, for instance those whose mental health would be adversely affected by a grant of limited leave rather than indefinite leave.[50]

11.29 If, of course, an FNP with ILR appeals against deportation on asylum grounds and succeeds, the position will remain as before (ie the FNP will retain ILR) unless the ILR is revoked. Revocation of ILR is dealt with at paras 12.130–12.133 and 19.66–19.75. However, once a valid deportation order has been served, if it is subsequently revoked then any previously held ILR is not automatically reinstated.[51]

11.30 Those recognised as refugees are entitled under the Qualification Directive to a number of benefits other than status itself, including the right to work[52] and undertake vocational training,[53] access to education,[54] access to welfare benefits[55] and healthcare,[56] freedom of movement within the member state[57] and access to integration facilities.[58] They are entitled to be granted a refugee travel document.[59]

11.31 States are also obliged to respect the principle of family unity for refugees.[60] UK practice is that family members of refugees who are already in the UK are granted residence permits in line with those granted to refugees, ie for five years and renewable.[61] Those abroad

---

49 HC 395 para 339Q(i); Home Office API on Refugee Leave.
50 Home Office API on Refugee Leave para 2.2, referring to Qualification Directive article 24; see *R (Thanigaikumaran) v Secretary of State for the Home Department* [2011] EWHC 1701 (Admin).
51 *R (Fitzroy George) v Secretary of State for the Home Department* [2011] EWHC 3247 (Admin).
52 Qualification Directive article 26(1); Immigration Rules para 344B.
53 Qualification Directive article 26(2).
54 Qualification Directive article 27.
55 Qualification Directive article 28.
56 Qualification Directive article 29.
57 Qualification Directive article 32.
58 Qualification Directive article 33.
59 Qualification Directive article 25; Refugee Convention article 28 and Schedule.
60 Qualification Directive article 23; UNHCR Handbook chapter VI and annex I.
61 Immigration Rules para 339Q(iii).

are entitled to apply for entry clearance to join the refugee, in particular spouses and civil partners where the marriage or civil partnership took place before the refugee left to seek asylum,[62] unmarried or same-sex partners who have been in a relationship for more than two years,[63] and children under the age of 18 who have not married or formed an independent life.[64] There is no requirement in these cases to show that the family member will be maintained and accommodated without recourse to public funds. In each case, the relative must show that they would not be excluded under article 1F of the Refugee Convention if they were to seek asylum themselves.

11.32 The Qualification Directive leaves it open to member states to decide whether to extend the principle of family unity to dependants other than spouses, partners and children,[65] and the domestic Immigration Rules do cater for this, but only where the dependant in question can be maintained and accommodated without recourse to public funds.[66]

11.33 Refugees may be joined by a spouse or partner where the relationship post-dates the refugee's departure for the UK, but only if they meet the requirements of the Immigration Rules applicable to those with ILR, which also include a requirement to show the availability of maintenance and accommodation and sufficient knowledge of English.[67] The contents of these provisions lie outside the scope of this book.

11.34 Chapter 19 looks at the benefits attaching to other forms of status, including humanitarian protection and discretionary leave, and compares them to those described above.

The refugee definition

11.35 The Refugee Convention lays down the definition of a refugee as being a person who:

> ... owing to well-founded fear of being persecuted for reasons of race, religion, nationality, membership of a particular social group or

---

62 Immigration Rules para 352A.
63 Immigration Rules para 352AA.
64 Immigration Rules para 352D.
65 Qualification Directive article 23(5).
66 Immigration Rules para 319X for a minor child who is not the child of the refugee; para 319V for a parent, grandparent or other close relative over the age of 18.
67 Immigration Rules para 319L onwards.

political opinion, is outside the country of his nationality and is unable or, owing to such fear, is unwilling to avail himself of the protection of that country; or who, not having a nationality and being outside the country of his former habitual residence as a result of such events, is unable or, owing to such fear, is unwilling to return to it.[68]

The elements of the refugee definition

11.36 Below, we give a brief outline of the principal concepts of the Refugee Convention as they are generally interpreted by the UK's courts.[69]

'Fear'

11.37 A refugee must, fundamentally, have a fear of being persecuted. A number of important issues arise from that simple requirement. A fear is necessarily forward-looking, and although it may – and is most likely to – stem from things which have happened in the past, it is neither necessary nor sufficient, for purposes of the refugee definition, that a person should have been persecuted in the past. However, that fear must be a well-founded one: that is to say, it must be a fear which is rooted in verifiable fact, as assessed not simply by the applicant but by an objective decision-maker. These concepts will now be explored in more detail below.

Protection rooted in future risk

11.38 A refugee must be at real risk of harm *in the future*. The Refugee Convention protects persons at risk of future persecution, whether or not they have suffered persecution in the past. Past persecution is likely to be a good indicator of the risk of future persecution,[70] but a person who is no longer at risk of ill treatment does not qualify for refugee status[71] (although, as we see in chapter 18, a person who is mentally ill as a consequence of past ill treatment may have a viable claim under the ECHR).

---

68 Refugee Convention article 1A.
69 The introduction to this section, at note 2, lists some of the leading academic works on refugee law.
70 Qualification Directive article 4(4); Immigration Rules para 339K.
71 UNHCR Handbook para 45; *Adan v Secretary of State for the Home Department* [1999] 1 AC 293.

'Well-founded'

11.39 The fear of persecution must be 'well-founded': it must be rooted in objective reality and does not depend on the perceptions of the applicant, however reasonable they might be.[72] Decision-makers should consider all available information which may bear on how a claimant may be treated if returned to his or her country.[73]

Refugees 'sur place'

11.40 The refugee's fear need not have arisen before he or she left the country of origin and a person need not have left with an intention to claim asylum abroad. A person may become a refugee while abroad due to changed circumstances in the country of origin. For example, a person may become wanted for prosecution while he or she is abroad, or may be imputed with hostile political opinions by attending political events or participating in political activities while abroad.[74] Such a person is known as a refugee 'sur place'.[75]

11.41 UK domestic law holds that where a person is at real risk of persecution for a convention reason owing to post-flight activities, he or she is a refugee even if those activities were engaged in purely for self-serving reasons to bolster a refugee claim.[76]

11.42 Even the fact of making an asylum claim may, in principle, found refugee status if the country of origin were to perceive that fact as a politically hostile act placing the refugee at real risk of persecution on return.[77]

---

72 *Sivakumaran v Secretary of State for the Home Department* [1988] AC 958.
73 Qualification Directive article 4.
74 Compare *BA (Demonstrators in Britain – risk on return) Iran CG* [2011] UKUT 36 (IAC), *TL and Others (sur place activities – risk) Burma CG* [2009] UKAIT 00017.
75 UNHCR Handbook paras 94–96; Immigration Rules HC 395 para 339P reflecting Qualification Directive article 5(1)–(2).
76 *Danian v Secretary of State for the Home Department* [2000] Imm AR 96. Qualification Directive article 5(3) suggests that states are entitled (but not required) to deny refugee status in these circumstances. As we discussed above at para 11.11, the autonomous meaning of the Refugee Convention must prevail over any lesser protection afforded by the Qualification Directive. The UK has (rightly we suggest, in the light of the terms of the Refugee Convention) chosen not to take the option offered at Qualification Directive article 5(3) and has not transposed this provision into domestic law. Otherwise, it has not been implemented by the UK and is in any event to be interpreted without prejudice to the Refugee Convention.
77 *R v Secretary of State for the Home Department ex p Mbanza* [1996] Imm AR 136.

11.43 A person who has broken his or her country's laws by departing it illegally or by staying outside it illegally (for example, by exceeding an exit permit) may be a refugee if the authorities impute the illegal activity to the person's political opinion and take hostile action against the person on that basis.[78]

'Persecution'

11.44 The UNHCR Handbook confirms that there is 'no universally accepted definition' of persecution. In the 1985 case of *Jonah*, it was held that 'persecuted' should be given its dictionary definition of 'subjected to injurious action or oppression'.[79] However, although this remains a valid starting point, in order to constitute persecution, the action or oppression must involve a certain minimum level of severity. In *Islam and Shah* Lord Hoffmann approved the formulation 'Persecution = Serious Harm + The Failure of State Protection',[80] and 'serious harm' is often used as a shorthand for what is required.

11.45 In *HJ and HT*, Lord Hope said:

> To constitute persecution for the purposes of the Convention the harm must be state sponsored or state condoned. Family or social disapproval in which the state has no part lies outside its protection. As Professor James C Hathaway in The Law of Refugee Status (1991), p 112 has explained, 'persecution is most appropriately defined as the sustained or systemic failure of state protection in relation to one of the core entitlements which has been recognised by the international community'.[81]

11.46 Article 9 of the Qualification Directive (reflected in RPNIP Regs 2006 reg 5) attempts a more detailed, but still non-exhaustive, definition:

> Acts of persecution
> 1. Acts of persecution within the meaning of article 1A of the Geneva Convention must:
>   (a) be sufficiently serious by their nature or repetition as to constitute a severe violation of basic human rights, in particular the rights from which derogation cannot be made under Article

---

78 UNHCR Handbook para 61; *OM (Cuba) v Secretary of State for the Home Department* [2004] UKIAT 00120.
79 *R v IAT ex p Jonah* [1985] Imm AR 7.
80 *Islam v Secretary of State for the Home Department; R v Immigration Appeal Tribunal ex p Shah* [1999] 2 AC 629, at 653; Lord Hoffmann derived this from the Gender guidelines for the determination of asylum claims in the UK, Refugee Women's Legal Group, July 1998.
81 *HJ (Iran) and HT (Cameroon) v Secretary of State for the Home Department* [2010] UKSC 31, [2010] 3 WLR 386 para 13.

15(2) of the European Convention for the Protection of Human Rights and Fundamental Freedoms;[82] or
   (b) be an accumulation of various measures, including violations of human rights which is sufficiently severe as to affect an individual in a similar manner as mentioned in (a).
2. Acts of persecution as qualified in paragraph 1, can, inter alia, take the form of:
   (a) acts of physical or mental violence, including acts of sexual violence;
   (b) legal, administrative, police, and/or judicial measures which are in themselves discriminatory or which are implemented in a discriminatory manner;
   (c) prosecution or punishment, which is disproportionate or discriminatory;
   (d) denial of judicial redress resulting in a disproportionate or discriminatory punishment;
   (e) prosecution or punishment for refusal to perform military service in a conflict, where performing military service would include crimes or acts falling under the exclusion clauses as set out in Article 12(2);
   (f) acts of a gender-specific or child-specific nature.

Agents (or actors) of persecution

11.47 Although persecution is often carried out by the state authorities, it may also be carried out by parties or organisations controlling the state or a substantial part of the territory of the state, or by 'non-state actors' (sometimes referred to as 'non-state agents').[83]

Sufficiency of protection

11.48 A fundamental principle of refugee law is 'the principle of surrogacy':

> The general purpose of the Convention is to enable the person who no longer has the benefit of protection against persecution for a Convention reason in his own country to turn for protection to the international community.[84]

11.49 Qualification Directive article 7 (reflected by RPNIP Regs 2006 reg 4) also defines those who can provide such protection: 'actors of protection' include the state and any party or organisation (including any international organisation) controlling the state or a substantial part of the state's territory. Protection is to be regarded as generally provided when such actors 'take reasonable steps to prevent the

---

82 These are ECHR articles 2, 3, 4(1) and 7 (footnote added).
83 Qualification Directive article 6.
84 *Horvath v Secretary of State for the Home Department* [2001] 1 AC 489 at 495.

persecution or suffering of serious harm by operating an effective legal system for the detection, prosecution and punishment' of acts of ill treatment. Whether *any* organisation controlling the territory of the state can be capable of providing protection is a matter of some controversy, however: in *Gardi* it was suggested by the Court of Appeal that 'the protection has to be that of an entity which is capable of granting nationality to a person in a form recognised internationally' and/or that 'protection can only be provided by an entity capable of being held responsible under international law'.[85] It may be that the Qualification Directive cannot be interpreted as watering down that principle.[86]

Internal relocation

11.50 Refugee status may be denied if a person has the option of relocating to another part of his or her country of origin (commonly known as the internal flight alternative or internal relocation).[87] The test is not only that the person should not have a well-founded fear of persecution in part of the country but also that he or she can reasonably be expected to stay there. The decision-maker must consider both the general circumstances prevailing in that part of the country and also the personal circumstances of the asylum applicant.[88] If it would be unduly harsh – or unreasonable – for a person to relocate, he or she must be recognised as a refugee.[89]

Convention reasons for persecution

11.51 A refugee's fear of persecution must be 'for reasons of race, religion, nationality, membership of a political social group or political opinion'. As expressed in *Islam and Shah*, the Refugee Convention

> ... is concerned not with all cases of persecution, even if they involve denials of human rights, but with persecution which is based on discrimination. And in the context of a human rights instrument, discrimination means making distinctions which principles of

---

85 See also *R (Vallaj) v Special Adjudicator* [2001] EWCA Civ 782, [2001] INLR 342.
86 See *K and Fornah v Secretary of State for the Home Department* [2007] 1 AC 412.
87 *R v Secretary of State for the Home Department ex p Robinson* [1998] QB 929; *Januzi v Secretary of State for the Home Department* [2006] UKHL 5, [2006] 2 AC 426; *AH (Sudan) v Secretary of State for the Home Department* [2007] UKHL 49, [2008] 1 AC 678.
88 HC 395 para 339O reflecting Qualification Directive article 8.
89 *Januzi v Secretary of State for the Home Department* [2006] UKHL 5, [2006] 2 AC 426.

fundamental human rights regard as inconsistent with the right of every human being to equal treatment and respect.[90]

11.52 A person will not qualify for refugee status unless he or she fears persecution for a reason stipulated by the Refugee Convention.[91] Victims of generalised warfare, economic collapse or natural disasters will not qualify for refugee status[92] (although they may now be able to qualify under ECHR article 3 or Qualification Directive article 15(c), see paras 13.6–13.41 and chapter 14 respectively).

11.53 The words 'for reasons of' imply only a broad linkage between the convention reason and the feared persecution. In *K and Fornah* Lord Bingham said:

> The ground on which the claimant relies need not be the only or even the primary reason for the apprehended persecution. It is enough that the ground relied on is an effective reason. The persecutory treatment need not be motivated by enmity, malignity or animus on the part of the persecutor, whose professed or apparent motives may or may not be the real reason for the persecution. What matters is the real reason.[93]

11.54 The Qualification Directive and RPNIP Regs 2006 reflect this principle. By Qualification Directive article 9(3), there must simply be 'a connection between' a convention reason and the acts of persecution.

11.55 The Qualification Directive also gives examples of what is included within the scope of each Refugee Convention reason. On the whole, the examples reflect existing English case-law and in some instances bring welcome clarity. Thus, it is now clear that religion as a convention reason includes abstention from religious acts and also the holding of non-theistic and atheistic beliefs.[94]

11.56 It has long been established that a person need not hold a political opinion to qualify for refugee status and that it is sufficient that the persecutors attribute or impute a political opinion to him or her.[95]

---

90 *Islam v Secretary of State for the Home Department; R v Immigration Appeal Tribunal ex p Shah* [1999] 2 AC 629 at 651A–B.
91 See, for example, *Islam v Secretary of State for the Home Department; R v IAT ex p Shah* [1999] 2 AC 629.
92 *Adan v Secretary of State for the Home Department* [1999] 1 AC 293.
93 *Secretary of State for the Home Department v K; Fornah v Secretary of State for the Home Department* [2006] UKHL 46, [2007] 1 AC 412; see also J Hathaway and M Foster 'The causal connection ("nexus") to a convention ground' 15 IJRL (2003) 461.
94 Qualification Directive article 10(1)(b).
95 *R (Sivakumar) v Secretary of State for the Home Department* [2001] EWCA Civ 1196, [2002] INLR 310; *Storozhenko v Secretary of State for the Home Department* [2001] EWCA Civ 895, [2002] Imm AR 329.

The Qualification Directive now clarifies that the persecutor's attribution of a characteristic to a person falls within the definition of all five of the convention reasons and is not limited to political opinion.[96]

11.57 The five Refugee Convention grounds are interpreted by Professor Hathaway and others so as to include in the class of refugees those who are persecuted because of their civil or political status. On this interpretation, refugees include persons who are persecuted on account of essential characteristics relating to who an individual is or what he or she believes.[97]

11.58 In *Islam and Shah*,[98] the House of Lords considered the meaning of 'a particular social group'[99] and held that the five convention reasons relate to 'immutable' characteristics which are either beyond the power of an individual to change or are so fundamental to identity or conscience that an individual ought not to be required to change them. It is also now clear that those persecuted for reason of sexual orientation may constitute part of a particular social group.[100] A family may be a particular social group in certain circumstances,[101] and, despite attempts by the tribunal and the courts to find to the contrary, it may even be the case that if family members of an individual are at risk of persecution, their association with the individual will constitute a Refugee Convention reason, even if the individual himself or herself is not being persecuted for a convention reason.[102]

Modifying behaviour

11.59 Decisions of the courts and tribunals were for a long time predicated on the notion that applicants could be denied refugee status if they would avoid persecution in the country of origin by modifying their

---

96 Qualification Directive article 10(2).
97 J Hathaway, *The law of refugee status*, Butterworths, 1991, p137.
98 *Islam v Secretary of State for the Home Department; R v Immigration Appeal Tribunal ex p Shah* [1999] 2 AC 629.
99 For further authoritative elaboration on the social group concept, see *K and Fornah v Secretary of State for the Home Department* [2006] UKHL 46, [2007] 1 AC 412.
100 RPNIP Regs 2006 reg 6(1)(e); Qualification Directive article 10(1)(d); see also *HJ (Iraq) and HT (Cameroon) v Secretary of State for the Home Department* [2010] UKSC 31, [2010] 3 WLR 386.
101 *K and Fornah v Secretary of State for the Home Department* [2006] UKHL 46, [2007] 1 AC 412.
102 *K and Fornah v Secretary of State for the Home Department* [2006] UKHL 46, [2007] 1 AC 412 paras 43–44, 67, 104–105, disapproving the approach of the Court of Appeal in *Quijano v Secretary of State for the Home Department* [1997] Imm AR 227.

behaviour, for example by acting 'discreetly'. Only if a person could show that they would in fact refuse to act discreetly – which was in practice a difficult thing to prove, unless they had a track record of, for instance, open political activism or religious proselytising – would they be entitled to refugee status.[103] That reasoning was particularly applied by the SSHD, tribunal and courts, to gay, lesbian, bisexual and transgender people. It has now been comprehensively demolished by the Supreme Court in *HJ (Iran) and HT (Cameroon)*, in which it was concluded, in relation to claimants who feared persecution for reason of sexual orientation, that the Refugee Convention protects the right to live openly as a gay man or lesbian, and therefore that if a person would conceal their sexuality out of a well-founded fear of persecution, they qualify for refugee status.[104] The underlying principle is applicable outside the context of persecution for sexuality:[105] for instance, the tribunal has recently applied it to religious persecution of Ahmadis[106] and the Court of Appeal has accepted that it applies to political opinion.[107]

'Outside country of his nationality'

11.60 Refugees must be outside the country of their nationality or habitual residence,[108] so that internally displaced persons are not Refugee Convention refugees.

The refugee definition and criminal conduct

11.61 A person does not fall outside the scope of the protection of the Refugee Convention simply because he or she has been convicted of a crime. Unless the threshold for exclusion is reached, a criminal who satisfies the refugee definition must be recognised as a refugee (exclusion is discussed at paras 12.7–12.74). However, particularly serious criminality, combined with a risk to the community of the

---

103 *Ahmed v Secretary of State for the Home Department* [2000] INLR 1.
104 *HJ (Iran) and HT (Cameroon) v Secretary of State for the Home Department* [2010] UKSC 31, [2010] 3 WLR 386.
105 *TM (Zimbabwe) v Secretary of State for the Home Department* [2010] EWCA Civ 916 para 38.
106 *MT (Ahmadi – HJ (Iran)) Pakistan* [2011] UKUT 00277 (IAC).
107 *RT (Zimbabwe) v Secretary of State for the Home Department* [2010] EWCA Civ 1285 para 37.
108 See *R (European Roma Rights Centre) v Immigration Officer, Prague Airport* [2004] UKHL 55, [2005] 2 AC 1.

Prosecution and persecution

11.62 Refugees may have been criminalised in their home country or country of habitual residence for attempting to exercise what would, in the UK and/or the EU, be considered as fundamental rights.[109] They may have been punished for a political or even for a recognised common law offence in a disproportionate or discriminatory manner or risk such punishment in the future. A body of jurisprudence has developed concerning the distinction between legitimate prosecution and persecution.

11.63 As the UNHCR Handbook makes clear,[110] persecution is not the same as prosecution and those who have fled their country of origin only to avoid punishment for a criminal offence do not normally qualify as refugees. However, it is also clear that excessive punishment for an offence may amount to persecution and also that prosecution for a Convention reason may in itself amount to persecution.[111] The Qualification Directive states that an act of persecution may include 'prosecution or punishment, which is disproportionate or discriminatory'[112] and that persecution may include 'denial of judicial redress resulting in a disproportionate or discriminatory punishment'.[113] In reaching a view on the nature of the treatment feared by the applicant, the decision-maker must look at the criminal justice system in the country of origin as a whole.[114]

---

109 Compare *Jain v Secretary of State for the Home Department* [2000] Imm AR 76, especially the concurring judgment of Evans LJ.

110 UNHCR Handbook para 56.

111 UNHCR Handbook para 57; see *R (Tientchu) v IAT* [2000] EWCA Civ 385; *HJ (Iran) v Secretary of State for the Home Department* [2010] UKSC 31, [2010] 3 WLR 386 para 17 (per Lord Hope, it 'may not be seriously in issue' that imprisonment or death penalty for being gay would be persecution; although note the surprising and somewhat troubling comment of Lord Walker at para 91 that it 'may be debatable' whether being sent to prison for a month for being gay would amount to persecution).

112 Qualification Directive article 9(2)(c); and see, adopting the same principle before the Qualification Directive came into force, *MI (Fair Trial – Pre-Trial Conditions) Pakistan CG* [2002] UKIAT 02239 para 25.

113 Qualification Directive article 9(2)(d).

114 *MI (Fair Trial – Pre-Trial Conditions) Pakistan CG* [2002] UKIAT 02239 para 24; compare *FS and others (Iran – Christian Converts) Iran CG* [2004] UKIAT 00303, para 163.

11.64 The UNHCR Handbook suggests that, in order to establish whether prosecution amounts to persecution, decision-makers should analyse the measure in question to determine whether it conforms to human rights standards. States parties can use their own national legislation and international human rights instruments as a reference point.[115] The UNHCR Handbook's approach is reflected in the case of *Islam and Shah* where Lord Hoffmann observed that the fact that the appellant would suffer discrimination in their country of origin:

> ... cannot be ignored merely on the ground that this would imply criticism of the legal or social arrangements in another country. The whole purpose of the Convention is to give protection to certain classes of people who have fled from countries in which their human rights have not been respected.[116]

Military service

11.65 Lord Bingham in *Sepet* held:

> There is compelling support for the view that refugee status should be accorded to one who has refused to undertake compulsory military service on the grounds that such service would or might require him to commit atrocities or gross human rights abuses or participate in a conflict condemned by the international community, or where refusal to serve would earn grossly excessive or disproportionate punishment.[117]

11.66 Thus it has been recognised that the real risk of punishment of a person who deserts an army rather than commit a grave violation of human rights gives rise to a valid asylum claim.[118]

11.67 Aside from that, however, a person who refuses to undertake compulsory military service is not a refugee if the law deals with all draft evaders in the same way and does not impose discriminatory punishment on certain groups.[119]

---

115 UNHCR Handbook paras 59–60.
116 [2004] EWCA Civ 69, [2004] 1 WLR 1825 at 43.
117 *Sepet v Secretary of State for the Home Department* [2003] UKHL 15, [2003] 1 WLR 856, para 8.
118 *BE (Iran) v Secretary of State for the Home Department* [2008] EWCA Civ 540, [2009] INLR 1.
119 *Sepet v Secretary of State for the Home Department* [2003] UKHL 15, [2003] 1 WLR 856.

The date at which refugee status is to be assessed

11.68 A person is a refugee if they meet the definition in the Refugee Convention at the date on which the determination of refugee status is made. It is not sufficient that they left their country of origin owing to a well-founded fear of persecution, if that fear no longer exists or is no longer well-founded.[120]

11.69 In appeals, the focus of the Tribunal's deliberations is the date of the hearing.[121] That is not to say that there must be a risk that the person would actually be persecuted on the date of decision: it is enough that there is a risk, on the date of decision, of persecution in the foreseeable future.[122]

Burden and standard of proof

11.70 Because the refugee definition is forward-looking – it raises questions of what may happen in the future and not just of what has happened in the past – the assessment of whether a person satisfies the definition raises 'questions not of hard fact but of evaluation'.[123] It is not a 'head-to-head litigation issue' involving two conflicting accounts but is rather 'an evaluation of the intrinsic and extrinsic credibility, and ultimately the significance, of the applicant's case'.[124] The question whether an asylum claimant has well founded fear of persecution for a convention reason 'should be looked at in the round, and all the relevant circumstances taken into account'.[125]

11.71 The burden lies on an asylum claimant to prove that he or she is a refugee and not on the state to show that he or she is not.[126] In spite of that, the Handbook suggests that, because of the difficulties a person

---

120 *Adan v Secretary of State for the Home Department* [1999] 1 AC 293, HL.
121 *Ravichandran v Secretary of State for the Home Department* [1996] Imm AR 97, CA; *Saad, Diriye and Osorio v Secretary of State for the Home Department* [2001] EWCA Civ 2008.
122 *Karanakaran v Secretary of State for the Home Department* [2000] 3 All ER 449, CA; the same test applies in the assessment of risk under ECHR article 3: see for instance *AS (Libya) v Secretary of State for the Home Department* [2008] EWCA Civ 289.
123 *Karanakaran v Secretary of State for the Home Department* [2000] 3 All ER 449 para 15.
124 *Karanakaran v Secretary of State for the Home Department* [2000] 3 All ER 449 para 18.
125 *Ravichandran* [1996] Imm AR 97, at 109.
126 UNHCR Handbook para 196.

fleeing persecution is likely to face in proving their case, 'the duty to ascertain and evaluate all the relevant facts is shared between the applicant and the examiner'.[127] Reflecting the gravity of the issues, the difficulty in locating probative evidence and the risks attaching to an erroneous decision, the standard of proof is lower than the balance of probabilities. In the landmark case of *Sivakumaran*, the House of Lords held that an asylum claimant must prove that there is a 'reasonable degree of likelihood' that he or she will be persecuted for one of the convention reasons.[128]

11.72 Adopting the formulation used in the context of extradition law,[129] the House of Lords made clear in *Sivakumaran* that other ways of expressing this standard are 'a reasonable chance', 'substantial grounds for thinking', or 'a serious possibility'.[130] A common way of expressing this is a 'real risk', in other words 'a real as opposed to a fanciful risk'.[131] That is in line with the test for showing a breach of the ECHR on removal.[132]

11.73 Although the exercise is not one of mathematically estimating the risk, it was said in *Sivakumaran*, by way of illustrating the level of risk required, that there was 'no room for the view that because an applicant had only a 10 per cent chance of being shot, tortured or otherwise persecuted he or she had no "well-founded fear" of the event happening'.[133] In similar vein, Sedley LJ said in *Batayav*[134] that:

> If a type of car has a defect which causes one vehicle in ten to crash, most people would say that it presents a real risk to anyone who drives it, albeit crashes are not generally or consistently happening.

127 UNHCR Handbook para 196.
128 *R v Secretary of State for the Home Department ex p Sivakumaran* [1988] AC 958, 994F, 1000F.
129 *R v Governor of Pentonville Prison ex p Fernandez* [1971] 1 WLR 987.
130 *R v Secretary of State for the Home Department ex p Sivakumaran* [1988] AC 958 at 994F–995B.
131 *MH (Iraq) v Secretary of State for the Home Department* [2007] EWCA Civ 852; in *HJ (Iran) and HT (Cameroon) v Secretary of State for the Home Department* [2010] UKSC 31, [2010] 3 WLR 386, Lord Dyson said at para 89 that '"[r]isk" is in my view the best word because ... it factors in both the probability of harm and its severity'.
132 In *Kacaj v Secretary of State for the Home Department* [2002] Imm AR 213, [2001] INLR 354 it was said that the test under both conventions – the Refugee Convention and the ECHR – was essentially the same.
133 *R v Secretary of State for the Home Department ex p Sivakumaran* [1988] AC 958, referring with approval to the decision of the United States Supreme Court in *INS v Cardozo-Fonseca* (1987) 34 LEd2d 434.
134 *Batayav v Secretary of State for the Home Department* [2003] EWCA Civ 1489, [2004] INLR 126.

11.74 Likewise, a relaxed standard of proof applies in assessing events that have occurred in the past, on which the risk of future persecution is likely to be based. The Immigration Appeal Tribunal in *Kaja* held that the assessment of whether a person has a well-founded fear of persecution is not a two-stage process in which the decision-maker finds facts on the balance of probabilities and then goes on to determine future risk on the basis of the facts so found. It is not only facts established as more likely than not to have occurred that must inform the assessment of future risk: all the evidence and the varying degrees of belief or disbelief must be considered, in order properly to evaluate the degree of future risk.[135] In the leading case of *Karanakaran*, the Court of Appeal analysed the decision in *Kaja* as meaning that:

> ... when assessing future risk decision-makers may have to take into account a whole bundle of disparate pieces of evidence:
> (1) evidence they are certain about;
> (2) evidence they think is probably true;
> (3) evidence to which they are willing to attach some credence, even if they could not go so far as to say it is probably true;
> (4) evidence to which they are not willing to attach any credence at all.
> The effect of Kaja is that the decision-maker is not bound to exclude category (3) evidence as he/she would be if deciding issues that arise in civil litigation.[136]

11.75 The court went on to explain further the effect of *Kaja*:

> This approach does not entail the decision-maker ... purporting to find 'proved' facts, whether past or present, about which it is not satisfied on the balance of probabilities. What it does mean, on the other hand, is that it must not exclude any matters from its consideration when it is assessing the future unless it feels that it can safely discard them because it has no real doubt that they did not in fact occur (or, indeed, that they are not occurring at present). Similarly, if an applicant contends that relevant matters did not happen, the decision-maker should not exclude the possibility that they did not happen (although believing that they probably did) unless it has no real doubt that they did in fact happen.

---

135 *Kaja v Secretary of State for the Home Department* [1995] Imm AR 1.
136 *Karanakaran v Secretary of State for the Home Department* [2000] 3 All ER 449.

The duty of non-refoulement

11.76 Article 33(1) of the Refugee Convention imposes a fundamental prohibition on 'refoulement':

> No Contracting State shall expel or return ('refouler') a refugee in any manner whatsoever to the frontiers of territories where his life or freedom would be threatened on account of his race, religion, nationality, membership of a particular social group or political opinion.

11.77 This is the key provision in the Refugee Convention's protective scheme and, as such, states parties are not permitted to make reservations in relation to it,[137] although there are exceptions to the principle under article 33(2), which are dealt with in detail at paras 12.75–12.96. Although the wording ('life or freedom would be threatened') might be seen as narrowing the definition of persecution in article 1A,[138] it is well established that the tests are the same and that the non-refoulement provision in article 33 applies to all those who are refugees under article 1 of the Refugee Convention.[139]

---

137 Refugee Convention article 42(1).
138 See paras 11.44–11.46 above.
139 *R v Refugee Convention ex p Sivakumaran* [1988] AC 958, 1000F.

CHAPTER 12

Exclusion, loss of protection and cessation under the Refugee Convention

12.1	**Introduction**
12.1	Exclusion
12.3	Loss of protection
12.6	Cessation
12.7	**The exclusion clauses**
12.7	Refugee Convention articles 1D and 1E
12.12	**Article 1F**
12.12	Overview
12.19	**Procedure**
12.19	Standard of proof
12.23	Burden of proof
12.24	No proportionality test
12.25	No requirement that the individual pose a present danger to the host state
12.26	**Article 1F(a)**
12.30	**Article 1F(b)**
12.30	Non-political crime
12.32	Serious crime

continued

12.36	Outside the country of refuge
12.46	**Article 1F(c)**
12.49	Article 1F(c) and terrorism
12.63	**Complicity for exclusion purposes**
12.66	Mens rea
12.71	Actus reus
12.74	When a person may be excluded under article 1F(c)
12.75	**Loss of protection from refoulement**
12.77	Article 32
12.78	Article 33(2)
12.80	Contrasting Refugee Convention article 33(2) with article 1F(b)
12.81	The test to be met under article 33(2)
12.84	The presumptions under NIAA 2002 s72
12.95	Definition of 'particularly serious crime'
12.97	Article 33(2), refugee status and residence permits
12.110	**Procedure on appeal to the IAC or SIAC in exclusion and loss of protection cases**
12.110	Certificates
12.113	Exclusion
12.119	Loss of protection
12.121	**Cessation**
12.125	Article 1C
12.126	European and domestic implementation of Refugee Convention article 1C
12.129	UNHCR's involvement in cessation decisions
12.130	Revocation of indefinite leave (ILR) to remain for cessation reasons
12.134	Approach to cessation
12.137	Voluntary re-availment of national protection
12.140	Voluntary re-establishment in the country where persecution was feared

Introduction

Exclusion

12.1 Not everyone who fulfils the criteria under article 1A of the Refugee Convention[1] will qualify for status as a refugee. Some do not qualify because they have engaged in crimes or other actions so serious that they are regarded as undeserving of Refugee Convention protection, and others because specific alternative means of protection exist. The provisions governing these, articles 1D, 1E and 1F of the Refugee Convention, are known as the 'exclusion clauses'.

12.2 In this chapter, we focus particularly on article 1F of the Refugee Convention, which excludes from refugee status people for whom there are serious reasons for considering that they have committed war crimes or crimes against humanity; serious non-political crimes outside the country where they are seeking asylum; and acts contrary to the purposes and principles of the UN, in particular acts of terrorism.

Loss of protection

12.3 In addition, even those recognised as refugees may be at risk of expulsion if they are deemed to be a threat to national security or, having committed a particularly serious crime, a danger to the community. Article 33(2) of the Refugee Convention, although not, strictly speaking, one of the exclusion clauses, is considered in this same chapter. This provision and the attempt to interpret it in domestic law through Nationality, Immigration and Asylum Act (NIAA) 2002 s72 are referred to in this chapter as 'loss of protection'.

12.4 Note that exclusion from the Refugee Convention and loss of protection do not preclude a person from successfully relying on European Convention on Human Rights (ECHR) article 3 (prohibition of torture or inhuman or degrading treatment or punishment) to resist deportation. This is because the protection afforded by article 3 is absolute: a person whose expulsion would breach article 3 cannot be expelled regardless of the gravity of their past actions. ECHR article 3 is considered at paras 13.6–13.41 and 18.4–18.52 (health cases).

12.5 However, where a person is excluded from Refugee Convention protection or is not entitled to protection from refoulement, he or she may be ineligible for humanitarian protection (a particular form of

---

1 The 1951 Convention Relating to the Status of Refugees and its 1967 Protocol.

status granted to those who cannot be expelled from the UK by operation of ECHR articles 2 or 3, or because of risks arising from armed conflict). Exclusion from humanitarian protection is considered at paras 19.18–19.25.

Cessation

12.6 Finally, in this chapter, we consider the 'cessation clauses' of the Refugee Convention which permit withdrawal of refugee status from those no longer considered to be at risk.

The exclusion clauses

Refugee Convention articles 1D and 1E

12.7 Articles 1D and 1E have limited application in practice, and raise no particular issues for FNPs.

12.8 In essence, article 1D provides that refugee status shall not be granted to a person receiving protection or assistance from UN agencies other than UNHCR, such as the United Nations Relief and Works Agency (UNRWA), which provides assistance, protection and advocacy for Palestinian refugees in the Middle East).[2]

12.9 Article 1E excludes from refugee status a person 'recognized by the competent authorities of the country in which he has taken residence as having the rights and obligations which are attached to the possession of nationality of that country', on the basis that such people are considered immune from refoulement and have rights similar to or greater than those conferred by refugee status.

12.10 Both articles are transposed into European law by article 12(1) of the Qualification Directive[3] and domestically by the Refugee or Person in Need of International Protection (Qualification) Regulations (RPNIP Regs) 2006[4] reg 7(1).

12.11 The use of article 1F is much more widespread and so it is the subject of the rest of this section.

---

2 For its interpretation, see UNHCR Handbook paras 142–143; *El-Ali v Secretary of State for the Home Department* [2002] EWCA Civ 1103, [2003] 1 WLR 95.

3 Council Directive 2004/83/EC of 29 April 2004 on minimum standards for the qualification and status of third country nationals or stateless persons as refugees or as persons who otherwise need international protection and the content of the protection granted; OJ L 304, 30/09/2004 ('Qualification Directive').

4 SI No 2170.

Article 1F

Overview

12.12 Article 1F states:

> The provisions of this Convention shall not apply to any person with respect to whom there are serious reasons for considering that:
> (a) he has committed a crime against peace, a war crime, or a crime against humanity, as defined in the international instruments drawn up to make provision in respect of such crimes;
> (b) he has committed a serious non-political crime outside the country of refuge prior to his admission to that country as a refugee;
> (c) he has been guilty of acts contrary to the purposes and principles of the United Nations.

12.13 The Qualification Directive adopts that definition at article 12(2), with the addition to (b) of words concerning 'particularly cruel actions' and to (c) of the words 'as set out in the Preamble and Articles 1 and 2 of the Charter of the United Nations'.

12.14 Article 12(3) of the Qualification Directive adds that the provisions apply 'to persons who instigate or otherwise participate in the commission of the crimes or acts mentioned therein'.

12.15 The application of article 1F is mandatory: states 'shall not' apply the Refugee Convention's provisions to those who fall within article 1F. This means that states must not recognise as refugees those who fall within the scope of article 1F.[5] Subject to other international obligations (such as ECHR article 3), a person excluded from refugee status can be sent to a country in which he or she will be persecuted. In *Gurung*, the Immigration Appeal Tribunal (IAT) stressed the mandatory nature of the exclusion clause and called the issue of exclusion 'an integral part of the refugee determination assessment'.[6] Although we refer in this chapter to certain passages of the *Gurung* judgment, it should be noted that the Supreme Court in *JS (Sri Lanka)* has cast doubt on aspects of that determination, suggesting that it should not 'be accorded the same oracular standing as it seems hitherto to have enjoyed'.[7]

---

5 *Bundesrepublik Deutschland v B and D* Joined Cases C-57/09 and C-101/09 [2011] Imm AR 190, [2011] INLR 133 para 115 (member states not entitled to grant refugee status to those excluded under article 12 of the Qualification Directive, but entitled to grant a different form of protection under domestic law).

6 *Gurung (Refugee exclusion clauses especially 1F(b)) Nepal CG* [2002] UKIAT 04870, [2003] INLR 133 para 38.

7 *R (JS (Sri Lanka)) v Secretary of State for the Home Department* [2010] UKSC 15 para 29.

12.16 Because article 1F sets out conditions for denying a humanitarian benefit, with potentially very serious results, it should be construed restrictively.[8]

12.17 The three limbs of article 1F(c) may overlap: a person may be excludable on more than one ground.[9] If so, the decision-maker may apply different limbs together or in the alternative.

12.18 Article 1F was intended to promote the objectives of the Refugee Convention by:

- ensuring that those who have committed gross violations of humanitarian law do not benefit from it, so entrenching humanitarian values;
- incentivising states to become signatories of the convention without fear that they would have to shelter war criminals and others who might jeopardise the state's security;
- ensuring that war criminals, and other serious criminals, cannot use the Refugee Convention to avoid legitimate prosecution in their own or another country.[10]

Procedure

Standard of proof

12.19 There must be 'serious reasons for considering' that a person falls within one of the exclusion clauses. The 'serious reasons' requirement reflects the grave consequences of exclusion.

12.20 The UNHCR has suggested that in deciding whether there are 'serious reasons for considering' that person is responsible for prohibited acts:

> ... the criminal standard of proof (eg beyond reasonable doubt in common law systems) need not be met. Thus, exclusion does not require a determination of guilt in the criminal justice sense. Nevertheless, in order to ensure that Article 1F is applied in a manner consistent with the overall humanitarian objective of the 1951 Convention, the

---

8 *Gurung (Refugee exclusion clauses especially 1F(b)) Nepal CG* [2002] UKIAT 04870, [2003] INLR 133 para 36; *R (JS (Sri Lanka)) v Secretary of State for the Home Department* [2010] UKSC 15 para 2.

9 See, for example, *Bundesrepublik Deutschland v B and D* Joined Cases C-57/09 and C-101/09 [2011] Imm AR 190, [2011] INLR 133 at paras 80–84, characterising terrorist acts as both 'serious non-political crimes' and acts contrary to the purposes and principles of the United Nations.

10 See, for example, J Hathaway, *The Law of Refugee Status*, Butterworths, 1991, pp214–229.

standard of proof should be high enough to ensure that bona fide refugees are not excluded erroneously. Hence, the 'balance of probabilities' is too low a threshold.[11]

12.21 That is not the approach of the domestic courts, which have held that the phrase, 'serious reasons for considering':

... sets a standard above mere suspicion. Beyond this, it is a mistake to try to paraphrase the straightforward language of the Convention: it has to be treated as meaning what it says.[12]

12.22 At the same time, however, the phrase:

... obviously imports a higher test for exclusion than would, say, an expression like 'reasonable grounds for suspecting'. 'Considering' approximates rather to 'believing' than to 'suspecting'.[13]

Burden of proof

12.23 The burden is on the receiving state to provide evidence justifying exclusion.[14] It is the UNHCR's view,[15] and the Canadian courts have specifically held,[16] that the burden is on the receiving state to show 'serious reasons for considering' that the individual has committed acts warranting exclusion. Primary, rather than secondary, evidence to support any allegation should be relied on by the state where available.[17]

---

11 'Background note on the application of the exclusion Clauses: article 1F of the 1951 Convention Relating to the Status of Refugees', UNHCR, 4 September 2003, para 107.
12 *Al-Sirri v Secretary of State for the Home Department* [2009] EWCA Civ 222, [2009] INLR 586 (sometimes cited as *YS (Egypt)*) para 33, cited with approval in *R (JS (Sri Lanka)) v Secretary of State for the Home Department* [2010] UKSC 15.
13 *R (JS (Sri Lanka)) v Secretary of State for the Home Department* [2010] UKSC 15 para 39; and see *Al-Sirri v Secretary of State for the Home Department* [2009] EWCA Civ 222, [2009] INLR 586 para 77.
14 *Gurung (Refugee exclusion clauses especially 1F(b)) Nepal CG* [2002] UKIAT 04870, [2003] INLR 133 at para 21; *Al-Sirri v Secretary of State for the Home Department* [2009] EWCA Civ 222, [2009] INLR 586 paras 27, 77.
15 UNHCR Guidelines on International Protection: Application of the Exclusion Clauses, Article 1F, 4 September 2003, HCR/GIP/03/05.
16 *Ramirez v Minister of Employment and Immigration* [1992] FC 306 (FCA) para 5, *Singh v Minister of Citizenship and Immigration* [2005] FCA 125, (2005) 253 DLR (4th) 606 para 23.
17 *Al-Sirri v Secretary of State for the Home Department* [2009] EWCA Civ 222, [2009] INLR 586 para 55.

No proportionality test

12.24 There is no proportionality test involved in the application of the exclusion clauses: that is, there is no need to weigh the risk to the applicant if expelled against the seriousness of the acts for which they are responsible.[18] An individual who satisfies the criteria for exclusion must be excluded from the Refugee Convention regardless of the gravity of the consequences of expulsion (although, as we have already seen, in practice, ECHR article 3 would in any event prevent expulsion to a real risk of serious harm).

No requirement that the individual pose a present danger to the host state

12.25 Exclusion is 'a penalty for acts committed in the past'.[19] It follows that it is not necessary that the individual should presently constitute a danger to the receiving state,[20] and that there is no concept of 'expiation' or 'rehabilitation': once responsibility for relevant acts is established to the requisite standard, it does not matter that they were committed long ago, or were unconnected to the asylum claim, or that the applicant has been punished by law for them.[21]

Article 1F(a)

12.26 The international instruments referred to in article 1F(a) include the 1948 Convention on the Prevention and Punishment of the Crime of Genocide and the 1949 Geneva Conventions for the Protection of Victims of War.[22] The starting point is now to be taken as the Rome Statute of the International Criminal Court.[23]

12.27 'War crimes' include willful killing, torture, intentional attacks on civilian targets, pillaging and enlisting child soldiers.[24] 'Crimes against

---

18 *Bundesrepublik Deutschland v B and D* Joined Cases C-57/09 and C-101/09 [2011] Imm AR 190, [2011] INLR 133 paras 106–111.
19 *Bundesrepublik Deutschland v B and D* Joined Cases C-57/09 and C-101/09 [2011] Imm AR 190, [2011] INLR 133 para 103.
20 *Bundesrepublik Deutschland v B and D* Joined Cases C-57/09 and C-101/09 [2011] Imm AR 190, [2011] INLR 133 paras 104–105.
21 See, for example, *KK (Article 1F(c)) Turkey* [2004] UKIAT 00101 para 91.
22 UNHCR Handbook annex VI.
23 *R (JS (Sri Lanka)) v Secretary of State for the Home Department* [2010] UKSC 15 para 8.
24 Statute of the International Criminal Court article 8.

humanity' include acts, committed as part of a widespread or systematic attack directed against civilians, such as murder, torture, rape and persecution of defined groups,[25] although the list given is not exclusive, and actions of a 'similar character' may also lead to exclusion.[26]

12.28 Taking part in military combat is, however, not a war crime, even if it includes killing government soldiers on behalf of a rebel movement.[27]

12.29 The question in article 1F(a) cases is frequently not whether the individual has personally committed such crimes, but whether his or her contribution to them – especially by way of membership of or involvement in a government, a military unit or a political movement whose members have been directly responsible – gives rise to individual responsibility. This is dealt with below at paras 12.63–12.73.

Article 1F(b)

Non-political crime

12.30 English case-law, in particular the decision of the House of Lords in *T v Immigration Officer*,[28] suggests that a crime will be considered 'political' if committed for a political purpose, that is 'with the object of overthrowing or subverting or changing the government of a state or inducing it to change its policy'.[29] The use of violence is not in itself incompatible with the advancement of a political cause: that much is clear from the use of the word 'non-political' in article 1F(b), implying the existence of a 'serious *political* crime'. However, there must be 'a sufficiently close and direct link between the crime and the alleged political purpose', and it will cease to count as political if the means are disproportionately violent to the political end.[30] On the facts of *T*, the applicant's objective – overthrowing the Government of Algeria – was political, but the connection between the means – the bombing of an airport in which ten members of the public were

---

25 Statute of the International Criminal Court article 7.
26 Statute of the International Criminal Court article 7(1)(k); and see *SK (Article 1F(a) – exclusion) Zimbabwe* [2010] UKUT 327 (IAC) (active participation in farm invasions in Zimbabwe leading to exclusion).
27 *PK (Sri Lanka – risk on return – exclusion clause) Sri Lanka* [2004] UKIAT 00089; and see *KJ (Sri Lanka) v Secretary of State for the Home Department* [2009] EWCA Civ 292 at 34, in the context of article 1F(c).
28 [1996] AC 742.
29 *T v Immigration Officer* [1996] AC 742 at 786–787.
30 *T v Immigration Officer* [1996] AC 742 at 787.

killed – and the end was held to be too remote: although the intention of the attack was claimed to be to strike at the economic interests of the country, it was held that it was bound to involve the deaths of innocent people, and the crime was held to be 'non-political'.[31]

12.31 Under the RPNIP Regs 2006 reg 7(2)(a), a 'serious non-political' crime includes 'a particularly cruel action, even if it is committed with an allegedly political objective'. While this reflects the language of article 12(2)(b) of the directive, the notion of a 'particularly cruel action' is new to domestic law and does not derive from the Refugee Convention itself.

Serious crime

12.32 The UNHCR Handbook suggests that:

> ... a 'serious' crime must be a capital crime or a very grave punishable act. Minor offences punishable by moderate sentences are not grounds for exclusion under Article 1F(b) even if technically referred to as 'crimes' in the penal law of the country concerned.[32]

More recent guidance from the UNHCR states that:

> In determining whether a particular offence is sufficiently serious, international rather than local standards are relevant. The following factors should be taken into account: the nature of the act, the actual harm inflicted, the form of procedure used to prosecute the crime, the nature of the penalty, and whether most jurisdictions would consider it a serious crime. Thus, for example, murder, rape and armed robbery would undoubtedly qualify as serious offences, whereas petty theft would obviously not.[33]

12.33 A leading commentator on the law of refugees, Guy Goodwin Gill, has observed in *The refugee in international law* that: 'Commentators and jurisprudence seem to agree, however, that serious crimes, above all, are those against physical integrity, life and liberty'.[34] However, in examining the higher category of 'particularly serious crime' for the purposes of loss of protection (see para 12.95 below) the Court of Appeal has stated, obiter, that particularly serious crime is not limited to offences against the person.[35]

---

31 *T v Immigration Officer* [1996] AC 742.
32 UNHCR Handbook, para 155.
33 UNHCR Guidelines on International Protection: Application of the Exclusion Clauses, article 1F, 4 September 2003, HCR/GIP/03/05 para 14.
34 G Goodwin Gill, *The refugee in international law*, OUP, 3rd edn, 2007, para 4.2.1.2.
35 *EN (Serbia) v Secretary of State for the Home Department* [2009] EWCA Civ 630, [2010] QB 633 para 47 per Stanley Burnton LJ.

12.34 The Home Office's Asylum Policy Instructions (API) on Exclusion suggest:

> An offence to which s72 of the [NIAA 2002] applies[36] will normally be regarded as 'serious'. An offence for which a person could expect to be sentenced to 1–2 years' imprisonment if it were committed in the UK may also qualify as 'serious'.[37]

12.35 No authority is cited for the Home Office's view and we suggest that it is incorrect, for the reasons given later in this chapter at paras 12.91–12.92 where we consider loss of protection.

Outside the country of refuge

12.36 On its face, article 1F(b) of the Refugee Convention applies only to a serious crime committed 'outside the country of refuge prior to ... admission to that country as a refugee'. That is, article 1F(b) would apply only to acts that take place before a person's entry into the country of refuge, while article 33(2) covers post-entry criminality:[38] the two provisions have to be seen together. That view is consistent with the intention of article 1F(b): if the drafters of the convention had intended to exclude *any* serious criminal from the convention, they could have simply omitted the words 'outside the country of refuge prior to his admission to that country as a refugee'. Professor Hathaway, another eminent academic on the law of refugees, has observed:

> The common law criminality exclusion disallows the claims of persons who are liable to sanctions in another state for having committed a genuine, serious crime, and who seek to escape legitimate criminal liability by claiming refugee status ... [I]t is simply a means of bringing refugee law into line with the basic principles of extradition law, by ensuring that important fugitives from justice are not able to avoid the jurisdiction of a state in which they may lawful face punishment
> ...
> [I]t follows from the linkage to extradition that the only allegations of criminality which are relevant to the application of this clause are those which involve acts committed outside a country of refuge, whether in the country of origin or while in transit to an asylum state ... Criminal activity in a state of refuge, on the other hand, is appropriately

---

36 That is, in essence, a conviction resulting in a sentence of at least two years or an offence specified by order of the SSHD. At present there is no secondary legislation to specify such offences. See paras 12.84–12.94 below.
37 API 'Exclusion: articles 1F and 33(2) of the Refugee Convention' para 2.3.
38 See *Pushpanathan v Canada* [1999] INLR 36 and *KK (Article 1F(c)) Turkey* [2004] UKIAT 00101 para 81.

adjudicated through due process of law, with recourse to expulsion or return if the refugee is consequently found to pose a security risk.[39]

12.37 The wording of article 1F(b) is opaque because a person who has committed a serious non-political crime is not, by definition, 'a refugee' in any event, and therefore cannot logically be said to have committed the crime before admission as such. It has been suggested by the Australian High Court that 'prior to his admission ... as a refugee' must mean prior to his 'putative admission as a refugee'[40] (in other words, simply 'before he arrived and sought asylum'), and in *KK Turkey* the Immigration Appeal Tribunal (IAT) similarly commented that '[i]f there are serious grounds for considering that such an act has been committed by the claimant *before* he reaches a place of refuge, then he is excluded'.[41] We suggest that this is the correct approach.

12.38 That approach has, however, come under strain in the UK's attempt to transpose the Qualification Directive into domestic law.

12.39 Article 12(2)(b) of the Qualification Directive uses the words:

... he or she has committed a serious non-political crime outside the country of refuge prior to his or her admission as a refugee; which means the time of issuing a residence permit based on the granting of refugee status.

12.40 We suggest that the effect of the gloss in the Qualification Directive ('which means the time of issuing a residence permit based on the granting of refugee status') is to exclude a person from refugee status under the Qualification Directive who arrives in the state of refuge and claims asylum but, while waiting for the determination of his or her claim, commits an offence in a third state. For example, an applicant arrives in the UK and claims asylum, but while awaiting the determination of his claim, travels to Holland and commits an offence. If the Qualification Directive indeed interprets exclusion as applying to a wider category of person than the Refugee Convention itself, this raises the question of whether a person may be granted refugee status under the Refugee Convention who would be excluded from such status under the Qualification Directive. We discussed this issue at para 11.11.

---

39 J Hathaway, *The Law of Refugee Status*, Butterworths, 1991, para 6.3.2, pp221–222 (with the numerous footnotes relating to the travaux préparatoires omitted).
40 *Minister for Immigration and Multicultural Affairs v Singh* [2002] HCA 7, para 5.
41 *KK (Article 1F(c)) Turkey* [2004] UKIAT 00101, para 80; emphasis in original.

12.41 RPNIP Regs 2006 reg 7(2) then offers a further gloss, stating that 'the reference to the crime being committed outside the country of refuge prior to his admission as a refugee shall be taken to mean the time up to and including the day on which a residence permit is issued'.

12.42 RPNIP Regs 2006 reg 7(2)(b) must as far as possible be interpreted compatibly with the Qualification Directive and we suggest it can be. The definition of the time of admission of a refugee does not alter the requirement that the offence be committed outside the country of refuge.

12.43 However, para 2.3.3 of the API on Exclusion gives RPNIP Regs 2006 reg 7(2)(b) the following interpretation:

> In the majority of cases this provision in [reg 7(2)(b)] will apply to crimes committed abroad but in some instances it could apply to crimes committed whilst seeking asylum in the UK up to the date that a residence permit is issued.

12.44 We suggest that this guidance in the API is unlawful. Nothing in the Qualification Directive, let alone the Refugee Convention, suggests that 'outside the country of refuge' is actually intended to mean 'inside the country of refuge (but while seeking asylum)'.

12.45 If, of course, RPNIP Regs 2006 reg 7(2)(b) had the meaning suggested in the API then it would inaccurately transpose the Qualification Directive and the Qualification Directive would need to be followed in any event: see the discussion of the primacy of EU law in the introduction to EU law at section B of this book.

Article 1F(c)

12.46 Article 1F(c) excludes those for whom there are serious reasons for considering that they are guilty of acts contrary to the purposes and principles of the United Nations.

12.47 The Supreme Court of Canada held in *Pushpanathan v Canada*[42] (rejecting the notion that an international drugs trafficker was excluded under article 1F(c)):

> In the light of the general purposes of the Convention, and the indications in the travaux préparatoires as to the relative ambit of Article 1F(a) and F(c), the purpose of Article 1F(c) can be characterized in the following terms: to exclude those individuals responsible for serious,

---

42 (1998) 6 BHRC 387, [1999] INLR 36, para 65.

12.48 Article 1F(c) applies not only to those who have committed past acts as state agents, but to those who have committed acts as private individuals, whether or not acting as part of a political movement.[43]

Article 1F(c) and terrorism

12.49 Terrorism is contrary to the purposes and principles of the United Nations, as the United Nations bodies have frequently stated.[44] However, the United Nations has provided no comprehensive definition of terrorism.

12.50 On 27 December 2001, the Council of the European Union adopted a Common Position[45] on the application of specific measures to combat terrorism. At article 1.3, so far as material, this defines an act of terrorism as:

> ... one of the following intentional acts, which, given its nature or its context, may seriously damage a country or an international organisation, as defined as an offence under national law, where committed with the aim of:
> (i) seriously intimidating a population, or
> (ii) unduly compelling a Government or an international organisation to perform or abstain from performing any act, or
> (iii) seriously destabilising or destroying the fundamental political, constitutional, economic or social structures of a country or an international organisation.

12.51 The 'intentional acts' referred to include a variety of acts including 'attacks upon a person's life which may cause death', 'attacks upon the physical integrity of a person', 'kidnapping or hostage taking', 'causing extensive destruction to a Government or public facility', hijacking, various actions related to nuclear, biological or chemical weapons, 'interfering with or disrupting the supply of water, power or any other fundamental natural resource, the effect of which is to endanger human life', and 'directing' or 'participating in the activities of a terrorist group'.

---

43 *KK (Article 1F(c)) Turkey* [2004] UKIAT 00101 para 20; *Al-Sirri v Secretary of State for the Home Department* [2009] EWCA Civ 222, [2009] INLR 586 para 39.
44 See, for example, Security Council Resolutions 1267, 1373, 1377 and 1624; and see *Bundesrepublik Deutschland v B and D* Joined Cases C-57/09 and C-101/09 [2011] Imm AR 190, [2011] INLR 133 paras 82–84.
45 Common Position 2001/931/CFSP, OJ 2001 L 344, p93.

12.52 Parliament has sought to give its own non-exhaustive definition to the purposes and principles of the United Nations. The Immigration Asylum and Nationality Act (IANA) 2006 s54 provides:

(1) In the construction and application of Article 1(F)(c) of the Refugee Convention the reference to acts contrary to the purposes and principles of the United Nations shall be taken as including, in particular–
(a) acts of committing, preparing or instigating terrorism (whether or not the acts amount to an actual or inchoate offence), and
(b) acts of encouraging or inducing others to commit, prepare or instigate terrorism (whether or not the acts amount to an actual or inchoate offence).
(2) In this section–
'the Refugee Convention' means the Convention relating to the Status of Refugees done at Geneva on 28th July 1951, and 'terrorism' has the meaning given by section 1 of the Terrorism Act 2000 (c. 11).

12.53 This attempt by parliament to unilaterally impose an interpretation on the Refugee Convention, however, has difficulties.

12.54 The first difficulty is that the Refugee Convention has one true meaning, which must be the same in all the signatory states. In *JS (Sri Lanka)*, Lord Brown observed that article 1F has 'an autonomous meaning to be found in international rather than domestic law'.[46]

12.55 The second difficulty is that the Terrorism Act (TA) 2000 provides a very broad definition of 'terrorism'. In essence, the definition in TA 2000 s1 amounts to the use or threat of serious violence to a person or serious damage to property, designed to influence the government or an international governmental organisation or to intimidate the public or a section of the public, for the purpose of advancing a political, religious, racial or ideological cause. Moreover, the use of firearms or explosives for advancing such a cause is defined in TA 2000 as terrorism, *whether or not it is intended to influence the government or intimidate the public.*[47] The actions taken may be outside the UK and the government that the 'terrorist' seeks to influence or the public that he or she seeks to threaten may also be outside the UK.

12.56 Thus TA 2000 defines ideologically motivated acts of serious criminal damage, aimed at intimidating a government or influencing the public, as terrorism. Its definition of terrorism is moreover so

46 *R (JS (Sri Lanka)) v Secretary of State for the Home Department* [2010] UKSC 15 para 2.
47 TA 2000 s1(3).

broad that it would appear to apply to virtually all acts of war. So, for example, the use of explosives or firearms by the anti-Gaddafi forces in Libya (or indeed the NATO forces) would almost certainly have amounted to 'terrorism' as defined in the TA 2000 s1.

12.57 In any event, IANA 2006 s54(2) must be read down to conform with article 12(2)(c) of the Qualification Directive. A third difficulty with parliament's attempt to unilaterally impose definitions arises out of the tension between the domestic definition and the terms of article 12(2)(c) of the Qualification Directive ('as set out in the Preamble and Articles 1 and 2 of the Charter of the United Nations'). It was conceded by the Home Office in *Al-Sirri* that 'this formula [in the Qualification Directive] does not go as wide as' TA 2000 s1; therefore, Sedley LJ held that:

> ... the adoption by s54(2) of the 2006 Act [IANA 2006] of the meaning of terrorism contained in the 2000 Act [TA 2000] has where necessary to be read down in an art. 1F case so as to keep its meaning within the scope of art 12(2)(c) of the Directive.[48]

12.58 Sedley LJ went on to say that 'terrorism here [ie in the context of article 1F(c)] means the use for political ends of fear induced by violence'.[49] We respectfully suggest that this is correct, and that definitions which omit the use of fear as a means in itself risk going too widely and encompassing actions which are plainly not contrary to the purposes and principles of the UN.

12.59 The preamble and articles 1 and 2 of the UN Charter are largely concerned with securing and maintaining *international* peace and harmony. For that reason, Sedley LJ also said in *Al-Sirri* that he saw 'the force of [the] submission that terrorism must have an international character or aspect in order to come within art 12 of the [Qualification] Directive'.[50] That view is supported by recent authority from the Grand Chamber of the Court of Justice of the European Union (CJEU),[51] although the Court of Appeal has elsewhere suggested

---

48 *Al-Sirri v Secretary of State for the Home Department* [2009] EWCA Civ 222, [2009] INLR 586 para 29; cited with approval in *SS (Libya) v Secretary of State for the Home Department* [2011] EWCA Civ 1457 para 24.
49 *Al-Sirri v Secretary of State for the Home Department* [2009] EWCA Civ 222, [2009] INLR 586 para 31.
50 *Al-Sirri v Secretary of State for the Home Department* [2009] EWCA Civ 222, [2009] INLR 586 para 32.
51 *Bundesrepublik Deutschland v B and D* Joined Cases C-57/09 and C-101/09 [2011] ImmAR 190, [2011] INLR 133 paras 82–84.

otherwise.[52] It was also held in *Al-Sirri* that it was not necessary, for purposes of article 1F(c), that the person concerned should be a state actor, someone who was 'in some tangible way using or abusing the powers of (or ordinarily deployed by) a sovereign state'.[53]

12.60 The Court of Appeal has held in *KJ (Sri Lanka)* that involvement in combat in the course of a civil war is not, in itself contrary to the purposes and principles of the UN: therefore a 'foot soldier' in the LTTE ('Tamil Tigers') in Sri Lanka would not, for that reason alone, fall to be excluded from under article 1F(c) (although the situation would clearly be different if they had, for instance, been involved in acts of violence against civilians).[54] The CJEU agreed in *B and D* that mere membership of an organisation which has been involved in armed struggle is insufficient to warrant exclusion.[55] However, in *SS (Libya)* it was said by the Court of Appeal that there was a distinction to be drawn between 'military action against a government' (which would not constitute terrorism) and violence 'directed at non-military targets, such as the police or government officials' (which, at least on the facts of that case, could constitute terrorism).[56] We respectfully suggest that it may not be possible, in all cases, to draw such a clear distinction in situations where the state is highly militarised or, for instance, the police are carrying out paramilitary duties.

12.61 It has also been held to be incorrect to exclude a member of an armed organisation (the PKK) who had acted primarily as a nurse,

---

52 In *DD (Afghanistan) v Secretary of State for the Home Department* [2010] EWCA Civ 1407 Pill LJ suggested at paras 62–63 that although 'consideration of the original Convention' lent support to UNHCR's views which 'would confine the application of the article to acts impinging on the international plane', nevertheless 'the UN Charter is a living instrument and ... the range of activities subsequently conducted under the auspices of the United Nations requires that the words be given a less limited construction'; however, neither *B and D* nor *Al-Sirri* seems to have been cited to the court.

53 *Al-Sirri v Secretary of State for the Home Department* [2009] EWCA Civ 222, [2009] INLR 586 paras 36-39; and see *Bundesrepublik Deutschland v B and D* Joined Cases C-57/09 and C-101/09 [2011] ImmAR 190, [2011] INLR 133, para 83.

54 *KJ (Sri Lanka) v Secretary of State for the Home Department* [2009] EWCA Civ 292, especially at paras 34 and 38; a suggestion that this conclusion was per incuriam was rejected in *SS (Libya) v Secretary of State for the Home Department* [2011] EWCA Civ 1457 paras 34–37.

55 *Bundesrepublik Deutschland v B and D* Joined Cases C-57/09 and C-101/09 [2011] ImmAR 190, [2011] INLR 133 para 99.

56 *SS (Libya) v Secretary of State for the Home Department* [2011] EWCA Civ 1457 para 41.

12.62 However, terrorism is not the only action which may fall within article 1F(c): in *DD (Afghanistan)*, taking part in armed activity against a UN-mandated force, the International Special Assistance Force (ISAF) in Afghanistan, was considered to be contrary to the purposes and principles of the UN.[58]

Complicity for exclusion purposes

12.63 A further difficulty in applying the exclusion clauses arises where the individual has been a member of an organisation responsible for war crimes or actions contrary to the purposes and principles of the UN, but is not said to have carried out such acts himself.

12.64 Mere membership of an organisation which has carried out relevant acts, among other activities, is not enough.[59] Nor even is 'mere passivity or continued involvement in the organisation after acquiring knowledge' of such acts.[60] What must be shown is a connection between the individual's actions and any crimes carried out by the organisation.

12.65 Neither the word 'committed' in articles 1F(a) and (b), nor the words 'guilty of' in article 1F(c), implies the need to show guilt to a criminal standard; 'guilty of' simply means 'responsible for'.[61]

Mens rea

12.66 In *JS (Sri Lanka)*, Lord Brown said that mens rea (the requisite state of mind) for the purposes of article 1F was to be defined in the following terms:

> ... when the accused is participating in (in the sense of assisting in or contributing to) a common plan or purpose, not necessarily to

---

57 *MH (Syria) v Secretary of State for the Home Department* [2009] EWCA Civ 226, especially para 37.
58 *DD (Afghanistan) v Secretary of State for the Home Department* [2010] EWCA Civ 1407.
59 *KJ (Sri Lanka) v Secretary of State for the Home Department* [2009] EWCA Civ 292 para 35.
60 *R (JS (Sri Lanka)) v Secretary of State for the Home Department* [2010] UKSC 15 para 56.
61 *Al-Sirri v Secretary of State for the Home Department* [2009] EWCA Civ 222, [2009] INLR 586 para 35.

commit any specific or identifiable crime but to further the organisation's aims by committing article 1F crimes generally, no more need be established than that the accused had personal knowledge of such aims and intended to contribute to their commission.[62]

12.67 Lord Brown concluded:

> Put simply, I would hold an accused disqualified under article 1F if there are serious reasons for considering him voluntarily to have contributed in a significant way to the organisation's ability to pursue its purpose of committing war crimes, aware that his assistance will in fact further that purpose.[63]

12.68 Lord Hope endorsed Lord Brown's approach, stressing the phrases 'in a significant way' and 'will in fact further that purpose', which, he said, provided 'the essential elements that must be satisfied to fix the applicant with personal responsibility'.[64]

12.69 It follows that mere membership of an organisation which is said to have carried out war crimes or acts of terrorism cannot by itself be a reason for exclusion.[65] Nor does the fact that the organisation is proscribed by the EU automatically lead to exclusion.[66]

12.70 The definition of the requisite mens rea for exclusion purposes is therefore wider (covering more states of mind) than the test for joint enterprise under domestic criminal law.

Actus reus

12.71 The relevant actus reus (the requisite wrongful act or omission) can include anyone providing funding or logistical support, or carrying out 'advance acts in support of terrorist activities'.[67] It is not necessary to identify, among crimes committed by the group, individual

---

62 *R (JS (Sri Lanka)) v Secretary of State for the Home Department* [2010] UKSC 15 para 37.
63 *R (JS (Sri Lanka)) v Secretary of State for the Home Department* [2010] UKSC 15 para 38.
64 *R (JS (Sri Lanka)) v Secretary of State for the Home Department* [2010] UKSC 15 para 49.
65 *KJ (Sri Lanka) v Secretary of State for the Home Department* [2009] EWCA Civ 292 para 35; *JS (Sri Lanka)* para 2 (where the point was 'common ground between the parties').
66 *Bundesrepublik Deutschland v B and D* Joined Cases C-57/09 and C-101/09 [2011] Imm AR 190, [2011] INLR 133 para 99.
67 *R (JS (Sri Lanka)) v Secretary of State for the Home Department* [2010] UKSC 15 paras 35, 47.

crimes in which the individual was specifically involved.[68] However, it is necessary to show that such crimes were in fact committed: the examination of the individual's personal role:

> ... inevitably involve[s] recognition of the ingredients of the offences in which he was said to be complicit and of what it was about the known behaviour of the [individual] that might be said to bring him to the requisite level of participation.[69]

It is necessary to show the 'personal guilt of the person in question',[70] which necessitates 'a close examination of the facts' in each case.[71]

12.72 The approach favoured by the tribunal in *Gurung*[72] and frequently followed by decision-makers since then – essentially of focussing on the nature of the organisation and seeking to place it on a 'continuum' of organisations ranging from those wholly dedicated to terrorism to those devoted to democracy which occasionally allow their standards to slip – was considered unhelpful in *JS (Sri Lanka)*.[73] In particular, the political motivation of the organisation to which the applicant is said to have belonged is irrelevant to whether its members may have committed war crimes or acted contrary to the purposes and principles of the UN.[74]

12.73 Instead, Lord Brown said that 'the determining factors in any case' were likely to be principally:

> (i) the nature and (potentially of some importance) the size of the organisation and particularly that part of it with which the asylum-seeker was himself most directly concerned, (ii) whether and, if so, by whom the organisation was proscribed, (iii) how the asylum-seeker came to be recruited, (iv) the length of time he remained in the organisation and what, if any, opportunities he had to leave it, (v) his position, rank, standing and influence in the organisation, (vi) his knowledge of the organisation's war crimes activities, and (vii) his own personal involvement and role in the organisation including

---

68 *R (JS (Sri Lanka)) v Secretary of State for the Home Department* [2010] UKSC 15 paras 38, 58.
69 *R (JS (Sri Lanka)) v Secretary of State for the Home Department* [2010] UKSC 15 para 58.
70 *KJ (Sri Lanka) v Secretary of State for the Home Department* [2009] EWCA Civ 292 para 35.
71 *R (JS (Sri Lanka)) v Secretary of State for the Home Department* [2010] UKSC 15 para 44.
72 *Gurung (Refugee exclusion clauses especially 1F(b)) Nepal CG* [2002] UKIAT 04870, [2003] INLR 133
73 *R (JS (Sri Lanka)) v Secretary of State for the Home Department* [2010] UKSC 15 paras 29–32.
74 *R (JS (Sri Lanka)) v Secretary of State for the Home Department* [2010] UKSC 15 para 32.

particularly whatever contribution he made towards the commission of war crimes.[75]

When a person may be excluded under article 1F(c)

12.74 In *RB (Algeria)*, the House of Lords held that a person may be excluded under article 1F(c) both before and after recognition as a refugee. If a refugee commits acts falling within this exclusion clause after recognition as a refugee, he or she stands to lose refugee status.[76] Article 1F(c) may also be invoked retrospectively, ie even if refugee status was granted after the relevant acts were committed.[77]

Loss of protection from refoulement

12.75 The preceding section of this chapter has dealt with the circumstances in which a person who would otherwise be recognised as a refugee is 'excluded' from such recognition.

12.76 Articles 32 and 33 of the Refugee Convention allow for the expulsion of refugees, in other words of those who *do* fall within the Refugee Convention but who represent a risk to national security or who have committed a serious offence and represent a danger to the community of the country of refuge and so are not protected from refoulement. In practice, however, under domestic law, the determination of whether a person has lost protection from refoulement under article 33(2) precedes the analysis of whether that person is a refugee so this loss of protection may affect both refugees and those who claim to be, but are not, refugees.

Article 32

12.77 Article 32 is rarely invoked and can be dealt with shortly. It provides that a refugee lawfully present in the country of refuge shall not be expelled 'save on grounds of national security or public order'. This has been deemed to apply to refugees who have been granted leave to remain and not to those awaiting a decision on their claims.[78] Hence

---

75 *R (JS (Sri Lanka)) v Secretary of State for the Home Department* [2010] UKSC 15 para 30.
76 *RB (Algeria) and others v Secretary of State for the Home Department* [2009] UKHL 10, [2010] 2 AC 110, paras 128–129, para 206.
77 Qualification Directive article 14(3)(a).
78 *Secretary of State for the Home Department v ST (Eritrea)* [2010] EWCA Civ 643.

the practice of removing asylum-seekers to safe third countries for their claims to be assessed there is not in breach of article 32.[79] Article 32 is without prejudice to article 33, which provides more comprehensive protection to those at risk of persecution, with some exceptions.

Article 33(2)

12.78 Article 33(1) is the provision of the Refugee Convention which supplies refugees with protection from expulsion or return to face persecution. The exceptions to that protection are set out in article 33(2), which requires consideration of whether the refugee is disqualified from international protection if:

- there are 'reasonable grounds' for considering him or her to be 'a danger to the security of the country [of refuge]'; or
- he or she is a person 'who, having been convicted by a final judgment of a particularly serious crime, constitutes a danger to the community of that country'.

12.79 It will be noted that 'reasonable grounds' applies only to the 'national security' limb of article 33(2) of the Refugee Convention: it is not sufficient for the SSHD reasonably to think that the individual presents a danger to the community: he or she must in fact present such a danger.[80]

Contrasting Refugee Convention article 33(2) with article 1F(b)

12.80 Article 33(2) of the Refugee Convention does not contain the same limitations of time and place as article 1F(b): it potentially applies wherever and whenever the 'particularly serious crime' was committed. However, the crimes covered by article 33(2) must be 'particularly' serious (whereas article 1F(b) does not use the word 'particularly'). Under article 33(2), the individual must, again in contrast to article 1F(b), pose a danger to the community. Article 33(2) is therefore primarily forward-looking, in contrast to article 1F(b).

---

79 *Secretary of State for the Home Department v ST (Eritrea)* [2010] EWCA Civ 643 para 44.
80 *IH (s72; 'Particularly Serious Crime') Eritrea* [2009] UKAIT 00012 para 14.

The test to be met under article 33(2)

12.81 The particularly serious crime and danger to the community are separate tests and the first needs to be fulfilled before the second comes into play.[81]

12.82 The burden of showing that the individual presents a danger to the community – and every other aspect of meeting the article 33(2) test – rests on the SSHD.[82]

12.83 There is no balance to be struck between the risk to the individual and the danger to the community, but as a result the IAT has held that the threshold is a high one:

> The effect of there being no balance in Article 33(2), as we conclude, is to emphasise that the tests for 'a particularly serious crime' and 'danger' must be higher than they would be if there were a balance to be undertaken. We have allowed for this in our conclusions on those issues. It is in particular the 'danger' threshold which would be affected by the risk on return to the refugee, if a balance were to exist and which we see as quite a high threshold in its absence.[83]

The presumptions under NIAA 2002 s72

12.84 NIAA 2002 s72 represents a further attempt by parliament to unilaterally impose an interpretation on provisions of the Refugee Convention.

12.85 Parliament has introduced presumptions that a person convicted in the UK and sentenced to a period of imprisonment of at least two years has committed a 'particularly serious crime' and constitutes 'a danger to the community' for the purposes of article 33(2) of the Refugee Convention.

12.86 NIAA 2002 s72(2) provides:

> A person shall be presumed to have been convicted by a final judgment of a particularly serious crime and to constitute a danger to the community of the United Kingdom if he is–
> (a) convicted in the United Kingdom, and
> (b) sentenced to a period of imprisonment of at least two years.

12.87 Equivalent provisions exist in NIAA 2002 s72(3) for those convicted outside the UK, with the proviso that the individual 'could have been sentenced to a period of imprisonment of at least two years had his conviction been a conviction in the United Kingdom of a similar offence'.

---

81 *EN (Serbia) v Secretary of State for the Home Department* [2009] EWCA Civ 630, [2010] QB 633 para 39.
82 *IH (s72; 'Particularly Serious Crime') Eritrea* [2009] UKAIT 00012 para 13.
83 *SB (Cessation and exclusion) Haiti* [2005] UKIAT 00036 para 84.

12.88 A period of imprisonment of at least two years does not include a suspended sentence (unless at least two years of the sentence are not suspended),[84] but does include a sentence in an institution other than a prison (including a hospital or an institution for young offenders)[85] or a sentence for an indeterminate period (provided that it may last for two years).[86] A person who has been sentenced to two years' or more imprisonment only by virtue of being sentenced to consecutive sentences which amount in aggregate to that period is not treated for these purposes as having been sentenced to at least two years' imprisonment.[87]

12.89 NIAA 2002 s72(4) provides a further presumption that a person has been convicted of a particularly serious crime and constitutes a danger to the community of the UK if 'he is convicted of an offence specified by order of the Secretary of State'. However, the order specifying 'particularly serious offences' made by the SSHD under NIAA 2002 s72(4)[88] was held by the Court of Appeal in *EN (Serbia)* to be ultra vires (outside the power conferred by the legislation), because it specified offences, including theft, which could not, without more, be regarded as 'particularly serious', contrary to parliament's intention.[89] No fresh order has been made.

12.90 It follows that the questions of whether in fact the applicant has been convicted of a 'particularly serious crime' and if so whether he or she constitutes a danger to the community are questions of fact to be determined in each case, taking into account the presumption in relation to those sentenced to more than two years' imprisonment under NIAA 2002 s72(2).

12.91 On its face, NIAA 2002 s72 appeared to create an irrebuttable presumption that a person sentenced to a period of imprisonment of at least two years had been convicted of a particularly serious crime, although the legislation made clear[90] that the presumption that such a person posed a danger to the community was rebuttable.

12.92 The Court of Appeal held in *EN (Serbia)* that an irrebuttable presumption would be contrary to article 14(4) of the Qualification

---

84 NIAA 2002 s72(11)(b)(i).
85 NIAA 2002 s72(11)(b)(ii).
86 NIAA 2002 s72(11)(b)(iii).
87 NIAA 2002 s72(11)(b)(ia).
88 Nationality, Immigration and Asylum Act 2002 (Specification of Particularly Serious Crimes) Order 2004 SI No 1910.
89 *EN (Serbia) v Secretary of State for the Home Department* [2009] EWCA Civ 630, [2010] QB 633 paras 81–83.
90 NIAA 2002 s72(6).

Directive. NIAA 2002 s72(2) must therefore be read down as creating *rebuttable* presumptions in respect of both the 'particularly serious crime' limb and the 'danger to the community' limb.

12.93 The presumptions under NIAA 2002 s72 will be rebutted if the individual can establish that he does not in fact constitute a danger to the community[91] or has not in fact been convicted of a particularly serious crime.

12.94 The presumptions under NIAA 2002 s72 do not apply while an appeal against conviction or sentence is possible or is pending.[92]

Definition of 'particularly serious crime'

12.95 Only a subset of crimes are 'serious', and only a small subset are 'particularly serious'. Nor can persistent low level offending be seen as amounting cumulatively to a 'particularly serious' crime.[93] However, whether an offence is 'particularly serious' needs to be seen in context, and a past history of offending may place an offence in that category when it would not be particularly serious if it stood on its own.[94] When considering whether a crime is 'particularly serious', it is necessary to take account of all the circumstances of the offence.[95] 'Particularly serious' does not simply mean 'exceptional', 'extreme' or 'grave'.[96] The Tribunal has said:

> Murder, rape, serious crimes of violence or public disorder may require little more to place them in the 'particularly serious' category. But that will be because nothing in the circumstances dilutes the justifiable conclusion reached. But not always: it is not difficult to envisage even for murder circumstances which might lead to a contrary view, for example the offence is an act of mercy killing. Likewise, there are crimes which, at first blush, do not necessarily seem to be 'particularly serious', for example theft. Theft is, of course, one of the scheduled crimes in the 2004 Order. By virtue of that Order, it is always a 'particularly serious crime' regardless of the circumstances of its commission. But, there may be a world of difference between

---

91 NIAA 2002 s72(6).
92 NIAA 2002 s72(7).
93 *SB (Cessation and exclusion) Haiti* [2005] UKIAT 00036 para 70.
94 *SB (Cessation and exclusion) Haiti* [2005] UKIAT 00036 paras 72–73; the offence which would not have been particularly serious if it stood in isolation was wounding; other offences committed by the appellant, including causing actual bodily harm, theft and possession of real or imitation firearms were not considered to fall within the relevant category.
95 *IH (s72; 'Particularly Serious Crime') Eritrea* [2009] UKAIT 00012, para 73.
96 *IH (s72; 'Particularly Serious Crime') Eritrea* [2009] UKAIT 00012, para 74.

the categorisation of a conviction for theft arising from a bank heist and one where the individual stole from a supermarket to feed his family. Both amount to the same crime, but only by looking at the circumstances can it properly be determined whether the crime was in fact 'particularly serious'.[97]

12.96 The 'danger to the community' will usually be, but does not have to be, causally connected to the conviction for a particularly serious crime.[98]

Article 33(2), refugee status and residence permits

12.97 Article 33(2) is not an exclusion clause: it does not mean that an individual is not a refugee, merely that they are not entitled to protection from refoulement.[99] We suggest that this means that, while a refugee remains in the country of refuge, they remain entitled to recognition as a refugee and to the benefits of refugee status other than protection from refoulement.

12.98 However, this is controversial, as we shall see below.

12.99 Confusion arises from article 14(4) of the Qualification Directive which states:

> Member states may revoke, end or refuse to renew the status granted to a refugee by a governmental, administrative, judicial or quasi-judicial body, when:
> (a) there are reasonable grounds for regarding him or her as a danger to the security of the member state in which he or she is present;
> (b) he or she, having been convicted by a final judgement of a particularly serious crime, constitutes a danger to the community of that member state.

12.100 Article 14(5) of the Qualification Directive continues:

> In situations described in paragraph 4, member states may decide not to grant status to a refugee, where such a decision has not yet been taken.

12.101 Article 14(6) goes on:

> Persons to whom paragraphs 4 or 5 apply are entitled to rights set out in or similar to those set out in Articles 3, 4, 16, 22, 31 and 32 and 33 of the Geneva Convention in so far as they are present in the member state.

---

97 *IH (s72; 'Particularly Serious Crime') Eritrea* [2009] UKAIT 00012, para 76.
98 *EN (Serbia) v Secretary of State for the Home Department* [2009] EWCA Civ 630, [2010] QB 633 para 46.
99 J Hathaway, *The law of refugee status*, Butterworths, 1991, p225, note 230; *SB (Cessation and exclusion) Haiti* [2005] UKIAT 00036 para 99.

12.102 Article 21 of the Qualification Directive provides:

Protection from refoulement
1. Member states shall respect the principle of non-refoulement in accordance with their international obligations.
2. Where not prohibited by the international obligations mentioned in paragraph 1, member states may refoule a refugee, whether formally recognised or not, when:
(a) there are reasonable grounds for considering him or her as a danger to the security of the member state in which he or she is present; or
(b) he or she, having been convicted by a final judgement of a particularly serious crime, constitutes a danger to the community of that member state.
3. Member states may revoke, end or refuse to renew or to grant the residence permit of (or to) a refugee to whom paragraph 2 applies.

12.103 The formulation in article 14(4) and (5) of the Qualification Directive is obscure, in part because, as discussed at para 11.24, refugee status is recognised (or declared), not granted by states.[100] If the intention of these provisions is simply to say that a *residence permit* does not *have to be* granted to a person falling within article 33(2) of the Refugee Convention, then they would appear to be otiose, since that is made clear in article 21(3) of the Qualification Directive.

12.104 If article 14(4) is intended to mean that a member state may treat a person as ceasing to be a refugee and ceasing to be entitled to *refugee status* and all its benefits in those circumstances, then we suggest that these provisions of the Qualification Directive are inconsistent with the Refugee Convention. A person in this position is still entitled to recognition as a refugee under the Refugee Convention even though the Qualification Directive may suggest otherwise.[101]

12.105 In *EN (Serbia)* Stanley Burnton LJ went still further, stating that article 14(5) of the Qualification Directive:

expressly authorises a member state to refuse refugee status to a person to whom [Article 14(4)] applies. Doubtless this is because the member states consider that the application of [Article 14(4)] is inconsistent with refugee status; a view with which I respectfully agree. Rules 334 and 339A of the Immigration Rules are consistent with this. It follows that if the tribunal finds that [an applicant] committed a particularly serious crime and that he constitutes a danger to the

---

100 Qualification Directive recital 14.
101 Compare *K and Fornah v Secretary of State for the Home Department* [2007] 1 AC 412 para 16, para 118; and see, among others, recitals (2), (3) and (16) of the Qualification Directive, affording primacy to the Refugee Convention.

community, he will not be entitled to refugee status even if his Convention rights preclude his removal.[102]

12.106 That passage was, however, expressly obiter, and, we respectfully suggest, incorrect. As we have discussed above at para 12.76, article 33(2) does not provide that committing a 'particularly serious crime' and posing a 'danger to the community' are inconsistent with refugee status, merely that this may prevent a person relying on protection from refoulement. Nor, in fact, do articles 14(4) or 14(5) of the Qualification Directive state that the commission of a particularly serious crime and posing a danger to the community are inconsistent with refugee status, because both provisions are discretionary ('may'): they permit refugee status to be retained even after such a crime. Indeed, article 14(6) of the Qualification Directive seems to confirm that the benefits that accrue to refugees under the Refugee Convention remain in place while the refugee remains on the territory of the member state concerned.

12.107 There is a further point which is that, arguably, those who are refugees, who have lost protection under the Refugee Convention but who cannot be expelled because of other international obligations (such as ECHR article 3) remain entitled to a residence permit. We set out this argument briefly below.

12.108 Article 24(1) of the Qualification Directive requires those granted status as refugees to be given a residence permit valid for at least three years. We suggest that 'refoulement' and 'international obligations' in article 21(1)–(2) of the Qualification Directive should be read as referring not only to the Refugee Convention but also to other international obligations, namely the ECHR, preventing forcible expulsion. The words 'where not prohibited by ... international obligations' in article 21(2) would be otiose if the international obligations referred to were only those in the Refugee Convention, since the rest of that provision reiterates the circumstances in which refugees can be refouled without breaching the Refugee Convention. If this is correct, where a person *is a refugee* but can nevertheless be refouled without breaching ECHR article 3, or some other international obligation, a residence permit can be (but does not have to be) withheld or revoked under article 21(3) of the Qualification Directive. But where refoulement would breach any of the state's international obligations (including, for example, ECHR article 3), and

---

102 *EN (Serbia) v Secretary of State for the Home Department* [2009] EWCA Civ 630, [2010] QB 633 para 113.

the person *is a refugee*, the entitlement to a residence permit persists under article 24(1) of the Qualification Directive.

12.109 Immigration Rules para 334(iv) provides that a person will not be 'granted asylum' in the UK if he or she, having been convicted by a final judgment of a particularly serious crime and poses a danger to the community of the UK. Paragraph 339A(x) likewise provides that 'a person's grant of asylum':

> ... will be revoked or not renewed if the Secretary of State is satisfied that having been convicted by a final judgment of a particularly serious crime he constitutes a danger to the community of the United Kingdom.

We suggest that these provisions within the Immigration Rules are arguably unlawful since:

- they fail to ensure that those who are refugees but have lost the protection from refoulement under the Refugee Convention remain recognised as refugees and entitled to the other benefits of such status under the Refugee Convention (see para 11.6 above);
- in addition, if the argument at para 12.108 above is correct, the Immigration Rules fail to ensure, contrary to articles 21(2) and 24(1) of the Qualification Directive, that those who are refugees, have lost the protection from refoulement under the Refugee Convention but who cannot be expelled because that would breach some other international obligation, retain their residence permit.

Procedure on appeal to the IAC or SIAC in exclusion and loss of protection cases

Certificates

12.110 IANA 2006 s55 entitles the Home Office to issue a certificate that article 1F or article 33(2) applies (in the latter case on national security grounds). In that case the Immigration and Asylum Chamber of the First Tier or Upper Tribunals (IAC) or SIAC is obliged to 'begin substantive deliberations' on the appeal by considering the certificate.

12.111 NIAA 2002 s72(9) likewise permits the SSHD to impose a certificate that the presumptions of having been convicted of a 'particularly serious crime' and of posing a 'danger to the community' apply to an individual, for the purposes of article 33(2) of the Refugee Convention. The IAC or SIAC must address the NIAA 2002 s72 certificate, including any issue as to whether the individual has in fact been convicted of a particularly serious crime and/or as to the presumption of dangerousness, at the beginning of the hearing of the appeal.[103]

12.112 Only after quashing any certificate made under IANA 2006 s55 or NIAA 2002 s72(9) may a substantive asylum appeal be considered. Usually, however, a person who brings a claim under the Refugee Convention will also have a claim under ECHR article 3, relying on the same evidence about risk on return. The ECHR article 3 claim and the evidence for it must be considered irrespective of the outcome of the consideration of the certificates. The immigration judge will usually therefore need to consider risk on return in any event.

Exclusion

12.113 If the Home Office considers that a person should be excluded from refugee status, the reasons for refusal letter (RFRL) should state the reasons for this. The applicant will then need to deal with exclusion on any appeal to the IAC or to SIAC in his or her witness statement and other evidence and in submissions.

12.114 The Tribunal has held that even if the Home Office has not raised the exclusion clauses, the immigration judge is entitled to do so, and indeed must do so if their applicability is '*Robinson* obvious': that is to say, it has 'a strong prospect of success if it is argued'.[104] In *AA Palestine* the Tribunal stated that 'what matters is not that the answer is obvious but that the question obviously arises'.[105] But immigration judges must ensure that both the applicant and the Home Office are given a fair opportunity to address the issue, if necessary by adjourning the appeal hearing.[106] Whether the issue 'obviously' arises depends on the facts, and the immigration judge is not required to take an exclusion point which the Home Office has failed to advance and which is not '*Robinson* obvious'.[107] An appellant may wish to ask for an adjournment for further preparation if the issue is raised

---

103 NIAA 2002 s72(10) and *TB (Jamaica) v Secretary of State for the Home Department* [2008] EWCA Civ 977, para 29.
104 *R v Secretary of State for the Home Department ex p Robinson* [1998] QB 929, [1997] 3 WLR 1162.
105 *AA (Exclusion clauses) Palestine* [2005] UKIAT 00104 para 44.
106 *Gurung* at para 48.
107 *MH (Syria) v Secretary of State for the Home Department* [2009] EWCA Civ 226 para 75.

unexpectedly at the hearing although, if it is obvious that an exclusion clause might apply, the request may not always be granted.[108]

12.115 Where an appellant's case reveals conduct that may give rise to exclusion, the legal representatives will have to consider whether to prepare evidence and submissions about exclusion even if this is not raised in the refusal letter. It may not be easy to justify preparing speculatively to answer a point not yet raised by the Home Office. An appropriate compromise may be, on careful instructions, to raise the issue at any pre-hearing review or case management review hearing on the basis that the exclusion clauses will be deemed not to be in issue unless the appellant is notified to the contrary in advance of the hearing.[109]

12.116 The Home Office does not need to consider whether an asylum claimant falls *within* the refugee definition (inclusion) before considering whether he or she falls under an exclusion clause (exclusion).

12.117 This means that the Home Office may decide that an exclusion clause applies, without considering the merits of the asylum claim.

12.118 In other cases, the Home Office refusal letter will set out other reasons for refusing the asylum claim – for instance that the applicant is not credible and/or that there is no risk of persecution – and then go on to add that the claimant is excluded.

Loss of protection

12.119 As concerns the presumptions under NIAA 2002 s72, the IAC or SIAC are again obliged to consider these where they potentially apply and will err if it does not[110] regardless of whether they have been raised in a Home Office reasons for refusal letter. Where the Home Office fails to raise article 33(2) of the Refugee Convention and loss of protection arguments in the reasons for refusal letter, tactical considerations will again arise for appellants and their representatives as to whether to nonetheless prepare on the point. The need to obtain clarification before the hearing may be less pressing in article 33(2) cases. This is because, where there is also an ECHR article 8 claim, or where an individual is challenging a decision to deport

---

108 *Gurung (Refugee exclusion clauses especially 1F(b)) Nepal CG* [2002] UKIAT 04870, [2003] INLR 133 paras 43 and 48.

109 This is what appears to have happened in the case of one of the appellants in *MH (Syria) v Secretary of State for the Home Department* [2009] EWCA Civ 226: see para 73.

110 *Mugwagwa (s72 – applying statutory presumptions) Zimbabwe* [2011] UKUT 00338 (IAC).

under the Immigration Act (IA) 1971 under para 364 of the Immigration Rules, the appellant and any legal representatives will almost invariably in any event need to prepare evidence on reoffending risk and any mitigating factors on the offence.

12.120 Checklists for evidence relevant to loss of protection arguments (specifically, for the purposes of rebutting the NIAA 2002 s72 presumptions of conviction of a particularly serious crime and dangerousness to the community) are dealt with in chapter 20.

Cessation

12.121 A refugee's circumstances may change so that he or she no longer needs the protection of the international community but can safely live again in his or her country of origin. In essence, a person may cease to be refugee.

12.122 As UNHCR has put it:

> Refugee status, as conceived in international law, is, in principle, a transitory phenomenon which lasts only as long as the reasons for fearing persecution in the country of origin persist.[111]

12.123 Article 1C of the Refugee Convention sets out the circumstances in which a person may cease to be a refugee. It is known as the cessation clause.

12.124 The cessation clause lays down exhaustive conditions. This means that the refugee's status is maintained until one of the cessation clauses can be invoked.

Article 1C

12.125 Article 1C states as follows:

> This Convention shall cease to apply to any person falling under the terms of Section A if:
> (1) He has voluntarily re-availed himself of the protection of the country of his nationality; or
> (2) Having lost his nationality, he has voluntarily re-acquired it; or
> (3) He has acquired a new nationality, and enjoys the protection of the country of his new nationality; or
> (4) He has voluntarily re-established himself in the country which he left or outside which he remained owing to fear of persecution; or

---

111 'The cessation clauses: guidelines on their application', UNHCR, Geneva, April 1999, para 1; and see *Saad, Diriye and Osorio v Secretary of State for the Home Department* [2001] EWCA Civ 2008, para 19.

(5) He can no longer, because the circumstances in connection with which he has been recognized as a refugee have ceased to exist, continue to refuse to avail himself of the protection of the country of his nationality;

Provided that this paragraph shall not apply to a refugee falling under Section A(I) of this Article who is able to invoke compelling reasons arising out of previous persecution for refusing to avail himself of the protection of the country of nationality;

(6) Being a person who has no nationality he is, because of the circumstances in connection with which he has been recognized as a refugee have ceased to exist, able to return to the country of his former habitual residence;

Provided that this paragraph shall not apply to a refugee falling under Section A(I) of this Article who is able to invoke compelling reasons arising out of previous persecution for refusing to return to the country of his former habitual residence.

European and domestic implementation of Refugee Convention article 1C

12.126 Article 1C is substantially adopted in article 11 of the Qualification Directive, with the proviso, as regards the provisions concerning changes of circumstances in the country of origin, that:

Member states shall have regard to whether the change of circumstances is of such a significant and non-temporary nature that the refugee's fear of persecution can no longer be regarded as well-founded.[112]

12.127 The Immigration Rules also make specific provision[113] for the revocation of or refusal to renew a grant of asylum, in terms which largely match article 1C, article 1F and/or article 33(2), but also include cases where 'misrepresentation or omission or facts, including the use of false documents, were decisive for the grant of asylum'.[114]

12.128 When a person's grant of asylum is revoked or not renewed, any limited leave which they have may be curtailed.[115] The person concerned must be informed in writing that the SSHD is reconsidering his qualification for refugee status and the reasons why, and is entitled

---

112 Qualification Directive article 11(2).
113 Immigration Rules para 339A.
114 Immigration Rules para 339A(viii), deriving from Qualification Directive article 14(3)(b).
115 Immigration Rules para 339B.

to an opportunity to submit, by way of a personal interview or a written statement, reasons why his refugee status should not be revoked.[116]

UNHCR's involvement in cessation decisions

12.129 Immigration Rules para 358C provides for UNHCR to be involved where the SSHD 'is considering revoking a person's refugee status'. The Policy, Guidance and Casework Instruction on Cancellation, Cessation and Revocation of Refugee Status states at para 2.4 that:

> It will also normally be appropriate to give the UNHCR an opportunity to comment on individual cases before a final decision is taken. There are certain situations where consultation on a case-by-case basis will not be necessary, but these are outlined in the appropriate place in this instruction.
>
> UKBA's default position is that UNHCR will be approached on every case.
>
> ...
>
> Consultation should take place after the individual concerned has had an opportunity to comment so that the UNHCR can take those representations into account when it prepares its own response.
> UNHCR should generally be allowed 15 working days within which to respond.

Revocation of indefinite leave (ILR) to remain for cessation reasons

12.130 The provisions of article 1C are also partly mirrored in NIAA 2002 s76(3), as regards those with ILR:

> The Secretary of State may revoke a person's indefinite leave to enter or remain in the United Kingdom if the person, or someone of whom he is a dependant, ceases to be a refugee as a result of–
> (a) voluntarily availing himself of the protection of his country of nationality,
> (b) voluntarily re-acquiring a lost nationality,
> (c) acquiring the nationality of a country other than the United Kingdom and availing himself of its protection, or
> (d) voluntarily establishing himself in a country in respect of which he was a refugee.

12.131 NIAA 2002 s76(3) reflects those limbs of article 1C which deal with situations brought about by the refugee: thus indefinite leave may not

---

116 Immigration Rules para 339BA.

be revoked under section 76 simply because the circumstances which led to the applicant being granted refugee status have changed.

12.132 By section 76(6), ILR may be revoked in respect of leave granted before the section came into force, but only in reliance on a refugee's action taken after the section came into force.

12.133 NIAA 2002 s76 is also dealt with more generally at paras 19.66–19.73.

Approach to cessation

12.134 The burden of proof in revocation of refugee status is on the state.[117] The various limbs of the cessation clause should be interpreted restrictively as the UNHCR has stated[118] and as has been accepted by the House of Lords.[119] The Tribunal has said that 'temporary changes in a situation of volatility do not suffice. Time should be allowed for the changes to consolidate, so as to show their durability'.[120] The European Court of Justice (ECJ) has held, in even more robust terms, that a

> ... change of circumstances will be of a 'significant and non-temporary' nature, within the terms of Article 11(2) of the Directive, when the factors which formed the basis of the refugee's fear of persecution may be regarded as having been permanently eradicated.[121]

12.135 The Policy, Guidance and Casework Instruction on Cancellation, Cessation and Revocation of Refugee Status also states at para 4.3 that the provisions relating to change of circumstances will 'normally' be invoked only 'where a Ministerial Statement has been issued announcing that significant and non-temporary changes have occurred in a country'.

12.136 Article 1C(5) relates only to those who have previously been recognised as refugees, so a person who claims asylum and is refused on the basis that the situation which caused her or him to leave cannot claim the benefit of article 1C(5).[122]

---

117 Qualification Directive article 14(2).
118 UNHCR Handbook para 116.
119 *In re B; R v Special Adjudicator ex p Hoxha* [2005] UKHL 19, para 65.
120 *SB (Cessation and exclusion) Haiti* [2005] UKIAT 00036 para 29.
121 *Abdulla v Bundesrepublik Deutschland* Joined Cases C-175/08, C176/08, C-178/08 and C-179/08 2 March 2010, para 73.
122 *R (Hoxha) v Special Adjudicator; R (B) v Immigration Appeal Tribunal* [2005] UKHL 19, [2005] 1 WLR 1063.

Voluntary re-availment of national protection

12.137 One of the more common reasons for cessation is that a person has voluntarily re-availed himself of the protection of his country of origin. Refugee status ceases because such a person is no longer 'unable or unwilling to avail himself of the protection of the country of his nationality', which is a requirement of refugee status under article 1A of the convention.

12.138 The UNHCR Handbook states:[123]

> If the refugee does not act voluntarily, he will not cease to be a refugee. If he is instructed by an authority, eg of his country of residence, to perform against his will an act that could be interpreted as a re-availment of the protection of the country of his nationality, such as applying to his Consulate for a national passport, he will not cease to be a refugee merely because he obeys such an instruction. He may also be constrained, by circumstances beyond his control, to have recourse to a measure of protection from his country of nationality. He may, for instance, need to apply for a divorce in his home country because no other divorce may have the necessary international recognition. Such an act cannot be considered to be a 'voluntary re-availment of protection' and will not deprive a person of refugee status.

12.139 The Handbook goes on to say:[124]

> In determining whether refugee status is lost in these circumstances, a distinction should be drawn between actual re-availment of protection and occasional and incidental contacts with the national authorities. If a refugee applies for and obtains a national passport or its renewal, it will, in the absence of proof to the contrary, be presumed that he intends to avail himself of the protection of the country of his nationality. On the other hand, the acquisition of documents from the national authorities, for which non-nationals would likewise have to apply – such as a birth or marriage certificate – or similar services, cannot be regarded as a re-availment of protection.

Voluntary re-establishment in the country where persecution was feared

12.140 This is the only limb of the cessation clause which is predicated on a refugee's return to his/her country of origin. Not every person who returns to his or her country will fall under the cessation clause. The evidence will need to show voluntary re-establishment (which

---

123 UNHCR Handbook para 120.
124 UNHCR Handbook para 121.

is more than mere presence in the country) and this may depend on factors such as:

- How long was the refugee's stay in his/her country of origin?
- What did the refugee do there?
- Did the refugee return there out of compelling personal reasons such as the illness or death of a close relative?
- Did the refugee have contact with the authorities, eg by paying taxes?
- Did the refugee live or work there without problems?
- Did the refugee intend to stay there permanently or just for a fixed period?

12.141 However, even a short visit to the refugee's country of origin may cause the Home Office to invoke a different part of article 1C, namely 1C(5), on the grounds that the refugee's willingness to return is evidence that the circumstances in connection with which he or she was recognised as a refugee have ceased to exist.

12.142 The Home Office's API on Revocation of Indefinite Leave indicates however, under the heading 'An explanation of s76(3)(a)–(d)' that this possibility ought to be approached with care by Home Office caseworkers:

> A lengthy stay would be the most obvious indicator of re-establishment. A short visit to the former country of persecution would not necessarily constitute 're-establishment' but a series of visits might. A longer visit will not amount to re-establishment if the refugee is conducting an exploratory visit. Such visits, whether via an official Explore and Prepare Programme where available or otherwise, are encouraged as an aid to resettlement.

12.143 The Home Office's Policy, Guidance and Casework Instruction on Cancellation, Cessation and Revocation of Refugee Status similarly envisages at para 4.2.4 that:

> If, for example, the visit is undertaken for exceptional reasons which have been approved (such as for a family funeral or to visit a sick relative) it will not be treated as re-establishment.
> Where approval has not been sought prior to travel the case should be considered on its own merits, taking into account factors such as the length and nature of the visit, and whether there have been any previous visits.

12.144 We suggest that the effect of the procedural safeguards set out in the Policy, Guidance and Casework Instruction on Cancellation, Cessation and Revocation of Refugee Status (quoted above at para 12.129) is that the SSHD is not entitled to raise cessation as an afterthought at the hearing of an appeal; nor is the tribunal entitled to raise cessation of its own motion. That is in contrast to the position with the exclusion clauses, as discussed above at para 12.114. Thus if the SSHD seeks to deport a recognised refugee, but cessation is not mentioned in the RFRL, we suggest that, subject to any exclusion or loss of protection issues, the tribunal must allow the appeal on grounds of asylum, and in a case involving 'automatic' deportation under UK Borders Act (UKBA) 2007 s32(5) must find that the appellant falls within the asylum exception at UKBA 2007 s33). Alternatively, the appeal would fall to be allowed as 'not in accordance with the law', on the basis that proper procedure relating to cessation had not been followed, leaving it open to the SSHD to make a further lawful decision, which would attract a further right of appeal.

CHAPTER 13
Relying on the ECHR in claims concerning 'intentional harm'

13.1	Introduction
13.6	**ECHR article 3**
13.7	Application in expulsion cases
13.10	Other consequences of the absolute nature of the prohibitions
13.15	Minimum level of severity
13.16	The prohibited ill treatment
	Torture • Inhuman or degrading treatment or punishment
13.23	Infliction of ill treatment by non-state agents
13.24	The death penalty: ECHR articles 2 and 3
13.33	Mental and physical health
13.34	Conditions of existence
13.40	The burden and standard of proof
13.42	**Reliance on other ECHR rights**
13.44	Other ECHR rights for which 'flagrant denial' is not required in a 'foreign' case
13.45	ECHR rights for which 'flagrant denial' must be shown in a 'foreign' case

Introduction

13.1 This chapter addresses claims under the European Convention on Human Rights (ECHR) in the context of 'intentional harm' claims – that is, allegations that a person would face serious harm after expulsion as a consequence of intentional acts or omissions by state or non-state agents. We focus in particular on ECHR article 3, which is of the widest application in such cases. We briefly also consider other protections to which the 'flagrancy' test does not apply (ECHR articles 2 and 4).

13.2 We go on to consider those ECHR rights to which a test of 'flagrant denial' of the right applies in 'foreign cases' that is, where the breach would occur in the country to which the individual is being expelled.

13.3 This chapter provides a summary overview only,[1] as a prelude to the discussion later in this book about issues which apply specifically to FNPs such as differential immigration status for FNPs who cannot be deported as a consequence of ECHR protections (see chapter 19). A detailed examination of the ECHR protections, and of controversial topics such as the reliability of diplomatic assurances in the context of expulsion, is beyond the scope of this book.

13.4 ECHR article 8 generally is dealt with separately in chapters 15–17. ECHR articles 3 and 8 in the context of mental and physical ill-health will be discussed in chapter 18.

13.5 The protection provided by the ECHR overlaps to a very significant degree with that provided by 'subsidiary protection' under the Qualification Directive.[2] Those who have no extant leave and who succeed in challenging their deportation under the ECHR are granted humanitarian protection or discretionary leave: see chapter 19.

---

1 For more detail, practitioners should consult specialist texts, such as: Lester, Pannick and Herberg, *Human rights law and practice*, LexisNexis Butterworths, 3rd edn, 2009; Clayton and Tomlinson, *The law of human rights*, 2nd edn, OUP, 2009; Ian Macdonald QC and Ronan Toal, *Macdonald's immigration law and practice*, LexisNexis Butterworths, 8th edn, 2010; Blake and Husain, *Immigration, asylum and human rights*, OUP, 2nd edn (forthcoming).
2 Council Directive 2004/83/EC of 29 April 2004 on minimum standards for the qualification and status of third country nationals or stateless persons as refugees or as persons who otherwise need international protection and the content of the protection granted; OJ L 304, 30/09/2004 ('Qualification Directive').

ECHR article 3

13.6 Article 3 ECHR states:

No one shall be subjected to torture or to inhuman or degrading treatment or punishment.

Application in expulsion cases

13.7 In the landmark judgment in *Soering*,[3] the issue was whether a state party to the ECHR could be fixed with responsibility for the ill treatment of an individual that would occur in another state (in that case, after extradition). The European Court of Human Rights (ECtHR) recalled that under article 1 of the ECHR, signatory states are bound to secure the rights and freedoms of the convention 'to everyone within their jurisdiction'. This jurisdictional limit is essentially territorial.[4] Signatories to the ECHR are not, generally, required to protect the rights of individuals in other states and are not required to impose human rights standards on states that are not parties to the ECHR.[5]

13.8 Nevertheless, as the ECtHR went on:

It would hardly be compatible with the underlying values of the Convention, that 'common heritage of political traditions, ideals, freedom and the rule of law' to which the Preamble refers, were a Contracting state knowingly to surrender a fugitive to another state where there were substantial grounds for believing that he would be in danger of being subjected to torture, however heinous the crime allegedly committed.[6]

The same would apply to a risk of inhuman or degrading treatment or punishment.[7] Consequently, liability under article 3 arises in relation to any action, including expulsion, which exposes an individual to prohibited ill treatment.[8]

13.9 *Soering* establishes that the extradition of an individual may breach article 3 where there are substantial grounds for believing that the individual faces a real risk of being subject to prohibited treatment. The ECtHR reached the same conclusion in the deportation context in *Cruz Varas v Sweden*.[9] Its approach was confirmed in cases such as

3 *Soering v UK* (1989) 11 EHRR 439.
4 *Soering v UK* (1989) 11 EHRR 439 para 86.
5 *Soering v UK* (1989) 11 EHRR 439 para 86.
6 *Soering v UK* (1989) 11 EHRR 439 para 86.
7 *Soering v UK* (1989) 11 EHRR 439 para 86.
8 *Soering v UK* (1989) 11 EHRR 439 para 91.
9 (1992) 14 EHRR 1.

Chahal v UK[10] and has now been applied by the ECtHR in numerous other expulsion cases,[11] as well as in the domestic courts.[12]

Other consequences of the absolute nature of the prohibitions

13.10 Because the prohibitions in article 3 are absolute,[13] they apply irrespective of any past misconduct or risks posed by the applicant and irrespective of the policy aims of the state.[14]

13.11 A person who has committed a criminal offence – however serious – remains entitled to the protection of ECHR article 3. Even in national security cases, there is no balancing exercise, as *Chahal*[15] made clear and as recently affirmed by the ECtHR in *Saadi v Italy*[16] and by the Court of Appeal in *AS (Libya)*.[17] Nor does an individual need to show any particular reason for the prohibited treatment.

13.12 The protection offered by ECHR article 3 is thus wider than the protection of the Refugee Convention, with its five qualifying reasons for persecution, exclusion clauses under article 1F and limitation on protection from refoulement for those who have been convicted of particularly serious crime under article 33(2).[18] Under ECHR article 3, it is a sufficient condition for non-expulsion that a person should be at real risk of prohibited treatment.

13.13 The absolute nature of the prohibition in ECHR article 3 also requires that decision-makers must give rigorous scrutiny to expulsion cases raising Article 3 issues. As the ECtHR has stated in *Chahal*

---

10 (1996) 23 EHRR 413.
11 See, for example, *Ahmed v Austria* (1997) 24 EHRR 278; *HLR v France* (1998) 26 EHRR 29; *Jabari v Turkey* [2001] INLR 136; *Sheekh v The Netherlands* (2007) 45 EHRR 50; *Saadi v Italy* (2009) 49 EHRR 30.
12 See, for example, *R (Ullah) v Special Adjudicator* [2004] UKHL 26, [2004] 2 AC 323; *R (Bagdanavicius) v Secretary of State for the Home Department* [2005] UKHL 38, [2005] 2 AC 668; *R (Wellington) v Secretary of State for the Home Department* [2008] UKHL 72, [2009] 1 AC 335; *AS (Libya) v Secretary of State for the Home Department* [2008] EWCA Civ 289, [2008] HRLR 28; *R (Nasseri) v Secretary of State for the Home Department* [2009] UKHL 23, [2010] 1 AC 1.
13 *Sufi and Elmi v UK* App Nos 8319/07 and 11449/07, 28 June 2011, para 212.
14 *R (Limbuela) v Secretary of State for the Home Department* [2005] UKHL 66.
15 *Chahal v UK* (1996) 23 EHRR 413.
16 *Saadi v Italy* (2009) 49 EHRR 30.
17 *AS (Libya) v Secretary of State for the Home Department* [2008] EWCA Civ 289, [2008] HRLR 28.
18 Compare chapter 12.

13.14 The domestic courts have also approved the notion of rigorous scrutiny.[20]

Minimum level of severity

13.15 In order to fall within the scope of ECHR article 3, ill-treatment must attain a minimum level of severity.[21] That will depend on all the circumstances of the case, such as the duration of the treatment, its physical or mental effects and, in some cases, the sex, age and state of health of the victim.[22]

The prohibited ill treatment

13.16 The distinction between torture on the one hand and inhuman or degrading treatment or punishment on the other hand derives 'principally from a difference in the intensity of the suffering inflicted',[23] but refers also to the question of whether the suffering inflicted is intentional. In a number of cases, the ECtHR has defined torture by reference in part to its purpose, such as obtaining information, inflicting punishment or intimidating the victim.[24] The distinction between torture and other treatment prohibited by article 3 recognises the special stigma of torture as attaching to 'deliberate inhuman treatment causing very serious and cruel suffering'.[25]

Torture

13.17 The judgment in *Soering* emphasises the abhorrence of torture in international human rights law:

19 *Chahal v UK* (1996) 23 EHRR 413 para 96.
20 For example, in *RB (Algeria) v Secretary of State for the Home Department* [2009] UKHL 10, [2010] 2 AC 110.
21 See, for example, *A and others v UK* (2009) 49 EHRR 29 para 127; *Rohde v Denmark* (2006) 43 EHRR 17 para 90; *Raninen v Finland* (1998) 26 EHRR 563 para 55; *Ireland v UK* (1979–80) 2 EHRR 25 para 162.
22 *Soering v UK* (1989) 11 EHRR 439 para 89, *A v UK* (2009) 49 EHRR 29 para 127.
23 *Ireland v UK* (1979–80) 2 EHRR 25 para 167.
24 For instance *Aksoy v Turkey* (1998) 25 EHRR 251 para 64; compare the definition in the United Nations Convention against Torture and Other Cruel, Inhuman or Degrading Treatment or Punishment, article 1.
25 *Ireland v UK* (1979–80) 2 EHRR 25 para 167; *Aksoy v Turkey* (1997) 23 EHRR 553 para 63.

This absolute prohibition of torture and of inhuman or degrading treatment or punishment ... shows that Article 3 ... enshrines one of the fundamental values of the democratic societies making up the Council of Europe.[26]

13.18 Findings of torture have included 'Palestinian hanging' (being suspended by the arms, tied together behind the back, causing severe pain and a period of paralysis of the arms), taking into account that the treatment was deliberately inflicted, for the purpose of obtaining admissions or information from the applicant;[27] a series of acts of physical and mental violence against a detainee including rape (the court commented that rape in detention by an official of the state is an 'especially grave and abhorrent form of ill treatment given the ease with which the offender can exploit the vulnerability and weakened resistance of his victim');[28] and the infliction of a large number of blows in detention of such intensity that marks were found over almost all of the applicant's body, together with other acts of violence, threats and humiliating taunts.[29]

13.19 In *Selmouni v France*, the ECtHR recalled that the ECHR is a living instrument which falls to be interpreted in the light of present-day conditions.[30] Owing to rising standards in the protection of human rights, acts which have in the past been classified as inhuman and degrading treatment may in the future be classified as torture.[31] Certain older ECtHR cases should therefore be treated with a degree of caution in so far as some treatment may not have been classified as torture which would be so classified today.

Inhuman or degrading treatment or punishment

13.20 In *A v UK*, the ECtHR summarised its established jurisprudence as follows:

> The Court has considered treatment to be 'inhuman' because, inter alia, it was premeditated, was applied for hours at a stretch and caused either actual bodily injury or intense physical or mental suffering. It has deemed treatment to be 'degrading' because it was such as to

---

26 *Soering v UK* (1989) 11 EHRR 439 para 88; and see the citations from international authority in the speech of Lord Bingham in *A and others v Secretary of State for the Home Department (No 2)* [2005] UKHL 71, [2006] 2 AC 221.
27 *Aksoy v Turkey* (1997) 23 EHRR 553 para 64.
28 *Aydin v Turkey* (1998) 25 EHRR 251 paras 83–87.
29 *Selmouni v France* (2000) 29 EHRR 403 paras 101–105.
30 See *Tyrer v UK* (1979–80) 2 EHRR 1 para 31.
31 *Selmouni v France* (2000) 29 EHRR 403 para 101.

Relying on the ECHR in claims concerning 'intentional harm' 243

arouse in the victims feelings of fear, anguish and inferiority capable of humiliating and debasing them. In considering whether a punishment or treatment was 'degrading' within the meaning of art.3, the Court will have regard to whether its object was to humiliate and debase the person concerned and whether, as far as the consequences are concerned, it adversely affected his or her personality in a manner incompatible with art.3. However, the absence of any such purpose cannot conclusively rule out a finding of a violation of art.3. In order for a punishment or treatment associated with it to be 'inhuman' or 'degrading', the suffering or humiliation involved must go beyond that inevitable element of suffering or humiliation connected with a given form of legitimate treatment or punishment.[32]

Punishment and life sentences

13.21 As the last quotation makes clear, ECHR article 3 is not engaged when the treatment does not go beyond the inevitable element of suffering, even humiliation, which accompanies legitimate punishment.[33] So, for example, a life sentence imposed on an adult is not in itself incompatible with article 3, even if there is no minimum term of unconditional imprisonment and even if there is only a limited possibility of parole. An irreducible life sentence – meaning a sentence without the possibility of a review that may lead to its commutation, remission or termination or to conditional release – may engage article 3. The question is whether there is any prospect of release.[34] In the context of extradition decisions, the House of Lords in *Wellington*[35] upheld the approach in *Kafkaris*, emphasising the high threshold for the engagement of article 3 and also that *Kafkaris* does not suggest that all irreducible life sentences will always violate article 3 irrespective of the crime for which they are imposed. *Wellington* also holds that the test of irreducibility will not be met even if the criteria for reduction of sentence are rarely met and even if reduction is solely a matter of executive discretion unsupervised by the courts.

---

32 *A and others v UK* (2009) 49 EHRR 29 para 127.

33 *A and others v UK* (2009) 49 EHRR 29 para 127; compare *Kafkaris v Cyprus* (2009) 49 EHRR 35 para 97, reflecting the ECtHR's settled case-law.

34 See *Kafkaris v Cyprus* (2009) 49 EHRR 35 paras 98–99 and cases cited there. *Kafkaris* was considered in *Babar Ahmad v UK* (2010) 51 EHRR SE6 (an admissibility decision of the ECtHR). Compare *de Boucherville v Mauritius* [2008] UKPC 37; 25 BHRC 433.

35 *R (Wellington) v Secretary of State for the Home Department* [2008] UKHL 72, [2009] 1 AC 335.

Prison conditions

13.22 While the usual concomitants of imprisonment cannot in themselves give rise to an issue under ECHR article 3, conditions of detention and imprisonment must be compatible with respect for human dignity and must not subject prisoners to avoidable distress or hardship.[36] If prison conditions do not meet these standards, they may amount to inhuman or degrading treatment.[37] Account must be taken of the cumulative effect of the conditions.[38] We discuss the application of article 3 in the context of imprisonment and detention in some detail at paras 36.57–36.74.

Infliction of ill treatment by non-state agents

13.23 A breach of article 3 may arise from a risk of ill-treatment by non-state agents:[39] 'However, it must be shown that the risk is real and that the authorities of the receiving state are not able to obviate the risk by providing appropriate protection'.[40] The approach of the House of Lords in *Bagdanavicius* was that in order to show a breach of article 3 in 'non-state agent cases', it had to be shown not only that there was a risk of serious harm, but also that 'the state has failed to provide reasonable protection'.[41] Where there is such a risk, but the state does provide reasonable protection, there is no breach of article 3. What is reasonable 'must be interpreted in a way which does not impose an impossible or disproportionate burden on the authorities'.[42]

The death penalty: ECHR articles 2 and 3

13.24 ECHR article 2 provides that:

> 1 Everyone's right to life shall be protected by law. No one shall be deprived of his life intentionally save in the execution of a sentence of a court following his conviction of a crime for which this penalty is provided by law.

---

36 *Kudla v Poland* (2002) 35 EHRR 11.
37 *Peers v Greece* (2001) 33 EHRR 1192; *Batayav v Secretary of State for the Home Department* [2003] EWCA Civ 1489, [2004] INLR 126.
38 *Dougoz v Greece* (2002) 34 EHRR 61 paras 45–46.
39 *HLR v France* (1997) 26 EHRR 29.
40 *HLR v France* (1997) 26 EHRR 29, para 40.
41 *R (Bagdanavicius) v Secretary of State for the Home Department* [2005] UKHL 38, [2005] 2 AC 668 para 24.
42 *Osman v UK* (1998) 29 EHRR 245 para 116 (an article 2 case: see *Bagdanavicius* at para 19).

2 Deprivation of life shall not be regarded as inflicted in contravention of this article when it results from the use of force which is no more than absolutely necessary:
   a in defence of any person from unlawful violence;
   b in order to effect a lawful arrest or to prevent the escape of a person lawfully detained;
   c in action lawfully taken for the purpose of quelling a riot or insurrection.

13.25 Article 1 of protocol 13 to the ECHR requires abolition of the death penalty in the states which are members of the Council of Europe.

13.26 A mandatory death sentence constitutes inhuman and degrading treatment contrary to ECHR article 3.[43]

13.27 In *Soering*, the applicant had not argued that a risk of being subject to the death penalty in itself violated his rights under the ECHR and the ECtHR commented that article 3 could not include a general prohibition of the death penalty since that would nullify the clear wording of article 2(1).[44] The issue was whether the risk that he would spend time on death row rendered his extradition in breach of ECHR article 3.[45]

13.28 However, the ECHR is a 'living instrument'[46] whose interpretation may change over time, and the approach of the ECtHR since *Soering* has developed significantly. In *Öcalan v Turkey*,[47] the ECtHR held that the imposition of the death penalty after an unfair trial would breach ECHR article 2 and article 3. It went on to hold in *Bader v Sweden* that if a state deports a person who is at risk of the death penalty as a result of a flagrant denial of a fair trial in the receiving state, there may be a breach of articles 2 or 3.[48]

13.29 In *Al-Saadoon v UK* the court went a step further.[49] It noted that protocol 13 to the ECHR, which requires abolition of the death penalty, had been signed and ratified by the UK, coming into force on 1 February 2004.[50]

---

43 *R (Wellington) v Secretary of State for the Home Department* [2008] UKHL 72, [2009] 1 AC 335 para 63; compare *de Boucherville v Mauritius* [2008] UKPC 37; 25 BHRC 433 para 17 and cases cited there (mandatory sentence of penal servitude for life constituting inhuman and degrading punishment).
44 *Soering v UK* (1989) 11 EHRR 439 para 103.
45 See paras 13.7–13.8.
46 *Tyrer v UK* (1979–80) 2 EHRR 1.
47 (2005) 41 EHRR 45.
48 (2008) 46 EHRR 13 para 42.
49 *Al-Saadoon v UK* (2010) 51 EHRR 9.
50 *Al-Saadoon v UK* (2010) 51 EHRR 9, para 117.

13.30 The ECtHR in *Al-Saadoon v UK* therefore held that the UK was not entitled to:

> ... enter into any arrangement or agreement which involved it in detaining individuals with a view to transferring them to stand trial on capital charges or in any other way subjecting individuals within its jurisdiction to a real risk of being sentenced to the death penalty and executed.[51]

13.31 However, having found 'that through the actions and inaction of the United Kingdom authorities the applicants have been subjected [for almost four years by the date of judgment] to the fear of execution by the Iraqi authorities' and that this caused 'psychological suffering' in breach of ECHR article 3,[52] the court declined to decide on the facts whether there had also been a breach of ECHR article 2.[53]

13.32 In principle a state has the same obligations not to expel a person to a second state from which he or she may in turn be expelled to a third state which may impose the death penalty.[54]

Mental and physical health

13.33 A breach of ECHR article 3 may arise where the actions of the state, including expulsion, risk resulting in suicide and/or the exacerbation of mental or physical illness.[55] This is dealt with in chapter 18.

Conditions of existence

13.34 In *N v UK* the ECtHR Grand Chamber had accepted that humanitarian conditions – in that case, relating to expulsion of a person with a serious, naturally occurring illness – could give rise to a breach of article 3 in very exceptional cases where the humanitarian grounds against removal were 'compelling'.[56]

---

51 *Al-Saadoon v UK* (2010) 51 EHRR 9, para 137.
52 *Al-Saadoon v UK* (2010) 51 EHRR 9, para 144.
53 *Al-Saadoon v UK* (2010) 51 EHRR 9, para 145.
54 *R (Bary) v Secretary of State for the Home Department* [2009] EWHC 2068 (Admin).
55 *Bensaid v UK* (2001) 33 EHRR 10; *J v Secretary of State for the Home Department* [2005] EWCA Civ 629, [2005] All ER (D) 359 (May); *Y and Z (Sri Lanka) v Secretary of State for the Home Department* [2009] EWCA Civ 362, [2009] HRLR 22, (2009) *Times* 5 May.
56 *N v UK* (2008) 47 EHRR 39, para 42; compare *D v UK* (1997) 24 EHRR 423.

13.35 In *MSS v Belgium and Greece*[57] the Grand Chamber of the ECtHR took an important step forward and recognised that ECHR article 3 might be breached by conditions of 'extreme material poverty'.[58] In that case, the applicant, while claiming asylum in Greece, had found himself in a 'particularly serious' situation, in that he had 'spent months living in a state of the most extreme poverty, unable to cater for his most basic needs: food, hygiene and a place to live', together with 'the ever-present fear of being attacked and robbed and the total lack of any likelihood of his situation improving'.[59] The Greek Government had failed to inform him of the possibilities of finding accommodation, and in practice he would have been unlikely to find any in any event.[60] Nor was it reasonable to expect that he would find work, because access to the job market was 'so riddled with administrative obstacles', and the applicant himself had 'personal difficulties due to his lack of command of the Greek language, the lack of any support network and the generally unfavourable economic climate'.[61] It was also relevant that the Greek authorities 'could have substantially alleviated his suffering' if they had determined his asylum claim promptly.[62]

13.36 It followed, in the Grand Chamber's view, that the conditions in Greece amounted to degrading treatment contrary to ECHR article 3:

> ... the victim of humiliating treatment showing a lack of respect for his dignity and that this situation has, without doubt, aroused in him feelings of fear, anguish or inferiority capable of inducing desperation. It considers that such living conditions, combined with the prolonged uncertainty in which he has remained and the total lack of any prospects of his situation improving, have attained the level of severity required to fall within the scope of Article 3 of the Convention.[63]

13.37 However, it was not just Greece which was in breach of ECHR article 3: Belgium had transferred the applicant to Greece for his asylum claim to be determined there, although the conditions for asylum-seekers in Greece were well known;[64] it followed that Belgium had 'knowingly exposed him to conditions of detention and living

---

57 App No 30696/09, 21 January 2011.
58 App No 30696/09 paras 252–263.
59 App No 30696/09 paras 254–245.
60 App No 30696/09 paras 257–259.
61 App No 30696/09 para 261.
62 App No 30696/09 para 262.
63 App No 30696/09 para 263.
64 App No 30696/09 para 366.

conditions that amounted to degrading treatment'[65] and was therefore in breach of ECHR article 3.[66]

13.38 The ECtHR then applied a similar approach in considering returns to Somalia in *Sufi and Elmi*.[67] The dire conditions in Somalia were held not only to be caused by drought, poverty or lack of state resources, but 'predominantly' by 'the direct and indirect actions of the parties to the conflict'.[68] The court appears to have drawn an important distinction between breaches of ECHR article 3 caused by naturally occurring phenomena, under which only 'very exceptional' cases will succeed, following *N v UK*,[69] and breaches caused predominantly by human agency, as to which a different test applies, set out in *MSS*[70] and summed up in *Sufi and Elmi* as requiring the decision-maker:

> ... to have regard to an applicant's ability to cater for his most basic needs, such as food, hygiene and shelter, his vulnerability to ill-treatment and the prospect of his situation improving within a reasonable time-frame.[71]

13.39 The precise dividing line between suffering caused by human actions and that caused by natural phenomena or by 'lack of resources' on the part of the state to which an individual is being expelled remains to be explored.

The burden and standard of proof

13.40 The standard of proof under ECHR article 3 is identical to the *Sivakumaran*[72] standard under the Refugee Convention,[73] which has been addressed at para 11.72: there must be substantial grounds for believing that there is a real risk of treatment contrary to ECHR article 3.[74] It is widely accepted that the 'reasonable degree of likelihood' test in *Sivakumaran* is substantially the same as the test of 'real risk'.[75]

65 App No 30696/09 para 367.
66 App No 30696/09 para 368.
67 App Nos 8319/07 and 11449/07, 28 June 2011.
68 App Nos 8319/07 and 11449/07 para 282.
69 See note 56 above.
70 App No 30696/09, 21 January 2011.
71 *Sufi and Elmi* App Nos 8319/07 and 11449/07, 28 June 2011 para 283.
72 *R v Secretary of State for the Home Department ex p Sivakumaran* [1988] AC 958.
73 *Kacaj* [2001] INLR 354; [2002] Imm AR 213.
74 *Soering v UK* (1989) 11 EHRR 439 para 88.
75 See eg *MA (Somalia) v Secretary of State for the Home Department* [2010] UKSC 49 para 13.

13.41 The burden of proof is on the applicant. However, once an applicant adduces evidence capable of proving that his or her expulsion will breach article 3, it is for the expelling state to 'dispel any doubts about it'.[76] In *RC v Sweden*, the court explained that this placed the onus on the state not only to dispel any doubts about whether the applicant had been tortured in the past, once prima facie evidence to that effect had been provided,[77] but also, once it was established that he had indeed been tortured, 'to dispel any doubts about the risk of his being subjected again to treatment contrary to Article 3 in the event that his expulsion proceeds'.[78]

Reliance on other ECHR rights

13.42 It is possible to challenge expulsion on the basis that there would be breaches *in the receiving country* of provisions of the ECHR other than articles 2 and 3.[79] A distinction is drawn in the case-law between those articles in respect of which it is necessary to show a risk, on expulsion, of a 'flagrant' breach of the right in question and those where it is not.

13.43 The House of Lords in *Ullah* drew a careful distinction between 'domestic cases' and 'foreign cases'. 'Domestic cases' are ones in which 'a state is said to have acted within its own territory in a way which infringes the enjoyment of a Convention right by a person within that territory'.[80] Domestic cases, for example, include those where exclusion or expulsion of a family member from the UK is alleged to breach ECHR article 8.[81] 'Foreign cases' are those:

> ... in which it is claimed that the conduct of the state in removing a person from its territory (whether by expulsion or extradition) to another territory will lead to a violation of the person's Convention rights in that other territory.[82]

---

76 *Saadi v Italy* (2009) 49 EHRR 30 para 129; *NA v UK* (2009) 48 EHRR 15 para 111.
77 *RC v Sweden* App No 41827/07, 9 March 2010, para 53.
78 *RC v Sweden* App No 41827/07, 9 March 2010, para 55.
79 *R (Ullah) v Special Adjudicator* [2004] UKHL 26, [2004] 2 AC 323.
80 *R (Ullah) v Special Adjudicator* [2004] UKHL 26, [2004] 2 AC 323 para 7.
81 *R (Ullah) v Special Adjudicator* [2004] UKHL 26, [2004] 2 AC 323 para 8.
82 *R (Ullah) v Special Adjudicator* [2004] UKHL 26, [2004] 2 AC 323 para 9.

Other ECHR rights for which 'flagrant denial' is not required in a 'foreign' case

13.44 ECHR article 4, the right not to be held in slavery or servitude, and not to be required to perform forced or compulsory labour, is an absolute right, like articles 2 and 3, meaning that interference with the right can never be justified. The House of Lords in *Ullah* observed that any claim based on a fear of such ill-treatment would probably succeed under article 3 in any event, but accepted that in theory a claim based on article 4 alone might succeed.[83] (We suggest, therefore, that it is unlikely that it will ever be necessary to rely on ECHR article 4 in isolation.)

ECHR rights for which 'flagrant denial' must be shown in a 'foreign' case

13.45 The appellants in *Ullah* argued that, even if they were not at risk of persecution so as to entitle them to refugee status, their rights to practise, preach and teach their religions would be so severely restricted in their respective countries that their removal would constitute an unlawful infringement of ECHR article 9 (the right to freedom of thought, conscience and religion). The House of Lords considered that essentially similar issues around removal arose under article 9 and a number of other articles of the convention.

13.46 Where reliance is placed on article 6, the right to a fair trial in a 'foreign' case, it must be shown that a person has suffered or risks suffering a flagrant denial of a fair trial in the receiving state.[84] The same test of 'flagrant' breach applies to article 5, the right to freedom from arbitrary detention[85] and article 7, freedom from retrospective punishment.[86]

13.47 As to qualified rights such as ECHR articles 8 or 9, Lord Bingham in *Ullah* quoted[87] with approval the decision of the Tribunal in *Devaseelan*:

---

83 *R (Ullah) v Special Adjudicator* [2004] UKHL 26, [2004] 2 AC 323 paras 16 and 41.
84 *R (Ullah) v Special Adjudicator* [2004] UKHL 26, [2004] 2 AC 323 paras 24 and 44; *Soering v UK* (1989) 11 EHRR 439 para 113.
85 *R (Ullah) v Special Adjudicator* [2004] UKHL 26, [2004] 2 AC 323 paras 24 and 43.
86 *R (Ullah) v Special Adjudicator* [2004] UKHL 26, [2004] 2 AC 323 para 45.
87 *R (Ullah) v Special Adjudicator* [2004] UKHL 26, [2004] 2 AC 323 para 24.

The reason why flagrant denial or gross violation is to be taken into account is that it is only in such a case – where the right will be completely denied or nullified in the destination country – that it can be said that removal will breach the treaty obligations of the signatory state however those obligations might be interpreted or whatever might be said by or on behalf of the destination state.[88]

13.48 The position with regard to ECHR articles 10 and 11 would logically be analogous to that under article 9.[89]

13.49 In *EM (Lebanon)*,[90] it was contended that a father would gain custody of his child, against the wishes of the mother (the appellant in that case) because of the operation and interpretation of sharia law by the courts in Lebanon. The House of Lords found a flagrant breach of ECHR article 8 on the grounds that the rigid and arbitrary patriarchal approach of the Lebanese legal system to child custody and the interests of mothers and children would, on the facts, mean that 'the very essence of [the child's] right to respect for his family life would be destroyed'[91] in a manner which was arbitrary and could not be justified.

13.50 The test in ECHR article 8 cases concerning separation from private or family life established in the UK is not one of 'flagrant' breach, because these are 'domestic' and not 'foreign' cases:[92] see the introduction to section D of this book, 'Other ECHR grounds for resisting deportation'.

---

88 *Devaseelan v Secretary of State for the Home Department* [2002] UKIAT 00702, [2003] Imm AR 1 para 111.
89 *R (Ullah) v Special Adjudicator* [2004] UKHL 26, [2004] 2 AC 323 para 48.
90 *EM (Lebanon) v Secretary of State for the Home Department* [2008] UKHL 64.
91 *EM (Lebanon) v Secretary of State for the Home Department* [2008] UKHL 64 para 46.
92 *R (Ullah) v Special Adjudicator* [2004] UKHL 26, [2004] 2 AC 323 paras 8 and 18.

CHAPTER 14
Article 15(c) of the Qualification Directive

14.1	Introduction
14.5	Definition
14.11	Approach of the ECJ (now the CJEU)
14.12	Approach of the domestic courts
14.16	Practical issues arising

Introduction

14.1 This chapter covers an innovation of the Qualification Directive[1] which has no antecedent in the Refugee Convention:[2] the provision in article 15(c) for a grant of humanitarian protection (HP) in cases where the risk arises from armed conflict.

14.2 Article 15(c) is dealt with briefly in this chapter because, although a ground for resisting deportation, it applies no differently to foreign national prisoners and former prisoners (FNPs) than to other foreign nationals resisting expulsion. As with article 3 of the European Convention on Human Rights (ECHR), the applicability of article 15(c) is not subject to considerations about the applicant's own conduct.

14.3 Article 15(c) will be of importance to FNPs from war zones, eg Iraq or Somalia, because it provides protection from serious harm arising from indiscriminate violence in the course of international or internal armed conflict.

14.4 The article 15(c) threshold is a high one: the level of generalised violence must be sufficiently high to show a real risk to civilians caught up in the conflict. Members of vulnerable groups may however be able to succeed on the basis that they would be particularly affected by the violence taking place in an armed conflict.

Definition

14.5 Article 2(e) of the Qualification Directive provides the following definition:

> '[P]erson eligible for subsidiary protection' means a third country national or a stateless person who does not qualify as a refugee but in respect of whom substantial grounds have been shown for believing that the person concerned, if returned to his or her country of origin, or in the case of a stateless person, to his or her country of former habitual residence, would face a real risk of suffering serious harm as defined in Article 15, and to whom Article 17(1) and (2) [exclusion from HP] do not apply, and is unable, or, owing to such risk, unwilling to avail himself or herself of the protection of that country.

---

1 Council Directive 2004/83/EC on minimum standards for the qualification and status of third country nationals or stateless persons as refugees or as persons who otherwise need international protection and the content of the protection granted.
2 The 1951 Convention Relating to the Status of Refugees and its 1967 Protocol.

14.6 Article 15 of the Qualification Directive defines 'serious harm' thus:

> Serious harm consists of:
> (a) death penalty or execution; or
> (b) torture or inhuman or degrading treatment or punishment of an applicant in the country of origin;
> or
> (c) serious and individual threat to a civilian's life or person by reason of indiscriminate violence in situations of international or internal armed conflict.

14.7 Qualification Directive article 15 subparagraphs (a) and (b) largely reflect ECHR articles 2 and 3 (which have been discussed at paras 13.6–13.41). Article 15(c), by contrast, has no direct analogue in the ECHR, although the European Court of Human Rights (ECtHR) has suggested that ECHR article 3 does 'offer comparable protection to that afforded under' article 15(c) of the Qualification Directive.[3]

14.8 As with ECHR articles 2 and 3, however, article 15(c) involves no proportionality test: its applicability is not subject to considerations about the public interest or the applicant's own conduct.

14.9 Article 15(c) is apparently intended to fill a lacuna in international protection which was discussed by the House of Lords in *Adan v Secretary of State for the Home Department*:[4]

> ... where a state of civil war exists, it is not enough for an asylum-seeker to show that he would be at risk if he were returned to his country. He must be able to show ... a differential impact. In other words, he must be able to show fear of persecution for Convention reasons over and above the ordinary risks of clan warfare.

14.10 Article 15(c) goes some way to ensuring that people who are affected by 'the ordinary risks' of warfare can gain international protection, if the effects are sufficiently serious, without having to show that they are more badly affected than others. However, a number of difficulties with the wording of article 15(c) have troubled the courts. How, for instance, can a threat be shown to be 'individual' if the violence is 'indiscriminate'? Is it intended that a 'threat' can in itself constitute 'serious harm'? Does the word 'conflict' imply a need for two or more parties to be fighting, or is it sufficient that the forces of the state, or of a single organisation, are responsible for 'indiscriminate violence' so as to threaten an individual's 'life or person'?

---

3 *Sufi and Elmi v UK* App Nos 8319/07 and 11449/07, 28 June 2011, para 226.
4 [1999] 1 AC 293; see also UN High Commissioner for Refugees (UNHCR) Handbook, para 164.

Approach of the ECJ

14.11 The leading case on the meaning of article 15(c) is the decision of the Grand Chamber of the ECJ in *Elgafaji*.[5] The court held, in essence:

- The protection provided by article 15(c) is wider than that provided by article 3 of the ECHR, whose contents are already covered by article 15(b) of the Qualification Directive.[6]
- The harm defined in article 15(c) is not limited to situations in which the applicant for subsidiary protection is specifically exposed to the risk of a particular type of harm', but covers 'a more general risk of harm'.[7]
- Article 15(c) is concerned with:
   ... harm to civilians irrespective of their identity, where the degree of indiscriminate violence characterising the armed conflict taking place ... reaches such a high level that substantial grounds are shown for believing that a civilian ... would, solely on account of his presence on the territory of that country or region, face a real risk of being subject to the serious threat [to his life or person].[8]
- Such circumstances are however, likely to be 'exceptional', given the stipulation in the recitals to the Qualification Directive that
   Risks to which a population of a country or a section of the population is generally exposed do normally not create in themselves an individual threat which would qualify as serious harm.[9]
- Although the test under article 15(c) means that the applicant is likely to be one of many to whom the risk applies, there is also a need to show a degree of individualised risk, by analogy with the other parts of article 15. The personal circumstances of the individual are always relevant, as provided for by article 4(3) of the Qualification Directive. That means that:
   ... the more the applicant is able to show that he is specifically affected by reason of factors particular to his personal circum-

---

5 *Elgafaji v Staatssecretaris van Justitie* Case C-465/07 [2009] 1 WLR 2100.
6 *Elgafaji v Staatssecretaris van Justitie* Case C-465/07 [2009] 1 WLR 2100 para 28.
7 *Elgafaji v Staatssecretaris van Justitie* Case C-465/07 [2009] 1 WLR 2100 paras 32–33.
8 *Elgafaji v Staatssecretaris van Justitie* Case C-465/07 [2009] 1 WLR 2100 para 35.
9 *Elgafaji v Staatssecretaris van Justitie* Case C-465/07 [2009] 1 WLR 2100 para 37, referring to recital 26 to the Qualification Directive; this formulation does not imply an additional requirement of exceptionality, but 'is simply stressing that it is not every armed conflict or violent situation which will attract the protection of article 15(c)': *QD (Iraq) v Secretary of State for the Home Department (UNHCR intervening)* [2009] EWCA Civ 620, [2011] 1 WLR 689 para 25.

stances, the lower the level of indiscriminate violence required for him to be eligible for subsidiary protection.[10]

- However, that is not the same as a requirement that the applicant be individually targeted for harm:

    ... the existence of a serious and individual threat to the life or person of an applicant for subsidiary protection is not subject to the condition that that applicant adduce evidence that he is specifically targeted by reason of factors particular to his personal circumstances.[11]

Approach of the domestic courts

14.12 Despite this elucidation, interpretation of article 15(c) remains complex and difficult, in part, the Court of Appeal noted in *QD (Iraq)*, because of poor drafting.[12] The Asylum and Immigration Tribunal (AIT) sought initially (before *Elgafaji*) to interpret it by reference to international humanitarian law (IHL), which relates to the protection of combatants and non-combatants from collateral harm during armed conflicts, and sought to derive from that the conclusion that the purpose of article 15(c) was to protect people from 'war crimes or other serious breaches of IHL'.[13] That analysis was rejected by the Court of Appeal on the grounds that IHL did not provide for a right to international protection and was not directly referred to in the Qualification Directive, and that the directive itself had to 'stand on its own legs and to be treated, so far as it does not expressly or manifestly adopt extraneous sources of law, as autonomous'.[14]

14.13 The Court of Appeal went on to note that although articles 2(e) and 15(c), read together, appear to mean that a 'real risk' of a 'threat' of serious harm would be sufficient to warrant a grant of subsidiary protection, that could not in fact have been the intention: what is needed is simply a real risk of serious harm arising from indiscriminate violence; the court gave as examples of the latter 'the placing of car bombs in market places' and 'snipers firing methodically at

---

10 *Elgafaji v Staatssecretaris van Justitie* Case C-465/07 [2009] 1 WLR 2100 para 39.
11 *Elgafaji v Staatssecretaris van Justitie* Case C-465/07 [2009] 1 WLR 2100 para 45.
12 *QD (Iraq) v Secretary of State for the Home Department (UNHCR intervening)* [2009] EWCA Civ 620, [2011] 1 WLR 689 para 19.
13 *KH (article 15(c) Qualification Directive) Iraq CG* [2008] UKAIT 00023, para 51.
14 *QD (Iraq) v Secretary of State for the Home Department (UNHCR intervening)* [2009] EWCA Civ 620, [2011] 1 WLR 689 para 18.

people in the streets'.[15] What article 15(c) is concerned with is 'serious threats of real harm'.[16]

14.14 However, 'conflict' does not necessarily imply more than one warring faction: it may be sufficient for the risk to arise from indiscriminate violence caused by a single faction, or by the state.[17] 'Civilian' in article 15(c) means a genuine non-combatant, not simply any person not in a uniformed armed force.[18] Despite the reference to 'exceptional' circumstances in *Elgafaji*, there is:

> ... no requirement that the armed conflict itself must be exceptional. What is, however, required is an intensity of indiscriminate violence – which will self-evidently not characterise every such situation – great enough to meet the test spelt out [in *Elgafaji*].[19]

14.15 The Court of Appeal summarised 'the critical question' as being:

> Is there in Iraq or a material part of it such a high level of indiscriminate violence that substantial grounds exist for believing that an applicant ... would, solely by being present there, face a real risk which threatens his life or person? By 'material part' we mean the applicant's home area or, if otherwise appropriate, any potential place of internal relocation.[20]

Practical issues arising

14.16 Although the courts have largely teased out the meaning of article 15(c) despite the opaque wording, the practical difficulties in applying the test in individual cases have not evaporated. Applicants seeking to establish a claim under article 15(c) must still show that they cannot reasonably be expected to relocate to a part of their country of origin where the risk from indiscriminate violence is less intense.[21]

---

15 *QD (Iraq) v Secretary of State for the Home Department (UNHCR intervening)* [2009] EWCA Civ 620, [2011] 1 WLR 689 para 27.
16 *QD (Iraq) v Secretary of State for the Home Department (UNHCR intervening)* [2009] EWCA Civ 620, [2011] 1 WLR 689 para 31.
17 *QD (Iraq) v Secretary of State for the Home Department (UNHCR intervening)* [2009] EWCA Civ 620, [2011] 1 WLR 689 para 35.
18 *QD (Iraq) v Secretary of State for the Home Department (UNHCR intervening)* [2009] EWCA Civ 620, [2011] 1 WLR 689 para 37.
19 *QD (Iraq) v Secretary of State for the Home Department (UNHCR intervening)* [2009] EWCA Civ 620, [2011] 1 WLR 689 para 36.
20 *QD (Iraq) v Secretary of State for the Home Department (UNHCR intervening)* [2009] EWCA Civ 620, [2011] 1 WLR 689 para 40.
21 Qualification Directive article 8(1); *HM and others (article 15(c)) Iraq CG* [2010] UKUT 331 (IAC) para 93.

As to what sort of threat would suffice, the Asylum and Immigration Tribunal (AIT) thought in *GS Afghanistan* that 'no precise definition that can be applied to the words "or person"'.[22] It agreed that the risk goes wider than simply a risk of death, but not as far as 'flagrant breaches of qualified rights, such as freedom of thought, conscience and religion'.[23] We suggest that a threat to a civilian's 'person' here covers a threat of physical injury[24] and is likely also, for sake of consistency, to include a threat of psychological harm.

14.17 The Immigration and Asylum Chamber of the Upper Tribunal (UT-IAC) has held that the assessment of risk must be 'both quantitative and qualitative' and must take into account 'a wide range of variables, not just numbers of attacks or deaths'.[25] Those variables may, 'provided that there is a sufficient although not necessarily exclusive causal nexus between the violence arising in the conflict and the harm suffered',[26] include the availability of state protection; the extent of criminal violence as a result of the absence of such protection; the extent of population displacement; and the destruction of means of living[27] (by which the tribunal appears to mean such necessities as housing, employment and health services). In *GS Afghanistan* it was held that indirect consequences of indiscriminate violence may be sufficient to bring a person within article 15(c), depending on the facts.[28] In that case, the AIT accepted that difficulties in the food supply in Afghanistan could in theory fall within article 15(c), but rejected the submission on the facts, on the grounds that they were caused, if anything, by 'targeted violence' between the factions rather than by indiscriminate violence, and that there was no 'satisfactory' evidence that the food supply would be any better if there were not a

---

22 *GS (article 15(c): indiscriminate violence) Afghanistan CG* [2009] UKAIT 00044 para 72.
23 *GS (article 15(c): indiscriminate violence) Afghanistan CG* [2009] UKAIT 00044 para 72.
24 This is supported by the fact that the German version of the Qualification Directive uses 'Unversehrtheit', meaning 'intactness' or 'freedom from injury', for the English word 'person'; the Danish uses 'fysiske integritet' and the Spanish 'integridad física' ('physical integrity' in each case). The French and several other versions use words equivalent to the English 'person'.
25 *HM and others (article 15(c)) Iraq CG* [2010] UKUT 331 (IAC) para 278ii.
26 *HM and others (article 15(c)) Iraq CG* [2010] UKUT 331 (IAC) para 92.
27 *HM and others (article 15(c)) Iraq CG* [2010] UKUT 331 (IAC) para 92.
28 *GS (article 15(c): indiscriminate violence) Afghanistan CG* [2009] UKAIT 00044 para 67.

war happening.²⁹ (We suggest that the first of these reasons seems to miss precisely the point of article 15(c), which is that violence which is 'targeted' as between the armed groups involved in the conflict may nonetheless be 'indiscriminate' in its effects on civilians. 'Indiscriminate' violence is not necessarily 'random' violence.)

14.18 In assessing the risk under article 15(c), it is important to distinguish between evidence of violence targeted at people because of their specific characteristics, such as their profession, religious adherence or sexuality, and evidence of violence capable of affecting people simply because of their presence as civilians within the affected area. Those with specific characteristics may be able to show that they are at risk both under the Refugee Convention and as persons 'specifically affected by reason of factors particular to [their] personal circumstances', under *Elgafaji*.³⁰ However, those at enhanced risk from indiscriminate violence cannot be limited to those also at risk of persecution for a Refugee Convention reason. In *GS Afghanistan*, the AIT sought to explain the point by illustration:

> The way in which an enhanced risk might arise for a group can best be demonstrated by example. If, say, the Taliban wanted to make a point about teachers continuing to teach girls, it may resolve to kill a teacher. It would not be any specific teacher but one who came into their sights. A teacher is of course not a combatant and an attempt to kill the first teacher they came across could be argued to demonstrate that teachers were then at enhanced risk of indiscriminate violence. Another possible example could be disabled people. If a bomber, or sniper, were to walk into a crowded marketplace, the public may well flee. A man with only one leg would move considerably more slowly and arguably as a result would be in a higher risk group than the general public.³¹

14.19 We suggest that the first of these hypothetical examples is perhaps better seen as an example of targeted persecution for reasons of religion, (imputed) political opinion and/or membership of a particular social group; the second is perhaps a clearer practical illustration of the concept of enhanced risk categories under article 15(c). Nevertheless, in order to show that a particular category of person is at enhanced risk, such that article 15(c) applies in circumstances

---

29 *GS (article 15(c): indiscriminate violence) Afghanistan CG* [2009] UKAIT 00044 para 69.
30 *HM and others (article 15(c)) Iraq CG* [2010] UKUT 331 (IAC) para 278iv, referring to *Elgafaji* para 39.
31 *GS (article 15(c): indiscriminate violence) Afghanistan CG* [2009] UKAIT 00044 para 134.

where the population as a whole is not so at risk, it is necessary to explain how and why that is the case. As a further example, in *HK Afghanistan*[32] it was argued that children were disproportionately affected by roadside blasts, air strikes, suicide attacks and crossfire between insurgents and government or foreign forces, but the tribunal declined to accept that the evidence demonstrated that children were any more at risk than adults.[33]

14.20 In *Sufi and Elmi* the ECtHR, albeit considering ECHR article 3 rather than article 15(c) of the Qualification Directive,[34] suggested that the following criteria provided an 'appropriate yardstick' (but not an 'exhaustive list') for considering the level of violence in Mogadishu, Southern Somalia:

> ... first, whether the parties to the conflict were either employing methods and tactics of warfare which increased the risk of civilian casualties or directly targeting civilians; secondly, whether the use of such methods and/or tactics was widespread among the parties to the conflict; thirdly, whether the fighting was localised or widespread; and finally, the number of civilians killed, injured and displaced as a result of the fighting.[35]

14.21 We suggest that a similar framework is likely to be of use in assessing whether the test in article 15(c) is made out.

---

32 *HK and others (minors – indiscriminate violence – forced recruitment by Taliban – contact with family members) Afghanistan CG* [2010] UKUT 378 (IAC).
33 *HK and others (minors – indiscriminate violence – forced recruitment by Taliban – contact with family members) Afghanistan CG* [2010] UKUT 378 (IAC) paras 21–26.
34 The ECtHR suggests that the tests under the two provisions are comparable: *Sufi and Elmi v United Kingdom* App Nos 8319/07 and 11449/07, 28 June 2011, para 226
35 *Sufi and Elmi v United Kingdom* App Nos 8319/07 and 11449/07, 28 June 2011, para 241 (referring to the AIT's decision in *AM & AM (armed conflict: risk categories) Somalia CG* [2008] UKAIT 00091).

SECTION D
Other ECHR grounds for resisting deportation

Chapter 15: The approach to be taken to ECHR article 8 by decision-makers   269

Chapter 16: ECHR article 8 and family and private life   279

Chapter 17: Proportionality in ECHR article 8 expulsion cases   293

Chapter 18: Resisting deportation on grounds of physical or mental illness under ECHR articles 3 and 8; *Quaquah* claims   323

Introduction to other ECHR grounds for resisting deportation

Organisation of this section

This section deals with commonly arising European Convention on Human Rights (ECHR) claims in expulsion cases other than those which concern the threat of 'intentional harm' after removal (already discussed in chapter 13).

Our primary focus is on ECHR article 8, which is of very widespread application in deportation cases, particularly for long-resident foreign national prisoners and former prisoners (FNPs). We begin with a discussion in chapter 15 of the approach that must be applied in ECHR article 8 expulsion cases by the Secretary of State for the Home Department (SSHD), tribunals and courts. We go on in chapter 16 to look at the circumstances in which protected family life and private life may be found to exist. Chapter 17 then examines the approach to be taken to proportionality in expulsion cases in general and in criminal deportation cases in particular.

In chapter 18 we then turn to the application of ECHR articles 3 and 8 in claims arising out of physical or mental ill-health. This section finishes with a review of '*Quaquah*' claims, that is, claims that the expulsion of a person who is litigating against the SSHD or one of its contractors would breach his or her rights to equality of arms under ECHR article 6.

ECHR article 8 rights and duties

ECHR article 8 provides:
> 1. Everyone has the right to respect for his private and family life, his home and his correspondence.
> 2. There shall be no interference by a public authority with the exercise of this right except such as is in accordance with the law and is necessary in a democratic society in the interests of national security, public safety or the economic well-being of the country, for the prevention of disorder or crime, for the protection of health or morals, or for the protection of the rights and freedoms of others.

ECHR article 8 protects individuals from unjustified interference or lack of respect for their family life, private life, home and correspondence. It imposes on states both a negative duty to refrain from unjustified interference with, and a positive duty to show respect for, protected rights[1] though the often elusive question of whether negative or positive obligations are at stake on should not affect the outcome.[2] Expulsion cases (such as deportation) concern the risk of an interference with ECHR article 8 rights by the expelling state.

We focus in this section on the right to respect for family and private life under ECHR article 8, which features prominently in challenges to deportation.

The rights protected under ECHR article 8(1) are qualified. An interference with these rights will not give rise to a breach of article 8 if it is justified under article 8(2) as being in accordance with the law, necessary in a democratic society and proportionate.

'Foreign' and 'domestic' ECHR article 8 cases

A 'domestic case' is one in which the breach complained of substantially occurs in the host country.[3] A 'foreign case' is one in which the breach of the right substantially takes place in the receiving state.[4]

In purely 'foreign cases', ECHR article 8 will only be breached if it can be shown that there is a real risk that expulsion would cause a 'flagrant denial of the very essence of the right' in the receiving state.[5] 'Flagrant denial' means 'complete denial or nullification' of the right.[6] Where a woman, if expelled to Lebanon, faced loss of custody of her son to her violent ex-partner, this was held to constitute a flagrant denial of her right to respect for her family life under ECHR article 8.[7]

Many expulsion cases will be a hybrid of 'foreign' and 'domestic' elements. There is no threshold test of 'flagrant denial' in hybrid

---

1 *Marckx v Belgium* (1979) 2 EHRR 33 para 31; *Abdulaziz, Cabales and Balkandali v UK* (1985) 7 EHRR 330 para 67; *X, Y and Z v UK* (1997) 24 EHRR 143 para 41.
2 *R (Quila) v Secretary of State for the Home Department* [2011] UKSC 45, [2011] 3 WLR 836 para 43
3 An example of a 'domestic case' would be the case of an immigrant who has formed a relationship with a person settled in the UK, where it is contended that expulsion from the UK would separate the couple and breach the immigrant's right to respect for his or her family life formed in the UK.
4 An example of a purely 'foreign' case would be the expulsion of an immigrant who contends that the conditions in his or her country of origin (for example, an inability to be open about sexual orientation) would be so severe as to breach ECHR article 8.
5 *R (Ullah) v Secretary of State for the Home Department* [2004] UKHL 26, [2004] 2 AC 323 paras 24 and 50.
6 *EM (Lebanon)* [2008] UKHL 64, [2009] 1 AC para 35.
7 *EM (Lebanon)* [2008] UKHL 64, [2009] 1 AC para 35.

cases.[8] An example of a hybrid case is the case of a mentally or physically ill immigrant whose expulsion would interrupt a course of medical treatment in the UK and would also potentially lead to a severe health deterioration in the receiving state, for example because of a lack of adequate treatment facilities there.[9]

---

8 *R (Razgar) v Secretary of State for the Home Department* [2004] UKHL 27, [2004] 2 AC 368 para 43 per Baroness Hale.
9 See the discussion of hybrid cases in *R (Ullah) v Secretary of State for the Home Department* [2004] UKHL 26, [2004] 2 AC 323 para 18 per Lord Bingham.

CHAPTER 15

The approach to be taken to ECHR article 8 by decision-makers

15.1	Introduction
15.2	The *Razgar* five-step test
15.5	Step 1(a): Is there a protected right?
15.6	Step 1(b): Is there an interference?
15.7	Step 2: Is ECHR article 8 engaged?
15.8	Step 3: Is the interference in accordance with the law?
15.13	Step 4: Is the interference necessary in a democratic society, ie justified by a pressing social need?
15.17	Step 5: Is the interference proportionate to the legitimate aim pursued?
15.22	**The role of the tribunal in ECHR article 8 appeals**
15.24	**Interaction between ECHR article 8 and Immigration Rules para 364**
15.27	**Burden and standard of proof**

Introduction

15.1 This chapter reviews the approach to be taken to European Convention on Human Rights (ECHR) article 8 claims in expulsion cases by the Secretary of State for the Home Department (SSHD), and the tribunals and courts. We start with the five step test described in *R (Razgar) v Secretary of State for the Home Department*[1] and clarifications of that test in subsequent case-law. We go on to consider the role of the tribunal in ECHR article 8 appeals, the interaction between ECHR article 8 and the Immigration Rules,[2] and the burden of proof to be applied when considering an ECHR article 8 claim.

The *Razgar* five-step test

15.2 A five step approach to be taken in ECHR article 8 cases was set out by Lord Bingham in *R (Razgar) v Secretary of State for the Home Department*:[3]

(1) Will the proposed removal be an interference by a public authority with the exercise of the applicant's right to respect for his private or (as the case may be) family life?
(2) If so, will such interference have consequences of such gravity as potentially to engage the operation of article 8?
(3) If so, is such interference in accordance with the law?
(4) If so, is such interference necessary in a democratic society in the interests of national security, public safety or the economic well-being of the country, for the prevention of disorder or crime, for the protection of health or morals, or for the protection of the rights and freedoms of others?
(5) If so, is such interference proportionate to the legitimate public end sought to be achieved?

15.3 As was confirmed by the House of Lords in *Huang v Secretary of State for the Home Department*[4] and by the Court of Appeal in *AG (Eritrea) v Secretary of State for the Home Department*,[5] ECHR article 8

---

1 [2004] UKHL 27, [2004] 2 AC 368 para 17; *Sen v The Netherlands* (2003) 36 EHRR 7.
2 HC 395.
3 [2004] UKHL 27, [2004] 2 AC 368 para 17; *Sen v The Netherlands* (2003) 36 EHRR 7 para 31.
4 [2007] UKHL 11, [2007] 2 AC 167.
5 [2007] EWCA Civ 801.

'raises no hurdles beyond those contained in the article itself'.[6] No extraneous tests or requirements (such as exceptionality) should be imported into ECHR article 8 by decision-makers other than, in a 'foreign case', the requirement to show 'flagrant denial' of the right.

15.4 Below, we discuss each of the *Razgar* steps in turn as they apply in all immigration cases, and in criminal deportation cases in particular before going on in the next chapters to consider family life, private life and proportionality in more detail.

Step 1(a): Is there a protected right?

15.5 The first step for a person making an ECHR article 8 claim is to establish that he or she has a protected article 8 right. In the immigration context, this will almost invariably involve establishing that the claimant has a family and/or private life in the UK.

Step 1(b): Is there an interference?

15.6 Having established the existence of a protected ECHR article 8 right, the article 8 claimant resisting expulsion must also show that expulsion would interfere with the protected right. Where it has been established that a person enjoys family and/or private life in the UK, expulsion will normally constitute an interference.[7]

Step 2: Is ECHR article 8 engaged?

15.7 The threshold for 'engaging' ECHR article 8 for applicants is not especially high.[8] Claimants who can show that an immigration decision would interfere with their protected article 8 rights will usually also be able to show that article 8 ECHR is engaged, save where any interference is minimal.[9] As Lord Wilson observed in *R (Quila) v*

---

6 [2007] EWCA Civ 801 para 25.
7 *AS (Pakistan) v Secretary of State for the Home Department* [2008] EWCA Civ 1118 at paras 15 and 18.
8 *Boultif v Switzerland* (2001) 33 EHRR 50 at paras 39–40; *R (Quila) v Secretary of State for the Home Department* [2011] UKSC 45, [2011] 3 WLR 836 para 43; *AG (Eritrea) v Secretary of State for the Home Department* [2007] EWCA Civ 801 at para 28 per Sedley LJ; *AS (Pakistan) v Secretary of State for the Home Department* [2008] EWCA Civ 1118 paras 15–18; *KR (Iraq) v Secretary of State for the Home Department* [2007] EWCA Civ 514; and *KD (Sri Lanka) v Secretary of State for the Home Department* [2007] EWCA Civ 1384.
9 *AS (Pakistan) v Secretary of State for the Home Department* [2008] EWCA Civ 1118 para 15.

Secretary of State for the Home Department in the context of British spouses, subjecting close family members to a choice of whether to live separately for years or to relocate, is 'a colossal interference' with the right to respect for family life.[10]

Step 3: Is the interference in accordance with the law?

15.8 Where ECHR article 8 is engaged, an interference will only be justified under ECHR article 8(2) if the interference is 'in accordance with the law'.

15.9 'The law' for the purposes of justification of interference with ECHR article 8 and other qualified ECHR rights includes not only statute but the common law,[11] the Immigration Rules[12] and policies governing the exercise of statutory powers.[13]

15.10 It is well established that a failure by the Home Office to apply and to follow (absent good reason) its own policy to a particular case is a public law error[14] and will render the immigration decision 'not in accordance with the law' for the purposes of an appeal under Nationality Immigration and Asylum Act (NIAA) 2002 s84(1)(e).[15] In these circumstances, the Immigration and Asylum Chamber of the First-tier and Upper Tribunals (IAC) is not confined to simply remitting the decision to be re-taken by the SSHD but (at least where the outcome of the proper application of the policy is clear) may itself apply the policy and allow or dismiss the appeal outright.[16]

---

10 *R (Quila) v Secretary of State for the Home Department* [2011] UKSC 45, [2011] 3 WLR 836 para 32.
11 *Dudgeon v UK* (1981) 4 EHRR 149 para 44.
12 HC 395, whose status has been discussed at paras 3.15 and 3.17.
13 *Lumba and Mighty v Secretary of State for the Home Department* [2011] UKSC 12, [2011] 2 WLR 671 paras 30 and 34–35; *R (Limbu) v Secretary of State for the Home Department* [2008] EWHC 2261 (Admin) para 44; *Nadarajah and Amirthanathan v Secretary of State for the Home Department* [2003] EWCA Civ 1768 para 54.
14 *Lumba and Mighty v Secretary of State for the Home Department* [2011] UKSC 12, [2011] 2 WLR 671 para 26.
15 *SL (Vietnam) v Secretary of State for the Home Department* [2010] EWCA Civ 225 para 33; *HH (Iraq) v Secretary of State for the Home Department* [2009] EWCA Civ 727; *R (S, H, Q) v Secretary of State for the Home Department* [2009] EWCA Civ 334; *AA (Afghanistan) v Secretary of State for the Home Department* [2007] EWCA Civ 12.
16 *AB (Jamaica) v Secretary of State for the Home Department* [2007] EWCA Civ 1302; *Fouzia Baig v Secretary of State for the Home Department* [2005] EWCA Civ 1246.

15.11 We suggest that a decision to deport which is unlawful under domestic law by reason of a failure without good reason to follow Home Office policy is also 'not in accordance with the law' for the purposes of ECHR article 8(2).[17] House of Lords authority supports that proposition.[18] The Asylum and Immigration Tribunal (AIT) has, however, held that a failure to follow Home Office policy does not render a decision 'not in accordance with the law' for article 8(2) purposes; we suggest that this wrong and based on the incorrect premise that Home Office policy does not constitute part of 'domestic law'.[19] Note that a failure by the Home Office to follow its own published policies may also render an interference disproportionate under ECHR article 8(2).[20]

15.12 The requirement that an interference be 'in accordance with law' refers not only to compliance with domestic law, but to the quality of law. The domestic law relied upon to justify the interference must be accessible and sufficiently precise to allow the individual, if necessary with appropriate advice- to reasonably foresee the legal consequences of her actions and regulate his or her conduct accordingly.[21]

---

17 Just as a failure without good reason to follow Home Office policy in the detention context renders the detention not in accordance with a procedure prescribed by law for ECHR article 5(1) purposes, see *Lumba and Mighty v Secretary of State for the Home Department* [2011] UKSC 12, [2011] 2 WLR 671 paras 30 and 34–35; *Nadarajah and Amirthanathan v Secretary of State for the Home Department* [2003] EWCA Civ 1768 para 54.

18 We suggest that *R (Munjaz) v Mersey Care Trust* [2005] UKHL 58, [2006] 2 AC 148 is conclusive House of Lords authority for the proposition that 'law' in the ECHR article 8 context has an autonomous meaning which comprehends policy (a Code of Practice may constitute law – see in particular paras 34, 91–92, 98,103).

19 In *AG (Kosovo) v Secretary of State for the Home Department* [2007] UKAIT 00082; we suggest that this aspect of *AG (Kosovo)* is wrong, conflicting as it does with the principle that policy forms part of the law for ECHR purposes, see note 18 above.

20 *R (Tozlukaya) v Secretary of State for the Home Department* [2006] EWCA Civ 379; *AB (Jamaica) v Secretary of State for the Home Department* [2007] EWCA Civ 1302; *R (S Afghanistan) v Secretary of State for the Home Department* [2007] EWCA Civ 546, the latter case concerned a deliberate decision not to apply a policy.

21 *R (Gillan) v Commissioner of Police of the Metropolis* [2006] UKHL 12, [2006] 2 AC 307 para 34 per Lord Bingham; *Gillan and Quinton v UK* (2010) 50 EHRR 45 paras 76–77.

Step 4: Is the interference necessary in a democratic society, ie justified by a pressing social need?

15.13 The question at this fourth stage is not whether the interference is generally necessary (that falls within the proportionality assessment at step 5) but whether the restriction on the primary right lies within one of the specified purposes,[22] namely

> ... in the interests of national security, public safety or the economic well-being of the country, for the prevention of disorder or crime, for the protection of health or morals, or for the protection of the rights and freedoms of others.[23]

15.14 In deportation cases, the 'legitimate aim' pursued by the state is usually the prevention of disorder or crime[24] but may also engage the protection of the economic well-being of the country (through maintenance of the system of immigration control).[25] In non-EEA national cases involving serious crimes, the public interest in deportation has been held (by the domestic courts) to include the deterrence of other offenders: see paras 17.72–17.78 below.

15.15 In administrative removal cases, the 'legitimate' aim pursued by the state is the requirements of immigration control (the right of states to control the entry and residence of non-nationals) and 'the maintenance of the integrity of the State's immigration policies':[26]

> In these cases, the legitimate aim is likely to be the economic well-being of the country in controlling immigration, although the prevention of disorder and crime and the protection of the rights and freedoms of others may also be relevant.[27]

15.16 Both deportation and administrative removal will usually be found to be 'necessary in a democratic society':

---

22 *VW (Uganda) and AB (Somalia) v Secretary of State for the Home Department* [2009] EWCA Civ 5 at para 23.
23 ECHR article 8(2).
24 *Boughanemi v France* (1996) 22 EHRR 228 at para 42; *Samaroo and Sezek v Secretary of State for the Home Department* [2001] EWCA Civ 1139 para 35; *N (Kenya) v Secretary of State for the Home Department* [2004] EWCA Civ 1094 para 54; *AS (Pakistan) v Secretary of State for the Home Department* [2008] EWCA Civ 1118 para 22.
25 See, for example, discussion in *R (Mansoor) v Secretary of State for the Home Department* [2011] EWHC 832 (Admin) para 34.
26 *Huang v Secretary of State for the Home Department* [2005] EWCA Civ 105, [2006] QB 1 para 4.
27 *ZH (Tanzania) v Secretary of State for the Home Department* [2011] UKSC 4, [2011] 2 WLR 148 para 18 per Lady Hale.

Where removal is proposed in pursuance of a lawful immigration policy, question (4) will almost always fall to be answered affirmatively. This is because the right of sovereign states, subject to treaty obligations, to regulate the entry and expulsion of aliens is recognised in the Strasbourg jurisprudence (see *Ullah* and *Do*, para 6) and implementation of a firm and orderly immigration policy is an important function of government in a modern democratic state. In the absence of bad faith, ulterior motive or deliberate abuse of power it is hard to imagine an adjudicator answering this question other than affirmatively.[28]

Step 5: Is the interference proportionate to the legitimate aim pursued?

15.17 Where ECHR article 8 is engaged in an expulsion case, the deciding question will usually be proportionality.

15.18 In *R (Daly) v Home Secretary*[29] Lord Steyn famously described the proportionality principle:

> The contours of the principle of proportionality are familiar. In *de Freitas v Permanent Secretary of Ministry of Agriculture, Fisheries, Lands and Housing* [1999] 1 AC 69 the Privy Council adopted a three stage test. Lord Clyde observed, at p 80, that in determining whether a limitation (by an act, rule or decision) is arbitrary or excessive the court should ask itself: 'whether: (i) the legislative objective is sufficiently important to justify limiting a fundamental right; (ii) the measures designed to meet the legislative objective are rationally connected to it; and (iii) the means used to impair the right or freedom are no more than is necessary to accomplish the objective.'

15.19 In *Razgar*[30] and again in *Huang*,[31] the House of Lords has emphasised that the proportionality assessment in the ECHR context:

> ... must always involve the striking of a fair balance between the rights of the individual and the interests of the community which is inherent in the whole of the Convention. The severity of the interference will call for careful assessment at this stage.

15.20 The approach taken to the proportionality assessment is similar for administrative removal and criminal deportation cases although

---

28 *R (Razgar) v Secretary of State for the Home Department* [2004] UKHL 27, [2004] 2 AC 368 para 19 per Lord Bingham.
29 [2001] 2 WLR 1622 at 1634.
30 *R (Razgar) v Secretary of State for the Home Department* [2004] UKHL 27, [2004] 2 AC 368 para 20 per Lord Bingham.
31 *Huang v Secretary of State for the Home Department* [2007] UKHL 11, [2007] 2 AC 167 para 19 per Lord Bingham.

additional factors apply in criminal deportation cases.[32] The weight to be given to the public interest may also differ: the public interest in expulsion is likely to be greater in a criminal deportation case concerning serious offending than it would be in an administrative removal case.[33]

15.21 We discuss proportionality in ECHR article 8 deportation cases in detail in chapter 17 below.

The role of the tribunal in ECHR article 8 appeals

15.22 As in other types of appeals before them, immigration judges of the IAC act as primary decision-makers in assessing proportionality under ECHR article 8(2): immigration judges are not exercising a secondary, reviewing function in relating to the SSHD's earlier decision, but forming their own judgment on the facts at the date of the hearing.[34]

15.23 However, in assessing proportionality in criminal deportation cases, immigration judges must give appropriate weight to the SSHD's policy on deportation and in particular (in non-EEA cases and, at least, in Immigration Act (IA) 1971 cases) to the SSHD's policy of using deportation as a deterrent measure for very serious crimes: see paras 17.72–17.78.

Interaction between ECHR article 8 and Immigration Rules para 364

15.24 The Immigration Rules at para 364 give guidance as to the exercise of the SSHD's discretion to deport in conducive deportation cases under the IA 1971.

15.25 Both the SSHD and the IAC must first consider whether an individual's deportation would breach the SSHD's obligations under the Human Rights Act 1998, including ECHR article 8, or the Refugee

---

32 *KB (Trinidad and Tobago) v Secretary of State for the Home Department* [2010] EWCA Civ 11 para 17.
33 *SS (India) v Secretary of State for the Home Department* [2010] EWCA Civ 388 para 54.
34 *Huang v Secretary of State for the Home Department* [2007] UKHL 11, [2007] 2 AC 167 para 11; *R (Quila) v Secretary of State for the Home Department* [2011] UKSC 45, [2011] 3 WLR 836 para 46

Convention.³⁵ Only in a case where deportation would not breach either convention should the decision-maker go on to consider Immigration Rules para 364.³⁶

15.26 The mere fact that an incorrect version of paragraph 364 of the Immigration Rules is applied where deportation is in any event foreseeable does not mean that a decision is 'not in accordance with the law' for ECHR article 8 purposes.³⁷

Burden and standard of proof

15.27 The burden is on the individual to show that article 8 is engaged. The burden then shifts to the state to justify the interference.³⁸ The Court of Appeal observed in *Chenge Miao v Secretary of State for the Home Department*³⁹ that:

> ... the assessment of proportionality is not a simple weighing of two cases against each other. It arises only when the claimant has established that he enjoys a protected right which is threatened with violation: at that point the burden shifts to the state to prove that the violation is nevertheless justified. To do this the state must show not only that the proposed step is lawful but that its objective is sufficiently important to justify limiting a basic right: that it is sensibly directed to that objective; and that it does not impair the right more than necessary.

15.28 The Supreme Court, in the context of assessing ECHR article 8(2) justification, has doubted that the civil standard of proof of the balance of probabilities is appropriate in 'in an evaluation which transcends matters of fact'.⁴⁰

---

35 The 1951 Convention Relating to the Status of Refugees and its 1967 Protocol ('Refugee Convention').
36 *EO (Turkey) v Secretary of State for the Home Department* [2007] UKAIT 00062.
37 *Onur v UK* (2009) 49 EHRR 38 para 51.
38 *R (Quila) v Secretary of State for the Home Department* [2011] UKSC 45, [2011] 3 WLR 836 para 44 per Lord Wilson with whom Lady Hale, Lord Phillips and Lord Clarke agreed; *Marcic v Thames Water Utilities Ltd* [2003] UKHL 66, [2004] 2 AC 42, para 37.
39 [2006] EWCA Civ 75 at para 12.
40 *R (Quila) v Secretary of State for the Home Department* [2011] UKSC 45, [2011] 3 WLR 836 para 44 per Lord Wilson with whom Lady Hale, Lord Phillips and Lord Clarke agreed.

CHAPTER 16
ECHR article 8 and family and private life

16.1	Introduction
16.4	**Family life**
16.4	General principles applicable to family life under ECHR article 8(1)
	Looking at the family as a whole • Factors to be considering when assessing the existence of family life • Duty to give reasons for findings as to existence or lack of family life • Relationships that do not amount to family life • Immigration status and family life • Potential family life • ECHR article 8, procedural obligations and contact proceedings
16.13	Different types of family relationships and family life under ECHR article 8(1)
	Family life between biological parent and child • Adoptive and foster parents and children • Family life between heterosexual spouses • Heterosexual unmarried partners • Same-sex partners • Family life between adults and their siblings or parents • Grandparents and minor grandchildren • Uncles, aunts, nieces and nephews and cousins
16.35	**Private life**
16.35	Scope of private life generally
16.36	Relationships and private life
16.37	Private life and social and economic relations
16.38	Composite family and private life cases

Introduction

16.1 This chapter reviews the circumstances in which protected family or private life for the purposes of European Convention on Human Rights (ECHR) article 8(1) may be found to exist.

16.2 This chapter begins with a review of the general principles applicable to a claim that family life exists. We then go on to consider the approach taken by the European Court of Human Rights (ECtHR) and the domestic courts to different types of relationships.

16.3 We then turn to private life, and to 'composite' claims engaging both the family and private life aspects of ECHR article 8(1).

Family life

General principles applicable to family life under ECHR article 8(1)

Looking at the family as a whole

16.4 The House of Lords in *Beoku-Betts* referred to 'the central point about family life, which is that the whole is greater than the sum of its individual parts'.[1] Thus, where the family consists of more than two people, the existence of family life should be considered as a whole. It is an error of law to consider a family as a series of discrete, relationships and then to determine whether family life exists for each distinct segment.[2]

Factors to be considering when assessing the existence of family life

16.5 The ECtHR has emphasised the fact-specificity of family life and the equal value of different models of family life:

> The existence or non-existence of 'family life' for the purposes of Article 8 is essentially a question of fact depending upon the real existence in practice of close personal ties.[3]
>
> Families differ widely, in their composition and in the mutual relations which exist between the members, and marked changes are

---

1 *Beoku-Betts (FC) v Secretary of State for the Home Department* [2008] UKHL 39, [2009] 1 AC 115 para 4.
2 *Zatoon Bi (Pakistan) v Secretary of State for the Home Department* [2009] EWCA Civ 834 para 41; see also *RG (Nepal) v Secretary of State for the Home Department* [2010] UKUT 273 (IAC) paras 19–20.
3 *Lebbink v The Netherlands* (2004) 40 EHRR 417 at para 36.

likely to occur over time within the same family. Thus there is no pre-determined model of family or family life to which article 8 must be applied. The article requires respect to be shown for the right to such family life as is or may be enjoyed by the particular applicant or applicants before the court, always bearing in mind (since any family must have at least two members, and may have many more) the participation of other members who share in the life of that family. In this context, as in most Convention contexts, the facts of the particular case are crucial.[4]

16.6 However, at odds with its professions of equal acceptance of distinct family models, the ECtHR has in practice taken a somewhat different approach to a) the nuclear family of legally and legitimately married spouses and minor children, and b) other family relationships. The ECtHR also has yet to accept the existence of family life between same-sex partners. We consider these different approaches at paras 16.13–16.18 and 16.24–16.27 below.

16.7 Where evidence must be shown of close family ties amounting to family life, the decision-maker must consider the degree of closeness enjoyed; whether there is a shared history; and prevalent cultural norms in the country of origin which may give additional importance to the family tie.[5]

Duty to give reasons for findings as to existence or lack of family life

16.8 It should not be presumed by decision-makers that more distant family relationships are incapable of giving rise to protected family life. As was emphasised by the Court of Appeal (in the context of family life between a healthy adult and his adult siblings),[6] decision-makers must assess the facts of each case and give adequate reasons for their findings as to the existence or lack of family life.

Relationships that do not amount to family life

16.9 Where a relationship or constellation of relationships does not meet the threshold for family life, it may nonetheless be protected as part of an individual's private life. The approach to be taken to relationships amounting to private life rather than family life is discussed at para 16.36.

---

4 *EM (Lebanon)* [2008] UKHL 64, [2009] 1 AC 1198 para 37.
5 *MT (Zimbabwe) v Secretary of State for the Home Department* [2007] EWCA Civ 455 in particular para 13.
6 *Senthuran v Secretary of State for the Home Department* [2004] EWCA Civ 950 para 15.

Immigration status and family life

16.10 Protected family life may exist between two people neither of whom have any leave to remain in the host country.[7] However, where the relationship is formed at a time that one (or even both) of the partners' immigration status was known to be precarious, the relationship may attract lesser protections – see paras 17.37–17.40 below. For the special considerations applicable to the family members of refugees, see para 17.22.

Potential family life

16.11 ECHR article 8 imposes a duty on states not only to refrain from interfering with existing family life but also to refrain from inhibiting the development of family life in the future.[8] ECHR article 8 therefore provides a degree of protection for intended family life. The ECtHR has found that article 8 may protect the potential relationships between a husband and wife who have not yet started to cohabit;[9] between a natural father and an 'illegitimate' child;[10] between adoptive parents and their adoptive child where the child had not yet been received;[11] and between a father and a child for whom the father was seeking a contact order.[12] Likewise, the Court of Appeal has recognised protected family life between two adult brothers, one of whom was severely mentally ill, who had lived together for only five weeks.[13] In *Singh v ECO-Delhi*,[14] the Court of Appeal also emphasised that article 8 protects the 'potential' for development of family life.[15]

---

7 *Krasniqi v Secretary of State for the Home Department* [2006] EWCA Civ 391 concerned a woman who enjoyed protected ECHR article 8 rights with her partner, also an asylum-seeker. Though *Krasniqi* was dealt with in the context of private life because it concerned a same-sex couple, the same approach would plainly apply to family life.
8 *R (Fawad and Zia Ahmadi) v Secretary of State for the Home Department* [2005] EWCA Civ 1721 para 18.
9 *Abdulaziz, Cabales and Balkandali v UK* (1985) 7 EHRR 330 para 62.
10 *Nylund v Finland* App No 7110/95 recognised this in principle, although family life was not found to exist on the facts of the case.
11 *Pini et al v Romania* (unreported, decision of 22 June 2004) para 143.
12 *Ciliz v The Netherlands* [2000] 2 FLR 469.
13 *R (Fawad and Zia Ahmadi) v Secretary of State for the Home Department* [2005] EWCA Civ 1721.
14 [2004] EWCA Civ 1075 paras 38 and 77.
15 However, as is made clear in *Singh* at 38, 'some degree of family life' must already be established, whether by biological parentage, or by the genuine beginnings of an informal adoption process etc.

ECHR article 8, procedural obligations and contact proceedings

16.12 ECHR article 8 incorporates procedural rights[16] including a right to participate meaningfully in contact proceedings. In *Ciliz v The Netherlands*[17] the expulsion of a man at the start of contact proceedings breached ECHR article 8 in that it precluded his meaningful participation in those proceedings. In *Ciliz v Netherlands*, the parent facing expulsion had committed no criminal offences; however, in *MS (Ivory Coast) v Secretary of State for the Home Department*[18] the Court of Appeal found it arguable that a woman's removal would breach article 8 where expulsion would prevent her participation in contact proceedings for her children, notwithstanding that she had been convicted of grievous bodily harm, actual bodily harm and cruelty against the same children.[19]

Different types of family relationships and family life under ECHR article 8(1)

Family life between biological parent and child

16.13 Family life exists between a mother and child which can only be broken in exceptional circumstances.[20]

16.14 The Supreme Court has, summarising the ECtHR's jurisprudence, suggested that a higher threshold applies to fathers than to mothers.[21] We suggest below that the approach taken by the ECtHR to the family life enjoyed by fathers and their children has been inconsistent.

16.15 The ECtHR has stated that mere biological kinship is not enough to establish the existence of family life between a father and child.[22]

---

16 See, for example, *McMichael v UK* (1995) 20 EHRR 205 paras 87 and 91; *R (B) v Crown Court at Stafford* [2006] EWHC 1645 (Admin), [2007] 1 WLR 1524.
17 [2000] 2 FLR 469.
18 [2007] EWCA Civ 133, [2007] Imm AR 538.
19 See also *AC (Turkey) v Secretary of State for the Home Department* [2009] EWCA Civ 377 in which the Court of Appeal upheld an Asylum and Immigration Tribunal (AIT) determination allowing an appeal against a refusal to revoke a deportation order. The deportation of a woman convicted of grievous bodily harm with intent who had regular contact with her child would breach ECHR article 8.
20 *Principal Reporter v K* [2010] UKSC 56, [2011] 1 WLR 18 para 36.
21 *Principal Reporter v K* [2010] UKSC 56, [2011] 1 WLR 18 para 36.
22 *Lebbink v The Netherlands* (2004) 40 EHRR 417 para 37. In that case, although the parents had never lived together and the father had not sought to recognise the child, protected family life was found to exist. Relevant factors were that

But the ECtHR has also repeatedly stated that, save in exceptional circumstances, family life exists between parents (generally, without distinguishing between mothers and fathers) and their minor biological children:[23]

> ... from the moment of the child's birth and by the very fact of it, there exists between him and his parents a bond amounting to 'family life', which subsequent events cannot break save in exceptional circumstances.[24]

16.16 Family life has in practice been found to exist between a father and child even where there is minimal or no evidence of close ties. For example, protected family life has been accepted by the ECtHR to exist:

- between a man and his minor child even where there was no evidence that the man had ever cohabited with the child's mother or provided for the child or enjoyed parental rights;[25]
- between a couple and their minor child, where the father had never lived with the child; the mother had been separated from the child for six years; and the separation from the child had been voluntary;[26]
- between a father and his minor child who had been separated for over seven years since the child was three months old but continued to maintain links through visits;[27] and
- between a father and child after the child had been taken into care.[28]

16.17 The factors to be considered where family life needs to be established between a father and child are summarised in *Khan v UK*[29] (where

> there had been a real relationship between the parents, the father had been present at the child's birth, had visited regularly, even changed her nappy a few times and babysat once or twice, and was in touch with the mother about the child's impaired hearing.

23 See discussion in *Singh v ECO (New Delhi)* [2004] EWCA Civ 1075, [2005] QB 608 para 21.
24 *Ahmut v The Netherlands* (1997) 24 EHRR 62, para 60. See also *Gul v Switzerland* (1996) 22 EHRR 93 para 32; *Berrehab v The Netherlands* (1998) 11 EHRR 322 para 21; *Hokkanen v Finland* judgment of 23 September 1994, Series A no 299-A, p19, para 54; *W v UK* (1987) 10 EHRR 29 para 59.
25 *Boughanemi v France* (1996) 22 EHRR 228; *Hendriks v The Netherlands* (1983) 5 EHRR 223.
26 *Sen v The Netherlands* (2003) 36 EHRR 7.
27 *Gul v Switzerland* (1996) 22 EHRR 93.
28 *W v UK* (1997) 10 EHRR 29 para 59.
29 (2010) 50 EHRR 47 para 34.

the ECtHR accepted the existence of family life between a man and his baby daughter despite not living together). Factors other than cohabitation which 'may also serve to demonstrate that a relationship has sufficient constancy to create de facto family ties' include:

> ... the nature and duration of the parents' relationship, and in particular whether they planned to have a child; whether the father subsequently recognised the child as his; contributions made to the child's care and upbringing; and the quality and regularity of contact.

16.18 ECHR article 8 protections are the same for a parent's relationship with his or her child regardless of whether the child is 'legitimate'.[30]

Adoptive and foster parents and children

16.19 Adoptive parent–child relationships have been held to constitute protected family life, both in the ECtHR[31] and in the domestic courts.[32] Where an adoption is valid under national and international law, ECHR article 8 has been held to protect planned family life between the adoptive parents and child even where close ties have not yet been formed.[33] Where the adoption is not legally valid, the existence of protected family life may still exist, particularly where close personal ties can be shown to exist.[34] The ECtHR has also held (in the context of determining whether there existed a right to see files relating to fostering arrangements) that fostering engages ECHR article 8.[35]

Family life between heterosexual spouses

16.20 Where couples are legally married and this is not a sham marriage, the ECtHR has presumed that protected family life exists. Family life has been found between legally married spouses even where the couple had not yet begun to cohabit.[36]

---

30 *Marckx v Belgium* (1979) 2 EHRR 330 para 31.
31 *X v Belgium and The Netherlands* (1975) 7 D&R 75; *X v France* (1982) 31 D&R 241; *Pini et al v Romania* [2005] 2 FLR 596, (2005) 40 EHRR 13.
32 *Singh v ECO (New Delhi)* [2004] EWCA Civ 1075, [2005] QB 608.
33 *Pini et al v Romania* paras 144–148.
34 *Singh v ECO (New Delhi)* [2004] EWCA Civ 1075, [2005] QB 608.
35 *Gaskin v UK* (1979) 2 EHRR 245. In R *(Mithokozisi) v Secretary of State for the Home Department* [2004] EWHC 2964 (Admin) the High Court found that a man did not have protected family life with his foster parents: however, the foster 'child' was 21 years old in that case.
36 *Abdulaziz, Cabales and Balkandali v UK* (1985) 7 EHRR 330 para 62; see also discussion in *Singh v ECO (New Delhi)* [2004] EWCA Civ 1075, [2005] QB 608 per Munby J at para 73; and in *A (Afghanistan) v Secretary of State for the Home Department* [2009] EWCA Civ 825 at paras 37–42.

Heterosexual unmarried partners

16.21 Where a couple has not married legally, the existence of protected family life under ECHR article 8(1) will depend on the nature of the couple's ties and their duration:

> When deciding whether a relationship can be said to amount to 'family life', a number of factors may be relevant, including whether the couple live together, the length of their relationship and whether they have demonstrated their commitment to each other by having children together or by any other means.[37]

16.22 So, for example, a couple who had undergone a marriage ceremony and believed themselves to be married enjoyed protected family life regardless of the fact that the marriage might be legally invalid.[38]

16.23 When assessing the existence of family life between an unmarried couple, cohabitation is an important factor but not a pre-requisite.[39]

Same-sex partners

16.24 The ECtHR has yet to recognise stable relationships between same-sex partners as constituting family life[40] and has instead dealt with these relationships under the rubric of private life.[41] The ECtHR has, however, recognised that there is growing international consensus that same-sex and heterosexual relationships should be treated equally.[42]

16.25 The domestic courts have declined to go further than the ECtHR in this respect and have yet to find that same-sex relationships constitute family life for the purposes of ECHR article 8.[43] However, the domestic courts have nonetheless repeatedly held that relationships between same-sex couples (even if falling under the 'private life' rubric) require protection analogous to that of heterosexual relationships. The House of Lords has, in the context of housing and social

---

37 *X, Y and Z v UK* (1997) 24 EHRR 143 para 36.
38 *Abdulaziz, Cabales and Balkandali v UK* (1985) 7 EHRR 330 para 63.
39 *Boyle v UK* (1988) 10 EHRR 425 at para 15(43); see also discussion in *Singh v ECO (New Delhi)* [2004] EWCA Civ 1075, [2005] QB 608 per Munby J at para 74. As to the importance of cohabitation, see *Lebbink v The Netherlands* (2004) 40 EHRR 417 at para 36.
40 The ECtHR and European Commission of Human Rights (ECommHR) declined to recognise same sex relationships as family life in *X v UK* (1983) 32 DR 220; *S v UK* (1986) 47 DR 274; *B v UK* (1990) 64 DR 278; *Estevez v Spain* (App No 56501/00) 10 May 2001. See likewise the ECJ in *Grant v South-West Trains* (1998) 3 BHRC 578.
41 *Roosli v Germany* App No 28118/95, 15 May 1996.
42 *JM v UK* [2011] 1 FLR 491; [2010] 3 FCR 648 paras 45–50.
43 *M v Secretary of State for Work and Pensions* [2006] UKHL 11, [2006] 2 AC 91.

welfare, held that a same-sex partner was capable of being a member of the original tenant's 'family' within the meaning of the Rent Act 1977;[44] and has made clear that the ties between a same-sex couple are no less close and merit no less protection than those between heterosexual partners:

> A homosexual couple, as much as a heterosexual couple, share each other's life and make their home together. They have an equivalent relationship.[45]

16.26 See likewise the powerful affirmation by the Supreme Court in *HJ (Iran) v Secretary of State for the Home Department*[46] (a case concerning Refugee Convention protections) of the equal respect to be accorded to same sex relationships.

16.27 In the immigration context, the Court of Appeal has taken the position that the relationship between a same-sex couple may be considered 'private life ... cognate with family life'.[47]

Family life between adults and their siblings or parents

16.28 The older ECtHR jurisprudence has recognised the relationship between healthy adults and their parents and siblings as constituting family life protected under ECHR article 8(1) even where:

- the adult did not live with his parents or siblings;[48] and
- the adult had formed a separate household and family.[49]

16.29 However, particularly in the more recent jurisprudence, the ECtHR and ECommHR have stated that the family ties between adults and their parents or siblings attract lesser protection unless there is 'evidence of further elements of dependency, involving more than the normal, emotional ties'.[50] The domestic courts have applied this test

---

44 *Fitzpatrick v Sterling Housing Association Ltd* [2001] 1 AC 27.
45 *Ghaidan v Godin-Mendoza* [2004] UKHL 30, [2004] 2 AC 557 at para 17.
46 [2010] UKSC 31, [2010] 3 WLR 386 in particular paras 14, 76.
47 *Krasniqi v Secretary of State for the Home Department* [2006] EWCA Civ 391.
48 *Moustaquim v Belgium* (1991) 13 EHRR 802 para 35; *Boujlifa v France* (2000) 30 EHRR 419 para 36; *El Boujaidi v France* (2000) 30 EHRR 223 para 33.
49 *Boughanemi v France* (1996) 22 EHRR 228 para 35.
50 *Benhebba v France* App No 53441/99, 10/07/2003 para 36; *Mokrani vFrance* (2003) 40 EHRR 123, para 33; *Advic v UK* (1995) 20 EHRR CD125; *S v UK* (1984) 40 DR 196; *Onur v UK* (2009) 49 EHRR 38 para 45. The principle is stated with particular stringency in *Slivenko v Latvia* (2004) 39 EHRR 24 para 97 and *Khan v UK* (2010) 50 EHRR 47 para 32: 'the Court has held that there will be no family life between parents and adult children unless they can demonstrate additional elements of dependence'.

for family life to relationships between adults and their siblings and parents[51] as well as to more extended family ties between adults.[52] This principle reflects the fact-specificity of 'family life' under ECHR article 8: it should not be taken to mean that protected family life cannot exist between healthy adults and their siblings or parents or extended family members.[53]

16.30 We suggest that 'more than the normal emotional ties' exist where an adult lives with his or her parents or siblings.[54] Overlapping with that consideration, the ECtHR Grand Chamber has found the existence of family life where a young adult had still formed no independent family of his own.[55]

16.31 The dependency may be by the applicant on his or her settled family members or vice versa.[56] The dependency may be largely financial[57] or may be emotional.[58]

---

51 *Kugathas v Secretary of State for the Home Department* [2003] EWCA Civ 31 para 19: 'Most of us have close relations of whom we are extremely fond and whom we visit, or who visit us, from time to time; but none of us would say on those grounds alone that we share a family life with them in any sense capable of coming within the meaning and purpose of Article 8'. See also *JB (India) v ECO* [2009] EWCA Civ 234 and *Odawey v ECO* [2011] EWCA Civ 840.

52 *Zatoon Bi (Pakistan) v Secretary of State for the Home Department* [2009] EWCA Civ 834; *MT (Zimbabwe) v Secretary of State for the Home Department* [2007] EWCA Civ 455.

53 *MT (Zimbabwe) v Secretary of State for the Home Department* [2007] EWCA Civ 455.

54 In *HK (Turkey) v Secretary of State for the Home Department* [2010] EWCA Civ 583, the Court of Appeal held at para 16 that 'normal family ties will exist between an adult child and his parents or other members of his family regardless of proximity and where they live'. We suggest that it follows that, where the adult continues to live with his or her parents or siblings, something more than the normal family ties exist and, as in *HK (Turkey)* family life is established. See likewise *RG (Nepal) v Secretary of State for the Home Department* [2010] UKUT 273 (UT) para 27, where Blake J sitting as President found family life between an adult son and his father where the son was still 'a dependent member of his family's household'. See likewise *Senthuran v Secretary of State for the Home Department* [2004] EWCA Civ 950.

55 *Maslov v Austria* [2009] INLR 47 para 62; see also *Osman v Denmark* App No 38058/09, judgment 14 June 2011, para 55; *Bousarra v France* App No 25672/07, judgment 23 September 2010 paras 38–39 (judgment currently available only in French).

56 *Kugathas v Secretary of State for the Home Department* [2003] EWCA Civ 31 per Arden LJ para 25; *Zatoon Bi (Pakistan) v Secretary of State for the Home Department* [2009] EWCA Civ 834.

57 *Zatoon Bi (Pakistan) v Secretary of State for the Home Department* [2009] EWCA Civ 834.

58 *MT (Zimbabwe) v Secretary of State for the Home Department* [2007] EWCA Civ 455 paras 13 and 26.

16.32   The Court of Appeal cautioned in *HK (Turkey)* against rigid notions of the significance of a person reaching the age of majority:

> undoubtedly he had family life while he was growing up and I would not regard it as suddenly cut off when he reached his majority.[59]

Grandparents and minor grandchildren

16.33   Where close personal ties exist, the relationship between a minor grandchild and grandparents has been found to be protected family life both in the ECtHR[60] and in the domestic courts[61] (though these relationships, even where amounting to family life, may attract lower protections than relationships within the nuclear family[62]).

Uncles, aunts, nieces and nephews and cousins

16.34   Particularly where the natural parents are absent, family ties have been held to exist between uncles and aunts and nieces and nephews, both in the ECtHR[63] and in the domestic courts.[64] Protected family life may also exist between adult cousins.[65]

Private life

Scope of private life generally

16.35   Private life as protected by ECHR article 8 is a broad concept, encompassing personal, social and economic relations; moral and physical integrity; personal identity including sexuality; personal information; and personal or private space. The first three of these aspects of private life feature prominently in immigration and deportation cases.

---

59 *HK (Turkey) v Secretary of State for the Home Department* [2010] EWCA Civ 583 para 16.
60 *Marckx v Belgium* (1979) 2 EHRR 330 para 45; *Bronda v Italy* (1998) 33 EHRR 81, para 50.
61 *R v Secretary of State for the Home Department ex p Mobin Jagot* (2000) Imm AR 414; see also obiter comments of the Supreme Court in *Principal Reporter v K* [2010] UKSC 56, [2011] 1 WLR 18 para 38.
62 *GHB v UK* [2000] EHRLR 545; see also obiter comments of the Supreme Court in *Principal Reporter v K* [2010] UKSC 56, [2011] 1 WLR 18 para 38.
63 *Boyle v UK* (1994) 19 EHRR 179; *Jucius and Juciuviene v Lithuania* (2008) 49 EHRR 70.
64 *R (Lekstaka) v IAT* [2005] EWHC 745 (Admin).
65 *MT (Zimbabwe) v Secretary of State for the Home Department* [2007] EWCA Civ 455.

Relationships and private life

16.36 Where the relationship between relatives is not accepted to amount to family life, it may nonetheless be protected private life.[66] The President of the Immigration and Asylum Chamber of the Upper Tribunal (UT-IAC) has suggested that in these circumstances, private life carries particular weight.[67] In an example of this approach, the Court of Appeal has treated a same-sex relationship as amounting to private life cognate with family life.[68]

Private life and social and economic relations

16.37 Private life encompasses the network of relations that a person has established such as work, education, friendships, reliance on medical or therapeutic services:

> ... the network of personal, social and economic relations that make up the private life of every human being.[69]

> ... the totality of social ties between settled migrants and the community in which they are living.[70]

> ... a right to personal development, and the right to establish and develop relationships with other human beings and the outside world.[71]

> Article 8 also protects the right to establish and develop relationships with other human beings and the outside world and can sometimes embrace aspects of an individual's social identity, it must be accepted that the totality of social ties between settled migrants and the community in which they are living constitutes part of the concept of 'private life' within the meaning of Article 8. Regardless of the existence or otherwise of a 'family life', the expulsion of a settled migrant therefore constitutes an interference with his or her right to respect for private life. It will depend on the circumstances of the particular case whether it is appropriate for the Court to focus on the 'family life' rather than the 'private life' aspect ...[72]

---

66 *Khan v UK* (2010) 50 EHRR 47 paras 32, 42, 43 and *Onur v UK* (2009) 49 EHRR 38 paras 45–46 where, in each case, the adult applicant had private life, although not family life, arising from his relations with his mother and adult siblings.
67 *RG (Nepal) v Secretary of State for the Home Department* [2010] UKUT 273 (IAC) para 25.
68 *Krasniqi v Secretary of State for the Home Department* [2006] EWCA Civ 391.
69 *Slivenko v Latvia* (2004) 39 EHRR 24 para 96.
70 *Onur v UK* (2009) 49 EHRR 38 para 46.
71 *Pretty v UK* (2002) 35 EHRR 1 para 61.
72 *Maslov v Austria* [2009] INLR 47 para 63.

There appears to be no reason in principle why this understanding of the notion of 'private life' should be taken to exclude the activities of a professional or business nature, since it is, after all, in the course of their working lives that the majority of people have a significant if not the greatest opportunity of developing relationships with the outside world.[73]

Composite family and private life cases

16.38 Many ECHR article 8 cases will combine both family and private life aspects, as was noted by the Immigration Appeal Tribunal (IAT) in the early guideline case on ECHR article 8, *Nhundhu and Chiwera v Secretary of State for the Home Department*:[74]

In the context of immigration and asylum cases, the Court has come to view the right to respect for private and family life as a composite right. This approach requires the decision-maker to avoid restricting himself to looking at the circumstances of 'family life' and to take into account also significant elements of the much wider sphere of 'private life': *Chorfi v Belgium* 7 August 1996, *Bouchelkia v France* judgment of 29 January 1997 (paragraph 41), *El Boujaidi v France* 26 September 1997 and *Mehemi v France* 26 September 1997 and *Nasri v France* (1996) 21 EHRR 458. One consequence of this approach is that a person may be able to establish a protected right under Article 8 either by reference to significant elements of family life or significant elements of private life or a mixture of both.

16.39 In a number of cases, mental ill-health has tipped the balance in the individual's favour in an ECHR article 8 family life case. In *HM (Malawi) v Secretary of State for the Home Department*,[75] the Administrative Court found that when assessing whether it is reasonable to expect other family members to relocate with the deportee, the impact of deportation on the health of the deportee and his or her family members is a 'potentially critical matter'. The medical condition of the deportee and family member, and the availability of treatment in the country of deportation would all be relevant. In *Krasniqi v Secretary of State for the Home Department*,[76] the Court of Appeal upheld a determination allowing the article 8 appeal of a profoundly mentally disturbed woman in a same-sex relationship with another asylum-seeker with whom she was rearing a child. The Court of

---

73 *Niemietz v Germany* (1992) 16 EHRR 97 para 29.
74 01TH00613 – CC-21729-2000, 1 June 2001 at para 26.
75 [2010] EWHC 1407 (Admin) para 490.
76 [2006] EWCA Civ 391.

Appeal found the effect on the appellant of the loss of the only people she considered to be her family would be exacerbated by her fragile mental and emotional state.[77] In *R (X) v Secretary of State for the Home Department*[78] the Administrative Court found arguable the case of a highly disturbed woman whose brother was settled in the UK: her dependency on her brother had been heightened by her history of trauma and fragile mental state and the feared consequences of the separation included suicide. The interplay between family life and mental and physical illness in ECHR articles 3 and 8 cases is discussed in further detail at paras 18.40–18.41.

---

77 [2006] EWCA Civ 391 para 33.
78 [2006] EWHC 1208 (Admin) in particular paras 49–50.

CHAPTER 17

Proportionality in ECHR article 8 expulsion cases

17.1	Introduction
17.2	**The proportionality assessment in family life expulsion cases generally**
17.2	Whether family life can reasonably be expected to be enjoyed elsewhere
17.7	No requirement to show 'insurmountable obstacles' to the enjoyment of family life elsewhere
17.13	Physical separation of a family
17.17	Severance of family life where family life cannot reasonably be expected to be enjoyed elsewhere
17.22	Family members of refugees
17.23	Rights of other family members
17.24	Best interests of the child
17.31	Where the settled family members are British citizens or other citizens of the EU – consequences of the *ZH (Tanzania)* and *Ruiz Zambrano* judgments
17.36	Further factors in the proportionality assessment in family life cases
17.37	**Factors relevant in proportionality assessment in both private and family life cases**
17.37	Family or private life formed while immigration status known to be precarious
17.41	Delay

continued

17.43	Length of residence in home state and 'home-grown criminals'
17.52	Conditions in the receiving state
17.54	Contribution to the community
17.55	**Additional proportionality considerations in criminal deportation cases**
17.55	The test to be applied
17.57	Gravity of offence
17.65	Risk of further offending
17.67	Deterrence and the expression of public revulsion
17.72	Deterrence and expression of public revulsion in deportation cases under the IA 1971
17.73	Deterrence and expression of public revulsion in 'automatic' deportation cases under the UKBA 2007
17.79	Time span of offending
17.80	Offences committed as a minor
17.85	Weight to be given to old offences; offences pre-dating a grant of leave to remain
17.86	The lapse of time since the commission of the index offence
17.89	Duration of the exclusion

Introduction

17.1 This chapter discusses the proportionality assessment under European Convention on Human Rights (ECHR) article 8, first as it generally applies in expulsion cases, then in the specific context of criminal deportation cases.

The proportionality assessment in family life expulsion cases generally

Whether family life can reasonably be expected to be enjoyed elsewhere

17.2 ECHR article 8 confers no right on individuals or families to choose where they live.[1] However, expulsion may breach the right to respect for family life under ECHR article 8, in particular where a family cannot reasonably be expected to enjoy their family life elsewhere than in the host state.[2]

17.3 In family life expulsion cases, where the proportionality stage is reached, the applicable test is that set out by the House of Lords in *Huang v Secretary of State for the Home Department*:

> ... the ultimate question for the appellate immigration authority is whether the refusal or leave to enter or remain [or decision to administratively remove or deport] in circumstances where the life of the family cannot reasonably be expected to be enjoyed elsewhere, taking full account of all considerations weighing in favour of the refusal [or decision to remove or deport] prejudices the family life of the appellant in a manner sufficiently serious to amount to a breach of the fundamental right protected by article 8.[3]

17.4 The Grand Chamber of the European Court of Human Rights (ECtHR) likewise clarified in its important guidance case on family life, proportionality and criminal offending, *Uner v The Netherlands*,[4]

---

1 *Abdulaziz, Cabales and Balkandali v UK* (1984) 6 EHRR 28 para 68; *Gül v Switzerland* (1996) 22 EHRR 93 para 38; and *Boultif v Switzerland* (2001) 33 EHRR 50 para 39.
2 See, for example, *Beljoudi v France* (1992) 14 EHRR 801; *Boultif v Switzerland* (2001) 33 EHRR 1179.
3 *Huang and Kashmiri v Secretary of State for the Home Department* [2007] UKHL 11, [2007] 2 AC 167 para 20.
4 (2007) 45 EHRR 14 para 75.

adopting and expanding the guidance set out earlier in *Boultif v Switzerland*:[5]

> ... the relevant criteria ... in order to assess whether an expulsion measure was necessary in a democratic society and proportionate to the legitimate aim pursued ...

include

> ... the seriousness of the difficulties which the spouse is likely to encounter in the country to which the country to which the applicant is to be expelled.

17.5 In short, the decision-maker must address two questions: whether the family members would in fact relocate and whether it would be reasonable for them to be expected to do so.[6]

17.6 If the family members will not in fact relocate, the decision-maker must address the fact that the likely consequence of deportation is separation rather than simply proceeding on the hypothetical basis that family life could be expected to be enjoyed elsewhere.[7] Where it is not clear what choices other family members will take if expulsion occurs (will the rest of the family really refuse to follow the expellee) the decision-maker is not required to form an educated guess as to what the other family members will in fact do. Rather, the decision-maker should recognise and evaluate the difficulty of the dilemma for the other family members.[8]

No requirement to show 'insurmountable obstacles' to the enjoyment of family life elsewhere

17.7 Reference has been made to 'insurmountable obstacles' to family life being enjoyed elsewhere, both in domestic case-law[9] and in the European Commission of Human Rights (ECommHR) and ECtHR's jurisprudence[10] on ECHR article 8. Until recently, 'insurmountable

---

5 (2001) 33 EHRR 1179.
6 *Valentin Batista v Secretary of State for the Home Department* [2010] EWCA Civ 896 paras 25–26.
7 *Valentin Batista v Secretary of State for the Home Department* [2010] EWCA Civ 896 paras 25–26.
8 *VW (Uganda) and AB (Somalia)* [2009] EWCA Civ 5 at para 42.
9 Most notably in *Mahmood v Secretary of State for the Home Department* [2001] 1 WLR 861 para 55 per Lord Phillips, then Master of the Rolls.
10 See, for example, *Poku v UK* (1996) 22 EHRR CD 94 para 3; *Konstatinov v The Netherlands* 16351/03, 26 April 2007, [2006] ECHR 336 (26 April 2007) at para 48; *Da Silva and Hoogkamer v The Netherlands* (2007) 44 EHRR 34 para 39; *Omoregie and others v Norway* [2009] Imm AR 170 para 66; *Nunez v Norway*,

17.8 obstacles' were often and erroneously understood, domestically, to impose a threshold test to a finding of a breach of ECHR article 8 in a family life case.

However, as the Court of Appeal has since clarified, there is no requirement in an ECHR article 8 family life case to show 'insurmountable obstacles' to the enjoyment of family life elsewhere. In *VW and AB (Somalia) v Secretary of State for the Home Department*, Sedley LJ stated:

> While it is of course possible that the facts of any one case may disclose an insurmountable obstacle to removal, the inquiry into proportionality is not a search for such an obstacle and does not end with its elimination. It is a balanced judgment of what can reasonably be expected in light of all the material facts.
>
> *EB (Kosovo)* now confirms that the material question in gauging the proportionality of a removal or deportation which will or may break up a family unless the family itself decamps is not whether there is an insuperable obstacle to this happening but whether it is reasonable to expect the family to leave with the appellant.[11]

17.9 The Court of Appeal has since reiterated that 'the Strasbourg court has not laid down any test of impossibility or exceptional difficulty':[12] it is an 'impermissible test'.[13]

17.10 The ECtHR's jurisprudence likewise makes clear that ECHR article 8 may be breached where there are serious obstacles to family life being enjoyed elsewhere, even though it is not impossible for other family members to follow the expellee to the receiving state.

17.11 In the case of *Amrollahi v Denmark*, where the EctHR held that the deportation of a heroin trafficker whose wife and children were Danish citizens was disproportionate, the EctHR found that there would be a breach of ECHR article 8 even if it were not impossible for the settled family to relocate:

App No 55597/09, judgment 28 June 2011, para 70. See also *Onur v the UK* (2009) 49 EHRR 38 para 60, referring to impossibility or exceptional difficulty.

11 [2009] EWCA Civ 5 paras 19 and 24.

12 *KB (Trinidad and Tobago) v Secretary of State for the Home Department* [2010] EWCA Civ 11 para 20; see also *JO (Uganda) and JT (Ivory Coast) v Secretary of State for the Home Department* [2010] EWCA Civ 10 paras 14–15 and 22–26 and *YD (Togo) v Secretary of State for the Home Department* [2010] EWCA Civ 214 paras 5, 17 and 18; *SS (India) v Secretary of State for the Home Department* [2010] EWCA Civ 388 paras 51–52.

13 *YD (Togo) v Secretary of State for the Home Department* [2010] EWCA Civ 214 para 18.

In these circumstances the Court accepts even if it is not impossible for the spouse and the applicant's children to live in Iran that it would, nevertheless, cause them obvious and serious difficulties ...[14]

17.12 In *Sezen v The Netherlands* the ECtHR found that it would be disproportionate to expel a man found to be in intentional possession of 52 kilos of heroin to Turkey because of the difficulties this would pose for his wife and children (themselves Turkish nationals and not refugees):

... the Court accepts that following the first applicant to Turkey would mean a radical upheaval for the second applicant [the spouse] and in particular for the couple's children ... and it finds that they cannot realistically be expected to do so [emphasis added].[15]

Physical separation of a family

17.13 As Lord Bingham stated in *Huang v Secretary of State for the Home Department*:

Human beings are social animals. They depend on others. Their family, or extended family, is the group on which many people most heavily depend, socially, emotionally and often financially. There comes a point at which, for some, prolonged and unavoidable separation from this group seriously inhibits their ability to live full and fulfilling lives.[16]

17.14 The ECtHR has been unimpressed by arguments that family members previously living together can maintain family life through occasional contact after expulsion:

The Court has previously held that domestic measures which prevent family members from living together constitute an inference with the right protected by Article 8 of the Convention and that to split up a family is an interference of a very serious order.[17]

---

14 App No 56811/00, 11 July 2002, para 41.
15 (2006) 43 EHRR 30 para 46.
16 [2007] UKHL 11, [2007] 2 AC 167 para 18.
17 *Sezen v The Netherlands* (2006) 43 EHRR 30 para 49. See also *Omojudi v UK* (2010) 51 EHRR 10, para 46, finding disproportionate the deportation of a sex offender who could maintain contact with his UK-based spouse and children by telephone and email. However, see by contrast *Onur v UK* (2009) 49 EHRR 38 para 58 and *Joseph Grant v UK* App No 10606/07, 5 June 1999, para 40 where it was considered that a father and daughter who had never lived together, could maintain contact by telephone and email after the father's expulsion. In both cases, the ECtHR indicated that the disruption to family life was less because the father and daughter had never lived together (the applicant in *Onur* had lived with another child but only briefly). The question

17.15 Thus, for example, the ECtHR has found expulsion disproportionate where the parent being expelled, formerly the primary carer, no longer had custody of the child and would be able to see the child during holidays.[18]

17.16 Blake J, sitting in the Administrative Court,[19] and also when sitting as President of the Immigration and Asylum Chamber of the Upper Tribunal (UT-IAC) has likewise observed of the Secretary of State for the Home Department's (SSHD's) 'wholly unrealistic' proposal for arrangements to maintain family life between an active parent and a young child:

> ... the internet and telephone calls do not substitute for the daily care, engagement and attendance on a young child that is the essence of family life in this context.[20]

Severance of family life where family life cannot reasonably be expected to be enjoyed elsewhere

17.17 The question of the reasonableness of another family member following the expellee is very important but not always decisive either way of the question of proportionality.

17.18 In *EB (Kosovo)*[21] Lord Bingham stated at para 12:

> ... it will rarely be proportionate to uphold an order for removal of a spouse if there is a close and genuine bond with the other spouse and that spouse cannot reasonably be expected to follow the removed spouse to the country of removal, or if the effect of the order is to sever a genuine and subsisting relationship between parent and child. But cases will not ordinarily raise such stark choices, and there is in general no alternative to making a careful and informed evaluation of the facts of the particular case. The search for a hard-edged or bright-line rule to be applied to the generality of cases is incompatible with the difficult evaluative exercise which article 8 requires.

---

of whether the family has experienced living together and if so for how long, is therefore likely to be key to the question of whether expulsion is proportionate where this will reduce contact to telephone contact. See likewise Blake J, President of the Upper Tribunal, Immigration and Asylum Chamber, in *LD (Zimbabwe) v Secretary of State for the Home Department* [2010] UKUT 278 (IAC) para 21.

18 *Nunez v Norway*, App. No 55597/09, judgment 28 June 2011, para 81.
19 *R (Mansoor) v Secretary of State for the Home Department* [2011] EWHC 832 (Admin) para 16.
20 *Omotunde (best interests – Zambrano applied – Razgar) Nigeria* [2011] UKUT 249 (IAC) para 29.
21 [2008] UKHL 41 para 12.

17.19 *EB (Kosovo)* is an administrative removal case and those comments 'may need to be qualified' in the context of criminal deportation.[22] This is because the public interest in the prevention of crime and disorder may be greater than the public interest in the maintenance of effective immigration controls.[23]

17.20 In the context of criminal deportation, the public interest in preventing crime and disorder may, in certain cases, be so great as to justify the severance of family ties:

> In some cases, the seriousness of the offence is so overwhelming as to trump all else.[24]
>
> ... it is possible in a case of sufficiently serious offending that the factors in favour of deportation will be strong enough to render deportation proportionate even if it does have the effect of severing established family ties.[25]

17.21 In *DS (India) v Secretary of State for the Home Department*[26] Rix LJ giving the sole judgment likewise held at para 30:

---

22 *KB (Trinidad and Tobago) v Secretary of State for the Home Department* [2010] EWCA Civ 11.

23 *SS (India) v Secretary of State for the Home Department* [2010] EWCA Civ 388 para 53. Note, however, that even in that case, which concerned a rape, the Court of Appeal was not convinced that the public interest in deportation would outweigh the hardship for the family consequent on deportation (para 55).

24 *HK (Turkey) v Secretary of State for the Home Department* [2010] EWCA Civ 583 para 28.

25 *JO (Uganda) and JT (Ivory Coast) v Secretary of State for the Home Department* [2010] EWCA Civ 10 para 27. For cases in which the gravity of the offences was capable of outweighing the fact that family ties would be severed, *see QJ Algeria v Secretary of State for the Home Department* [2010] EWCA Civ 1478; *R (Sezek and Samaroo) v Secretary of State for the Home Department* [2001] EWCA Civ 1139. For a case in which minor but persistent offending was capable of outweighing the fact of the severance of family ties, see *AS (Pakistan) v Secretary of State for the Home Department* [2010] EWCA Civ 816. However, both the *Sezek and Samaroo* and the *AS (Pakistan)* cases concern rationality challenges: they are not authority that deportation in these circumstances is proportionate, merely authority that a decision to deport (or to dismiss a deportation appeal) in these circumstances may be rational. The cases cited above predate the Supreme Court's guidance in *ZH (Tanzania) v Secretary of State for the Home Department* [2011] UKSC 4, [2011] 2 WLR 148 on the requirement to consider the best interests of the child in ECHR article 8 expulsion cases. Article 8 expulsion cases involving children predating *ZH (Tanzania)* should be treated with caution; but even after *ZH (Tanzania)*, deportation has been found proportionate even in circumstances where it would sever family ties between parent and child: *Lee v Secretary of State for the Home Department* [2011] EWCA Civ 348 para 27.

26 [2009] EWCA Civ 544.

A finding that it was unreasonable to expect a wife or family to accompany a deportee does not in itself answer the question of proportionality. Rather, it sets up an important factor on the route to a conclusion about overall proportionality. If it would be reasonable for a wife to accompany her husband, then the interference in family life is that much the less. If it would be unreasonable, then the interference would be that much the more. However, where the scales ultimately fall will depend on the overall evaluation of every factor in the balance. In the present case a critical factor is the serious offence ...

Family members of refugees

17.22 Where it is proposed to expel a person who enjoys family life with a recognised refugee, the decision-maker must take as her starting point that the refugee cannot reasonably be expected to return to his or her home country. This approach should be taken whether the refugee was granted status in his or her own right or as the dependant of another refugee. However, this presumption may be rebutted by evidence that the refugee can in fact return.[27]

Rights of other family members

17.23 The decision-maker must take other family members' rights into account when assessing proportionality under ECHR article 8 in family life cases. That is, the impact of the SSHD's immigration decision (such as a decision to refuse leave to enter; to administratively remove; or to deport) on the appellant's family members is relevant to the proportionality assessment:[28]

> The right to respect for the family life of one necessarily encompasses the right to respect for the family life of others, normally a spouse or minor children, with whom that family life is enjoyed.[29]

---

27 *AB (Democratic Republic Congo) v Secretary of State for the Home Department* [2007] EWCA Civ 1422.
28 *Beoku-Betts (FC) v Secretary of State for the Home Department* [2008] UKHL 39, [2009] 1 AC 115. For the application of that principle in the deportation context, see *AS (Pakistan) v Secretary of State for the Home Department* [2008] EWCA Civ 1118 and *AF (Jamaica) v Secretary of State for the Home Department* [2009] EWCA Civ 240.
29 *Beoku-Betts (FC) v Secretary of State for the Home Department* per Lady Hale at para 4.

Best interests of the child

17.24 The best interests of the child *must* be treated as a primary consideration in any ECHR article 8 expulsion case which concerns:

- expulsion of a child along with a principal;[30]
- expulsion of a principal where this entails separation from a child;[31]
- expulsion of a minor where the minor is the principal expellee;[32] or
- expulsion in consequence of offences committed as a minor even where the expellee is no longer a minor.[33]

17.25 The mandatory nature of the best interests consideration has been emphasised by the ECtHR Grand Chamber in *Uner v The Netherlands*[34] and *Maslov v Austria*[35] and by the Supreme Court in *ZH (Tanzania)*.[36]

17.26 The requirement to treat the best interests of the child as a primary consideration is derived from article 3 of the UN Convention on the Rights of the Child (UNCRC) to which, as an international human rights instrument, the ECtHR has regard when interpreting the scope of convention protections.[37] See paras 4.7–4.13 for a discussion of the distinct but related statutory duty under Borders, Citizenship and Immigration Act (BCIA) 2009 s55 to have regard to the best interests of the child. On the special considerations applicable to British citizen children, see paras 17.31–17.35 below.

17.27 Where ECHR article 8 is engaged and BCIA 2009 s55 applies, a failure to have regard to the best interests of the child as a primary consideration contrary to BCIA 2009 s55 will render a decision not in accordance with the law for ECHR article 8(2) purposes.[38]

---

30 *Uner v The Netherlands* [2006] ECHR 873.
31 *Boultif v Switzerland* (2001) 33 EHRR 1179.
32 *Jakupovic v Austria* (2003) 38 EHRR 595.
33 *Maslov v Austria* [2009] INLR 47 para 75.
34 (2007) 45 EHRR 14 para 58.
35 [2009] INLR 47 para 82.
36 [2011] UKSC 4, [2011] 2 WLR 148 para 21 per Lady Hale.
37 See discussion in *ZH (Tanzania) v Secretary of State for the Home Department* [2011] UKSC 4, [2011] 2 WLR 148 para 21 per Lady Hale For an example of this approach see *Maslov v Austria* [2009] INLR 47 paras 82–83 finding a duty to promote the rehabilitation of juvenile offenders.
38 *ZH (Tanzania) v Secretary of State for the Home Department* [2011] UKSC 4, [2011] 2 WLR 148 para 24 per Lady Hale; see also *LD (Zimbabwe) v Secretary of State for the Home Department* [2010] UKUT 278 (IAC) para 3.

17.28 Quite apart from the BCIA 2009 s55 duty, in ECHR article 8 cases the best interests of the child necessarily carry great weight in the proportionality assessment under article 8(2). The Supreme Court in *ZH (Tanzania)* was emphatic that the misconduct of the parents facing expulsion should not detract from the weight to be given to the best interests of a minor child:

> It would be wrong in principle to devalue what was in their best interests by something for which they could in no way be held to be responsible.[39]

17.29 Thus in *ZH (Tanzania)*, the public interest in the expulsion of a woman who had an 'appalling' immigration history[40] could be outweighed by the best interests of the child. Likewise, the ECtHR has held that ECHR article 8 would be breached by the expulsion of a mother notwithstanding a previous criminal conviction and very bad immigration history, and notwithstanding that the father had custody of the children.[41]

17.30 The same best interests test applies in criminal deportation cases as in administrative removal cases, although the risk posed by a parent to the public may carry greater weight (as a countervailing consideration) than the threat posed to a country's economic interests by a failure to maintain immigration control.[42]

Where the settled family members are British citizens or other citizens of the EU – consequences of the *ZH (Tanzania)* and *Ruiz Zambrano* judgments

17.31 In *ZH (Tanzania)*, the Supreme Court was emphatic that the fact that the minor dependent child of a proposed expellee is a British citizen 'will hardly ever be less than a very significant and weighty factor against moving children who have that status to another country'.[43]

---

39 *ZH (Tanzania) v Secretary of State for the Home Department* [2011] UKSC 4, [2011] 2 WLR 148 para 44 per Lord Hope.
40 *ZH (Tanzania) v Secretary of State for the Home Department* [2011] UKSC 4, [2011] 2 WLR 148 para 5.
41 *Nunez v Norway* App No 55597/09, judgment 28 June 2011.
42 *ZH (Tanzania) v Secretary of State for the Home Department* [2011] UKSC 4, [2011] 2 WLR 148 para 28 per Lady Hale; see also *Lee v Secretary of State for the Home Department* [2011] EWCA Civ 348 para 27 where deportation was found proportionate notwithstanding that it would sever family ties between parent and child.
43 Para 41 per Lord Hope.

17.32 In *Ruiz Zambrano*,[44] the Grand Chamber of the Court of Justice of the European Union (CJEU) went considerably further. The far-reaching ramifications of the *Zambrano* judgment have been discussed in more detail at paras 10.4–10.16 but the main points relevant to ECHR article 8 are summarised below.

17.33 In *Ruiz Zambrano*, the Grand Chamber of the CJEU found that it would breach article 20 of the Treaty on the Functioning of the European Union (TFEU) to deny a right of residence to third country parents where the consequence would be that their child, a citizen of the European Union (EU), would have to leave the territory of the EU.

17.34 As we have seen at para 17.3 above, it is a key element of the ECHR article 8(2) proportionality assessment in family life cases whether a settled family member can reasonably be expected to follow the deportee abroad. We suggest that, following *Ruiz Zambrano*, it will never be reasonable for ECHR article 8(2) purposes to expect a settled person to relocate outside the EU to follow an expellee outside the territories of the EU where the settled person is a British citizen or the citizen of another EU member state. It may also be unreasonable to expect a British citizen to leave the UK. Note, however, that where it is unreasonable to expect the settled family member to relocate, this is important but not always decisive on ECHR article 8(2) and may be defeated by serious offending by the proposed expellee – see paras 17.17–17.21 above.

17.35 We suggest that different considerations arise where the EU citizen family member is a minor dependent child or another person who is dependent on the third country national expulsee and will *have to* follow the expellee out of the EU area, that is, where a situation of constructive expulsion from the EU area arises. Although it remains to be seen how the *Ruiz Zambrano* principles will apply in the context of criminal deportation, the constructive expulsion for the EU citizen from the EU area may breach TFEU article 20 in many if not all such cases, so that the deportation of the third country national principal would not be in accordance with the law and would be disproportionate for ECHR article 8(2) purposes.

---

44 *Ruiz Zambrano v Office National de l'emploi* Case C-34/09.

Further factors in the proportionality assessment in family life cases

17.36 A wide range of factors must be considered when assessing the proportionality of an interference with right to respect for family life under ECHR article 8:

> Matters such as the age and vulnerability of the applicant, the closeness and previous history of the family, the applicant's dependence on the financial and emotional support of the family, the prevailing cultural traditions and conditions in the country of origin and many other factors may all be relevant.[45]

Factors relevant in proportionality assessment in both private and family life cases

Family or private life formed while immigration status known to be precarious

17.37 Where private or family life has been forged by an immigrant in the UK in the knowledge that his or her immigration status was precarious, this may militate against a finding that the interference caused by expulsion is disproportionate.[46]

17.38 In criminal deportation cases, the issue of precariousness may arise where the proposed deportee formed private or family life while he or she had no leave to enter or remain in the UK. The issue of precariousness may also arise for a proposed deportee (whether or not he or she has leave to enter or remain) who is aware[47] of liability to

---

45 *Huang v Secretary of State for the Home Department* [2005] EWCA Civ 105, [2006] QB 1 para 18.

46 On family life, see *Mahmood v Secretary of State for the Home Department* [2001] 1 WLR 840 and *R (Jeneba Boima) v Secretary of State for the Home Department* [2007] EWHC 2579 (Admin). In the ECtHR, see *Abdulaziz, Cabales and Balkandali v UK* (1985) 7 EHRR 471 para 68; *Omoregie v Norway* [2009] Imm AR 170 paras 59–65 where the state's positive obligations were lessened by fact that relationships formed at time prospects known to be precarious. On private life, see *RU (Sri Lanka) v Secretary of State for the Home Department* [2008] EWCA Civ 753 and *KD (Sri Lanka) v Secretary of State for the Home Department* [2007] EWCA Civ 1384.

47 In a sharp extension of the 'precariousness' principle, the ECtHR in *Khan v UK* (2010) 50 EHRR 47 para 46 attached 'no decisive weight' to the applicant's relationship with his girlfriend, because this had begun while the applicant was in prison – even though at that point, no deportation action against him had been initiated. Notably, in *Khan v UK*, while the ECtHR declined to attach 'decisive' weight to the relationship in these circumstances, so that the relationship was not in itself sufficient to tilt the balance in the applicant's favour,

deportation (because of receipt of a court recommendation for deportation; or because of receipt of a Home Office notification of liability to deportation or intention to deport[48]).

17.39 But ECHR article 8 is frequently found to be breached notwithstanding that immigration status was known to be precarious at the time that article 8(1) rights were established.[49] For example, where there has been delay by the SSHD, the fact that the immigrant forged ties knowing his or her immigration status to be precarious will carry less importance: immigrants forced to wait will almost inevitably forge ties.[50]

17.40 In addition, in *ZH (Tanzania)* the Supreme Court has decisively rejected the notion that decision-makers may give lesser weight to the best interests of children born to parents whose status was precarious at the time that the relationship was formed or the child conceived.[51] Similarly, the ECtHR has found a breach of ECHR article 8, where the expulsion of a mother who had married and had children knowing that she had illegally re-entered the host-state after an earlier deportation would not be in the children's best interests.[52] Domestic jurisprudence on precariousness where children are involved predating *ZH (Tazania)* must be treated with great caution.

Delay

17.41 In *EB Kosovo v Secretary of State for the Home Department*, the House of Lords confirmed that, while there is no right to a decision within any given period of time,[53] prolonged delays by the SSHD may be relevant in ECHR article 8 cases in that:

> the relationship formed part of the applicant's overall circumstances leading to a finding that the his expulsion would breach his rights under ECHR article 8.

48 See, for example, *Onur v UK* (2009) 49 EHRR 38 para 59, giving lesser weight to family ties forged while the applicant and his partner knew that he had been previously warned of his liability to deportation.
49 See, for example, *Krasniqi v Secretary of State for the Home Department* [2006] EWCA Civ 391 where both parties to the relationship were asylum-seekers; *AB (Jamaica) v Secretary of State for the Home Department* [2007] EWCA Civ 1302 where the refusal of a marriage application to an overstayer breached ECHR article 8 since her British husband – met while she was an overstayer – could not reasonably be expected to follow her to her home country.
50 *EB (Kosovo)* [2008] UKHL 41, [2009] 1 AC 1159 paras 15 and 37.
51 *ZH (Tanzania) v Secretary of State for the Home Department* [2011] UKSC 4, [2011] 2 WLR 148 para 44 per Lord Hope, see also Lady Hale at para 20.
52 *Nunez v Norway*, app. No. 55597/09, judgment 28 June 2011, paras 74, 84-85.
53 *EB (Kosovo) v Secretary of State for the Home Department* [2008] UKHL 41, [2009] 1 AC 1159 para 27.

- the applicant may, during the delay period, develop family and/or private life in the UK;
- while it is normally a factor weighing against an individual applicant in the proportionality assessment if he or she entered into a relationship knowing his or her immigration status to be precarious this may carry less weight if the applicant, after suffering long delays, has come to expect that he or she will not be removed;[54]
- '[d]elay may reduce the weight otherwise to be accorded to the requirements of firm and fair immigration control, if the delay is shown to be the result of a dysfunctional system which yields unpredictable, inconsistent and unfair outcomes'.[55]

17.42 Delay in criminal deportation cases is considered at paras 17.86–17.88 below.

Length of residence in home state and 'home-grown criminals'

17.43 Where the foreign national spent formative childhood years in the host state, this is a powerful factor against exclusion or expulsion being found to be proportionate, including in cases of deportation for serious criminal offences. In *Maslov v Austria*,[56] the Grand Chamber of the ECtHR held:

> ... for a settled migrant who has lawfully spent all or the major part of his or her childhood and youth in the host country very serious reasons are required to justify expulsion.

17.44 The principled basis for the special status of those who spend formative years in the host state was explained by the Grand Chamber of the ECtHR in *Uner v The Netherlands*:[57]

> ... the rationale behind making the duration of a person's stay in the host country one of the elements to be taken into account lies in the assumption that the longer a person has been residing in a particular country the stronger his or her ties with that country and the weaker the ties with the country of his or her nationality will be. Seen against that background, it is self-evident that the Court will have regard to

---

54 *EB (Kosovo) v Secretary of State for the Home Department* [2008] UKHL 41, [2009] 1 AC 1159 paras 15 and 37.
55 *EB (Kosovo) v Secretary of State for the Home Department* [2008] UKHL 41, [2009] 1 AC 1159 paras 16 and 27; see also *Akaeke v Secretary of State for the Home Department* [2005] EWCA Civ 947.
56 [2009] INLR 47 para 75.
57 (2007) 45 EHRR 14 para 58.

the special situation of aliens who have spent most, if not all, their childhood in the host country, were brought up there and received their education there [emphasis added].

This principle that 'very serious reasons' are required to justify the expulsion or exclusion of a person who has spent formative years in the host state has been applied by the ECtHR to find a breach of ECHR article 8 even where the foreign national had, after eight formative years in the host state, spent two years outside the host state.[58]

17.45 Failure by a tribunal or court to have regard to the fact that a proposed expellee has been in the UK since childhood is an error of law.[59]

17.46 The Grand Chamber of the ECtHR in *Maslov v Austria* referred to long term 'lawful residence'. However, as the Court of Appeal has held, even if a person is in the UK unlawfully, the fact that the person has been in the country since childhood 'is still a weighty consideration in the Article 8 balancing exercise'. The fact that a person is in the UK without leave is not a reason to disregard the guidance in *Maslov v Austria* concerning the position of those in the UK since early childhood or (see further below) those who committed their criminal offences as juveniles.[60]

17.47 In a number of cases including those involving serious offenders, the ECtHR has taken the view that the expulsion of foreign national offenders who were born in the host country or who came to the host country as very young children is disproportionate. For example:

- A repeat offender who had committed a series of offences including assault and battery, aggravated theft and possession of arms; but had been born in the host country and had no links to his

---

58 *Osman v Denmark*, App. no. 38508/09, judgment 14 June 2011 paras 65, 68 and 77.

59 *MW (Democratic Republic of the Congo) v Secretary of State for the Home Department* [2011] EWCA Civ 1240 paras 24 and 29; *JO (Uganda) and JT (Ivory Coast) v Secretary of State for the Home Department* [2010] EWCA Civ 10 para 52; *MJ (Angola) v Secretary of State for the Home Department* [2010] EWCA Civ 557 para 40; *HM (Iraq) v Secretary of State for the Home Department* [2010] EWCA Civ 1322 paras 33–34. See also *Radovanovic v Austria* (2005) 41 EHRR 6 para 33 where the ECtHR stated that 'the applicant's family ties and the social ties he established in the host country by receiving his schooling and by spending the decisive years of his youth there are to be taken into account'.

60 *JO (Uganda) and JT (Ivory Coast) v Secretary of State for the Home Department* [2010] EWCA Civ 10 paras 31 and 52.

country of nationality save for his nationality. His wife was a national of the host country.[61]
- A repeat offender who had committed a series of offences including gang rape. He had lived in the host country since the age of five and was deaf and dumb; his parents and siblings lived in the host country and some had acquired its nationality.[62]
- A drug trafficker, convicted of conspiracy to import 142 kilos of hashish. He had been born in the host state and had his parents, siblings, wife and minor children there. His only link to his country of nationality was the nationality itself.[63]
- A man convicted of conspiracy to import heroin, who had been in the UK since the age of three; his parents, siblings, girlfriend and child lived in the UK.[64]
- A man convicted of robbery and damage to property. He had lived in the host state since the age of two and his wife was a national of the host state.[65]
- A repeat offender who had committed numerous offences of aggravated theft and robbery (as an adolescent); he had arrived in the host state aged two; and had returned to his home country only twice.[66] His parents and siblings all lived in the host country.

17.48 The domestic courts have likewise emphasised the importance of a person spending their formative years in the UK. *IM (Zambia) v Secretary of State for the Home Department*[67] the Court of Appeal upheld the Asylum and Immigration Tribunal's (AIT's) finding that the long residence of the proposed deportee (convicted of statutory rape of a minor) constituted an exceptional factor under Immigration Rules para 364 precluding deportation. In *Yousuf v Secretary of State for the Home Department*[68] the Court of Appeal noted that:

> ... for someone who has lived here since the age of eleven or twelve and has no family left in his country of origin, deportation may well be akin to exile.

---

61 *Beljoudi v France* (1992) 14 EHRR 801.
62 *Nasri v France* (1995) 21 EHRR 458.
63 *Mehemi v France* (2000) 30 EHRR 739.
64 *Khan v UK* (2010) 50 EHRR 47.
65 *Boultif v Switzerland* (2001) 33 EHRR 1179.
66 *Moustaquim v Belgium* (1991) 13 EHRR 802.
67 [2008] EWCA Civ 944.
68 [2008] EWCA Civ 394 para 18.

17.49 In *HK (Turkey)*,[69] Sedley LJ emphasised the special nature of the ties formed in the UK during childhood:

> Fifteen years spent here as an adult are not the same as fifteen years spent here as a child. The difference between the two may amount the difference between enforced return and exile. Both are permissible by way of deportation, but the necessary level of compulsion is likely to be very different.

17.50 However, there is no absolute protection from expulsion for long-term immigrants born or raised in the host country.[70] Where the offence is particularly serious,[71] or where the immigrant has retained ties with his or her country of origin[72] the ECtHR has found the expulsion of a foreign national offender to be proportionate.

17.51 Nor, conversely, should it be thought that young adults who have spent a relatively short part of their youth in the UK cannot succeed in their ECHR article 8 claims. See, for example, *AA v UK*[73] in which the ECtHR held that the deportation of a young adult for a rape committed as a minor would be disproportionate, notwithstanding that he had committed the crime two years after his arrival in the UK.

Conditions in the receiving state

17.52 Circumstances of feared persecution or extreme deprivation which do not meet the ECHR article 3 threshold may nonetheless tilt the

---

69 [2010] EWCA Civ 583 para 35.
70 *Uner v The Netherlands* (2007) 45 EHRR 14 para 55.
71 In *Uner v The Netherlands* (2007) 45 EHRR 14 the expulsion of a Turkish national who had lived in the Netherlands since the age of 12 was proportionate: the offence was manslaughter. In *El Boujaidi v France* (2000) 30 EHRR 223, the exclusion of a man convicted of heroin trafficking was proportionate notwithstanding that he had lived in France since the age of seven and his parents and siblings lived there. In *Boujlifa v France* (2000) 30 EHRR 419, the expulsion of a man convicted of offences of armed robbery was proportionate notwithstanding that he had lived primarily in France since the age of five and his parents and siblings were resident there. In *Benhebba v France* App No 53441/99 10/07/2003, expulsion was proportionate notwithstanding that the applicant had lived in France since the age of five and his parents and siblings lived there. He had a string of convictions including drugs possession and armed robbery. In *Kaya v Germany* [2007] 2 FCR 527, [2007] Imm AR 802, the expulsion of a man who had been convicted of attempted aggravated trafficking in human beings and battery was proportionate notwithstanding that he had been born in Germany.
72 *Boughanemi v France* (1996) 22 EHRR 228.
73 App No 8000/08, judgment 20 September 2011.

balance in favour of the applicant in the ECHR article 8 proportionality balancing exercise. See for example *Nhundhu and Chiwera* para 54:

> ... an appellant whose private and family life ties in the UK were not on their own strong enough to give rise to a violation of article 8 could nevertheless succeed under that article if removal would expose him or her to a real risk of significant harms or serious obstacles, albeit harms falling below the article 3 threshold.[74]

17.53 However, see the introduction to this section on the distinction between foreign, domestic and hybrid cases.

Contribution to the community

17.54 In the context of administrative removal, it has been accepted that an individual's contribution to the community is relevant to the proportionality balancing exercise under ECHR article 8(2) though this is likely to affect the outcome only in a minority of cases.[75] We suggest that the same consideration applies to the assessment of the public interest in criminal deportation cases,[76] although the greater weight given to the prevention of crime and disorder is likely to mean that positive considerations of contribution to the community are rarely decisive.

Additional proportionality considerations in criminal deportation cases

The test to be applied

17.55 In criminal deportation cases, the proportionality assessment involves the balance between the applicant's right to respect for his or her private and family life on the one hand, and the prevention of disorder

---

74 IAT 0ITH00613-CC-21729-2000; see also *LD (Zimbabwe) v Secretary of State for the Home Department* [2010] UKUT 278 (IAC) Blake J sitting as President of the Upper Tribunal (Immigration and Asylum Chamber).

75 *UE (Nigeria) and others v Secretary of State for the Home Department* [2010] EWCA Civ 795 paras 35, 36.

76 See *AS (Pakistan) v Secretary of State for the Home Department* [2008] EWCA Civ 1118 para 22 and *UE (Nigeria) and others v Secretary of State for the Home Department* [2010] EWCA Civ 795 paras 19–20.

or crime on the other.[77] While additional factors apply, the general approach to be taken to the proportionality assessment in criminal deportation cases is similar to that in administrative removal cases, and the courts' guidance on the proportionality assessment issued in the context of administrative removal remains applicable with some qualifications to criminal deportation.[78]

17.56 In *Uner v The Netherlands*,[79] the ECtHR Grand Chamber gave important guidance for the assessment of proportionality in a criminal expulsion or exclusion case, listing the following factors to be considered:

- the nature and seriousness of the offence committed by the applicant;
- the length of the applicant's stay in the country from which he or she is to be expelled;
- the time elapsed since the offence was committed and the applicant's conduct during that period;
- the nationalities of the various persons concerned;
- the applicant's family situation, such as the length of the marriage, and other factors expressing the effectiveness of a couple's family life;
- whether the spouse knew about the offence at the time when he or she entered into a family relationship;
- whether there are children of the marriage, and if so, their age; and
- the seriousness of the difficulties which the spouse is likely to encounter in the country to which the applicant is to be expelled.

...

- the best interests and well-being of the children, in particular the seriousness of the difficulties which any children of the applicant are likely to encounter in the country to which the applicant is to be expelled; and
- the solidity of social, cultural and family ties with the host country and with the country of destination.

---

77 *Boughanemi v France* (1996) 22 EHRR 228 at para 42; *Samaroo and Sezek v Secretary of State for the Home Department* [2001] EWCA Civ 1139, [2001] UKHRR 1150 para 35; *N (Kenya) v Secretary of State for the Home Department* [2004] EWCA Civ 1094, [2004] INLR 612 para 54.
78 *KB (Trinidad and Tobago) v Secretary of State for the Home Department* [2010] EWCA Civ 11.
79 (2007) 45 EHRR 14 at para 57.

Gravity of offence

17.57 The more serious the offence, the greater the public interest in deportation. However, even where there is serious past offending or a risk of further serious offending, the circumstances of the case may render deportation disproportionate. The ECtHR has found expulsion or exclusion to be a breach of ECHR article 8 even in cases involving very serious offenders[80] and recidivist offenders.[81]

17.58 The ECtHR has treated certain offences as especially serious, including manslaughter;[82] drugs trafficking;[83] possession of drugs with intent to supply;[84] and living off the earnings of prostitution with aggravating circumstances.[85]

17.59 The ECtHR has drawn a clear distinction between violent and non-violent property offences, treating the former only as serious.[86] The ECtHR has also drawn a clear distinction between drugs offences linked to trafficking and supply (treated as serious in the ECtHR case-law), and drugs offences of pure possession for personal consumption:[87]

> It is true that in the sphere of drug dealing the Court has shown understanding of the domestic authorities' firmness as regards those actively involved in the spread of this scourge (see, for instance, *Dalia v France*, judgment of 19 February 1998, Reports 1998-I, p. 92, [s] 54, and *Baghli v France*, no. 34374/97, [s] 48, ECHR 1999-VIII). However, it has not taken the same approach as regards those convicted of drug consumption (see *Ezzouhdi*, cited above, [s] 34).

---

80 *Nasri v France* (1995) 21 EHRR 458 (involvement in gang rape) ; *Mehemi v France* (2000) 30 EHRR 739 (conspiracy to import 142 kilos of hashish); *Boujlifa v France* (2000) 30 EHRR 419 (armed robbery); *Sezen v The Netherlands* (2006) 43 EHRR 30 possession of 52 kilos of heroin; *Bousarra v France* App No 25672/07, judgment 23 September 2010 (false imprisonment, extortion of funds, sale of drugs, use of a firearm, judgment currently available only in French).

81 *Beljoudi v France* (1992) 14 EHRR 801 (offences included assault and battery; aggravated theft; acquisition and possession of arms).

82 *Uner v The Netherlands* (2007) 45 EHRR 14.

83 *El Boujaidi v France* (2000) 30 EHRR 223.

84 *Benhebba v France* App No 53441/99, 10/07/2003. Where drugs are for personal use, this attracts lesser opprobrium – *Joseph Grant v UK* App No 10606/07, 5 June 1999, para 38.

85 *Boughanemi v France* (1996) 22 EHRR 228.

86 *Jakupovic v Austria* (2003) 38 EHRR 595; *Maslov v Austria* [2009] INLR 47 para 81.

87 *Maslov v Austria* [2009] INLR 47 para 80.

17.60 A similar distinction has been drawn by the European Court of Justice (ECJ) in cases involving interference with the free movement rights of EEA nationals and their family members.[88]

17.61 The ECtHR has repeatedly taken the length (or brevity) of prison sentences imposed to be indicative of the seriousness of the offence.[89] Where offences were so minor that the offender had not been imprisoned, the ECtHR has found expulsion to be disproportionate.[90]

17.62 However, the Court of Appeal has warned that where a person has been recommended for deportation by a court, immigration judges should be wary of treating the imprisonment portion of the sentence as indicative of seriousness (or lack of it) in isolation. Distinct portions of a sentence (the court recommendation and the prison sentence) must be viewed as a whole.[91]

17.63 The best indication of the gravity of an offence is the judge's sentencing remarks in relation to the individual's conviction for that offence. The gravity attached to the offence by the sentencing judge should be neither inflated nor deflated by IAC and Home Office, although decision-makers and courts considering deportation are entitled to themselves have regard to the circumstances of the offence, including the light these shed on the risk of reoffending.[92]

17.64 There are no hurdles extraneous to the ECHR article 8 test itself to be crossed for it to be shown that deportation is proportionate in a family life criminal offending case: it is not necessary to show that the gravity of the offence was 'overwhelming' or made deportation 'virtually inevitable'.[93]

Risk of further offending

17.65 The ECtHR Grand Chamber has emphasised in *Maslov v Austria* that the assessment of risk of further offending is at the heart of the ECHR article 8 balancing exercise in criminal expulsion and exclusion cases (and is inherent in the article 8(2) justification itself – 'the

---

88 See discussion in *HB v Secretary of State for the Home Department* [2008] EWCA Civ 806.
89 See, for example, *Radovanovic v Austria* (2005) 41 EHRR 635; *Omojudi v UK* (2010) 51 EHRR 10 para 44.
90 *Yildiz v Austria* (2003) 36 EHRR 553.
91 *EO (Turkey) v Secretary of State for the Home Department* [2007] UKAIT 00062.
92 *HK (Turkey) v Secretary of State for the Home Department* [2010] EWCA Civ 853 paras 28, 34.
93 *AR (Pakistan) v Secretary of State for the Home Department* [2010] EWCA Civ 816 para 13.

prevention of crime or disorder'). The fundamental question is 'the extent to which the applicant can be expected to cause disorder or to engage in criminal activities'.[94]

17.66 For a further application of that principle, see *Omojudi v UK*,[95] where the ECtHR engaged in a detailed analysis of the pattern and causation of offending, finding in that case (where the applicant had convictions for offences of dishonesty and for sexual assault) that there was no 'underlying problem' or pattern of offending. See likewise *AA v UK* in which the ECtHR found that the deportation of a man who had, as a minor, engaged in a gang-rape, would be disproportionate having regard to, among other points, his subsequent rehabilitation.[96]

Deterrence and the expression of public revulsion

17.67 General deterrence and the expression of public revulsion at particular offences are not generally identified in ECHR article 8 or in the ECtHR's jurisprudence as justifying interference with private or family life.[97]

17.68 Nonetheless, the domestic courts have repeatedly emphasised that in non-EEA national cases involving multiple serious crimes, the public interest in deportation includes the deterrence of other offenders and the expression of public revulsion at serious crimes. The leading domestic case on deterrence remains *N (Kenya)* in which the Court of Appeal held:[98]

> Where a person who is not a British citizen commits a number of very serious crimes, the public interest side of the balance will include importantly, although not exclusively, the public policy need to deter and to express society's revulsion at the seriousness of the criminality.
> ... for very serious crimes, a low risk of re-offending [by the individual] is not the most important public interest factor.

---

94 *Maslov v Austria* [2009] INLR 47 at para 70. See also consideration of risk of reoffending in *Khan v UK* (2010) 50 EHRR 47 para 41; and in *AA v UK* App No 8000/08, judgment 20 September 2011 para 68.
95 (2010) 51 EHRR 10 para 42.
96 App No 8000/08, judgment 20 September 2011 para 58.
97 See discussion in *RG (Nepal) v Secretary of State for the Home Department* [2010] UKUT 273 (IAC), per Blake J sitting as President of UT-IAC, para 31. However, see *Nunez v Norway* app. no. 55597/09, judgment 28 June 2011, para 71 referring to expulsion as an important deterrent measure.
98 [2004] EWCA Civ 1094 paras 64–65.

17.69 The Court of Appeal in *OH (Serbia)*, distilling the *N (Kenya)* principles, identified three facets of the public interest to be considered in deportation cases. These were:

1) the risk of re-offending but this was 'in the case of very serious crimes, not the most important facet';
2) 'the need to deter foreign nationals from committing serious crimes by leading them to understand that, whatever the other circumstances, one consequence of them may well be deportation'; and
3) 'the role of a deportation order as an expression of society's revulsion at serious crimes and in building public confidence in the treatment of foreign citizens who have committed serious crimes'.[99]

17.70 The public interest in deterrence is diminished in less serious and non-intentional offences.[100] It is very serious offences which will warrant deportation irrespective of further offending risk.[101] Deportation where there is no risk of reoffending and in consequence of a lesser offence may not be proportionate to the aim pursued.[102]

17.71 As we have discussed at paras 9.14–9.15, factors of general deterrence are irrelevant where the individual facing deportation is an EEA national or his or her family member.[103]

---

99 *OH (Serbia) v Secretary of State for the Home Department* [2008] EWCA Civ 694, [2009] INLR 109 per Wilson J at para 15. Endorsed in the 'automatic' deportation context in *RU (Bangladesh) v Secretary of State for the Home Department* [2011] EWCA Civ 651 para 36.

100 *AS (Pakistan) v Secretary of State for the Home Department* [2008] EWCA Civ 1118 para 22. See likewise discussion in *RG (Nepal) v Secretary of State for the Home Department* [2010] UKUT 273 (IAC), Blake J sitting as President of UT-IAC, para 34.

101 See discussion in *RG (Nepal) v Secretary of State for the Home Department* [2010] UKUT 273 (IAC) paras 33, 39.

102 *RG (Nepal) v Secretary of State for the Home Department* [2010] UKUT 273 (IAC) paras 40(i), 44.

103 Citizens Directive (Directive 2004/38/EC on the right of citizens of the European Union and their family members to move and reside freely within the territory of the EU) article 27(2); Immigration (European Economic Area) Regulations (EEA Regs) 2006 SI No 1003 reg 21 (5)(b) and (d); *Nazli v Stadt Nurnberg* Case C-340/97 [2000] ECR 1-957 para 59; *Bonsignore v Stadt Koln* Case 67/74 [1975] ECR 297; *Calfa* Case C-348/96 [1999] ECR I-11.

Deterrence and expression of public revulsion in deportation cases under the IA 1971

17.72 In assessing proportionality in deportation cases under the Immigration Act (IA) 1971, immigration judges must give appropriate weight to (but need not defer to[104]) the SSHD's policy on deportation and in particular (in non-EEA cases) to the SSHD's policy of using deportation as a deterrent measure for very serious crimes:[105]

> ... while the tribunal is in no sense merely reviewing or in literal terms hearing an appeal against the Secretary of State's decision, it is considering matters of public policy upon which the Secretary of State's current view is of considerable evidential weight.[106]

Deterrence and expression of public revulsion in 'automatic' deportation cases under the UKBA 2007

17.73 Deterrence and the expression of public revulsion for serious crime form part of the 'public good' to which the UK Borders Act (UKBA) 2007[107] deems the deportation of those defined as 'foreign criminals' to be conducive.[108]

17.74 Therefore, in 'automatic' deportation cases, the deterrent/ expression of public revulsion aspects of the public interest:

- must still be considered by the executive when performing the proportionality balancing exercise on considering an ECHR article 8 claim; and
- must be acknowledged and given due weight by the tribunal or court hearing a subsequent appeal.[109]

---

104 See the rejection of the notion of deference in ECHR article 8 cases in *Huang and Kashmiri v Secretary of State for the Home Department* [2007] UKHL 11, [2007] 2 AC 167 para 16 and in *R (Quila) v Secretary of State for the Home Department* [2011] UKSC 45, [2011] 3 WLR 836 para 46.

105 *N (Kenya) v Secretary of State for the Home Department* [2004] EWCA Civ 1094 paras 64 and 83; *OH (Serbia) v Secretary of State for the Home Department* [2008] EWCA Civ 694, [2009] INLR 109 at para 15; *JS (Colombia) v Secretary of State for the Home Department* [2008] EWCA Civ 1238; *OP (Jamaica)* [2008] EWCA Civ 440; *DS (India) v Secretary of State for the Home Department* [2009] EWCA Civ 544 para 37; *AC (Turkey) v Secretary of State for the Home Department* [2009] EWCA Civ 377 para 14.

106 *Yousuf v Secretary of State for the Home Department* [2008] EWCA Civ 394 para 11.

107 Section 32(4).

108 See paras 5.12–5.13 and *RU (Bangladesh) v Secretary of State for the Home Department* [2011] EWCA Civ 651 para 36.

109 *RU (Bangladesh) v Secretary of State for the Home Department* [2011] EWCA Civ 651 paras 36 and 40.

17.75 However, as has been held by the UT-IAC presided over by Sedley LJ, and again when presided over by Blake J, in 'automatic' deportation cases under UKBA 2007, no special or separate weight need be given to the executive's views of where the public interest lies.[110] This is because, by contrast to deportation under the IA 1971, proceeding with 'automatic' deportation against a particular individual under UKBA 2007 is not a matter for the SSHD's discretion, let alone the result of any executive policy that a particular category of offence requires deterrence or the expression of revulsion through deportation.[111] Rather, proceeding with 'automatic' deportation is the result of parliament's enactment of the 'automatic' deportation provisions in UKBA 2007.[112]

17.76 The question of the weight to be given to the public interest in deterrence and the expression of public revulsion in cases under UKBA 2007 remains to be decided.[113] The Court of Appeal has stated, obiter, that although the executive's policy has been superseded by parliament's intervention, the policy factors identified in *OH (Serbia)* were if anything reinforced by parliament's enactment of the 'automatic' deportation legislation.[114]

17.77 But, as Blake J, sitting as President of the UT-IAC has warned, the criteria for 'automatic' deportation should not be confused with the type of offences so serious as to warrant deportation irrespective of reoffending risk.[115]

---

110 *Secretary of State for the Home Department v MK* [2010] UKUT 281 at para 25; see also obiter comments in *Secretary of State for the Home Department v BK* [2010] UKUT 328 at para 24. Both cases presided over by Sedley LJ. See also *Omotunde (best interests – Zambrano applied – Razgar) Nigeria* [2011] UKUT 249 (IAC) paras 34–35 per Blake J sitting as President of UT-IAC.

111 As we have discussed in detail at paras 5.12–5.30, in 'automatic' deportation cases under the UKBA 2007 s32(5) the SSHD must make a deportation order provided the threshold criteria are met, unless one of the specified exceptions or exemptions to liability to deportation in section 33 applies.

112 See discussion in *Secretary of State for the Home Department v MK* [2010] UKUT 281 para 23; *Secretary of State for the Home Department v BK* [2010] UKUT 328 at para 24, both cases presided over by Sedley LJ.

113 *RU (Bangladesh) v Secretary of State for the Home Department* [2011] EWCA Civ 651 para 39.

114 *AP (Trinidad and Tobago) v Secretary of State for the Home Department* [2011] EWCA Civ 551 para 44 per Carnwath LJ; endorsed in *RU (Bangladesh) v Secretary of State for the Home Department* [2011] EWCA Civ 651 at para 39.

115 *RG (Nepal) v Secretary of State for the Home Department* [2010] UKUT 273 (IAC) para 39; *Omotunde (best interests – Zambrano applied – Razgar) Nigeria* [2011] UKUT 249 (IAC) para 35.

17.78　　The President of the UT-IAC has also indicated that offences of serious intentional violence or sexual misconduct, importing or dealing in Class A drugs and people trafficking are offences where deportation as a measure to deter others 'may have particular efficacy'.[116]

Time span of offending

17.79　　Linked to the question of offending risk, where there have been long periods during which an offender manages to stay out of trouble (even if he or she subsequently re-offends) this militates against a finding that deportation is proportionate.[117] Conversely, where offences have been committed repeatedly over a long period this will weigh in favour of deportation being found proportionate.[118]

Offences committed as a minor

17.80　　Offences committed as a minor should be given less weight when assessing the public interest in expulsion or exclusion.[119]

17.81　　The decision-maker in an expulsion case must have regard to the best interests of the child where the expulsion decision is based on offences committed as a minor, even if the foreign national offender is no longer a minor at the time of the expulsion.[120] As we have already seen at para 17.26, article 3(1) of the UNCRC, which informs the interpretation of ECHR article 8, requires regard to be had to the best interests of the child. The best interests requirement must in turn be interpreted in light of UNCRC article 40(1) recognising 'the desirability of promoting the child's reintegration and the child's assuming a constructive role in society'. Expulsion should therefore be a 'last resort' for juvenile or former juvenile offenders.

17.82　　Thus the Grand Chamber of the ECtHR held in *Maslov v Austria*:[121]

116　*Omotunde (best interests – Zambrano applied – Razgar) Nigeria* [2011] UKUT 249 (IAC) para 38(5) per Blake J sitting as President of UT-IAC.
117　See discussion in *Omojudi v UK* (2010) 51 EHRR 10 para 42, distinguishing the circumstances of that case from *Joseph Grant v UK* App No 10606/07, 5 June 1999.
118　*Omoregie and others v Norway* [2009] Imm AR 170 para 40.
119　*Maslov v Austria* [2009] INLR 47 para 72; *Moustaquim v Belgium* (1991) 13 EHRR 802, para 44; *Radovanovic v Austria* (2005) 41 EHRR 6 para 35.
120　See, for example, *AA v UK*, App No 8000/08, judgment 20 September 2011 para 60, finding disproportionate the expulsion of a young adult for his participation in a gang rape at the age of 15.
121　[2009] INLR 47 paras 82 and 83.

The Court considers that where offences committed by a minor underlie an exclusion order regard must be had to the best interests of the child.

The Court considers that, where expulsion measures against a juvenile offender are concerned, the obligation to take the best interests of the child into account includes an obligation to facilitate his or her reintegration ... In the Court's view this aim will not be achieved by severing family or social ties through expulsion, which must remain a means of last resort in the case of a juvenile offender.

17.83 It is an error of law to disregard the ECtHR's guidance 'about the significance of the age at which criminal offences were committed'.[122]

17.84 This principle concerning juvenile offending has been applied by the Court of Appeal to a person who had committed the majority of his offences below the age of 21.[123]

Weight to be given to old offences; offences pre-dating a grant of leave to remain

17.85 Where a proposed deportee has indefinite leave to remain (ILR), the weight given to offences predating the grant of ILR may be substantially reduced or even, where there is no pattern of offending to which those offences are relevant, disregarded.[124] However, while the grant of indefinite leave to remain may show that prior offences did not generate concern at the time, there is no general principle which dictates that such offences should always be disregarded.[125] In some cases, the Home Office may have granted ILR in ignorance of the offence.[126]

The lapse of time since the commission of the index offence

17.86 Where a significant period of time has lapsed since the commission of the index offence, and in particular where there has been a delay between release from imprisonment and the decision to expel or exclude the

---

122 *JO (Uganda) and JT (Ivory Coast) v Secretary of State for the Home Department* at para 52.
123 *MJ (Angola) v Secretary of State for the Home Department* [2010] EWCA Civ 557 paras 40 and 42.
124 *Omojudi v UK* (2010) 51 EHRR 10 para 42 – there the ECtHR disregarded all offences committed prior to the grant of indefinite leave to remain.
125 *R (HM Malawi) v Secretary of State for the Home Department* [2010] EWHC 1407 (Admin).
126 See, for example, *AA v UK*, App No 8000/08, judgment 20 September 2011 para 61.

offender, this militates against the measure being found proportionate.[127] The ECtHR Grand Chamber stated in *Maslov v Austria*:[128]

> ... the fact that a significant period of good conduct elapses between the commission of the offences and the deportation of the person concerned necessarily has a certain impact on the assessment of the risk which that person poses to society.

17.87 The Court of Appeal has likewise held that where a proposed deportee has been at liberty and of good behaviour since his deportation, this weighs heavily against deportation (*Yousuf v Secretary of State for the Home Department*[129]). A failure to have regard to the lapse of time since the offence and the proposed deportee's conduct during that period is a material error of law (*HM (Iraq) v Secretary of State for the Home Department*).[130]

17.88 However, while relevant to proportionality, the mere fact of a long delay before issuing a notice of decision to deport does not render that decision otherwise than 'in accordance with the law' for ECHR article 8 purposes.[131] See also para 17.41 above on delay generally.

Duration of the exclusion

17.89 The ECtHR has repeatedly held that the longer the period of exclusion from the host country faced, the heavier the justification required from the state for the interference:[132]

> ... the duration of an exclusion measure is to be considered as one factor among others (see, as cases in which the unlimited duration of a residence prohibition was considered as a factor supporting the conclusion that it was disproportionate, *Ezzouhdi*, cited above, [s]35; *Yilmaz v Germany*, no 52853/99, [ss]48–49, 17 April 2003; and *Radovanovic*, cited above, [s]37; see, as cases in which the limited duration of a residence prohibition was considered as a factor in favour of its proportionality, *Benhebba*, cited above, [s]37; *Jankov v Germany* (dec.), no 35112/92, 13 January 2000; and *Üner*, cited above, [s]65).

17.90 As seen in paras 1.48 and 7.30, those who are deported from the UK are barred from re-entering the UK while the deportation order

127 See, for example, *Sezen v The Netherlands* (2006) 43 EHRR 30 para 44; *AA v UK*, App No 8000/08, judgment 20 September 2011 paras 62–63, 66 and 68.
128 [2009] INLR 47 para 90.
129 [2008] EWCA Civ 394 paras 17, 18 and 33.
130 [2010] EWCA Civ 1322 para 34.
131 *Onur v UK* (2009) 49 EHRR 38 para 52.
132 *Maslov v Austria* [2009] INLR 47 para 98. See also *Khan v UK* (2010) 50 EHRR 47 para 48; *Omojudi v UK* (2010) 51 EHRR 10 para 46.

17.91 remains in force. Moreover, the duration of the exclusion has been significantly lengthened under rule 391 of the Immigration Rules (as amended on 9 June 2008[133]) (see para 7.15).

A failure properly to direct oneself to the likely duration of the exclusion or to have regard to the duration of the exclusion as a relevant factor may amount to a material error of law.[134] However, the mere fact that an immigration judge has not mentioned rule 391 is not a material error of law.[135]

---

133 Statement of Changes in the Immigration Rules HC 607.
134 *NB (Jamaica) v Secretary of State for the Home Department* [2010] EWCA Civ 824 para 13; *AS (Pakistan) v Secretary of State for the Home Department* [2008] EWCA Civ 1118 para 27.
135 *Reid v Secretary of State for the Home Department* [2010] EWCA Civ 138 para 38.

CHAPTER 18

Resisting deportation on grounds of physical or mental illness under ECHR articles 3 and 8; *Quaquah* claims

18.1	Introduction
18.4	ECHR article 3 and health
18.6	ECHR article 3 claims based on physical ill-health and deprivation of care in the expulsion context
18.6	The foundational ECtHR authority: *D v UK*
18.12	The application of those principles in *N (Uganda) v Secretary of State for the Home Department* and *N v UK* (the '*N* litigation')
18.19	Exceptions to the N approach in HIV/AIDS cases and other cases of severe physical ill-health
18.20	Treatment received by a person with leave to remain
18.25	Ostracism, humiliation or deprivation of basic rights
18.26	Deliberate action by state or non-state agents to withhold medical treatment
18.27	Impact on third parties compounding the suffering of the principal
18.29	ECHR article 3, mental ill-health and suicide risk

continued

323

18.29	Foundational ECtHR case on mental ill-health, suicide risk and deprivation of care: *Bensaid v UK*
18.31	The leading domestic case: *J v Secretary of State for the Home Department*
18.35	**Possible exceptions to the *D v UK* and *N* approach in mental illness and suicide cases**
18.35	Mental illness and suicide risk arising from expulsion itself rather than deprivation of care
18.40	Family
18.42	'Domestic' cases
18.43	A history of past persecution
18.44	**Anxious scrutiny in mental health and suicide cases generally**
18.48	**Further issues arising in mental health and suicide risk cases**
18.48	A subjective fear of return can suffice
18.50	'Effective mechanisms'
18.53	**ECHR article 8 and mental and physical illness**
18.53	Private life and health
18.56	The relationship between ECHR article 3 and article 8 in health claims
18.59	***MSS v Belgium and Greece* and *Sufi and Elmi v UK*: a modified approach?**
18.60	**ECHR article 6 and '*Quaquah* claims'**

Introduction

18.1 This chapter primarily concerns the circumstances in which the European Convention on Human Rights (ECHR) will prevent the expulsion of a mentally or physically ill person. The expulsion of the physically or mentally ill may give rise to a real risk of inhuman or degrading treatment contrary to ECHR article 3, or amount to an unlawful interference with the right to respect for private life, contrary to ECHR article 8. This chapter first discusses the development of the jurisprudence and the high thresholds that have been set for such claims to date. We then consider how important developments in the approach of the European Court of Human Rights (ECtHR) to economic and social rights in *MSS v Belgium*[1] and *Sufi and Elmi v UK*[2] may affect ECHR claims by the physically and mentally ill.

18.2 At the end of this chapter, we discuss briefly claims (sometimes referred to by practitioners as '*Quaquah* claims') that expulsion of a person engaged in civil litigation against the Home Office or its private contractors would breach his or her rights under ECHR article 6.

18.3 ECHR article 3 in the context of serious harm arising out of intentional acts (which we refer to in this book as 'intentional harm' grounds) has been discussed separately in chapter 13. ECHR article 8 generally has been discussed in chapters 15–17.

ECHR article 3 and health

18.4 The ECtHR, in an important extension of the interpretation of the ECHR article 3 protections, has accepted that:

> The suffering which flows from naturally occurring illness, physical or mental, may be covered by Article 3, where it is, or risks being, exacerbated by treatment, whether flowing from conditions of detention, expulsion or other measures, for which the authorities can be held responsible.[3]

18.5 Below, we review the principal case-law developments from the ECtHR and domestic courts on health and ECHR article 3 in the expulsion context.

---

1 (2011) 53 EHRR 2.
2 App Nos 8319/07 and 11449/07 judgment 28 June 2011.
3 *Pretty v UK* (2002) 35 EHRR 1 para 52.

ECHR article 3 claims based on physical ill-health and deprivation of care in the expulsion context

The foundational ECtHR authority: *D v UK*

18.6 In the landmark case of *D v UK*, an AIDS sufferer faced deportation from the UK following his release on licence from a sentence of imprisonment for drugs importation.

18.7 In finding that his expulsion would violate ECHR article 3, the ECtHR's judgment broke new ground. The court observed that, in its previous case-law, the expelling state's responsibility under article 3 had arisen in the context of intentional acts of public authorities in the receiving country or intentional acts of non-state bodies where the authorities were unable to provide protection. However, the ECtHR held:

> Aside from these situations and given the fundamental importance of Article 3 in the convention system, the Court must reserve to itself sufficient flexibility to address the application of that Article in other contexts which might arise. It is not therefore prevented from scrutinising an applicant's claim under Article 3 where the source of the risk of proscribed treatment in the receiving country stems from factors which cannot engage either directly or indirectly the responsibility of the public authorities of that country, or which, taken alone, do not in themselves infringe the standards of that Article. To limit the application of Article 3 in this manner would be to undermine the absolute character of its protection. In any such contexts, however, the Court must subject all the circumstances surrounding the case to a rigorous scrutiny, especially the applicant's personal situation in the expelling State.[4]

18.8 Emphasising the 'very exceptional circumstances' of the case and the 'compelling humanitarian considerations', the court found that implementation of the expulsion decision would amount to inhuman treatment contrary to ECHR article 3.[5]

18.9 The ECtHR relied on a number of factors to reach its conclusions. The applicant was in the advanced stages of a terminal illness. His limited quality of life derived from his medical treatment in the UK and from the assistance of a charitable organisation. Removal would 'further reduce his already limited life expectancy and subject him to acute mental and physical suffering'.[6] It had not been demonstrated

---

4 *D v UK* (1997) 24 EHRR 423, para 49.
5 *D v UK* (1997) 24 EHRR 423, paras 53–54.
6 *D v UK* (1997) 24 EHRR 423 para 52.

that he would be guaranteed a suitable hospital bed in St Kitts. He would have no moral or social support there whereas in the UK he had been counselled to prepare for death.[7] The UK had also assumed responsibility for his treatment:

> The Court also notes in this respect that the respondent State has assumed responsibility for treating the applicant's condition since August 1994. He has become reliant on the medical and palliative care which he is at present receiving and is no doubt psychologically prepared for death in an environment which is both familiar and compassionate. Although it cannot be said that the conditions which would confront him in the receiving country are themselves a breach of the standards of Article 3, his removal would expose him to a real risk of dying under most distressing circumstances and would thus amount to inhuman treatment.

18.10 The ECtHR observed that the considerations in the case 'must be seen as wider in scope than the question whether or not the applicant is fit to travel back'.[8] *D v UK* nevertheless emphasised that there is generally no right to remain for the purpose of medical or other social assistance.[9]

18.11 The domestic courts have commented that *D v UK* represents an 'extension of an extension' of state obligations under ECHR article 3.[10] Cases such as *Soering v UK*[11] had extended the responsibility of signatory states to circumstances in which they were expelling a person to a real risk of prohibited treatment in another state, after expulsion. *D v UK* drew on the principle of *Soering* and extended it to cases where the anticipated harm after expulsion stems not from deliberate acts but from naturally occurring illness. It has been said that *D v UK* is best regarded as the 'paradigm case' for the extension of ECHR article 3 to health issues rather than as laying down exact criteria for the sort of exceptionality that may engage human rights obligations in this context.[12]

---

7 *D v UK* (1997) 24 EHRR 423 paras 51–53.
8 *D v UK* (1997) 24 EHRR 423 para 53.
9 *D v UK* (1997) 24 EHRR 423 para 54.
10 See, for example, *N v Secretary of State for the Home Department* [2005] UKHL 31; [2005] 2 AC 296 at paras 23 and 87.
11 See the discussion at paras 13.7–13.9.
12 *N v Secretary of State for the Home Department* [2005] UKHL 31, [2005] 2 AC 296 at para 48.

The application of those principles in *N (Uganda) v Secretary of State for the Home Department* and *N v UK* (the 'N litigation')

18.12 In *N v Secretary of State for the Home Department*, the appellant was a Ugandan national suffering from advanced AIDS. She had been repeatedly raped in Uganda but had not succeeded in her asylum claim because she was not at risk of intentional harm if returned. While under treatment in the UK, her medical condition had stabilised: if she continued to have access to medical treatment in the UK, she was likely to live for decades. However, if expelled to Uganda, she would be unable to afford the necessary anti-retroviral treatment, and would suffer discomfort, pain and death within one or two years.

18.13 The House of Lords found that her expulsion would not breach ECHR article 3. *D v UK* was distinguished: in that case, the applicant was already dying. Lord Nicholls held:

> ... the Strasbourg court has constantly reiterated that in principle aliens subject to expulsion cannot claim any entitlement to remain in the territory of a contracting state in order to continue to benefit from medical, social and other forms of assistance provided by the expelling state. Article 3 imposes no such 'medical care' obligation on contracting states. This is so even where, in the absence of medical treatment, the life of the would-be immigrant will be significantly shortened. But in D, unlike the later cases, there was no question of imposing any such obligation on the United Kingdom. D was dying, and beyond the reach of medical treatment then available.[13]

18.14 In considering the effect of *D v UK*, Baroness Hale held:

> In my view, therefore, the test, in this sort of case, is whether the applicant's illness has reached such a critical stage (ie he is dying) that it would be inhuman treatment to deprive him of the care which he is currently receiving and send him home to an early death unless there is care available there to enable him to meet that fate with dignity.[14]

Baroness Hale also recognised that:

> There may, of course, be other exceptional cases, with other extreme facts, where the humanitarian considerations are equally compelling. The law must be sufficiently flexible to accommodate them.[15]

---

13 *N v Secretary of State for the Home Department* [2005] UKHL 31, [2005] 2 AC 296 para 15.
14 *N v Secretary of State for the Home Department*, [2005] UKHL 31, [2005] 2 AC 296 para 69. See also Lord Hope at para 50 and Lord Brown at para 94.
15 *N v Secretary of State for the Home Department* [2005] UKHL 31, [2005] 2 AC 296 para 70.

18.15 Lord Brown observed that cases such as these concerned the state's positive obligations to take steps to prevent treatment contrary to ECHR article 3 (by continuing to provide treatment) rather than negative obligations (to refrain from expelling):[16]

> D really did concern what was principally a negative obligation, not to deport D to an imminent, lonely and distressing end. Not so the more recent cases including the present one. Given the enormous advances in medicine, the focus now is rather on the length and quality of the applicant's life than the particular circumstances of his or her death. In these cases, therefore, the real question is whether the state is under a positive obligation to continue treatment on a long-term basis.[17]

18.16 N's application was dismissed by the Grand Chamber of the ECtHR in *N v UK*. The Grand Chamber there reiterated the 'very exceptional' and 'compelling' threshold for such cases:

> Aliens who are subject to expulsion cannot in principle claim any entitlement to remain in the territory of a contracting state in order to continue to benefit from medical, social or other forms of assistance and services provided by the expelling state. The fact that the applicant's circumstances, including his life expectancy, would be significantly reduced if he were to be removed from the contracting state is not sufficient in itself to give rise to breach of Art 3. The decision to remove an alien who is suffering from a serious mental or physical illness to a country where the facilities for the treatment of that illness are inferior to those available in the contracting state may raise an issue under Art 3, but only in a very exceptional case, where the humanitarian grounds against the removal are compelling.[18]

18.17 However, the Grand Chamber observed that other cases might reach the *D v UK* threshold:

> The Court does not exclude that there may be other very exceptional cases where the humanitarian considerations are equally compelling. However, it considers that it should maintain the high threshold set in *D v United Kingdom* and applied in its subsequent case law, which it regards as correct in principle, given that in such cases the alleged future harm would emanate not from the intentional acts or omissions of public authorities or non-state bodies, but instead from a naturally occurring illness and the lack of sufficient resources to deal with it in the receiving country.[19]

---

16 *N v Secretary of State for the Home Department* [2005] UKHL 31, [2005] 2 AC 296 para 88.
17 *N v Secretary of State for the Home Department* [2005] UKHL 31, [2005] 2 AC 296 para 93.
18 *N v UK* (2008) 47 EHRR 39, para 42.
19 *N v UK* (2008) 47 EHRR 39, para 43.

18.18 The *N* litigation establishes that the expulsion of a person who would otherwise enjoy a substantial life expectancy to a country where he or she will be unable to afford the same life-saving medication will not of itself breach ECHR article 3, even where the result would be severely reduced life expectancy. The circumstances must be 'very exceptional' and 'compelling'. The Grand Chamber in *N v UK* also observed that although that litigation concerned AIDS, the same principles would apply to other types of cases concerning naturally occurring mental or physical illness and the need for specialist treatment:

> ... the same principles must apply in relation to the expulsion of any person afflicted with any serious, naturally occurring physical or mental illness which may cause suffering, pain and reduced life expectancy and require specialised medical treatment which may not be so readily available in the applicant's country of origin or which may be available only at substantial cost.[20]

Exceptions to the N approach in HIV/AIDS cases and other cases of severe physical ill-health

18.19 Limited exceptions may be carved out from the *N* approach to health cases. In particular, it is noteworthy that the *N* litigation did not address the approach to be applied where: 1) the individual had received medical treatment while in the UK with leave to remain; 2) the medical effects of loss of treatment are compounded by societal discrimination or ostracism; 3) the absence of medical treatment in the state to which expulsion is proposed *is* the result of deliberate action by state or non-state agents; or 4) the deterioration in an individual's ill-health following expulsion will severely affect others, in turn compounding the suffering of the principal. We discuss the available case-law on some of these questions below.

Treatment received by a person with leave to remain

18.20 Many foreign national prisoners and former prisoners (FNPs) will have accrued long periods of continuous leave to remain before facing deportation proceedings. For this group, there is an important exception to the *N* approach. The very high *N* threshold does not apply to those who have been continuously lawfully present in the

20 *N v UK* (2008) 47 EHRR 39, para 45.

18.21 *D v UK* and the *N* litigation concerned people who had no leave to remain in the UK while they received their treatment or indeed at any point.[21] That was emphasised in *ZT (Zimbabwe)* where Buxton LJ observed of the appellant before him:

> Ms ZT is in exactly the same position as was Ms N. Ms ZT never had any right to be in this country, and absent the present proceedings any permissive presence here would have been terminated nearly five years ago.[22]

18.22 *JA (Ivory Coast) v Secretary of State for the Home Department* concerned two women who had entered the UK lawfully and subsequently were diagnosed as HIV positive. They were granted leave to remain under an earlier Home Office policy, specifically in order to obtain medical treatment. Home Office policy then changed following the *N* litigation and they were refused a renewal of their leave: they appealed on ECHR article 8 grounds. Giving the judgment of the Court of Appeal, Sedley LJ found that the particularly high exceptionality threshold applied in *D v UK* and *N v UK* did not apply to a continuously lawful entrant:

> JA's is a markedly different case. Her position as a continuously lawful entrant places her in a different legal class from N, so that she is not called upon to demonstrate exceptional circumstances as compelling as those in *D v United Kingdom*.[23]

18.23 Nor, however, did the fact of having continuous leave to remain automatically entitle the appellants in *JA (Ivory Coast)* to stay in the UK for treatment. One appellant, who would on the evidence be able to access medical treatment in her country of origin, lost her appeal on grounds that it would inevitably fail before the tribunal. The other appellant's case was remitted to the tribunal to reconsider, applying the correct threshold test.

18.24 Note also that it makes no difference whether a person contracted HIV before or after arrival in the UK.[24]

---

21 See discussion in *JA (Ivory Coast) v Secretary of State for the Home Department* [2009] EWCA Civ 1353, [2010] Imm AR 381 para 21.
22 *ZT (Zimbabwe) v Secretary of State for the Home Department* [2005] EWCA Civ 1421 para 20.
23 *JA (Ivory Coast) v Secretary of State for the Home Department* [2009] EWCA Civ 1353, [2010] Imm AR 381 para 25.
24 *ZT (Zimbabwe) v Secretary of State for the Home Department* [2005] EWCA Civ 1421 paras 19–20.

Ostracism, humiliation or deprivation of basic rights

18.25 In *ZT (Zimbabwe)*, Buxton LJ indicated obiter that the ECHR article 3 threshold might be reached where an AIDS sufferer would experience ostracism, humiliation or deprivation of basic rights after expulsion:

> I can envisage a case in which the particular treatment afforded to an AIDS sufferer on return, in terms of ostracism, humiliation, or deprivation of basic rights that was added to her existing medical difficulties, could create an exceptional case in terms of the guidance given by Baroness Hale of Richmond ...[25]

Deliberate action by state or non-state agents to withhold medical treatment

18.26 The Court of Appeal[26] and subsequently the Immigration and Asylum Chamber of the Upper Tribunal (UT-IAC)[27] considered whether conditions in Zimbabwe might meet the *ZT (Zimbabwe)* threshold, and specifically considered allegations of a politicisation of access to medical treatment and of discrimination against HIV sufferers. However, on the evidence, the appellants in those cases were found not to be at real risk of discriminatory denial of medication or other treatment in breach of ECHR article 3. It remains the case, in our view, that deliberate withholding of medical treatment could constitute a breach of article 3, and could also, if motivated by a convention reason, constitute persecution for purposes of the Refugee Convention.[28]

Impact on third parties compounding the suffering of the principal

18.27 In *CA v Secretary of State for the Home Department*, the Court of Appeal found that there had been no error of law in a decision by an adjudicator allowing an appeal under ECHR article 3 by a Ghanaian national

---

25 *ZT (Zimbabwe) v Secretary of State for the Home Department* [2005] EWCA Civ 1421 para 18.
26 *BK (Zimbabwe) v Secretary of State for the Home Department* [2008] EWCA Civ 510.
27 *RS (Zimbabwe) v Secretary of State for the Home Department* [2010] UKUT 363 (IAC).
28 *RS (Zimbabwe) v Secretary of State for the Home Department* [2010] UKUT 363 (IAC) para 129.

whose unborn child risked being born with HIV if special precautions, available in the UK but not in Ghana, were omitted. Laws LJ, with whom the other members of the court agreed, observed that the suffering to a mother of watching her child sicken and perhaps die might be greater than that to which the mother would be exposed by her own illness:

> It seems to me obvious simply as a matter of humanity that for a mother to witness the collapse of her newborn child's health and perhaps its death may be a kind of suffering far greater than might arise by the mother's confronting the self-same fate herself.[29]

18.28 Those considerations would now be reinforced, in an ECHR article 8 case, by the *Beoku-Betts* principle that the rights of third parties must be considered when expelling a principal[30] (see para 17.23) and, in a case involving a child, by the requirement to treat the best interests of the child as a primary consideration (see paras 17.24–17.30).

ECHR article 3, mental ill-health and suicide risk

Foundational ECtHR case on mental ill-health, suicide risk and deprivation of care: *Bensaid v UK*

18.29 A similarly high threshold has been applied to cases concerning a need for mental health treatment. The founding ECtHR authority on mental health and expulsion, *Bensaid v UK*, concerned a schizophrenic applicant, who had been on temporary admission and reliant on anti-psychotic medication and specialist psychiatric treatment in the UK. Mr Bensaid asserted that if expelled to Algeria, he would be unable to afford or reliably access the medication necessary to prevent a relapse and possible self-harm. The ECtHR accepted that the suffering that a relapse might cause to Mr Bensaid could in principle engage ECHR article 3.[31] The court observed that article 3 would not be breached by a mere difference in standards of treatment[32] and went on to apply the test of whether the case disclosed 'exceptional circumstances' of the type seen in *D v UK* (see paras 18.6–18.11

---

29 *CA v Secretary of State for the Home Department* [2004] EWCA Civ 1165, [2004] Imm AR 640 para 26.
30 *Beoku-Betts v Secretary of State for the Home Department* [2008] UKHL 39, [2009] 1 AC 115.
31 *Bensaid v UK* (2001) 33 EHRR 10 para 37.
32 *Bensaid v UK* (2001) 33 EHRR 10 para 38.

above).[33] The case failed on the facts. There was insufficient evidence that Mr Bensaid would in fact be deprived of the necessary treatment in Algeria:

> The Court finds that the risk that the applicant will suffer a deterioration in his condition if he is returned to Algeria and that, if he did, he would not receive adequate support or care is to a large extent speculative.[34]

18.30 Also relevant was the fact that Mr Bensaid risked relapse even if he remained in the UK.[35]

The leading domestic case: *J v Secretary of State for the Home Department*

18.31 The domestic courts have also considered the circumstances in which suicide risk exacerbated by or consequent on expulsion may breach ECHR article 3.

18.32 In the leading case of *J v Secretary of State for the Home Department*, an immigration adjudicator had determined that the applicant had no well-founded fear of persecution under the Refugee Convention. The applicant maintained that he had a fear of return to Sri Lanka to the extent that he would commit suicide after expulsion. The Court of Appeal drew a distinction between cases where the risk of suicide arose while still in the UK ('domestic cases') and cases where the risk arose after expulsion ('foreign cases'[36]):

> In cases such as the present case the risk of a violation of article 3 or 8 must be considered in relation to three stages. By reference to the claim made in this case, these are: (i) when the appellant is informed that a final decision has been made to remove him to Sri Lanka; (ii) when he is physically removed by airplane to Sri Lanka; and (iii) after he has arrived in Sri Lanka. In relation to stage (i), the case is plainly a domestic case. In relation to stage (iii), it is equally clearly a foreign case. The classification of the case in relation to stage (ii) is less easy. Since in practice arrangements are made by the Secretary of State in suicide cases for an escort it is safer to treat this as a domestic case.[37]

---

33 *Bensaid v UK* (2001) 33 EHRR 10 para 40.
34 *Bensaid v UK* (2001) 33 EHRR 10 para 39.
35 *Bensaid v UK* (2001) 33 EHRR 10 para 38.
36 See the discussion of 'foreign' and 'domestic' cases at paras 13.42–13.43.
37 *J v Secretary of State for the Home Department* [2005] EWCA Civ 629, [2005] Imm AR 409 para 17.

18.33 Dismissing the appeal, the Court of Appeal treated the case before it as a 'foreign' one and laid down six principles which can be summarised as follows:[38]

1) The treatment must reach the minimum level of severity.[39]
2) There must be a causal link between the threatened expulsion and the risk of ill treatment under ECHR article 3.[40]
3) '[I]n the context of a foreign case, the article 3 threshold is particularly high simply because it is a foreign case. And it is even higher where the alleged inhuman treatment is not the direct or indirect responsibility of the public authorities of the receiving state, but results from some naturally occurring illness, whether physical or mental'[41] (applying *D v UK* and *Bensaid*).
4) Suicide cases can in principle found a claim to remain in the UK under ECHR article 3 (applying *Bensaid*).[42]
5) It will be important to consider whether the applicant's fear of return to the receiving state is objectively based. If the fear is not well-founded, expulsion is less likely to give rise to a breach of ECHR article 3.[43]
6) It will also be important to consider whether the UK or the receiving state has 'effective mechanisms' to reduce the risk of suicide which may avoid a breach of article 3: the presence of such mechanisms will weigh heavily against the article 3 claim.[44]

The Court of Appeal went on to observe that in 'domestic' cases, the third principle will be absent, but the others apply equally and the sixth is of particular significance.[45]

18.34 The *J v Secretary of State for the Home Department* principles have since been repeatedly applied by tribunals and courts.[46]

---

38 *J v Secretary of State for the Home Department* [2005] EWCA Civ 629, [2005] Imm AR 409 paras 26–32.
39 Ibid para 26.
40 Ibid para 27.
41 Ibid para 28.
42 Ibid para 29.
43 Ibid para 30.
44 Ibid para 31.
45 Ibid para 33.
46 See eg *R (Tozlukaya) v Secretary of State for the Home Department* [2006] EWCA Civ 379, [2006] Imm AR 417; *CN (Burundi) v Secretary of State for the Home Department* [2007] EWCA Civ 587. In the extradition context, see eg *R (Prosser) v Secretary of State for the Home Department* [2010] EWHC 845 (Admin), [2010] ACD 57; *Jansons v Latvia* [2009] EWHC 1845 (Admin).

Possible exceptions to the *D v UK* and *N* approach in mental illness and suicide cases

Mental illness and suicide risk arising from expulsion itself rather than deprivation of care

18.35 Although the ECtHR in *Bensaid v UK* applied the high threshold of *D v UK* in the context of mental health and suicide risk, *Bensaid v UK* concerned the effects of losing the specialist care and medication on which the applicant had become reliant in the UK. Likewise, when the ECtHR Grand Chamber in *N* indicated that the *N* principles were of application to other forms of illness, the Grand Chamber was still discussing cases concerning a deprivation of specialist care (see para 18.18 above). There has therefore been some debate as to the test to be applied in mental health and suicide risk cases where the risk arises from expulsion itself. As we briefly explain below, the domestic courts have thus far settled on the view that the test in such cases, remains that applied in *D v UK* and *N*.

18.36 In *G v Secretary of State for the Home Department*[47] the *D v UK* and *N* test was said to apply in suicide cases. In *Tozlukaya* v *Secretary of State for the Home Department*, Richards LJ (with whom the other members of the court agreed) noted the distinction between the suicide risk case before it and the *D v UK, N v UK* line of authority. He said, in comments subsequently endorsed elsewhere by the Court of Appeal,[48] that:

> One material difference is that the risk in the present context arises not just from the person's removal to a place where the condition is likely to worsen, but from the direct impact on that person's mental health of the decision to remove. Nonetheless the similarities are in my view more important than the differences.[49]

18.37 The test applied by the Court of Appeal in *Tozlukaya* (another 'foreign' case[50]), in language derived from *J v Secretary of State for the Home Department*,[51] was a high one, namely to:

---

47 *G v Secretary of State for the Home Department* [2006] EWCA Civ 771 para 14.
48 *AJ (Liberia) v Secretary of State for the Home Department* [2006] EWCA Civ 1736, para 15.
49 *Tozlukaya* v *Secretary of State for the Home Department* [2006] EWCA Civ 379, [2006] Imm AR 417, para 62.
50 *R (Tozlukaya) v Secretary of State for the Home Department* [2006] EWCA Civ 379, [2006] Imm AR 417 para 69.
51 *J v Secretary of State for the Home Department* [2005] EWCA Civ 629, [2005] Imm AR 409 para 26.

... ask whether removal would be an 'affront to fundamental humanitarian principles'.[52]

18.38 In *RA (Sri Lanka)* (again a 'foreign' case) Richards LJ, with whom the rest of the Court of Appeal agreed, subsequently held that the approach to be taken to a claim of suicide risk on expulsion was materially identical to that in *D v UK* and in *N*:

> There has been some debate in our domestic case-law as to the extent to which cases of mental illness, in particular where it is said that removal will give rise to a risk or increased risk of suicide, are analogous to cases of physical illness for the purposes of the application of article 3 ... [counsel for the appellant] contended that a material difference exists between the two types of case, since in the suicide risk case the very act of expulsion causes or may cause a deterioration in the applicant's condition whereas in the HIV/AIDS situation it is the loss of assistance or services currently enjoyed that gives rise to the issue under article 3. Whilst there may be factual differences between the two types of case, the passage I have quoted from *N v United Kingdom* makes clear, as it seems to me, that the same principles are to be applied to them both. Nor do I detect any important difference of approach in the domestic cases on suicide risk.[53]

18.39 We respectfully suggest that this reasoning, in so far as it relies on the Grand Chamber judgment in *N v UK*, is difficult. As we have already seen at para 18.18 above, the Grand Chamber suggested that the test elaborated in *N* could be applied to other cases concerning reliance on 'specialised medical treatment which may not be so readily available in the applicant's country of origin or which may be available only at substantial cost'.[54]

Family

18.40 The availability of family members to care for the sick individual after expulsion is a relevant factor in determining whether a health case crosses the ECHR article 3 threshold. The question of whether a person would be left to sicken and die in isolation (in a physical health case) or to face their terror and disturbance alone (in a mental health and suicide risk case), has weighed heavily with the courts. For example, in *D v UK* the ECtHR observed the lack of evidence

---

52 *R (Tozlukaya) v Secretary of State for the Home Department* [2006] EWCA Civ 379, [2006] Imm AR 417 para 64.
53 *RA (Sri Lanka) v Secretary of State for the Home Department* [2008] EWCA Civ 1210 para 49.
54 *N v UK* (2008) 47 EHRR 39 para 45.

of moral or social support that would await the applicant, in finding that he could not be expelled to St Kitts without breaching his rights under ECHR article 3.[55] Conversely, the applicant in *N v UK* who could be returned without such a breach appeared to have family members in Uganda.[56] Likewise, the unsuccessful applicant in *Bensaid v UK* had family in Algeria.[57]

18.41 A similar approach can be seen in the domestic authorities. The unsuccessful applicant in *J v Secretary of State for the Home Department* had been found to have family in Sri Lanka.[58] There was evidence in *J v Secretary of State for the Home Department* that those family members might, since the determination that was under appeal, have perished in the tsunami. That fresh evidence was irrelevant to the question of whether there had been any error of law at first instance. Nonetheless, the Court of Appeal expressed 'great concern' over the risk that 'this might cause a serious deterioration in the appellant's mental health or render him significantly more vulnerable' and indicated that the position of the family members should be ascertained before the Secretary of State for the Home Department (SSHD) attempted to remove J.[59] The unsuccessful applicant in *Tozlukaya*[60] faced expulsion alongside her family and so would not be isolated after expulsion. The unsuccessful applicant in *RA (Sri Lanka)* was found to have family available to care for him if he were expelled.[61] Conversely, the successful applicants in *Y (Sri Lanka)* had lost many family members to the tsunami and the only relative with whom they were in contact was a UK resident, leaving it unlikely that anyone would be able to help them access whatever medical care might be available in Sri Lanka.[62]

55 *D v UK* (1997) 24 EHRR 423 para 2(e). See also the Grand Chamber's judgment in *N v UK* (2008) 47 EHRR 39 at paras 33 and 42, discussing the lack of family support as a feature of *D v UK*.
56 *N v UK* (2008) 47 EHRR 39 para 48.
57 *Bensaid v UK* (2001) 33 EHRR 10 para 20. The ECtHR in that case found that the suggestion that the family would not support the mentally ill applicant because of their religious beliefs was speculative, para 39.
58 *J v Secretary of State for the Home Department* [2005] EWCA Civ 629, [2005] Imm AR 409 para 63.
59 *J v Secretary of State for the Home Department* [2005] EWCA Civ 629, [2005] Imm AR 409 para 73.
60 *R (Tozlukaya) v Secretary of State for the Home Department* [2006] EWCA Civ 379.
61 *RA (Sri Lanka) v Secretary of State for the Home Department* [2008] EWCA Civ 1210, see paras 37–39.
62 *Y (Sri Lanka) and Z (Sri Lanka) v Secretary of State for the Home Department* [2009] EWCA Civ 362, [2009] HRLR 22 paras 43–45.

'Domestic' cases

18.42 *Bensaid v UK, J v Secretary of State for the Home Department, Tozlukaya* and *RA (Sri Lanka)* are all 'foreign' cases. *J v Secretary of State for the Home Department* itself is authority for the proposition that a lower threshold test must apply to a 'domestic' case, that is one where the risk of suicide may materialise before expulsion (para 18.33 above).[63] However, *J v Secretary of State for the Home Department* also indicates that the availability of 'effective mechanisms' is particularly important in 'domestic' cases and that tribunals and courts considering suicide risk cases are entitled to take notice of the arrangements the UK puts in place to minimise such risk before and during removal.[64] We discuss the question of 'effective mechanisms' at paras 18.50–18.52 below.

A history of past persecution

18.43 The Court of Appeal has indicated in *Y (Sri Lanka)* that where a person's mental health is fragile, and his or her fears of return acute because of a history of past persecution, the *D v UK* and *N* approach should be modified. In such cases, the real cause of the harm is not naturally occurring illness but intentional action by the receiving state. In *Y (Sri Lanka)* the appellants had been subjected to past torture in Sri Lanka and (albeit without objective foundation) had an acute fear of being returned there:

> ... in contrast with what is envisaged at the end of §43 of *N*, the anticipated self-harm would be the consequence of the acts of the Sri Lankan security forces, not of a naturally occurring illness. It would be, if it were to occur, the product of fear and humiliation brought about by the brutality to which both appellants were subjected before they fled.[65]

---

63 See also the *obiter dicta* of Sedley LJ in *KH (Afghanistan) v Secretary of State for the Home Department* [2009] EWCA Civ 1354 para 37.
64 *J v Secretary of State for the Home Department* [2005] EWCA Civ 629, [2005] Imm AR 409 paras 33 and 62.
65 *Y (Sri Lanka) and Z (Sri Lanka) v Secretary of State for the Home Department* [2009] EWCA Civ 362, [2009] HRLR 22 para 50.

Anxious scrutiny in mental health and suicide cases generally

18.44 Despite the high threshold in mental health and suicide risk cases generally, the Court of Appeal has been emphatic that such claims can succeed and has been sometimes prepared to remit such cases where the tribunal has failed to properly address its mind to the evidence or law.[66] In *Y (Sri Lanka)* the Court of Appeal allowed outright on ECHR article 3 grounds the appeals of the two highly traumatised appellants who, having previously been subjected to torture, were so terrified that they would, if expelled to Sri Lanka, be unwilling or unable to access medical care.[67]

18.45 As Sedley LJ drily observed in the latter case, decision-makers should not take the approach that until a person has actually killed himself or come close to doing so, an ECHR article 3 claim based on mental ill-health and suicide risk cannot succeed:

> ... the mode of reasoning in the present case (which is far from unique) is such that no art. 3 'foreign' claim based on a risk of suicide is likely ever to succeed. Indeed Hughes LJ in *AJ (Liberia) v Home Secretary* [2006] EWCA Civ 1736 remarked on the fact that, so far as the reported cases went, none ever had. The reasoning is that, since Y had made no attempt at suicide despite more than one refusal of his asylum claim, and since Z's attempt at suicide had not been seriously life-threatening, and since both would ex hypothesi find on return that their fears, even if genuine, are now groundless, there is no real risk that return will impel either appellant to commit suicide. The effect is that, apart from an asylum-seeker who actually commits suicide, only one who comes close enough to succeeding to manifest a serious intent is going to be regarded as presenting a serious risk of suicide on return.[68]

18.46 Nor, as Sedley LJ warned in *Y (Sri Lanka)*, is it permissible for decision-makers to 'cherry-pick' psychiatric evidence.[69]

18.47 In cases raising mental health, just as in cases raising physical health, tribunals and courts must consider on a case sensitive analysis

---

66 *CN (Burundi) v Secretary of State for the Home Department* [2007] EWCA Civ 587 para 28; *AJ (Liberia) v Secretary of State for the Home Department* [2006] EWCA Civ 1736.
67 *Y (Sri Lanka) and Z (Sri Lanka) v Secretary of State for the Home Department* [2009] EWCA Civ 362, [2009] HRLR 22.
68 *Y (Sri Lanka) and Z (Sri Lanka) v Secretary of State for the Home Department* [2009] EWCA Civ 362, [2009] HRLR 22 para 36.
69 *Y (Sri Lanka) and Z (Sri Lanka) v Secretary of State for the Home Department* [2009] EWCA Civ 362, [2009] HRLR 22 para 34.

the extent of the illness and risks to the individual;[70] and whether this particular individual would have access to appropriate medication and treatment after expulsion (not merely its generic availability).[71]

Further issues arising in mental health and suicide risk cases

A subjective fear of return can suffice

18.48   In *Y (Sri Lanka)*, the Court of Appeal considered the fifth principle in *J*, namely the effect of a person's fear of ill-treatment in the receiving state even where the fear is not objectively warranted. The issue was distilled by Sedley LJ:

> If a fear of ill-treatment on return is well-founded, this will ordinarily mean that refoulement (if it is a refugee convention case) or return (if it is a human rights case) cannot take place in any event. In such cases the question whether return will precipitate suicide is academic. But the principle leaves an unfilled space for cases like the present one where fear of ill-treatment on return, albeit held to be objectively without foundation, is subjectively not only real but overwhelming. There is no necessary tension between the two things. The corollary of the final sentence of §30 of *J* is that in the absence of an objective foundation for the fear some independent basis for it must be established if weight is to be given to it. Such an independent basis may lie in trauma inflicted in the past on the appellant in (or, as here, by) the receiving state: someone who has been tortured and raped by his or her captors may be terrified of returning to the place where it happened, especially if the same authorities are in charge, notwithstanding that the objective risk of recurrence has gone.[72]

18.49   Sedley LJ (with whom the other members of the court agreed) held therefore that an ECHR article 3 claim based on the mental ill-health and suicide risk arising out of a fear of future ill-treatment could succeed, even though that fear was not objectively well-founded.[73]

---

70   *CN (Burundi) v Secretary of State for the Home Department* [2007] EWCA Civ 587 para 20.
71   *AJ (Liberia) v Secretary of State for the Home Department* [2006] EWCA Civ 1736; *RA (Sri Lanka) v Secretary of State for the Home Department* [2008] EWCA Civ 1210, [2009] Imm AR 320, para 45.
72   *Y (Sri Lanka) and Z (Sri Lanka) v Secretary of State for the Home Department* [2009] EWCA Civ 362, [2009] HRLR 22 paras 14–15.
73   *Y (Sri Lanka) and Z (Sri Lanka) v Secretary of State for the Home Department* [2009] EWCA Civ 362, [2009] HRLR 22 para 16.

'Effective mechanisms'

18.50 In *Tozlukaya v Secretary of State for the Home Department*, the Court of Appeal reiterated the importance of the sixth of the *J v Secretary of State for the Home Department* principles ('effective mechanisms') but rejected the SSHD's argument that a suicide risk claim must fail where the receiving state (in that case Germany) could be expected to comply with its own obligations under ECHR article 3:

> We are concerned here not just with the risk of harm in the receiving state, but also with the risk of harm in the removing state; and in each case the risk arises not from the action of third parties but from the direct impact of the decision to remove on the person's mental health. Moreover, and more fundamentally, the line of authority that establishes that article 3 can in principle apply in a case of suicide risk also shows that the application of article 3 does not depend on an actual or notional breach of any Convention obligation by the receiving state.[74]

18.51 In *Y (Sri Lanka)*, the Court of Appeal also considered the sixth principle. In that case, the appellants were so traumatised and fearful that they would not be able to access any care that was available on return, so that the existence of local hospitals could not materially attenuate the risk of suicide.[75] *Y (Sri Lanka)* demonstrates that generally 'effective mechanisms' in the state to which a person is being expelled are of little consequence if they will be ineffective for the individual being expelled.

18.52 Finally, distinct issues relating to 'effective mechanisms' arise in 'domestic cases', that is, where it is asserted that there is a real risk of suicide prior to expulsion. *J v Secretary of State for the Home Department*[76] indicates that the tribunals and courts are entitled to take notice of the arrangements that the SSHD puts in place to minimise risks when expelling the vulnerable. The SSHD has a published policy, contained in the Immigration Directorate Instructions (IDIs), concerning steps to be taken to minimise the risk of suicide or self-harm, both in detention and during expulsion.[77] The 'domestic'

---

74 *R (Tozlukaya) v Secretary of State for the Home Department* [2006] EWCA Civ 379, [2006] Imm AR 417 para 57.
75 *Y (Sri Lanka) and Z (Sri Lanka) v Secretary of State for the Home Department* [2009] EWCA Civ 362, [2009] HRLR 22 paras 61 and 64.
76 *J v Secretary of State for the Home Department* [2005] EWCA Civ 629, [2005] Imm AR 409 para 62.
77 IDIs chapter 1 section 10 para 8.16 onwards. Available at www.ukba. homeoffice.gov.uk/sitecontent/documents/policyandlaw/IDIs/idischapter1/section10/section10.pdf?view=Binary.

element of a suicide risk cases will be unlikely to succeed unless it can be shown that the measures generally adopted by the SSHD would not be effective for the particular individual or that there are deficiencies in the implementation of the SSHD's policy.

ECHR article 8 and mental and physical illness

Private life and health

18.53 As we have already seen at para 16.35, the concept of private life includes moral and physical integrity, and 'those features which are integral to a person's identity or ability to function socially as a person'.[78]

18.54 ECHR article 8 therefore protects the right to respect for one's health, including mental health.[79] In *Bensaid v UK* (discussed at paras 18.29–18.30 above), the ECtHR held that:

> Mental health must also be regarded as a crucial part of private life associated with the aspect of moral integrity. Article 8 protects a right to identity and personal development, and the right to establish and develop relationships with other human beings and the outside world. The preservation of mental stability is in that context an indispensable precondition to effective enjoyment of the right to respect for private life.[80]

18.55 The ECtHR in *Bensaid v UK* went on to consider whether Mr Bensaid's expulsion would breach his rights under ECHR article 8 although that claim again foundered on the facts.

The relationship between ECHR article 3 and article 8 in health claims

18.56 The effects of expulsion on physical or mental health may be relied on to resist expulsion under ECHR article 8, even if the facts do not meet the ECHR article 3 threshold:

---

78 *Razgar v Secretary of State for the Home Department* [2004] UKHL 27, [2004] 2 AC 368 para 9.
79 For examples of ECHR article 8 claims in the mental health context, see *R (Razgar) v Secretary of State for the Home Department* [2004] UKHL 27, [2004] 2 AC 368; *CN (Burundi) v Secretary of State for the Home Department* [2007] EWCA Civ 587; *AJ (Liberia) v Secretary of State for the Home Department* [2006] EWCA Civ 1736.
80 *Bensaid v United Kingdom* (2001) 33 EHRR 10 para 47.

... reliance may in principle be placed on article 8 to resist an expulsion decision, even where the main emphasis is not on the severance of family and social ties which the applicant has enjoyed in the expelling country but on the consequences for his mental health of removal to the receiving country. The threshold of successful reliance is high, but if the facts are strong enough article 8 may in principle be invoked.

... the rights protected by article 8 can be engaged by the foreseeable consequences for health of removal from the United Kingdom pursuant to an immigration decision, even where such removal does not violate article 3, if the facts relied on by the applicant are sufficiently strong.[81]

There is no fixed relationship between Art 3 and Art 8. Typically a finding of a violation of the former may make a decision on the latter unnecessary; but the latter is not simply a more easily accessed version of the former. Each has to be approached and applied on its own terms, and [counsel for the SSHD] is accordingly right not to suggest that a claim of the present kind must come within Art 3 or fail.[82]

18.57 *JA (Ivory Coast)*, the facts of which were discussed at paras 18.22–18.23 above, is an example of a case in which an applicant suffering from AIDS successfully relied on ECHR article 8 to resist expulsion (and did not pursue ECHR article 3 at all, at least by the time the case reached the Court of Appeal[83]).

18.58 However, it will often be difficult for a health case which cannot succeed under ECHR article 3 to succeed under article 8. The high threshold test of 'compelling humanitarian grounds', applied by the House of Lords in *N v Secretary of State for the Home Department*[84] to an ECHR article 3 physical health (HIV/AIDS) case has been applied to a number of ECHR article 8 health cases by the domestic courts.[85] Moreover, many health cases will be 'foreign cases' (where the alleged breach would take place in the receiving state) and are thus subject to a higher threshold test of flagrant denial.

---

81 *Razgar v Secretary of State for the Home Department* [2004] UKHL 27, [2004] 2 AC 368 paras 9–10; the same point is made in *AJ (Liberia) v Secretary of State for the Home Department* [2006] EWCA Civ 1736 para 26 and in *R (Tozlukaya) v Secretary of State for the Home Department* [2006] EWCA Civ 379, [2006] Imm AR 417 para 75; see also *Bensaid v UK* (2001) 33 EHRR 10 para 46.
82 *JA (Ivory Coast)* [2009] EWCA Civ 1353, [2010] Imm AR 381 para 17.
83 *JA (Ivory Coast)* [2009] EWCA Civ 1353, [2010] Imm AR 381 para 11.
84 [2005] 2 WLR 1124 per Lord Hope of Craighead at para 50; see also Baroness Hale of Richmond at para 69.
85 *RA (Sri Lanka) v Secretary of State for the Home Department* [2008] EWCA Civ 1210 para 50; *BK (Zimbabwe) v Secretary of State for the Home Department* [2008] EWCA Civ 510 para 17.

MSS v Belgium and Greece and *Sufi and Elmi v UK*: a modified approach?

18.59 Two recent judgments, *MSS v Belgium and Greece*[86] and *Sufi and Elmi v UK*,[87] mark powerful interventions by the ECtHR in the arena of resources. The facts of these two cases, and their implications in challenges arising out of poor living conditions after expulsion, have been addressed at paras 13.35–13.38. Both cases recognise that ECHR article 3 may be breached by the expulsion of a person to harmful conditions in the receiving state which arise from a lack of resources. *MSS v Belgium and Greece* additionally compels the Council of Europe's member states (in that instance, both Belgium, the expelling state, and Greece, the receiving state) to devote more resources to the care of destitute and dependent foreign nationals. Yet neither case applies the high thresholds of *D v UK* or *N v UK*. It remains to be seen whether these developments will herald any shift in approach to health cases.

ECHR article 6 and '*Quaquah* claims'

18.60 Finally, while a full discussion of ECHR article 6 is beyond the scope of this book, we mention briefly here claims that a person's expulsion while pursuing civil litigation against the Home Office would breach the UK's obligations under ECHR article 6. These are often referred to as '*Quaquah* claims', after the case in which the point was first argued.

18.61 The applicant in *Quaquah*[88] successfully challenged a decision by the SSHD refusing to set aside directions set for his removal while he was pursuing a claim for damages in malicious prosecution against the Home Office and its private contractors. The claim was brought on the grounds, among others, that the SSHD had failed to consider that the applicant's expulsion would breach his right to adequate time and facilities to prepare his case, and to equality of arms, principles enshrined both in the Civil Procedure Rules 1998 (CPR) 1.1.2 and in ECHR article 6(3)(b) (which was accepted to apply also to civil proceedings). Turner J observed:

---

86 (2011) 53 EHRR 2.
87 App Nos 8319/07 and 11449/07, judgment 28 June 2011.
88 CO/4738/98, 15 December 1999, Turner J, [2000] HRLR 325.

The application was put on the basis that it would diminish the Applicant's prospects of success in his civil proceedings if he could not have ready access to the solicitor whom he has instructed in those proceedings. There are numerous stages in the course of civil proceedings at which a party needs to be in communication with his advisers for the purpose of providing adequate instructions and being able to respond to requests from the other parties. As a consequence, if the applicant were now to be removed to Ghana he would suffer great disadvantage in the preparatory stages of the litigation.

18.62 Granting the claim, Turner J held that:

This was not just a simple straightforward case of infringement of a private right by a private individual. The case may be one in which the agencies of the state (the Group 4 custodians) have breached, in the public sphere, duties which they owed to those who were held in the Detention Centre and for which the respondent (the decision-maker) had the overall legal responsibility. It is also contended, that the Secretary of State is liable for the torts committed by the Group 4 guards. In pursuit of his right the Applicant is entitled to have adequate time and facilities for the preparation of his (case). The decision under challenge was calculated, as I have said not intentionally, to interfere with that 'minimum' right.

18.63 However, in the light of improving communications, such claims are now unlikely to succeed in practice unless it can be demonstrated:

a) that the nature of the underlying claim requires the applicant's presence in the UK to give detailed instructions (establishing this may require a witness statement from the solicitor in the civil claim); and also

b) communications in the country of expulsion are so poor that they could not be maintained by internet or phone; and/or

c) something in the applicant's individual circumstances (such as a risk of being destitute and homeless after expulsion or mental ill-health) makes the gathering of long-distance instructions impracticable. This may require expert evidence.

18.64 If the underlying civil claim is one which would be severely hampered by the claimant's inability to give oral evidence at trial, then a deportation order may provide a compelling argument against expulsion pending the final outcome of the trial, since, once enforced, re-entry is prohibited.

SECTION E

Immigration status for FNPs who cannot be deported

CHAPTER 19

Immigration status for FNPs who cannot be deported

19.1	Introduction
19.5	Humanitarian protection and discretionary leave
19.7	**Humanitarian protection (HP)**
19.7	Definition
19.11	Domestic implementation
19.13	Contents of humanitarian protection
19.18	Exclusion from humanitarian protection
	Domestic interpretation of the criteria for exclusion from Humanitarian Protection
19.26	Leave to remain under humanitarian protection
19.28	Cessation of subsidiary protection/humanitarian protection
19.31	**Discretionary Leave (DL)**
19.34	'Exclusion' in discretionary leave cases
19.36	Duration of grants of discretionary leave and 'active review'
	Standard grants of discretionary leave • 'Non-standard' grants of discretionary leave
19.56	**Leave outside the Rules**
19.61	**Special Immigration Status**
19.66	**Revocation of indefinite leave to remain where individual cannot be deported**
19.76	**Power to deprive a dual national of citizenship**

Introduction

19.1 This chapter examines the immigration status of foreign national prisoners and former prisoners (FNPs) who are not deported other than for reasons arising under the Refugee Convention (refugee status has been discussed at paras 11.28–11.33). There are three broad topics in this chapter.

19.2 First, the primary focus of this chapter is an examination of the forms of status available to foreign nationals who do not have other leave to remain, nor refugee status, but have succeeded in showing that their expulsion would breach the European Convention on Human Rights (ECHR) or the Qualification Directive.[1] These types of status, known as humanitarian protection (HP) and discretionary leave (DL), may themselves be affected by the past commission of serious crimes.

19.3 Second, this chapter examines the circumstances in which an immigrant who (for example on ECHR, Refugee Convention[2] or Qualification Directive article 15(c) grounds) cannot lawfully be deported and still has indefinite leave to remain (ILR), may have ILR revoked. The revocation of ILR for a person who has ceased to be a refugee has been considered separately at paras 12.130–12.132.

19.4 Finally and more briefly, this chapter considers other forms of immigration status, and also a group who are not strictly speaking FNPs: the rare circumstances in which dual nationals may lose their British citizenship.

Humanitarian protection and discretionary leave

19.5 HP is a relatively new form of status, introduced with effect from 1 April 2003,[3] and aimed at providing protection from expulsion for certain categories of person who are at risk of serious abuses of human rights but do not fall within the Refugee Convention. It derives from the provisions relating to 'subsidiary protection' in the Qualification Directive.

---

1 Council Directive 2004/83/EC of 29 April 2004 on minimum standards for the qualification and status of third country nationals or stateless persons as refugees or as persons who otherwise need international protection and the content of the protection granted; OJ L 304, 30/09/2004 ('Qualification Directive').
2 The 1951 Convention Relating to the Status of Refugees and its 1967 Protocol ('Refugee Convention').
3 See Asylum Policy Instructions (API) on Humanitarian Protection, 'Introduction'.

19.6   HP is itself complemented by a status known as DL, which applies to other categories of person who cannot be expelled for human rights reasons. Some of those eligible for DL are subject to significant restrictions if they have been excluded from refugee status or have committed offences.

Humanitarian protection (HP)

Definition

19.7   The Qualification Directive creates a status known as 'subsidiary protection', defined as follows:

> '[P]erson eligible for subsidiary protection' means a third country national or a stateless person who does not qualify as a refugee but in respect of whom substantial grounds have been shown for believing that the person concerned, if returned to his or her country of origin, or in the case of a stateless person, to his or her country of former habitual residence, would face a real risk of suffering serious harm as defined in Article 15, and to whom Article 17(1) and (2) do not apply, and is unable, or, owing to such risk, unwilling to avail himself or herself of the protection of that country.[4]

19.8   Article 17 of the Qualification Directive deals with exclusion of certain people from HP, and is discussed below.

19.9   Article 15 of the Qualification Directive defines 'serious harm' thus:

> Serious harm consists of:
> (a) death penalty or execution; or
> (b) torture or inhuman or degrading treatment or punishment of an applicant in the country of origin;
> or
> (c) serious and individual threat to a civilian's life or person by reason of indiscriminate violence in situations of international or internal armed conflict.

19.10   Subparagraphs (a) and (b) largely reflect ECHR articles 2 and 3,[5] although as has been pointed out by the Court of Appeal in *QD (Iraq)*, article 15(a) surprisingly omits any reference to unlawful killing.[6]

---

4   Qualification Directive article 2(e).
5   Discussed at paras 13.6–13.28.
6   *QD (Iraq) v Secretary of State for the Home Department* (UNHCR intervening) [2009] EWCA Civ 620, [2011] 1 WLR 689 para 13.

Domestic implementation

19.11 The Immigration Rules at para 339C[7] provide as follows, essentially implementing the passages above from the Qualification Directive:

> A person will be granted humanitarian protection in the United Kingdom if the Secretary of State is satisfied that:
> (i) he is in the United Kingdom or has arrived at a port of entry in the United Kingdom;
> (ii) he does not qualify as a refugee as defined in regulation 2 of The Refugee or Person in Need of International Protection (Qualification) Regulations 2006;
> (iii) substantial grounds have been shown for believing that the person concerned, if he returned to the country of return, would face a real risk of suffering serious harm and is unable, or, owing to such risk, unwilling to avail himself of the protection of that country; and
> (iv) he is not excluded from a grant of humanitarian protection.
> Serious harm consists of:
> (i) the death penalty or execution;
> (ii) unlawful killing;
> (iii) torture or inhuman or degrading treatment or punishment of a person in the country of return; or
> (iv) serious and individual threat to a civilian's life or person by reason of indiscriminate violence in situations of international or internal armed conflict.

19.12 The contents and meaning of article 15(c) – as reflected in the final subparagraph of paragraph 339C – have been dealt with separately in chapter 14.

Contents of humanitarian protection

19.13 It will be noted from the extracts above that:

- As with subsidiary protection under article 2(e) of the Qualification Directive, HP under the Immigration Rules is granted only to those who do not qualify as refugees: HP and refugee status are thus closely related and parallel, but mutually exclusive.
- Most of the forms of 'serious harm' listed in para 339C would also constitute persecution for purposes of the Refugee Convention and would make an applicant eligible for refugee status if there was a Refugee Convention reason[8] for the persecution. Most of those who qualify for HP rather than refugee status, other than

---

7 HC 395.
8 Under Refugee Convention article 1A; see Qualification Directive article 10.

those who qualify under article 15(c), will therefore do so on the basis that they would be refugees but for the fact that there is no Refugee Convention reason for the persecution.[9]

- The omission of 'unlawful killing' from the definition in article 15(a) of the Qualification Directive is rectified in the UK by the inclusion of the term in the Immigration Rules.[10]
- However, the definition of persecution under the Refugee Convention[11] is wider than that of serious harm under article 15(c): see paras 11.44–11.46 and chapter 14.

19.14 In addition, it is the Home Office's position that the definition of 'serious harm' in article 15 is intended to exclude cases where the 'treatment' feared would arise solely from the effects of illness:[12]

> Where a person claims that their return would be in breach of Article 3 of the ECHR because of their medical condition, they are not in need of international protection and are not eligible for Humanitarian Protection. The breach of Article 3 arises because the healthcare available to the applicant in the UK is not available in the country of return and because of the applicant's own exceptional circumstances. Individuals who cannot return for this reason may qualify for Discretionary Leave ...[13]

19.15 We suggest that this is questionable, since there is nothing in the Qualification Directive which limits the words 'inhuman or degrading treatment' in article 15(b) to treatment which is deliberately caused, rather than to treatment arising from serious illness together with a lack of available care. (It is well-established in the case-law of the European Court of Human Rights (ECtHR) that 'suffering which flows from naturally occurring illness, physical or mental' may constitute 'treatment' for purposes of article 3;[14] see para 18.4 for the fuller discussion.) Recital 9 to the Qualification Directive states that those 'who are allowed to remain in the territories of the member states for reasons not due to a need for international protection but on a discretionary basis on compassionate or humanitarian grounds, fall outside the scope of this Directive', but that does not explain the

---

9 This is also the view expressed in the API on Humanitarian Protection, 'Introduction'. See paras 11.51–11.58 for a discussion of Refugee Convention reasons.
10 Immigration Rules para 339C, second subpara (ii).
11 Qualification Directive article 9.
12 Compare *N v UK* (2008) 47 EHRR 39. See discussion of these cases in chapter 18.
13 API on Humanitarian Protection, section headed 'Medical cases'.
14 See, for example, *N v UK* (2008) 47 EHRR 39 para 29.

19.16 Many of the concepts which apply to the assessment and grant of refugee status (see chapter 11) also apply to HP: for example, the Qualification Directive applies the same concepts of 'sur place' protection needs,[15] perpetrators ('actors of persecution or serious harm'),[16] sufficiency of protection[17] and internal relocation[18] as apply to the Refugee Convention. The 'assessment of facts and circumstances' is also to be carried out in the same way as in an application for refugee status.[19]

19.17 The parallel functions of refugee status and HP are underlined by the comment in the API on Humanitarian Protection that '[a]n asylum claim will always be deemed to be a claim for Humanitarian Protection' and that HP must always be considered alongside refugee status.[20]

Exclusion from humanitarian protection

19.18 Individuals otherwise eligible for HP can be excluded from it under article 17 of the Qualification Directive, which provides:

> Exclusion
> 1. A third country national or a stateless person is excluded from being eligible for subsidiary protection where there are serious reasons for considering that:
> (a) he or she has committed a crime against peace, a war crime, or a crime against humanity, as defined in the international instruments drawn up to make provision in respect of such crimes;
> (b) he or she has committed a serious crime;
> (c) he or she has been guilty of acts contrary to the purposes and principles of the United Nations as set out in the Preamble and Articles 1 and 2 of the Charter of the United Nations;
> (d) he or she constitutes a danger to the community or to the security of the member state in which he or she is present.

---

15 Qualification Directive article 5.
16 Qualification Directive article 6.
17 Qualification Directive article 7.
18 Qualification Directive article 8.
19 Qualification Directive article 4.
20 API on Humanitarian Protection, section headed 'Granting or refusing humanitarian protection'.

2. Paragraph 1 applies to persons who instigate or otherwise participate in the commission of the crimes or acts mentioned therein.
3. Member states may exclude a third country national or a stateless person from being eligible for subsidiary protection, if he or she prior to his or her admission to the member state has committed one or more crimes, outside the scope of paragraph 1, which would be punishable by imprisonment, had they been committed in the member state concerned, and if he or she left his or her country of origin solely in order to avoid sanctions resulting from these crimes.

19.19 Article 17(3) seems intended to ensure that individuals are not eligible for protection under the Qualification Directive solely on the basis of punishment for criminality. That does not mean that the individual could be returned if the punishment involved the death penalty, or torture or inhuman or degrading treatment, since that would be contrary to articles 2 and 3 of the ECHR respectively: it merely means that the individual would not benefit from the social protections provided by the Qualification Directive. (In the UK, such individuals are likely to qualify for DL: see paras 19.31–19.47 below.)

19.20 There is substantial overlap between the provisions of article 17 and the exclusion clauses[21] and the 'loss of protection' clause[22] in the Refugee Convention. The latter have been considered in detail in chapter 12 although there are some differences, notably:

- Qualification Directive article 17(1)(b) is very similar to Refugee Convention article 1F(b), with the difference, at least in the English version of the Qualification Directive,[23] that the 'serious crime' does not need to be 'non-political'; nor does it make a difference where or when the crime is said to have been committed.
- Qualification Directive article 17(1)(d) is very similar to Refugee Convention article 33(2), except that it is not necessary, in respect of HP, to show that the individual has been convicted of an offence in order for the 'danger to the community' provision to apply.[24]

---

21 Refugee Convention article 1F(a)–(c).
22 Refugee Convention article 33(2).
23 The French version of article 17(1)(b) has, for 'serious crime', 'un crime grave de droit commun' – which is the same as the wording used for 'serious non-political crime' in Qualification Directive article 12(2)(b) and Refugee Convention article 1F(b). Thus it would seem that article 17(1)(b) may in fact have been intended to cover the same offences as article 12(2)(b), and the reason for the difference in the English-language version (ie omitting the word 'non-political' in article 17(1)(b)) is unclear.
24 Compare the discussion of Refugee Convention article 33(2) at paras 12.78–12.83.

Domestic interpretation of the criteria for exclusion from Humanitarian Protection

19.21 The provisions of Qualification Directive article 17 are essentially reproduced in paragraph 339D of the Immigration Rules.

19.22 However, as we shall see below, the Secretary of State for the Home Department's (SSHD's) policies, which are contained in the APIs arguably go considerably further in who they purport to exclude than do the Qualification Directive or the Immigration Rules. We suggest that the SSHD's API on Humanitarian Protection may be unlawful insofar as it concerns exclusion.

19.23 The API on Humanitarian Protection contains a section headed 'Exclusion criteria'. The material part of this reproduces the contents of Immigration Rules para 339D, but then goes on to add the following gloss:

> A 'serious crime' for these purposes is:
> - one for which a custodial sentence of at least twelve months has been imposed in the United Kingdom; or
> - a crime considered serious enough to exclude the person from being a refugee in accordance with Article 1F(b) of the Convention ...; or
> - conviction for an offence listed in an order made under section 72 of the Nationality, Immigration and Asylum Act 2002 ...
>
> People who may represent 'a danger to the community or to the security of the UK' include:
> - those included on the Sex Offenders Register ...
> - those whose presence in the United Kingdom is deemed not conducive to the public good by the Secretary of State, for example on national security grounds, because of their character, conduct or associations.
> - those who engage in one or more unacceptable behaviours (whether in the UK or abroad).
>
> The list of unacceptable behaviours includes using any means or medium including:
> - writing, producing, publishing or distributing material
> - public speaking including preaching
> - running a website or
> - using a position of responsibility such as teacher, community or youth leader to express views which:
>   - foment, justify or glorify terrorist violence in furtherance of particular beliefs
>   - seek to provoke others to terrorist acts
>   - foment other serious criminal activity or seek to provoke others to serious criminal acts, or foster hatred which may lead to inter-community violence in the UK.

This list is indicative, not exhaustive.

A person may also be regarded as a danger to the community or to the security of the United Kingdom in the light of their character, conduct or associations, insofar as this is not covered by the categories listed above ...

19.24 As to what constitutes a serious crime, as discussed at para 12.92, it was held in *EN (Serbia)*[25] that an irrebuttable presumption in Nationality, Immigration and Asylum Act (NIAA) 2002 s72 that any crime resulting in a sentence of two years or more was 'particularly serious' would be contrary to article 14(4) of the Qualification Directive. It might have been thought to follow that an irrebuttable presumption, arising from policy, that a crime resulting in a sentence of one year is so 'serious' as to warrant exclusion must also be unlawful. However, it was held in *Mayaya* that an irrebuttable presumption that a crime is 'serious' where it has resulted in a sentence of 12 months' imprisonment was not unlawful, because 'the criminal courts do not pass sentences of 12 months or more for offences which are not serious'.[26] There was no unlawful fettering of the SSHD's discretion under Immigration Act (IA) 1971 s3(1) as to the grant of leave to remain, because 'a 12 months' sentence threshold is a reliable and rational measure of seriousness, which has been set by a court'.[27]

19.25 Those potentially eligible for, but excluded from, HP cannot be expelled from the UK, because their expulsion would almost certainly breach ECHR articles 2 and/or 3, and will still qualify for DL, see paras 19.31–19.47 below.

Leave to remain under humanitarian protection

19.26 As with recognised refugees,[28] those given HP in the UK are entitled to residence permits valid for five years, at the end of which they can apply for ILR. ILR may be granted earlier if the person is accepted to be vulnerable and to have special needs.[29]

---

25 *EN (Serbia) v Secretary of State for the Home Department* [2009] EWCA Civ 630, [2010] QB 633.
26 *R (Mayaya and others) v Secretary of State for the Home Department* [2011] EWHC 3088 (Admin) para 42.
27 *R (Mayaya and others) v Secretary of State for the Home Department* [2011] EWHC 3088 (Admin) para 46.
28 See para 11.28.
29 API on Humanitarian Protection, section headed 'Leave to be granted'; compare Qualification Directive article 20.

19.27 The rights of those granted HP are broadly similar to those granted refugee status, as set out at paras 11.28–11.31. Although the Qualification Directive allows for differences in the treatment of those with HP, in comparison with refugees,[30] these have generally not been implemented by the UK, which makes almost identical provision for those with HP and those with refugee status.[31] A travel document may be granted to a person with HP, but not as of right, as with a refugee, but only:

- 'where that person is unable to obtain a national passport or other identity documents which enable him to travel'; or
- where it would be possible to obtain a national passport but the applicant 'can show that he has made reasonable attempts to obtain a national passport or identity document and there are serious humanitarian reasons for travel';[32] and
- not if 'compelling reasons of national security or public order otherwise require'.[33]

Cessation of subsidiary protection/humanitarian protection

19.28 Article 16 of the Qualification Directive provides for cessation of subsidiary protection in terms analogous to those in article 11(1)(e) of the Qualification Directive, which in turn corresponds to article 1C(5) of the Refugee Convention:

> Article 16
> 1. A third country national or a stateless person shall cease to be eligible for subsidiary protection when the circumstances which led to the granting of subsidiary protection status have ceased to exist or have changed to such a degree that protection is no longer required.
> 2. In applying paragraph 1, member states shall have regard to whether the change of circumstances is of such a significant and non-temporary nature that the person eligible for subsidiary protection no longer faces a real risk of serious harm.

19.29 It will be noted, however, that, in contrast to the Refugee Convention, there is no concept of withdrawing subsidiary protection on the basis that the applicant has re-established himself or herself in the country of origin or re-availed himself or herself of the protection of

---

30 Compare Qualification Directive article 26(3), article 28(2).
31 Compare Immigration Rules para 344B, para 352FA.
32 Immigration Rules para 344A(iii).
33 Immigration Rules para 344A(ii).

the country of nationality. Nonetheless, steps which would fall within Qualification Directive article 11 and/or Refugee Convention article 1C may be relevant to whether 'the circumstances which led to the granting of subsidiary protection status have ceased to exist or have changed to such a degree that protection is no longer required', as expressed in article 16(1) of the Qualification Directive.

19.30 HP may also be revoked or not extended if the person granted it 'misrepresented or omitted facts, including the use of false documents, which were decisive to the grant of humanitarian protection'.[34]

Discretionary Leave (DL)

19.31 As indicated above, certain categories of FNP are likely to fall outside the provisions of the Refugee Convention and Qualification Directive, while being entitled to remain in the UK on the basis that their rights under the ECHR will be breached. These include:

- those who have a well-founded fear of being persecuted and/or who have a real risk of being subjected to serious harm, but who are excluded from refugee status and/or HP for reasons of criminality;
- refugees who do not benefit from the non-refoulement provision in article 33(1) of the Refugee Convention because they fall within article 33(2);[35]
- those who are not at risk of persecution or serious harm, but cannot be expelled for other reasons, notably because it would breach ECHR article 8 on the basis of private or family life;
- those who are not at risk of persecution or serious harm, but whose removal would be contrary to ECHR articles 3 and/or 8 on medical grounds or on grounds that they would be returning to inhumane conditions, eg through lack of water, food or basic shelter;
- unaccompanied asylum-seeking children who are not eligible for refugee status or HP but cannot be removed because no reception arrangements exist for them.

Such individuals are granted DL, a form of leave to remain which is in many cases subject to very severe restrictions.

---

34 Immigration Rules para 339G(v).
35 But see paras 12.97–12.109.

19.32 DL is granted according to the provisions of the SSHD's API on Discretionary Leave. DL exists entirely outside the Immigration Rules. At the time of writing, the API had been removed from the SSHD's website and replaced with a statement that it was 'currently being updated'. References to the API in this chapter are to the version dated 27 October 2009, which is the most recent version accessible via the UK Government Web Archive[36] and which we take to be that still applicable as of the date of writing.

19.33 The API contains seven sets of criteria for a grant of DL:

- *Cases where return would breach ECHR article 8.* The API suggests that:
  Where the return of an individual would involve a breach of Article 8 of the ECHR ... on the basis of family life established in the UK, they should be granted Discretionary Leave.

[It is unclear what would be granted if it were the right to respect for private life which would be breached by removal, but we suggest that the SSHD would probably grant DL in those circumstances, as the individual would fall into the fifth category, 'Other cases where return would breach the ECHR', below.]

- *Cases where return would breach ECHR article 3 but where HP is not applicable.* The most obvious example, other than cases falling into the next two categories, is a case where a person is at risk of serious harm but is excluded from both refugee status and HP (see paras 19.18–19.19 above). According to the SSHD's 'Interim guidance on Article 1F: Restricted discretionary leave', effective from 2 September 2011, such people are generally to be given leave to remain for short periods and subject to stringent conditions, which are discussed below.
- *Medical cases.* This applies to the relatively rare cases where it is established that it would be a breach of ECHR article 3 to remove a person from the UK on the basis of their medical condition.[37]
- *Severe humanitarian conditions.* The API says:
  There may be some extreme cases (although such cases are likely to be rare) where a person would face such poor conditions if returned – eg absence of water, food or basic shelter – that removal could be a breach of the UK's Article 3 obligations. Discretionary Leave should

---

36 See http://webarchive.nationalarchives.gov.uk/20110413124310/http://www.ukba.homeoffice.gov.uk/sitecontent/documents/policyandlaw/asylumpolicyinstructions/apis/discretionaryleave.pdf?view=Binary.
37 Although see para 19.15 above for our reservations about the SSHD's view that such a person would not qualify for HP.

not be granted if the claimant could avoid the risk of suffering by leaving the UK voluntarily.

[It is unclear to us in what circumstances a person would be able to obtain food or water which was not otherwise available in a time of humanitarian crisis simply by leaving the UK voluntarily.]

- *Other cases where return would breach the ECHR.* This is said in the API to apply to:

    ... cases where the breach would not give rise to a grant of Humanitarian Protection and is not covered [in the other categories] above. For example, where return would result in a flagrant denial of the right in question in the person's country of origin.

    See paras 13.45–13.48 for a discussion of the circumstances in which this might be the case.

- *Unaccompanied asylum-seeking children.* Children who have claimed asylum but have been refused are deemed to qualify for DL if there are inadequate reception arrangements available in their own country.[38] Detailed guidance on handling asylum claims and applications for DL by children lies outside the scope of this book.[39]

- *Other cases.* This applies to cases where there might be considered to be 'compelling' reasons for not removing a person who has claimed asylum. The circumstances in which this might be deemed to be the case are left open by the API.

'Exclusion' in discretionary leave cases

19.34 Applicants may be 'excluded' from DL. This is a misnomer: they may still recive DL but the duration of leave and the waiting period for ILR is different from that in 'non-excluded' DL cases, see paras 19.42–19.45 below. So-called 'exclusion' in DL cases[40] is covered in a section of the API headed 'Applicants excluded from refugee status, humanitarian protection or discretionary leave', which reads in part:

---

38 See API on Processing Asylum Applications from Children.
39 See in particular *Working with refugee children: current issues in best practice* and *Resources guide for practitioners working with refugee children*, both published by the Immigration Law Practitioners Association, May 2011, available at www.ilpa.org.uk.
40 In fact we suggest that this is a misnomer, as those in this category are not being 'excluded' from DL, merely granted a shorter period of leave than they would otherwise get.

Exclusion from Discretionary Leave
The grounds for exclusion from Humanitarian Protection will apply to Discretionary Leave ... A person who is excluded from Discretionary Leave will be expected to leave the UK. Where neither enforced nor voluntary return is possible without material prejudice to the rights protected under this instruction [ie rights protected under the ECHR], Discretionary Leave will usually be granted for six months.

19.35 The same 'exclusion' criteria as appear in Immigration Rules para 339D (based on Qualification Directive article 17, as interpreted in the API on Humanitarian Protection) are thus transposed into the API. Those affected are granted a shorter period of DL than they would otherwise be entitled to, as appears in the next section.

Duration of grants of discretionary leave and 'active review'

Standard grants of discretionary leave

19.36 The API provides that it 'will normally be appropriate to grant' those eligible for DL three years' leave to remain and states that:

Where an extension of leave is sought after a period of Discretionary Leave the request will be subject to an active review. A person will not become eligible for settlement until they have completed six years' Discretionary Leave.[41]

19.37 'Active review' involves a review of the individual's continuing eligibility for DL whenever she or he applies for an extension. The process is defined in the API in the following terms, so far as material:

Extension requests will normally be the subject of an active review, to decide whether the person still qualifies for Discretionary Leave (or any other form of leave that is requested). This review will take account of the information on the extension request form, present country information and any other information of which we are aware and which is relevant to the claim, including any relevant information provided at the time of the original grant of Discretionary Leave ...
The nature of the active review will depend on the reasons why Discretionary Leave was granted. It may, for example, involve consideration of the current family situation of the applicant, the conditions in the country of origin, whether reception arrangements for a child are

---

41 API on Discretionary Leave, under heading 'Key points'; and see heading 'Duration of grants of discretionary leave', subheading 'Standard period for different categories of discretionary leave'.

still unavailable or whether there is still a barrier to the return of an excluded person.[42]

19.38 Those granted DL have access to welfare benefits and can work,[43] but are expected to apply for a national passport rather than a Home Office travel document, unless it has been accepted that they are in fear of the authorities of their country of nationality.[44] In the latter case, they may apply for a Home Office Certificate of Identity.[45] The same applies if they can show that they have been formally and unreasonably refused a national passport.[46]

19.39 The API on Discretionary Leave is silent on the position of family members of those on DL.[47] However, the usual practice, presumably on the basis of the UK's obligations under ECHR article 8, is to grant dependants leave to remain, usually for the same period and on the same conditions (eg as to employment, where applicable) as the principal applicant, assuming of course that they do not have independent claims for instance under the Refugee Convention or the ECHR.

'Non-standard' grants of discretionary leave

19.40 Shorter periods of leave may be suitable in particular circumstances, according to the API, 'where it is clear from the individual circumstances of the case that the factors leading to Discretionary Leave being granted are going to be short lived'.[48] Examples given are where the family member with whom the applicant is connected is expected to leave the UK within 12 months, or 'where a grant of leave is appropriate to enable a person to stay in the UK to participate in a court case'.[49]

---

42 API on Discretionary Leave, under heading 'Applications for further leave'.
43 API on Discretionary Leave, under heading 'Key points'.
44 API on Discretionary Leave, under heading 'Granting or refusing discretionary leave in asylum cases'.
45 API on Discretionary Leave, under heading 'Issuing of travel documents'.
46 API on Discretionary Leave, under heading 'Issuing of travel documents'.
47 It simply says, under the heading 'Key points': 'refer to Asylum Complex Advice Team via a senior caseworker'.
48 API on Discretionary Leave, under heading 'Duration of grants of discretionary leave', subheading 'Non-standard grant periods'.
49 API on Discretionary Leave, under heading 'Duration of grants of discretionary leave', subheading 'Non-standard grant periods'; compare *MS (Ivory Coast) v Secretary of State for the Home Department* [2007] EWCA Civ 133.

Unaccompanied children

19.41 Unaccompanied child asylum-seekers who are not eligible for refugee status or HP, or for DL under any of the other categories, are granted DL until the point where they are aged 17 years six months, or for three years, whichever is the shorter.[50] For some nationalities, specified in the relevant Operational Guidance Note on the country in question, to be found on the SSHD's website, the grant will be until the age of 17 years six months, or for *one* year, whichever is the shorter.[51] (Before 1 April 2007, it was the practice to grant DL until the individual's 18th birthday, see discussion at paras 4.37–4.39.[52])

'Exclusion' cases

19.42 The API on DL provides for shorter periods of leave (and therefore more frequent 'active review') in cases of 'exclusion' from DL:

> Excluded from Humanitarian Protection or Discretionary Leave – six months. This period applies to the first grant and any subsequent grants following an active review.

19.43 However, it is clear from the API that there is a discretion to grant longer periods of leave in 'excluded' cases than six months, since it states that in 'exclusion' cases 'Discretionary Leave will *usually* be granted for six months' (emphasis added).[53]

19.44 As to ILR (or 'settlement'), the API currently provides that:

> A person will normally become eligible for consideration for settlement after completing six continuous years of Discretionary Leave. However, where a person is covered by one of the exclusion categories they will not become eligible for consideration for settlement until they have completed ten continuous years of Discretionary Leave.

It goes on:

> Where a person who is subject to the grounds of exclusion has completed ten years of Discretionary Leave they may be denied settlement where Ministers decide in the light of all the circumstances of the case, that the person's presence in the United Kingdom is not conducive to the public good (this may be decided in the individual circumstances

---

50 API on Discretionary Leave, under the heading 'Duration of grants of discretionary leave', subheading 'UASCs'.
51 API on Discretionary Leave, under the heading 'Duration of grants of discretionary leave', subheading 'UASCs'.
52 API on Discretionary Leave, under the heading 'Duration of grants of discretionary leave', subheading 'UASCs'.
53 API on Discretionary Leave, under heading 'Applicants excluded from refugee status, humanitarian protection or discretionary leave', subheading 'Exclusion from discretionary leave'.

of a case, or for a category of cases). Reasons for this decision should be given. A further period of Discretionary Leave should be granted where it is not possible to remove the person. In such a case, for so long as the individual remains in the United Kingdom, a fresh decision will need to be taken at least every three years on whether settlement should continue to be denied.

19.45 The requirement to wait at least ten years before ILR is considered, is blanket in its terms in the most recent draft of the API at the time of writing. The rigid ten-year waiting period in the API was declared in *Mayaya* to be unlawful in that it fettered the SSHD's discretion as to when to grant ILR.[54] The SSHD will therefore need to consider ILR applications on their merits even where an 'excluded' person seeks ILR before ten years of DL have elapsed. It has also been suggested by Collins J that there must be a limit to the length of time for which the SSHD can rely on past criminality in order to deny a person ILR.[55] Lengthy delay in determining the original claim may also be relevant to the length of time for which it is reasonable to defer a grant of ILR.[56]

Lawfulness of the six-month discretionary leave policy and of its application

19.46 A policy of granting only six months' DL to remain at a time to those excluded from HP has been found to be generally lawful by the Administrative Court.[57] (That case concerned a convicted hijacker, and, understandably, did not challenge the designation of certain offences as 'serious' and warranting exclusion.)

19.47 However, the restrictions resulting from a decision of the SSHD to grant DL for only six months have been accepted, at least cumulatively, to be capable of constituting an interference in the individual's

---

54 *R (Mayaya and others) v Secretary of State for the Home Department* [2011] EWHC 3088 (Admin) para 53 (a declaration was granted in the accompanying Order).
55 *R (N) v Secretary of State for the Home Department* [2009] EWHC 1581 (Admin) para 22.
56 *R (N) v Secretary of State for the Home Department* [2009] EWHC 1581 (Admin) para 25.
57 *R (N) v Secretary of State for the Home Department* [2009] EWHC 1581 (Admin) paras 20–22.

private life.[58] These restrictions include the inability to travel abroad,[59] disadvantages in the employment market arising from the short length of stay and problems in obtaining mortgages, mobile phone contracts etc.[60] The SSHD's position is 'that the justification for giving discretionary leave at six-monthly intervals is self-evident; that is that it allows a review, not only of the claimant's circumstances but also the conditions in the state in question'.[61] In *Mayaya* the policy was said by the SSHD to have:

> ... a twofold precautionary function: to review behaviour and any renewed criminal activity, and to ensure that the need for international protection has not passed, or that article 8 ECHR is no longer engaged, such that removal can proceed. The public is entitled to reassurance that the right to remain in the United Kingdom is kept under review.[62]

In other words, the SSHD is entitled to reconsider on a regular basis whether the individual should continue to be permitted to remain in the UK. In consequence, it has been accepted by the courts, on the facts of the cases so far considered, that the interference is proportionate to a legitimate aim,[63] although with the proviso that applications for extensions of DL are dealt with promptly[64] (which in practice they are frequently not, calling into question the rationale of the policy as allowing for regular review of the individual's circumstances). It has also been held that it might be possible to show that an individual is encountering serious difficulties as a result of the short grant of leave which would render the imposition of the policy disproportionate.[65]

---

58 *R (C) v Secretary of State for the Home Department* [2008] EWHC 2448 (Admin) paras 37–39; *R (Boroumand) v Secretary of State for the Home Department* [2010] EWHC 225 (Admin) para 84.
59 By virtue of the Immigration (Leave to Enter and Remain) Order 2000 SI No 1161 article 13.
60 *R (C) v Secretary of State for the Home Department* [2008] EWHC 2448 (Admin) para 37.
61 *R (C) v Secretary of State for the Home Department* [2008] EWHC 2448 (Admin) para 36.
62 *R (Mayaya and others) v Secretary of State for the Home Department* [2011] EWHC 3088 (Admin) para 33.
63 *R (C) v Secretary of State for the Home Department* [2008] EWHC 2448 (Admin) para 39.
64 *R (Boroumand) v Secretary of State for the Home Department* [2010] EWHC 225 (Admin) para 85.
65 *R (Boroumand) v Secretary of State for the Home Department* [2010] EWHC 225 (Admin) para 86.

Restricted discretionary leave for those excluded from the Refugee Convention under article 1F

19.48 With effect from 2 September 2011, the SSHD introduced 'Interim Guidance' on 'Restricted Discretionary Leave' for those who are excluded under article 1F of the Refugee Convention, but whose rights under ECHR article 3 prevent their removal. The Interim Guidance states that:

> Such cases should usually only be granted Restricted Discretionary Leave to remain for a maximum of six months at a time, with some or all of the following restrictions:
> - a condition restricting the person's employment or occupation in the United Kingdom;
> - a condition restricting where the person can reside;
> - a condition requiring the person to report to an immigration officer or the Secretary of State at regular intervals; and
> - a condition prohibiting the person studying at an education institution.[66]

19.49 Such individuals will also be 'referred by UK Border Agency to the Independent Safeguarding Authority (ISA) to consider whether the individuals concerned should be barred from working/volunteering in ISA-regulated fields'.[67]

19.50 The Interim Guidance states that the SSHD may impose either a total ban on employment ('exceptionally in cases posing a particularly high public protection risk') or 'a condition not to take any employment or engage in any business unless the [SSHD] has given prior consent in writing'.[68] Consent to work will be given or withheld on a case-by-case basis, dependent on the individual facts[69], but '[the] presumption is that a person excluded from the [Refugee] Convention under Article 1F should not be permitted to work or volunteer in any of the roles that require a standard or enhanced CRB [Criminal Records Bureau] check'.[70] Residence requirements may be imposed, again on a case-by-case basis, in order, for instance, to facilitate proposed removal or to ensure that the individual concerned does not 'seek to use his influence within the community to intimidate others or to exert undue influence'.[71] It is said that excluded individuals should 'generally be subject to a condition which prevents them from

---

66 Interim guidance on Article 1F: Restricted discretionary leave, para 1.4.
67 Interim guidance on Article 1F: Restricted discretionary leave, para 1.4.
68 Interim guidance on Article 1F: Restricted discretionary leave, para 3.1.
69 Interim guidance on Article 1F: Restricted discretionary leave, para 3.5.
70 Interim guidance on Article 1F: Restricted discretionary leave, para 3.6.
71 Interim guidance on Article 1F: Restricted discretionary leave, para 4.

undertaking a course of study, whether by attending in person or remote learning',[72] because this, it is claimed, 'underlines the temporary nature of the leave' and 'reduces pressure on public finances and, for privately funded courses, ensures that the person does not occupy course spaces that would otherwise be taken up by British Citizens or regular migrants'.[73]

19.51 It is also said in the Interim Guidance that:

> The policy imposes a short period of leave and appropriate conditions while removal options continue to be pursued. Cases excluded from refugee protection continue to be a priority for removal even where removal cannot currently be enforced. Such cases will remain under close review by UK Border Agency and will be removed at the earliest opportunity. These reviews will be conducted at six monthly intervals as a minimum, at the time when the Restricted DL expires.[74]

19.52 The rationale for the additional restrictions is said to be:

- the 'public interest in maintaining the integrity of immigration control';
- the need to 'ensure that UK Border Agency is able to monitor where an individual lives and works and/or prevent access to positions of influence or trust'; and
- the need to support 'the principle that those excluded from refugee status, including war criminals, cannot establish a new life in the UK and [to support] our broader international obligations'.[75]

19.53 The period of six months is chosen deliberately, because '[a] grant of leave for longer than six months permits a person to leave the UK and to be readmitted during the validity of their grant of leave'[76] and it 'would be at odds with the aim of this policy to permit such a person to re-enter the UK'.[77]

19.54 As to dependants, it is said:

> Where dependants have not made a protection claim in their own right, they should be granted leave in line with the main applicant. It is generally not appropriate to impose similar restrictions as apply

---

72 Interim guidance on Article 1F: Restricted discretionary leave, para 6.
73 Interim guidance on Article 1F: Restricted discretionary leave, para 6.1.
74 Interim guidance on Article 1F: Restricted discretionary leave, para 1.5.
75 Interim guidance on Article 1F: Restricted discretionary leave, para 1.6.
76 By virtue of the Immigration (Leave to Enter and Remain) Order 2000 SI No 1161 article 13.
77 Interim guidance on article 1F: Restricted discretionary leave, para 2.

to the main applicant. The restrictions applied should be at the minimum level necessary to maintain contact with the case.[78]

19.55 At the time of writing, it is too early to anticipate how this policy will be applied in practice to those excluded from article 1F and their dependants, or what form any further changes to the overall DL policy (currently withdrawn, see para 19.32 above) may take. It is sufficient at this point to note that the Interim Guidance clearly raises issues of whether the restrictions on individual rights are necessary or proportionate, whether they are justified by evidence and how they logically bear on the legitimate aim pursued. It may be particularly vulnerable to challenge if delays within the Home Office mean that the SSHD fails in her avowed aim of conducting an active review no less frequently than every six months.

Leave outside the Rules

19.56 The SSHD retains a general discretion to grant leave to remain outside the Immigration Rules and outside any policy.[79] That power was exercised before 1 April 2003 by a grant of exceptional leave to remain (ELR), a status granted to a wide range of people, including those granted leave to remain on the basis of their ECHR rights. Since the abolition of ELR from 1 April 2003, the SSHD operates that discretion, on a narrow basis, under a policy headed 'leave outside the Rules' (LOTR).[80]

19.57 Paragraph 2.1 of this policy suggests that one category of person to whom this would apply will be those benefitting from so-called 'concessions' outside the Immigration Rules, ie policies applying to particular groups of people, often small in number. These are very unlikely to be relevant to FNPs and most concessions have in any event been incorporated within the Immigration Rules.

19.58 Paragraph 2.2 of the policy says, more germanely to FNPs, that LOTR should be granted 'only for genuinely compassionate and circumstantial reasons, or where it is deemed absolutely necessary to allow someone to enter/remain in the UK, when there is no other available option'.

19.59 What 'circumstantial reasons' means is not clear; it may be intended to have the implication of 'taking into account all the circumstances'.

---

78 Interim guidance on article 1F: Restricted discretionary leave, para 10.
79 Compare *R (Acan) v IAT* [2004] EWHC 297 (Admin).
80 Immigration Directorate Instructions (IDIs) chapter 1 section 14.

(Earlier, the LOTR policy adopts the even more strangulated phrase 'reasons that are particularly compelling in circumstance'.[81]) Either way, it seems clear that the SSHD envisages only a limited number of cases qualifying in unusual compassionate circumstances where there is no breach of the ECHR.

19.60 LOTR may be granted 'for a specified period for the necessary duration of stay required'[82] – in other words, the duration of the leave granted will be fact-specific and will vary from case to case – although

> ... there may be a very small number of instances where it is considered appropriate to grant indefinite LOTR [ie ILR] because the particular compelling circumstances of the individual case are such that it is almost certain that there will be no change in circumstances within five years.[83]

Special Immigration Status

19.61 Part 10 of the Criminal Justice and Immigration Act (CJIA) 2008 (not yet in force, and with no commencement date appointed as of the time of writing) would create a special immigration status for 'designated persons', defined as 'foreign criminals' who are liable to deportation, but whose removal from the UK would be in breach of their convention rights.[84] Members of the family of such people can also be 'designated'.[85] 'Foreign criminal' for these purposes is defined as anyone who is not a British citizen[86] and who:

- falls within the conditions set out in NIAA 2002 s72(2)(a)–(b) or s72(3)(a)–(c), ie that they have been convicted in the UK of an offence and sentenced to imprisonment for at least two years[87] or convicted outside the UK and received a similar sentence, and could have been sentenced to at least two years' imprisonment if they had been convicted in the UK;[88]
- falls within the conditions set out in NIAA 2002 s72(4)(a) or (b), ie that they have been convicted of an offence set out in an order

---

81 IDIs chapter 1 section 14 para 1.2.
82 IDIs chapter 1 section 14 para 3.2.
83 IDIs chapter 1 section 14 para 3.3.
84 CJIA 2008 s130(2).
85 CJIA 2008 s130(3).
86 CJIA 2008 s131(1)(a).
87 Compare NIAA 2002 s72(2).
88 Compare NIAA 2002 s72(3). CJIA 2008 s131(2).

made by the SSHD or a similar offence committed abroad[89] and has been sentenced to a period of imprisonment;[90] or
- falls within article 1F of the Refugee Convention, ie is excluded from the Refugee Convention.[91]

19.62 As to those falling within the conditions in NIAA 2002 s72, it would under this new statutory provision not be a question of a presumption, rebuttable or otherwise, applying to the individual:[92] it will be sufficient that the factual conditions set out in the various subparas of section 72 apply. If they do, the person may be designated by the SSHD, with the consequences explained below. Nor is it clear whether it will be necessary that the person should present a danger to the community, since under NIAA 2002 s72 that is a presumption triggered by meeting the conditions in s72(2)(a)–(b) or in s72(3)(a)–(c), rather than being one of the conditions themselves.

19.63 Exceptions are made for those with the right of abode in the UK[93] or if the SSHD 'thinks that an effect of designation would breach' the Refugee Convention or the person's rights under the EU treaties.[94] (The effect of the latter provision would appear to be that refugees and those exercising EU Treaty rights in the UK cannot be designated[95].)

19.64 If brought into force, those granted special immigration status would exist in a kind of legal twilight, being treated as neither having leave to enter or remain,[96] nor as asylum-seekers or former asylum-seekers,[97] nor as in breach of immigration laws.[98] They could be subject to conditions restricting their residence or employment or requiring them to report to the police or immigration authorities.[99] They could be subject to electronic monitoring.[100] Failure, without reasonable excuse, to abide by any such conditions would be a

---

89 CJIA 2008 s131(3)(a); see para 12.89 for a discussion of the finding in *EN (Serbia) v Secretary of State for the Home Department* [2009] EWCA Civ 630, [2010] QB 633 that the order made under NIAA 2002 s72(4) was ultra vires.
90 CJIA 2008 s131(3)(b).
91 CJIA 2008 s131(4); see paras 12.7–12.74 for a discussion of exclusion.
92 CJIA 2008 s131(5).
93 CJIA 2008 s130(4).
94 CJIA 2008 s130(5).
95 Compare CJIA 2008 s136(1)(d), providing for designation to lapse if the person is notified of a right of residence under the EU treaties.
96 CJIA 2008 s132(1).
97 CJIA 2008 s132(2)(b).
98 CJIA 2008 s132(2)(c).
99 CJIA 2008 s133(1)–(2).
100 CJIA 2008 s133(3).

summary offence punishable by a fine or by imprisonment for up to 51 weeks.[101] Limited support would be provided to such people on the same basis as asylum-seekers.[102] There is no apparent limit on the length of time for which a person could be designated: designation ends only where the person is granted leave to enter or remain;[103] is notified of a right of residence under the EU Treaties;[104] leaves the UK;[105] or is made the subject of a deportation order under IA 1971 s5.[106] (In our view, given that Treaty rights derive directly from EU law and not from any decision on the part of the domestic authorities,[107] it is highly unlikely that a person who in fact had a right of residence under the EU treaties could lawfully be designated simply because the SSHD had not yet notified him or her of that right.)

19.65 These provisions, if brought into force, would be draconian. Measures designed for the relatively short-term support of asylum-seekers would be imposed on individuals indefinitely, and could also by extension be imposed on family members who were themselves innocent of any wrongdoing. It remains to be seen whether the imposition of such stringent conditions on designated persons, especially ones who were not responsible for the conduct leading to the designation in the first place, would be considered proportionate or otherwise lawful by the courts.

Revocation of indefinite leave to remain where individual cannot be deported

19.66 NIAA 2002 s76 provides the SSHD with the power to revoke a person's ILR in certain circumstances, even if that person cannot be removed. Section 76(1) provides for revocation of ILR 'if the person (a) is liable to deportation but (b) cannot be deported for legal reasons'.

19.67 The phrase 'for legal reasons' is not defined, but apparently means 'because it would be unlawful to do so', ie principally on the basis

---

101 CJIA 2008 s133(5)–(6).
102 CJIA 2008 ss134–135; see Sue Willman and Stephen Knafler QC, *Support for asylum-seekers and other migrants*, LAG, 2009.
103 CJIA 2008 s136(1)(a).
104 CJIA 2008 s136(1)(b).
105 CJIA 2008 s136(1)(c).
106 CJIA 2008 s136(1)(d).
107 See, for example, the decision of the ECJ in *Germany v Sagulo* [1977] ECR 1495; [1977] 2 CMLR 585; (1977) *Times* 3 August.

that it would be in breach of the UK's obligations under the Refugee Convention and/or the ECHR. A person is 'liable to deportation' in the circumstances described in the IA 1971 s3(5) and (6), ie if the SSHD 'deems his deportation to be conducive to the public good', if he belongs to the family of a person who has been ordered to be deported, or if 'he is convicted of an offence for which he is punishable with imprisonment and on his conviction is recommended for deportation by a court'.[108]

19.68 Those whose ILR is revoked on this basis are likely to be granted DL unless they are refugees, in which case they would appear still to be eligible for the longer grant of leave consequent on refugee status.[109] The SSHD's API on Revocation of ILR suggests that:

> An example of when such action might be appropriate would be where we have pursued action under section 72 of the NIA Act 2002 because a refugee has committed a particularly serious crime, and is considered a danger to the community, but deportation has been prevented by the ECHR. In such a circumstance it would normally be appropriate to revoke the Indefinite Leave under section 76(1) and replace it with Temporary Admission/Release or with short periods of Discretionary Leave, until removal becomes possible.
> In some circumstances the person should not be granted further leave, for example where there is a realistic prospect of removal in the very near future, or where the applicant will not leave as opposed to cannot leave eg inability to document because the subject is not prepared to co-operate. For those whose indefinite leave is not replaced with leave there will be no entitlement to public funds, unless failure to provide support would constitute a breach of the ECHR.

19.69 The ECtHR has held in a number of cases[110] that ECHR article 8 requires some form of residence permit to be granted to those lawfully in the territory of a state, and we suggest that temporary admission cannot be regarded as constituting a residence permit. It remains to be seen whether the UK's obligations under ECHR article 8 can be reconciled with leaving a person for long periods on temporary admission who cannot lawfully be expelled in circumstances where ILR has been revoked, or where special immigration status is conferred (if the statutory provisions for special immigration status are brought into force).

---

108 NIAA 2002 s76(4), applying IA 1971 s3(5) and (6).
109 Qualification Directive article 24, and compare article 21.
110 For example, *Mendizabal v France*, App No 51431/99 (judgment available in French only); *Sisojeva v Latvia* (2007) 45 EHRR 33.

19.70 NIAA 2002 s76(2), which is of less direct interest to FNPs, provides for ILR to be revoked where it was obtained by deception and the person, although 'liable to removal because of the deception', 'cannot be removed for legal or practical reasons'. The API says that examples of 'practical reasons' would include 'where there is no physical means of return or where there are problems with documenting the individual'.[111]

19.71 NIAA 2002 s76(3), which deals with revocation of ILR on grounds relating to cessation of refugee status, has already been examined at paras 12.130–12.133.

19.72 Revocation in all these circumstances remains at the discretion of the SSHD. The API on Revocation of Indefinite Leave offers very limited guidance on the circumstances in which it would not be appropriate to revoke ILR, stating that '[c]ompelling circumstances may exist where as a matter of policy a person's indefinite leave should not be revoked'.[112] The only concrete example given is 'Length of time spent in the UK', but this is said to be irrelevant in section 76(1) cases (legal bar to removal of person liable to be deported), because 'length of time spent in the UK will not constitute a bar to revocation of IL[R] because length of time spent in the UK will have been taken into account in deciding whether the person should be deported'.[113] This appears to us to be incorrect. Section 76(1) comes into play when a person becomes 'liable to be deported' under IA 1971 s3, not when a decision has been made to deport them under IA 1971 s5. Determining liability to deportation does not involve taking account of length of residence: it is simply a question of whether the preconditions in IA 1971 s3(5) and (6), set out above, are met. We suggest that this aspect of the policy appears to leave the SSHD, unlawfully, incapable of factoring in length of residence when deciding how to exercise her discretion in a NIAA 2002 s76(1) revocation case.

19.73 As to section 76(2) cases (ILR obtained by deception), the API suggests that residence in the UK for 14 years or more 'may constitute a compelling reason' for not revoking ILR, 'in line with the Rules on

---

111 API on Revocation of Indefinite Leave, section 76 of the Nationality, Immigration and Asylum Act 2002, heading 'How to deal with a case where s76 applies'.
112 API on Revocation of Indefinite Leave, heading 'Compelling Reasons for not Revoking IL [sic]'.
113 API on Revocation of Indefinite Leave.

19.74 ILR may be regained once revoked, 'based on the policy applicable to the limited leave granted':[116] in other words, if DL has been granted, for instance, then the provisions for the grant of ILR to a person with DL (explained above) will apply.

Long Residence'.[114] while in section 76(3) cases, five years 'will normally constitute a compelling reason'.[115]

19.75 There is a right of appeal to the Immigration and Asylum Chamber of the First-tier Tribunal (FTT-IAC) against revocation of ILR.[117] Appeals to the FTT-IAC are discussed in chapter 21.

Power to deprive a dual national of citizenship

19.76 Lastly in this chapter, we draw attention to a provision which would make a person who was not originally an FNP into an FNP. This is section 40 of the British Nationality Act 1981 (as amended by Immigration Asylum and Nationality Act 2006 s56), which permits the SSHD to deprive a person of British citizenship (or other citizenship status, such as British overseas territory citizenship), if satisfied 'that deprivation is conducive to the public good'.

19.77 This power may not be invoked if the result would be to make the individual stateless:[118] in other words, it applies only to dual nationals. It applies even to those who were entitled to British citizenship, as of right, at birth. (The concept that the government might be entitled to deprive such a person of their citizenship reminds us of Berthold Brecht's suggestion that the East German Government, having lost confidence in its citizens, might find it easier to dissolve the people and choose another.)

19.78 There is also a power to deprive a person of citizenship (regardless of whether it would make them stateless) if they acquired citizenship by way of naturalisation or registration, and that application was materially tainted by fraud, false representation or concealment of a material fact.[119]

---

114 Immigration Rules para 276B(i)(b).
115 API on Revocation of Indefinite Leave, section 76 of the Nationality, Immigration and Asylum Act 2002, heading 'Compelling Reasons for not Revoking IL [sic]'.
116 API on Revocation of Indefinite Leave, heading 'Terms and conditions of stay'.
117 NIAA 2002 s82(2)(f).
118 IANA 2006 s40(4).
119 IANA 2006 s40(3).

SECTION F

Representations, evidence and appeals

Chapter 20: Representations, evidence and preparing appeals 381

Chapter 21: Appeals in the IAC 399

Chapter 22: Restriction and loss of appeal rights in deportation and revocation cases 437

Chapter 23: The Special Immigration Appeals Commission and its procedures 445

Introduction to representations, evidence and appeals

Organisation of this section

In chapter 20, we set out practical guidance on making claims and preparing appeals in cases concerning deportation and the revocation of deportation orders. Procedures governing appeals in the Immigration and Asylum Chamber of the First-tier or Upper Tribunals (collectively referred to here as the IAC) are then summarised in chapter 21. We then go on to examine in chapter 22 the circumstances in which certificates can be imposed which restrict or altogether curtail appeal rights. Finally, in chapter 23, we provide an overview of appeals in the Special Immigration Appeals Commission (SIAC).

We do not discuss public funding in this book. At the time of writing, sweeping legal aid cuts are proposed and it is too early to anticipate future funding arrangements with any precision.

Who can provide immigration services

Only a person falling within one or more of the following categories may offer immigration advice and representation:

- those registered with the Office of the Immigration Services Commissioner (OISC);[1]
- members of the Law Society (of England, Northern Ireland or Scotland), the General Council of the Bar, the Institute of Legal Executives or the Faculty of Advocates;[2]
- those authorised to provide immigration services by the Law Society, the Institute of Legal Executives or the General Council of the Bar;[3]
- those who have an equivalent qualification in another European Economic Area (EEA) state to any of the above;[4]
- those permitted to provide equivalent advice or services in another EEA state;[5] and

---

1 Immigration and Asylum Act (IAA) 1999 s84(2)(a). For a list of registered providers and a list of specifically prohibited providers of immigration services, see the OISC website: www.oisc.gov.uk.
2 IAA 1999 ss84(2)(b) and 85.
3 IAA 1999 ss84(2)(ba) and 86Q.
4 IAA 1999 s84(2)(c).
5 IAA 1999 s84(2)(d).

- those acting on behalf of and under supervision of a person falling within any of the above categories.[6]

Thus (although they may not receive public funding for it) non-immigration Law Society member solicitors, and caseworkers supervised by them, are not precluded from providing advice and representation on immigration matters to foreign national prisoners and former prisoners (FNPs). However, immigration law is a specialised and fast-changing area and we suggest that, wherever possible, specialist immigration practitioners should undertake representations against deportation or for revocation of a deportation order, any ensuing appeals and judicial reviews of certificates that curtail or restrict appeal rights.

All solicitors and caseworkers doing publicly funded immigration and asylum work beyond a probationary period must be accredited under the Immigration and Asylum Accreditation Scheme. Accreditation is encouraged but not mandatory for solicitors and caseworkers doing privately-funded immigration and asylum work. Accreditation is subdivided into three levels of escalating complexity. Accreditation to Level 2 is required to make representations about deportation to the UK Border Agency. Accreditation to Level 3 is required to act in a bail application or appeal in the First-tier Tribunal, Immigration and Asylum Chamber (FTT-IAC), or to undertake specialist asylum casework.

---

6 IAA 1999 s84(2)(e).

CHAPTER 20

Representations, evidence and preparing appeals

20.1　Introduction

20.2　Making representations against deportation

20.5　Special considerations in 'automatic' deportation cases under the UKBA 2007

　　　Box 20.1: Checklist for representations against deportation

20.11　Evidence

　　　Box 20.2: Evidence checklist in claims relying on the Citizens Directive and EEA Regs 2006

　　　Box 20.3: Materials checklist in 'intentional harm' cases: asylum, ECHR article 3 and Qualification Directive article 15(c) claims

　　　Box 20.4: Evidence checklist in ECHR article 8 claims

20.12　Information and evidence on past offending and future offending risk

　　　Box 20.5: Useful sources of information and evidence on past offending and future offending risk

20.14　Instructing experts

　　　Box 20.6: Guidance from the Senior President of the Tribunals on instructing experts

20.16　Preparing a trial bundle for an appeal in the IAC

　　　Box 20.7: Guidance from the Senior President of the Tribunals on preparing bundles

Introduction

20.1 This chapter focuses on the practical aspects of bringing claims and preparing appeals in the deportation context. We first discuss making representations against deportation. We then provide non-exhaustive checklists of types of evidence that may be relevant in the most common types of claim in deportation cases, with a particular emphasis on how to locate documents relating to past offending and future offending risk for foreign national prisoners and former prisoners (FNPs). Finally, we reproduce guidance given by the Senior President of the Tribunals, Carnwath LJ, on the instruction of experts and the preparation of trial bundles.

Making representations against deportation

20.2 Those being considered for deportation should be invited to make representations, by way of a form or a letter from the Home Office as to why they should not be deported. In 'automatic' deportation cases under the UK Borders Act (UKBA) 2007 cases, FNPs should be invited to state whether they fall within any of the exceptions to 'automatic' deportation.[1]

20.3 However, Home Office practice on seeking representations from proposed deportees remains erratic. The effect is to place the onus on potential deportees (who may be unrepresented and against whom an 'automatic' deportation order may be made at any time[2]) to anticipate the possibility of deportation and the timing of the decision, and to raise any reasons why they fall within the exceptions to 'automatic' deportation[3] and should not be deported under the Immigration Act (IA) 1971 either.[4]

20.4 Where no representations have been invited by the UK Border Agency, and it appears likely that the FNP will be the subject of deportation action (for example, because he or she received a sentence of imprisonment of 12 months or more[5]) and the FNP wishes to contest

---

1 Under UKBA 2007 s33. The UK Border Agency should normally in automatic deportation cases invite representations on form ICD 0350AD.
2 UKBA 2007 s34(1).
3 The exceptions are set out at UKBA 2007 s33.
4 See the discussion at para 3.13 and chapter 3, note 9.
5 The catalyst for the making of an 'automatic' deportation order under UKBA 2007 s32 unless one of the exceptions under s33 applies.

deportation, we suggest that FNPs and their legal representatives should, where possible, take the initiative and make representations against deportation. We suggest that such representations should, where possible, be made *at least* three months before the completion of the criminal custodial term. This is in order to lessen the risks of a lengthy period of administrative detention after completion of the criminal custodial term while the Home Office belatedly considers whether to deport[6] and the risks of a deportation decision being taken without prior consideration of representations.

Special considerations in 'automatic' deportation cases under the UKBA 2007

20.5 In the context of 'automatic' deportation, it is particularly important that any asylum or European Convention on Human Rights (ECHR) claim should be put in detail and that the collection and submission of evidence should occur at an early stage. The merits of such a claim may determine whether or not the individual has an in-country right of appeal to the Immigration and Asylum Chamber of the First-Tier Tribunal (FTT-IAC). See paras 5.43–5.46 and 21.17–21.24 in which we discuss in-country rights of appeal in 'automatic' deportation cases.

20.6 For the purposes of founding in-country appeal rights, an asylum or ECHR claim should be made to the Secretary of State for the Home Department (SSHD).[7]

20.7 FNPs may receive, without prior warning, notice that an 'automatic' deportation order has been made under UKBA 2007, together with out-of-country appeal forms. If the FNP has a viable claim which gives rise to an in-country right of appeal, namely an asylum, ECHR or (where the FNP is an EEA national or the family member of an EEA national) an EU law claim,[8] and has yet to make it, we suggest that the appropriate course of action is to:

---

6 UKBA 2007 s36(1)(a) permits administrative detention while the SSHD 'considers' whether the criteria for 'automatic' deportation are met.
7 Nationality, Immigration and Asylum Act (NIAA) 2002 s113 defines asylum and human rights claims as 'a claim made by a person to the Secretary of State at a place designated by the Secretary of State ...'. That part of the definition of 'asylum claim' and 'human rights claim' will fall away if and when Immigration Asylum and Nationality Act 2006 s12(1) and (2) come into force, amending NIAA 2002 s113. However, see *R (Jisha) v Secretary of State for the Home Department* [2010] EWHC 2043 (Admin) finding that a 'human rights claim' had been made in grounds of appeal to the predecessor tribunal, the Asylum and Immigration Tribunal (AIT).
8 NIAA 2002 s92(4).

a) make the claim immediately to the SSHD in writing;
b) invite the SSHD to revoke the 'automatic' deportation order[9] on the basis that the FNP falls within an exception to 'automatic' deportation;[10] and
c) lodge an in-country appeal in the FTT-IAC (appeal forms can be downloaded from the Ministry of Justice website[11]) enclosing copies of the claim.

20.8 The consequence will usually be that the SSHD will revoke the 'automatic' deportation order[12] for the purposes of considering the claims, which will mean that there is no appeal pending before the FTT-IAC. If the SSHD refuses the new claims, she may then issue a further 'automatic' deportation order (and may make a 'clearly unfounded' certificate on the asylum and ECHR claims).

20.9 If a 'clearly unfounded' certificate is imposed under NIAA 2002 s94, there will be no in-country right of appeal in reliance on the asylum or ECHR claim; if a 'one-stop' certificate has been imposed under NIAA 2002 s96, there will be no right of appeal at all in reliance on those claims. A challenge to such certificates may only be brought by judicial review.[13]

20.10 In summary, those potentially liable to 'automatic' deportation under UKBA 2007 face serious prejudice if inadequate, late, or no representations are made. This is not only because, as we have seen above, these representations may determine whether there is an in-country right of appeal. It is also because where representations are submitted late so that the SSHD makes an 'automatic' deportation order only to revoke (and then possibly reinstate it) or where a certificate is imposed which is then challenged in judicial review, these delays (and any delays while bringing a judicial review against a certificate) may prolong any period of administrative detention after sentence completion.

9 Under UKBA 2007 s32(6)(a).
10 Under UKBA 2007 s33.
11 See: www.justice.gov.uk/global/forms/hmcts/tribunals/immigration-and-asylum/index.htm.
12 Under UKBA 2007 s34(4).
13 See discussion in chapter 22.

Box 20.1: Checklist for representations against deportation

	Type of case	Consider
1)	All deportation cases	Is the individual exempt from deportation under the IA 1971 provisions[14] (eg British citizenship or a right of abode,[15] long-term residence of a Commonwealth citizen[16])? Would deportation breach the individual's rights under the ECHR, the Refugee Convention, EU law or the Council of Europe Convention against Trafficking?
2)	'Discretionary' deportation cases under the IA 1971	Is this a case in which the discretion should not be exercised to deport? For example, is there anything that renders this case exceptional under Immigration Rules para 364 or any Home Office policy which precludes or militates against deportation?[17] Would deportation breach Borders, Citizenship and Immigration Act (BCIA) 2009 s55?[18]
3)	'Automatic' deportation cases under the UKBA 2007	Does the individual fall within the other numbered exceptions to 'automatic' deportation under UKBA 2007, namely that the person was under 18 at the time of conviction,[19] is subject to extradition proceedings,[20] or is subject to specified orders or directions under mental health legislation?[21]

14 These exemptions also apply to 'automatic' deportation under the UKBA 2007, see paras 5.23–5.24
15 IA 1971 s3(5) and (6).
16 IA 1971 s7.
17 See chapter 46 concerning Immigration Rules HC395 paragraph 364 and Home Office policies relevant to deportation.
18 BCIA 2009 s55 has been discussed at paras 4.7–4.33. In a strange lacuna, it is not an exception to 'automatic' deportation under the UKBA 2007 that deportation would breach the SSHD's duties under BCIA 2009 s55. However, in many if not all cases where BCIA 2009 s55 arises, deportation will also engage ECHR article 8 (breach of which is a statutory exception to 'automatic' deportation under UKBA 2007 s33(2)(a)). We therefore suggest that BCIA 2009 s55 points can be made as part of representations under ECHR article 8.
19 UKBA 2007 s33(3).
20 UKBA 2007 s33(5).
21 UKBA 2007 s33(6).

Evidence

20.11 Below, we provide non-exhaustive checklists of evidence that may be appropriate in the most common types of cases:
   a) when making representations to the SSHD against deportation or for revocation; and
   b) when bringing an appeal in the Immigration and Asylum Chamber of the First-tier or Upper Tribunal (IAC) against a deportation decision or against a refusal to revoke a deportation order.

Box 20.2: Evidence checklist in claims relying on the Citizens Directive[22] and EEA Regs 2006

	Type of case	Consider whether the following are available
1)	All	Evidence relating to the risk of further offending and any diminution of that risk since the index offence. See box 20.5 below.
2)	Where the proposed deportee is an EEA national	• A copy of any registration certificate or document certifying permanent residence for the proposed deportee; • in the absence of such documentation, evidence of his or her EEA nationality (passport or identity document copy).
3)	Where the proposed deportee is an EEA national asserting a right of permanent residence in the absence of a document certifying this, or where asserting residence for ten or more years	• Evidence of EEA nationality; • evidence of the length and continuity of residence; • evidence of exercise of any rights of freedom of movement.

---

22 Directive 2004/38/EC on the right of citizens of the European Union and their family members to move and reside freely within the territory of the EU.

	Type of case	Consider whether the following are available
4)	Where the proposed deportee is the 'family member' of an EEA national[23]	A copy of any EEA family permit, residence card or permanent residence card for the proposed deportee. In the absence of such documentation: • evidence of the principal's EEA nationality (see (2) above); • evidence of principal's exercise of rights of freedom of movement; • evidence of the family tie (eg marriage, civil partnership, birth certificates; witness evidence); • evidence of duration and continuity of residence together and in the UK; • evidence of any other EU law rights exercised.
5)	Where the proposed deportee is the 'extended family member' of an EEA national[24]	Additionally to 1) and 4) above: • where the individual relies on EEA Regs 2006 reg 8(2), evidence that the proposed deportee was the dependant or member of the of the EEA national's household in the country from which he or she has come (eg witness evidence, photos, any bank statements or other documentary evidence); • where the individual relies on EEA Regs 2006 reg 8(3) evidence, preferably from a medical expert, of the serious health problem of the proposed deportee, and evidence (from an expert and/or witness evidence) as to why this strictly requires the personal care of the EEA national principal; • where the individual relies on EEA Regs 2006 reg 8(5), evidence of the closeness and duration of the relationship with the EEA national principal (eg witness evidence, any evidence of cohabitation such as bills and tenancy agreements, electronically dated photos and videos).

---

23 As defined in Citizens Directive article 2(2) and Immigration (European Economic Area) Regulations (EEA Regs) 2006 SI No 1003 reg 7(1)(a).
24 As defined in Citizens Directive article 3(2) and EEA Regs 2006 reg 8.

Box 20.3: Materials checklist in 'intentional harm' cases: asylum, ECHR article 3 and Qualification Directive[25] article 15(c) claims

	Type of case	Consider whether the following are available
1)	All	Reported cases on a similar point from the Immigration and Asylum Chamber of the Upper Tribunal (UT-IAC), or from the predecessor tribunals (the Asylum and Immigration Tribunal (AIT) or, more rarely, the Immigration Appeal Tribunal (IAT)), and in particular country guidance cases marked 'CG' may be critical. Tribunal country guidance cases, unless superseded by other country guidance or binding authority and unless displaced by subsequent evidence are treated as authoritative by the IAC on the matters with which they deal.[26] Reported tribunal cases and country guidance cases are available on the Ministry of Justice (MoJ) website.[27]
		Generic country background evidence concerning conditions and risk factors in the country of proposed expulsion. Useful sources include the UK Border Agency's own Country of Origin Information Service;[28] any relevant US State Department reports; any relevant reports by respected human rights organisations such as Amnesty International and Human Rights Watch; and any relevant UN High Commissioner for Refugees (UNHCR) position papers.[29]

25 Council Directive 2004/83/EC on minimum standards for the qualification and status of third country nationals or stateless persons as refugees or as persons who otherwise need international protection and the content of the protection granted ('Qualification Directive').
26 Immigration and Asylum Chambers of the First-Tier Tribunal and the Upper Tribunal Practice Direction 10 February 2010 para 12.2.
27 See www.judiciary.gov.uk/media/tribunal-decisions/immigration-asylum-chamber.
28 See: www.ukba.homeoffice.gov.uk/policyandlaw/guidance/coi/.
29 Also relevant are the Operational Guidance Notes issued by the UK Border Agency to its own caseworkers. These indicate how the UK Border Agency will generally approach specific types of cases from the countries from which claimants most frequently originate. These are not always reliable in their analysis of the law and do not bind independent tribunals. Available on http://www.bia.homeoffice.gov.uk/sitecontent/documents/policyandlaw/countryspecificasylumpolicyogns/.

	Type of case	Consider whether the following are available
2)	Wherever possible	Detailed witness statement from the applicant explaining past history and the reasons for claiming to be at risk in the future.
3)	Where the credibility of the account of past events is, or is likely to be, in dispute	Is there evidence which can corroborate the individual's account of past events: • expert scarring or psychiatric evidence? • documentary evidence? • witness evidence from others? In addition to 1) above: • is there further evidence which tends to show that the individual's account is plausible in the country context? • are there news reports or indications, for example from human rights and monitoring organisations, of broadly similar incidents? • is it possible to obtain a country expert's report to comment on this?
4)	Where risk on return is disputed by the Home Office even in the event that the account of past events is accepted as credible (most cases)	In addition to 1) above: • where feasible to obtain, the evidence of a country expert may be important in assessing the risks to an individual appellant, including any issues of sufficiency of protection or an internal flight alternative.
5)	In asylum cases where article 33(2) and the Refugee Convention and NIAA 2002 s72[30] may apply	• Are there mitigating circumstances in the offence which may demonstrate that the individual has not committed a particularly crime? If so, the judge's sentencing remarks (and of course any judgment of the Court of Appeal on appeal) and witness evidence are likely to be needed on this point. • Is there evidence relating to the risk of further offending and any diminution of that risk since the index offence? See box 20.5 below.

---

30 See paras 12.78–12.96 of this book.

Box 20.4: Evidence checklist in ECHR article 8 claims

	Type of case	Consider whether the following are available
1)	All ECHR article 8 cases	Evidence relating to the risk of further offending and any diminution of that risk since the index offence. See box 20.5 below.
2)	Where an FNP has resided in the UK for a long period	Home Office documents or passport copies showing length of residence and immigration status. In the absence of such documents, and where police records do not themselves establish length of stay in the UK: • witness statements; • bank statements; • evidence from the Driver and Vehicle Licensing Agency (DVLA), HM Revenue and Customs, landlords, employers and GPs; • educational certificates; • evidence of any past involvement with social services.
3)	In all family life cases	• Evidence of the immigration status or, where appropriate, citizenship, of the family members; • evidence of the existence and nature of the family ties, including any special dependency. For example, witness evidence, photographs and videos, birth and marriage certificates, proof of any cohabitation and evidence of any custodial arrangements or custody proceedings for separated children; • evidence of any relevant impact of deportation on other family members.
4)	In a family life case where there has been a long period of imprisonment during which family contact has been maintained	Evidence of maintained family contact during imprisonment, including witness statements, copies of cards and letters, copies of extracts from the prison visitors' log, copies of prison phone records showing calls made by the applicant to his or her home.

	Type of case	Consider whether the following are available
5)	In family life cases involving children	• Evidence relating to the best interests of the child, including witness evidence where appropriate and, where possible, evidence from an independent social worker; evidence from teachers and any involved social services professional of the impact on children of accompanying the deportee or being separated from the deportee.
6)	In a family life case where it is claimed that family life cannot reasonably be expected to be enjoyed elsewhere	• Evidence of any reasons why settled family members cannot reasonably be expected to relocate. For example, evidence of the professional, family and educational ties of the proposed deportee's close family members (including evidence of any children in full-time education); • evidence of the existence of any separated children of the proposed deportee and his or her partner and their custodial arrangements or any custody proceedings; • evidence of refugee status or humanitarian protection status of close family members; and • evidence of any serious medical or special educational or other needs of close family members which could not be met elsewhere.
7)	In family life cases where there is any special medical or emotional vulnerability or need on the part of a family member	• Evidence of any vulnerability or need (from GP/teachers/social services and/or an expert); • evidence, where possible from an expert source, of the impact on the family member of either accompanying or being separated from the deportee.
8)	ECHR article 8 case where the FNP has any particular vulnerability	Evidence, where possible from an expert, of any vulnerability on the FNPs part, and of the impact of deportation.
9)	ECHR article 8 private life cases	Evidence of any social, professional and educational ties to the UK, including witness evidence and documentary evidence of employment, tax payments, educational achievements.

Information and evidence on past offending and future offending risk

20.12 Note that where an appeal or bail application is pending, the IAC may direct (or be invited to direct) that details of an FNP's criminal record and risk assessments by the probation authorities be obtained by the SSHD.[31]

20.13 The National Offender Management Service (NOMS), which incorporates both the prison and probation services,[32] is usually the best source of information about an FNP's past offending history and risk assessments. NOMS is required to retain core inmate files for prisoners who were sentenced to three months or more for six years from their date of discharge or the date of last action on the files, whichever is the latest (and for prisoners serving life sentences, until after their deaths).[33] Many of the documents discussed below may be sought through a written request by the FNP or those acting for the FNP to the current or most recent prison establishment, the sentencing court, or the FNP's Offender Manager (OM) at NOMS. In addition, and more likely to yield documents though this will usually take at least 40 days, a formal Subject Access request may be made under the Data Protection Act (DPA) 1998 to NOMS.[34] We discuss requests for personal data under the DPA 1998 at paras 42.12–42.14.

Box 20.5: Useful sources of information and evidence on past offending and future offending risk

	Type of case	Consider whether the following are available.
1)	All cases where future offending risk is in issue	An expert report may, where feasible, be commissioned from an independent forensic psychologist or psychiatrist for the purposes of the claim or appeal.

---

31 This is specifically recognised in Presidential Guidance Note No 1 of 2011, Bail Guidance for Immigration Judges para 12.
32 See discussion at para 24.3.
33 PSO 9025, archiving and retention policy, Annex E sets out document retention periods.
34 PSO 9020 sets out NOMS policies on responding to requests under the Data Protection Act 1998.

Representations, evidence and preparing appeals 393

	Type of case	Consider whether the following are available.
2)	Wherever there has been a conviction	• Sentencing judge's remarks; • certificate of conviction; and • list of previous convictions from Police National Computer (PNC). Where the UK Border Agency has not already obtained and supplied copies (see para 20.12 above), the three documents listed above may sometimes be obtained from NOMS, or, often with difficulty, from the sentencing court or previous criminal solicitors. Any judgment of the Court of Appeal where there was an appeal against conviction or sentence.
3)	Where a sentence of imprisonment was imposed	Copies of pre-sentencing reports may be obtained from NOMS. OASys (Offender Assessment System) assessments should be available for those sentenced to periods of imprisonment of 12 months or more.[35] FNPs are entitled to see their own OASys assessments save in exceptional circumstances and these may be obtained from NOMS. Any prison probation or prison psychological reports. FNPs are entitled to see their own (save that obtaining psychological reports may be subject to the approval of a medical practitioner) and these may be obtained from NOMS. Evidence of any offending behaviour courses completed in prison, and any comments from trainers on the FNPs progress may, sometimes, be obtained from the most recent prison establishment or NOMS if the FNP has not retained them. Evidence of any past adjudications or lack of them may be obtained from the most recent prison establishment or NOMS.

35 See discussion of these reports at paras 24.14–24.21. OASys assessments will be conducted for all young offenders sentenced to 4 weeks or more; automatic conditional release offenders (12 months and over but less than 4 years); discretionary release offenders (4 years or more); all offenders sentenced under the Criminal Justice Act 2003 to 12 months or more; all life sentence offenders; all recalled offenders if their time in custody after recall would be one year or more.

	Type of case	Consider whether the following are available.
4)	Where there has been Parole Board involvement in a decision over the FNP's release from prison[37]	The parole dossier and copies of written reasons for parole decisions should be available. A parole dossier should include a summary of the index offence; a list of previous convictions; an OASys report; information on the prisoner's progress in custody;[38] any medical or psychological reports undertaken for the parole decision; parole assessment reports from the Home Probation Officer and from the Seconded Probation Officer; and written reasons for previous parole decisions. A copy of the parole dossier and of the latest parole decision can be obtained by request, whether informally or by a Subject Access request under the Data Protection Act 1998 from the prison where the FNP is currently or was last held. It can also be obtained directly from NOMS. It can also be obtained by Subject Access request from the Parole Board, though this retains parole dossiers only for a limited period.[39]
5)	Where an FNP is still in prison or on licence	Evidence from the FNP's Offender Manager (OM) at NOMS. Wherever there has been an FTT-IAC bail application, OMs should complete a pro forma setting out any risk assessments on the FNP, including any OASys score; this risk assessment is disclosable to the FNP and his or her legal representatives. If no such pro forma has been completed, it is at the discretion of individual OMs whether to respond to a request for information from the FNP or his or her legal representatives for an IAC appeal.[40]

36 See para 26.11 for which cases are dealt with by the Parole Board.
37 Including details of any adjudications, details of any courses completed and reports from the prison wing manager, personal officer and other prison staff.
38 The Parole Board retains dossiers in life and extended sentence cases for nine months only. In other cases, dossiers are returned to the Ministry of Justice on completion of the review unless any further action is being undertaken by the Parole Board following the review: Parole Board for England and Wales Freedom of Information Publication Scheme, which can be found at http://www.justice.gov.uk/downloads/global/foi-requests/parole-board-foi-publication-scheme.pdf.
39 Probation Circular PC 32/2007. This can now be found annexed to the Bail Guidance for Immigration Judges, Presidential Guidance Note No.1 of 2011, at http://www.justice.gov.uk/downloads/guidance/courts-and-tribunals/tribunals/immigration-and-asylum/lower/bail-guidance-immigration-judges.pdf.

	Type of case	Consider whether the following are available.
6)	Where the FNP has spent a period of liberty since the index offence	Evidence of the FNP's conduct during the period spent at liberty (eg witness statements; letter from the FNP's OM; evidence of any offending behaviour courses, addiction treatment or counselling undertaken while at liberty).

Instructing experts

20.14 Below, we reproduce extracts from guidance issued by Carnwath LJ, the Senior President of the Tribunals, on expert evidence.[40] The guidance was issued in the context of appeals to the IAC but is applicable with minor modification to expert evidence in other contexts. Those instructing an expert may find it useful to forward this guidance to the expert.

Box 20.6: Guidance from the Senior President of the Tribunals on instructing experts

> A party who instructs an expert must provide clear and precise instructions to the expert, together with all relevant information concerning the nature of the appellant's case, including the appellant's immigration history, the reasons why the appellant's claim or application has been refused by the respondent and copies of any relevant previous reports prepared in respect of the appellant.
> ...
> It is the duty of an expert to help the Tribunal on matters within the expert's own expertise. This duty is paramount and overrides any obligation to the person from whom the expert has received instructions or by whom the expert is paid.
> ...
> Expert evidence should be the independent product of the expert uninfluenced by the pressures of litigation.
> ...
> An expert should assist the Tribunal by providing objective, unbiased opinion on matters within his or her expertise, and should not assume the role of an advocate.
> ...
> An expert should consider all material facts, including those which might detract from his or her opinion.
> ...

40 Immigration and Asylum Chambers of the First-Tier Tribunal and the Upper Tribunal, Practice Direction 10 February 2010 para 10.

An expert should make it clear:–
(a) when a question or issue falls outside his or her expertise; and
(b) when the expert is not able to reach a definite opinion, for example because of insufficient information.

If, after producing a report, an expert changes his or her view on any material matter, that change of view should be communicated to the parties without delay, and when appropriate to the Tribunal.

...

An expert's report should be addressed to the Tribunal and not to the party from whom the expert has received instructions.

...

An expert's report must:–
(a) give details of the expert's qualifications;
(b) give details of any literature or other material which the expert has relied on in making the report;
(c) contain a statement setting out the substance of all facts and instructions given to the expert which are material to the opinions expressed in the report or upon which those opinions are based;
(d) make clear which of the facts stated in the report are within the expert's own knowledge;
(e) say who carried out any examination, measurement or other procedure which the expert has used for the report, give the qualifications of that person, and say whether or not the procedure has been carried out under the expert's supervision;
(f) where there is a range of opinion on the matters dealt with in the report:
  (i) summarise the range of opinion, so far as reasonably practicable, and
  (ii) give reasons for the expert's own opinion;
(g) contain a summary of the conclusions reached;
(h) if the expert is not able to give an opinion without qualification, state the qualification; and
(j) contain a statement that the expert understands his or her duty to the Tribunal, and has complied and will continue to comply with that duty.

...

An expert's report must be verified by a Statement of Truth as well as containing the statements required in paragraph 10.9(h) and (j).

...

The form of the Statement of Truth is as follows:–
'I confirm that insofar as the facts stated in my report are within my own knowledge I have made clear which they are and I believe them to be true, and that the opinions I have expressed represent my true and complete professional opinion'.

20.15 Instructions to experts are not privileged, although there can be no cross-examination of an expert in the IAC on the content of the instructions without the IAC's permission.[41]

---

41 Immigration and Asylum Chamber of the First-Tier Tribunal and the Upper Tribunal Practice Direction, 10 February 2010, para 10.12.

Preparing a trial bundle for an appeal in the IAC

20.16 Below, we reproduce extracts from guidance issued by Carnwath LJ, the Senior President of the Tribunals, on the preparation of trial bundles.[42] This is applicable to the IAC only: distinct guidance is given in the Civil Procedure Rules[43] for evidence in judicial review proceedings and appeals to the Court of Appeal.

Box 20.7: Guidance from the Senior President of the Tribunals on preparing bundles

> The best practice for the preparation of bundles is as follows:–
> (a) all documents must be relevant, be presented in logical order and be legible;
> (b) where the document is not in the English language, a typed translation of the document signed by the translator, and certifying that the translation is accurate, must be inserted in the bundle next to the copy of the original document, together with details of the identity and qualifications of the translator;
> (c) if it is necessary to include a lengthy document, that part of the document on which reliance is placed should, unless the passages are outlined in any skeleton argument, be highlighted or clearly identified by reference to page and/or paragraph number;
> (d) bundles submitted must have an index showing the page numbers of each document in the bundle;
> (e) the skeleton argument or written submission should define and confine the areas at issue in a numbered list of brief points and each point should refer to any documentation in the bundle on which the appellant proposes to rely (together with its page number);
> (f) where reliance is placed on a particular case or text, photocopies of the case or text must be provided in full for the Tribunal and the other party; and
> (g) large bundles should be contained in a ring binder or lever arch file, capable of lying flat when opened.
> ...
> Bundles should contain all the documents that the Tribunal will require to enable it to reach a decision without the need to refer to any other file or document. The Tribunal will not be assisted by repetitious, outdated or irrelevant material.
> ...
> It may not be practical in many appeals to require there to be an agreed trial bundle but it nevertheless remains vital that the parties inform each other at an early stage of all and any documentation upon which they intend to rely.
> ...
> The parties cannot rely on the Tribunal having any prior familiarity with any country information or background reports in relation to the case in question. If either party wishes to rely on such country or background information, copies of the relevant documentation must be provided.

---

42 Immigration and Asylum Chambers of the First-Tier Tribunal and the Upper Tribunal, Practice Direction 10 February 2010 para 18.
43 CPR Part 52, Practice Direction, para 15.4.

CHAPTER 21
Appeals in the IAC

21.1	Introduction
21.4	The statutory framework
21.8	Statutory grounds of appeal to the FTT-IAC
21.10	Not in accordance with the Immigration Rules; discretion should have been exercised differently under the Immigration Rules
21.11	Not in accordance with the law
21.13	Human rights and Refugee Convention grounds
21.17	In-country and out-of country appeals
21.25	One-stop notices and one-stop statements
21.30	Suspensory nature of an appeal
21.34	The First-tier Tribunal and the Upper Tribunal
21.37	Starting an appeal in the FTT-IAC
21.37	Time-limits
21.40	Calculation of time
21.41	Extensions of time
21.42	Contents of the appeal notice
21.44	Evidence and procedure in the FTT-IAC: a brief summary
21.51	Case management review hearings
21.55	Adjournments

continued

21.57	Appeal hearings in the FTT-IAC
21.60	Where the Home Office is unrepresented
21.61	Order of proceedings
21.69	Challenging a determination of the FTT-IAC on a point of law
21.72	Errors of law
21.75	Review by the FTT-IAC of its own decision
21.78	'Excluded decisions'
21.79	Applying to the FTT-IAC for permission to appeal to the UT-IAC
21.82	Renewing the application for permission to appeal to the UT-IAC ('second applications')
21.91	Challenging a refusal of permission to appeal by the UT-IAC
21.99	Powers of the UT-IAC on determining an appeal
21.101	Procedure of the UT-IAC on appeal
21.110	Grounds of appeal in the UT-IAC
21.113	Hearings in the UT-IAC
21.120	Seeking permission to appeal from the UT-IAC on a second appeal
21.123	Time limits
21.127	Extensions of time
21.128	Application notice
21.129	Applicable test
21.131	Review by the UT-IAC of its own decisions
21.134	Procedure after a grant of permission by UT-IAC to appeal to the Court of Appeal
21.136	Making an application for permission to appeal in the Court of Appeal
21.140	Abandonment and 'final determination' of appeals

Introduction

21.1 This chapter discusses appeals to the Immigration and Asylum Chamber of the First-tier Tribunal (FTT-IAC) and the Upper Tribunal (UT-IAC), referred to collectively here as the IAC. We examine the statutory framework for these appeals before providing an overview of IAC forms and procedures. At the end of this chapter, applications for permission to appeal to the Court of Appeal are briefly discussed.

21.2 Detailed analysis of the law concerning appeals on points of law and the law of evidence lies outside the scope of this book, as do the detail of procedures for appeals in the Court of Appeal and any consideration of onward appeals to the Supreme Court and European Court of Human Rights (ECtHR).

21.3 Appeals to the Special Immigration Appeals Commission (SIAC) are dealt with separately in chapter 23.

The statutory framework

21.4 For the purposes of foreign national prisoners and former prisoners (FNPs), the relevant immigration decisions appealable to the FTT-IAC are:

- a decision under the Immigration Act (IA) 1971 to make a deportation order;[1]
- a decision that the criteria for 'automatic' deportation[2] under the UK Borders Act (UKBA) 2007 are met;[3]
- a decision that concerns a person's removal from the UK under the Immigration (European Economic Area) Regulations 2006 (EEA Regs) 2006;[4]
- a refusal to revoke a deportation order;[5]
- revocation[6] of indefinite leave to remain;[7]
- a decision to remove a person unlawfully in the UK (an overstayer);[8]

---

1 Nationality, Immigration and Asylum Act (NIAA) 2002 s82(2)(j).
2 Under UK Borders Act 2007 s32(5).
3 NIAA 2002 s82(3A).
4 SI No 1003 reg 2(1).
5 NIAA 2002 s82(2)(k).
6 NIAA 2002 s76.
7 NIAA 2002 s82(2)(f).
8 NIAA 2002 s82(2)(g).

- a decision to remove an illegal entrant;[9]
- a decision by the Secretary of State for the Home Department (SSHD) to make an order depriving a person of his or her citizenship;[10] and
- a decision[11] to deprive a person of the right of abode in the UK.[12]

21.5 We focus in this chapter on appeals arising from the first four of the above immigration decisions, these being the most common.

21.6 Note that removal directions and deportation arrangements (defined at paras 6.17–6.18 of this book) may not be appealed to the IAC. The only challenge that may be brought against removal directions or deportation arrangements is by way of judicial review.

21.7 Note also that (save in circumstances highly unlikely to arise for an FNP[13]) the right of appeal is not against the refusal of an asylum claim but against the immigration decision which is associated with that refusal.

Statutory grounds of appeal to the IAC

21.8 An appeal to the FTT-IAC may be brought on any of the grounds listed under NIAA 2002 s84:
a) that the decision is not in accordance with the Immigration Rules;[14]
b) that the decision is unlawful by virtue of Race Relations Act (RRA) 1976 s19B (or Race Relations (Northern Ireland) Order 1997 article 20A);[15]
c) that the decision is unlawful under the Human Rights Act (HRA) 1998 as being incompatible with the appellant's rights under the European Convention on Human Rights (ECHR);[16]

---

9 NIAA 2002 s82(2)(h).
10 British Nationality Act 1981 s40A.
11 Under IA 1971 s2A.
12 NIAA 2002 s82(2)(b).
13 Under NIAA 2002 s83 there is a right of appeal to the IAC against the refusal of an asylum claim where leave to enter or remain has been granted for a period exceeding one year – in one grant or in the aggregate of several grants of leave.
14 NIAA 2002 s84(1)(a). See paras 3.15 and 3.17 for a discussion of the status of the Immigration Rules HC 395.
15 NIAA 2002 s84(1)(b).
16 NIAA 2002 s84(1)(c).

d) that the appellant is an European Economic Area (EEA) national or a member of the family of an EEA national and the decision breaches the appellant's rights under the Community Treaties in respect of entry to or residence in the UK;[17]
e) that the decision is otherwise not in accordance with the law;[18]
f) that the person in taking the decision should have exercised differently a discretion conferred by the immigration rules;[19]
g) that removal of the appellant from the UK in consequence of the immigration decision would breach the UK's obligations under the Refugee Convention[20] or would be unlawful under the HRA 1998 as being incompatible with the appellant's ECHR rights.[21]

21.9 Below, we set out distinct considerations for particular grounds of appeal where these are not self-evident.

Not in accordance with the Immigration Rules; discretion should have been exercised differently under the Immigration Rules

21.10 There is no discretionary exercise in, and the Immigration Rules do not apply to, a decision that the 'automatic' deportation provisions of UKBA 2007 apply. Likewise, the Immigration Rules do not apply to decisions made under the EEA Regs 2006. Therefore, where a decision is made under UKBA 2007 s32(5) that the criteria for 'automatic' deportation apply, or where a decision is made under the EEA Regs 2006 (eg a decision to expel on public policy or public security grounds or a refusal to revoke a deportation order) no appeal may be brought on the grounds listed at NIAA 2002 s84(1)(a) or (f)).

Not in accordance with the law

21.11 This wide ground of appeal encompasses failures to comply with domestically enforceable law, other than those already set out in the grounds at NIAA s84(1)(a)–(d) (ie other than failures to comply with the Immigration Rules; with RRA 1976 s19B; with HRA 1998 s6 or

---

17 NIAA 2002 s84(1)(d).
18 NIAA 2002 s84(1)(e).
19 NIAA 2002 s84(1)(f).
20 The 1951 Convention Relating to the Status of Refugees and its 1967 Protocol ('Refugee Convention').
21 NIAA 2002 s84(1)(g).

with the EC treaties). The concept of 'not in accordance with the law' includes:
- failure to apply an applicable government policy (considered in more detail below);
- other public law errors eg breach of legitimate expectation;
- breach of primary legislation (eg decision to deport a person who is exempt from deportation).

21.12 A failure by the Home Office to apply, or without good reason, to follow, its own policy will render an immigration decision 'not in accordance with the law' for the purposes of NIAA 2002 s84(1)(e).[22] In these circumstances, the IAC may remit the decision to be re-taken by the SSHD with proper regard to the relevant policy or (at least where the outcome of the proper application of the policy is clear) may itself apply the policy and allow or dismiss the appeal outright.[23] Likewise, a decision in breach of the SSHD's duties under Borders, Citizenship and Immigration Act (BCIA) 2009 s55 in relation to children will not be in accordance with the law for the purposes of NIAA 2002 s84(1)(e).[24]

Human rights and Refugee Convention grounds

21.13 NIAA 2002 s84(1)(g) asserts that the appellant's rights under the ECHR or Refugee Convention would be breached by expulsion in consequence of the immigration decision. This ground may be relied on, for example, to contest deportation.

21.14 Where a person is bringing an appeal on ECHR grounds from outside the UK or where there is no expulsion in issue (for example, because the person cannot lawfully be deported but now faces a decision to revoke his or her indefinite leave to remain) the appropriate ground of appeal is NIAA 2002 s84(1)(c). NIAA 2002 s84(1)(c) asserts that the immigration decision is unlawful under HRA 1998 as being incompatible with the appellant's ECHR rights.

21.15 Refugee Convention issues may still be raised in the context of an out-of-country appeal, by relying on grounds that the decision is not in accordance with the Immigration Rules (subject to the point at

---

22 See discussion at paras 3.17–3.18.
23 *AB (Jamaica) v Secretary of State for the Home Department* [2007] EWCA Civ 1302; *Fouzia Baig v Secretary of State for the Home Department* [2005] EWCA Civ 1246.
24 See discussion at para 4.32.

para 21.10 above) and/or not in accordance with the law (NIAA 2002 s84(1)(a) and (e)).[25]

21.16 Nothing prevents appellants from relying on NIAA 2002 s84(1)(c) and (g) in combination[26] and in practice, it is sufficient for the Grounds of Appeal to state that the decision is contested 'on ECHR grounds' rather than specifying a particular statutory provision.

In-country and out-of country appeals

21.17 The question of whether there is an in-country right of appeal or only an out-of-country right of appeal to the FTT-IAC is of great importance to appellants. As Sedley LJ noted in *BA (Nigeria) and PE (Cameroon) v Secretary of State for the Home Department*:[27]

> The fact is that, especially but not only where credibility is in issue, the pursuit of an appeal from outside the United Kingdom has a degree of unreality about it. Such appeals have been known to succeed, but only in the rarest of cases. The reason why the Home Office is insistent on removal pending appeal wherever the law permits it is that in the great majority of cases it is the end of the appeal.

21.18 Under NIAA 2002 s92, there are a number of immigration decisions against which an appeal may always be brought from within the UK (unless appeal rights are lost altogether through certification under NIAA 2002 s96 or EEA Regs 2006 reg 26(5), see paras 22.14–22.23). In other cases, the norm is that an appeal may only be brought to the FTT-IAC from outside the UK unless certain criteria apply.

21.19 For the purposes of FNPs, the relevant immigration decisions which can always[28] be appealed while still in the UK are:
- a decision to revoke indefinite leave to remain; and
- a decision to make a deportation order under the IA 1971.

21.20 Other immigration decisions (for the purposes of this book, a decision that the criteria for 'automatic' deportation are met; a refusal to revoke a deportation order; a decision to deprive a person of the right

---

25 Because Asylum and Immigration Appeals Act (AIAA) 1993 s2 prohibits the Immigration Rules from laying down any practice which would be contrary to the Refugee Convention.
26 This will be appropriate when challenging a decision which is not an expulsion decision but which may lead to expulsion (eg deprivation of citizenship).
27 [2009] EWCA Civ 119.
28 Save where certified under NIAA 2002 s96 or EEA Regs 2006 reg 26(5).

of abode) will only be appealable in-country if one or more of the following criteria are met:

- the person has made an ECHR claim while in the UK;[29]
- the person has made an asylum claim while in the UK;[30]
- the person is an EEA national or the family member of an EEA national and makes a claim to the SSHD that the decision breaches his or her rights under the EC treaties in respect of entry to or residence in the UK.[31]

21.21 Note that a decision that the criteria for 'automatic' deportation under the UKBA 2007 are met has been specifically excluded from the class of immigration decisions that are always[32] appealable in the UK.[33]

21.22 The asylum or ECHR claim should be made to the SSHD.[34] However, there is Administrative Court authority indicating that raising asylum or human rights grounds of appeal in the appeal notice to the Tribunal may suffice as an asylum or human rights claim for the purposes of founding an in-country right of appeal.[35]

21.23 A person cannot rely on a purely historic asylum or ECHR claim (ie a claim already determined adversely to the individual and which has no nexus to the immigration decision now appealed) to show that he or she 'has made an asylum or human rights claim, while in the United Kingdom'.[36] Where the person has made a previous asylum or human rights claim, there is no requirement that the current 'asylum or human rights claim' should have passed the fresh claim threshold[37] as defined in Immigration Rules para 353.

---

29 NIAA 2002 s92(4)(a).
30 NIAA 2002 s92(4)(a).
31 NIAA 2002 s92(4)(b).
32 Unless certified under NIAA 2002 s96 or EEA Regs 2006 reg 26(5).
33 NIAA 2002 s82(3A).
34 NIAA 2002 s113 defines 'asylum claim' and 'human rights' claim as ' a claim made by a person to the Secretary of State at a place designated by the Secretary of State...'. That part of the definition of 'asylum claim' and 'human rights claim' will fall away if and when Immigration Asylum and Nationality Act (IANA) 2006 s12(1) and (2) come into force, amending NIAA 2002 s.113.
35 *R (Jisha) v Secretary of State for the Home Department* [2010] EWHC 2043 (Admin) para 25.
36 *R (Etame) v Secretary of State for the Home Department* [2008] EWHC 1140 (Admin). This aspect of the *Etame* judgment was undisturbed in the subsequent appeal in the Court of Appeal and Supreme Court.
37 *BA (Nigeria) and PE (Cameroon) v Secretary of State for the Home Department* [2009] UKSC 7, [2010] 1 AC 444. Note, however, that there is statutory provision, not brought into force, which may reverse this. If IANA 2006 s12 is brought into force, this would amend NIAA 2002 s113 so that 'asylum claim'

21.24 However, once there is an in-country right of appeal to the FTT-IAC (eg because the appellant is an EEA national and has made an EU law claim) any of the grounds of appeal listed in NIAA 2002 s84 can be relied upon in the in-country appeal.

One-stop notices and one-stop statements

21.25 The so-called 'one-stop' system is designed to compel individuals to make their claims as early as possible and where possible resolve in one appeal all their reasons for wishing to enter, remain or not be expelled from the UK and to deter staggered applications or claims.

21.26 A one-stop warning is a written notice from the SSHD to a person who has made an application to enter or remain in the UK[38] or, more relevantly for FNPs, a person in respect of whom an immigration decision has been or may be taken.[39] The one-stop warning requires the person to state, among other points, any grounds on which he should not be removed from or required to leave the UK.[40] The one-stop notice may be served on an FNP along with the immigration decision and appeal forms.

21.27 A one-stop statement is a statement of additional grounds filed in response to a one-stop notice. The one-stop statement may be filed and served at any time: there is no deadline. Failure, without good reason, by an individual to provide all his or her reasons in response to a one-stop warning may result in a later application being certified under NIAA 20002 s96(2) with the consequence that appeal rights are lost. This form of certification is discussed in more detail in the next chapter.

21.28 Thus, for example, where an FNP has made an application for revocation or an asylum claim and this has been refused, the one-stop statement should set out any further grounds not contained in the earlier application.

21.29 When determining an appeal, the IAC is required to consider any NIAA 2002 s84 grounds which are raised in the one-stop statement into account, even where the statement was made after the commencement of the appeal.[41]

and 'human rights claim' are defined to exclude claims which do not meet the fresh claim threshold.
38 NIAA 2002 s120(1)(a).
39 NIAA 2002 s120(1)(b).
40 NIAA 2002 s120(2)(c).
41 NIAA 2002 s85(2) and (3).

Suspensory nature of an appeal

21.30 While a person has an appeal pending under NIAA 2002 s82(1), he or she can neither be removed from the UK nor be required to leave the UK.[42]

21.31 A discretionary deportation order under IA 1971 cannot be made while a NIAA 2002 s82(1) appeal could be brought (ignoring any possibility of an appeal out of time with permission)[43] or is pending.[44] However, this suspensory effect does not apply where the SSHD certifies that the decision to make a deportation order was made on grounds that expulsion is in the interests of national security.[45] In such cases, any appeal lies to SIAC. SIAC appeals are discussed in chapter 23. Once a discretionary deportation order under IA 1971 is signed (and we suggest it must also be served, see paras 1.48–1.50 above) this invalidates any existing leave to enter or remain in the UK.[46]

21.32 By contrast, an 'automatic' deportation order under UKBA 2007 s32(5) may be made while an appeal could be brought or is pending.[47] However, an 'automatic' deportation order does not invalidate existing leave to enter or remain as long as a NIAA 2002 s82(1) appeal could be brought (ignoring any possibility of an appeal out of time with permission) or is pending.[48]

21.33 An appeal is pending during the period beginning when it is 'instituted' and ending when it is finally determined, withdrawn or abandoned or when it 'lapses'[49] because it has been certified under NIAA 2002 s96, s97 or s98.[50] An appeal is not finally determined as long as:

- an application for permission to appeal to the UT-IAC or the Court of Appeal could be made or is awaiting determination;[51]
- permission to appeal to the UT-IAC or the Court of Appeal has been granted and the appeal is awaiting determination;[52] or

---

42 NIAA 2002 s78.
43 NIAA 2002 s79(1)(a).
44 NIAA 2002 s79(1)(b).
45 NIAA 2002 s97A(2)(a).
46 IA 1971 s5(1).
47 NIAA 2002 s79(3).
48 NIAA 2002 s79(3).
49 NIAA 2002 s104(1).
50 NIAA 2002 s99.
51 NIAA 2002 s104(2)(a).
52 NIAA 2002 s104(2)(b).

- an appeal has been remitted by the UT-IAC or Court of Appeal and is awaiting determination.[53]

The First-tier Tribunal and the Upper Tribunal

21.34 The Tribunals, Courts and Enforcement Act (TCEA) 2007 s3 created a new unified tribunals structure dealing with diverse jurisdictions, including immigration. There are two tiers: the First-tier and the Upper Tribunal, each organised into chambers according to subject matter. In this book, we refer simply to 'IAC' when we are referring to the Immigration and Asylum Chambers of *both* the First-tier and Upper Tribunals.

21.35 The FTT-IAC hears appeals against immigration decisions (see the definition of immigration decisions at para 21.4 above) at first instance, save for those dealing with national security (as to which, see chapter 23).

21.36 A dissatisfied party may then appeal, with permission, on a point of law from the FTT-IAC to the UT-IAC.

Starting an appeal in the FTT-IAC

Time-limits

21.37 An in-country appeal to the FTT-IAC is instituted[54] by filing a notice of appeal on form IAFT-1[55] with the IAC. The deadline for bringing an in-country appeal is:

- if the person is detained under Immigration Act powers at the time of being served with notice of the immigration decision, five working days after being served with notice of the immigration decision;[56] and
- otherwise, ten working days after being served with notice of the immigration decision.[57]

---

53 NIAA 2002 s104(2)(c).
54 Asylum and Immigration Tribunal (Procedure) Rules 2005 SI No 230 (AIT (Procedure) Rules 2005) r6(1).
55 Appeal forms should be supplied by the SSHD along with the immigration decision giving rise to the right of appeal but copies can also be downloaded from the Ministry of Justice website at: www.justice.gov.uk/global/forms/hmcts/tribunals/immigration-and-asylum/index.htm.
56 AIT (Procedure) Rules 2005 r7(1)(a).
57 AIT (Procedure) Rules 2005 r7(1)(b).

21.38 An appeal to the FTT-IAC from outside the UK (save against a decision by an Entry Clearance Officer to refuse entry clearance) is instituted[58] by filing a notice of appeal on form IAFT-3 with the FTT-IAC. The deadline for bringing an out-of-country appeal is:

- where the person was in the UK at the time that the decision was made but he or she is precluded by a provision of the NIAA 2002 (eg certification under NIAA 2002 s94) from appealing from within the UK, 28 calendar days after his or her departure from the UK;[59]
- otherwise, 28 calendar days after being served with notice of the immigration decision.[60]

21.39 The notice of appeal must reach the FTT-IAC before expiry of the deadline for appealing. However, a person who is detained under IA powers may file his or her appeal notice by serving notice on the person who has custody.[61] The custodian is then required to endorse the notice with the date on which it was served and then forward it to the FTT-IAC within two days.[62]

Calculation of time

21.40 When calculating time-periods in the FTT-IAC, the period is to be calculated by excluding the date on which the period begins (eg the date of service of the immigration decision).[63] If the period ends on a non-business day, the act is done in time if it is done on the next business day.[64]

Extensions of time

21.41 The FTT-IAC has jurisdiction to extend the time for filing the notice of appeal if satisfied that it would be unjust not to do so.[65] Any notice of appeal filed late should state the reasons why the application was filed late. Where the FTT-IAC refuses to extend time on a late application, the remedy is judicial review.

---

58 AIT (Procedure) Rules 2005 r6(1).
59 AIT (Procedure) Rules 2005 r7(2)(a)(i).
60 AIT (Procedure) Rules 2005 r7(2)(a)(ii).
61 AIT (Procedure) Rules 2005 r6(3)(b).
62 AIT (Procedure) Rules 2005 r6(5).
63 AIT (Procedure) Rules 2005 r57(1)(a).
64 AIT (Procedure) Rules 2005 r57(2).
65 AIT (Procedure) Rules 2005 r10(5).

Contents of the appeal notice

21.42 The notice of appeal must specify the appellant's name and address; the name and address of any representative; the grounds of appeal and reasons in support of those grounds (see below); and, insofar as is practicable, list any documents on which the appellant intends to rely as evidence in the appeal.[66] The notice of appeal must be signed and dated by the appellant or his or her representative[67] and must, if reasonably practicable, by accompanied by a copy of the notice of the immigration decision which is being appealed.[68] The appeal form asks appellants to specify whether they wish to have an oral hearing or to have their case determined on the papers: an oral hearing is more advantageous for appellants.

21.43 Reasons should be given in the appeal notice for reliance on each ground of appeal, briefly explaining how the statutory grounds relate to the facts of the case. Grounds of appeal can be varied subsequently with the permission of the FTT-IAC;[69] however, it is preferable to include grounds of appeal which are later discarded if irrelevant than to omit them and have to seek permission to amend later.

Evidence and procedure in the FTT-IAC: a brief summary

21.44 Detailed analyses of rules of evidence and procedure in the FTT-IAC are outside the scope of this book. Below, we deal with points that are of very wide application. Important sources of evidence for appeals and representations, trial bundles and the instruction of experts have been discussed separately in chapter 20.

21.45 The FTT-IAC may allow oral, documentary or other evidence to be given of any fact which appears to be relevant, even if that evidence would be inadmissible in a court of law.[70] This means that there is, for instance, no rule against hearsay and no strict rule requiring evidence to be given in a particular format.

21.46 The FTT-IAC may, and generally does, issue directions requiring the parties to file and serve statements, paginated and indexed

---

66 AIT (Procedure) Rules 2005 r8(1).
67 AIT (Procedure) Rules 2005 r8(3).
68 AIT (Procedure) Rules 2005 r8(2).
69 AIT (Procedure) Rules 2005 r14.
70 AIT (Procedure) Rules 2005 r51(3).

bundles, skeleton arguments and other documents within given time-frames before the hearing.[71] The standard directions issued by both tiers of the IAC are that:[72]

(a) not later than 5 working days before the full hearing (or 10 days in the case of an out-of-country appeal) the appellant shall serve on the Tribunal and the respondent:
  (i) witness statements of the evidence to be called at the hearing, such statements to stand as evidence in chief at the hearing;
  (ii) a paginated and indexed bundle of all the documents to be relied on at the hearing with a schedule identifying the essential passages;
  (iii) a skeleton argument, identifying all relevant issues including human rights claims and citing all the authorities relied upon; and
  (iv) a chronology of events;
(b) not later than 5 working days before the full hearing, the respondent shall serve on the Tribunal and the appellant a paginated and indexed bundle of all the documents to be relied upon at the hearing, with a schedule identifying the relevant passages, and a list of any authorities.

21.47 In cases concerning FNPs, the SSHD will usually be directed to adduce the sentencing remarks of the criminal court and certificates of conviction.

21.48 The FTT-IAC must not direct an unrepresented party to do something unless satisfied that he is able to comply with the direction.[73]

21.49 The AIT (Procedure) Rules 2005 stipulate that the FTT-IAC must not consider written evidence which has not been filed and served in accordance with directions unless satisfied there are good reasons to do so.[74]

21.50 The FTT-IAC can vary the time limits for complying with directions.[75] Applications to the FTT-IAC for further time should, wherever possible be made before expiry of the original time limit. Once the time limit for complying with the original direction has expired, the AIT (Procedure) Rules 2005 stipulate that time will be extended by the FTT-IAC 'if it considers that there are exceptional reasons for doing so'.

---

71 AIT (Procedure) Rules 2005 r45(e).
72 Immigration and Asylum Chamber of the First-Tier Tribunal and the Upper Tribunal Practice Direction 10 February 2010 para 7.5.
73 AIT (Procedure) Rules 2005 r45(5).
74 AIT (Procedure) Rules 2005 r51(4).
75 AIT (Procedure) Rules 2005 r45(4)(c).

Case management review hearings

21.51 Either tier of the IAC may provide for a case management review hearing (CMRH) to be held before the full hearing[76] where the appellant (or in the UT-IAC, the party who was the appellant at first instance) is in the UK and has an in-country right of appeal.[77]

21.52 If a party does not appear and is unrepresented at a CMRH, and the IAC is satisfied that the party or representative has been given notice of date time and place of the hearing and there is no good reason for the absence, the appeal may be determined in his absence.[78]

21.53 The CMRH is an opportunity for the parties to seek clarification of each other's positions in the appeal and the IAC's assistance, for example in obtaining disclosure of documents from the other. It is also an opportunity to highlight any likely difficulties with complying with timescales and additional practical requirements (such as evidence needing to be heard by video-link[79]). In practice, however, the SSHD often fails to engage constructively with these hearings or to comply with directions made.

21.54 At the CMRH, appellants should make any application for permission to vary their grounds of appeal or reasons in support of those grounds and provide particulars of any witnesses whose oral or written evidence will be relied on at the full hearing; both parties should provide a draft of any specific directions sought.[80] At the end of the CMRH the IAC should provide the parties with a written list of issues agreed to be relevant to the determination of the appeal and any concessions made at the CMRH by either party.[81]

---

76 For the First-tier Tribunal, the AIT (Procedure) Rules 2005 r45(4)(d)(ii) and for the Upper Tribunal, the Tribunal Procedure (Upper Tribunal) Rules 2008 SI No 2698 r5(3)(f).
77 Immigration and Asylum Chamber of the First-Tier Tribunal and the Upper Tribunal Practice Direction 10 February 2010 para 7.1.
78 AIT (Procedure) Rules 2005 r19(1); Immigration and Asylum Chamber of the First-tier Tribunal and the Upper Tribunal Practice Direction 10 February 2010 para 7.2.
79 The FTT-IAC has the power to hear evidence, or conduct a hearing by video-link, see the AIT (Procedure) Rules 2005 r45(4)(i).
80 Immigration and Asylum Chamber of the First-Tier Tribunal and the Upper Tribunal Practice Direction 10 February 2010 para 7.3.
81 Immigration and Asylum Chamber of the First-Tier Tribunal and the Upper Tribunal Practice Direction 10 February 2010 para 7.8.

Adjournments

21.55 The AIT (Procedure) Rules 2005 stipulate that the FTT-IAC must not adjourn the hearing of an appeal unless satisfied that the appeal cannot otherwise justly be determined.[82] In particular, the FTT-IAC must not adjourn a hearing on the application of a party in order to produce more evidence unless satisfied that the evidence relates to a matter in dispute in the appeal; it would be unjust to determine the appeal without permitting the party a further opportunity to produce the evidence and a satisfactory explanation has been provided for any failure to comply with directions for the production of the evidence.[83] A party applying for an adjournment must show good reason why an adjournment is necessary, produce evidence of any fact or matter relied on in support of that application and if practicable notify all other parties of the application.[84]

21.56 Applications for the adjournment of appeals in either tier of the IAC should be made not later than 5pm one working day before the date of the hearing; otherwise, 'save in the most exceptional circumstances' the IAC will require the party seeking the adjournment to attend the hearing. But even where properly made, an application for an adjournment may be refused and the party seeking the adjournment should always check with the IAC whether it has been granted.[85]

Appeal hearings in the FTT-IAC

21.57 Hearings of the FTT-IAC are normally open to the public. However, the FTT-IAC has power to exclude any or all members of the public from any hearing or part of the hearing if it is necessary in the interests of public order or national security or to protect the private life of a party or the interests of a minor.[86]

21.58 Appeals in the FTT-IAC are heard by a single judge of the FTT-IAC or by a panel of two to three members, at least one of whom must be a judge of the FTT-IAC[87] (the others being lay members).

---

82 AIT (Procedure) Rules 2005 r21(2).
83 AIT (Procedure) Rules 2005 r213.
84 AIT (Procedure) Rules 2005 r21(1).
85 Immigration and Asylum Chambers of the First Tier Tribunal and the Upper Tribunal, Practice Direction 10 February 2010 para 9.
86 AIT (Procedure) Rules 2005 r54.
87 Immigration and Asylum Chambers of the First Tier Tribunal and the Upper Tribunal, Practice Direction 10 February 2010 para 2.1.

21.59 The Home Office is usually represented before the FTT-IAC by a Presenting Officer or 'HOPO' (a civil servant) though in more complex appeals the Home Office may instruct the Treasury Solicitor and Counsel. Not infrequently, the Home Office fails to appear at all. A failure to appear by the Home Office, while frequently deprecated by the immigration judiciary, does not prevent the Home Office from appealing a decision adverse to it by the FTT-IAC.

Where the Home Office is unrepresented

21.60 The predecessor of the IAC, the Asylum and Immigration Tribunal (AIT), in the past set out guidelines (the *Surendran* guidelines[88]) to try to avoid procedural unfairness in circumstances where the Home Office is unrepresented. Among other points, these guidelines remind the tribunal in these circumstances to put to the appellant any matters of credibility, and that the tribunal should itself point out to the appellant or his or her representative any obvious difficulties or contradictions that arise in the papers, but should avoid stepping into an inquisitorial role itself. However, the AIT subsequently emphasised that these 'are guidelines and guidance; they are not rules of law. They are not a strait-jacket'.[89]

Order of proceedings

21.61 Hearings in the FTT-IAC will usually begin with some discussion to identify live issues, followed by the calling of witness evidence on behalf of the appellant. The appellant is ordinarily called first. Witnesses other than the appellant will normally be asked to remain outside the court room until the FTT-IAC is ready to hear their evidence.

21.62 Appellants and other witnesses are not required to give oral evidence and they and their representatives may choose not to tender the appellant for cross-examination. However, generally, appellants and all important witnesses of fact whose evidence is in dispute should give oral evidence since evidence not tested in cross-examination is usually given less weight, adverse inferences may be drawn from a witness' failure to give oral evidence (unless a good reason is

---

88 *Surendran v Secretary of State for the Home Department*, 12 July 1999 HX/70901/98, reproduced in *MNM (Surendran guidelines for Adjudicators) Kenya* 00TH02423, [2000] UKIAT 00005.

89 *WN (DRC) v Secretary of State for the Home Department* [2004] UKIAT 00213 para 29 per Ouseley J.

provided); and an immigration judge is likely to have a better 'feel' for a witness that he or she has heard. Exceptions to that general approach might include circumstances in which there is medical or psychiatric evidence to the effect that a witness is so traumatised that giving evidence would adversely affect his or her health. Where evidence is not in dispute, there may be no need to call the appellant or other witnesses. There will rarely be good reason to do so where the only effect would be to enable the Home Office to question previously accepted evidence.

21.63 Where expert evidence has been obtained (see the discussion at paras 20.14–20.15) and the expert's evidence is central to the appeal and remains in dispute, appellants and their representatives should consider calling the expert to give oral evidence if resources permit.

21.64 The IAC Practice Direction states that the norm is that witness evidence stands as the evidence in chief at the hearing (meaning that the only oral evidence heard would be cross-examination by the other party or his representative) although 'there may be cases in which it will be appropriate for appellants or witnesses to have the opportunity of adding to or supplementing their witness statements'.[90] In practice, although witnesses should not repeat the contents of their witness statements, it is often useful for witnesses to provide clarification or additional detail in oral evidence.

21.65 Each witness on behalf of the appellant will then be cross-examined by the Home Office's representative.

21.66 In the very rare cases where the Home Office itself wishes to rely on witness evidence, the Home Office witnesses will then give their evidence in chief, to be cross-examined by the appellant or his representative.

21.67 After completion of the parties' evidence, the Home Office representative makes oral submissions on the law and evidence, followed by the appellant's representative. If no oral evidence has been heard, the order of submissions is traditionally reversed, so that the appellant's representative goes first, although in these cases the appellant should get the final word after the HOPO has made submissions.

21.68 The FTT-IAC in deportation appeals will usually 'reserve' its decision, notifying the parties later in writing of its decision and reasons for it.

---

90 Immigration and Asylum Chambers of the First-tier Tribunal and the Upper Tribunal, Practice Direction 10 February 2010 para 7.7.

Challenging a determination of the FTT-IAC on a point of law

21.69 An appeal lies to the UT-IAC against all decisions of the FTT-IAC other than 'excluded decisions'.[91] 'Excluded' decisions are discussed further below at para 21.78.

21.70 Appeals to the UT-IAC may only be brought on points of law.[92] Errors of law are briefly discussed at para 21.72 below.

21.71 However, as we see at para 21.78, before an appeal reaches the UT-IAC, there is a filter mechanism whereby the FTT-IAC decides whether to review the determination itself.

Errors of law

21.72 To challenge successfully a decision made by the IAC, it is not enough that the reviewing or appellate tribunal or court disagrees with the decision. The decision will only be set aside if it contains a material error of law. Important guidance on errors of law was given by the Court of Appeal in *R (Iran) v Secretary of State for the Home Department*. Brooke LJ, giving the judgment of the Court, provided a non-exhaustive list of material errors of law:[93]

> It may be convenient to give a brief summary of the points of law that will most frequently be encountered in practice:
> i) Making perverse or irrational findings on a matter or matters that were material to the outcome ('material matters');
> ii) Failing to give reasons or any adequate reasons for findings on material matters;
> iii) Failing to take into account and/or resolve conflicts of fact or opinion on material matters;
> iv) Giving weight to immaterial matters;
> v) Making a material misdirection of law on any material matter;
> vi) Committing or permitting a procedural or other irregularity capable of making a material difference to the outcome or the fairness of the proceedings;
> vii) Making a mistake as to a material fact which could be established by objective and uncontentious evidence, where the appellant and/or his advisers were not responsible for the mistake, and where unfairness resulted from the fact that a mistake was made.[94]

---

91 TCEA 2007 s11.
92 TCEA 2007 s11(1).
93 [2005] EWCA Civ 982, [2005] Imm AR 535 para 9.
94 As to error of fact amounting to error of law, see also *E and R v Secretary of State for the Home Department* [2004] EWCA Civ 49, [2004] QB 1044 para 66.

21.73 A full discussion of errors of law is beyond the scope of this book: we strongly recommend that those seeking to challenge a decision made by IAC should, where possible, refer to specialist immigration texts and/or the full discussion of errors of law by the Court of Appeal in *R (Iran)*.

21.74 As the above list indicates, the error of law must be material: a decision will not be set aside if the result would inevitably have been the same notwithstanding the error.[95]

Review by the FTT-IAC of its own decision

21.75 The FTT-IAC has jurisdiction to review its own decisions[96] save for 'excluded decisions'.[97] This power is rarely used in practice and we discuss it only briefly here.

21.76 When the FTT-IAC receives an application for permission to appeal to the UT-IAC, it must, within ten days of receipt of the application, decide whether to review the decision itself,[98] but can only undertake a review if satisfied that there was an error of law in the decision.[99]

21.77 On carrying out a review, the FTT-IAC may correct accidental errors in the decision or in the record of the decision;[100] amend its reasons[101] or set the determination aside.[102] Where the FTT-IAC sets a determination aside, it can either re-determine the appeal itself or refer it to the UT-IAC.

'Excluded decisions'

21.78 Certain decisions of the FTT-IAC are 'excluded' from appeal to the UT-IAC. With one minor exception, these are also 'excluded' from

---

95 *R (Iran) v Secretary of State for the Home Department* [2005] EWCA Civ 982, [2005] Imm AR 535 para 10.
96 TCEA 2007 s9(1).
97 For these purposes, a decision to set aside an earlier decision is not an excluded decision but it can be reviewed to the extent of correcting accidental errors (TCEA 2007 s9(9)).
98 AIT (Procedure) Rules 2005 r25(3).
99 AIT (Procedure) Rules 2005 r26(1).
100 TCEA 2007 s9(4)(a).
101 TCEA 2007 s9(4)(b).
102 TCEA 2007 s9(4)(c).

review by the FTT-IAC[103] and may be challenged only in judicial review. We mention here only those 'excluded' decisions relevant to FNPs in the deportation and detention contexts:

- refusals of bail;[104]
- procedural, ancillary or preliminary decisions in appeals against immigration decisions;[105]
- a decision by the FTT-IAC to review, or not to review its own earlier decision;[106]
- a decision by the FTT-IAC not to take action in light of the review of its earlier decision;[107]
- a decision by the FTT-IAC to set aside an earlier decision of the tribunal[108] (this is an excluded decision only for the purposes of an appeal to UT-IAC; it may be reviewed by the FTT-IAC but only to the extent of correcting accidental errors[109]);
- a decision by the FTT-IAC to refer or not to refer a matter to the UT-IAC;[110] or
- a decision that has already been set aside by the FTT-IAC.[111]

Applying to the FTT-IAC for permission to appeal to the UT-IAC

21.79 An application for permission to appeal to the UT-IAC must first be made on form IATF-4[112] to the FTT-IAC. The application must identify the decision of the UT-IAC to which it relates; identify the alleged error or errors of law; and state the result that is sought.[113]

21.80 An application made by an appellant who is in the UK must be made no later than five business days[114] after the deemed date of

---

103 See para 21.75.
104 Appeals (Excluded Decisions) Order 2009 SI No 275 (as amended by SI 2010 No 41) article 2(b).
105 Appeals (Excluded Decisions) Order 2009 (as amended by SI 2010 No 41) article 3(m).
106 TCEA 2007 s11(d)(i).
107 TCEA 2007 s11(d)(ii).
108 TCEA 2007 s11(d)(iii).
109 TCEA 2007 s9(9).
110 TCEA 2007 s11(d)(iv).
111 TCEA 2007 s11(e).
112 Available on the website of the Ministry of Justice, see note 55 above.
113 AIT (Procedure) Rules 2005 r24(5).
114 Defined in AIT (Procedure) Rules 2005 r2.

receipt of the written reasons for the FTT's decision.[115] Where the appellant is outside the UK, the application must be made no later than 28 days after the deemed date of receipt.[116] The FTT-IAC has jurisdiction to extend time if satisfied that 'by reason of special circumstances it would be unjust not to do so'.[117]

21.81 If the FTT-IAC decides not to review the decision itself, or reviews the decision and decides to take no action in relation to the decision or part of it, it must consider whether to grant permission to appeal to the UT-IAC.[118]

Renewing the application for permission to appeal to the UT-IAC ('second applications')

21.82 An application for permission to appeal can be made to the UT-IAC if the FTT-IAC has refused permission to appeal or refused to admit an application for permission to appeal.[119]

21.83 The application to the UT-IAC for permission to appeal to itself should be made to the UT on form IAUT-1, which is available on the Ministry of Justice website.[120] The application must state the name and address of the appellant and any representatives, the address for service of documents, the grounds relied on and whether the appellant wants the application to be dealt with at a hearing.[121] The President of the Upper Tribunal has indicated that oral hearings of permission applications should be rare and that, given time constraints on the UT-IAC, permission should be granted when in doubt, rather than adjourn the application for an oral hearing.[122] In practice, the UT-IAC appears to invariably determine these applications on the papers.

21.84 A copy of any written record of the decision and any separate statement of reasons, and of the notice of the FTT-IAC's refusal of

---

115 AIT (Procedure) Rules 2005 rr24(2), 57(1)(b).
116 AIT (Procedure) Rules 2005 r24(3).
117 AIT (Procedure) Rules 2005 r24(4)(a).
118 AIT (Procedure) Rules 2005 r25(2).
119 Tribunal Procedure (Upper Tribunal) Rules 2008 SI No 2968 r21(2).
120 See www.justice.gov.uk/global/forms/hmcts/tribunals/immigration-and-asylum/upper/index.htm.
121 Tribunal Procedure (Upper Tribunal) Rules 2008 r21(4).
122 Blake J Guidance Note 1 of 2011 para 26.

permission to appeal (or of refusal to admit the application for permission to appeal) must be enclosed.[123]

21.85 Appellants should beware of the very short deadlines for in-country appeals. Where the appellant is in the UK, the application must be received by the UT-IAC no later than seven working days after the date on which notice of the FTT-IAC's refusal of permission was sent to the appellant,[124] unless the notice of decision is sent electronically or delivered personally, in which case the application for permission to appeal must be received by the UT-IAC no later than five working days after the date on which notice of the FTT-IAC's refusal of permission was sent to the appellant.[125] Note, therefore, that detained FNPs who are delivered personally with the refusal of permission to appeal from the FTT-IAC will have only five working days to get the notice of appeal to the UT-IAC.

21.86 Where the appellant is outside the UK at the time of making the application, the application must be received by the UT-IAC no later than 56 days after the date on which notice of the FTT-IAC's refusal of permission was sent to the appellant[126] (unless that notice of refusal was electronically or personally delivered in which case the application must be received by the UT-IAC no later than 28 days after the date on which notice of the FTT-IAC's refusal of permission was sent to the appellant[127]).

21.87 The UT-IAC has discretion to extend time.[128] Where the application for permission to appeal to the UT-IAC is made out of time, the application notice must include a request for an extension of time and the reason why time limits were not complied with.[129]

21.88 Where a dissatisfied party has lodged an appeal, the respondent (who may of course be the individual, having succeeded in the FTT-IAC) may provide a response to a notice of appeal.[130] Any response must be provided within one month of the date on which the respondent was sent notice that permission to appeal had been granted[131] and if later than this must include a request for an extension of time

---

123 Tribunal Procedure (Upper Tribunal) Rules 2008 r214.
124 Tribunal Procedure (Upper Tribunal) Rules 2008 r21(3)(aa)(i).
125 Tribunal Procedure (Upper Tribunal) Rules 2008 r21(3A)(a).
126 Tribunal Procedure (Upper Tribunal) Rules 2008 r21(3)(ab).
127 Tribunal Procedure (Upper Tribunal) Rules 2008 r21(3A)(c).
128 Tribunal Procedure (Upper Tribunal) Rules 2008 r5(3)(a).
129 Tribunal Procedure (Upper Tribunal) Rules 2008 r21(6)(a).
130 Tribunal Procedure (Upper Tribunal) Rules 2008 r24(1A).
131 Tribunal Procedure (Upper Tribunal) Rules 2008 r24(2).

and the reason why the response was not provided in time.[132] The response must be in writing and state the name and address of the respondent and any representatives and an address for documents; and must state whether the respondent opposes the appeal and the grounds on which the respondent relies, including any grounds on which the respondent was unsuccessful in the tribunal below but intends to rely in the proceedings.[133]

21.89 The appellant (who may be the SSHD or the individual depending on the outcome in the tribunal below) may in turn provide a reply to the response. The reply must be in writing and sent or delivered to the UT-IAC so that it is received within one month of the date on which the UT-IAC sent a copy of the response to the appellant.[134]

21.90 The President of the Upper Tribunal has warned immigration judges of the UT-IAC to take an anxious, or generous, approach to second applications for permission to appeal to the UT-IAC:

> Wherever life, limb or liberty may be placed in jeopardy or important human rights may not be respected, the approach of the higher courts on judicial review has been to scrutinise anxiously the decision below to ensure that it is in no way flawed. Judges deciding whether to grant permission to appeal should adopt no less stringent an approach (in the context of 'second applications', a refusal of permission is final and so the application may be the last opportunity for a judicial remedy).[135]

And:

> Whilst the existence of reasonable prospects of success is a relevant criterion to apply to the grant of permission, it is not a precondition for its grant. A point of law may be of such general importance as to justify the grant of leave even though the prospects of the appellant succeeding may not be substantial.[136]

Challenging a refusal of permission to appeal by the UT-IAC

21.91 The UT-IAC is a superior court of record[137] and thus has the power to set precedent but its non-appealable decisions (including a refusal

---

132 Tribunal Procedure (Upper Tribunal) Rules 2008 r24(4).
133 Tribunal Procedure (Upper Tribunal) Rules 2008 r24(3).
134 Tribunal Procedure (Upper Tribunal) Rules 2008 r25.
135 Blake J Guidance Note 1 2011, July 2011, para 8.
136 Blake J Guidance Note 1 2011, July 2011, para 14.
137 TCEA 2007 s3(5).

by UT-IAC of permission to appeal) may nonetheless be judicially reviewed.[138]

21.92 The Supreme Court in *R (Cart) v Upper Tribunal*[139] considered the test to be applied in a judicial review of a refusal by the Upper Tribunal of permission to appeal to the Upper Tribunal. The Supreme Court found that the test in such cases was the same test applicable to 'second appeals' from the Upper Tribunal.

21.93 A 'second appeal' is an appeal to the Court of Appeal from a decision of the Upper Tribunal on appeal from the First-tier Tribunal (that is, it is an appeal from a determination which was itself made on appeal from an earlier determination). Delegated legislation stipulates that permission to appeal to the Court of Appeal from the Upper Tribunal on a second appeal shall not be granted unless:

(a) the proposed appeal would raise some important point of principle or practice; or
(b) there is some other compelling reason for the relevant appellate court to hear the appeal.[140]

21.94 Having approved the application of that 'more restrained approach' to judicial review of the Upper Tribunal's decisions, the Supreme Court in *Cart* went on to state that this test:

... is capable of encompassing both the important point of principle affecting large numbers of similar claims and the compelling reasons presented by the extremity of the consequences for the individual.[141]

And:

... might include (i) a case where it is strongly arguable that the individual has suffered ... 'a wholly exceptional collapse of fair procedure' or (ii) a case where it is strongly arguable that there has been an error of law which has caused truly drastic consequences.[142]

And in the linked Scottish case of *Eba v Advocate General for Scotland* Lord Hope stated:

Underlying the first of these concepts is the idea that the issue would require to be one of general importance, not one confined to the

---

138 *R (Cart) v Upper Tribunal* [2011] UKSC 28, [2011] 2 WLR 36 para 43.
139 [2011] UKSC 28, [2011] 2 WLR 36.
140 Appeals from the Upper Tribunal to the Court of Appeal Order 2008 SI No 2834 article 2.
141 *R (Cart) v Upper Tribunal* [2011] UKSC 28, [2011] 2 WLR 36, para 57, per Baroness Hale of Richmond with whom the other members of the court agreed.
142 *R (Cart) v Upper Tribunal* [2011] UKSC 28, [2011] 2 WLR 36, para 131, per Lord Dyson, with whom Baroness Hale, Lord Hope, Lord Rodger and Lord Brown agreed.

petitioner's own facts and circumstances. The second would include circumstances where it was clear that the decision was perverse or plainly wrong or where, due to some procedural irregularity, the petitioner had not had a fair hearing at all.[143]

21.95 However, the Court of Appeal, after *Cart*, set out its own interpretation of the second appeals test in the context of three applications for permission to appeal from the UT-IAC to the Court of Appeal. Carnwath LJ giving the judgment of the Court on permission in *PR (Sri Lanka), SS (Bangladesh) and TC (Zimbabwe)*[144] stated:

> ... 'compelling' means legally compelling, rather than compelling, perhaps from a political or emotional point of view, although such considerations may exceptionally add weight to the legal arguments.

21.96 The Administrative Court has since held that the *PR (Sri Lanka)* test applies to judicial reviews of a refusal by the UT-IAC of a permission to appeal to the UT-IAC.[145]

21.97 The effect of *PR (Sri Lanka)* (if it does indeed apply also on judicial review) is to make it difficult either to seek judicial review of a decision of the UT-IAC to refuse permission to appeal to itself, or to obtain permission to appeal to the Court of Appeal from a substantive decision of the UT-IAC, even where fundamental rights are at stake. Although the impact of the judgment has yet to be worked out in practice at the time of writing, it appears that only cases involving an important point of principle or practice (which means a new point and not just an existing point which has been wrongly applied[146]), or cases with high prospects of success, where there has been a 'plainly wrong' decision in the FTT-IAC (see *Eba*, quoted above at para 21.94) or where there has been a 'collapse of fair procedure' would be granted permission.[147] It may also be a relevant factor where an appeal has been re-made de novo (meaning afresh) by the UT-IAC, so that in effect there has been only one level of judicial consideration[148]

---

143 *Eba v Advocate General* [2011] UKSC 29, [2011] 3 WLR 149 para 48, endorsed by the other members of the Supreme Court in *Cart* [2011] UKSC 28, [2011] 2 WLR 36.
144 [2011] EWCA Civ 988.
145 *R (Khan) v Secretary of State for the Home Department and the Upper Tribunal* [2011] EWHC 2763 (Admin).
146 *Uphill v BRB (Residuary) Ltd* [2005] EWCA Civ 60, applying the same test under Access to Justice Act 1999 s55.
147 *PR (Sri Lanka) v Secretary of State for the Home Department* [2011] EWCA Civ 988 para 35.
148 *PR (Sri Lanka) v Secretary of State for the Home Department* [2011] EWCA Civ 988 para 53.

(the Court of Appeal did not decide whether it would also be relevant if the applicant had won before the FTT-IAC, only to lose on appeal by the SSHD, but we suggest that it should[149]).

21.98 We respectfully suggest that the Court of Appeal's approach in *PR (Sri Lanka)* is difficult to reconcile with the conclusion in *Cart*, that extreme 'consequences for the individual' may present 'compelling' reasons for granting permission.

Powers of the UT-IAC on determining an appeal

21.99 Where the UT-IAC sets aside a decision of the FTT-IAC, it can:
- remit the case back to the FTT-IAC with directions for its reconsideration[150] (it may, for example, direct that the case be heard by members of the FTT-IAC who did not make the decision now set aside[151]); or
- re-make the decision itself[152] in which circumstances it may make its own findings of fact[153] and has power to make any decision which the FTT-IAC could have made.[154]

21.100 The Senior President has said in his Practice Statements that the UT-IAC will generally re-make the decision itself rather than remitting to the FTT-IAC unless 'the effect of the error has been to deprive a party before the First-tier Tribunal of a fair hearing' or there are 'highly compelling reasons' for remitting it.[155] It remains to be seen whether this practice may be modified in light of the acute difference for the purposes of onward appeals, between, on the one hand, cases remitted after a finding of an error of law to the FTT-IAC (so that the second appeals test does not apply to an onward appeal from the next decision), and on the other, cases where the UT-IAC has re-decided the case itself (so that the stringent second appeals test, discussed at paras 21.93–21.98 above, applies to any onward appeal).

---

149 Compare the stress in *PR (Sri Lanka)* at para 41 on cases where the applicant 'has failed twice' before the FTT-IAC and UT-IAC.
150 TCEA 2007 s12(2)(b)(i).
151 TCEA 2007 s12(3)(a).
152 TCEA 2007 s12(2)(b)(ii).
153 TCEA 2007 s12(4)(b).
154 TCEA 2007 s12(4)(a).
155 Practice Statements, Immigration and Asylum Chambers of the First-Tier Tribunal and the Upper Tribunal, Carnwath LJ, 10 February 2010, no 7.

Procedure of the UT-IAC on appeal

21.101 Where permission to appeal to the UT-IAC has been granted, the UT-IAC may list a case management review hearing.[156]

21.102 The UT-IAC may make directions as to the issues on which it wishes to hear evidence and submissions; the nature of evidence or submissions; and the way in which evidence is to be given.[157] The UT-IAC may also make anonymity orders and orders prohibiting the disclosure or publication of documents relating to the proceedings or of any matter likely to lead members of the public to identify a person who the UT-IAC considers should not be identified.[158] It also has the power to summons witnesses to attend a hearing (usually on 14 days' notice) and to order any person to answer any question or produce any documents in their possession which relate to any issue in the proceedings.[159] The UT-IAC may also require a party or another person to provide documents, information or submissions to it.[160] The general rule is that hearings in the UT-IAC are in public[161] however, the UT-IAC may give directions that part or all of an appeal should be heard in private.[162]

21.103 The UT-IAC may make directions of its own motion or on the application of one of the parties, that application being made orally at a hearing or in writing.[163] A failure to comply with directions does not of itself render the proceedings void or any step in the proceedings;[164] however, the UT-IAC does have powers to impose sanctions for such failures. Most relevantly, the UT-IAC has the power to exclude evidence which was not provided within the time allowed by a direction[165] (or where it would otherwise be unfair to admit the evidence).

21.104 Like the FTT-IAC, the UT-IAC has the power to hear evidence which would be inadmissible in a civil trial.[166] The UT-IAC also has the power to hear evidence that was not heard by the Tribunal

---

156 See the discussion of these hearings at paras 12.51–12.29 above.
157 Tribunal Procedure (Upper Tribunal Rules) 2008 SI No 2968 r15(1).
158 Tribunal Procedure (Upper Tribunal Rules) 2008 r14.
159 Tribunal Procedure (Upper Tribunal Rules) 2008 r16(1).
160 Tribunal Procedure (Upper Tribunal Rules) 2008 r5(3)(d).
161 TCEA 2007 s37(1).
162 TCEA 2007 s37(2).
163 Tribunal Procedure (Upper Tribunal Rules) 2008 r6.
164 Tribunal Procedure (Upper Tribunal Rules) 2008 r7(1).
165 Tribunal Procedure (Upper Tribunal Rules) 2008 r15(2)(b)(i).
166 Tribunal Procedure (Upper Tribunal Rules) 2008 r15(2)(a)(i).

below.[167] Often fresh evidence will be important because the appellant's personal circumstances or (where relevant) the security or human rights situation in the country of return may have changed. Fresh evidence may also go to the question of whether the Tribunal below erred in law,[168] or, more commonly, be relied on in relation to the re-making of the decision by the UT-IAC in the event that it decides that the FTT-IAC erred in law.

21.105 Where a party seeks to rely on fresh evidence in the UT-IAC *to demonstrate an error of law* by the FTT-IAC, the *Ladd v Marshall* test will apply. The *Ladd v Marshall* test asks whether the evidence could with reasonable diligence have been obtained in the earlier proceedings, whether the evidence would have had an important effect on the earlier proceedings and whether the evidence is apparently credible, although the *Ladd v Marshall* principles must be applied with some flexibility in the asylum context (and we suggest also the context of fundamental rights).[169]

21.106 A party wishing to rely on fresh evidence in the UT-IAC must file a notice of its intention to do so with the UT-IAC and serve the notice also on the other party.[170] Where no timetable has been specified by the UT-IAC, this notice should be given as soon as practicable after permission has been granted.[171] The fresh evidence itself (for example an expert report) may be submitted at a later date. However, in deciding whether to consider fresh evidence, the UT-IAC 'must have regard to whether there has been unreasonable delay in producing that evidence'.[172]

21.107 The notice of intention to rely on fresh evidence must indicate the nature of the evidence and explain why it was not submitted to the FTT-IAC.[173] The notice must also explain whether the evidence is sought to be adduced:

a) in connection with the issue of whether the FTT-IAC made an error of law; or

---

167 Tribunal Procedure (Upper Tribunal Rules) 2008 r15(2)(a)(ii).
168 See para 21.72 and note 94 of this chapter for the exacting test for an error of fact amounting to an error of law.
169 *E and R v Secretary of State for the Home Department* [2004] EWCA Civ 49, [2004] QB 1044 para 88.
170 Tribunal Procedure (Upper Tribunal Rules) 2008 r15(2A)(a).
171 IAC Practice Direction 10 February 2010, Carnwath LJ, para 4.1.
172 Tribunal Procedure (Upper Tribunal Rules) 2008 r15(2A)(b).
173 Tribunal Procedure (Upper Tribunal Rules) 2008 r15 (2A)(a)(ii).

b) in connection with the re-making of the decision by the UT-IAC in the event of the FTT-IAC decision being set aside.[174]

The notice must also clearly indicate whether the party seeks to adduce the evidence at the error of law hearing, whether it includes oral evidence, and if so give a time estimate.[175]

21.108 The UT-IAC has power to adjourn a hearing.[176] See para 21.56 above concerning the timing of adjournment applications in both tiers of the IAC.

21.109 The discussion at para 21.46 above concerning standard directions and trial bundles is equally applicable to UT-IAC.

Grounds of appeal in the UT-IAC

21.110 Nothing in primary legislation or in the Tribunal Procedure (Upper Tribunal Rules) 2008 indicates that an appeal before the UT-IAC is limited to those grounds of appeal which were raised in the notice of appeal or indeed on which permission to appeal was granted. The TCEA 2007 simply provides that there is a 'right of appeal to the Upper Tribunal on any point of law arising from a decision made by the First-Tier Tribunal other than an excluded decision'.[177] However, there is an indication in the delegated legislation that the UT-IAC may impose limitations or conditions on the grant of permission to appeal.[178]

21.111 It remains to be seen how the UT-IAC and higher courts will approach the question of whether an appeal to the UT-IAC can be confined to the grounds raised or the grounds on which permission was granted. The President of the Upper Tribunal has himself indicated that immigration judges considering applications for permission to appeal should look beyond the grounds of appeal and have power to consider any point arising from the decision if justice requires it.[179] The UT-IAC is in any event always under an obligation, at least in an appeal brought on Refugee Convention or ECHR grounds, to consider any points of law which, although not raised in the Grounds of Appeal, are 'obvious', in the sense of having 'a

---

174 IAC Practice Direction 10 February 2010, Carnwath LJ para 4.2.
175 IAC Practice Direction 10 February 2010, Carnwath LJ paras 4.3 and 4.5.
176 Tribunal Procedure (Upper Tribunal Rules) 2008 r5(3)(h).
177 TCEA 2007 s11(1).
178 Tribunal Procedure (Upper Tribunal Rules) 2008 r22(2)(a).
179 Blake J, Guidance Note 1 of 2011 paras 9–11.

strong prospect of success if ... argued'.[180] This principle is generally regarded as relating only to points favourable to applicants, with an exception for matters relating to exclusion from the Refugee Convention (as to which, see para 12.114).[181]

21.112 We would caution, however, that parties who wish to rely on a point not raised in their grounds of appeal should amend their grounds of appeal as early as possible, notwithstanding the absence of any express provision in the primary or delegated legislation for such amendments, and, if seeking to reopen a ground on which permission was refused, should give notice to the tribunal and to the opposing party of their intention to do so. Likewise, where a point is raised in a hearing which was not in the grounds of appeal on which permission was granted, the opposing party should be given time, and an adjournment if necessary, to address it.

Hearings in the UT-IAC

21.113 In the UT-IAC, the Home Office is usually represented by a presenting officer (see para 21.59 above) although the Treasury Solicitor and Treasury Counsel may be instructed in more complex cases.

21.114 At the hearing of the appeal in the UT-IAC, the UT-IAC will first consider whether there was an error of law in the decision of the FTT-IAC such that the decision should be set aside.[182] The UT-IAC will generally hear submissions first from the appealing party, then from the responding party.

21.115 Where it is satisfied that the original decision should be set aside, the UT-IAC will then consider whether to re-make the decision itself by reference to the FTT-IAC's findings of fact and any new documentary evidence submitted which is reasonably practicable to adduce for consideration at that hearing.

21.116 The parties should therefore be ready, unless specific directions have been given to the contrary, for the UT-IAC to proceed directly after finding an error of law to re-make the decision on the documents before it, unless further oral evidence is required.[183] This makes it critical to:

180 *R v Secretary of State for the Home Department ex p Robinson* [1997] 3 WLR 1162.
181 *R v Secretary of State for the Home Department ex p Robinson* [1997] 3 WLR 1162.
182 Under TCEA 2007 s12(2)(a).
183 IAC Practice Direction 10 February 2010, Carnwath LJ, para 3.

a) make an application, where appropriate, for permission to rely on any relevant fresh evidence; (see 21.106 above) and
b) put the UT-IAC on notice where oral evidence will be needed in the event that the Tribunal proceeds to remake the decision itself.

Standard practice in the UT-IAC currently is that the UT-IAC will decide in before the hearing whether or not it is likely that, if an error of law is found, it will proceed immediately to re-make the decision, and will issue directions accordingly.

21.117 Where it is not reasonably practicable for the UT-IAC to remake the decision immediately on finding an error of law, it will give written reasons for its finding that there has been an error of law, and adjourn the hearing, to recommence either before a differently constituted or the same panel, to consider the evidence.[184]

21.118 Where the UT-IAC hears oral evidence, the procedure is the same as that already described above at paras 21.60–21.68 in respect of the FTT-IAC.

21.119 Alternatively, the UT-IAC may remit the matter back to the FTT-IAC, and may give directions as to its reconsideration, including a direction that the case be heard by a different panel or procedural directions.[185]

Seeking permission to appeal from the UT-IAC on a second appeal

21.120 Second appeals have already been defined at para 21.93 above. An appeal on a point of law lies from the UT-IAC to the Court of Appeal (or, in Scotland, the Court of Session, or in Northern Ireland, the Court of Appeal of Northern Ireland).[186]

21.121 However, there is no right of appeal against an 'excluded' decision of the UT-IAC. For these purposes, an 'excluded' decision is a decision by the UT-IAC on permission to appeal from the FTT-IAC;[187] a decision by the UT-IAC on whether to review or the action to take in light of a review, of the FTT-IAC;[188] a decision of the UT-IAC that has

---

184 IAC Practice Direction 10 February 2010, Carnwath LJ, paras 3.4 and 3.6.
185 TCEA 2007 s12.
186 TCEA 2007 s13.
187 TCEA 2007 s13(8)(c).
188 TCEA 2007 s13(8)(d).

already been set aside;[189] and any procedural, ancillary or preliminary decision made in relation to certain appeals.[190] Most importantly for the purposes of FNPs, procedural, ancillary or preliminary decisions are 'excluded' where these are made in relation to an appeal under NIAA 2002 s82 (which covers appeals against a decision to deport or a decision refusing to revoke a deportation order) or an appeal under the EEA Regs 2006 reg 26 (appeals against 'EEA decisions').

21.122 Permission to appeal from a decision of the UT-IAC must first be sought from the UT-IAC. Only if permission is refused by the UT-IAC, may permission to appeal be sought from the Court of Appeal.[191] We discuss applications for permission to appeal in the Court of Appeal further below at paras 21.36–21.39.

Time limits

21.123 Note that time for appealing from the UT-IAC begins to run when the UT-IAC (or where appropriate the SSHD) *sends* the written notice of decision; notification of amended reasons for, or correction of, the decision following a review; or notification that an application for the decision to be set aside has been unsuccessful.[192]

21.124 Where the applicant is in the UK at the time that the application is made, the application for permission to appeal from the UT-IAC must be brought within 12 working days of time beginning to run[193] (or, if the notice of decision is served electronically or delivered personally, ten working days[194]).

21.125 However, where the applicant is in detention at the time that the application is made, the application must be brought within seven working days of time beginning to run[195] (or, if the notice of decision is served electronically or delivered personally, five working days[196]).

21.126 Where the applicant is outside the UK at the time that the application is made, the application for permission to appeal from the UT-IAC must be brought within 38 calendar days of time beginning to

---

189 TCEA 2007 s13(8)(e).
190 Appeals (Excluded Decisions) Order 2009 article 3(m).
191 TCEA 2007 s13(5).
192 Tribunal Procedure (Upper Tribunal Rules) 2008 rr3 and 3A.
193 Tribunal Procedure (Upper Tribunal Rules) 2008 r3B(a)(i).
194 Tribunal Procedure (Upper Tribunal Rules) 2008 r3C(a).
195 Tribunal Procedure (Upper Tribunal Rules) 2008 r3B(ii).
196 Tribunal Procedure (Upper Tribunal Rules) 2008 r3C(b).

run[197] (or, if the notice of decision is served electronically or delivered personally, ten working days[198]).

Extensions of time

21.127 The UT-IAC has discretion to extend time.[199] Any application for permission to appeal made out of time should be accompanied by a request for an application for an extension of time and reasons why the application was not made in time.[200]

Application notice

21.128 There is no specific form on which applications for permission to appeal from the UT-IAC to the Court of Appeal should be made. The application should be made in writing[201] and must:
 a) identify the decision of the tribunal to which it relates;
 b) identify the alleged error or errors of law in the decision; and
 c) state the result the party making the application is seeking.[202]

Applicable test

21.129 We have already discussed above at paras 21.92–21.98 the guidance of the Supreme Court and Court of Appeal on the test to be applied on second appeals. Note that this more exacting test for second appeals does not apply where the decision of the UT-IAC was itself made on appeal from the AIT (the predecessor tribunal).[203] Where the decision considered by the UT-IAC was made by the AIT, the test for permission is simply whether there are real prospects of success or some other compelling reason why the appeal should be heard.[204]

21.130 See also the discussion of errors of law at para 21.72 above.

---

197 Tribunal Procedure (Upper Tribunal Rules) 2008 r3B(b).
198 Tribunal Procedure (Upper Tribunal Rules) 2008 r3C(c).
199 Tribunal Procedure (Upper Tribunal Rules) 2008 r5(3)(a).
200 Tribunal Procedure (Upper Tribunal Rules) 2008 r44(6)(a).
201 Tribunal Procedure (Upper Tribunal Rules) 2008 r44(1).
202 Tribunal Procedure (Upper Tribunal Rules) 2008 r44(7).
203 *FA (Iraq) v Secretary of State for the Home Department* [2010] EWCA Civ 827 paras 7 and 8 (undisturbed on appeal to the Supreme Court).
204 Civil Procedure Rules 1998 (CPR) 52.3(6).

Review by the UT-IAC of its own decisions

21.131 Again (just as in an appeal from FTT-IAC to UT-IAC) there is a rarely-used filter 'review' stage in an appeal from the UT-IAC to the Court of Appeal. The UT-IAC has the power to review, on its own initiative, or on receiving an application for permission to appeal to the Court of Appeal, a decision of the UT-IAC other than an 'excluded' decision.[205] 'Excluded' decisions for these purposes have already been defined at para 21.121 above.[206]

21.132 The UT-IAC may only undertake such a review if:
a) when making the decision, the UT-IAC overlooked a legislative provision or binding authority which could have had a material effect on the decision;[207] or
b) since the UT-IAC's decision, a court has made a decision which is binding on the UT and which, had it been made before the UT-IAC's decision, could have had a material effect on it.[208]

21.133 On a review, the UT-IAC may correct accidental errors in the decision or in a record of the decision;[209] amend reasons given for the decision;[210] or set the decision aside.[211] If the UT-IAC sets a decision aside, it must re-decide the matter[212] and when re-deciding the matter, may make its own findings of fact.[213]

Procedure after a grant of permission by UT-IAC to appeal to the Court of Appeal

21.134 The UT-IAC may grant permission to appeal to the Court of Appeal on all grounds or only on limited grounds.[214]

---

205 TCEA 2007 s10(1)–(2).
206 For the purposes of review, the UT-IAC may review its own decision, on an earlier review, to set aside a decision of the FTT-IAC, but only to the extent of correcting accidental errors in the decision or in the record of the decision: TCEA 2007 s10(7).
207 Tribunal Procedure (Upper Tribunal Rules) 2008 r45(1)(a).
208 Tribunal Procedure (Upper Tribunal Rules) 2008 r45(1)(b).
209 TCEA 2007 s10(4)(a).
210 TCEA 2007 s10(4)(b).
211 TCEA 2007 s10(4)(c).
212 TCEA 2007 s10(5).
213 TCEA 2007 s10(6).
214 Tribunal Procedure (Upper Tribunal Rules) 2008 r45(5).

21.135 Where the UT-IAC grants permission to appeal to the Court of Appeal, the successful applicant must file an appellant's notice in the Court of Appeal within 14 calendar days of being served with notice of the grant of permission, and must serve a copy of the appellant's notice on the respondent and on the Upper Tribunal within a further seven working days.[215] The appellant's notice is form N161 which is available on the HM Courts website.[216] The appellant's notice must be accompanied by the specific documents listed at CPR Practice Direction 52 para 5.6(2)(a)–(f) but the appellant need not file any appeal bundle. On being served with the appellant's notice, the UT-IAC sends to the Court of Appeal copies of the documents which were before the tribunal when it considered the appeal.[217]

Making an application for permission to appeal in the Court of Appeal

21.136 Where the UT-IAC refuses permission to appeal from itself on a second appeal, the applicant may renew his or her application for permission to appeal to the Court of Appeal. The application for permission to appeal must be made on an appellant's notice within 14 calendar days of being served with the refusal of permission to appeal of the UT-IAC.[218] The same requirements for service, documents and bundles then apply as described at para 21.35 above. The Court of Appeal has power to extend time for seeking permission to appeal[219] but will expect to see good reason for so doing.

21.137 The application for permission to appeal will first be considered on the papers by a single Lord Justice of Appeal. Where permission to appeal is refused on the papers, there is usually a right to orally renew the application in the Court of Appeal. The application to make oral submissions should be made within seven working days of being served with the refusal of permission.[220] When a legally represented applicant is orally renewing an application for permission to appeal, the applicant's advocate must file an 'Advocate's Statement' at least

---

215 CPR PD 52 para 21.7(3)–(4).
216 See http://hmctscourtfinder.justice.gov.uk/HMCTS/GetForm.do?court_forms_id=388.
217 CPR PD 52 para 21.7(5).
218 CPR PD 52 para 21.7(3).
219 CPR 3.1(2)(a).
220 CPR 52.3(5).

four days before the hearing, informing the court and respondent of the points he or she intends to pursue and explaining why permission is still pursued notwithstanding the refusal of permission on the papers and (where the applicant is publicly funded) confirming that a copy of the refusal of permission has been forwarded to the Legal Services Commission.[221]

21.138 The exception to the usual entitlement to orally renew applications for permission in the Court of Appeal is that the single Lord Justice of Appeal considering the application on the papers has the power to indicate that an application is 'totally without merit', and to order that the application for permission may not be orally renewed.[222]

21.139 There is no onward appeal to the Supreme Court from a refusal of permission to appeal by the Court of Appeal.

Abandonment and 'final determination' of appeals

21.140 Where a person brings an appeal under NIAA 2002 s82 while he or she is still in the UK, the appeal in the IAC is treated as abandoned if he or she leaves the UK.[223]

21.141 Likewise, a person bringing an appeal under NIAA 2002 s82 who is granted leave to enter or remain in the UK[224] is treated as having abandoned the appeal in the IAC unless the appeal is brought on Refugee Convention grounds and the individual is granted a period of leave of over 12 months (or the appeal is brought on Race Relations Act grounds) and gives notice that he or she intends to pursue the appeal.[225] This applies not only to appeals in the tribunal but also to appeals in the Court of Appeal.[226]

21.142 In certain types of appeals, an appeal is treated as finally determined where a deportation order is made against the appellant. Most significantly for FNPs, this applies where the appeal is against a decision to revoke indefinite leave to remain.[227]

---

221 CPR PD 52 para 4.14A.
222 CPR 52.3(4A).
223 NIAA 2002 s104(4).
224 NIAA 2002 s104(4A).
225 NIAA 2002 s104(4B) and (4C).
226 *LB (Jamaica) v Secretary of State for the Home Department* [2011] EWCA Civ 1420.
227 NIAA 2002 ss104(5) and 82(2)(f).

CHAPTER 22

Restriction and loss of appeal rights in deportation and revocation cases

22.1	Introduction
22.4	**Loss of in-country appeal rights**
22.4	'Clearly unfounded' certificates
22.10	Third-country certificates
22.14	**Loss of all appeal rights**
22.14	'One-stop' certification under NIAA 2002 s96
22.23	Certificate under EEA Regs reg 26(5)
22.24	**Summary**

Introduction

22.1 This chapter reviews the circumstances in which rights of appeal to the Immigration and Asylum Chamber of the First-tier Tribunal (FTT-IAC) may be restricted or lost through certification in deportation and revocation cases. We focus on certification under Nationality, Immigration and Asylum Act (NIAA) 2002 s94(2) ('clearly unfounded' certificates) and s96 ('one-stop' certificates). These forms of certification are likely to be particularly significant in the context of 'automatic' deportation and applications for revocation of a deportation order. Third country certification are discussed only briefly here since this will have very limited application to foreign national prisoners and former prisoners (FNPs).

22.2 Appeals to the Special Immigration Appeals Commission (SIAC) are discussed separately in chapter 23. Note that certification under NIAA 2002 s96, discussed in this chapter, applies to appeals to SIAC as well as appeals to the FTT-IAC.[1]

22.3 For a brief overview of judicial review procedures which may be used to challenge certification, see paras 42.16–42.71.

Loss of in-country appeal rights

'Clearly unfounded' certificates

22.4 Where an asylum or human rights claim has been certified under NIAA 2002 s94 as 'clearly unfounded', no in-country appeal can be brought to the FTT-IAC in reliance on that claim unless and until the certificate is quashed in judicial review proceedings.

22.5 The House of Lord has held in respect of predecessor legislation on 'manifestly unfounded' certificates that the test for the imposition of a certificate is 'whether the allegation is so clearly without substance that the appeal would be bound to fail'.[2] The test for a 'clearly unfounded' certificate has been held to be identical;[3] and it has been held that a claim may only be certified as 'clearly unfounded' if 'the claim cannot on any legitimate view succeed'.[4]

---

1 Special Immigration Appeals Commission Act 1997 s2(2)(i).
2 *R (Yogathas) v Secretary of State for the Home Department* [2003] 1 AC 920.
3 *ZT (Kosovo)* [2009] UKHL 6, per Lord Hope.
4 *R (L) v Secretary of State for the Home Department* [2003] EWCA Civ 25, [2003] 1 WLR 1230.

22.6 In addition, if an asylum or human rights claimant is entitled to reside in one of the countries listed under NIAA 2002 s94(4), then the Secretary of State for the Home Department (SSHD) is required to certify the claim unless satisfied that the claim is not clearly unfounded. Likewise, in third country cases, where a person makes a claim that his or her rights under the European Convention on Human Rights (ECHR) would be breached by removal to a listed safe third country of which he or she is not a national or citizen, the SSHD is required to certify the claim as clearly unfounded unless satisfied that the claim is not clearly unfounded.[5] However, the test to be applied by the SSHD (and by any court reviewing the certificate) in respect of the listed countries is no different from the general 'clearly unfounded' test under NIAA 2002 s94(2).[6] The claim can only be certified if it cannot on any legitimate view succeed, whether or not the asylum or human rights claimant is from one of the listed countries.

22.7 In *R (Razgar) v Secretary of State for the Home Department*, Lord Bingham of Cornhill held, in respect of predecessor 'manifestly unfounded' legislation, that when a certificate is challenged in judicial review, the test to be applied by a court was wednesbury review with a requirement of anxious scrutiny but:

> ... the reviewing court must, as it seems to me, consider how an appeal would be likely to fare before an adjudicator, as the tribunal responsible for deciding the appeal if there were an appeal. This means that the reviewing court must ask itself essentially the questions which would have to be answered by an adjudicator.[7]

22.8 In *ZT (Kosovo) v Secretary of State for the Home Department*[8] the House of Lords was split as to the nuances of the approach to be taken by a court where a 'clearly unfounded' certificate imposed under NIAA 2002 s94 is challenged by judicial review. Lord Phillips took the view that the court must ask itself the same question that the SSHD is required to ask herself:

> ... if any reasonable doubt exists as to whether the claim may succeed then it is not clearly unfounded ... [I]f the court concludes that a claim has a realistic prospect of success when the Secretary of State has

---

5 Asylum and Immigration (Treatment of Claimants etc) Act (AITCA) 2004 Sch 3 para 5(4).
6 AITCA 2004 Sch 3 para 5(4).
7 [2004] UKHL 27, [2004] 2 AC 368, para 17.
8 [2009] UKHL 6, [2009] 1 WLR 348.

reached a contrary view, the court will necessarily conclude that the Secretary of State's view was irrational.[9]

Lord Brown of Eaton under Heywood agreed: the approach was a *Wednesbury* review with an additional requirement of anxious scrutiny but:

> ... if the Court concludes that an appeal to the [Asylum and Immigration Tribunal] AIT might succeed, it must uphold the challenge and allow such an in-country appeal to be brought.[10]

Lords Hope and Carswell emphasised that the approach was one of review, applying a standard of anxious scrutiny. Lord Neuberger took an intermediate position finding that, while it was hard to conceive of circumstances in which the SSHD's certificate could stand notwithstanding that the court concluded that the claim had realistic prospects of success, there was no hard and fast rule to preclude this.

22.9 A certificate under NIAA 2002 s94 has no effect if imposed after an in-country appeal to the FTT-IAC has been instituted.[11]

Third-country certificates

22.10 Third-country certificates are likely to be of limited application in FNP cases and we discuss them only briefly here. These certificates will be relevant where the FNP has never had leave to enter or remain in the UK and makes an asylum or ECHR claim in the UK having previously passed through another country deemed a safe third country.

22.11 An asylum or human rights claim may be certified on third-country grounds under AITCA 2004 Sch 3 Part 2 where the SSHD proposes to remove the person to a country of which the person is not a national or a citizen and which is one of a list of safe states[12] (currently Iceland, Norway and the EU member states other than the UK) or another state added to the list of safe third countries by secondary

---

9 *ZT (Kosovo) v Secretary of State for the Home Department* [2009] UKHL 6, [2009] 1 WLR 348, para 23.
10 *ZT (Kosovo) v Secretary of State for the Home Department* [2009] UKHL 6, [2009] 1 WLR 348 para 75.
11 *AS Somalia v Secretary of State for the Home Department* [2009] EWCA Civ 114.
12 The legislation which deems conclusively certain states to be safe was successfully challenged before the Grand Chamber of the CJEU in *NS v Secretary of State for the Home Department and ME and Others v Refugee Applications Commissioner and Minister of Justice, Equality and Reform* Cases C-411/10 and C-493/10 judgment on 21 December 2011, and is likely to be substantially amended.

legislation.[13] This applies to an asylum claim or human rights claim brought on the basis that onward removal from the third country to another country would breach the individual's rights under the Refugee Convention[14] or ECHR.[15] The certification of the asylum claim or human rights claim on third country grounds prevents that claim from founding an in-country right of appeal.[16] The third-country certificate will usually be accompanied by a 'clearly unfounded' certificate on any further human rights claim.[17] Where both the asylum and human rights claims are so certified, neither the asylum nor the human rights claim can be relied upon to found an in-country right of appeal unless and until the certificates are quashed by judicial review.

22.12 A certificate under AITCA 2004 Sch 3 Part 2 has no effect if imposed after an in-country appeal to the FTT-IAC has been instituted.[18]

22.13 NIAA 2002 s94(7) goes further: it allows a statutory presumption of safety to be applied to any third country. The statutory presumption of safety is that the country is a place where a person's life and liberty is not threatened by reason of his race, religion, nationality, membership of a particular social group or political opinion and is a place from which a person will not be sent to another country otherwise than in accordance with the Refugee Convention. The SSHD certifies in an individual case that there is no reason to believe that the person's ECHR rights will be breached in that country. Again, this certificate has the effect that neither an asylum nor human rights claim can be relied upon to found an in-country right of appeal unless and until the certificate is quashed by judicial review.

Loss of all appeal rights

'One-stop' certification under NIAA 2002 s96

22.14 The 'one-stop' certificate, which penalises those who seek to rely on a matter which could have been raised earlier, is even more draconian in its effects than those certificates considered above. Where a

---

13 There is no secondary legislation designating further safe third countries at the time of writing.
14 The 1951 Convention Relating to the Status of Refugees and its 1967 Protocol.
15 AITCA 2004 Sch 3 para 5(3).
16 AITCA 2004 Sch 3 para 5(2).
17 AITCA 2004 Sch 3 para 5(4) and (5).
18 *AS Somalia v Secretary of State for the Home Department* [2009] EWCA Civ 114.

claim is certified under NIAA 2002 s96, the individual has no right of appeal to the FTT-IAC, whether in-country or out-of-country, unless and until the certificate is quashed by judicial review.

22.15 'One-stop' certification could, for example, preclude any appeal by a person who, having failed to raise a matter in an earlier appeal against a decision to deport (or, having been notified of the right of appeal but failed to bring an appeal at all) then tries to raise the same matter in an application for revocation of the deportation order.

22.16 'One-stop' certification is not limited to human rights or asylum claims: a certificate under NIAA 2002 s96 could be imposed on a claim by an EEA national or an EEA national's family member that an immigration decision breaches EU law.

22.17 A certificate may be imposed under NIAA 2002 s96 if either:

- the individual was notified of a right of appeal against an earlier immigration decision and the claim or application which the individual now seeks to make relies on a matter which could have been raised in the earlier appeal (whether or not that appeal was actually brought);[19] or
- the individual received a one-stop notice (under NIAA 2002 s120) in relation to a previous immigration decision or application and the claim or application which the individual now seeks to make relies on a matter which could have been made in a one-stop statement made in response to the one-stop notice.[20]

22.18 However, there is a 'defence' to such certification: the certificate must not be imposed if, in the opinion of the SSHD or the immigration officer, there is a satisfactory reason for the matter not being raised earlier.[21]

22.19 Detailed guidance on certification under NIAA 2002 s96 has been provided in *R (J) v Secretary of State for the Home Department*:[22]

> Under Section 96 (1) and (2) before the Secretary of State can lawfully decide to certify, she has to go through a four stage process. First she must be satisfied that the person was notified of a right of appeal under Section 82 against another immigration decision (Section 96(1)) or that the person received a notice under Section 120 by virtue of an application other than that to which the new decision relates or by virtue of a decision other than the new decision (Section 96(2)). Second she must conclude that the claim or application to which the

---

19 NIAA 2002 s96(1).
20 NIAA 2002 s96(2).
21 NIAA 2002 s96(1)(c) and (2)(c).
22 [2009] EWHC 705 (Admin) para 106.

new decision relates relies on a matter that could have been raised in an appeal against the old decision (Section 96(1)(b)) or that the new decision relates to an application or claim which relies on a matter that should have been but has not been raised in a statement made in response to that notice (Section 96(2)(b)). Third she must form the opinion that there is no satisfactory reason for that matter not having been raised in an appeal against the old decision (Section 96(1)(c)) or that there is no satisfactory reason for that matter not having been raised in a statement made in response to that notice (Section 96(2)(c)). Fourth she must address her mind to whether, having regard to all relevant factors, she should exercise her discretion to certify and conclude that it is appropriate to exercise the discretion in favour of certification.

22.20 *R (J)* clarifies that at both the third and fourth stages of the decision process, the SSHD must, if certifying an asylum or ECHR article 3 claim under NIAA 2002 s96, give anxious scrutiny to the consequences of certification. In addition, at the fourth stage (in which the SSHD must consider her discretion as to whether to certify) the SSHD must have regard to the underlying merits of the claim and, if certifying an asylum or ECHR article 3 claim:

> ... those circumstances [which must be considered by the SSHD] would ordinarily include the fact that the claim is an asylum claim and/or an Article 3 claim, the risk of persecution death and/or torture if the claimant is returned on the basis of a refusal which the Secretary of State has determined would have a realistic prospect of being overturned on appeal, the fact of that determination and the reasons for it, whether the Secretary of State rejected the second claim on the merits robustly or only with difficulty and on balance.[23]

22.21 Stadlen J warned that 'one-stop' certification must be used cautiously in the context of asylum and ECHR article 3 claims because:

> Although Section 96 has, in my view, a legitimate purpose of creating an incentive for claimants to be open and honest in their original claims, the power of certification is not designed to punish those who lie through misguided fear of telling the truth, by exposing them to a real risk of persecution, death or torture.[24]

22.22 A certificate under NIAA 2002 s96 has no effect where imposed after an appeal has been instituted to the FTT-IAC.[25]

---

23 [2009] EWHC 705 (Admin) para 140.
24 [2009] EWHC 705 (Admin) para 140.
25 NIAA 2002 s96(7).

Certificate under EEA Regs reg 26(5)

22.23 There exists a further power of certification specifically designed to prevent repetitive appeals in the context of EU law claims. Under the Immigration (European Economic Area) Regulations (EEA Regs) 2006[26] reg 26(5), the SSHD may certify a ground where it has been considered in a previous appeal brought under the EEA Regs 2006 or under NIAA 2002 s81, with the effect that no appeal at all may be brought under the EEA Regs 2006 in reliance on that ground.

Summary

22.24 The position on appeal rights can be summarised as follows:
1) Where the immigration decision appealed against is a decision to revoke indefinite leave to remain or a 'discretionary' decision to deport under the Immigration Act 1971, the appeal to the FTT-IAC may be brought from within the UK.
2) Where the immigration decision appealed against is a decision that the criteria for 'automatic' deportation under UK Borders Act 2007 are met; a refusal to revoke a deportation order; or a decision to deprive a person of the right of abode in the UK, the decision can only be appealed to the FTT-IAC from within the UK if certain criteria are met. The criteria for an in-country right of appeal against these immigration decisions are that:
    a) the appellant has made an asylum or human rights claim in the UK which has a nexus to the present immigration decision and the asylum or human rights claim has not been certified as 'clearly unfounded' nor certified on third country grounds (although it need not meet the fresh claim threshold); or
    b) the appellant is an EEA national or the family member of an EEA national and makes a claim that the immigration decision breaches EU law.

22.25 However, in respect of any of the above immigration decisions, if the claim or application is certified under NIAA 2002 s96 or EEA Regs 2006 reg 26(5) all appeal rights (both in- and out-of-country) are lost.

---

26 SI No 1003.

CHAPTER 23

The Special Immigration Appeals Commission and its procedures

23.1	Introduction
23.2	The establishment of SIAC
23.5	**SIAC's jurisdiction**
23.5	Former jurisdiction under ATCSA 2001
23.11	Current jurisdiction
23.19	**In-country and out-of-country appeals**
23.20	**Closed material and special advocates**
23.34	**Legality of the use of closed evidence in substantive deportation appeals**
23.46	**The procedure for disclosure**
23.52	**Exculpatory review**
23.56	**Burden and standard of proof**
23.58	**Detainee reporting**
23.59	**The progress of deportation appeals in SIAC**
23.71	**Consideration of deportation appeals**
23.73	Assessment of risk to national security
23.78	Assessment of safety on return

continued

23.81	**SIAC's determination**
23.83	**Bail**
23.90	Bail conditions
23.95	Variation of bail conditions
23.96	Challenging SIAC's bail decisions
23.97	**Appeal from SIAC**
23.98	Permission to appeal
23.99	The appeal

Introduction

23.1 This chapter deals with appeals to the Special Immigration Appeals Commission (SIAC) and is particularly relevant to foreign national prisoners and former prisoners (FNPs) who face expulsion from the UK on the ground that they present a risk to the UK's national security. As considered in chapter 1, a foreign national may be deported on the ground that deportation is conducive to the public good.[1] Any appeal against a decision to deport on 'conducive' grounds lies in general to the Immigration and Asylum Chamber of the First-tier tribunal (FTT-IAC) under Nationality, Immigration and Asylum Act (NIAA) 2002 s82.[2] However, some 'conducive' cases do not generate appeal rights to the FTT-IAC but to SIAC. This chapter concentrates on appeals against a decision to deport, but much of its content is relevant to other kinds of appeal in SIAC.[3] Practitioners should consult SIAC's comprehensive website which includes a database of its judgments and decisions.[4] The SIAC judgments mentioned and cited in this chapter can be found on that website.[5]

The establishment of SIAC

23.2 SIAC was established by the Special Immigration Appeals Commission Act (SIACA) 1997 s1.[6] It is now (according to the amended statute) a superior court of record.[7] The SIACA 1997 was enacted in response to the judgment of the European Court of Human Rights

---

1 Immigration Act (IA) 1971 s3(5)(a).
2 See chapter 21.
3 For SIAC's approach in appeals against a refusal to revoke a deportation order, see *T v Secretary of State for the Home Department* (SC/31/2005), 22 March 2010. For the approach in cases where the SSHD has directed that the exclusion of a person from the UK is conducive to the public good, see *EV v Secretary of State for the Home Department* (SC/67/2008) 7 April 2009.
4 See www.justice.gov.uk and follow the links.
5 In this chapter, unlike the rest of the book, we refer to individual appellants as 'he' as accurately reflecting the position in SIAC.
6 SIAC came into being on 3 August 1998: Special Immigration Appeals Commission Act 1997 (Commencement No 2) Order 1998 SI No 1892 article 2.
7 SIACA 1997 s1(3) added by Anti-terrorism, Crime and Security Act (ATCSA) 2001 s35; 14 December 2001. For an overview of SIAC's status and jurisdiction, see *R (Cart) v Upper Tribunal; R (U) v Special Immigration Appeals Commission; R (C) v Same* [2009] EWHC 3052 (Admin), [2010] 2 WLR 1012. Compare *R (Cart) v Upper Tribunal; R (MR (Pakistan)) v Same* [2011] UKSC 28, [2011] 3 WLR 107.

(ECtHR) in *Chahal v UK*[8] which had considered a non-statutory procedure for the review of deportation decisions in national security cases contained in previous immigration rules.[9] Under that procedure, deportation decisions were reviewed by an advisory panel (sometimes referred to as 'the three wise men'). The Secretary of State for the Home Department (SSHD) could withhold evidence from the applicant; and an applicant was not permitted legal representation. The panel gave advice to the SSHD but the advice was not disclosed to the applicant nor was it binding. The ECtHR in *Chahal* held that this procedure did not provide a review of detention by a court as required by European Convention on Human Rights (ECHR) article 5(4):

> The Court recognises that the use of confidential material may be unavoidable where national security is at stake. This does not mean, however, that the national authorities can be free from effective control by the domestic courts whenever they choose to assert that national security and terrorism are involved. The Court attaches significance to the fact that, as the intervenors pointed out in connection with Article 13, in Canada a more effective form of judicial control has been developed in cases of this type. This example illustrates that there are techniques which can be employed which both accommodate legitimate security concerns about the nature and sources of intelligence information and yet accord the individual a substantial measure of procedural justice.[10]

23.3 The ECtHR also found that the UK was in breach of the right to an effective remedy under ECHR article 13. The advisory procedure, together with the availability of judicial review, provided an inadequate remedy because there was insufficient independent scrutiny of the applicant's claim that his deportation would breach ECHR article 3.[11]

23.4 As a result, SIAC was formed with statutory jurisdiction bestowed by SIACA 1997[12] and by the Special Immigration Appeals Commission (Procedure) Rules 2003.[13] Appeals to SIAC are heard by

---

8 (1996) 23 EHRR 413.
9 HC 251 para 157. For a description of this procedure and the establishment of SIAC, see eg *W (Algeria) v Secretary of State for the Home Department* [2010] EWCA Civ 898.
10 (1996) 23 EHRR 413 para 131.
11 (1996) 23 EHRR 413 paras 140-155.
12 In European Economic Area (EEA) cases, SIACA 1997 is applicable by virtue of the Immigration (European Economic Area) Regulations (EEA Regs) 2006 SI No 1003 reg 28(8).
13 SI No 1034 as amended; the rules are made under SIACA 1997 s5.

constitutions of three members, at least one of whom must hold or have held high judicial office[14] or be or have been a member of the Judicial Committee of the Privy Council; and at least one of whom must be or have been a judge of the FTT-IAC or the Upper Tribunal (UT-IAC).[15] The third member is likely to be someone with experience of national security matters, as described in *Secretary of State for the Home Department v M*,[16] though this is not required by statute. SIAC has a chairman appointed by the Lord Chancellor.[17] The chairman or, in his absence, another member nominated by the chairman must preside at sittings of SIAC and report its decisions.[18] SIAC has the power to grant bail.[19]

SIAC's jurisdiction

Former jurisdiction under ATCSA 2001

23.5 In addition to its jurisdiction in immigration appeals, SIAC was the forum for challenging detention under Part 4 of ATCSA 2001. This statutory regime (now repealed) rested on the UK's derogation from the right to liberty and security provided by ECHR article 5(1). Derogation from obligations under the ECHR is permitted under article 15(1), which stipulates the conditions that must be satisfied for a lawful derogation to take place. ECHR article 15(1) states:

> In time of war or other public emergency threatening the life of the nation any High Contracting Party may take measures derogating from its obligations under this Convention to the extent strictly required by the exigencies of the situation, provided that such measures are not inconsistent with its other obligations under international law.

---

14 Defined in Part 3 of the Constitutional Reform Act 2005 as including (among others) a judge of the Supreme Court, Court of Appeal and High Court.
15 SIACA 1997 Sch 1 para 5. Members of SIAC are appointed by the Lord Chancellor: SIACA 1997 Sch 1 para 1.
16 [2004] EWCA Civ 324, [2004] 2 All ER 863 para 2. See also *Secretary of State for the Home Department v Rehman* [2003] 1 AC 153 (CA) para 11; *AS (Libya) and DD (Libya) v Secretary of State for the Home Department* [2008] EWCA Civ 289, [2008] HRLR 28 para 18.
17 SIACA 1997 Sch 1 para 2.
18 SIACA 1997 Sch 1 para 6.
19 SIACA 1997 s3.

23.6 After the terrorist attacks in the United States on 11 September 2001, the UK derogated from the obligations of ECHR article 5(1)[20] and established a regime for the indefinite detention of foreign nationals under Part 4 of ATCSA 2001.

23.7 The objective of these measures was to permit the detention of terror suspects who could neither be expelled from the UK nor detained under immigration law. As chapter 13 describes, a person cannot lawfully be expelled from the UK if there are substantial grounds for believing that he would, in the receiving country, face a real risk of ill treatment contrary to ECHR article 3. Nor can a person with leave to remain in the UK be detained under immigration powers unless he is subject to the deportation process and unless the detention is reasonably necessary for the process of deportation to be effected, as expounded by the leading case of *R v Governor of Durham Prison ex p Hardial Singh*.[21] In addition, indefinite detention of foreign nationals falls outside the scope of ECHR article 5(1)(f) and so (in the absence of a lawful derogation from article 5(1)) will breach the SSHD's obligations under the Human Rights Act (HRA) 1998 s6.

23.8 The UK's derogation from article 5(1) and the enactment of Part 4 of ATCSA 2001 marked an attempt to render lawful the indefinite detention of foreign nationals without charge or trial. More specifically, under the ATCSA 2001, the SSHD was able to certify that a person was a 'suspected international terrorist'[22] which permitted his detention under IA 1971 if he could not be deported from the UK by reason of ECHR article 3 or other legal or practical considerations.[23] Appeal against a certificate lay to SIAC which was also empowered to carry out periodic reviews of certificates. SIAC had the power to grant bail to those detained pursuant to a certificate.[24]

23.9 In *A and others v Secretary of State for the Home Department*,[25] the House of Lords considered the UK's derogation and the scheme of detention under Part 4 of ATCSA 2001. In relation to the derogation, their Lordships refused to interfere with the government's conclusion that there was a public emergency threatening the life of the nation within the meaning of ECHR article 15(1).[26] They held,[27]

---

20 Human Rights Act 1998 (Designated Derogation) Order 2001 SI No 3644.
21 [1984] 1 WLR 704. See chapter 33 for full treatment.
22 ATCSA 2001 s21.
23 ATCSA 2001 s23.
24 ATCSA 2001 ss24–26.
25 [2004] UKHL 56, [2005] 2 AC 68; known colloquially as 'the Belmarsh case'.
26 Lord Hoffmann dissenting.
27 Lord Walker dissenting.

however, that the derogation was disproportionate and did not satisfy the conditions of ECHR article 15 because it was not strictly required by the exigencies of the situation. In addition, detention under Part 4 of ATCSA 2001, which did not make provision for the detention of British terror suspects, discriminated against foreign nationals in such a way as to breach ECHR article 14 read with article 5. Hence ATCSA 2001 s23 was incompatible with the ECHR and a declaration of incompatibility[28] was made to this effect. The scheme lapsed under statutory instrument in March 2005 and in the same month it was repealed by primary legislation.[29] The parts of the SIAC (Procedure) Rules 2003 which governed the scheme have been repealed and this part of SIAC's work has disappeared.

23.10 In *A and others v UK*,[30] the ECtHR Grand Chamber considered the cases of a group of those who had been detained under ATCSA 2001. It held that the UK's derogation from ECHR article 5(1) was invalid as being disproportionate because it discriminated unjustifiably between nationals and non-nationals. The indefinite detention of a number of the applicants was therefore in breach of ECHR article 5(1). The ECtHR Grand Chamber also held that a number of the applicants had suffered a violation of ECHR article 5(4) because their detention had been upheld by SIAC in reliance on closed material. Some of the applicants were awarded compensation under ECHR article 5(5).

Current jurisdiction

23.11 SIAC has jurisdiction over appeals against decisions which would be appealable to the FTT-IAC save that they raise the interests of national security or some other protected public interest. In essence, the SSHD will certify the decision on national security or other public interest grounds, causing appeal to lie to SIAC.[31] As in other 'conducive' deportation appeals, the appellant need not have a criminal conviction.[32]

---

28 Under HRA 1998 s4(2).
29 Anti-terrorism, Crime and Security Act 2001 (Continuance in force of sections 21 to 23) Order 2004 SI No 751; Prevention of Terrorism Act 2005 s16.
30 (2009) 49 EHRR 29.
31 Nationality, Immigration and Asylum Act (NIAA) 2002 s97; EEA Regs 2006 reg 28; British Nationality Act (BNA) 1981 s40A.
32 See the discussion at para 1.9 above.

23.12 Under the relevant statutory provisions,[33] the grounds for certification are that:
- the decision was taken wholly or partly (or given wholly or partly in accordance with a direction of the SSHD which identifies the person to whom the decision relates) in the interests of national security; or
- the decision was taken wholly or partly (or given wholly or partly in accordance with a direction of the SSHD which identifies the person to whom the decision relates) in the interests of the relationship between the UK and another country; or
- the decision was taken wholly or partly in reliance on information which in the SSHD's opinion should not be made public in the above interests or otherwise in the public interest.

23.13 Decisions which may be certified are:
- an immigration decision under NIAA 2002 s82(1);
- the rejection of an asylum claim under NIAA 2002 s83(2);
- the decision to curtail or to refuse to extend limited leave following a decision that a person is not a refugee under NIAA 2002 s83A;
- EEA decisions (as defined by the EEA Regs 2006 reg 2);
- a decision to deprive a person of citizenship under the British Nationality Act (BNA) 1981 s40.[34]

23.14 Save in cases of deprivation of citizenship, the decision to certify must be taken by the SSHD acting in person.[35] If the certificate is issued while an appeal to the tribunal is pending, the appeal will lapse and a person will have the right to commence an appeal in SIAC.[36]

23.15 The available grounds of appeal to SIAC are the same statutory grounds applicable to appeals in the FTT-IAC under NIAA 2002 s84.[37] Other provisions of NIAA 2002 also apply to SIAC proceedings, including the matters to be considered on an appeal, the grounds on which an appeal must be allowed and the power to give directions

---

33 See note 31 above.
34 SIACA 1997 ss2 and 2B; EEA Regs 2006 reg 28. For discussion of BNA 1981 s40, see *R (Hicks) v Secretary of State for the Home Department* [2005] EWHC 2818 (Admin), [2006] ACD 47 and (on appeal) *Secretary of State for the Home Department v Hicks* [2006] EWCA Civ 400, [2006] INLR 203.
35 NIAA 2002 s97(4); EEA Regs 2006 reg 28(5). BNA 1981 has no equivalent provision in relation to deprivation of citizenship.
36 NIAA 2002 s99; SIACA 1997 s2; EEA Regs 2006 reg 28.
37 See chapter 21 for the discussion of those grounds. Applicable to SIAC appeals by virtue of SIACA 1997 s2(2)(e).

for the purpose of giving effect to a decision to allow an appeal.[38] An appeal against the rejection of an asylum claim is to be treated as abandoned if the appellant leaves the UK.[39]

23.16 SIAC has power to review the SSHD's decision on questions of fact and law.[40] In deportation appeals, there are usually two aspects to the proceedings. SIAC will determine whether a person is a danger to national security and, if so, will then consider whether his expulsion is lawful. Both practitioners and SIAC have adopted the term 'safety on return' to describe the assessment of whether a person, if expelled, is at risk of ill treatment in breach of his human rights. In determining the issue of safety on return, the same framework of the Refugee Convention,[41] Qualification Directive,[42] ECHR and Immigration Rules applies in SIAC as applies in all challenges to expulsion. The same general principles of law will apply.

23.17 A number of SIAC's powers may be exercised by the chairman alone or by a single member, including extensions of time for appealing to SIAC, giving directions at a hearing or in writing, deciding applications for leave to vary grounds of appeal, deciding applications for leave to appeal to the Court of Appeal, bail decisions, deciding applications by the SSHD for leave to amend or supplement closed material, making orders for failure to comply with directions, issuing a witness summons and ordering that two or more proceedings

---

38 NIAA 2002 ss85, 86 and 87. Other statutory provisions applicable to SIAC appeals are: IA 1971 ss3C and 3D (continuation of leave pending appeal); NIAA 2002 s78 (no removal while appeal pending), s79 (no deportation order while appeal pending) (but see also NIAA 2002 s97A(2) by which section 79 does not apply where the SSHD certifies that the decision to make a deportation order was taken in the interests of national security), s96 (disallowing new appeals where there has been an earlier right of appeal), s104 (defining when an appeal is pending), s105 (notice of immigration decision).
39 SIACA 1997 s2(4).
40 Compare *Secretary of State for the Home Department v Rehman* [2001] UKHL 47, [2003] 1 AC 153 para 11.
41 The 1951 Convention Relating to the Status of Refugees and its 1967 Protocol ('Refugee Convention').
42 Council Directive 2004/83/EC on minimum standards for the qualification and status of third country nationals or stateless persons as refugees or as persons who otherwise need international protection and the content of the protection granted ('Qualification Directive').

23.18 Appeal from SIAC's final determinations lies to the Court of Appeal.[44] There is no right of appeal against the grant or refusal of bail. Appeals against interlocutory and preliminary rulings will need to await SIAC's final determination of the case, as there is no appeal right 'until after SIAC has finally completed its task'.[45] Unless and until SIAC issues a decision that is dispositive of the appeal, no right of further appeal accrues.[46]

In-country and out-of-country appeals

23.19 SIACA 1997 enables a person to appeal to SIAC from within the UK in the same circumstances as a person can appeal in-country to the FTT-IAC.[47] However, the Immigration, Asylum and Nationality Act (IANA) 2006 introduced limitations to in-country rights of appeal by inserting section 97A into NIAA 2002 which has the effect of qualifying SIACA 1997.[48] By virtue of SIACA 1997 s97A, the right of appeal against deportation in national security cases is non-suspensive save in respect of human rights claims and claims by EEA nationals under EU law.[49] Even in human rights cases, the SSHD may certify that a person's removal from the UK would not breach the ECHR. There is an in-country right of appeal against the issue of the certificate.[50] At present, there is little case-law to shed light on the application of SIACA 1997 s97A or on SIAC's general approach to it.

---

43 SIAC (Procedure) Rules 2003 r5. The same rule allows anything of an administrative nature to be done by a member of SIAC's staff. It is, for example, very common for variations to bail conditions to be decided by a member of SIAC on the papers and for the decision to be conveyed to the parties by letter from a member of the SIAC staff.
44 SIACA 1997 s7. In Scotland, appeal lies to the Court of Session.
45 *Al-Jedda v Secretary of State for the Home Department* [2010] EWCA Civ 212 para 69.
46 *LO (Jordan) v Secretary of State for the Home Department* [2011] EWCA Civ 164.
47 SIACA 1997 s2(5).
48 NIAA 2002 s97A is inserted by the IANA 2006 s7(1). It came into force on 31 August 2006 (Immigration, Asylum and Nationality Act 2006 (Commencement No 2) Order 2006 SI No 2226 Sch 1 article 3).
49 NIAA 2002 s97A makes no exception for asylum claims.
50 NIAA 2002 s97A(3).

Closed material and special advocates

23.20 SIACA 1997 enables proceedings to take place without the appellant being given the full evidence upon which the SSHD relies and without the appellant and his legal representatives being present.[51] At the core of SIAC procedures is the distinction between open material, seen by SIAC and all parties, and 'closed material', seen only by SIAC, the Home Office and the special advocate representing the interests of the appellant.[52] The Home Office may not rely on closed material unless a special advocate has been appointed.[53] The special advocate's role is set down in the SIAC (Procedure) Rules 2003 r35. He or she must 'represent the interests of the appellant' by:

- making submissions to SIAC at any hearings from which the appellant and his representatives are excluded;
- adducing evidence and cross-examining witnesses at any such hearings; and
- making written submissions to SIAC.

23.21 In short, the special advocate will seek to maximise disclosure to the appellant in the open case and will represent the appellant's interests during the sessions dealing with closed material from which the appellant and his lawyers will be excluded.

23.22 The special advocate will be a security cleared barrister appointed by the Attorney-General.[54] Special advocates are serviced by lawyers in the Special Advocates Support Office (SASO), which is located in the Treasury Solicitor's Department. SASO has produced an Open Manual which is a guide to the special advocate's role, available on the website of the Attorney-General's Office.[55]

23.23 As a matter of practice, the Attorney-General is willing to appoint two special advocates for cases in SIAC, a leader (who need not be a QC) and a junior.[56] The appellant is able to select his special advocate from a list of those who are members of the Attorney's panel. As

---

51 SIACA 1997 s5(3).
52 SIACA 1997 ss5(3) and 6; SIAC (Procedure) Rules 2003 r37. Where the SSHD relies on closed material, he or she must file with SIAC and serve on the special advocate a statement of reasons for objecting to its disclosure: SIAC (Procedure) Rules 2003 r37(3)(b).
53 SIAC (Procedure) Rules 2003 r37(2).
54 SIACA 1997 s6; SIAC (Procedure) Rules 2003 r34. In Scotland, the special advocate is appointed by the Lord Advocate.
55 See www.attorneygeneral.gov.uk.
56 This chapter will use the statutory term 'special advocate' albeit that there may be more than one in practice.

23.24 Members of SASO are a mixture of security cleared lawyers and staff supporting special advocates in relation to closed matters, and non-security cleared lawyers and staff providing support before a special advocate receives the closed material. The open team will continue to deal with the appellant's legal representatives and with general administrative matters which do not touch on the SSHD's closed case, after the special advocate has received the closed material.

23.25 Although representing the appellant's interests, the special advocate is not a party to the proceedings.[58] Nor as a matter of law is the special advocate responsible to the person whose interests he or she is appointed to represent.[59] A special advocate cannot be responsible to the appellant because he or she cannot take instructions from the appellant after receipt of the closed material. The special advocate will need to use judgment, discretion and common sense in deciding how to present the appellant's case in the absence of instructions but is bound to represent the appellant's interests and will be likely to give very great weight to any expressed wishes of the appellant. It is important for appellants to be advised that they remain free to communicate with the special advocate about the progress of the proceedings at any time, provided that the communication is made through the appellant's legal representative and in writing; it is only the special advocate who cannot communicate with the appellant after receipt of the closed material.[60]

23.26 The special advocate system has been controversial but has been increasingly used in contexts other than SIAC.[61] A number of statutes make provision for special advocates in the national security context, most notably the Prevention of Terrorism Act (PTA) 2005

---

57 R (Murungaru) v Secretary of State for the Home Department [2008] EWCA Civ 1015, [2009] INLR 180 para 14. See also Tariq v Home Office [2011] UKSC 35, [2011] 3 WLR 322 paras 42–59.

58 SIAC (Procedure) Rules 2003 r32 which stipulates that the parties are the appellant, the SSHD and, where he gives notice that he wishes to be treated as a party, the UK representative of the UN High Commissioner for Refugees (UNHCR).

59 SIACA 1997 s6(4).

60 SIAC (Procedure) Rules 2003 r36(6).

61 For a summary of the history and nature of the role, see Malik v Manchester Crown Court [2008] EWHC 1362 (Admin), [2008] 4 All ER 403; R (Murungaru) v Secretary of State for the Home Department [2008] EWCA Civ 1015, [2009] INLR 180.

under which special advocates represent the interests of persons who challenge control orders.[62] Special Advocates have also been appointed in cases which do not have a national security context but which have raised issues of public interest immunity, most notably (outside criminal cases) in proceedings before the Parole Board and in wardship proceedings in the Family Division of the High Court.[63] It is impermissible for closed material and special advocates to be deployed, for example, in claims for damages in tort.[64]

23.27 While the UK has made extensive use of special advocates, they have also been used in Canada and New Zealand. Following the Supreme Court of Canada's ruling in *Charkaoui v Canada (Citizenship and Immigration)*,[65] the Canadian parliament amended the Immigration and Refugee Protection Act 2001 to introduce into immigration proceedings a system of special advocates similar to the UK's system.[66] Canada has already used special counsel in proceedings before the Security and Intelligence Review Committee (SIRC)[67] and in the Arar Inquiry.[68]

23.28 The special advocate in SIAC cases may communicate with the appellant and his representative at any time prior to receipt of the closed material. Thereafter, the special advocate is bound not to communicate with any person about any matter connected with the proceedings except that he or she may communicate with:

- SIAC;
- the SSHD and those acting for the SSHD;

---

62 See especially *Secretary of State for the Home Department v MB* [2007] UKHL 46, [2008] 1 AC 440; *R (JJ) v Secretary of State for the Home Department* [2007] UKHL 45, [2008] 1 AC 385; *Secretary of State for the Home Department v AF (No 3)* [2009] UKHL 28, [2010] 2 AC 269. In the context of employment legislation, see *Tariq v Home Office* [2011] UKSC 35, [2011] 3 WLR 322.
63 *R (Roberts) v Parole Board* [2005] UKHL 45, [2005] 2 AC 738; *Re T (Wardship: Impact of Police Intelligence)* [2009] EWHC 2440 (Fam), [2010] 1 FLR 1048. See also *Roberts v Nottinghamshire Healthcare NHS Trust* [2008] EWHC 1934, where a special advocate was appointed on a non-statutory basis in an application under Part 8 of the Civil Procedure Rules 1998 (CPR) for disclosure of a psychological report under the Data Protection Act (DPA) 1998.
64 *Al Rawi v Security Service* [2011] UKSC 34, [2011] 3 WLR 388 para 150.
65 [2007] 1 SCR 350, 2007 SCC 9.
66 An Act to amend the Immigration and Refugee Protection Act (certificate and special advocate) and to make a consequential amendment to another Act SC 2008, c 3 / LC 2008, ch 3. See *Re Almrei*, 2009 FC 1263, [2009] FCJ No 1579.
67 The committee monitors the activities of the Canadian Security Intelligence Service.
68 See, for example, M Code and K Roach 'The Role of the Independent Lawyer and Security Certificates' (2006) 52 Crim LQ 85.

- the Attorney-General and those acting for the Attorney-General (which includes lawyers at SASO who instruct special advocates); and
- any other person (save for the appellant and his representative) with whom it is necessary to communicate in relation to administrative matters.[69]

23.29 In addition, the special advocate may seek SIAC's permission to communicate with the appellant or his legal representative or any other person. SIAC must notify the SSHD of any such request from the special advocate and the SSHD can lodge objection to the request on public interest grounds. SIAC will then take a decision.[70]

23.30 Given that the SSHD will see all requests, the special advocate is unable to take confidential instructions from the appellant after he or she has received the closed material. In addition, communications from the special advocate to the appellant cannot touch on sensitive information. These factors limit the scope for communication after the special advocate has received the closed material.

23.31 In practice, the special advocate may usually without controversy communicate with the permission of SIAC on matters such as the following:

- *Procedural matters.* For example, a party seeks an extension of time for service of evidence. The special advocate may consent to or oppose the extension and may wish to let the appellant know of his or her view. Administrative matters (such as counsel's availability) as well as agreement to draft directions and general case timetabling need not amount to a communication from the special advocate about the case and so may be dealt with directly by the open lawyer in SASO.
- *The special advocate's actions.* For example, the appellant makes a written application to vary his bail conditions. The special advocate may also wish to make written submissions and may seek time from SIAC to do so. The special advocate may wish to inform the appellant that he or she will be making written submissions within the time permitted by SIAC.
- *Grounds of appeal.* If an appeal has been dismissed, the special advocate may take the view that there are closed grounds of appeal to the Court of Appeal. The special advocate may through SASO wish to inform the appellant to this effect, ask whether the

---

69 SIAC (Procedure) Rules 2003 r36(3).
70 SIAC (Procedure) Rules 2003 r36(4)–(5).

appellant wishes to appeal on closed grounds and, if so, request that the appellant lodge a notice of appeal to which the closed grounds may thereafter be appended. It may well not be possible for the special advocate to indicate the nature of the grounds of appeal to the appellant.

23.32 As mentioned, the appellant is free to communicate with the special advocate after the latter has received the closed material but this must be done through the appellant's legal representative and in writing. The special advocate must not reply unless SIAC has granted permission to reply, save that the special advocate may without permission acknowledge receipt of the communication to the appellant's legal representative.[71]

23.33 The appellant may wish to meet his special advocate to discuss the case in order that the special advocate may act from the greatest possible degree of knowledge of the case and of the appellant's wishes. The special advocate is free to communicate with the appellant and his lawyers until receiving the closed material and one or more meetings may take place until this point. In certain instances, the special advocate may be prevented from meeting an appellant because the special advocate has already seen closed material from a previous case which is likely to be used again in relation to the appellant's case (such as common country of origin information). The appellant may in these circumstances either choose a special advocate who has not seen any relevant closed material or may decide to forego communication with the special advocate on the basis that he wishes to have someone with experience in cases deploying that evidence. Where two special advocates are appointed, it is possible for the appellant to select one with whom he may communicate and one who is experienced in the evidence. There is no requirement for both special advocates to receive the closed evidence at the same time. If there are matters that remain to be discussed with the appellant, one special advocate may receive the closed material and commence work on it while the other remains free to communicate with the appellant. In these circumstances, the special advocates will not communicate with each other until both have received the closed material.

---

71 SIAC (Procedure) Rules 2003 r36(6)(b).

Legality of the use of closed evidence in substantive deportation appeals

23.34 SIAC has described its consideration of closed material in the following way:

> We see the closed material upon which the Security Service recommends to the Secretary of State that the decision under appeal should be made, together with any subsequently generated or discovered closed material deployed to support or undermine that decision. If, in their opinion, the Special Advocates consider that the closed material produced is insufficient to permit SIAC to determine the outcome of the appeal justly, they can and do seek further closed disclosure. Further, SIAC itself is required by Rule 4(3) of the Special Immigration Appeals Commission (Procedure) Rules 2003 to satisfy itself that the material available to it enables it properly to determine the proceedings. Our closed judgments are invariably founded on a close analysis of this material. The Security Service witness has three principal functions: to explain and justify to SIAC the collective Security Service view about the case of an individual appellant and about particular aspects of it; to respond to challenges to that assessment by the Special Advocates (and, where possible, by the open advocates); and to make such further enquiries as the Special Advocates and SIAC may require in the course of the hearing.[72]

23.35 SIAC does 'not generally require that the witness has been personally involved in the investigation into the individual appellant in whose case he or she gives evidence'.[73]

23.36 In *MT (Algeria) v Secretary of State for the Home Department*,[74] the Court of Appeal upheld the legality of the use of closed evidence to assess and determine the issue of safety on return. It was argued before the Court of Appeal that the absolute nature of article 3, and the fundamental values which it enshrines, imports a procedural element into the determination of whether expulsion would breach article 3. However, the court held that *Chahal*[75] (on which reliance was placed):

> ... says nothing to mandate any particular form of scrutiny, indeed envisages that the scrutiny may not even be by a court, and gives no

---

72 *LO v Secretary of State for the Home Department* (SC/73/2009) 4 March 2010 para 5.
73 *LO v Secretary of State for the Home Department* (SC/73/2009) 4 March 2010 para 5.
74 *MT (Algeria), RB (Algeria) and U (Algeria) v Secretary of State for the Home Department* [2007] EWCA Civ 808, [2008] QB 533.
75 *Chahal v UK* (1996) 23 EHRR 413.

support at all for the suggestion that article 3 requires the applicant to be present throughout.[76]

23.37 It was also argued that the use of closed evidence breached the fundamental principle of legality in English law. The court held that, when parliament passed the statutory scheme for the use of closed evidence, it confronted what it was doing. It held that there were no grounds for supposing that the full implications of the statute passed unnoticed in the democratic process. The courts should therefore not interfere with the scheme enacted by parliament. Secondary alternatives (conducting the proceedings in camera, with the appellant present but not the press or public; or allowing an appellant's open advocates to have the sensitive material without sharing it with their client) were also rejected on a number of grounds.

23.38 After the Court of Appeal handed down its judgment, the House of Lords gave judgment on the lawfulness of the use of closed evidence in control order cases under PTA 2005. In *Secretary of State for the Home Department v MB*,[77] one of the issues was whether the SSHD's reliance on closed evidence to make a control order breached ECHR article 6. The majority (Lord Hoffmann dissenting) held that reliance on closed evidence will breach ECHR article 6 if the controlled person is not afforded a substantial measure of procedural justice. The use of a special advocate does not automatically cure injustice. Baroness Hale, Lord Carswell and Lord Brown read down the statutory disclosure provisions so that, if a fair trial cannot be achieved without further disclosure, the court may direct that the SSHD cannot rely on the material which, if crucial to the SSHD's decision, will render the control order flawed and liable to be overturned.

23.39 The issue then arose whether the procedural safeguards laid down by *MB* were applicable to substantive deportation appeals in SIAC. There is European and domestic case-law to the effect that ECHR article 6 does not apply to expulsion cases because these do not concern the determination of civil rights and obligations or of a criminal charge under ECHR article 6(1).[78] On this basis, it was argued that the control order cases can be distinguished from deportation appeals in SIAC and standards of procedural fairness under article 6 do not carry over into the deportation cases. This distinction

---

76 *MT (Algeria), RB (Algeria) and U (Algeria) v Secretary of State for the Home Department* [2007] EWCA Civ 808, [2008] QB 533 para 12.
77 [2007] UKHL 46, [2008] 1 AC 440.
78 See, for example, *Maaouia v France* (2001) 33 EHRR 42; *MNM v Secretary of State for the Home Department* [2000] INLR 576.

was upheld by SIAC as a preliminary issue in *OO v Secretary of State for the Home Department*.[79]

23.40 Subsequently, in *RB (Algeria)*,[80] the House of Lords considered whether the use of closed material was lawful in relation to the question of safety on return. The House of Lords held that the SIAC (Procedure) Rules 2003 r4 (which mandates that SIAC should ensure that information is not disclosed contrary to the public interest)[81] is permitted under the rule-making power of SIACA 1997 and that SIAC's procedures provide a fair balance between the need to protect the public interest and the need to provide applicants with a fair hearing. Deportation proceedings do not engage civil rights and thus do not engage ECHR article 6. Consequently, control order proceedings can be distinguished. SIAC's procedures breach neither the ECHR nor common law principles of fairness.

23.41 The House of Lords also drew a distinction between control order proceedings and SIAC proceedings on the basis that in the former the SSHD has formulated a case against the controlled person of which he will be unaware unless it is disclosed in the open material; whereas in SIAC proceedings the appellant will normally be aware of the factors that place him at risk of human rights violations in his country of origin and will himself rely on them. Even if the appellant is unaware of factors that make his return dangerous (such as the particular reasons why the authorities in his country of origin seek to detain him), this does not mean that the SSHD's case cannot be rebutted. As expressed by Lord Phillips of Worth Matravers, 'where safety on return is in issue it is not likely to be critically important for the advocate advancing the case of the deportee to be able to obtain input from the deportee in relation to the evidence that the deporting state wishes to remain closed'[82] so that 'ignorance on the part of the deportee of the closed material is unlikely to prejudice the conduct of his case'.[83] The ratio of *MB* therefore did not apply to deportation appeals.

---

79 *OO v Secretary of State for the Home Department (Preliminary Issue (MB) judgment)* (SC/51/2006) 27 June 2008.
80 [2009] UKHL 10, [2010] 2 AC 110.
81 See para 23.46 below.
82 *RB (Algeria) v Secretary of State for the Home Department* [2009] UKHL 10, [2010] 2 AC 110 para 98.
83 *RB (Algeria) v Secretary of State for the Home Department* [2009] UKHL 10, [2010] 2 AC 110 para 100.

23.42 Further important cases followed. In *A and others v UK*[84] (referred to above at para 23.10), the ECtHR Grand Chamber held that SIAC procedures enabling the SSHD to deploy closed evidence in appeals against certification and detention under ATCSA 2001 Part 4 breached article 5(4) 'unless the detainee was provided with sufficient information about the allegations against him to enable him to give effective instructions to the special advocate'.[85] Where the open material 'consisted purely of general assertions and SIAC's decision to uphold the certification and maintain the detention was based solely or to a decisive degree on closed material, the procedural requirements of article 5(4) would not be satisfied'.[86] Soon afterwards, in *Secretary of State for the Home Department v AF (No 3)*[87] the House of Lords held that the ECtHR's approach is applicable in control order proceedings.[88]

23.43 The ratio of *AF (No 3)* will not apply to deportation cases because the question for SIAC in deportation appeals does not engage ECHR article 6. However, the question remained after *AF (No 3)* whether the common law required a similar degree of disclosure in deportation appeals. The Court of Appeal considered this question in *W (Algeria) v Secretary of State for the Home Department*,[89] and held that the common law does not require disclosure of material beyond that which the SIAC (Procedure) Rules 2003 r38, coupled with r4, will yield. The court concluded that, unlike in control order cases, fairness in deportation appeals does not require an irreducible minimum of disclosure of information about the risk which a person poses to national security.

23.44 The courts have also to date rejected arguments relying on the incidental or consequential interference with civil rights (such as the right to respect for private and family life under ECHR article 8) brought about by expulsion decisions. Such an effect does not mean that article 6 ECHR is engaged. It is 'the nature of the proceedings' that determines the applicability of ECHR article 6, not the effects of

---

84 (2009) 49 EHRR 29.
85 *A v UK* (2009) 49 EHRR 29 para 220.
86 *A v UK* (2009) 49 EHRR 29 para 220.
87 *Secretary of State for the Home Department v AF (No 3)* [2009] UKHL 28, [2010] 2 AC 269.
88 See also *Secretary of State for the Home Department v BC* [2009] EWHC 2927 (Admin), [2010] 1 WLR 1542; *AN v Secretary of State for the Home Department* [2010] EWCA Civ 869.
89 *W (Algeria) v Secretary of State for the Home Department* [2010] EWCA Civ 898.

the proceedings.[90] The further and different argument that ECHR article 8 in itself generates a procedural requirement for disclosure to the extent of ECHR article 5(4) and article 6 has also failed. While ECHR article 8 incorporates procedural requirements, they are less muscular than the procedural aspects of ECHR article 5 or 6 and they are satisfied by the statutory scheme under which SIAC operates.[91] The question whether a citizen of the EU facing expulsion has the right at least to a gist of the closed evidence against him as part of effective judicial protection under the Citizens Directive[92] has been referred to the Court of Justice of the European Union (CJEU).[93]

23.45 SIAC has held that the approach in *MB* is inapplicable in appeals against deprivation of citizenship on the basis that ECHR article 6 is not engaged.[94] In *W (Algeria)*,[95] the Court of Appeal concluded that there was no analogous right for the appellant to place material before SIAC that had been withheld from the SSHD.

The procedure for disclosure

23.46 Procedure rules must have regard to 'the need to secure that information is not disclosed contrary to the public interest'.[96] The SIAC (Procedure) Rules 2003 r4 mandates that SIAC 'shall secure' that information is not disclosed contrary to the interests of:

- national security;
- the international relations of the UK;
- the detection and prevention of crime; or
- in any other circumstances where disclosure is likely to harm the public interest.

---

90 See, for example, *RB (Algeria)* [2007] EWCA Civ 808, [2008] QB 533 paras 175, 178 and 228. Compare *Maaouia v France* (2001) 33 EHRR 42 para 38.
91 *IR (Sri Lanka) v Secretary of State for the Home Department* [2011] EWCA Civ 704, (2011) *Times* 26 August.
92 Directive 2004/38/EC. See especially articles 30 and 31. For general discussion of the Citizens Directive, see chapters 8 and 9.
93 *ZZ v Secretary of State for the Home Department* [2011] EWCA Civ 440.
94 Decided as a preliminary issue in *Al Jedda v Secretary of State for the Home Department* (SC/66/2008) 22 October 2008.
95 *W (Algeria) v Secretary of State for the Home Department* [2010] EWCA Civ 898.
96 SIACA 1997 s5(6)(b).

23.47 Subject to its duty to prevent disclosure contrary to the public interest, SIAC must satisfy itself that the material before it enables it properly to determine the proceedings.[97]

23.48 A key function of the special advocate is to endeavour to convert evidence from the closed to the open case, thus enabling the appellant to know more of the case against him and giving him an opportunity to deal with it. On the face of rule 4, there is no balancing exercise: the protection of the public interest as set out in the rule prevails over openness. Unless the special advocate persuades SIAC that disclosure is not contrary to the public interest, SIAC will not order disclosure.

23.49 As a matter of practice, the special advocate may search for open sources of information with a view to mounting the argument that closed evidence is not sensitive because it has already found its way to the public domain. The special advocate may also argue that closed evidence should be summarised in the open case[98] or disclosed subject to redaction.[99] The appellant is entitled to an explanation of the grounds (other than legal professional privilege) of any redaction in the open material which must be filed in un-redacted form with SIAC.[100]

23.50 The procedure for disclosure of closed material into the open case is set out in the SIAC (Procedure) Rules 2003 rr37 and 38. This process is core to SIAC proceedings. Under rule 38, having received the closed material, the special advocate will file and serve on the SSHD a written submission containing any requests for onward disclosure of closed material to the appellant. The SSHD will consider the special advocate's requests and make a written reply. The special advocate may in turn reply to the SSHD.

23.51 As a matter of practice, there will then usually be a meeting between the special advocate and counsel or solicitor for the SSHD where negotiations take place with a view to reaching agreement on material which should pass from the closed to the open case. Any outstanding points of dispute go to a hearing, for which the special advocate and the SSHD must under SIAC (Procedure) Rules 2003 r38(4)(c) file with SIAC a schedule identifying the issues. SIAC must uphold the SSHD's objection to disclosure where it considers that disclosure would be contrary to the public interest. If SIAC over-

---

97 SIAC (Procedure) Rules 2003 r4(3).
98 Commonly known as a 'gist'.
99 SIAC (Procedure) Rules 2003 r38(8).
100 SIAC (Procedure) Rules 2003 r38A.

rules the SSHD's objection, the SSHD is not required to disclose the material to the appellant. However, if the SSHD does not disclose it, SIAC may direct that the SSHD shall not rely on the material. If the material is exculpatory, SIAC may direct that the SSHD shall not rely on such points or shall make concessions or take other steps as SIAC may specify.[101]

Exculpatory review

23.52 The Home Office must carry out an exculpatory review in every case before SIAC. Under the SIAC (Procedure) Rules 2003 r2, 'exculpatory material' means material which adversely affects the SSHD's case or supports the appellant's case. The nature of the appellant's case should be widely interpreted as including all that is relevant to the risk of ill treatment prohibited by article 3, so that the SSHD ought to disclose 'anything touching on that general issue', whether or not it relates to any specific argument made by the appellant.[102]

23.53 Under the SIAC (Procedure) Rules 2003 r10, the SSHD must file any exculpatory material of which he or she is aware at the stage of filing a statement opposing the appeal. In addition, under rule 10A, where the appellant serves a statement, the SSHD must then make a reasonable search for exculpatory material and notify the appellant of the extent of that search. If the full notification includes information which cannot be disclosed in the open case, the special advocate must also be notified.

23.54 The factors relevant in deciding the reasonableness of a search include:

- the number of documents involved;
- the nature and complexity of the proceedings;
- whether the documents are in the control of the Secretary of State;
- the ease and expense of retrieval of any particular document; and
- the significance of any document which is likely to be located during the search.[103]

---

101 SIAC (Procedure) Rules 2003 r38(6)–(9).
102 *MT (Algeria) v Secretary of State for the Home Department* [2007] EWCA Civ 808, [2008] QB 533 para 136. See also *DD and AS v Secretary of State for the Home Department* (SC/42 and 50/2005) 27 April 2007 paras 415–427.
103 SIAC (Procedure) Rules 2003 r10A(3).

23.55 The duty to undertake an exculpatory search continues until the appeal has been determined.[104] In practice, this means that the SSHD may serve successive tranches of material. Exculpatory material is subject to the disclosure procedure under rules 37 and 38 as much as any other material.

Burden and standard of proof

23.56 As described in chapter 13, the burden lies on an appellant to prove that his expulsion would breach ECHR article 3. The standard of proof is whether there are substantial grounds for believing that the individual faces a real risk of being subject to ill treatment contrary to article 3.[105] Where other articles of the ECHR are raised, such as articles 5 and 6 and 'foreign' article 8 cases,[106] the 'flagrant breach' test will apply, as described in chapter 13.

23.57 The burden and standard of proof in asylum cases is considered in chapter 11. Appellants in SIAC may appeal on the grounds that their expulsion would breach the Refugee Convention but they are unlikely to succeed on this basis unless they defeat the national security case against them: otherwise, they are likely to lose the benefit of non-refoulement under article 33(2) of the Refugee Convention.[107] They may, depending on the facts, fall within one of the Refugee Convention's exclusion clauses.[108]

Detainee reporting

23.58 In *A and others v Secretary of State for the Home Department (No 2)*,[109] the House of Lords held that the rules which permit SIAC to receive evidence not admissible in a court of law do not displace the normal

---

104 SIAC (Procedure) Rules 2003 r10A(10)–(11).
105 *Chahal v UK* (1996) 23 EHRR 413; *Saadi v Italy* [2008] Imm AR 519; *AS (Libya) v Secretary of State for the Home Department* [2008] EWCA Civ 289, [2008] HRLR 28. For the proper application of the *Chahal* test, see *MT (Algeria) v Secretary of State for the Home Department* [2007] EWCA Civ 808, [2008] QB 533 at 162 and chapters 9 and 13.
106 The difference between 'foreign' and 'domestic' cases is described at para 13.43; see *R (Ullah) v Special Adjudicator* [2004] UKHL 26, [2004] 2 AC 323.
107 See paras 12.75–12.79.
108 See chapter 12.
109 [2005] UKHL 71, [2006] 2 AC 221.

exclusionary rule applied in courts for evidence obtained by torture. Evidence must be excluded if, following 'such diligent inquiries into the sources that it is practicable to carry out', SIAC concludes that it was on balance of probabilities obtained by torture.[110] SIAC will therefore need to investigate evidence if it emanates from a person who is in detention in a country which has a record of abusing detainees. There is little case-law on the nature and extent of the investigation which SIAC must undertake, because the SSHD may choose not to rely on detainee reporting 'for pragmatic reasons'.[111] It may not always be clear whether evidence has emanated from a person in detention. Those representing appellants in SIAC should, if in doubt, ask the SSHD's solicitor to seek instructions as to the source of the potentially tainted evidence. A submission that a court is not entitled to take into account any evidence or information adverse to an appellant's case arising out of or to do with the unlawful detention of other individuals has been rejected by SIAC.[112]

The progress of deportation appeals in SIAC

23.59 Appeal lies against a decision to make a deportation order under the NIAA s82(2)(j) and is commenced by giving notice of appeal under the SIAC (Procedure) Rules 2003 r7. The notice is filed with SIAC or, if the appellant is in immigration detention, it may be served on the person having custody of him. If filed with SIAC, the notice must at the same time be served on the SSHD. If served on the appellant's gaoler, the gaoler must forward the notice to SIAC, and SIAC must serve it on the SSHD.

23.60 Under the SIAC (Procedure) Rules 2003 r8, the time limit for giving notice of appeal is five days after the appellant is served with the notice of decision if the appellant is in detention, and ten days otherwise. When the appellant is outside the UK, the time limit is 28 days after service of the notice of decision. If the appellant is entitled only to an out-of-country appeal, the time limit is 28 days after departure from the UK. Where there has been an appeal in the IAC which has

---

110 *A and others v Secretary of State for the Home Department (No 2)* [2005] UKHL 71, [2006] 2 AC 221 para 121.
111 *DD and AS v Secretary of State for the Home Department* (SC/42 and 50/2005) 27 April 2007 para 20; *Othman v Secretary of State for the Home Department* (SC/15/2005) 26 February 2007 para 73.
112 *XX v Secretary of State for the Home Department* (SC/61/2007) 10 September 2010.

lapsed owing to the issue of a certificate under NIAA 2002 s97, a further notice of appeal to SIAC must be given not later than five days after service of the notice that the previous appeal has lapsed for an appellant in detention, ten days otherwise and 28 days if the appellant is outside the UK. SIAC may extend the time limit for starting an appeal if 'satisfied that by reason of special circumstances it would be unjust not to do so'.[113] This is the same test as applies to extension of time for appealing to the FTT-IAC.[114]

23.61 Under the SIAC (Procedure) Rules 2003 r9, the notice of appeal must set out the grounds for appeal and give reasons in support of those grounds. A copy of the notice of decision must be attached to the notice of appeal, together with any other document that has been served on the appellant containing reasons for the decision. The grounds of appeal may subsequently be amended with the leave of SIAC.[115]

23.62 The next stage in proceedings is a directions hearing under the SIAC (Procedure) Rules 2003 r9A. This may be a discrete hearing or it may take place at the same time as a bail application. If the special advocate has been appointed, he or she may be present.[116] It is sensible for the special advocate to attend. It is also sensible for the directions hearing to take place before the special advocate has received the closed material, so that he or she can freely communicate with the appellant and his representatives on procedural and timetabling matters. It is good practice for the parties, together with the special advocate, to prepare draft directions for the assistance of SIAC. Key directions under rule 9A will include the dates on or by which:

- the SSHD should file and serve the statement of evidence on which he or she relies in opposition to the appeal, together with any exculpatory material of which the SSHD is at that stage aware. As a matter of practice, the SSHD usually files and serves a statement containing both the evidence relied on to oppose the appeal and any initial exculpatory material. This statement will, as a matter of practice, be lodged before the appellant files any evidence;
- the appellant should file and serve the statement of evidence on which he seeks to rely in support of his appeal. This will include any witness statements;

---

113 SIAC (Procedure) Rules 2003 r8(5).
114 Asylum and Immigration Tribunal (Procedure) Rules 2005 SI No 230 r10(5).
115 SIAC (Procedure) Rules 2003 r11.
116 SIAC (Procedure) Rules 2003 r9A(1).

- the SSHD should file and serve any evidence in reply to the appellant's statement of evidence, together with any further exculpatory material. As explained above,[117] it is after the appellant has filed a statement that the SSHD is under a duty to undertake an exculpatory review. As a matter of practice, where the appellant lodges a statement, the SSHD will thereafter lodge a further statement dealing with the appellant's statement and including the results of the exculpatory review;
- the SSHD should file and serve closed material on the special advocate;
- the special advocate should file and serve on the SSHD his or her written submissions on disclosure under the SIAC (Procedure) Rules 2003 r38;
- the SSHD should under the SIAC (Procedure) Rules 2003 r38 file and serve on the special advocate a response to the special advocate's submissions on disclosure;
- the hearing should take place under the SIAC (Procedure) Rules 2003 r38 to determine any matters in dispute between the SSHD and the special advocate relating to disclosure;
- the SSHD should file and serve amended statements which take account of any additional disclosure to be made to the appellant in consequence of the SIAC (Procedure) Rules 2003 r38 process;
- skeleton arguments should be filed and served;
- the hearing of the appeal should take place.

23.63 Both the appellant and the special advocate may apply for a direction that the SSHD files further information about the case.[118] The special advocate may conveniently make any appropriate requests in the same document as his or her disclosure submissions under the SIAC (Procedure) Rules 2003 r38, so that they are dealt with at the same time.

23.64 SIAC has an additional, general power to give oral or written directions under the SIAC (Procedure) Rules 2003 r39. It also has a general power to adjourn proceedings.[119] It is not uncommon for the parties and the special advocate to seek directions on matters arising after the first directions hearing and before the substantive hearing. On a day-to-day basis, it is often convenient to seek directions through correspondence with SIAC, although an oral hearing may be desirable to resolve more complex applications for directions. The

117 Para 23.53.
118 SIAC (Procedure) Rules 2003 r10A(5).
119 SIAC (Procedure) Rules 2003 r42.

SIAC (Procedure) Rules 2003 contain sanctions for breach of directions.[120] Procedural errors such as a failure to comply with a procedure rule do not invalidate any step taken in the proceedings unless SIAC so orders.[121]

23.65 Where the closed material is itself redacted on grounds other than those of legal professional privilege, the SSHD must file the material with SIAC in un-redacted form, together with an explanation of the redactions, so that SIAC can give independent scrutiny to the appropriateness of the redactions and their extent.[122]

23.66 Any hearing under the SIAC (Procedure) Rules 2003 r38 will be closed to the appellant and his representatives[123] but the rule 38 hearing is sometimes combined with a further directions hearing which the appellant's representatives may attend.

23.67 An appellant may withdraw his appeal orally or in writing. An appeal will be treated as withdrawn if the SSHD notifies SIAC that the decision under appeal has itself been withdrawn.[124] SIAC may strike out a notice of appeal if it appears to disclose no reasonable grounds for bringing the appeal or it appears to be an abuse of process. SIAC may strike out the SSHD's reply to the appeal if it appears to disclose no reasonable grounds for defending the appeal.[125]

23.68 An appeal will be determined at a hearing unless:

- it falls to be abandoned or finally determined by operation of SIACA 1997 s2(4)[126] or NIAA 2002 ss104(4)–(4C) and 104(5);[127]
- it is withdrawn;
- the SSHD consents to it being allowed; or
- the appellant is outside the UK or it is impracticable to give him notice of a hearing and, in either case, he is unrepresented.[128]

23.69 SIAC will serve a notice of hearing on the parties and the special advocate.[129] Appeals raising common issues may be heard together.[130] If the SSHD has served closed material, the appeal hearing will

---

120 SIAC (Procedure) Rules 2003 r40.
121 SIAC (Procedure) Rules 2003 r53.
122 SIAC (Procedure) Rules 2003 r37(4A).
123 SIAC (Procedure) Rules 2003 r38(5).
124 SIAC (Procedure) Rules 2003 r11A.
125 SIAC (Procedure) Rules 2003 r11B.
126 Para 23.15 above.
127 Para 21.33 above.
128 SIAC (Procedure) Rules 2003 r12.
129 SIAC (Procedure) Rules 2003 r41.
130 SIAC (Procedure) Rules 2003 r46.

involve open sessions attended by the parties and the special advocates and closed sessions attended only by the SSHD and the special advocate.[131] As a matter of practice, open sessions generally precede closed sessions, so that the special advocate is able to learn and understand how the appellant is putting his final case to SIAC which may affect the way in which the special advocate conducts the closed case. However, there is no statutory requirement for the open sessions to be held prior to closed sessions. Typically, evidence relating to national security issues (open and closed) is heard first and evidence relating to safety on return (open and closed) is heard second. After that, open closing submissions take place followed by closed closing submissions.

23.70 SIAC has the power to issue a summons requiring any person in the UK to attend a hearing as a witness and at the hearing to answer questions or produce documents which relate to an issue in the case.[132] There are specific provisions in the SIAC (Procedure) Rules 2003 governing the filing and service of documents and the calculation of time.[133]

Consideration of deportation appeals

23.71 SIAC has (like the Immigration and Asylum Chamber of the First-tier and Upper Tribunals (IAC)) wide powers to receive evidence.[134] It may receive evidence that would not be admissible in a court of law. Evidence may be oral, in writing or in documentary form. These powers enable SIAC to adopt informal and flexible procedures in relation to the reception of evidence, consistent on the one hand with the grave human rights issues at stake for the appellant and on the other hand with the interests of national security which SIAC must uphold. However, it is open to SIAC to place less weight on written evidence than on oral evidence tested in cross-examination.

23.72 Unlike the practice in the IAC, the SSHD has to date called oral evidence in SIAC cases as a matter of course. A witness is called to deal with the national security case against the appellant. A further

---

131 SIAC (Procedure) Rules 2003 r43.
132 SIAC (Procedure) Rules 2003 r45.
133 Rules 49 and 51.
134 SIAC (Procedure) Rules 2003 r44. For evidence which may have been obtained by torture, see para 23.58.

witness is called to give evidence on the issue of safety on return in deportation cases.

Assessment of risk to national security

23.73 In assessing the risk posed by an appellant to national security, the House of Lords held in the leading case of *Rehman* that the interests of national security are not limited to actions against the UK. Actions against a foreign state or against the community of nations may be capable indirectly of affecting the security of the UK.[135] It follows that a person who is found to have undertaken terrorist activities outside the UK may be treated as a risk to national security. The SSHD is moreover entitled to take a preventive or precautionary approach: there is no requirement to wait until a person becomes a direct threat to the UK or carries out harmful activities before seeking to deport him as being conducive to the public good.[136]

23.74 It is clear from *Rehman* that the question whether a person's deportation is conducive to the public good is a matter of judgment or assessment.[137] The SSHD is therefore entitled to have regard to all the information in his or her possession. A decision that a person's presence in the UK is a risk to national security need not rely only on material that is proved on the balance of probabilities. The concept of a standard of proof in assessing future risk is 'not particularly helpful'; nor should risk be assessed by 'taking each allegation seriatim and deciding whether it has been established'.[138] Nevertheless, if specific acts are relied on by the SSHD, they must be proved on the balance of probability.[139]

23.75 In *Y v Secretary of State for the Home Department*, SIAC held that the question whether a person is a danger to national security is 'ultimately one of the evaluation or assessment of risk, a risk that someone will do acts in the future which are a danger to national security'. Allegations which are not proved on the balance of probabilities

---

135 *Secretary of State for the Home Department v Rehman* [2001] UKHL 47, [2003] 1 AC 153.
136 *Secretary of State for the Home Department v Rehman* [2001] UKHL 47, [2003] 1 AC 153 paras 17 and 22.
137 *Secretary of State for the Home Department v Rehman* [2001] UKHL 47, [2003] 1 AC 153 para 22.
138 *Secretary of State for the Home Department v Rehman* [2001] UKHL 47, [2003] 1 AC 153 para 56 per Lord Hoffmann.
139 *Secretary of State for the Home Department v Rehman* [2001] UKHL 47, [2003] 1 AC 153 paras 23 and 29.

cannot be wholly removed from SIAC's assessment: 'all sorts of pieces of information require to be evaluated'.[140]

23.76 In assessing whether an appellant is a risk to national security, SIAC will weigh the evidence for itself but will show deference to the SSHD to the extent that it will give due weight to the SSHD's assessment and conclusions in light of the latter's political responsibilities and expertise in matters affecting the UK's security. As expressed by Lord Slynn, the SSHD is:

> ... undoubtedly in the best position to judge what national security requires even if his decision is open to review. The assessment of what is needed in the light of changing circumstances is primarily for him.[141]

23.77 Lord Hoffmann's speech[142] emphasises judicial deference in relation to the assessment of the interests of national security. His speech nevertheless confirms that the question whether an appellant's deportation will breach ECHR article 3 is a matter for SIAC.[143]

Assessment of safety on return

23.78 In SIAC appeals concerning the government's policy of 'deportation with assurances', the SSHD has called witnesses on safety on return from the Foreign and Commonwealth Office (FCO) with diplomatic experience.[144] These witnesses have given evidence about the bilateral negotiations which led to the assurances. They have also given evidence of the state of diplomatic relations between the UK and the country to which the appellants have stood to be deported as an aspect of the evidence relating to whether the foreign state has political incentive to adhere to assurances. Even non-diplomatic issues (of the sort which are part of the ordinary assessment of country of origin conditions in asylum and human rights cases) have been the subject of evidence from FCO sources. An individual witness may

140 SC/36/2005, 24 August 2006, para 123.
141 *Secretary of State for the Home Department v Rehman* [2001] UKHL 47, [2003] 1 AC 153 para 26.
142 *Secretary of State for the Home Department v Rehman* [2001] UKHL 47, [2003] 1 AC 153 paras 33–62.
143 *Secretary of State for the Home Department v Rehman* [2001] UKHL 47, [2003] 1 AC 153 para 54.
144 *Y v Secretary of State for the Home Department* (SC/36/2005) 24 August 2006; *Othman v Secretary of State for the Home Department* (SC/15/2005) 26 February 2007; *DD and AS v Secretary of State for the Home Department* (SC/42 and 50/2005) 27 April 2007; *XX v Secretary of State for the Home Department* (SC/61/2007) 10 September 2010.

express not only his or her own view but the collective view of the FCO.[145] The SSHD may supplement the witness evidence with ordinary country of origin information such as the Home Office's own Country of Origin Information Service reports.[146]

23.79 SIAC must consider the question of safety on return for itself and does not simply adopt a reviewing function such as in judicial review proceedings.[147] There is no place for SIAC to show constitutional deference to FCO evidence. Rather, the views of an FCO witness are 'entitled to weight according to the expertise, experience and cogency with which they were expressed'.[148]

23.80 However, the assessment of risk under ECHR article 3 'is a question of evaluation and prediction based on evidence' such that 'the executive enjoys no constitutional prerogative'.[149] As in any other deportation case, the responsibility for findings of fact rests on SIAC alone and so it need not accept every part of the FCO evidence.[150] Whether SIAC accepts or rejects FCO evidence, the Court of Appeal will interfere with SIAC's findings of fact only if they contain an error of law.[151]

SIAC's determination

23.81 SIAC must give a written determination of its decisions.[152] On substantive appeals, where the SSHD has relied on closed material, it will give an open and a closed judgment.[153] Prior to the appellant receiving the open judgment, it is served on the SSHD and on the

145 *DD and AS v Secretary of State for the Home Department* (SC/42 and 50/2005) 27 April 2007 para 324.
146 Available at www.ukba.homeoffice.gov.uk/policyandlaw/guidance/coi/.
147 *AS (Libya) v Secretary of State for the Home Department* [2008] EWCA Civ 289, [2008] HRLR 28 paras 33, 41 and 50.
148 *AS (Libya) v Secretary of State for the Home Department* [2008] EWCA Civ 289, [2008] HRLR 28 para 33, adopting SIAC's formulation in *DD and AS v Secretary of State for the Home Department* (SC/42 and 50/2005) 27 April 2007 para 321. See also *Othman v Secretary of State for the Home Department* (SC/15/2005) 26 February 2007 paras 339–343.
149 *Secretary of State for the Home Department v Rehman* [2001] UKHL 47; [2003] 1 AC 153 para 54, per Lord Hoffmann.
150 *AS (Libya) v Secretary of State for the Home Department* [2008] EWCA Civ 289, [2008] HRLR 28 paras 33 and 50.
151 SIACA 1997 s7(1); *AS (Libya) v Secretary of State for the Home Department* [2008] EWCA Civ 289, [2008] HRLR 28 para 3.
152 SIAC (Procedure) Rules 2003 r47(3).
153 SIAC (Procedure) Rules 2003 r47(4).

special advocate. The SSHD is permitted five days to check the open judgment and to apply to SIAC for the judgment to be amended if it is considered to contain material which should not be open. The special advocate may oppose any application to remove material from the open judgment and SIAC may determine the application with or without a hearing.[154] It is unusual, to say the least, that the appellant is therefore the last to know the result of his own appeal. The SSHD generally tries to mitigate this imbalance and to minimise any litigation advantage by not permitting Treasury Counsel or the Treasury Solicitor to see the draft judgment at the checking stage.

23.82 Conversely, the special advocate may make an application to SIAC that material in the closed judgment can be placed in the open judgment without harm to the public interest.[155] This may be done either before or after the appellant has received the open judgment: there is no time limit. There is separate provision for amendment of orders and determinations to correct clerical errors and other accidental slips and omissions.[156]

Bail

23.83 SIAC has jurisdiction to grant bail under the IA 1971 in cases where:
- the SSHD has certified that a person's detention is necessary in the interests of national security;
- a person is detained following a decision to refuse leave to enter the UK on the ground that exclusion is in the interests of national security;
- a person is detained following a decision to make a deportation order against him on national security grounds.[157]

23.84 SIAC has held that the procedural guarantees of ECHR article 6(1), and hence the requirements of *MB*,[158] do not apply to bail proceedings.[159] The Divisional Court has also held that ECHR article 6 does

154 SIAC (Procedure) Rules 2003 r48.
155 SIAC (Procedure) Rules 2003 r47.
156 SIAC (Procedure) Rules 2003 r54.
157 SIACA 1997 s3. The provisions of IA 1971 Sch 2 apply to the extent that they are set out in and modified by the SIACA 1997 Sch 3, as discussed by SIAC in *U v Secretary of State for the Home Department* (SC/32/2005) 29 July 2011.
158 *Secretary of State for the Home Department v MB* [2007] UKHL 46, [2008] 1 AC 440.
159 *Othman v Secretary of State for the Home Department* (SC/15/2005) 2 December 2008.

not apply to bail proceedings.[160] However, the procedural guarantees of ECHR article 5(4) do apply, such that a decision to refuse bail will breach the applicant's human rights if he does not have sufficient disclosure of the evidence against him to be able to give effective instructions to his special advocate.[161] It does not matter whether the bail proceedings precede or follow SIAC's judgment on the substantive deportation appeal: for the purposes of bail, the applicant must be able to give effective instructions to his special advocate even if the upshot is that the SSHD cannot rely on an extant, substantive judgment of SIAC that the applicant poses a threat to national security because the judgment was based on closed material.[162]

23.85 There is no statutory test for the grant or refusal of bail. SIAC has nevertheless consistently considered two principal factors – the risk to national security and the risk of absconding. SIAC expressed the question as follows in *A and others v Secretary of State for the Home Department*:

> Are we satisfied that there is a real risk that, if released on bail, subject to whatever conditions may be imposed, an applicant would abscond, in the sense of not turning up to the hearing as required, and are we satisfied that there would be a real risk to national security if he were meanwhile on such bail, whether having absconded or even if he had not absconded?[163]

23.86 Some doubt has been cast on this approach by the decision in *U, XC, UF v Secretary of State for the Home Department*.[164] In that decision, SIAC observed that the Divisional Court's judgment in *Cart* means that SIAC can no longer refuse bail on the basis of evidence which is contained substantially or determinatively in the closed material. SIAC commented that it may be difficult to assess the risk to national security and the risk of absconding on the basis of open material only. In cases where the assessment of these two risks is difficult on the open material, SIAC will not start with a presumption of detention but will adopt a precautionary approach, meaning that it is 'unlikely' to grant bail but will insist on a tight timetable for appeals as being, in its view, the way to avoid arbitrary or prolonged detention.[165]

160 *R (BB (Algeria)) v SIAC* [2011] EWHC 2129 (Admin), [2011] UKHRR 997.
161 *R (Cart) v Upper Tribunal; R (U) v Special Immigration Appeals Commission; R (C) v Same* [2009] EWHC 3052 (Admin), [2010] 2 WLR 1012.
162 *R (BB (Algeria)) v SIAC* [2011] EWHC 336 (Admin), [2011] ACD 48.
163 SC/33/34/35/36/37/38/39, 20 October 2005 para 11. See also *Othman v Secretary of State for the Home Department* (SC/15/2005) 2 December 2008.
164 SC/77/2009, SC/80/2009, SC/32/2005 21 December 2009.
165 SC/77/2009, SC/80/2009, SC/32/2005 21 December 2009, para 7.

23.87 However, there has to date been little indication of the nature or extent of the precautionary approach. In *M1 v Secretary of State for the Home Department*,[166] SIAC expressed the view that its bail jurisdiction is in a state of flux and that even the precautionary approach set out in the paragraph above may not be lawful. In the same case, while expressing the view that there is currently not much guiding principle, SIAC went on to list six points of principle or practice that seem to be established in bail proceedings that precede a substantive appeal. In summary:

1) It is wrong to form or express a firm view in bail proceedings about material that will be relied on by either party at the substantive appeal.
2) The SSHD must provide sufficient information in the open case to enable the applicant to give effective instructions to his special advocate.
3) The best interests of any children involved must be treated as a primary consideration.[167]
4) Respect must be shown for the rights of any family members involved, under ECHR article 8.
5) The *Hardial Singh* principles must be applied.[168]
6) There is no presumption for or against bail. This sixth principle was expressed tentatively in the absence of argument on the point.

23.88 Bail applications follow the procedures set down by Part 6 of the SIAC (Procedure) Rules 2003. Applications must be made in writing and contain the particulars specified by the SIAC (Procedure) Rules 2003 r29, including the grounds of the application and, where a previous application has been made, full details of any change in circumstance which has occurred since the refusal. A person's success on appeal – either before SIAC or before the Court of Appeal – may constitute a change of circumstances pending the outcome of further appeal by the SSHD.[169] While the continued detention of a successful appellant is lawful pending further appeal, SIAC may give significant weight to an appellant's success.[170]

---

166 SC/101/10 28 February 2011.
167 See chapter 4.
168 *R v Governor of Durham Prison ex p Hardial Singh* [1984] 1 WLR 704.
169 *O v Secretary of State for the Home Department* (SC/15/2005) 8 May 2008.
170 *O v Secretary of State for the Home Department* (SC/15/2005) 8 May 2008 para 10.

23.89 When a bail application is filed, SIAC must as soon as reasonably practicable serve a copy on the SSHD and fix a hearing. If the application is to be contested, the SSHD must file a written statement of reasons for objecting to bail.[171] In addition, if the SSHD seeks to rely on closed material, a closed statement of objections will be served on SASO and a special advocate will attend the hearing to represent the interests of the appellant. The SIAC (Procedure) Rules 2003 rr37 and 38 will apply and the special advocate may request that material in the closed statement is disclosed to the appellant. Apart from disclosure issues, the hearing will proceed in open and closed session. SIAC must give written notice of its decision and any reasons for the decision that can be stated openly.[172] It may give closed reasons for its decision but this is not required by the SIAC (Procedure) Rules 2003.

Bail conditions

23.90 Bail may be granted subject to sureties and to the applicant's own recognizance.[173] SIAC must also set and include in its written decision the conditions of bail. In practice, bail conditions in national security cases are generally of a wholly different nature and magnitude to those bail conditions commonly imposed by the FTT-IAC. They may amount to a deprivation of liberty under ECHR article 5(1) and may thus be even more stringent than the obligations imposed under a non-derogating control order.[174]

23.91 Commonly imposed conditions, relevant both to containment of the risk to national security and to the risk of absconding,[175] include:

- Curfew: the applicant must remain at home other than for a daily period specified by SIAC.
- Bail boundary: when outside the home, the applicant may be required to remain within an area defined on a map as specified by SIAC.
- Tagging: the applicant may be required to wear an electronic monitoring tag.

---

171 SIAC (Procedure) Rules 2003 r30.
172 SIAC (Procedure) Rules 2003 r30(4).
173 SIAC (Procedure) Rules 2003 r30(6).
174 *O v Secretary of State for the Home Department* (SC/15/2005) 8 May 2008; *A and others v Secretary of State for the Home Department* SC/33/34/35/36/37/38/39, 20 October 2005 para 16.
175 *A and others v Secretary of State for the Home Department* SC/33/34/35/36/37/38/39, 20 October 2005 para 17.

- Communications with the outside world: the applicant may be required to limit entry to his home to persons listed in the bail order (such as family members, his solicitor and medical professionals) and thereafter to obtain the SSHD's permission for any other visitors to the home. There may be restrictions or a ban on having a computer and other communications equipment in the home. The applicant may also be prohibited from any form of contact with specific persons, listed in the bail order.
- In order that compliance with bail conditions may be monitored, an applicant may be required to grant access to his home to the UK Border Agency, the police and any company monitoring his tagging.

23.92 Despite the stringency of control order conditions, SIAC is not bound to accept that bail conditions on control order terms will meet the risk to national security in any particular case. SIAC has held that the control order system represents a means of balancing risk to national security and liberty where detention is not available. The same balance need not be struck where there is a statutory power to detain. It is a matter of assessing the circumstances of each case.[176]

23.93 SIAC has also held that assessment of the risk of absconding is restricted to absconding within the UK. However, the risk of an appellant going abroad is relevant to the risk to national security:

> ... the risk of clandestine departure abroad in order to carry out activities which would present a risk to national security is relevant and the risk of clandestine departure abroad is allied to a closely-associated risk of a clandestine return to the UK. That latter can be very relevant to the assessment of the risk to national security created by absconding pending the hearing.[177]

23.94 Given the potential complexity of bail conditions and the potential consequences of breach, it is important for an applicant's lawyers to explain to him the terms of a bail order in detail, so that they are fully understood.

Variation of bail conditions

23.95 An applicant may apply to have his conditions of bail varied. For example, if an applicant's GP or solicitor is outside his bail boundary,

---

176 *A and others v Secretary of State for the Home Department* SC/33/34/35/36/37/38/39, 20 October 2005 paras 19–22.
177 *A and others v Secretary of State for the Home Department* SC/33/34/35/36/37/38/39, 20 October 2005 para 24.

he will need SIAC's permission to attend appointments. Similarly, he will need permission from SIAC to attend religious activities falling within the curfew hours. SIAC has adopted a standard form which ought to be completed as part of any application for a variation. Some variations may be sought and granted in writing. More complex or controversial variations will require determination at a hearing. It is open to applicants refused variation of bail on paper to renew the application at a hearing.

Challenging SIAC's bail decisions

23.96 There is no right of appeal against SIAC's bail decisions. SIAC is not however immune from judicial review and so its bail decisions may be challenged in the Administrative Court. It has nevertheless been emphasised that, given the sensitivity of the issues before SIAC which require fine judgments, the Administrative Court is unlikely to interfere with SIAC's decisions on *Wednesbury* grounds: some sharp-edged error of law will be required.[178] SIAC's expertise and experience means that it is 'generally wise' for the appellate courts not to interfere with its decisions on bail.[179]

Appeal from SIAC

23.97 An appeal lies from a final determination of SIAC to the Court of Appeal on a question of law material to the determination.[180]

Permission to appeal

23.98 The Lord Chancellor may make procedure rules governing applications to SIAC for leave to appeal under SIACA 1997 s8. The current procedure is contained in the SIAC (Procedure) Rules 2003 r27. An application for permission to appeal is made in the first instance to SIAC. If the appellant seeks to appeal, he must file the application not later than five days after service of SIAC's determination if he is in immigration detention and otherwise not later than ten days. If

---

178 *R (Cart) v Upper Tribunal; R (U) v Special Immigration Appeals Commission; R (C) v Same* [2009] EWHC 3052 (Admin), [2010] 2 WLR 1012; reiterated in *R (U) v Special Immigration Appeals Commission* [2010] EWHC 813 (Admin).
179 *R (BB (Algeria)) v SIAC* [2011] EWHC 2129 (Admin), [2011] UKHRR 997 para 13.
180 SIACA 1997 s7. Appeal in Scotland lies to the Court of Session.

the SSHD seeks to appeal, the application for permission must be filed no later than ten days after receipt of the determination. SIAC may extend time if it is satisfied that 'by reason of special circumstances, it would be unjust not to do so'. This is the same test as that for extending time for appeals to SIAC.[181] The application for permission to appeal must state the grounds of appeal and must be served on every other party. SIAC may decide the application without a hearing unless it considers that special circumstances make a hearing necessary or desirable. If SIAC refuses permission to appeal, a party can renew his or her application in the Court of Appeal in accordance with the CPR Part 52.

The appeal

23.99 The Court of Appeal does not review SIAC's judgment on its merits but will decide only whether there has been an error of law.[182] In appeals from SIAC, the approach of the Court of Appeal to intervention will recognise that SIAC is a specialist tribunal, as expressed by Lord Slynn in *Rehman*:

> On an appeal the Court of Appeal and your Lordships' House no doubt will give due weight to the conclusions of the Commission, constituted as it is of distinguished and experienced members, and knowing as it did, and as usually the court will not know, of the contents of the 'closed' evidence and hearing. If any of the reasoning of the Commission shows errors in its approach to the principles to be followed, then the courts can intervene.[183]

23.100 The Court of Appeal will be reluctant to interfere with SIAC's decisions unless it is 'quite clear' that it has misdirected itself in law as expounded in the context of tribunal appeals by Baroness Hale in *AH (Sudan) v Secretary of State for the Home Department*[184] and as applied to SIAC appeals by *AS (Libya)*.[185] In determining whether SIAC has made such an error, the court will consider the judgment of SIAC as a whole.[186]

---

181 See para 23.60 above.
182 *RB (Algeria) v Secretary of State for the Home Department* [2009] UKHL 10, [2009] 2 WLR 512.
183 *Secretary of State for the Home Department v Rehman* [2003] 1 AC 153, CA para 26.
184 [2007] UKHL 49, [2007] 3 WLR 832 para 30.
185 [2008] EWCA Civ 289, [2008] HRLR 28 paras 15–19.
186 *AS (Libya) v Secretary of State for the Home Department* [2008] EWCA Civ 289, [2008] HRLR 28 para 19.

PART II

Prison law

SECTION G
The prison and sentencing system

Chapter 24: Prison institutions, legislation and policy   489

Chapter 25: Complaints and supervision   499

Chapter 26: Sentences   507

Introduction to the prison and sentencing system

Part II of this book is concerned with how and in what conditions foreign nationals serve criminal sentences. Immigration detention (including immigration detention in prisons) is dealt with separately at Part III.

In this section, we provide an introduction to general prison law, as a prelude to a more detailed discussion in the following section of issues of particular concern to foreign national prisoners. A detailed analysis of prison law lies outside the scope of this book.[1] We start in chapter 24 with an overview of the institutions of the prison system, and the legislative and policy framework, as well as a summary of important risk assessment tools and arrangements. We then go on in chapter 25 to the complaints and supervision mechanisms that apply to all those held in prisons. Finally, in chapter 26 we summarise the different sentences that may be imposed.

---

1 For a more comprehensive examination of prison law see Creighton and Arnott, *Prisoners: law and practice*, LAG, 2009; and for the procedures of the Parole Board see Arnott and Creighton, *Parole Board hearings: law and practice*, 2nd edn, LAG, 2010.

CHAPTER 24
Prison institutions, legislation and policy

24.1	Introduction
24.2	The organisation of the prison and probation systems
24.5	Statutory and policy framework
24.5	Prisons
24.10	Probation
24.12	Prisons and other places of detention
24.14	Risk assessment: OASys
24.22	Multi-Agency Public Protection Arrangements

Introduction

24.1 This chapter summarises the structure and legislative and policy framework of the prison system, as well as risk assessment tools and risk management arrangements in general use.

The organisation of the prison and probation systems

24.2 Until May 2007, the Home Office had responsibility both for the management of prisons and the criminal justice system and for immigration and the expulsion of foreign nationals. Those roles have been split. The Ministry of Justice (MoJ) was created in May 2007, following the announcement by the then Home Secretary, John Reid, that the Home Office was 'unfit for purpose' in the wake of the foreign national prisoners (FNP) furore. The Secretary of State for Justice (SSJ) became responsible for the control and maintenance of the prison system,[1] and for the provision of probation services.[2]

24.3 However, the day-to-day management and commissioning of prison and probation services is delegated by the SSJ to the National Offender Management Service (NOMS). NOMS is an executive agency of the MoJ that operates under a framework document last amended in April 2011,[3] and has since April 2008 incorporated the Prison and Probation Services.

24.4 The Prison Service is an agency within NOMS and has responsibility for management of prisons and young offender institutions (YOIs). The Prison Service also manages on behalf of the UK Border Agency two immigration removal centres.

---

1 Prison Act (PA) 1952 ss1 and 4 – see also Secretary of State for Justice Order 2007 SI No 2128.
2 Offender Management Act (OMA) 2007 s2.
3 'National Offender Management Service: Agency Framework Document', MoJ, April 2011. See www.justice.gov.uk/downloads/publications/corporate-reports/noms/NOMS_framework%202011.pdf.

Statutory and policy framework

Prisons

24.5 The basic legal framework for the management of prisons is contained in the PA 1952. This gives the SSJ responsibility for the management of prisons,[4] provides for the appointment of various roles within prisons including the governor,[5] and provides that prisoners are in the lawful custody of the governor and may be held in any prison.[6] PA 1952 also sets out offences relating to prisons,[7] but otherwise contains little detail on how prisons should be managed.

24.6 There are currently 11 contracted out prisons operated by the private sector.[8] These have a director who is employed by the private contractor, and a controller who is an MoJ employee.[9] Together they carry out the functions of the governor in publicly run prisons.[10] Private prisons are broadly subject to the same statutory, policy and regulatory framework as other prisons. The SSJ has the power to take over the management of a private prison in circumstances where the director has lost effective control.[11]

24.7 More comprehensive provisions on how prisons are managed are contained in the Prison Rules (PR) 1999.[12] These provide the statutory basis for areas including:

- the classification of prisoners – which allows the allocation of prisoners to different security categories[13] (see paras 27.10–27.27 below);
- incentives and earned privileges (IEP) schemes;[14]
- temporary release (see paras 28.4–28.11 below);

---

4 PA 1952 ss1 and 4 – although in practice this is delegated to NOMS.
5 PA 1952 s7.
6 PA 1952 ss12–13.
7 PA 1952 ss39–40F.
8 Created under Criminal Justice Act (CJA) 1991 s84. See www.justice.gov.uk/about/hmps/contracted-out.htm.
9 CJA 1991 s85(1).
10 CJA 1991 s87(2) – in the remainder of this section references to the Governor should be take to refer to the Director and/or Controller as appropriate.
11 CJA 1999 s88.
12 Issued under PA 1952 s47 – SI No 728 as amended. Similar rules with some important differences apply to YOIs: Young Offender Institution Rules 2000 SI No 3371 as amended.
13 PR 1999 r7.
14 PR 1999 r8 – PSI 11/2011 provides the central policy on the IEP system.

- the Prison Service complaints procedure (see paras 25.3–25.14 below);
- religion;[15]
- medical care;[16]
- provisions to do with welfare and work in prisons;[17]
- restrictions on communications with the outside world;[18]
- searching;[19]
- segregation and use of force;[20]
- offences against prison discipline.[21]

24.8 As delegated legislation, the Prison Rules 1999 will be can be declared unlawful if they purport to bestow more power than authorised by the PA 1952 itself.[22]

24.9 The Prison Service also issues detailed policies on most areas of prison management. These are known as Prison Service Orders (PSOs) and Prison Service Instructions (PSIs).[23] These provide the most detailed guidance on prison regimes and decision-making. As with other centrally issued guidance the courts will expect individual prisons to follow these unless there are cogent reasons not to, and they are capable of creating for prisoners a legitimate expectation that, subject to their amendment, they will be followed.[24] In relation to some issues (such as incentives and privileges schemes, and searching) individual prisons are required to have their own local policies and disclosure of these may need to be sought when considering the lawfulness of decisions.

---

15 PR 1999 rr13–19.
16 PR 1999 rr20–22.
17 PR 1999 rr23–31.
18 PR 1999 rr34–39.
19 PR 1999 r41; policy on searches of the person is in PSI 48/2010.
20 PR 1999 r45-49; policy on segregation is in PSO 1700, and on use of force in PSO 1600.
21 PR 1999 rr51–61; policy on the prison discipline system is in PSI 47/2011.
22 For example, see *R v Secretary of State for the Home Department ex p Leech (No 2)* [1994] QB 198.
23 These can be accessed at www.justice.gov.uk/guidance/prison-probation-and-rehabilitation/index.htm.
24 *R v Secretary of State for the Home Department ex p Hargreaves* [1997] 1 WLR 906. The courts have so far refused in the prison context to accept that a policy can create a substantive legitimate expectation that may survive a change in policy.

Probation

24.10 Although the SSJ has ultimate responsibility for the provision of probation services[25] these are in fact delivered by regional Probation Trusts created by OMA 2007. Probation services are also centrally managed by the NOMS agency. Policy guidance is issued to Probation Trusts in the form of Probation Instructions (PIs),[26] and probation officers are required to meet Offender Management National Standards.[27]

24.11 Prisoners will have allocated to them an Offender Manager (OM) whose function is to manage the sentence and will be responsible for producing the pre-sentence report and other key documents such as assessments of risk to the public upon which the UK Border Agency may rely in decision-making (see paras 24.14–24.21 below). OMs also supervise prisoners once they are released on licence and are responsible for making recommendations for recall to prison during the currency of the sentence. OMs are not located in prisons, although probation officers are seconded to work in prisons and may contribute to reports completed on prisoners. Those aged under 18 who receive custodial sentences are not allocated OMs but are supervised by officers from youth offender teams (YOTs).[28]

Prisons and other places of detention

24.12 There are, at the time of writing, 137 adult prisons and YOIs in England and Wales. Of these, 126 are run by the public sector by the Prison Service, and 11 are contracted out and run by private companies.[29] YOIs generally hold those aged between 18 and 21. There are 14 women-only prisons. Prisons vary from the high security category, designed to hold those assessed as the most dangerous prisoners (including all those given Category A status – see para 27.11 below), to open prisons, where prisoners are able to develop links with the outside world in preparation for release.

---

25 OMA 2007 s2(1).
26 Previously these were issued as Probation Circulars (PCs).
27 'National Standards for the Management of Offenders in England and Wales', NOMS, MoJ, 5 April 2011. Available at www.justice.gov.uk/downloads/publications/corporate-reports/MoJ/national-standards-management-offenders-2011.pdf.
28 Established under the Crime and Disorder Act 1988 s39.
29 Under CJA 1991 s84.

24.13 The allocation of under-18 year olds to custody is administered by the Youth Justice Board[30] (YJB). This group can be held, depending upon an assessment of their vulnerability, either in secure children's homes which are run either by local authorities or private contractors, in one of the four secure training centres (STCs) which are all contracted out, or in YOIs. Only 17-year-old females should be held in YOIs, and then only in dedicated units.

Risk assessment: OASys

24.14 The primary tool for assessing the risk posed by prisoners used by the Prison and Probation Services is known as OASys (Offender Assessment System).[31] It is designed to be used throughout the sentence to provide a means by which management and release decisions can be informed by an assessment both of reconviction, and of the risk of harm posed by the prisoner. It is computer-based and although the primary duty on completing the risk assessment rests with the OM, it can also be updated by prison staff.

24.15 OASys is completed by reference both to documentary evidence and an interview with the prisoner by a probation officer. The risk of reconviction is assessed through an actuarial tool (the Offender Group Reconviction Scale, or OGRS3) under which the risks of reconviction within two years of release for the prisoner are assessed. It is based on static factors (such as number of previous convictions). In short, the OGRS3 score indicates:

> ... the probability that offenders with a given history of offending will be reconvicted within two years of sentence or release if sentenced to custody. It does not define the probability that a particular offender will be reconvicted.[32]

24.16 OASys also incorporates the General Re-offending Predictor (OGP). This measure incorporates both the calculation of static risk (under OGRS3) and scores on those dynamic factors (factors which may change) which the MoJ say research using OASys data has shown to be most predictive of non-violent reconviction (for example, drug

---

30 Created by CDA 1988 s41.
31 See PSO 2205, the OASys Manual, and the Public Protection Manual version 4.0 chapter 9.
32 *R (Schmelz) v IAT* [2003] EWHC 1859 (Admin).

misuse, accommodation, employability, lifestyle, thinking and behaviour).[33]

24.17 A separate predictor of violence, the OASys Violence Predictor (OVP), is now also included in the OASys assessment. This also incorporates the actuarial assessment of reconviction and dynamic factors and is intended to inform the assessment of risk of harm (see para 24.19 below).

24.18 In addition, the OM will carry out his or her own risk assessment of the harm posed by the prisoner. This does involve a subjective assessment and *in principle* at least includes an evaluation of dynamic factors (such as age or response to offending behaviour courses).

24.19 The levels of risk of harm used by OASys are:

- *Low:* Current evidence does not indicate likelihood of causing serious harm.
- *Medium:* There are identifiable indicators of risk of serious harm. Potential to cause harm but unlikely to do so unless there is a change of circumstances.
- *High:* Identifiable indicators of risk of serious harm. Potential event could happen at any time and impact would be serious.
- *Very high:* Imminent risk of serious harm. Potential event is more likely than not to happen imminently. The impact would be serious.

24.20 Thus OASys risk of harm categories should address both the gravity of any further offending, and the likelihood or imminence of further offending.

24.21 Problematically, probation officers frequently have little regard to the second function of the assessment (likelihood or imminence). Those who have committed serious offences are frequently assessed by probation officers as posing a high risk of harm solely because of the nature of the index offence, on the basis that if they did re-offend, however unlikely this might be, the consequences would be serious.

Multi-Agency Public Protection Arrangements

24.22 There is now a statutory duty on the police, probation trusts and the Prison Service to work together to establish arrangements to assess and manage the risks posed by serious sexual and violent offenders.[34]

---

33 Ministry of Justice Research Summary 2/2009.
34 CJA 2003 ss325–326.

A wide range of other public bodies have a statutory to co-operate in these arrangements, including social services departments, NHS trusts, local authorities and social landlords.[35] From 20 July 2011 the UK Border Agency has been added to this list of bodies with a duty to co-operate.[36]

24.23 These arrangements are known as Multi-Agency Public Protection Arrangements (MAPPA). There is statutory guidance[37] on how the various public bodies should operate MAPPA.[38] There is now a specific electronic database which holds details of all those managed under MAPPA.[39] The policy identifies three categories of offender that will be managed under MAPPA:[40]

- *Category 1* – offenders who are required to register under the sex offender registration requirements.
- *Category 2* – violent and other sexual offenders – where the sentence is 12 months or more for a specified offence.[41]
- *Category 3* – other dangerous offenders – those assessed as posing a risk of serious harm which requires inter-agency management, but who do not come within the first two categories.

24.24 The guidance then requires those responsible for MAPPA to apply one of three levels of management to such offenders:[42]

- *Level 1* – ordinary agency management. This is where it is considered that the supervising agency alone (such as the Probation Service) is able to manage the risk. Other agencies might be involved but the offender will not be referred to a MAPPA meeting.
- *Level 2* – where the offender is considered to pose a high risk of serious harm which needs co-operation between agencies.
- *Level 3* – where the offender is considered to pose a high or very high risk of serious harm, which require 'close co-operation at a

---

35 CJA 2003 s325(3) and (6).
36 Co-operation in Public Protection Arrangements (UK Border Agency) Order 2011 SI No 1733.
37 Issued under CJA 2003 s325(8).
38 It can be found in chapter 1 of the 'Public Protection Manual' issued by NOMS, available at www.justice.gov.uk/guidance/prison-probation-and-rehabilitation/public-protection-manual.htm.
39 Violent and Sexual Offenders Register or ViSOR – MAPPA Guidance 2009 para 2.5.
40 MAPPA Guidance 2009 section 4.
41 Those contained in CJA 2003 Sch 15.
42 MAPPA Guidance 2009 section 10.

senior level'. This level will also be applied regardless of risk if there is a 'high likelihood of media scrutiny'.

24.25 Only those at MAPPA levels 2 and 3 are considered to require active agency management. Assignment to MAPPA level 2 or 3 in practice requires offenders' cases to be referred to regular MAPPA meetings,[43] where decisions will be made on how risk should be managed and how information should be shared between agencies. MAPPA meetings make recommendations as to additional licence conditions for those released from their sentence. The NOMS Public Protection manual includes a specific section on FNPs[44] which includes guidance on information sharing, and also confirms the expectation that MAPPA level 2 or 3 offenders who are detained at the end of their sentence will be detained in prisons rather than Immigration Removal Centres.

---

43 MAPPA Guidance 2009 section 11.
44 Public Protection Manual Version 4.0 January 2009 chapter 7.

CHAPTER 25

Complaints and supervision

25.1	**Introduction**
25.3	**Complaints**
25.8	**The Prisons and Probation Ombudsman**
25.15	**Supervision of prisons**
25.15	Independent Monitoring Boards
25.16	Her Majesty's Chief Inspector of Prisons
25.19	International supervision

Introduction

25.1 This chapter summarises the system of complaints and supervision applicable to all those held in prisons. Complaints procedures may provide prisoners with a prompt means of seeking redress for unfair treatment. In addition, as noted in para 42.7, although an actionable claim may be brought without prior recourse to internal complaints or any relevant ombudsman, there is a growing expectation in the courts, particularly in low-value cases concerning maladministration, that such schemes should be utilised before court proceedings are considered.

25.2 The Prison Service complaints procedure described below applies not only to serving prisoners, but to immigration detainees held in prisons, although complaints about UK Border Agency decisions will need to go through the UK Border Agency complaints procedure. The complaints procedures applicable in Immigration Removal Centres (IRCs) are described separately at paras 39.53–38.83

Complaints

25.3 Both prisons and young offender institutions (YOIs) are required to operate a system of requests and complaints.[1] The complaints system discussed here relates solely to issues relating to imprisonment.

25.4 There is a detailed policy on requests and complaints.[2] Requests and complaints should be treated separately. The policy suggests that prisoners' requests should first be dealt with on the wing, and a written procedure for this is not mandatory.[3] If a request does not resolve the prisoner's concern then it should be dealt with through the formal complaints process.

25.5 Prison Service Order (PSO) 2510 states that complaints should normally be made within three months of the incident complained of although there is discretion to extend this time limit.[4] There are four forms that are used in the complaints process:

- *COMP 1: for first stage complaints.* This is normally responded to at prison officer level. The policy suggests that there should be

---

1 Prison Rules 1999 SI No 728 r11; Young Offender Institution Rules 2000 SI No 3371 r8.
2 PSO 2510 deals with complaints, and Prison Service Instruction (PSI) 10/2011 with requests.
3 PSI 10/2011 para 3.1.
4 PSO 2510 para 6.4.1.

a response to a stage 1 complaint within three weekdays, or ten weekdays if it involves a complaint against a member of staff or regarding another prison.
- *COMP 1A: for second stage and third stage complaints.* A second stage complaint should be responded to at management level. A third stage complaint should be responded to at governor level. Stage 2 and 3 complaints should be responded to within seven weekdays, or ten if the complaint is about a member of staff or involves another prison.
- *COMP 2: for confidential matters.* The confidential access procedure enables prisoners to direct a complaint to, for example, the governor. This may be appropriate where the prisoner wishes to bypass a response from the wing because the complaint raises issues about treatment by the wing staff. If the recipient of the form considers that the matter is inappropriate for this procedure then the prisoner will be told to use the normal procedure. Confidential complaints should be submitted in a sealed envelope. A confidential complaint should be responded to within seven weekdays.
- *ADJ 1: in order to challenge governors' disciplinary decisions.*

25.6 Forms should be freely available to prisoners. Importantly for foreign national prisoners (FNPs), the policy requires there to be provision of information about the complaints system in languages other than English where necessary, and prisoners can submit complaints in their own language.[5] Complaints that raise issues of race discrimination should be referred to the prison's race relations liaison officer (RRLO).[6]

25.7 Probation Trusts have their own complaints procedures which need to be exhausted before complaints can be made to the Prisons and Probation Ombudsman (PPO).

The Prisons and Probation Ombudsman

25.8 A prisoner who has been through the Prison Service complaints procedure and remains dissatisfied may complain to the PPO. The PPO will generally not consider a complaint until internal prison,

---

5 PSO 2510 para 6.5.
6 PSO 2510 para 12.1.

probation or UK Border Agency complaints procedures have been exhausted.[7]

25.9 The first PPO was appointed in 1994 as a response to Lord Woolf's recommendation in his report into the riot at HMP Strangeways. The office of the PPO now has a broad remit which includes investigating complaints against the Prison Service, the Probation Service and since October 2006 complaints made by those held in immigration removal centres. The PPO's remit excludes ministerial decisions and clinical decisions.[8] The office also is now responsible for investigating deaths in prisons, YOIs, IRCs and while under escort managed by the UK Border Agency for which the remit is wider as it includes clinical matters.

25.10 The PPO's office has no statutory basis, and this has led to concerns over its independence from the Ministry of Justice (MoJ). The PPO also can only make recommendations which are not binding on the executive if complaints are upheld and has no enforcement powers.

25.11 The time limit for making a complaint to the PPO is three months of receiving a 'substantive reply' from the relevant organisation.[9] The PPO will not generally accept complaints where there has been a delay of more than 12 months between the complainant becoming aware of the relevant facts and submitting their case to the PPO, unless the delay has been the fault of the relevant authority and the PPO considers that it is appropriate to do so. However, the PPO has discretion to investigate complaints where there is good reason for the delay, or where the issues raised are so serious as to override the time factor.[10]

25.12 Where the PPO does investigate a complaint, the Terms of Reference state that the PPO may seek to resolve the matter in whatever way he or she sees most fit, including by mediation.[11] Accordingly, a formal report may not be produced in each case. As noted above at para 25.10, if a complaint is upheld, then recommendations will be made which are not binding on the appropriate body, but which in most cases are accepted.[12]

---

7 Guidance on making complaints to the PPO is contained in PSI 58/2010.
8 See PPO Terms of Reference, available at www.ppo.gov.uk/terms-of-reference.html.
9 PPO Terms of Reference para 21.
10 PPO Terms of Reference paras 22–23.
11 PPO Terms of Reference para 24.
12 PPO Terms of Reference paras 27–28.

25.13 Investigations into deaths in custody are managed slightly differently by the PPO. The Terms of Reference require the PPO to investigate deaths in:[13]

- prisons, YOIs and secure training centres (STCs);
- approved premises (hostels holding those released on licence);
- IRCs, Short Term Holding Facilities (STHFs) and under immigration escort;
- court buildings.

25.14 The PPO will always issue an investigation into a death in custody and the remit of the investigation is wider. Since clinical matters will be investigated. The Terms of Reference state that the aims of a PPO investigation into a fatal incident are to:[14]

- establish the circumstances and events surrounding the death, especially regarding the management of the individual by the relevant authority or authorities within remit, but including relevant outside factors;
- examine whether any change in operational methods, policy, practice or management arrangements would help prevent a recurrence;
- in conjunction with the NHS where appropriate, examine relevant health issues and assess clinical care;
- provide explanations and insight for the bereaved relatives;
- assist the Coroner's inquest – fulfil the investigative obligation arising under European Convention on Human Rights (ECHR) article 2 ('the right to life'), by ensuring as far as possible that the full facts are brought to light and any relevant failing is exposed, any commendable action or practice is identified, and any lessons from the death are learned.

Supervision of prisons

Independent Monitoring Boards

25.15 The Secretary of State for Justice (SSJ) is required to appoint an Independent Monitoring Board (IMB) for each prison[15] whose function is to 'pay frequent visits to the prison and hear any complaints which

---

13 PPO Terms of Reference para 29.
14 PPO Terms of Reference para 31.
15 Prison Act (PA) 1952 s6(2) – these used to known as Boards of Visitors.

may be made by the prisoners and report to the Secretary of State any matter which they consider it expedient to report'.[16] The Prison Rules 1999 contain duties on IMBs, including to hear prisoners' complaints and check on prison conditions.[17] The IMBs' role in dealing with prisoners' complaints is not part of the formal complaints procedure. IMBs for individual prisons are required to produce annual reports.[18] The role of IMBs in IRCs is discussed separately at paras 39.84–39.90.

Her Majesty's Chief Inspector of Prisons

25.16 The Office of Her Majesty's Chief Inspector of Prisons (HMCIP) is created by statute which imposes a duty to inspect prisons and report upon conditions and the treatment of prisoners.[19] This duty has also been extended to IRCs, short-term holding facilities, and conditions of immigration escorting arrangements.[20] HMCIP can also be directed by the Secretary of State to investigate and report on specific issues.[21]

25.17 HMCIP's role is therefore not to investigate the individual complaints of prisoners or detainees, but to investigate conditions generally. Reports are therefore produced both on individual institutions and services, and also on thematic issues.[22] The Chief Inspector has also published a set of 'Expectations', which set out the criteria against which inspections are carried out in respect of police custody, prisons, immigration detention, and the imprisonment of young people.[23] These are very useful as they reference relevant domestic and international standards in relation to conditions of detention.

25.18 There is a Chief Inspector of Probation responsible for inspections of probation services.[24]

---

16 PA 1952 s6(3).
17 PR 1999 rr77–78.
18 PR 80, the reports are available at www.justice.gov.uk/about/imb.htm.
19 PA 1952 s5A(2).
20 PA 1952 s5(5A) and (5B).
21 PA 1952 s5A(4).
22 These are available at www.justice.gov.uk/publications/inspectorate-reports/hmi-prisons/index.htm.
23 'Inspections guidance: inspection and appraisal criteria', available at www.justice.gov.uk/guidance/inspection-and-monitoring/hmi-prisons/inspections-guidance/inspection-and-appraisal-criteria.htm.
24 Criminal Justice and Courts Services Act 2000 s6.

International supervision

25.19 The Committee for the Prevention of Torture (CPT) which is administered by the Council of Europe was established by article 1 of the European Convention for the Prevention of Torture.[25] The UK is a signatory to the convention and is therefore subject to period inspection by the CPT, which includes inspections of the conditions of detention. The CPT has issued a set of standards,[26] and the Council of Europe has also issued the European Prison Rules.[27] These standards are not binding in domestic law. Nonetheless, these standards set out accepted international minimum standards and will be relevant, for example, when assessing the proportionality of standards applied in the UK.

25.20 The United Nations has also issued Standard Minimum Rules for the Treatment of Prisoners. The Optional Protocol to the UN Convention against Torture[28] (OPCAT) has also created a monitoring regime for conditions of detention. The UK ratified OPCAT in December 2003. OPCAT provides for visits and inspections to be made of signatory states. It also requires that States designate a 'national preventive mechanism' (NPM) to carry out visits to places of detention, to monitor the treatment of and conditions for detainees and to make recommendations regarding the prevention of ill-treatment.

25.21 The UK's NPM is currently made up of 18 visiting or inspecting bodies which visit prisons, police custody, immigration detention centres, children's secure accommodation and mental health institutions. The NPM is co-ordinated by HMCIP and issued its first annual report in February 2011.[29]

---

25 European Convention for the Prevention of Torture and Inhuman or Degrading Treatment or Punishment, CPT/Inf/C (2002) 1 at www.cpt.coe.int/en/documents/ecpt.htm.
26 See www.cpt.coe.int/en/about.htm.
27 See https://wcd.coe.int/wcd/ViewDoc.jsp?id=955747.
28 See www2.ohchr.org/english/law/cat-one.htm.
29 'The UK's National Preventive Mechanism', available at www.justice.gov.uk/about/hmi-prisons/preventive-mechanism.htm.

CHAPTER 26

Sentences

26.1	Introduction
26.3	Types of prison sentence
26.4	**Determinate sentences**
26.4	Determinate sentences for adults
26.5	Determinate sentences for children
26.6	**Indeterminate sentences**
26.7	Types of indeterminate sentence that can currently be imposed
26.8	**Extended sentences**
26.9	**The meaning of the term 'liable to removal from the UK'**
26.11	**Procedures for release**
26.11	Procedures for release – the Parole Board
	The Parole Board
26.12	Procedures for release – determinate sentences
	Consideration by the Parole Board • Release criteria for those not liable to removal • Release criteria for those liable to removal • Refusal of release on parole licence
26.20	Procedures for release – indeterminate sentences
26.23	**New legislative proposals for FNPs 'liable to removal'**

Introduction

26.1 Foreign nationals are liable to the same range of sentences of imprisonment[1] as British citizens save that, as part of their sentences, foreign nationals may be recommended for deportation. Criminal court recommendations for deportation have been discussed separately in chapter 2. As set out below, the principal difference in relation to the sentencing of foreign nationals who are 'liable to removal' from the UK is how such sentences are administered.

26.2 The sentencing framework in England and Wales is extremely complicated, since a wide range of sentencing options are available depending upon the date of the offence, the date and length of sentence and the level of risk the offender is assessed as posing to the public. The purpose of this chapter is to provide an overview of the sentences available to the criminal court, and of the release dates in respect of those sentences.

Types of prison sentence

26.3 In summary there are three types of custodial sentence that can be imposed by the criminal court:
1) *Determinate, or fixed-term, sentences.* These are sentences where the term of imprisonment is primarily imposed as punishment.
2) *Indeterminate, or life, sentences.* These sentences are made up of a 'minimum term' that must be served as punishment, following which the prisoner will be detained until the Parole Board decides that the risk they pose is low enough for release on licence.
3) *Extended sentences.* These are a hybrid between determinate and indeterminate sentences and are made up of a custodial term, equivalent to the determinate sentence that would have been imposed for the offence, and an extension period, during which the offender is on licence in the community. The extension period is imposed for public protection rather than punishment.

---

1 Community sentences are outside the scope of this book.

Determinate sentences

Determinate sentences for adults[2]

26.4 Calculating release dates for prisoners with determinate sentences has become increasingly complicated as successive legislative schemes are layered onto each other.[3] Below, we set out a brief outline of the statutory framework for release dates:

- Determinate sentences imposed for offences committed prior to 4 April 2005:
  - If the sentence is for less than 12 months the prisoner is released unconditionally after serving six months.[4]
  - If the sentence is for 12 or more months, but less than four years, then the prisoner is released automatically at the half-way point, on licence[5] until the three-quarter point.[6]
  - If the sentence is for four or more years then, unless the sentence is for a specified sexual or violent offence,[7] the prisoner is released automatically at the half-way point, on licence until the end of the whole sentence.[8] If the offence is so specified then release at the half-way point is dependent upon a recommendation of the Parole Board.[9] Where the Parole Board recommends release, this is on licence until the three-quarter point.[10] If the Parole Board does not direct release the prisoner will be automatically released at the two-thirds point, on licence to the three-quarter point.[11]

---

2 Although sentences imposed on those aged 18 but under 21 are technically sentences of detention rather than imprisonment – see Powers of Criminal Courts (Sentencing) Act (PCC(S)A) 2000 s96, they are with some minor distinctions administered in the same way – see Criminal Justice Act (CJA) 2003 s237.

3 In *R (Noone) v Governor of HMP Drake Hall and another* [2010] UKSC 30 Lord Judge noted at para 78 that it appeared there had by the time of that judgment been 55 Acts of Parliament altering the rules of criminal justice since 1997 with the result that 'elementary principles of justice have come ... to be buried in the legislative morass'.

4 CJA 1991 s33(1)(a).
5 That is, under supervision by the Probation Service.
6 CJA 1991 s33(1)(b).
7 Those contained in CJA 2003 Sch 15.
8 CJA 1991 ss33(1A), 35(1A) and 37ZA(1).
9 CJA 1991 ss33(1B) and 35(1).
10 CJA 1991 s37(1).
11 CJA 1991 ss33(2) and 37(1).

- Determinate sentences imposed for offences committed on or after 4 April 2005:
  - If the sentence is for less than 12 months the prisoner is released unconditionally after serving six months.[12]
  - If the sentence is for 12 months or more then the prisoner is released automatically at the half-way point, on licence to the end of the sentence.[13]

Determinate sentences for children

26.5 For those aged under 18 at the time of conviction the normal determinate sentence will be a Detention and Training Order.[14] The maximum sentence is 24 months and generally half is spent in custody and half in the community. Where the offence would attract a maximum term of 14 years for someone 18 or over, a longer determinate sentence may be imposed[15] which is then subject to the same release date as would as apply to determinate sentences for adults (see para 26.4 above).

Indeterminate sentences

26.6 There are now a number of indeterminate sentences available to the court. However, all indeterminate sentences have the following features in common:
- The prisoner must serve at least a minimum term, which is set by the sentencing court to reflect the appropriate period of imprisonment for punishment.[16]
- The prisoner will only be released at the end of the minimum term if the Parole Board is satisfied that it is no longer necessary for the protection of the public that the prisoner should be

---

12 CJA 1991 s33(1)(a).
13 CJA 2003 ss244(3)(a) and 249(1).
14 Imposed under PCC(S)A 2000 s100.
15 PCC(S)A 2000 s91.
16 Set under CJA 2003 s269 and Sch 21 where a life sentence is imposed for murder, and under PCC(S)A 2000 s82A where an indeterminate sentence is imposed in for other offences.

detained.[17] If the Parole Board does not direct release then the prisoner can be detained indefinitely until the test for release is met, although the Parole Board will continue to review detention at least every two years.[18] However, proposed legislation would change this in relation to foreign national prisoners (FNPs): see para 26.23 below.
- If the Parole Board directs release then this is (with the exception of the indeterminate sentence for public protection, discussed at para 26.7 below) on licence for life.

Types of indeterminate sentence that can currently be imposed

26.7 The types of indeterminate sentence that can currently be imposed are as follows:
- The mandatory life sentence for murder.[19] The sentencing court has no discretion when sentencing for murder and must impose a life sentence. This means, that unlike with all other kinds of indeterminate sentence, the court does not make an assessment that the offender is dangerous.
- For offences committed prior to 4 April 2005:
  - A discretionary life sentence[20] as long as imprisonment for life is the maximum sentence available, and the court considers that the offence is grave enough to justify a very long sentence, and the offender is dangerous.[21]

---

17 Crime (Sentences) Act (C(S)A) 1997 s28(5)–(6) only the risk of further offences occasioning serious harm is capable of justifying continuing detention, because it is this kind of risk to the public that the life sentence is intended to address – see, for example, *Stafford v UK* (2002) 35 EHRR 32 paras 70–80.
18 C(S)A 1997 s28(7).
19 Those 21 and over have this sentence imposed under Murder (Abolition of Death Penalty) Act 1965 s1. Those between 18 and 21 are given what is known as custody for life under PCC(S)A 2000 s93. Under 18-year-olds are sentenced to what is known as detention at Her Majesty's Pleasure (HMP) under PCC(S)A 2000 s90.
20 PCC(S)A 2000 s80.
21 *R v Chapman* [2000] 1 Cr App R 77.

- An 'automatic life sentence'[22] where a second serious offence[23] is committed and the sentencing court considers that the offender is dangerous.[24]
- Where the offender commits serious specified sexual or violent offence(s)[25] on or after 4 April 2005,[26] and the court considers both that there is a significant risk of the offender causing serious harm by the commission of further specified offences, the sentencing court is required to impose either a life sentence or an indeterminate sentence for public protection (IPP). A life sentence should be imposed if the seriousness of the offence(s) is such to justify life imprisonment.[27] If not, then the IPP sentence should be imposed as long as the offence is sufficiently serious to warrant a minimum term of at least two years.[28] The only practical difference between the two types of sentence is that an offender who has been released from an IPP can apply to cancel the licence after ten years in the community.[29]

Extended sentences

26.8 As noted above at para 26.3, an extended sentence is made up of a custodial term, which is equivalent to the normal determinate sentence applicable to the offence, together with an extended period of licence to be served in the community.

- *Where the offence is committed on or after 30 September 1998 but before 4 April 2005*: the court can impose on adults an extended sentence for sexual or violent offences where the court considers

---

22 Also known as the 'two-strikes' life sentence, imposed under PCC(S)A 2000 s109.
23 Those contained in PCC(S)A 2000 s109(5).
24 *R v Offen (No 2)* [2000] 1 WLR 253.
25 Those contained in CJA 2003 Sch 15.
26 The provisions of the CJA 2003 introduced on this date removed the power of the sentencing court to impose a discretionary life sentence under PCC(S)A 2000 s80, or an automatic life sentence under PCC(S)A 2000 s109.
27 CJA 2003 s225(2), where the offender is under 18 an equivalent sentence of detention for life can be imposed: CJA 2003 s226(2). See *R v Lang and others* [2005] EWCA Crim 2864 for how sentencing courts are to apply these powers.
28 CJA 2003 s225(3); the equivalent sentence for those under 18 is imposed under CJA 2003 s226(3). The requirement for at least a two-year minimum term was introduced on 14 July 2008 in order to reduce the number of prisoners receiving such sentences.
29 C(S)A 1997 s31A.

that the normal period on licence would be inadequate.[30] The prisoner's release date will be calculated by reference to the length of the custodial term in the same way as set out in at para 26.4 above. The prisoner is then on licence in the community until the end of the extension period.[31]

- *Where the offence is committed on or after 4 April 2005*: the court can impose an extended sentence for a specified sexual or violent offence,[32] on those both over and under 18, where the court considers that there is a significant risk of the offender causing serious harm by the commission of further such offences.[33] The prisoner is automatically released at the halfway point of the custodial term, on licence until the end of the extension period.[34]

The meaning of the term 'liable to removal from the UK'

26.9 A key statutory determinant in how FNPs are treated in terms of the administration of criminal sentences is whether they are 'liable to removal' from the UK. This has a specific statutory definition and not all FNPs are 'liable to removal'. An FNP is only 'liable to removal' if he or she:[35]

- is liable to deportation under Immigration Act (IA) 1971 s3(5) and has been notified of a decision to make a deportation order;
- has been recommended for deportation by a court under IA 1971 s3(6);
- has been notified of a decision to refuse him or her leave to enter the UK;
- is an illegal entrant within the meaning of IA 1971 s33(1); or
- is liable to administrative removal under Immigration and Asylum Act (IAA) 1999 s10.

---

30 PCC(S)A 2000 s85.
31 CJA 1991 s44(3)
32 The specified offences are contained in CJA 2003 Sch 15, and are serious if they are punishable, in the case of a person aged 18 or over, with ten years' imprisonment or more: CJA 2003 s224(2)(b).
33 CJA 2003 ss227 and 228.
34 CJA 2003 s247(2) – although those sentenced prior to 14 July 2008, when amendments were made to the CJA 2003 by the Criminal Justice and Immigration Act (CJIA) 2008, are only released at the half-way point of the custodial term where the Parole Board recommends.
35 CJA 1991 s46 and CJA 2003 s259.

26.10 Important statutory provisions in the Immigration Acts on deportation and administrative removal have been discussed at chapter 1.

Procedures for release

Procedures for release – the Parole Board

The Parole Board

26.11 The Parole Board derives its statutory powers from the CJA 2003.[36] Its functions in relation to the release and recall of prisoners are in summary:

- The Parole Board is responsible for deciding whether indeterminate sentence prisoners should be released after completion of their minimum term,[37] and also whether such prisoners should be re-released if recalled from licence by the Secretary of State for Justice (SSJ).[38] It will only make decisions to release an indeterminate sentence prisoner after an oral hearing to which the Parole Board Rules 2011 apply.[39] Article 5(4) of the European Convention on Human Rights (ECHR) applies to reviews of the detention of those serving indeterminate sentences on and after expiry of the minimum term.[40] Accordingly, prisoners may seek compensation under ECHR article 5(5) if there is unjustified delay in convening a hearing.[41]
- In relation to determinate sentence, and extended sentence prisoners it makes decisions as to initial release only in a limited class of cases (see paras 26.12–26.13 below). When deciding on the initial release of determinate sentence prisoners, ECHR article 5(4) is not engaged.[42] The Board will generally make such decisions on the basis of a dossier and the prisoners written representations.
- Recalled determinate sentence prisoners, who are not subsequently re-released by the SSJ, have their cases referred to the Parole Board.[43] Where the case is referred to the Board the review

---

36 CJA 2003 Sch 19.
37 C(S)A 1997 s28(5)–(6).
38 C(S)A 1997 s32(5).
39 SI No 2947.
40 For example, see *Stafford v UK* (2002) 35 EHRR 32.
41 *R (Faulkner) v Secretary of State for Justice* [2011] EWCA Civ 349.
42 *R (Black) v Secretary of State for Justice* [2009] UKHL 1.
43 CJA 2003 ss254–256A.

does engage ECHR article 5(4).[44] The Board may hold an oral hearing to consider the release and recall of determinate sentence prisoners where it considers that fairness requires this.[45]

Procedures for release – determinate sentences

26.12 As noted above, most prisoners serving determinate sentences are released automatically at the half-way point of the sentence (subject of course to any decision to detain under IA 1971 powers). The exceptions are prisoners serving sentences of four or more years[46] imposed for specified offences committed before 4 April 2005, and extended sentence prisoners whose offences were committed on or after 4 April 2005 but before 14 July 2008. These prisoners are only eligible for release at the half-way point of the sentence or custodial period, and the decision as to whether to release is made by the Parole Board.

26.13 Historically, determinate sentenced prisoners who were liable to removal did not have their cases referred to the Parole Board because the decision on conditional release was by statute reserved to the SSJ. However, two prisoners challenged this position on the basis that the differential treatment mandated by the statutory framework was unlawfully discriminatory in breach of ECHR article 14 in conjunction with article 5. The House of Lords upheld the challenge and made a declaration of incompatibility in relation to the relevant statutory provision.[47] The law was subsequently amended in July 2008 so that those liable to removal now have their cases referred to the Parole Board in the same way as other prisoners.[48]

Consideration by the Parole Board

26.14 Detailed policies concerning the referral of cases to the Parole Board of determinate sentence cases are contained in Prison Service Order

---

44 *R (Smith and West) v Parole Board* [2005] UKHL 1.
45 The Parole Board's Practice Guidance on when it will hold oral hearings is available at www.justice.gov.uk/downloads/guidance/prison-probation-and-rehabilitation/parole-board/Practice_guidance_for_oral_hearings.doc.
46 Or serving an extended sentence where the custodial term is four or more years.
47 *R (Headley and Hindawi) v Secretary of State for the Home Department* [2006] UKHL 54.
48 CJA 1991 s35.

(PSO) 6000.[49] In outline, a dossier of reports is prepared which is disclosed to the prisoner so that written representations can be made to the Parole Board. If fairness requires it (for example the case raises issues of contested fact) the Board may hold an oral hearing, but in the vast majority of determinate sentence cases the Board makes its decision on the papers. The parole process for determinate sentence prisoners should begin six months before the parole eligibility date.

Release criteria for those not liable to removal

26.15 The test for release to be applied by the Parole Board is set out in statutory directions issued by the SSJ. The directions applicable to those who are *not* liable to removal[50] state that the Parole Board should:

> ... consider primarily the risk to the public of a further offence being committed at a time when the prisoner would otherwise be in prison and whether any such risk is acceptable.

This level of risk 'must be balanced against the benefit' of early release.

Release criteria for those liable to removal

26.16 Prison Service policy from November 2011 states that:

> Foreign national prisoners cannot opt out of the parole process. Governors must ensure that those parole eligible prisoners who are not removed early under ERS are referred to the Parole Board for consideration for release on parole in the same way as other parole eligible determinate sentence prisoners (in line with PSO 6000). The parole dossier must contain any relevant UKBA paperwork relating to the prisoner's immigration status and progress towards their removal or deportation. In cases where the prisoner has no home address or previous place of residence in the UK – and therefore does not have an Offender Manager from the 'home' area – the report that is normally provided by the Offender Manager is not required. If the prisoner's immigration status changes during the course of the parole process, the prison must notify the Parole Board.[51]

---

49 PSO 6000 chapter 5 – guidance on the contents of the dossier is at appendix d to the chapter. For a full account of the determinate sentence parole process see Arnott and Creighton *Parole Board hearings: law and practice*, 2nd edn, LAG, 2010.

50 'Directions to the Parole Board under Section 32(6) of the Criminal Justice Act 1991', Parole Board, May 2004. Available at http://tna.europarchive. org/20110206085921/http://www.paroleboard.gov.uk/policy_and_guidance/ secretary_of_states_directions/directions_may_2004/.

51 PSI 59/2011 para 5.4.

This suggests that when considering whether to release on licence those who are liable to removal, the Parole Board should apply the same test it applies to other prisoners (we have referred to that test at para 26.15 above). Note that this marks a shift: previously, the courts had indicated that the Parole Board should, when considering parole for an FNP who was liable to removal, apply the criteria which historically pertained when the SSJ had the power to make the release decision.[52] There is a potential anomaly for FNPs eligible for the Early Removal Scheme (ERS, discussed at paras 28.31–28.44 below) who are not removed prior to their Parole Eligibility Date. It appears that the Parole Board is required to apply a higher test for release on parole from the Parole Eligibility Date, even for a person liable to removal who, it is presumed, will be deported, than would have been applied in removing the same prisoner under the ERS in the 270 days prior to that point (as we shall see at paras 28.40–28.41, FNPs can only be refused early removal on limited grounds). We suggest that this anomaly may be susceptible to legal challenge.

Refusal of release on parole licence

26.17 If parole is refused, then PSO 6000[53] confirms that there will be an entitlement to annual reviews until the automatic release date is reached. There is no appeal against the Parole Board's decision, which can only be challenged by way of judicial review in the Administrative Court. Judicial review generally is discussed at paras 42.16–42.70.

26.18 Where a determinate sentenced FNP who is liable to removal is released, the FNP will be issued with a licence. The licence will confirms that, if the FNP is not released immediately because detained under IA 1971 powers, should they be released into the UK during the currency of the licence, the FNP should immediately report to the supervising probation officer.[54] This requirement immediately to report also applies to an FNP detained under Immigration Act powers who is subsequently released on bail by an immigration judge or by the UK Border Agency itself.

26.19 Once released, determinate sentence prisoners remain liable to recall for breach of their licences for the duration of the licence (which

---

52 *R (Hindawi) v Secretary of State for Justice* [2011] EWHC 830 (QB); *R (Ismailaj) v Parole Board* [2011] EWHC 1020 (Admin).
53 PSO 6000 para 5.9.2.
54 See sample licences at PSI 59/2011 Annex K. PSI 65/2011 also imposes duties on the releasing prison to ensure that the probation service is informed of any release during the licence period.

for sentences of more than 12 months imposed for offences committed on or after 4 April 2005 will be the entirety of the sentence).[55]

Procedures for release – indeterminate sentences

26.20 Release from indeterminate sentences is now administered in the same way whatever the type of indeterminate sentence. Where the minimum term is of sufficient length, there will be a referral to the Parole Board in advance of the minimum term's expiry, in order to consider whether a transfer to open conditions in preparation for release is appropriate.[56]

26.21 Preparation for the review by the Parole Board at the expiry of the minimum term is governed by a detailed policy, PSO 6010, termed the 'generic parole process'. Normally PSO 6010 envisages a six-month process during which a dossier of reports is prepared and disclosed to the prisoner who can then make representations to the Parole Board. The Parole Board will then consider whether the matter should proceed to an oral hearing at which a release direction or recommendation for open conditions can be made.[57] Oral hearings before the Parole Board are governed by the Parole Board Rules 2011.[58]

26.22 If the case does proceed to an oral hearing, then any decision of the Parole Board to release is binding on the SSJ, and the prisoner will be released on licence.[59] The Parole Board will not direct release unless satisfied that the prisoner no longer poses a substantial risk of committing further offences of serious harm.[60] In cases where it is clear that the prisoner will be deported if released, the Board is required to consider risk to the public outside the UK.[61] If not released by the Board, indeterminate sentenced prisoners are entitled to periodic reviews by the Board at no greater than two-year intervals.[62] Those

---

55 CJA 2003 s254.
56 For a full account see Arnott and Creighton *Parole Board hearings: law and practice*, 2nd edn, LAG, 2010, chs 10–11.
57 The policy on when the Parole Board will grant an oral hearing is available at www.justice.gov.uk/guidance/prison-probation-and-rehabilitation/parole-board/oral-hearings.htm.
58 SI No 2947.
59 C(S)A 1997 s28(5).
60 *R v Parole Board ex p Bradley* [1991] 1 WLR 134.
61 *R v Parole Board ex p White* (1994) *Times* 30 December QBD.
62 C(S)A 1997 s28(7).

released on licence remain liable to recall to prison for life,[63] unless they are serving an IPP sentence and have successfully applied for cancellation of the licence after ten years in the community. Recalls will be referred to the Board which again has the power to direct re-release.

New legislative proposals for FNPs 'liable to removal'

26.23 Important changes are proposed by the Legal Aid, Sentencing and Punishment of Offenders Bill. The proposed legislation (at clause 100) would remove the role of the Parole Board in determining whether indeterminate sentence prisoners who are 'liable to removal' (as defined above) are released, and give power to the SSJ to remove the lifer from prison for the purpose of deportation or removal from the UK on expiry of the minimum term. If introduced, the new statutory power to release for the purpose of expulsion would arise regardless of the risk the FNP was assessed as posing. The clause confirms that while in the UK, such prisoners will still be liable to be detained pursuant to the sentence.

63 C(S)A 1997 s32.

SECTION H
Foreign national (serving) prisoners

Chapter 27: Management of FNPs in prisons   525

Chapter 28: Temporary and early release, early removal   539

Chapter 29: Repatriation of prisoners   555

Chapter 30: Mental health legislation and FNPs   567

Introduction to foreign national (serving) prisoners

Foreign nationals in the prison system

As at 30 September 2011 there were a total of 11,076 foreign national prisoners (FNPs) held in prisons, some 11.8 per cent of the total prison population at that date of 87,501.[1]

The treatment and management of FNPs serving sentences in prisons has been of concern for many years. The Chief Inspector of Prisons produced a thematic review on the issue in July 2006,[2] which identified three primary issues of concern: family contact, immigration (principally the UK Border Agency's lack of communication and delay) and language. The report made recommendations to the UK Border Agency including that prisons should have allocated immigration officers to whom enquiries could be directed, that immigration decisions should be made earlier in the sentence, and that prison staff should be trained in how to deal with immigration paperwork. One of the recommendations made to the Prison Service was that there should be a national policy for the management and support of FNPs, with a foreign national co-ordinator in each prison. The focus of the recommendations was clearly on the unmet needs of FNPs.

The research that informed that thematic review was carried out before the FNP political furore of spring 2006 (already described in the Introduction to this book). The Chief Inspector issued a follow up report in February 2007[3] in which she observed of those events:

> As a consequence, all foreign nationals were assumed to be deportable. Foreign nationals who had been in open conditions, or were on licence in the community, were returned to closed prisons, even if their behaviour had been exemplary. The trawl was so undiscriminating that it included some British citizens (who are not deportable in any circumstances), Irish and EEA nationals (who are deportable only in limited circumstances), and those who had committed only minor offences, but had lengthy residence and family ties only in the UK. Moreover, the absence of proper systems, which had led to the original crisis, left the immigration authorities entirely unable to cope with the volume of

---

1 www.justice.gov.uk/publications/statistics-and-data/prisons-and-probation/oms-quarterly.htm.
2 'Foreign national prisoners: a thematic review', HM Inspectorate of Prisons, July 2006. Available at www.justice.gov.uk/downloads/publications/inspectorate-reports/hmipris/foreignnationals-rps.pdf.
3 'Foreign national prisoners: A follow-up report', HM Inspectorate of Prisons, January 2007. Available at www.justice.gov.uk/downloads/publications/inspectorate-reports/hmipris/foreign_nationals_follow-up1-rps.pdf.

work now created. As a consequence, foreign nationals, suddenly and unexpectedly threatened with deportation, also found it impossible to find out what was happening to them, and were held in prisons and immigration removal centres far past their sentence expiry dates, even those who were desperate to return home. Their presence significantly contributed to the prison overcrowding crisis of late 2006.[4]

The Chief Inspector found that this had resulted in an increased prevalence of self-harm among FNPs.

Policies implemented since May 2006 have focussed on the targeting of those eligible for deportation and removal from the UK, rather than on the needs of FNPs, despite occasional reliance on those needs as a justification for policy changes. These changes have involved attempts both to ensure that FNPs are identified early and located in designated prisons to facilitate UK Border Agency processing, and amendments to the statutory and policy framework for early release to enable the removal of FNPs from the UK at earlier points in their sentence (see paras 28.31–28.32) and their repatriation without consent (see paras 29.7–29.8 below).

Organisation of this section

We start by looking at how FNPs are managed in the prison estate, including security categorisation and allocation, before turning to other issues of specific concern to FNPs, namely temporary and early release, early removal, and the repatriation of prisoners.

---

4 'Foreign national prisoners: A follow-up report', HM Inspectorate of Prisons, January 2007, p5.

CHAPTER 27
Management of FNPs in prisons

27.1	**Introduction**
27.4	**The Service Level Agreement**
27.8	**Local policies for managing FNPs**
27.9	**FNPs held on remand**
27.10	**Categorisation and allocation**
27.11	**Categorisation**
27.12	Remand prisoners
27.13	Categorisation of women and young offenders
27.14	Categorisation following conviction
27.16	Categorisation of FNPs
27.21	FNPs who are detained in prison at the end of a sentence
27.22	Challenging a categorisation decision
27.23	**Allocation**
27.24	The 'Rationalisation Plan'
27.28	**Communication between prisons and the UK Border Agency**
27.29	Communication when an FNP is serving the sentence
27.36	Communication when an FNP remains detained under Immigration Act powers
27.38	**The IS91 detention authority form**
27.40	**Release of FNPs**
27.43	**Communication with embassies**

Introduction

27.1 This chapter concerns the management of foreign national prisoners (FNPs) in the prison system. We consider security categorisation and allocations to different types of prisons, and the particular issues affecting FNPs in this context.

27.2 We will refer extensively to Prison Service Instruction (PSI) 52/2011, Prison Service policy which provides guidance to prisons on particular aspects of decision-making relevant to FNPs. This policy replaced the previous guidance, Prison Service Order (PSO) 4630, in November 2011.

27.3 As we see in this section and in paras 28.12–28.30 on Home Detention Curfew (HDC), the standard steps in progression through the sentence are often complicated or even blocked for FNPs, in turn impeding preparations for re-integration into the community on release. This is of particular concern where FNPs have strong grounds for remaining in the UK and will not in fact be expelled.

The Service Level Agreement

27.4 In May 2009 a Service Level Agreement (SLA) was agreed between the National Offender Management Service (NOMS) in the Ministry of Justice (MoJ), which became responsible for the management of prisons on its creation in 2007, and the UK Border Agency which aimed to 'support the effective management and speedy removal of Foreign National Prisoners'.[1] This SLA created a Foreign National Prisoners Board to oversee the joint working by the two departments. It also set out the reciprocal expectations between the two departments.

27.5 On the UK Border Agency side, the SLA sets out the expectations that it will seek to reduce the numbers of prisoners detained in prisons solely under immigration powers, and that it will provide information to the MoJ on numbers of such prisoners, and provide identification of which prisoners the UK Border Agency are to seek to detain and remove. Where the sentence length allows, the SLA includes an expectation that the UK Border Agency will begin consideration of removal 18 months before the earliest date of release.

27.6 On the side of the MoJ, the SLA includes expectations that the MoJ will provide information about FNPs liable for deportation,

---

1 Available at www.irr.org.uk/pdf2/FNP_SLA.pdf.

27.7 pass on records such as security and medical records when they are transferred to the immigration detention estate,[2] and assist in collecting documentation and attempts to document FNPs. The SLA therefore supplements the duties the Prison Service has under its own policies in relation to providing information to the UK Border Agency (see further at paras 27.28–27.37 below).

27.7 The SLA includes a 'Protocol for the Management of Detainees held in Prison Custody and Movement of Detainees between the NOMS and UK Border Agency Estate'. This includes similar criteria for holding immigration detainees in prisons to those contained in the UK Border Agency detention policy. The SLA also includes a 'Rationalisation Plan' aimed at concentrating FNPs in a smaller number of prisons (see paras 27.28–27.37 below).

Local policies for managing FNPs

27.8 All prisons were previously required by PSO 4630 to have a local policy for managing FNPs. This mandatory requirement was removed when PSI 52/2011 replaced PSO 4630.[3]

FNPs held on remand

27.9 On reception into a prison, FNPs who are held on remand should be provided with information on applying for bail from the criminal courts in the same way as any other prisoner, although information provided to the court should confirm their nationality and immigration status if known.[4]

Categorisation and allocation

27.10 Categorisation and allocation are the two procedures that determine where a prisoner is held. Categorisation refers to the process by which the appropriate security category for the prisoner is determined. Once

---

2 Although these should be returned to the Prison Service on the release or removal of the detainee.
3 PSI 52/2011 para 1.8.
4 PSI 52/2011 paras 2.27–2.30.

Categorisation

27.11 Categorisation[5] will broadly depend on an assessment of three factors, namely likelihood of escape; risk to the public; and any control problems that the prisoner may pose.[6] Adult male prisoners can be categorised as:[7]

- *Category A* (and such prisoners are also designated either standard, high or exceptional escape risk). These are prisoners whose escape would be highly dangerous to the public, the police or the security of the state, and for whom the aim must be to make escape impossible. Such prisoners are held in high security prisons and are subject to a wide range of security measures. The detailed policy on how prisons should identify prisoners that might be made Category A, and the review procedures for decision-making in such cases is now contained in Prison Service Instruction (PSI) 3/2010.
- *Category B.* These are prisoners for whom the very highest conditions of security are not necessary but for whom escape must be made very difficult.
- *Category C.* These are prisoners who cannot be trusted in open conditions but who do not have the resources and will to make a determined escape attempt.
- *Category D.* These are prisoners who can be reasonably trusted in open conditions.

Remand prisoners

27.12 Prisoners on remand can be placed in Category A or given restricted status, but otherwise are not formally given a security category but

---

5 See Prison Rules (PR) 1999 SI No 728 r7, Young Offender Institution Rules 2000 SI No 3371 r4, PSI 3/2010 (in relation to Category A), PSI 39/2011 in relation to women prisoners, and PSI 40/2011 in relation to adult male offenders. For a full analysis of categorisation procedures and how such decisions may be challenged see Creighton and Arnott, *Prisoners: law and practice*, LAG, 2009.
6 PSI 40/2011 para 1.1.
7 PSI 40/2011 para 2.1.

will normally be held in closed conditions (adult males will normally be held in Category B prisons).[8]

Categorisation of women and young offenders

27.13 There are fewer categories for women prisoners, young offenders and under 18-year-olds held in prisons or young offender institutions (YOIs).[9] Although in principle such prisoners can be made Category A, in practice they normally given what is called 'restricted status' instead,[10] which is reserved for those whose escape would present a serious risk to the public and who are required to be held in designated secure accommodation. Otherwise women, young offenders and those aged under 18 will be categorised as either suitable for open or closed conditions only.[11]

Categorisation following conviction

27.14 On conviction, the holding prison will make a decision on the appropriate security category on the basis of centrally issued guidance.[12] This guidance requires periodic review of categorisation decisions.

27.15 Responsibility for categorisation decisions lies with the holding prison, except those relating to Category A/restricted status and decisions as to whether indeterminate sentence prisoners should go to open conditions. Category A decisions are made by the Directorate of High Security Prisons in National Offender Management Service (NOMS). Decisions relating to whether indeterminate sentence prisoners should go open conditions are normally made only following a recommendation of the Parole Board.

Categorisation of FNPs

27.16 Categorisation decisions other than those relating to Category D are made without particular reference to the nationality or immigration status of the prisoner. However, Prison Service policy proceeds on the basis that where FNPs are facing deportation, this may increase

---

8 PSO 4600 para 1.3.
9 Secure Children's Homes and secure training centres (STCs) do not apply security categories to the children that they hold.
10 See PSI 3/1010.
11 PSI 39/2011 para 2.1.
12 PSI 39/2011 for women prisoners and PSI 40/2011 for adult males.

the risk of them absconding from open prisons, which by their nature have comparatively low levels of perimeter and internal security.[13]

27.17 FNPs are eligible for consideration for Category D and allocation to open conditions, subject to the holding prison adopting certain procedures before making such decisions.

27.18 Under MoJ policy, if an FNP meets the criteria for consideration for deportation (see para 27.30 below), then before a decision to downgrade to Category D can be made the prison must send a prescribed form[14] to the Criminal Casework Directorate (CCD) at the UK Border Agency. This form requests information as to whether any enforcement action is being pursued against the prisoner and whether the UK Border Agency have any intelligence or information which would assist in assessing suitability for open conditions (such as family ties strong community links).[15] Unless the prison receives confirmation from the UK Border Agency that deportation is not being pursued, then it must make the categorisation decision on the assumption that deportation will take place.[16] The policy now states that prisons must not make a decision to transfer such prisoners to open conditions without a UK Border Agency response.

27.19 PSO 4630 on foreign national prisoners previously stated that:

> Each case must be individually considered on its merits but the need to protect the public and ensure the intention to deport is not frustrated is paramount. Category D will only be appropriate where it is clear that the risk is very low.[17]

The inclusion in PSO 4630 of a policy aim of preventing frustration of the deportation process was held to be lawful on the basis that there is potentially a link between absconding risk and the threat of deportation.[18] However, despite the use of the term 'paramount' in the policy, the prison was always required to exercise discretion in each individual case.[19]

27.20 That policy has now been replaced with PSI 52/2011. The new policy states that:

---

13 PSI 52/2011 paras 2.20–2.25.
14 Form CCD3 at Annex B to PSI 52/2011.
15 And failure to consult UK Border Agency will invalidate a decision favourable to the prisoner – see *R (Manhire) v Secretary of State for Justice* [2009] EWHC 1788 (Admin) at 29–30.
16 PSI 52/2011 para 2.23.
17 PSO 4630 para 14.4.
18 *R (Omoregbee) v Secretary of State for Justice and another* [2011] EWCA Civ 559.
19 *R (Omoregbee) v Secretary of State for Justice and another* [2011] EWCA Civ 559 para 11.

All foreign national prisoners may be considered for categorization and subsequent allocation to open conditions.

PSI 52/2011 states that FNPs sentenced to less than 12 months 'must be included in consideration for allocation to open conditions ...'.[20] However, the policy also states that FNPs sentenced to 12 months or more imprisonment must be referred to the UK Border Agency and in this latter class of cases:

> ... the individual risk must be assessed on the assumption that deportation will take place unless a decision not to deport has already been taken by the UKBA ... A response must be received from UKBA if Category D is being considered and establishments cannot make such a decision without receiving a response from UKBA.[21]

The requirement to take into account the UK Border Agency's view as to suitability for Category D in cases which have been referred to the UK Border Agency for deportation consideration is problematic. Some prisons have (even under the preceding policy) effectively delegated the responsibility for the decision on allocation to open conditions to the UK Border Agency, treating the UK Border Agency's views as binding. We suggest that such an approach may be an unlawful delegation of powers, and contrary to parliament's intentions, since the statutory framework provides that the decision should be made by the prison governor or (in a contracting prison, the controller) on behalf of the Secretary of State for Justice (SSJ).[22] Even where prisons have not treated the UK Border Agency's view as binding, there have been many cases where insufficient weight has been given to other relevant factors, such as family ties in the UK, that suggest a low risk of absconding[23] in making categorisation decisions for FNPs. In addition, as we observe at note 31 below, there are certain differences between the criteria for referral to the UK Border Agency as described in prison policy and the UK Border Agency's own policy on criteria for deportation consideration. We suggest that where an FNP does not meet the UK Border Agency's criteria for deportation consideration, and is not the subject of a deportation decision, it may be unlawful to assess him or her for categorisation 'on the assumption that deportation will take place'.

---

20 PSI 52/2011 para 2.22.
21 PSI 52/2011 para 2.23.
22 See the facts of *R (Gyamfi) v Secretary of State for Justice* [2010] EWHC 349 (Admin).
23 *R (Manhire) v Secretary of State for Justice* [2009] EWHC 1788 (Admin); *Abel Oge-Denge v Secretary of State for Justice* [2011] EWHC 266 (Admin).

FNPs who are detained in prison at the end of a sentence

27.21 Although unconvicted prisoners are normally held in 'local prisons', that is Category B prisons that serve courts, there is no requirement to transfer FNPs to such conditions at the end of their sentence where they have been held in more relaxed conditions during the sentence. However if the prisoner is held in a prison which does not normally hold unconvicted prisoners they may only continue to be held there under Immigration Act (IA) 1971 powers if they expressly consent.[24] See also the discussion at paras 38.14–38.15.

Challenging a categorisation decision

27.22 Decisions to refuse downgrading security category can be challenged through the Prison Service complaints procedure (see paras 25.3–25.14) and thereafter pursued with the Prisons and Probation Ombudsman (PPO). They can also be challenged in judicial review proceedings.

Allocation

27.23 The decision as to the particular institution to which a prisoner will be allocated will follow the decision as to the appropriate security category. Low-risk prisoners may be immediately assessed as suitable to open conditions. Higher-risk prisoners will, where appropriate, progress towards open conditions as risks are assessed as reducing as a result, for example, of completion of offending behaviour courses.

The 'Rationalisation Plan'

27.24 The SLA agreed between NOMS and the UK Border Agency in May 2009 (see the Introduction to this section) set out measures by which certain FNPs would be allocated to particular prisons with embedded UK Border Agency staff in order to 'improve joint working throughout the removals process'.[25] This policy of concentrating FNPs in certain prisons is referred to in the SLA as the 'Rationalisation Plan'.

---

24 PSI 52/2011 para 2.66; PR 1999 r7(2).
25 SLA Annex F. See also PSI 40 Annex B paras 18 to 28 and Annex H.

27.25 The Rationalisation Plan only applies to male adult category B and C prisons. The Rationalisation Plan created two FNP-only prisons, HMP Canterbury and HMP Bullwood Hall. It also created six regional 'hub' prisons with embedded UK Border Agency teams at HMP Risley, HMP Hewell, HMP Morton Hall, HMP The Mount, HMP The Verne and HMP Wormwood Scrubs. It also created a larger number of 'spoke' prisons, without embedded UK Border Agency teams, but with specific protocols for joint working with UK Border Agency staff including sharing of information. The Rationalisation Plan states that FNPs with more than a month, but less than three years to serve will be transferred to these hub and spoke prisons.

27.26 When the Rationalisation Plan was introduced there was widespread concern that a blanket policy was being applied to transfer eligible FNPs to hub and spoke prisons, without consideration of individual circumstances, such as family ties or any offending behaviour work an FNP may have been undertaking in the holding prison. Several prisoners issued claims for judicial review challenging decisions to transfer them; these judicial reviews were withdrawn because the MoJ agreed that these particular prisoners' transfers would not proceed without representations as to individual circumstances being considered.[26]

27.27 The Equality and Human Rights Commission (EHRC) also brought a challenge to the Rationalisation Plan on grounds that the SSJ had not had due regard to the duties to eliminate race and disability discrimination,[27] in that no adequate equality impact assessments had been carried out before the SLA was implemented. This challenge succeeded, although by the time of the full hearing the SSJ had completed impact assessments after the event, which satisfied the court that the statutory duties had belatedly been complied with.[28]

---

26 See *R (EHRC) v Secretary of State for Justice and Secretary of State for the Home Department* [2010] EWHC 147 (Admin) paras 19–22.
27 Race Relations Act 1976 s71; Disability Discrimination Act 2005 s49A.
28 *R (EHRC) v Secretary of State for Justice and Secretary of State for the Home Department* [2010] EWHC 147 (Admin).

Communication between prisons and the UK Border Agency

27.28 As noted in the introduction to this section, a series of measures were introduced following the furore in late April 2006, when it transpired that a large numbers of FNPs had been released by the Prison Service on completion of their custodial sentences without being considered for deportation by the UK Border Agency.

Communication when an FNP is serving the sentence

27.29 PSI 52/2011 states that prisons should notify the UKBA at first reception of all foreign nationals (both EEA and non-EEA nationals), dual nationals and those whose nationality is unclear 'to facilitate efficient and timely case consideration' by the UK Border Agency.[29]

27.30 Prison policy states that the following categories of FNP must be referred to the UK Border Agency's CCD within five working days of sentence.[30]

- All those recommended for deportation by a court.
- All foreign nationals (EEA and non-EEA nationals) sentenced to 12 months' or more imprisonment (except Irish citizens).[31]
- All non-EEA nationals sentenced to less than 12 months but where the current sentence plus one or two previous sentences within the last five years (taking account of the most significant sentences during the period) total 12 months or more.
- All non-EEA nationals who receive a custodial sentence for a drug offence (except possession only cases).

27.31 Dual nationals are included because in very exceptional circumstances the UK Border Agency may seek to deprive a dual national of British citizenship (see paras 19.76–19.78).

---

29 PSI 52/2011 para 2.7.
30 PSI 52/2011 para 2.8 on the form at Annex A to the PSI.
31 Note that there are differences between prison policy as to who should be referred to the UK Border Agency for deportation consideration, and the UK Border Agency's own policy as to who should be considered for deportation, in particular for EEA nationals. Whereas PSI 52/2011 para 2.8 indicates that EEA nationals (other than Irsih citizens) should, like non-EEA nationals, be referred for deportation consideration if they are serving sentences of 12 months or more. But UK Border Agency policy states at EIG chapter 11, para 11.2.1 that EEA nationals should be considered for deportation if serving a custodial sentence of 24 months or more, unless the conviction was of a specified drug, sex or violent offence. See chapter 9 para 9.82 above.

27.32   PSI 52/2011 states that the details of Irish nationals should only be notified to the UK Border Agency where there is a criminal court recommendation for deportation or where there are exceptional circumstances justifying consideration for deportation.[32]

27.33   The prison is always required, where relevant, to confirm to the UK Border Agency whether the sentencing court recommended deportation, and to provide a copy of the prisoner's previous convictions.[33] Where the UK Border Agency require further information before deciding whether to proceed with deportation, for example when dealing with EEA nationals, it will seek this from the prisoner's Offender Manager (OM) in the Probation Service.[34] The UK Border Agency may also seek further information from the holding prison during the sentence, such as reports and assessments completed that are relevant to risk.[35]

27.34   In order to prevent FNPs being released without consideration for deportation by the UK Border Agency, prisons are required to make checks with CCD 48 hours before release to confirm whether an IS 91 (authority to detain under immigration powers) is to be issued.[36]

27.35   The UK Border Agency may also approach the prisoner's OM in the Probation Service for up-to-date information on the assessed risk of harm and likelihood of re-conviction, in the lead up to the due release date. OMs are required to co-operate with such requests.[37]

Communication when an FNP remains detained under Immigration Act powers

27.36   FNPs who complete their criminal custodial term should also be referred to CCD with confirmation of the position, and such prisoners should also be the subject of weekly updates to PMS if they remain in IA 1971 powers after completion of their sentence.[38]

27.37   The UK Border Agency may also seek information from NOMS for detention reviews where an FNP has entered immigration detention. OMs are also instructed to provide such information to UK

---

32 PSI 52/2011 para 2.5 – these will be where the offences relate to national security or serious risk to the public – see Annex H to the PSI.
33 PSI 52/2011 para 2.10.
34 PSI 52/2011 para 2.18 and Probation Circulars 11/2007 and 32/2007.
35 See para 27.35.
36 PSI 52/2011 para 2.55.
37 PC 32/2007 para 6 – a pro-forma for such information is at Annex A of the Circular.
38 PSI 52/2011 para 2.64.

Border Agency for use in bail summaries where FNPs are detained under immigration powers beyond their release date.[39] Where an FNP applies for immigration bail during the currency of their licence period, the fact that they are unable to claim benefits must not be used by the Probation Service as a justification for claiming that they cannot be accommodated in approved premises (that is a probation hostel).[40]

The IS91 detention authority form

27.38 As we discuss at paras 31.35–31.36, there is a power to 'dual detain' an FNP who is being administratively removed, so that the prisoner is simultaneously detained under Immigration Act and criminal justice powers. However, there is no power of 'dual detention' in criminal deportation cases (in criminal deportation cases the prisoner is either held under Immigration Act powers or criminal justice powers).

27.39 Whether a prisoner is being 'dual detained' or purely detained under criminal justice powers, the UK Border Agency will often issue an IS91 detention authority form (or a letter authorising detention under Immigration Act powers) for FNPs. (These detention authority forms and letters are discussed in detail at paras 35.6–35.7.) These forms and letters authorise the detention of the FNP under Immigration Act powers (on completion of the criminal custodial term if for the purposes of deportation). In practical terms, the IS91 form warns the prison authorities that the FNP should not simply be released from prison on being granted bail (if a remand prisoner) or on completing the custodial term (if a serving prisoner).

Release of FNPs

27.40 If a remand FNP is granted criminal bail or acquitted, or if a serving FNP completes the custodial part of his or her criminal sentence, the FNP must be released unless there is a (lawful) detention authority from the UK Border Agency authorising his or her detention under IA 1971 powers.[41] Continued detention without such authorisation

---

39 PC 32/2007 para 6.
40 Approved Premises Handbook 2009 para 8.6.
41 PSI 52/2011 paras 2.31–2.36.

from the UK Border Agency lacks lawful authority and amounts to false imprisonment.

27.41 In these cases, where the prisoner is released, prisons should contact the UK Border Agency's CCD through NOMS with details to assist the Home Office in later locating the prisoner in the community.[42] Likewise where the prisoner is sentenced to a term which gives rise to an immediate release date due to time spent on remand.

27.42 As published MoJ policy recognises, a prison may only hold a foreign national after his or her due release date where there has been a decision by the SSHD to detain under Immigration Act powers and notification of that decision has been served on the individual.[43]

Communication with embassies

27.43 There are two mechanisms which require prisons to provide information to embassies and consulates of foreign national prisoners: individual bi-lateral agreements and the Vienna Convention on Consular Relations 1962. The Prison Service has issued guidance on these duties.[44]

27.44 Prisons are required to inform FNPs on first reception of their right to consular notification, so as to allow consular officials to visit and provide support.

27.45 Where there is a bi-lateral agreement with the country of the prisoner's nationality then the consulate must be informed of the prisoner's location, personal details and details relating to the offence.[45] The UK Border Agency detention policy states that such notification should not take place where there the prisoner has made a claim for asylum, or where there is an indication that an asylum claim might be forthcoming.[46]

27.46 Where there is no bi-lateral agreement, the Vienna Convention provides that consular notification should not take place unless the prisoner requests or consents to this.[47] Where a prisoner has agreed to contact with their consular officials then they have a right to visit, correspond and arrange for legal representation.[48]

42 PSI 52/2011 para 2.35.
43 PSI 52/2011 paras 2.33 and 2.62.
44 PSI 52/2011 section 3.
45 A list of countries is at Annex M to PSI 52/2011.
46 Enforcement Instructions and Guidance (EIG) chapter 55 para 55.18.
47 Vienna Convention article 36(1)(b).
48 Vienna Convention article 36(1)(c).

CHAPTER 28

Temporary and early release, early removal

28.1	Introduction
28.4	Release on Temporary Licence (ROTL)
28.12	Early release from sentence into the community – Home Detention Curfew (HDC)
28.14	Statutory exclusions from HDC
28.16	Groups of person statutorily eligible but presumed unsuitable for HDC
28.17	Those for whom there is a presumption in favour of release on HDC
28.18	The time window for HDC
28.20	The HDC consideration process
28.23	Refusal of HDC
28.25	Recall from HDC
28.27	FNPs and HDC
28.31	**The Early Removal Scheme (ERS)**
28.33	Early removal in CJA 1991 cases
28.34	Early removal in CJA 2003 cases
28.35	Eligibility and consideration for early removal
28.44	Return to the UK after release on ERS
28.45	**The Facilitated Returns Scheme (FRS)**

Introduction

28.1 In chapter 26 we considered how serving prisoners may become entitled to automatic release (on completing the custodial part of their sentence) or eligible for consideration for release by the Parole Board.

28.2 This chapter considers three other mechanisms by which prisoners serving sentences may be released, prior to the normal dates for release from the sentence:

- temporarily into the community (Release on Temporary Licence (ROTL));
- on a long-term basis into the community before completion of the criminal custodial term (Home Detention Curfew (HDC) – which is only available to those serving determinate sentences); or
- on condition that they are immediately removed or deported (Early Removal Scheme (ERS) – again which only applies to those serving determinate sentences).

28.3 In recent years, an important development for foreign national prisoners (FNPs) has been the introduction and widening of means by which they can be released early in order to be administratively removed or deported from the UK (Early Removal). The corollary of this is that FNPs are often refused the benefit of any early release into the community in the UK (ROTL and HDC). As with decisions on categorisation for open conditions (see para 27.20) these refusals are are not infrequently unlawful. This is particularly problematic because ROTL and HDC are important steps in the preparation of a prisoner for his or her final release into the community. Many FNPs are denied these, notwithstanding that they will not realistically be removed or deported from the UK.

Release on Temporary Licence (ROTL)

28.4 The Prison Rules (PR) 1999[1] and Young Offender Institution (YOI) Rules 2000[2] provide that during the custodial part of a prison sentence, prisoners may be released on temporary licence into the community for specific purposes.[3] Prison Service Order (PSO) 6300 sets

---

1 SI No 728.
2 SI No 3371.
3 PR 1999 r9, YOI Rules 2000 r5.

out the policy concerning ROTL. There are four types of temporary release under PSO 6300:

1) *Resettlement day release:* this is used where prisoners are working during the day outside prison, for attending interviews and maintaining family ties.
2) *Resettlement overnight release:* this allows prisoners to spend time including overnight stays at their proposed release address in preparation for resettlement in the community.
3) *Childcare resettlement leave:* this is for prisoners who can demonstrate that they have sole caring responsibility for a child under 16.
4) *Special purpose licence:* for occasions such as funerals and outside medical appointments.

28.5 Although in some circumstances ROTL can be granted from closed prisons, generally ROTL is only available to those who are considered suitable for Category D status. PSO 6300 makes clear that it is open to FNPs to apply for ROTL.[4]

28.6 Only FNPs whose immigration status allows them to work or study will be allowed temporary release for these purposes, although those without such permission are able to undertake unpaid community work from prison.[5]

28.7 PSO 6300 stipulates that FNPs who are court recommended for deportation or have been served with a notice of intention to deport or a deportation order can only be released on ROTL once the prison has sought the comments of the Criminal Casework Directorate (CCD) within the UK Border Agency on a prescribed form. The CCD advice is not binding and the decision as to whether to grant ROTL remains with the governor or controller in private prisons.[6]

28.8 Where an FNP meets the criteria for referral to the CCD for deportation (see para 27.30) but is not the subject of a court recommendation for deportation and has not been served with notice of intention to deport, PSO 6300 specifies that unless CCD has made a decision that the prisoner will not be deported, the presumption when making the decision on ROTL must be that deportation action will proceed on completion of the sentence.[7] There is no requirement to seek UK Border Agency's comments in these cases.[8] PSO 6300

---

4 PSO 6300 para 5.5.
5 PSO 6300 para 5.5.1.
6 PSO 6300 para 5.5.2.
7 As with decisions on transfer to open conditions, see paras 28.31–28.44 below.
8 PSO 6300 para 5.5.3.

states that the need to protect the public is 'paramount'; therefore the presumption that deportation will take place will be a significant factor for governors to consider when assessing the risk that a prisoner will not comply with the temporary licence.[9]

28.9 However, there must always be an individualised assessment by the Prison Service. See by analogy *R (Omoregbee) v Secretary of State for Justice and another*[10] in which the use of the term 'paramount' in another PSO, in the context of security categorisation, was held to leave the prison service with a duty of individualised consideration in each case (see para 27.19 above).

28.10 As with decisions on transfers to open conditions, and HDC decisions (see paras 28.12–28.30 below) there is a common problem that prison governors improperly delegate the ROTL decision to the UK Border Agency by either refusing to make a decision without the UK Border Agency view, or by treating that view as binding. We suggest that this approach may be an unlawful delegation or fettering of discretion and that prison governors should be reminded that that they are required to exercise their own discretion.

28.11 PSO 6300 confirms that those detained solely under Immigration Act (IA) 1971 powers are not eligible for ROTL, although in such cases, release on compassionate grounds can in principle be sought from the UK Border Agency.[11]

Early release from sentence into the community – Home Detention Curfew (HDC)

28.12 HDC is a scheme, initially introduced in 1999,[12] that allows for early release on an electronic tag. The purpose of HDC as described in the main policy relating to its administration, PSO 6700, 'is to manage more effectively the transition of offenders from custody back into the community' and so 'for most eligible prisoners HDC must be viewed as a normal part of his or her progression through the sentence'.[13] Many FNPs face considerable or insurmountable obstacles to accessing HDC.

---

9 PSO 6300 para 5.5.4.
10 [2011] EWCA Civ 559 para 11.
11 PSO 6300 para 5.5.9.
12 By amendments to the CJA 1991 made by the Crime and Disorder Act 1998.
13 PSO 6700 para 1.4.

28.13 The HDC scheme is complex and what follows only provides an overview.[14] HDC is available to prisoners serving sentences administered both under the Criminal Justice Acts (CJA) 1991 and 2003 and the schemes are broadly similar.

Statutory exclusions from HDC

28.14 The legislative scheme sets out those who are statutorily excluded from HDC.[15] Importantly, those who are 'liable to removal' within the meaning of CJA 1991 or CJA 2003 excluded from consideration for release on HDC (instead they are eligible for the ERS – see paras 28.31–28.44 below). The statutory definition of persons 'liable to removal' has been discussed at para 26.9.

28.15 As well as excluding those liable to removal, there are a number of other statutory exclusions, for example, those serving extended sentences and those subject to sex offender notification requirements. HDC is only available to those serving fixed term sentences. Those serving sentences of four or more years administered under CJA 1991 are also statutorily excluded.

Groups of person statutorily eligible but presumed unsuitable for HDC

28.16 As well as the statutory exclusions, there are policy restrictions that affect eligibility for release on HDC. Certain categories of prisoner are by policy 'presumed unsuitable' for HDC: these prisoners will not be granted HDC unless the governor considers that there are exceptional circumstances justifying release.[16] As we shall see in more detail at para 28.28 below, importantly Prison Service Instruction (PSI) 52/2011 imposes a presumption of unsuitability for HDC on foreign national prisoners who are not statutorily excluded from HDC because they have not been served with any decision to deport, but who have been notified by the SSHD that they are being considered for deportation. In addition:

---

14 For a full account see Creighton and Arnott, *Prisoners: law and practice*, LAG, 2009, paras 11.94–11.117. Prison Service guidance on the scheme is contained in PSO 6700.
15 CJA 1991 s46 and CJA 2003 s259.
16 General guidance on 'exceptional circumstances' is contained in PSI 31/2006.

- those serving sentences of four or more years administered under CJA 2003 are not statutorily excluded but are by policy 'presumed unsuitable' for HDC;
- prisoners serving sentences for certain offences, including most sexual offences and serious violent offences.[17]

Those for whom there is a presumption in favour of release on HDC

28.17 For those serving less than 12 months there is a presumption in favour of release on HDC. This requires governors to release those serving at least three months but less than 12 months on HDC unless there are 'exceptional and compelling reasons not to'.[18] However, those serving sentences for violent, sexual or drugs offences are excluded from this presumption in favour of release.[19] If excluded from presumptive HDC, statutorily eligible prisoners should still be considered under the standard HDC procedures.

The time window for HDC

28.18 To be eligible for HDC prisoners must be serving a sentence of at least three months if the sentence is administered under CJA 1991, or 12 weeks if administered under CJA 2003, and there are minimum periods that a prisoner is required to serve before release.[20] Broadly, prisoners must have served at least one month of the sentence or one quarter of the sentence, whichever is longer, before he or she will be eligible for HDC.

28.19 The maximum period of release on HDC is 135 days ending at the half-way point of the sentence, which would be the normal release date.[21] In practice this means that the HDC period ranges from about two weeks for a three-month sentence, to the full 135 days for an 18-month or longer sentence.

---

17 The list of presumed unsuitable offences is contained in PSI 31/2003 Annex A.
18 Guidance on this scheme is contained in PSI 19/2002.
19 PSI 19/2002 Annex A.
20 See CJA 1991 s34A(4)(a) and CJA 2003 s246(2) – PSI 31/2003 contains a summary.
21 CJA 1991 s34A(3)–(4); CJA 2003 s246(1)–(2) – the minimum period is 30 days in CJA 1991 and four weeks in the CJA 2003.

The HDC consideration process

28.20 On reception to prison, the HDC eligibility date should be calculated by the prison and prisoners should be invited to complete a form giving details of their proposed accommodation ten weeks before their eligibility date.[22] The accommodation must have an electricity supply so that electronic monitoring equipment can be installed.[23] Those without their own addresses can be released to accommodation supplied by private contractors.[24]

28.21 The prison then considers whether an enhanced risk assessment is required (see para 28.22 below). If release on HDC is authorised by the governor then the prisoner should be informed as soon as possible.[25] The Offender Manager (OM), the police and the contractor responsible for the tagging should be notified 14 days before the proposed release.[26]

28.22 A prisoner who applies for HDC may be subject to an enhanced risk assessment if it is considered that that there is a high risk of further sexual or violent offences.[27]

Refusal of HDC

28.23 As HDC is considered to be a normal part of progression through a sentence in most cases, where a prisoner is eligible the grounds they should only be refused where:[28]

- there is an unacceptable risk to the victim or the public;
- there is a likelihood of reoffending;
- there is no suitable address;
- it is not considered that the prisoner will abide by the curfew conditions;
- there is less than 14 days for the curfew to run.

---

22 PSO 6700 para 5.1.1.
23 PSO 6700 para 5.17.1.
24 This is provided by Stonham housing – see PSI 34/2010.
25 PSO 6700 para 7.1.
26 PSO 6700 para 8.1.
27 PSO 6700 para 5.3.3.
28 PSO 6700 para 5.13.3. Where governors believe the release of an otherwise eligible prisoner would 'seriously damage public confidence in the scheme', the case should be referred to the Chief Executive of NOMS for the final decision – PSI 31/2006 para 20.

28.24 Where HDC is refused the prisoner is informed and should be given reasons.[29] The refusal can be appealed through the Prison Service complaints procedure[30] (see paras 25.3–25.14), including a complaint to the Prisons and Probation Ombudsman (PPO).

Recall from HDC

28.25 Those released on HDC can be recalled if they fail to comply with the curfew conditions or if it is no longer possible to monitor the curfew at the specified address.[31] A decision to recall for these reasons is reviewed by the Public Protection Unit at the National Offender Management Service (NOMS), and the prisoner can make representations,[32] and if the recall is upheld then the prisoner will released at the normal date of release (the half-way point of the sentence). If the prisoner is recalled during the curfew period under the normal recall provisions for determinate sentence prisoners, that is on risk to the public grounds, then their cases will be referred to the Parole Board under the same procedure that applies to recall from licence once the curfew period has expired (see para 26.11 below).

28.26 The fact that recall from HDC for breach of the curfew conditions is reviewed by the Secretary of State for Justice (SSJ), rather than the Parole Board, has been held not to breach article 5(4) of the European Convention on Human Rights (ECHR) on the basis that there is a distinction between the entitlement to release on licence at the half-way point of the sentence, and the discretionary scheme to release early on electronic tag before that half-way point has been reached.[33] For similar reasons, unreasonable delays in considering applications for release on HDC have not been held to breach ECHR article 5(4)[34] or (1).[35]

29 PSO 6700 para 7.2.
30 PSO 6700 para 7.10.
31 CJA 1991 s38A; CJA 2003 s255.
32 PSO 6700 para 9.7.1.
33 *R (McAlinden) v Secretary of State for Justice* [2010] EWHC 1557 (Admin).
34 *Mason v Ministry of Justice* [2008] EWHC 1787 (QB).
35 *R (Francis) v Secretary of State for Justice and Secretary of State for the Home Department* [2011] EWHC 1271 (Admin) at para 41 – the breach of the public law duty to exercise the discretion to release the prisoner on HDC during the normal custodial period of the sentence did not give rise to either a breach of ECHR article 5(1), or a claim in false imprisonment. Similarly where the interference with the prisoner's ECHR article 8 rights did not go beyond that inevitably caused by the lawful detention, there could be no claim for a breach of article 8. This judgment is under appeal at the time of writing.

FNPs and HDC

28.27 FNPs as a class are not statutorily excluded from HDC: only those who are 'liable to removal' as defined at para 26.9 above are so excluded. Thus FNPs who are neither faced with administrative removal nor have been served with any decision to deport are not statutorily excluded (even if the SSHD is considering whether to deport them). These FNPs are entitled to consideration for HDC.[36]

28.28 However, PSI 52/2011, adopted on 18 November 2011, states that FNPs who have been notified by the SSHD that they are 'liable to deportation'[37] and under consideration for deportation (though no decision to deport has yet been served) should be presumed to be unsuitable for HDC unless there are exceptional circumstances justifying release. These FNPs should be given a risk assessment for HDC[38] but the decision-maker is instructed to proceed on the basis of an assumption that the FNP will be deported at some point after release from prison.[39] This regime appears to leave the SSHD little incentive to make decisions to deport sufficiently early in an FNP's sentence to permit release on HDC where the SSHD decides against deportation or where the Tribunal allows an appeal against a decision to deport. Merely notifying an FNP that he or she is being considered for deportation will in most cases preclude release on HDC, and in 'automatic' deportation cases will also give rise to a statutory power for the SSHD to detain after sentence completion.[40] There is a risk that the SSHD will frequently delay making decisions to deport until even after sentence completion. FNPs with strong cases against deportation and their legal representatives may wish to press the SSHD for an early decision on deportation to avoid losing the opportunity of release on HDC.

28.29 The justification given in PSI 52/2011 for this presumption of unsuitability for FNPs under consideration for deportation is that the purpose of HDC is resettlement (since FNPs who are to be deported do not require resettlement). It remains to be seen what type of case

---

36 As is now expressly recognised in PSI 52/2011 para 2.46.
37 Not to be confused with the statutory term 'liable to removal' defined at para 26.9 above. In deportation cases, 'liability to removal' arises only after a decision to deport has been made and served on the individual.
38 PSI 52/2011 para 2.47 states that these prisoners 'may' be risk assessed. We suggest that any statutorily eligible prisoner must be risk assessed for HDC: to do otherwise would unlawfully fetter the governor's discretion to release.
39 PSI 52/2011 para 2.47.
40 Under UKBA 2007 s36(1)(a).

will be found sufficiently 'exceptional' to justify a grant of HDC to an FNP who is presumed unsuitable, or whether the policy itself will be found lawful. The example given in PSI 52/2011 for exceptional circumstances warranting release of such an FNP is 'where UKBA has confirmed that deportation is unlikely to be effected for the foreseeable future, and they do not intend to detain the prisoner on release from prison'.[41] Since, as reported by the Independent Chief Inspector of the UK Border Agency, the UK Border Agency appears to be administratively detaining some 97% of FNPs after sentence completion, sometimes for prolonged periods[42] that would set a very high bar for FNPs seeking HDC. We suggest that where there are significant obstacles to an FNP's deportation, whether legal (for example where an FNP enjoys special protections from expulsion as a long-resident EEA national) or practical (such as known problems with the route of return or with travel documentation for a particular country) so that the FNP is likely to require resettlement in the community after sentence completion, this is apt to constitute an 'exception' justifying a grant of HDC notwithstanding ongoing deportation deliberations by the SSHD. In these circumstances, we suggest that, as well as pressing for an early decision on deportation from the SSHD, FNPs and their representatives may wish to make early representations as to exceptional circumstances justifying HDC to the prison governor and to the MoJ.

28.30 However, there is a significant further barrier contained in PSI 52/2011 for FNPs seeking HDC. For many FNPs who are still serving their sentence, the SSHD will issue a form IS91 (a detention authority form) authorising the FNP's detention under Immigration Act powers after sentence completion. The Divisional Court in *R (Francis) v Secretary of State for Justice and Secretary of State for the Home Department* confirmed that the IS91 form is not a statutory bar to HDC.[43] But the Divisional Court went on to hold in the same case that the SSJ was entitled to operate a policy of not granting HDC to FNPs issued with a detention authority by the SSHD. This latter aspect of the judgment of the Divisional Court in *Francis* is under appeal at the time of writing on grounds that to allow a detention authority issued by the SSHD to act as a complete bar

---

41 PSI 52/2011 para 2.47.
42 A Thematic Inspection of how the UK Border Agency manages foreign national prisoners, February – May 2011, Executive Summary paras 7 to 8.
43 [2011] EWHC 1271 (Admin). The Divisional Court declared that an earlier policy, PSO 4630 para 11.1 which stated erroneously that the IS91 form was a statutory bar to release on HDC, was unlawful.

(albeit not statutory) to release on HDC for an FNP who is statutorily eligible for HDC would (a) amount to an unlawful delegation of discretion to grant HDC from the SSJ to the SSHD; (b) amount to an unlawful fetter of the SSJ's discretion; and (c) deprive FNPs of the opportunity to seek bail from the Immigration and Asylum Chamber of the First-tier Tribunal. (This is because immigration bail could be sought by an FNP nominally 'released' on HDC only to be redetained under Immigration Act powers, but not by an FNP who remains detained under criminal justice powers having been refused HDC.) PSI 52/2011, issued after the Divisional Court's judgment in *Francis*, states that FNPs issued with an IS91 form 'should be advised that they are unsuitable for HDC because they cannot meet the criteria to be released into the community for resettlement purposes at present but that suitability for HDC will be reassessed if the IS91 is withdrawn'.[44] The policy is silent as to whether such FNPs should be given a substantive risk assessment for HDC. The Court of Appeal in *Francis* will determine whether the SSJ is entitled to impose, by policy, such an extra-statutory complete bar to HDC for FNPs issued with an IS91 form. If the lawfulness of such a policy is upheld, the only route to HDC for an FNP issued with an IS91 form would be to challenge, by judicial review or habeas corpus, the SSHD's decision to detain the FNP under Immigration Act powers.

The Early Removal Scheme (ERS)

28.31 CJA 2003 introduced the ERS,[45] which was initially envisaged as a counterpart to HDC for those who are liable to removal from the UK. The impetus to increase the numbers of FNPs removed from the UK has resulted in a number of changes that now mean that the ERS is of significantly wider application than HDC for FNPs.

28.32 The legislative scheme now provides that the SSJ may release FNPs serving fixed term sentences, including extended sentences, who are liable to removal from the UK, up to 270 days early solely for the purpose of deportation or removal from the UK.[46]

---

44 PSI 52/2011 para 2.48.
45 CJA 1991 s46A; CJA 2003 s260.
46 CJA 1991 s46A(1); CJA 2003 s260(1).

Early removal in CJA 1991 cases

28.33 For those serving sentences administered under CJA 1991 (ie sentences imposed for offences committed prior to 4 April 2005) where the sentence is less than three years the prisoner is required to serve at least a quarter of the sentence before being released. For longer sentences the eligibility for early release is 270 days less than half the sentence.[47]

Early removal in CJA 2003 cases

28.34 For sentences administered under CJA 2003 (for offences committed on or after 4 April 2005) then the maximum eligibility for early release is 270 days less than half the sentence, with the proviso that the prisoner must serve at least a quarter of the sentence.[48]

Eligibility and consideration for early removal

28.35 When the ERS was first introduced, there were a number of statutory exclusions. These were removed by amendments to the legislative provisions in 2008, at the same time that the maximum period of early release was increased to 270 days. Thus PSI 59/2011, the Prison Service policy on the ERS, now confirms that:

> ERS is mandatory; all determinate sentenced FNPs who are liable to removal must be considered under the scheme, subject to eligibility checks.[49]

28.36 Prisoners cannot opt out of the ERS and prisons are required to process all those who are eligible.[50] However, prisoners can only be removed under the ERS if the UK Border Agency is able to effect their removal during the ERS eligibility period (which ends at the normal statutory release date, that is the half-way point of the sentence or custodial term in extended sentence cases). CCD will confirm to the prison on the CCD referral form (see paragraph 27.30) whether the prisoner can be removed within the ERS eligibility period.[51]

---

47 CJA 1991 s46A(5).
48 CJA 2003 s260(2).
49 PSI 59/2011 para 1.2.
50 PSI 59/2011 para 1.16.
51 PSI 59/2011 para 4.9.

28.37 Release under ERS will be refused where the prisoner is facing outstanding criminal charges, or has a further term of imprisonment to serve, for example in respect of a confiscation order.[52]

28.38 Other common reasons why early removal will not be possible are a lack of travel documents for the prisoner or an outstanding immigration appeal. Where ERS is refused, the prisoner will be informed of the reasons.[53]

28.39 Prison Service policy previously distinguished between those eligible prisoners who were 'presumed suitable' for the ERS, and those who were required to undergo an 'enhanced risk assessment'. Essentially all prisoners were 'presumed suitable' other than those serving sentences administered under CJA 1991 of four or more years[54] for a sexual or violent offence contained in CJA 2003 Sch 15.[55] The enhanced risk assessment was carried out by the Public Protection Unit in NOMS, and if release on the ERS was refused, the prisoner would then be considered for release by the Parole Board at the halfway point of the sentence. However, the need for an enhanced risk assessment for prisoners convicted of sexual or violent offences was removed in February 2011,[56] and this has now been confirmed in PSI 59/2011.

28.40 PSI 59/2011 sets out exceptional types of cases in which governors should consider refusing release under ERS:

- clear evidence that the prisoner is planning further crime, including plans to evade immigration control and return to the UK unlawfully;
- evidence of violence or threats of violence, in prison, on a number of occasions;
- dealing in class A drugs in custody;
- serving a sentence for terrorism or a terrorism related offence;
- other matters of similar gravity relating to public safety;[57]

---

52 PSI 59/2011 para 2.5. ERS may be considered in confiscation order cases where the default term is very short – para 2.6.
53 PSI 59/2011 para 2.9.
54 Including those serving an extended sentence for such an offence where the custodial term is four or more years.
55 PSO 6000 para 9.7.
56 This was effected by a NOMS Note to Governors dated February 2011 pending the issuing of PSI 59/2011.
57 PSI 59/2011 para 2.8

- if the prison is considering releasing a prisoner convicted of terrorism related offences then the NOMS Extremism Unit should be consulted before the decision is made.[58]

28.41 Further, where the governor considers that that the prisoner's early removal 'may seriously undermine public confidence in the scheme' the case must be referred to the Chief Executive of the NOMS who will take the final decision. PSI 59/2011 indicates that such cases 'will be exceptional' and so the numbers are anticipated to be small. This group include FNPs who have been involved in a notorious crime or crime of particular concern to the public.[59]

28.42 Prisoners may complain about decisions to refuse release under the ERS through the normal Prison Service complaints procedure (see paras 25.3–25.12) including a complaint to the PPO.[60] Such decisions can also be challenged by way of judicial review.

28.43 As with HDC, the statutory scheme for ERS is expressed as giving the SSJ a discretion as to whether to grant early release. This has led the courts to reject arguments that there is a legal entitlement to release under the ERS during the eligibility period. Accordingly, an unreasonable delay in processing consideration for release under ERS has been held not to give rise to any claim for false imprisonment or breach of ECHR article 5.[61]

Return to the UK after release on ERS

28.44 Any prisoner released and removed under the ERS who returns to the UK during the currency of the sentence is unlawfully at large. He or she is liable to be arrested and required to serve a period equivalent to the period between the date they were removed from the UK and the normal release date (the half-way point of the sentence), or until the sentence expiry date, whichever is shorter.[62]

---

58 PSI 59/2011 para 2.12
59 PSI 59/2011 paras 2.14–2.16.
60 PSI 59/2011 4.22.
61 *R (Christian) v Secretary of State for the Home Department* [2006] EWHC 2152 (Admin).
62 CJA 2003 s261; CJA 1991 s46B.

The Facilitated Returns Scheme (FRS)

28.45 The FRS was first introduced in 2006 and seeks to encourage FNPs to consent to deportation or removal from the UK by financial incentive. It is not a mechanism of early release in itself. FNPs can only benefit from it to achieve release prior to the normal release date from the sentence in conjunction with the ERS (see above) or repatriation (see chapter 29). It is also open to those who have completed the custodial term of their sentence and are detained solely under immigration powers, although at that stage its terms are now less generous.

28.46 To apply for FRS, an FNP needs to be a non-EEA national who has been convicted and is serving, or has served a custodial sentence in a UK prison, who is liable to administrative removal or deportation and for whom deportation arrangements or removal directions have not yet been set. Removal directions and deportation arrangements are the actual directions which specify the means (eg the flight) by which the individual will be expelled, and the date and place to which they will expelled.

28.47 Prisoners who participate in the FRS are either administratively removed or deported. For those FNPs who are serving a determinate custodial sentence, the FRS scheme normally works in conjunction with the ERS. Those who apply for FRS are expected to co-operate with the documentation process.

28.48 The only way FNPs can take advantage of the FRS prior to the ERS eligibility date is through an application to be repatriated. This means that they will be required to serve their sentence in the receiving state rather than being released.

28.49 Changes to the FRS scheme were made from 1 October 2010.[63] Now if an FNP agrees to voluntary repatriation or otherwise applies for FRS while still serving a sentence, they will receive a maximum of £1,500 if removed. FNPs who apply for FRS after they have served their custodial sentence will receive a maximum of £750. This includes £500 on a pre-paid cash card which will be given to the FNP at the airport at the time of his or her departure from the UK.

28.50 FRS is administered by the International Organization for Migration (IOM). Those removed having made applications after 1 October 2010 should contact the IOM in the receiving state who will then

---

63 For details see PSI 52/2011 paras 2.104–2.106. The new arrangements replaced the earlier version of the scheme which provided for a smaller cash payment on release together with £4,500 payable in kind for re-integration purposes such training or business start-up costs.

contact the FRS team in the UK Border Agency who will arrange for the remaining money to be placed on the cash card that was given to the FNP on the date they left the UK.

28.51 The FRS team will take applications from FNPs if they are interested in the scheme, by fax through the assistance of their prison officer, UK Border Agency staff or directly by telephone where they can speak to a member of the team. Once the application details have been taken, the FRS Team will check the form and will write to the prisoner to inform them whether they have been accepted onto the scheme. An FNP should receive a response from the FRS Team in writing within 72 hours of receipt of their application. If their application is rejected they will be informed of the reason. If a decision cannot be made at the time the application is received then they will be sent an acknowledgment slip and informed of the decision as soon as possible.

28.52 It is very important to note that participation in the FRS means the withdrawal of any outstanding appeals or applications for leave to remain in the UK. An FNP will only be accepted onto the FRS scheme if he or she completes and signs the UK Border Agency disclaimer form confirming that they wish to withdraw any appeals or outstanding barriers to removal. It is also important to note that an FNP who is liable to deportation and then participates in the FRS scheme is actually being deported, meaning that the prisoner is prohibited from returning to the UK unless or until the deportation order is revoked.

28.53 The FRS scheme and other similar schemes for co-operation with return are also discussed more generally at paras 6.8–6.16.

CHAPTER 29

Repatriation of prisoners

29.1	Introduction
29.3	Repatriation of Prisoners Act 1984
29.6	Bi-lateral and multi-lateral prisoner transfer agreements
	Table 29.1: Information of states with which the UK has prisoner transfer agreements
29.7	Consent of the prisoner
29.9	Criteria for repatriation
29.10	Applying for repatriation
29.12	The basis of the transfer
29.15	Additional Protocol to the Council of Europe Convention on the Transfer of Sentenced Persons
29.18	The EU Framework Decision
29.22	Challenges to repatriation decisions
29.26	Foreign national prisoners transferred to the UK
29.27	Colonial Prisoners Removal Act 1884
29.28	International Criminal Court Act 2001

Introduction

29.1 Foreign national prisoners (FNPs) may apply to be repatriated to their own country to complete their sentence. Prisoner repatriation is not a form of early release, and should not be confused with the Early Removal Scheme (ERS) discussed in the preceding section. Unlike a prisoner removed from the UK under the ERS (and unlike a prisoner who is solely deported or administratively removed), a repatriated prisoner will continue to serve, in his or her own country, the sentence imposed by the court. However, a repatriated prisoner who is subject to a deportation order will be prohibited from re-entering the UK in the same way as someone deported solely pursuant to that order.

29.2 This chapter examines the various means by which FNPs may either apply to be repatriated, or in some cases be repatriated without their consent. The limited circumstances in which foreign nationals may be transferred to the UK to serve their sentences are also examined.

Repatriation of Prisoners Act 1984

29.3 The transfer of FNPs to other countries to serve their sentences is governed by the Repatriation of Prisoners Act (RPA) 1984 as amended. This provides that repatriation warrants can only be issued where the UK is a party to international arrangements with the receiving state, both the Secretary of State for Justice (SSJ) and the 'appropriate authority' in the receiving state agree to the transfer and, where the relevant international agreement requires the prisoner's consent, that consent has been obtained.[1]

29.4 A warrant under the RPA 1984 cannot be issued unless the SSJ is satisfied that all reasonable steps have been taken to inform the prisoner in writing and in his or her own language of the substance of the relevant international agreement, and the effect of the warrant.[2] Where the consent of the prisoner is required by the international agreement, this must be given by the prisoner him or herself, or by an 'appropriate person' if by reason of the age, or physical or mental condition the SSJ considers it inappropriate for the prisoner to make

---

1 RPA 1984 s1(1).
2 RPA 1984 s1(4).

the decision themselves.[3] Consent withdrawn after the issue of a warrant does not affect its validity.[4]

29.5 The transfer warrant itself provides the lawful basis for the removal of the prisoner from the UK, and for their delivery to the appropriate authority in the receiving state.[5] The original sentence of the court which is the authority for detention at the time of issuing the warrant remains in effect after removal from the UK, so as to provide for re-detention during its currency should the prisoner return to the UK.[6] The SSJ has power to vary the order of imprisonment in such circumstances to take into account time spent out of UK, and the impact of domestic release arrangements.[7]

Bi-lateral and multi-lateral prisoner transfer agreements

29.6 The UK is party to two multi-state agreements providing for prisoner repatriation, the Council of Europe Convention on the Transfer of Sentenced Persons[8] and the Commonwealth Scheme for the Transfer of Convicted Offenders.[9] The UK has also entered into number of bilateral agreements with individual states on prisoner repatriation, not all of which are in force.[10] For the list of all states that at the time of writing have prisoner transfer agreements under these various arrangements see Table 29.1.

---

3 RPA 1984 s1(5).
4 RPA 1984 s1(6).
5 RPA 1984 s2(1).
6 RPA 1984 s2(2).
7 RPA 1984 s2(4).
8 CETS 112 – the list of states, which is not limited to members of Council of Europe, which have ratified the Convention is at http://conventions.coe.int/Treaty/Commun/ChercheSig.asp?NT=112&CM=8&DF=02/07/2011&CL=ENG.
9 The Commonwealth Scheme is in practice only used to transfer prisoners to Grenada – see Roisin Mulgrew, 'The international movement of prisoners', Criminal Law Forum 2011 22(1), 103–143.
10 A list of the states with which the UK has prisoner transfer agreements, and their status, can be accessed at www.fco.gov.uk/en/publications-and-documents/treaties/treaty-texts/prisoner-transfer-agreements.

Table 29.1: Information of states with which the UK has prisoner transfer agreements given in a written parliamentary answer at 28 February 2011, column WA266

Territories with which the UK has prisoner transfer agreements		
Albania	France	Netherlands
America	Georgia	Nicaragua
Andorra	Germany	Nigeria
Anguilla	Ghana	Norway
Antigua and Barbuda	Greece	Pakistan
Armenia	Grenada	Panama
Australia	Hong Kong	Peru
Austria	Honduras	Poland
Azerbaijan	Hungary	Portugal
Bahamas	Iceland	Russia
Barbados	India	Romania
Belgium	Ireland	Rwanda
Bermuda	Israel	Samoa
Bolivia	Italy	San Marino
Bosnia Herzegovina	Japan	Serbia
Brazil	Korea	Slovakia
British Virgin Island	Latvia	Slovenia
Bulgaria	St Laos	Spain
Canada	Lesotho	Sri Lanka
Chile	Libya	Lucia
Cook Islands	Liechtenstein	Suriname
Costa Rica	Lithuania	Sweden
Croatia	Luxembourg	Switzerland
Cuba	Macedonia	Thailand
Cyprus	Malawi	Tonga
Czech Republic	Malta	Trinidad and Tobago
Denmark	Mauritius	Turkey
Ecuador	Mexico	Ukraine
Egypt	Moldova	Venezuela
Estonia	Montenegro	Vietnam
Finland	Morocco	Vietnam

Territories that have prisoner transfer agreements with the UK	
Aruba	Henderson, Ducie and Oeno
Bouvet Island	Montserrat
British Indian OT	Peter I Island
Cayman Islands	Pitcairn
Dutch Antilles	Queen Maud Land Faroe Islands
Falkland Islands	St Helena and Dependencies
Gibraltar	Sovereign Base Areas of Akratri and Dhekelia (Cyprus)

Consent of the prisoner

29.7 Until recent changes to RPA 1984[11] the consent of the prisoner was always required before a repatriation warrant could be issued. The Council of Europe Convention on the Transfer of Sentenced Persons, and most bilateral agreements, do require the consent of the prisoner. However increasingly the UK government is seeking to negotiate bi-lateral agreements that allow for transfers without the prisoner's consent and, as noted below, the Additional Protocol to the Council of Europe Convention, and the EU Framework Decision 2008/909 allow for no consent transfers in particular circumstances. It is anticipated that these new no consent arrangements will significantly increase the number of FNPs repatriated to their country of nationality.[12]

29.8 The SSJ in a parliamentary answer has confirmed that it is government policy to negotiate agreements that do not require the prisoner's consent with the objective of 'significantly reducing the foreign prisoner population in UK detention and so the burden on the UK taxpayer'.[13] At the time of writing there are few bi-lateral agreements in force that permit no-consent transfers, and as yet no transfers have in fact taken place under them. For the position under the Additional Protocol and EU Framework decision, see paras 29.15–29.17 below.

Criteria for repatriation

29.9 The precise conditions for the issue of a warrant will depend upon the applicable international agreement. However the usual requirements (such as those contained in the Council of Europe Convention on the Transfer of Sentenced Persons under which most transfers are effected[14]) are:

- the prisoner is a national of the receiving state;[15]
- the sentence is final and so is not subject to appeal;

11 Introduced by Police and Justice Act 2006 s44.
12 The numbers of repatriations that take place has always been relatively small – in 2010, 48 prisoners were transferred out of the UK, and 89 into the UK: *Hansard* Debates HL col WA267, 28 February 2011.
13 *Hansard* Debates HC col 410W, 1 March 2011.
14 Article 3 of the Council of Europe Convention on the Transfer of Sentenced Persons.
15 The explanatory report to the Council of Europe Convention on the Transfer of Sentenced Persons (para 20) confirms that there is some flexibility about

- the offence giving rise to the sentence is an offence in the receiving country;
- there are at least six months of the sentence outstanding, or the sentence is indeterminate (some bi-lateral agreements require at least 12 months); and
- both the sentencing and receiving state consent to the transfer.

Applying for repatriation

29.10 Guidance on making applications for repatriation is provided in Prison Service Instruction (PSI) 52/2011 paras 2.81–2.94. Prisoners who meet the criteria but who have outstanding criminal proceedings against them in the UK will not be considered for transfer until those proceedings have been resolved. Prisoners with outstanding Confiscation Orders will be required to satisfy those orders or be subject to a term of imprisonment in default before repatriation will be considered.

29.11 An application to be repatriated must be made on specified form[16] which will be forwarded to the Cross Border Transfer Section in NOMS. The process which involves consultation with the other state involved can take some time. If the receiving state is willing to accept the prisoner it provides details of how it intends the sentence should be administered. If these are agreed by the Cross Border Transfer Section then the transfer warrant will be prepared for the date of the agreed transfer.

The basis of the transfer

29.12 There are two bases upon which states can agree that the sentence is administered after transfer:
1) *Continued enforcement:*[17] the receiving state is bound by the legal nature and duration of the sentence. This may be subject to the

> this, so that prisoners with established roots through permanent residence in the administering state may be considered for repatriation. However, in one case where a British citizen sought transfer to the Netherlands on this basis the application was refused primarily as, if on transfer the sentence was reduced then on his release there would be nothing to stop him returning to the UK at a time when had he continued to serve the sentence here he would have remained in prison – *R (Shaheen) v Secretary of State for Justice* [2008] EWHC 1195 (Admin).
>
> 16 At Annex T to PSI 52/2011.
> 17 See article 9 of the Council of Europe Convention on the Transfer of Sentenced Persons.

principle that if the sentence exceeds the maximum sentence available for the offence in the receiving state, then it will be reduced to that maximum but no less.[18]

2) *Conversion of sentence:*[19] the receiving state will effectively re-sentence the prisoner according to its own laws although it will be bound by the findings of fact made by the court in the sentencing state, must deduct time already served and must not increase the sentence.

29.13 When the UK first ratified the Council of Europe Convention on the Transfer of Sentenced Persons, the UK Government issued a declaration stating that it intended only to consent to prisoner transfers into the UK on the basis of continued enforcement.[20] In relation to transfers out of the UK, the position is more flexible and so whether continued enforcement or conversion is applied will depend on the particular agreement reached with the state concerned. Bi-lateral agreements will specify the basis upon which the sentence will be administered after transfer. Once transferred the enforcement of the sentence becomes the responsibility of the receiving state, which may (as RPA 1984 does for prisoners transferred to the UK[21]) apply its own early release provisions to the term.

29.14 The Council of Europe Convention on the Transfer of Sentenced Persons and some bi-lateral agreements allow for the receiving state to grant the prisoner a pardon or amnesty after transfer, although only the sentencing state retains the ability to review the judgment itself.[22] There is obviously a tension between these two principles, but it has been held in a case involving a prisoner transferred from Bulgaria to the UK that it is not a breach of the prohibition on the receiving state reviewing the judgment for it to grant a pardon on the

---

18 For examples of this principle in relation to transfers of British nationals to the UK, see *R v Secretary of State for the Home Department ex p Read* [1989] AC 1014 and *R (Willcox) v Secretary of State for Justice* [2009] EWHC 1483 (Admin). In *Willcox* the court refused to interfere with a warrant that required the claimant to serve a sentence of over 29 years for an offence that on its facts would have attracted a four- to five-year sentence in the UK, as the sentence was still less than the maximum available in the UK.

19 Article 11 of the Council of Europe Convention on the Transfer of Sentenced Persons.

20 Although the effect of CJA 2003 s273 is that those sentenced to life terms abroad will have their cases referred to the High Court on transfer to the UK for the setting of the minimum term – see *Re Soyege* [2005] EWHC 2648 (QB).

21 RPA 1984 Sch 1.

22 Articles 12–13 of the Council of Europe Convention.

basis of an alleged miscarriage of justice. This is because the power to pardon is an executive rather than a judicial process.[23]

Additional Protocol to the Council of Europe Convention on the Transfer of Sentenced Persons

29.15 RPA 1984 also includes provisions that give effect to the Additional Protocol to the Council of Europe Convention on the Transfer of Sentenced Persons which was ratified by the UK on 17 July 2009 and came into force on 1 November 2009.[24] The Additional Protocol establishes mechanisms to prevent offenders fleeing to their own country in order to avoid having to complete a sentence imposed abroad. Where an offender is sentenced in one contracting state, and then flees to another contracting state of which they are a national, the former state can request that the latter enforce the sentence.[25]

29.16 The Additional Protocol does not require the prisoner to consent to the issue of a warrant for this purpose.[26] RPA 1984 as amended allows the SSJ, where there are reasonable grounds for believing that a person has committed an offence abroad, to apply for a warrant from a designated district judge to arrest and detain that person while consideration is given as to whether to enforce the sentence.[27]

29.17 A further provision introduced by the Additional Protocol permits repatriation of prisoners without their consent in certain circumstances. This allows a sentencing state, where either the sentence itself provides for the deportation of the offender, or where there is a subsequent administrative decision to deport in light of the offence, to request that the state of which the prisoner is a national receive them to enforce the sentence. If this request is accepted then the consent of the prisoner is not required although the opinion of the sentenced person must be taken into account.[28] The Additional Protocol

---

23 *R (Shields) v Secretary of State for Justice* [2008] EWHC 3102 (Admin).
24 A list of the 35 states which have ratified the Additional Protocol is available at http://conventions.coe.int/Treaty/Commun/ChercheSig. asp?NT=167&CM=8&DF=02/07/2011&CL=ENG.
25 Convention on the Transfer of Sentenced Prisoners (Additional Protocol) CETS 167 article 2, and RPA 1984 s4A – for example, in seemingly the first use of this power by the UK, the enforcement of a sentenced prisoner who had absconded from an open prison in England was transferred to Austria, where he had fled – see *Hansard* Debates HC col 122W, 5 July 2010.
26 Additional Protocol article 2(3).
27 RPA 1984 ss4D and 4E.
28 Additional Protocol article 3.

allows states to opt out of this provision.[29] But for the issue of the prisoner's consent the process of issuing the warrant for repatriation will be as set outat paras 29.3–29.5 above.

The EU Framework Decision

29.18 From 5 December 2011 EU Framework Decision 2008/909/JHA[30] will replace the Council of Europe Convention on the Transfer of Sentenced Persons and Additional Protocol in relation to repatriation of prisoners between EU member states.[31]

29.19 Like the Additional Protocol to the Council of Europe Convention on the Transfer of Sentenced Persons, in cases where the prisoner has fled the sentencing jurisdiction, EU Framework Decision 2008/909/JHA allows for transfer of responsibility for enforcing the sentence without consent.[32] The same provisions of RPA 1984 referred to in para 29.16 above will allow for arrest and detention pending the decision on the transfer of responsibility.

29.20 The EU Framework Decision 2008/909/JHA marks a development in *requiring* the receiving state to accept the transfer subject to limited exceptions, for example where the sentence relates to conduct that would not be an offence in the receiving state.[33] Under EU Framework Decision 2008/909/JHA, unlike under the Additional Protocol, there is also a requirement to apply the principle of continued enforcement of the sentence, although any sentence that exceeds the maximum available in the receiving state will be reduced to that maximum.[34]

29.21 The EU Framework Decision 2008/909/JHA requires the prisoner's consent unless the transfer is to a member state in which they live, or to which they will be deported on release. If transfer of responsibility for enforcing the sentence involves repatriating the prisoner from the sentencing state then their opinion needs to be taken into account.[35]

---

29 Additional Protocol article 3(6).
30 '[O]n the application of the principle of mutual recognition to judgments in criminal matters imposing custodial sentences or measures involving deprivation of liberty for the purpose of their enforcement in the European Union.'
31 EU Framework Decision 2008/909/JHA article 26(1).
32 EU Framework Decision 2008/909/JHA article 6(2).
33 EU Framework Decision 2008/909/JHA article 9.
34 EU Framework Decision 2008/909/JHA article 8.
35 EU Framework Decision 2008/909/JHA article 6(3).

Challenges to repatriation decisions

29.22 Prisoners may seek to challenge either refusals to repatriate at their request, or decisions to repatriate against their will. In relation to the former, in light of the government policy as set out at para 29.8, it would seem that there would be little reason for the UK authorities to refuse requests from eligible prisoners. However, there may be reluctance to agree to transfers where by application of the conversion principle, the prisoner will end up serving a markedly shorter sentence in their home state.[36]

29.23 With transfers under the Council of Europe Convention on the Transfer of Sentenced Persons, even where the UK itself agrees to repatriation, the UK cannot force the receiving state to accept the prisoner for repatriation. The situation may be different under the EU Framework Decision 2008/909/JHA, under which states can only refuse to accept eligible transfers on specified grounds and there are specified time limits for accepting responsibility and effecting the transfer.[37]

29.24 Where a prisoner is seeking to resist repatriation without their consent, for example on the basis of long residence or the existence of family ties in the sentencing state, then the grounds for such challenges are likely to be similar to those in deportation cases. Prison Service policy states that where prisoners have been identified as suitable for repatriation against their consent they should be informed of this, given the opportunity to seek legal advice, and, normally, given 28 days to make representations against the decision.[38] Importantly the arrangements contained in EU Framework Decision 2008/909/JHA are described as having the aim of 'facilitating the social rehabilitation of the sentenced person'[39] and so any proposed non-consensual transfer that frustrates this aim would be outside its scope.

29.25 There is an obvious concern that the use of no consent repatriation warrants will be used to circumvent a prisoner's right to challenge decisions affecting their right to remain in the UK under immigration laws. For example if a prisoner is appealing against a decision to deport, or a refusal to revoke a deportation order, on human rights

---

36 This, together with the possibility of return to the UK following the completion of the sentence as the prisoner was a British citizen, was one of the reasons for the refusal in *R (Shaheen) v Secretary of State for Justice* [2008] EWHC 1195 (Admin).
37 EU Framework Decision 2008/909/JHA articles 12 and 15.
38 PSI 52/2011 para 2.90.
39 EU Framework Decision 2008/909 article 3(1).

grounds, it would be improper to seek to repatriate them on a no consent basis before the final determination of the appeal.

Foreign national prisoners transferred to the UK

29.26 The above provisions deal with the circumstances in which FNPs are removed from the UK to serve their sentences in the countries of their nationality. However, there are a limited set of circumstances in which foreign nationals will be transferred to the UK to serve their sentences.

Colonial Prisoners Removal Act 1884

29.27 The Colonial Prisoners Removal Act 1884 allows for the transfer of prisoners sentenced in British territories to the UK to serve the sentence. This legislation is used primarily to transfer to the UK those given long sentences in territories such as the Cayman Islands, where there are no suitable prison facilities. There are few transfers under this legislation.

International Criminal Court Act 2001

29.28 More importantly, the International Criminal Court Act (ICCA) 2001 provides for the transfer to the UK of those convicted by the International Criminal Court (ICC) in The Hague to serve their sentences.[40] The Act also provides that those sentenced by other UN war crimes tribunals may similarly be transferred to the UK.[41] The UK has entered into bilateral agreements to facilitate such transfers with the ICC,[42] the International Criminal Tribunal for the Former Yugoslavia[43] and the Special Court for Sierra Leone.[44]

29.29 The transfer to the UK of prisoners sentenced by these tribunals requires the agreement of the SSJ,[45] however the consent of

---

40 ICCA 2001 ss42–48.
41 ICCA 2001 ss77 and 77A.
42 See ww.icc-cpi.int/NR/rdonlyres/C540B3EF-F3FF-4AD0-93F5-DA85E96B1522/0/ICCPres040107ENG.pdf.
43 See www.icty.org/x/file/Legal%20Library/Member_States_Cooperation/enforcement_agreement_uk_11_03_04_en.pdf.
44 See www.sc-sl.org/LinkClick.aspx?fileticket=kKfMQr9KsuA%3d&tabid=176.
45 ICCA 2001 s42(1).

the prisoner is not required.[46] The agreements require time spent in detention before transfer to be taken into account and prohibit modification of the sentence by the UK. Prisoners are to be held in conditions applicable to domestic prisoners, and each agreement requires access for inspection of conditions for transferees by the European Committee for the Prevention of Torture (CPT).

29.30 Once in the UK, such prisoners are, subject to important exceptions set out at para 29.31 below, to be treated for all purposes as if they had been sentenced in the UK.[47] Accordingly, the provisions of the Prison Rules 1999 and any applicable policies, for example in relation to categorisation and prison discipline, will apply. The very specific offending history of such prisoners will sometimes make application of these policies problematic. For example, a prisoner convicted of war crimes by the ICTY successfully challenged a refusal to downgrade him from Category A status on the basis that insufficient consideration had been given, notwithstanding the seriousness of the crimes, to the likelihood of any ongoing risk of re-offending in the light of those offences' historical specificity. Further, it was not rational to assess risk by reference to a failure to complete offending behaviour programmes, when no such programmes were available in light of the nature of the offences.[48]

29.31 These transferred prisoners are not eligible for release on temporary licence, and the provisions on early release on licence do not apply.[49] The bilateral agreements with the tribunals therefore reserve the decision-making on whether transferred prisoners should be released early to those tribunals themselves.[50] The practice adopted in relation to the one prisoner transferred under ICTY who has reached his nominal release date (the half-way point of the sentence) was for reports to be prepared by the holding prison and sent to the tribunal to determine whether release should be granted.

---

46 Although the ICC agreement requires the UK to take into account the views of the sentenced person.
47 ICCA 2001 s42(4).
48 *R (Krstic) v Secretary of State for Justice* [2010] EWHC 2125 (Admin).
49 ICCA 2001 Sch 7 para 3.
50 Article 8 of the ICTY and SCSL agreements; and article 9 of the ICC agreement.

CHAPTER 30
Mental health legislation and FNPs

30.1	Introduction
30.5	The Mental Health Act 1983
30.7	Hospital orders and interim hospital orders
30.11	Restriction orders
30.13	Hospital directions and limitation directions
30.14	Transfer directions: prisoners
30.17	Transfer directions: immigration detainees
30.19	Restriction directions
30.20	Remittal from hospital to prison or to a detention facility: prisoners
30.23	Remittal from hospital to prison or to a detention facility: prisoners
30.24	Access to the First-tier Tribunal (Mental Health)
30.25	Restricted patients
30.34	After-care
30.37	The relationship between MHA 1983 and deportation

Introduction

30.1 In this chapter, we provide an overview of mental health legislation as it may affect foreign nationals who are still serving their sentence, and foreign nationals who are detained under Immigration Act (IA) 1971 powers.

30.2 A growing number of cases have concerned serving foreign national prisoners and immigration detainees suffering from mental disorder and the complex overlap between prison, mental health and immigration legislation.

30.3 We will refer to the provisions of Part III of the Mental Health Act (MHA) 1983 applying to prisoners and detainees who suffer from mental disorder[1] and which make provision for the transfer of prisoners and immigration detainees to and from hospital.[2]

30.4 A detailed overview of the statutory regime applying to detention under the MHA 1983 is outside the scope of this book.[3] Our focus is on the relationship between criminal sentences and hospital orders made by the criminal court, and the circumstances in which prisoners and detainees may be transferred to hospital during a criminal sentence or when detained under IA 1971 or the UK Borders Act (UKBA) 2007.

The Mental Health Act 1983

30.5 MHA 1983, and therefore Part III, applies to persons suffering from 'mental disorder' as defined in section 1 of the Act. Under that sec-

---

1 For the principal guidance on performance of duties generally under MHA 1983, see 'Code of Practice Mental Health Act 1983', Department of Health (DoH), May 2008; available at www.dh.gov.uk/en/Publicationsandstatistics/ Publications/PublicationsPolicyAndGuidance/DH_084597. The Code of Practice is made pursuant to MHA 1983 s118. Chapter 33 of the Code deals with prisoners. For cross-departmental guidance on hospital transfers, see the DoH's 'Good Practice Procedure Guide. The transfer and remission of adult prisoners under MHA 1983 ss47 and 48'; www.dh.gov.uk/en/ Publicationsandstatistics/Publications/PublicationsPolicyAndGuidance/DH_ 125767. For Prison Service materials, see the Indeterminate Sentence Manual (PSO 4700), chapter 15; Prison Service Order (PSO) 6000, chapter 11; and Prison Service Instruction (PSI) 50/2007.

2 In MHA 1983 Part III, as in Part II, any reference to a hospital includes a 'registered establishment' so that private hospitals are included: see MHA 1983 ss34(1) and (2), 55(5) and 145(1).

3 For detailed analysis see Richard Jones, *Mental Health Act manual*, 14th edn, Sweet & Maxwell, which is regularly updated.

tion, a mental disorder means 'any disorder or disability of the mind'. By section 1(2A), learning disability is excluded from the definition, save in certain circumstances. The provisions of MHA 1983, including the scheme for the transfer of prisoners and detainees to hospital, apply only to those suffering from mental disorder within the statutory meaning.[4] It will be contrary to article 5(1)(e) of the European Convention on Human Rights (ECHR) to detain a person 'unless it can be shown that the patient is suffering from a mental disorder that warrants detention'.[5]

30.6 A different statutory scheme applies to persons who lack capacity, which is not the same as mental disorder.[6] The law relating to mental capacity lies outside the scope of this book and specialist texts should be consulted.[7]

Hospital orders and interim hospital orders

30.7 Part III of the MHA 1983 opens with provisions for criminal courts to remand accused persons to hospital for reports or for treatment.[8] As regards convicted persons, under MHA 1983 s37, the Crown Court or a magistrates' court may make a hospital order as a substitute for imposing a sentence of imprisonment.[9] A number of conditions laid down by section 37 must be satisfied before a hospital order may be made:

- The court must be satisfied, on the written or oral evidence of two registered medical practitioners,[10] that the offender is suffering from mental disorder of a nature of degree which makes it appropriate for him or her to be detained in hospital for medical treatment and appropriate medical treatment is available.

---

4 Guidance on the definition of mental disorder is provided by the 'Code of Practice Mental Health Act 1983', DoH, May 2008, chapter 3.
5 *R (H) v London North and East Region Mental Health Review Tribunal* [2001] EWCA Civ 415; [2002] QB 1 at 31.
6 Mental Capacity Act 2005 as amended by the Mental Capacity Act 2007.
7 See, for example, A Weereratne and others, *The Mental Capacity Act 2005*, LexisNexis, 2008.
8 MHA 1983 ss35 and 36.
9 A hospital order cannot be imposed where a person has been convicted of an offence the sentence for which is fixed by law: MHA 1983 s37(1). Section 37 does not therefore apply to persons convicted of murder who receive a mandatory life sentence.
10 For requirements as to medical evidence under MHA 1983 Part III, see s54.

- The court must be of the opinion, having regard to all the circumstances, that a hospital order is the most suitable method of disposal.
- The court must be satisfied, by appropriate written or oral evidence, that a hospital place is available within 28 days of the hospital order.

30.8 Under MHA 1983 s37, the convicted person must be transferred to the hospital named in the hospital order save by reason of an emergency or other special circumstances, in which case the Secretary of State for Justice (SSJ) may direct admission to another hospital.

30.9 Under MHA 1983 s38, a court may make an interim hospital order before making a hospital order or sentencing the offender in some other way which enables a period of assessment in order to ascertain whether a hospital order is appropriate.

30.10 A sentence of imprisonment does not in itself breach a mentally disordered person's rights under ECHR article 3 because MHA 1983 contains a regime for transferring prisoners to hospital. This regime (dealt with below) may prevent suffering and deterioration in a person's mental health that might otherwise amount to inhuman or degrading treatment or punishment under ECHR article 3.[11] However, in chapter 36, we consider the circumstances in which conditions of detention, including the detention of the mentally ill, may breach ECHR articles 3, 5 or 8.

Restriction orders

30.11 Under MHA 1983 s41, a hospital order may be supplemented by a restriction order. Such an order has no existence independently of a hospital order: it is not a separate means of disposing of a case before the courts.[12] A Crown Court may make a restriction order if it appears to the court that it 'is necessary for the protection of the public from serious harm'.[13] At least one registered medical practitioner must give oral evidence to the court before an order is made.[14] The restrictions are as follows:

- A restriction order means that the special restrictions set out in MHA 1983 s41(3) apply to the confinement of the offender in

11 *R v Drew* [2003] UKHL 25.
12 *R v Birch* (1990) 90 Cr App R 78 at 210.
13 MHA 1983 s41(1).
14 MHA 1983 s41(1) and (2).

hospital. None of the provisions of MHA 1983 Part II relating to the duration, renewal and expiration of authority for the detention of patients apply to a person subject to a restriction order. Such a person will continue to be liable to be detained by virtue of the relevant hospital order until he or she is duly discharged in accordance with the statutory provisions for discharge that apply to patients subject to a restriction order.
- A restricted patient cannot be the subject of a community treatment order.
- The provisions for applications to the First-tier Tribunal (Mental Health) (FTT-MH) under MHA 1983 ss66 and 69 do not apply. Specific provisions apply to restricted patients.[15]
- A patient may only take leave of absence from hospital and may only be transferred to another hospital with the consent of the SSJ. Consent is also required for an order discharging the patient from hospital under MHA 1983 s23.[16]

30.12 Under MHA 1983 s42(1), the Secretary of State for Justice (SSJ) may direct that the patient cease to be subject to a restriction order and, under section 42(2), may also discharge a restricted patient from hospital either absolutely or conditionally at any time. A person discharged absolutely ceases to be liable to be detained under the hospital order and the restriction order ceases to have effect. Conditional discharge means that the restriction order may continue in force and renders a person liable to be recalled to hospital by warrant of the SSJ.

Hospital directions and limitation directions

30.13 By virtue of MHA 1983 s45A, it is now also possible for the Crown Court to sentence a person to imprisonment but to direct that he or she be detained in hospital (called a hospital direction) with a further direction that the offender be subject to the MHA 1983 s41 restrictions (called a limitation direction).[17] An offender subject to such directions must be treated in the same way as a person subject to a transfer direction coupled with a restriction direction, dealt with

---

15 See para 30.25.
16 MHA 1983 s23 concerns the discharge of patients under Part II. Other provisions of MHA 1983 Part II apply with modifications to restricted patients by virtue of MHA 1983 s41(3) and Sch 1 Part II.
17 See *R v Cooper* [2010] EWCA Crim 2335 and cases cited there.

below. Subject to any application to the FTT-MH,[18] he or she will remain in hospital until transferred to prison by the direction of the SSJ or released on licence.[19]

Transfer directions: prisoners

30.14 A mentally disordered person who is serving a sentence of imprisonment may at any time be transferred to hospital under MHA 1983 s47.[20] Transfers and hospitalisation following transfer attract the protection of ECHR article 5(1)(a) and (e).[21] There is no obligation to detain a person of unsound mind in a hospital unless objective medical expertise establishes that confinement in a suitable therapeutic environment is warranted.[22]

30.15 Under MHA 1983 s47, in order for a transfer to take place, the SSJ must be satisfied by reports from at least two registered medical practitioners that the prisoner is suffering from mental disorder of a nature or degree which makes it appropriate for him or her to be detained in a hospital for medical treatment. Appropriate treatment must also be available. In reaching a decision, the SSJ must have regard to the public interest and all the circumstances of the case. The transfer will be effected by a warrant directing that a person be removed to and detained in the hospital specified in the direction. A direction under section 47 is called a 'transfer direction'. It is important that, when the direction is made, a hospital place is available because a transfer direction ceases to have effect after 14 days. The effect of a transfer direction is the same as a hospital order under MHA 1983 s37.

30.16 It has been held that:

> ... once the prison service have reasonable grounds to believe that a prisoner requires treatment in a mental hospital in which he may be detained, the SSJ is under a duty expeditiously to take reasonable steps to obtain appropriate medical advice, and if that advice confirms

---

18 See para 30.25.
19 See MHA 1983 ss45B(2) and 50(5).
20 See, for example, *R (South West London and St George's Mental Health NHS Trust) v W* [2002] All ER (D) 62 (Aug); *R (D) v Secretary of State for the Home Department* [2004] EWHC 2857 (Admin); [2005] MHLR 17.
21 Compare *R (IR) v Shetty* [2003] EWHC 3022 (Admin) at 8.
22 *R (IR) v Shetty* [2003] EWHC 3022 (Admin), citing relevant European Court of Human Rights (ECtHR) case-law.

the need for transfer to a hospital, to take reasonable steps within a reasonable time to effect that transfer.[23]

Transfer directions: immigration detainees

30.17 The provisions for the transfer to hospital of prisoners other than those serving a sentence of imprisonment are contained in MHA 1983 s48. They apply expressly to persons detained under IA 1971 or under Nationality, Immigration and Asylum Act (NIAA) 2002 s62.[24] As under section 47, the SSJ must be satisfied by reports from at least two registered medical practitioners that the detainee is suffering from mental disorder of a nature or degree which makes it appropriate for him or her to be detained in a hospital for medical treatment. Section 48 imposes an apparently additional test to that under section 47, namely that the need for such treatment is 'urgent'.[25] Appropriate treatment must also be available. In addition, the SSJ must be satisfied that the detainee is in urgent need of hospital treatment. A direction under section 48 is also called a 'transfer direction'. In the same way as a transfer direction under section 47, it is important that, when the direction is made, a hospital place is available because the direction ceases to have effect after 14 days. As under section 47, the effect of a transfer direction is the same as a hospital order.

30.18 A continuing authority to detain under immigration powers is required for transfer under MHA 1983 s48. In some circumstances it might be appropriate to request release from immigration detention (for example where it is clear that continuing immigration detention is contrary to the UK Border Agency policy on detaining those with mental illness at Enforcement Instructions and Guidance (EIG) para 55.10, see the discussion at paras 34.27–34.32), in order to allow

---

23 See *R (D) v Secretary of State for the Home Department* [2004] EWHC 2857 (Admin); [2005] MHLR 17 at 33.
24 MHA 1983 s48(2)(d) – there is an apparent lacuna in the legislation in that section 48 has not been amended to include detention under UK Borders Act (UKBA) 2007 s36(1), the power to detain while the Home Secretary considers whether the automatic deportation provisions apply.
25 MHA 1983 s48(1)(b) – The Reed Committee was concerned that the requirement for 'urgent' treatment was interpreted too narrowly and recommended that the section 'should be applied where a doctor would recommend in patient treatment if a person were seen as an out-patient in the community'. This interpretation was accepted in the previous version of the DoH policy on section 48 transfers, but is not mentioned in the current version – see note 1 above.

voluntary admission to hospital, or admission for assessment under MHA 1983 s2. The advantage of this is that the detainee will not be transferred back to immigration detention once it is considered that in-patient hospital treatment is no longer required. Another advantage is that patients transferred under section 48 will normally also be the subject of a restriction direction. If released from immigration detention and admitted under section 2 for assessment, the patient will not be subject to such restrictions.

Restriction directions

30.19 Under MHA 1983 s49, where a transfer direction is given, the SSJ may also make a 'restriction direction'.[26] This is a direction that a transferred person shall be subject to the special restrictions contained in MHA 1983 s41. A restriction direction has the same effect as a restriction order made by the Crown Court (under section 41) in relation to a person subject to a hospital order[27] but a person subject to a restriction direction may be returned to prison or detention if discharged from hospital.[28] While a person is subject to a restriction direction the responsible clinician must examine him or her and report to the SSJ at least annually. Every report must contain such particulars as the SSJ may require.

Remittal from hospital to prison or to a detention facility: prisoners

30.20 The return of offenders from hospital to prison is governed by MHA 1983 s50. Where the prisoner has been transferred to hospital and is the subject of a restriction direction, the SSJ may before the prisoner's release date be notified by the responsible clinician, any other approved clinician or the FTT-MH that the prisoner no longer requires treatment in hospital for mental disorder or that no effective treatment for the disorder can be given in the hospital to which he or she has been removed. This has been called the 'treatability test'.[29]

---

26 In certain circumstances, not including immigration detainees, the SSJ must make a restriction direction: MHA 1983 s49(1).
27 See para 30.11.
28 See MHA 1983 ss50–53.
29 *R (M) v Nottinghamshire Healthcare NHS Trust* [2002] EWCA Civ 1728; [2003] 1 All ER 784 at 36; mentioned in *R (IR) v Shetty* [2003] EWHC 3022 (Admin) at 36.

30.21 After being notified by the responsible clinician, the SSJ may direct that the prisoner be remitted to any prison in which he or she might have been detained if not removed to hospital. The prisoner will then continue to serve his or her sentence in the usual way. The transfer direction and the restriction direction cease to have effect on the prisoner's arrival in prison.

30.22 The SSJ may alternatively exercise any power to release the prisoner on licence (or discharge him or her under supervision) which would have been exercisable if the prisoner had been remitted to prison. When this power is exercised, the transfer direction and the restriction direction cease to have effect upon release or discharge. Under MHA 1983 s50(2), a restriction direction ceases to have effect in any event on a person's release date.[30]

Remittal from hospital to prison or to a detention facility: prisoners

30.23 In relation to immigration detainees, a transfer direction ceases to have effect on the expiration of the period during which a detainee would, if he or she had not been removed to hospital, be liable to be detained. Where an immigration detainee is the subject of a transfer direction and a restriction direction, the SSJ may be notified by the responsible clinician, by any other approved clinician or by the FTT-MH that the detainee no longer requires treatment in hospital for mental disorder or that no effective treatment for the disorder can be given in the hospital to which he or she has been removed. The SSJ may then direct that the detainee be remitted to any place where he or she might have been detained if not removed to hospital. The transfer direction and the restriction direction cease to have effect when the detainee arrives at the place of detention.[31] Where an immigration detainee was transferred to hospital because his or her mental health had deteriorated in detention, there may be concerns about return to the conditions which caused such deterioration. In such circumstances it is incumbent on the UK Border Agency to consider whether continued detention is consistent with its own policy on detaining the mentally ill at EIG para 55.10 and otherwise reasonable and ECHR compliant. See the discussion at paras 34.37–34.32 and chapter 36.

30 For calculation of the release date, see MHA 1983 s50(3)–(4).
31 MHA 1983 s53.

Access to the First-tier Tribunal (Mental Health)

30.24 A person who is an unrestricted patient or a community patient may be discharged at any time without the intervention or involvement of the FTT-MH under an order for discharge by the responsible clinician, the hospital managers or (subject to any barring order under MHA 1983 s25) the nearest relative.[32] The SSJ may at any time discharge a restricted patient from hospital either absolutely or conditionally with no tribunal involvement.[33] Unrestricted patients, restricted patients and community patients also have certain rights of access to the FTT-MH.

Restricted patients

30.25 There are discrete provisions that apply to a person who is a restricted patient,[34] defined in MHA 1983 s79 as being a patient subject to a restriction order, limitation direction or restriction direction. A restricted patient detained in a hospital may apply to the FTT-MH in the period between six months and 12 months from the date of the relevant hospital order, hospital direction or transfer direction and then in any subsequent period of 12 months. The SSJ may at any time refer the case of a restricted patient to the FTT-MH and is under a duty to refer a case which has not been considered by a tribunal within the last three years.[35]

30.26 The FTT-MH has no general discretion to direct the discharge of restricted patients. Its various statutory powers and duties are contained in MHA 1983 ss73–75. These provisions enable both the absolute and the conditional discharge of restricted patients.[36] A direction for conditional discharge may be deferred for appropriate discharge arrangements to be put into place.[37]

30.27 MHA 1983 s73 deals with patients subject to a hospital order under MHA 1983 s37 who have also been made subject to a restriction order

---

32 MHA 1983 s23 and 'Code of Practice Mental Health Act 1983', DoH, May 2008, chapter 29.
33 MHA 1983 s42(2). See para 30.12.
34 MHA 1983 s72(7) disapplies s72(1) in the case of restricted patients except as provided in ss73–74.
35 MHA 1983 s71.
36 There is no provision for the conditional discharge of patients who are not restricted.
37 MHA 1983 s73(7) applied to s74 discharges by s74(6).

under section 41. The criteria for absolute discharge are the same as the conditions for the discharge of unrestricted patients under section 72(1)(b) and are the same criteria that must be satisfied before a person can be detained under section 3.[38] In addition, the tribunal must be satisfied that it is not appropriate for the patient to remain liable to be recalled to hospital for further treatment, which would require a conditional discharge. Where a patient is absolutely discharged, he or she is no longer liable to be detained under the hospital order and the restriction order ceases to have effect.

30.28 The FTT-MH must direct a patient's conditional discharge when the criteria for discharge under section 72(1)(b) are established but the tribunal is not satisfied that it is not appropriate for the patient to remain liable to be recalled to hospital for further treatment. Where a patient is conditionally discharged, he or she must comply with conditions imposed by the tribunal at the time of discharge or subsequently by the SSJ. A conditionally discharged patient is liable to be recalled to hospital by the SSJ. If his or her restriction order ceases to have effect, the patient will be deemed (unless previously recalled) to have been absolutely discharged and will no longer be liable to be detained by virtue of the hospital order.[39]

30.29 MHA 1983 s74 deals with the powers and duties of tribunals in relation to patients subject to limitation directions or restriction directions.[40] The FTT-MH has no general power to discharge such patients, because they remain subject to other powers of imprisonment, custody or detention. Instead, the FTT-MH must notify the SSJ whether, in its opinion, the patient would, if subject to a restriction order, be entitled to be absolutely or conditionally discharged under section 73. If the FTT-MH notifies the SSJ that the patient would be entitled to be conditionally discharged, it may recommend that in the event that discharge does not take place, the patient should continue to be detained in hospital.

30.30 After the FTT-MH has given notification to the SSJ, there is a period of 90 days for the SSJ to give notice to the tribunal that the patient may be discharged. If the SSJ gives notice to the FTT-MH, the tribunal must direct that the patient be discharged, either absolutely or conditionally. If the SSJ does not give notice to the tribunal within the 90 day period, the managers of the hospital shall, unless the

---

38 *R (H) v London North and East Region Mental Health Review Tribunal* [2001] EWCA Civ 415; [2002] QB 1 at 20.
39 MHA 1983 s73.
40 This will include restricted prisoners and immigration detainees transferred to hospital under MHA 1983 ss47 and 48.

tribunal has made a recommendation under MHA 1983 s74(1)(b), transfer the patient to a prison or other institution in which the patient might have been detained if he or she had not been removed to hospital. Under section 74(5), the relevant hospital direction and limitation direction cease to have effect when the patient arrives at the prison.

30.31 A person who is subject to a recommendation under MHA 1983 s74(1)(b) remains subject to a restriction or limitation direction but has the benefit of being able to apply to the Parole Board provided that he or she would otherwise be entitled to apply if not detained in hospital. If the Parole Board make a direction or recommendation for the patient's release from the custodial part of the prison sentence, the restriction direction or limitation direction ceases to have effect at the time when he or becomes entitled to be released. Release will take place from hospital into the community.[41]

30.32 There is a different provision for immigration detainees. If, in the case of a patient who is subject to a transfer direction under section 48, the tribunal notifies the SSJ that the patient would be entitled to be absolutely or conditionally discharged, the SSJ must direct that the patient be remitted to detention, save where the tribunal has made a recommendation under section 74(1)(b). The relevant transfer and restriction directions will cease to have effect when the patient arrives at the detention facility.

30.33 The effect of absolute and of conditional discharge under MHA 1983 s74 is the same as under s73. Where a patient is absolutely discharged, he or she is no longer liable to be detained under the hospital or transfer direction and the limitation direction or restriction direction ceases to have effect. Where a patient is conditionally discharged, he or she must comply with conditions imposed by the tribunal at the time of discharge or subsequently by the SSJ. A conditionally discharged patient is liable to be recalled to hospital by the SSJ. If his or her limitation or restriction direction ceases to have effect, the patient will be deemed (unless previously recalled) to have been absolutely discharged and will no longer be liable to be detained by virtue of the relevant hospital direction or transfer direction.[42]

---

41 MHA 1983 s74(5A).
42 MHA 1983 s73(3)–(6) as applied by s74(6).

After-care

30.34 The following patients are entitled to after-care services under MHA 1983 s117,[43] if they cease to be detained and leave hospital:
- those detained for treatment under MHA 1983 s3;
- those detained under a hospital order;
- those transferred to hospital under a hospital direction;
- those transferred to hospital under a transfer direction under MHA 1983 s47; and
- those transferred to hospital under a transfer direction under MHA 1983 s48.

30.35 There is no statutory definition of after-care services and no express provision as to their scope. The term is not however apt to cover a general raft of social services or community care. It is limited to services that are 'necessary to meet a need arising from a person's mental disorder' to be distinguished from 'common needs' such as the need for work or housing per se.[44]

30.36 The duty to provide such services falls on the Primary Care Trust or Local Health Board together with the local social services authority.[45] In each case, the relevant trust, board and social services authority will be the one for the area in which the patient is resident or to which he or she is sent on discharge from hospital.[46] These providers must work in co-operation with relevant voluntary agencies. The duty to provide after-care services continues until such time as the providers are satisfied that the person concerned is no longer in need of such services.[47] After-care is not a form of support that falls to be

---

43 For useful commentary on after-care services, see Jones, pp465–480.
44 *R (Mwanza) v London Borough of Greenwich and London Borough of Bromley* [2010] EWHC 1462 (Admin) at 64–65 (strictly speaking, this conclusion is obiter dictum as permission to bring a judicial review claim under section 117 was formally refused at a rolled-up hearing on grounds of delay: see para 92). For further gloss of after-care services, see cases cited in *Mwanza* at 68–74.
45 MHA 1983 s117(2), s145(1). See further, 'Code of Practice Mental Health Act 1983', DoH, May 2008, chapter 27. After-care services must continue throughout the period that a person remains subject to a community treatment order: MHA 1983 s117(2).
46 MHA 1983 s117(3). For recent treatment of section 117(3), see *R (M) v London Borough of Hammersmith and Fulham and others* [2010] EWHC 562 (Admin).
47 MHA 1983 s117(2).

withheld on grounds of immigration status.[48] The duty is therefore not affected by a person's irregular or unlawful status.[49]

The relationship between MHA 1983 and deportation

30.37 An FNP who is the subject of a hospital order or guardianship order under MHA 1983 s37, a hospital direction under section 45A or a transfer direction under section 47 will fall within one of the exceptions from 'automatic' deportation under the provisions of the UK Borders Act (UKBA) 2007.[50]

30.38 However, there is no bar in principle to the SSJ discharging a person from hospital in order for the Secretary of State for the Home Department (SSHD) to effect expulsion from the UK. A person subject to a hospital order and a restriction order may be discharged conditionally under MHA 1983 s42(2)[51] where the sole condition is that the person submits to the removal process.[52]

30.39 Even a person who continues to need treatment may be lawfully expelled by a combination of the exercise of discretion by SSJ under the provisions for discharge within MHA 1983 and the removal or deportation powers of the SSHD under IA 1971.[53] Nevertheless, the SSJ must exercise discretion in accordance with public law principles and ECHR obligations.

30.40 The SSHD's decision to remove or deport will attract a right of appeal to the Immigration and Asylum Chamber of the First-tier Tribunal (FTT-IAC) (see chapter 21) at which ECHR arguments concerning the individual's mental health needs can be raised (see paras 18.29–18.58) and also applicable policies concerning the expulsion of the mentally ill or suicidal (see para 18.52).

---

48 See NIAA 2002 s54 and Sch 3.
49 Confirmed by *R (Mwanza) v London Borough of Greenwich and London Borough of Bromley* [2010] EWHC 1462 (Admin) at 7.
50 UKBA 2007 s33(6). See chapter 5, in particular para 5.30.
51 See para 30.12.
52 *MJ (Angola) v Secretary of State for the Home Department* [2010] EWCA Civ 557, [2010] 1 WLR 2699.
53 See 'Foreign national restricted patients – guidance on repatriation', MoJ, 25 March 2009; available at www.justice.gov.uk/downloads/guidance/prison-probation-and-rehabilitation/mentally-disordered-offenders/guidance-repatriation.pdf.

30.41 In addition, there is a rarely-used power under MHA 1983 s86 which enables the SSHD to remove from the UK a patient who is detained for treatment or under a hospital order or under any order having the effect of a hospital order and who is neither a British citizen nor a Commonwealth citizen having the right of abode in the UK.[54] To exercise this power the SSHD must be satisfied that proper arrangements have been made for the patient's removal, and for the patient's care and treatment in the receiving jurisdiction, and that removal is in the interests of the patient. If these conditions are satisfied, SSHD may authorise the removal of the patient from the place where he or she is receiving treatment to another country. The SSHD must not remove a patient except with the approval of FTT-MH.[55]

30.42 The power to remove under MHA 1983 s86 is distinct from SSHD's powers of immigration control under the IA 1971. The MHA 1983 s86 power does not apply only to those who satisfy the conditions for expulsion under immigration law. For example, a friend or relative may request SSHD to remove an incapacitated patient from detention in hospital to his or her country of origin and the section 86 scheme may be used to achieve this even in cases where the patient has limited or indefinite leave to remain. In contrast, there is no power to remove a person under the IA 1971 at the request of a third party even if removal is in a patient's best interests and so expulsion under the IA 1971 cannot be founded on third party wishes.

30.43 The MHA 1983 section 86 power in principle extends to forcible expulsion. However, it is published Home Office policy that the SSHD will not use the MHA 1983 s86 power unless the Home Office is 'first approached by the patient's medical adviser'.[56]

30.44 The powers bestowed on the SSHD under MHA 1983 s86 and expulsion powers under immigration legislation (primarily IA 1971) may both be applicable. The courts have held that the SSHD may in principle use its expulsion powers under the IA 1971 to expel a patient without having to use simultaneously the powers under the MHA 1983 s86. Thus, the IA 1971 powers can be used to expel a person who is subject to compulsory in-patient treatment under MHA 1983 which will consequently be disrupted.[57] When exercising powers under IA 1971, the SSHD must nevertheless have regard to a

---

54 The right of abode is governed by IA 1971 s2(1)(b).
55 MHA 1983 s86(3).
56 IDIs Chapter 1 Section 8 4.2
57 *R (X) v Secretary of State for the Home Department* [2001] 1 WLR 740.

patient's mental illness and the prospect of care and treatment in the country to which he or she is to be expelled.[58]

30.45 The courts have not yet examined the question of whether the section 86 power can be exercised in the context of forcible expulsion, without an immigration decision being made under the IA 1971. We suggest that where a person would have had a full-merits appeal against an immigration decision to the FTT-IAC prior to expulsion (see chapter 21) that right of appeal cannot be bypassed for patients by the SSHD refraining from making an immigration decision. As we have already seen, wherever the SSHD seeks to exercise the MHA 1983 s86 power, the FTT-MH must determine whether the statutory preconditions for use of the power are made out, including whether removal is in the interests of the patient and that proper arrangements for the patient's care and treatment have been made. If the SSHD can proceed without an immigration decision so that the expulsion decision is only to be reviewed by the FTT-MH then it may be that the FTT-MH would be required to provide a full merits appeal, in which it would consider not only arguments under the ECHR, but potentially wider issues, for example, under the Refugee Convention[59] and EU law.

30.46 Under MHA 1983 s91, orders and directions under Part III cease to have effect when a person is removed by virtue of section 86, save where a person is subject to a hospital order coupled with a restriction order. In this latter type of case, the orders continue in force and they will apply to the patient if he or she returns to England and Wales. If a person is expelled under immigration legislation, section 91 will not be applicable.

---

58 *MJ (Angola) v Secretary of State for the Home Department* [2010] EWCA Civ 557, [2010] 1 WLR 2699 at 28.
59 The 1951 Convention Relating to the Status of Refugees and its 1967 Protocol.

PART III

Immigration detention

It is a fair summary of history to say that the safeguards of liberty have frequently been forged in controversies involving not very nice people.

United States v Rabinowitz, 339 US 56, 69 (1950) (Frankfurter, J, dissenting)

SECTION I
The power to detain

Introduction to the power to detain

Immigration detention is subject to fewer statutory safeguards than detention within the criminal justice system. There is no statutory time limit on the duration of immigration detention[1] and there is no provision for automatic court reviews of the lawfulness of the detention.[2] In practice, the onus is on immigration detainees to make their own bail applications. This is more difficult than it might seem. Quite apart from impediments of language or knowledge of rights faced by many immigration detainees, HM Inspector of Prisons has repeatedly noted the lack of access to adequate legal advice for immigration detainees, and, particularly for those held in prisons, the lack of access to immigration officers or adequate information or documentation concerning their cases.[3] The problem is likely to worsen in the light of legal aid cuts, and the closure, in 2010 and 2011, of the two principal providers of publicly funded immigration legal services in immigration removal centres.[4]

---

1 This is by contrast with the UK's European partners. The European Parliament and the Council of the European Union on 16 December 2008 adopted Directive 2008/115 on common standards and procedures in member states for returning illegally staying third country nationals ('Return Directive'); the deadline for transposition is 24 December 2010. The Return Directive imposes time limits on the detention of illegally staying immigrants. The initial time limit of six months may be extended for a further 12 months in cases of lack of co-operation by the third-country national concerned or delays in obtaining the necessary documentation for third countries. Many European countries already imposed shorter time limits prior to the Return Directive. The UK has opted out of the Return Directive. Ireland, which also opted out of the Directive, already has shorter time limits for immigration detention. Denmark, which had initially opted out, has now effectively opted in to the Return Directive.

2 The Immigration and Asylum Act 1999 s44 had introduced a right to two automatic references to the magistrates' court for bail. These provisions were never brought into force and were repealed by the Nationality, Immigration and Asylum Act 2002 s68.

3 HM Inspector of Prisons *Foreign nationals, a thematic review*, July 2006 and *Foreign nationals, a follow up report*, January 2007. Available at http://inspectorates.homeoffice.gov.uk/hmiprisons/thematic-reports1.

4 Refugee and Migrant Justice and the Immigration Advisory Service.

CHAPTER 31

Statutory powers of immigration detention

31.1	Introduction
31.6	**Detention powers under IA 1971**
31.7	Detention powers in deportation cases under IA 1971
31.10	Meaning of 'pending'
31.11	Cases where no statutory power to detain arises
31.12	**Deportation and detention powers under UKBA 2007**
31.17	UKBA 2007 s36 detention and the steps in the deportation process
	Detention under UKBA 2007 s36(1)(a) • *Detention under UKBA 2007 s36(1)(b)*
31.34	Detention under UKBA 2007 s36(2) once an 'automatic' deportation order has been made
31.35	**No dual detention for deportation under IA 1971 or under UKBA 2007**
31.37	*R (Khadir)* and statutory powers of detention

Introduction

31.1 Until recently, the statutory powers of immigration detention were contained in the Immigration Act (IA) 1971 Schs 2 and 3 (though those statutory provisions were amended and supplemented by subsequent legislation). A distinct, parallel immigration detention regime has been established under the UK Borders Act (UKBA) 2007, discussed further below.

31.2 Statutory powers of detention are, on their face, very wide. It is relatively rare to encounter a case in which a period of immigration detention is unlawful by reason that there was no power to detain on the express terms of the statute.

31.3 However, those statutory powers are not unfettered. The Secretary of State for the Home Department's (SSHD's) powers of detention are circumscribed by the common law, including the duty to comply with the *Hardial Singh* principles (these are principles concerning the permissible purpose and reasonable duration of detention in expulsion cases, discussed in detail in chapter 33), and, absent good reason for not so doing, with Home Office policy (discussed in chapter 34). The SSHD's detention powers are also limited by article 5 of the European Convention on Human Rights (ECHR) as discussed in chapter 36. Many detention challenges concern cases where the power to detain has been unlawfully exercised.

31.4 Below, we consider the powers of detention for deportation under IA 1971 and under UKBA 2007. This chapter finishes with a discussion of *R (Khadir) v Secretary of State for the Home Department* in which the House of Lords emphasised that the fact that in a given case there existed a statutory power to detain did not mean that it was reasonable or lawful to exercise that power in the circumstances.[1]

31.5 The question of whether any of those statutory powers of detention should be construed as imposing a presumption of detention, in particular in cases of detention pursuant to a court recommendation under IA 1971 Sch 3 para 2(1), is addressed at paras 32.31–32.40 in the next chapter.

---

1 *R (Khadir) v Secretary of State for the Home Department* [2005] UKHL 39, [2006] 1 AC 207 paras 31 and 32.

Detention powers under IA 1971

31.6 The SSHD's powers of immigration detention under IA 1971 can be broadly summarised as follows:

- Persons subject to immigration control can be detained pending examination and a decision on whether to grant, cancel or refuse leave to enter.[2]
- Persons subject to immigration control who have been refused leave to enter, or whose leave has been cancelled; or illegal entrants or overstayers; and persons reasonably suspected of falling in these categories can be detained pending a decision over whether to remove, and pending removal.[3] Similarly, persons who have not observed a condition attached to their limited leave to enter; persons who have used deception in seeking leave to remain; persons whose indefinite leave to remain has been revoked; and their family members who are not British citizens; and persons reasonably suspected of falling within these categories can be detained pending a decision over whether to remove, and pending removal.[4]
- Persons whom the SSHD considers should be deported for the public good or who are the subject of a criminal court's recommendation for deportation can be detained pending steps in the deportation procedure.[5]

Detention powers in deportation cases under IA 1971

31.7 In relation to those in the last group (deportation), the SSHD's detention powers under IA 1971 are contained in Schedule 3 (as amended by subsequent legislation). These are the detention powers relevant to foreign national former prisoners (FNPs) facing deportation under IA 1971. The SSHD may detain a person:

- in respect of whom a recommendation for deportation has been made by a court and remains in force, pending the making of a deportation order;[6]

---

2 IA 1971 Sch 2 para 16(1) and (1A).
3 IA 1971 Sch 2 paras 8, 9, 12–14 and 16(2).
4 Immigration and Asylum Act (IAA) 1999 s10(1) and (7).
5 IA 1971 Sch 3 para 2(1)–(3).
6 IA 1971 Sch 3 para 2(1).

- who has received notice of a decision to make a deportation order pending the making of the deportation order[7] or to whom a notice of a decision to make a deportation order is 'ready to be given';[8] or
- against whom a deportation order is in force, pending their removal or departure from the UK.[9] The Administrative Court has clarified that the deportation order must be served on the individual in order to trigger the power to detain.[10]

31.8 As a consequence of an amendment to IA 1971 Sch 3 para 2(4) introduced by the Immigration Asylum and Nationality Act (IANA) 2006 s53, a person for whom there is a notice of a decision to make a deportation order 'ready to be given' is liable to detention. This does not permit prolonged detention of a person on the basis that there is a notice of intention to deport which could potentially be served. This amendment is only for the purposes of IA 1971 Sch 2 para 17(1), which empowers a constable or immigration officer to make an arrest without warrant. The effect of the amendment is that a person may be arrested without warrant where there is a notice of intention to deport 'ready to be given to him'. Detention thereafter will only be lawful if the notice of intention to deport is served (or if the person has already been recommended for deportation by a court or has a deportation order in force against him or her). Ministerial statements at the time of the passage of this legislation indicate that the purpose of this provision is to ensure the lawfulness of an arrest made where the arresting officer does not have to hand the notice of intention to deport.[11]

31.9 The requirements of authorisation for detention under each limb of IA 1971 Sch 3 para 2 are discussed at paras 35.3–35.4.

---

7 IA 1971 Sch 3 para 2(2).
8 IA 1971 Sch 3 para 2(4) as amended by IANA 2006 s53.
9 IA 1971 Sch 3 para 2(3) (as amended by IAA 1999 s54(3)).
10 *R (S) v Secretary of State for the Home Department* [2011] EWHC 2120 (Admin) paras 151–159.
11 'The clause confirms that the power of arrest in deportation cases is available when notice of intention to deport is ready but has not yet been given to a prospective deportee. The clause will ensure that immigration officers and constables can continue to seek a warrant to enter named premises in order to search for and arrest a prospective deportee and serve him with a notice of decision to deport': Tony McNulty MP, Minister of State, Standing Committee E, 8th sitting, 27 October 2005 pm, col 279.

Meaning of 'pending'

31.10 Statutory powers of detention under IA 1971 are expansively drafted. The powers of detention include a power to detain a person 'pending' examination, administrative removal or deportation. Each of these processes may in some cases take years. The House of Lords in *Khadir*[12] held that the word 'pending' simply means 'until'. In expulsion cases, the statutory power to detain therefore remains: 'so long as the Secretary of State remains intent on removing [or deporting] the person and there is some prospect of achieving this'. We discuss the *Khadir* judgment in more detail below at paras 31.37–31.39.

Cases where no statutory power to detain arises

31.11 Examples of cases where no statutory power to detain arises under IA 1971 Sch 3 are:

- where a person is detained ostensibly for the purposes of deportation but there is no power in law to deport that person (for example, because he or she is British or is otherwise exempt from deportation;[13] or because the courts have allowed the individual's appeal against deportation and there is no further appeal from the SSHD);
- where the steps in the deportation process which are express conditions precedent for detention powers under IA 1971 have not occurred (for example, where the person is ostensibly detained for deportation but is not the subject of a court recommendation for deportation and no notice of decision to deport has been given or no deportation order served[14]).

---

12 *R (Khadir) v Secretary of State for the Home Department* [2005] UKHL 39 para 32.
13 As to the approach taken by the court where detention is challenged on this basis, the High Court may decline to determine whether a detainee is liable to or exempt from deportation where the Tribunal is shortly to determine the issue: *R (Oswald Thomas) v Secretary of State for the Home Department* [2009] EWHC 1008 (Admin).
14 See *R (S) v Secretary of State for the Home Department* [2011] EWHC 2120 (Admin) paras 151–159, where there was no power to detain under IA 1971 Sch 3 para 2(3) because the deportation order was not served.

Deportation and detention powers under UKBA 2007

31.12 The UKBA 2007 significantly expands the SSHD's powers of immigration detention.

31.13 As was discussed in some detail in chapter 5, the UKBA 2007 introduces a new system of 'automatic' deportation for foreign national offenders. Foreign national offenders who meet certain criteria will be designated as 'foreign criminals'.[15] The criteria are that the individual is a foreign national who is convicted in the UK of an offence and sentenced to either (Condition 1) a period of imprisonment of at least 12 months; or (Condition 2) a period of imprisonment of any length for an offence defined by secondary legislation as 'particularly serious'. The statutory provisions relating to the first group of 'foreign criminals' (Condition 1) came into force on 1 August 2008;[16] but those relating to the second group (Condition 2) are not in force.

31.14 An 'automatic' deportation order must be made for these 'foreign criminals'[17] unless the individual is exempt from all deportation or certain exceptions apply. The exceptions include[18] cases where the SSHD believes that deportation would breach the individual's rights under the Refugee Convention,[19] the ECHR[20] or European Community (EC) law.[21] 'Foreign criminals' will then have a right of appeal to the Immigration and Asylum Chamber of the First Tier Tribunal (FTT-IAC) against the automatic deportation order.[22] The 'automatic' deportation order will not take effect in revoking any extant leave to enter or remain in the UK until these appeals have been exhausted.[23] However, in many cases, the foreign national offender will only be able to exercise his or her appeal to FTT-IAC from outside the UK, after expulsion.[24]

---

15 UKBA 2007 s32(1).
16 UK Borders Act 2007 (Commencement No 3 and Transitional Provisions) Order 2008 SI No 1818 para 2.
17 UKBA 2007 s32(5).
18 For a full discussion of the exemptions and exceptions see paras 5.23–5.30.
19 The 1951 Convention Relating to the Status of Refugees and its 1967 Protocol ('Refugee Convention'). UKBA 2007 s33(2)(b).
20 UKBA 2007 s33(2)(a).
21 UKBA 2007 s33(4).
22 Nationality, Immigration and Asylum Act (NIAA) 2002 s82(2)(j), as added by UKBA 2007 s35.
23 UKBA 2007 s35(4).
24 See discussion at paras 5.43–5.46.

31.15 The 'automatic' deportation provisions (in relation to Condition 1) have retrospective effect. The SSHD may impose 'automatic' deportation orders on those convicted before the passing of the UKBA 2007 who were in custody or subject to a suspended sentence at the time of commencement on 1 August 2008.[25] Notwithstanding a lacuna in the wording of the transitional provisions, 'automatic' deportation and associated detention powers have been found to apply also to those convicted between the passing of the UKBA 2007 and its entry into force.[26]

31.16 Associated with this new 'automatic' deportation regime are new powers of immigration detention which we discuss below.

UKBA 2007 s36 detention and the steps in the deportation process

31.17 Under UKBA 2007 s36(1)(a), the SSHD has a power to detain a person who has served a period of imprisonment, while the SSHD 'considers' whether the 'automatic' deportation provisions apply.[27] This detention power arises where the UKBA 2007 s32(5) decision (that the individual is liable to 'automatic' deportation) has not yet been made. Once the SSHD 'thinks' (ie decides) that a foreign national former prisoner satisfies the criteria for deportation under UKBA 2007 s32(5), then UKBA 2007 s36(1)(b) permits detention pending the making of the deportation order, upon which any further detention pending the enforcement of the order is permitted under UKBA 2007 s36(2).

31.18 Note that the SSHD's caseworkers must inform the detainee exactly which part of UKBA 2007 s36 is relied on to justify the detention. It is not enough for the SSHD to state (as is unfortunately currently common UK Border Agency practice) that a person is detained 'under UKBA 2007 s36(1)'. A person is entitled to know under exactly which statutory provision she is detained.[28] It has been held at Administrative Court level that a failure by the SSHD to specify the correct limb under UKBA 2007 s36(1) under which a detainee is held

---

25 UK Borders Act 2007 (Commencement No 3 and Transitional Provisions) Order 2008 SI No 1818 para 3.
26 *R (Rashid Hussein) v Secretary of State for the Home Department* [2009] EWHC 2492 (Admin); *AT (Pakistan) and JT (Pakistan) v Secretary of State for the Home Department* [2010] EWCA Civ 567.
27 UKBA 2007 s36(1)(a).
28 See *R (Rashid Hussein) v Secretary of State for the Home Department* [2009] EWHC 2492 (Admin) at para 41.

Detention under UKBA 2007 s36(1)(a)

31.19 As was seen above at paras 31.7–31.8, the pre-existing powers of detention for deportation under IA 1971 Sch 3 allow the SSHD to detain only where specific steps in the deportation process have already occurred. By contrast, UKBA 2007 s36(1)(a) uncouples the power to detain from the steps in the deportation process. The power to detain arises under UKBA 2007 s36(1)(a) *before* the decision as to liability to deportation has been taken.[30]

31.20 There is an ambiguity as to what conditions must be met for the SSHD's exercise of her detention powers under UKBA 2007 s36(1)(a). Below, we discuss three possible interpretations of the UKBA 2007 s36(1)(a) detention power.

31.21 The first and narrowest interpretation of the detention power is that the detention power arises only where a) a person is a 'foreign criminal' as defined under UKBA 2007 s32(1), that is he or she is a foreign national sentenced to a period of imprisonment of at least 12 months;[31] and b) the individual is not exempt from all deportation as a long resident Irish or Commonwealth national, diplomat or crewmember.[32] That is, being a 'foreign criminal' as defined in UKBA 2007 s36(1) and being non-exempt from deportation[33] are statutory conditions precedent for the lawful exercise of the power to detain. On this construction, the deliberations which take place during section 36(1)(a) detention concern only the UKBA 2007 s33 numbered exceptions (exceptions 1–6[34]). We suggest that this narrowest construction is correct. It is consistent with the wording of

---

29 *R (NXT) v Secretary of State for the Home Department* [2011] EWHC 969 (Admin) para 124.
30 It has been argued, unsuccessfully, at High Court level, that the UKBA 2007 s36(1)(a) detention power, which permits detention while liability to deportation is determined, is incompatible with the requirement under ECHR article 5(1)(f) that proceedings with a view to deportation must be in progress (*R (Rashid Hussein) v Secretary of State for the Home Department* [2009] EWHC 2492 (Admin)).
31 Condition 1 at UKBA 2007 s32(2), the only condition presently in force.
32 These exemptions, contained in IA 1971 ss7 and 8, apply also to 'automatic' deportation by operation of UKBA 2007 s33(1)(b).
33 But not the application of the numbered exceptions at UKBA 2007 s36(2)–(7).
34 Contained at UKBA 2007 s33(2)–(6A).

the statute[35] and with the principle that statutory provisions conferring powers of executive detention must be 'strictly and narrowly' construed.[36]

31.22 On a second, wider, construction of the UKBA 2007 s36(1)(a) detention power, the SSHD's deliberations would concern not only the application of the numbered exceptions to 'automatic' deportation but also the question of exemptions from discretionary as well as 'automatic' deportation as a diplomat, seaman or long-resident Commonwealth or Irish national.[37]

31.23 On a third, wider still construction of the UKBA 2007 s36(1)(a) detention power, any person who had served a period of imprisonment[38] – even a British citizen – could be lawfully be detained under UKBA 2007 s36(1)(a) while the SSHD considered whether the individual was in fact a 'foreign criminal'. The SSHD has, on at least one occasion, argued for this widest construction.[39]

31.24 We suggest that the second and third interpretations of the UKBA 2007 s36(1)(a) detention power set out above are impermissibly wide. Notably there exists no statement of parliamentary intention to empower the SSHD to detain for deportation those statutorily exempt by their status, for example, British citizens or international diplomats, an astonishing omission if so drastic an extension of the SSHD's powers of administrative detention had been intended.

31.25 Whichever construction prevails, we suggest that UKBA 2007 s36(1)(a) is a bridging provision. Section 36(1)(a) allows the SSHD a grace period after completion of a criminal custodial term during which to make a decision over liability to deportation where it has not

---

35 Section 36(1)(a) permits detention 'while the Secretary of State considers whether section 32(5) applies'. Under section 33(1)(a), section 32(4) and (5) 'do not apply' where one of the numbered exceptions applies. However, distinct language is used for the other exemptions: section 33(1)(b) that section 32(4) and (5) 'are subject to' the exemptions from deportation in IA 1971 for long-resident Commonwealth or Irish nationals or international diplomats. Section 32(1), setting out the criteria for 'foreign criminal' status likewise makes no reference to 'applies'.

36 *In re Wasfi Suleiman Mahmood* [1995] Imm AR 311, 314; *In Re SC (Mental Patient: Habeas Corpus)* [1996] QB 599, 603 and *Tan Te Lam and others v Superintendant of Tai A Chau Detention Centre* [1997] AC 97, 111.

37 The exemptions contained in IA 1971 ss7 and 8, apply also to 'automatic' deportation by operation of UKBA 2008 s33(1)(b).

38 The only express condition for detention under UKBA 2007 s36(1).

39 *R (Rashid Hussein) v Secretary of State for the Home Department* [2009] EWHC 2492 (Admin) para 44(i). Nicol J observed that the SSHD's argument would amount to 'a dramatic extension of the law' but did not consider it necessary to decide the point in that case.

been possible to make the decision during the currency of the sentence (eg because the person had been released almost immediately after sentence because of time previously served on remand). The government assured parliament during the passage of the UK Borders legislation that 'automatic' deportation orders would, 'whenever possible' be made before the completion of the custodial part of the criminal sentence:

> It is perfectly reasonable to expect the Home Office to undertake the issue of deportation orders in advance and substantially in advance of somebody being released from custody.[40]
>
> I fully realise that noble Lords feel queasy about what they view as an open-ended power to detain. Who would not? It is an understandable reaction, and I am no different in that regard. I can provide some reassurance that the provision is not designed to allow the Secretary of State to detain people indefinitely; that is not its objective. Deportation action will, whenever possible, be commenced while the criminal sentence is being served. In those circumstances, it will not be necessary to use these powers. My guess is that that will cover the majority of circumstances. However, there will be cases where, for example, a person who appears to meet the criteria for automatic deportation is eligible for immediate release by the sentencing court because he has already served the sentence while on remand. That happens from time to time. In such circumstances, it is vital to have a power to detain while the Secretary of State considers whether automatic deportation applies. I am sure that noble Lords will understand why that might be the case. This will help to remove the risk of the offender absconding, thereby affording an extra level of public protection from potential harm. I am sure that we can imagine the sorts of cases where that would be especially important.[41]

31.26 Where an individual is detained for a protracted period under UKBA 2007 s36(1)(a) in the absence of active steps by the SSHD to pursue deportation or the resolution of any prior asylum, ECHR or EU law claims, detention may be unlawful. This is particularly so where there is no good reason why the question of liability to 'automatic' deportation, including the resolution of any asylum claim, was not determined during the currency of the criminal custodial term.[42]

---

40 Liam Byrne MP, Minister for Immigration, Citizenship and Nationality: UK Borders Bill Committee, Thirteenth Sitting, *Hansard* HC Debates col 438, 20 March 2007.
41 Lord Bassam of Brighton, Minister of State, *Hansard* HL Report cols 661–662. 16 October 2007 :
42 *R (Rashid Hussein) v Secretary of State for the Home Department* [2009] EWHC 2492 (Admin) para 52.

31.27 The *Hardial Singh* principles, which protect individuals against unreasonably protracted administrative detention (discussed in detail in chapter 33 below) apply with minor modifications to UKBA 2007 s36(1)(a) detention.[43] In particular, detention cannot lawfully be maintained once it becomes apparent that either resolution of the question of whether any of the UKBA 2007 s33 exceptions apply, or any subsequent deportation, or both, will take more than a reasonable time.[44] In addition, the SSHD is under a duty to act with reasonable diligence and expedition to determine whether any of the section 33 exceptions applies.[45]

Detention under UKBA 2007 s36(1)(b)

31.28 The UKBA 2007 s36(1)(b) detention power arises once a decision has been made under UKBA 2007 s32(5) that the person is liable to automatic deportation[46] but before the 'automatic' deportation order has been made.

31.29 In practice, Home Office caseworkers are making the decision that UKBA 2007 s32(5) applies and simultaneously making 'automatic' deportation orders. The UKBA 2007 s36(1)(b) detention power is therefore being used rarely, if at all, at the time of writing.

31.30 We suggest that the detention power under UKBA 2007 s36(1)(b) is a further bridging provision permitting detention for a short time only after the UKBA 2007 s32(5) decision, while the minister's signature is obtained and the 'automatic' deportation order served on the proposed deportee. Although there is no statutory time-limit on the making of an 'automatic' deportation order,[47] delays in making such an order against a detained person once the decision has been made under UKBA 2007 s32(5) are likely to be considered unreasonable, contrary to the *Hardial Singh* principles.

31.31 As with the UKBA 2007 s36(1)(a) detention power, litigation is to be anticipated over the conditions precedent for the lawful exercise of the UKBA 2007 s36(1)(b) detention power.

---

43 *R (Rashid Hussein) v Secretary of State for the Home Department* [2009] EWHC 2492 (Admin) para 44.
44 *R (Rashid Hussein) v Secretary of State for the Home Department* [2009] EWHC 2492 (Admin) para 44(iii).
45 *R (Rashid Hussein) v Secretary of State for the Home Department* [2009] EWHC 2492 (Admin) para 44(iv).
46 *R (Rashid Hussein) v Secretary of State for the Home Department* [2009] EWHC 2492 (Admin) para 41.
47 UKBA 2007 s34(1) provides that the Secretary of State is entitled to make an 'automatic' deportation.

31.32 We suggest that the UKBA 2007 s36(1)(b) power may only be exercised where: a) the person is a 'foreign criminal' as defined under UKBA 2007 s32(1); b) none of the exemptions to deportation in the IA 1971 (which also preclude 'automatic' deportation by operation of UKBA 2007 s33(1)) applies; and c) the SSHD has made a decision under UKBA 2007 s32(5) that the individual is liable to 'automatic' deportation. We suggest that these are conditions precedent for the power to detain and that an error as to the existence of one of the above conditions vitiates the authority to detain. If the SSHD, for example, proceeds with 'automatic' deportation against a British citizen then (however reasonably held the SSHD's erroneous belief that the person is a foreign national) there is no power to detain and any decision to detain is *ultra vires* (that is, beyond the SSHD's powers).

31.33 A further question arises concerning the legality of detention under UKBA 2007 s36(1)(b) or s36(2) where it subsequently transpires that the individual falls within one of the numbered exceptions to 'automatic' deportation under UKBA 2007. We suggest that an error by the SSHD as to the application of one of the numbered exceptions (under UKBA 2007 s33(2)–(6)) will render the detention unlawful if, but only if, the SSHD's decision was tainted by material public law error. If there is no material public law error in the UKBA's finding that an individual is not, for example, a refugee,[48] a subsequent disagreement as to merit, and the mere fact of a subsequent favourable refugee finding by the appellate tribunal does not retrospectively render unlawful the detention.[49] However, if the SSHD has acted unreasonably, for example proceeding with 'automatic' deportation, notwithstanding undisputed evidence that the individual is still a minor[50] we suggest that detention pursuant to that decision, under UKBA 2007 s36(1)(b) or s36(2) will be unlawful. This approach is consistent with *Lumba and Mighty*[51] in which the Supreme Court has held that a decision to detain is vitiated by material public law error.[52]

---

48 And therefore covered by exception 1, UKBA 2007 s33(2)(b).
49 A similar approach was taken to detention under the IA 1971 in *OM (Algeria) v Secretary of State for the Home Department* [2010] EWHC 65 (Admin) paras 62–63.
50 And therefore covered by exception 2, UKBA 2007 s33(3).
51 *R (Lumba and Mighty) v Secretary of State for the Home Department* [2011] UKSC 12, [2011] 2 WLR 671.
52 This is a more flexible approach than that taken in *R (Kullas) v Secretary of State for the Home Department* [2009] EWHC 735 (Admin) para 6. The claimant in *Kullas* challenged his past detention under the IA 1971 on grounds that the immigration officer had failed to appreciate the strength of his ECHR article

Detention under UKBA 2007 s36(2) once an 'automatic' deportation order has been made

31.34 Under UKBA 2007 s36(2), once an 'automatic' deportation order has been made, the SSHD 'shall' exercise her powers of immigration detention 'unless' she thinks it 'inappropriate' to do so. On its face, UKBA 2007 s36(2) appears to establish a statutory presumption of detention where an 'automatic' deportation order has been made. Similarly worded provisions in the IA 1971 have been read down, at High Court level, as containing no presumption of detention.[53] But, as we explain further below at paras 32.34–32.37, it is unclear whether or to what extent that declaration remains good law: the law is currently opaque as to whether such provisions do establish a presumption of detention. We suggest that under UKBA 2007 s36(2), as under the equivalent power in IA 1971 Sch 3 para 2(3), the deportation order must be served on the individual to trigger the power to detain (see para 31.7 above).

No dual detention for deportation under IA 1971 or under UKBA 2007

31.35 A person held under those detention powers in the Immigration Acts relating to examination and administrative removal[54] may simultaneously be detained under criminal justice powers, sometimes referred to as 'dual detention'.

31.36 However, where a person is detained for the purposes of deportation, there can be no 'dual detention': a person is either detained under criminal justice powers or under the Immigration Acts for

---

8 claim. Nicol J considered that liability for false imprisonment could only be established if bad faith or irrationality were shown on the part of the decision-maker. We respectfully suggest that Nicol J's test requires modification in the light of *Lumba and Mighty*.

53 IA 1971 Sch 3 para 2(1) states that a person 'shall ... be detained ... unless ...'. The passage in parentheses in Sch 3 para 2(3) states that a person 'shall continue to be detained unless ...'. In *Sedrati, Buitrago-Lopez and Arangatu v Secretary of State for the Home Department* [2001] EWHC (Admin) 418, Moses J as he then was, declared, by mutual agreement of the parties, that there was no presumption of detention in Sch 3 para 2. In *R (Lumba and Mighty) v Secretary of State for the Home Department* [2011] UKSC 12, [2011] 2 WLR 671, Lord Dyson at para 55 stated that 'in relation to paragraph 2(2) and (3), therefore, so far as it goes, the declaration granted by Moses J is correct'.

54 Those detention powers have been summarised at para 31.6.

deportation. In detention for deportation under IA 1971 Sch 3 para 2, this is clear from the language of the statute itself.[55] The language of UKBA 2007 s36 is slightly less clear but the Administrative[56] and Divisional Court[57] have both confirmed that there is no power of dual detention under UKBA 2007 s36.

R (Khadir) and statutory powers of detention

31.37 Although not a detention case, the House of Lords' judgment in *R (Khadir) v Secretary of State for the Home Department*[58] is relevant to the courts' approach to the extent of the statutory power to detain. The appellant in *Khadir* was an Iraqi Kurd who had been on temporary admission for over four years. The appellant challenged the Secretary of State's refusal to grant him exceptional leave to enter, claiming that since he could not be removed (there was then no safe route to Northern Iraq) he was not 'liable to be detained' 'pending removal' under IA 1971,[59] and therefore could not be granted temporary admission.[60] The House of Lords widely construed the power to detain 'pending' a decision on whether to set removal directions and 'pending' removal.[61] Notwithstanding that there was no route of removal for K, he remained a person liable to detention, and thus could be granted temporary admission by the SSHD rather than leave to remain. The word 'pending' in the statutory power to detain in administrative removal cases meant no more than 'until' and:

> So long as the Secretary of State remains intent on removing the person and there is some prospect of achieving this, paragraph 16 authorises detention meanwhile.[62]

---

55 IA 1971 Sch 3 paras 2(1) and (2) each specify that they apply only to a person who is not 'detained in pursuance of the sentence or order of the court'.
56 *R (Aitouaret) v Secretary of State for the Home Department* [2010] EWHC 3136 (Admin) para 22.
57 *R (Francis) v Secretary of State for the Home Department* [2011] EWHC 1271 (Admin) para 12.
58 [2005] UKHL 39, [2006] 1 AC 207.
59 IA 1971 Sch 2 para 16(2).
60 Under IA 1971 Sch 2 para 21 (which permits the grant of temporary admission to persons liable to be detained under Sch 2 para 16).
61 IA 1971 Sch 2 para 16(2). This statutory provision confers a power to detain in administrative removal cases.
62 *R (Khadir) v Secretary of State for the Home Department* [2005] UKHL 39 para 32.

31.38 But the House of Lords in *Khadir* emphasised the distinction between the existence of a statutory power to detain and the circumstances in which it would be reasonable to exercise that power:

> ... it surely goes without saying that the longer the delay in effecting someone's removal the more difficult it will be to justified his continued detention meanwhile. But that is by no means to say that he does not remain 'liable to detention' ...
>
> ... plainly it may become unreasonable actually to detain the person pending a long delayed removal (ie throughout the whole period until removal is finally achieved). But that does not mean that the power has lapsed.[63]

31.39 *Khadir* is authority for the proposition that the power to detain may exist even in circumstances where it would be unreasonable, by reference to the *Hardial Singh* principles, to exercise that power. We respectfully suggest that this may need to be revisited: that proposition is difficult to reconcile with the Supreme Court's subsequent holding in *Lumba and Mighty* that a decision to detain flawed by material public law error is a nullity. *Lumba and Mighty* clarifies that a power unreasonably exercised is no power: whether the SSHD seeks to exercise a power for which the statutory conditions precedent are unmet, or whether she seeks to exercise that power unreasonably, she is acting ultra vires, that is, outside her powers.[64] This aspect of *Lumba and Mighty* is discussed at paras 32.5 and 32.10–32.11 below.

---

63 *R (Khadir) v Secretary of State for the Home Department* [2005] UKHL 39 paras 31 and 32.
64 See also *D v Home Office* [2005] EWCA Civ 38, [2006] 1 WLR 1003, para 111.

SECTION J
Restrictions on the power to detain

Chapter 32: Core common law principles generally applicable to deprivation of liberty   609

Chapter 33: The *Hardial Singh* principles   629

Chapter 34: Home Office detention policy   651

Chapter 35: Procedural requirements in immigration detention   673

Chapter 36: The ECHR and detention   683

Chapter 37: Detention in CCD cases involving children   713

Introduction to limitations on the power to detain

Circumstances in which immigration detention is unlawful – a short summary

Immigration detention will be unlawful if:
- statutory provisions bearing on the decision to detain have been breached;
- the decision to detain is vitiated by a material public law error, that is, a public law error bearing directly on the decision. An example of such a public law error would be a failure, without good reason, to follow applicable policy where the aspect of the policy that has been breached relates sufficiently closely to the decision to detain. Another example would be breach of the *Hardial Singh* principles – principles delimiting the reasonable exercise of the power to detain in the expulsion context; or
- the detention otherwise breaches European Convention on Human Rights (ECHR) restrictions on the power to detain.

Essential sources and organisation of the following chapters

General common law limitations on the exercise of the power to detain, and the *Hardial Singh* principles are discussed in chapters 32 and 33 respectively.

Published Home Office policy on the criteria for detention, now set out at chapter 55 of the Enforcement Instructions and Guidance (EIG), and the legal effects of non-compliance are discussed in chapter 34.

Procedural requirements for immigration detention are set out both in Home Office policy and (where the detention is in an immigration removal centre) in the Detention Centre Rules 2001. These procedural requirements, and the legal consequences of non-compliance are discussed in chapter 35.

The application of the ECHR protections in the context of detention is discussed in chapter 36.

Special limitations on the power to detain in cases involving children are discussed in chapter 37.

CHAPTER 32

Core common law principles generally applicable to detention

32.1 Introduction

32.2 Equal protection of the law for immigrants

32.3 The burden is on the detainer to justify the detention in legal proceedings

32.6 The executive's powers of detention must be strictly construed

32.10 The legality of a decision to detain or maintain detention is vitiated by a material public law error

32.14 The tort of false imprisonment is established without proof of special damage

32.17 No causation defence in liability for the detainer

32.21 Material and non-material public law error

32.22 An intermediary category of public law error?

32.24 Causation and damages

32.26 Duty to give reasons for detention

32.30 There is no good faith defence for the detainer

32.31 Whether the Immigration Acts contain a presumption of detention

continued

32.31 A policy of normally detaining a specified category of person is permissible
32.32 Ongoing debate as to interpretation of Immigration Acts
Construction of the power to detain in court recommendation cases

32.41 The courts' role when assessing the lawfulness of administrative detention

Introduction

32.1 This chapter provides an overview of core common law principles generally applicable to deprivation of liberty. We include in this chapter a discussion of the controversial issue of how those principles apply in cases of court recommendations to deport under the Immigration Act (IA) 1971 Sch 3 para 2(1). The *Hardial Singh* principles (which specifically concern the executive deprivation of liberty of immigrants pending their expulsion) are discussed separately in chapter 33. A further duty imposed by the common law, that of compliance with published Home Office detention policy, is considered separately in chapter 34; procedural safeguards, whether imposed directly by the common law or through policy, are discussed in chapter 35.

Equal protection of the law for immigrants

32.2 General principles safeguarding individual liberty apply to immigrants as they do to British citizens. As the House of Lords stated in *R v Home Secretary ex p Khawaja*:[1]

> Every person within the jurisdiction enjoys the equal protection of our laws. There is no distinction between British nationals and others. He who is subject to English law is entitled to its protection.

And as the Court of Appeal stated in *ID and others v the Home Office*:[2]

> ... although people like the present claimants are described in the statute as being 'liable to detention' so that they can be subjected to administrative detention under the authority of an immigration officer without any reference to a court of law, English law will remain jealous of their right to liberty and will scrutinise with care the legality of any executive act that deprives them of that liberty.
> In the last resort I see no reason why an immigrant deprived of his liberty by an unlawful decision of an immigration officer should go uncompensated by reason of practical concerns about administrative convenience.

---

1 [1984] AC 74 per Lord Scarman at pp111–112.
2 [2005] EWCA Civ 38, [2006] 1 WLR 1003 at paras 76 and 131.

The burden is on the detainer to justify the detention in legal proceedings

32.3 It is a fundamental common law principle that in legal proceedings, every detention (other than that ordered by judge) is prima facie unlawful. Once it is established that a detention occurred, the burden is on the detainer to justify the detention as lawful. Lord Atkin's famous dissenting speech in *Liversidge v Anderson*[3] stated:

> In English law, every imprisonment is prima facie unlawful and ... it is for a person directing imprisonment to justify his act. The only exception is in respect of imprisonment ordered by a judge ...

See also *R (Abbassi) v Secretary of State for Foreign and Commonwealth Affairs*:[4]

> The underlying principle, fundamental in English law, is that every imprisonment is prima facie unlawful ... This principle applies to every person, British citizen or not, who finds himself within the jurisdiction of the court.

The point was again confirmed by Lord Dyson in *R (Lumba and Mighty) v Secretary of State for the Home Department*.[5]

32.4 It used to be thought that the burden of proof was on the detainer to establish the existence of the power to detain but that the burden then passed back to the claimant to show that the exercise of the power had been unlawful.[6] Other authorities, however, held that the burden of proof as to the lawful exercise of the power to detain also rested on the detainer.[7]

32.5 We suggest that the Supreme Court judgment in *Lumba and Mighty* settles the dispute and establishes that the burden is on the detainer not only to point to the statutory basis for the detention but to establish the lawful exercise of the power to detain. The Supreme

---

3 [1942] AC 206, at 245, subsequently accepted as correct not only on the point of construction of the wartime regulations but 'in its declaration of English legal principle' (per Lord Scarman, *Khawaja* [1984] AC 74 at 110, also *R v Inland Revenue Commissioners ex p Rossminster Ltd* [1980] AC 952, 1011, 1025).
4 [2002] EWCA Civ 1598, [2003] UKHRR 76 para 60.
5 *R (Lumba and Mighty) v Secretary of State for the Home Department* [2011] UKSC 12, [2011] 2 WLR 671 paras 42, 44, 65.
6 *Al-Fayed v Commissioner of Police for the Metropolis* [2004] EWCA Civ 1579 para 83(4).
7 *Tan Te Lam v Superintendent of Tai A Chau Detention Centre* [1997] AC 97, 114; *R (SK) v Secretary of State for the Home Department* [2008] EWCA Civ 1204, [2009] 1 WLR 1527 para 32 (a point not disturbed by the Supreme Court) and, since *Lumba and Mighty*, *R (MS) v AIT and Secretary of State for the Home Department* [2011] EWCA Civ 938 para 32.

Court's judgment in *Lumba and Mighty* confirms, as *Anisminic*[8] established, that there are no distinct categories of legal error. Wrongful exercise of jurisdiction, like excess of jurisdiction, renders a decision, including a decision to detain a nullity.[9] It follows that there is no principled basis for taking a different approach on burden of proof to an error of exercise of jurisdiction than to an error of excess of jurisdiction. We suggest therefore that (as the courts have on occasions held[10]) the Secretary of State for the Home Department (SSHD) bears the burden of establishing, for example, compliance with the *Hardial Singh* principles including providing specific evidence relating to the expected timescale for removal.

The executive's powers of detention must be strictly construed

32.6 As the Supreme Court reaffirmed in *Lumba and Mighty*,[11] it is an established principle that the courts should strictly and narrowly construe general statutory powers whose exercise restricts fundamental rights.

32.7 That principle has been emphasised repeatedly in the context of the administrative detention of immigrants. In *Khawaja*,[12] Lord Bridge of Harwich stated that the courts should always:

> ... regard with extreme jealousy any claim by the executive to imprison a citizen without trial and allow it only if it is allowed by the statutory language relied on.

---

8 *Anisminic Ltd v Foreign Compensation Commission* [1969] 2 AC 147, [1969] 2 WLR 163.
9 See in particular *R (Lumba and Mighty) v Secretary of State for the Home Department* [2011] UKSC 12, [2011] 2 WLR 671 per Lord Dyson para 66, Lord Kerr para 247.
10 The approach taken in *SK (Zimbabwe) v Secretary of State for the Home Department* [2008] EWCA Civ 1204, [2009] 1 WLR 1527 para 32. This point was not disturbed on appeal in the Supreme Court. See also *MI (Iraq) and AO (Iraq) v Secretary of State for the Home Department* [2010] EWHC 764 (Admin) paras 61–62; and *R (C) v Secretary of State for the Home Department* [2010] EWHC 1089 (Admin) paras 36 and 38.
11 *R (Lumba and Mighty) v Secretary of State for the Home Department* [2011] UKSC 12, [2011] 2 WLR 671 Lord Dyson at para 53.
12 [1984] AC 74, 122.

32.8 In *Re Wasfi Suleiman Mahmood*,[13] Laws J, as he then was, held:

> While of course, Parliament is entitled to confer powers of administrative detention without trial, the courts will see to it that where such a power is conferred, the statute that confers it will be strictly and narrowly construed and its operation and effect will be supervised by the court according to high standards.

32.9 The Privy Council held in *Tan Te Lam v Tai A Chau Detention Centre* that:[14]

> ... the courts ... should be slow to hold that statutory provisions authorise administrative detention for unreasonable periods or in unreasonable circumstances.[15]

The legality of a decision to detain or maintain detention is vitiated by a material public law error

32.10 A decision to detain or to maintain detention is nullified not only by a breach of statutory conditions precedent for detention but also by a material public law error.[16]

32.11 As the Supreme Court held in *Lumba and Mighty*, the test for a vitiating public law error is that 'the breach of public law must bear on and be relevant to the decision to detain';[17] 'the breach of public law duty must be material to the decision to detain and not to some other aspect of the detention and it must be capable of affecting the result- which is not the same as saying that the result would have been different had there been no breach'.[18] The Supreme Court again

---

13 [1995] Imm AR 311.
14 [1997] AC 97.
15 [1997] AC 97 at 111.
16 Mohammed-Holgate v Duke [1984] AC 437, 443; *R (Lumba and Mighty) v Secretary of State for the Home Department* [2011] UKSC 12, [2011] 2 WLR 671, see in particular Lord Dyson para 66, Lord Kerr para 247; *R (Kambadzi) v Secretary of State for the Home Department* [2011] UKSC 23, [2011] 1 WLR 1299 paras 40, 49.
17 *R (Lumba and Mighty) v Secretary of State for the Home Department* [2011] UKSC 12, [2011] 2 WLR 671 per Lord Dyson para 68, see also Lord Collins para 219 and Lord Kerr para 219.
18 *R (Lumba and Mighty) v Secretary of State for the Home Department* [2011] UKSC 12, [2011] 2 WLR 671 per Lady Hale para 207; *R (Kambadzi) v Secretary of State for the Home Department* [2011] UKSC 23, [2011] 1 WLR 1299 per Lady Hale para 69.

confirmed in *R (Kambadzi) v Secretary of State for the Home Department*[19] that this is the correct test.

32.12 Material public law errors include, but are not confined to, breaches of the *Hardial Singh* principles (discussed in chapter 33). Another example of a vitiating public law error is a breach of published detention policy[20] or the application of an unlawful detention policy[21] (where the detention policy is sufficiently closely related to the authority to detain to qualify the SSHD's discretion to detain[22]). As the Supreme Court clarified in *Kambadzi*, detention can also be rendered unlawful by a material public law error which is purely procedural (such as a failure to carry out the detention reviews required by policy).[23]

32.13 Although these have not yet been the subject of decided authority at the time of writing, other classic grounds of *Wednesbury* review, including breach of natural justice and a failure to have regard to relevant considerations, may clearly also amount to material public law errors vitiating the legality of a decision to detain.

The tort of false imprisonment is established without proof of special damage

32.14 As the Supreme Court's judgment in *Lumba and Mighty* again confirms:[24]

> Trespassory torts (such as false imprisonment) are actionable per se regardless of whether the victim suffers any harm ... By contrast, an action on the *case* (of which a claim in negligence is the paradigm example) regards damage as the essence of the wrong.

---

19 *R (Kambadzi) v Secretary of State for the Home Department* [2011] UKSC 23, [2011] 1 WLR 1299, see Lord Hope paras 41–42, Lady Hale para 69, Lord Kerr para 88.
20 *R (Lumba and Mighty) v Secretary of State for the Home Department* [2011] UKSC 12, [2011] 2 WLR 671; *R (Kambadzi) v Secretary of State for the Home Department* [2011] UKSC 23, [2011] 1 WLR 1299.
21 *R (Lumba and Mighty) v Secretary of State for the Home Department* [2011] UKSC 12, [2011] 2 WLR 671.
22 *R (Kambadzi) v Secretary of State for the Home Department* [2011] UKSC 23, [2011] 1 WLR 1299, para 51 per Lord Hope.
23 See in particular Lady Hale paras 71–72.
24 *R (Lumba and Mighty) v Secretary of State for the Home Department* [2011] UKSC 12, [2011] 2 WLR 671 Lord Dyson para 64; see also *R (Kambadzi) v Secretary of State for the Home Department* [2011] UKSC 23, [2011] 1 WLR 1299 per Lord Hope para 55.

32.15 It follows that liability may be established for false imprisonment even if the victim is unaware of being detained.[25]

32.16 This has significant consequences for the detention of infants: the SSHD does not escape liability for an otherwise unlawful detention because the detainee is so young as to be unaware of the detention.

No causation defence in liability for the detainer

32.17 Where a decision to detain is flawed by an error which has the effect of rendering the decision to detain a nullity (such as a material public law error or a breach of a statutory condition precedent) the detainer cannot escape liability for false imprisonment by showing that had the error had not been committed, the individual would inevitably have been detained lawfully in any event.

32.18 The causation issue gained prominence with the litigation around the Home Office's secret detention policy for foreign national prisoners and former prisoners (FNPs). Between circa 25 April 2006 and 9 September 2008, unknown to the courts, detainees or their lawyers, the Home Office operated an unpublished policy of detaining FNPs who had completed their criminal custodial terms on a blanket or near blanket basis. During the same period, the Home Office's published policy contained a presumption in favour of release (see the discussion in the introduction to this book). A key question that arose for the courts in the litigation around that hidden policy was whether FNPs to whom it had been applied had been unlawfully detained, notwithstanding that they would have inevitably been detained even under the lawful published policy.

32.19 As the Supreme Court held in *Lumba and Mighty*, reversing a line of erroneous authority in the lower courts,[26] there is no causation ingredient in the tort of false imprisonment.[27] It would be inimical to the rule of law for a detainer to escape the consequences of his unlawful acts by showing that he would have made the correct decision if

25 See *Murray v Ministry of Defence* [1988] 1 WLR 692 at 703A–B.
26 *SK (Zimbabwe) v Secretary of State for the Home Department* [2008] EWCA Civ 1204; *R (Abdi) and others v Secretary of State for the Home Department* [2008] EWHC 3166 (Admin); *WL and KM v Secretary of State for the Home Department* [2010] EWCA Civ 111, [2010] 1 WLR 2168; we suggest that by implication *R (Anam) v Secretary of State for the Home Department* [2010] EWCA Civ 1140 is also wrongly decided.
27 That followed from the principles that the legality of a decision to detain is vitiated by material public law error and that the tort of false imprisonment is actionable without proof of special damage.

he had put his mind to it.[28] So, in the secret policy cases, liability is established on the detainee showing that the unlawful policy was applied to him; there is no additional requirement to show that the secret policy caused the detention.

32.20   Likewise, the Supreme Court in *Kambadzi* held that a detainee whose detention was not reviewed as required by the lawful published policy is, without more, unlawfully detained. The SSHD would be liable for false imprisonment for the periods that the detention was not reviewed, notwithstanding that detention would inevitably have continued even with the requisite reviews.[29]

Material and non-material public law error

32.21   Not every public law error or even breach of statute will render detention unlawful. The error must be 'material' to the decision to detain in the sense of being 'capable of affecting the result, which is not the same as saying that the result would have been different had there been no breach'.[30] 'The essential question must be whether there is an adequate connection between compliance with the duty and the lawfulness of the detention.'[31] Where a requirement is breached or disregarded which can have no bearing on the decision to detain, such as a policy or even statutory requirement concerning detention conditions, the public law error is immaterial and the lawfulness of the detention is unaffected.[32] As Lady Hale stated in *Kambadzi*:

> A clear distinction can be drawn between a requirement which goes to whether or not a person is detained and a requirement which goes to the conditions under which a person is detained.[33]

---

28   *R (Lumba and Mighty) v Secretary of State for the Home Department* [2011] UKSC 12, [2011] 2 WLR 671, see in particular paras 62, 66, 175, 221 and 242.

29   *R (Kambadzi) v Secretary of State for the Home Department* [2011] UKSC 23, [2011] 1 WLR 1299 per Lord Hope para 54, per Lady Hale para 74, per Lord Kerr paras 88–89.

30   *R (Lumba and Mighty) v Secretary of State for the Home Department* [2011] UKSC 12, [2011] 2 WLR 671 per Lady Hale para 207; *R (Kambadzi) v Secretary of State for the Home Department* [2011] UKSC 23, [2011] 1 WLR 1299 per Lady Hale para 69.

31   *R (Kambadzi) v Secretary of State for the Home Department* [2011] UKSC 23, [2011] 1 WLR 1299 para 80 per Lord Kerr.

32   *R (Lumba and Mighty) v Secretary of State for the Home Department* [2011] UKSC 12, [2011] 2 WLR 671 per Lord Dyson para 68.

33   *R (Kambadzi) v Secretary of State for the Home Department* [2011] UKSC 23, [2011] 1 WLR 1299 per Lady Hale para 71.

An intermediary category of public law error?

32.22 Obiter dicta from Lady Hale in *Kambadzi* suggest that there is an intermediary category of public law error. Breach of certain procedural requirements, whether imposed by statute or policy, does not render the detention unlawful irrespective of whether the substantive grounds for the detention exist. In this intermediary category, causation is still relevant to liability and the detention will only be rendered unlawful if the error caused the detention. The example given by Lady Hale in *Shepherd Masimba Kambadzi*[34] was the requirement in the Detention Centre Rules 2001[35] r34 that detainees in Immigration Removal Centres (IRCs) be given a medical examination within 24 hours. This will be discussed in more detail below at paras 34.33–34.36.

32.23 We suggest that another example of an error in this intermediary category would be a failure to carry out a detention review at the correct grade. The Supreme Court has held that where the sole flaw in the detention review was that it had not been conducted at the correct grade, this was not a material public law error.[36] We suggest that where it can be shown that the failure to review at the correct grade was causative of the detention, the ensuing detention, until properly reviewed, will be unlawful.

Causation and damages

32.24 In a case concerning public law error, once liability is established, causation does go to quantum of damages. If the detainee has suffered no loss by reason of a vitiating public law error in the decision to detain, the detainee is not entitled to substantial damages in the basic award, only nominal damages (ie £1).[37] It remains an open question whether any different approach will be taken to quantum where liability arises because there was no power to detain.

---

34 *R (Kambadzi) v Secretary of State for the Home Department* [2011] UKSC 23, [2011] 1 WLR 1299, per Lady Hale paras 70–71.
35 SI No 238.
36 *R (Kambadzi) v Secretary of State for the Home Department* [2011] UKSC 23, [2011] 1 WLR 1299 per Lord Hope para 60, citing Lord Dyson in *Lumba and Mighty* at para 68.
37 *R (Lumba and Mighty) v Secretary of State for the Home Department* [2011] UKSC 12, [2011] 2 WLR 671, see in particular paras 95, 237 and 252.

32.25 Where liability has been established but the detainer seeks to escape paying substantial damages by arguing that there was an alternative lawful basis on which the detainee would have been detained, who bears the burden of proof and what standard should be applied? At the time of writing, these questions have not been expressly addressed by the Supreme Court. We discuss the role of causation in the award of damages, and decisions of the lower courts since *Lumba and Mighty*, at paras 44.9–44.15 below.

Duty to give reasons for detention

32.26 We suggest that a failure to give reasons for detention at least at the outset will, without more, render the detention unlawful until such time as reasons are given. Below, we set out the convoluted litigation history on the point.

32.27 The House of Lords in *Christie and Leachinsky*[38] found an arrest unlawful where reasons had not been given, notwithstanding that there were lawful grounds for arrest. The House of Lords in *Saadi v Secretary of State for the Home Department*[39] subsequently found that a failure to give accurate reasons to fast track immigration detainees did not affect the legality of their detention. However, *Christie and Leachinsky* does not appear to have been cited in *Saadi* and the reasons point in *Saadi* is in any event obiter.[40] *Christie and Leachinsky* remains good law and received powerful endorsement from the Supreme Court in *Lumba and Mighty*[41] and we suggest that it is this approach that must be followed in the immigration detention cases.[42] The failure to give reasons can be seen as breach of an

---

38 [1947] AC 573, see in particular Viscount Simon at 588H.
39 [2002] UKHL 41, [2002] 1 WLR 3131 per Lord Slynn para 48.
40 See discussions in *R (Lumba and Mighty) v Secretary of State for the Home Department* [2011] UKSC 12, [2011] 2 WLR 671 per Lord Dyson para 84; *R (Kambadzi) v Secretary of State for the Home Department* [2011] UKSC 23, [2011] 1 WLR 1299 per Lord Hope para 45.
41 *R (Lumba and Mighty) v Secretary of State for the Home Department* [2011] UKSC 12, [2011] 2 WLR 671 per Lord Dyson at para 76, Lord Walker at para 185, Lady Hale at paras 201 and 211, Lord Collins para 221, Lord Phillips para 327, and Lord Brown and Lord Rodger para 345. See also *R (Kambadzi) v Secretary of State for the Home Department* [2011] UKSC 23, [2011] 1 WLR 1299 per Lady Hale at paras 72–73.
42 For the application of this approach in the immigration detention context, see *R (Faulkner) v Secretary of State for the Home Department* [2005] EWHC 2567 (Admin). Note, however, that Lord Walker at in *R (Lumba and Mighty) v Secretary of State for the Home Department* [2011] UKSC 12, [2011] 2 WLR 671

implied statutory condition precedent; or as an unlawful exercise of the power to detain, it matters not which.[43]

32.28 However, the Court of Appeal stated in *R (MS) v Secretary of State for the Home Department*, citing *Saadi*, that the giving of a wrong reason did not vitiate the legality of detention.[44] The appellant in *MS* was told, correctly, that he was being held in the Detained Fast Track because his claim could be speedily decided;[45] but he was not told the true reasons why it was believed that his claim could be speedily determined[46] and while all other correspondence with the detainee referred to the Detained Fast Track, one letter then referred erroneously to a separate detention procedure.[47] We suggest that, just as in *Saadi* (see para 32.27 above) the ratio of the Court of Appeal's judgment in *MS* concerns the reasonableness of the decision to place the appellant in the Detained Fast Track (identified as 'the sole issue' in the case) rather than the giving of accurate reasons for detention.[48] The question of whether the giving of a false reason could vitiate the legality of the detention does not appear to have been argued by the appellant or SSHD[49] and there is no indication that *Christie and Leachinsky* was cited in the Court of Appeal. Just as the comments of the House of Lords in *Saadi* on the giving of reasons were obiter, as the Supreme Court subsequently confirmed,[50] so too we suggest the comments of the Court of Appeal in *MS* on the same point were obiter.

32.29 Subsequently, the Administrative Court in *R (Raed Salah Mahajna) v Secretary of State for the Home Department*[51] held detention to

para 185 distinguished *Christie and Leachinsky* from *Saadi* on the basis that the statutes governing immigration detention required no giving of reasons.

43 See discussion in *R (Lumba and Mighty) v Secretary of State for the Home Department* [2011] UKSC 12, [2011] 2 WLR 671 per Lord Dyson para 77 per Lady Hale para 201.

44 *R (MS) v AIT and Secretary of State for the Home Department* [2011] EWCA Civ 838 para 49.

45 *R (MS) v AIT and Secretary of State for the Home Department* [2011] EWCA Civ 838 paras 12, 18, 19.

46 *R (MS) v AIT and Secretary of State for the Home Department* [2011] EWCA Civ 838 para 47.

47 *R (MS) v AIT and Secretary of State for the Home Department* [2011] EWCA Civ 838 para 49.

48 *R (MS) v AIT and Secretary of State for the Home Department* [2011] EWCA Civ 838 paras 24 and 32.

49 See *R (MS) v AIT and Secretary of State for the Home Department* [2011] EWCA Civ 838 paras 25–28 summarising the arguments.

50 See footnote 40 above.

51 [2011] EWHC 2481 (Admin).

Core common law principles generally applicable to detention 621

be unlawful for the period during which no adequate reasons were given. Where the detainee was not given reasons for his detention in a language he understood, and the SSHD had not shown good reasons for that failure, this was sufficient to render the detention unlawful.[52] It was not enough to give a detainee an IS91R (reasons for detention) form in a language he did not understand.[53] Nor was the problem rectified by sending a copy of the IS91R form to the detainee's solicitors if they did not have the opportunity to translate it to him, since the knowledge of the solicitors could not be imputed to the detainee.[54] Nor was it any defence for the SSHD that the detainee had not requested the reasons for his detention: 'Neither at common law nor under the Convention is the obligation to provide this information dependent on a prior request from the detainee'.[55] It was not enough to tell the detainee the statutory power under which he was being held, nor was it enough to tell him that he was being detained for deportation: he should have been informed not just of the purpose of the detention but also the factual basis for it (in that case, because his deportation was believed to be imminent).[56] As to the content of the reasons requirement, Nicol J held in *Mahajna*:

> I accept that what is required in any particular situation is fact sensitive and dependent on all the relevant circumstances. That may influence the amount of information which can be conveyed at the point of arrest. But even so, at that point the person concerned must be told something as to why the arrest is taking place (see Lewis). What he is told must relate to the factual as well as the legal position (see Taylor) ... Rights under the common law and the Convention are intended to be real rights and confer real benefits. The Claimant was entitled to know, at least in the broadest terms, why he was being arrested.[57]

---

52 *R (Raed Salah Mahajna) v Secretary of State for the Home Department* [2011] EWHC 2481 (Admin) para 57.
53 *R (Raed Salah Mahajna) v Secretary of State for the Home Department* [2011] EWHC 2481 (Admin) para 59.
54 *R (Raed Salah Mahajna) v Secretary of State for the Home Department* [2011] EWHC 2481 (Admin) para 60.
55 *R (Raed Salah Mahajna) v Secretary of State for the Home Department* [2011] EWHC 2481 (Admin) para 59.
56 *R (Raed Salah Mahajna) v Secretary of State for the Home Department* [2011] EWHC 2481 (Admin) paras 54 and 59.
57 *R (Raed Salah Mahajna) v Secretary of State for the Home Department* [2011] EWHC 2481 (Admin) para 54. The cases referred to by Nicol J are *Lewis v Chief Constable of South Wales Constabulary* [1991] 1 All ER 206 and *Taylor v Chief Constable of Thames Valley* [2004] 1 WLR 3155, from the context of police detention.

There is no good faith defence for the detainer

32.30 False imprisonment is a tort of strict liability. Where a detention lacks lawful justification, it is no defence that the detainer acted in good faith. In *R v Governor of Brockhill Prison ex p Evans (No 2)*, the House of Lords found that where a prison governor had, in good faith and applying the law as it was then understood to be, miscalculated a prisoner's release date, the prison governor was nonetheless liable to pay damages for false imprisonment:

> Imprisonment involves the infringement of a legally protected right and therefore must be justified. If it cannot be lawfully justified, it is no defence for the defendant to say that he believed that he could justify it.[58]

Whether the Immigration Acts contain a presumption of detention

A policy of normally detaining a specified category of person is permissible

32.31 The Supreme Court in *Lumba and Mighty*[59] has, following the earlier House of Lords judgment in *R (Saadi) v Secretary of State for the Home Department*,[60] decided that the executive may lawfully adopt a policy describing a 'normal practice' of detaining a specified category of people. The issue arose in *Lumba and Mighty* because the executive had briefly, from 9 September 2008 until 22 January 2009, adopted a published policy which presumed in favour of detaining FNPs who met the criteria for deportation under Immigration Act powers post sentence completion.

Ongoing debate as to interpretation of Immigration Acts

32.32 *Lumba and Mighty* has left open the question of whether any of the statutory powers of detention under the IA 1971 themselves contain a presumption in favour of detention or are neutral.[61] The question

---

58 *R v Governor of Brockhill Prison ex p Evans (No 2)* [2001] 2 AC 19, per Lord Hobhouse at 42E–F.
59 Per Lord Dyson para 54, with whom there was no disagreement on the issue of presumption of liberty.
60 [2002] UKHL 41, [2002] 1 WLR 3131.
61 See in particular Lord Dyson at para 55.

of the correct interpretation of similarly worded provisions in the UKBA 2007[62] has also yet to be decided. Note that the question of whether there is a presumption of detention in the statute (applicable to the executive when deciding administratively whether to detain) is distinct from the question of burden of proof in legal proceedings (in which the detainer bears the burden of justifying the detention).[63]

32.33 We explain in some more detail below the convoluted recent history of litigation around the question of the correct interpretation of the detention provisions in the IA 1971.

Construction of the power to detain in court recommendation cases

32.34 The terms of IA 1971 Sch 3 para 2(1) appear on their face to create a presumption of detention for those who have been recommended for deportation by a court.[64] It had previously been held, in the immigration detention context, at High Court level, that there is no presumption of detention in the IA 1971. In *Sedrati, Buitrago-Lopez and Arangatu v Secretary of State for the Home Department*.[65] Moses J as he then was issued a declaration by consent to the effect that IA 1971 Sch 3 para 2 does not contain a presumption of detention, apparently although not explicitly reading down those provisions under the Human Rights Act 1998 s3 and European Convention on Human Rights (ECHR) article 5. *Sedrati* was then followed in other Administrative Court cases.[66]

32.35 The Administrative Court then held in *Choy* that IA 1971 Sch 3 paras 2(1) and (3) imposed a presumption of detention. The Administrative Court in Choy further held (following obiter dicta of the Court of Appeal in *WL and KM v Secretary of State for the Home Department*[67])

62 UKBA 2007 s36(2), like IA 1971 Sch 3 para 2(1) and (3) (the passage in parentheses), appears on its face to create a presumption of detention.
63 *R (Lumba and Mighty) v Secretary of State for the Home Department* [2011] UKSC 12, [2011] 2 WLR 671 per Lord Dyson paras 42–44.
64 IA 1971 Sch 3 para 2(1) provides: 'Where a recommendation for deportation made by a court is in force in respect of any person ... he shall, unless the court by which the recommendation is made ... be detained pending the making of a deportation order in pursuance of the recommendation, unless the Secretary of State directs him to be released pending further consideration of his case or he is released on bail.'
65 [2001] EWHC Admin 418.
66 *R (Vovk and Datta) v Secretary of State for the Home Department* [2006] EWHC 3386 (Admin) and *R (Abdi) v Secretary of State for the Home Department* [2008] EWHC 3166 (Admin).
67 [2010] EWCA Civ 111, [2010] 1 WLR 2168 para 88.

that a person detained after a court recommendation for deportation was excluded from claiming damages for false imprisonment.[68] We respectfully suggest that the Administrative Court's judgment in *Choy* erroneously conflates two distinct issues (the question of whether the statute creates any presumption of detention, and the question of whether the SSHD, in detaining a person in pursuit of a court recommendation is required to do so lawfully)[69]. At least as concerns the notion that those who are the subject of a court recommendation for deportation cannot claim in false imprisonment after detention under IA 1971 Sch 3 para 2(1), we suggest that *Choy* is inconsistent with *Lumba and Mighty*,[70] as are a number of other Administrative Court authorities which take the same approach. See para 32.38 below.

32.36 In *Lumba and Mighty*, Lord Dyson, giving the sole judgment of the Supreme Court on the presumption issue, held that neither ECHR article 5 nor the common law prohibited the adoption of a policy of normally detaining a certain class of person, provided that the *Hardial Singh* principles were observed, and each case was individually considered.[71] As to the statute and *Sedrati*, Lord Dyson stated:[72]

> Whatever the position may be in relation to paragraph 2(1) and the parenthesis in paragraph 2(3), paragraph 2(2) and the remainder of paragraph 2(3) do not create any presumption. They simply give the Secretary of State a discretion to detain. In relation to paragraph 2(2) and (3) therefore, so far as it goes, the declaration granted by Moses J [in *Sedrati*] is correct.

32.37 That statement of the law in *Lumba and Mighty* leaves open the question of whether the declaration in *Sedrati* (which referred to all of IA 1971 Sch 3 para 2) was correct as to those parts of the statute whose language on its face ostensibly does create a presumption of detention (that is, IA 1971 Sch 3 para 2(1) and the passage in parentheses of para 2(3)). It has been suggested at Administrative Court level since *Lumba and Mighty* that *Sedrati* is, in its entirety, still good law

---

68 *R (Choy) v Secretary of State for the Home Department* [2011] EWHC 365 (Admin) para 22.
69 A modified approach was then taken in *R (BA) v Secretary of State for the Home Department* [2011] EWHC 2748 (Admin), finding that those detained under IA 1971 Sch 3 para 2(1), were the subject of a presumption in favour of detention but could still claim in false imprisonment. See para 32.39 below.
70 *R (Lumba and Mighty) v Secretary of State for the Home Department* [2011] UKSC 12, [2011] 2 WLR 671.
71 *R (Lumba and Mighty) v Secretary of State for the Home Department* [2011] UKSC 12, [2011] 2 WLR 671 per Lord Dyson para 53.
72 Para 55.

and that IA 1971 Sch 3 para 2(1) contains no presumption in favour of detention.[73] Subsequently, Lord Kerr in *Kambadzi* referred to a presumption in favour of release.[74]

32.38 In any event, Lord Dyson's judgment in *Lumba and Mighty*[75] does clarify that, contrary to the obiter dicta of the Court below in *WL and KM*[76] no part of the IA 1971 ousts the *Hardial Singh* principles, the obligation to consider each detainee's case individually, or the entitlement to claim damages in false imprisonment.[77] We respectfully suggest that it follows that the approach taken in *Choy* is wrong in law[78] as is the approach taken in other Administrative Court cases which applied the Court of Appeal's obiter dicta from *WL and KM*.[79] It follows too that the same duties of individuated consideration and compliance with the *Hardial Singh* principles, and entitlement to damages in false imprisonment where these are breached, also apply to similarly worded detention powers in the UKBA 2007.[80]

32.39 At the time of writing, there remains conflicting Administrative Court authority on how IA 1971 Sch 3 para 2(1) should be interpreted. On one view, discussed in *Vovk and Datta v Secretary of State for the Home Department*, the statute itself at IA 1971 sch 3 para 2(1) authorises detention, but this is only for a short, bridging period following the completion of a criminal custodial term. On this analysis, the

---

73 *R (Jaswinder Singh) v Secretary of State for the Home Department* [2011] EWHC 1402 (Admin) para 13.
74 in *R (Lumba and Mighty) v Secretary of State for the Home Department* [2011] UKSC 12, [2011] 2 WLR 671, para 81.
75 See in particular para 53.
76 The Court of Appeal in *R (WL and KM) v Secretary of State for the Home Department* [2010] EWCA Civ 111, [2010] 1 WLR 2168 para 88 held, obiter, that under IA 1971 Sch 3 para 2(1), the authority for detention was provided by the criminal court's recommendation for deportation, so obviating the need for a fresh decision by the SSHD to detain.
77 See also See *R (Jaswinder Singh) v Secretary of State for the Home Department* [2011] EWHC 1402 (Admin) para 15.
78 In *R (Choy) v Secretary of State for the Home Department* [2011] EWHC 365 (Admin) para 22 Bean J, following the obiter dicta from the Court of Appeal in *WL and KM* at para 88, held that a person recommended for deportation by a criminal court was barred from claiming damages in false imprisonment not only while detained under IA 1971 Sch 3 para 2(1) but also thereafter when detained under para 2(3).
79 *R (MXL) v Secretary of State for the Home Department* [2010] EWHC 2397 (Admin), para 29; *AE Libya* [2011] EWHC 154 (Admin) paras 104–105; *R (Rangwani) v Secretary of State for the Home Department* [2011] EWHC 516 (Admin) para 51 (obiter); *R (Solomon) v Secretary of State for the Home Department* [2011] EWHC 3075 (Admin) paras 38–42.
80 UKBA 2007 s36(2).

purpose of the bridging provision is to ensure that those who are subject to a court recommendation for deportation are not released where there is no, or only a minimal, period of imprisonment to be served after the imposition of the sentence and court recommendation for deportation, for example, where a sentence is deemed served because of the period in remand. After that short bridging period, the SSHD must authorise continued detention.[81] Similarly, Collins J held in *R (Jaswinder Singh) v Secretary of State for the Home Department* that the requirement for authority to detain from the SSHD is an implied term of that statutory detention power.[82] A different approach was then taken in *R (BA) v Secretary of State for the Home Department*. In that case, the Administrative Court found that there was a statutory 'duty to detain' in court recommendation cases under IA 1971 Sch 3 para 2(1), but that this was subject to a discretion for the SSHD as to whether to release. The 'statutory warrant for detention' would be 'destroyed' by a failure to comply with the *Hardial Singh* principles, in which case the tort of false imprisonment would be made out and damages would be available.[83]

32.40 However, the Administrative Court went on to hold in *R (BA) v Secretary of State for the Home Department* that a policy breach could not give rise to the tort of false imprisonment in a case of detention pursuant to a court recommendation for deportation. The court considered that a policy breach did not, unlike a breach of the *Hardial Singh* principles, undermine the 'statutory warrant for detention'.[84] We respectfully suggest that *BA* is incorrectly decided at least insofar as concerns the effect of a policy breach in an IA 1971 Sch 3 para 2(1) case. The reasoning in *BA* is difficult because a) breach of the *Hardial Singh* principles is a form of public law error[85] and there is no principled reason why another form of public law error such as

---

81 *R (Vovk and Datta) v Secretary of State for the Home Department* [2006] EWHC 3386 (Admin).

82 *R (Jaswinder Singh) v Secretary of State for the Home Department* [2011] EWHC 1402 (Admin) para 15 where Collins J considered that for detention under IA 1971 Sch 3 para 2(1) there had to be 'a positive decision by the Secretary of State that steps will be taken to follow up the recommendation and to put it into effect'.

83 *R (BA) v Secretary of State for the Home Department* [2011] EWHC 2748 (Admin) paras 131–142, 148–149, 157.

84 *R (BA) v Secretary of State for the Home Department* [2011] EWHC 2748 (Admin) paras 157, 206.

85 See the discussion in *R (Lumba and Mighty) v Secretary of State for the Home Department* [2011] UKSC 12, [2011] 2 WLR 671, per Lord Dyson para 30, per Lady Hale paras 198–199, Lord Kerr para 248.

a breach of policy should not have the same effect; b) *Lumba and Mighty* and *Kambadzi* are high authority that compliance with public law duties, including the duty to comply with published detention policy absent good reason for deviating from it, may be treated as statutory condition precedents for the executive's exercise of detention powers or the exercise of the discretion to release;[86] c) if there is an implied statutory duty for the SSHD to consider release in all court recommendation cases, it is unclear why, applying the principle of strict construction of executive detention powers, a failure to exercise that duty properly or at all should not vitiate the 'statutory warrant to detain'.

The courts' role when assessing the lawfulness of administrative detention

32.41 When assessing the lawfulness of an administrative detention undeer the *Hardial Singh* principles, the court acts as primary decision-maker. That is, when hearing challenges to the lawfulness of a detention (whether the claim is brought by way of private law action, application for habeas corpus, or claim for judicial review) the court *does not* exercise a supervisory, review function (of assessing whether the SSHD's decision to detain was within a range of reasonable responses) but rather forms its own judgment of the lawfulness of the detention.[87] However, this does not absolve the court of its duty to supervise the detainer's decison-making and its compliance with other public law requirements, as the judgments in *Lumba and Mighty* and *Kambadzi* both demonstrate.

32.42 However, on matters on which the SSHD has special expertise, in particular the assessment of progress of negotiations with a foreign government, the court will be slow to second-guess the SSHD's views.[88]

---

86 See in particular *R (Kambadzi) v Secretary of State for the Home Department* [2011] UKSC 23, [2011] 1 WLR 1299 paras 71–73.

87 *Youssef v Home Office* [2004] EWHC 1884 (QB) at para 62; *R (A) v Secretary of State for the Home Department* [2007] EWCA Civ 804 at paras 62 and 71–72.

88 *R (MH) v Secretary of State for the Home Department* [2010] EWCA Civ 1112 at para 67; *R (NXT) v Secretary of State for the Home Department* [2011] EWHC 969 (Admin) para 113. An example in which the court did 'second guess' the Home Office's view on the progress of negotiations is *Youssef v the Home Office* [2004] EWHC 1884 (QB).

32.43 When hearing an appeal in a detention challenge, where no oral evidence was heard in the court below, the Court of Appeal is entitled to decide the legality of the detention for itself rather than limiting itself to the traditional appellate role. Where the impugned detention is ongoing, the Court of Appeal is entitled to consider up to date facts and evidence[89] and may dispense with the need for a fresh application for habeas corpus.[90] However, this will not always be appropriate.[91]

---

89 *R (Lumba and Mighty) v Secretary of State for the Home Department* [2011] UKSC 12, [2011] 2 WLR 671 para 145 per Lord Dyson.

90 *Tan Te Lam and others v Superintendent of Tai A Chau Detention Centre* [1997] AC 97 at 116; *R (I) v Secretary of State for the Home Department* [2002] EWCA Civ 888; [2003] INLR 196 at para 25; *R (M) v Secretary of State for the Home Department* [2008] EWCA Civ 307, paras 15, 19; *AS (Sudan) v Secretary of State for the Home Department* at para 7.

91 *R (Lumba and Mighty) v Secretary of State for the Home Department* [2011] UKSC 12, [2011] 2 WLR 671 para 145 per Lord Dyson.

CHAPTER 33

The *Hardial Singh* principles

33.1	Introduction
33.3	**The landmark case and the four principles**
33.5	First *Hardial Singh* principle: detention must not be used for any purpose other than that for which the statutory power is given
33.9	Second *Hardial Singh* principle: detention should not exceed the period that is reasonable
33.14	Third *Hardial Singh* principle: there must be a realistic prospect of expulsion within a reasonable period
33.18	Fourth *Hardial Singh* principle: the Home Office must exercise reasonable diligence and expedition in effecting removal
33.19	**Factors bearing on the reasonable duration of detention for *Hardial Singh* purposes**
33.20	Offending risk and the Court of Appeal's judgment in (A) Somalia
33.23	Absconding risk
33.27	Time spent in detention pursuing challenges to expulsion
33.29	A detainee's refusal to repatriate voluntarily
33.35	Other forms of non-co-operation by a detainee
33.43	Mental illness
33.47	Serious medical conditions generally
33.48	Disability
33.49	Previous refusals of bail

Introduction

33.1 In *R v Governor of Durham Prison ex p Hardial Singh*,[1] guiding principles were set out for the lawful exercise[2] of the executive's power to detain for expulsion. In essence, *Hardial Singh* held that:

> ... such detention was permissible only for such time as was reasonably necessary for the process of deportation to be carried out. Thus there was no warrant for the long-term or indefinite detention of a non-UK national whom the Home Secretary wished to remove.[3]

Although the *Hardial Singh* principles were developed in the context of detention for deportation under the Immigration Act (IA) 1971 Sch 3, they are equally applicable in the context of detention for administrative removal under IA 1971 Sch 2.[4] And, as discussed at para 31.27, these principles also apply, with minor modification, to detention for 'automatic' deportation under UKBA 2007 s36.

33.2 In this chapter, we first provide an overview of the principles themselves before discussing in more detail specific factors which may affect the assessment of the reasonable period for detention.

The landmark case and the four principles

33.3 *Hardial Singh*[5] concerned a burglar, sentenced to a total of two years' imprisonment, and who had been administratively detained for just under five months. He had previously absconded from prison. Negotiations over travel documentation had been fruitless through no fault of the detainee's. Woolf J as he then was found that the claimant should be released unless it could be shown that he was due to be deported 'within a very short time indeed'.

---

1 [1984] 1 WLR 704.
2 *Khadir* [2005] UKHL 39, [2006] 1 AC 207, described the *Hardial Singh* line of authority as concerning the exercise of the power to detain rather than its existence per Lord Simon Brown para 33. But see Lord Kerr's analysis in *R (Kambadzi) v Secretary of State for the Home Department* [2011] UKSC 23, [2011] 1 WLR 1299 para 83, viewing the *Hardial Singh* principles as an implied limitation on the statutory power to detain.
3 Lord Bingham's summary, *A and others v Secretary of State for the Home Department* ('the Belmarsh case') [2004] UKHL 56, [2005] 2 AC 68 para 8.
4 See, for example, *R (S, C and D) v Secretary of State for the Home Department* [2007] EWHC 1654 (Admin).
5 [1984] 1 WLR 704.

33.4   The *Hardial Singh* principles have been approved at the highest level[6] including by the Supreme Court in *Lumba and Mighty*.[7] These principles were authoritatively distilled by Dyson LJ, as he then was, in *R (I) v Secretary of State for the Home Department*,[8] in a summary which received emphatic endorsement in *Lumba and Mighty*[9] as follows:

> (i) The Secretary of State must intend to deport the person and can only use the power to detain for that purpose;
> (ii) The deportee may only be detained for a period that is reasonable in all the circumstances;
> (iii) If, before the expiry of the reasonable period, it becomes apparent that the Secretary of State will not be able to effect deportation within that reasonable period, he should not seek to exercise the power of detention;
> (iv) The Secretary of State should act with the reasonable diligence and expedition to effect removal.

Principles (ii) and (iii) are conceptually different ... there may be circumstances where, although a reasonable period has not yet expired, it becomes clear that the Secretary of State will not be able to deport the detained person within a reasonable period. In that event, principle (iii) applies.

First *Hardial Singh* principle: detention must not be used for any purpose other than that for which the statutory power is given

33.5   The purpose of the power to detain under IA 1971 Sch 3 is 'to enable the machinery of deportation to be carried out',[10] that is to enable

---

6 *Tan Te Lam v Tai A Chau Detention Centre* [1997] AC 97; *A and others v Secretary of State for the Home Department* [2004] UKHL 56, [2005] 2 AC 68, para 8; *R (Khadir) v Secretary of State for the Home Department* [2005] UKHL 39, [2006] 1 AC 207 para 33.

7 *R (Lumba and Mighty) v Secretary of State for the Home Department* [2011] UKSC 12, [2011] 2 WLR 671, Lord Dyson para 25, Lord Hope para 171, Lord Walker para 189, Lady Hale para 198, Lord Kerr para 250, implicitly Lord Collins at para 219, Lord Brown and Lord Rodger para 362 and, albeit with disagreement as to their scope, Lord Phillips at para 261.

8 [2002] EWCA Civ 888, [2003] INLR 196, paras 46–47.

9 *R (Lumba and Mighty) v Secretary of State for the Home Department* [2011] UKSC 12, [2011] 2 WLR 671 paras 25, 102, 171, 189. See also *R (Kambadzi) v Secretary of State for the Home Department* [2011] UKSC 23, [2011] 1 WLR 1299 para 12.

10 *R v Governor of Durham Prison ex p Hardial Singh* [1984] 1 WLR 704, 706D; see also *R (Lumba and Mighty) v Secretary of State for the Home Department* [2011] UKSC 12, [2011] 2 WLR 671 per Lord Dyson at para 24, per Lord Hope at paras 172 and 174, per Lady Hale para 198.

the making of a deportation order[11] and then the enforcement of the deportation order.[12]

33.6 By analogy, the power to detain under UKBA 2007 s36(1)(a) can only be used where the Secretary of State intends to deport and for the purposes of examining whether one of the exceptions in UKBA 2007 s33 applies;[13] and the powers of detention under section 36(1)(b) and (2) can only be used for the purposes of making and enforcing the deportation order respectively.

33.7 Detention cannot be used for a unlawful collateral purpose. It is unlawful to detain, for example, solely:

- to secure a detainee's attendance as a witness in a coming trial;[14]
- to prevent a suicidal detainee from harming himself on release;[15]
- to investigate whether arrangements can be made for the detainee's transfer into detention in the country to which he is being deported;[16] or
- to deprive the detainee of access to legal advice and to the courts before expulsion.[17]

33.8 There is controversy as to whether the prevention of offending is a lawful purpose of immigration detention. In *Lumba and Mighty*,[18] Lord Phillips, dissenting alone on this point, suggested that if offending risk could be the determinant factor in how long it was reasonable to detain a foreign national prisoner (FNP), why should it not be the determinant, even sole reason, for detaining him in the first place?[19] Lord Phillips considered that while deportation was pending, it was lawful to detain an FNP to prevent re-offending or because he would pose a security risk if at large.[20] The other members of the

11 Where a person is detained under IA 1971 Sch 3 paras 2(1) or (2).
12 Where a person is detained under IA 1971 Sch 3 para 2(3).
13 *Rashid Hussein v Secretary of State for the Home Department* [2009] EWHC 2492 (Admin) para 44(i).
14 *R (Asghar and another) v Governor of Richmond Remand Centre* [1971] 1 WLR 129.
15 *R (AA) v Secretary of State for the Home Department* [2010] EWHC 2265 (Admin) para 40.
16 *R (HXA) v Secretary of State for the Home Department* [2010] EWHC 1177 (QB).
17 *R (Karas and Miladinovic) v Secretary of State for the Home Department* [2006] EWHC 747 (Admin) para 81.
18 *R (Lumba and Mighty) v Secretary of State for the Home Department* [2011] UKSC 12, [2011] 2 WLR 671.
19 *R (Lumba and Mighty) v Secretary of State for the Home Department* [2011] UKSC 12, [2011] 2 WLR 671 per Lord Phillips para 282.
20 *R (Lumba and Mighty) v Secretary of State for the Home Department* [2011] UKSC 12, [2011] 2 WLR 671 para 284.

Supreme Court robustly rejected Lord Phillips's proposed approach as an impermissible extension of the *Hardial Singh* principles and of the statutory purpose of detention.[21] However, when addressing the relevance of offending risk to the permissible duration of detention, Lord Dyson went on to state that the detention power could be construed broadly as a power which could be exercised to further the objects of deportation, that is public protection.[22] We suggest that these comments by Lord Dyson were directed to the second *Hardial Singh* principle, the relevance of offending risk to the reasonable duration of detention, and did not detract from the majority's emphatic rejection of the notion that, when interpreting the first *Hardial Singh* principle, detention could be effected for the sole or primary purpose of public protection. In *R (Raed Salah Mahajna) v Secretary of State for the Home Department*,[23] however, the Administrative Court held that offending risk was a permissible purpose of deportation where the Secretary of State for the Home Department (SSHD) still intended to deport. We respectfully suggest that the Administrative Court's conclusions on this point in *Mahajna* are difficult to differentiate from Lord Phillips' position, which was rejected by the majority in *Lumba and Mighty*.

Second *Hardial Singh* principle: detention should not exceed the period that is reasonable

33.9 There are no hard-edged rules as to how long is too long for detention: the reasonable duration of detention is fact-specific,[24] although this does not mean that useful guidance cannot be derived from earlier cases.[25] At High Court level, it has at times been suggested that certain cases were approaching the outer limits of the permissible

---

21 *R (Lumba and Mighty) v Secretary of State for the Home Department* [2011] UKSC 12, [2011] 2 WLR 671 paras 23 and 25 per Lord Dyson, paras 173–174 (with whose judgment Lord Brown and Lord Rodger agreed, para 362) ; per Lord Hope; per Lady Hale at para 198, per Lord Kerr at para 250.
22 *R (Lumba and Mighty) v Secretary of State for the Home Department* [2011] UKSC 12, [2011] 2 WLR 671 paras 106–109.
23 [2011] EWHC 2481 (Admin) paras 34–35.
24 *R (Davies) v Secretary of State for the Home Department* [2010] EWHC 2656 (Admin) para 45; *R (NAB) v Secretary of State for the Home Department* [2010] EWHC 3137 (Admin) para 78.
25 *R (Sino) v Secretary of State for the Home Department* [2011] EWHC 2249 (Admin) paras 59–60.

period.[26] Elsewhere, the Court of Appeal has held similar or longer periods of detention to be lawful, although, as we discuss further below, some of the latter authorities should be approached with caution because of the erroneous approach taken to a refusal of voluntary repatriation.[27]

33.10 With that caveat as to the fact-specificity of permissible periods of detention, there has been notable 'inflation' in periods of detention found reasonable since the earlier cases. See the facts of *Hardial Singh* at para 33.3 above. In *Re Wasfi Suleman Mahmod*,[28] in which Laws J, as he then was, granted a writ of habeas corpus to a convicted drugs offender who had been sentenced to four years' imprisonment and had thereafter been administratively detained for ten months awaiting deportation. In *R (I) v Secretary of State for the Home Department*, the detention for 17 months of a convicted sex offender was found to have exceeded the reasonable period. More recently, considerably longer periods of detention have been found lawful.[29]

33.11 In *R (I) v Secretary of State for the Home Department*, Dyson LJ as he then was set out a non-exhaustive list of factors relevant to the assessment of the reasonable period.[30] He subsequently cited this passage with approval in *Lumba and Mighty*:[31]

> ... the length of the detention; the nature of the obstacles standing in the path of the SSHD preventing a deportation; the diligence, speed and effectiveness of the steps taken by the SSHD to surmount such obstacles; the conditions in which the detained person is being kept;

---

26 In *R (Bashir) v Secretary of State for the Home Department* [2007] EWHC 3017 (Admin) para 21, Mitting J held that: '23 months on any view must be at or near to the top of the period during which detention can lawfully occur'. In *R (Wang) v Secretary of State for the Home Department* [2009] EWHC 1578 (Admin) para 27, Mitting J stated that a 30-month detention was 'right at the outer limit of the period of detention which can be justified on *Hardial Singh* principles except in the case of someone who has in the past committed very serious offences and who may go on to commit further offences or who poses a risk to national security'.

27 *R (A) Somalia v Secretary of State for the Home Department* [2007] EWCA Civ 804, (2007) *Times* 5 September, finding lawful a period of three years and ten months for a child rapist. This is arguably no longer good law – see discussion at para 33.21 below. See also *R (MH) v Secretary of State for the Home Department* [2010] EWCA Civ 1112 upholding the judgment of the Administrative Court finding a detention of 38 months lawful for a recidivist offender.

28 [1995] Imm AR 311.

29 See footnote 27 above.

30 [2002] EWCA Civ 888, [2003] INLR 196 para 48.

31 *R (Lumba and Mighty) v Secretary of State for the Home Department* [2011] UKSC 12, [2011] 2 WLR 671 paras 104–105.

the effect of the detention on him and his family; the risk that if he is released from detention he will abscond; and the danger that, if he is released, he will commit criminal offences.

33.12 The Immigration and Asylum Chamber of the First-tier Tribunal (FTT-IAC) has meanwhile issued guidance to immigration judges determining bail applications which is of some relevance in challenges in the higher courts to the legality of detention:

> Each case turns on its own facts and must be decided in light of its particular circumstances. However, it is generally accepted that detention for three months would be considered a substantial period of time and six months a long period. Imperative considerations of public safety may be necessary to justify detention in excess of six months.[32]

33.13 Further below, at paras 33.19–33.49, we discuss factors relevant to the assessment of the reasonable period (whether one is considering a historic period of detention under the second *Hardial Singh* principle or considering prospectively whether there is a realistic prospect of expulsion within a reasonable period under the third *Hardial Singh* principle).

Third *Hardial Singh* principle: there must be a realistic prospect of expulsion within a reasonable period

33.14 There may be situations where, although the reasonable period for detention has not yet expired, it becomes clear that the SSHD will not be able to deport the detained person within a period that is reasonable in all the circumstances, having regard in particular to the time that the person has already spent in detention.[33] Once it becomes clear that there is no realistic prospect that deportation will take place within a reasonable time, continued detention is unlawful.[34]

33.15 The question of the requisite degree of certainty, if any, over prospects of future expulsion remains to be settled. In certain cases both at High Court and Court of Appeal level, detention has been found

---

32 Bail Guidance for Immigration Judges, Presidential Guidance Note No 1 of 2011 FTT-IAC 11 July 2011 para 18.
33 *R (Lumba and Mighty) v Secretary of State for the Home Department* [2011] UKSC 12, [2011] 2 WLR 671 per Lord Dyson at para 103; *R (I) v Secretary of State for the Home Department* per Dyson LJ para 47.
34 *R (Lumba and Mighty) v Secretary of State for the Home Department* [2011] UKSC 12, [2011] 2 WLR 671 per Lord Dyson para 103.

to have become unlawful for want of a timescale for expulsion;[35] in others, detention has been found lawful notwithstanding the lack of any timescale for expulsion.[36]

33.16 In cases decided before *Lumba and Mighty*, the Court of Appeal has indicated that there is a sliding scale, with those detainees who pose higher risks of offending or expulsion requiring lesser prospects of removal (or no certain prospects of expulsion at all) to justify continued detention.[37] In *R (MH) v Secretary of State for the Home Department*,[38] the Court of Appeal held that:

> There can, however, be a realistic prospect of removal without it being possible to specify or predict the date by which, or period within which, removal can reasonably be expected to occur and without any certainty that removal will occur at all.

33.17 We suggest that it is a logical corollary of the requirement that expulsion occur within a reasonable period that there must always be a predicted period within which expulsion can be effected. This approach has been taken in certain cases in the Administrative Court[39] and

---

35 *R (I) v Secretary of State for the Home Department* [2002] EWCA Civ 888; *R (A, MA, B, ME) v Secretary of State for the Home Department* [2007] EWHC 142 (Admin); *R (Bashir) v Secretary of State for the Home Department* [2007] EWHC 3017 (Admin); *R (IO) v Secretary of State for the Home Department* [2008] EWHC 2596 (Admin); *R (MA and TT) v Secretary of State for the Home Department* [2010] EWHC 2350 (Admin).

36 *A (Somalia) v Secretary of State for the Home Department* [2007] EWCA Civ 804, but see Keene LJ at para 82; *R (M) v Secretary of State for the Home Department* [2008] EWCA Civ 307; *R (MH) v Secretary of State for the Home Department* [2010] EWCA Civ 1112 para 65; *R (MMH) v Secretary of State for the Home Department* [2007] EWHC 2134 (Admin); *R (Qaderi) v Secretary of State for the Home Department* [2008] EWHC 1033 (Admin); *R (MM) v Secretary of State for the Home Department* [2010] EWHC 3288 (Admin).

37 *A (Somalia) v Secretary of State for the Home Department* [2007] EWCA Civ 804 para 45 per Toulson LJ and para 82 per Keene LJ; *R (MH) v Secretary of State for the Home Department* [2010] EWCA Civ 1112 paras 64 and 65; *R (Sino) v Secretary of State for the Home Department* [2011] EWHC 2249 (Admin) para 65.

38 [2010] EWCA Civ 1112 para 65, per Richards LJ, with whom Etherton and Longmore LJJ agreed.

39 '[F]or continued detention to be lawful, two questions have to be capable of being answered. First, by when does the Secretary of State expect to be able to deport A? Secondly, what is the basis for that expectation?' *R (A, MA, B, ME) v Secretary of State for the Home Department* [2007] EWHC 142 (Admin) para 16, followed in *R (IO) v Secretary of State for the Home Department* [2008] EWHC 2596 (Admin) para 48 where detainee was released because there was 'an uncertain expectation rather than a reasonable expectation of being able to deport the claimant'. Followed also in *R (Jammeh) v Secretary of State for the Home Department* [2010] EWHC 1091 (Admin) para 31. But see the

now finds support in recent dicta in *Lumba and Mighty*, where Lord Dyson stated that in the *Hardial Singh* assessment:

> A convenient starting point is to determine whether, and if so when, there is a realistic prospect that deportation will occur.[40]

Fourth *Hardial Singh* principle: the Home Office must exercise reasonable diligence and expedition in effecting removal

33.18 Undue delay by the Home Office in taking steps towards deportation may render detention unlawful.[41] Dilatory conduct by the Home Office will militate still more strongly in favour of release where it is known that a detainee's health is being adversely affected.[42] Delays by the Home Office are also commonly treated as a further factor bearing on the reasonable duration of detention. See the passage from *R (I) v Secretary of State for the Home Department* cited at para 33.11 above.[43] The Administrative Court has also observed that:

> ... an earlier failure to act with reasonable diligence and expedition may well mean that it is reasonable to expect that the Secretary of State should act thereafter with greater diligence and expedition than she might otherwise reasonably be expected to do. Thus, even if that failure does not itself make detention unlawful subsequently, it may affect what a reasonable period in such a case would be.[44]

---

interpretation of that paragraph by the Court of Appeal in *R (MH) v Secretary of State for the Home Department* [2010] EWCA Civ 1112 para 65.

40 *R (Lumba and Mighty) v Secretary of State for the Home Department* [2011] UKSC 12, [2011] 2 WLR 671 per Lord Dyson para 103. For Administrative Court authority on the point since *Lumba and Mighty* see *R (Mounir Raki) v Secretary of State for the Home Department* [2011] EWHC 2421 (Admin) para 44, where the Administrative Court found detention unlawful in the absence of 'substantial or compelling evidence as to (a) the prospect of deportation occurring at all or (b) the timespan for removal'.

41 See, for example, *R (NAB) v Secretary of State for the Home Department* [2010] EWHC 3137 (Admin) para 76; *R (Belmihoub) v Secretary of State for the Home Department* [2011] EWHC 2044 (Admin); *R v Special Adjudicator and Secretary of State for the Home Department ex p B* [1998] Imm AR 182, [1998] INLR 315.

42 *R (Belmihoub) v Secretary of State for the Home Department* [2011] EWHC 2044 (Admin) paras 67–69.

43 See also *R (Kambadzi) v Secretary of State for the Home Department* [2011] UKSC 23, [2011] 1 WLR 1299, obiter dicta of Lady Hale at para 64: 'if the Secretary of State is dragging his feet then the period may become unreasonable'.

44 *R (Sino) v Secretary of State for the Home Department* [2011] EWHC 2249 (Admin) para 69.

Factors bearing on the reasonable duration of detention for *Hardial Singh* purposes

33.19 Below, we look at specific factors which bear on the assessment of the reasonable period (for the purposes of the second and third *Hardial Singh* principles).

Offending risk and the Court of Appeal's judgment in (A) Somalia

33.20 The risk that a detainee will re-offend if released, and the gravity of any reoffending, is relevant to the assessment of the reasonable duration of detention. The Court of Appeal has repeatedly so held[45] and the Supreme Court reaffirmed the point in *Lumba and Mighty*.[46]

33.21 The Court of Appeal's judgment in *A (Somalia)*[47] marked a watershed in the courts' approach to long-term immigration detention for deportation in criminal cases, particularly those involving serious reoffending risks. But we respectfully suggest that *A (Somalia)* should be treated with caution in light of the clarification of the law provided by *Lumba and Mighty*. *A (Somalia)* concerned a Somali national who had previously been sentenced to eight years' imprisonment for the rape and indecent assault of a 13-year-old girl. The appellant posed a high risk of further sexual offending if released. He had refused to sign a document to the effect that he was prepared to return to Somalia voluntarily. By the time his case came before the Court of Appeal, A had been in immigration detention for three years and ten months after the completion of his criminal custodial term. For just over 19 months of that period, there had been no prospect of enforced removal to Somalia. The Court of Appeal held that the claimant had been lawfully detained throughout. The two critical issues in the Court of Appeal's judgment were the risk of further offending, and the claimant's refusal to accept voluntary repatriation to Somalia. However, as is discussed below at paras 33.29–33.34, the Supreme Court in *Lumba and Mighty* subsequently clarified that one of those two core issues – a refusal voluntarily to repatriate – is of

---

45 *R (I) v Secretary of State for the Home Department* [2002] EWCA Civ 888, [2003] INLR 196 paras 29 and 53; *R (A) Somalia v Secretary of State for the Home Department* [2007] EWCA Civ 804, (2007) *Times* 5 September paras 55, 82; *R (M) v Secretary of State for the Home Department* [2008] EWCA Civ 307 paras 14, 37.
46 *R (Lumba and Mighty) v Secretary of State for the Home Department* [2011] UKSC 12, [2011] 2 WLR 671 per Lord Dyson, paras 108–110 and 121.
47 [2007] EWCA Civ 804, (2007) *Times* 5 September.

limited relevance per se, if any.[48] It is therefore arguable that *(A) Somalia* would now be decided differently.

33.22 In any event, offending risk does not justify indefinite detention.[49] The courts have found that the permissible period of detention has been exceeded (or that detention was no lawful in light of the lack of a reasonable timescale for expulsion) even for recidivist or serious criminal offenders[50] and for suspected international terrorists.[51]

Absconding risk

33.23 The risk that a detainee would abscond if released is also relevant to the assessment of the reasonable period of detention. The Court of Appeal so held.[52] The Supreme Court in *Lumba and Mighty* again confirmed the importance of absconding risk: absconding would frustrate the purpose of the detention power of effecting deportation.[53]

---

48 Per Lord Dyson at para 127.
49 See, in the context of suspected international terrorists, *A and others v Secretary of State for the Home Department* [2004] UKHL 56, [2005] 2 AC 68, Lord Bingham para 8.
50 See *R (Abdi) v Secretary of State for the Home Department* [2011] EWCA Civ 242 in which the Court of Appeal considered detention of a serial offender (whose offences included indecent assault, robbery, burglary, assault on a police officer and a drugs offence – see the first instance judgment of Davis J in *R (Abdi) v Secretary of State for the Home Department* [2009] EWHC 1324 (Admin) ('Abdi 2')). The detention was found to have become unlawful after 24 months because there was no realistic prospect of removal within a reasonable period. See also *R (H) v Secretary of State for the Home Department* [2005] EWHC 1702 (Admin) in which the High Court found that a man who had raped a minor and who had spent two years and four months in immigration detention had been detained for an unreasonably long period and must be released.
51 In *Youssef and the Home Office* [2004] EWHC 1884 (QB) the detention of a suspected international terrorist was found to have become unlawful after ten months, by which time, in the light of fruitless negotiations with the Egyptian authorities, it should have been clear that there was no realistic prospect of deportation. See also note 49 above. By contrast, see *R (Q) v Secretary of State for the Home Department and Governor of HMP Long Lartin* [2006] EWHC 2690 (Admin) in which the Divisional Court declined to grant an order for the release of a suspected international terrorist who had been held for 14 months in immigration detention, having regard, among other points, to the national security risks posed if release were granted, and also to the 'real possibility' in that case of an early resolution to the problem of travel documentation.
52 *R (I) v Secretary of State for the Home Department* paras 29 and 48 ; *R (A) Somalia v Secretary of State for the Home Department* [2007] EWCA Civ 804, (2001) *Times* 5 September paras 54 and 82; *R (M) v Secretary of State for the Home Department* [2008] EWCA Civ 307 para 14, 37.
53 *R (Lumba and Mighty) v Secretary of State for the Home Department* [2011] UKSC 12, [2011] 2 WLR 671 per Lord Dyson para 121.

33.24 However, absconding risk is also not a trump card. In a passage which he subsequently cited with apparent approval in *Lumba and Mighty* in the Supreme Court[54] Dyson LJ as he then was warned in *R (I) v Secretary of State for the Home Department* that:

> ... the relevance of the likelihood of absconding, if proved, should not be overstated. Carried to its logical conclusion it could become a trump card that carried the day for the Secretary of State in every case where such a risk was made out regardless of all other considerations, not least the length of the period of detention. That would be a wholly unacceptable outcome where human liberty is at stake.

33.25 In short, as Dyson LJ stated in *R (M) v Secretary of State for the Home Department*:[55]

> However grave the risk of absconding and re-offending, there must come a time when it can no longer be said that detention is reasonable.

33.26 The courts have therefore been willing to order the release of those posing a significant risk of absconding on grounds that their detention had exceeded the reasonable period.[56]

Time spent in detention pursuing challenges to expulsion

33.27 There is no exclusionary rule by which periods spent in detention during the pursuit of legal challenges to expulsion, should be excluded from consideration for *Hardial Singh* purposes.[57] The question of the

---

54 *R (Lumba and Mighty) v Secretary of State for the Home Department* [2011] UKSC 12, [2011] 2 WLR 671 per Lord Dyson para 123.
55 *R (M) v Secretary of State for the Home Department* [2008] EWCA Civ 307 para 37.
56 See, for example, *R (Wang) v Secretary of State for the Home Department* [2009] EWHC 1578 (Admin); *R (Daq) v Secretary of State for the Home Department* [2009] EWHC 1655 (Admin); *R (A, MA, B, ME) v Secretary of State for the Home Department* [2007] EWHC 142 (Admin); *R (Bashir) v Secretary of State for the Home Department* [2007] EWHC 3017 (Admin). See also facts of *Hardial Singh* itself (in which the applicant had previously absconded from prison); likewise *R (S) v Secretary of State for the Home Department* [2011] EWHC 2120 (Admin) in which the applicant succeeded in his detention challenge despite having previously absconded.
57 The Court of Appeal and Supreme Court decisively rejected such an exclusionary rule in two judgments handed down in quick succession (and which do not therefore refer to each other): *R (Abdi) v Secretary of State for the Home Department* [2011] EWCA Civ 242 paras 40–46; and *R (Lumba and Mighty) v Secretary of State for the Home Department* [2011] UKSC 12, [2011]

approach to be taken to time spent detained while pursuing appeals is fact sensitive and a question of weight rather than any hard-edged exclusionary rule.[58] Much more weight should be given to detention during a period when a detained person is pursuing a meritorious appeal than to detention during a period when a hopeless appeal is being pursued.[59] Minimal weight will be attached to periods spent detained while pursing 'a hopeless' appeal.[60] Where a claim has been certified, this is an indication on its face that it is unmeritorious while orders for reconsideration or a grant of permission to the Court of Appeal are indicative of merit.[61]

33.28 The duty of the SSHD to consider whether deportation can be effected within a reasonable period exists from the outset of detention, not merely from the date on which appeal rights are exhausted.[62] Detention may become unlawful because there is no realistic prospect of expulsion within a reasonable period, where the sole reason for the delay in expulsion is that the detainee's actual or likely legal challenges. That is the case whether the detainee is pursuing appeals or a judicial review or has obtained a rule 39 interim measure from the European Court of Human Rights (ECtHR)[63] prohibiting his expulsion, or even that he would inevitably obtain such an

---

2 WLR 671 per Lord Dyson paras 115–121. Both the Court of Appeal in *Abdi* (para 45) and the Supreme Court in *Lumba and Mighty* (paras 115 and 121) approved the approach taken by Davis J at first instance in *R (Abdi) v Secretary of State for the Home Department* [2009] EWHC 1324 (Admin) ('*Abdi 2*').

58 *R (Lumba and Mighty) v Secretary of State for the Home Department* [2011] UKSC 12, [2011] 2 WLR 671 para 121; *R (Abdi) v Secretary of State for the Home Department* [2011] EWCA Civ 242 para 44.

59 *R (Lumba and Mighty) v Secretary of State for the Home Department* [2011] UKSC 12, [2011] 2 WLR 671 para 121, *R (Abdi) v Secretary of State for the Home Department* [2011] EWCA Civ 242 para 44.

60 *R (Lumba and Mighty) v Secretary of State for the Home Department* [2011] UKSC 12, [2011] 2 WLR 671 para 121; *R (M) v Secretary of State for the Home Department* [2008] EWCA Civ 307 para 31; *AS (Sudan) v Secretary of State for the Home Department* [2009] EWCA Civ 1518 para 15.

61 *R (Lumba and Mighty) v Secretary of State for the Home Department* [2011] UKSC 12, [2011] 2 WLR 671 para 120.

62 *R (HXA) v Secretary of State for the Home Department* [2010] EWHC 1177 (QB) para 73.

63 Rule 39 of the Rules of the Court of the European Court of Human Rights, which allow the ECtHR 'to indicate to the parties any interim measure which it considers should be adopted in the interests of the parties or of the proper conduct of the proceedings before it'. In the deportation context, these refer to indications that a person should not be deported.

interim measure from the ECtHR if he applied for it.[64] However, the mere intimation that a detainee may initiate proceedings challenging expulsion with suspensory effect, or even the SSHD's knowledge that the ECtHR would grant the detainee a rule 39 interim measure prohibiting expulsion if the detainee sought it, are not in themselves sufficient to render detention unlawful.[65]

A detainee's refusal to repatriate voluntarily

33.29 There are two principal forms of refusal to co-operate with the expulsion process[66] (although the case-law has commonly conflated them). The first is a refusal to avail oneself of one of the schemes offered by the Home Office (see chapter 6) to leave the UK voluntarily, on which the Supreme Court gave guidance in *Lumba and Mighty*. The second form is a refusal to comply with travel documentation process by a detainee who does not have his passport, which is discussed at paras 33.35–33.42 below.

33.30 The refusal to repatriate voluntarily is of no relevance where the detainee is still pursuing proceedings challenging expulsion (unless the proceedings are an abuse). Nor can it be held against a detainee that he is refusing to repatriate voluntarily where return is impossible for other extraneous reasons.[67]

33.31 The refusal to repatriate voluntarily may be indicative of an absconding risk, which itself is relevant to the reasonable period of detention as we have seen at para 33.23 above. However, no automatic inference of absconding risk can be drawn from a refusal to repatriate voluntarily: it is necessary to look at the history and particular circumstances of each detainee.[68] It is for the SSHD to demonstrate

---

64 *R (Abdi) v Secretary of State for the Home Department* [2011] EWCA Civ 242 paras 51–56; *R (MM Somalia) v Secretary of State for the Home Department* [2009] EWHC 2353 (Admin) paras 34 and 37; *R (A) v Secretary of State for the Home Department* [2010] EWHC 808 (Admin) para 84; *CM (Somalia) v Secretary of State for the Home Department* [2010] EWHC 640 (Admin) para 31.
65 *R (AR) v Secretary of State for the Home Department* [2011] EWCA Civ 857 para 23.
66 See distinction drawn in *R (Lumba and Mighty) v Secretary of State for the Home Department* [2011] UKSC 12, [2011] 2 WLR 671 para 122.
67 *R (Lumba and Mighty) v Secretary of State for the Home Department* [2011] UKSC 12, [2011] 2 WLR 671 per Lord Dyson para 127. See also *R (Mounir Raki) v Secretary of State for the Home Department* [2011] EWHC 2421 (Admin) para 45(ii) finding that a detainee could not have his refusal to voluntarily repatriate held against him where in any event extraneous reasons prevented expulsion.
68 *R (Lumba and Mighty) v Secretary of State for the Home Department* [2011] UKSC 12, [2011] 2 WLR 671 per Lord Dyson para 123.

that it is right to infer absconding risk from a refusal to repatriate voluntarily in a given case.[69]

33.32 The Supreme Court held in *Lumba and Mighty* that where no absconding risk is to be inferred, a refusal to repatriate voluntarily is of limited significance if any as a free-standing reason.[70] In short, the Supreme Court has left open the argument that a refusal to repatriate voluntarily is entirely irrelevant where no absconding risk is to be inferred from the refusal. Arguably, since the purpose of the power to detain under IA 1971 Sch 3 is 'to enable the machinery of deportation to be carried out'[71] and deportation refers only to enforced expulsion, a failure to repatriate voluntarily is irrelevant to the purpose of the statutory detention power unless absconding risk (which would frustrate the purpose of the power) can properly be inferred. Earlier authorities make the point that it would be an improper use of the power to detain to deploy it to compel a person to agree to voluntary departure.[72]

33.33 In any event, *Lumba and Mighty* clarifies that a refusal to repatriate voluntarily is not a 'trump card' enabling the SSHD 'to continue to detain until deportation can be effected, whenever that may be'.[73]

33.34 The Supreme Court's judgment in *Lumba and Mighty* therefore casts great doubt on if not overturns an earlier line of case-law[74] in which lesser or no weight was given to periods of detention deemed

---

69 *R (Lumba and Mighty) v Secretary of State for the Home Department* [2011] UKSC 12, [2011] 2 WLR 671 per Lord Dyson, para 123, endorsing his own earlier dicta in *R (I) v Secretary of State for the Home Department* [2002] EWCA Civ 888 [2003] INLR 196 para 54.

70 *R (Lumba and Mighty) v Secretary of State for the Home Department* [2011] UKSC 12, [2011] 2 WLR 671 per Lord Dyson paras 128, 144.

71 *R v Governor of Durham Prison ex p Hardial Singh* [1984] 1 WLR 704, 706D; see also *R (Lumba and Mighty) v Secretary of State for the Home Department* [2011] UKSC 12, [2011] 2 WLR 671 per Lord Dyson at para 24, per Lord Hope at paras 172 and 174, per Lady Hale para 198.

72 *R (Bashir) v Secretary of State for the Home Department* [2007] EWHC 3017 (Admin) para 16; *MI (Iraq) and AO (Iraq)* [2010] EWHC 764 (Admin) para 52.

73 *R (Lumba and Mighty) v Secretary of State for the Home Department* [2011] UKSC 12, [2011] 2 WLR 671 para 128.

74 The Privy Council in *Tan Te Lam v Superintendent of Tai A Chau Detention Centre* [1997] AC 97 at 114–115 had considered it a 'factor of fundamental importance' 'that the detention is self-induced by reason of the failure to apply for voluntary repatriation', though there, the statutory context in Hong Kong made a refusal of voluntary repatriation a mandatory relevant consideration. See also *A (Somalia)* para 54 in which a refusal to repatriate voluntarily was treated as a 'decisive factor' because 'the loss of liberty involved in the individual's continued detention is a product of his own making'.

to be self-induced because the detainee was refusing voluntary repatriation.

Other forms of non-co-operation by a detainee

33.35 The other main form of non-co-operation is a refusal by a person who lacks a valid passport to co-operate with the obtaining of travel documents to enable return.

33.36 This was not specifically addressed by the Supreme Court in *Lumba and Mighty*, but three broad principles emerge from the Supreme Court's judgment in *Lumba and Mighty* which are relevant to all forms of non-co-operation. First, where the non-co-operation has no causal effect on the length of detention because the detainee in any event cannot be expelled for extraneous reasons (such as an outstanding legal challenge to expulsion) non-co-operation per se cannot be held against the detainee.[75] Second, where absconding risk is asserted, it is for the SSHD to establish that non-co-operation is indicative of an absconding risk.[76] Third, non-co-operation is never a trump card: it does not enable the SSHD to 'continue to detain until deportation can be effected, whenever that may be'.[77]

33.37 In judgments postdating *Lumba and Mighty*, the Administrative Court has held that:

> Thus in my judgment it is likely, other things being equal, that a reasonable period for the detention of an individual who does not co-operate in obtaining a travel document may be well be longer than it will be in the case of individual who co-operates. Similarly it is likely, other things being equal, that a reasonable period may be still longer in the case of an individual who seeks to frustrate efforts to obtain one by supplying false or misleading information (leading to false hopes of obtaining, and unsuccessful attempts to obtain, a travel document). Nonetheless, although an individual who has only himself to blame for his detention being prolonged by virtue of his own conduct may not attract sympathy, in my judgment his conduct cannot be regarded as providing a trump card justifying his detention indefinitely. The Secretary of State may not detain a person pending deportation for

---

75 *R (Lumba and Mighty) v Secretary of State for the Home Department* [2011] UKSC 12, [2011] 2 WLR 671 per Lord Dyson para 127.
76 *R (Lumba and Mighty) v Secretary of State for the Home Department* [2011] UKSC 12, [2011] 2 WLR 671 per Lord Dyson para 123, endorsing his own earlier dicta in *R (I) v Secretary of State for the Home Department* [2002] EWCA Civ 888, [2003] INLR 196 para 54.
77 *R (Lumba and Mighty) v Secretary of State for the Home Department* [2011] UKSC 12, [2011] 2 WLR 671 per Lord Dyson, para 128.

more than a reasonable period even in the case of an individual who is deliberately seeking to sabotage any efforts to deport him.[78]

And likewise that:

A finding that a detainee has been uncooperative may incline a Court to lengthen the timespan over which it would regard continued detention to be lawful, but where no realistic prospect of deportation within any timeframe can be demonstrated, such indulgence does not assist the Defendant.[79]

33.38 Earlier authorities make the similar point that the fact that an individual is prolonging his or her own detention by a refusal to co-operate does not justify indefinite detention.[80] If there is no realistic deportation, the statutory power ceases to exist:

There must come a time when such a sterile tactic as merely sitting and waiting while repeatedly urging [the detainee] to change his mind, in the full expectation that he would not, ceases to be detention genuinely for the purposes of deportation.[81]

Once an impasse has been reached, the individual should be released.[82] It has also been said that in the absence of an absconding or re-offending risk, it would be wrong to prolong detention purely as a consequence of the detainee's refusal to co-operate with the documentation or expulsion process.[83]

---

78 R (Sino) v Secretary of State for the Home Department [2011] EWHC 2249 (Admin) para 56.
79 R (Mounir Raki) v Secretary of State for the Home Department [2011] EWHC 2421 (Admin) para 45(iii).
80 R (I) v Secretary of State for the Home Department [2002] EWCA Civ 888, [2003] INLR 196 paras 51–53; R (SK) v Secretary of State for the Home Department [2008] EWHC 98 (Admin) para 95; R (FR) Iran v Secretary of State for the Home Department [2009] EWHC 2094 (QB); R (Wang) v Secretary of State for the Home Department [2009] EWHC 1578 (Admin); R (HY) v Secretary of State for the Home Department [2010] EWHC 1678 in particular para 29; R (NAB) v Secretary of State for the Home Department [2010] EWHC 3137 (Admin) in particular para 42; R (BE) v Secretary of State for the Home Department [2011] EWHC 690 (Admin).
81 R (NAB) v Secretary of State for the Home Department [2010] EWHC 3137 (Admin), para 76.
82 R (Oppong) v Secretary of State for the Home Department [2008] EWHC 2596 (Admin).
83 R (A) v Secretary of State for the Home Department [2007] EWCA Civ 804 at paras 53 and 79; R (BE) v Secretary of State for the Home Department [2011] EWHC 690 (Admin) para 154.

33.39 The ECtHR[84] has likewise held that where expulsion is simply an impossibility because of non-co-operation, detention can no longer be justified under ECHR article 5(1)(f) as detention of a person against whom action is being taken with a view to deportation. See para 36.21.

33.40 We also suggest that where a detainee has an outstanding legal challenge against expulsion on Refugee Convention[85] or ECHR article 3 grounds that the detainee's expulsion would put him or her at risk from the receiving state agents, a refusal to cooperate with the travel documentation process (and so with the home authorities) cannot be held against the detainee. Conversely, the Court of Appeal has held that where a detainee has exhausted his or her asylum and ECHR appeals and is failing to co-operate, the fact that the country to which he or she would be returning is chaotic or war-torn is irrelevant.[86]

33.41 Not all behaviour that impedes or delays travel documentation can be counted as non-co-operation or obstruction.[87] An honest error in completing a bio-data form cannot be counted as non-co-operation even if it delays the documentation process.[88]

33.42 Where no attempt has been made to prosecute the detainee under Asylum and Immigration (Treatment of Claimants etc) Act 2004 s35 for failure to co-operate with the documentation process, this may be relevant in rebutting allegations of non-co-operation.[89]

---

84 *Milolenko v Estonia* (App No 10664/05, 8 October 2009) where the applicant could not be removed because he persistently refused to sign an application for a passport or temporary travel document.
85 The 1951 Convention Relating to the Status of Refugees and its 1967 Protocol ('Refugee Convention').
86 In the context of voluntary repatriation, *A (Somalia)* [2007] EWCA Civ 804 paras 56 and 57.
87 For examples of behaviour not deemed obstructive, see *R (H) v Secretary of State for the Home Department* [2005] EWHC 1702 (Admin) paras 33–38, a disputed nationality case; and *R (A, MA, B, ME) v Secretary of State for the Home Department* [2007] EWHC 142 (Admin) para 15 concerning a lack of identifying documents.
88 *R (A, MA, B, ME) v Secretary of State for the Home Department* [2007] EWHC 142 (Admin) paras 37–38.
89 *R (A, MA, B, ME) v Secretary of State for the Home Department* [2007] EWHC 142 (Admin) para 15.

Mental illness

33.43 Mental illness is a relevant factor when considering the reasonableness of a period of past or future detention.[90] The Court of Appeal has stated that:

> ... if it is shown that a person's detention has caused or contributed to his suffering mental illness, this is a factor which in principle should be taken into account in assessing the reasonableness of the length of the detention. But the critical question in such cases is whether facilities for treating the person whilst in detention are available so as to keep the illness under control.[91]

33.44 However, in determining the lawfulness of a period of past or future detention, a detainee's mental illness must be balanced against other factors, including the risks of re-offending and absconding.[92]

33.45 Note that, aside from the relevance of mental illness to the *Hardial Singh* assessment, mental illness in a detainee may be relevant to the question of whether detention is compliant with published Home Office policy. This is discussed at paras 34.27–34.31.

---

90 See *R (Lumba and Mighty) v Secretary of State for the Home Department* [2011] UKSC 12, [2011] 2 WLR 671 per Lady Hale para 218.

91 *R (M) v Secretary of State for the Home Department* [2008] EWCA Civ 307 where ongoing detention was lawful for a depressed and suicidal man. There was no medical evidenced that the appellant in that case was unfit for detention. However, see *R (MMH) v Secretary of State for the Home Department* [2007] EWHC 2134 (Admin) where the immigration detention of a foreign national offender who had repeatedly attempted to self-harm was unlawful being contrary to published Home Office policy. See also *R (Wang) v Secretary of State for the Home Department* [2009] EWHC 1578 (Admin) and *R (Daq) v Secretary of State for the Home Department* [2009] EWHC 1655 (Admin) where the detainee's mental ill-health was relevant to the a finding that the *Hardial Singh* principles had been breached. See likewise *R (Belmihoub) v Secretary of State for the Home Department* [2011] EWHC 2044 (Admin) paras 67–69 where a combination of dilatory conduct by the Home Office and the detainee's mental ill-health rendered detention unlawful.

92 *R (MC) Algeria v Secretary of State for the Home Department* [2010] EWCA Civ 347. This authority should be approached with caution. We respectfully suggest that the findings on policy and causation have been overruled by the Supreme Court's judgment in *R (Lumba and Mighty) v Secretary of State for the Home Department* [2011] UKSC 12, [2011] 2 WLR 671. For comprehensive Administrative Court guidance postdating *Lumba and Mighty* on the approach to be taken to mental illness in detention, see *R (S) v Secretary of State for the Home Department* [2011] EWHC 2120 (Admin) para 171, followed in *R (BA) v Secretary of State for the Home Department* [2011] EWHC 2748 (Admin).

33.46 A suicidally depressed detainee cannot be detained on the basis of a need to protect the detainee from himself: that would be detention for an unlawful collateral purpose.[93] See para 33.7 above.

Serious medical conditions generally

33.47 As with mental illness, where a detainee suffers from a serious medical condition of a physical nature, this may be relevant both to the *Hardial Singh* assessment[94] and to the question of whether Home Office policy has been complied with (see paras 34.27–34.31).

Disability

33.48 Where a detainee suffers from a disability and the detainee's needs are not adequately met in detention so that the detainee is suffering substantial hardship as a consequence of detention, this may 'tip the balance into unlawfulness' for the purposes of the *Hardial Singh* reasonableness assessment.[95] A detainee's disability may also be relevant to the question of whether detention is compliant with Home Office policy, see paras 34.27–34.32.

Previous refusals of bail

33.49 The fact that a person has previously been refused bail is not determinative of the legality of the detention at the time of the refusal. The Administrative Court has warned that a refusal of bail should not be given undue weight.[96]

---

93 *R (AA) v Secretary of State for the Home Department* [2010] EWHC 2265 (Admin) at para 40.

94 *R (T) v Secretary of State for the Home Department* [2011] EWHC 370 (Admin) – this authority should be treated with caution because it treats a failure to comply with Home Office policy as insufficient to render detention unlawful, an approach we suggest has been overruled by *Lumba and Mighty*, see note 92 above. However, see also *R (MD and others) v Secretary of State for the Home Department* [2011] EWCA Civ 1238 in which (case of MD) even an interruption during detention of anti-retroviral medication for an HIV positive detainee which was likely to have led to the development of anti-retroviral resistance, with severe consequences for his life expectancy after expulsion, did not render detention unlawful. See discussion at para 34.20.

95 *R (BE) v Secretary of State for the Home Department* [2011] EWHC 690 (Admin) particular para 180. This authority should be treated with caution. See notes 92 and 94 above.

96 *MI (Iraq) and AO (Iraq) v Secretary of State for the Home Department* [2010] EWHC 764 (Admin) para 50; *R (Rangwani) v Secretary of State for the Home*

33.50 This is because bail is not a determination of the legality of detention, whether at common law, or for ECHR article 5(4) purposes.[97] In addition, while similar factual questions will be considered (such as absconding risk, offending risk and the degree of any non-co-operation) an immigration judge hearing a bail application may have considerably less documentary evidence before her than a High Court judge subsequently hearing a claim for judicial review.[98]

Department [2011] EWHC 516 (Admin) para 17. See also the more extreme statement that a refusal of bail is irrelevant to the legality of detention in *R (HXA) v Secretary of State for the Home Department* [2010] EWHC 1177 (QB) para 74. Many successful claimants in detention challenges have previously been refused bail. See, for example, *R (Vovk and Datta) v Secretary of State for the Home Department* [2006] EWHC 3386 (Admin) para 62; *R (Bashir) v Secretary of State for the Home Department* [2007] EWHC 3017 (Admin) paras 5–6.

97 *R (Lumba and Mighty) v Secretary of State for the Home Department* [2011] UKSC 12, [2011] 2 WLR 671 per Lord Dyson para 118; *Zamir v UK* (1983) 40 DR 42 at 59, para 109. See also Bail Guidance for Immigration Judges, Presidential Guidance Note No 1 of 2011 FTT-IAC 11 July 2011 para 5.

98 *R (HXA) v Secretary of State for the Home Department* [2010] EWHC 1177 (QB) para 74; *R (MA and TT) v Secretary of State for the Home Department* [2010] EWHC 2350 (Admin) paras 15 and 58.

CHAPTER 34

Home Office detention policy

34.1	Introduction
34.6	The legal status of policy
34.8	The question of causation in the policy context
34.11	The detail of Home Office detention policy
34.11	Sources
34.12	Detention policy in flux
34.15	The policy referred to below
34.18	General principles, applicable to all detainees (whether Criminal Casework Directorate cases or not)
34.19	Permissible reasons for detention
34.20	Factors that the SSHD's caseworkers must consider when deciding whether to detain or maintain detention
34.23	Those who should only be detained in the most or very exceptional circumstances
	Minors • Adults who should only be detained in very exceptional circumstances • Interplay with the Detention Centre Rules 2001 • Claims concerning the detention of the seriously mentally ill; those suffering from serious medical conditions; and the seriously disabled • Claims concerning the detention of torture victims
34.37	Special criteria for detention in CCD cases
34.39	The process of considering detention in CCD cases
34.47	More serious offences

continued

34.52 Those with British or EEA national spouses
34.54 Other common examples of policy breaches in FNP cases
34.55 The secret detention policy for FNPs

Introduction

34.1 Home Office detention policy places a further limitation on the Secretary of State for the Home Department's (SSHD's) exercise of her detention powers. It is now well established that detention is unlawful where the SSHD has failed to consider, or failed without good reason to follow, applicable published Home Office policy going to the decision to detain.[1]

34.2 Detention has been found unlawful on the basis that detention was contrary to, or disregarded, Home Office policy:

- on no longer treating removal as 'imminent' where judicial review proceedings have been threatened;[2]
- on the general length of detention and on the detention of families with children;[3]
- on the detention of disputed minors;[4]
- on the detention of a person for whom there exists independent evidence of torture or for whom, had the required medical reviews taken place, such independent evidence would have come to light;[5]
- on the provision of malaria prophylaxis to children prior to departure;[6]

---

1 *R (Shepherd Masimba Kambadzi) v Secretary of State for the Home Department* [2011] UKSC 23, [2011] 1 WLR 1299; *R (Lumba and Mighty) v Secretary of State for the Home Department* [2011] UKSC 12, [2011] 2 WLR 671; *D v Home Office* [2005] EWCA Civ 38, [2006] 1 WLR 1003 para 111; *Nadarajah and Amirthanathan v Secretary of State for the Home Department* [2003] EWCA Civ 1768.

2 *Nadarajah and Amirthanathan v Secretary of State for the Home Department* [2003] EWCA Civ 1768.

3 *R (Konan) v Secretary of State for the Home Department* [2004] EWHC 22 (Admin); *R (S, C and D) v Secretary of State for the Home Department* [2007] EWHC 1654 (Admin); *R (Suppiah) v Secretary of State for the Home Department* [2011] EWHC 2 (Admin); *R (FM) v Secretary of State for the Home Department* [2011] EWCA Civ 807.

4 *R (I and O) v Secretary of State for the Home Department* [2005] EWHC 1025 (Admin).

5 *R (D and K) v Secretary of State for the Home Department* [2006] EWHC 980 (Admin) and *R (B) v Secretary of State for the Home Department* [2008] EWHC 364 (Admin). Note that these cases deal also with a failure by the SSHD to follow the requirements of the Detention Centre Rules 2001 SI No 238.

6 *R (Nukajam) v Secretary of State for the Home Department* [2010] EWHC 20 (Admin). See the discussion of that policy at para 6.24 above. However, see also *R (FM) v Secretary of State for the Home Department* [2011] EWCA Civ 807 in which the detention of a mother and her children was found to be lawful notwithstanding delays that were inherent in the provision of malaria prophylaxis.

- on the detention of the mentally ill;[7]
- on the presumption of liberty;[8]
- on the provision of regular detention reviews.[9]

34.3 Published Home Office detention policy is also relevant to bail. Immigration judges have been directed to have regard to it in determining bail applications in the Immigration and Asylum Chamber of the First-tier Tribunal (FTT-IAC).[10]

34.4 In a detention challenge, the interpretation of polices are a matter for the court rather than solely for the SSHD.[11]

34.5 In this chapter, we first review the legal status of policy, then the question of whether there is any need to show that the policy breach was causative of the detention. The rest of the chapter is devoted to the content of Home Office detention policy itself and common examples of policy breaches. We attempt to providew practical guidance on choice of remedy, fora and the appropriate defendant in chapter 42.

The legal status of policy

34.6 Public authorities are required to comply, absent good reason for not so doing, with their own published policies.[12]

---

7 *R (MMH) v Secretary of State for the Home Department* [2007] EWHC 2134 (Admin); *R (T) v Secretary of State for the Home Department* [2010] EWHC 668 (Admin); *R (S) v Secretary of State for the Home Department* [2011] EWHC 2120 (Admin).

8 *R (Lumba and Mighty) v Secretary of State for the Home Department* [2011] UKSC 12, [2011] 2 WLR 671.

9 *R (Kambadzi) v Secretary of State for the Home Department* [2011] UKSC 23, [2011] 1 WLR 1299.

10 Bail Guidance for Immigration Judges, Presidential Guidance Note No 1 of 2011, FTT-IAC, 11 July 2011 para 7.

11 *R (MD) v Secretary of State for the Home Department* [2011] EWCA Civ 1238, para 12; see also *R (BA) v Secretary of State for the Home Department* [2011] EWHC 2748 (Admin) para 161.

12 *R (Kambadzi) v Secretary of State for the Home Department* [2011] UKSC 23, [2011] 1 WLR 1299 per Lord Hope paras 36 and 43, Lady Hale at para 73, Lord Kerr at para 85. *R (Lumba and Mighty) v Secretary of State for the Home Department* [2011] UKSC 12, [2011] 2 WLR 671 per Lord Dyson para 30, per Lady Hale para 210, per Lord Collins para 221, per Lord Phillips para 313, per Lord Brown and Lord Rodger paras 347(4) and 351; *R (Saadi) v Secretary of State for the Home Department* in the Court of Appeal [2001] EWCA Civ 1512, [2002] 1 WLR 356, per Lord Philips MR para 7; *Re McFarland* [2004] UKHL 17, [2004] 1 WLR 1289, per Lord Steyn para 24.

34.7 Policy is not, in the domestic sense of the word, 'law' since it can be departed from with good reason.[13] However, since compliance is a public law duty, policy forms part of the 'law' for the purposes of detention 'in accordance with a procedure prescribed by law under ECHR article 5(1)[14] and interference 'in accordance with the law' under ECHR article 8(2). Policy must therefore have the quality of 'law' for ECHR purposes and be adequately accessible and should enable those affected by it reasonably to foresee the consequences of their actions.[15]

The question of causation in the policy context

34.8 Causation has been discussed in more detail at paras 32.17–32.23. A breach of, or failure without good reason to have regard to, applicable published detention policy, will give rise to unlawful detention and the tort of false imprisonment, provided that the policy relied on is sufficiently closely related to the authority for detention.[16] In such cases, there is no need to show causation (in the sense that but for the breach detention would not have occurred).[17] We suggest that any policy which concerns suitability for detention, or other criteria and considerations to be applied in decisions over detention, or the detention review process by those criteria and considerations are applied, falls into this category.[18]

---

13 *R (Kambadzi) v Secretary of State for the Home Department* [2011] UKSC 23, [2011] 1 WLR 1299 per Lord Hope para 36, Lord Kerr para 87.

14 *R (Lumba and Mighty) v Secretary of State for the Home Department* [2011] UKSC 12, [2011] 2 WLR 671 per Lord Dyson paras 30 and 32; *Nadarajah and Amirthanathan v Secretary of State for the Home Department* [2003] EWCA Civ 1768 para 54; *R (Munjaz) v Mersey Care Trust* [2005] UKHL 58, [2006] 2 AC 148 paras 34, 91–92, 98, 103.

15 *R (Lumba and Mighty) v Secretary of State for the Home Department* [2011] UKSC 12, [2011] 2 WLR 671 per Lord Dyson para 32; *Nadarajah and Amirthanathan* paras 54 and 64–67.

16 *R (Kambadzi) v Secretary of State for the Home Department* [2011] UKSC 23, [2011] 1 WLR 1299 per Lord Hope para 27.

17 *R (Lumba and Mighty) v Secretary of State for the Home Department* [2011] UKSC 12, [2011] 2 WLR 671; *R (Kambadzi) v Secretary of State for the Home Department* [2011] UKSC 23, [2011] 1 WLR 1299.

18 See *R (Kambadzi) v Secretary of State for the Home Department* [2011] UKSC 23, [2011] 1 WLR 1299 per Lady Hale para 71 distinguishing 'a requirement which goes to whether or not a person is detained' from requirements concerning detention conditions.

34.9 Conversely, the breach or disregard of a policy which can have no bearing on the decision to detain does not affect the legality of detention. Examples would include policies concerning detention conditions[19] or policies concerning places of detention.

34.10 But (see paras 32.22–32.23 above) there may be an intermediary category of requirements whose breach or disregard will only render detention unlawful where the error caused the detention.[20]

The detail of Home Office detention policy

Sources

34.11 The Enforcement Instructions and Guidance (EIG) formerly known as the Operational Enforcement Manual (OEM) are the primary source of published Home Office policy on immigration detention.[21] The EIG and OEM have been supplemented (and on occasion contradicted) by ministerial statements.

Detention policy in flux

34.12 For over two years the Home Office also maintained parallel, unpublished detention policies for FNPs. The hidden policies, applied by Home Office caseworkers from circa 25 April 2006, imposed near blanket detention on FNPs after sentence completion. Meanwhile, the published OEM chapter 38 and EIG chapter 55 continued to refer to a presumption in favour of release. It was not until late June 2008 that the existence of the unpublished policies emerged.[22]

---

19 *R (Lumba and Mighty) v Secretary of State for the Home Department* [2011] UKSC 12, [2011] 2 WLR 671 per Lord Dyson para 68; *R (Kambadzi) v Secretary of State for the Home Department* [2011] UKSC 23, [2011] 1 WLR 1299 per Lady Hale para 71.

20 *R (Kambadzi) v Secretary of State for the Home Department* [2011] UKSC 23, [2011] 1 WLR 1299, obiter dicta of Lady Hale paras 70–71.

21 The EIG are frequently amended by the Home Office. For the latest version, see the UK Border Agency website, www.bia.homeoffice.gov.uk/policyandlaw/guidance/enforcement/.

22 The Home Office then argued the secret policy litigation that its secret policy had not been a blanket policy but rather one that presumed in favour of detention. This was incorrect. In fact, as the Home Office later conceded in the Supreme Court in *R (Lumba and Mighty) v Secretary of State for the Home Department* [2011] UKSC 12, [2011] 2 WLR 671, the secret policy had been a blanket or near blanket policy rather than a rebuttable presumption of detention.

34.13 On 9 September 2008, with no fanfare, the Home Office introduced a radical change to its published policy on immigration detention. EIG chapter 55 was amended to refer to a presumption of detention for those detained for deportation.[23]

34.14 The EIG was again amended on 22 January 2009.[24] In the post 22 January 2009 EIG chapter 55, references to a presumption of detention were removed and references to the presumption of liberty for all detainees re-inserted.[25]

The policy referred to below

34.15 Below, we describe only Home Office detention policy as it stands at the time of writing.[26] Note, however, that earlier versions of the EIG and OEM remain important when seeking to establish whether a past period of detention accorded with published Home Office policy.

34.16 We discuss here only those elements of the policy most relevant to FNPs. The separate detention regime for asylum-seekers held for the fast-tracking of their claims is highly unlikely to be applied to FNPs and it is not discussed here.

34.17 Applicable procedural requirements, some of which are contained in policy, are discussed in chapter 35. Policies relating to places and to conditions of detention are dealt with separately in chapters 38 and 39 respectively.

---

23 The Supreme Court in *R (Lumba and Mighty) v Secretary of State for the Home Department* [2011] UKSC 12, [2011] 2 WLR 671 found that the SSHD had been entitled to operate a published policy presuming in favour of detention, in so far as it described a 'normal practice' of detaining a certain class, provided that individuated consideration was given to each case and provided that the policy complied with the *Hardial Singh* principles. Per Lord Dyson paras 42, 52–53, see discussion at paras 32.31–32.39 above.

24 The policy was amended in response to the conclusion of Davis J at first instance in the unpublished policy litigation, in *R (Abdi) v Secretary of State for the Home Department* [2008] EWHC 3166 (Admin) that it was unlawful to have a policy of a presumption in favour of detention. The true position that later emerged in the Supreme Court in *Lumba and Mighty* was that a) the secret policy had been a near blanket policy rather than one of presumption; but b) the SSHD had been entitled to operate a published policy that presumed in favour of detention.

25 In *R (Abdi) v Secretary of State for the Home Department* [2009] EWHC 1324 (Admin) the Administrative Court found that the revised policy was lawful. That aspect of the judgment was not appealed.

26 Current as of 1 January 2012.

General principles, applicable to all detainees (whether Criminal Casework Directorate cases or not)[27]

34.18 EIG chapter 55 contains a presumption of liberty and an apparent necessity test for all immigration detention:

> ... the [1998] White Paper confirmed that there was a presumption in favour of temporary admission or release and that, wherever possible, we would use alternatives to detention ... These criteria ... were reiterated in the 2002 White Paper ... They currently represent stated policy on the use of detention.[28]
>
> ...
>
> Detention must be used sparingly, and for the shortest period necessary.[29]

Permissible reasons for detention

34.19 The six permissible reasons for detention under the EIG are:
1) likelihood of absconding if granted temporary admission or release;
2) lack of sufficient reliable information to decide on whether to grant temporary admission or release;
3) imminent removal from the UK;
4) need for detention while alternative arrangements are made for the detainee's care;
5) release not considered conducive to the public good; and
6) (in fast track cases only) the application may be decided quickly using fast-track procedures.[30]

Factors that the SSHD's caseworkers must consider when deciding whether to detain or maintain detention

34.20 The EIG lists 14 factors which may form the basis of the decision to detain:

1) the individual does not have enough close ties (eg family or friends) to make it likely that he or she will stay in one place;

---

27 Some of the criteria below apply in modified form to fast-track detention, which we do not discuss in this book.
28 EIG chapter 55 para 55.1.
29 EIG chapter 55 para 55.1.3.
30 EIG chapter 55 para 55.6.3.

2) the individual has previously failed to comply with conditions of stay, temporary admission or release;
3) the individual has previously absconded or escaped;
4) (for fast-track cases only) on initial consideration it appears that the individual's case is one which can be decided quickly;
5) the individual has used or attempted to use deception in a way which leads the immigration service to consider he or she may continue to deceive;
6) the individual has failed to give satisfactory or reliable answers to an Immigration Officer's enquiries;
7) the individual has not provided satisfactory evidence of his or her identity, nationality or lawful basis to be in the UK;
8) the individual has previously failed or refused to leave the UK when required to do so;
9) the individual is a young person without the care of a parent or guardian;
10) the individual's health gives serious cause for concern on grounds of his or her own well-being and/or public health or safety;
11) the individual is excluded from the UK at the personal direction of the SSHD;
12) the individual is detained for national security;
13) the individual's previous unacceptable character, conduct or associations; and
14) (for very short-term detention only) detention is reasonably necessary to take fingerprints because the individual has failed to provide these voluntarily.[31]

34.21 EIG chapter 55 also emphasises the need for careful, individualised consideration before deciding to detain or to maintain detention:

> All relevant factors must be taken into account when considering the need for initial or continued detention, including:
> - What is the likelihood of the person being removed and, if so, after what timescale?
> - Is there any evidence of previous absconding?
> - Is there any evidence of a previous failure to comply with conditions of temporary release or bail?
> - Has the subject taken part in a determined attempt to breach the immigration laws? (eg entry in breach of a deportation order, attempted or actual clandestine entry).
> - Is there a previous history of complying with the requirements of immigration control? (eg by applying for a visa, further leave, etc).

31 EIG chapter 55 para 55.6.3.

- What are the person's ties with the United Kingdom? Are there close relatives (including dependants) here? Does anyone rely on the person for support? Does the person have a settled address/employment?
- What are the individual's expectations about the outcome of the case? Are there factors such as an outstanding appeal, an application for judicial review or representations which afford incentive to keep in touch?
- Is there a risk of offending or harm to the public (this requires consideration of the likelihood of harm and the seriousness of the harm if the person does offend)?
- Is the subject under 18?
- Has the subject a history of torture?
- Has the subject a history of physical or mental ill health?[32]

34.22 The published policy also emphasises elsewhere the importance of considering any outstanding claims or appeal rights which afford an incentive to stay in touch if released:

> It is not an effective use of detention space to detain people for lengthy periods if it would be practical to effect detention later in the process once any rights of appeal have been exhausted. A person who has an appeal pending or representations outstanding might have more incentive to comply with any restrictions imposed, if released, than one who is removable.[33]

Those who should only be detained in the most or very exceptional circumstances

Minors

34.23 EIG chapter 55 sets a very high threshold for the detention of unaccompanied minors. They 'must only ever be detained in the most exceptional circumstances and then only normally overnight, with appropriate care, while alternative arrangements for their care and safety are made'. However, those criteria are somewhat relaxed in Criminal Casework Directorate (CCD) cases. The Family Returns Panel is discussed in chapter 37, as is the detention of unaccompanied minor FNPs.

---

32 EIG chapter 55 para 55.3.1.
33 EIG chapter 55 para 55.1.3.

Adults who should only be detained in very exceptional circumstances

34.24 EIG chapter 55 also lists other groups who should only be detained in very exceptional circumstances. However, a special caveat applies in CCD cases:

> In CCD cases the risk of further offending or harm to the public must be carefully weighed against the reason why the individual may be unsuitable for detention. There may be cases where the risk of harm to the public is such that it outweighs factors that would otherwise normally indicate that a person was unsuitable for detention.[34]

34.25 The categories of person who are 'normally considered suitable for detention only in very exceptional circumstances whether in dedicated immigration accommodation or in prisons' are as follows:

- 'the elderly, especially where significant or constant supervision is required which cannot be satisfactorily managed in detention';[35]
- pregnant women (except where 'removal is imminent and medical advice does not suggest confinement before the due removal date');[36]
- 'those suffering from serious medical conditions which cannot satisfactorily be managed within detention';[37]
- 'those suffering from serious mental illness which cannot be satisfactorily managed within detention';[38]
- 'those where there is independent evidence that they have been tortured';[39]
- 'people with serious disabilities which cannot be satisfactorily managed within detention';[40]
- 'persons identified by the Competent authorities as victims of trafficking'.[41]

---

34 EIG chapter 55 para 55.10.
35 EIG chapter 55 para 55.10.
36 EIG chapter 55 para 55.9.1; but see also the differently worded criteria at para 55.10. Note that somewhat different criteria apply to the detention of pregnant women in the detained fast-track at Yarlswood: they may be held until 24 weeks pregnant.
37 EIG chapter 55 para 55.10.
38 EIG chapter 55 para 55.10.
39 EIG chapter 55 para 55.10.
40 EIG chapter 55 para 55.10.
41 EIG chapter 55 para 55.10.

Interplay with the Detention Centre Rules 2001[42]

34.26 Those bringing claims challenging detention in an immigration removal centre (IRC) on the basis of serious mental illness, serious medical conditions, serious disability or the torture evidence policy should familiarise themselves with relevant requirements imposed by delegated legislation, the Detention Centre Rules 2001, as well as by executive orders. The delegated legislation and executive orders governing conditions in IRC's are discussed in detail in chapter 39. Most pertinently, the Detention Centre Rules 2001 at r34 impose a requirement to provide each detainee with a physical and mental examination within 24 hours of admission to an IRC, by a medical practitioner[43] (of at least GP qualifications[44]). Rule 35 of the Detention Centre Rules 2001 imposes a duty on the medical practitioner to report to the manager of the IRC on the case of any detained person whose health is likely to be injuriously affected by continued detention or any conditions of detention[45] and on the case of any detained person he or she suspects of having suicidal intentions[46] or is concerned may have been the victim of torture.[47] As long as the medical practitioner suspects that a detainee has suicidal intentions, the detainee must remain under special observation.[48] See para 34.36 below for a discussion of the legal consequences of breach of these requirements.

Claims concerning the detention of the seriously mentally ill; those suffering from serious medical conditions; and the seriously disabled

34.27 Detention in breach of or in disregard of stated Home Office policy concerning the seriously mentally ill, those suffering from serious medical conditions and the seriously disabled is unlawful.[49] It used

---

42 SI No 238.
43 Detention Centre Rules 2001 r34(1).
44 Detention Centre Rules 2001 r33(1).
45 Detention Centre Rules 2001 r35(1).
46 Detention Centre Rules 2001 r35(2).
47 Detention Centre Rules 2001 r35(3).
48 Detention Centre Rules 2001 r35(2).
49 In the context of serious mental illness, see *OM (Nigeria)* [2011] EWCA Civ 909; *R (MMH) v Secretary of State for the Home Department* [2007] EWHC 2134 (Admin); *R (T) v Secretary of State for the Home Department* [2010] EWHC 668 (Admin); *R (S) v Secretary of State for the Home Department* [2011] EWHC 2120 (Admin). In the context of serious medical conditions, see *R (TN) Vietnam v Secretary of State for the Home Department* [2010] EWHC 2184 (Admin). In

to be thought that such errors would only render detention unlawful if the error had caused the decision to detain in a given case.[50] *Lumba and Mighty*[51] overrules that line of case-law.

34.28 Since the detention policy on the detention of those suffering serious mental illness, medical conditions or having a serious disability concerns the criteria for suitability for detention, it is sufficient for the purposes of liability that the public law error was material. That is: a) the detainee was suffering from serious mentally illness or a serious medical condition or was seriously disabled so that this policy was applicable; and b) the policy was disregarded or incorrectly applied. Liability is established irrespective of c) whether the correct application of the policy would have led to release.[52] However, causation will be relevant to damages[53] – see paras 32.24–32.25 above.

34.29 The courts have considered that serious offending and very high absconding risks may constitute 'very exceptional circumstances' justifying the detention under Immigration Act powers of those who would otherwise be considered unsuitable.[54] However, the Administrative Court has also emphasised that where a person falls in the category of person suitable for detention only in 'very exceptional circumstances', the SSHD should not approach the case as if merely

---

the context of serious disability, see *R (BE) v Secretary of State for the Home Department* [2011] EWHC 690 (Admin). However, these authorities should be approached with caution. The findings on causation and policy breaches, have, we suggest, been overruled by the Supreme Court's judgment in *Lumba and Mighty*.

50 See, for example, in the context of mental illness: *MC (Algeria) v Secretary of State for the Home Department* [2010] EWCA Civ 347 paras 50–52; *R (Anam) v Secretary of State for the Home Department* [2010] EWCA Civ 1140; in the context of serious medical conditions *R (T) v Secretary of State for the Home Department* [2011] EWHC 370 (Admin) and *R (TN) (Vietnam) v Secretary of State for the Home Department* [2010] EWHC 2184 (Admin); and in the context of disability see: *R (BE) v Secretary of State for the Home Department* [2011] EWHC 690 (Admin) paras 169–171.

51 *R (Lumba and Mighty) v Secretary of State for the Home Department* [2011] UKSC 12, [2011] 2 WLR 671.

52 *OM (Nigeria)* [2011] EWCA Civ 909 para 21 (by concession); *R (S) v Secretary of State for the Home Department* [2011] EWHC 2120 (Admin) paras 132, 173.

53 *OM (Nigeria)* [2011] EWCA Civ 909 paras 22–24; *R (S) v Secretary of State for the Home Department* [2011] EWHC 2120 (Admin) para 223.

54 *R (Anam) v Secretary of State for the Home Department* [2009] EWHC 2496 (Admin) paras 52 and 55, a point undisturbed on appeal; *MC (Algeria) v Secretary of State for the Home Department* [2010] EWCA Civ 347 para 44. Both these authorities should be approached with caution: we suggest that they have been overruled by the Supreme Court's judgment in *Lumba and Mighty* insofar as they address causation.

the usual presumption of liberty in the policy needed to be displaced: 'significantly weighty countervailing considerations' are required to justify detention.[55] Even where a person poses high risks of absconding and of violent offending, those factors will not necessarily outweigh the risk posed to the individual's mental health by detention.[56] In any event, as we have seen in the preceding paragraph, the question of whether a person *would* have been released had the policy been properly applied (including the weighing of different factors militating for and against release) does not go to liability, though it may be relevant to quantum of damages.

34.30 The Court of Appeal has held that the term 'suffering from' in the policy (concerning serious mental illness and medical conditions) requires that the person must be 'seriously affected' by the illness and that the illness is not 'satisfactorily managed'[57]. The consequence of this interpretation, in *R (MD) v Secretary of State for the Home Department*, was that a person with HIV/AIDS who had missed his antiretroviral medication with likely severe consequences for his health, and who had been found unfit to fly, was not unlawfully detained in breach of the policy.[58]

34.31 However, when deciding whether to detain, the SSHD must consider whether the person would, if detained, 'suffer from' a serious mental illness or medical condition which would not be satisfactorily managed, even if the person is relatively well at the time that the decision to detain is taken. The SSHD cannot take a 'laissez-faire' approach of seeing whether health deteriorates once in detention[59]. The Administrative Court has also clarified that the SSHD is under a duty, where it is on notice that a detainee suffers from mental illness, to make inquiries and where possible seek relevant medical records[60] (both as a logical consequence of Home Office policy and in order to comply with the UK's obligations under ECHR articles 3 and 8[61]).

---

55 *R (S) v Secretary of State for the Home Department* [2011] EWHC 2120 (Admin) para 85(v).
56 *R (S) v Secretary of State for the Home Department* [2011] EWHC 2120 (Admin) para 182.
57 *R (MD) v Secretary of State for the Home Department* [2011] EWCA Civ 1238, paras 13–14.
58 *R (MD) v Secretary of State for the Home Department* [2011] EWCA Civ 1238, case of MD, paras 46, 49, 51.
59 *R(BA) v Secretary of State for the Home Department* [2011] EWHC 2748 (Admin) paras 183–184.
60 *R (S) v Secretary of State for the Home Department* [2011] EWHC 2120 (Admin) paras 65, 68 and 208.
61 See discussion of ECHR articles 3 and 8 in the detention context in chapter 36.

34.32 Where the SSHD in deciding to detain or to maintain detention fails to address his or her mind to the question of whether a disabled person's needs can satisfactorily be managed in the detention stage, this may also breach Disability Discrimination Act 1995 s49A.[62]

Claims concerning the detention of torture victims

34.33 As we have already seen, those for whom there is independent evidence of torture are another group treated by stated Home Office policy as suitable for detention 'only in very exceptional circumstances' subject to the caveat in CCD cases that this must be weighed against the risk of harm to the public. Detention in disregard or breach of this policy is unlawful.[63] Our comments at para 34.31 above, concerning the weighing of factors militating for and against detention and the duty to make enquiries at least once a person is in detention[64] apply equally to the torture evidence policy.

34.34 The torture evidence policy concerns suitability for detention, and thus is directly related to the authority to detain. We therefore suggest that disregard or breach of the torture evidence policy is sufficient, without more, to render detention unlawful.

34.35 *R (D and K) v Secretary of State for the Home Department*[65] and *R (B) v Secretary of State for the Home Department*[66] concerned asylum-seekers detained without any or any adequate initial medical screening. Had the required medical screening taken place as required by Detention Centre Rules 2001 r34, independent evidence would have emerged corroborating the asylum-seekers' claims of past torture. The claimants' detention past the date when, had the required medical screening taken place, they would have been released was found to be unlawful. *Lumba and Mighty*[67] subsequently clarified that breach of a policy which bears on the decision to detain is sufficient

---

62 *R (BE) v Secretary of State for the Home Department* [2011] EWHC 690 (Admin) para 165.
63 *R (D and K) v Secretary of State for the Home Department* [2006] EWHC 980 (Admin); *R (B) v Secretary of State for the Home Department* [2008] EWHC 364 (Admin).
64 In *HK (Turkey) v Secretary of State for the Home Department* [2007] EWCA Civ 1357, the Court of Appeal rejected the submission that the SSHD was under a duty to check for evidence of torture before making the decision to detain in the fast track, where a person had made an allegation of torture.
65 [2006] EWHC 980 (Admin).
66 [2008] EWHC 364 (Admin).
67 *R (Lumba and Mighty) v Secretary of State for the Home Department* [2011] UKSC 12, [2011] 2 WLR 671.

to render detention unlawful. In obiter dicta in *Kambadzi*,[68] Baroness Hale approved *R (D and K)* and indicated that a breach of the procedural requirement in Detention Centre Rules 2001 r34 would not, without more, render detention unlawful[69] (see the fuller discussion at para 32.22).

34.36 We suggest that the correct position in torture evidence cases is as follows:

- A failure to carry out a medical examination within 24 hours as required by Detention Centre Rules 2001 r34 (so that the Home Office never had the necessary information or notice of a problem to consider its own policy) is not in itself sufficient to establish liability for unlawful detention.[70] In these circumstances, liability will only be established if: i) the failure to medically examine was material, in that the detainee was a person in respect of whom there was independent evidence of torture; and ii) the error caused the detention in that the medical examination would have led to release in all the circumstances.
- Where, as in a) above, causation is relevant to liability, the burden is on the detainer to establish that the error was not causative. See paras 32.3–32.5 above.
- However, where the Home Office had the necessary information (or was put on notice of a problem and then failed to make the necessary inquiries[71]) but failed to consider or properly apply published Home Office policy concerning the detention of victims of torture, it is sufficient that the error was material (in that the detainee was a person in respect of whom there was independent evidence of torture). There is no further requirement of causation before liability is established. Causation will be relevant only to the quantum of damages.

---

68 *R (Kambadzi) v Secretary of State for the Home Department* [2011] UKSC 23, [2011] 1 WLR 1299.
69 [2011] UKSC 23, [2011] 1 WLR 1299 para 70.
70 See Lady Hale's obiter dicta in *R (Kambadzi) v Secretary of State for the Home Department* [2011] UKSC 23, [2011] 1 WLR 1299 para 70.
71 See the discussion in *R (S) v Secretary of State for the Home Department* [2011] EWHC 2120 (Admin) paras 65, 68 and 208.

Special criteria for detention in CCD cases

34.37 EIG chapter 55 makes distinct provision for CCD cases, that is, foreign national former offenders who meet the criteria for consideration for deportation.[72]

34.38 The policy for deciding to detain or maintain detention in CCD cases is set out in convoluted and prolix terms. In summary, the policy:

- maintains the presumption of liberty for CCD cases;
- asserts (although the evidential basis for this is unclear) that the absconding risk may be higher in deportation cases;
- states that the imperative of protecting the public from harm requires special emphasis to be placed on the risk of offending upon release;
- states that in CCD cases, the presumption of liberty will often be outweighed by the risks of absconding and reoffending; and
- reminds caseworkers that detention is unlawful where it would exceed the period reasonably necessary for removal, although the assessment of reasonableness in any given case is affected by the offending and absconding risks posed by the individual.[73]

The process of considering detention in CCD cases

34.39 The EIG sets out the way in which CCD caseworkers should approach the decision over whether to detain or maintain detention.

34.40 The first step in the consideration of detention or release is the question of the timing of removal: 'If removal is imminent then detention or continued detention will usually be appropriate'. Imminent removal is defined in the policy as there being travel documentation, no legal barriers to removal, removal directions in place, and removal to occur within four weeks.[74] If removal is not imminent, caseworkers are directed to consider whether removal has been

---

72 For the deportation criteria for non-EEA nationals, see para 3.6. For the deportation criteria for EEA nationals, see para 9.82.
73 EIG chapter 55 paras 55.1.2, 55.1.3, 55.3.A.
74 In *R (FM) v Secretary of State for the Home Department* [2011] EWCA Civ 807 para 50, the Court of Appeal found that the 'imminence' requirement placed no more onerous restriction on the SSHD than did the *Hardial Singh* principles. We respectfully suggest that a) this is difficult to reconcile with binding authority establishing that policy itself restricts the SSHD's exercise of the power to detain; and b) imminence cannot be synonymous with *Hardial Singh* reasonableness since this would mean that in some cases, removal within, for example, a year's time would still be 'imminent'. That would be

delayed by the detainee's refusal to cooperate with the travel documentation process: non-cooperation is a factor 'weighing strongly against release'.[75]

34.41 If removal is not imminent (and there is no significant non-cooperation by the detainees) the second step for CCD caseworkers is to consider absconding risk if the detainee is released:

> Individuals with a long history of failing to comply with immigration control or who have made a determined attempt to breach the UK's immigration laws would normally be assessed as being unlikely to comply with the terms of release on restrictions. Examples of this would include multiple attempts to abscond or the breach of previous conditions, and attempts to frustrate removal (not including the exercise of appeal rights). Also relevant is where the person's behaviour in prison or IRC (if known) has given cause for concern. The person's family ties in the UK and their expectations about the outcome of the case should also be considered. If there is an above average risk of absconding, detention or continued detention will usually be appropriate. Where the individual has complied with attempts to re-document them but difficulties remain due to the country concerned, this should not be viewed as non-compliance by the individual.[76]

34.42 The third step is the assessment of harm to the public. The harm-risk assessment should in the first instance be carried out by the National Offender Management Service (NOMS) rather than by immigration officers. The process of liaison between the UK Border Agency and NOMS has been discussed at paras 27.36–27.37. However, if there is no Offender Assessment System (OASys) or pre-sentence report available, the UK Border Agency 'case owner' may make the risk assessment.[77] In practice, and particularly in cases where there was no Parole Board involvement in release from criminal custody and/ or of long-term immigration detention, there will often be no up-to-date NOMS risk assessment. The prospect of untrained UK Border Agency staff making offending risk assessments which affect the duration of administrative detention is concerning, not least in the light of the oddities in the guidance that they have been given (see in particular paras 34.47–34.49 below).

34.43 The revised EIG provides general guidance for case owners making such a risk assessment:

> inconsistent with the terms of the policy and with the ordinary meaning of the word 'imminent'.

75 EIG chapter 55 para 55.3.2.4.
76 EIG chapter 55 para 55.3.2.5.
77 EIG chapter 55 para 55.3.2.6.

Factors relevant to this will be the nature of the original offence, any other offences committed, record of behaviour in prison and or IRC and general record of compliance. A PNC check should always be made ... Those with a long record of persistent offending are likely to be rated in the high or medium risk. Those with a low level, one-off conviction and, with a good record of behaviour otherwise are likely to be low risk.[78]

34.44 Home Office detention policy distinguishes between 'more serious offences' and 'less serious offences'. On its face, EIG chapter 55 appears to direct Home Office caseworkers that, in the absence of a NOMS assessment, a conviction of one of a list of specified offences is indicative of a 'high risk' of further offending.[79] These 'more serious' offences are considered further below.

34.45 It is Home Office policy that (having 'passed' the initial steps) 'those assessed as low or medium risk' should 'generally' be considered for release on a 'rigorous contact management' regime[80] (the EIG suggests twice weekly reporting and electronic monitoring in such cases[81]).

34.46 Personal compassionate circumstances should also be considered; as should any reasons given by an immigration judge of the tribunal for refusing bail.[82]

More serious offences

34.47 Annexed to EIG chapter 55 is a list of offences deemed 'more serious'. That policy in relation to the 'more serious offences' has been unsuccessfully challenged at High Court level.[83]

34.48 The list of 'more serious' offences is long and amorphous, ranging from self-evidently serious offences to summary offences to acts which now no longer constitute criminal offences at all (buggery and gross indecency between males). It is in places very vague ('other possession of weapons'; 'other miscellaneous sexual offences'). The list includes:

- drugs offences save for simple possession;
- offences of violence against the person (from common assault involving no injury to murder);

---

78 EIG chapter 55 para 55.3.2.8.
79 EIG chapter 55 para 55.3.2.8.
80 EIG chapter 55 para 55.32.11.
81 EIG chapter 55 para 55.20.5.2.
82 EIG chapter 55 paras 55. 3.2.11 and 55.3.2.13.
83 *R (Abdi) v Secretary of State for the Home Department* [2009] EWHC 1324 (Admin) para 9.

- child cruelty or neglect (child abandonment or abduction);
- weapons offences (no definition provided in the list but apparently including all possession offences);
- harassment offences;
- sexual offences (from 'miscellaneous sexual offences' to rape of a child under 13). All those presently on the sex offenders register are required to be treated as serious offenders, even if the sex offence is not the most recent conviction;
- property offences (all robbery offences; all burglary offences relating to domestic property; profiting from or concealing knowledge of the proceeds of crime);
- criminal damage (arson only);
- public order offences (riot, violent disorder);
- other miscellaneous offences (kidnapping, blackmail, absconding from lawful custody).

34.49 EIG chapter 55 states, without apparent evidential basis, that conviction of any of the listed offences may be indicative of a high absconding risk as well as indicative of high offending risk.[84] Offending and absconding risks, particularly where assessed as high, weigh against release,[85] may justify a longer period of detention and may outweigh factors such as mental illness which would otherwise lead to release.[86]

---

84 'A conviction for one of the more serious offences is strongly indicative of the greatest risk of harm to the public and a high risk of absconding': EIG chapter 55 para 55.3.A. 'Where there is a conviction for an offence on the [serious offences] list the nature of the offence is such that the person presents a high risk [of future harm] ... Such high risk offences should be given particularly substantial weight when assessing reasonableness to detain': EIG chapter 55 para 55.3.2.8.
85 'In practice, release is likely to be appropriate only in exceptional cases. This does not mean, however, that individuals convicted of offences on the list can be detained indefinitely and regardless of the effects on their dependents': EIG chapter 55 para 55.3.2.1. 'So, in practice, it is likely that a conclusion that such a person should be released would only be reached where there are exceptional circumstances which clearly outweigh the risk of public harm and which mean detention is not appropriate': EIG chapter 55 para 55.3.A.
86 'Caseworkers must balance against the increased risk, including the particular risk to the public from re-offending and the risk of absconding in the individual case, the types of factors normally considered in non-FNP detention cases, for example, if the detainee is mentally ill or if there is a possibly disproportionate impact on any dependent child under the age of 18 from continued detention. Caseworkers are reminded that what constitutes a "reasonable period" for these purposes will generally be longer than in non-criminal cases, or in less serious criminal cases ...': EIG chapter 55 para 55.3.A.

34.50 Notably, the EIG provides no guidance to caseworkers as to how to deal with those convicted in the past of serious offences, whose most recent offence giving rise to the potential or actual deportation proceedings is a lesser offence. The exception is sex offences, where caseworkers are directed to treat anyone as a serious offender who is presently on the sex offenders register, even if the sex offence is not the most recent offence.[87]

34.51 We suggest that a mechanistic approach by CCD caseworkers to the 'more serious' offences list, equating such a conviction with high offending risk without regard to individual factors indicative of lower risk (such as the 'one-off' nature of a serious offence, a diminution in the gravity of offending over time, or successful completion of offending behaviour courses or good behaviour in prison), would be unlawful. So too would be a practice of equating a conviction of such offences with high absconding risk without regard to individual factors indicative of lower risk (such as a history of compliance with temporary admission or bail, ties in the community, and outstanding claims or appeals which give an incentive to comply with conditions of release). The common law requirement of individualised assessment has been emphasised by the Supreme Court in *Lumba and Mighty*;[88] and the proportionality requirement in ECHR articles 5 and 8 also entails an individualised assessment of suitability for detention.

Those with British or EEA national spouses

34.52 In non-CCD cases, special caution must be exercised on detaining those with British or European Economic Area (EEA) national spouses. However, the policy goes on to state that:

> In CCD cases, the fact that the FNP is the spouse of a British Citizen or EEA national should not prevent detention.[89]

34.53 The family members of EEA nationals may enjoy special protections from expulsion and so too may the family members of dependent citizens of the European Union, as has already been seen in chapters 9 and 10 respectively. The policy should not be interpreted as

---

87 List of 'crimes where release from immigration detention or at the end of custody would be unlikely', annexed to EIG chapter 55.
88 *R (Lumba and Mighty) v Secretary of State for the Home Department* [2011] UKSC 12, [2011] 2 WLR 671 per Lord Dyson at para 53.
89 EIG chapter 55 para 55.9.2.

permitting the detention of those FNPs for whom there is no realistic prospect of deportation because of the operation of EU law.

Other common examples of policy breaches in FNP cases

34.54 We have already discussed at paras 34.27–34.26 above claims relating to the policy concerning the seriously mentally ill, those with serious medical conditions, the seriously disabled, and those for whom there is independent evidence of torture. At paras 35.30–35.33, we will examine the remedial consequences of a failure to comply with detention review requirements set out in published Home Office policy.

The secret detention policy for FNPs

34.55 The Home Office operated a secret blanket or near blanket detention policy for FNPs between circa 25 April 2006 and 9 September 2008.[90] A person to whom this unlawful detention policy was applied will, without more, be able to establish that he or she was unlawfully detained, but will only be entitled to substantial damages if the secret policy caused the detention.[91]

---

90 See Introduction to this book.
91 *R (Lumba and Mighty) v Secretary of State for the Home Department* [2011] UKSC 12, [2011] 2 WLR 671. See also application in *R (Sino) v Secretary of State for the Home Department* [2011] EWHC 2249 (Admin).

CHAPTER 35

Procedural requirements in immigration detention

35.1	Introduction
35.3	**Initial detention authorisation**
35.6	Detention authority forms including the IS91
35.8	Levels of detention authority
35.10	**Reasons for detention**
35.13	Content and form of the reasons
35.17	Consequences of a failure to give reasons for detention
35.22	**Notification of entitlement to bail**
35.25	**Risk assessment in all immigration detention cases**
35.27	**Detention reviews**
35.30	Legal consequences of a failure to properly carry out detention reviews
35.34	**Authorisation before release**
35.35	**Medical reviews**

Introduction

35.1 This chapter looks at the procedural requirements that apply where a person is detained under Immigration Act powers and considers the legal consequences of failure to comply with these requirements.

35.2 The detention of those detained for deportation is managed by the Criminal Casework Directorate (CCD) within the UK Border Agency of the Home Office whether they are held in Immigration Removal Centres (IRCs) or in prisons.

Initial detention authorisation

35.3 The authorisation of detention by the Secretary of State for the Home Department (SSHD) is an express statutory requirement for detention under the Immigration Act (IA) 1971 for a person given notice of intention to deport[1] and for a person who is the subject of a deportation order.[2] Such authorisation is also an express statutory requirement for all detention under the UK Borders Act (UKBA) 2007, whether the SSHD is considering whether the 'automatic' deportation provisions apply,[3] thinks they apply[4] or has made an 'automatic' deportation order.[5]

35.4 The exception is that there is no express statutory requirement for the SSHD's authority to detain in court recommendation cases. IA 1971 Sch 3 para 2(1), which permits detention in court recommendation cases, makes no express reference to the authority of the SSHD. The position in court recommendation cases remains controversial at the time of writing and has already been discussed at paras 32.34–32.40.

35.5 At least in cases other than court recommendation cases, lack of any lawful authority to detain will render detention unlawful, whether or not there are substantive grounds to justify the detention.[6]

---

1 IA 1971 Sch 3 para 2(2) referring to detention 'under the authority of' the SSHD.
2 IA 1971 Sch 3 para 2(3) referring to detention 'under the authority of' the SSHD.
3 UKBA 2007 s36(1)(a) referring to detention 'under the authority of' the SSHD.
4 UKBA 2007 s36(1)(b) referring to detention 'under the authority of' the SSHD.
5 UKBA 2007 s36(2). This applies the power of detention under IA 1971 Sch 3 para 2(3) which itself can only be exercised 'under the authority of' the SSHD.
6 *R (Lumba and Mighty) v Secretary of State for the Home Department* [2011] UKSC 12, [2011] 2 WLR 671; *R (Kambadzi) v Secretary of State for the Home Department* [2011] UKSC 23, [2011] 1 WLR 1299, see in particular paras 50–52 and 54 per Lord Hope, and paras 82 and 88 per Lord Kerr.

Detention authority forms including the IS91

35.6 In practice, the authority to detain may appear in a number of formats: a form simply headed 'authority for detention' is sometimes provided or a letter confirming authority to detain. There is also an IS91 'detention authority' form which Home Office policy requires be issued for every detained person (including children).[7]

35.7 Detaining bodies are under instructions not to accept into immigration detention individuals for whom no IS91 is held:[8] the exception is when a person is held at a police station where there is no immigration service presence in which case the IS91 must be faxed to the police station. Where the person is held in a prison, Prison Service Instruction (PSI) 52/2011 likewise stipulates that an IS91 must be held by the prison.[9] Only one IS91 is issued for each continuous period of detention: the form is passed from one detaining authority to the next when a detainee is transferred. However, where a new risk assessment (form IS91RA – see paras 35.25–35.26 further below) has been completed, in which case a new IS91 will be issued.

Levels of detention authority

35.8 The Enforcement Instructions and Guidance (EIG) requires that initial CCD detention be authorised at least at senior caseworker level, and *before* the person enters CCD detention.[10]

35.9 However, a failure to authorise detention at the correct grade of seniority is not in itself sufficient to render detention unlawful – see the discussion at paras 32.22–32.23.

Reasons for detention

35.10 The government committed in its 1998 white paper[11] that written reasons would be given to immigration detainees at the start of their detention and monthly thereafter. This remains current Home Office policy as set out in EIG chapter 55; it is also Home Office policy to

---

7 EIG chapter 55 para 55.6.2.
8 EIG chapter 55 para 55.6.2.
9 PSI 52/2011 para 2.62.
10 EIG chapter 55 para 55.5.2.
11 Fairer, faster and firmer – a modern approach to immigration and asylum para 12.7.

provide written reasons for detention more often if circumstances change.[12]

35.11 The Detention Centre Rules 2001, which apply to all those held in IRCs, likewise provide at rule 9 that every detained person will be provided with written reasons for detention at the start of the detention and monthly thereafter.

35.12 The common law also imposes a duty to give reasons in detention cases generally[13] including immigration detention cases.[14]

Content and form of the reasons

35.13 It is not enough to give reasons for detention: the reasons for detention must be correctly stated. This is clear from the EIG;[15] and, we suggest, from the common law;[16] as well as from the ECtHR's jurisprudence on European Convention on Human Rights (EHCR) article 5(2).[17]

35.14 It is Home Office practice to provide immigration detainees with a 'reasons for detention' form. IS91R consists of a checklist, where the appropriate box(es) can be ticked. However, in CCD cases, form ICD 1913 (letter format) is now issued instead of form IS91R; and in automatic deportation cases, form ICD 1913AD will be issued.

35.15 The reasons for detention form is itself an important source of Home Office policy, listing the permissible reasons for detention. The six permissible reasons for detention under the EIG[18] and the factors to be taken into consideration,[19] have been listed at paras 34.19–34.20 above.

35.16 The Home Office may also provide immigration detainees with a letter setting out more fully the reasons for their detention. Monthly detention updates are normally provided to detainees on form IS151F.

12 EIG chapter 55 paras 55.6 and 55.6.3.
13 *Christie v Leachinsky* [1947] AC 573, see in particular Viscount Simon at 588H.
14 *R (Faulkner) v Secretary of State for the Home Department* [2005] EWHC 2567 (Admin); *R (Raed Salah Mahajna) v Secretary of State for the Home Department* [2011] EWHC 2481 (Admin); see also the discussion at paras 32.26–32.29 and 35.17 below.
15 'It should be noted that the reasons for detention given could be subject to judicial review. It is therefore important that they are always justified and correctly stated': EIG chapter 55 para 55.6.3.
16 See the detailed discussion at paras 32.26–32.29.
17 *Saadi v the UK* App No 13229/03, 29 January 2008 paras 84–85.
18 EIG chapter 55 para 55.6.3.
19 EIG chapter 55 para 55.6.3.

Consequences of a failure to give reasons for detention

35.17 House of Lords authority, *Christie and Leachinsky*,[20] establishes that, at common law, a failure to give reasons renders the underlying detention unlawful. The House of Lords in *Saadi v Secretary of State for the Home Department*[21] subsequently stated that a failure to give accurate reasons did not vitiate the legality of detention but *Christie and Leachinsky* does not appear to have been cited. In *Lumba and Mighty*,[22] the Supreme Court confirmed that *Christie and Leachinsky* remained good law[23] and that the dicta of the House of Lords in *Saadi* were obiter.[24] See *R (Raed Salah Mahajna) v Secretary of State for the Home Department*[25] in which a detention under Immigration Act powers was found unlawful for want of reasons. We have suggested that recent *dicta* in the Court of Appeal in *R (MS) v Secretary of State for the Home Department*,[26] again apparently without reference to *Christie and Leachinsky*, but citing *Saadi* and to the same effect, are also obiter. See the more detailed discussion at paras 32.26–32.29. However, where the failure to give reasons did not cause the detention (in that the person would inevitably have been detained lawfully if given reasons) this is likely to reduce quantum. See the discussion on causation and quantum at paras 32.24–32.25.

35.18 A failure promptly to give accurate reasons for detention will breach ECHR article 5(2). In *Saadi v the UK*,[27] where accurate reasons for detention were not given promptly, the ECtHR Grand Chamber found that there had been a breach of article 5(2).

35.19 A failure by the Home Office to provide any or any accurate reasons for detention may also impede a challenge to the lawfulness

---

20 *Christie v Leachinsky* [1947] AC 573, see in particular Viscount Simon at 588H.
21 [2002] UKHL 41, [2002] 1 WLR 3131 per Lord Slynn para 48.
22 *R (Lumba and Mighty) v Secretary of State for the Home Department* [2011] UKSC 12, [2011] 2 WLR 671.
23 *R (Lumba and Mighty) v Secretary of State for the Home Department* [2011] UKSC 12, [2011] 2 WLR 671 per Lord Dyson at para 76; Lord Walker at para 185; Lady Hale at paras 201, 211; Lord Collins para 221; Lord Phillips para 327; and Lord Brown and Lord Rodger para 345. See also *R (Kambadzi) v Secretary of State for the Home Department* [2011] UKSC 23, [2011] 1 WLR 1299 per Lady Hale at paras 72–73.
24 See discussions in *R (Lumba and Mighty) v Secretary of State for the Home Department* [2011] UKSC 12, [2011] 2 WLR 671 per Lord Dyson para 84; *R (Kambadzi) v Secretary of State for the Home Department* [2011] UKSC 23, [2011] 1 WLR 1299 per Lord Hope para 45.
25 [2011] EWHC 2481 (Admin).
26 [2011] EWCA Civ 838 para 49.
27 (2008) 47 EHRR 17; [2008] Imm AR 368.

of detention by a detainee and therefore also give rise to a breach of ECHR article 5(4).[28] Article 5(4) provides that any person deprived of his or her liberty by arrest or detention shall be entitled to take proceedings by which the lawfulness of his or her detention shall be decided upon speedily by a court and his or her release ordered if the detention is not lawful.

35.20 There is a right to 'compensation' for a breach of ECHR article 5(2) or (4). ECHR article 5(5) provides a right to compensation for 'everyone who has been the victim of arrest or detention in contravention of this Article' and makes no distinction between the distinct ECHR article 5 subparagraphs for the purpose of this award of compensation. However, for purely procedural breaches, the compensation need not be financial.[29]

35.21 See the fuller discussion of ECHR article 5 at paras 36.4–36.46.

Notification of entitlement to bail

35.22 For an unrepresented detainee, a failure to give the reasons for detention form often has the added consequence that the detainee is not informed of the right to seek bail. Attached to the reasons for detention form should normally be an explanation for detainees of their entitlement to apply for immigration bail from the Immigration Service or from the FTT-IAC and contact details for certain legal advisers for assistance in these applications.

35.23 It is stated Home Office policy that detainees should be informed of their bail rights (using an interpreter where necessary).[30]

35.24 Arguably,[31] notification of the entitlement to bail is so fundamental a procedural safeguard that its breach may affect the legality of the underlying detention at common law. See paras 34.8–34.10 for a discussion of the legal consequences of policy breaches. Additionally, where the underlying detention is unlawful for some other reason, a failure to inform a detainee of his or her entitlement to seek immi-

---

28 *Garcia Alva v Germany* App No 23541/94, 13 February 2001, para 39.
29 In *Saadi v UK* App No 13229/03, 29 January 2008 at para 89, the Grand Chamber did not award damages for the breach of ECHR article 5(2), treating its own findings as just satisfaction for the breach. See likewise *Wassink v The Netherlands* (1990) 22 EHRR 820 para 41, where a purely procedural breach of ECHR article 5(1) gave rise to no financial compensation.
30 EIG chapter 55 para 55.6.3.
31 Particularly in the light of the importance given by the law to the provision of reasons for detention (to enable a detainee to seek release) – see paras 32.26–32.29.

gration bail may found a claim for aggravated damages. Finally, a failure to notify a detainee of his right to seek bail may breach ECHR article 5(4).

Risk assessment in all immigration detention cases

35.25 It is Home Office policy, under the EIG,[32] that a risk assessment should be completed (on form IS91RA) for each person who is to be detained under Immigration Act powers. The form should be forwarded to the Detainee Escorting and Population Management Unit (DEPMU) or the Family Detention Unit (family cases) for the purposes of assessing and allocating appropriate detention location. Risk factors should be identified in advance of detention where possible through a 'planned operation/visit'. Where it is not possible to complete a risk assessment in advance of detention (the examples given by the EIG are where a person has been arrested or picked up 'in the field') the risk assessment should be completed as soon as possible and in all cases 'no later than 24 hours after entry into detention at a police station and always before entry into the Immigration detention estate is sought'.[33] The duty to assess risk is ongoing: where new risk factors come to light, a new IS91RA form should be completed and sent to DEPMU or the Family Detention Unit.

35.26 In practice, IS91RA forms are often left blank by the immigration service. We suggest that risk assessments may fall in the intermediary category of procedural requirement, breach of which renders detention unlawful unless the SSHD can show that detention would in any event have ensued (see the discussion at paras 32.22–32.23 above). In any event, where a detainee is held who should not have been detained under the Home Office's own policies concerning the vulnerable, a failure by the Immigration Service to complete the IS91RA adequately or at all may furnish important evidence that relevant considerations were not taken into account before the decision to detain or to maintain detention was reached.

32 EIG chapter 55 para 55.6.1.
33 EIG chapter 55 para 55.6.1.

Detention reviews

35.27 It is published Home Office policy that detention should be regularly reviewed by officials at escalating levels in the CCD hierarchy. Often missed in long-term detention cases, detention reviews are an essential procedural safeguard. The Supreme Court has held that detention reviews are 'fundamental to the propriety of continued detention',[34] and that they are 'not only commendable; they are necessary', indicating that even if the policy did not require detention reviews, the common law would require them.[35] The review can be considered to be an implied aspect of the SSHD's statutory duty to authorise detention: the detention reviews are the means by which the authority to detain is renewed.[36] The review is also a public law duty, being the means by which the continued legality of detention is ensured, as well as an obligation imposed by policy.[37]

35.28 It is important to note that detention review requirements have been modified over time. Since 9 September 2008, the EIG contains scaled-down review requirements for those detained by the CCD (by contrast to other immigration detainees). CCD cases (other than unaccompanied minor FNPs, see para 37.30) even at the outset of detention, must now only be reviewed monthly. Those in CCD detention used to be entitled to reviews at the 24-hour, 7-day, 14-day and 21-day stages of detention. Non CCD cases are still entitled to these more frequent reviews at the outset of detention.

35.29 The EIG seeks to justify the distinct review regime for CCD cases on the basis that where immigration detainees come from prison 'their personal circumstances have already been taken into account by the UK Border Agency when the original decision to detain was made'.[38] That reasoning is questionable, not least since the new scaled-back review requirements appear to apply to all those in CCD detention (not just those detained directly after the completion of a criminal custodial term) and may be open to challenge.

---

34 *R (Kambadzi) v Secretary of State for the Home Department* [2011] UKSC 23, [2011] 1 WLR 1299 per Lord Hope para 51 and per Lady Hale at para 73, approving the dicta of Munby J at first instance.

35 *R (Kambadzi) v Secretary of State for the Home Department* [2011] UKSC 23, [2011] 1 WLR 1299 para 51 per Lord Hope.

36 *R (Kambadzi) v Secretary of State for the Home Department* [2011] UKSC 23, [2011] 1 WLR 1299 paras 52 and 54 per Lord Hope, para 87 per Lord Kerr.

37 *R (Kambadzi) v Secretary of State for the Home Department* [2011] UKSC 23, [2011] 1 WLR 1299 para 51 per Lord Hope, para 73 per Lady Hale, paras 84–85 per Lord Kerr.

38 EIG chapter 55 para 55.8.

Legal consequences of a failure to properly carry out detention reviews

35.30 A person whose detention is not reviewed with the regularity required by published Home Office detention policy is, without more, unlawfully detained for the period that his detention is not reviewed, until the next review. However, if detention would have continued lawfully even if reviewed, there is no loss and the detainee will only be entitled to nominal damages.[39]

35.31 As concerns ongoing detention, in principle, during the period for which the detention is not reviewed, a detainee is entitled to habeas corpus. There are, however, significant practical obstacles to release on this basis. First, obtaining copies of Home Office files or documents is often a slow process (see the discussion of disclosure at paras 42.12–42.15), and many detainees will be unaware of whether their detention is being been reviewed. Second, if the Home Office rectifies the error by carrying out a review before the court hearing or indeed before the court gives judgment, then (provided that the review is itself substantively lawful and the detention is otherwise justified) the illegality will be purely historic and the detainee will not be entitled to release.[40]

35.32 A review which is flawed by a material error (for example, material errors of fact) also, without more, renders detention unlawful.[41]

35.33 Where the flaw in the detention review is purely a failure to review at the correct grade of seniority, this is not of itself a material public law error and does not vitiate the legality of the detention.[42] We suggest that this may fall in the intermediary category of procedural

---

39 *R (Kambadzi) v Secretary of State for the Home Department* [2011] UKSC 23, [2011] 1 WLR 1299.

40 This occurred at first instance in the case of *R (Kambadzi) v Secretary of State for the Home Department* [2011] UKSC 23, [2011] 1 WLR 1299, also known as *SK (Zimbabwe) v Secretary of State for the Home Department* [2008] EWHC 98 (Admin), see paras 125–134. Having found that the detention had been unlawful for the periods it had not been reviewed, Munby J declined to order release because he had received a fresh lawful detention review from the Home Office before giving judgment.

41 As occurred in *R (Kambadzi) v Secretary of State for the Home Department* [2011] UKSC 23, [2011] 1 WLR 1299, see paras 26 and 60.

42 *R (Lumba and Mighty) v Secretary of State for the Home Department* [2011] UKSC 12, [2011] 2 WLR 671 per Lord Dyson para 68; *R (Kambadzi) v Secretary of State for the Home Department* [2011] UKSC 23, [2011] 1 WLR 1299 per Lord Hope para 60.

error[43] discussed above at paras 32.22–32.23, which is not of itself sufficient to render detention unlawful, but would do so if the error had caused the detention (in that another official could properly have reached a different view).

Authorisation before release

35.34 A decision to release a time served FNP must be approved at Assistant Director level and authorised by the Chief Executive of the UK Border Agency or a board member deputising in his or her absence.[44] The distinct position for the release of a 'serious criminal' to rejoin a family with dependent children under 18 is discussed at para 37.20.

Medical reviews

35.35 The special requirements in IRCs for medical screening within two hours of arrival, and for medical examination within 24 hours, and the consequences of breach of those requirements, have been discussed at paras 34.33–34.36 above.

---

43 See *R (Kambadzi) v Secretary of State for the Home Department* [2011] UKSC 23, [2011] 1 WLR 1299 per Lady Hale paras 70–71.
44 EIG chapter 55 para 55.8.

CHAPTER 36
The ECHR and detention

36.1	Introduction
36.4	**ECHR article 5**
36.5	An unqualified right
36.6	'Deprivation of liberty'
36.8	**ECHR article 5(1)**
36.10	'In accordance with a procedure prescribed by law'
36.13	Protection from arbitrary detention
36.17	ECHR article 5(1) and detention conditions
36.18	**ECHR article 5(1)(f) detention**
36.19	The second limb of ECHR article 5(1)(f) – detention for expulsion
	Deportation proceedings 'in progress' • Detention for a reasonable period • Flaws in the expulsion decision • No necessity test (for now)
36.34	The relationship between the Hardial Singh principles, domestic policy and ECHR article 5(1)(f)
36.37	**ECHR article 5(2)**
36.41	**ECHR article 5(4)**
36.46	**ECHR article 5(5)**
36.47	**ECHR article 3**
36.48	Positive and negative obligations
36.50	The minimum level of severity

continued

36.55	Inhuman or degrading treatment
36.57	Conditions of detention
	Detention conditions for asylum-seekers • Detention in conditions inappropriate for a particular detainee • Defective medical care in detention • Inappropriate to 'wait and see' • Detention of the mentally and physically ill
36.71	Injuries and mental ill health sustained in custody: burden of proof
36.74	ECHR article 3 and the requirement to release
36.75	**ECHR article 8**
36.76	Private life aspects
36.79	Family life aspects
	Correspondence • Positive and negative obligations • Treatment falling short of the ECHR article 3 threshold • Limitations on rights consequent on imprisonment • Justification and proportionality
36.95	**ECHR article 14**
36.104	**Breaches of the ECHR resulting from a detention contractor's actions or omissions**

Introduction

36.1 This section examines the most common instances of the application of the protections under the European Convention on Human Rights (ECHR) in challenges to immigration detention.

36.2 The primary focus of this chapter is on the protection against arbitrary deprivation of liberty in ECHR article 5 and the related European Court of Human Rights (ECtHR) jurisprudence.

36.3 We go on to consider claims that detention amounts to inhuman or degrading treatment under ECHR article 3; or an unjustified interference with the rights protected by ECHR article 8. The chapter ends with an overview of ECHR article 14.

ECHR article 5

36.4 ECHR article 5 provides, insofar as is relevant to immigration detention:

Everyone has the right to liberty and security of person.

1. No one shall be deprived of his liberty save in the following cases and in accordance with a procedure prescribed by law:

...

(f) the lawful arrest or detention of a person to prevent his effecting an unauthorized entry into the country or of a person against whom action is being taken with a view to deportation or extradition.

2. Everyone who is arrested shall be informed promptly, in a language which he understands, of the reasons for his arrest and the charge against him.

...

Everyone who is deprived of his liberty by arrest or detention shall be entitled to take proceedings by which the lawfulness of his detention shall be decided speedily by a court and his release ordered if the detention is not lawful.

Everyone who has been the victim of arrest or detention in contravention of the provisions of this article shall have an enforceable right to compensation.

An unqualified right

36.5 The right to liberty under ECHR article 5 is an unqualified right – it may only be derogated from in the exceptional circumstances (war or public emergency threatening the life of the nation) defined in ECHR article 15 and there is no such derogation by the UK at present:

The point about the right not to be deprived of one's liberty under Article 5.1 is that, subject to the exceptions, it is unqualified ... Only in time of war or 'public emergency threatening the life of the nation' may the government derogate from the Convention, suspend habeas corpus and imprison people without trial.[1]

'Deprivation of liberty'

36.6 ECHR article 5 protects individuals deprived of their liberty; it is not engaged by mere restriction on liberty.[2]

36.7 The classic forms of deprivation of liberty include detention in prison, police cell or an immigration removal centre. However, deprivation of liberty may take many other forms:

> The difference between deprivation of and restriction upon liberty is ... merely one of degree or intensity, and not one of nature or substance.

To assess whether there has been a deprivation of liberty, it may be necessary to examine 'a whole range of criteria such as the type, duration, effects and manner of implementation of the measure in question'.[3] Detention has been held to include immigrants being held in the transit zone of an airport for a protracted period (even though the asylum-seeker claimants were to some extent left to their own devices and 'free to leave' by leaving the country) while awaiting a determination of their asylum claim.[4]

ECHR article 5(1)

36.8 Detention will breach ECHR article 5(1) unless it meets the following test:[5]

i) Is the detention lawful under domestic law?
ii) Is the law under which the detention was authorised sufficiently accessible and precise for an individual to foresee the consequences?

---

1 *R (JJ) v Secretary of State for the Home Department* [2007] UKHL 45, [2008] 1 AC 385 per Lord Hoffmann para 35.
2 *Engel v The Netherlands (No 1)* (1976) 1 EHRR 647.
3 *Guzzardi v Italy* (1980) 3 EHRR 333 paras 92–93.
4 *Amuur v France* (1996) 22 EHRR 533, para 42.
5 See test set out by *R v Governor of Brockhill Prison ex p Evans (2)* [2001] 2 AC 19 per Lord Hope of Craighead at 38.

iii) Does detention fall within one of the permissible categories of detention under Article 5 (1) ECHR and is detention otherwise non-arbitrary and proportionate.

36.9 Below, we consider distinct elements of that test.

'In accordance with a procedure prescribed by law'

36.10 To comply with ECHR article 5(1), detention must comply with the substantive and procedural[6] rules of domestic law.[7]

36.11 Domestic 'law' for ECHR purposes does not comprise only statutory law. Domestic 'law' includes common law restrictions on the exercise of the power to detain, including the public law requirement that the SSHD, absent good reason for not so doing, follow published Home Office policy (see the discussion at para 34.7). Detention contrary to published Home Office policy has therefore been held to breach ECHR article 5(1).[8]

36.12 To have the quality of 'law' for the purposes of justifying detention under ECHR article 5(1), the domestic law under which detention is authorised must be sufficiently accessible and precise to enable the individual to foresee the consequences of his or her actions and possible restrictions that will ensue.[9]

Protection from arbitrary detention

36.13 Detention must also comply and be consistent with the requirements and objectives inherent in ECHR article 5(1) itself. The primary purpose of the protections set out in ECHR article 5(1) is to protect individuals from arbitrary detention.[10] The concept of arbitrariness

---

6 For an example of a failure to meet a purely procedural obligation in domestic law giving rise to a breach of ECHR article 5(1), see *Wassink v The Netherlands* (Series A/185-A) 1990, para 27.

7 *Winterwerp v The Netherlands* (1979) 2 EHRR 387 paras 39 and 45; *Bozano v France* (1986) 9 EHRR 297 at para 54; *Weeks v UK* (1987) 10 EHRR 293 at para 42; *Benham v UK* (1996) 22 EHRR 293.

8 *Nadarajah and Amirthanathan v Secretary of State for the Home Department* [2003] EWCA Civ 1768, see discussion at paras 32.40 and 34.1–34.2.

9 *R v Governor of Brockhill Prison ex p Evans* (2) [2001] 2 AC 19 per Lord Hope of Craighead at 38; see also *Sunday Times v UK* (1979) 2 EHRR 245; *Zamir v UK* (1983) 40 D & R 42, paras 90–91.

10 *Amuur v France* (1996) 22 EHRR 533 at para 42; *Mitunga v Belgium* App No 13178/03 para 96; *Saadi v UK* App No 13229/03, 29 January 2008 para 67; *Winterwerp v The Netherlands* (1979) 2 EHRR 387, para 37; *Amuur*, cited above, para 50; *Chahal v UK* (1996) 23 EHRR 413, para 118.

extends beyond lack of compliance with national law: a deprivation of liberty may be lawful under domestic law but still arbitrary and contrary to ECHR article 5(1).[11]

36.14 ECHR article 5(1) sets out an exhaustive list of the exceptions in which deprivation of liberty is permissible: if a detention falls outside those exceptions the detention is arbitrary and contrary to ECHR article 5(1).[12] The exceptions must be narrowly construed.[13]

36.15 Examples of arbitrariness contrary to ECHR article 5(1) are:

- where the order to detain or the execution of the detention do not genuinely conform with the restrictions set out in the relevant ECHR article 5(1) subparagraph;[14]
- where, despite complying with the letter of national law, there has been an element of bad faith or deception on the part of the authorities;[15]
- where there is no (or no adequate) relationship between the ground of permitted deprivation of liberty relied on and the place and conditions of detention;[16] and
- where the detention exceeds the period reasonably necessary for the purpose pursued.[17]

36.16 The prohibition on arbitrary detention under ECHR article 5(1) also includes a requirement that detention should not be disproportionate.[18] As we discuss further below, current ECtHR and domestic jurisprudence holds that the proportionality requirement applies

---

11 *Saadi v UK* (2008) 47 EHRR 17 Grand Chamber para 67.
12 *Witold Litwa v Poland* (2000) 33 EHRR 1267 para 49.
13 *Quinn v France* (1995) 21 EHRR 529 para 42; *Van der Leer v The Netherlands* (1990) 12 EHRR 567 para 22; *Wassink v The Netherlands* (Series A/185-A) 1990, para. 24.
14 *Winterwerp v The Netherlands* (1979) 2 EHRR 387, para 39; *Bouamar v Belgium* (1988) 11 EHRR 1; *O'Hara v UK* (2002) 34 EHRR 32.
15 *Bozano v France* (1986) 9 EHRR 297; *Conka v Belgium* (2002) 34 EHRR 1298.
16 *Bouamar v Belgium* at para 50; *Aerts v Belgium* (1986) 9 EHRR 297 at para 46; *Enhorn v Sweden* (2005) 41 EHRR 30 at para 42; *A and others v UK* (2009) 49 EHRR 29 at para 164; *Mayeka v Belgium* (2008) 46 EHRR 23.
17 *Vasileva v Denmark* (2003) 40 EHRR 27 at para 37; *McVeigh and others v UK* (1981) 5 EHRR 71 309; *Saadi v UK* (2008) 47 EHRR 17 para 74; *A and others v UK* (2009) 49 EHRR 29 para 164.
18 *Engel v The Netherlands (No 1)* (1976) 1 EHRR 647, para 58; *Tsirlis and Kouloumpas v Greece* (1997) 25 EHRR 198, para 56; *Witold Litwa v Poland* (2000) 33 EHRR 1267, para 78. The duration of the detention is a relevant factor in striking such a balance (*Vasileva v Denmark* (2003) 40 EHRR 27; *McVeigh and others v UK* (1983) 5 EHRR 71).

differently in ECHR article 5(1)(f), although there are indications of a shift at ECtHR level.

ECHR article 5(1) and detention conditions

36.17 Conditions of detention will only very rarely render a detention unlawful under ECHR article 5(1). However, 'there must be some relationship between the ground of permitted deprivation of liberty relied on and the place and conditions of detention'.[19] Thus, for example, the detention of an unaccompanied minor in an immigration detention centre for adults has been held to breach ECHR article 5(1).[20] Conversely, the Court of Appeal found that detention in a prison rather than an Immigration removal Centre did not breach ECHR article 5.[21]

ECHR article 5(1)(f) detention

36.18 Immigration detention potentially falls within the ambit of ECHR article 5(1)(f). The first limb of article 5(1)(f) recognises the power of domestic authorities to detain immigrants while making a decision on whether to grant (or cancel existing) leave to enter or remain (we refer to these as 'examination cases'). The second limb of article 5(1)(f) recognises the power of domestic authorities to detain immigrants pending their expulsion – covering, in the UK context, administrative removal and deportation as well as extradition (we refer to these as 'expulsion cases'). Our focus is on the second limb, which almost invariably is the relevant limb in immigration detention cases for foreign national former prisoners (FNPs).

The second limb of ECHR article 5(1)(f) – detention for expulsion

Deportation proceedings 'in progress'

36.19 Detention under the second limb of article 5(1)(f) is only permissible where action is being taken towards expulsion and with due diligence:

---

19 *Aerts v Belgium* (2000) 29 EHRR 50 para 46.
20 *Mitunga v Belgium* App No 13178/03 para 102.
21 *R (Dritan Krasniqi) v Secretary of State for the Home Dewpartment* [2011] EWCA Civ 1549.

Any deprivation of liberty under Article 5 para. 1 (f) will be justified only for as long as deportation proceedings are in progress. If such proceedings are not prosecuted with due diligence, the detention will cease to be permissible under Article 5 para. 1 (f).[22]

36.20 The ECtHR's jurisprudence makes clear that a purely aspirational or excessively vague expectation of expulsion is not enough. A 'realistic prospect' of expulsion test was applied by the Grand Chamber of the ECtHR in *A and others v UK*. That case concerned detainees who had been held without charge and without prospect of deportation at HMP Belmarsh under the Anti-Terrorism Crime and Security Act 2001:

> One of the principal assumptions underlying the derogation notice, the 2001 Act and the decision to detain the applicants was, therefore, that they could not be removed or deported 'for the time being' ... There is no evidence that during the period of the applicants' detention there was, except in respect of the second and fourth applicants, any realistic prospect of their being expelled without this giving rise to a real risk of ill-treatment contrary to Article 3 ... In these circumstances, the Court does not consider that the respondent Government's policy of keeping the possibility of deporting the applicants 'under active review' was sufficiently certain or determinative to amount to 'action ... being taken with a view to deportation'.[23]

36.21 In *Mikolenko v Estonia* the mere expectation of a legal change was insufficient to justify detention in circumstances where expulsion could not be effected without the applicant's cooperation, which he was unwilling to give. The detention breached ECHR article 5(1) notwithstanding that the reason why the applicant could not be expelled was his own non-cooperation which, under the domestic legal regime, was required. The ECtHR concluded:

> The foregoing considerations are sufficient to enable the Court to conclude that the grounds for the applicant's detention – action taken with a view to his deportation – did not remain valid for the whole period of his detention due to the lack of a realistic prospect of his expulsion and the domestic authorities' failure to conduct the proceedings with due diligence. There has accordingly been a violation of Article 5(1) of the Convention.[24]

---

22 *Chahal v UK* (1997) 23 EHRR 413 at para 113. See also *Slivenko v Latvia* (2004) 2 FCR 28 (Grand Chamber) at para 146; *Quinn v France* (1996) 21 EHRR 529 para 48; *Saadi v UK* (2008) 47 EHRR 17 at para 72.
23 (2009) 49 EHRR 29 para 167.
24 App No 10664/05, 8 October 2009, paras 66 and 68. See also *Massoud v Malta* App No 24340/08, judgment 27 July 2010 para 69; and *M v Bulgaria* App No 41416/08, judgment 26 July 2011 paras 70–75.

Detention for a reasonable period

36.22 The limitation on the duration of detention extends beyond a requirement that the expelling state exercise due diligence (see para 36.19 above): the duration must be reasonably required. In *Saadi v UK*, the ECtHR Grand Chamber stated:

> ... the length of the detention should not exceed that reasonably required for the purpose pursued.[25]

36.23 As in domestic law, the question of whether a reasonable period of detention has been exceeded for ECHR article 5(1)(f) purposes is fact specific. In the 'exceptional circumstances' of *Chahal v UK* (a suspected international terrorist) and where the UK authorities had acted with due diligence, a detention of over six years was found to be justified. However, in *Quinn v France*,[26] a detention of almost two years for extradition where the national authorities had not shown due diligence was held to breach ECHR article 5(1). Likewise, in *A and others v UK*, nine suspected international terrorists were found to have been unlawfully detained. For those applicants found to have been unlawfully detained in that case, the longest detention had lasted for three years and 83 days, and the shortest detention had lasted for 17 months. *Chahal* was distinguished by the ECtHR Grand Chamber in *A and others* on the basis that in *Chahal*, the UK government had 'actively and diligently pursued' deportation action.[27]

36.24 Albeit detention time limits are not mandatory under ECHR article 5(1)(f), the ECtHR has found time limits to be an important safeguard against arbitrary detention. In a series of cases, the ECtHR has found that in the absence of clear legal provisions, among other safeguards, setting up time limits for detention for expulsion, the deprivation of liberty was not circumscribed by adequate safeguards against arbitrariness, namely *Ismoilov and others v Russia*;[28] *Muminov v Russia*;[29] *Abdolkhani and Karimnia v Turkey*;[30] *ZNS v Turkey*;[31] *Tehrani and others v Turkey*;[32] *Charahili v Turkey*;[33] *Alipour and Hosseinzagdan*

---

25 *Saadi v UK* (2008) 47 EHRR 17 para 74.
26 (1995) 21 EHRR 529.
27 *A and others v UK* (2009) 49 EHRR 29 paras 169–170.
28 (2009) 49 EHRR 1128 para 140.
29 App No 42502/06, judgment 11 December 200 paras 121–122.
30 App No 30471/08, judgment 22 September 2009, paras 133 and 135.
31 App No 21896/08, judgment 19 January 2010, para 56.
32 App Nos 32940/08, 41626/08, 43616/08, 13 April 2010, para 70.
33 App No 46605/07, judgment 13 April 2010, para 66.

v Turkey;[34] *Dbouba v Turkey*;[35] *Massoud v Malta*.[36] In *Massoud v Malta*, the ECtHR observed that the consequence of a lack of such safeguards was 'indeterminate detention'.[37] This development may prove important for the UK. The UK is now alone among the members of the EU in having no time limits for the administrative detention of immigrants whether or not they have committed criminal offences (see introduction to Section I, note 1).

Flaws in the expulsion decision

36.25 Detention may be lawful under article 5(1)(f) notwithstanding that the underlying decision of the state to expel the individual was itself unlawful.[38] Note, however, that in domestic law, at least in relation to detention under IA 1971 Sch 3, if there is no power in law to deport (eg because the proposed deportee is British) then there is no power to detain.[39] As we have already seen, detention that is unlawful in domestic law will also breach ECHR article 5(1).

36.26 In addition, if the decision to expel was itself an abuse of power,[40] or, as we have already seen above if due diligence has not been shown by the state in pursuing the expulsion,[41] the detention may breach ECHR article 5(1)(f).

No necessity test (for now)

36.27 The ECtHR Grand Chamber in *Chahal* found that detention under the second limb of article 5(1)(f) need not be 'necessary':

> Article 5 para. 1 (f) (art. 5-1-f) does not demand that the detention of a person against whom action is being taken with a view to deportation be reasonably considered necessary, for example to prevent his committing an offence or fleeing.[42]

---

34 App Nos 6909/08, 12792/08, 28960/08, judgment 13 July 2010, para 57.
35 App No 15916/09, judgment 13 July 2010, para 50.
36 App No 24340/08, judgment 27 July 2010, para 71.
37 App No 24340/08, judgment 27 July 2010, para 71.
38 *Kolompar v Belgium* (1992) 16 EHRR 197; *X v UK* (1977) 12 DR 207 ECommHR; *Z v The Netherlands* (1984) 38 DR 145 ECommHR; *Quinn v France* (1995) 21 EHRR 529 at para 19; *Zamir v UK* (1983) 40 DR 42, ECommHR; *Chahal v UK* (1997) 23 EHRR 413 para 112.
39 See discussion at paras 31.20–31.24 for the position under UKBA 2007 s36.
40 *Bozano v France* (1986) 9 EHRR 297.
41 See para 36.19.
42 *Chahal v UK* (1997) 23 EHRR 413 para 112.

36.28 The ECtHR Grand Chamber in *Saadi v UK* held that the tests for arbitrariness and proportionality in examination and expulsion cases under the two limbs of ECHR article 5(1)(f) are the same and reiterated that there was no necessity test.[43]

36.29 In short, whereas the proportionality test under ECHR article 5(1) *generally* implies a necessity test and consideration of less restrictive measures, these authorities hold that an attenuated proportionality test applies to the detention of immigrants under article 5(1)(f).

36.30 The ECtHR Grand Chamber in *Saadi v UK*[44] and *A and others v UK*[45] has stated that the proportionality test in article 5(1)(f) cases merely requires that detention should not exceed the period that is reasonably required for the purpose pursued.

36.31 In taking this approach, the ECtHR has parted ways with other international human rights law. The analogue of ECHR article 5 in International Covenant of Civil and Political Rights (ICCPR) article 9, does include a full proportionality test and applies equally to the detention of immigrants, as the UN Human Rights Committee has repeatedly held.[46]

36.32 There are, however, signs that the ECtHR may be moving towards the adoption of a full necessity test in ECHR article 5(1)(f). In a number of recent judgments concerning article 5(1)(f), various sections of the ECtHR have applied a test of whether less restrictive alternatives exist to detention.[47]

36.33 In any event, even where ECHR article 5(1) does not itself require the imposition of a necessity test, where domestic law requires it, so too will article 5(1). The ECtHR held in *Rusu v Austria*:[48]

> It follows that while the necessity of detention with a view to expulsion is not required by the wording of Article 5 [s] 1 (f) of the Convention, it may be required under the domestic law to which that provision refers.

---

43 *Saadi v UK* (2008) 47 EHRR 17 at paras 72–73.
44 *Saadi v UK* (2008) 47 EHRR 17 at para 73.
45 *A and others v UK* (2009) 49 EHRR 29 paras 163 and 164.
46 See, for example, *A v Australia* CCPR/C/59/D/560/1993, 30 April 1997, para 9.2.
47 *Mikolenko v Estonia* App No 10664/05, 8 October 2009 at para 67; *Massoud v Malta* App No 24340/08, judgment of 27 July 2010 at para 68; *Raza v Bulgaria* App No 31465/08, 11 February 2010 at para 74; *Rusu v Austria* (2009) 49 EHRR 28 at para 58.
48 (2009) 49 EHRR 28 at para 54.

The relationship between the *Hardial Singh* principles, domestic policy and ECHR article 5(1)(f)

36.34 The *Hardial Singh* principles (common law principles governing the exercise of the power to detain, see chapter 33) may go further than ECHR article 5(1)(f) itself. In *R (Shepherd Masimba Kambadzi) v Secretary of State for the Home Department,* Lord Simon Brown and Lord Rodger suggested that the *Hardial Singh* test did incorporate a necessity test: there was a need to show a risk of absconding or reoffending.[49]

36.35 Further, domestic policy, save in fast track cases, appears to impose a necessity requirement. See paras 34.18 and 34.19 above.

36.36 As we have already seen above, detention must comply with domestic 'law' if it is to comply with ECHR article 5(1). Since domestic policy save in fast track cases incorporates a necessity requirement (and so too may the *Hardial Singh* principles) we suggest that, in the context of detention for expulsion in the UK, detention which is unnecessary will indeed breach ECHR article 5(1)(f). See also para 36.33 above.

ECHR article 5(2)

36.37 The ECtHR Grand Chamber stated in *Saadi v UK*:[50]

> Article 5 (2) contains the elementary safeguard that any person arrested should know why he is being deprived of his liberty. This provision is an integral part of the scheme of protection afforded by Article 5: by virtue of paragraph 2 any person arrested must be told, in simple, non-technical language that he can understand, the essential legal and factual grounds for his arrest, so as to be able, if he sees fit, to apply to a court to challenge its lawfulness in accordance with Article 5(4).

36.38 The question of whether adequate reasons have been given and 'promptly' is fact-specific. In *Conka v Belgium*,[51] the ECtHR found no violation of ECHR article 5(2) where the applicant was given broad reasons for his detention when he was detained, and written reasons were supplied two days later. In *Fox, Campbell and Hartley*,[52] giving reasons within seven hours after arrest was accepted to be 'prompt'.

---

49 [2011] UKSC 23, [2011] 1 WLR 1299 para 94.
50 (2008) 47 EHRR 17, para 51.
51 (2002) 34 EHRR 1298.
52 (1990) 13 EHRR 157.

In *Saadi v UK*,[53] the ECtHR Grand Chamber found that a 76-hour delay in providing accurate reasons for detention did not meet the requirement that reasons be given 'promptly'.

36.39 In the immigration detention context, ECHR article 5(2) may be breached by failure to comply with the requirements of secondary legislation and Home Office policy in respect of giving reasons for detention. Rule 9 of the Detention Centre Rules 2001[54] requires that written reasons for detention be given to a person 'at the time of his initial detention'. Home Office policy as set out in the Enforcement Instructions and Guidance (EIG) states that form IS91R (the reasons for detention checklist):

> ... must be served on every detained person at the time of their initial detention ... It is important that the detainee understands the contents of the IS91R. If he does not understand English, officers should ensure that the form's contents are interpreted. Failure to do so could lead to successful challenge under the Human Rights Act (Article 5(2) of the ECHR refers).[55]

36.40 Where the failure to give reasons has meant that the detainee had insufficient information to understand the basis of his or her detention and to mount an effective challenge to detention, then a failure to give reasons may give rise to a breach of ECHR article 5(4)[56] and may also render the detention arbitrary in breach of ECHR article 5(1).

ECHR article 5(4)

36.41 ECHR article 5(4) requires that those deprived of their liberty be allowed to speedily obtain judicial supervision and a decision as to the lawfulness of their detention.[57] The judicial supervision must be capable of leading, where appropriate, to the detainee's release.[58]

36.42 ECHR article 5(4) incorporates procedural guarantees albeit these guarantees are not uniform to all contexts.[59] ECHR article 5(4) proceedings must be adversarial and must always ensure 'equality

---

53 (2008) 47 EHRR 17.
54 SI No 238.
55 EIG chapter 55 para 55.6.3.
56 *Garcia Alva v Germany* App No 23541/94, 13 February 2001 para 39.
57 *De Wilde, Ooms and Versyp v Belgium*, judgment of 18 June 1971, Series A no 12, at 76.
58 *Slivenko v Latvia* [GC], App No 48321/99, at 158, ECHR 2003-X.
59 *Garcia Alva v Germany* App No 23541/94, 13 February 2001 para 39; *A and others v UK* (2009) 49 EHRR 29 paras 203–204 and 217.

of arms' between the parties.[60] Where there is reliance on closed material and a special advocate procedure, the detainee must have sufficient information about the allegations against him to give effective instructions.[61]

36.43 ECHR article 5(4) may be breached notwithstanding that the underlying detention is lawful under ECHR article 5(1).[62]

36.44 The requirements of ECHR article 5(4) are not met by the possibility of applying for bail.[63] When an immigration judge of the tribunal considers a bail application, he or she is not determining (and has no power to determine) the lawfulness of the underlying detention.[64] Nonetheless, the domestic courts have taken the approach that bail proceedings must meet the requirements of procedural fairness set out in ECHR article 5(4).[65]

36.45 In the immigration detention context, a failure to provide a person with form IS91R (the 'reasons for detention' checklist) may give rise to a breach of ECHR article 5(4). Written reasons for detention may assist the detainee in challenging the lawfulness of his or her detention in the High Court.[66]

ECHR article 5(5)

36.46 ECHR article 5(5) provides a right to compensation to any person detained or arrested in breach of any of the subparagraphs ECHR article 5(1)–(4).[67] ECHR article 5(5) applies where there has been a breach of ECHR article 5 regardless of whether the detention was lawful under domestic law.[68] The compensation must be a legally

---

60 *A and others v UK* (2009) 49 EHRR 29 para 204; *Reinprecht v Austria* App No 67175/01, para 31.
61 *A and others v UK* (2009) 49 EHRR 29 para 220.
62 *Douiyeb v The Netherlands* (2000) 30 EHRR 790.
63 *Zamir v UK* (1983) 40 DR 42, ECommHR para 59.
64 *R (Konan) v Secretary of State for the Home Department* [2004] EWHC 22 (Admin) para 30.
65 *Othman v Secretary of State for the Home Department* SC/15/2005, Mitting J in Special Immigration Appeals Commission (SIAC) and *R (Cart) v Upper Tribunal* [2009] EWHC 3052 (Admin), [2010] 2 WLR 1012 in the Divisional Court.
66 By analogy, see *Garcia Alva v Germany* App No 23541/94, 13 February 2001 para 39 where a failure to provide a detainee with the information necessary to challenge his detention gave rise to a breach of ECHR article 5(4).
67 *Wassink v The Netherlands* (Series A/185-A) 1990.
68 *Brogan v UK* (1988) 11 EHRR 117.

binding award.[69] However, the compensation need not always be financial: the ECtHR has, for procedural breaches of ECHR article 5, found that its own judgment constitutes just satisfaction and compensation.[70] In certain cases, the ECtHR has been prepared to award damages only where causation of detention is shown (ie where it is shown that but for the breach, the person would not have been deprived of his or her liberty).[71]

ECHR article 3

36.47 ECHR article 3 has already been discussed in some detail in the context of challenges to expulsion generally (paras 13.6–13.41) and specifically in the context of challenges to expulsion by the mentally or physically ill (paras 18.4–18.52). Here, we review the application of ECHR article 3 in detention challenges.

Positive and negative obligations

36.48 Detention engages the negative obligation on states to refrain from inflicting serious harm on persons within their jurisdiction. Detention also engages the positive obligation on states to take measures designed to ensure that individuals within their jurisdiction are not subjected to treatment contrary to ECHR article 3.[72] The positive obligation of states under ECHR article 3 includes a duty to take reasonable steps of which the authorities had or ought to have had knowledge.[73]

36.49 The preventative obligations on the state are particularly high insofar as they concern those in state custody.[74]

The minimum level of severity

36.50 ECHR article 3 will be engaged only where the treatment complained of reaches a minimum level of severity. The assessment of whether

---

69 *Brogan v UK* (1988) 11 EHRR 117.
70 *Wassink v The Netherlands* (Series A/185-A) 1990, para 41; *Nikolova v Bulgaria* App No 31195/96, para 76; *A and others v UK* (2009) 49 EHRR 29 para 250.
71 *Nikolova v Bulgaria* para 76; *A and others v UK* (2009) 49 EHRR 29 para 252.
72 See, for example, discussion in *Mayeka v Belgium* (2008) 46 EHRR 23 para 53; and *Keenan v UK* (2001) 33 EHRR 38 para 112.
73 *Z v UK* [2002] 34 EHRR 3.
74 *Ribitsch v Austria* (1996) 21 EHRR 573 para 34.

36.51 It is relevant to the assessment of whether treatment has attained the minimum level of severity whether 'its object is to humiliate and debase the person concerned'.[76]

36.52 It will also be relevant to the severity assessment whether the treatment complained of adversely affected the victim's personality.[77]

36.53 As a result of the special obligations of states towards those they detain, ECHR article 3 will be breached by lesser ill-treatment towards detainee than might be required to cross the threshold for those at liberty. The Court of Appeal has observed that:

> We tend to think of obligations under art 3 in terms of extreme violence, deprivation or humiliation. Convention jurisprudence however makes clear that depending on the circumstances art 3 may be engaged by conduct that falls below that high level. Two circumstances that have been identified as imposing special obligations on the state are that the subject is dependent on the state because he has been deprived of his liberty; and that he is young or vulnerable. That is the uniform jurisprudence of the ECtHR ...[78]

36.54 However, in the detention context, it is also relevant to note that:

> .. the suffering and humiliation involved must in any event go beyond that inevitable element of suffering or humiliation connected with a given form of legitimate treatment or punishment.[79]

Inhuman or degrading treatment

36.55 ECHR article 3 complaints in the UK detention context will usually concern inhuman or degrading treatment. These have been defined at para 13.20 of this book. The meaning of 'treatment' specifically has been considered at para 18.4.

---

75 *Raninen v Finland* (1998) 26 EHRR 563 at para 55. See also para 13.15 of this book.
76 *Keenan v UK* (2001) 33 EHRR 38 para 109.
77 *Keenan v UK* (2001) 33 EHRR 38 para 109; see also *Ilascu v Moldova and Russia* (2005) 40 EHRR 46 (Grand Chamber) para 427.
78 *R (C) v Secretary of State for Justice* [2008] EWCA Civ 882 at para 58 per Buxton LJ, with whom Tuckey and Keene LJJ agreed.
79 See, for example, *Kudla v Poland* App No 30210/96, judgment 26 October 2000; *Ilascu v Moldova and Russia* (2005) 40 EHRR 46 Grand Chamber para 428.

36.56 There is no requirement that the inhuman treatment or the suffering entailed in such treatment be intentionally inflicted.[80] Likewise there is no requirement for degrading treatment that the humiliation or debasement be intentionally inflicted.[81]

Conditions of detention

36.57 Below, we give examples of circumstances in which the ECHR article 3 threshold may be crossed purely by poor detention conditions. In practice, detention conditions in the UK will relatively rarely be so poor as to breach ECHR article 3 of themselves, without any additional element of excessive prolongation, vulnerability on the part of the detainee, or improper purpose.

36.58 The Grand Chamber of the ECtHR has held that:

> Article 3 requires the State to ensure that every prisoner is detained in conditions which are compatible with respect for his human dignity, that the manner and method of the execution of the measure do not subject him to distress or hardship of an intensity exceeding the unavoidable level of suffering inherent in detention ...[82]

36.59 The assessment of whether the minimum level of severity is crossed involves fine questions of degree. Detention conditions may amount to inhuman or degrading treatment contrary to ECHR article 3, in circumstances where prisoners are held in extremely overcrowded and filthy conditions;[83] or given inadequate food;[84] or where food and medical treatment are withheld.[85] Detention in solitary confinement for legitimate security purposes will not in itself ECHR article 3;[86] however, very protracted solitary confinement under poor conditions may do so,[87] as would complete sensory and social isolation.[88] Merely having to use a receptacle which is not a toilet is not in itself a breach of ECHR article 3;[89] but having to relieve oneself in the presence

---

80 *Ireland v UK* (1978) 2 EHRR 25 para 167.
81 *V v UK* (1999) 30 EHRR 121 at 71; *Pretty v UK* (2002) 35 EHRR 1 para 52.
82 *Ilascu v Moldova and Russia* (2005) 40 EHRR 46 (Grand Chamber) para 428.
83 *Modarca v Moldova* App No 14437/05 10 August 2007 para 68; see also *Kalashnikov v Russia* (2003) 36 EHRR 34 at para 102.
84 *Moisejevs v Latvia,* App No 64846/01, 15 June 2006.
85 *Cyprus v Turkey* (1982) 4 EHRR 482, 541.
86 See for example *R (N) v Secretary of State for the Home Department* [2009] EWHC 1921 (Admin).
87 *Ilascu v Moldova and Russia* (2005) 40 EHRR 46 (Grand Chamber) para 432.
88 *Ilascu v Moldova and Russia* (2005) 40 EHRR 46 (Grand Chamber) para 432.
89 See discussion in *Greens* [2011] CSOH 79.

of other detainees or officers[90] or in a bucket even for a single-cell occupant[91] may be. Strip searches do not in themselves breach ECHR article 3; but a strip search carried out under inappropriate conditions or for a punitive motive may breach ECHR article 3.[92]

Detention conditions for asylum-seekers

36.60 As to conditions for the detention of asylum seekers, the ECtHR Grand Chamber in *MSS v Belgium* provided the following helpful summary of circumstances in which ECHR article 3 had been found to be breached:

> ... confining an asylum seeker to a prefabricated cabin for two months without allowing him outdoors or to make a telephone call, and with no clean sheets and insufficient hygiene products, amounted to degrading treatment within the meaning of Article 3 of the Convention (see *SD v Greece*, no. 53541/07, [ss] 49 to 54, 11 June 2009). Similarly, a period of detention of six days, in a confined space, with no possibility of taking a walk, no leisure area, sleeping on dirty mattresses and with no free access to a toilet is unacceptable with respect to Article 3 (ibid., [s] 51). The detention of an asylum seeker for three months on police premises pending the application of an administrative measure, with no access to any recreational activities and without proper meals has also been considered as degrading treatment (see *Tabesh v Greece*, no. 8256/07, [ss] 38 to 44, 26 November 2009). Lastly, the Court has found that the detention of an applicant, who was also an asylum seeker, for three months in an overcrowded place in appalling conditions of hygiene and cleanliness, with no leisure or catering facilities, where the dilapidated state of repair of the sanitary facilities rendered them virtually unusable and where the detainees slept in extremely filthy and crowded conditions amounted to degrading treatment prohibited by Article 3 (see *AA v Greece*, no. 12186/08, [ss] 57 to 65, 22 July 2010).[93]

36.61 In *MSS v Belgium*, the ECtHR Grand Chamber went on to find that the applicant's conditions of detention in a Greek detention centre for asylum-seekers had breached ECHR article 3. He had only been held there for four days on one occasion, a week on another.[94] However, the conditions were extreme. The asylum-seekers' area was rarely unlocked; asylum-seekers forced to drink from the toilets for lack of

---

90 *Kehayov v Bulgaria* App No 41035/98, judgment 18 January 2005.
91 *Malechkov v Bulgaria* App No 57830/00, judgment 28 September 2007.
92 *Iwanczuk v Poland* (2004) 38 EHRR 8.
93 *MSS v Belgium* (2011) 53 EHRR 2 para 222.
94 *MSS v Belgium* (2011) 53 EHRR 2 para 232.

access to a drinking fountain; there were insufficient beds so that asylum-seekers were sleeping on the bare floor; and a lack of sufficient ventilation so that cells were unbearably hot. There was no soap or toilet paper and there were severe restrictions in access to toilets so that detainees had to urinate in plastic bottles to empty later.[95]

36.62 The ECtHR Grand Chamber considered it an aggravating factor that the applicant, having been detained without reasons,[96] would have felt his detention to be arbitrary, an experience with which feelings of inferiority and anxiety were often associated.[97] It was a further aggravating feature of the detention that he was an asylum-seeker:

> ... the Court must take into account that the applicant, being an asylum seeker, was particularly vulnerable because of everything he had been through during his migration and the traumatic experiences he was likely to have endured previously.[98]
> ... the applicant's distress was accentuated by the vulnerability inherent in his situation as an asylum seeker.[99]

Detention in conditions inappropriate for a particular detainee

36.63 Detention in conditions inappropriate for a particular detainee's vulnerabilities, such as disability or age, may breach ECHR article 3. The detention of a paraplegic in the UK a non-adapted police cell and then prison amounted to degrading treatment contrary to ECHR article 3.[100] The detention of an unaccompanied five-year-old child in a Belgian detention centre for adults was found to amount to inhuman treatment contrary to ECHR article 3.[101] However, this principle has also been applied in less extreme contexts, such as the detention in a Belgian detention centre for just over a month of children alongside their mother.[102] Likewise, while handcuffing in itself does not breach ECHR article 3,[103] the unnecessary handcuffing of physically ill prisoners may amount to inhuman or degrading treatment contrary to ECHR article 3.[104]

---

95 *MSS v Belgium* (2011) 53 EHRR 2 paras 230–231.
96 *MSS v Belgium* (2011) 53 EHRR 2 paras 225–226.
97 *MSS v Belgium* (2011) 53 EHRR 2 para 233.
98 *MSS v Belgium* (2011) 53 EHRR 2 para 232.
99 *MSS v Belgium* (2011) 53 EHRR 2 para 233.
100 *Price v UK* App No 33394/96, judgment 10 October 2001.
101 *Mayeka v Belgium* (2008) 46 EHRR 23.
102 *Muskhadzhiyeva v Belgium* App No 41442/07, judgment 19 January 2010.
103 *Raninen v Finland* (1998) 26 EHRR 563 at paras 55 and 56.
104 *Moiusel v France* (2004) 38 EHRR 34; *R (Graham) v Secretary of State for the Home Department* [2007] EWHC 2940 (Admin). For decisions in the domestic

Defective medical care in detention

36.64 ECHR article 3 requires states to 'protect the physical well being of persons deprived of their liberty'.[105] While ECHR article 3 does not impose a general obligation to release an individual on health grounds or place a detainee in a civil hospital,[106] the state must ensure that:

> ... given the practical demands of imprisonment, his health and well-being are adequately secured by, among other things, providing him with the requisite medical assistance.[107]

36.65 Thus in *Paladi v Moldova*,[108] the ECtHR Grand Chamber found a violation of ECHR article 3 where a severely ill remand prisoner had not received the medical care he needed, initially receiving only emergency treatment, and then receiving treatment but missing sessions on various occasions because the necessary equipment for his treatment was missing at the hospital where he was taken.

36.66 Delay in providing medical assistance may also cause a breach of ECHR article 3.[109] In *R(MD) v Secretary of State for the Home Department*, Arden LJ left it open that a three day interruption in the availability of antiretrovirals for an HIV positive detainee, which might have led to the development of antiretroviral resistance, with dire consequences for life expectancy if expelled, might breach ECHR article 3.[110]

Inappropriate to 'wait and see'

36.67 State authorities may not 'wait and see' whether treatment contrary to ECHR article 3 occurs.[111] In *R (Limbuela) v Secretary of State for the Home Department*, the House of Lords held that the SSHD was under an obligation to act where there was an 'imminent prospect' of a breach of ECHR article 3.[112]

---

context that handcuffing did not breach a cancer patient's ECHR rights, see *R (Faizovas) v Secretary of State for Justice* [2009] EWCA Civ 373; *R (Spinks) v Secretary of State for the Home Department* [2005] EWCA Civ 275.

105 *Khudobin v Russia* (2009) 48 EHRR 22 para 93; *Keenan v UK* (2001) 33 EHRR 38 para 110.
106 *Kudla v Poland* App No 30210/96, judgment 26 October 2000, para 93.
107 *Kudla v Poland* App No 30210/96, judgment 26 October 2000, para 94; *Farbtuhs v Lithuania* App No 4672/02, judgment 2 December 2004, para 51.
108 App No 39806/05, judgment 10 March 2009.
109 *Hurtado v Switzerland*, Series A No. A-280, 26 January 2004.
110 *R (MD) v Secretary of State for the Home Department* [2011] EWCA Civ 1238, para 55.
111 *R (S) v Secretary of State for the Home Department* [2011] EWHC 2120 (Admin) para 208.
112 [2005] UKHL 66, [2006] 1 AC 396 para 62.

Detention of the mentally and physically ill

36.68 The ECtHR has confirmed that:

... the authorities are under an obligation to protect the health of persons deprived of liberty. The lack of appropriate medical treatment may amount to treatment contrary to Article 3. In particular, the assessment of whether the treatment or punishment concerned is incompatible with the standard of Article 3 has, in the case of mentally ill persons, to take into consideration their vulnerability and their inability, in some cases, to complain coherently or at all about how they are being affected by any particular treatment.[113]

36.69 As the Administrative Court has summarised:

It is clear that the prison authorities must take cognisance of specific features of the prisoner when handling him, including any mental illness of which they have notice – a matter which may render unlawful treatment otherwise acceptable in the case of a healthy prisoner. Increased vigilance is required where the prisoner has particular vulnerability or weakness.[114]

36.70 As we have already seen at para 18.4, treatment which causes or exacerbates severe mental or physical ill-health may breach ECHR article 3. Thus in *R (S) v Secretary of State for the Home Department* the Administrative Court found that the detention under Immigration Act powers of a mentally ill FNP breached ECHR article 3. Article 3 had been breached both in its negative aspects (in that S had been subjected to degrading treatment as the detention caused his mental health to severely deteriorate) and positive aspects (in that the SSHD had failed to put in place adequate safeguarding procedures and had failed to follow even those procedures that were in place).[115] That case was then followed in *R (BA) v Secretary of State for the Home Department*, in which ECHR article 3 was breached where a detainee suffering from a psychotic illness and refusing food and fluids was met with 'a combination of bureaucratic inertia, and lack of communication and co-ordination between those who were responsible for his welfare'.[116]

---

113 *Keenan v UK* (2001) 33 EHRR 38 para 110.
114 *R (N) v Secretary of State for the Home Department* [2009] EWHC 1921 (Admin) para 101.
115 *R (S) v Secretary of State for the Home Department* [2011] EWHC 2120 (Admin) paras 210–217.
116 *R (BA) v Secretary of State for the Home Department* [2011] EWHC 2748 (Admin) para 237.

Injuries and mental ill health sustained in custody: burden of proof

36.71 The burden is on the state to explain physical injuries sustained in detention:

> The Court considers that where an individual is taken into police custody in good health but is found to be injured at the time of release, it is incumbent on the State to provide a plausible explanation of how those injuries were caused, failing which a clear issue arises under Article 3 of the Convention.[117]

36.72 Likewise, the onus is on the detaining state to explain a deterioration in the mental health of a person in custody.[118]

36.73 Indeed, a mentally ill detained person may be found to have suffered a breach of ECHR article 3 even where it cannot be established that detention caused a deterioration in his or her mental health:

> ... treatment of a mentally-ill person may be incompatible with the standards imposed by Article 3 in the protection of fundamental human dignity, even though that person may not be capable of pointing to any specific ill-effects.[119]

ECHR article 3 and the requirement to release

36.74 A breach of ECHR article 3 in a case of ongoing detention will not necessarily compel immediate release if the breach can be remedied while the detainee remains in custody.[120]

ECHR article 8

36.75 ECHR article 8 in the expulsion context has been considered in detail in chapters 15–17 above. Here, we review the application of article 8 in the detention context only.

---

117 *Selmouni v France* (2000) 29 EHRR 403 para 87; *Bazorkina v Russia* (2008) 46 EHRR 15 at para 105.
118 *Keenan v UK* (2001) 33 EHRR 38 para 110.
119 *Keenan v UK* (2001) 33 EHRR 38 para 112.
120 *Aleksanyan v Russia* (2011) 52 EHRR 18, paras 136–138.

Private life aspects

36.76 The broad notion of private life includes, for example, concepts of personal autonomy.[121] Thus the right to respect for private life is engaged by detention.[122]

36.77 Private life includes the right to associate with others, so that, for example, segregation has been found to engage ECHR article 8,[123] as has a highly restrictive security regime for Category A prisoners (in that case, held on remand).[124]

36.78 Private life also includes physical integrity, so that, for example, the adoption of a new regime for the use of force against minors held in secure training centres has been found to engage ECHR article 8,[125] as has illness sustained as a result of detention.[126] In *R (Malcom) v Secretary of State for Justice*,[127] the Court of Appeal accepted that deprivation of time in open air for a prisoner (and especially a segregated prisoner) might in principle engage ECHR article 8, though it was not engaged on the facts of that case.

Family life aspects

36.79 In the immigration detention context, it has been observed that the detention of a parent (whether with the children or splitting the family) will almost invariably engage the right to respect for family life.[128]

36.80 Allocation to a prison too far for family to visit has been found to engage ECHR article 8;[129] restrictions on family visits have also been found to engage ECHR article 8,[130] as have restrictions on the

---

121 See discussion in *R (Wood) v Commissioner of Police of the Metropolis* [2009] HRLR 25 paras 21–22.
122 *Raninen v Finland* (1998) 26 EHRR 563 para 63; see also *McFeeley v UK* (1981) 3 EHRR 161 para 91.
123 *McFeeley v UK* (1981) 3 EHRR 161.
124 *R (Bary) v Secretary of State for Justice and Governor of HMP Long Lartin* [2010] EWHC 587 (Admin) paras 130–131.
125 *R (C) v Secretary of State for Justice* [2008] EWCA Civ 882, [2009] QB 657.
126 *R (S, C and D) v Secretary of State for the Home Department* [2007] EWHC 1654 (Admin) in particular para 82.
127 [2011] EWCA Civ 1538 paras 26 and 29.
128 *R (MXL and others) v Secretary of State for the Home Department* [2010] EWHC 2397 (Admin) para 82.
129 *Ouinas v France* (1990) 65 DR 265; but see also *McCotter v UK* (1993) 15 EHRR CD 98 pp98–99 finding that there is no right for a prisoner to be imprisoned near his family.
130 *Nowicka v Poland* App No 30218/96, judgment 3 December 2002 paras 73–77.

conjugal rights of prisoners;[131] and the UK regime for the removal of babies from imprisoned mothers.[132]

Correspondence

36.81 ECHR article 8 protects the right to respect for private correspondence. Censorship and other restrictions on or impediments to prisoners' correspondence have been found to engage ECHR article 8.[133] However, the regime for prisoners' telephone calls has been found not to engage ECHR article 8, particularly where there is an adequate regime for written correspondence.[134]

Positive and negative obligations

36.82 In the detention context, ECHR article 8 imposes not only negative but also positive obligations. The ECtHR has observed that:

> The Court recalls that, although the object of Article 8 is essentially that of protecting the individual against arbitrary interference by the public authorities, it does not merely compel the State to abstain from such interference. In addition to this primarily negative undertaking, there may be positive obligations inherent in an effective respect for private and family life. These obligations may involve the adoption of measures designed to secure respect for private and family life even in the sphere of the relations of individuals between themselves. The boundaries between the State's positive and negative obligations under Article 8 do not lend themselves to precise definition. The applicable principles are nonetheless similar. In particular, in both instances regard must be had to the fair balance to be struck between the competing interests.

36.83 The positive obligations include the duty to facilitate the enjoyment of family life by prisoners. The ECtHR has held:

> The Court observes that any detention which is lawful for the purposes of Article 5 of the Convention entails by its nature a limitation on private and family life. However, it is an essential part of a prisoner's right to respect for family life that the prison authorities assist him in maintaining contact with his close family ...[135]

---

131 *X v UK* (1975) 2 DR 105; *Messina No 2 v Italy* App No 25498/94, 28 December 2000, paras 61–62.
132 *R (P and Q) v Secretary of State for the Home Department* [2001] EWCA Civ 1151; [2001] 1 WLR 2002.
133 *Herczegfalvy v Austria* (1993) 15 EHRR 437.
134 *AB v The Netherlands* (2003) 37 EHRR 48; *R (RD) v Secretary of State for the Home Department* [2008] EWCA Civ 676.
135 *Messina No 2 v Italy* App No 25498/94, 28 December 2000, para 61.

36.84 ECHR article 8 also incorporates procedural obligations, including, where appropriate, the involvement of an individual in decision-making which will affect his or her protected rights.[136] Thus, for example, ECHR article 8 protects the right to participate meaningfully in contact proceedings.[137] Decisions affecting rights protected by ECHR article 8(1) (such as an administrative decision to detain) must also be made through a mechanism that ensures an effective proportionality assessment.[138]

Treatment falling short of the ECHR article 3 threshold

36.85 As with other contexts, treatment relating to detention which does not reach the ECHR article 3 threshold may nonetheless breach ECHR article 8.[139]

Limitations on rights consequent on imprisonment

36.86 The ECtHR has rejected the notion that there are wide implied limitations on prisoners' rights:

> The court accepts, moreover, that the 'necessity' for interference with the exercise of the right of a convicted prisoner to respect for his correspondence must be appreciated having regard to the ordinary and reasonable requirements of imprisonment. The 'prevention of disorder or crime', for example, may justify wider measures of interference in the case of such a prisoner than in that of a person at liberty. To this extent, but to this extent only, lawful deprivation of liberty within the meaning of article 5 does not fail to impinge on the application of article 8.[140]

36.87 The same is of course true in the common law (see, for example, Lord Bingham's famous speech in *R (Daly) v Secretary of State for the Home Department*[141]).

---

136 *Tysiac v Poland* (2007) 45 EHRR 42 at 115; *X v Croatia* App No 11223/04, judgment 17 July 2008 at para 49.
137 *Ciliz v The Netherlands* [2000] 2 FLR 469; *MS (Ivory Coast) v Secretary of State for the Home Department* [2007] EWCA Civ 133; [2007] ImmAR 538.
138 *Taliadorou and Stylianou v Cyprus* App Nos 39627/05 and 39631/05, judgment 16 October 2008 at para 55.
139 *Raninen v Finland* (1998) 26 EHRR 563 para 63.
140 *Golder v UK* (1975) 1 EHRR 524 para 45; see likewise *Hirst v UK* (2006) 42 EHRR 41 paras 69–70; *Dickson v UK* (2006) 44 EHRR 419 para 70.
141 [2001] UKHL 26, [2001] 2 AC 532, para 5.

Justification and proportionality

36.88 The ECtHR Grand Chamber in *Dickson v UK* has defined two grounds on which interference with prisoners' rights may properly be justified: first, that the interference is the 'necessary and inevitable consequence' of imprisonment; or second that there is an adequate link between the interference and the circumstances of the individual prisoner. Fear of offending public opinion is not a permissible justification for interference:

> ... a person retains his or her Convention rights on imprisonment, so that any restriction on those rights must be justified in each individual case. This justification can flow, inter alia, from the necessary and inevitable consequences of imprisonment or (as accepted by the applicants before the Grand Chamber) from an adequate link between the restriction and the circumstances of the prisoner in question. However, it cannot be based solely on what would offend public opinion.[142]

36.89 Since the restriction of liberty itself engages the right to respect for private life, where the underlying detention itself is unlawful, there will almost invariably, if not always, be a breach of ECHR article 8 because the interference will lack justification:

> ... of course, if the detention is unlawful it is difficult to envisage circumstances in which there would not be a breach of Article 8 since the detention, itself, would constitute an unacceptable infringement of a person's right to private life.[143]

36.90 Below, we consider the position where the underlying detention is lawful.

36.91 It is uncontroversial that where the interference with rights protected by ECHR article 8 extends beyond the 'necessary and inevitable consequence' (see para 36.88 above) on detention, ECHR article 8 may be breached notwithstanding that the underlying detention is lawful.

36.92 A difficulty arises where the interference is said to be the 'necessary and inevitable consequence' of detention or imprisonment which is itself lawful.

36.93 The Divisional Court has held, obiter, in the context of a challenge to a refusal of Home Detention Curfew (HDC), that even if the refus-

---

142 *Dickson v UK* (2008) 46 EHRR 41, Grand Chamber, para 68; as to the point that offence caused to public opinion is not justification, see also *Hirst v UK* (2006) 42 EHRR 41, para 70.
143 *R (Suppiah) v Secretary of State for the Home Department* [2011] EWHC 2 (Admin) para 189.

al of HDC had been unlawful, there would be no breach of ECHR article 8 unless the underlying prison sentence (which the prisoner continued to serve in default of HDC) was also unlawful.[144] At the time of writing, that judgment is under appeal on a number of grounds, among others that where the state fails to lawfully operate an early release scheme (or any other special scheme it has put in place to minimise disruption to private or family life[145]) restrictions experienced in the subsequent detention are not the inevitable and necessary restrictions and limitations consequent on imprisonment.

36.94 We suggest also that 'necessary and inevitable consequence' should not be interpreted as meaning the consequences normally associated with imprisonment in that country. Rather, the ECtHR now applies a strict proportionality test requiring exploration of less restrictive alternatives. Thus, the ECtHR Grand Chamber in *Dickson v UK* stated, finding that a blanket ban on arrangements for the artificial insemination prisoners' partners breached ECHR article 8:

> Whilst the inability to beget a child might be a consequence of imprisonment, it is not an inevitable one, it not being suggested that the grant of artificial insemination facilities would involve any security issues or impose any significant administrative or financial demands on the State.[146]

ECHR article 14

36.95 Less commonly than the ECHR rights discussed above, detainees may rely on ECHR article 14. This provides that:

> The enjoyment of the rights and freedoms set forth in this Convention shall be secured without discrimination on any ground such as sex, race, colour, language, religion, political or other opinion, national or social origin, association with a national minority, property, birth or other status.

36.96 ECHR article 14 prohibits discrimination in the enjoyment of the other ECHR rights and freedoms. Therefore article 14 is not a general prohibition on discrimination but 'parasitic': article 14 claims can only be brought in respect of the 'substantive' ECHR rights.

---

144 *R (Diana Francis) v Secretary of State for Justice* [2011] EWHC 1271 (Admin) para 43.
145 See, for example, the Mother and Baby Units regime discussed in *R (P and Q) v Secretary of State for the Home Department* [2001] EWCA Civ 1151, [2001] 1 WLR 2002.
146 *Dickson v UK* (2008) 46 EHRR 41, Grand Chamber, para 74.

However, there is no need to show that the 'substantive' right has been breached, merely that the facts fall 'within the ambit' of the 'substantive' right.

36.97 ECHR article 14 prohibits indirect as well as direct discrimination in the enjoyment of ECHR rights:

> ... a general policy or measure that has disproportionately prejudicial effects on a particular group may be considered discriminatory notwithstanding that it is not specifically aimed at that group.[147]

36.98 ECHR article 14 not only prohibits differential treatment, it prohibits treating those who are different identically and failing to make necessary adjustments.[148] ECHR article 14 does not prohibit, and may in some circumstances require, positive discrimination.[149]

36.99 The list of prohibited grounds of discrimination in ECHR article 14 is not exhaustive. 'Other status' includes immigration status.[150] Certain grounds have been said to require 'very weighty reasons' to justify differential treatment (sometimes referred to as 'suspect reasons'), namely sex, nationality,[151] sexual orientation and birth status ('legitimate' or otherwise). As for discrimination on grounds of 'race, colour or ethnic origins', the ECtHR Grand Chamber has said:

> Racial discrimination is a particularly invidious kind of discrimination and, in view of its perilous consequences, requires from the authorities special vigilance and a vigorous reaction. It is for this reason that the authorities must use all available means to combat racism, thereby reinforcing democracy's vision of a society in which diversity is not perceived as a threat but as a source of enrichment. The Court has also held that no difference in treatment which is based exclusively or to a decisive extent on a person's ethnic origin is capable of being objectively justified in a contemporary democratic society built on the principles of pluralism and respect for different cultures.[152]

36.100 The comparator in an ECHR article 14 claim is persons in an analogous position, that is 'persons in relevantly similar situations'.[153]

---

147 *DH v Czech Republic* (2008) 47 EHRR 3 Grand Chamber, para 175.
148 *Thlimmenos v Greece* (2001) 31 EHRR 15.
149 *DH v Czech Republic* (2008) 47 EHRR 3 Grand Chamber, para 175.
150 *A and others v Secretary of State for the Home Department* ('the Belmarsh case') [2004] UKHL 56, [2005] 2 AC 68 para 49.
151 The ECtHR in *Gaygusuz v Austria* (1997) 23 EHRR 364 warned that 'very weighty reasons would have to be put forward before the Court could regard a difference of treatment based exclusively on the ground of nationality as compatible with the Convention'.
152 *DH v Czech Republic* (2008) 47 EHRR 3 Grand Chamber para 176.
153 *Zarb Adami v Malta* (2006) 44 EHRR 49 para 71.

36.101 Article 14 ECHR will breached if there is no 'objective and reasonable justification' for the differential treatment or if there is 'no reasonable relationship of proportionality between the means employed and the aim sought to be realised'.[154] The onus is on the state to establish the justification for differential treatment.

36.102 The test for breach of article 14 was distilled in *A and others v Secretary of State for the Home Department* ('the Belmarsh case') by Lord Bingham:

> The question is whether persons in an analogous or relevantly similar situation enjoy preferential treatment, without reasonable or objective justification for the distinction, and whether and to what extent differences in otherwise similar situations justify a different treatment in law.

36.103 Lord Bingham went on to approve a series of questions:[155]

> (1) Do the facts fall within the ambit of one or more of the Convention rights? (2) Was there a difference in treatment in respect of that right between the complainant and others put forward for comparison? (3) If so, was the difference in treatment on one or more of the proscribed grounds under article 14? (4) Were those others in an analogous situation? (5) Was the difference in treatment objectively justifiable in the sense that it had a legitimate aim and bore a reasonable relationship of proportionality to that aim?[156]

Breaches of the ECHR resulting from a detention contractor's actions or omissions

36.104 Because the SSHD owes positive duties under towards those detained on the SSHD's authority, the SSHD may be liable where detainees' ECHR article 3 or article 8 rights are breached even if the immediate cause was the actions or omissions of a private contractor. Thus the Administrative Court found in *R (S) v Secretary of State for the Home Department*, a case concerning the detention of a mentally ill FNP, that even if defects could be attributed to the detention centre contractors, legal responsibility for ensuring compliance with ECHR article 3 rested with the SSHD.[157]

---

154 *Belgian Linguistic Case* (1968) 1 EHRR 252 para 10.
155 Derived from *R (S) v Chief Constable of the South Yorkshire Police* [2004] 1 WLR 2196 para 48.
156 [2004] UKHL 56, [2005] 2 AC 68 para 50.
157 *R (S) v Chief Constable of the South Yorkshire Police* [2004] 1 WLR 2196 para 221.

36.105 See likewise *R (S, C and D) v Secretary of State for the Home Department* where a small child detained in an IRC developed rickets and anaemia notwithstanding that those conditions had been foreseeable and preventable in light of his eating difficulties. The Administrative Court found the SSHD liable for a breach of the child's ECHR article 8 right to respect for his physical integrity.[158] Dismissing the SSHD's attempt to blame the healthcare contractor, Wynn Williams J stated:

> The question for my consideration is whether the D's right to physical integrity was infringed when he was detained at the behest of the Defendant. If it was, the Defendant, as the public authority responsible for the detention and compliance with Article 8, must be responsible in law for the infringement.

36.106 However, as we shall see in more detail at para 43.22, private contractors may also be liable for breaches of the Human Rights Act 1998.[159]

---

158 [2007] EWHC 1654 (Admin) in particular para 82.
159 See discussion at *Quaquah v Group 4* TLQ 340/01 23 May 2001 para 15.

CHAPTER 37

Detention in CCD cases involving children

37.1	Introduction
37.3	The BCIA 2009 s55 duty and the *Every Child Matters* statutory guidance
37.5	Legal consequences of a failure to have regard to the best interests of the child as a primary consideration
37.8	Home Office policy and the new statutory duty
37.10	**Family Returns Panel**
37.11	**Children's Champion**
37.12	**Split families**
37.13	Internal CCD instructions
37.20	Releasing a 'serious criminal' to a family including dependent minors
37.21	**Unaccompanied minor FNPs**
37.22	**Families with children**
37.22	Exploration of alternatives to enforced expulsion
37.25	'Pre-departure accommodation'
37.27	Detention at Tinsley House Immigration Removal Centre
37.28	Mother and Baby Units
37.29	Time limits on detention of families with children
37.30	Reviews in detained family cases

Introduction

37.1 The Coalition government announced on 12 May 2010 its intention to end the detention of children under Immigration Act powers.[1] However, as we see below, some detention of children, both unaccompanied and with their families, continues nonetheless.

37.2 This chapter considers the detention of unaccompanied minor foreign national former prisoners (FNPs) and also of families with children (families in which there is one or more dependent child aged under 18). The chapter also considers the more commonly encountered situation of a detained parent separated from a child (referred to below as 'split families').

The BCIA 2009 s55 duty and the *Every Child Matters* statutory guidance

37.3 Since 2 November 2009, any decision to detain under Immigration Act powers which impacts on a child, whether because the child is being detained, or because the parent is being detained and so separated from a child, is subject to the requirements of the Borders, Citizenship and Immigration Act (BCIA) 2009 s55.[2] The new statutory duty stipulates that such decisions must be taken with regard to the need to safeguard and promote the welfare of children in the UK and to the statutory code of practice, *Every Child Matters* which in turn requires that the best interests of the child be treated as a primary consideration.

37.4 The best interests of the child principle, the requirements of BCIA 2009 s55 and the statutory code of practice have been discussed in detail in chapter 4.

---

1 Confirmed in Prime Minister's statement of 25 May 2010 (*Hansard* HC, col 25, May 2010).
2 See *ZH (Tanzania) v Secretary of State for the Home Department* [2011] UKSC 4, [2011] 2 WLR 148 paras 25–26 and *R (NXT and others) v Secretary of State for the Home Department* [2011] EWHC 969 (Admin).

Legal consequences of a failure to have regard to the best interests of the child as a primary consideration

37.5 Since at least the coming into force of BCIA 2009 s55,[3] a detention decision in a case involving a child which is taken without regard to the best interests of the child is flawed by material public law error (failure to have regard to a relevant consideration)[4] and, we suggest, will render the detention unlawful.[5] This is so where children are themselves detained[6] or where a parent is separated from a child by detention.[7]

37.6 In addition, where a decision to deport a parent affecting a child has been taken without regard to these considerations, the consequent detention of the adult may be rendered unlawful.[8]

37.7 Independent of the new statutory duty, ECHR article 5 requires that the best interest of the child be treated as a primary consideration in detention cases involving children. The principle that the best interests of the child must be treated as a primary consideration in actions concerning children derives from the UN Convention on the Rights of the Child (UNCRC) article 3. As discussed at para 17.26, the ECHR protections must be read in the light of other international human rights instruments, including the UNCRC. The Administrative Court has thus accepted, long before the coming into force of the BCIA 2009 s55 duty and in the context of the detention of a family with children, that ECHR article 5 must be read in the light of UNCRC article 3.[9]

---

3 See chapter 4 note 8 on earlier interim measures in force since 6 January 2009. See also para 37.7 below on the principles of ECHR article 5 independent of the statutory duty.
4 *ZH (Tanzania) v Secretary of State for the Home Department* [2011] UKSC 4, [2011] 2 WLR 148, para 24; *R (TS) v Secretary of State for the Home Department* [2010] EWHC 2614 (Admin) para 24.
5 See the discussion of material pubic law errors and detention at paras 32.10–32.13 and 32.17–32.21.
6 *R (Suppiah and others) v Secretary of State for the Home Department* [2011] EWHC 2 (Admin); *R (FM) v Secretary of State for the Home Department* [2011] EWCA Civ 807.
7 *R (MXL) v Secretary of State for the Home Department* [2010] EWHC 2397 (Admin).
8 *R (SM) v Secretary of State for the Home Department* [2011] EWHC 338 (Admin).
9 *R (S, C and D) v Secretary of State for the Home Department* [2007] EWHC 1654 (Admin) para 41. For a reiteration of the same principle since BCIA 2009 s55 came into force, see *R (Suppiah and others) v Secretary of State for the Home Department* [2011] EWHC 2 (Admin) para 148.

Home Office policy and the new statutory duty

37.8 It is published Home Office policy that where detention involves or impacts on children under the age of 18, reviewing officers 'must demonstrably have regard to the need to safeguard and promote the welfare of children'.[10] Notwithstanding that the published detention policy currently does not state that the best interests of the child must be treated as a primary consideration, the policy has been found to comply with BCIA 2009 s55.[11] Unpublished internal instructions to caseworkers in Criminal Casework Directorate (CCD) cases go further, as we see below at paras 37.13–37.19.

37.9 Reviewing officers in all cases concerning children should have received training on children's issues (ie Tiers 1 and 2 of Keeping Children Safe).[12]

Family Returns Panel

37.10 Since 1 March 2011, the UK Border Agency has established an independent Family Returns Panel to advise on the method of expulsion of families with children (but not decisions as to whether to expel) and on the use of detention[13] in certain cases involving children. The purpose of the panel is to ensure compliance with the UK Border Agency's duties under BCIA 2009 s55. The members of the panel include a UK Border Agency official, an official from the Department of Education, individuals with a background in local authority children's services/social work, and a medical doctor. The 'presumption' is that the Family Return Panel's advice will be followed.[14]

Children's Champion

37.11 The Children's Champion is a senior UK Border Agency official whose role is to advise the UK Border Agency's Chief Executive on

---

10 Enforcement Instructions and Guidance (EIG) chapter 55 para 55.8, see also para 55.1.1.
11 *R (Suppiah and others) v Secretary of State for the Home Department* [2011] EWHC 2 (Admin) para 210.
12 EIG chapter 55 para 55.8.
13 EIG chapter 55 para 55.9.4 notes that the Family Returns Panel advises on the use but not the place of detention.
14 UK Border Agency document: *The independent family return panel, how it will work*; EIG chapter 45.

compliance with the BCIA 2009 s55 duty, to advise UK Border Agency staff on cases involving children and to identify areas of concern. The role is now a requirement of the *Every Child Matters* statutory Code of Practice.[15] The Children's Champion's views are weighty albeit not determinative: a failure to have regard to the views of the Children's Champion is an error of law which may vitiate the legality of detention.[16]

Split families

37.12 Where a decision is taken to detain a parent separately from a child or maintain that detention, published Home Office policy requires that:

> ... the impact of the separation must be considered carefully. Any information concerning the children that is available or can reasonably be obtained must be considered.[17]

Internal CCD instructions

37.13 However, an internal process instruction to CCD caseworkers, 'Parental Responsibilities and continued detention of FNPs',[18] places considerably more onerous duties on the CCD. Because this is not (at time of writing) published, we cite it below in some detail. By the time this book is published, this version of the CCD instruction will no longer be in force: it remains to be seen what replaces it. We suggest that the contents of the unpublished policy provide helpful guidance as to the proper approach.

37.14 The unpublished CCD instruction states that where an FNP is being considered for immigration detention at the end of the criminal custodial sentence, the CCD case owner must check whether the FNP has parental responsibility for a child under the age of 18. When in doubt of a claim of parental responsibility, the case owner should

---

15 Every Child Matters statutory guidance paras 2.9, 2.12.
16 *R (MXL and others) v Secretary of State for the Home Department* [2010] EWHC 2397 paras 41–42; *R (NXT) v Secretary of State for the Home Department* [2011] EWHC 969 (Admin) para 144. Conversely, see *R (Bizimana) v Secretary of State for the Home Department* [2011] EWHC 1200 (Admin) para 37 in which the Children's Champion had advised that a family split would not breach ECHR article 8.
17 EIG chapter 55 para 55.1.4.2.
18 PC No 11, issued on 10 January 2011, valid until 10 July 2011.

make further checks. The case owner should then assess whether any family relationships are subsisting, for example by consulting prison visiting records. If there has been no contact between the FNP and child, the reason should be sought. In addition:

> Case Owners must contact Local Authority Children's Services to find out if they have any involvement in each case. All decisions taken regarding ongoing separation from their parents or removal of children of FNPs must fully take into account comments from Children's Services including any information about child protection issues or possible risks to the children from the parent in prison and any information about the effect on the child's welfare as a result of the parent's absence.

37.15 'Case Owners must ensure that they obtain a full picture of the FNPs family' – this includes determining whether the FNP was the main or sole carer, or whether the other parent is in custody (in which case 'special consideration' is required), who is presently caring for the child and whether there are any formal orders (such as custody or care orders) providing a basis for that care; the number of children, their ages and any special needs. Where it is established that an FNP has entered into an informal foster arrangement, the UK Border Agency must inform the Local Authority Children's Services. The impact on individual children must be considered:

> ... for example young children may forget who a parent is if any subsisting relationship is not carefully managed and older children may be affected by the absence of parental guidance in areas such as bullying or physical development.

37.16 The case owner must then assess the FNPs own history and current situation:

> In family cases, whilst not a determining factor, the Case Owner must consider whether the need to care for children and access services such as education and healthcare will mitigate the risk of absconding in individual cases.
>
> ...
>
> To meet the Section 55 duty Case Owners must consider where the best interests of children lie. Where there is a subsisting relationship between the parent and child and unless there are child protection concerns, this will almost always be in the liberty of the parent. Where this is the case staff must consider whether there are lawful grounds on which the best interests of the child can be overridden. This means that the case owner must balance the risk to the public and the risk of absconding which the individual poses against the potential impact of the detention of the parent on the child, taking account of the unique factors in each case.

37.17 Where the effect of detaining the FNP would be that a child would have been taken into local authority care, the FNP should not be detained:

> The UK Border Agency has made a commitment that it will not detain both parents or a single parent where that decision will result in a child being taken into care.

37.18 Any decision to detain which would split a parent from a child must be referred to the Office of the Children's Champion for advice. Any such decision must be approved by the CCD Director.

37.19 Where the FNP is detained and the children remain at liberty, the Internal Process Communication requires case owners to consider measures to maintain contact between the FNP and child. This may include arranging supervised 'socialisation' meetings in a detention centre prior to departure, where the family is being deported together to refamiliarise child and parent, or where the family is being split, to say goodbye.

Releasing a 'serious criminal' to a family including dependent minors

37.20 Where it is proposed to release a 'serious criminal' (see paras 34.47–34.51 above) to rejoin a family which includes dependent children under 18, it is published Home Office policy that advice should be sought from the Office of the Children's Champion and that a referral to the relevant local authority's children's service is 'likely'.[19]

Unaccompanied minor FNPs

37.21 An unaccompanied minor FNP who has completed a custodial sentence may, under Home Office policy, continue to be detained in the juvenile secure estate 'in exceptional circumstances where it can be shown that they pose a serious risk to the public and a decision to deport or remove has been taken'. Such detention should only occur on the advice of the Family Returns Panel, and is subject to a requirement of ministerial authorisation.[20]

---

19 EIG chapter 55 para 55.3.2.2.
20 EIG chapter 55 paras 55.5.3 and 55.9.3.

Families with children

Exploration of alternatives to enforced expulsion

37.22 Families with children who are in the community and facing expulsion should normally be offered assisted return (see paras 6.10–6.12 above), then 'required return', with at least two weeks' notice within which to make their own arrangements for return; before moving to 'ensured return' (ie enforced return).

37.23 However, it is Home Office policy that in cases where a family considered to pose such an absconding risk that they are 'almost certain' not to comply with other means, or to pose a 'high risk' to the public, voluntary means of return need not be exhausted before 'ensured return'.[21]

37.24 Wherever it is proposed to remove a family, the UK Border Agency must submit a plan for an 'ensured return' and submit it to the Family Return Panel.

'Pre-departure accommodation'

37.25 On 16 December 2010, the family centre at Yarlswood, previously the main Immigration Removal Centre (IRC) holding families with children, was closed. However, the UK Border Agency announced its intention to introduce 'family-friendly' 'pre-departure accommodation' 'with an entirely different look and feel from existing immigration removal centres'.[22]

37.26 It has been said that 'pre-departure accommodation' will be used 'as a last resort for those few families who resolutely fail to co-operate with other ensured return options'.[23] Such detention will be on the advice of the Family Return Panel. In August 2011, 'pre-departure' accommodation, The Cedars, opened in Pease Pottage near Gatwick Airport, amid concerns that the promise to end the detention of children had been broken.

---

21 EIG chapter 45.
22 Announcement from David Wood, the UK Border Agency Strategic Director for Criminality and Detention, on the outcome of the review into ending the detention of children (16 December 2010).
23 Announcement from David Wood, the UK Border Agency Strategic Director for Criminality and Detention, on the outcome of the review into ending the detention of children (16 December 2010).

Detention at Tinsley House Immigration Removal Centre

37.27 In 'very rare' cases where a family is believed to pose a 'significant risk to the public' such that the family cannot safely be detained in 'pre-departure accommodation', they may be detained at Tinsely House. Such detention will be on the advice of the Family Return Panel but also requires ministerial authorisation.[24]

Mother and Baby Units

37.28 Where a mother and baby are already in a Mother and Baby Unit at a prison, they may remain in that unit on sentence completion pending deportation. Such detention will be on the advice of the Family Return Panel.[25]

Time limits on detention of families with children

37.29 The same time limits apply to family detention wherever the family is detained.[26] Detention of families with children is limited to 72 hours 'except in exceptional circumstances where stays will be strictly limited to a maximum of one week and linked to a specific return date'. Ministerial authority will be required to extend the stay to seven days.[27]

Reviews in detained family cases

37.30 CCD cases involving the detention of children must be reviewed at the seven-day, ten-day and 14-day stages, and every 14 days thereafter. Owing to the seven-day limit on the detention of families with children, these review requirements should in practice only apply to the detention of minor FNPs, as the published policy acknowledges.[28]

---

24 EIG chapter 55 para 55.9.4.
25 EIG chapter 55 para 55.9.4.
26 EIG chapter 55 para 55.9.4.
27 EIG chapter 55 para 55.9.4.
28 EIG chapter 55 para 55.8.

SECTION K
Places and conditions of detention; complaints

Chapter 38: Places of immigration detention 727

Chapter 39: Conditions of detention in Immigration Removal Centres and complaints 737

Introduction to places and conditions of detention

In this section, we consider the safeguards concerning the places and conditions in which individuals may be detained under Immigration Act powers.

Where there is an ongoing failure to meet requirements concerning places or conditions of detention, detainees may seek injunctive or declaratory relief by way of judicial review to obtain transfer to appropriate accommodation or appropriate conditions of detention.

At common law, being held in an unlawful location (or in poor detention conditions) is normally insufficient to render the underlying detention unlawful.[1] But inappropriate detention location and poor detention conditions, where they adversely affect the detainee, may be contributing factors rendering the detention unreasonable in all the circumstances.[2] Note also that where liability is established for past unlawful detention, an inappropriate place of detention or poor detention conditions may found a claim for aggravated damages. Aggravated damages are discussed at paras 44.30–44.37.

As we have seen in chapter 36, places and conditions of detention may in certain circumstances, give rise to a breach of the European Convention on Human Rights (ECHR) articles 3 or 8. Claims arising out of inappropriate places or conditions of detention will rarely give rise to a breach of ECHR article 5,[3] although 'there must be some relationship between the ground of permitted deprivation of liberty relied on and the place and conditions of detention'.[4]

---

1 *R (Lumba and Mighty) v Secretary of State for the Home Department* [2011] UKSC 12, [2011] 2 WLR 671 para 68 per Lord Dyson; *R (Kambadzi) v Secretary of State for the Home Department* [2011] UKSC 23, [2011] 1 WLR 1299 para 71 per Lady Hale. For application in the context of transfer from an IRC to prison, see *Rashford v Home Office* [2010] EWHC 2200 (QB) para 14; *R (Rangwani) v Secretary of State for the Home Department* [2011] EWHC 516 (Admin) para 71 in which decisions on transfer did not affect the legality of detention.
2 See for example *R(I) v SSHD* [2002] EWCA Civ 888, [2003] INLR 196 para 18; *R v Governor of Durham Prison ex p Hardial Singh* [1984] 1 WLR 704 at 705.
3 See for example *R (Driton Krasniqi) v SSHD* [2011] EWCA Civ 1459, finding that detention in a prison rather than an immigration removal centre did not breach ECHR article 5.
4 *Aerts v Belgium* (2000) 29 EHRR 50 para 46.

CHAPTER 38

Places of immigration detention

38.1	Introduction
38.4	Places of detention permitted under the Immigration (Places of Detention) Direction 2009
38.5	Detention in prisons for those held under sole Immigration Act powers
38.12	Prison regime for those in sole immigration detention
38.16	Challenging the conditions under which an immigration detainee is held in prison
38.17	**Decisions over transfer**
38.21	Challenging a transfer decision
38.23	**Detention in police stations**

Introduction

38.1 This chapter considers the places where a person detained under sole Immigration Act powers[1] can lawfully be held.

38.2 We begin with an overview of permissible places of detention. The vast majority of immigration detention for criminal deportation occurs at Immigration Removal Centres (IRCs), prisons and (on a short-term basis only) police stations. We go on to review in some detail the circumstances and conditions in which immigration detainees can be held in prisons and in police stations. The legal consequences of detention in inappropriate places have been discussed in the introduction to this section.

38.3 Relevant sources of law and policy on places of detention are:

- Immigration (Places of Detention) Direction 2009. This is an executive Direction made under the Immigration Act (IA) 1971 Sch 2 para 18(1).[2] The Direction is not delegated legislation nor otherwise subject to parliamentary scrutiny and does not have the force of statute.
- Published Home Office detention policy, now set out in chapter 55 of the Enforcement Instructions and Guidance (EIG).
- Where a person is held in a prison, the Prison Rules 1999, Prison Service Orders (PSOs) and Prison Service Instructions (PSIs) will also apply. The Prison Rules 1999 are delegated legislation made under the Prison Act 1952 s47. PSOs and PSIs are guidance for the implementation of the Prison Rules and do not have statutory force.[3]

---

1 As is discussed at paras 31.35–31.36, whereas those held for examination or administrative removal may be simultaneously detained under criminal justice and Immigration Act powers, there is no power of 'dual detention' in deportation cases. A person may only be detained under Immigration Act powers for the purposes of deportation after completion of any period of custody ordered by a criminal court.
2 Applied to detention for deportation under IA 1971 Sch 3 by para 2(4) of that Schedule; and applied to detention under for 'automatic deportation' under UK Borders Act (UKBA) 2007 s36(1) by UKBA 2007 s36(4). By an oddity of drafting, this Direction does not apply to detention under UKBA 2007 s36(2).
3 See paras 24.9 for more detail.

Places of detention permitted under the Immigration (Places of Detention) Direction 2009

38.4 The Immigration (Places of Detention) 2009 Direction permits detention for the purposes of 'discretionary deportation' under IA 1971 Sch 3 or 'automatic' deportation under UKBA 2007 s36(1)[4] in the following places:[5]

- any hospital, young offender institution (YOI), prison, remand centre or in the case of a person under the age of 18, any 'place of safety';[6] or
- IRCs.

And for short term detention only,[7] in:

- any police station;
- any place specifically provided for the purposes of detention at any port;
- any place used by an immigration officer for the purpose of his or her functions;
- in a control zone or supplementary control zone;[8]
- any short-term holding facility;[9] or

---

4 See note 2 above.
5 Immigration (Places of Detention) Direction 2009 para 3(2).
6 Defined at Immigration (Places of Detention) Direction 2009 para 2: '"place of safety" has, in England and Wales, the same meaning as in the Children and Young Persons Act 1933, in Scotland, the same meaning as in the Children (Scotland) Act 1995 and, in Northern Ireland, means a home provided under Part VII of the Children (Northern Ireland) Order 1995, any police station, any hospital or surgery, or any other suitable place, the occupier of which is willing temporarily to receive a person under the age of 18'.
7 For five consecutive days (extended to seven days if at the end of five days directions are set for removal within a further two days): Immigration (Places of Detention) Direction 2009 para 4. However, published Home Office policy sets more stringent standards, see paras 38.23–38.24 below.
8 Areas where the officers of another state are permitted to carry out immigration control functions. These are defined in the Channel Tunnel (International Arrangements Order) 1993 SI No 1813; Channel Tunnel (Miscellaneous Provisions) Order 1994 SI No 1405; Nationality, Immigration and Asylum Act 2002 (Juxtaposed Controls) Order 2003 SI No 2818.
9 This is defined in Immigration and Asylum Act 1999 s147 and means a place used for the detention of detained persons for a period of not more than seven days 'or for such other period as may be prescribed'.

- premises where immigration appeals[10] are heard or specially provided for the purposes of detention in the vicinity of such premises.

Detention in prisons for those held under sole Immigration Act powers

38.5 In the white paper *Fairer, Faster, Firmer* of July 2002[11] and the Parliamentary Answer of Minister Beverley Hughes on 26 January 2004,[12] the government committed to ending the routine use of prison for immigration detention, though prisons would continue to hold immigration detainees where this was necessary 'for reasons of security and control'.

38.6 It is published Home Office policy that people held in sole immigration detention should only be held in prison 'when they present risk factors that indicate they pose a serious risk to the stability of immigration removal centres or to the safety of others being held there'.[13] The policy provides a non-exhaustive list of risk factors indicating that a person should be held in a prison rather than in an IRC. However, a person may be held in prison even where none of the listed factors are present, where other risk factors make detention in the more relaxed conditions of an IRC inappropriate. The list of risk factors has been broadened since earlier drafts of the policy and, at the time of writing, covers:

- National security cases – where there is specific verifiable intelligence that person is a member of a terrorist group or has been engaged in/planning terrorist activities;
- Criminality – those detainees who have been involved in serious offences involving the importation and/or supply of Class A Drugs, committed serious offences involving violence, or committed serious sexual offences requiring registration on the sex offenders' register[14], those who are subject to MAPPA levels 2 and

---

10 Under Nationality, Immigration and Asylum Act 2002 Part V; Anti-terrorism, Crime and Security Act 2001 Part IV; or under the Special Immigration Appeals Commission Act 1997.
11 *Fairer, Faster, Firmer* July 2002, para 12.13.
12 *Hansard* HC Debates col 606W, 30 January 2004.
13 EIG chapter 55 para 55.10.1.
14 This aspect of the policy has been upheld on challenge *R (Rangwani) v Secretary of State for the Home Department* [2011] EWHC 516 (Admin) para 58.

3[15] and/or there is a threat to members of the public if the detainee remains within the UK Border Agency estate;
- Behaviour during custody – where an immigration detainee's behavior whilst either in an IRC or prison custody makes them unsuitable for the IRC estate, ie numerous proven adjudications for violence or incitement to commit serious disorder which could undermine the stability of the IRC estates;
- Security – where the detainee has escaped from prison, police, immigration custody, escort or planned or assisted others to do so;
- Control – engagement in, planning or assisting others to engage in/ plan serious disorder.[16]

38.7 In addition, a time-served foreign national former prisoner (FNP) who is undergoing specialist in-patient medical care that is not available in the IRC estate may be held in a prison on 'health grounds'. This may include mothers who have recently given birth and are held in a Mother and Baby Unit of a prison (though see chapter 37 on the strict criteria for the detention of children). FNPs held in prisons on these grounds should be transferred to the IRC estate when medically fit for transfer.[17]

38.8 The relevant prison policies on immigration detention in prison are now contained in PSI 52/2011, which largely repeats the risk factors already discussed at para 38.6 above. PSI 52/2011[18] also adds to the indicators of suitability for immigration detention in prison the following:
- those convicted of sexual offending involving a minor or identified whilst serving as prisoners as posing a risk of serious harm to minors; those identified whilst serving as prisoners as being subject to harassment procedures;[19]
- those last categorised as Category B prisoners.

15 These are supervision arrangements made for the highest risk offenders. Level 2 refers to violent or other sex offenders; level 3 refers to other high risk offenders.However, for several months after April 2010, DEPMU operated internally, and inconsistently with the published policy, a blanket ban on the transfer of certain level 1 MAPPA offenders. See discussion in *AE (Libya) v Secretary of State for the Home Department* [2011] EWHC 154 (Admin) in particular para 86.
16 EIG chapter 55 para 55.10.1.
17 EIG chapter 55 para 55.10.1.
18 PSI 52/2011 para 2.69.
19 Ie prisoners who have been convicted or charged with offences under the Protection from Harassment Act 1997 or who have been subjected to a restraining order or injunction under the Act. For further detail, see PSO 4400 chapter 2.

38.9 Conversely, PSI 52/2011 also contains significant caveats to the risk categories:

> Detainees sentenced to less than 12 months for a sexual offence should not be presumed unsuitable to transfer on this basis alone, but in all such cases consideration should be given to the specifics of the offence and any previous sexual offending when making an assessment.[20]
>
> Detainees convicted of violent offences should not be presumed unsuitable for transfer on this basis alone, but in all such cases consideration should be given to the specifics of the offending and behaviour whilst in custody when making an assessment.[21]
>
> Individual circumstances might indicate that a detainee who would initially appear unacceptable might on assessment, present an acceptable risk to warrant transfer to an IRC.[22]
>
> It should be assumed that any ex-prisoner who had been deemed suitable for transfer to open conditions, irrespective of offence or length of sentence, will be acceptable to an IRC.[23]

38.10 A decision to keep a detainee in prison rather than in an IRC for his or her own safety, where the detainee was at risk from other detainees, has been held to be lawful.[24]

38.11 It has been held that in deciding whether a detainee should be held in prison, the Secretary of State for the Home Department (SSHD) is entitled to take into account confidential police intelligence of alleged criminal activity for which the detainee has not been convicted.[25]

Prison regime for those in sole immigration detention

38.12 PSI 52/2011 states at para 2.66:

> Persons detained only under immigration powers must be treated as an unconvicted prisoner with the same status and privileges.

38.13 Persons held in prison under sole immigration detention should not, without their explicit consent, share cells with convicted prisoners. This is set out at Prison Rules 1999 r7(b):

---

20 PSI 52/2011 para 2.69.
21 PSI 52/2011 para 2.69.
22 PSI 52/2011 para 2.70.
23 PSI 52/2011 para 2.71.
24 *R (T) v Secretary of State for the Home Department* [2007] EWHC 3074 (Admin), in particular paras 42–43.
25 *R (McFarlane) v Secretary of State for the Home Department* [2010] EWHC 3081 (Admin) para 30.

Unconvicted prisoners shall under no circumstances be required to share a cell with a convicted prisoner.

38.14 In addition, sole immigration detainees should, where reasonably possible, be kept out of contact with convicted prisoners unless they have consented to share residential accommodation or to participate in any activity with convicted prisoners.[26] Under PSO 4600[27] paras 1.4–1.6, unconvicted prisoners (a category which includes immigration detainees) must not be required to share a cell with a convicted prisoner without the explicit consent of the unconvicted prisoner. PSO 4600 also provides that:[28]

> ... sharing activities with convicted prisoners is acceptable, providing such activities are supervised and on the understanding that this enables unconvicted prisoners to have a better choice of activities, education and work than they would if they were kept segregated. Should the prisoner object to sharing activities, he/she must not be forced to do so.

38.15 However, prison policy makes provision for immigration detainees who consent to this, to be held in prisons which normally do not hold unconvicted prisoners. PSI 52/2011 states at para 2.66:

> Where a prisoner is held beyond the end of his custodial sentence in a prison which does not normally hold unconvicted prisoners, consideration may be given to enable the prisoner to remain where (s)he is. The prisoner must be made aware that (s)he will be held with convicted prisoners and his/her agreement must be recorded ... Where an immigration detainee opts to be held with convicted prisoners, all reasonable efforts must be made to accommodate the privileges to which unconvicted prisoners are entitled. However, it remains a matter for the Governor to determine whether or not it is appropriate for the prisoner to remain in convicted conditions.

Challenging the conditions under which an immigration detainee is held in prison

38.16 It has been stated, obiter, that a challenge to the conditions on which an immigration detainee is held in prison (for example, being held in a cell with convicted prisoners or in a Category A prison) should be directed to the Secretary of State for Justice or the Prison Governor

---

26 Prison Rules 1999 r7(a).
27 This PSO deals with Unconvicted, Unsentenced and Civil Prisoners.
28 EIG chapter 55 para 55.10.1.

rather than to the SSHD.[29] However, where the challenge is to the failure to transfer to an IRC and the conditions of detention in prison are pleaded as a reason for transfer, the challenge is properly brought against the SSHD[30] (see para 38.21 below).

Decisions over transfer

38.17 Decisions over transfers from prisons to IRCs are taken by the DEPMU within the Home Office.

38.18 It is published Home Office policy that:

... all cases who have completed a prison sentence will be assessed by DEPMU on an individual basis as to whether they should remain in prison or be transferred to an IRC.[31]

38.19 At least those time-served FNPs who are subject to MAPPA arrangements and remain in prison[32] should then be risk assessed on an individual basis monthly to determine their suitability for transfer to an IRC.

38.20 Any individual may request a transfer from prison to an IRC, and, if rejected by DEPMU, will be given reasons for this decision.[33]

Challenging a transfer decision

38.21 The appropriate course when seeking transfer from prison to IRC is to write to DEPMU and request it. Likewise, DEPMU can be asked to stop or reverse a transfer which would, for example, impede the detainee's access to legal advice. A refusal (or a failure to respond)

---

29 *R (MH) v Secretary of State for the Home Department* [2009] EWHC 2506 (Admin) para 123, not challenged in the subsequent appeal; see discussion in *R (McFarlane) v Secretary of State for the Home Department* [2010] EWHC 3081 (Admin) para 43.
30 *R (McFarlane) v Secretary of State for the Home Department* [2010] EWHC 3081 (Admin) para 44.
31 *R (Rangwani) v Secretary of State for the Home Department* [2011] EWHC 516 (Admin) para 30.
32 The requirement for a monthly risk assessment is referred to in Detention Service Order (DSO) 12/2007 on MAPPA arrangements but that has been interpreted to mean a requirement for a monthly risk assessment on an individual basis 'of all time served FNPs remaining in prison': *AE (Libya) v Secretary of State for the Home Department* [2011] EWHC 154 (Admin) para 101.
33 EIG chapter 55 para 55.10.1; see also *Rashford v Home Office* [2010] EWHC 2200 (QB) para 14.

by DEPMU can be judicially reviewed (the defendant being the SSHD).[34]

38.22 On one view, which we suggest is correct, DEPMU's transfer decisions attract no deference since the risk assessment is not an expert assessment.[35] However, conflicting authority holds that the court should be slow to second-guess transfer decisions.[36]

Detention in police stations

38.23 It is Home Office policy that immigration detainees should:

> ... preferably only spend one night in police cells, with a normal maximum of two nights. In exceptional cases, a detainee may spend up to 5 nights continuously in a police cell (7 nights if removal directions have been set for within 48 hours of the 5th night).[37]

38.24 Detention beyond two nights in a police cell must be authorised by an Inspector or Senior Executive Officer:

> ... who must take into account the UK Border Agency duty of care for detainees and the likelihood that police cells do not provide adequate facilities for this purpose in the long term.[38]

---

34 *Rashford v Home Office* [2010] EWHC 2200 (QB) para 14; *AE (Libya) v Secretary of State for the Home Department* [2011 EWHC 154 (Admin) para 83.
35 *R (Rangwani) v Secretary of State for the Home Department* [2011] EWHC 516 (Admin) para 52; *AE (Libya) v Secretary of State for the Home Department* [2011 EWHC 154 (Admin) para 83.
36 *R (McFarlane) v Secretary of State for the Home Department* [2010] EWHC 3081 (Admin) paras 12, 26.
37 EIG chapter 55 para 55.13.2.
38 EIG chapter 55 para 55.13.2.

CHAPTER 39

Conditions of detention in Immigration Removal Centres and complaints

39.1	Introduction
39.6	**Conditions of detention**
39.6	Maximisation of freedom of movement, minimisation of restrictions
39.8	Access to legal advice
39.9	Access to immigration officers
39.11	Searches
39.12	Detainees' property and clothing
39.14	Facilities
39.16	Hygiene
39.17	Access to activities and open air
39.20	Correspondence and visits
39.24	Medical care
39.29	Medical examination and consequent reports
39.35	Suicide and self-harm
39.41	Incentives schemes
39.42	Removal from association and temporary confinement
39.47	Use of force and use of control and restraint in IRCs
39.51	Mandatory drugs and alcohol testing in IRCs

continued

39.52 Complaints
39.52 The Prisons and Probation Ombudsman
39.53 Internal complaints
Centralised complaints body: the Detention Services Customer Service Unit • Subject matter of complaints; who can complain • The complaint form • Timescale for making the complaint • Timescales for responding to complaints • Investigative responsibilities • Duty to investigate all serious misconduct complaints • Refusing to deal with complaints from certain detainees • Potential outcomes, including ex gratia payments • Internal record keeping of complaints • Assault and other criminal allegations

39.84 Independent Monitoring Board
39.91 Complaints and subsequent litigation

Introduction

39.1 Immigration Removal Centres (IRCs) are detention centres for those detained under sole Immigration Act powers. They are run by private security firms on contract to the Home Office[1] or, directly, by HM Prison Service. Contracted-out IRCs are now the norm.

39.2 The primary sources of guidance and regulation for conditions in IRCs are as follows:

- The Detention Centre Rules 2001:[2] these are delegated legislation made under the Immigration and Asylum Act (IAA) 1999.[3]
- The Detention Services Operating Standards Manual for Immigration Service Removal Centres ('the Operating Standards'):[4] published in January 2005, the Operating Standards set out the standards and means by which contractors should meet their duties under the Detention Centre Rules 2001.
- Detention Services Orders (DSOs) issued on specific topics.[5]
- The Handling Complaints Manual, issued in June 2011.[6]

The Operating Standards, DSOs and Handling Complaints Manual are statements of Home Office policy and have no statutory force.

39.3 This chapter sets out particularly important and commonly encountered aspects of those rules and policies relating to detention conditions.

39.4 The legal consequences of deficiencies in detention conditions in IRCs generally have been discussed in the introduction to this section. The exception to the usual principle that poor conditions of detention

---

1 As permitted under Immigration and Asylum Act 1999 s148.
2 SI No 238.
3 Immigration and Asylum Act 1999 ss148(3), 149(6), 152(2) and (3), 153 and 166(3); Schs 11 and 13 para 2, Sch 12 paras 1–3.
4 Available on the UK Border Agency website: www.ukba.homeoffice.gov.uk/sitecontent/documents/managingourborders/immigrationremovalcentres/.
5 Useful DSOs include: Detention Services Order 11/2006 (Immigration Escorting and STHF Searching Policy); Detention Services Order 02/2007 (Use of handcuffs in cases subject to medical escort); Detention Services Order 03/2008 (Special Illnesses and Conditions); Detention Services Order 08/2008 (Guidelines on the use of handcuffs on detainees under escort); Detention Services Order 09/2008 (Detainees' Property); Detention Services Order 12/2008 Reporting and communicating of Incidents; Detention Services Order 13/2008 (Complaints) and the annexed Handling Complaints Manual; Detention Services Order 14/2008 (Recording of Injuries). DSOs are available on the Home Office website at www.ukba.homeoffice.gov.uk/sitecontent/documents/policyandlaw/detention-services-orders/.
6 This is annexed to Detention Services Order 13/2008 (Complaints). See Home Office website at www.ukba.homeoffice.gov.uk/sitecontent/documents/policyandlaw/detention-services-orders/.

do not undermine the legality of detention at common law is that where there has been a failure to carry out medical examinations or reviews which, if properly carried out and their results properly communicated, would have disclosed that the detainee was unsuitable for detention, this will give rise to the tort of false imprisonment. We have discussed this in some detail at paras 34.33–34.36.

39.5 This chapter ends with an examination of the UK Border Agency's internal complaints procedures applicable in IRCs.

Conditions of detention

Maximisation of freedom of movement, minimisation of restrictions

39.6 IRCs must provide detainees with as much freedom of movement and association as possible. The Detention Centre Rules 2001[7] state that

> ... the purpose of detention centres shall be to provide for the secure but humane accommodation of detained persons in a relaxed regime with as much freedom of movement and association as possible, consistent with maintaining a safe and secure environment, and to encourage and assist detained persons to make the most productive use of their time, whilst respecting in particular their dignity and the right to individual expression.[8]

The Detention Centre Rules 2001 also state that:

> Due recognition will be given at detention centres to the need for awareness of the particular anxieties to which detained persons may be subject and the sensitivity that this will require, especially when handling issues of cultural diversity.[9]

39.7 Security must be maintained in an IRC, 'but with no more restriction than is required for safe custody and well ordered community life'.[10]

Access to legal advice

39.8 Within 24 hours of arrival in an IRC, detainees must be advised of their right to legal representation and how they can obtain it.[11]

---

7 SI No 238.
8 Detention Centre Rules 2001 r3(1).
9 Detention Centre Rules 2001 r3(2).
10 Detention Centre Rules 2001 r39(1).
11 Operating Standards section 1:3.

Detainees who cannot read or write or for whom there is no booklet concerning legal representation in their own language must be assisted by the IRC staff in obtaining legal representation.[12]

Access to immigration officers

39.9 Detainees must be seen by an immigration officer for an induction interview within 72 hours of arrival at an IRC.[13]

39.10 Unless there are dedicated surgeries at the IRC, detainees must be seen within 24 hours of asking to see a representative of the Immigration Service.[14] When a detainee asks for information about his or her case, Immigration Service staff at the IRC must respond to the request within 24 hours or, if there is a delay, respond within 24 hours advising the detainee of the delay.[15]

Searches

39.11 Detainees must be searched by an officer on arrival in an IRC and may also be searched subsequently as directed by the IRC manager or by the Secretary of State for the Home Department (SSHD).[16] The search must be conducted 'in as seemly a manner as is consistent with discovering anything concealed'[17] and any stripping must not be in sight of any other detainee or any officer or other person of the opposite sex.[18]

Detainees' property and clothing

39.12 Detainees are entitled to keep their own property, other than cash, 'save where such retention is contrary to the interests of safety or security or is incompatible with the storage facilities provided at the centre'.[19]

---

12 See www.ukba.homeoffice.gov.uk/sitecontent/documents/managingourborders/immigrationremovalcentres/.
13 Operating Standards section 1:15.
14 Operating Standards section 1:14.
15 Operating Standards section 1:14.
16 Detention Centre Rules 2001 r7(1).
17 Detention Centre Rules 2001 r7(2).
18 Detention Centre Rules 2001 r7(3).
19 Detention Centre Rules 2001 r6.

39.13 Detainees may wear their own clothes in IRCs, provided these are suitable and sufficiently clean.[20] Further, 'where required all detained persons shall be provided with clothing adequate for warmth and health'.[21]

Facilities

39.14 The Detention Centre Rules 2001 provide that:
> No room shall be used as sleeping accommodation for a detained person unless the Secretary of State has certified that:–
> (a) its size, lighting, heating, ventilation and fittings are adequate for health;
> (b) it has adequate storage facilities (consistent with interests of security and safety); and
> (c) it allows the detained person to communicate at any time with an officer.[22]

39.15 The following furniture and fittings must be provided and detainees' rooms and dormitories must be large enough to contain them:
- a bed (there must be space for a single bed even if bunk beds are used);
- use of a table, chair, pinboard, mirror and waste bin;
- curtains.[23]

Hygiene

39.16 Every detained person must be provided with facilities for a daily bath or shower.[24] On arrival at an IRC, each detainee must be given a pack of toiletries to meet immediate needs and this must include a comb, toothbrush and toothpaste, soap, deodorant, shampoo, razor and sanitary wear.[25]

---

20 Detention Centre Rules 2001 r12(1).
21 Detention Centre Rules 2001 r12(2).
22 Detention Centre Rules 2001 r15(2).
23 Operating Standards section 1:4.
24 Detention Centre Rules 2001 r16(2).
25 Operating Standards section 1:11.

Access to activities and open air

39.17 All detainees must be:

> ... provided with an opportunity to participate in activities to meet, as far as possible, their recreational and intellectual needs and the relief of boredom.[26]

39.18 Programmes of educational classes must be provided at all IRCs.[27] The IRC must provide educational activities amounting to at least 25 hours per week. Education must be provided at least 50 weeks of the year.[28] Every IRC must have a library which meets a variety of linguistic and cultural needs.[29] All detainees must be given the opportunity to participate in sports and health related activities[30] and the IRCs' physical education centre must be open at least 30 hours a week, 52 weeks a year.[31] Where the manager of an IRC provides the opportunity, detainees may undertake paid activities at rates approved by the SSHD.[32] Recreational facilities must as a minimum include access to satellite television, music CDs, foreign videos and games including electronic games.[33]

39.19 All detainees must be given the opportunity to spend at least one hour in the open air daily;[34] this can only be refused 'in exceptional circumstances where necessary in the interests of safety or security'.[35]

Correspondence and visits

39.20 Save where restrictions are justified in the interests of security or safety, detainees are entitled to enjoy family life with their family members living outside the IRC[36] and with other people and agencies based outside the IRC.[37]

---

26 Detention Centre Rules 2001 r17(1).
27 Detention Centre Rules 2001 r17(6).
28 Operating Standards Instructions section 1:5.
29 Detention Centre Rules 2001 r17(8).
30 Detention Centre Rules 2001 r17(7).
31 Operating Standards section 1:7.
32 Detention Centre Rules 2001 r17(3)–(4).
33 Operating Standards section 1:7.
34 Detention Centre Rules 2001 r18(1).
35 Detention Centre Rules 2001 r18(2).
36 Detention Centre Rules 2001 r26(1).
37 Detention Centre Rules 2001 r26(2).

39.21 Detainees must be given access to a telephone within 12 hours of arrival at an IRC.[38] They must have access to telephones for at least 14 hours a day, including during normal active periods.[39]

39.22 Detainees can send at their own expense and receive as many letters and faxes as they wish.[40] Where a detainee does not have the necessary funds, the SSHD 'may' (but is not required to) bear the postage expense of a 'reasonable number of letters'[41] and 'must' bear the postage expense of any letter to the tribunals, higher courts or European Court of Human Rights (ECtHR) or Court of Justice of the European Union. A communication to and from a detainee may not be opened, read or stopped unless:

> ... the manager has reasonable cause to believe that its contents may endanger the security of the detention centre or the safety of others or are otherwise of a criminal nature or where it is not possible to determine the addressee or sender without opening the correspondence;[42]

in which case the detainee must be given the opportunity to be present while the correspondence is opened or read and must be given reasons in advance.[43]

39.23 Detainees may receive as many visits as they wish 'within such reasonable limits and subject to such reasonable conditions as the SSHD may direct, either generally or in a particular case'.[44] These visits must take place within sight of, but out of the hearing of, an officer unless the SSHD directs otherwise.[45] Legal advisers and representatives of detainees 'shall be afforded reasonable facilities for interviewing him in confidence, save that any such interview may be in the sight of an officer'.[46]

Medical care

39.24 Each IRC must have a healthcare team including a 'medical practitioner' trained as a GP[47] and qualified nurses.[48] In practice, the

---

38 Operating Standards section 1:11.
39 Operating Standards section 1:20.
40 Detention Centre Rules 2001 r27(1).
41 Detention Centre Rules 2001 r27(2).
42 Detention Centre Rules 2001 r27(4).
43 Detention Centre Rules 2001 r27(5).
44 Detention Centre Rules 2001 r28(1).
45 Detention Centre Rules 2001 r28(2)–(3).
46 Detention Centre Rules 2001 r30.
47 Detention Centre Rules 2001 r33(1)–(2).
48 Operating Standards section 1:37.

healthcare services are usually provided by a distinct healthcare contractor. Where the IRC is itself contracted out, the healthcare team's contract is with the private contractor operating the IRC rather than with the Home Office.

39.25 IRC healthcare teams are required to provide primary care services, including the 'observation, assessment, and management and care of detainees with mental health care needs'.[49] Where a detainee presents 'serious mental health needs' or has other specialist needs, the healthcare team must facilitate access to secondary care and specialist services where these are required.[50]

39.26 All IRC medical staff must attend training relevant to the identification of the mentally ill and of those detainees who may be victims of torture.[51]

39.27 The medical practitioner must obtain 'so far as reasonably practicable' any previous medical records located in the UK for a detainee[52] and when the detainee leaves the IRC must ensure these records are forwarded as appropriate.[53]

39.28 A detainee is entitled to request attendance by an outside registered medical practitioner or dentist provided that the detainee meets the cost; the manager 'is satisfied that there are reasonable grounds for the request'; and the attendance of the outside practitioner is in consultation with the IRC's medical practitioner.[54] 'Reasonable facilities' must be provided to permit examination of a detainee by a registered medical practitioner in connection with legal proceedings.[55]

Medical examination and consequent reports

39.29 Each IRC must ensure that staff employed in the admissions process have been trained to recognise behaviour and signs that indicate anxiety, distress or risk of self-harm.[56]

39.30 On arrival in an IRC, each detainee must be given a medical screening within two hours including an assessment of risks of self-

---

49 Operating Standards section 1:37.
50 Operating Standards section 1:37.
51 Operating Standards section 1:34.
52 Detention Centre Rules 2001 r33(8).
53 Detention Centre Rules 2001 r33(9).
54 Detention Centre Rules 2001 r33(7).
55 Detention Centre Rules 2001 r33(11).
56 Operating Standards section 1:10.

harm or suicide.[57] These initial medical screenings may be carried out by a nurse.

39.31 In addition, each detainee must be given a medical examination within 24 hours of admission to an IRC provided that he or she consents.[58] This examination must be conducted by a 'medical practitioner' (that is, a person of at least GP qualifications).[59] The purpose of this examination is:

> ... to identify any immediate and significant mental or physical health needs, the presence of a communicable disease and whether the individual may have been the victim of torture.[60]

The 24-hour medical examination must be sufficiently thorough to furnish independent evidence of torture in an appropriate case.[61]

39.32 The medical practitioner must report to the IRC manager:

- 'on the case of any detained person whose health is likely to be injuriously affected by continued detention or any conditions of detention';[62]
- on the case of any person suspected of having suicidal intentions (in which case the detainee must be put on special observation);[63] and
- 'on the case of any detained person who he is concerned may have been the victim of torture'.[64]

Copies of these reports must be sent 'without delay' by the IRC manager to the SSHD[65] and in any event, within 24 hours to the caseworking office with responsibility for reviewing that detainee's detention.[66] It has been held that to comply with Detention Centre Rules 2001 r35, the report should be from the medical practitioner and include details of the mental or physical examination or state of the detainee.[67] However, the SSHD's pro forma for such reports does

---

57 Operating Standards section 1:10.
58 Detention Centre Rules 2001 r34(1).
59 Detention Centre Rules 2001 rr33(1) and 34(1).
60 Operating Standards section 1:36.
61 *R (D and K) v Secretary of State for the Home Department* [2006] EWHC 980 (Admin) at paras 50, 53.
62 Detention Centre Rules 2001 r35(1).
63 Detention Centre Rules 2001 r35(2).
64 Detention Centre Rules 2001 r35(3).
65 Detention Centre Rules 2001 r35(4).
66 Detention Service Order 03/2008 Special Illnesses and Conditions.
67 *E v Home Office*, Claim No 9CL01651, 10 June 2010, Central London County Court, para 30.

not ask for these details to be enclosed or attached.[68] It is difficult to see how the very brief information required on the form can properly inform the decision whether to maintain detention or release and strongly arguable that the current procedure falls short of the requirements of Detention Centre Rules 2001 r35.

39.33 The Detention Centre Rules 2001 further provide that:

> ... the medical practitioner shall pay special attention to any detained person whose mental condition appears to require it, and make any special arrangements (including counselling arrangements) which appear necessary for his supervision or care.[69]

39.34 Detention has been found to be unlawful where:

a) no (or no adequate) medical examination had taken place within 24 hours of admission; and
b) had the requisite medical examination taken place, this would have disclosed evidence of torture; such that
c) the detainee should have been released under the SSHD's policy concerning the detention under Immigration Act powers of victims of torture, have been released.

The leading cases on this point, *R (D and K) v Secretary of State for the Home Department* [70] and *R (B) v Secretary of State for the Home Department*[71] and applicable legal principles have been discussed at paras 34.33–34.36.

Suicide and self-harm

39.35 Each IRC must have in place systems for ensuring that information about detainees showing signs of vulnerability is recorded and relayed to the healthcare team and others responsible for the care of the detainee.[72]

39.36 It is the duty of IRC staff to bring any concerns they have about the physical or mental health of a detainee to the attention of the healthcare staff.[73]

39.37 IRCs must now apply the Assessment Care in Detention and Teamwork (ACDT) self-harm reduction strategy.

---

68 The Pro Forma Rule 35 notice is annexed to Detention Service Order 03/2008 Special Illnesses and Conditions.
69 Detention Centre Rules 2001 r35(5).
70 [2006] EWHC 980 (Admin).
71 [2008] EWHC 364 (Admin).
72 Operating Standards section 1:10.
73 Detention Centre Rules 2001 r45(4).

The introduction of ACDT still requires all staff to be responsible for the prevention of detainee suicide and self-harm.[74]

All IRC staff must be trained in the use of suicide and self-harm prevention[75] procedures, including recognising those who may be at risk, receiving both basic and refresher training.[76] All IRC staff in contact with detainees, including the chaplaincy team, resettlement, education and training, catering, healthcare, and all escort staff etc must be trained to at least ACDT Foundation level.[77]

39.38 Healthcare Managers must be trained to ACDT Case Manager level. All healthcare staff and mental health in-reach teams working in IRCs must be trained to ACDT foundation level:

> Healthcare Managers must ensure all healthcare staff (as above) are aware of the importance of sharing risk and care information with staff from other disciplines, informed that this does not contradict professional guidelines, and do share such information with those managing individual detainees.[78]

39.39 Each IRC should have its own ACDT policy statement setting out protocols for communications concerning those on ACDT plans.[79]

> In the event of any incident of self-harm or whenever a member of staff believes a detainee is at risk of suicide or self-harm, an ACDT Plan must (where there is not one open already) be opened.

In the case of transfer of a detainee on an open ACDT plan, escorts, Detainee Escorting and Population Management Unit (DEPMU) and the receiving establishment must be informed of the ACDT plan.

> When receiving detainees with open ACDT documents staff should talk to the detainee and to escort staff, to check whether the risk is current or historical.[80]

---

74 Detention Services Order 06/2008 Assessment Care in Detention and Teamwork.
75 The Operating Standards refer to Prison Service F2052SH procedures, but those have now been replaced by the Assessment Care in Detention and Teamwork (ACDT) self-harm reduction strategy.
76 Operating Standards section 1:73.
77 Detention Services Order 06/2008 Assessment Care in Detention and Teamwork.
78 Detention Services Order 06/2008 Assessment Care in Detention and Teamwork.
79 Detention Services Order 06/2008 Assessment Care in Detention and Teamwork.
80 Detention Services Order 06/2008 Assessment Care in Detention and Teamwork.

Conditions of detention in IRCs and complaints 749

39.40 Where a detainee on an open ACDT plan is being prepared for release, a pre-release 'CAREMAP' should be produced, including action to link the detainee to external organizations to provide support after release:

> The aim is to ensure the discharged at-risk detainee receives at least comparable support to that they have received in the establishment.[81]

Incentives schemes

39.41 IRCs may operate incentives and privileges schemes[82] under which access to certain additional privileges is given or withdrawn according to the detainee's behaviour. Decisions must be based on patterns of behaviour and not generally on a single incident unless it is especially serious. Reasons for the decision must be recorded and notified to detainees who must be informed of their right to challenge decisions under the internal complaints procedure.[83]

Removal from association and temporary confinement

39.42 There is a power to remove detainees from association:

> ... where it appears necessary in the interests of security or safety that a detained person should not associate with other detained persons, either generally or for particular purposes.

In contracted-out IRCs, the power to remove from association is exercised by the SSHD,[84] although the power can be exercised by a manager on the SSHD's behalf 'in cases of urgency' in which case the manager must then notify the SSHD of the removal from association as soon as possible.[85] A detainee must not be removed from association for longer than 24 hours without authorisation from the SSHD.[86] The authorisation for removal from association must not exceed 14 days.[87] The detainee must be given reasons within two hours of removal from association.[88] Removal from association must be terminated if the medical practitioner so advises on medical

---

81 Detention Services Order 06/2008 Assessment Care in Detention and Teamwork.
82 Detention Centre Rules 2001 r19.
83 Operating Standards section 1:42.
84 Detention Centre Rules 2001 r40(1).
85 Detention Centre Rules 2001 r40(2).
86 Detention Centre Rules 2001 r40(3).
87 Detention Centre Rules 2001 r40(4).
88 Detention Centre Rules 2001 r40(5).

grounds.[89] During every day of removal from association, the detainee must be visited by the IRC manager, the medical practitioner and (in a contracted-out IRC) an officer of the SSHD.[90]

39.43 Where a detainee may be at risk of self-harm or suicide, removal from association 'must only be used as a last resort' and must be with the authority of the contract monitor (in contracted-out centres) or the centre manager (in directly managed centres).[91]

39.44 Detainees are entitled to request their own removal from association.[92]

39.45 There also exists a distinct power to confine temporarily in special accommodation a detainee who is 'refractory or violent'. However, temporary confinement must not be used as a punishment, nor after the detainee has ceased to be refractory or violent.[93] In a contracted-out IRC, this power is exercised by the SSHD,[94] but 'in cases of urgency' the power to confine temporarily may be exercised by the IRC manager on the SSHD's behalf, in which case the IRC manager must inform the SSHD of this as soon as possible.[95] A person must not be temporarily confined for longer than 24 hours without the SSHD's authorisation.[96] Each order for temporary confinement can last for a maximum of three days;[97] the detainee must be given a copy of the order, including the reasons for the temporary confinement, before the 27th hour of temporary confinement.[98] A person in temporary confinement must be visited by the IRC manager, the medical practitioner and, at a contracted-out IRC, an officer of the SSHD at least once daily.[99]

39.46 The ECHR principles applicable to segregation and confinement have been discussed at paras 36.59 and 36.78.

---

89 Detention Centre Rules 2001 r40(7).
90 Detention Centre Rules 2001 r40(9).
91 Operating Standards section 1:51.
92 Operating Standards section 1:51.
93 Detention Centre Rules 2001 r42(1).
94 Detention Centre Rules 2001 r42(1).
95 Detention Centre Rules 2001 r42(2).
96 Detention Centre Rules 2001 r42(3).
97 Detention Centre Rules 2001 r42(4).
98 Detention Centre Rules 2001 r42(5).
99 Detention Centre Rules 2001 r42(8).

Use of force and use of control and restraint in IRCs

39.47 Force must only be used as a last resort.[100] A detainee custody officer must not use force 'unnecessarily' against a detainee and, where force is necessary, 'no more force than is necessary shall be used'.[101] Officers must not act in a manner deliberately calculated to provoke a detainee.[102] Every use of force must be recorded by the manager and reported to the SSHD.[103] Force may only be used by members of IRC staff who have received Prison Service training (or training by Prison Service certified instructors) in the use of force.[104] Where force has been used, the detainee must be seen by healthcare staff 'as soon as practicable' afterwards.[105]

39.48 There exists also a separate power to order that a detainee be placed under special control or restraint 'where this is necessary to prevent the detained person from injuring himself or others, damaging property or creating a disturbance'.[106] The only permissible grounds for special control or restraint are for the above purposes and 'for safe custody, to give effect to directions lawfully given for his removal from the United Kingdom, or on medical grounds by direction of the medical practitioner'.[107]

39.49 Special control or restraint must be 'of a pattern authorised by the Secretary of State' and must be 'used in such manner and under such conditions as the Secretary of State may direct'.[108]

39.50 Special control or restraint must not be used as a punishment.[109] In a contracted-out IRC, the power of special control or restraint is exercised by the SSHD[110] but in cases of urgency, can be exercised by the IRC manager on the SSHD's behalf after which the manager must inform the SSHD without delay.[111] A detainee must not be kept under special control and restraint without written authorisation from an officer of the SSHD (as opposed to an officer of the

---

100 Operating Standards section 1:76.
101 Detention Centre Rules 2001 r41(1).
102 Detention Centre Rules 2001 r41(1).
103 Detention Centre Rules 2001 r41(3).
104 Operating Standards section 1:76.
105 Operating Standards section 1:76.
106 Detention Centre Rules 2001 r43(1).
107 Detention Centre Rules 2001 r43(10).
108 Detention Centre Rules 2001 r.43(12).
109 Detention Centre Rules 2001 r43(11).
110 Detention Centre Rules 2001 r43(1).
111 Detention Centre Rules 2001 r43 (2).

detention centre).[112] Special control or restraint must not be used for longer than necessary.[113] The medical practitioner must be informed of such an order without delay[114] and any recommendation against special control or restraint by the medical practitioner must be followed by the IRC manager.[115] The detainee must be given a copy of the order for special control or restraint, including reasons for the order and a specification of its duration,[116] no later than the 27th hour of the application of the special control or restraint.[117] A detainee must be visited by the IRC manager, medical practitioner and (in a contracted out IRC) an officer of the SSHD at reasonable intervals during every 24 hour period of special control or restraint.[118]

Mandatory drugs and alcohol testing in IRCs

39.51 Under the IAA 1999,[119] the SSHD may issue authorisations for mandatory drugs and alcohol testing in specified IRCs. Where such an authorisation has been issued, a detainee custody officer has the power to require a detainee to provide a sample of urine, breath or another type of sample specified in the authorisation. The officer must have 'reasonable grounds for believing' that the detainee has a controlled drug or alcohol in his or her body.[120]

Complaints

The Prisons and Probation Ombudsman

39.52 The mandate of the Prisons and Probation Ombudsman (PPO) covers IRCs as well as prisons. Detainees must exhaust the relevant internal complaints procedure before making a complaint to the PPO. Any complaint to the PPO must be made within three months of receiving the substantive reply in the internal complaints procedure. The PPO is discussed separately and in detail at paras 25.8–25.14.

---

112 Detention Centre Rules 2001 r43(5).
113 Detention Centre Rules 2001 r43(5).
114 Detention Centre Rules 2001 r43(3).
115 Detention Centre Rules 2001 r43(4).
116 Detention Centre Rules 2001 r43(6).
117 Detention Centre Rules 2001 r43(7).
118 Detention Centre Rules 2001 r43(9).
119 IAA 1999 Sch 12 para 2.
120 Detention Centre Rules 2001 r44(3).

Internal complaints

39.53 The complaints procedure discussed below applies to those who are being detained in the UK Border Agency detention estate, whether in an IRC, short-term holding facility or holding room, or who are being escorted under a UK Border Agency contract. It does not cover those who are detained in prisons or police cells.[121]

Centralised complaints body: the Detention Services Customer Service Unit

39.54 The Detention Centre Rules 2001 require that IRCs have an internal complaints procedure[122] and inform detainees of it within 24 hours of their arrival at the IRC.[123]

39.55 The handling of complaints for all IRCs (other than local minor complaints) has now been centralised and is largely the responsibility of the Detention Services Customer Service Unit (DS CSU).[124] The Complaints Handling Manual, issued in June 2011,[125] is essential reading for anyone making an internal complaint concerning an IRC.

Subject matter of complaints; who can complain

39.56 The complaints procedure applies to services and staff conduct in IRCs and during escort. It does not, for example, apply to immigration decisions, Home Office policy or to failures to provide disclosure in response to Data Protection Act 1998 requests.[126]

39.57 Complaints are accepted from: detainees who suffered the problem complained of; detainees' legal representatives; parents or guardians complaining on behalf of a child; those who personally witnessed an event or other service complained of; members of the Independent Monitoring Board (IMB); and members of staff with whom a detainee has directly raised an issue.[127] In certain instances, complaints are also accepted from third parties.[128] Complaints from

---

121 Handling of Complaints Guidance Manual section 1c.
122 Detention Centre Rules 2001 r38.
123 Operating Standards section 1:22.
124 DS CSU: fax no: +44 (0)20 8603 8030, email: Detentionservicescomplaints@homeoffice.gsi.gov.uk.
125 See para 39.2 footnote 6 for web reference.
126 Handling of Complaints Guidance Manual section 3k.
127 Handling of Complaints Guidance Manual section 1d.
128 Handling of Complaints Guidance Manual section 6m.

MPs are not dealt with under this procedure, although an MP complaint which describes serious misconduct by IRC staff should be referred to the Professional Standards Unit (PSU).[129]

The complaint form

39.58 It is the responsibility of the UK Border Agency Manager (or another appointed UK Border Agency officer) at each IRC to ensure that there are complaint forms (DCF 9 forms) and complaints boxes available.[130] Detainees with language or literacy difficulties should be assisted by IRC staff or members of the IMB in completing the complaints form if requested.[131] Complaints should be dealt with even if not on the DCF 9 form and even if written in a language other than English.[132] While anonymity may hamper investigation, anonymous complaints should 'in so far as possible' be dealt with by the same mechanisms as other complaints.[133]

Timescale for making the complaint

39.59 The complaint should be made within three months of the incident or circumstances complained of.[134] However, 'an investigation may be conducted into a complaint outside this period if it is considered that there are exceptional circumstances to warrant one'.[135]

Timescales for responding to complaints

39.60 The UK Border Agency Manager is required to ensure that the complaints boxes are emptied daily and that completed complaints forms are forwarded within six hours (other than forms relating to clinical matters) to the DC CSU.[136]

39.61 It is the responsibility of the Customer Services Manager at the IRC to ensure that any complaint of serious misconduct against an IRC staff member made verbally by a detainee is brought to the attention of the UK Border Agency manager 'at the earliest opportunity'.[137]

---

129 Handling of Complaints Guidance Manual section 3k.
130 Handling of Complaints Guidance Manual section 2b.
131 Handling of Complaints Guidance Manual section 3d.
132 Handling of Complaints Guidance Manual section 3d.
133 Handling of Complaints Guidance Manual section 3h(j).
134 Handling of Complaints Guidance Manual section 3i.
135 Handling of Complaints Guidance Manual section 6j.
136 Handling of Complaints Guidance Manual section 2b.
137 Handling of Complaints Guidance Manual section 2f.

39.62 Within two working days of receipt of a complaint, the DC CSU must record the complaint on its database, allocate it for investigation and categorise the complaint as:
  a) service delivery (complaints relating to services of the UK Border Agency or a supplier without referring to matters of personal conduct of an individual officer – eg administrative delays, lost property; standard of the physical environment);
  b) minor misconduct; or
  c) serious misconduct.[138]

39.63 Examples of serious misconduct include: repeated instances of minor misconduct offences; 'offensive personal behaviour including verbal abuse'; 'swearing or using threatening or intimidating behaviour'; 'false statements and concealment of errors'; 'failure to carry out proper procedures'; any form of discrimination; any form of harassment or bullying; computer misuse; seeking sexual favours; physical assault; serious negligence.[139]

39.64 Within two days of receiving the complaint from the DC CSU, the investigating officer should send the complainant an acknowledgment of the complaint.[140]

39.65 The complainant should be given a substantive response by the investigator within the following timescales:
  a) for a service delivery matter in an IRC, within ten working days of allocation of the complaint;
  b) for a service delivery matter occurring in a short-term holding facility or while under escort, within 15 working days of allocation of the complaint;
  c) for a minor misconduct matter, within 15 working days of allocation of the complaint.[141]

39.66 Complaints relating to clinical treatment or care are forwarded to the IRC Healthcare Manager.[142] The complainant is to be given a substantive response by a Healthcare Manager or the Escorting Contract Manager within 15 days of receipt of the complaint, save where the healthcare facilities are provided by a local Primary Care Trust in which case the timescales are not guaranteed.[143]

---

138 Handling of Complaints Guidance Manual section 3h.
139 Handling of Complaints Guidance Manual section 3h(iii).
140 Handling of Complaints Guidance Manual section 3i.
141 Handling of Complaints Guidance Manual section 3i.
142 Handling of Complaints Guidance Manual section 6b(i)i.
143 Handling of Complaints Guidance Manual section 3i.

39.67 The PSU has responsibility for the handling of complaints of serious misconduct. In complaint of serious misconduct, PSU will send an acknowledgment letter within two days of receipt telling the complainant to submit any further evidence within seven days. The PSU has a 'target' of 12 weeks from receipt of the complaint to its substantive response.[144]

39.68 However, the Handling of Complaints Manual states that:

> ... there may be exceptional reasons why a complaint cannot be concluded within the given timescales, particularly where the complaint is complex or the investigation relies on reports required from outside agencies. In such cases, revised timescales should be agreed with the DS CSU in advance, and the detainee sent an interim response providing a new timescale for completion.[145]

Investigative responsibilities

39.69 All service delivery complaints and minor misconduct complaints are investigated by the IRC operator or the UK Border Agency Manager.

39.70 All serious misconduct complaints (see para 36.93 above) are referred by the DC CSU to the UK Border Agency's PSU for investigation. Where the allegation concerns serious matters of security or corruption, the PSU may refer the complaint to the UK Border Agency's Security and Anti Corruption Unit (SACU). The PSU should automatically refer any criminal allegations identified in serious misconduct complaints to the local Police, and should obtain a crime reference number and pass this information on to the detainee or their legal representative upon request.[146]

39.71 Complaints that involve an arguable breach of ECHR article 2 or 3 should be brought to the attention of the duty Director of Detention Services.[147]

Duty to investigate all serious misconduct complaints

39.72 Serious misconduct complaints should never be closed without an investigation even where circumstances limit the ability to investigate.[148]

---

144 Handling of Complaints Guidance Manual section 4e(iii).
145 Handling of Complaints Guidance Manual section 3i.
146 Handling of Complaints Guidance Manual section 3e.
147 Handling of Complaints Guidance Manual section 3h(v).
148 Handling of Complaints Guidance Manual section 4g(ii).

Refusing to deal with complaints from certain detainees

39.73 Where a complainant's actions are threatening, abusive or offensive behaviour, or the complainant is so 'unreasonably persistent' as to hinder the investigation of other complaints, the complainant should be warned; if the behaviour persists, the UK Border Agency may decide to restrict its contact including not investigating a complaint.[149] However, see para 39.72 above.

Potential outcomes, including ex gratia payments

39.74 The UK Border Agency Area Manager or Escorting Contract Monitor may recommend to the relevant UK Border Agency Assistant Director the suspension or revocation of the detainee custody officer or escort officer's certification which enables them to work with detainees.[150]

39.75 There is no statutory scheme for payments arising out of complaints in IRCs, but:

> ... where an investigation demonstrates that a detainee has suffered actual financial or material loss because of the actions or negligence of a member of staff (eg lost or damaged property), the supplier should consider making an ex-gratia payment on an extra-statutory basis.[151]

39.76 Ex gratia payments will only be made for non-financial losses in 'very exceptional circumstances'. However, a 'consolatory' payment for distress should be made where serious or persistent errors have been made and the CSU is reasonably satisfied that this caused distress.[152]

39.77 The standard of proof applied as to whether loss has been suffered by the detainee is the balance of probabilities.[153]

> The rationale behind any decision whether or not to make a payment, and the amount to be offered must be clearly documented to show the information and factors considered when reaching a decision.[154]

39.78 Ex gratia payments will normally only be considered where an application for an ex gratia payment has been submitted within three months of the conclusion of the investigation. The conclusion of the investigation is when the complainant is notified of the outcome of

---

149 Handling of Complaints Guidance Manual section 6i.
150 Handling of Complaints Guidance Manual section 4e(ii).
151 Handling of Complaints Guidance Manual section 7a.
152 Handling of Complaints Guidance Manual section 7b.
153 Handling of Complaints Guidance Manual section 7b.
154 Handling of Complaints Guidance Manual section 7a.

the complaint by the UK Border Agency or a private contractor or the PPO, whichever occurs last.[155]

Internal record keeping of complaints

39.79 Detainees and their legal representatives should be able to access records for the individual detainee (through Subject Access requests under the Data Protection Act 1998 s7) and may be able to obtain generic detention centre documents through requests for information under the Freedom of Information Act 2000 and litigation disclosure.

39.80 The IRC Customer Services Manager and UK Border Agency Manager must ensure that there is a full audit trail of any complaint including any supporting evidence, including the investigation report, and that these are retained for six years from the conclusion of the investigation. Prior to the destruction of the local file, this documentation should be forwarded for linking to the main Home Office file.[156]

39.81 Each IRC should have a complaints database. Maintaining that database is the responsibility of the IRC's Customer Services Manager and the UK Border Agency Manager.[157] The IRC Customer Services Manager must also maintain a register of informal complaints.

39.82 The IRC Customer Services Manager must also ensure that a record is kept of all officers who have allegations of both minor and serious misconduct made against them by detainees. Where an officer receives more than three complaints in any rolling 12-month period this should immediately be reported to the UK Border Agency manager.[158]

Assault and other criminal allegations

39.83 The IRC Customer Services Manager must ensure that detainees who allege they have been assaulted – whether by another detainee or a member of staff – are given a medical examination, which records any injuries, and subject to the agreement of the detainee, are photographed. The records of the examination and photographs should be placed on the detainee's medical file.[159] Where a detainee alleges

---

155 Handling of Complaints Guidance Manual section 7b.
156 Handling of Complaints Guidance Manual section 2f.
157 Handling of Complaints Guidance Manual sections 2f and 3e.
158 Handling of Complaints Guidance Manual section 2f.
159 Handling of Complaints Guidance Manual section 2f; see also Detention Services Order 14/2008 Recording of injuries and reporting of allegations to the police.

assault by a member of staff, the detainee must be informed of the informal complaint procedure.[160] Where a detainee alleges that he or she is the victim of a crime, whether by a member of the IRC staff, an escort officer, another detainee, a UK Border Agency official or the staff of another IRC, the contractor must inform the UK Border Agency Manager and contact the police.[161]

Independent Monitoring Board

39.84 IMBs used to be known as 'Visiting Committees' and are still referred to as such in the legislation. IMBs have long existed in prisons – IMBs in prisons have a distinct statutory basis and have been discussed separately at para 25.15.

39.85 IAA 1999[162] established a requirement that each IRC must have its own IMB and that each member of the IMB for that IRC is able to enter the IRC at any time and have free access to every part of it and to all its detainees.

39.86 At least one IMB member should visit the IRC weekly.[163] They may interview any detainee out of the sight and hearing of detention custody officers.[164]

39.87 The IMBs have specific safeguarding duties towards detainees who are in vulnerable situations. Where a use of force is planned, the Chair or another designated member of the IMB must be notified 24 hours or as soon as reasonably practicable in advance but the use of force need not be delayed for the IMB member to attend.[165] The IRC Duty Manager must notify the Chair or designated member of the IMB within two hours of any removal from association, temporary confinement, use of force, use of special control and restraint or any serious incident in the IRC.[166] One of the IMB's members must visit any detained person who is subject to a) removal from association;[167] b) temporary confinement;[168] or c) special control or restraint. In the

---

160 Detention Services Order 14/2008 Recording of injuries and reporting of allegations to the police.
161 Detention Services Order 14/2008 Recording of injuries and reporting of allegations to the police.
162 IAA 1999 s152.
163 Detention Centre Rules 2001 r63(1).
164 Detention Centre Rules 2001 r63(2).
165 Detention Service Order 02/2011 on Independent Monitoring Boards para 39.
166 Detention Service Order 02/2011 on Independent Monitoring Boards paras 39 and 40.
167 Detention Centre Rules 2001 r62(1)(a).
168 Detention Centre Rules 2001 r62(1)(b).

latter case, the first visit must be made within 24 hours of the person being made subject to special control or restraint.[169] The IMB must also enquire into any report made to them, whether or not by a member of the committee, that a detained person's mental or physical health is likely to be injuriously affected by detention.[170]

39.88 During the management of any serious or critical incidents (which includes 'any concerted indiscipline active or passive') in an IRC, a single IMB member should be allowed to attend the silver command room as an observer.[171] The IMB National Council has agreed that its members should make themselves and any contemporaneous notes available for any subsequent management review or investigation[172] and we suggest that these should also be available in litigation.

39.89 IMB members must hear complaints from detainees[173] insofar as those fall within its remit. The IMB's remit does not include matters directly relating to immigration status, with the following exception. IMB members can consider any aspect of the immigration status of a detainee that causes them concern 'in so far as it affects the detained person's continued detention'.[174] The IMB must 'immediately' report to the SSHD any abuse which comes within its knowledge[175] and we have seen above (see para 39.57 the IMB can make complaints on a detainee's behalf through the UK Border Agency's internal complaints procedure.

39.90 An IRC's IMB should receive a copy of final reports on serious misconduct from the PSU[176] unless the complaint concerns a clinical or medical matter or the detainee has indicated that she or he does not wish the IMB to be kept informed.[177]

Complaints and subsequent litigation

39.91 Where a detainee has suffered personal injury or other actionable damage in an IRC, there is no legal requirement to bring an internal complaint or a complaint to the IMB or to the PPO before bringing a legal claim.

169 Detention Centre Rules 2001 r62(1)(c).
170 Detention Centre Rules 2001 r62(1)(4).
171 Detention Service Order 02/11 on Independent Monitoring Boards para 33.
172 Detention Service Order 02/11 on Independent Monitoring Boards para 37.
173 Detention Centre Rules 2001 rr38(1), 62(2).
174 Detention Centre Rules 2001 r61(5)–(6).
175 Detention Centre Rules 2001 r61(4).
176 Handling of Complaints Guidance Manual section 2g.
177 Handling of Complaints Guidance Manual section 2k.

SECTION L
Bail

Chapter 40: Powers of immigration bail and release on a restriction order 765

Chapter 41: Applying for bail or release on a restriction order 779

Introduction to bail

Organisation of this section

This section examines the law governing bail and restriction orders as they apply to persons detained for deportation, whether under the Immigration Act (IA) 1971 or UK Borders Act (UKBA) 2007. In chapter 40, we discuss the powers of the Secretary of State for the Home Department (SSHD) and Immigration and Asylum Chamber of the First-tier Tribunal (FTT-IAC) to grant bail or release on a restriction order. The practicalities of applying for bail or release on a restriction order and considerations in FTT-IAC bail hearings are then dealt with in chapter 41. Particular considerations arising in applications made in the Special Immigration Appeals Commission (SIAC) for bail have been dealt with separately in chapter 23.

Legal consequences of bail or a refusal of bail

Bail is not a determination of the legality of detention, whether at common law, or for the purposes of article 5(4) of the European Convention on Human Rights (ECHR).[1] The FTT-IAC's Bail Guidance for Immigration Judges tells immigration judges that they should assume that bail applicants are lawfully detained, although 'it will be a good reason to grant bail if for one reason or another continued detention might well be successfully challenged elsewhere'.[2]

In short:

- The test for bail is not whether detention is unlawful but usually the lower test of whether (assuming there is a power to detain) detention should be maintained in the particular circumstances of the case.
- Bail is not an alternative remedy that must be sought before judicially reviewing the lawfulness of a person's detention.
- The fact that a person has been refused bail is relevant to any subsequent detention challenge but does not preclude the person from subsequently establishing that he or she was unlawfully detained at the time.[3]

---

1 *R (Lumba and Mighty) v Secretary of State for the Home Department* [2011] UKSC 12, [2011] 2 WLR 671 per Lord Dyson para 118; *Zamir v UK* (1983) 40 DR 42 at 59, para 109.
2 Bail Guidance for Immigration Judges, Presidential Guidance Note No 1 of 2011 FTT-IAC 11 July 2011 para 5.
3 See discussion at paras 33.49–33.50 above.

- The requirement under ECHR article 5(4) that a detainee must be entitled to take proceedings by which the lawfulness of his detention shall be speedily decided by a court is not exhausted by the right to seek bail.[4]
- However, bail proceedings must meet the requirements of procedural fairness set out in ECHR article 5(4).[5]

Sources of law and guidance

Important sources of law and guidance on bail considered in this section are:
- the statutory provisions governing bail: IA 1971 Sch 2 paras 22–24, 29–34 and the statutory provisions which apply those bail powers to cases of detention for deportation, namely IA 1971 Sch 3 paras 2(4A) and 3 and UKBA 2007 s36(4).
- published Home Office policy, namely Enforcement Instructions and Guidance (EIG) chapters 55 (detention policy) and 57 (bail).
- the guidance issued to immigration judges by the President of the FTT-IAC, namely the Bail Guidance for Immigration Judges, Presidential Guidance Note No 1 of 2011 FTT-IAC 11 July 2011. Although non-binding, immigration judges should have regard to it and may need to give reasons for departing from it.[6] This is available on the Ministry of Justice (MoJ) website: we strongly recommend that bail applicants and their representatives familiarise themselves with it.[7]

---

4 *Zamir v UK* (1983) 40 DR 42 at 59 (para 109).
5 *R (Cart) v Upper Tribunal* [2009] EWHC 3052 (Admin), [2010] 2 WLR 1012.
6 Bail Guidance for Immigration Judges, Presidential Guidance Note No 1 of 2011 FTT-IAC 11 July 2011 para 3.
7 It is available at www.justice.gov.uk/downloads/guidance/courts-and-tribunals/tribunals/immigration-and-asylum/lower/bail-guidance-immigration-judges.pdf.

CHAPTER 40
Powers of immigration bail and release on a restriction order

40.1	Introduction
40.3	**Statutory powers of bail**
40.4	General powers of bail
40.8	Bail in principle
	Bail where appeal is pending
40.13	**Sureties**
40.15	**Conditions of bail**
40.17	Residence
40.18	Electronic monitoring
40.24	**Breach of conditions**
40.26	Forfeiture and re-detention after the grant of bail
40.32	**Bail from immigration judges of the Immigration and Asylum Chamber of the Upper Tribunal**
40.33	**Bail powers of the Administrative Court and Court of Appeal**
40.36	**Release directed by the criminal courts**
40.38	**Release on a restriction order**
40.43	**Home Office policy concerning authorisation for bail and restriction orders**

Introduction

40.1 A person detained for deportation may be granted bail by the Secretary of State for the Home Department (SSHD) (a power delegated to his or her Inspectors and caseworkers) or the Immigration and Asylum Chamber of the First-tier Tribunal (FTT-IAC), or, in certain circumstances, by an immigration officer or a police officer.

40.2 In addition, the SSHD has a power, instead of detaining or on granting release, to impose restriction orders on most people who are liable to be detained for deportation. (In examination and administrative removal cases, the equivalent powers are temporary admission for those not detained, and temporary release for those released after being detained.)

Statutory powers of bail

40.3 The primary statutory powers to grant bail are contained in Immigration Act (IA) 1971 Schs 2 and 3. These bail powers apply not only to those detained for deportation under the IA 1971 but also to those detained for 'automatic' deportation under the UK Borders Act (UKBA) 2007.[1]

General powers of bail

40.4 Any person who has been in the UK for at least seven days and who is detained may be released on bail.[2] Earlier restrictions on bail for persons liable to deportation were lifted in 2003.[3]

40.5 For the first eight days of detention (the eight days are calculated as beginning on the first day of detention) a person who is detained for deportation may be released on bail by the SSHD,[4] by an immigration officer of at least the rank of Chief Immigration Officer (CIO) or by the FTT-IAC.[5] After the expiry of the eight-day period, only the

---

1 UKBA 2007 s36(4).
2 IA 1971 Sch 2 para 22(1A) and (1B). The requirement that the person should have been in the UK for at least seven days applies only to new arrivals seeking leave to enter.
3 By Immigration and Asylum Act (IAA) 1999 s54.
4 IA 1971 Sch 3(5) and (6). Applied to 'automatic' deportation cases by operation of UKBA 2007 s36(4).
5 IA 1971 Sch 3 para 2(4A) and Sch 2 para 22(1A). Applied to 'automatic' deportation cases by operation of UKBA 2007 s36(4).

SSHD and FTT-IAC have the power to grant bail: the immigration officer only has the power to grant bail if acting on behalf of the SSHD.[6]

40.6 However, where the detainee has an appeal pending under Nationality, Immigration and Asylum Act (NIAA) 2002 Part V, separate bail powers apply: see paras 40.9–40.12 below.

40.7 When granting bail, the SSHD, CIO or immigration judge must take a recognizance (or, in Scotland, a bail bond) and require the individual to appear at a time and place specified in writing or to appear at a time and place to be notified later by an immigration officer.[7] A recognizance is a sum of money which the detainee forfeits if he or she fails to appear as required. In practice, the recognizance is often a token low sum (eg £5[8] or £10) and no proof of ability to pay is required.

Bail in principle

40.8 The SSHD, CIO and FTT-IAC have a power to grant provisional bail, that is, to fix the amount and conditions of bail for bail to be taken at a later date by a specified person.[9] This is commonly referred to as 'bail in principle'. As we shall see in the next chapter, immigration judges have received guidance to the effect that they should grant bail in principle where the risk factors have all been considered but the actual mechanics of release on bail cannot be met immediately.[10]

Bail where appeal is pending

40.9 Separate but similar powers exist to release a person on bail pending[11] his or her in-country appeal.[12] This bail power may be exercised by the SSHD, by an immigration officer of at least CIO rank (although

6 NIAA 2002 s68.
7 NIAA 2002 s68.
8 The figure suggested in the Home Office's own published policy on bail, EIG chapter 57 para 57.6.1.
9 IA 1971 Sch 3 para 2(4A) and Sch 2 para 22(3). Applied to 'automatic' deportation cases by operation of UKBA 2007 s36(4).
10 Bail Guidance for Immigration Judges, Presidential Guidance Note No 1 of 2011 FTT-IAC 11 July 2011 paras 45–50.
11 The definition of a 'pending' appeal is provided at NIAA 2002 s104. An appeal is still pending while any application for permission to appeal or appeal or application for reconsideration or reconsideration could still be brought in time.
12 IA 1971 Sch 3 para 3 and Sch 2 para 29(1). Applied to 'automatic' deportation cases by operation of UKBA 2007 s36(4).

after the first eight days of detention, this power can only be exercised by an immigration officer if acting on behalf of the SSHD[13]) or by the FTT-IAC, and also by a police officer of at least inspector rank.[14] Identical provisions for taking a recognizance (or in Scotland, a bail bond)[15] and provisional bail[16] apply.

40.10 This bail power applies to any person who has an appeal pending under NIAA 2002 Part 5. It therefore applies to any person who has an appeal against a decision to deport,[17] has an appeal pending against an automatic deportation order made under the UKBA 2007,[18] or has an appeal pending against a refusal to revoke a deportation order.[19]

40.11 Special statutory considerations apply when the FTT-IAC is determining a bail application from a person who has an appeal pending.[20] The FTT-IAC is not 'obliged' to release an appellant if it appears to the FTT-IAC that the appellant has previously failed to comply with bail; that the appellant is likely to commit an offence unless retained in detention; that the release of the appellant would be likely to cause a danger to public health; that the appellant is suffering from a mental disorder and his continued detention is necessary in his own interests or for the protection of any other person; or that the appellant is under 17 and necessary satisfactory arrangements for care on release have not yet been made. Arguably, these provisions establish a statutory presumption of release where an appeal is pending.[21] As we have already noted at paras 32.32–32.37 above, the Supreme

---

13 NIAA 2002 s68.
14 IA 1971 Sch 3 para 3 and Sch 2 para 29(2). Applied to 'automatic' deportation cases by operation of UKBA 2007 s36(4).
15 IA 1971 Sch 3 para 3 and Sch 2 para 29(2), (3) and (5). Applied to 'automatic' deportation cases by operation of UKBA 2007 s36(4).
16 IA 1971 Sch 3 para 3 and Sch 2 para 29(6). Applied to 'automatic' deportation cases by operation of UKBA 2007 s36(4).
17 An appeal brought under NIAA 2002 s82(2)(j).
18 This is an appeal under NIAA 2002 Part 5 by operation of NIAA 2002 s82(3A) as inserted by UKBA 2007 s35(3).
19 An appeal brought under NIAA 2002 s82(2)(k).
20 IA 1971 Sch 2 para 30(2). Applied to 'discretionary' deportation cases by IA 1971 Sch 3 para 3 and to 'automatic' deportation cases by operation of UKBA 2007 s36(4).
21 We suggest that the Bail Guidance for Immigration Judges, Presidential Guidance Note No 1 of 2011 FTT-IAC 11 July 2011 is incorrect in stating at para 26 (without reference to these statutory provisions) that there is 'no statutory presumption in favour of release in immigration detention cases'.

Court's judgment in *Lumba and Mighty*[22] leaves open the question of statutory presumptions of release or detention.

40.12 In addition, a supplementary restriction ostensibly applies where a person is released on bail pending an appeal. The IA 1971 provides that an appellant may not be released under this bail power without the consent of the SSHD if directions for the person's removal from the UK are presently in force or if the power to set such directions is presently exercisable.[23] Since removal directions can be set wherever a person has any appeal pending,[24] on its face this provision has the curious effect that wherever a person with an appeal pending is granted bail, the SSHD's consent is required before release. This provision, if relied on by the SSHD, would be open to strong challenge as contravening the decisions of independent courts and tribunals.

Sureties

40.13 Sureties may be taken when granting bail (but not when releasing a person on a restriction order). There is no statutory requirement that a person have sureties in order to be released on bail.[25] The approach to be taken by the FTT-IAC and courts to sureties is discussed at paras 41.55–41.58.

40.14 The recognizance offered by a surety is only paid (save in Scotland) if forfeited. It is unlawful for the SSHD, the FTT-IAC or the criminal courts to require sureties to deposit sums of money with the court, Home Office or with solicitors as a condition of bail.[26] The exception is Scotland, where bail bonds may be required.[27]

---

22 *R (Lumba and Mighty) v Secretary of State for the Home Department* [2011] UKSC 12, [2011] 2 WLR 671.
23 IA 19712 Sch 3 para 3 and Sch 2 para 30(1). Applied to 'automatic' deportation cases by operation of UKBA 2007 s36(4).
24 NIAA 2002 ss77(4) (a) and 78(3)(a).
25 IA 1971 Sch 3 para 2(4A) and Sch 2 para 22(2). Applied to 'automatic' deportation cases by operation of UKBA 2007 s36(4).
26 Asylum and Immigration Tribunal (AIT) Practice Direction 6 of June 2003.
27 EIG chapter 57 para 57.6.4.

Conditions of bail

40.15 Where bail is granted under Immigration Act powers, a date and place must be set where the person released will answer bail:[28] this is sometimes known as the primary bail condition. In practice, where an immigration appeal is pending and the FTT-IAC grants bail, the primary condition will be to answer bail to the FTT-IAC usually at the appeal hearing.[29] Where no appeal is pending, the bail applicant will be required to surrender to an Immigration Officer, usually at the reporting centre nearest to the bail address.[30]

40.16 Secondary bail conditions (restrictions as to reporting, residence, employment, and electronic monitoring) are imposed to secure compliance with the primary condition.[31] Bail may be granted without any secondary conditions[32] although this is rare in practice as we shall see in the next section.

Residence

40.17 There is no requirement to have a bail address. This is reflected in the Asylum and Immigration Tribunal (Procedure) Rules 2005[33] which require that bail applications state the address where the applicant would reside if granted bail 'or, if he is unable to give such an address, the reason why an address is not given'.[34] However, as is discussed in more detail at para 41.4, in practice it is often vital to have at least a temporary bail address.

---

28 IA 1971 Sch 3 para 2(4A) and Sch 2 para 22(1A); where an appeal is pending, Sch 3 para 3 and Sch 2 para 29(2). Applied to 'automatic' deportation cases by operation of UKBA 2007 s36(4).
29 Bail Guidance for Immigration Judges, Presidential Guidance Note No 1 of 2011 FTT-IAC 11 July 2011 para 35.
30 Bail Guidance for Immigration Judges, Presidential Guidance Note No 1 of 2011 FTT-IAC 11 July 2011 paras 32–33.
31 IA 1971 Sch 3 para 2(4A) and Sch 2 para 22(2); where an appeal is pending, Sch 3 para 3 and Sch 2 para 29(5). Applied to detention under UKBA 2007 s36(1) by operation of UKBA 2007 s36(4).
32 Bail Guidance for Immigration Judges, Presidential Guidance Note No 1 of 2011 FTT-IAC 11 July 2011 para 36.
33 SI No 230.
34 Asylum and Immigration Tribunal (Procedure) Rules 2005 SI No 230 r38(2)(d).

Electronic monitoring

40.18 For those who are the subject of a restriction order or who are granted bail and who are 18 or over, the Asylum and Immigration (Treatment of Claimants etc) Act (AITCA) 2004 introduced a power to impose electronic monitoring in combination with a residence requirement[35] or in lieu of a reporting requirement[36] and wherever immigration bail is granted.[37]

40.19 Electronic monitoring can take three forms. The first, used only in lower risk cases, is requiring individual to report by telephone from a specified landline at a specified address at a specified time using biometric voice recognition software. The second, the most prevalent for those liable to be detained for deportation, is requiring an individual to wear a tag and which enables the Home Office to ensure that the person is at a specified address at specified times. This is often associated with a curfew requiring the individual to remain at his or her address during specified times for monitoring.[38] The third and most intrusive, but not yet widely implemented, form of electronic monitoring would require an individual to wear a satellite tracking device to allow his or her whereabouts to be continually monitored.

40.20 Since November 2005, it is no longer Home Office policy to seek the individual's consent before imposing electronic monitoring.[39]

40.21 Notwithstanding that it is frequently argued for the Home Office in bail and detention challenges that electronic monitoring does not offer an adequate method to control individuals who pose an absconding risk, the Minister of State for Immigration has said that:

> Electronic monitoring provides the Immigration Service with a real alternative to detention while allowing them to manage the risk of non-compliance with reporting and residence restrictions according to the specific circumstances of a case.[40]

It is also published Home Office policy that the appropriate conditions for the release of a person liable to deportation but whose

---

35 AITCA 2004 s36(2).
36 AITCA 2004 s36(3).
37 AITCA 2004 s36(4).
38 Curfews may be imposed under AITCA 2004 s36(5).
39 *Hansard* HC Debates, col 87WS, 13 March 2006, Minister for Immigration, Citizenship and Nationality, Tony McNulty MP.
40 *Hansard* Debates, col 87WS, 13 March 2006, Minister for Immigration, Citizenship and Nationality, Tony McNulty MP.

detention cannot be justified throughout the time taken for deportation are twice-a-week reporting and electronic tagging.[41]

40.22 On a bail application in the FTT-IAC, the Home Office must substantiate any request for electronic monitoring conditions and satisfy the Immigration Judge that those conditions are indeed required.[42]

40.23 Where an electronic monitoring condition is imposed, the individual may remain in detention while the UK Border Agency makes electronic monitoring arrangements for a period not exceeding two days after the date on which bail is granted.[43] The Guidance issued to Immigration Judges of the FTT-IAC suggests that they specify that if the electronic monitoring arrangements have not been effected within those two working days, the detainee should be released on reporting conditions.[44]

Breach of conditions

40.24 Failure to comply, without reasonable excuse, with a residence or reporting condition or of electronic monitoring requirements[45] is a criminal offence punishable on summary conviction with a fine of not more than level 5 or imprisonment of not more than six months or both.[46]

40.25 However, in practice, breach of a condition of bail or of a restriction order, as with absconding, will usually simply lead to revocation of any bail and re-detention under Immigration Act powers[47] rather than prosecution.

---

41 EIG chapter 55 para 55.20.5.1.
42 Bail Guidance for Immigration Judges, Presidential Guidance Note No 1 of 2011 FTT-IAC 11 July 2011 para 37(vi).
43 Electronic Monitoring, Revised Policy issued by Deputy President of the AIT Ms Arfon-Jones on 14 August 2008, now attached to the Bail Guidance for Immigration Judges, Presidential Guidance Note No 1 of 2011 FTT-IAC 11 July 2011 as Annex 5.
44 Bail Guidance for Immigration Judges, Presidential Guidance Note No 1 of 2011 FTT-IAC 11 July 2011, Annex 8.
45 Under AITC 2004 s36 (2)–(3) a requirement of electronic monitoring may be treated as if it were a breach of a reporting or residence restriction.
46 IA 1971 s24(1)(e).
47 IA 1971 Sch 2 para 24(1), and, in pending appeals cases, para 33(1), applied to deportation cases under IA 1971 by Sch 3 paras 2(4A) and 3. Applied to UKBA 2007 s36(1) 'automatic' deportation cases by UKBA 2007 s36(4).

Forfeiture and re-detention after the grant of bail

40.26 Immigration officers and police officers have the power to arrest without warrant a person released on bail where there are reasonable grounds to suspect that the individual will breach, is breaking or has broken a condition of bail (whether a primary or secondary condition); or where a surety gives written notification that the person is likely to fail to answer bail (ie break the primary condition) and the surety asks to be relieved of his or her obligations. A person so arrested must be brought within 24 hours before a justice of the peace or the FTT-IAC to determine whether to direct detention or release.[48] The test of likelihood of breaching conditions for these purposes is equivalent to the 'substantial grounds for believing' test for revoking criminal bail under the Bail Act 1976 Sch 1 para 2.[49]

40.27 The FTT-IAC does not have the power to revoke bail (ie to order re-detention) although a person who attends a bail hearing having failed to comply with conditions of reporting or residence may be re-detained by an immigration officer or police officer at the hearing.

40.28 The FTT-IAC has the power to declare that a recognizance for the principal person released or for a surety has been forfeited where the person breaches the primary bail condition by failing to appear at the required time and date to answer bail; forfeiture is enforced by a magistrates' court.[50] There is no power of forfeiture for breach of secondary conditions.[51]

40.29 AITCA 2004 amended IA 1971 so that the SSHD has the power to re-detain a person whose release has been directed by a criminal court or who has been granted bail in the tribunal or higher courts where the individual has been recommended for deportation;[52] or where the individual is the subject of a discretionary decision to deport under IA 1971.[53] There is also a power of re-detention for a

---

48 IA 1971 Sch 3 para 2 (4A) and Sch 2 para 24. In cases where there is a pending appeal, IA 1971 Sch 3 para 3 and Sch 2 para 33. Applied to 'automatic' deportation cases by operation of UKBA 2007 s36(4).

49 Held in the context of SIAC's power to revoke bail: *Othman v Secretary of State for the Home Department* SC/15/2005, Mitting J in SIAC.

50 IA 1971 Sch 3 para 2(4A) and Sch 2 para 23. In cases where there is a pending appeal, IA 1971 Sch 3 para 3 and Sch 2 para 31. Applied to 'automatic' deportation cases by operation of UKBA 2007 s36(4).

51 Bail Guidance for Immigration Judges, Presidential Guidance Note No 1 of 2011 FTT-IAC 11 July 2011 para 64.

52 IA 1971 Sch 3 para 2(1) as amended by AITCA 2004 s34.

53 IA 1971 Sch 3 para 2(2) as amended by AITCA 2004 s34.

person who is the subject of a deportation order under IA 1971[54], and to a person who had, before his release on bail, been detained under UKBA 2007 s36(1).[55]

40.30 Finally, there remains the general power for police and immigration officers to arrest without warrant a person liable to detention[56] which may be used where, for example, a person previously released on bail has now had directions set for their removal.

40.31 Re-detention by the SSHD after a grant of bail from the FTT-IAC or a court would probably be considered arbitrary and in breach of ECHR article 5 unless either there was a material change of circumstances since the earlier grant of bail, or the court or tribunal granting bail or directing release had not been fully appraised of the facts.

Bail from immigration judges of the Immigration and Asylum Chamber of the Upper Tribunal

40.32 Immigration judges of the Immigration and Asylum Chamber of the Upper Tribunal (UT-IAC) are also immigration judges of the FTT-IAC.[57] When considering bail, they are sitting as judges of the FTT-IAC.[58] However, it will usually be appropriate for a bail application to be made to a judge of the UT-IAC only where the applicant's appeal is being heard by the UT-IAC or where a hearing before the UT-IAC is imminent.[59]

Bail powers of the Administrative Court and Court of Appeal

40.33 The High Court has inherent jurisdiction to release individuals on bail: this power may be exercised ancillary to other proceedings, for

---

54 IA 1971 Sch 3 para 2(3).
55 UKBA 2007 s36(4).
56 IA 1971 Sch 2 para 17; applied to cases where there is a decision to deport or deportation order by IA 1971 Sch 3 para 2(4). Applied to 'automatic' deportation cases by operation of UKBA 2007 s36(4).
57 Tribunals, Courts and Enforcement Act (TCEA) 2007 s4(1)(c).
58 Practice Directions of the Immigration and Asylum Chambers 10 February 2010 para 13.3.
59 Practice Directions of the Immigration and Asylum Chambers 10 February 2010 para 13.4.

example for a detainee who has brought a claim for judicial review.[60] An appeal against a refusal of bail in the High Court lies to the Court of Appeal.[61]

40.34 Likewise, the Court of Appeal has jurisdiction to grant bail where an appeal is pending before it from the IAC or from the High Court.[62]

40.35 In determining a bail application, the High Court and Court of Appeal exercise original jurisdiction. That is, the bail hearing is not a review of the SSHD's decision to detain.[63] (This is distinct from circumstances in which judicial review is sought of a decision of the FTT-IAC to refuse bail, in which case the higher Courts exercise a review jurisdiction.) Bail hearings in the High Court are discussed in more detail at paras 42.63–42.64.

Release directed by the criminal courts

40.36 A convicted person recommended for deportation under the IA 1971 may have his or her release directed by the criminal court making the recommendation,[64] or, where he or she appeals against the conviction or the recommendation, by the court hearing the appeal even if the recommendation is upheld.[65] Where a person has been recommended for deportation and the Crown Court, Court of Appeal, High Court of the justiciary (in Scotland) or the Crown Court or Court of Appeal in Northern Ireland decides to release that person, the court may direct that the person be subject to restrictions as to residence, employment or occupation, reporting or electronic monitoring.[66]

40.37 The UKBA 2007 also makes separate provision that a court determining an appeal against conviction or sentence has the power to direct the release[67] of a person who is detained for 'automatic'

---

60 *R (Turkoglu) v Secretary of State for the Home Department* [1988] QB 398.
61 Senior Courts Act 1981 s16.
62 Under Senior Courts Act 1981 s15(3).
63 See *R (Mehmet Sezek) v Secretary of State for the Home Department* [2001] EWCA Civ 795, [2002] 1 WLR 348.
64 IA 1971 Sch 3 para 2(1).
65 IA 1971 Sch 3 para 2(1A).
66 IA 1971 Sch 3 para 4; power to impose electronic monitoring AITCA 2004 s36.
67 UKBA 2007 s36(3).

deportation, whether before[68] or after[69] the making of an 'automatic' deportation order.

Release on a restriction order

40.38 A restriction order is similar to bail, save that a restriction order can only be imposed by the SSHD and no sureties can be required.

40.39 Any person who has been detained for deportation under IA 1971[70] may be the subject of a restriction order imposed by the SSHD (in lieu of detention or when releasing a person who has already been detained).[71]

40.40 The position for those liable to detention under UKBA 2007 is more complex. A person who is detained before the making of an 'automatic' deportation order under UKBA 2007 may be the subject of a restriction order imposed by the SSHD, whether in lieu of detention or on release from detention,[72] while the SSHD 'considers' whether the 'automatic' deportation provisions apply[73] or where the SSHD 'thinks' that the 'automatic' deportation apply.[74] However, once an 'automatic' deportation order is made under UKBA 2007, a distinct power of detention applies.[75] There are no provisions for the release on a restriction order by the SSHD of a person detained after the making of an 'automatic' deportation order. Therefore, restrictions can only be imposed on a person against whom an 'automatic' deportation order has been made if that person is released under the distinct bail powers discussed above at paras 40.3–40.5 and 40.9–40.12.

40.41 When releasing under a restriction order, the SSHD can impose restrictions as to residence, employment or occupation, and as to

---

68 Under UKBA 2007 s36(1).
69 Under UKBA 2007 s36(2).
70 Under IA 1971 Sch 3 para 2, ie a person who is the subject of a court recommendation to deport, of a decision to deport under IA 1971, or of a deportation order under IA 1971.
71 IA 1971 Sch 3 para 2(5)–(6).
72 IA 1971 Sch 3 para 2(5) as applied by UKBA 2007 s36(5).
73 UKBA 2007 s36(1)(a).
74 UKBA 2007 s36(1)(b).
75 UKBA 2007 s36(2).

reporting to the police or to an immigration officer. The restrictions must be notified in writing.[76]

40.42 Restrictions imposed by the SSHD may be subsequently varied by the SSHD or by an immigration officer.[77] The fact that release on a restriction order has been granted does not prejudice a later exercise of the power to detain that person[78] although re-detention absent a change of circumstances (such as new removal directions being set) may be found to be arbitrary.

Home Office policy concerning authorisation for bail and restriction orders

40.43 There is now a requirement in published Home Office policy to seek the authority of the Chief Executive of the UK Border Agency (or a board member deputising in his or her absence) before the UK Border Agency releases on restriction or decides not to detain a time-served foreign national former prisoner.[79]

---

76 IA 1971 Sch 2 para 2(5), applied to those detained under UKBA 2007 s36(1) by UKBA 2007 s36(5).
77 NIAA 2002 s62(4).
78 IA 1971 Sch 2 para 21(1).
79 EIG chapter 55 para 55.3.2.2.

CHAPTER 41
Applying for bail or release on a restriction order

41.1	Introduction
41.5	**Applications to the Home Office for release**
41.14	**Bail applications in the FTT-IAC**
41.14	The bail address
41.16	NASS accommodation
41.24	Offering suitable sureties
41.28	The bail applicant's instructions and evidence
41.32	The bail application
41.34	Listing
41.35	Seeking an in-person bail hearing where necessary
41.36	The bail summary and the National Offender Management Service pro forma
41.40	Burden of proof at a bail hearing
41.42	Standard of proof at a bail hearing
41.43	Evidence from the Home Office
41.44	Issues to be considered by the FTT-IAC at a bail hearing
41.51	Procedure at the bail hearing
41.55	Sureties in the FTT-IAC
41.59	Bail in principle
41.60	Bail for those still on the licence period
41.64	The bail decision
41.67	**Challenging a refusal of bail**

continued

41.68	**Further bail applications**
41.70	**Bail renewal**
41.72	**Bail variation**

Introduction

41.1 The test for bail from the Immigration and Asylum Chamber of the First-tier Tribunal (FTT-IAC) has been summarised in this way in guidance to immigration judges:

> In essence, an Immigration Judge will grant bail where there is no sufficiently good reason to detain a person and lesser measures can provide adequate alternative means of control. An Immigration Judge will focus in particular on the following three criteria (which are in no particular order) when deciding whether to grant immigration bail.
> a. The reason or reasons why the person has been detained.
> b. The length of the detention to date and its likely future duration.
> c. The likelihood of the person complying with conditions of bail.[1]

41.2 This chapter reviews practical steps to be taken when:

- applying for release on a restriction order or bail from the Secretary of State for the Home Department (SSHD) or bail from a Chief Immigration Officer (CIO) (referred to below jointly as applications to the Home Office for release); and
- preparing and presenting a bail application in the FTT-IAC.

41.3 This chapter also considers the burden and standard of proof and the approach to evidence in FTT-IAC bail hearings.

41.4 Bail in the Special Immigration Appeals Commission (SIAC) has been dealt with separately in chapter 23.

Applications to the Home Office for release

41.5 There is no requirement to apply for release from the Home Office before seeking bail in the FTT-IAC. However, aside from the (relatively slim) chances of succeeding, these applications may assist detainees in subsequent applications for bail in the FTT-IAC or detention challenges in the higher courts by prompting disclosure of more information about the reasons for detention (or, if the Home Office fails to respond, demonstrating inertia on the part of the detaining authority).

41.6 Applications for release from the Home Office should address those points which, under published policy, Home Office caseworkers are required to consider:

---

1 Bail Guidance for Immigration Judges, Presidential Guidance Note No 1 of 2011 FTT-IAC 11 July 2011 para 4.

... the likelihood of the applicant failing to appear when required; the period of time likely to elapse before any conclusive decision is made or outstanding appeal is disposed of; the diligence, speed and effectiveness of the steps taken by the Immigration Service to effect removal; any special reason for keeping the person detained ...; [and in bail applications only] the reliability and standing of sureties ...[2]

41.7 Where the risk of absconding or offending is low, applications should invite the Home Office to follow its own published policy, namely:

If an individual is unlikely to abscond and there is no other reason to detain him, you should normally grant temporary release. Each case should be assessed on its individual merits but you should consider the person's family, social and economic background and his immigration history. Despite an adverse background/history, a CIO or the Secretary of State may grant bail where sufficient and satisfactory sureties are produced.[3]

41.8 Where the Home Office – in monthly detention updates to the detainee, in response to earlier applications or in previous bail hearings – has relied on contentious assertions to justify detention (eg disputed allegations of obstruction, or repeated assertions that removal is imminent) the Home Office should be asked to provide evidence and particulars.

41.9 Applications for release should also address any compassionate factors, including any impact of the detention on the detainee or third parties. Claims that a detainee's mental or physical health is adversely affected should, where possible, be substantiated with medical evidence. Where children are adversely affected by the detention decision, applicants and their representatives should be alert to the duties owed by the SSHD to children under the British Citizenship and Immigration Act (BCIA) 2009 s55.[4]

41.10 The application should set out proposed release arrangements, including any bail address, any invitation to the Home Office to consider electronic tagging and (when seeking bail) any sureties offered.

41.11 As seen at para 40.13, sureties cannot be required when releasing a person on a restriction order. However, in relation to bail, it is stated Home Office policy that sureties are normally required.[5]

---

2 Enforcement Instructions and Guidance (EIG) chapter 57 para 57.5.
3 EIG chapter 57 para 57.5.1.
4 See discussion at paras 37.5–37.7.
5 EIG chapter 57 para 57.6.1.

Home Office policy also sets out stringent criteria for suitable sureties for bail.[6] Under Home Office policy, the surety should be:

- over 18;
- able to show that he or she has enough disposable income or assets to pay the sum offered as surety;
- settled in the UK (save in exceptional cases where a surety with no or limited leave to remain in the UK will be accepted);
- a householder, or at least well-established in the place where he or she lives;
- free of any criminal record (although there is a discretion to accept sureties with criminal records);
- a person who has not come to adverse notice on other immigration matters (in particular, has not stood bail for a person who absconded);
- a person with a personal connection with the applicant or be acting on behalf of an organisation which has an interest in the applicant's welfare;[7]
- a person with 'some credible reason' for acting as a surety (ie not a professional surety);
- able to show that he or she will be able to control the applicant if released (eg through geographical proximity).

41.12 We suggest that only the first two of the above criteria are mandatory requirements of any sureties that are to be offered; the rest, however, offer useful guidance to bail applicants and their representatives.

41.13 It is stated Home Office policy to seek high levels of recognizance from sureties. While stating that 'each case should be assessed on its individual merits', caseworkers are told that 'a figure of between £2,000 and £5,000 per surety will normally be appropriate' and that it is 'justifiable to fix bail' or to suggest to the FTT-IAC that it be fixed at a larger sum if the applicant has a strong financial incentive to remain in the UK.[8] The Home Office policy of setting levels of surety is arguably unlawful: the question for the decision-maker should be whether the sum offered is sufficiently high to provide adequate incentive for a particular surety, in the light of his or her means, to control the individual on bail. An affluent surety should provide a higher level of recognizance than a surety who is a single parent on benefits.

---

6 EIG chapter 57 para 57.6.2.
7 EIG chapter 57 para 57.6.2.
8 EIG chapter 57 para 57.6.1.

Bail applications in the FTT-IAC

The bail address

41.14 Although there is no statutory requirement of a residence condition when granting bail (see para 40.17), bail will rarely be granted without a specified address or at least evidence of a firm offer of an address from the National Asylum Support Service (NASS) or another respected organisation.

41.15 Where a private residence or the council accommodation occupied by another is proposed, it is helpful, where possible, to provide evidence of the size of the accommodation and evidence that the bail applicant would be able to live there if released (eg copy of a tenancy agreement; letter from landlord; letter from council for council accommodation).

NASS accommodation

41.16 Accommodation may be granted by the SSHD via the NASS to a bail applicant who is an asylum seeker or dependent of an asylum-seeker and who it appears may be destitute.[9] NASS support and accommodation may also be granted to a failed asylum-seeker or the dependant of a failed asylum-seeker who appears to the SSHD to be destitute and who meets one or more of a set of stringent conditions. The conditions for support to a failed asylum-seeker or his or her dependent are that he or she:

- is taking all reasonable steps to leave the UK;
- is unable to leave the UK by reason of a physical impediment to travel or some other medical reason;
- is unable to leave the UK because in the opinion of the SSHD there is no currently viable route of return available;
- has made a claim for judicial review in relation to the asylum claim and has been granted permission to proceed; or
- the provision of accommodation is necessary to avoid a breach of the person's rights under the European Convention on Human Rights (ECHR).[10]

---

9 Immigration and Asylum Act (IAA) 1999 s98.
10 IAA 1999 s4(2) and (3); Immigration and Asylum (Provision of Accommodation to Failed Asylum Seekers) Regulations 2005 SI No 930 reg 3(2).

41.17 Most usefully for bail applicants, there is a further power for the SSHD to grant accommodation via NASS to a person who is 'released on bail from detention under any provision of the Immigration Acts'.[11] Those released on bail may be granted accommodation regardless of whether they have made any previous asylum application.[12] It is stated Home Office policy that where a person meets the criteria for release on bail but has no address, or has an address which is not suitable for required electronic monitoring, the person may be released into NASS accommodation, whether or not he or she is an asylum-seeker.[13] The SSHD has a power to make payments to those released on bail for the purposes of enabling them to comply with reporting restrictions.[14]

41.18 The SSHD has accepted that she has a duty 'to use reasonable endeavours to provide a bail address if the person concerned would otherwise be likely to remain in detention'.[15]

41.19 The Chief Adjudicator's Guidance Notes on Bail of May 2003 suggested that in circumstances where there was evidence of the NASS grant of accommodation but no address was yet provided, adjudicators (now immigration judges) might grant bail subject to the following residence requirement:

> To reside at such accommodation as is directed by NASS in accordance with the terms and conditions of support given, and to notify the IAA, the Chief Immigration Officer and the Secretary of State for the Home Department of the address of such accommodation within 24 hours of being provided with it.[16]

41.20 Although that guidance has since been replaced, we suggest that this remains a reasonable solution in circumstances where NASS has agreed to provide an address in principle but has failed to specify an address before the bail hearing.

41.21 The UK Border Agency and the Asylum and Immigration Tribunal (AIT) (now FTT-IAC) subsequently established a protocol on 13 March 2009[17] whereby the UK Border Agency agreed that it would:

---

11 IAA 1999 s4(1)(c).
12 The relevant asylum support bulletin is 64 – this bulletin was under review at the time of writing.
13 EIG chapter 55 para 55.20.5.5.
14 Nationality, Immigration and Asylum Act (NIAA) 2002 s69.
15 *R (Razai and others) v Secretary of State for the Home Department* [2010] EWHC 3151 (Admin) para 26.
16 Chief Adjudicator's Guidance Notes on Bail of May 2003.
17 Attached to the Bail Guidance for Immigration Judges, Presidential Guidance Note No 1 of 2011, 11 July 2011 at Annex 4.

- provide the tribunal with an address prior to the bail hearing from a list of initial accommodation providers;
- ensure that the successful bail applicant would stay in the initial accommodation for at least 48 hours prior to dispersal; and
- apply on the papers to the tribunal for variation of the bail conditions once the bail applicant had moved to the new address.

41.22 However, as later emerged, the SSHD from January 2010 operated an unpublished policy concerning accommodation for those convicted of murder, violence, sexual offences, drugs offences bar minor possession or who fell under MAPPA (Multi-Agency Public Protection Arrangements) level 2 or 3 arrangements,[18] or indeed who had a history of property damage. That unpublished policy, which emerged in the *R (Razai and others) v Secretary of State for the Home Department*[19] litigation permitted UK Border Agency case owners in such cases to decide that neither initial nor dispersal accommodation was appropriate. This in practice led to significant delays for the provision of NASS accommodation for serious offenders. The policy was found to be lawful[20] but to have been operated unfairly.[21]

41.23 A failure by the SSHD to make a decision on whether to provide accommodation under IAA 1999 s4 is susceptible to judicial review (only an actual positive refusal to accommodate will generate a right of appeal to the FTT (Social Entitlement Chamber)).[22] The SSHD must inform the individual of a decision, even a provisional decision, that he or she is unsuitable for initial accommodation and give at least the gist of the reasons.[23]

Offering suitable sureties

41.24 As we have seen in para 40.13, there is no statutory requirement of sureties when seeking bail. However, sureties may offer crucial assistance in obtaining bail.

---

18 See paras 24.22–24.25 for an explanation of MAPPA.
19 [2010] EWHC 3151 (Admin).
20 *R (Razai and others) v Secretary of State for the Home Department* [2010] EWHC 3151 (Admin) para 100.
21 *R (Razai and others) v Secretary of State for the Home Department* [2010] EWHC 3151 (Admin) para 111(vii).
22 *R (Razai and others) v Secretary of State for the Home Department* [2010] EWHC 3151 (Admin) para 62.
23 *R (Razai and others) v Secretary of State for the Home Department* [2010] EWHC 3151 (Admin) para 85.

41.25 The key questions for the FTT-IAC in assessing the suitability of a surety will be whether the surety has the means to pay in the event of forfeiture and whether the surety is sufficiently reliable and close to the bail applicant to control the applicant on release. The Home Office's own checklist for sureties, set out above, provides a useful guide to the characteristics of the ideal surety[24] but, as to the non-mandatory requirements, should not deter bail applicants from offering less rosy sureties if no others are available. Bail Guidance to the immigration judiciary now states that:

> A surety who has no immigration status, regular address, means of subsistence or knowledge of the applicant may well be unsuitable to act as such, as will a surety who has criminal convictions that are not spent.[25]

41.26 The responsibilities and obligations of a surety (to contact the police and/or immigration service in the event that the bail applicant breaches or is likely to breach a condition) and the risks of forfeiture must be explained to the surety. The surety should be told to seek independent legal advice if in doubt.

41.27 As to the sum to be offered, see para 41.58.

The bail applicant's instructions and evidence

41.28 Instructions should be taken well in advance of the hearing date, not only to collect any relevant evidence but because most bail hearings are now conducted by video-link, with detainees able to speak to their representatives only for ten minutes by video-link[26] before the start of the hearing.

41.29 Witness statements are increasingly important in bail applications given the time pressures imposed by video link bail applications. Documentary, witness and even expert evidence may also be vital, where available and appropriate, to address the following points:

- *Risk of further offending and any reduction in risk since the index offence.* Consider obtaining evidence of courses completed in prison; probation reports; OASys (Offender Assessment System)

---

24 These and further criteria for sureties are set out in the Home Office's own guidance to caseworkers, EIG chapter 57 para 57.6.2.
25 Bail Guidance for Immigration Judges, Presidential Guidance Note No 1 of 2011 FTT-IAC 11 July 2011 para 41.
26 Bail Guidance for Immigration Judges, Presidential Guidance Note No 1 of 2011 FTT-IAC 11 July 2011, Annex 6 'Guidance Note to the Judiciary about video link hearings'.

assessments; and if possible a report from a forensic psychologist or psychiatrist. See chapter 20 above, box 20.5 for a more detailed discussion of evidence of offending risk.

- *Any previous compliance with conditions of temporary admission, temporary release, release on licence and/or immigration or criminal bail.* Where there has been compliance, consider obtaining witness statements from the applicant and others to show this; confirmation by letter from solicitors representing the applicant in criminal proceedings of past compliance with criminal bail; and, where possible, confirmation from the probation officer of compliance with licence conditions and probation requirements.
- *Any barriers to removal.* Where there is an outstanding application or legal challenge, this should be shown by documentation, and the question of whether any legal challenge is expedited (and any anticipated timescale for resolution) should be addressed. Where ther are difficulties in obtaining travel documents, consider seeking evidence from organisations such as the Bail for Immigration Detainees charity on the time generally taken to secure travel documents for the applicant's destination country.
- *Rebuttal where appropriate of any inaccurate allegations of non cooperation.* Consider seeking witness evidence from the applicant and copies of any signed bio-data forms.
- *Rebuttal where appropriate of any inaccurate allegations of past absconding.* Where, as occurs not infrequently, there is a dispute as to whether a bail applicant previously absconded, consider whether there is evidence that the applicant remained in contact with the Home Office and/or remained living at the same address while allegedly having absconded.
- *Any ties in the UK that would promote compliance with bail.* Where the applicant has family members, consider obtaining witness statements and securing their attendance at the hearing; where the applicant has resided for a long time in the UK or even at the same address, establish this by documentary evidence.
- *Any plans on release that would promote compliance with bail.* Where a bail applicant has plans for the future which promote stability and tend to reduce offending or absconding risk, such as an offer or plan of employment for an applicant who is entitled to work, or plans to enter counselling or a drugs testing programme, or any studies, this should be evidenced as far as possible by documentation and/or witness evidence.
- *Licence conditions.* Where the applicant is still on licence, a copy should be provided by the applicant if it has not already been

produced by the Home Office. The licence may help to demonstrate an additional source of control if the applicant is released, see paras 41.61–41.63 below.
- *Any compassionate circumstances or special vulnerability.* If third parties such as children are adversely affected by the applicant's detention, this should be shown by witness evidence and, where appropriate and possible, medical or expert social work evidence. Where the applicant is suffering adverse mental or physical health effects from detention, the applicant's detention centre or prison health records should, where possible, be sought to evidence this, and expert evidence obtained where feasible.

41.30 For a more detailed discussion of sources of documentary and expert evidence in criminal deportation cases generally, see chapter 20.

41.31 On receipt of the bail summary, the bail applicant's instructions should be taken carefully on the facts alleged in the bail summary, checking in particular for any inaccuracies. See para 41.38 below.

The bail application

41.32 Applications for FTT-IAC bail are made by lodging form B1.[27] Applicants must provide:
- their full name;
- date of birth;
- date of arrival in the UK;
- the address where detained;
- an indication of whether any appeal is pending before the Immigration and Asylum Chamber of the First-tier Tribunal (IAC);
- the proposed release address, or if unable to provide such an address, the reason why;
- where the applicant is aged 18 or over, an indication of whether he or she is willing if required to cooperate with electronic monitoring;
- the amount of the recognizance in which he or she will agree to be bound;
- the full names, addresses, occupations and dates of birth of any sureties and the amounts of the recognizances which they are offering;

---

27 Available on the Ministry of Justice (MoJ) website: www.justice.gov.uk/global/forms/hmcts/tribunals/immigration-and-asylum/index.htm.

- the grounds of the bail application and, if an earlier application was refused, full details of any change of circumstances since that refusal; and
- whether an interpreter will be required and if so which language or dialect.[28]

The application form must be signed by the applicant or his or her representative, or if the applicant is a child or otherwise lacks capacity, the person acting on their behalf.[29]

41.33 Failure to provide on the bail form the full details of a proposed release address or the full details of proposed sureties is likely to lead to an adjournment or, where the hearing proceeds, a bail refusal. In principle at least, the UK Border Agency carries out security checks on proposed bail addresses and sureties and thus must be given sufficient time to carry these out.

Listing

41.34 On receiving the application form, the FTT-IAC are required 'as soon as reasonably practicable' to serve a copy of the application on the SSHD and fix a date for a hearing. The tribunal's own Practice Direction states that 'if practicable', the fixing of the hearing should take place within three working days of the receipt of the bail application;[30] this target is frequently missed.

Seeking an in-person bail hearing where necessary

41.35 Many bail hearings are now conducted by video-link. We discuss the logistics of video-link hearings further below at para 41.51. The tribunal has indicated that where there are exceptional circumstances that make video-link inappropriate, representatives should make representations and submit evidence to that effect to the Resident Senior Immigration Judge at the hearing centre.[31] No guidance has been issued as to what constitute exceptional circumstances. We suggest that in cases which are unusually factually, evidentially or legally complex and require longer time than the norm, or which involve

28 Asylum and Immigration Tribunal (Procedure) Rules 2005 r38(2).
29 Asylum and Immigration Tribunal (Procedure) Rules 2005 r38(3).
30 Practice Directions of the Immigration and Asylum Chambers of the First-tier Tribunal and the Upper Tribunal, Carnwath LJ 10 February 2010, para 13.1.
31 Refugee Council and BID: 'Bail hearings by video link' March 2008; see also Bail Guidance for Immigration Judges, Presidential Guidance Note No 1 of 2011 FTT-IAC 11 July 2011 Annex 6 para 7.

particularly vulnerable detainees whose evidence may be impaired if given by video-link, applicants and representatives may wish to seek an in-person bail hearing.

The bail summary and the National Offender Management Service pro forma

41.36 The Asylum and Immigration Tribunal (Procedure) Rules 2005[32] provide that 'if the SSHD wishes to contest an application, [she] must file with the Tribunal and serve on the applicant a written statement of [her reasons] for doing so' no later than 2pm on the business day before the hearing, or if the SSHD was served with notice of the bail hearing less than 24 hours before that time, as soon as reasonably practicable.[33] We suggest that it logically follows from the terms of the delegated legislation (the SSHD 'must' file a bail summary if she wishes to contest the application) that if the SSHD fails to comply with the requirement to provide a bail summary, he or she should not be allowed to contest bail. However, current Bail Guidance to the immigration judiciary envisages that immigration judges may be able to 'infer reasons for detention from other available sources'.[34]

41.37 In preparing the bail summary for a criminal deportation case, the SSHD (in practice her Criminal Casework Directorate (CCD)) should normally seek input from the National Offender Management Service (NOMS). This input is provided to the CCD by the bail applicant's offender manager at NOMS on a pro forma[35] and should address the risks of reoffending and reconviction, including any OASys results; as well as the bail applicant's known history of compliance (or lack of it) with bail and licence conditions; and any NOMS comments on bail conditions. NOMS offender managers are specifically directed to exclude confidential information (such as information that might compromise victim safety) from the pro forma. NOMS guidance states that the pro forma should be made

32 SI No 230.
33 Asylum and Immigration Tribunal (Procedure) Rules 2005 r39(2).
34 Bail Guidance for Immigration Judges, Presidential Guidance Note No 1 of 2011 FTT-IAC 11 July 2011 para 6.
35 'Request for offender management information on a foreign national prisoner'.

available by Home Office Presenting Officers (HOPOs) to bail applicants and their solicitors.[36]

41.38 It is vital for those representing bail applicants to take careful instructions on the bail summary before the hearing since it may contain inaccuracies and omit important information. Where a detainee confidently contests an allegation made in the bail summary (eg an allegation that he or she is obstructing travel documentation) or where a questionable fact is asserted in the bail summary (eg an assertion that deportation will now take place within a specified time) representatives may wish to write to the Home Office Presenting Officers' Unit before the hearing asking for evidence of the contested fact.

41.39 Home Office caseworkers are directed not to oppose bail where a person is deemed appropriate for bail, but to seek the imposition of restrictions.[37] In practice, however, it appears that bail is almost invariably opposed in FNP cases.

Burden of proof at a bail hearing

41.40 The burden of proof to justify detention in a bail application lies on the SSHD. We have discussed the burden of proof in detention challenges generally at paras 32.3–32.5: the detainer bears the burden of showing power to detain and showing that the power has been exercised lawfully. Albeit not a challenge to the underlying legality of the detention, the same principle applies in bail.

41.41 Current Bail Guidance to the immigration judiciary is, we respectfully suggest, less clear than it could be. The current guidance states (correctly) that:

> ... bail should not be refused unless there is good reason to do so, and it is for the respondent to show what those reasons are ...[38]

and:

> ... the immigration authorities will have to show that the reasons for detention remain connected to the pending investigation [where

---

36 Probation Circular 32/2007 'Management of Foreign National Prisoners: Licences, Bail Hearings, Releases from Immigration Detention and Deportation'. This can now be found at Annex 3 to the Bail Guidance for Immigration Judges, Presidential Guidance Note No 1 of 2011 FTT-IAC 11 July 2011.
37 EIG chapter 55 para 55.3.2.14.
38 Bail Guidance for Immigration Judges, Presidential Guidance Note No 1 of 2011 FTT-IAC 11 July 2011 para 26.

detention is pending the making of an immigration decision] and/or removal.[39]

However, the Guidance also states that 'attempts to apply a strict burden of proof may be misleading'.[40] We suggest that this caveat is unnecessary.[41]

Standard of proof at a bail hearing

41.42   The current Bail Guidance for immigration judges states that the standard of proof is 'whether there are substantial grounds for believing that detention should be maintained'.[42] As earlier guidance to the immigration judiciary explained, this standard, derived from the Bail Act 1976 applicable to criminal bail, is 'higher than the balance of probabilities but less than the criminal standard of proof'.[43]

Evidence from the Home Office

41.43   The bail summary constitutes the SSHD's pleadings, and does not constitute evidence. Where the SSHD has provided no documentary or witness evidence of a disputed fact, and the only evidence heard is that of the bail applicant denying the fact, it is strongly arguable that the fact should be considered not proven. The Chief Adjudicator's Guidance Note on Bail of May 2003 stated:

> If allegations in the bail summary are contested in evidence then the Secretary of State should adduce evidence, including any documents relevant to the decision to detain, to support such allegations.

---

39 Bail Guidance for Immigration Judges, Presidential Guidance Note No 1 of 2011 FTT-IAC 11 July 2011 para 17.
40 Bail Guidance for Immigration Judges, Presidential Guidance Note No 1 of 2011 FTT-IAC 11 July 2011 para 27.
41 This passage of the Bail Guidance perhaps confuses the bail context, in which individual liberty is at stake and the detainer holds many of the informational and evidential cards, with the asylum and ECHR appeal context, in which burdens of proof and ordinary adversarial rules indeed do not apply strictly since the parties in principle have a joint interest in ensuring that fundamental rights are not breached, and the asylum applicant, on whom the burden formally lies, may lack much of the information and evidence to make his or her case.
42 Bail Guidance for Immigration Judges, Presidential Guidance Note No 1 of 2011 FTT-IAC 11 July 2011 para 29.
43 Chief Adjudicator's Guidance Note on Bail May 2003.

Issues to be considered by the FTT-IAC at a bail hearing

41.44 The primary issue to be considered by the FTT-IAC in a bail application is whether the applicant, if released subject to any conditions that may be imposed, would answer bail. As the current Bail Guidance for Immigration Judges states:

> Immigration Judges should grant bail where a less intrusive alternative to immigration detention is sufficient to protect the relevant public interest. Detention will be neither necessary nor proportionate if release on bail is likely to be sufficient to ensure that the person concerned attends hearings, reports when required, and does not commit offences.[44]

41.45 Where removal is imminent, this may militate against a finding that the applicant would comply if released. Conversely, settled ties or outstanding applications or appeals will weigh in favour of a finding that compliance is likely. Also, as the current Bail Guidance states:

> An Immigration Judge is likely to give significant weight to a person's previously good record of complying with immigration control and maintaining contact with the immigration authorities because this history will provide a reasonable ground for believing that the person is likely to comply with bail conditions.[45]

41.46 The FTT-IAC will also consider the SSHD's reasons for detention. As the current Bail Guidance for immigration judges states:

> The judge must consider the weight to be given to the reasons why a person is detained. The judge will be considering whether in totality the reasons given are proportionate to the need to continue to detain. The judge may also want to consider whether the reasons given are consistent with any UK Border Agency instructions governing the use of detention, as a failure to follow policy may seriously undermine the case for detention.[46]

41.47 The current Bail Guidance also explains that 'a person cannot be subject to immigration detention merely because they pose a risk of harm to the public or because there may be a risk of reoffending'.[47] However, the FTT-IAC will (and where there is an appeal pending, must

---

44 Bail Guidance for Immigration Judges, Presidential Guidance Note No 1 of 2011 FTT-IAC 11 July 2011 para 21.
45 Bail Guidance for Immigration Judges, Presidential Guidance Note No 1 of 2011 FTT-IAC 11 July 2011 para 23.
46 Bail Guidance for Immigration Judges, Presidential Guidance Note No 1 of 2011 FTT-IAC 11 July 2011 para 7.
47 Bail Guidance for Immigration Judges, Presidential Guidance Note No 1 of 2011 FTT-IAC 11 July 2011 para 10.

by statutory provision[48]) have regard to the risk of further offending and consequences of any further offending in a criminal deportation case.[49]

41.48 The SSHD must also demonstrate that the reasons for detention remain connected to its statutory purpose (in the cases of FNPs, almost invariably deportation). As the current Bail Guidance states:

> If the immigration authorities cannot demonstrate this connection, then an Immigration Judge should grant bail as continued detention may well be unlawful. Where there is some continued connection but the detention has become prolonged the weight that would otherwise be given to the allegation that detention is necessary in the interests of immigration control should diminish when assessing whether detention remains proportionate.[50]

41.49 The length of detention that has already elapsed and the likely duration of detention before deportation can be effected is also, therefore an important consideration. Current Bail Guidance to the immigration judiciary states that:

> Each case turns on its own facts and must be decided in light of its particular circumstances. However, it is generally accepted that detention for three months would be considered a substantial period of time and six months a long period. Imperative considerations of public safety may be necessary to justify detention in excess of six months.[51]
> ...
> Detention of over a year has been held to be proportionate where there is a high risk of the applicant causing serious harm to the public. On the other hand, a period of weeks might be disproportionate where one of the effects of detention is to keep a parent apart from young children.[52]

41.50 As seen in the introduction to this section, a bail application is not a challenge to the legality of the detention. Challenges to the legality of an ongoing detention should be advanced in the High Court by way of a claim for judicial review or an application for habeas corpus:

---

48 IA 1971 Sch 3 para 3 and Sch 2 para 30(2). Applied to detention under UK Borders Act (UKBA) 2007 s36(1) pending the making of an 'automatic' deportation order by operation of UKBA 2007 s36(4).
49 Bail Guidance for Immigration Judges, Presidential Guidance Note No 1 of 2011 FTT-IAC 11 July 2011 para 10.
50 Bail Guidance for Immigration Judges, Presidential Guidance Note No 1 of 2011 FTT-IAC 11 July 2011 para 17.
51 Bail Guidance for Immigration Judges, Presidential Guidance Note No 1 of 2011 FTT-IAC 11 July 2011 para 18.
52 Bail Guidance for Immigration Judges, Presidential Guidance Note No 1 of 2011 FTT-IAC 11 July 2011 para 20.

these detention challenges are discussed in chapter 42. However, since courts and tribunals are prohibited by the Human Rights Act (HRA) 1998 s6 from acting in a way which is incompatible with an ECHR right, the FTT-IAC is arguably prohibited from refusing bail where it considers that the underlying detention is unlawful and thus contrary to ECHR article 5. In practice, many of the arguments concerning bail overlap with those concerning the legality of detention, as the current Bail Guidance recognises.

Procedure at the bail hearing

41.51 Since the spring of 2008, many bail hearings in the tribunal have been conducted by video-link from prisons and Immigration Removal Centres (IRCs). Representatives will normally only have ten minutes before the hearing[53] to take instructions from bail applicants by video-link: this is particularly problematic given that Home Office bail summaries are only required to be provided on the afternoon before the bail hearing and frequently are served late. Bail hearings from prisons are allotted 45 minutes of time; the video-link often terminates abruptly once the time has elapsed, even part-way through the bail application. The Refugee Council, Bail for Immigration Detainees and the Immigration Law Practitioners' Association have expressed serious concerns that video-link hearings cause grave prejudice to bail applicants. See para 41.35 above concerning applications for in-person hearings where necessary.

41.52 Although the order of proceedings is at the immigration judge's discretion, the Chief Adjudicator's Guidance Note of May 2003 suggested that the bail hearing should proceed in three stages and this approach is still followed by many immigration judges:

First, is this a case where bail is right in principle, subject to suitable conditions if necessary? Second, are sureties necessary? Third, are the sureties and recognizances offered satisfactory? If you indicate bail is right in principle, make it clear that your decision is subject to there being suitable and satisfactory conditions and sureties if you are going to require them.

41.53 Particularly if no witness statements have been provided, it will usually be vital to call oral evidence from the bail applicant on any aspect of the bail summary which he or she contests.

---

53 Bail Guidance for Immigration Judges, Presidential Guidance Note No 1 of 2011 FTT-IAC 11 July 2011 Annex 6.

Applying for bail or release on a restriction order

41.54 A bail applicant or his or her representative from may withdraw the bail application at any point until the immigration judge makes his or her decision.

Sureties in the FTT-IAC

41.55 Sureties should only be required by the FTT-IAC where necessary to secure compliance with the primary condition of answering bail. The courts have held that sureties should not be required where unnecessary:[54]

> Clearly it would be wrong to require sureties, if there were no need for sureties, but where one reaches a situation where one cannot otherwise be sure that the obligations will be observed, Parliament has rightly provided that that extra ammunition is available to a Special Adjudicator dealing with these matters if, in fact, that will have the consequence that a person who might not otherwise be granted his liberty will be granted it.[55]

41.56 The current Bail Guidance likewise reminds immigration judges that sureties:

> ... should not be an automatic requirement and the Judge must have due regard to the fact that people recently arrived in the country may have nobody to whom they could expect to stand surety for them.[56]

41.57 We have already discussed the suitability of different sureties at paras 41.11–41.12 above. As the current Bail Guidance reminds immigration judges:

> A surety need not reside at the same address as the applicant, and the degree of supervision that the surety may seek to exercise to ensure that the applicant attends when required is a matter for the surety in the light of the risk of the loss of the recognisance.[57]

41.58 As to the sum offered in surety, the FTT-IAC should not have 'tariff sums' in mind as minimum acceptable levels of surety, but should always have regard to the financial ability of the individual surety: £100 offered by a millionaire is not the same as £100 offered by

---

54 *R v Secretary of State for the Home Department ex p Minteh (Lamin)* (unreported) judgment 8 March 1997, CA.
55 *R v Secretary of State for the Home Department ex p Brezinski and Glowacka* (unreported), judgment 19 July 1996, per Kay J.
56 Bail Guidance for Immigration Judges, Presidential Guidance Note No 1 of 2011 FTT-IAC 11 July 2011 para 38.
57 Bail Guidance for Immigration Judges, Presidential Guidance Note No 1 of 2011 FTT-IAC 11 July 2011 para 39.

a single parent on benefits with only £120 in savings. The Chief Adjudicator's Guidance Note of May 2003 gave the following guidance to decision-makers, which we suggest remains apposite:

(a) it must be realistic in the sense that it must be well within the resources of the surety, and not so high as to be prohibitive;
(b) it must be assessed in relation to the means of the surety alone;
(c) it must be sufficient to satisfy you that it will ensure that the applicant and the surety will meet their obligations;
(d) it must be realisable in the event of forfeiture.

...

The amount of the recognizance must be fixed with regard to the surety's means, but it must always be an adequate and sufficient sum to secure attendance. There is no tariff figure and the sums involved are always a matter for the individual adjudicator.

Bail in principle

41.59 Where the immigration judge is satisfied that, if a particular condition is met, bail is appropriate, bail may be granted in principle subject to that condition being satisfied. See para 40.8. The Bail Guidance for Immigration Judges now tells them:

... there may be occasions where although an Immigration Judge can fully assess the risks and decide that bail should be granted in principle, release cannot be immediate because information is missing to complete the conditions to be imposed. It is undesirable that bail should be refused in these circumstances or that hearing time is spent on repeat applications on the same point. In appropriate cases therefore bail can be granted in principle and the applicant detained until such time as the information is provided to the Judge's satisfaction when release can be effected.

...

Where an Immigration Judge would grant bail and order release but for the fact that a relevant document is not available, the judge may grant bail in principle and order that release should be delayed for 48 hours for the document to be produced. If the document is produced to the Tribunal within the set period, and is satisfactory, the order for release can be completed without any further hearing. The grant of bail may be signed by the same or by a different judge.[58]

---

58 Bail Guidance for Immigration Judges, Presidential Guidance Note No 1 of 2011 FTT-IAC 11 July 2011 paras 45 and 47.

Bail for those still on the licence period

41.60   Where the bail applicant is still on the licence period of his or her last criminal sentence, the terms imposed by the licence are additional to and independent from any bail conditions imposed by the FTT-IAC.

41.61   At the bail hearing, the FTT-IAC's attention should be drawn to the additional controls and incentives for compliance imposed by the licence: a person released during his or her licence period risks recall to prison if he or she breaches the good behaviour conditions or probationary reporting conditions that are standard to most licences.

41.62   In these cases, the bail applicant should be re-issued with the licence before the FTT-IAC bail hearing (by the prison establishment or IRC where the bail applicant is held) and told the arrangements for reporting to NOMS if released. The pro forma letter for licencees normally requires them to report to NOMS by 5pm on the day of release, or, if that is not possible, by 2pm on the day after release.[59] In any event, the Home Office Presenting Officer should have a copy of the licence even if the bail applicant does not, and this should be shown to the FTT-IAC to ensure that the conditions of bail (such as reporting to the immigration service) do not conflict with those of the licence (such as reporting to NOMS on the same date).

41.63   As the current Bail Guidance to the immigration judiciary recognises, 'Stringent bail conditions may not be necessary if there is already an obligation to report to a probation officer regularly'.[60]

The bail decision

41.64   The FTT-IAC must serve written notice of its decision on the parties and on the person having custody of the applicant[61] (eg the manager of a contracted-out detention centre).

41.65   Where bail is granted, the notice must include the conditions of bail and the amount in which the applicant and any sureties agree to be bound.[62] The person having custody of the applicant must release him or her upon being served with a notice of the decision to grant

---

59 Probation Circular 32/2007 'Management of Foreign National Prisoners: Licences, Bail Hearings, Releases from Immigration Detention and Deportation'. Now annexed to the Bail Guidance for Immigration Judges, Presidential Guidance Note No 1 of 2011 FTT-IAC 11 July 2011.
60 Bail Guidance for Immigration Judges, Presidential Guidance Note No 1 of 2011 FTT-IAC 11 July 2011 para 14.
61 Asylum and Immigration Tribunal (Procedure) Rules 2005 r39(3).
62 Asylum and Immigration Tribunal (Procedure) Rules 2005 r39(4).

bail and being satisfied that any recognizances required as a condition of bail have been entered into.[63]

41.66 Where bail is refused, the notice must include reasons for the refusal.[64]

Challenging a refusal of bail

41.67 A refusal of bail can only be challenged by way of a claim for judicial review. While such a challenge might be useful in overturning any findings of fact that were unreasonably made[65] (which otherwise risked prejudicing further bail applications) it must be noted that, on its own, a challenge to a bail refusal will only lead to a quashing of that decision. Unless combined with a challenge to the lawfulness of the underlying detention, or unless combined with a bail application in the High Court, such a judicial review will not lead to the detainee's release.

Further bail applications

41.68 There are in principle no limits on how many times or with what frequency a person may seek bail from the FTT-IAC or from the SSHD. However, an immigration judge hearing a bail application will have regard to the reasons given by other immigration judges on any previous refusals. Once bail has been refused, a change of circumstances will normally need to be shown before bail is granted on a subsequent application. A passage of time, particularly with little progress towards deportation, is itself a relevant change of circumstances.

41.69 Current Bail Guidance indicates that in certain circumstances, on a renewed bail application, the FTT-IAC will restrict the length of a further bail hearing, the evidence that will be heard and the opportunity for the applicant to have a period of consultation by video-link. The first condition for the imposition of such restrictions by the FTT-IAC is that bail was refused in the FTT-IAC after a full hearing within the previous 28 calendar days. The second condition is that the fresh application raises no new evidence and no new ground of bail.[66]

63 Asylum and Immigration Tribunal (Procedure) Rules 2005 r41.
64 Asylum and Immigration Tribunal (Procedure) Rules 2005 r39(5).
65 For a discussion of the scope of judicial review, see paras 42.25–42.31
66 Bail Guidance for Immigration Judges, Presidential Guidance Note No 1 of 2011 FTT-IAC 11 July 2011 para 66.

Bail renewal

41.70 As already seen at para 40.27, the FTT-IAC has no power to revoke bail. Thus, where a person complies with the primary condition of appearing for his or her bail renewal hearing, the FTT-IAC must renew bail unless the person is re-detained at the hearing by an immigration or police officer. Where secondary conditions have been breached and the person is not re-detained, the FTT-IAC may impose more stringent conditions.

41.71 Where the primary condition is breached (the person on bail fails to appear at the required place and time), the FTT-IAC has power to find that part or all of the recognizance offered by the person on bail and any surety is forfeit. Forfeiture has been discussed at para 40.26.

Bail variation

41.72 The FTT-IAC may vary bail where bail has been granted by the tribunal and an appeal is pending. In all other circumstances, responsibility for variation lies with an Immigration Officer.[67]

41.73 The FTT-IAC may vary bail conditions on application or of its own motion. Variation of bail conditions may be sought from the FTT-IAC:

- *on the papers:* where the request is to vary the residence address, reporting conditions or electronic monitoring, the FTT-IAC will wish to know the SSHD's view, so that Home Office consent should first be sought before writing to the FTT-IAC. Where the parties agree, the variation will normally be granted on the papers, where they cannot, a bail variation hearing will normally be listed;[68] or
- *at a bail renewal or variation hearing:* a request to change sureties will normally require a hearing.[69]

---

[67] Bail Guidance for Immigration Judges, Presidential Guidance Note No 1 of 2011 FTT-IAC 11 July 2011 para 54.
[68] Bail Guidance for Immigration Judges, Presidential Guidance Note No 1 of 2011 FTT-IAC 11 July 2011 paras 56–57.
[69] Bail Guidance for Immigration Judges, Presidential Guidance Note No 1 of 2011 FTT-IAC 11 July 2011 para 58.

PART IV

Remedies

SECTION M
Remedies

Chapter 42: Choice of jurisdiction   809

Chapter 43: Causes of action   839

Chapter 44: Damages   849

Introduction to remedies

Part IV of this book is concerned with judicial remedies. We provide an overview only and focus on aspects likely to be of wide application in claims brought by foreign national prisoners and former prisoners (FNPs). Detailed consideration of the applicable law and procedure on remedies are beyond the scope of this book and we encourage practitioners to consult specialist texts.[1]

Chapter 42 concerns choice of jurisdiction, that is, the different procedures by which FNPs can bring legal challenges. Statutory appeals against deportation decisions and other immigration decisions have already been considered separately in chapters 21 (appeals in the Immigration and Asylum Chamber of the First Tier and Upper Tribunals (IAC)) and 23 (appeals to Special Immigration Appeals Commission (SIAC)).

Causes of action in civil proceedings are discussed separately in chapter 43 and damages are discussed in chapter 44.

Note also that the various complaints procedures through which FNPs might seek to seek redress for their treatment have been addressed in chapters 25 on prisons and 39 on Immigration Removal Centres (IRCs).

---

1 On judicial review see Fordham, *Judicial review handbook*, 5th edn, Hart Publishing, 2008; Manning, *Judicial review proceedings: a practitioner's guide*, 2nd edn, LAG, 2004. On civil claims see Harrison, Cragg and Williams, *Police misconduct: legal remedies*, 4th edn, LAG, 2005; Clayton and Tomlinson, *Civil actions against the police*, Sweet & Maxwell, 2005; *Clerk and Lindsell on torts*, 20th edn, Sweet & Maxwell, 2010. On habeas corpus see Farbey and Sharpe, *The law of habeas corpus*, 3rd edn, OUP, 2011.

CHAPTER 42
Choice of jurisdiction

42.1	Introduction
42.5	**Litigation generally**
42.5	Civil Procedure Rules and the overriding objective
42.8	Pre-action protocols
42.11	Offers to settle
42.12	Obtaining documents prior to proceedings
42.16	**Judicial review**
42.19	Who can be challenged by way of judicial review?
42.23	Which decisions and omissions can be challenged in judicial review?
42.25	On what grounds can judicial review be brought?
42.32	Who can bring a claim for judicial review?
42.34	Other participants
42.36	Remedies in judicial review
42.39	The pre-action protocol in judicial review
42.44	The claim form and time limits in judicial review
42.46	Issuing the claim
42.51	The duty of candour in judicial review
42.53	The permission stage
42.59	Post permission
42.61	Amending a claim form in light of fresh decisions

continued

42.62	Interlocutory applications for directions and disclosure
42.63	Interim remedies and bail
42.66	The full hearing
42.70	Appeals
42.72	**Habeas corpus**
42.74	Choosing between habeas corpus and judicial review
42.80	Bringing an application for a writ of habeas corpus
42.82	**Private law claims**
42.83	Burden of proof
42.84	Who can be sued?
42.87	Remaining in the UK to pursue a claim
42.88	Which court?
42.90	Limitation periods
42.92	Jury trials
42.93	Pre-action correspondence
42.94	Procedure in civil claims
42.99	**Choosing between a civil claim for damages and judicial review**

Introduction

42.1 There are broadly two types of proceedings that may be brought by FNPs to challenge unlawful treatment:

1) *Public law challenges – judicial review and habeas corpus.* Judicial review is the means by which the High Court supervises the lawfulness of conduct and decision-making by public bodies and lower courts. As we shall see at para 42.18, the Upper Tribunal now also has jurisdiction to hear certain claims for judicial review. Habeas corpus, applications for which are also brought initially in the High Court, is a particular form of proceeding primarily concerned with ending unlawful detention.
2) *Private law challenges* – these are primarily claims brought to seek compensation for past unlawful treatment.

42.2 There is frequently an overlap between these different jurisdictions. For example: a) challenges to ongoing detention may be brought as in judicial review or habeas corpus or both simultaneously see para 42.81 below; b) in respect of a past detention, representatives and applicants may need to choose between judicial review and private law remedies, see paras 42.99–42.102 below; c) a claim challenging a detention may start as a judicial review but then be transferred to continue as private law proceedings once release has occurred. See para 42.69 below.

42.3 Historically, a rigid distinction was drawn between private and public law matters so that it has been held to be an abuse to seek to challenge public law decisions in private law proceedings, so circumventing the shorter time limits and permission requirement applicable in judicial review proceedings.[1] However, the rigidity of this distinction has diminished. If the purpose of a challenge is to vindicate private law rights, then a claim may be brought by ordinary private law action even if this involves a challenge to a public law decision.[2] Specifically, in the context of challenges to immigration detention, it has been held that a challenge may be brought by way of either judicial review or a civil claim for damages.[3]

42.4 We begin this chapter with an overview of issues arising in litigation generally, before providing brief summaries of procedures in public law and private law challenges. We discuss at paras 42.74– 42.79 the choice between judicial review and habeas corpus jurisdictions when challenging an ongoing detention. This chapter closes

1 *O'Reilly v Mackman* [1983] 2 AC 237.
2 *ID v Home Office* [2005] EWCA Civ 38, [2006] 1 WLR 1003 para 105.
3 *ID v Home Office* [2005] EWCA Civ 38, [2006] 1 WLR 1003 paras 105–109.

with a discussion of the choice between judicial review and civil actions for damages when challenging a historic wrong.

Litigation generally

Civil Procedure Rules and the overriding objective

42.5 Civil cases, whether brought as public or private law challenges, are governed by the Civil Procedure Rules 1998 (CPR) which are regularly updated.[4] The CPR have as an overriding objective of 'enabling the court to deal with cases justly'.[5] This objective is further defined as including considerations of finite court resources, and the need to ensure that claims are dealt with in a way that is proportionate to the issues involved and the value of the claim, but also with the need of ensuring that the parties are on an equal footing.[6]

42.6 The CPR therefore places an expectation on parties that litigation is to be viewed as a last resort. They are expected to attempt to settle disputes where possible without litigation. Hence the importance of compliance with the pre-action protocols, and consideration of pre-action offers to settle, failure to comply or engage with which may lead to adverse consequences, see para 42.39 below.

42.7 There is no general requirement to pursue internal complaints mechanisms or to complain to an ombudsman prior to proceeding in judicial review, habeas corpus or tort. However, in maladministration cases concerning low sums of potential damages, the courts will consider whether adequate reasons have been given for failing to pursue less costly avenues of redress such as internal complaints or a complaint to an ombudsman.[7] Likewise, in a maladministration case where negligence is claimed, the courts will be particularly slow to find a duty of care where there are alternative methods of redress to the courts.[8]

---

4 See www.justice.gov.uk/guidance/courts-and-tribunals/courts/procedure-rules/civil/index.htm.
5 CPR 1.1(1).
6 CPR 1.1(2).
7 *R (Anufrijeva) v Southwark LBC and another* [2004] QB 1124 para 81(iii).
8 *Home Office v Mohammed* [2011] EWCA Civ 351 at 25–27.

Pre-action protocols

42.8 There are now a number of pre-action protocols that apply to various types of litigation (including judicial review, see paras 42.39–42.43 below) which potential claimants are expected to follow before issuing court proceedings.[9] Where there is no specific pre-action protocol (for example in false imprisonment) there is a general Practice Direction on pre-action conduct[10] which sets out some key expectations of parties before court proceedings are brought. These include sending the defendant a letter before claim setting out the basis of the case, with a summary of the facts, an explanation of what the claimant seeks from the defendant, the documents that will be relied upon, and details of any proposed alternative dispute resolution if appropriate. The defendant should be given an opportunity to reply and the parties should then consider their positions in order to consider whether proceedings can be avoided.

42.9 There will be situations where proceedings need to be issued urgently (for example, due to a limitation period that is about to expire, or where judicial review proceedings are being issued to challenge an ongoing detention). In such circumstances claimants should at least attempt to comply with the spirit of the CPR by sending a letter of claim where possible, even if this gives a very short period to respond before proceedings are issued.

42.10 There is no pre-action protocol in habeas corpus.

Offers to settle

42.11 The principle that parties should seek to avoid unnecessary litigation, which is implicit in the CPR's overriding objective, also means that where proceedings have begun, that the parties should continue to attempt where possible to settle claims. Accordingly CPR Part 36 contains a set of provisions that incentivise both parties to make offers of settlement with sanctions for unreasonable refusals to compromise. Briefly summarised, if an offer to settle is rejected, and the party that has rejected the offer fails to achieve a better result at trial, then they will have to pay the costs of the other party from the date of the offer, with interest.[11]

---

9 See www.justice.gov.uk/guidance/courts-and-tribunals/courts/procedure-rules/civil/menus/protocol.htm.
10 Available at www.justice.gov.uk/guidance/courts-and-tribunals/courts/procedure-rules/civil/index.htm.
11 CPR 36.14.

Obtaining documents prior to proceedings

42.12 Under the Data Protection Act (DPA) 1998 there is a right to request copies of personal data.[12] Where legal proceedings are contemplated or ongoing, DPA 1998 s7 provides a means of fairly prompt access (subject to limited exceptions) of the wide range of documentation that an organisation may hold on an individual. Requests for disclosure under DPA 1998 are known as subject access requests. They must be made in writing and different organisations have their own forms and require different levels of proof of identity before processing a request. The maximum fee for processing a subject access request is £10, or £50 in relation to medical records where manual and electronic records are being disclosed.[13] Disclosure under DPA 1998 should take place within 40 days, although that period is unfortunately often exceeded.[14]

42.13 Private contractors, such as those that run immigration detention centres or provide immigration escorts, are covered by DPA 1998 although the UK Border Agency has stated that it views itself as the data controller for these subcontractors.[15] Accordingly subject access requests to UK Border Agency should include, where relevant, documents held by such sub-contractors. Subject access requests to the UK Border Agency should be made to the Data Protection Unit, UK Border Agency, Lunar House, 40 Wellesley Road, Croydon CR9 2BY, with a cheque payable to 'The Home Office Accounting Officer' together with copy of proof of identity, and the Home Office Reference number.[16]

42.14 Complaints about levels of disclosure or delays in complying with the DPA 1998's requirements can be made to the Information Commissioner's Office.[17]

42.15 In some cases it might be appropriate to seek disclosure of non-personal data, such as statistical information or details of undisclosed policies. Such information can be sought under the Freedom

---

12 DPA 1998 s7.
13 Data Protection (Subject Access) (Fees and Miscellaneous Provisions) Regulations 2000 SI No 191.
14 DPA 1998 s7(10).
15 UK Border Agency letter to Immigration Law Practitioners' Association (ILPA) 1 September 2011.
16 See UK Border Agency guidance at www.ukba.homeoffice.gov.uk/navigation/personal-data/.
17 See www.ico.gov.uk.

of Information Act (FOIA) 2000.[18] There is not generally a fee for such requests.[19]

Judicial review

42.16 Judicial review is the jurisdiction by which the higher courts supervise the public law acts and omissions of public bodies and tribunals. Judicial review is not an appeal, and generally does not provide a means to challenge the underlying merits of a decision (although the approach in human rights cases will be different – see para 42.31 below, as will the approach taken in detention challenges, see para 32.41). The general rule in judicial review is that the court will consider whether the decision has been lawfully made.

42.17 Claims for judicial review have historically been brought in the Administrative Court division of the High Court.[20] The procedure for applying for judicial review is now contained in CPR Part 54.[21]

42.18 Statutory changes permit judicial review claims to be determined by the Upper Tribunal, by virtue of the Tribunals, Courts and Enforcement Act (TCEA) 2007.[22] The Borders, Citizenship and Immigration Act (BCIA) 2009 s53 has amended the Senior Courts Act (SCA) 1981 s31A so that judicial review of decisions not to treat submissions as amounting to a fresh asylum or human rights claim are now decided in the Immigration and Asylum Chamber of the Upper Tribunal (UT-IAC). The grounds and procedures described below for judicial review generally apply whether a claim for judicial review is brought in the Administrative Court or UT-IAC.

Who can be challenged by way of judicial review?

42.19 Judicial review can be brought against public bodies in the performance of their public functions, and in respect of the decisions of lower courts and tribunals. Thus the decision-making or conduct of

---

18 FOIA 2000 s1.
19 For guidance on FOI requests to UK Border Agency see www.ukba.homeoffice.gov.uk/navigation/foi/.
20 SCA 1981 s31.
21 See www.justice.gov.uk/guidance/courts-and-tribunals/courts/procedure-rules/civil/contents/parts/part54.htm. The MoJ website also includes the practice directions relevant to each part of the CPR.
22 TCEA 2007 ss15–19; G Mitchell, 'Judicial Review, But Not As We Know It: Judicial Review in the Upper Tribunal' [2010] JR 122.

42.20 The position can be more complicated where a government department contracts out its functions to a private company. Whether the private company is amenable to judicial review will depend upon the level of statutory underpinning of the activities that are contracted out. For example, the contracting out of a duty purely to provide accommodation might not render the contractor amenable to judicial review in respect of those functions.[23] By contrast, a company contracted to run an immigration detention centre was successfully challenged in relation to its failure to ensure that the requirements of the Detention Centre Rules 2001[24] were met in relation to the medical examination of detainees.[25]

42.21 Even if the body is clearly a public one, it is only its public functions that are amenable to judicial review. Private law rights, such as the enforcement of contractual obligations against public authorities, cannot be pursued through judicial review.

42.22 For the test for 'public authority' applicable in Human Rights Act (HRA) 1998 claims, see para 43.22.

Which decisions and omissions can be challenged in judicial review?

42.23 The CPR defines a claim for judicial review as a means to review the lawfulness of an enactment, or a decision, action or failure to act in relation to the exercise of a public function.[26]

42.24 In relation to enactments:

- The courts can determine whether an Act of Parliament is compatible with EU law, and if it is not give precedence to the EU law.[27]
- They can also, in respect of primary legislation, make a declaration that a provision is incompatible with rights under the European

---

23 *R v Servite Houses ex p Goldsmith* (2001) 33 HLR 35.
24 SI No 238.
25 *R (D and K) v Secretary of State for the Home Department and others* [2006] EWHC 980 (Admin) – in the same case the judge considered that the company subcontracted to provide healthcare in the centre was not amenable to judicial review, as their activities were 'delineated by its contractual obligations' and so lacked sufficient statutory underpinning.
26 CPR 54.1(2).
27 *R v Secretary of State for Transport ex p Factortame (No 2)* [1990] 1 AC 603.

Convention on Human Rights (ECHR).[28] This declaration does not affect the validity of the provision in question.

- Secondary legislation (such as statutory instruments such as the Detention Centre Rules 2001, or the Prison Rules 1999[29]) can be declared unlawful on the same grounds as other decisions and the same applies to policies contained in documents such as Prison Service Orders (PSOs) and Prison Service Instructions (PSIs).

On what grounds can judicial review be brought?

42.25 There are a wide range of bases upon which the court might decide that the decision or policy adopted by a public body is unlawful. One classic formulation of the grounds upon which a claim might be brought was made by Lord Diplock in a 1985 case involving a challenge to a trade union ban in GCHQ:

> Judicial review has I think developed to a stage today when without reiterating any analysis of the steps by which the development has come about, one can conveniently classify under three heads the grounds upon which administrative action is subject to control by judicial review. The first ground I would call 'illegality,' the second 'irrationality' and the third 'procedural impropriety.'
>
> ...
>
> By 'illegality' as a ground for judicial review I mean that the decision-maker must understand correctly the law that regulates his decision-making power and must give effect to it. Whether he has or not is par excellence a justiciable question to be decided, in the event of dispute, by those persons, the judges, by whom the judicial power of the state is exercisable.
>
> By 'irrationality' I mean what can by now be succinctly referred to as 'Wednesbury unreasonableness' (*Associated Provincial Picture Houses Ltd v Wednesbury Corporation* [1948] 1 KB 223). It applies to a decision which is so outrageous in its defiance of logic or of accepted moral standards that no sensible person who had applied his mind to the question to be decided could have arrived at it ...
>
> I have described the third head as 'procedural impropriety' rather than failure to observe basic rules of natural justice or failure to act with procedural fairness towards the person who will be affected by the decision. This is because susceptibility to judicial review under this head covers also failure by an administrative tribunal to observe procedural rules that are expressly laid down in the legislative instrument

---

28 HRA 1998 s4.
29 SI No 728.

by which its jurisdiction is conferred, even where such failure does not involve any denial of natural justice.

42.26 That classic formulation of the grounds for judicial review is not exhaustive and there may be considerable overlap between the grounds.[30]

42.27 Claims broadly under the head of illegality will include those where the defendant exceeds its statutory power, takes irrelevant considerations into account or ignores relevant ones, takes a decision with an improper purpose, or otherwise misuses its discretion. Of particular importance in the immigration detention context has been the role of policy.[31] As discussed in detail in chapter 34, it is a public law error where a decision-maker fails, without good reason, to apply its own stated policy,[32] or applies an undisclosed policy that conflicts with a published one.

42.28 In some cases the adopted policies themselves have been held to be unlawful.[33] A common error which will render a policy unlawful is where the policy, being set out in blanket terms, fetters a discretion which is afforded to the executive under statute. While the executive is entitled to adopt policies setting out the criteria it will apply for the exercise of its discretion, the policy may not be rigid and the executive must always remain open to new arguments in individual cases.[34]

42.29 Irrationality has traditionally been difficult to establish since it requires the court to review the substance of the decision, rather than the decision-making process. The hurdle is a high one: that no reasonable decision-maker properly directing himself or herself on the facts, law and evidence could have taken the decision in question. This limited way in which the court will review the decision itself is arguably of less importance given the expanding ways in which the

---

30 For a comprehensive analysis of grounds upon which judicial review may be brought see M Fordham QC *Judicial review handbook*, Hart Publishing, 5th edn, 2008.
31 *R (Lumba and Mighty) v Secretary of State for the Home Department* [2011] UKSC 12, [2011] 2 WLR 671 provides the authoritative analysis of where policy breaches might give rise to unlawfulness.
32 This has been relevant in a series of challenges to the detention of those with mental illness in breach of the Home Office's own policy – see, for example, *R (S) v Secretary of State for the Home Department* [2011] EWHC 2120 (Admin).
33 For example, in *R (Medical Justice) v Secretary of State for the Home Department* [2010] EWHC 1925 (Admin).
34 *British Oxygen v Board of Trade* [1971] AC 610 per Lord Reid at 625D. See also *R (Lumba and Mighty) v Secretary of State for the Home Department* [2011] UKSC 12, [2011] 2 WLR 671 at para 21.

substance of decisions can be challenged, for example in challenges under HRA 1998 (see para 42.31 below).

42.30 Claims involving procedural fairness will commonly involve situations where decisions are taken without proper disclosure to the claimant, and without a proper opportunity to make representations before such decisions are taken.[35]

42.31 The entry into force of HRA 1998 has significantly broadened the reach of judicial review. It is unlawful for public bodies to act in such a way as to breach the rights under the ECHR incorporated by the HRA 1998[36] and such breaches can be challenged through judicial review. When determining whether there has been a breach of ECHR rights the court will, where appropriate, decide itself whether there has been a breach on consideration of proportionality.[37]

Who can bring a claim for judicial review?

42.32 A court may not grant permission to make an application for judicial review unless the claimant has sufficient interest in the matter to which the claim relates.[38] For individual claimants this will rarely be an issue: someone directly affected by a decision will have sufficient interest.

42.33 A publicly minded citizen may also have standing to challenge government decisions, even where not directly affected.[39] Similarly public interest groups may have standing to challenge decisions relevant to their campaigns.[40] See para 43.21 for the distinct test for standing in claims brought under HRA 1998.

Other participants

42.34 The person (or body) bringing the judicial is known as the claimant, and the body being challenged as the defendant. Claims should also

---

35 *R v Secretary of State for the Home Department ex p Doody* [1993] 1 AC 531.
36 HRA 1998 s6.
37 *R (Daly) v Secretary of State for the Home Department* [2001] 2 AC 532.
38 SCA 1981 s31(3).
39 Lord Rees Mogg's challenge to the decision to ratify the Maastricht Treaty was not unsuccessful because he did not have standing – *R v Secretary of State for Foreign and Commonwealth Affairs ex p Rees Mogg* [1994] QB 552.
40 For example *R (Medical Justice) v Secretary of State for the Home Department* [2010] EWHC 1925 (Admin) – a successful challenge to a UK Border Agency policy on removal without proper notice.

be served on any interested party.[41] The CPR defines an 'interested party' as any person 'who is directly affected by the claim'.[42] This has been held to mean affected by reason of the grant of a remedy.

42.35 Public interest groups may wish to make third party interventions in judicial review claims and such interventions are permitted under the CPR.[43] It may assist a claimant's case to encourage such an organisation to provide support in appropriate cases. Applications should be made at the earliest opportunity to avoid delaying the substantive hearing.[44]

Remedies in judicial review

42.36 The remedies (and more than one remedy may be sought in a claim) that can be sought in a claim for judicial review are:[45]

- A quashing order – this overturns the decision under challenge and will require the defendant to consider remaking the decision.
- A prohibiting order – this is appropriate where the claimant is seeking to in advance to prevent the defendant making what would be an unlawful decision.
- A mandatory order – this is an order requiring the defendant to do something, for example to make a decision where there has been improper delay in doing so.

42.37 These three remedies are based on the former 'prerogative writs' and can only be sought in judicial review proceedings. The following remedies are available in both judicial review and other civil proceedings:

- a declaration – as to the scope of the unlawful conduct of the defendant;
- an injunction – that prohibits further unlawful conduct;
- damages (although a claim for judicial review may not be used to seek damages alone, and damages are only available in judicial review if they could have been awarded in an ordinary claim[46]);

---

41 CPR 57(b).
42 CPR 54(2)(1)(f).
43 CPR 54.17.
44 PD 54 para 13.5.
45 SCA 1981 s31; CPR 54(2), (3).
46 SCA 1981 s31(4); CPR 54(3)(2).

- the claimant can also seek interim relief under CPR Part 25 pending the full hearing of the claim, including bail, considered at para 42.64 below.

42.38 Remedies in judicial review are discretionary, so that even if the claimant establishes that a decision is unlawful, relief may be withheld. Common examples of when this will happen is where the issue has become academic, where there has been a failure to use adequate alternative remedies, or where there has been undue delay and granting relief would cause hardship, prejudice or would be detrimental to good administration.[47] The claimant's own conduct may also affect whether relief is granted (for example, failure to act in good faith or disclose relevant information). However, in detention challenges, there is very little if any room for the discretionary refusal of a remedy.

The pre-action protocol in judicial review

42.39 There is a pre-action protocol for judicial review[48] with which the claimant should normally (and save in urgent cases) comply. Failure to comply without good reason may have costs implications, or even affect the granting of remedies.

42.40 The pre-action protocol for judicial review requires the sending of a pre-action letter to the defendant identifying the matter to be challenged, summarising the grounds of challenge and specifying the action sought and the timeframe for a response.

42.41 The suggested timeframe is that 14 days should be given to respond, and proceedings should normally not be issued until that period has passed. However, as we have already indicated at para 42.9 above, there will be urgent cases (for example, where there is a challenge to an ongoing deprivation of liberty) in which the claimant will have good reasons to abridge the time given for the defendant's response to a few days or even (in the most urgent cases, such as one involving imminent expulsion) a few hours.

42.42 Note that compliance with the pre-action protocol does not alter the time limit of three months for filing the claim form. if proceedings need to be issued before compliance with the pre-action protocol, the claim form has a space in which to explain why the pre-action protocol was not followed.

---

47 SCA 1981 s31(6).
48 See www.justice.gov.uk/guidance/courts-and-tribunals/courts/procedure-rules/civil/contents/protocols/prot_jrv.htm.

42.43 The pre-action protocol for judicial review states that where the judicial review involves an immigration, asylum or nationality case, the letter of claim should be sent to UK Border Agency's Judicial Review Unit, St Anne's House, 20–26 Wellesley Road, Croydon CR9 2RL. For most other government departments, letters of claim should be sent to the Treasury Solicitor at One Kemble Street, London WC2B 4TS.

The claim form and time limits in judicial review

42.44 A claim form for judicial review must be filed promptly and in any event within three months of the date on which the grounds to make the claim first arose.[49] Note that a claim brought within three months may, in certain circumstances, still be considered not to have been filed promptly. The CPR states that the parties cannot by agreement extend the period.[50] The court may agree to extend time, but will only do so where there is good reason for the delay. The time limit runs from the date of the impugned decision, rather than the date on which the claimant learned of the decision, although the latter might obviously be relevant to whether there is good reason to extend time.

42.45 In cases involving challenges to lengthy periods of unlawful detention it is generally accepted that where the claim is brought during the detention or promptly after release, periods more than three months prior to the issue of the claim may still be challenged by judicial review.[51]

Issuing the claim

42.46 The claim form in judicial review proceedings is N461,[52] The claim form must contain a detailed statement of the facts relied on and grounds for bringing the claim (normally in a separate document), must specify precisely which acts or omissions are challenged, and must include any application to extend time, and any application for

---

49 CPR 54(5)(1).
50 CPR 54(5)(2).
51 For a stark example in *R (Sino) v Secretary of State for the Home Department* [2011] EWHC 2249 (Admin) the court held, in a case issued in 2010 that detention since July 2006 had been unlawful.
52 Forms for civil proceedings including judicial review are available at www.justice.gov.uk/guidance/courts-and-tribunals/courts/procedure-rules/civil/menus/forms.htm.

directions.[53] The claim form must be accompanied by any written evidence in support of the application to extend time, a copy of the order or decision under challenge, copies of documents upon which the claimant seeks to rely, any relevant statutory material, and a list of essential reading.[54] The claim form should confirm whether any claim under HRA 1998 is being brought.[55]

42.47 If a matter requires urgent consideration by the court, form N463 should also be completed. This form should set out the reasons why the matter is urgent and briefly summarise the relief that is sought and why. The form can be used to ask the court to vary the normal timetable for the defendant's response to the claim form.[56] Form N463 needs to be faxed to the defendant together with the claim form prior to filing at court.

42.48 Specific guidance for the contents of a judicial review bundle is provided at CPR PD 54A paras 5.6–5.9. Two copies of the paginated bundle must be lodged with the court on issue[57] together with the issue fee of and the public funding certificate if any. A copy of the bundle must be served on the defendant and interested parties within seven days of the date of issue[58] together with any notice of issue of the public funding certificate (and the claimant should then file a certificate of service with the Administrative Court so that it knows when the papers can be considered by the single judge).

42.49 Specific provisions apply where the judicial review is issued to challenge removal directions. CPR PD 54A requires the claimant in such cases to include a copy of the removal directions, any available document which includes the UK Border Agency's summary of the case, and the claimant's detailed grounds for bringing the claim.[59]

42.50 If those served wish to take part in the proceedings, they must file an acknowledgement of service, which should also include summary grounds for opposing the claim, within 21 days of service of the bundle including the claim form,[60] and serve it on the claimant as soon as practicable and in any event within seven days of filing.[61] Although the CPR does not provide for a response to the acknowledgement of

---

53 PD 54A para 5.6.
54 PD 54 para 5.7.
55 PD 54 para 5.3.
56 See Practice Statement [2002] 1 WLR 810.
57 PD 54 para 5.9.
58 CPR 54.7.
59 PD 54A para 18.2.
60 CPR 54.8(2)(a).
61 CPR 54.8(2)(b).

service, the claimant should consider whether to put in any further short submissions dealing with fresh matters raised in the summary grounds.

The duty of candour in judicial review

42.51 In judicial review proceedings, there is a duty on the parties to make full and frank disclosure and disclose all material facts, including those adverse to the claimant's case. Improper failure to give proper disclosure will give grounds for refusing permission or relief at the end of the case (and may have costs implications).

42.52 The duty of candour also applies to the defendant, especially at the post-permission stage, when filing detailed grounds for resisting claims (see below). The Home Office in particular has been criticised in a significant number of cases in recent years over its failure to properly discharge its duty of candour in judicial review proceedings. Where inadequate disclosure is made by a public authority, the courts may draw adverse inferences against the defendant.[62] In the light of repeated criticisms by the court in judicial reviews involving government departments, the Treasury Solicitor has issued internal guidance on how public authorities' duty of candour to the court should be discharged.[63] This is a very useful resource – we suggest that practitioners should familiarise themselves with it.

The permission stage

42.53 A single judge will then decide whether to grant permission on the papers.[64] The test for permission is whether the court is satisfied that there is an arguable case that a ground for judicial review exists which merits full investigation.[65]

42.54 If permission is refused the application can be renewed for an oral hearing on form 86B.[66] A publicly funded claimant and his or her representatives should notify the Legal Services Commission of

---

62 For example, see *I and others v Secretary of State for the Home Department* [2010] EWCA Civ 727 at para 55; *R (Sino) v Secretary of State for the Home Department* [2011] EWHC 2249 (Admin) paras 26–34.
63 See www.tsol.gov.uk/Publications/Scheme_Publications/Guidance_on_ Discharging_the_Duty_of_Candour.pdf.
64 PD 54 para 8.4.
65 *R v LAB ex p Hughes* (1992) 5 Admin LR 623.
66 CPR 54.12(2).

42.55 The defendant ordinarily appears and contests oral permission hearings in the Administrative Court (unlike those in the Court of Appeal). Permission hearings ordinarily last approximately 30 minutes, and parties should notify the court listing office if longer is likely to be required.

42.56 If permission is refused after an oral hearing, in a civil matter the claimant can apply to the Court of Appeal for permission within seven days.[67]

42.57 A defendant who has complied with the pre-action protocol may be able to claim costs of preparing the summary grounds if permission is refused at an oral hearing[68] notwithstanding the provision that where a defendant does attend the permission hearing costs will not normally be awarded against the claimant.[69]

42.58 If a judicial review involves a particular issue of public interest the court has jurisdiction to make a protective costs order.[70]

Post permission

42.59 If permission is granted then, unless the claim has been expedited, the defendant and any person wishing to contest the claim has 35 days from the service of the order granting permission to file detailed grounds for contesting the claim together with any written evidence.[71] The claimant must pay a court fee on the granting of permission.[72]

42.60 Once permission is granted the claimant should generally reconsider the merits of the claim in light of the defendant's detailed grounds and evidence, and consider whether there is sufficient merit to justify continuing (this will normally be a requirement of any public funding certificate). The claimant may wish to consider whether any further evidence should be submitted at this stage. Further evidence at the post-permission stage will normally be allowed provided that the parties have had time to respond. The claimant should also consider whether further grounds of challenge need to be brought

---

67 CPR 52.15.
68 *R (Mount Cook Land Ltd) v Westminster CC* [2003] EWCA Civ 1346.
69 PD 54 para 8.6.
70 *R (Corner House Research) v SS for Trade and Industry* [2005] 1 WLR 260.
71 CPR 54.14.
72 Fees are on form EX50 available at http://justice.gov.uk/guidance/courts-and-tribunals/courts/fees/index.htm

(permission to add grounds not included in the permission application will be required from the court[73]).

Amending a claim form in light of fresh decisions

42.61 Frequently, a public authority will issue further decisions in a case after the initial claim for judicial review has been lodged. If the claimant wishes to challenge those fresh decisions, the claimant should amend the claim form. The general rule is that where the underlying issue remains the same and new decisions are made, the existing claim form should be amended rather than a fresh claim issued.[74] As we have already seen at para 42.60 above, the court's permission to amend grounds of review is required where permission has already been granted.

Interlocutory applications for directions and disclosure

42.62 Interlocutory applications for directions and disclosure are possible but still relatively rare since judicial review is not primarily concerned with establishing facts.[75] However, the need to establish whether convention rights have been breached may in some circumstances require a level of merits review such that cross examination of witnesses is necessary.[76] Likewise, where detention is in issue and facts are in dispute, the Administrative Court has indicated that in judicial review proceedings it may be appropriate to provide for detailed disclosure and hear oral evidence.[77]

Interim remedies and bail

42.63 As noted above, the court in judicial review claims can order interim relief pending the full hearing.[78] There is a specific provision in the CPR that the court may stay the proceedings under review when

---

73 CPR 54.15.
74 *R v Secretary of State for the Home Department ex p Alabi* [1998] COD 103.
75 PD 54 para 21.1 states that disclosure (beyond that in the detailed grounds and evidence) is not required unless the court orders otherwise.
76 *R (Wilkinson) v RMO Broadmoor Hospital and others* [2002] 1 WLR 419.
77 *R (MH) v Secretary of State for the Home Department* [2009] EWHC 2506 (Admin) at para 7. See also general discussion of cross-examination in judicial review proceedings in *R (Al-Sweady) v Secretary of State for the Home Department* [2009] EWHC 2387 (Admin) paras 19–20.
78 See generally CPR Part 25.

granting permission.[79] An application for interim relief, including bail should be included on form N463 when an application for urgent consideration by the court is made and a draft order should be attached to the form.[80] This form must be sent to the defendant and interested parties to inform them of the application so that they might make representations.[81]

42.64 The High Court has inherent jurisdiction to grant bail.[82] On an appeal from the High Court, the Court of Appeal has all the authority and jurisdiction of the High Court[83] and thus also has jurisdiction to grant bail. Older authorities suggested that the function of the court in determining a bail application was *Wednesbury* review of the decision to detain;[84] later authorities clarified that the court on considering bail exercises original jurisdiction and conducts a full merits review[85] but still indicated that it would attach importance to the Secretary of State for the Home Department's (SSHD's) reasons for detaining.[86] It now being established law that the courts act as primary decision-makers in assessing the lawfulness of detention, owing no defence to the SSHD save on specific matters of her expertise such as the progress of diplomatic negotiations,[87] we suggest that the same approach must apply to bail and indeed, that is the approach which

---

79 CPR 54.10(2).
80 Practice Statement (Administrative Court: Listing and urgent cases) [2002] 1 WLR 810 para 3.
81 Practice Statement (Administrative Court: Listing and urgent cases) [2002] 1 WLR 810 at para 5.
82 *R v Secretary of State for the Home Department ex p Turkoglu* [1998] 1 QB 398 at 401B.
83 Senior Courts Act (formerly Supreme Court Act) 1981 s15(3). See also discussion in *R v Secretary of State for the Home Department ex p Turkoglu* [1998] 1 QB 398 at 401G.
84 *Vilvarajah v Secretary of State for the Home Department* [1990] Imm AR 457.
85 *R v Secretary of State for the Home Department ex p Kelso* [1998] INLR 603, QBD, approved in *R (Doku) v Secretary of State for the Home Department* (C/2000/3360, 30 November unreported, CA).
86 *R (Sezek) v Secretary of State for the Home Department* [2001] INLR 675 para 22.
87 *R (A) v Secretary of State for the Home Department* [2007] EWCA Civ 804 at paras 62 and 71–72. See, for example, Keene LJ at 71: 'It is to my mind a remarkable proposition that the courts should have only a limited role where the liberty of the individual is being curtailed by administrative detention. Classically the courts of this country have intervened by means of *habeas corpus* and other remedies to ensure that the detention of a person is lawful, and where such detention is only lawful when it endures for a reasonable period, it must be for the court itself to determine whether such a reasonable period has been exceeded ...' See also discussion at para 32.41.

is now being taken in practice.[88] Bail should be sought by using the N463 form to seek an urgent hearing, on notice to the defendant.

42.65 Aside from bail the most common form of interim relief sought in immigration cases will be a stay on removal pending the claim.[89] Other examples might include seeking an order that a mentally ill detainee is not transferred back to a detention centre from a hospital. In cases seeking such interim relief the court will consider firstly whether there is at least a prima facie case, and then consider the 'balance of convenience',[90] that is it will aim to take the course that appears to pose the least risk of injustice.

The full hearing

42.66 Once the time limit for filing detailed grounds has passed the Administrative Court Office will notify the parties that the case is ready for listing and counsel's clerk will be contacted in order to agree a date for the hearing.[91]

42.67 Once the case is listed the claimant's representatives must file and serve a skeleton argument together with a paginated bundle of all relevant documents for the hearing not less than 21 days before the date of the hearing.[92] The bundle will be that relied on for the permission stage together with the order granting permission and any other orders, the detailed grounds of resistance and any evidence relied upon by the defendant, and any further evidence put in by the claimant.

42.68 The hearing of a claim for judicial review is normally by a single judge in open court. Subject to the considerations at para 42.31 above, judicial review hearings rarely determine issues of fact and so commonly last no more than a day.

42.69 Where the Administrative Court resolves a public law issue that then gives rise to a claim for damages, it may then transfer the claim to the appropriate court to continue as a normal civil claim with appropriate directions.[93] In practice, claims for judicial review concerning past detention are often determined on liability in the

---

88 See, for example, *R (Polanco) v Secretary of State for the Home Department* [2009] EWHC 826 (Admin).
89 See *R (Madan) v Secretary of State for the Home Department* [2007] EWCA Civ 770 at 17 for the principles that apply in such cases.
90 A principle derived from the private law case of *American Cyanamid v Ethicon (No 1)* [1975] AC 396.
91 See Practice Statement [2002] 1 WLR 810.
92 PD 54 para 15.1 – for content of skeletons 15.3, and PD 16.1.
93 CPR 54.20.

Administrative Court (with any appropriate declarations made at that stage) and then transferred to a Master of the Queen's Bench Division for the assessment of damages if these cannot be agreed by the parties in the interim. However, where causation of damage is in issue (and thus where it remains to be determined whether nominal or substantial damages are available, see the discussion at paras 44.9–44.15) the Administrative Court is likely to decide this question itself[94]. The Administrative Court may also itself assess damages.[95]

Appeals

42.70 Where a claim for judicial review in respect of a civil matter is dismissed, the onward appeal lies to the Court of Appeal.[96] Permission to appeal should ordinarily be sought from the Administrative Court at the time that judgment is handed down (or if there is no attendance at the handing down, on the papers before judgment is handed down) although a party may request an extension of time within which to seek permission from the Administrative Court.[97] Where permission to appeal is refused in the Administrative Court (or where the applicant simply bypasses the option of seeking permission from the Administrative Court) permission to appeal may be sought from the Court of Appeal.[98] The application for permission to appeal in the Court of Appeal should be brought within the time specified, if any, by the lower court, or alternatively within 21 days of the date of judgment in the court below.[99] See paras 21.136–21.139 for more detail on steps to be taken in applications for permission to appeal in the Court of Appeal (note, however, that the time limits referred to in that chapter differ since they concern applications for permission to appeal from the Upper Tribunal).

42.71 Where the judicial review concerns a criminal matter, the appeal lies directly to the Supreme Court if the Administrative Court certifies

---

94 See, for example, *R (Sino) v Secretary of State for the Home Department* [2011] EWHC 2249 (Admin) and *R (OM) v Secretary of State for the Home Department* [2011] EWCA Civ 909.
95 See for example *PB v Secretary of State for the Home Department* [2008] EWHC 364 (Admin) before Kenneth Parker QC.
96 CPR Part 52 deals with appeals. CPR 52.15 deals specifically with appeals against refusals of permission.
97 PD 52 para 4.3A(1).
98 CPR 52.3.2.
99 Under CPR Part 52 rule 52.4(2)(b).

a point of general public importance and either it, or the House of Lords, grants permission to appeal.

Habeas corpus

42.72 Habeas corpus is an ancient and constitutionally important remedy by which a claim can be issued to obtain the release of anyone unlawfully restrained. Its procedure is governed by Rules of the Supreme Court (RSC) Order 54, which is now incorporated to Schedule 1 to the CPR.[100]

42.73 Although its common use is to challenge an ongoing detention, habeas corpus may be available to challenge restraint which does not amount to actual loss of liberty, possibly including challenges to bail conditions imposed on a released person.[101]

Choosing between habeas corpus and judicial review

42.74 The utility of habeas corpus as a remedy has been controversial in recent years. It has been held that judicial review affords sufficient protection in cases of ongoing unlawful detention, especially since there are now specific provisions for dealing with urgent claims involving loss of liberty[102] (through use of the N463 procedure).

42.75 Judicial review remedies are certainly considerably broader. The sole remedy available in habeas corpus proceedings is the writ for the production of the detainee, by contrast to the array of remedies in judicial review proceedings discussed at paras 42.36–42.37 above. Thus, while either judicial review or habeas corpus may assist a person challenging an ongoing detention, once released (subject to the caveat at para 42.73 above), only judicial review proceedings or private law proceedings can assist the former detainee in seeking declaratory relief and damages for the historic detention.

42.76 In addition, the grounds on which habeas corpus can be sought may be more limited than the grounds on which one can seek release by way of judicial review. Habeas corpus has been held to be

---

100 See www.justice.gov.uk/guidance/courts-and-tribunals/courts/procedure-rules/civil/contents/schedule1/rscorder54.htm.
101 See the discussion in Farbey and Sharpe, *The law of habeas corpus*, 3rd edn, OUP, 2011, ch 8.
102 See, for example, *R v Oldham Justices ex p Cawley* [1997] QB 1 at 16 and 19 per Simon Brown LJ as he then was. See also the ALBA lecture given by Simon Brown LJ, 'Habeas Corpus' a new chapter, ALBA, 23 November 1999.

inappropriate where the real challenge is to an underlying administrative decision, such as a refusal of leave to enter, rather than to the lawfulness of the detention itself.[103]

42.77 It was also previously thought that habeas corpus was appropriate only in cases where there was no power to detain, as opposed to a challenge to the exercise of the statutory discretion to detain.[104] However, we suggest that these distinctions between jurisdictional error cases and wrongful exercise of power cases have now been blurred by two (rather contradictory) legal developments:

- as the Supreme Court confirmed in *Lumba and Mighty*,[105] there are no distinct categories of legal error: wrongful exercise of jurisdiction, like excess of jurisdiction, renders a decision a nullity;[106] and
- in *Khadir*,[107] the House of Lords held that the *Hardial Singh* line of cases concerned the *exercise* of the power to detain under the Immigration Acts rather than the *existence* of the power. This is a difficult distinction in light of 1) above; but in any event, *Hardial Singh*[108] itself was a habeas corpus case, as were *Re Wasfi Suleman Mahmod*[109] and *Tan Te Lam*[110] (other authorities in that same line).

42.78 The question of when habeas corpus is available remains to be re-examined in light of those authorities. We suggest that in light of these developments, habeas corpus may be available not only in 'no statutory power' cases but in cases where the exercise of the power to detain is flawed by a breach of the *Hardial Singh* principles, a material public law error (see the discussion at para 32.10 above) or a breach of ECHR article 5(1).

42.79 Habeas corpus retains four procedural advantages over judicial review, the first two of which are particularly important:

---

103 *R v Secretary of State for the Home Department ex p Muboyayi* [1991] 3 WLR 704.
104 See, for example, *R v Secretary of State for the Home Department ex p Cheblak* [1991] 1 WLR 890, 984 C–E per Lord Donaldson MR.
105 *R (Lumba and Mighty) v Secretary of State for the Home Department* [2011] UKSC 12, [2011] 2 WLR 671.
106 [2011] UKSC 12, [2011] 2 WLR, see in particular Lord Dyson para 66, Lord Kerr para 247.
107 [2005] UKHL 39, [2006] 1 AC 207 para 33.
108 [1984] 1 WLR 704.
109 [1995] Imm AR 311.
110 [1997] AC 97.

- There is no permission requirement when seeking habeas corpus in the Administrative Court. (We respectfully suggest that, if judicial review is to be offered as a full alternative to habeas corpus, the Courts should be slow indeed to refuse permission to seek judicial review in a challenge concerning an ongoing detention. At present, however, the courts do, at least in some instances, refuse permission to seek judicial review in such cases.)
- Where habeas corpus is refused in the Administrative Court, an appeal lies as of right to the Court of Appeal. There is again no permission requirement.
- If an applicant is released at first instance on habeas corpus, any appeal by the defendant can only serve to clarify the law, not to redetain.
- The writ of habeas corpus issues as of right whereas, as discussed at para 42.38 above, judicial review remedies are discretionary. However, it is difficult to conceive of circumstances in which the courts would find, in judicial review, that an ongoing detention was still unlawful as of the date of judgment but decline to order release.[111]

Bringing an application for a writ of habeas corpus

42.80 An application for a writ of habeas corpus should be directed against the person with physical custody of a detainee (rather than, as in judicial review, the authority which decided upon the detention). For example, if an immigration detainee is held in a prison, a claim for judicial review challenging the detention under Immigration Act powers would be directed against the SSHD who gave the authority to detain, but a claim for a writ of habeas corpus would be issued against the Prison Governor.

42.81 Claims challenging ongoing detention may be issued as both a claim for judicial review and habeas corpus (see for example *R (I) v Secretary of State for the Home Department*[112] where the claim was brought in judicial review as well as habeas corpus). In such cases, the application for a writ of habeas corpus may be included on form N461 as one of the remedies sought. Note that if proceeding simultaneously in judicial review and habeas corpus, there will usually need to be two defendants, for the reasons explained in the preceding

---

111 See *R v Oldham Justices ex p Cawley* [1997] QB 1 at 19A–D per Simon Brown LJ as he then was.
112 [2002] EWCA Civ 888, [2003] INLR 196, paras 46–47.

paragraph (although in practice, the defendants are likely to be jointly represented by counsel in court). Although the High Court may in principle grant a writ of habeas corpus without a hearing, the normal course is that an urgent hearing will be listed, on notice to the defendant, to consider whether the writ should be granted.

Private law claims

42.82 Private law claims, also known as civil claims or civil actions, are brought to challenge past conduct, and the main remedy sought is compensation. They involve establishing a civil wrong, or 'tort' against the defendant. There are also causes of action that have a statutory basis.

Burden of proof

42.83 The normal principle in civil claims is that the burden of proof is on the claimant who is required to establish their case applying the civil standard, that is the balance of probabilities. An exception to this rule is that in false imprisonment claims, where the claimant alleges that detention has been unlawful, it is for the defendant to establish that it was not.[113]

Who can be sued?

42.84 Civil claims can be brought any body with a legal identity, individuals, government departments, statutory bodies and private companies. Choosing the correct defendant can be difficult and in factually complicated situations there might be a number of defendants. For example, where a person is unlawfully detained by the UK Border Agency, assaulted by staff in the detention centre run by a private company, and provided with inadequate treatment by the contracted out healthcare provider there will be three defendants. Human rights claims can only be brought against public authorities and hybrid public authorities (see below at para 43.22).

---

113 *R (Lumba and Mighty) v Secretary of State for the Home Department* [2011] UKSC 12, [2011] 2 WLR 671 at para 44. See also discussion at paras 32.3–32.5.

42.85 The Minister for the Civil Service must publish a list of government departments that can be named in civil claims against the state and proceedings must be brought against one of those departments.[114]

42.86 Where the wrongful conduct is carried out by individuals, for example where assaults are alleged against officers of an institution, then if the wrong is so closely connected with the employment that it is fair to hold the employer vicarious liable, then the claim can be brought against that employer.[115] In most cases civil claims in the detention context will rely on this principle.

Remaining in the UK to pursue a claim

42.87 'Quaquah' claims that a person should not be removed from the UK while his or her claim is pending have been discussed at paras 18.60–18.64.

Which court?

42.88 Where the value of the claim is assessed at more than £25,000, or £50,000 in personal injury cases, it should be brought in the High Court.[116] In addition, even for lower value claims, a claim with a significant public law element or complex subject matter might appropriately be brought in the High Court (for example, a claim which seeks declaratory relief in respect of an unlawful policy, since declarations can be granted in the High Court in civil proceedings but not in the County Court).

42.89 Discrimination claims for compensation only must be brought in the county court,[117] although this does not prevent discrimination

---

114 Crown Proceedings Act 1947 s17(1) and (3) – the list was most recently updated on 23 September 2009 and is available at www.tsol.gov.uk/contact_us.htm – whereas in a judicial review a claim would be brought against the SSHD, as the person with ultimate responsibility for discharge of the department's public functions, private law claims are brought against 'The Home Office'.
115 *Lister v Hesley Hall Ltd* [2002] 1 AC 214 para 781.
116 The High Court and County Courts Jurisdiction Order 1991 arts 4A and 5, see also CPR PD 7A.
117 Equality Act (EA) 2010 s114. Decisions relating to the entitlement of a person to enter or remain in the UK which have, or could have been, challenged in immigration appeals can not be the subject of further proceedings in the county court EA 2010 s115.

claims being brought as part of a wider challenge in judicial review proceedings.[118]

Limitation periods

42.90 Limitation periods for civil claims generally are governed by the Limitation Act (LA) 1980. LA 1980 does not affect the normal time limit for bringing judicial review proceedings. Where (as in discrimination or human rights claims), other legislation provides a specific limitation for bring a claim, LA 1980 does not apply.[119]

42.91 LA 1980 provides that:
- The limitation period for claims involving personal injuries, which include psychiatric injury, is three years from the date of the cause of action accruing, or, if later, the date of knowledge of the person injured.[120]
- This period can be extended by the court where it considers it equitable to do so.[121]
- Where the claim is for injuries, including psychiatric injuries, this three-year limitation period applies whether or not the claim for negligence or intentional conduct such as assaults and false imprisonment.[122]
- Where damages for personal injuries are not sought, the normal limitation period for claims in tort is six years, which the court does not have discretion to extend.[123]

Jury trials

42.92 Where a claim is brought for false imprisonment, there is a right for the trial to be heard by a jury 'unless the court is of opinion that the trial requires any prolonged examination of documents or accounts or any scientific or local investigation which cannot conveniently be made with a jury'.[124] An application for a claim to be heard by a jury must be made within 28 days of the service of the defence.[125] In

---

118 EA 2010 s113(3)(a).
119 LA 1980 s39.
120 LA 1980 s2(4).
121 LA 1980 s33.
122 *A v Hoare* [2008] 1 AC 844.
123 LA 1980 s2.
124 SCA 1981 s69(1); County Courts Act 1984 s64(3).
125 CPR 26.11.

immigration detention cases, the sometimes inflammatory nature of media coverage should be taken into account in considering whether a claim would benefit from a jury.

Pre-action correspondence

42.93 The overriding objective of the CPR applies both to civil claims and judicial review and so compliance where possible with the pre-action practice direction, or any relevant specific pre-action protocol is important. The pre-action protocols in civil claims provide much longer periods for responding to letters before claim (for example the pre-action protocol in personal injury claims states that defendants should be given three months to respond[126]). However, claims should still be issued within the relevant limitation period, and the imminence of expiry of such a period will be a reason to request an earlier response. Pre-action correspondence also affords claimants an important opportunity to seek specific pre-action disclosure.

Procedure in civil claims

42.94 Those considering bringing a civil claim should consult CPR Part 7 which sets out the procedure for conducting civil claims, and associated Practice Directions. A detailed analysis of civil procedure is outside the scope of this book. Below, we provide a cursory summary only, emphasising that it is very far from complete.

42.95 Claims are started by the claimant requests the court to issue a claim form.[127] Unless the claimant is entitled to remission of the fee the court requires a fee to be paid, the level of which is dependent on the value of the claim. The claim form should be issued within the earliest of the limitation periods for any cause of action included. The claim form is a prescribed form.[128]

42.96 Once the claim form is issued, it must be served on the defendant within four months.[129] When the claim form is served, it should be accompanied by a fuller document setting out the particulars of claim, or the particulars of claim should be served within 14 days.[130]

126 Personal Injury Pre-Action Protocol para 2.11.
127 CPR Part 7.
128 Form N1 – forms for civil claims are available at www.justice.gov.uk/guidance/courts-and-tribunals/courts/procedure-rules/civil/menus/forms.htm.
129 CPR 7.5.
130 CPR 7.4.

42.97 A claimant can seek anonymity in proceedings (and this applies equally to judicial review) where the court 'considers non-disclosure necessary to protect the interests of that party'.[133] This may be appropriate in relation to vulnerable claimants, or even where there are concerns over potential inflammatory media reaction to the claim which might put the claimant at risk. In such cases in publicly accessible court documents and reports, the claimant will only be identified by initials.

42.98 The defendant, if the claim is not conceded, will file a defence to the claim.[134] The court will then list a case management conference when directions for the future conduct of the claim to trial will be ordered. The CPR provides for means by which the parties can seek further clarification of the opponent's case,[135] the rules by which parties are required to provide disclosure of documents and other material relevant to the claim,[136] exchange of witness statements[137] and expert evidence.[138]

Choosing between a civil claim for damages and judicial review

42.99 As we have seen at para 42.37 above, a claim solely for damages cannot be brought in judicial review proceedings and must be brought as a civil claim. However, a claim for damages may be combined with

---

131 CPR 3.1(2)(f).
132 CPR 7.6.
133 CPR 39.2(4).
134 CPR 15.
135 CPR 18.
136 CPR 31.
137 CPR 34.
138 CPR 35.

42.100 In civil claims the primary remedy being sought is financial compensation (although in appropriate cases other remedies such as declarations,[139] or injunctions[140] may be sought).

42.101 Civil claims are better suited to resolving cases where disputed facts are key to establishing liability. This is because the procedure for civil claims under the CPR includes detailed requirements on disclosure and inspection,[141] exchange of witness statements,[142] clarification of areas of dispute[143] and, where the case reaches this point, oral evidence at trial (although, as we have seen at para 42.62 above, the Administrative Court is increasingly open to borrowing procedures, including cross-examination, more commonly associated with civil claims). Conversely, judicial review is likely to be preferable where there are few disputes of fact and these can be resolved by reference to documents.

42.102 Choice of remedy may be dictated by questions of timing. As we have seen, the limitations period for civil claims (six years, save for personal injury claims in which a three-year limit applies) are far more generous than the three-month outer time limit for issuing a claim in judicial review. However, for a claimant who seeks a speedy result, the more lugubrious and procedurally far more complex nature of civil proceedings may be less attractive than the relatively streamlined judicial review process.

---

139 CPR 40.20.
140 SCA 1981 s37; CCA 1984 s38.
141 CPR Part 31.
142 CPR Part 32.
143 CPR Part 18, also Notices to admit under rule 32.18.

CHAPTER 43

Causes of action

43.1	Introduction
43.4	**Trespass to the person**
43.5	Assault and battery
43.9	False imprisonment
43.13	**Misfeasance in public office**
43.15	**Negligence**
43.19	**Breach of statutory duty**
43.20	**Human rights claims**
43.28	**Claims under the Data Protection Act 1998**
43.29	**Discrimination claims**

Introduction

43.1 This chapter considers the most common causes of action arising for foreign national prisoners (FNPs) in civil proceedings, some of which may also be raised in judicial review.

43.2 We begin with a description of 'torts', that is, civil wrongs, which are usually brought in private law. It then goes on to consider other types of claim (Human Rights Act (HRA) 1998 claims, Data Protection Act (DPA) 1998 claims and discrimination claims) which are actionable both in private and public law proceedings.

43.3 We provide no more than a brief overview. Useful practitioners' texts have been mentioned in the introduction to this section.

Trespass to the person

43.4 This is the umbrella term for claims in assault, battery and false imprisonment. These are intentional torts. They are actionable without proof of damage meaning that a person may bring a claim in trespass even if he or she suffered no loss by the tort.[1]

Assault and battery

43.5 The meaning of assault in tort is different to that in criminal law or the general understanding of the word. Accordingly:

> An assault is an act which causes another person to apprehend the infliction of immediate, unlawful force on his person; a battery is the actual infliction of unlawful force on another person.[2]

43.6 In the immigration and prison contexts, cases of assault and battery frequently arise where it is alleged that excessive force has been used, for example in attempts at removal by escort contractors, or where detainees are placed in segregation.[3] It will often be the case that the word of the detainee is set against multiple mutually corroborating accounts of officers who will say that any force used was reasonable. Such claims are therefore often difficult, particularly where the detainee's own credibility may have been impugned in previous criminal sentencing remarks, a conviction for an offence of

---

1 *Co-operative Group (CES) Ltd v Pritchard* [2011] EWCA Civ 329.
2 *Collins v Wilcock* [1984] 1 WLR 1772 at 1177B.
3 See Medical Justice's report 'Outsourcing Abuse', 2008, available at www.medicaljustice.org.uk/content/view/411/88/.

dishonesty, or an adverse determination of an immigration appeal. Where available CCTV footage, early accounts on use of force documentation, contemporaneous medical records, and expert forensic medical evidence showing that injuries sustained are consistent with excessive use of force, may be very be useful.

43.7 If use of force is admitted by the defendant then the burden of proof of proving that the force, or level of force, used was lawful is on the defendant.[4] Even where use of force is not admitted it is incumbent on the state to provide a plausible explanation for how any injuries sustained in custody occurred.[5]

43.8 Note that since any unwanted touching (other than that which occurs in the normal course of daily life) without lawful justification is a battery,[6] technical battery claims may arise wherever there is physical contact with a detainee in the course of, for example, an unlawful removal, an unjustified search[7] or where the underlying detention is itself unlawful. However, damages for such technical batteries are likely to be nominal or low.

False imprisonment

43.9 False imprisonment is defined as 'the unlawful imposition of constraint upon another's freedom of movement from a particular place'.[8] Imprisonment does not refer just to being locked in a room or institution, as being confined by physical force or threats may also give rise to a claim. The fact that the detainee is unaware of his or her imprisonment, for example is asleep for its duration, does not affect the establishment of this tort.[9]

43.10 False imprisonment is a tort of strict liability. This means that if the detention is unlawful a claim can be brought even though the detainer is acting in good faith and does not believe they are acting unlawfully.[10] However the tort does require that the Defendant is directly responsible and intended the imprisonment. This therefore

---

4 *Ashley v Chief Constable of Sussex Police* [2006] EWCA Civ 1085 para 22.
5 *Selmouni v France* (1999) 29 EHRR 403, para 87, Grand Chamber. See also *Keenan v UK* (2001) 33 EHRR 38 para 40.
6 *Collins v Wilcock* [1984] 1 WLR 1172 at 1177.
7 *Wainwright v Home Office* [2003] UKHL 53.
8 *Wainwright v Home Office* [2003] UKHL 53.
9 *Murray v Ministry of Defence* [1988] 1 WLR 692 703B – although in such circumstances only nominal damages may be awarded.
10 This was the position of the Governor who incorrectly calculated the prisoner's sentence in *R v Governor of Brockhill Prison ex p Evans (No 2)* [2001] 2 AC 19.

requires a positive act, rather than an omission unless there is a specific duty to act.[11]

43.11 Where a person is being detained lawfully, the conditions in which they are held will normally not render that detention unlawful so as to found a claim for false imprisonment.[12] Similarly, although a detainee or prisoner may be free to move around an institution under normal circumstances, an unlawful decision to segregate them, if made by or on behalf of the detaining authority, will not render the underlying detention (whether under criminal justice or Immigration Act powers) unlawful,[13] although this may be actionable in misfeasance or ECHR article 8; see paras 43.13–43.14 and 43.20–43.27 below. Forced confinement within the institution by another detainee or a member of staff acting without proper authority can however give rise to a claim in false imprisonment.[14]

43.12 In the FNP context, claims for damages for false imprisonment will lie where detention has breached the *Hardial Singh* principles or where the detention is in breach of the Home Office's policy or where the decision to detain has otherwise been made in breach of public law principles. Less commonly, there will be cases where the statutory power to detain does not exist at all. See the detailed discussion in section J of this book.

Misfeasance in public office

43.13 This tort is made out public officer exercises his or her power specifically intending to injure the claimant, or when the officer acts with knowledge of, or with reckless indifference to, the illegality of their act and in the knowledge of, or with reckless indifference to, the probability of causing injury to the claimant. Subjective recklessness in the sense of not caring whether the act is illegal or whether the consequences happen is sufficient, and a deliberate omission

---

11 *Iqbal v Prison Officers Association* [2010] 2 WLR 1054.
12 *R v Deputy Governor of Parkhurst Prison ex p Hague, Weldon v Home Office* [1992] 1 AC 58 – although conditions and treatment in prison may establish other torts or claims for breaches of human rights.
13 *R v Deputy Governor of Parkhurst Prison ex p Hague, Weldon v Home Office* [1992] 1 AC 58.
14 *Iqbal v Prison Officers Association* [2010] 2 WLR 1054, which involved a claim against the Prison Officers' Association for periods prisoners were confined to their cells because of an unlawful strike – it failed on the facts because of the court's finding that generally omissions will not give rise to claims for false imprisonment.

involving an actual decision not to act might also give rise to liability.[15] However, manifest incompetence, or carelessness, in the exercise of their power is not in itself sufficient to establish misfeasance, in the absence of proof of reckless indifference.[16] The burden is on the claimant to establish the requisite mental state of the officer and this makes claims in misfeasance particularly difficult.

43.14 Unlike trespass claims, in misfeasance claims the claimant must prove loss to establish the claim.[17] This may be financial loss, or personal or psychiatric injury. Loss of liberty has been held to be sufficient damage to enable a claim for misfeasance to be brought, and this (unlike in false imprisonment claims) may include the comparative loss of liberty brought about by a change in the conditions of imprisonment.[18] Accordingly a claim in misfeasance may be brought where prison officers deliberately exceed their powers by maliciously segregating a prisoner, notwithstanding the unavailability of false imprisonment as a remedy.[19]

Negligence

43.15 To establish a claim for negligence the claimant must establish four elements:
1) that the defendant owes a duty of care to the claimant;
2) breach of that duty;
3) a causal connection between the defendant's breach and the damage caused;
4) that the damage caused is reasonably foreseeable.

43.16 Common examples of claims for negligence by prisoners and detainees are where injury is caused by a failure to maintain a safe environment (where the correct defendant would be the body responsible

---

15 *Three Rivers District Council and others v Governor and Company of the Bank of England* [2003] 2 AC 1.
16 *Muuse v Secretary of State for the Home Department* [2010] EWCA Civ 453; *Malcolm v Home Office* [2010] EWHC 3389 (QB).
17 *Watkins v Secretary of State for the Home Department and others* [2006] 2 AC 395 – where a claim brought by a prisoner who alleged his legal correspondence had been opened in breach of the Prison Rules 1999 r39 failed as he had not suffered any loss or damage.
18 *Karagozlu v Commissioner of Police for the Metropolis* [2007] 1 WLR 1881 – where the loss was established in circumstances where the claimant had been transferred from an open to a closed prison.
19 *Racz v Home Office* [1994] 2 AC 45.

for managing the institution); where property is lost or damaged; or where inadequate medical treatment causes injury (where the correct defendant will be the healthcare provider). In some circumstances, where a prisoner or detainee is injured by another, the detaining authority may be liable in for negligent supervision.[20]

43.17 Note, however, that the courts have been reluctant to find a duty of care in negligence claims arising out of maladministration by the Home Office in the immigration context. It has been held that there was no claim in negligence against the Home Office where the claimant was detained due to an administrative error, the reasoning being that the immigration officers concerned were carrying out statutory functions inconsistent with owing a duty of care in negligence.[21]

43.18 In other cases, the availability of alternative redress has been held to be a relevant consideration. The Court of Appeal accordingly upheld a strike out of a claim in negligence in respect of delay in granting indefinite leave to remain, because a complaint could have been made to the Parliamentary Commissioner, who could recommend payment of compensation.[22] This may be contrasted with a case where the wife of a refugee admitted to the UK was wrongly refused benefits, resulting in losses which could only be recovered by way of damages, the circumstances of which were considered sufficient to found a claim.[23]

Breach of statutory duty

43.19 A wide variety of statutory provisions impose duties on public bodies. Whether a person who suffers loss due to a failure to properly carry out such a statutory duty can seek compensation as a result is complicated. The general approach of the courts has been to look at the purpose of the statutory framework, in order to ascertain whether there was any intention to impose liability to individuals for loss. For

---

20 For an example of a successful claim in the prison context, see *Hartshorn v Home Office* [1999] Prison LR 4; for an unsuccessful one, see *Stenning v Home Office* [2002] EWCA Civ 793.
21 *W v Home Office* [1997] Imm AR 302 – although the claimant would have been able to bring a claim in false imprisonment, and such an error may also give rise to a claim under DPA 1998.
22 *Home Office v Mohammed* [2011] EWCA Civ 351.
23 *R (Kanidagli) v Secretary of State for the Home Department* [2004] EWHC 1585 (Admin).

example it has been held that the Prison Rules 1999 were not intended to give rise to claims to individual prisoners for their breach.[24]

Human rights claims

43.20 Claims under HRA 1998 may be brought in conjunction with other causes of action or as freestanding claims. Among other ways of proceeding with HRA 1998 claims, these can be brought in judicial review and in civil claims for damages.

43.21 Claims under HRA 1998 may only be brought by someone who 'is (or would be) a victim of the unlawful act'.[25]

43.22 A claim under HRA 1998 may only be brought against a 'public authority',[26] or any other organisation 'certain of whose functions are of a public nature'.[27] Whether a body is carrying out public functions which may be challenged under HRA 1998 involves similar considerations as the question of whether such a body is amenable to judicial review (see paras 42.19–42.21). However, the test is slightly different in that it has been held that the purpose of HRA 1998 is to enable rights and remedies, previously only available by recourse to the European Court of Human Rights (ECtHR), to be enforced by domestic courts. Accordingly the key issue is whether the body is carrying out a function of government which would engage the responsibility of the UK before the ECtHR. Immigration Removal Centres (IRCs) and detention escort agencies exercising their functions in relation to detainees have been found to be hybrid public authorities for the purposes of HRA 1998 claims.[28]

43.23 There is authority that where treatment in a contracted out detention breaches rights under the ECHR, that the SSHD remains responsible under HRA 1998 even where the treatment is carried out by the contractor.[29]

43.25 Claims made under HRA 1998 must be brought before the end of one year beginning with the date on which the act complained

---

24 *R v Deputy Governor of Parkhurst Prison ex p Hague* [1992] 1 AC 58 – although such breaches may of course be challenged by way of judicial review.
25 HRA 1998 s7(1).
26 HRA 1998 s6(1).
27 HRA 1998 s6(3)(b) and (5).
28 *Quaquah v Group 4 Securities Ltd (No 2)* [2001] Prison LR 318 para 15.
29 *R (MT) v Secretary of State for the Home Department and others* [2008] EWHC 1788 (Admin) para 49; *S and others v Secretary of State for the Home Department* [2007] EWHC 1654 (Admin) para 82.

of took place, or such longer period as the court or tribunal considers equitable having regard to all the circumstances. However, those time limits are subject to any rule imposing a stricter time limit in relation to the procedure in question[30] so that, for example, an HRA 1998 claim made in judicial review proceedings is still subject to the outer time limit of three months. Where the breach is a continuing one, the period runs from the last day of that continuing act.[31]

43.26 Damages may be awarded by the domestic courts for the breach of a Convention right incorporated by HRA 1998, provided that the court is satisfied that such an award is necessary to afford 'just satisfaction'. In determining the level of damages the court is required to take into account the principles applied by the ECtHR when making such awards.[32] In practice, awards made under HRA 1998 are frequently lower than those awarded under the common law. Note in particular that exemplary damages are not available under the HRA 1998. Indeed, the finding of a breach of the ECHR may itself be found to amount to 'just satisfaction', without need for monetary compensation.[33]

43.27 ECHR articles 3, 5, 8 and 14 claims in the detention context have been discussed in chapter 36. ECHR article 3 and 8 claims in the context of resisting deportation have been discussed separately in chapters 13 and 15–18.

Claims under the Data Protection Act 1998

43.28 DPA 1998 imposes broad duties on those who hold personal data, including the duty to ensure it is accurate and up to date.[34] Where a breach of this requirement causes damage, a claim for compensation can be made which will include a claim for compensation for any distress caused.[35] It is a defence that such care as in all the circumstances was reasonably required to maintain accurate data was taken.[36] Where a failure by the UK Border Agency to update records causes loss, such as a longer period of detention, then adding a claim

---

30 HRA 1998 s7(5).
31 *Home Office v Mohammed* [2011] EWCA Civ 351 para 5.
32 HRA 1998 s8.
33 *R (Greenfield) v Secretary of State for the Home Department* [2005] UKHL 14.
34 DPA 1998 Sch 1 Part 1 para 4.
35 DPA 1998 s13(1)–(2).
36 DPA 1998 s13(3).

under DPA 1998 may be appropriate.[37] Claims under DPA 1998 can be brought in either the High Court or county court[38] subject to the value of the claim (see para 42.88). DPA 1998 does not impose a limitation period for such claims and so they should be brought within six years, or three years where the damage includes personal or psychiatric injury (see 42.91 above).

Discrimination claims

43.29 The Equality Act (EA) 2010 now provides the basis for claims for discrimination. Discrimination law is particularly complex and what follows is the briefest of summaries.

43.30 EA 2010 includes a public sector equality duty that requires public authorities to have due regard to the need to eliminate discrimination.[39] Predecessors to the current statutory duty have been held to require public bodies to properly assess the potentially discriminatory impact of legislative or policy changes before implementing such changes.[40]

43.31 EA 2010's provisions apply in different ways to the protected characteristics of age, disability, gender reassignment, marriage and civil partnership, pregnancy and maternity, race, religion or belief, sex, and sexual orientation.[41]

43.32 Prohibited conduct under EA 2010 includes direct discrimination,[42] indirect discrimination[43] and the failure to make reasonable adjustments for those with disabilities.[44]

43.33 Claims for discrimination under EA 2010 may not be brought after the end of the period of six months starting with the date of the act to which the claim relates, or such other period as the court

---

37 Although this might not add anything more than a claim for false imprisonment – see *Muuse v Secretary of State for the Home Department* [2010] EWCA Civ 453.
38 DPA 1998 s15(1).
39 EA 2010 s149.
40 For example, *R (C) v Secretary of State for Justice and another* [2008] EWCA Civ 882.
41 EA 2010 s4.
42 EA 2010 s13, where a person is treated less favourably due to a protected characteristic.
43 EA 2010 s19, where an act or practice impacts disproportionately to the disadvantage of those with a protected characteristic.
44 EA 2010 s20.

thinks just and equitable.[45] If the claim is referred to the Equality and Human Rights Commission, the period within which the claim must be brought is extended to nine months or other such period as the court thinks just and equitable.[46]

43.34 Discrimination claims for compensation are brought in the county court.[47] In such proceedings the court has the power to grant any remedy that could be sought in judicial review proceedings, or other civil claim,[48] and, by contrast with normal civil claims, can award compensation for injured feelings in addition to any other award.[49] However, breaches of the EA 2010 can also be raised in judicial review claims, where relief other than compensation is being sought.[50]

---

45 EA 2010 s118(1).
46 EA 2010 s118(4).
47 EA 2010 s114.
48 EA 2010 s119(2).
49 EA 2010 s119(4). For guidance on appropriate bands for awards for injury to feelings under the previous sex discrimination legislation, see *Vento v Chief Constable of West Yorkshire Police* [2002] EWCA Civ 1871.
50 EA 2010 s113(3)(a).

CHAPTER 44

Damages

44.1	Introduction
44.9	Nominal or substantive damages?
44.17	The basic award for loss of liberty
44.30	Aggravated damages
44.38	Exemplary damages
44.48	Settlements in civil actions

Introduction

44.1 This chapter provides a brief overview of damages that may be available in judicial review and in civil claims.

44.2 Damages to compensate losses that have a specific monetary value are known as special damages. These may, for example, include property, lost wages, lost pension or benefit rights and medical, travel and other expenses.

44.3 Damages to compensate losses which have no precise monetary value are known as general damages. These may, for example, include damages to compensate for loss of liberty, or for pain, suffering and loss of amenity. Where wrongful conduct causes personal injury (including psychiatric injury), the courts will be guided by the *Judicial Studies Board's guidelines for the assessment of damages in personal injury cases*,[1] as well as by earlier awards in cases of broadly similar injury and circumstances (including the age of the claimant). The level of other general damages awards will be primarily guided by precedent.

44.4 Aggravated damages, which form part of general compensatory damages, may be added where the 'basic' compensatory award is insufficient to compensate for the harm caused to the claimant by the defendant's unlawful acts. In addition to the compensatory award, the courts may grant exemplary damages to punish specific categories of conduct by defendants.

44.5 Since late April 2006 when the Home Office significantly expanded the use of immigration detention for foreign national former prisoners (FNPs), the vast majority of damages claims brought by FNPs have challenged unlawful detention under Immigration Act powers. This chapter therefore focuses on damages available in claims concerning loss of liberty. Issues relating to the quantification of personal injury claims (which are often associated with false imprisonment claims, particularly in the form of claims that detention caused psychiatric injury) and special damages which may flow from such claims are beyond the scope of this book.

44.6 We begin by considering the current controversy over the circumstances in which only a nominal compensatory award should be granted in a false imprisonment claim in private law proceedings or an unlawful detention challenge in public law proceedings. We then consider, in cases where a substantial award is made, levels of basic awards for loss of liberty, and awards for aggravated damages.

1 10th edn, OUP, September 2010.

Finally, we consider the circumstances in which an award of exemplary damages may be made, and the level of such awards.

44.7 Aggravated and exemplary damages are available not only in false imprisonment claims in private law and challenges to unlawful detention in public law but also in other claims (although exemplary damages are not available in Human Rights Act (HRA) 1998 claims). Our comments on the general principles governing aggravated and exemplary damages therefore have broader application, although in examples given below of specific awards, we focus exclusively on the immigration detention context.

44.8 The figures given in this chapter are the sums awarded at the time of judgment only: any adjusted figures given now would rapidly have become outdated by further inflation. We emphasise that it is *critical* to adjust for inflation when considering awards made in earlier cases.[2] Note in particular that the guideline sums from the landmark case of *Thompson and Hsu v Commissioner of Police for the Metropolis*[3] given here are the original figures, would be very significantly higher if given an inflation uplift, and, as the Court of Appeal subsequently confirmed, must be adjusted for inflation.[4]

Nominal or substantive damages?

44.9 There is an ongoing debate over the circumstances in which a nominal rather than substantial compensatory award should be made to an individual who has been detained unlawfully. The majority of the Supreme Court in *Lumba and Mighty*[5] held that only nominal damages of £1 should be awarded where, had the defendant exercised the power to detain lawfully, the claimant would inevitably have been detained in any event. The claimant would not be entitled to substantial damages, having suffered no loss.[6]

44.10 However, the Supreme Court did not expressly address the questions of the applicable burden of proof and standard of proof where

---

2 See the Bank of England's 'Inflation calculator' at www.bankofengland.co.uk/education/inflation/calculator/flash/index.htm.
3 [1998] QB 498.
4 *MK (Algeria) v Secretary of State for the Home Department* [2010] EWCA Civ 980 para 9.
5 *R (Lumba and Mighty) v Secretary of State for the Home Department* [2011] UKSC 12, [2011] 2 WLR 671.
6 [2011] UKSC 12, [2011] 2 WLR 671.

the detainer argues that the claimant suffered no loss so that only nominal damages should be awarded.

44.11 There are compelling arguments that the burden of proof is on the detainer to establish the alternative lawful basis of detention for the purposes of nominal damages. *Lumba and Mighty* confirms that for the purposes of liability in false imprisonment the burden of proof is on the detainer not only to establish the existence but also the lawful exercise of the power to detain.[7] We suggest that the burden must also be on the detainer to establish the alternative justification for detention at the quantum stage, namely that detention would have ensued had the detention power been lawfully exercised. We suggest too that the normal principle at the quantum stage (which is that a claimant bears the burden of establishing that he has suffered loss) cannot apply where the defendant is seeking to benefit from a hypothetical scenario (what would have happened if the defendant had lawfully exercised the detention power).

44.12 Thus the Court of Appeal in obiter dicta has stated:
It seems to me that on normal compensatory principles it would be for a claimant to prove his loss on the balance of probabilities. It well may be that in circumstances such as these the burden shifts to the defendant to prove that the claimant would and could have been detained if the power of detention had been exercised lawfully.[8]

44.13 However, the Administrative Court has held the burden of proof to fall on the claimant to show that he would not have been detained had the power to detain been lawfully exercised.[9] At the time of writing, it remains to be seen which view will prevail.

44.14 In *Lumba and Mighty*, the express finding of those favouring nominal damages was that this was because detention was *inevitable* in any event.[10] This would be in line with the test applied in public law where a remedy may be denied because but for that error, the same result would *inevitably* have ensued; and would also be consistent with the established principle that where a fundamental constitutional right has been breached, the courts should be very slow to

---

7 See detailed discussion at paras 32.3–32.5.
8 *R (OM) v Secretary of State for the Home Department* [2011] EWCA Civ 909 para 23 per Richards LJ with whom Ward and Hughes LJJ agreed.
9 *R (Sino) v Secretary of State for the Home Department* [2011] EWHC 2249 (Admin) paras 88–89.
10 Lord Dyson para 169, with whom Lord Collins agreed at para 237, Lord Kerr para 253 see also Lady Hale discussing that reasoning at para 209.

deny a remedy on the basis that the breach made no difference to the outcome.[11]

44.15 However, at the time of writing, both the Court of Appeal in obiter dicta[12] and the Administrative Court[13] have favoured a lower threshold test whereby if, on the balance of probabilities, the individual would have been detained in any event, then he or she will be entitled only to nominal damages.

44.16 Below, we consider basic damages and aggravated damages in cases where substantial damages are available. At the end of this chapter, we consider exemplary damages (which may be available whether the compensatory award was nominal or substantial).

The basic award for loss of liberty

44.17 *Thompson and Hsu v Commissioner of Police for the Metropolis*[14] remains the guideline case on damages for false imprisonment, as was confirmed by the Court of Appeal in *Miller v Independent Assessor*.[15] The Court of Appeal has also provided more recent guidance on quantum in the context of immigration detention in *Muuse v Secretary of State for the Home Department*[16] and *MK (Algeria) v Secretary of State for the Home Department*.[17]

44.18 Where substantial damages are awarded, the level of the basic award will depend on a wide range of factors including (but not exclusively): the length of detention; whether the period of detention was unlawful from the outset; the conditions of the detention; any special vulnerability of the detainee; and the impact of the detention on the claimant.

44.19 An exhaustive examination of the authorities on the appropriate value of claims is beyond the scope of this book. Below, we refer to

---

11 See, in the context of natural justice, *R v Chief Constable Thames Valley Police ex p Cotton* [1990] IRLR 344 at para 60 per Bingham LJ as he then was.
12 *R (OM) v Secretary of State for the Home Department* [2011] EWCA Civ 909 para 23 per Richards LJ with whom Ward and Hughes LJJ agreed.
13 *R (Sino) v Secretary of State for the Home Department* [2011] EWHC 2249 (Admin) para 88; *R (BA) v Secretary of State for the Home Department* [2011] EWHC 2748 (Admin) paras 158 to 160.
14 [1998] QB 498.
15 [2009] EWCA Civ 609.
16 [2010] EWCA Civ 453.
17 [2010] EWCA Civ 980.

44.20 Lord Woolf recommended in *Thompson and Hsu* that the first hour of loss of liberty should be compensated with an award of approximately £500 while 24 hours of false imprisonment would entitle a claimant to £3,000.

44.21 However, damages for loss of liberty will decrease as time in detention progresses: the difficulty has been in determining the rate at which damages decline.

44.22 In *MK (Algeria) v Secretary of State for the Home Department*[18] Laws LJ distilled guidance for the basic award:

> There are three general principles which should be born in mind: 1) the assessment of damages should be sensitive to the facts and the particular case and the degree of harm suffered by the particular claimant: see the leading case of *Thompson v Commissioner of Police* [1998] QB 498 at 515A and also the discussion at page 1060 in *R v Governor of Brockhill Prison ex parte Evans* [1999] QB 1043; 2) Damages should not be assessed mechanistically as by fixing a rigid figure to be awarded for each day of incarceration: see *Thompson* at 516A. A global approach should be taken: see *Evans* 1060 E; 3) While obviously the gravity of a false imprisonment is worsened by its length the amount broadly attributable to the increasing passage of time should be tapered or placed on a reducing scale. This is for two reasons: (i) to keep this class of damages in proportion with those payable in personal injury and perhaps other cases; and (ii) because the initial shock of being detained will generally attract a higher rate of compensation than the detention's continuance: *Thompson* 515 E–F.

44.23 The basic award for loss of liberty will also vary according to whether the detention was unlawful from the start (in which case the detainee will need to be compensated for the initial shock of detention – the clang of the prison doors) or whether it was preceded by a period of lawful detention.

44.24 Thus, in *R (E) v Secretary of State for the Home Department*,[19] an interim award of £4,000 was made for a two- to three-day period of unlawful detention under Immigration Act powers where the claim (which Mitting J considered bound to succeed if it went to trial) was for detention that was unlawful from the start.

44.25 In *Re Udu and Nyenty*[20] the High Court of Justice in Northern Ireland relied on *Thompson and Hsu* to award £12,500 (to the claimant

18 [2010] EWCA Civ 980 para 8.
19 [2006] EWHC 2500 (Admin).
20 [2008] NIQB 157.

Nyenty) for a period of seven days' unlawful detention under Immigration Act powers which was unlawful from the start. Although the finding of liability in *Udu and Nyenty* was subsequently overturned by the Court of Appeal in Northern Ireland,[21] no criticism was made of the level of damages and we suggest that it still provides a useful benchmark for damages awards in cases where detention is unlawful from the outset.

44.26 In *MK (Algeria) v Secretary of State for the Home Department*, the Court of Appeal awarded £12,500 for 24 days' unlawful detention, for an adult man, no particular vulnerability, detention having become unlawful after the first four days of detention.

44.27 In *Muuse v Home Office*[22] £25,000 in basic damages was awarded in the High Court to an adult man, no particular vulnerability, who had been unlawfully detained for 128 days (this figure was undisturbed on appeal). The claimant there had previously been lawfully imprisoned for 147 days under criminal justice powers. While the *immigration* detention was unlawful from the start in *Muuse*, the claimant in that case was found to be entitled to no award for the initial shock of detention nor for 'the experience that first time custody can bring', having, on the contrary had 'considerable prior experience of custody'.[23]

44.28 In *R (B) v Secretary of State for the Home Department*[24] £32,000 in basic damages was awarded to an adult woman and former torture victim who had been unlawfully detained for six months. The claimant in *B* had previously been detained lawfully for a two-week period.

44.29 By contrast with all of the above awards, in *R v Governor of Brockhill Prison ex p Evans (No 2)*,[25] the House of Lords upheld an award by the Court of Appeal of £5,000 for a 59-day detention for a prisoner whose release date had been erroneously calculated. In arriving at that low figure, the Court of Appeal had taken into account that i) the two-month period of unlawful detention had been preceded by a two-year lawful detention; ii) at the time, the prisoner was unaware that she was being unlawfully detained; iii) the prisoner had been willing to jeopardize her own liberty since she had committed a series of

---

21 [2007] NICA 48.
22 [2009] EWHC 1886 (QB).
23 *Muuse v Secretary of State for the Home Department* [2010] EWCA Civ 453 para 111.
24 [2008] EWHC 3189 (Admin), cited with approval in *Miller v Independent Assessor* [2009] EWCA Civ 609.
25 [2001] 2 AC 19.

disciplinary offences while in prison. The Court of Appeal specifically discouraged attempts to try to calculate a daily or weekly rate from this award and emphasised that this case was fact-specific.[26] In *R (NAB) v Secretary of State for the Home Department*[27] the Administrative Court has recently referred to the 'rough daily rate' upheld by the House of Lords in *Evans (2)*: it is not clear whether the Administrative Court in *NAB* was aware of the Court of Appeal's warning, in *Evans (2)* against precisely such an exercise. In *NAB*, the Administrative Court then proceeded to reach its own overall assessment of damages by reference to a flat daily rate,[28] an exercise which we suggest is impermissible. The Court of Appeal's guidance in both *Thompson and Hsu* and *MK (Algeria)* is that the basic award for loss of liberty is to be calculated on a tapering scale. As we have seen at para 44.22 above, the Court of Appeal in *MK (Algeria)* specifically warned against 'fixing a rigid figure to be awarded for each day of incarceration'. We respectfully suggest that the approach and award in *NAB* should not be followed. In that case, proceeding on the basis of a daily rate, having regard to the claimant's lengthy periods of prior lawful detention and having regard also to the claimant's own failure through his detention to co-operate with the travel documentation process, so prolonging his detention, £6,150 was awarded for 82 days' unlawful detention.

Aggravated damages

44.30 In *Thompson and Hsu v Commissioner of Police for the Metropolis*, Lord Woolf stated that aggravated damages:

> ... can be awarded where there are aggravating features about the case which would result in the plaintiff not receiving sufficient compensation for the injury suffered if the award were restricted to a basic award. Aggravating features can include ... the way the litigation and trial are conducted.[29]

---

26 [1999] QB 1043 p1060.
27 [2011] EWHC 1191 (Admin) para 17.
28 [2011] EWHC 1191 (Admin) para 19.
29 *Thompson and Hsu v Commissioner of Police for the Metropolis* [1998] QB 498 at 516.

44.31 Aggravated damages may be appropriate where the manner of the commission of the wrongful conduct injured the claimant's proper feelings of dignity and pride.[30]

44.32 They may also be awarded to reflect the court's disapproval of the way in which the defendant has conducted the defence.[31]

44.33 In *Thompson and Hsu*, Lord Woolf went on to state that aggravated damages were unlikely to be less than £1,000 or more than double the amount of basic damages.

44.34 In *MK (Algeria)*, aggravated damages of £5,000 were awarded where the Home Office had 'acted in a blinkered and high-handed manner' by detaining a man who had been entitled to rely on his wife's rights of residence under EC law.

44.35 In *Muuse v Secretary of State for the Home Department*, aggravated damages of £7,500 were awarded to a Dutch national detained on the erroneous premise that he was a Somali national, and whose repeated protestations concerning his nationality were ignored and who faced expulsion to Somalia, a country with which he had few connections.

44.36 In *R (B) v Secretary of State for the Home Department* aggravated damages of £6,000 were awarded to reflect the defendant's maintenance of an unjustified defence, failure to show due diligence and failure to follow his own stated policy concerning the detention of victims of torture.

44.37 In *E v Home Office*,[32] £10,000 in aggravated damages were awarded where there had been multiple points during the detention at which the claimant should have been released; where it was a 'serious aggravating factor' that the claimant, a victim of torture, had not been offered the necessary counselling at the Immigration Removal Centre (IRC) where she was held; where the claimant had been detained in undignified circumstances without a change of clothes; where the Home Office had failed to call evidence from the decision-makers directly involved in the case; and where the Home Office had been deficient in its conduct of the litigation and attempts to reach settlement.

---

30 *Rookes v Barnard* [1964] AC 1129 at para 1221.
31 *Thompson and Hsu v Commissioner of Police for the Metropolis* [1998] QB 498 at 517; *R (Lumba and Mighty) v Secretary of State for the Home Department* [2011] UKSC 12, [2011] 2 WLR 671 para 165 per Lord Dyson.
32 Central London County Court, Claim No 9CL01651, 10 June 2010.

Exemplary damages

44.38 More rarely, exemplary damages may be awarded. These are not compensatory but punitive damages.

44.39 Exemplary damages are awarded to mark oppressive, arbitrary or unconstitutional action by the servants of the government, or where the defendant's conduct has been calculated to make a profit.[33]

44.40 The courts have described exemplary damages as having three purposes:[34]

- to punish the defendant;
- to deter similar conduct;
- to express the court's disapproval and thereby to 'serve a useful purpose in vindicating the strength of the law'.[35]

44.41 It is appropriate to award exemplary damages arising out of false imprisonment whether or not misfeasance is made out, as the Home Office conceded and the Court of Appeal clarified in *Muuse v Home Office*.[36] *Muuse v Home Office* further confirms[37] that there are no requirements extraneous to those of 'oppressive, arbitrary or unconstitutional' conduct sufficiently 'outrageous' that exemplary damages are called for to mark disapproval, to deter and to vindicate the strength of the law. There is no need to show malice, fraud, insolence, cruelty or other similar specific conduct.

44.42 Among the points found to justify an award of exemplary damages in *Muuse* were the detention of the individual without good cause and adequate explanation, disregard of established procedures, the failure of the SSHD's junior officers to consider evidence in their own possession, their failure to ascertain whether detention was necessary pending deportation and the failure to act speedily once it became clear that the individual should be released; and threatened deportation to a failed state.[38]

44.43 It had previously been thought that poor conduct of litigation was punishable in exemplary damages, but in *Lumba v Mighty* Lord

---

33 *Rookes v Barnard* [1964] AC 1129.
34 *Rookes v Barnard* [1964] AC 1129 at 1228; *Kuddus v Chief Constable of Leicestershire* [2002] AC 122 at 63, 65 per Lord Nicholls and 75, 79 per Lord Hutton; *A v Bottrill* [2003] 1 AC 449 at para 22; *Whiten v Pilot insurance Co* [2002] 1 SCR 595, 2002 SCC 18 at para 68.
35 *Rookes v Barnard* [1964] AC 1129 per Lord Devlin at 1226.
36 [2010] EWCA Civ 453 para 67.
37 [2010] EWCA Civ 453 para 71.
38 [2010] EWCA Civ 453 paras 66 and 73.

Dyson indicated that disapproval of conduct of litigation should be marked by an appropriate order for costs or by an increased award of aggravated damages.[39]

44.44 Exemplary damages may be awarded even if the basic award is only one of nominal damages.[40] In *Lumba and Mighty* itself, exemplary damages were not awarded, Lord Dyson, with whom the other members of the Supreme Court agreed on this point referred to the following points:

- The courts below had found against the appellants on exemplary damages and their judgments were not, on this point, plainly wrong so as to justify intervention by an appellate court.[41]
- There were potentially large numbers of claimants, not all of whom were before the court.[42] Note, however, that this was not treated as a factor which would always preclude an award of exemplary damages.
- Serious allegations had been made against government officials – but they had not been heard nor had the allegations been tested in evidence.[43]
- The Court of Appeal in the case below had been entitled to give some weight to the fact that the appellants could have been lawfully detained.[44] We respectfully suggest that this is difficult to reconcile with Lord Dyson's recognition in the same case[45] that exemplary damages may be awarded where only nominal basic damages are available, and with the punitive rather than compensatory nature of exemplary damages.

44.45 The *Thompson and Hsu* guidelines recommend £5,000 as the minimum figure for exemplary damages; conduct would have to be 'particularly deserving of condemnation' for an award of £25,000 to be

---

39 R (Lumba and Mighty) v Secretary of State for the Home Department [2011] UKSC 12, [2011] 2 WLR 671 para 165.
40 R (Lumba and Mighty) v Secretary of State for the Home Department [2011] UKSC 12, [2011] 2 WLR 671 para 101 per Lord Dyson.
41 R (Lumba and Mighty) v Secretary of State for the Home Department [2011] UKSC 12, [2011] 2 WLR 671 para 166 per Lord Dyson.
42 R (Lumba and Mighty) v Secretary of State for the Home Department [2011] UKSC 12, [2011] 2 WLR 671 para 167.
43 R (Lumba and Mighty) v Secretary of State for the Home Department [2011] UKSC 12, [2011] 2 WLR 671 para 168.
44 R (Lumba and Mighty) v Secretary of State for the Home Department [2011] UKSC 12, [2011] 2 WLR 671 para 166.
45 R (Lumba and Mighty) v Secretary of State for the Home Department [2011] UKSC 12, [2011] 2 WLR 671 para 101.

44.46 In *Muuse v Home Office*, already discussed above, an award of £27,500 was made to the claimant. That award was upheld in the Court of Appeal, albeit the Court of Appeal observed that a higher award might have been justified.[46]

44.47 In *E v Home Office*, discussed above at para 44.37, an award of £25,000 was made in exemplary damages. The flaws in *E v Home Office* primarily concerned non-compliance by the defendant with its policy and procedures on the detention of torture victims.

Settlements in civil actions

44.48 Out of court settlements may differ significantly from the awards we have cited in this chapter. On the one hand, claimants may settle for lower sums because of urgent need for money, concerns over litigation risk (the risk that if the case proceeds to trial the claimant will lose altogether) or a desire to avoid the difficult experience of trial. Conversely, by being alert in negotiations to the defendant's concerns, for example the avoidance of setting a new precedent on a point of law, damaging publicity, or additional costs, claimants may achieve out of court settlements that are substantially higher than court awards in comparable cases.

---

46 [2010] EWCA Civ 453 para 84.

Index

Appeal rights
  loss and restriction *see* Loss and restriction of appeal rights
Appeals
  judicial review 42.70,42.71 *see also* Judicial review
Appeals to IAC 21.1–21.142
  abandonment 21.140
  appealable decisions 21.4
  application for permission to appeal in Court of Appeal 21.136–21.139
  challenging determination on point of law 21.69–21.74
  challenging refusal of permission to appeal by UT-IAC 21.91–21.98
    'more restrained approach' 21.94
    'second appeal' 21.93–21.97
    test to be applied 21.92
  final determination 21.141,21.142
  First-tier Tribunal 21.34–21.36
    adjournments 21.55, 21.56
    appeal hearings 21.57–21.68
    calculation of time 21.40
    case management review hearings 21.51–21.54
    contents of appeal notice 21.42,21.43
    directions 21.46–21.50
    evidence 21.44–21.56
    extensions of time 21.41
    procedure 21.44–21.56
    starting appeal 21.37–21.43
    time-limits 21.37–21.39
  grounds of appeal in UT-IAC 21.110–21.112

hearings in First-tier Tribunal 21.57–21.68
  decision 21.68
  expert evidence 21.63
  Home Office submissions 21.67
  HOPO 21.59
  Home Office unrepresented, where 21.60
  oral evidence 21.62
  order of proceedings 21.61–21.68
  panel 21.58
  public 21.57
  witness evidence 21.64–21.66
hearings in UT-IAC 21.113–21.119
  decision 21.116, 21.117
in-country 21.17–21.24
  one-stop notices 21.25–21.29
  one-stop statements 21.25–21.29
  out-of-country 21.17–21.24
procedure after grant of permission to appeal to Court of Appeal 21.134, 21.135
review by FTT-IAC of own decision 21.75–21.77
review by UT-IAC of own decision 21.131–21.133
rights of 1.4
seeking permission to appeal from UT-IAC 21.120–21.130
  applicable test 21.129, 21.130
  application notice 21.128
  excluded decision 21.121
  extensions of time 21.127
  time limits 21.123–21.126

Appeals to IAC *continued*
  statutory framework 21.4
  statutory grounds 21.8, 21.9
    discretion should have been
      exercised differently under
      Immigration Rules 21.10
    human rights 21.13–21.16
    not in accordance with
      Immigration Rules 21.10
    not in accordance with law
      21.11, 21.12
    Refugee Convention
      21.13–21.16
  suspensory nature of appeal
    21.30–21.33
    automatic deportation order,
      and 21.31
    discretionary deportation order
      21.31
  trial bundles 20.16, 20.7
  UT-IAC, appeal to 21.34–21.36,
    21.69–21.71
    application for permission
      21.79–21.81
    approach to second
      applications 21.90
    errors of law 21.72–21.74
    excluded decisions 21.78
    form IAUT-1 21.83
    reviewing application for
      permission 21.82–21.90
    second application 21.82–21.90
    short deadlines for in-country
      appeals 21.85
  UT-IAC, powers of 21.99, 21.100
  UT-IAC procedure 21.101–21.109
    directions 21.102, 21.103
    evidence 21.104
    fresh evidence 21.106, 21.107
Article 3 13.6–13.41, 36.47–36.74
  application in expulsion cases
    13.09
  burden and standard of proof
    13.40–13.41
  conditions of detention
    36.57–36.70
    asylum-seekers 36.60–36.62
    defective medical care
      36.64–36.66
    inappropriate for particular
      detainee 36.63
    inappropriate to 'wait and *see*'
      36.67
    mentally and physically ill
      36.68–36.70
  conditions of existence
    13.34–13.39
  death penalty, and 13.24–13.32
  infliction of ill treatment by non-
    state agents 13.23
  inhuman or degrading treatment
    13.20–13.22, 36.55, 36.56
    prison conditions 13.22
    punishment and life sentences
      13.21
  injuries and mental ill health
    sustained in custody: burden
    of proof 36.71–36.73
  mental and physical health 13.33
  minimum level of severity 13.15,
    36.50–36.54, 36.59
  other consequences 13.10–13.14
  positive and negative obligations
    36.48, 36.49
  prohibited ill treatment
    13.16–12.22
  requirement to release 36.74
  torture 13.17–13.19
Article 5 36.4–36.7
  deprivation of liberty 36.6, 36.7
  unqualified right 36.5
Article 5(1) 36.8–36.17
  detention conditions, and 36.17
  'in accordance with procedure
    prescribed by law'
    36.10–36.12
  protection from arbitrary
    detention 36.13–36.16
Article 5(1)(f) detention 36.18–36.36
  deportation proceedings in
    progress 36.19–36.21
  detention for reasonable period
    36.22–36.24
  flaws in expulsion decision 36.25,
    36.26
  no necessity test 36.27–36.33
Article 5(2) 36.37–36.40
  adequate reasons 36.38–36.40

Index 863

Article 5(4) 36.41–36.45
Article 5(5) 36.46
Article 8 36.75–36.94
  approach to, 15.1–15.28
    burden and standard of proof 15.27–15.28
    Immigration Rules para 364, and 15.24–15.27
    Razgar five-step test 15.1, 15.2–15.21
    role of the tribunal in appeal 15.22–15.23
  family life aspects 16.4–16.34, 36.79, 36.80
    adoptive and foster parents and children 16.19
    adults and their siblings or parents, between 16.28–16.32
    biological parent and child 16.13–16.18
    contact proceedings, and 16.12
    different types of family relationships 16.13–16.34
    duty to give reasons for findings 16.8
    factors to consider 16.5–16.7
    general principles 16.4–16.12
    grandparents and minor grandchildren 16.33
    heterosexual spouses 16.20
    heterosexual unmarried partners 16.21–16.23
    immigration status, and 16.10
    looking at the family as a whole 16.4
    potential family life 16.11
    procedural obligations, and 16.12
    relationships that do not amount to family life 16.9
    same-sex partners 16.24–16.27
    uncles, aunts, nieces and nephews and cousins 16.34
  justification 36.88–36.94
  limitations on rights consequent on imprisonment 36.86, 36.87
  positive and negative obligations 36.82–36.84
  private life aspects 16.34, 36.76–36.78
    composite cases 16.38–16.39
    private life and social and economic relations 16.37
    relationships and private life 16.36
    scope generally 16.35
  proportionality *see* Proportionality in article 8 cases
  treatment falling short of article 3 threshold 36.85
Article 14 36.95–36.103
  discrimination 36.95–36.103
  'other status' 36.99
Assault and battery 43.5–43.8
Automatic deportation 5.1–5.56
  appeals 5.43
    in-country 5.47–5.50
    obstacles to 5.44–5.46
    out-of-country 5.51–5.56
  automatic deportation orders
    effect 5.40
    made 5.37
  custodial sentences, and 5.18 – 5.21
    consecutive sentences 5.19
    detention 5.20
    is convicted and is sentenced, meaning 5.21
    suspended sentences 5.18
  exemptions 5.21–5.30
    all deportation 5.23
    long-resident Commonwealth and Irish nationals 5.24
    under UKBA 2007 5.25–5.30
  foreign criminal, meaning 5.12–5.14
  legislative response 5.2
  Immigration Act 1971, under 5.31–5.36
    family members 5.31
    foreign criminals 5.34
    not foreign criminals 5.32
  liable, who is 5.12
  misnomer 5.3
  no private law action for failure to issue 5.22
  timetable for entry into force 5.8

Automatic deportation *continued*
    transitional provisions 5.10
    two statutory deportation
        regimes, differences 5.6–5.7
    UK Borders Act 2007 5.4

Bail 40.1–40.43
    Administrative Court, powers
        40.33–40.35
    appeal pending, where 40.9–40.12
    applications in FTT-IAC
        41.14–41.69
        address 41.14, 41.15
        applicant's instructions and
            evidence 41.28–41.31
        application 41.32–41.33
        bail in principle 41.59
        bail summary 41.36
        burden of proof at hearing
            41.40, 41.41
        challenging refusal 41.67
        compliance 41.44, 41.45
        decision 41.64–41.66
        evidence from Home Office
            41.43
        further applications 41.68,
            41.69
        issues to be considered at
            hearing 41.44–41.50
        length of detention 41.49
        listing 41.34
        NASS accommodation
            41.16–41.23
        National Offender
            Management Service pro
            forma 41.36–41.39
        persons still on licence period
            41.60–41.63
        procedure at hearing
            41.51–41.54
        reasons for detention
            41.46–41.48
        renewal 41.70, 41.71
        seeking in-person hearing
            41.35
        standard of proof at hearing
            41.42
        sureties 41.24–41.27,
            41.55–41.58

    variation 41.72, 41.73
    breach of conditions 40.24–40.31
        forfeiture 40.26–40.31
        re-detention 40.26–40.31
    conditions 40.15–40.23
        breach 40.24–40.31
        electronic monitoring
            40.18–40.23
        residence 40.17
    Court of Appeal, powers
        40.33–40.35
    general powers 40.4–40.7
    Home Office detention policy,
        and 34.3
    Home Office policy 40.43
    immigration judges of UT-IAC,
        from 40.32
    in principle 40.80–40.12
    judicial review, and 42.63–42.65
    notification of entitlement to
        35.22–35.24
    powers to grant 40.1, 40.2
    release directed by criminal
        courts 40.36, 40.37
    release on restriction order
        40.38–40.42
    SIAC *see* SIAC
    statutory powers 40.3–40.12
    sureties 40.13, 40.14, 41.11–41.13,
        41.24–41.27, 41.55–41.58
    test for 41.1
Best interests of the child 4.7–4.33
    article 8, and 17.24–17.30
    ascertaining 4.20
    Borders Citizenship and
        Immigration Act 2009 s55
        4.8–4.10
        consequences of failure to have
            regard to 4.30
    British citizens
        best interests of 4.22
        expulsion of parents of 4.23
    Every Child Matters 4.11–4.13
    meaning of 4.19
        'have regard to' 4.29
        'primary consideration'
            4.14–4.18
    new statutory duty 4.7

parent's wrongdoing, effect of 4.24
safeguarding and promoting the welfare of the child 4.25
statutory code of practice 4.11–4.13
timely resolution 4.33
UNCRC, reliance on other aspects of 4.27
Breach of statutory duty 43.19

Canada
special advocates 23.27
Causation
Home Office detention policy, and 34.8–34.10
liability for detainer, and 32.17–32.20
damages, and 32.24, 32.25
Causes of action 43.1–43.34
Certificate under EEA Regs reg 26(5)
loss of appeal rights, and 22.23
Children
best interests of see Best Interests of children
detention of see Detention of children
Children's Champion 37.11
Choice of jurisdiction 42.1–42.102
Civil claims see Private law claims
Civil Procedure Rules 42.5–42.11
offers to settle 42.11
overriding objective 42.5
pre-action protocols 42.8–42.10
Clearly unfounded certificates
loss of appeal rights, and 22.4–22.9
Common law principles applicable to deprivation of liberty 32.1–32.43
burden on detainer to justify detention 32.3–32.5
Lumba and Mighty 32.5
causation and damages 32.24, 32.25
court's role when assessing lawfulness of administrative detention 32.41–32.43

duty to give reasons for detention 32.26–32.29
no adequate reasons 32.29
wrong reason 32.28
equal protection of law for immigrants 32.2
executive's powers of detention must be strictly construed 32.6–32.9
false imprisonment
special damage, and 32.14–32.16
legality of decision vitiated by material public law error 32.10–32.13
material and non-material public law error 32.21–32.23
intermediary category 32.22, 32.23
no causation defence in liability for detainer 32.17–32.20
no good faith defence for detainer 32.30
presumption of detention in Immigration Acts, whether 32.31–32.40
Administrative Court Authority 32.39, 32.40
construction of power to detain in court recommendation cases 32.34–32.40
Lumba and Mighty 32.36–32.38
ongoing debate as to interpretation 32.32
policy of normally detaining specified category of person 32.31
Complaints
Immigration Removal Centres see Immigration Removal Centres
Conducive deportation 1.7–1.9
allegations and evidence used at trial abroad 1.14
character and associations, basis of 1.13
criminal conviction, without 1.9
leave obtained by deception 1.11–1.12

Conducive deportation *continued*
  offences committed abroad, based on 1.10
Court of Appeal
  appeal from SIAC 23.18, 23.97–23.100
  application for permission to appeal in 21.136–21.139
  procedure after grant of permission to appeal by UT-IAC 21.134, 24.135

Damages 44.1–44.48
  aggravated 44.4, 44.7, 44.30–44.37
  basic award for loss of liberty 44.17–44.29
  exemplary 44.4, 44.7, 44.38–44.47
  general 44.3
  nominal 44.9–44.16
    burden of proof 44.11–44.15
  settlements in civil actions 44.48
  special 44.2
  substantive 44.9–44.16
  unlawful detention, and 44.5
Data Protection Act 1998 43.28
Deaths in custody
  investigation into 25.13, 25.14
Deportation
  arrangements 6.17–6.22
  certain overstayers 1.25–1.26
  considered, who is 3.5–3.8
  co-operation with 6.13–6.16
  delays for medical treatment 6.23–6.25
  discretionary 1.2
  exemptions 1.5
    British citizens 1.27–128
    diplomats and international functionaries 1.41–1.42
    long-resident Irish and Commonwealth nationals 1.34–1.37
    meaning of ordinarily resident 1.38–1.40
    others with a right of abode 1.29–1.33
  family members 1.15–1.16
  circumstances in which deportation order will cease to have effect 1.20
  definition of family member under Immigration Act 1971 s3(5)(b) 1.17
  immigration rules and limitations on power to deport 1.21
  relevant factors in decision whether to deport 1.23–1.24
  settled in UK, meaning 1.22
  time limits 1.18–1.19
  issuing decision to 3.47–3.48
  orders
    revocation of *see* Revocation of deportation orders
  paying for 6.22
  process of consideration 3.9–3.14
  representation against *see* Representations against deportation
  resisting on grounds of illness *see* Resisting deportation on grounds of illness
  Detention Centre Rules 2001
    physical and mental examination 34.26
Detention of children 37.1–37.30
  BCIA 2009 s55 duty 37.3–37.9
    Home Office policy, and 37.8, 37.9
    legal consequences of failure to have regard to best interests of child 4.30, 37.5–37.7
  Children's Champion 37.11
  Every Child Matters 37.3–37.9
  families with children 37.22–37.30 *see also* Families with children
  Family Reforms Panel 37.10
  split families 37.12–37.20
    internal CCD instructions 37.13–37.19
    releasing 'serious criminal' to family including dependent minors 37.20
  unaccompanied minor FNPs 37.21

Index 867

Detention reviews 35.27–35.33
  legal consequences of failure to properly carry out 35.30–35.33
Detention Services Customer Service Unit 39.54, 39.55
Discretionary leave 19.5–19.6, 19.31–19
  active review 19.37
  duration of grants 19.36–19.55
  exclusion 19.34–19.35
  non-standard 19.40–19.55
    exclusion cases 19.42–19.45
    lawfulness of 6 month leave policy 19.46–19.47
    Refugee Convention and 19.48–19.55
    restrictions on discretionary leave 19.48–19.55
    unaccompanied children 19.41
  standard 19.36–19.39
Discrimination claims 43.29–43.34
Dual nationality 19.76– 19.78

Early release 28.1–28.3
Early Removal Scheme (ERS) 28.31–28.44
  CJA 1991 cases 28.33
  CJA 2003 cases 28.34
  complaints about decisions 28.42
  consideration 28.35–28.43
  eligibility 28.35–28.43
  exceptional and compelling reasons for refusing 28.40
  'presumed suitable' 28.39
  return to UK after release on 28.44
Electronic monitoring 40.18–40.23
Embassies
  communication with 27.43–27.46
Entry in breach of a deportation order 7.30–7.31, 9.79
Error of law
  meaning 21.72–21.74
EU law
  acquisition of permanent rights of residence 8.41–8.45
  Citizen's Directive 8.1–8.4
  EEA Regs 2006 8.1–8.4
  entitled to reside in the UK, who is 8.6
  administrative formalities 8.10
  qualified persons 8.9
  EU citizens 8.5
  EEA nationals 4.3, 8.5
  family members 8.11–8.15
    British citizens, of 8.36–8.39
    dependants', 'personal care' and 'durability' 8.24–8.27
    dual nationals of 8.40
    extended family members 8.19–8.24
    other relatives 8.18–8.29
    protection 8.32–8.35
    right of permanent residence 8.46–8.48
    right of residence for 8.30–8.40
    rights of extended family members 8.28–8.29
    students and their family members 8.16–8.17
European Convention on Human Rights 36.1–36.106
  article 3 13.6–13.41, 36.47–36.74
    application in expulsion cases 13.09
    asylum-seekers 36.60–36.62
    burden and standard of proof 13.40–13.41
    conditions of detention 36.57–36.70
    conditions of existence 13.34–13.39
    death penalty, and 13.24–13.32
    defective medical care 36.64–36.66
    inappropriate for particular detainee 36.63
    inappropriate to 'wait and see' 36.67
    infliction of ill treatment by non-state agents 13.23
    inhuman or degrading treatment 13.20–13.22, 36.55, 36.56
    injuries and mental ill health sustained in custody: burden of proof 36.71–36.73

European Convention on Human Rights, article 3 *continued*
   mental and physical health 13.33
   mentally and physically ill 36.68–36.70
   minimum level of severity 13.15, 36.50–36.54, 36.59
   other consequences 13.10–13.14
   positive and negative obligations 36.48, 36.49
   prison conditions 13.22
   prohibited ill treatment 13.16–12.22
   punishment and life sentences 13.21
   requirement to release 36.74
   torture 13.17–13.19
 article 5 36.4–36.7
   deprivation of liberty 36.6, 36.7
   unqualified right 36.5
 article 5(1) 36.8–36.17
   detention conditions, and 36.17
   ' in accordance with procedure prescribed by law' 36.10–36.12
   protection from arbitrary detention 36.13–36.16
 article 5(1)(f) detention 36.18–36.36
   deportation proceedings in progress 36.19–36.21
   detention for reasonable period 36.22–36.24
   flaws in expulsion decision 36.25, 36.26
   no necessity test 36.27–36.33
 article 5(2) 36.37–36.40
   adequate reasons 36.38–36.40
 article 5(4) 36.41–36.45
 article 5(5) 36.46
 article 8 36.75–36.94
   adoptive and foster parents and children 16.19
   adults and their siblings or parents, between 16.28–16.32 approach to, 15.1–15.28
   biological parent and child 16.13–16.18
   burden and standard of proof 15.27–15.28
   composite cases 16.38–16.39
   contact proceedings, and 16.12
   different types of family relationships 16.13–16.34
   duty to give reasons for findings 16.8
   factors to consider 16.5–16.7
   family life aspects 16.4–16.34, 36.79, 36.80
   general principles 16.4–16.12
   grandparents and minor grandchildren 16.33
   heterosexual spouses 16.20
   heterosexual unmarried partners 16.21–16.23
   Immigration Rules para 364, and 15.24–15.27
   immigration status, and 16.10
   justification 36.88–36.94
   limitations on rights consequent on imprisonment 36.86, 36.87
   looking at the family as a whole 16.4
   positive and negative obligations 36.82–36.84
   potential family life 16.11
   private life and social and economic relations 16.37
   private life aspects 16.34, 36.76–36.78
   procedural obligations, and 16.12
   proportionality *see* Proportionality in article 8 cases
   Razgar five-step test 15.1, 15.2–15.21
   relationships and private life 16.36
   relationships that do not amount to family life 16.9
   role of the tribunal in appeal 15.22–15.23
   same-sex partners 16.24–16.27

Index 869

scope generally 16.35
treatment falling short of article 3 threshold 36.85
uncles, aunts, nieces and nephews and cousins 16.34
article 14 36.95–36.103
  breaches resulting from detention contractor's actions or omissions 36.104–36.106
  detention, and 36.1–36.106
  discrimination 36.95–36.103
  flagrant denial required, 13.45–13.50
  flagrant denial not required 13.44
  'other status' 36.99
  Qualification Directive, and 13.5
  reliance on 13.42–13.43
Evidence 20.11–20.13
  checklist in claims relying on Citizens Directive and EEA Regs 2006 Box 20.2
  checklist in ECHR article 8 claims Box 20.4
  expert *see* Expert evidence
  future offending risk 20.12, 20.13
    sources of information Box 20.5
  materials checklist in 'intentional harm' cases Box 20.3
  past offending 20.12, 20.13
    sources of information Box 20.5
Expert evidence 20.14, 20.15
  cross-examination 20.15
  guidance from Senior President of Tribunals Box 20.6
Expulsion of EEA nationals and family members
  applicable principles 9.6–9.8
    first level of protection 9.9–9.20
      genuine, present and sufficiently serious threat affecting fundamental interest 9.12–9.13
      measures based exclusively on personal conduct 9.14–9.16
      particularly serious past offences 9.17–9.18
      proportionality 9.19–9.20
      public security, public security or public health grounds 9.9–9.11
  calculation of qualifying periods 9.32–9.47
  calculating duration of 'legal' residence: starting point 9.38
  continuity of residence 9.39–9.41
  deportation orders, and 9.1
  delay in enforcing 9.74
  general principles 9.6–9.8
  generic term 9.1, 9.3
  Home Office *see* Home Office policies
  immigration detention against whom action is being taken 9.75–9.78
  legal residence
    litigation history 9.36–9.37
    meaning 9.32–9.35
    time spent in prison 9.42–9.47
  procedure and practice 9.48–9.5
    appeals 9.55–9.67
    appeals to SIAC 5.60–5.62
    certification 5.65–9.67
    exemptions 9.50–9.51
    grounds 9.57
    in-country and out-of-country appeals 9.58–5.59
    Irish nationals 9.51
    notification of decisions 9.52
    proof 5.63–6.64
    relationship between EEA Regs 2006, IA 1971 and UKBA 2007 9.48–9.49
    required judicial remedies 9.53
  second level of protection 9.24–9.24
    application in criminal court recommendation cases 9.24
    serious grounds of public policy or public security 9.22–9.23

Expulsion of EEA nationals and family members *continued*
  third level of protection 9.25–9.31
    imperative grounds of public security 9.26–9.29
    legal residence requirement 9.30
    previous ten years 9.31
Expulsion of non-EU citizens 10.2, 10.4–10.16
  countervailing considerations 10.13–10.14
  have to leave, when does EU citizen 10.12
  Ruiz Zambrano and
    third-country national parents of British children or other EU citizens 10.5–10.6
    other third-country national family members of British or other EU citizens 10.7–10.11
  TFEU article 20 10.4
  ECHR article 8, and 10.15, 10.16

Facilitated Returns Scheme (FRS) 6.13–6.17, 28.45–28.53
  administration of 28.50
  applications 28.51
  effect of participation 28.52
  eligibility 28.46
  nature of 28.45
False imprisonment 43.9–43.12
  special damage, and 32.14–32.16
Families with children 37.22–37.30
  detention at Tinsley House Immigration Removal Centre 37.27
  exploration of alternatives to enforced expulsion 37.22–37.24
  mother and baby units 37.28
  pre-departure accommodation 37.25, 37.26
  reviews in detained family cases 37.30
  time limits on detention 37.29
Family Returns Panel 37.10
Foreign nationals in the prison system 27.1–27.46
  allocation 27.10, 27.23–27.27
    Rationalisation Plan 27.24–27.27
  categorisation 1.1, 27.10,27.11
    challenging decision 27.22
    conviction, following 27.14, 27.15
    deportation, and 27.16–27.20
    young offenders 27.13
    PSO 4630 27.19
    remand prisoners 27.12
    women 27.13
  category A 27.11
  category B 27.11
  category C 27.11
  category D 27.11
  communication between prisons and UKBA 27.28–27.37
    FNP serving sentence, when 27.29–27.35
    FNP detained under Immigration Act powers, where 27.36,27.37
  detained in prison at end of sentence 27.21
  embassies, communication with 27.43–27.46
  IS91 detention authority form 27.38,27.39
  local policies 27.8
  management 27.1–27.46
  release 27.40–27.42
  remand, held on 27.9, 27.12
  Service Level Agreement 27.4–27.7
    expectations 27.5, 27.6
Future offending risk
  information and evidence 20.12, 20.13, Box 20

Habeas corpus 42.72 - 42.81
  application for 42.80, 42.81
  judicial review, and 42.74–42.79
***Hardial Singh* principles** 33.1–33.50
  approval of 33.4
  detention must not be used for any purpose other than statutory power 33.5–33.8
    prevention of offending 33.8

unlawful collateral purpose 33.7
detention should not exceed reasonable period 33.9–33.13
 bail applications 33.12
 factors relevant to assessment 33.11
 inflation in periods of detention 33.10
facts 33.3
Home Office must exercise reasonable diligence and expedition 33.18
reasonable duration of detention 33.19–33.50
 absconding risk 33.23–33.26
 (A) Somalia 33.20–33.22
 detainee's refusal to reptriate voluntarily 33.29–33.34
 disability 33.48
 mental illness 33.34–33.46
 non-co-operation by detainee 33.35–33.42
 offending risk 33.20–33.22
 outstanding legal challenge, where 33.40
 previous refusals of bail 33.49, 33.50
 refusal to cooperate with obtaining travel documents 33.35–33.39
 serious medical conditions 33.47
 time spent in detention persuing challenges to expulsion 33.27, 33.28
realistic prospect of expulsion within reasonable period 33.14–33.17
 requisite degree of certainty 33.15–33.17
Her Majesty's Chief Inspector of Prisons (HMCIP) 25.16–25.18
Home Detention Curfew 28.12–28.30
 consideration process 28.20–28.22
 FNPs, and 28.27–28.30
 'liable to removal' 28.28

Prison Service Policy 28.29, 28.30
groups of persons stautorily eligible but presumed unsuitable 28.16
presumption in favour of 28.17
purpose of 28.12
recall from 28.25, 28.26
refusal of 28.23, 28.24
statutory exclusions 28.14, 28.15
time window for 28.18, 28.19
Home Office detention policy 34.1–34.55
 adults who should only be detained in very exceptional circumstances 34.24, 34.25
 bail, and 34.3
 causation, and 34.8–34.10
 claims concerning detention of torture victims 34.33–34.36
 examples of breaches 34.54, 34.55
 factors that SSHD's caseworkers must consider 34.20–34.22
 flux 34.12–34.14
 general principles 34.18–34.36
 interplay with Detention Centre Rules 2001 34.26
 legal status 34.6, 34.7
 minors 34.23
 necessity test 34.18
 permissible reasons for detention 34.19
 presumption of liberty 34.18
 secret detention policy for FNPs 34.55
 serious medical conditions, those suffering from 34.27–34.32
 seriously disabled persons 34.27–34.32
 seriously mentally ill persons 34.27–34.32
 special criteria for detention in CCD cases 34.37–34.53
  assessment of harm to public 34.42–34.45
  consideration of abconding risk 34.41
  more serious offences 34.47–34.51

Home Office detention policy,
  special criteria for detention in
  CCD cases *continued*
    personal compassionate
      circumstances 34.46
    persons with British or EEA
      national spouses 34.52, 34.53
    policy 34.38
    process of considering
      detention 34.39–34.46
    timing of removal 34.40
  unlawful detention, and 34.2
  unpublished 34.12
Home Office policies
  deportation of EEA nationals and
    their family members
    9.80–9.88
    cases that will be referred 9.82
    deportation consideration,
      when begins 9.80
    incorporation of a presumption
      of deportation 9.84
    information sought 9.81
    interpretation of protection
      from expulsion 9.83
    Irish nationals 9.85–9.86
    revocation of 9.87–9.88
  Immigration Act 1971 3.28–3.3
    deportation of the elderly 3.32
    different types of offences and
      convictions 3.28–3.29
    relevant factors and exceptional
      circumstances 3.30
  previously applicable to
    deportation under the IA
    1971 3.34–3.46
    DP3/96 3.40–3.46
    legal consequences of a
      withdrawn policy 3.35–3.36
    war zones policy 3.37–3.39
  relevant to the deportation of
    children 4.34–4.44
    former seven-year concession
      4.40
    splitting families 4.34–4.36
    unaccompanied minors 4.37
Hospital orders 30.7–30.10
Human rights
  appeal to IAC, and 21.13–21.16

Human rights claims 43.20–43.27
  damages 43.26
  public authority 43.22, 43.24
Humanitarian protection 19.5–19.6,
  19.7–19
  cessation 19.28–19.30
  contents 19.13–19.17
  definition 19.7–19.10
  domestic implementation
    19.11–19.12
  exclusion from 19.18–19.25
    domestic interpretation
      19.21–19.25
  leave to remain 19.26–19.27

Immigration detention 31.1–31.39
  common law, and 31.3
  common law principles *see*
    Common law principles
    applicable to deprivation of
    liberty
  dual detention for deportation,
    none 31.35, 31.36
  IA 1971 31.6–31.11
    cases where no statutory power
      31.11
    deportation cases 31.7–31.9
    pending, meaning 31.10
  procedural requirements *see*
    Procedural requirements in
    immigration detention
  R (Khadir) 31.37–31.39
  statutory powers 31.1–31.39
  UKBA 2007 31.12–31.34
    'automatic' deportation, and 5.
      4, 31.13, 31.14, 31.15
    'automatic' deportation order
      made, where 31.34
    conditions 31.20–31.24
    "foreign criminals" 31.13,
      31.14
    Hardial Singh principles 31.27
    information to detainee 31.18
    s36 (1)(a) 31.19–31.27
    s36 (1)(b) 31.28–31.33
    steps in deportation process,
      and 31.17–31.33
Immigration Removal Centres
  39.1–39.91

access to activities and open air
    39.17–39.19
access to immigration officers
    39.9, 39.10
access to legal advice 39.8
complaints 39.52–39.91
  assault 39.83
  criminal allegations 39.83
  Detention Services Customer
    Service Unit 39.54, 39.55
  duty to investigate all serious
    misconduct complaints 39.72
  ex gratia payments 39.74–39.78
  form 39.58
  internal 39.53–39.83
  internal record keeping
    39.79–39.82
  investigative responsibilities
    39.69–39.71
  potential outcomes 39.74–39.78
  Prisons and Probation
    Ombudsman 39.52
  refusing to deal with
    complaints from certain
    detainees 39.73
  subject matter 39.56, 39.57
  subsequent litigation, and
    39.91
  timescale for making 39.59
  timescales for responding
    39.60–39.68
  who can complain 39.56, 39.57
conditions of detention
    39.1–39.91
correspondence 39.20–39.23
detainees' property and clothing
    39.12, 39.13
facilities 39.14, 39.15
hygiene 39.16
incentives scheme 39.41
Independent Monitoring Board
    39.84–39.90
mandatory drugs and alcohol
    testing 39.51
maximisation of freedom of
    movement 39.6, 39.7
medical care 39.24–39.28
medical examination 39.29–39.34
medical reports 39.29–39.34

minimisation of restrictions
    39.6, 39.7
removal from association
    39.42–39.46
searches 39.11
self-harm 39.35–39.40
sources of guidance and
    regulation for conditions
    39.2
suicide 39.35–39.40
temporary confinement
    39.42–39.46
use of control and restraint
    39.47–39.50
use of force 39.47–39.50
visits 39.20–39.23
Immigration Rules 3.20
  amended 3.23–3.24
  old 3.21–3.22
  relevant factors 3.25–3.26
  requirement of consistency 3.27
Indefinite leave to remain
  revocation where individual
    cannot be deported
    19.66–19.75
Independent Monitoring Board
    39.84–39.90
Initial detention authorisation
    35.3–35.9
  forms 35.6, 35.7
  levels of 35.8, 35.9
Interim hospital orders 30.7–30.10
IS91 detention authority form 27.38,
    27.39

Judicial review 42.16–42.71
  amending claim form in light of
    fresh decisions 42.61
  appeals 42.70, 42.71
  bail 42.63–42.65
  civil claim for damages, and
    42.99–42.102
  claim form 42.44, 42.45
  decisions which can be
    challenged 42.23, 42.24
  duty of candour 42.51, 42.52
  full hearing 42.66–42.69
  grounds 42.25–42.31
  habeas corpus, and 42.74, 42.79

Judicial review *continued*
    HRA 1998, and 42.31
    illegality 42.25, 42.27, 42.28
    interested parties 42.34
    interim remedies 42.63–42.65
    interlocutory applications for
        directions and disclosure
        42.62
    irrationality 42.25, 42.29
    issuing claim 42.46–42.50
    omissions which can be
        challenged 42.23, 42.24
    permission stage 42.53–42.58
    post permission 42.59–42.60
    pre-action protocol 42.39–42.43
    procedural fairness 42.30
    remedies 42.36–42.38
    third party interventions 42.35
    time limits 42.44, 42.45
    what can be challenged
        42.19–42.22
    who can bring claim 42.32, 42.33

Kluxen 2.2–2.3

Leave
    outside rules 19.56–19.60
Litigation 42.5–42.15
    obtaining documents prior to
        proceedings 42.12–42.15
Loss and restriction of appeal rights
    22.1–22.25
    certificate under EEA Regs reg 26
        (5) 22.23
    clearly unfounded certificates
        22.4–22.9
    in-country appeal rights
        22.4–22.13
Loss of all appeal rights 22.14–22.23
    one-stop certification under NIAA
        2002 s 96 22.14–22.22
    third-country certificates
        22.10–22.13

Mental Health Act 1983 30.5, 30.6
    access to First-tier Tribunal
        (Mental Health) 30.24
    after-care 30.34–30.36
    deportation, relationship with
        30.37–30.46
    appeal, right of 30.40
    expulsion from UK 30–38,
        30–39
    immigration control, and 30.42
    section 86 30.41–30.45
    section 91 30.46
    hospital directions 30.13
    limitation directions 30.13
    remittal from hospital to prison
        or detention facility:
        prisoners 30.20–30.22, 30.23
    restricted patients 30.25–30.33
    conditional discharge 30.28
    discharge, effect 30.33
    immigration detainees 30.32
    Parole Board, and 30.31
    powers and duties of tribunals
        30.29, 30.30
    restriction directions 30.19
    restriction orders 30.11–30.12
    transfer directions: immigration
        detainees 30.17, 30.18
    transfer directions: prisoners
        30.14–30.16
    treatability test 30.20
Mental health legislation 30.1–30.46
Ministry of Justice 24.2
Minors
    detention in most or very
        exceptional circumstances
        34.23
    statutory powers 4.4–4.7
Misfeasance in public office 43.13,
    43.14
**Multi-agency public protection
    arrangements** 24.22–24.25
    categories of offender 24.23
    levels of management 24.24,
        24.25

**National Offender Management
    Service (NOMS)** 24.3
    source of information, as 20.13
National security
    assessment of risk to 23.73–23.77
Negligence 43.15–43.18

Index 875

OASys (Offender Assessment
    System) 24.14–24.21
  levels of risk of harm 24.19
  OGP 24.16
  OGRS 3 24.15
  OUP 24.17
  probation officers, and 24.21
One-stop certification under NIAA
    2002 s96
  loss of appeal rights, and
    22.14–22.22
One-stop statement 21.27
One-stop warning 21.26

Parole Board 26.11 – 26.22
  functions 26.11
Past offending
  information and evidence 20.12,
    20.13, Box 20.5
Places of immigration detention
  38.1–38.24
Prison service 24.4
Prison system
  organisation 24.2– 24.4

Prisons
  Committee for the Prevention of
    Torture (CPT) 25.19
  complaints 25.3–25.7
    forms 25.5, 25.6
    policy 25.4
    time limit 25.5
  contracted out 24.6
  Independent Monitoring Boards
    25.15
  internal supervision 25.19– 25.21
  NPM 25.20, 25.21
  OASys 24.14– 24.21 *see also* OA
    Sys
  OM 24.11
  OPCAT 25.20
  policy framework 24.5– 24.11
  Prison Rules 1999 24.7
  PSIs 24.9
  PSOs 24.9
  risk assessment 24.14– 24.21
  statutory framework 24.5– 24.11
  supervision 25.15– 25.21

Prisons and Probation Ombudsman
  25.8–25.14, 39.52
  investigation into deaths in
    custody 25.13, 25.14
  remit 25.9
  resolution of complaint 25.12
  time limit for complaint to 25.11
Private law challenges 42.1– 42.3
Private law claims 42.82– 42.102
  anonymity 42.97
  burden of proof 42.83
  claim form 42.95, 42.96
  courts 42.88, 42.89
  judicial review, and 42.99–42.102
  jury trials 42.92
  limitation periods 42.90, 42.91
  pre-action correspondence 42.93
  procedure 42.94–42.98
  remaining in UK to pursue claim
    42.87
  who can be sued 42.84–42.86
Probation
  statutory framework 24.10
Probation system
  organisation 24.2–24.4
Procedural requirements in
    immigration detention 2.8,
    35.1–35.35
  authorisation before release 35.34
  detention reviews *see* Detention
    reviews
  full inquiry 2.9
  Immigration (Places of
    Detention) Direction 2009
    38.4
  initial detention authorisation
    35.3–35.9
    see also Initial detention
      authorisation
  medical reviews 35.35
  notification of entitlement to bail
    35.22–35.24
  police stations 38.23, 38.24
  prisons 38.5–38.16
    challenging conditions 38.16
    health grounds 38.7
    police intelligence 38.11
    regime 38.12–38.15
    risk factors 38.6

Procedural requirements in immigration detention, prisons *continued*
  transfer 38.9
  reasons for detention 2.10, 35.10–35.21
  see also Reasons for detention
  risk assessment 35.25, 35.26
  sources of law and policy 38.3
  transfer, decisions over 38.17–38.20
    challenging 38.21, 38.22
  written notice 2.8
Proportionality in article 8 cases 17.2–17.91, 36.88–36.94
  assessment 17.2–17.36
    best interests of the child 17.24–17.30
    family members of refugees 17.22
    further factors 17.36
    enjoyed elsewhere 17.2–17.6
    no requirement to show 'insurmountable obstacles' to enjoyment elsewhere 17.7–17.12
    physical separation 17.13–17.16
    rights of other family members 17.23
    settled family members are British citizens 17.31–17.35
    severance where not enjoyed elsewhere 17.17–17.22
  criminal deportation 17.55–17.91
    deterrence and the expression of public revulsion 17.67–17.71
    duration of exclusion 17.89–17.91
    gravity of offence 17.57–17.64
    minor, offences committed as a 17.80–17.84
    risk of further offending 19.65
    test 17.55–17.56
    time lapse since index offence 17.86–17.88
    time span of offending 17.79
    under the UKBA 2007 17.73–17.78
    under the IA 1971 17.72
    weight to give to old offences 17.85
  relevant factors 17.37–17.54
    conditions in the receiving state 17.52–15.53
    contribution to the community 17.54
    delay 17.41–17.42
    length of residence in home state and home-grown criminals 17.43–17.51
    life formed while immigration status known to be precarious 17.37–17.40
Public authority
  meaning 43.22, 43.24
Public law challenges 42.1–42.3

Qualification Directive
  article 15(2)
    approach of the domestic courts 14.12–14.15
    approach of the ECJ 14.11
    definition 14.5–14.10
    importance of 14.3–14.5
    practical issues arising 14.16–14
  European Convention on Human Rights, and 13.5

Reasons for detention 35.10–35.21
  consequences of failure to give 35.17–35.21
  content 35.13–35.16
  form 35.13–35.16
Recommendations for deportation
  challenging 2.19–2.20
  Courts 2.4
  passport offences, for 2.15–2.18
  subject to, who may be 2.5
Refugee Convention
  appeal to IAC, and 21.13–21.16
  brief history 11.4–11.5
  brief overview 11.6
  burden 11.70–11.75
  cessation 12.6, 12.121–12.144
    approach 12.134–12.136
    article 1C 12.125

Index 877

European and domestic
   implementation of article 1C
   12.1126–12.128
revocation of indefinite leave
   12.130– 12.133
voluntary re-availment of
   national protection
   12.137–12.139
voluntary re-establishment in
   the country where
   persecution was feared
   12.140–12.144
UNHCR's involvement in
   cessation decisions 12.129
criminal conduct, and
   11.61–11.67
   military service 11.65–11.67
   prosecution and persecution
      11.62–11.64
date status assessed 11.68–11.69
definition of refugee 11.35
duty of non-refoulement
   11.76–11.77
elements 11.36–11.60
   convention reasons for
      persecution 11.51–11.59
   fear 11.37
   outside country of his
      nationality 11.60
   persecution 11.44–11.50
   protection rooted in future risk
      11.38
   refugees 'sur place'
      11.40–11.43
   well-founded 11.39
exclusion 12.1–12.2, 12.7–12.74
   actus reus 12.71–12.74
   articles 1D and 1E 12.7–12.11
   article 1F 12.12–12.18
   article 1F(a) 12.26
   article 1F(b) 12.30–12.45
   article 1F(c) 12.46–12.62
   burden of proof 12.23
   clauses 12.7–12.11
   complicity for exclusion
      purposes 12.63–12.65
   mens rea 12.66–12.70
   no proportionality test 12.24

   no requirement that individual
      poses danger to the host state
      12.25
   non-political crime 12.30–12.31
   outside the country of refuge
      12.36–12.45
   procedure 12.19–12.25
   serious crime 12.32–12.35
   standard of proof 12.19–12.22
   terrorism, and 12.49–12.62
loss of protection 12.3–12.5,
   12.75–12.120
   article 32 12.77
   article 33(2) 12.78–12.79
   article 1F(b) 12.80
   particularly serious crime,
      meaning of 12.95–12.96
   presumptions under NIAA
      2002 s72 12.84–12.94
   refoulement, from
      12.75–12.109
   refugee status and residence
      permits 12.97–12.109
   test 12.81–12.83
partial incorporation into
   domestic law 11.18–11.23
procedure on appeal in exclusion
   cases 12.110–12.120
   certificates 12.110
   exclusion 12.113–12.118
   loss of protection
      12.119–12.120
Qualification Directive, and
   11.10–11.17
   measures transposing into
      domestic law 11.13–11.17
recognition as a refugee
   11.24–11.34
   domestic procedures
      11.25–11.27
   grants of leave 11.28–11.34
standard of proof 11.70–11.75
UNHCR 11.7–11.9

Release
   applications to Home Office
      41.5–41.13
   compassionate factors 41.9
   points to be addressed 41.6

Release *continued*
  criminal courts, directed by 40.36, 40.37
  restriction order, on 40.38–40.42
Release on temporary licence (ROTL) 28.4–28.11
  delegation of decision to UKBA 28.10
  deportation action, and 28.7, 28.8
  individualised assessment by Prison Service 28.9
  types of temporary release 28.4
Repatriation of prisoners 29.1–29.31
  Additional Protocol to Council of Europe Convention on Transfer of Sentenced Persons 29.15–29.17
  applying for 29.10, 29.11
  basis of transfer 29.12–29.14
  bi-lateral transfer agreements 29.6–29.8
  challenges to decisions 29.22–29.25
  consent 29.7, 29.8
  continued enforcement 29.12, 29.13, 29.14
  conversion of sentence 29.12
  criteria for 29.9
  EU Framework Decision 29.18–29.21
  FNPs transferred to UK 29.26–29.31
    Colonial Prisoners Removal Act 1884 29.27
    International Criminal Court Act 2001 29.28–29.31
  multilateral transfer agreements 29.6–29.8
  RPA 1984 29.3–29.5
  status with UK prisoner transfer agreements Table 29.1
  warrants 29.3, 29.4, 29.5
Representations against deportation 20.2–20.10
  checklist Box 20.1
  evidence 20.11–20.13
  FNP, and 20.4
  Home Office practice 20.3
  special considerations in 'automatic' deportation cases 20.5–20.10
  'clearly unfounded' certificate 20.8, 20.9
  in-country appeal rights, and 20.6, 20.7
  prejudice, and 20.10
  revocation of order 20.8
Resisting grounds of deportation on grounds of illness
  ECHR article 3
    Bensaid v UK 18.29–18.30
    D v UK 18.6–18.11
    health, and 8.4–18.5
    J v Secretary of State for the Home Department 18.31–18.34
    mental ill-health and suicide risk, and 18.29
    N (Uganda) v Secretary of State for the Home Department and N v UK (the 'N litigation') 8.12–8.18
    physical ill-health and deprivation of care, and 18.6–18.18
  ECHR article 6, and 18.60–18.64
  ECHR article 8 18.53–18.59
    article 3, and 18.56–18.58
    MSS v Belgium and Greece and Sufi and Elmi v UK 18.59
    private life and health 18.53–18.55
  exceptions in HIV/AIDS cases and other cases of severe physical ill-health 8.19–8.28
    deliberate withholding of medical treatment 18.26
    impact on third parties 18.27–18.28
    ostracism, humiliation or deprivation of basic rights 18.25
    treatment received by a person with leave to remain 18.20–18.24
  mental illness and suicide
    anxious scrutiny 18.44–1847

arising from expulsion itself
rather than deprivation of
care 18.35–18.39
domestic cases 18.42
effective mechanisms
18.50–18.52
exceptions 18.35–18.43
family 18.40–18.41
further issues 18.48–18.52
history of past persecution
18.43
subjective fear of return can
suffice 18.48–18.49
'*Quaquah* claims' 18.60–18.64
Restriction order
Home Office policy 40.43
release on 40.38–40.42
Revocation of deportation orders
7.2–7.4, 7.11–7.29, 9.67–9.73
after enforcement
current immigration rules
7.14–7.18
old immigration rules 7.13
appeal against refusal to revoke
7.29, 9.73
consequences 7.25–7.26
immediate 9.71–9.72
notification 7.27–7.28
representations for 7.23–7.24
under IA 1971 7.11
under UKBA 2007
in-country 7.19–7.21, 9.68–9.70
out-of-country 7.22, 9.68–9.70

Safety to return
assessment of 23.78–23.80
Secretary of the State for the Home Department (SSHD)
approach taken 2.21–2.23
decision-making process 4.1
Sentences 26.1–26.23
determinate 26.3, 26.4, 26.5
adults 26.4
children 26.5
consideration by Parole Board
26.14
procedure for release
26.12–26.19

refusal of release on parole
licence 26.17–26.19
release criteria for those liable
to removal 26.16
release criteria for those not
liable to removal 26.15
extended 26.8
foreign nationals 26.1
framework 26.2
indeterminate 26.3, 26.6, 26.7
common features 26.6
procedures for release
26.20–26.22
types 26.7
'liable to removal from the UK'
26.9
Parole Board *see* Parole Board
prison, types of 26.3
determinate 26.3
extended 26.3, 26.8
fixed-term 26.3
indeterminate 26.3, 26.6
life 26.3
procedures for release
26.11–26.22
determinate sentences
26.12–26.19
indeterminate sentences
26.20–26.22
new legislative proposals for
FNPs liable to removal 26.23
relevant and irrelevant
considerations for the
sentencing court 2.11–2.14
essential test 2.11
irrelevant considerations 2.12
special considerations 2.14
Settlements
civil actions, in 44.48
Sources of guidance: Immigration Rules and Home Office policies
3.15–3.16
Home Office policies as 'law' for
the purposes of the European
Convention on
Human Rights 3.17–3.19
Special advocates 23.20–23.33
Canada 23.27
communication 23.28–23.32

Special advocates *continued*
   grounds of appeal 23.31
   procedural matters 23.31
   special advocate's actions 23.31
  national security context 23.26
  meeting appellant 23.33
  Open Manual 23.22
  role 23.21, 23.22
  SASO 23.22, 23.24
  selection 23.23
  SIAC, and 23.20–23.33
  status 23.25

Special Immigration Appeals Commission (SIAC) 23.1–23.100
  appeal from 23.18, 23.97–23.100
   permission 23.98
  bail 23.83–23.96
   applications 23.88
   challenging decisions 23.96
   conditions 23.90–23.94
   ECHR article 6(1), and 23.84
   factors for grant or refusal 23.85–23.87
   hearing 23.89
   jurisdiction 23.83
   precautionary approach 23.86, 23.87
   risk of absconding 23.91–23.93
   variation of conditions 23.95
  burden of proof 23.56, 23.57
  closed evidence
   consideration 23.34
   control order proceedings, and 23.41, 23.42
   deportation cases, and 23.43
   ECHR article 6, and 23.38, 23.44
   legality of use in substantive deportation appeals 23.34–23.45
   procedural safeguards 23.39
   safety on return, and 23.40
  closed material 23.20–23.33
  consideration of deportation appeals 23.71–23.80
   assessment of risk to national security 23.73–23.77
   oral evidence 23.72
   powers to receive evidence 23.71
   safety on return, assessment of 23.78–23.80
  detainee reporting 23.58
  determination 23.81, 23.82
  disclosure, procedure for 23.46–23.51
   special advocate, and 23.48, 23.49, 23.51
  establishment 23.2–23.4
  exculpatory review 23.52–23.55
   search, reasonableness of 23.54
  jurisdiction 23.5–23.18
   current 23.11–23.18
   decisions which may be certified 23.13
   derogation from ECHR article 5(1), and 23.6–23.10
   former jurisdiction under ATCSA 001 23.5–23.10
   grounds for certification 23.12
   grounds of appeal 23.15
   review of decision of SSHD 23.16
  in-country appeals 23.19
  out-of-country appeals 23.19
  powers 23.17
  progress of deportation appeals in 23.59–23.70
   adjournment 23.64
   determination of appeal 23.68
   directions hearing 23.62–23.64
   notice of appeal 23.59, 23.60, 23.61
   notice of hearing 23.69
   withdrawal 23.67
  special advocates *see* Special advocates
  standard of proof 23.56, 23.57
  website 23.1

Special immigration status 19.61–19.65

Split families *see* Detention of children

Sureties 40.13, 40.14, 41.11–41.13, 41.24–41.27
  FTT-IAC, in 41.55–41.58

Termination of deportation order
7.1, 7.6–7.10
ceases to have effect 7.6–7.9
invalid from outset 7.10
Third-country certificates
loss of appeal rights, and 22.10–22.13
Timing and effect of deportation order under Immigration Act 1971 1.43–1.44
effect 1.48–1.50
in-country rights of appeal 1.43–1.44
timing of 1.45–1.47
Torture victims
claims concerning detention 34.33–34.36
Torts 43.2
Trespass to the person 43.4–43.12
Trial bundles
appeals to IAC 20.16

Turkish Association Agreement cases 10.3, 10.17–10.22
family members 19.22
workers 19.20–19.21

Voluntary deportation
alternative to deportation 6.8
assisted voluntary return through International Organization for Migration 6.10
supervised departure 6.9
automatic, and 5.3 *see* Automatic deportation
discretionary, and 5.3 *see* Discretionary deportation
incentives 6.5–6.7
requirement person still in the UK 6.4